84 SERMONS ON

THE SONG OF SOLOMON

BY CHARLES HADDON SPURGEON

Copyright © 2020
Eric Stewart and Gary Morris
All rights reserved.
ISBN: 979-8-55-894256-9

CONTENTS

Chapter 1

Chapter 2

Chapter 3

Chapter 4

Chapter 5

AN EXPOSITION AND 13 SERMONS
ON CHAPTER 1

1. AN EXPOSITION OF CHAPTER 1

THIS evening, we will read from the one Book of the Bible which is wholly given up to fellowship. I allude to the Book of Canticles. This Book stands like the tree of life in the midst of the garden, and no man shall ever be able to pluck its fruit, and eat from it, until first he has been brought by Christ past the sword of the cherubim, and led to rejoice in the love which has delivered him from death. The Song of Solomon is only to be comprehended by the men whose standing is within the veil. The outer court worshippers, and even those who only enter the court of the priests, think the Book a very strange one; but those who come very near to Christ can often see in this Song of Solomon the only expression which their love to their Lord desires.

Verses 1-2. *The song of songs, which is Solomon's. Let him kiss me with the kisses of his mouth: for thy love is better than wine.*

The Person here alluded to is not named; this omission is very common and usual to all-absorbing love. The spouse is thinking so much of Christ Jesus her Lord that it is not necessary for her to name him; she cannot make a mistake, and, she is so oblivious of all beside that she does not think of them, or of those who would ask, "Who is this of whom you speak?" The communion is so close between herself and her Lord that his name is left out: "Let *him* kiss me." By the kiss is to be understood that strange and blessed manifestation of love which Christ gives from himself to his children. Inasmuch as the word "kisses" is in the plural, the spouse asks that she may have the favour multiplied; and inasmuch as she mentions the "mouth" of her Bridegroom, it is because she wishes to receive the kisses fresh and warm from his sacred Person.

"For thy love is better than wine." It is better in itself, for it is more costly. Did it not flow out in streams of blood from a better winepress than earth's best wine has ever known? It is better, too, in its effects; more exhilarating, more strengthening, and it leaves no bad results.

Verse 3. *Because of the savour of thy good ointments thy name is as ointment poured forth, therefore do the virgins love thee.*

The spouse surveys all the attributes of Christ, and she compares them with separate and precious ointments. Christ is anointed as Prophet, Priest and King, and, in each of these anointings, he is a source of sweetness and fragrance to his people. But as if jealous of herself for having talked of the "ointments" when she should have spoken of him, she seems to say, "Your very name is as an alabaster box when it is opened, and the odour of the precious spikenard fills the room."

Jesus, the very thought of thee
With sweetness fills my breast.

(Bernard of Clairvaux)

"Thy name is as ointment poured forth", and the spouse adds, as a note of commendation, "Therefore do the virgins love thee."

4. *Draw me, we will run after thee:*

She feels, perhaps, as you do now, beloved brethren, heavy of heart. She cannot fly, nor go to reach her Lord; but her heart longs after him, so she cries, "Draw me, we will run after thee." While she prays the prayer, others feel it suitable to them also, so they join

5

with her. When Christ draws us, we do not walk*, but "run" after him. There is no heavy going then. When Christ draws us, how swiftly we fly, as the dove to the dovecote, when Jesu's grace entices us.

Running soon brings the spouse to her Lord; for notice the next clause —

4. *The king hath brought me into his chambers.*

It is done: "The King hath brought me into his chambers." Come to him in prayer, and perhaps, while you are yet speaking, he will hear; while you are musing, the fire will burn, and you will be able to say, "Yes, he has brought me near to himself, to the retired chamber where I may be alone with him, to the chamber of riches and delights, where I may feast with him."

4. *We will be glad and rejoice in thee,*

This is the sure result of getting into the inner chamber with Christ.

4. *We will remember thy love more than wine: the upright love thee.*
Not only the just in heart, those pure and lowly ones who, wherever the Lamb leads, from his footsteps they ne'er depart, but the upright, those who love moral excellence and virtue, they must love Christ. Now the singer's note changes:

5. *I am black,*

Ah, my soul, how true is that of you! "I am black" —

5. *But comely.*

Oh, glorious faith that can, through the blackness, still see the comeliness! We are comely when covered with the righteousness of Christ, though black in ourselves. "I am black, but comely".

5. *O ye daughters of Jerusalem, as the tents of Kedar,* smoke-dried, foul, filthy, poverty-stricken.

5. *As the curtains of Solomon.*

Bedecked with embroidery made with gold and silver threads, and fit for a king's tent, so strangely mixed is the nature of the believer: "black but comely", "as the tents of Kedar, as the curtains of Solomon."

6. *Look not upon me, because I am black, because the sun hath looked upon me.*

Perhaps you are afraid, beloved, that the Master should look at you, for you feel yourself so unworthy.

6. *My mother's children were angry with me.*

You have been persecuted until your spirit is broken.

6. *They made me the keeper of the vineyards.*

6

Perhaps you have been put to some ignoble work; you have toiled under the whip of the law; but you have a worse sorrow even than this, for you have to add —

6. *But mine own vineyard have I not kept.*

The Scriptures

You are conscious that you are restrained in prayer, and that you have neglected searching (the Word,) and that you have not lived as near to God as you ought; and all this seems to make you feel as if you could not come into close communion with Christ. Come, my brother, my sister, shake off your unbelief; may the Master shake it off from you! Then once again you can change the note, as the spouse does here —

7. *Tell me, O thou whom my soul loveth, where thou feedest, where thou makest thy flock to rest at noon: for why should I be as one that turneth aside by the flocks of thy companions?*

There are other shepherds, though they are false ones, and these pretend to be companions of Christ. But why should we turn aside to them? And yet we shall, O our Beloved One, unless you tell us where to follow you, and how to abide close by your side, or tell us where you make your flock rest at noon! Here comes the answer —

8. *If thou know not, O thou fairest among women.*

Just note that; she said that she was black, but Christ says that she is the fairest among women; in fact, there is a passage in the Song where he twice over calls her fair:

Lo! thou art fair, lo! thou art fair,
Twice fair art thou, I say;
My grace, my righteousness becomes
Thy doubly-bright array.

(Ralph Erskine)

O you faithful ones, what joy is contained in this encomium which your Lord gives to you!" If you do not know, O fairest among women,

8. *Go thy way forth by the footsteps of the flock, and feed thy kids beside the shepherds' tents.*
There are two ways of finding Christ. First, follow after true believers; most of you know some experienced Christians, so follow their footsteps and you will find their God. Or else, go to the shepherds' tents; wait on the ministry of the Word, for the Lord is often pleased to manifest himself to his people when they are willing to hear what messages he sends through his ambassadors.

9. *I have compared thee, O my love, to a company of horses in Pharaoh's chariots.*

True believers are as strong, as noble, and as beautiful as the horses in Pharaoh's chariot, which were renowned throughout all the world. Let us be like those horses, let us all pull together, let us draw the great chariot of our King behind us, let us be content to wear his harness, that we may be partakers of his splendid triumph.

10. *Thy cheeks are comely with rows of jewels, thy neck with chains of gold.*
Christ here praises his Church. Orientals were in the habit of wearing jewels in such abundance that their cheeks were covered with them, and then they multiplied the chains of gold around their necks; and the graces which Christ gives to his people, and especially

Trinity

the various parts of his own finished work, become to them like rows of jewels and chains of gold.

11. *We will make thee borders of gold with studs of silver.*

Jesus

As if Father, Son, and Holy Spirit all work together to make the believer perfectly beautiful.

12-13. *While the king sitteth at his table, my spikenard sendeth forth the smell thereof. A bundle of myrrh is my well-beloved unto me.*

Not a sprig, mark you, but a bundle of myrrh.

13. *He shall lie all night betwixt my breasts.*

Christ, as a bundle of myrrh, shall always be near our hearts, so that every life-pulse shall come from him.

14. *My beloved is unto me as a cluster of camphire in the vineyards of Engedi.*

He is not, I say again, one sprig or spray of camphire, but a cluster of it. The spouse, you see, multiplies figures to describe her Bridegroom; and even when she has done so, she cannot reach the height of his glory.

Nor earth, nor seas, nor sun, nor stars,
Nor heaven, his full resemblance bears;
His beauties we can never trace,
Till we behold him face to face.

(Isaac Watts)

16. *Behold, thou art fair, my love; behold, thou art fair; thou hast doves' eyes.*
So Christ speaks of his Church; she has the soft, mild, tender eyes of a dove. Besides, she has the discerning eye by which the dove can distinguish between carrion and fit food; and then she has a clear eye like that of the dove. You know that the dove, or pigeon, when it is taken far away from home, and wants to reach its cote, flies round and round till it gets up high, and then it looks for miles, perhaps for hundreds of miles, till it tracks with unerring eye its own resting-place, or some familiar landmark, and then, with cutting wing, it flies through the air till it reaches its home. So, every believer should have doves' eyes — eyes that can see from earth to heaven, and see Christ in his glory, even when his cause is disowned by men.

16-17. *Behold, thou art fair, my beloved, yea, pleasant: also our bed is green. The beams of our house are cedar, and our rafters of fir.*

We have the word "rafters" here, but it should be "galleries." The "bed" expresses the near fellowship which Christ has with his people. The "house" is a larger expression, and perhaps denotes the whole Church; and the "galleries" signify the ordinances of grace. You notice that these are made of unrotting wood, the one of cedar and the other of fir; and truly, dear friends, in closing our reading, we can say of our Lord, as did Isaac Watts in his adaption of the Song of Solomon 1:2-5, 12-13, 17:

Let him embrace my soul, and prove
Mine interest in his heavenly love:
The voice that tells me, "Thou art mine"

8

Exceeds the blessings of the vine.

Jesus, allure me by thy charms,
My soul shall fly into thine arms,
Our wandering feet thy favours bring
To the fair chambers of the King.

Though in ourselves deformed we are,
And black as Kedar tent appear,
Yet when we put thy beauties on,
Fair as the courts of Solomon.

While at his table sits the King,
He loves to see us smile and sing;
Our graces are our best perfume,
And breathe like spikenard round the room.

As myrrh new bleeding from the tree,
Such is a dying Christ to me;
And while he makes my soul his guest,
My bosom, Lord, shall be thy rest.

No beams of cedar or of fir
Can with thy courts on earth compare;
And here we wait until thy love
Raise us to nobler seats above.

2. BETTER THAN WINE
NO. 2459

A SERMON AT THE METROPOLITAN TABERNACLE, NEWINGTON ,
ON LORD'S-DAY EVENING, JUNE 2ND, 1872

"Thy love is better than wine." (Song of Solomon 1:2)

THE Scriptural emblem of wine, which is intended to be the symbol of the richest earthly joy, has become desecrated in process of time by the sin of man. I suppose, in the earlier ages when the Word of God was written, it would hardly have been conceivable that there could have existed on the face of the earth such a mass of drunken men and women as now pollute and defile it by their very presence. Nowadays, man is not content with the wine that God makes, but he manufactures some for himself of which he cannot partake, at least in any abundance, without becoming drunk. Redeem the figure in our text if you can, and go back from the drinking customs of our own day to more primitive and purer times, when the ordinary meal of a man was very similar to that which is spread upon this communion table — bread and wine — of which men might partake without fear of evil effects; but do not use the metaphor as it would now be understood amongst the mass of mankind, at least in countries like our own.

"Thy love is better than wine." In considering these words in the spirit in which the inspired writer used them, I shall try, first of all, to show you that *Christ's love is better than wine because of what it is not*; and, secondly, that *it is better than wine because of what it is*. Next, we will examine the marginal reading of the text, which teaches us something about *Christ's love in the plural*: "Thy loves are better than wine." And then, lastly, we will come back to the version we have before us, in which we shall see *Christ's love in the singular*, for the love of Christ, even when it is put in the plural, is always one. Though there are many forms of it, it is evermore the same love.

I. First, then, I want to prove to you that CHRIST'S LOVE IS BETTER THAN WINE BECAUSE OF WHAT IT IS NOT.

It is so, firstly, *because it can be taken without question*. There may be, and there always will be in the world, questions about wine. There are some who will say — and wisely say — "Let it alone." There are others who will exclaim, "Drink of it abundantly"; while a third company will say, "Use it moderately". But there is no question among upright men about partaking to the full of the love of Christ. There will be none of the godly who will say, "Abstain from it"; and none who will say, "Use it moderately"; but all true Christians will choose the words of the Heavenly Bridegroom himself: "Drink, yea, drink abundantly, O beloved." (Song 5:1) The wisdom of imbibing freely of the love of Christ shall never be questioned even by the pure spirits in heaven; this is the wine which they themselves quaff in everlasting bowls at the right hand of God, and the Lord of glory himself bids them drink it to the full. This is the highest delight of all who know Christ, and have been born again by the regenerating power of the Holy Spirit. This is our greatest joy while here below, and we can never have too much of it. Yes, we may even swim in this sea of bliss, and there will be none who dare to ask any one of us, as they did Elijah, "What doest thou here?" (1 Kings 19:9, 13) Many delightful things, many earthly joys, many of the pleasures of this world, are very questionable enjoyments. Christians had better keep away from everything about which their consciences are not perfectly clear; but all our consciences are clear concerning the Lord Jesus and our heart's love for him; so that, in this respect, his love is better than wine.

Christ's love is also better than wine *because it is to be had without money*. Many a man has beggared himself, and squandered his estate, through his love of worldly pleasure, and especially his fondness for wine; but the love of Christ is to be had without money. What does the Scripture say? "Come, buy wine and milk without money and without price." (Is. 55:1) The love of Christ is unpurchased; and I may add that it is unpurchasable. Solomon says, in this book, "If a man would give all the substance of his house for love, it would utterly be contemned [despised]" (Song 8:7), and we may as truly say, "If a man would give all the substance of his house for the love of Christ, it would be utterly contemned." The love of Jesus comes to his people freely, not because they deserve it, or ever will deserve it; not because, by any merits of their own, they have won it, or by any prayers of their own, they have secured it. It is a spontaneous love; it flows from the heart of Christ because it must come like a stream that leaps from an ever-flowing fountain. If you ask why Jesus loves his people, we can give no other reason than this: "Because it seemed good in his sight." (Lk. 10:21)

Christ's love is the freest thing in the world — free as the sunbeam, free as the mountain torrent, free as the air. It comes to the child of God without purchase and without merit; and in this respect it is better than wine.

Again, Christ's love is better than wine *because it is to be enjoyed without cloying*. The sweetest matter on earth, which is for a while pleasant to the taste, sooner or later cloys upon the palate. If you find honey, you cannot soon eat too much of it, because you will no longer relish its sweetness. But the love of Jesus never yet cloyed upon the palate of a new-born soul. He who has had most of Christ's love cries, "More! More! More!" If ever there was a man on earth who had Christ's love in him to the full, it was holy Samuel Rutherford; yet you can see in his letters how he laboured for suitable expressions while trying to set forth his hungering and thirsting after the love of Christ. He says he floated upon Christ's love like a ship on a river, and then he quaintly asks that his vessel may founder, and go to the bottom, till that blessed stream shall flow right over the masthead of his ship. He wanted to be baptised into the love of Christ, and flung into the ocean of his Saviour's love; and this is what the true Christian ever longs for. No lover of the Lord Jesus has ever said that he has had enough of Christ's love. After Madame Guyon [Jeanne Marie B. de la Mothe] had spent many a day and many a month in the sweet enjoyment of the love of Jesus, she penned most delicious hymns concerning it; but they are all full of craving after more, and there is no indication that she wished for any change of affection to her Lord, or any change in the object of her affection. She was satisfied with Christ, and longed to have more and more of his love. Ah, you poor drunkard! You may put away the cup of devils because you are satiated with its deadly draught; but never did he who drinks of the wine of Christ's love become satiated or even content with it; he ever desires more and yet more of it.

Further, Christ's love is better than wine *because it is without lees*. All wine has something in it which renders it imperfect and liable to corruption; there is something that will have to settle, something that must be skimmed off the top, something that needs refining down. So is it with all the joys of earth; there is sure to be something in them that mars their perfection. Men have sought out many inventions of mirth and pleasure, amusement and delight, but they have always found some hitch or flaw somewhere. Solomon gathered to himself all manner of pleasant things that are the delight of kings; and he gives us a list of them in the Book of Ecclesiastes (2:4-8):

"I made me great works; I builded me houses; I planted me vineyards: I made me gardens and orchards, and I planted trees in them of all kind of fruits: I made me pools of water, to water therewith the wood that bringeth forth trees: I got me servants and maidens, and had servants born in my house; also I had great possessions of great and

11

small cattle above all that were in Jerusalem before me: I gathered me also silver and gold, and the peculiar treasure of rings and of the provinces: I got me men singers and women singers, and the delights of the sons of men, as musical instruments, and that of all sorts."

But his verdict concerning all of them was, "Behold, all was vanity and vexation of spirit." (2:11) But he who delights himself in the love of Christ will tell you that he finds no vanity and vexation of spirit there, but everything to charm and rejoice and satisfy the heart. There is nothing in the Lord Jesus Christ that we could wish to have taken away from him; there is nothing in his love that is impure, nothing that is unsatisfactory. Our precious Lord is comparable to the most fine gold; there is no alloy in him; no, there is nothing that can be compared with him, for "He is altogether lovely" (Song 5:16), all perfections melted into one perfection, and all beauties combined into one inconceivable beauty. Such is the Lord Jesus, and such is his love for his people without anything of imperfection needing to be removed.

The love of Christ, too, blessed be his name! is better than wine *because it will never, as wine does, turn sour*. In certain stages of its development, and under certain influences, the sweet ferments, and vinegar is formed instead of wine. Oh, through what fermentations Christ's love might have passed if it had been capable of being acted upon by anything from without! Oh, how often, beloved, have we grieved him! We have been cold and chill towards him when we ought to have been like coals of fire. We have loved the things of this world, we have been unfaithful to our Best-beloved, we have suffered our hearts to wander towards other lovers; yet never has he been soured toward us, and never will be. Many waters cannot quench his love, neither can the floods drown it. He is the same loving Saviour now as ever he was, and such he always will be, and he will bring us to the rest which remains for the people of God. Truly, in all these respects, because there are none of these imperfections in his love, it is better than wine.

Once more, Christ's love is better than wine *because it produces no ill effects*. Many are the mighty men who have fallen down slain by wine. Solomon says:

"Who hath woe? who hath sorrow? who hath contentions? who hath babbling? who hath wounds without cause? who hath redness of eyes? They that tarry long at the wine; they that go to seek mixed wine." (Prov. 23:29-30)

But who was ever slain by the love of Christ? Who was ever made wretched by this love? We have been inebriated with it, for the love of Christ sometimes produces a holy exhilaration that makes men say, "Whether in the body, or out of the body, I cannot tell." (2 Cor. 12:3) There is an elevation that lifts the soul above all earthly things, and bears the spirit up beyond where eagles soar, even into the clear atmosphere where God communes with men. There is all that sacred exhilaration about the love of Christ; but there are no evil effects arising from it. Whoever will may drink from this golden chalice, and he may drink as much as he will, for the more he drinks, the stronger and better he shall be.

Oh, may God grant to us, dear friends, to know the love of Christ, which passes knowledge! I feel sure that, while I am preaching on such a theme as this, I must seem to some here present to be talking arrant nonsense, for they have never tasted of the love of Jesus. But those who have tasted of it will, perhaps, by my words, have many sweet experiences called to their minds, which will refresh their spirits, and set them longing to have new draughts of this all-precious love which infinitely transcends all the joys of earth. This, then, is our first point: Christ's love is better than wine because of what it is not.

II. But, secondly, CHRIST'S LOVE IS BETTER THAN WINE BECAUSE OF WHAT IT IS.

Let me remind you of some of the uses of wine in the East. Often, it was employed as a medicine, for *it had certain healing properties.*

The good Samaritan, when he found the wounded man, poured into his wounds "oil and wine". (Lk. 10:34) But the love of Christ is better than wine; it may not heal the wounds of the flesh, but it does heal the wounds of the spirit. Do not some of you remember when your poor heart was gashed through by the dagger of Moses, when you felt the wounds caused by the law, the deadly wounds that could not be healed by human hands? Then, how sweetly did that wine of Christ's love come streaming into the gaping wounds! There were such healing drops as this: "Come unto me, all ye that labour and are heavy laden, and I will give you rest" (Mat. 11:28); or such as this, "The blood of Jesus Christ his Son cleanseth us from all sin" (1 Jn.1:7); or this, "All manner of sin and blasphemy shall be forgiven unto men" (Mat. 12:31); or this, "He that believeth on him is not condemned" (Jn. 3:18); or this, "Look unto me, and be ye saved all the ends of the earth, for I am God, and there is none else" (Is. 45:22). I cannot, perhaps, quote the text that dropped like wine and oil into your wounds; but I remember well the text that dropped into mine. The precious vial of wine that healed up all my wounds as in a moment, and made my heart whole, was that text I quoted last, "Look unto me, and be ye saved, all the ends of the earth." Wine made by man cannot be medicine to a broken heart, nor can it heal a wounded spirit; but the love of Jesus Christ can do this, and do it to perfection.

Wine, again, was often *associated by men with the giving of strength*. Now, whatever strength wine may give or may not give, certainly the love of Jesus gives strength, and strength mightier than the mightiest earthly force; for when the love of Jesus Christ is shed abroad in a man's heart, he can bear a heavy burden of sorrow. If he could have the load of Atlas piled upon his shoulders, and if he could have all the cares of all the world pressing upon his heart, yet, if he had the love of Christ in his soul, he would be able to bear the load. The love of Christ helps a man to fight the battles of life; it makes life, with all its cares and troubles, a happy one; it enables a man to do great exploits, and makes him strong for suffering, strong for self-sacrifice, and strong for service. It is wonderful in reading the history of the saints to notice what the love of Christ fitted them to do; I might almost say that it has plucked up mountains, and cast them into the sea, for things impossible to other men have become easy enough to men on fire with the love of Christ. What the Church of Christ wants just now to strengthen her is more love to her Lord, and her Lord's love more fully enjoyed in the souls of her members; there is no strengthening influence like it.

Wine was also frequently used as a *symbol of joy*; and certainly, in this respect, Christ's love is better than wine. Whatever joy there may be in the world (and it would be folly to deny that there is some sort of joy which even the basest of men know), yet the love of Christ is far superior to it. Human joy derived from earthly sources is a muddy, dirty pool at which men would not drink did they know there is a stream sweeter, cooler, and far more refreshing. The love of Jesus brings a joy that is fit for angels, a joy that we shall have continued to us even in heaven itself, a joy which makes earth like to heaven; it is therefore far better than wine.

It is better than wine, once more, for *the sacred exhilaration which it gives*. I have already spoken of this; the love of Christ is the grandest stimulant of the renewed nature that can be known. It enables the fainting man to revive from his swooning; it causes the feeble man to leap up from his bed of languishing; and it makes the weary man strong again. Are you weary, brother, and sick of life? You only need more of Christ's love shed abroad in your heart. Are you, dear brother, ready to faint through unbelief? You only need more of

13

Christ's love, and all shall be well with you. I would to God that we were all filled with it to the full, like those believers were on the day of Pentecost, of whom the mockers said that they were full of new wine. Peter truly said that they were not drunk, as men supposed, but that it was the Spirit of God and the love of Christ filling them with unusual power and unusual energy, and therefore men did not know what it was. God grant to us also this great power, and Christ shall have all the glory of it!

III. But now passing rapidly on, for our time is flying, the marginal reading of our text is in the plural: "Thy loves are better than wine", and this teaches us that CHRIST'S LOVE MAY BE SPOKEN OF IN THE PLURAL because it manifests itself in so many ways.
I ask all renewed hearts that have been won to Jesus, the virgin souls that follow him "whithersoever he goeth" (Rev. 14:4), to walk with me in imagination over the sacred tracks of the love of Christ.

Think, beloved, of *Christ's covenant love*, the love he had for us before the world was. Christ is no new lover of his people's souls; but he loved them before the day-star knew its place, or the planets began their mighty revolutions. Every soul whom Jesus loves now, he loved forever and ever. What a wondrous love was that — infinite, unbounded, everlasting — which led him to enter into covenant with God that he would bear our sins, and suffer our penalties, that he might redeem us from going down into the pit! Oh, the covenant love of Jesus! Some dear souls are afraid to believe this truth; let me persuade them to search the Scriptures till they find it, for, of all the doctrines of Holy Writ, I know of none more full of consolation to the heart when rightly received than the great foundation truths of Divine Predestination and Personal Election. When we see that we were eternal, chosen in Christ, eternally given to Christ by his Father, eternally accepted in the Beloved, and eternally loved by Christ, then shall we say, with holy gratitude, "Such love as this is better than wines on the lees...well refined." (Is 25:6)

Think next, beloved, of *Christ's forbearing love* — the love which looked upon us when we were born, and saw us full of sin, and yet loved us — the love which saw us when we went astray from the womb speaking lies — the love which heard us speak profanely, and think wickedly, and obstinately disobey, yet loved us all the while. Let the thought of it ravish your heart as you sing:

He saw me ruined in the fall,
Yet loved me, notwithstanding all:
He saved me from my lost estate,
His loving-kindness, oh, how great!

(Samuel Medley)

Thus were we the subjects of Christ's electing love and forbearing love. Yes! But the sweetness to us was when we realised *Christ's personal love*, when at last we were brought to the foot of his cross, humbly confessing our sins. May I ask you who can go back to that happy moment? There you lay at the cross-foot, broken in pieces, and you thought there was no hope for you; but you looked up to the crucified Christ, and those blessed wounds of his began to pour out a stream of precious blood upon you, and you saw that he was wounded for your transgressions, that he was bruised for *your* iniquities, that the chastisement of your peace was upon him, and that with his stripes *you* were healed. (Is. 53:5) That very instant, your sins were all put away; you gave one look of faith to the bleeding Saviour, and every spot and speck and stain of your sin were all removed, and your guilt was forever pardoned.

14

When you first felt *Christ's forgiving love*, I will not insult you by asking whether it was not better than wine. Oh, the unutterable joy, the indescribable bliss you felt when Jesus said to you, "I have borne your sins in my own body on the tree, I have carried the great load of your transgressions, I have blotted them out like a cloud, and they are gone from you forever!" That was a love that was inconceivably precious; at the very recollection, our heart leaps within us, and our "soul doth magnify the Lord" (Lk. 1:46)

Since that glad hour, we have been the subjects of *Christ's accepting, love*, for we have been "accepted in the Beloved" (Eph. 1:6). We have also had *Christ's guiding love*, and *providing love*, and *instructing love*. His love in all manner of ways has come to us, and benefited and enriched us. And, beloved, we have had *sanctifying love*; we have been helped to fight this sin and that sin, and to overcome them by the blood of the Lamb. The Spirit of God has been given to us so that we have been enabled to subdue this ruling passion, and overcome that evil power. The Lord has also given us *sustaining love* under very sharp troubles. Some of us could tell many a story about the sweet upholding love of Christ — in poverty, or in bodily pain, or in deep depression of spirits, or under cruel slander, or reproach. His left hand has been under our head while his right hand has embraced us. We have almost courted suffering itself by reason of the richness of the consolation which suffering times have always brought with them. He has been such a precious, precious, precious Christ to us, that we do not know how to speak well enough of his dear name.

Then let us reflect with shame upon *Christ's enduring love to us*. Why, even since we have been converted, we have grieved him times without number! As I have already reminded you, we have often been false to him, we have not loved him with the love which he might well claim from us; yet Christ has never cast us away, but still to this moment he smiles upon us, his own brethren whom he has bought with blood, and to each one of us he says, "I have graven thee upon the palms of my hands. (Is. 49:16) I have espoused thee unto myself forever. I will never leave thee, nor forsake thee." He uses the most kind and endearing terms towards us to show that his love will never die away. Glory be to his holy name for this! Is not his love better than wine?

There is one word I must not leave out, and that is, *Christ's chastening love*. I know that many of you who belong to him have often smarted under his chastening hand, but Christ never smote you in anger yet. Whenever he has laid the cross on your back, it has been because he loved you so much that he could not keep it off. He never took away a joy without meaning by it to increase your joy, and it was always done for your good. Perhaps we cannot at present say that the Lord's chastising love has always been sweet to us, but we shall say it one day, and I think I must say it now. I bless my dear Master for everything he has done to me, and I can never tell all that I owe to the anvil and the hammer and the fire and the file. Blessed be his name that many of us can say, "Before I was afflicted I went astray, but now have I kept thy Word." Therefore will we put in Christ's chastising love among the rest of his loves, and say of it, "This love also is better than wine." We would sooner have the chastisements of God than the pleasures of the world; we would rather have God's cup full of gall than the devil's cup full of the sweetest wine he ever made. We prefer to take God's left hand instead of the world's right hand, and would sooner walk with God in the dark than walk with the world in the light. Will not every Christian say that?

Beloved, there are other forms of Christ's love yet to be manifested to you. Do you not sometimes tremble at the thought of dying? Oh, you shall have — and you ought to think of it now — you shall have special revelations of *Christ's love in your dying moments*. Then you shall say, like the governor of the marriage feast at Cana, "Thou hast kept the good wine until now." I believe we have hardly any conception of what comfort the Lord

15

pours into his people's souls in their dying moments. We do not need those comforts yet, and we could not bear them now; but they are laid up in store, and when we need them, they will be brought out, and then shall our spirits find that the Lord's promise is fulfilled, "As thy days, so shall thy strength be." (Deut. 33:25)

And then — but perhaps I had better be silent upon such a theme — when the veil is drawn, and the spirit has left the body, what will be the bliss of *Christ's love to the spirits gathered with him in glory?*

Oh, for the bliss of dying,
My risen Lord to meet!
Oh, for the rest of lying
Forever at His feet!

Oh, for the hour of seeing,
My Saviour face to face!
The hope of ever being
In that sweet meeting-place.

Jesus, O King of glory
I soon shall dwell with Thee
I soon shall sing the story
Of Your great love to me.

(Charitie Lees Smith)

Or, as Dr. Watts puts it,

Millions of years my wondering eyes
Shall o'er thy beauties rove;
And endless ages I'll adore
The glories of thy love.

Then think of *the love of the day of our resurrection*, for Christ loves our bodies as well as our souls; and, arrayed in glory, these mortal bodies shall rise from the tomb. Oh, the bliss of being like our Lord, and being with him when he comes in all the splendour of the Second Advent, sitting as assessors with him to judge the world, and to judge even the angels! And then to be in his triumphal procession, when he shall ascend to God, and deliver up the kingdom to the Father, and the Mediatorial system shall be ended, and God shall be all in all! And then to be forever, forever, forever, "for ever with the Lord" with no fear of the soul dying out, with no dread of the false doctrine of annihilation, like a grim spectre ever crossing our blissful pathway! With a life coeval with the life of God, and an immortality divinely given, we shall outlast the sun; and when the moon grows pale, and wanes for ever, and this old earth and all that is therein shall be burned up, yet still shall we be forever with him. Truly, his love is better than wine, it is the very essence of heaven, it is better than anything that we can conceive. God grant us foretastes of the loves of heaven in the present realisation of the love of Jesus, which is the self-same love, and through which heaven itself shall come to us!

IV. Now I must have just a few minutes for my last point, and that is, CHRIST'S LOVE IN THE SINGULAR — a theme which might well suffice for half a dozen sermons at the very least. Look at the text as it stands: "Thy love is better than wine."

Think, first, of *the love of Christ in the cluster*. That is where the wine is first. We talk of the grapes of Eshcol; but these are not worthy to be mentioned in comparison with the love of Jesus Christ as it is seen, in old eternity, in the purpose of God, in the covenant of grace, and afterwards, in the promises of the Word, and in the various revelations of Christ in the types and symbols of the ceremonial law. There I see the love of Christ in the cluster. When I hear God threatening the serpent that the seed of the woman should bruise his head, and when, later on, I find many prophecies concerning him who is mighty to save, I see the wine in the cluster, the love of Christ that is really there, but not yet enjoyed. What delight it gives us even to look at the love of Christ in the cluster!

Next, look at *the love of Christ in the basket*, for the grapes must be gathered and cast into the basket before the wine can be made. I see Jesus Christ living here on earth amongst the sons of men — gathered, as it were, from the sacred vine, and like a cluster thrown into the basket. Oh, the love of Jesus Christ in the manger of Bethlehem, the love of Jesus in the workshop of Nazareth, the love of Jesus in his holy ministry, the love of Jesus in the temptation in the wilderness, the love of Jesus in his miracles, the love of Jesus in his communion with his disciples, the love of Jesus in bearing shame and reproach for our sakes, the love of Jesus in being so poor that he had not where to lay his head, the love of Jesus in enduring such contradiction of sinners against himself! I cannot hope to enter into this great subject; I can only point it out to you, and pass on. There is, first, Christ's love in the cluster; and next, there is Christ's love in the basket. Think of it, and as you think of it, say, "It is better than wine."

But oh, if your hearts have any tenderness towards him, think of *the love of Christ in wine-press*. See him there, when the cluster in the basket begins to be crushed. Oh, what a crushing was that under the foot of the treader of grapes when Christ sweat as it were great drops of blood, and how terribly the great press came down again and again, when he gave his back to the smiters, and his cheeks to them that plucked off the hair, and did not hide his face from shame and spitting! But oh, how the red wine flowed from the wine-press, what fountains there were of this precious sweetness, when Jesus was nailed to the cross, suffering in body, depressed in spirit, and forsaken by his God! "Eloi, Eloi, lama sabachthani?" (Mk. 15:34) These were the sounds that issued from the wine-press, and how terrible and yet how sweet they are! Stand there, and believe that all your sins were borne by him, and that he suffered what you ought to have suffered, and, as your Substitute, was crushed for you:

O thou who didst thy glory leave
Apostate sinners to retrieve
From Adam's deadly fall,
Me thou hast purchased with a price,
Nor shall my crimes in judgment rise,
For Thou hast borne them all.

Jesus was punished in my stead,
Without the gate my Surety bled
To expiate my sin:
On earth the Godhead deigned to dwell,
And made of infinite avail
The sufferings of the Man.

And was He for such rebels given?
He was; the incarnate King of heaven
Did for His foes expire:
Amazed, O earth, the tidings hear;

17

He bore that we might never bear
His Father's righteous ire.

Ye saints, the Man of Sorrows bless,
The God for your unrighteousness
Appointed to atone:
Praise Him, till with the heavenly throng,
Ye sing the never ending song,
And see Him on His throne.

(Augustus Montague Toplady)

Yes, beloved, Christ's love in the wine-press is better than wine.

Now I want you to think of *the love of Christ in the flagon*, where his precious love is stored up for his people — the love of his promises, given to you; the love of his providence, for he rules for you; the love of his intercession, for he pleads for you; the love of his representation, for he stands at the right hand of the Father as the Representative of his people; the love of his union with his people, for you are one with him, he is the Head, and you are the members of his body; the love of all that he is, and all that he was, and all that he ever shall be, for in every capacity and under all circumstances he loves you, and will love you without end. Think of his rich love, his abundant love towards his people. I call it love in the flagon, this love of his to all the saints which he has stored up for them.

And then, beloved, not only think of, but enjoy, *the love of Christ in the cup*, by which I mean his love to *you*. I always feel, when I get to this topic, as if I would rather sit down, and ask you to think it over, than try to talk to you about it; this theme seems to silence me. I think it is like the poet James Thomson says:

Come, then, expressive silence, muse his praise.

Love to *me*! Dear child of God, do think of it in this way; let me speak for you. "He loves *me*! He, a King, loves me! A King? The King of kings, HE loves *me*! God, very God of very God, loves me!" Strange conjunction this between the Infinite and a worm! We have heard and read romantic stories of the loves of emperors to poor village maidens, but what of these? Worms were never raised so high above their meaner fellow-worms as the Lord Jesus is above us. If an angel loved an emmet [ant], there would be no such difference as when Jehovah-Jesus loves us. Yet there is no fact beneath heaven, or in heaven, that is so indisputable as this fact, that he loves us if we are his believing people. For this, we have the declaration of inspiration; no, brethren, we have more even than that to confirm it beyond all question, for we have his own death upon the cross. He signed this document with his own blood in order that no believer might ever doubt its authenticity. "Herein is love." "Behold what manner of love" there is in the cross! What wondrous love is there! Oh, then, let us have Christ's love in the cup, the love that we may daily drink, the love that we may personally drink just now at this moment, the love which shall be all our own, as if there were no others in the world, and yet a love in which ten thousand times ten thousand have an equal share with ourselves.

God bless you, dear friends, and give you to drink of this wine! And if any here do not know the love of Jesus Christ, I pray the Lord to bring them to know it. May he renew their heart, and give them faith in him, for whosoever believes that Jesus is the Christ is born of God. "He that believeth on him is not condemned." (Jn. 3:18) His great gospel word is, "He that believeth and is baptized shall be saved." (Mk. 16:16) May the Lord confirm this word by his Spirit for our Lord Jesus Christ's sake! Amen.

18

3. THE MEMORY OF CHRIST'S LOVE

NO. 2294

AT THE METROPOLITAN TABERNACLE, NEWINGTON
ON LORD'S-DAY EVENING, NOV. 2ND, 1890
AT AN EVENING COMMUNION SERVICE

"We will remember thy love more than wine: the upright love thee."
(Song of Solomon 1:4)

I DO not think I can preach tonight; I feel so weary, and worn, and ill. Still, I can talk to you a little concerning the great love of Christ. If I were dying, I think I could speak upon that theme; and oh, when we rise again, how we shall talk forever and ever about Christ's love! This will be our endless theme throughout the eternal ages, "His great love wherewith he loved us, even when we were dead in sins." (Eph. 2:5)

I have taken for a text the last two sentences in the Song of Solomon, the first chapter, and the fourth verse: "We will remember thy love more than wine: the upright love thee."

This is a night for remembering Christ's love. The communion-table spread before us, the sacred feast to which we are about to come, is meant to recall to our minds our Saviour's words, "This do in remembrance of me...This do ye, as oft as ye drink it, in remembrance of me." (1 Cor. 11:25) But, while we remember Christ, the central thought in our minds shall be that of which Paul wrote, "...who loved me, and gave himself for me." (Gal. 2:20) We will, above all things else tonight, remember his love. Have any of you been forgetting it?

Is it long since you had an hour's real enjoyment in meditating upon the love of Christ? Then, beloved, come tonight, and renew your vows; begin again your fellowship; and make this firm a resolve, "We will remember our Lord; we will remember his love tonight!" May the Holy Spirit, who brings everything to remembrance whatever Christ has said to us (Jn. 14:26), help us now to remember him! For him to remember us, when he comes to his kingdom, will be our heaven. For us to remember him, though he has gone away to his kingdom, shall be a little heaven to us tonight.

As I am able, I will talk to you briefly, first, upon the preparations for the holy memory mentioned in our text. We shall find them in the verse in which the text is embedded: "Draw me, we will run after thee: the king hath brought me into his chambers: we will be glad and rejoice in thee." When we have considered the preparations for the holy memory here referred to, I will speak on the divine subject of this holy memory: "We will remember thy love more than wine." Then, thirdly, we will meditate upon the divine product of this holy memory: "The upright love thee, love thee because they remember thy love.

I. First, then, dear friends, as I may be helped by the Holy Spirit, I would remind you of THE PREPARATIONS FOR THIS HOLY MEMORY. Here they are.

The first word is, "Draw me." Lord, I would fain come to you; but, like Mephibosheth, I am lame in both my feet. I would fain fly to you, but my wings are broken; if, indeed, I ever had any. I cannot come to you. I lie inert and dead and powerless. So the first preparation is, "Draw me." It is a sweet, gracious, efficacious exercise of divine power that I need and entreat. I do not say, "Drive me", but "draw me". I do not say, "Throw me there, or force me yonder", but, "Lord, draw me. Whilst thou dost draw, I shall have liberty left to run: draw me, we will run after thee."

19

We do not need to be born again; we who are believers in Christ have had that miracle wrought in us already. We are not asking now for pardon and justification; as believers in Christ, we have these priceless boons already. What we want is the gentle influence of the Holy Spirit to attract us nearer to Christ; so each one cries to the Lord, "Draw me". We are not dead; we are quickened and made alive. Our very pain and anguish, because we are not able to come to Christ as we would, prove that we are alive. I commend this prayer to you, "Lord, draw me; draw me." It is the work of Christ to draw. "I, if I be lifted up from the earth, will draw all men unto me." (Jn. 12:32) It is the work of the Father. "No man can come to me," said Christ, "except the Father which hath sent me draw him." (Jn. 6:44) It is the work of the Spirit of God to draw a soul towards Christ. I pray this for myself, and I trust that you will pray with me, "Come, Sacred Spirit, and draw us nearer to Christ; enliven our hopes; incline our hearts; arouse our desires; and then help us to yield our whole being to your gracious influences!"

If thou hast drawn a thousand times,
Oh, draw me, Lord, again!
Around me cast Thy Spirit's bands,
And all my powers constrain!

(Benjamin Beddome)

That, then, is the first preparation for the holy memory mentioned in our text — divine drawing: "Draw me."

Notice, next, that this verse says, "Draw me, we will run after thee." I like the change in the pronouns, as though I should pray tonight, "Lord, draw me; I am the most weighted, the heaviest of all your children in this congregation; but draw me, we will run after you. All my brothers and sisters will run at once if you draw me. If you draw the most burdened one towards yourself, all the rest will come to you at a rapid rate." Do you not feel, my dear brother or sister, as if you could use this expression? Lord, if you will draw me, all my fellow-members will be running with me; yet they will not outstrip me in their eagerness to reach you, for we will together run after you. Therefore, draw me, my gracious Lord!

If we would be fully prepared to remember Christ, we must get into this running pace: "Draw me: we will run after thee." Be quick, my soul, be quick about heavenly things! Creep, if you will, about your worldly business; but run after thy Lord. Oh, that we all might attain the running pace tonight! Oh, that we might speed along towards our Lord with that strong, impetuous desire which will not let us rest till we are close to him: "Draw me, we will run after you."

Divine drawing is the first preparation for the holy memory; then next comes speedy running.

Now, in the further preparation, if you read the verse through, you will find that an answer comes to the prayer directly it is uttered: "The king hath brought me into his chambers." Then what I asked for, I have obtained at once; and I have received more than I asked for. I prayed, "Draw me", and he has carried me bodily. "The king hath brought me into his chambers." I did but pray that I might come a little nearer to my Lord; but he has brought me into his secret places, into his withdrawing rooms. He has brought me where he brings his bride. He has brought me where he receives his courtiers. The King has brought me into his chambers; and now I see how truly royal he is. The King has done it. *The* King, not a king; but that King, who is King of all kings, the most royal of all monarchs, "the Prince of the kings of the earth" (Rev. 1:5), even my Lord Jesus "hath brought me into his chambers."

20

How quickly this was done! I want you to believe, beloved, that it could be done just as quickly in your case. Pray, "Lord, draw me. I feel as if I were coming to the communion-table quite unfit to come." Is that what you say? Then pray, "Draw me", and in a moment, before the prayer is uttered, you shall find yourself not only drawn, but actually brought into the secret place of fellowship. "The king hath brought me into his chambers." "Or ever I was aware, my soul made me like the chariots of Amminadab." (Song 6:12) I know, and some of you know, unhappily, what it is to feel very cold and lifeless; but I also know, and some of you know, what it is to become full of life, full of love, full of joy, full of heavenly rapture, in a single moment. You who could only creep begin to run. You who could only sigh begin to sing. I want it to be so with every one of you, dearly beloved, tonight. And you, who think you are forgotten, shall be remembered tonight, at any rate. You who have almost forgotten what a real, hallowed time of communion means, may learn it over again tonight, as you cry, "Draw me, we will run after thee: the king hath brought me into his chambers."

Thus we have had three preparations for the holy memory mentioned in our text: drawing, running, and bringing.

There is only one more preparation for remembering Christ, and that is to feel gladness and joy in him: "We will be glad and rejoice in thee." Come, take those ashes from your head, you who are sighing by reason of affliction! Come, unbind that sackcloth, and throw it aside, you who have lost fellowship with God, and are consequently in the dark! Christ is yours if you believe in him. He has given himself to you, and he loves you. Rejoice in that blessed fact.

Remember who he is, and what he is: very God of very God, yet perfect man, God in human nature, Immanuel, God with us, glorified now in the highest heavens, though once, for our sakes, he sank down into the very depths of death and the grave. Bless his dear name. Be glad and rejoice in him.

Now, I pray you, let your mouth be filled with laughter, your tongue with singing, and your heart with holy ecstasy, as you think of who your Well-beloved is, how great he is, and what greatness he puts upon you by virtue of his union with you. We cannot very well remember Christ as we should while we carry about with us a heavy heart. Come, sad spirit, be glad in the Lord! "Rejoice in the Lord alway: and again I say, Rejoice." (Phil. 4:4) If ever a human soul had reason to rejoice, it must be the soul that believes in Christ. If ever there were any of the sons of Adam who had cause to be glad, and to clap their hands with holy mirth, it is the men who have found Christ to be their salvation, and their all in all.

These, then, are the preparations for the holy memory of which our text speaks. If they be well made, you will have no difficulty in remembering Christ's love tonight.

II. So now, in the second place, as I may be strengthened, I would like to speak about THE DIVINE SUBJECT OF THIS HOLY MEMORY: "We will remember thy love."

First, we will remember the fact of Christ's love. What a wonderful thing it is that the Son of God should love us! I do not wonder so much that he should have any love for you; but I am lost in wonder at the fact that he has any love for me, even for me. Does not each believer feel that the wonder of wonders must ever be that the Lord Jesus Christ loves him? He was in glory, wanting nothing. He was in his Father's bosom, enjoying ineffable delight. If he wanted to cast his eyes of love on any of his creatures, there were myriads of bright spirits before the throne. But, no, he must look down, down, down, to earth's dunghills, and find out us who were utterly unworthy of his regard. Then he might have

21

pitied us, and left us in our lost estate; but it could not be so with one who has such a heart as our dear Saviour has; he must needs love us. What it is for God to love, God only knows. We faintly guess, by the love that burns in our bosom towards the objects of our affection, what the love of God must be. The love of God must be a mighty passion. I use the word because I know no better; I am conscious that it is not the right one, for human language is too feeble to describe divine love.

Stronger his love than death or hell;
Its riches are unsearchable:
The first-born sons of light
Desire in vain its depths to see;
They cannot reach the mystery
The length, and breadth, and height.

(Charles Wesley)

Oh, the love of Christ! It must ever be the wonder of wonders that Jesus Christ, the darling of the heavens, should have set the eyes of his affection upon men of mortal mould, on sinful men, on me! That, to me, is the climax. We will remember the fact of Christ's love.

But we will remember, also, the character of Christ's love. What a love it was! He loved us before the foundation of the world. With the telescope of his prescience, he foresaw our existence, and he loved us when we had no being. Then he struck hands with the great Father, and entered into covenant on our behalf, and engaged that he would stand sponsor for us, and redeem us from the ruin of our sin. Oh, the love, the love, the everlasting love of Christ! He has never left off loving us from the very first. All through the ages before the world was, and through the centuries in which the world has existed, he has loved his chosen every moment, and loved them to the full. Can you drink in the sweetness of that thought? Oh, I pray you, remember the antiquity and the constancy of the love of Christ to his people! "We will remember thy love."

It was unmerited love, which had no reason in us for it to light upon.

What was there in you that could merit esteem,
Or give the Creator delight?
'Twas even so, Father', you ever must sing,
Because it seemed good in thy sight.'

(Richard Keen)

He loved us because he would love us. It was the sovereignty of his love that made him love those whom he chose to love. He loved them freely, without anything in them, or that would ever be done by them, to deserve his love. But he loved fully as well as freely; he loved intensely, divinely, immeasurably. You know your love for your child; yet it is but a feeble spark compared with the great sun of Christ's love to you. You know your love for your husband; yet it is a tiny rill compared with the ocean of Christ's love to his people. Beloved, turn over the wondrous qualities of the love of Christ to you, and say, as you sit at the communion-table tonight, "We will remember your love, for we cannot forget it. We will remember your love, for the joyous theme forces itself upon us. We will remember your love more than wine."

We will also remember the deeds of Christ's love. It is a grand story; but I cannot stay to tell it to you tonight. You know how, in the fullness of time, the Son of God came out of the glory, and alighted on a stall where the horned oxen fed. He who had made all worlds was hanging at a woman's breast, for he was made flesh that he might save us from our sins. "Herein is love!" (1 Jn. 4:10) See him living a laborious life, going about doing good, despised, maligned, yet ever ready to give still greater grace and mercy to the unworthy. You know his life, the wondrous life of Christ. "Herein is love." At last, he gave himself up in agony even to a bloody sweat. He gave his back to the smiters, and his cheeks to them that plucked off the hair; he hid not his face from shame and spitting. And then he gave himself, his hands to the nails, his feet to the cross and the cruel iron, his side to the lance, his body to the tomb, his soul to depart to his Father. "Herein is love." I wish I could preach upon this theme as it deserves to be proclaimed. Oh, that I knew how to speak of the dying love of Christ! The angels desire to look into the mystery of the love of Jesus; but even they cannot compass its immeasurable height and depth and length and breadth. Will not each of us, who are the objects of it, remember his dying love?

When to the cross I turn mine eyes,
And rest on Calvary
O Lamb of God! my sacrifice!
I must remember thee.

Remember thee, and all thy pains,
And all thy love to me;
Yea, while a breath, a pulse remains,
Will I remember thee!

(James Montgomery)

But Jesus rose from the grave. He rose with the same love; he ascended with the same love; he lives with the same love, pleading for us. He loves us now; and he will come for us in love. Love shall give him wings to fly down to earth again. He will reign here; but not without his people. "The Lord of hosts shall reign in mount Zion, and in Jerusalem, and before his ancients gloriously." (Is. 24:23) He will reign forever in love. Evermore, throughout the life to come, and the ages that shall never end, Christ will rest in his love; he will rejoice over his people with joy, he will joy over them with singing. He will also give them to share his glory, and to sit upon his throne, and to reign with him forever and ever.

Oh, what a theme is this, the deeds of Christ's love! In trying to talk of it, I feel like a poor schoolboy standing here, speaking on a subject he loves. Oh, that there were a Milton, or someone of Miltonic calibre, to tell out the story of this great love of Christ! Yet, maybe, the theme is better with my poor description than it would be with the loftiest words of men because you are more likely to forget the description, and remember the love that cannot be described; whereas, had my discourse been filled with lofty and worthy diction, you might have forgotten the theme and remembered the speaker.

I would like you, brothers and sisters, tonight, to remember the proofs of Christ's love. You were far off, but he sought you, and brought you back. You were deaf, but he called you, and opened your ear to hear his loving call. You came trembling and afraid, but he cheered you; and in a moment he took your burden from you and set you free. Do you remember it?

Dost mind the place, the spot of ground,
Where Jesus did thee meet?

(Ralph Erskine)

23

I remember, tonight, the place where first I saw the Lord; I know it to a yard. Some of you cannot speak as definitely as that, and you need not blush because you cannot. Did Jesus come to you? Did he forgive your sins? Did he comfort you with his love? Then remember it tonight. Never mind about dates and places; but remember his love.

Since Jesus first came to you, and saved you, many a time you have been in trouble, and he has comforted you. You have been in labour, and he has sustained you. You have been in disrepute, but he has honoured you. Alas, you have proved yourself unworthy of his love; but he has forgiven your backslidings. You have wandered from him, but he has restored you. Remember his great love.

No word of mine will, I fear, help you much; but let your memory begin to run over the pages of your diary. Turn over the leaves that record your Lord's favour to you. Are there not some pages with great crosses upon them which you made in the day of trouble, and other crosses which you made in the hour of your deliverance when Jesus came to your relief? Oh, remember his love, remember his love more than wine!

I will not detain you on this point any longer; although there was much more I wanted to say. Only, brothers and sisters, if I cannot talk to you, do the thing that we are thinking about. Do remember Christ and his great love. Do now, before you partake of the emblems of his broken body and his shed blood, get to him. You may forget everything else if you like; but I charge you remember Christ's love. There, fling overboard every other recollection, however precious! Let the golden ingots go; but hold you fast to the true lading of the ship, her real cargo, the love with which Christ has loved us. Do remember that, and sit still, and enjoy the blessed memory.

Before I come to the last division of my subject, I should like to ask whether there are any here who cannot remember Christ's love because they never knew it. Is that your case, my dear friend, over yonder? Let me remind you of the lepers of whom we have been reading, and then let me recall to your minds God's ancient law concerning the man suffering from leprosy. When he was brought for the high priest to examine him, the high priest looked him up and down, from the crown of his head to the sole of his foot, and said to the leper, "Here is a place still on your breast where thy flesh is perfectly clean"; and the leper said, "Yes, I am pleased to see that it is so." But the high priest replied, "You are unclean, you must not go into the house of the Lord, or associate with the people." Then there came another, and he searched him all over, and said, "Here, upon this part of your leg, there is a sound place still." Said the other, "Yes, I have often thought what a good sign it was." Said the high priest, "You also are unclean. Go to your separate house, and abide there." Then there came one poor man who was white all over, and the high priest said to him, "Have you any clean places?" "No, my lord, not one; examine me, and see"; and the high priest looked, and there was not a clean spot on him where you could have put a pin's point. The leprosy was all over him, he was saturated all through with the deadly virus, and foul with the loathsome disease; and there he stood, and cowered and trembled before the high priest. Then the high priest said to him, "Behold, you are clean; when you have performed the ceremony required by the law, you may go home to your house, and to the house of your God, for you are clean." There was a medical reason, I suppose, for this law; the mischief had thrown itself out, it had come out to the shin, the disease was fully developed, and would soon be removed. But, whatever may have been the medical reason, such was the law; and if I am addressing anybody here who feels, "There is nothing good about me; I am unclean, unclean, unclean, from the crown of my head to the sole of my foot; and the lowest place in hell is my desert", then, my friend, the grace of God has begun to work in you. Now that you are emptied, God will begin to fill you. Trust in the atoning sacrifice of his dear Son, and you shall have the assurance that you also are the subject of his saving grace; his love shall be shed abroad in your heart by the Holy Spirit, and you shall join with us in remembering that great love with which he has loved us.

III. The last thing upon which I have to speak to you is this, THE DIVINE PRODUCT OF THIS HOLY MEMORY: "The upright love thee."

So it seems, then, that if we remember Christ, we shall have a respect for his people. His people are the upright; and she, who speaks in the sacred Canticle, here looks round upon them and says, "The upright love you, and that commends you to me; for if those who are of a chaste spirit love you, much more should I." I think, if you feel as I do sometimes, you would be glad to be sure that you were even the least in God's house. We know the upright love Christ, and we love the upright because they do so; and we esteem Christ because the better men are, the more they think of him. Is it not so? But sometimes we are afraid we are not among the number of the chosen ones. "The upright love thee." Lord, am I one of the upright? Our hymn by Augustus Charles Thomson puts it like this, even concerning heaven:

There ye that love my Saviour sit,
There I would fain have place,
Among your thrones, or at your feet,
So I might see his face.

Would we not gladly sit at the feet of the very least of his people if we might but love Christ? They love him. I know how you look around tonight, and you say, "There sits Brother So-and-so, he loves Christ; there is Mistress So-and-so, who is so busy in the service of her Lord; she loves Christ. And that dear man [Mr. William Olney], whose death we still commemorate by these sad memorials around the pulpit, he loved Christ" "Ah, well!" you say, "I wish I loved him, too, and that I were among the upright in character, who truly admire him." Seek that blessing, dear friends, for it is to be had if you seek it aright. Seek it, for the love of Christ will make you love the upright, and foster in you an esteem for them. I do not like to hear Christian people speak ill of one another; and I do not like to hear Christian people speak ill of the Church. If Christ loves her, and is married to her, woe to you if you find fault with my Master's bride! He does not love those who do not love his chosen. Have a great love for the people of God, even the poorest of them. Count them to be the aristocrats of the world, the blood-royal of the universe, the men and women who have angels to be their servants, and who are made kings and priests unto God. If you remember Christ, you will remember his people. If you remember his love, you will feel a love towards them, God grant that you may do so!

One thing more and I have done. In remembering Christ's love as the upright do, we shall grow upright. I believe that God blesses trouble to our sanctification, and that he can bless joy to the same end; but I am sure of this, that the greatest instrument of sanctification is the love of Jesus. One asked what he should think of to make him holy, and his friend answered, "Think of death." It is wise to talk with the grave, the mattock, and the shroud; but the living love of Christ has a sanctifying power that even thoughts of death have not. One has said, "If you would grow holy, think of the punishment of sin, the pit that God has dug for the wicked. It will make you tremble at the thought of sin, and cause you to flee from it as from an arch-destroyer." This is true; but still, if you would grow in grace fast, and become holy rapidly, this is the best theme for your meditation: "We will remember thy love." If you remember Christ's love, you will be lifted up from your crookedness, and made straight, and will be put among the upright, who love the Lord.

Come, then, let us join tonight in sweet thoughts of love to Christ. The sermon is short, but the subject is long; and you have now an opportunity for coming to the communion-table,

25

and thinking out that theme which I have started for you: "The love of Christ for me, the love of Christ for me." Then follow it up with this: "Oh, my poor love to Christ!" Think, dear friends, if you remember your own love to Christ, what a small thing it is to remember. His great love is like the sun in the heavens. Your love — well, you have to put on your spectacles before you can see it; it is so small a thing. God grant it may grow tonight; and, at the communion-table, may you have such a visitation from Christ, such delightful fellowship with him, that you may be able to sing again the hymn that you were singing by young William Ralph Featherstone, when I was obliged to retire for a while from the platform:

My Jesus, I love thee, I know thou art mine,
For thee all the follies of sin I resign;
My gracious Redeemer, my Saviour, art thou,
If ever I loved thee, my Jesus, 'tis now.

I will love thee in life, I will love thee in death,
And praise thee as long as thou lendest me breath;
And say when the death-dew lies cold on my brow,
'If ever I loved thee, my Jesus, 'tis now.'

May you sing it now, and be able to sing it when the death-dew lies cold on your brow! The Lord be with you, for Jesus' sake. Amen.

4. A REFRESHING CANTICLE
NO. 2794

AT NEW PARK STREET CHAPEL, SOUTHWARK
ON A LORD'S-DAY EVENING, IN THE WINTER OF 1860

"We will remember thy love more than wine." (Song of Solomon 1:4)

THE Hebrew word for "love" here is in the plural: "We will remember thy loves." Do not think, however, that the love of Jesus is divided, but know that it has different channels of manifestation. All the affections that Christ has, he bestows upon his Church; and these are so varied that they may well be called "loves" rather than "love". The Septuagint translation is "We will remember thy breasts." Jacques-Benigne Bossuet, and many of the Romanist expositors who have brought much sanctity of thought and fervent appreciation of heart to bear upon this superlative Song, dilate very sweetly upon the word "breasts" as it appears in the Latin Vulgate. I am disposed to be content with our own Version, with the alteration of one letter: "We will remember thy loves more than wine." By this expression we must understand, of course, all the love of Jesus, from the beginning even to the end; or, rather, to that eternity which has no end. We will remember those acts of love of which we have heard with our ears, and our fathers have declared to us. It has been told us by inspired prophets, and God has revealed it to us in his Word by his Spirit, that Jesus Christ loved us from before the foundation of the world. We believe that his love is no passion of modern date — no mere spasm of pity. It is as ancient as his glory, which he had with the Father before the world was, one of the things of eternity. This love divine is not a spring that welled up only a few days ago, but it an everlasting fountain which has never ceased to flow. We will remember, O Jesus, that love of yours which was displayed in the council chamber of eternity, when, on our behalf, you interposed as the Daysman and Mediator; when you struck hands with your Father, and became our Surety, taking us as your betrothed! We will remember that love which moved you to undertake a work so burdensome to accomplish, an enterprise which none but yourself could ever have achieved. We will remember the love which suggested the sacrifice of yourself; the love which, until the fullness of time, mused over that sacrifice, and longed for the hour of which, in the volume of the Book it was written of you, "Lo, I come." (Is. 40:7; Heb. 10:7, 9) We will remember your love, O Jesus, as it was manifested to us in your holy life, from the manger of Bethlehem to the garden of Gethsemane! We will track you from the cradle to the grave, for every word and every deed of yours was love. You, wherever you walked, scattered loving-kindnesses with both hands. As it is said of your Father, "God is love" (1 Jn. 4:8, 16), so, surely, you are love, O Jesus! The fullness of the Godhead dwells in you (Col, 2:9); the essence of love, nothing else but love is your incarnate Person.

And especially, O Jesus, will we remember your love to us upon the cross! We will view you as you come from the garden of your agony, and from the hall of your flagellation [flogging]. We will gaze upon you with your hands and your feet nailed to the accursed tree. We will watch you when you could, if you had willed it, have saved yourself; but when you did, nevertheless, you give up your strength, and bow yourself downward to the grave that you might lift us up to heaven. We will remember you love which you manifested through your poor, bleeding hands and feet and side.

We will remember this love of yours till it invigorates and cheers us "more than wine" — the love of which we have heard, which you have exercised since your death, the love of your resurrection, the love which prompts you continually to intercede before your Father's throne, that burning lamp of love which will never let you hold your peace until your chosen ones are all safely housed, and Zion is glorified, and the spiritual Jerusalem is settled on her everlasting foundations of light and love in heaven. We will remember all

27

your love, from its beginning in the eternal past to the eternity that is to come; no, we will try to project our thoughts and imagination, and so to remember that, long as eternity shall continue, even forever and for evermore, so long shall your love exist in all its glory, undiminished in its lustre or its force. "We will remember thy love more than wine." Nor is this all the love we have to remember. Though we ought to recollect what we have heard, and what we have been taught, I think the spouse means more than this. "We will remember thy loves" — not only what we have been told, but what we have felt. Come, dear hearers, let each one of you speak for yourselves; or, rather, do you think of this for yourselves, and let me speak of it for you. I will remember your love, O Jesus; your love to me when I was a stranger, wandering far from God; the love which restrained me from committing deadly sin, and withheld my hand from self-destruction! I will remember the love which tracked me in my course — "When Satan's blind slave, I sported with death."

I will remember the love which held back the axe when Justice said, "Cut it down; why let it cumber the ground?" I will remember the love that took me into the wilderness, and stripped me there of all my self-righteousness, and made me feel my weight of guilt, and the burden of my iniquity. Especially will I remember the love which said to me, "Come unto me, and I will give thee rest." (Mat. 11:28) I cannot forget that matchless love which, in a moment, washed my sins away, and made my spotted soul white as the driven snow. Can you forget, my brothers and sisters, that happiest of days when Jesus first whispered to you, "I am thine, and thou art mine"? I can never forget the transporting hour when he spoke thus to me; it is as fresh in my memory now as if it had only happened this afternoon. I could sing of it if it were right to stop a sermon for a sonnet; I could sing of that love, passing all measure, which took my soul, and washed it in the precious blood of Jesus, and then clothed it in the spotless robe of his righteousness. O love divine, yours excels all other loves, that you could deal with such a rebellious, traitorous worm, and make that worm an heir of heaven! But we have more love than this to recollect — all the love that we have felt since then. I will remember the valley of Baca (Ps. 84:6) and the hill Mizar (Ps. 42:6); nor shall my soul forget those chambers of fellowship where you have unveiled yourself to me. If Moses had his cleft in the rock where he could see the back parts of his God (Ex. 33:22), we also have had our clefts in the rock, where we have seen the full splendours of the Godhead in the Person of Christ. Did David remember the tracks of the wild goat where he was hunted on the mountains — the cave of Adullam, and the land of Jordan, and of the Hermonites? We, too, can remember spots equally dear to these in blessedness. "The Lord hath appeared of old unto me, saying, Yea, I have loved thee with an everlasting love: therefore with loving-kindness have I drawn thee." (Jer. 31:3) Christian, can you not recollect the sweet exchanges there have been between yourself and your Lord, when you have left your griefs at his feet, and borne away a song? Can you not remember some happy seasons when you went to him empty and came away full? Is your heart heavy just now? It has not always been so. There have been times when, like David, you could dance before the Lord; times of holy merriment when, like Miriam, you could strike your timbrel, and say to those around you, "Sing ye to the Lord, for he hath triumphed gloriously". (Ex. 15:21) You have another, another, for he has linked his arm in yours, and walked along with you; and there have been other times when your head has been upon his bosom (Jn. 13:23), and you could feel his heart beating with warm love to thee. Thus, then, in the summary of Christ's loves, which I will now humbly endeavour to pass in review, it will be necessary for me to mention, not only the love we have heard about, but the love we have felt and enjoyed. Do not suppose, dear brothers and sisters, that I am able to refresh your memories upon this sacred subject. It is the Holy Spirit's work to assist you in that matter; but I do trust that the resolution contained in our text will be formed in the heart of every one of you, "We will remember thy loves more than wine", and that you will have the grace to carry out that resolution.

28

I. Here then, beloved, we have A RESOLUTION POSITIVELY EXPRESSED: "We will remember thy love."

Why does the spouse speak so positively? Because she is inspired; she is not like Simon Peter when he said, "Although all shall be offended, yet will not I." (Mk 14:29) She is speaking the truth, for she will not forget the love of her Lord. Why is that? For one very good reason: because she cannot. If the Church could forget Christ's love to her, she would do so. She is such a forgetful wife that all her Husband's affections would be lost upon her, were it possible. But that cannot be; there is something about the love of Christ that makes it adhere to those upon whom it is bestowed; we cannot forget it. It enters into the heart, like wine that seasons the cask, and the scent of it abides. It pervades the soul; it imbues every faculty; it brings the secret thoughts into obedience to Christ; it flows through every vein of hope and fear, passion and desire. So the spouse could truthfully say to her Lord, "We will remember thy love." The virtue was not in her constancy, but in the tenacity of his affection, therefore she could not help remembering it.

What is there in the love of Christ that will compel us to remember it? The things that we recollect best are of certain kinds.

Some that we remember best have been sublime things. When we have stood, for the first time, where we could see a lofty mountain, whose snowy summit pierced the thick ebony clouds, we have said, "We shall never forget this sight." When Alexander von Humboldt, the great traveller, had his first view of the vast prairies of North America, he declared that he could never forget the sensations of that moment. I can imagine how Dr. David Livingstone, when he first came in sight of the magnificent falls which he discovered, might well say, "To my dying day, I shall hear the rushing of that tremendous stream of water." I can myself remember an unusually violent thunderstorm when the lightning flew across the heavens, flash after flash, without a moment's pause, as though a thousand suns were dashing through the sky. I recollect the consternation of men and women when a neighbouring house was smitten by the lightning, and burnt with a terrific blaze, which could scarcely be seen by reason of the brightness of the lightning. My recollection of that terrible scene will never depart from me. The sublimity of what we have seen often causes us to remember it. So is it with the love of Christ. How it towers to heaven! And mark how brightness succeeds brightness, how flash follows after flash of love unspeakable and full of glory! There is no pause, no interval of darkness or blackness, no chasm of forgetfulness. Its sublimity compels us to remember its manifestation.

Again, we are pretty sure to recollect unusual things. If asked whether we recollected that the sun had risen, we might say, "It is not a matter of memory at all. I feel certain that it did, though I did not see it." But if asked if we ever saw an eclipse, "Oh, yes!" we reply, "We recollect that; we remember watching it, and, how disappointed we were because it was not so dark as we expected it to be." Many people do not notice the stars much, but who forgets the comet? Everybody recollects that phenomenon of nature because it is unusual. When we see something strange, uncommon, out of the ordinary, the memory at once fixes upon it and holds it fast. So is it with the love of Christ. It is such an extraordinary thing, such a marvellous thing, that the like was never known. Ransack history, and you cannot find its parallel. There is but one love that is like it, that is the love of the Father to his only-begotten Son. Besides this, there is nothing to which we can compare the love of Christ to his people. That constellation of the cross is the most marvellous that is to be seen in the spiritual sky; the eye, once spellbound by its charms, must retain its undying admiration because it is the greatest wonder of wonders and miracle of miracles which the universe has ever seen.

29

Sometimes, too, things which are not important in themselves are fixed on the memory because of certain circumstances that happen in association with them. The country people often say, if you ask them whether they recollect such-and-such a year, "Ah, master! It was the year of the hard frost, wasn't it?" Another time they will say, "Why, yes! That was the year when the blight fell upon our gardens, and all our potatoes were of no use, and we were nearly starved that winter. Circumstances help to make us recollect facts. If something particular in politics should happen on our birthday, or our wedding day, or on some other notable occasion, we should say, "Oh, yes! I recollect that; it happened the day I was married, or the day So-and-so was buried." Now, we can never forget the love of Christ because the circumstances were so peculiar when, for the first time, we knew anything at all about it. We were plunged in sin and ruin; we were adrift on the great sea of sin, we had no hope, we were ready to sink, and no shore was near; but Jesus came and saved us. We can never forget those circumstances; with some of us, they were truly awful, beyond all description. Therefore, we cannot forget the time when Jesus' love first dawned upon our minds.

I think, my dear friends, I might give you twenty reasons why it would be impossible for the children of God to forget the love of Christ to them; but above and beyond every other reason is this one: Christ will not let his people forget his love. If, at any time, he finds them forgetful, he will come to them and refresh their memories. If all the love they have ever enjoyed should be forgotten by them, he will give them some fresh manifestations of love. "Have you forgotten my cross?" he asks. "Then I will cause you to remember it afresh, for at my table I will manifest myself to you as I have not done of late. Do you forget what I did for you in the council chamber of eternity? Then I will remind you of it, for you still need a Counsellor, and I will come to your relief just when you are at your wits' end, and I will give you wisdom. Have you forgotten that I called you to myself when you were a stranger! I will bring you back from your wanderings, and then you will recollect me again." Mothers do not let their children forget them if they can help it. If her boy has gone to Australia, and he does not write home, his mother writes to him, "Has my John forgotten his mother?" Then there comes back a sweet epistle, which lets the mother know that the gentle hint she gave him was not lost. So is it with Christ. He often says to one of his forgetful children, "What! Is your heart cold to him who loved you so much that he could not live in heaven without you, but must needs come to earth, go out into the wilderness, up to the cross, and down to the grave, in order to find you?" Be sure that he will have our hearts; prone to wander, he knows that they are, and we feel it ourselves, but he will have them. Oh, that he would drive the nail of the cross right through your hearts that it might be forever fastened there! Painful might the process be; some sharp affliction might rend your flesh; yet, if that would bring you near your Lord, and keep you near him, you might thank him even for the affliction, and love him all the more because of it.

II. Now let us advance another step, and look at THE COMPARATIVE RESOLUTION: "We will remember thy love more than wine."

Why is "wine" mentioned here? I take it to be used here as a figure of speech. The fruit of the vine represents the chief of earthly luxuries. "I will remember thy love more than the choicest or most exhilarating comforts that this world can give me." We have many things which we might compare to wine, in the good and in the bad sense, too — good, because it cheers and comforts and invigorates; bad, because, when we rely upon it, it intoxicates and overthrows, and casts down to the ground. We very readily remember the good things of earth for a season. When creature comforts abound with us, and we have happy and merry days, we recollect them; and when nights of darkness come upon us, we remember the days of our brightness, and we talk of them. It is so with the widow bereaved of her husband; she remembers the days of her happiness when the partner of her joys was with her; she recollects his affectionate words, and his sweet deeds of love. In the case of the mother bereaved of her child, she recalls the love that child had to her, and the solace it was to her when her little one slept on her bosom. Have you become poor? Then the "wine" that you recollect is the wealth you once possessed. You remember how you had no need to tramp over weary miles, and to shiver in the wintry cold. Now that your pain has come, you recollect your former joy, and it makes your present pain all the more painful. This "wine" may be, to a minister, the joy of being successful; and there may come to him days when his chapel will be half-empty, and then he will look back, with regret, upon the joys he once possessed. The spouse says, "We will remember your love more than all earthly comforts." She cannot help doing so; if she could, she would recollect the world rather than heaven; she would have a remembrance of creature comforts, and she would be forgetful of her Lord.

The fact is the impression which the love of Christ makes on the true believer is far greater and deeper than the impression which is made by anything earthly. Mere mortal joys write their record on the sand, and their memory is soon effaced; but Christ's love is like an inscription cut deep into marble, and the remembrance of it is deeply engraved in our hearts. The joy of the creature is something like a lithograph cut lightly on the stone; when the stone is cleaned, the picture is gone; but the love of Christ is like the steel engraving, it is deeply cut, and cannot be easily erased. Earthly joys tread with light feet, and leave but a faint impression; but the love of Christ treads into the very core of our soul at every footstep, and therefore it is that we remember it better than we remember any earthly pleasure. Earthly comforts, too, like wine, leave but a mingled impression. In the cup of joy there is a dash of sorrow. There is nothing we have here below which is not somewhat tainted with grief. Solomon has warned us against the sparkling wine: "Look not thou upon the wine when it is red, when it giveth his colour in the cup, when it moveth itself aright. At the last it biteth like a serpent, and stingeth like an adder." (Prov. 23:31-32) Even friendship, the very cream of joy, trembles on the confines of disappointment, as it is written, "Cursed be the man that trusteth in man, and maketh flesh his arm." (Jer. 17:5) But in Christ's love there is nothing for you ever to regret; when you have enjoyed it to the full, you cannot say that there has been any bitterness in it. When you have come forth from the secret chamber of communion with your Lord, you have realised the purity of his love, there has been nothing to qualify your enjoyment of it. When you have been to a party of your friends, you have said, "I have been very happy, but — I could not enjoy myself there six days in a week"; but when you have been with Christ, you have felt that you could enjoy yourself in that way to all eternity; you could not have too much of such fellowship, for there was nothing in it to mar your happiness. True, there is the remembrance of your sin, but that is so sweetly covered by your Lord's forgiveness and graciousness, that his love is indeed better than wine. It has had all the good effects of wine, and none of its bad results. Equally true is it that the remembrance of earth's comforts, of which wine is the type, must be but transient. If the sinner could live many days, and have much wealth, would he remember it when he entered the unseen world? Ah, he might remember it, but it would be with awful sighs and sobs! You know how Abraham spoke, across the great gulf, to the rich man in hell: "Son, remember that thou in thy lifetime receivedst thy good things, and likewise Lazarus evil things: but now he is comforted, and thou art tormented." (Lk. 16:25) But we can say of the love of Christ that it is better than wine, for we shall rejoice to remember it in eternity.

There, on a green and flowery mount,
Our weary souls shall sit,
And with transporting joys recount...

(Isaac Watts)

What shall we recount? Dr. Watts says,

The labours of our feet.

— but I don't think so; I believe we shall recount the labours of him who lived and died for us. That is what we will talk about in heaven; sure I am that this is the theme of all the music and songs of Paradise.

Jesus, the Lord, their harps employs,
Jesus, my Love, they sing!
Jesus, the life of all our joys
Sounds sweet from every string.

(Isaac Watts)

Do you not see, then, why this comparison is made in our text? We remember Christ's love more than the best earthly comforts because they make but a feeble impression, a mingled impression, a marred impression, and their impression, at best, is but transient; but the love of Christ is remembered as something that is better than wine.

I have to hurry over these different points; but if you enjoy hearing about this subject as much as I delight in preaching it, you would not mind listening to me all night long, and I should not mind preaching right through the night. Surely, this is a theme that sets one's tongue at a happy liberty. "My tongue is the pen of a ready writer" (Ps. 45:1) if I can but feel the love of Christ shed abroad in my heart.

III. Now, thirdly, I am to speak of THE PRACTICAL EFFECTS OF REMEMBERING CHRIST'S LOVE.

If we remember the love of Christ to us, the first practical effect will be that we shall love him. Can I remember your love to me, O my sweet Lord, and not love you in return? Surely Dr. Watts was right when he wrote,

Come, Holy Spirit, heavenly Dove,
With all thy quickening powers,
Come, shed abroad a Saviour's love,
And that shall kindle ours.

True is it, O Jesus, that there is no light of love in our hearts except the light of your love! It is the holy fire from your altar that must kindle the incense in the censer of our hearts. There is no living water to be drawn out of these dry wells; you, O Jesus, must supply them from the bubbling spring in your own heart! When my heart is conscious of your love, it loves you in return.

Another practical effect of remembering Christ's love will be love for the brethren. When we remember Christ's love as we ought, we shall not meet one of Christ's brethren without falling in love with him directly. Christ has some very poor brethren, and some very unhandsome ones. David sent to enquire whether there were any left of the house of Saul to whom he might show kindness for Jonathan's sake. Ziba told him that Jonathan had a son named Mephibosheth who was lame on his feet. What did David do when he heard this? Did he say, "I will have nothing to do with him; I do not want a lame fellow like that stumbling about my palace"? Oh, no! He might be lame on his feet, but he was Jonathan's son; so David sent for him, and said to him, "Thou shalt eat bread at my table continually." (2 Sam. 9:7) Did you ever know one of Christ's beloved who was lame on his feet? There is a little lameness somewhere or other about all of them; and if we only love those saints who are very holy, it will seem as if we only loved them for their own sakes; but if we love

Christ's deformed and crippled children, that looks like loving them for his sake. And, I think, if you could remember what a clumsy child you were yourself, you would not look with such disdain on any of God's other children. Ministers have much to bear in connection with some of their people. One man's judgement is so keen that you are always afraid of saying something amiss in his presence; another man's temper is so hot that you cannot meddle with him for fear you should provoke a quarrel. Another man is so worldly that, although he has the grace of God in his heart, it seems to be only like a spark in damp tinder. Christ has many very unseemly children; yet if we can but see that they are Christ's, if they have only a small likeness to him, we love them directly for his sake, and are willing to do what we can for them out of love for him. The remembrance of the love of Christ to us will, I repeat, always kindle in us a love towards all the brethren.

The next effect will be holy practice. When we remember the love of Christ for us, we shall hate sin. Feeling that he has bought us with his precious blood, we shall abhor the very name of iniquity. When Satan tempts us, we shall each one say, "Get away, for I will have nothing to do with you; I remember Christ's love for me." Have you never heard the story of the Indian woman who, when she was enticed by some great chief who wished to lead her astray gave to him this noble answer: "I know no one in the world to be beautiful or attractive but my husband"? So will the believer say, when he is tempted, "I know of nothing that is good but Christ; I know of no one who is so fair as he; so begone, black Satan, my heart is given wholly to Christ, and I will have nothing to do with you."

Another effect of remembering the love of Christ will be repose of heart in a time of trouble. When we have, for a while, lost the light of God's countenance; when we are like the apostle in that great storm at sea, and are in a place where two seas meet, and our vessel is already broken by the violence of the waves; when darkness increases our fears, or daylight reveals fresh dangers, then is it specially sweet to remember the love of our Lord. In such a time as that, the tried believer can say, "He loved me once, and his love never changes. Though I cannot now see the light of his countenance, I know that he is still the same as he ever was. I remember the garden of delights where he revealed his love to me, and the banqueting house where he gave me such choice fare; and I feel persuaded that he has not forgotten his poor spouse, but that he will come to her again, and once more lift her out of the mire, set her feet upon a rock, put a new song into her mouth, and establish her goings." (Ps. 40:2) A constant remembrance of Christ's love for us will always make us cheerful, dutiful, and holy. Dear Lord, grant us this boon; for if you will enable us to remember your love more than wine, you will give us all good things in one. Let your good Spirit but keep us up to this good resolution, and we shall be both holy and happy, honouring you and rejoicing in you.

IV. Lastly, I would put before you A FEW PRACTICAL SUGGESTIONS AS TO PRESERVING A DEEPER AND MORE SINCERE REMEMBRANCE OF CHRIST'S LOVE than you have done so far.

The old Puritan divines frequently compared their hearers with the Egyptian dog that ran to the Nile and drank, and then ran away. They came up to the meeting-house, and heard the minister, took a little sip of the gospel, which sufficed them, and then they were off. One preacher said that he wished they were like the fishes; not come and lap at the stream, as the dog did, but swim in it, and live in it. There are too many in this age who are content with hearing a little of Christ's love; a sip by the way is all that they seem to need. But it would be far better if you could come up to Samuel Rutherford's ideal: "I would have my soul sunk over its masthead in a sea of love to Christ. I would be sunken fifty fathoms deep in the mighty shoreless ocean of his love, so that there might be nothing left of me, and that I might be swallowed up in love to Christ, and in Christ's love to me." I expect, dear brothers and sisters, that your complaint is that you cannot recollect good

33

things as you want to. I know very well how you feel. You hear a sermon, and become, for a while, absorbed in holy meditation; but you have to return to your shop early tomorrow morning, and you only quitted it as late as twelve o'clock on Saturday night. There are six days for the world, and only one for heaven; it is no wonder that you find the sermon so difficult to remember. You remind me of a person going out into a garden on a dark night carrying a lighted candle. If the wind should blow, there is such a careful shielding of the light with the hand lest it should be blown out. In like manner, it is but a feeble light that you bear away from the public ministry, and there are ten thousand winds blowing around you, trying to put it out. You must indeed be careful to keep it alight all the week in your recollection. Let me give you a little practical advice as to how you may keep constantly in your mind a remembrance of Jesus Christ's love.

One of the first things I would recommend to you is frequent meditation. See if you cannot more often get a quarter of an hour all alone, that you may sit down and turn over and over again the love of Christ for you. Remember that souls grow more by meditation than by anything else. The cattle go round the fields and crop the grass; that is like hearing the Word. But, afterwards, they lie down in a quiet corner and chew the cud; that is like meditating upon what we have heard. Get a quarter of an hour, if you can, to masticate and digest the Word. "A quarter of an hour!" says someone; "why, I could not get five minutes!" I would not be hard with you, dear brother, but I think you could; days can sometimes be pulled out either at one end or at the other. If you cannot lengthen the day at the night end, cannot you pull it out at the morning end? Is there not a possibility of a little saving of time at some hour during the day? You will do none the less work for allowing time for meditation and prayer. Our old proverb says, "Prayer and provender hinder no man's journey"; and I believe that prayer and meditation hinder no man's work. Do try to get a little time to think about your soul. What, so much time to be occupied with this dusty, sinful world, and so little time to be devoted to that which relates to heaven! So much time to be employed concerning meat and drink and clothes, and so little time to be given to thoughts of our precious Saviour and all his loveliness! Do get a little time alone, beloved, for that will help to keep you right. You would not forget your Master's love nearly as much as you do if you would secure more time for meditation upon it.

Another means of remembering Christ's love is this: take care that you are not content with what you knew of Christ's love yesterday. You want to know a little more about it today, and you ought to know still more about it tomorrow. Some Christians do not commune with their Lord nearly as often as they ought; I wonder how they manage to live on in such a fashion. They get a little manna once a month and they try to live on that until another month comes round. They meet with their Saviour, perhaps, at the communion table — and not always then — and they are content to live from day to day without having fellowship with him. Be not one of that order of Christians. Seek for daily — no, more than that — continual communion with the Lord Jesus Christ. You are to pray for daily bread; then, surely, he who bade you do that must mean that you should seek to be fed daily with himself, who is the Bread of heaven. I do not like to hear people talk about what they knew of Jesus five or six years ago, unless they can also tell something of what they know of him now. What would you think of a wife who said, "My husband spoke kindly to me some years ago; and I saw him five years ago, but I have not seen him since"? You would say, "How can the woman live, if she is a loving wife, without seeing her husband? Is he in the same house with her, and yet has he not spoken to her all that while? The Lord Jesus is always near to you, and do you mean to say that you can live without fellowship with him? Yes, you can, for some of you do; but I pray you not to live so any longer, for it is a poor, starving way of dragging on a miserable existence. You have just enough religion to make you wretched; you have not enough to make you happy; so get a great deal more of it. Drink deeply at the heavenly spring of fellowship. If you learn a

34

little more about Christ every day, you will not be likely to forget what you already know of him.

Then, again, as another way of keeping in your heart what you do know — take care, when you have a sense of Christ's love, that you let it go down deeply. If there were a nail so placed that it would slacken its hold a little every day for six days, if I had the opportunity of driving it in the first day, I would try to drive it in right up to the head, and to clinch it. So, if you have not much time for fellowship and communion with Christ, if you have only a short season for meditation, try to drive the nail well home. Do not be content with merely thinking about Christ; seek to see him before your eyes as manifestly crucified. See him as he groans in the garden, and do not be content unless you can groan with him. See him as he hangs upon the cross, and do not rest satisfied until you can feel that you are crucified with him. Realise your fellowship with him as he rises from the tomb, for this will help very much to keep you right.

I heard the story of a man who was passing by a house where a poor idiot lad, with a piece of sandpaper, was scouring away at a brass plate. The man asked what he was doing, and he replied, "I am trying to scour the name out." "Ah!" said the other, "you may scour away as long as you like, but you will never be able to do that." And so, I think, I see the devil scouring away at some of you, trying to get the name of Jesus out of your heart. Scour away, Satan, if you like; but you will never get it out, for it is too deeply cut. If Christ's name is engraved upon your heart, Satan may try to get it out, but he will never succeed in doing so; it will never be obliterated, but will shine all the more brightly for his attempts to remove it.

Let me add one more direction. When any of you meet together, it is always a good thing to make Christ the theme of your conversation. Oh, what a deal of idle gossip there is even on Sundays! Many people do not go out on Sunday afternoon, so they must talk about something. They do not like to talk about their trade; that would be too secular, they fancy. They do not like to talk about strictly sacred things; that might appear hypocritical, they think. So they begin, "Have you ever heard So-and-so preach?" "Yes, I did once." "Did you like him?" So, from one, they go on to others, and ministers and their sermons become the bones that they pick on Sunday afternoons. They feel that they must have some theme for their conversation not quite sacred, nor wholly secular. I would advise you to talk more about the Lord Jesus Christ than you have been used to do; you will be less likely to forget his love if you are often talking of him. Let the music of his name ring in your ears all the day long; and if you would have it ring in your ears, it must ring from your tongue. Whenever you have the opportunity, tell out the marvellous story of his great love to you; so will your own memory be refreshed, and others, listening to your testimony, will also get a large, and, it may be, an everlasting blessing.

May God now grant to you, my dear hearers, that you retain a sense of Christ's love to you, if you have ever enjoyed it! If you never have, may God now give it to you! If you have never come to Christ, come to him now. Remember that Jesus loves sinners. Those who are now farthest from him, when they once return to him they will know that he loves them. If you "take with you words", and come to him groaning and sighing, he will not cast you out. He stands now with open arms, and freely invites you. Come to him, I beseech you. As his ambassador, I entreat you to come; if you do so, he will fold you in his bosom. All that the heirs of heaven can have, you shall have. All that the glorified saints are now enjoying shall yet be your privilege also. You shall one day walk with Christ in white, and see his face, and be with him in Paradise, and be blessed throughout eternity.

May God grant us his grace now, that our text may become the cheerful sonnet of our experience: "We will remember thy love more than wine."

5. REJOICING AND REMEMBERING
NO. 2641

AT THE METROPOLITAN TABERNACLE, NEWINGTON
ON LORD'S-DAY EVENING, APRIL 4TH, 1886
A COMMUNION SERVICE

"We will be glad and rejoice in thee, we will remember thy love more than wine."
(Song of Solomon 1:4)

IT is a very blessed habit of saints who have grown in grace to enter into actual conversation with the Well-beloved. Our tort [fault] is not so much speaking of him as speaking *to* him: "We will be glad and rejoice in thee, we will remember thy love more than wine." Of course, in prayer and in praise, we speak to God; but I suggest that we should seek to have much more of intense and familiar intercourse with the Lord Jesus Christ than most of us at present enjoy. I find it good sometimes in prayer to say nothing, but to sit or kneel quite still, and to look up to my Lord in adoring silence; and then sometimes to talk to him, not asking anything of him, but just speaking familiarly with Jesus, realising him to be present, and waiting to hear him speak until some precious word of his from Scripture comes into my soul as with living accents newly-spoken by those dear lips which are as lilies dropping sweet-smelling myrrh. The French have a word which they use concerning that conversation which is common among those who love one another, or are on terms of intimate friendship; they call it *tutoyage* when they say "thee" and "thou" to one another, instead of the more formal language used towards strangers. I like that form of expression that is used in our text, and delight to meet with souls that are brought into so rapt a state of fellowship with Christ that they can speak to him in this familiar fashion, "We will be glad and rejoice in thee, we will remember thy love more than wine."

If you, dear friends, have not lately conversed with Jesus, do so now in the quietness of your own spirit. Think that his shadow is over you; do not let it be mere imagination, but let it be what is better far than that, a true realising faith, for if he be present where two or three are met together in his name, rest assured that he is not absent where this great assembly of his people has come together to commemorate his passion and his death. You are here, blessed master; we are sure that you are, and we worship you, and speak with you, as really as if we could see you with that vesture on, woven from the top throughout — as truly as if we saw you now lifting that beloved pierced hand, and laying it upon us; and we would say to you from the bottom of our hearts, "We will rejoice and be glad in thee, we will remember thy love more than wine." This text is not so much for me to explain, dear friends, as for you to enjoy. Forget all about the preacher, but take the text, and part it among yourselves; and extract as much as you can of its spiritual nourishment, and feed on it.

I. As you do so, you will notice, first, that we have here A DOUBLE RESOLVE: "We will be glad and rejoice in thee, we will remember thy love more than wine."

I may say of that resolve that it is, first, *a necessary resolve*, for it is not according to human nature to rejoice in Christ, it is not according to the tendency of our poor fallen state to remember his love. There must be an act of the will with regard to this resolve; let us will it now: "We *will* be glad and rejoice in thee, we *will* remember thy love more than wine." There are so many things that try to come in between our souls and our Saviour, so many sorrows that would prevent our rejoicing in him, so we must be resolved to be glad in him whatever our sorrows may be. Down with you, sorrows! Down with you! We have said to the Lord that we will be glad and rejoice in him, and we mean to prove our words to be true. Then there are so many troubling thoughts that come flying in to mar our full

36

fellowship with our Lord. However tightly windows may be closed, and doors shut, these thoughts will find an entrance, and we get remembering the sick child at home, or some care that has afflicted us during the week. Oh, but, Lord, we will not remember these things now! We say to you from our hearts, "We *will* — we *will* — we *will* remember thy love." Away with you, care, sorrow, grief, away with you! Come to me, O Holy Spirit, and help me now to have a happy time, to be glad and rejoice in my Lord — and to have a holy time to remember His love, and to remember nothing beside! You must will it most intensely, dear friends, or it will not come to pass. It is not sufficient merely to walk into a place of worship, and put ourselves into a posture of devotion, and then imagine that, doing whatever is proper to the place and the hour, we shall have fellowship with Jesus. Oh, no, beloved; oh, no! We must worship him in spirit and in truth, not in fiction and in sham; not mechanically, as though we could have true fellowship with him without earnest and intense desire. No, there must be these two utterances of our holy resolve: "We will be glad and rejoice in thee, we will remember thy loves more than wine."

And truly, dear friends, as this resolve is necessary, it is also *a right and proper resolve*. Should we not be glad and rejoice in Christ?

Why should the children of a King
Go mourning all their days?

(Isaac Watts)

Why should the children of the bride-chamber fast while the Bridegroom is with them? (Mat. 9:15; Mk. 2:19; Lk. 5:34) With such a Husband as we have in Christ, should not the spouse rejoice in him? Would it be becoming for a heart that is married to Christ to be in any other condition than that of rejoicing in him? I know you have many things in which you cannot rejoice; well, let them go. But you can rejoice in him — in his Person, in his work, in his offices, in his relationships, in his power, in his glory, in his first advent, in his second advent. Surely, these are not things that can be thought of without delightful emotion; it is most proper that we should be glad and rejoice in our Lord. There ought to be a reduplication of our joy; we should joy in him and then rejoice in him, we should "be glad and rejoice" in him (Rev. 19:7). It is most proper that we should be glad in the Lord, and what can be more proper than that we should remember him? What a shame it is that we ever forget him! His name should be so deeply engraved on our hearts that we cannot forget him. Let us remember his love, for surely, if there is anything that we ought ever to remember; it is that undying love which is our choicest portion on earth, and which will be the main constituent of our highest bliss in heaven. Then, by the help of God's Spirit, let us make this resolve at this moment. Whatever we may do when we get out of this building, at any rate for the next half-hour, let us resolve to stand by this double declaration, "We will rejoice, and we will remember."

Do you not think also that this resolution, if we carry it out, will be *very helpful to ourselves?* What a help it is to a Christian to be glad in the Lord! I know what it is to be depressed; I do not suppose there is anyone in this place who knows what it is to be cast down so low as I sometimes am. Then I feel that there is no help for me, and no hope of my living and working, except I can get out of that sad condition, and get to be glad in the Lord; and I cry, "My heart, my heart, what are you at?" "Why art thou cast down, O my soul? And why art thou disquieted within me? Hope in God: for I shall yet praise him, who is the health of my countenance, and my God." (Ps. 42:11, 43:5) There is no way of getting right out of the Stygian bog of the Slough of Despond like rejoicing in the Lord. If you try to rejoice in yourself, you will have a poor reason for joy; but if you rejoice and be glad in the Lord, you have the real, abiding, unchanging source of joy; for he who rejoices in Christ rejoices in him who is "the same yesterday, and today, and for ever" (Heb. 13:8);

37

and he may always rejoice in him. Come, then, and for your own good hang up the sackbut, and take down the psaltery; put away the ashes. What if men call this season "Lent"? We will keep no Lent tonight; this is our Easter time, our Lord has risen from the dead and is among us, and we will rejoice in him. Come, beloved, surely it is time that, for a while at least, we forget our pain and griefs and all the worries of this weary world; and, for one, I must, I will, be glad and rejoice in my Lord, and I hope many of you will join with me in this happy occupation, which will be helpful to yourselves.

Certainly, it will also be *for the good of others*. I think that believers do much harm if they allow their depression of spirit to be too conspicuous. There is another meaning besides the first one to that text, "Thou, when thou fastest, anoint thine head, and wash thy face; that thou appear not unto men to fast." (Mat. 6:17) But if you can get right out of your sorrow, and can actually rejoice in the Lord, and if you can so remember him as to be glad and rejoice in him, you will allure many to the fair ways of Christ, which else will be evil spoken of if you go mourning all your days. Come, you weak ones, come and feast on bread that can make you strong. Come, you whose eyes are red with weeping; take a handkerchief that shall dry your tears, and make your eyes as bright as diamonds. Remember Christ, and be glad and rejoice in him. Angels round the throne can have no higher joy than this; and they cannot enter as fully into it as you can, for he has not loved them even as he has loved you.

Never did angels taste above,
Redeeming grace and dying love.

(Isaac Watts)

This, then, is what I earnestly commend to you, this double resolve, that we should all truly say to our Lord, "We will be glad and rejoice in thee, we will remember thy love more than wine." But, dear friends, *we cannot carry out the resolve without the help of the Holy Spirit*. Therefore, let us breathe it unto the Lord in prayer; and, as we tell him what we mean to do, let us each one add, "Draw me, O Lord; then I will run after you. Help me to come to you; manifest yourself to me, and then I will be glad and rejoice in you."

II. Now I want to go a step further, and say that I think the resolve of the text is A SUITABLE RESOLVE FOR THIS OCCASION: "We will be glad and rejoice in thee, we will remember thy love more than wine."

We are most of us coming to the communion table to eat of the bread and to drink of the cup in remembrance of our Master's dying love. Surely, now is the hour, if ever in our lives, to be glad and rejoice in him, and to remember him, for the object of this supper is *to commemorate his dying love*. It is idle, and worse than idle, to come to Christ's table if you do not remember him; what good can it do you? The use that it is to the spectator is that you show Christ's death "till he come"; but if there be not in the spectator any thought of that death, of what use is the sight of the table with its sacred vessels? And if you yourself do not think of Christ, of what avail to you are the emblems of a forgotten or an unknown Lord? No, we are to commemorate his death; so let us in our hearts rejoice in him, and remember him. Well did we sing just now:

Jesus, when faith with fixèd eyes,
Beholds thy wondrous sacrifice,
Love rises to an ardent flame,
And we all other hope disclaim.

Hence, O my soul, a balsam flows

To heal thy wounds, and cure thy woes;
Immortal joys come streaming down,
Joys like his griefs, immense, unknown.

(Benjamin Beddome)

Recollect, next, that in coming to this communion table we also *commemorate the results of Christ's death*. One result of our Lord's death is that he gives food to His people; his body broken has become bread for our souls, yes, it is food indeed. His blood, which was shed for many for the remission of sins has become drink indeed. By his death, Christ has given us life; and by the completion of his great redeeming work, and by his ever-living intercession, he has given us bread and wine by which that life may be sustained. He has finished it all, and he has gone into the glory to secure the results of his finished work. Sitting around his table, we are reminded of all this; the bread is ready, the cup is filled. We have nothing to do to prepare the feast; all we have to do now is to come and partake of it, and feed even to the full on heavenly food. So, dear friends, if we come to this table in a right spirit, we must rejoice in our Lord, and we must remember his love.

I think also that there is this further reason why we should rejoice in our Lord and remember his love, because at this table *the commemoration is made by our Lord to be a feast*. They miss the meaning of the Lord's Supper when they kneel around what they call an "altar". The very point of the supper is that it should be taken while sitting around a table. It is not meant to be an adoration, it is a communion; we come here that we may have fellowship with him who sat at the table with his disciples, and made them to be his companions at his last supper. Joy is becoming at a royal feast. What, will you come to the King's table with sorrowful countenances? Will ye come sadly to see what he has brought you? Now that he has prepared the bread and wine as a feast for your souls, will you come here hanging your heads like bulrushes? No, but let this be your resolution, "We will be glad and rejoice in thee, we will remember thy love more than wine." Do kings make feasts, do they lift high the flowing bowl, are there shouts of joy and exultation at their banquets? And shall it be that this world's poor vine, whose juice is often to men like the wine of Gomorrah, shall bring even the semblance of joy superior to ours when we drink of the wine that comes from the Vine of God, and the clusters that Christ hath trodden in the winepress? No; higher far be your joy than ever came to them that have made merry at earthly feasts. More delightful, more intense, more real, more true be your hallowed ecstasies than anything that wine or wealth can ever bring. "We will be glad and rejoice in thee, we will remember thy love more than wine." O God, help us to carry out this resolution! It seems to me to be specially right and proper and fit, when we come to this high festival of the Church of God that we should rejoice in the Lord, and remember his love.

Let us also recollect that, when we come to the table of our Lord, *we commemorate a very happy union*. Our text speaks in the plural: "*We* will be glad and rejoice in thee, *we* will remember thy love more than wine." I do not know how you feel, brothers and sisters, but I should not like to go to heaven alone. If nobody else will go on pilgrimage, Christian must set out by himself, and march along towards the Celestial City until he finds a suitable fellow-pilgrim. But I like best to go with Christiana, and Mercy, and the children, and as a company together. Though I should enjoy fellowship with my Lord if I were his only loved one, yet it greatly increases my joy as I look at the faces of many of you whom I have known a score of years, and with whom I have lived in such happy union year after year. Many of you who were once "in the gall of bitterness, and in the bond of iniquity" (Acts 8:23) have been plucked, like brands out of the burning, through the preaching of the gospel in this pulpit; and it seems such a happy thing for us to be communing together around the table of our Lord.

Some of you, my dear venerable brothers and sisters, will soon be home; come, we will be glad and rejoice in our Lord, will we not? Before you quite go away from us, join us in another holy song; give us another of your patient, quiet, happy, restful looks. One dear sister went home this morning at twelve o'clock, while we were worshipping here. I am sure that her spirit is now rejoicing before the throne, and some of you will be going soon; but, till you do, we will rejoice and be glad together, will we not? We will take the cup of blessing still at the Lord's Table, whatever our infirmities and sorrows may be; and we will remember him until we drink the new wine in our Father's kingdom above. And you men and women in the very midst of the battle of life, with all your trials and struggles, we will stand shoulder to shoulder, will we not? We are one in Christ, and there is between us a bond of union that can never be snapped; it binds us for time and eternity. We came to this communion table to eat and drink, not each one for himself only, but each one in fellowship with all the rest; and this ought to make us glad. If I am not glad about myself, I will be glad to think that you are glad. If I have a heavy burden to carry, I will be glad that you have not; and if you have a burden, and I have not, try to be glad that I have not one; or, if you have one, and I have another, let us rejoice that we both have the same God to help us to carry them, and let us believe that, as our days, so shall our strength be. (Deut 33:25)

What a joy it adds to this festival when we see the young folk coming among us, the sons and daughters of God's people being brought into the church! Do you not notice how dear Mr. William Olney, whenever he prays for a blessing upon our ministry, always breaks out into thanksgiving to God that all his family have been brought to Christ? There are many others of us who can praise the Lord for the same favour, and it is a great joy to us. Yes, Lord, we will remember your love — husband and wife, sons and daughters, and some of us can say grandchildren, too — we will all come clustering around your table, and together we will remember your sweet love to our fathers, and to ourselves, and to our children. We cannot help remembering it, and rejoicing and being glad in it.

I must give you just one more thought on this point. It does not become us to gather at this communion table with a heavy heart when we recollect that *it is not only a commemoration, but an anticipation*. We are to do this "till he come." (1 Cor. 11:26) Did I not try this morning [See Metropolitan Tabernacle Pulpit, No. 1,894: "The Two Appearings and the Discipline of Grace"] to sound the trumpet of his coming? It would not have startled me if he had come while we were assembled, and I was speaking of "the glorious appearing of the great God and our Saviour Jesus Christ." (Tit. 2:13) Nor should it startle any of you, if, in the dead of this very night, while you are in your beds, you should hear the cry, "Behold, the Bridegroom cometh" (Mat. 25:6), for he may come at any moment, and he will come "in such an hour as ye think not". (Mat. 24:24) Let us leap up at the remembrance of this gladsome hope. We are coming to the table, keeping up the memorial of our Lord's first appearing in the fond hope and sure belief of that second appearing, when the righteous shall shine forth as the sun in the kingdom of their Father. Therefore, let us keep the feast with high hope. With joy-notes sound aloud the silver trumpet of the great jubilee; and as you come to the table, let your hearts be glad in the Lord, whose love you specially remember at this hallowed festival.

III. I will close in a very few minutes, but I must dwell for a brief space upon what I meant to make my third point concerning this double resolve — LET US CARRY IT OUT.

That ought always to be the practical conclusion to every sermon — let us carry it out. We have said to our Lord in the language of the text, "We will be glad and rejoice in thee, we will remember thy love more than wine". Very well, now let us carry out this resolve.

"We will remember thy love". Dear Saviour, what we have to remember is *your love* — your love in old eternity, or ever the earth was, your prescient love proclaims:

Awake, my soul, in joyful lays,
And sing thy great Redeemer's praise;
He justly claims a song from thee,
His loving-kindness, oh, how free!

He saw me ruined in the Fall,
Yet loved me, notwithstanding all;
He saved me from my lost estate,
His loving-kindness, oh, how great!

(Samuel Medley)

We remember the love of your espousals when you espoused your people to yourself, and resolved that, whatever might be the lot of your elect, you would share it with them. The Lord Jesus made up his mind that he would be one with his Church; for this purpose, he left his Father that he might be one with his bride. I shall get into great deeps if I go much further in speaking about Christ's love.

"We will remember thy love" — that love which, having once begun, has never wavered, never diminished, never stopped.

Love, so vast that nought can bound;
Love, too deep for thought to sound;
Love, which made the Lord of all
Drink the wormwood and the gall.
Love, which led him to the cross,
Bearing there unuttered loss;
Love, which brought him to the gloom
Of the cold and darksome tomb.

Love, which will not let him rest
Till his chosen all are blest;
Till they all for whom he died
Live rejoicing by his side.

(Albert Midlane)

We remember the love which Jesus bore in his heart right up into the glory at the right hand of the Father; that love which is still as great as when he hung on Calvary to redeem us to himself. The wonderful part of all this to me is that it should be the love of such a one as Christ. That ever so divine a Person should set his love on us is very wonderful. I can understand my mother's love, I can understand my child's love, I can understand my wife's love; but I cannot understand Christ's love. Oh, brothers, we are nothings, we are nobodies; yet this glorious Everybody, this All in All, actually set his love upon us! Suppose that all the holy angels had loved us, and that all God's redeemed had loved us; all put together, it would be only so many grains of dust that would not turn the scale; but Christ's love is a mountain, no, more than all the mountains in the universe. I know of nothing compared with it.

That is the first way in which we are to carry out this double resolve; we are to remember and to rejoice in Christ's love.

41

Next, let each one of us say to Christ, "I will remember thy love *to me*." Brothers and sisters, I can believe in Christ's loving you; but there are times when it seems a great mystery that he should ever have loved me. I can truly say that, often, I have felt that if I might sit at the feet of the poorest, meanest, least of God's servants, and serve them, I would count it a heaven to do it if I did but feel sure of Christ's love to my own soul. I see so many beauties in my brothers and my sisters that I can admire the grace of God in them; but, often, I see and feel so many imperfections in myself that I can only wonder that ever Christ should have loved me. I suppose that each of you feels the same. I am sure that you do if you are in a right state of heart, for, truth to tell, there is no beauty in any of us that he should desire us, and there is no excellence in any of us that could have made it worth his while to die for us. "God commendeth his love toward us, in that, while we were yet sinners, Christ died for us" (Rom. 5:8) "When we were yet without strength, in due time Christ died for the ungodly" (Rom. 5:6) and died for us as ungodly. Come, then, will you not be glad and rejoice that ever Christ should have loved you? Will you not be glad and rejoice, and yet wonder all the while, that ever it should have been possible for him to draw you "with cords of a man, with bands of love" (Hos. 11:4), and bring you into living, loving, everlasting union with himself?

Still, even that is not all. The text does not merely speak about Christ's love, and Christ's love to me, but it talks about *Christ himself*. "We will be glad and rejoice in thee" — not only in his love, but in himself. Do try, dear friends, to let your thoughts dwell upon Christ, his complex Person — God and man — and all the wonders that lie wrapped up in Immanuel, God with us. Your work, Lord, is fair; but the hand that did the work is fairer still. All your designs of love are full of splendour, but what shall we say of the mind that first gave creation to those designs? The glance, the look of love, which you have given me, is blessed; but oh, those eyes of yours, those eyes which are brighter than the stars of the morning! The Lord Jesus is better than everything that comes from him; if his gifts are infinitely precious then what must he himself be? Come, then, beloved, and let us be glad and rejoice in him, and let us remember his love more than wine.

The text says "*we will remember*", but some of you cannot remember because you do not know. A man cannot remember what he has never heard of, or seen, or known. But, brothers and sisters, *let us remember what we do know of Christ's love*. I remember the first day I ever tasted of his love consciously to myself. Ah, but I look back, and think of the rivers of love that came streaming down to me when I did not even know that I was receiving them! And I remember that many days have passed since first I could give back the glance of love in return for his love to me. But oh, what his love to me since then has been! His love in sickness, in sorrow, in labour, in backsliding, in prayer, in tears, in unbelief, in faith, in varyings and changings as many as the changes of the moon! Yet, his love has always been the same. What a book some of you could write concerning Christ's love to you if you had but a facile pen! What a story some of you could tell of Christ's love if some guest could be detained while you told out the wondrous story! I sometimes think within myself that, if all the interesting things that are written in all the works of fiction could be put together, I could surpass them all in the literal simple facts of a common life like mine; and I believe that many of God's people here could say the same. A Christian's life is full of interest. Last Thursday night, I called the life of a Christian a cluster of Koh-i-noors, threaded on a string of divine faithfulness, and I am sure that it is so:

Give to our God immortal praise;
Mercy and truth are all His ways:
Wonders of grace to God belong,
Repeat His mercies in your song.

42

(Isaac Watts)

Repeat his mercies as you remember them, and be glad and rejoice in him even more than in the mercies that come from him.

In conclusion, I would say that I think the people of God, in gathering to the communion table, should try to *be glad and rejoice their Lord, and in nobody else, and to remember him, and nothing else*. Let all be a blank except what Christ has written on your memory; let all be a blank except where that dear face appears —

The head that once was crowned with thorns,

as Thomas Kelly puts it, but —

Is crowned with glory now.
A royal diadem adorns
The mighty Victor's brow.

Think only of him. Put the glass to your eye, and shut out all the rest of the landscape, and let that glass take nothing within its circle but just the face of the Well-beloved which we soon hope to see without a cloud between. God bless you, dear friends! I wish that all of you understood this truth of which I have been speaking. Some of you do not; may the Lord lead you to do so, for there is no life like that which is spent at Jesu's feet, and no joy like that which comes from our dear Lord. I wish you knew it. Believe on him, and you shall know it, and shall know it at once. Amen.

6. SELF-HUMBLING AND SELF-SEARCHING
NO. 990

A SERMON ON LORD'S-DAY MORNING, JANUARY 15TH, 1871,
AT THE METROPOLITAN TABERNACLE, NEWINGTON

"Look not upon me, because I am black, because the sun hath looked upon me: my mother's children were angry with me, they made me the keeper of the vineyards; but mine own vineyard have I not kept." (Song of Solomon 1:6)

FROM where do I draw my text but from the very fountain of love? And to whom shall I address my discourse but to the friends of the bridegroom? You must have warm hearts, quick sensibilities, lively emotions, to interpret the sayings and sympathise with the tender notes of this most sacred song. I suppose that the history of the statues in St. Paul's Cathedral, from year to year, would not be remarkably interesting. They are placed on their pedestals; they stand there quietly; and unless some terrible convulsion should occur, probably that will be the whole of their history for many years to come, as it has been for many years past. During the time in which anyone of those statues has stood there, however, the history of any one human person has been chequered with all sorts of incidents, happy and sorrowful. Aches and pains, joys and rejoicings, depressions and exultations, have alternated in the living; but in the cold marble there has been no such change. Many of you in this house know little of what are the experiences of God's people. If you hear of their anxieties and encouragements, their temptations and deliverances, their inward conflicts and spiritual triumphs, their gloomy depressions and cheerful exultations — all those things seem to you as an idle tale. The living, the living, shall know the secret; but unto the mere professor, this thing is not revealed. My subject, which will be mainly addressed to God's working people — to such as are really serving him — will appear to have very little bearing upon any here present who do not understand the spiritual life, and they will probably think that the evening to them is wasted. Just this word at the outset, however, I would drop in your ears. If you do not know anything of spiritual life, what will you do at the end of your natural life? If there be no work of God's Spirit upon your soul, and you are a stranger to the living experience of God's children, what will be your portion forever? It must be divided to you with the unbelievers. Are you prepared to receive it? Are you willing that this should be your eternal destiny? Are you not, rather, alarmed? Are you not made anxious and desirous if by any means you may pass into that better, truer, state of life? Considering its boundless interests, notwithstanding all the present struggles and sorrows it may entail on you, do you not wish to know and prove what spiritual life means? I pray God you may. Let me remind you that the gospel preached to you is still available for your quickening; and whoever believes in Christ Jesus is born of God, and is possessor of that spiritual life.

Now, in conducting the people of God to a special survey of our text, "Look not upon me, because I am black", our first remark shall be this: *the fairest Christians are the most shamefaced with regard to themselves*. The person who says, "Look not upon me, because I am black", is described by some one else in the eighth verse as the "fairest among women." Others, who thought her the fairest of the fair, spoke no less than the truth when they affirmed it; but in her own esteem she felt herself to be so little fair, and so much uncomely, that she besought them not even to look upon her. Why is it that the best Christians depreciate themselves the most?

Is it not because they are most accustomed to look within? They keep their books in a better condition than those unsafe tradesmen, the counterpart of mere professors, who think themselves "rich and increased in goods" (Rev. 3:17) when they are on the very

44

verge of bankruptcy. The Christian in his right state tests himself to see whether he be in the faith. He values too much his own soul to go on blindly. He knows that *Heedless* and *Toobold* are always bad pilots, so he sets *Caution* and *Self-examination* at the helm. He cries to God, "Search me, O God, and know my heart". (Ps. 139:23) He is accustomed to examine his actions and his motives — to pass his words and his thoughts in review. He does not live the life of one who goes recklessly on, but he stops and considers his ways, and looks well to the state of everything within him "to have always a conscience void of offense toward God and toward men." (Acts 24:16) Solomon says, "The wise man looks to the state of his flocks and his herds" (and it is no marvel if any one suffers loss who neglects this counsel. But he also says, "Keep thy heart with all diligence, for out of it are the issues of life" (Prov. 4:23), and it is quite certain that he who fails in this exercise is liable to every kind of moral disorder. In his anxiety to be pure from evil, the godly man will be eager to notice, and quick to detect, the least particle of defilement; and for this reason he discovers more of his blackness than any other man is likely to see. He is no blacker, but he looks more narrowly, and therefore sees more distinctly the spots on his own character.

The genuine Christian, also, tries himself by a higher standard. The professor, if he be as good as another professor, is well content. He estimates himself by a comparison with his neighbours. He has no standard but that of ordinary commonplace Christianity. Far otherwise is it with the believer who walks near to God; he asks himself "What manner of persons ought we to be, in all holy conversation and godliness?" (2 Pet. 3:11) He knows the law to be spiritual, and therefore he judges many things to be sinful which others wink at; and he counts some things to be important duties which others regard as trifles. The genuine Christian sets up no lower standard than perfection. He does not judge himself by others, but by the exact measure of the divine requirements, by the law of God, and especially by the example of his Lord and Master; and when he thus sets the brightness of the Saviour's character side by side with his own, then it is that he cries out, "Look not upon me, for I am black." The mere professor never does this: he neither scrutinises himself nor observes his Master with close heed and strained attention, desiring to ascertain the truth; but he flatters himself in his own eyes, and goes on presumptuously. Not so the genuine Christian; he hides his face, sighs in secret, and cries before God, because he is not what he wants to be; not what his Lord was; not fully conformed to Christ in all things; and just because these short-comings grieve and vex his righteous soul, he cries, "Look not upon me, for I am black." All the while he may be of the highest type of Christian, yet he is not so in his own esteem. He may be a star to others, but he is a blot, as he thinks, to himself. In God's esteem he is "accepted in the Beloved" (Eph.1:6), but in his own esteem he seems to himself to be full of all manner of evil, and he cries out against it before his Lord.

Another reason why the fairest Christians are generally those that think themselves the blackest is that they have more light. A person may seem to be very fair in the dark, very fair in the twilight; but when the light gets strong, and the eye is strengthened to perceive, then it is that spots that were not noticed before are soon discovered. You have, perhaps, a handkerchief that has looked to you extremely white; so it has been in comparison with other linen: but one day, when there has been a fall of snow, you have laid your handkerchief side by side with the snow, and you have seen that it was very far from the whiteness you imagined. When the light of God comes into the soul, and we see what purity really is, what holiness really is, then it is the contrast strikes us. Though we might have thought we were somewhat clean before, when we see God in his light we see light, and we abhor ourselves in dust and ashes. Our defects so appal our own heart, that we marvel they do not exhaust his patience.

45

The better Christian a man is, the more abashed he always feels; because to him sin is so exceedingly hateful, that what sin he sees in himself he loathes himself far more than others do. The ungodly man would condone very great sin in himself, though he might know it to be there; it would not disturb him. But the Christian, being another sort, having a love for holiness and a hatred for sin, cannot bear to see the smallest speck of sin on himself: he knows what it is. There are persons living before the public eye, and jealous of popularity, who appear quite indifferent to the good opinion of the sovereign in whose kingdom they dwell; there are other persons, favourites at court, who would lie awake at night tossed to and fro in fear if they thought that something had been reported to the sovereign's ear that was disloyal. A man who does not fear God will break all his laws with an easy conscience, but one who is the favourite of heaven, who has been indulged to sit at royal banquets, who knows the eternal love of God to him, cannot bear that there should be any evil way in him that might grieve the Spirit and bring dishonour to the name of Christ. A very little sin, as the world calls it, is a very great sin to a truly awakened Christian. I ask you now, dear hearers (most of you are members of this or of other churches), do you know what it is to fret because you have spoken an unadvised word? Do you know what it is to smite upon your breast because you were angry? — justly provoked, perhaps, but still, being angry, you spoke unadvisedly. Have you ever gone to a sleepless couch because in business you have let fall a word, or have done an action which, upon mature deliberation, you could not justify? Does the tear never come from your eye because you are not like your Lord, and have failed where you hoped to succeed? I would give little for your godliness if you know nothing of this. Repentance is as much a mark of a Christian as faith itself. Do not think we have done with repenting when we come to Christ and receive the remission of our sins by the blood that once atoned. No; we shall repent as long as we sin, and as long as we need the precious blood for cleansing. While there is sin, or a proneness to any kind of sin, lurking in us, the grace of God will make us loathe the sin and humble ourselves before the Most High on account of it.

Now, I think our text seems to say just this: there were some that admired the church. They said she was fair. She seemed to say, "Don't say it; you don't know what I am, or you would not praise me." Oh, there is nothing that brings a blush to a genuine Christian's face like praising him; for he feels — "Praise such a heap of dirt as I? Give any credit to such a worthless worm as I? No; do not cast admiring glances at me! Do not say, 'That man has many virtues and many excellences!' Look not upon me, for I am black." Are there not some who will imitate any Christian — and be very right in doing so — any Christian who is eminently godly and holy? There will be many who will follow in his footsteps. I think I see such a man turn round to his followers, and say: "Do not look at me; do not copy me. I am black. Copy a better model, even Jesus. If I follow in his footsteps, follow me; but inasmuch as I have gone astray like a lost sheep, follow the shepherd; do not follow my example." Every Christian, in proportion as he lives near to God, will feel this self-abasement, this lowliness of heart; and if others talk of admiring or of imitating him, he will say, "Look not upon me, for I am black." And as he thus, in deep humility, begs that he be not exalted, he will often desire others that they would not despise him. It will come into his mind, "Such-and-such a man of God is a Christian indeed; as he sees my weakness, he will contemn [despise] me. Such-and-such a disciple of Christ is strong; he will never be able to bear with my weakness. Such-and-such a Christian woman does, indeed, adorn the doctrine of God her Saviour; but, as for me, alas! I am not what I ought to be, nor what I would be. Christian of God, do not look upon me with scorn. I will not say that you have motes in your own eyes; I have a beam in mine. Do not look upon me too severely. Judge me not harshly. If you do look at me, look to Christ for me, and pray that I may be helped; 'for I am black, because the sun has looked upon me.'"

46

Still I would have you beware of affecting anything that you do not feel. Humility itself may be counterfeited with much ostentation. Wherever there is anything like cant, as it is practised by some people who depreciate themselves but do not mean it, it is loathsome to the last degree. I recollect a very proud man, certainly twice as proud as he was high, who used to pray for himself as "God's poor dust." There was nothing, I am sure, about his conduct and conversation that entitled him to use any such expression. I have heard of a monk who said he was full of sin — he was as bad as Judas; and when somebody said, "That is true", he turned round and said, "What did I ever do that you should say so?" The effrontery of the arrogant is not more odious than the servility of the sycophant. There is a great deal of self-abnegation which is not genuine; it is the offspring of self-conceit, and not of self-knowledge. Much that we say of ourselves would mightily offend our vainglory if anybody else said the same of us. Oh, let us beware of mock humility! At the same time, the more of the genuine article we have the better, and the more truthfully we can cry out to God's people, "Look not upon me, because I am black", the more clear will it be that we are, after all, amongst the fairest.

But I pass on. The most diligent Christian — let this stand for the second observation — *the most diligent Christian will be the man most afraid of the evils connected with his work*. "Evils connected with his work!" says one. "Does work for God have evils contingent upon it?" Yes; but for every evil connected with the work of God, there are ten evils connected with idleness. No, all you professors who are doing nothing are wearing yourselves out faster by rust than you could have done by honest wear. But, you see, in the case of our text, there was evil connected with work. She had been made a keeper of the vineyards; and having to trim the vines, the sun had shone upon her, and she says, "Look not upon me, because I am black, because the sun has looked upon me." The blackness that she confessed was a blackness occasioned by her having to bear the burden and heat of the day.

And now I speak to such as live in active service, doing the work of God. Dear brethren, there are certain evils connected with our lifework, coming from the sun that looks upon us, which we should confess before our heavenly Father. I speak now only to the workers. I have known some whom the sun has looked upon in this respect; their zeal has grown cold through non-success. You went out first of all as a Christian, full of fire and life. You intended to push the church before you, and drag the world after you. Perhaps you thought that you were going to work a Reformation almost as great as that of Luther. Well, much of that was of the flesh, though beneath the surface there was an earnest zeal for God which was eating you up. But you have been mixed up with Christians for some years of a very cool sort. Use the thermometer tonight. Has not the spiritual temperature gone down in your own soul? Perhaps you have not seen many conversions under your ministry; or, in the class which you conduct, you have not seen many children brought to Jesus? Do you feel you are getting cool? Then wrap your face in your mantle tonight! And say: "Look not upon me, for in losing my zeal I am black, for the sun has looked upon me." Perhaps it has affected you in another way, for the sun does not bring freckles out on all faces in the same place. Perhaps it is your temper that has grown sour? When you joined the church, you felt all love, and you expected, as you had a right to do, that everybody would reciprocate the same feeling; it may be that since then you have had to do battle against contentions. You have been in a part of the church where there has been a strife, not altogether for the faith once delivered to the saints, but something of a party feeling was mixed with it, and you have had to take some share in it. And perhaps you have gradually acquired a carping, critical habit, so that where you used to enjoy the Word, you are now all for judging the preacher. You are not so much a feeder upon the Word, as a mere taster of the dishes, to see if you cannot find some fault with their flavour. Wrap your face again, I beseech you, in your mantle. Again bow before God, and say: "Look not upon me, because I am black; the sun has looked upon me. In my service for God I have

47

been impaired." Perhaps, dear friend, you have suffered in another way! I sometimes suffer in this respect very materially. The Christian's walk ought to be calm, peaceful, quiet, unruffled. Leaving everything with the Lord, and awaiting his will, our peace should be like a river. But you know that, when there is much to be done in God's service, there is a very strong temptation to want to push this and that thing forward with undue haste. Or if it does not move quickly at the rate you wish, there is a temptation to be sad, careful, and anxious; to be, in fact, like Martha, cumbered with much service. When you get into that condition, it is an injury to yourself, and really prejudicial to your own work; for they serve Christ best who commune with him most, and broken fellowship means broken strength.

Yet this is often our trouble; our energies are exhausted by worry more than by work. Part of our duty is neglected through unexpected cares that have distracted our thoughts. Pardon me, if I transfer the thing to myself in a figure. Say that this Tabernacle wants all my vigilance concentrated upon its welfare. Then there is another matter that wants instant attention at the same time. Here is a soul seeking Christ; here is another backsliding; here is a brother falling to ears with a brother. Innumerable things crowd upon one's view, and clamour for immediate investigation till one gets disturbed and troubled. "Look not upon me, because I am black; because the sun has looked upon me. The work I have engaged in for you has brought me into the sun and burnt my face." It ought to be bright and fair with fellowship; it is soiled and begrimed with service.

Sometimes this evil of sun-burning will come in the shape of joy taken away from the heart by weariness. I do not think, dear brethren, any of us are weary of God's work. If so, we never were called to it. But we may get weary *in* it. You recollect, some of you, here — I speak to such as often preach the gospel — how happy you were when first you were permitted to open your mouth for Christ! Oh, what a joy it was! What a pleasure! How you threw your whole soul into it! There was no sleepiness and dullness in your sermon then. But now, year after year, year after year, your brain gets weary, and though the spirit is willing, the flesh is weak. The joy you once had in service was your strength, and it has somewhat gone from you. The toil is more irksome when the spirits are less buoyant. Well, I would advise you to confess this before God, and ask for a medicine to heal you. You have needs get your joy back, but first you must acknowledge that you have lost it. Say, "I am black, because the sun has looked upon me." On the other hand, it is a bad result of a good work when our humility is injured by it.

Place a Christian in a position where he has to do much for Christ, and is much thought of and set by: let him have great success, and the tendency will be for him to compliment himself as though he were some great one. You cannot reap great sheaves for the Master without this temptation coming over your soul. What a glorious workman you are, and what a great reward your soul will have for having done so well! It is the sun looking upon you, taking away the fairness of your humility, freckling and blackening your face with a pride that is obnoxious to God. This ought to be confessed at once, and heartily repented of. I do not think I shall attempt to go through the list of all the matters that might come out of Christian service. It will suffice me to say, I am afraid that in many cases our motives get mixed. Pure and simple at first in our service, we may get at last to serve Christ only because it is our office to do so. Woe to the man that preaches only because he is a minister, and does not preach because he loves Christ! We may also get to be self-reliant. It is a great mercy for God's ministers when they tremble on going into the pulpit, even though they have been accustomed to preach for twenty years.

Martin Luther declares that he never feared the face of man; and all who knew him would bear witness that it was even so; yet he said he never went up the stairs of the pulpit at Wittenberg but he felt his knees knock together with fear lest he should not be faithful to God and his truth. When we begin to rely upon ourselves, and think we can do it, and our

48

experience and our practice will suffice to bear us safely through the next discourse without help from on high, then the sun has looked upon us and blackened our face indeed, and the time of our usefulness draws to a close. Come, Christian people, brothers and sisters, thankful though I am that I can address so large a number who are engaged in the Master's work, I beseech you, let us go together to the footstool of the heavenly grace, confess there our blackness, and own that much of it has come upon us even while we were engaged in the service of God.

In the third place, *the most watchful Christian is conscious of the danger of self-neglect*. That is the next part of our text. "...they made me the keeper of the vineyards; but mine own vineyard have I not kept."

Solemnly, let me speak again to my brethren who are seeking to glorify Christ by their lives. I came some time ago on a sermon by that famous divine, Mr. Henry Melville, which consists all through of one solitary thought, and one only image well worked out. I will give you the pith of what took some eight pages to get through. He supposes a man to be a guide in Switzerland. It is his duty to conduct travellers in that country through the sublime passes, and to point out to them the glories of the scenery, and the beauties of the lakes, and streams, and glaciers, and hills. This man, as he continues in his office, almost inevitably gets to repeat his descriptions as a matter of course; and everybody knows how a guide at last comes to "talk book", and just iterate words which do not awaken any corresponding feeling in his own mind. Yet when he began, perhaps it was a sincere love of the sublime and the beautiful that led him to take up the avocation of a guide; and at first it really was to him a luxury to impart to others what he had felt amidst the glories of nature; but as, year after year, to hundreds of different parties, he had to repeat much the same descriptions, call attention to the same sublimities, and indicate the same beauties, it is almost impossible but that he should get to be at last a mere machine. Through the hardening tendency of custom, and the debasing influence of gain, his aptest descriptions and most exquisite eulogies came to be of no greater account than the mere language of a hireling. This thought I will not work out *in extenso* [in detail] as that famous preacher has done, but I give it to you as a cutting, which may germinate if planted in the garden of your heart. Every worker for Christ is deeply concerned in the application of this parable, because the peril of self complacency increases in precisely the same ratio as the zeal of proselytising. When counselling others, you think yourself wise. When warning others, you feel yourself safe. When judging others, you suppose yourself above suspicion. You began the work with a flush of ardour; it may be with a fever of enthusiasm; a sacred instinct prompted, and a glowing passion moved you. How will you continue it? Here is the danger — the fearful danger — lest you do it mechanically, fall into a monotony, continue in the same train, and use holy words to others with no corresponding feeling in your own soul. May we not stir up others to devout emotions and yet our own hearts fail to burn with the sacred fire? Oh, may it not be easy for one to stand as a signpost on the road to heaven, and never stir himself? Every preacher who judges himself aright knows that this is the risk he incurs; and I believe the same danger in a measure threatens Christians in every form of work in which they occupy themselves for Christ.

Dear friends, beware of reading the Bible for other people. Get your own text — your own morsel of marrow and fatness — out of Scripture; and do not be satisfied to be sermon-making or lesson-making for your class in the Sunday-school. Feed on the Word yourselves, or else your own vineyard will not be kept. When you are on your knees in prayer, pray for others by all means; but, oh, let private prayer be kept up with a view to your own edification and your own growth in grace as well. Do not preach the Saviour's blood, and yet be without the blood mark on yourselves. Do not tell of the fountain, and yet go unwashed. Do not point to heaven, and then turn your back on it and go down to hell. Fellow-workers, look to yourselves, lest, after having preached to others, you yourselves should be cast away. Your neighbours certainly, but yourselves also; the children in your class certainly, your own children at home certainly; but look to yourselves also, oh, you that are workers in God's house, lest ye keep the vineyards of others and your own vineyards are not kept. It is very possible for a man to get to dislike the very religion to which he feels bound still by force of custom to go on teaching to others. "Is that possible?" says one. Alas, that it is! Have you never heard of the flower-girl in the streets? What is her occupation! I dare say some girls like her have passed by and seen her with a great basket full of violets, and said: "What a delightful occupation, to have that fragrant smell for ever near to one!" Yes, but there was one girl who sold them, and said she hated the smell of violets. She had got to loathe them, and to think that there was no smell in the world so offensive because they were always under her nostrils all day, and taken home to her little scanty room at night; and having nothing but violets around her, she hated them altogether. And I do believe that there are persons without the grace of Christ in their hearts who keep on talking about grace, and mercy, and practicing prayer, and yet in their heart of hearts they hate the very fragrance of the name of Jesus, and need that there should come upon them an awakening out of their sleep of presumption and hypocrisy, to make them know that, though they thought they were the friends of God, they were, after all, his enemies. They were mere keepers of other men's vineyards, but their own vineyards had gone to ruin.

Our last reflection is of the deepest importance. The most conscientious Christian will be the first to enquire for the antidote, and to use the cure. What is the cure? The cure is found in the verse next to my text. "Look not upon me, because I am black, because the sun hath looked upon me. They made me the keeper of the vineyards; but mine own vineyard have I not kept." What is next? "Tell me, O thou whom my soul loveth, where thou feedest, where thou makest thy flock to rest at noon: for why should I be as one that turneth aside by the flocks of thy companions?" See, then, you workers, if you want to keep up your freshness, and not to get blackened by the sun under which you labour, go to your Lord again — go and talk to him. Address him again by that dear name, "Thou whom my soul loveth." Ask to have your first love rekindled; strive after the love of your espousals. There are men in married life who seem to have forgotten that they ever loved their wives; but there are others concerning whom the hymn is true —

And as year rolls after year,
Each to other still more dear.

(Isaac Watts)

So there are some Christians who seem to forget that they ever loved the Saviour; but I will believe there are others in whom that love deepens and becomes more fervent as each year passes over their heads. If any of you are at fault in this, do not give sleep to your eyelids tonight till you have renewed your espousal love. Thy Lord recollects it, if you do not, for he says: "I remember thee, the kindness of thy youth, the love of thine espousals, when thou wentest after me in the wilderness, in a land that was not sown." (Jer. 2:2) You did some wild things in those early days. You were a great deal more zealous than wise; but, though you look back upon that with censure, Christ regards it with delight. He wishes you were now as you were then. Perhaps today you are not quite cold to him. Do not flatter yourself on that account; for he has said, "I would thou wert cold or hot." (Rev. 3:15) It is just lukewarmness that he loathes most of all, and he has threatened to spue the lukewarm out of his mouth. Oh, to be always full of love to him! You will never come to any harm by working for him then; your work will do you good. The sweat of labour will even make your face the fairer. The more you do for souls, the purer, and the holier, and the more Christian will you be if you do it with him. Keep up the habit of sitting at his feet like Mary, as well as serving him with Martha. You can keep the two together;

50

they will balance each other, and you shall not be barren or unfruitful, neither shall you fall into the blackness which the sun is apt to breed.

Oh for more nearness to Christ, more love to Christ, and closer communion with him! Did you notice what the spouse said: "Tell me, O thou whom my soul loveth, where thou feedest?" (Song 1:7) I suppose her object was to go and feed with him. Look to the feeding of your own soul, Christian. When a man says, "I have a hard day's work to do, I shall have no time to eat", you know full well that he is losing time where he thinks he gains it; for if he does not keep himself in good repair he will sicken by-and-by, and, in the long run, he will do less than if he gave himself due pause. So is it with your soul. You cannot give out a vital energy which you have not got in you healthy and vigorous; and if you have not got power from God in your own soul, power cannot come out of you, for it is not there. Do, therefore, feed upon Christ. Or do you feel yourself like that guide of whom we spoke just now? Has the routine of service blunted your sensibilities, till you gaze unmoved on those objects of beauty and marvel that should awaken every passion and thrill every nerve of your being? Ask then in what way he might keep up his interest in the lakes and the mountains? Would it not be well for him, occasionally, at any rate, to take a lonely journey to find out new features in the gorgeous scenery or to stand in solitude, and see the hills in a fresh light, or mark the forest trees in different states of the weather; so that he might again renew his own sensations of admiration, and of gratitude to God for having created such sublimities? Then I can readily believe his enthusiasm would increase rather than abate by an increasing familiarity with the landscape.

And you, worker for God, you must go to God alone; feed on precious truth for yourself; dig into the deep things of God and enrich your own spirit. Thus you may serve God as much as ever you did: you will come to no harm from it. Did you notice that she also asked: "Tell me where thou makest thy flock to rest at noon?" Rest is what the worker wants. Where is the rest of Christ's flock but in his own dear bosom? Where is there repose, but in his own fidelity, in the two immutable things wherein it is impossible for God to lie — the oath and the promise? Oh, never turn away from that rest! Turn into it again, tonight, beloved. As for me, I feel I want my Saviour more than ever I did. Though I have preached his gospel now these five-and-twenty years and more, I need still to come and cling to his cross as a guilty sinner, and find "life for a look at the crucified One", just as I did at first. Oh that God's grace may ever keep the most ardent among us always faithful with our own soul, abiding in the Lord, and rejoicing in him!

I have done. This is my word to workers. Let me only say to you for whom there has seemed nothing in the sermon, if you are not workers for Christ you are workers against him. "He that is not with me is against me; and he that gathereth not with me scattereth abroad." (Mat. 12:30) O souls, why should you stand out against the Saviour? Why should you resist him? Bleeding out his life for his enemies, the mirror of disinterested love, what is there in him that can make you fight against him? Drop your weapons, man! Drop them tonight, I charge you by the living God! And come now, ask pardon through the precious blood, and it shall be given you. Seek a new heart, and a right spirit. The Holy Spirit will work it. From this, night come a worker for Christ. The church wants you. The armies of Christ need recruiting. Take the proffered blessing and become a soldier of the cross; and may the Lord build up his Zion by many of you who were not his people aforetime, but of whom it is said: "And it shall come to pass, that in the place where it was said unto them, Ye are not my people, there it shall be said unto them, Ye are the sons of the living God." (Hos. 1:10)

7. THE UNKEPT VINEYARD: OR, PERSONAL WORK NEGLECTED
NO. 1936

A SERMON DELIVERED ON LORD'S DAY EVENING,
SEPTEMBER 19TH, 1886
AT THE METROPOLITAN TABERNACLE, NEWINGTON

**"They made me the keeper of the vineyards; but mine own vineyard
have I not kept." (Song of Solomon 1:6)**

The text is spoken in the first person singular — "They made me". Therefore, let the preaching tonight be personal to you, dear friends: personal to the preacher first, and then to each one of this mixed multitude. May we at this hour think less of others than of ourselves! May the sermon be of practical value to our own hearts! I do not suppose that it will be a pleasing sermon: on the other hand it may be a saddening one. I may bring unhappy memories before you; but let us not be afraid of that holy sorrow which is health to the soul. Since the spouse in this text speaks of herself, "They made me the keeper of the vineyards; but mine own vineyard have I not kept", let each one of us copy her example, and think of our own selves.

The text is the language of complaint. We are all pretty ready at complaining, especially about other people. Not much good comes of picking holes in other men's characters; and yet many spend hours in that unprofitable occupation. It will be well for us, at this time, to let our complaint, like that of the text, deal with ourselves. If there is something wrong at home, let the father blame himself; if there is something wrong with the children, let the mother look to her own personal conduct as their instructor. Do not let us lend out our ears, but let us keep them at home for our own use. Let us clear out an open passage to the heart, so that everything that is said shall go down into the spirit, and purify our inner man. Let us from the heart make the confession — "They made me the keeper of the vineyards; but mine own vineyard have I not kept." Let us make the text practical. Do not let us be satisfied to have uttered the language of complaint; but let us get rid of the evils which we deplore. If we have been wrong, let us labour to be right. If we have neglected our own vineyard, let us confess it with due humiliation; but let us not continue to neglect it. Let us ask of God that holy results may flow out of our self-lamentations, so that before many days we may begin to keep our own vineyards carefully by the grace of God; and then we shall better carry out the office of keeper of the vineyards of others, if we are called to such an employment.

There are two things upon which I am going to dwell at this time. The first is, that there are many Christian people — I hope they are Christian people — who will be compelled to confess that the greater part of their life is spent in labour which is not of the highest kind, and is not properly their own. I shall find out the worker who has forgotten his heavenly calling. And when I have done with this case — and I am afraid that there will be much about it that may touch many of us — I shall then take a more general view, and deal with any who are undertaking other works, and neglecting their own proper vocation.

I. First, then, let me begin with THE CHRISTIAN MAN WHO HAS FORGOTTEN HIS HIGH AND HEAVENLY CALLING.

In the day when you and I were born again, my brethren, we were born for God. In the day when we saw that Christ died for us, we were bound henceforth to be dead to the world. In the day when we were quickened by the Holy Spirit into newness of life, that life was bound to be a consecrated one. For a thousand reasons it is true that, "Ye are not your own: ye are bought with a price." (1 Cor. 6:19-20) The ideal Christian is one who has been

52

made alive with a life which he lives for God. He has risen out of the dominion of the world, the flesh, and the devil. He reckons that "if one died for all, then were all dead: and that he died for all, that they which live should not henceforth live unto themselves, but unto him which died for them, and rose again." (2 Cor 5:14-15) This you will not deny. Christian friends, you admit that you have a high, holy, and heavenly calling!

Now, let us look back. We have not spent our life idly: we have been forced to be keepers of the vineyards. I hope I am not addressing anybody here who has tried to live without employment and labour of some kind. No, we have worked, and we have worked hard. Most men speak of their wages as "hard-earned," and I believe that in many cases they speak the bare truth. Many hours in the day have to be spent upon our occupations. We wake up in the morning, and think of what we have to do. We go to bed wearied at night by what we have done. This is as it should be, for God did not make us that we might sport and play, like leviathan in the deep. Even in Paradise, man was bidden to dress the garden. There is something to be done by each man, and especially by each Christian man.

Come back to what I began with. In the day when we were born again, as many of us as are new creatures in Christ Jesus, we began to live for God and not for ourselves. Have we carried out that life? We have worked, we have even worked hard; but the question comes to us: What have we worked for? Who has been our master? With what object have we toiled? Of course, if I have been true to my profession as a Christian, I have lived and worked for God, for Christ, for the kingdom of heaven. But has it been so? And is it so now? Many are working very hard for wealth, which means, of course, for self, that they may be enriched. Some are working simply for a competence, which means, if it goes no farther, it is still for self. Others work for their families, a motive good enough in its way, but still only an enlargement, after all, of self. To the Christian there must always be a far higher, deeper, purer, truer motive than self in its widest sense; or else the day must come when he will look back on his life, and say, "They made me the keeper of the vineyards; but mine own vineyard" — that is, the service of Christ, the glory of him that bought me with his blood — "have I not kept." It seems to me to be a terrible calamity to have to look back on twenty years, and say, "What have I done in all those twenty years for Christ? How much of my energy has been spent in striving to glorify him? I have had talents: how many of those talents have been used for him who gave them to me? I have had wealth, or I have had influence. How much of that money have I spent distinctly for my Lord? How much of that influence have I used for the promotion of his kingdom?" You have been busy with this notion and that motive and the other endeavour; but have you lived as you will wish to have lived when you stand at his right hand amid his glories? Have you so acted that you will then judge yourself to have lived well when your Lord and Master shall come to call you to account? Ask yourself, "Am I an earnest labourer together with God, or am I, after all, only a laborious trifler, an industrious doer of nothing, working hard to accomplish no purpose of the sort for which I ought to work, since I ought to live unto my Lord alone?" I invite all my fellow servants to take a retrospect, and just see whether they have kept their own vineyards. I suppose that they have worked hard. I only put the question: Have they kept their own vineyards? Have they served the Lord in all things?

I am half afraid to go a step farther. To a very large degree, we have not been true to our own professions: our highest work has been neglected, for we have not kept our own vineyards. In looking back, how little time has been spent by us in communion with God! How little a part of our thoughts has been occupied with meditation, contemplation, adoration, and other acts of devotion! How little have we surveyed the beauties of Christ, his Person, his work, his sufferings, his glory! We say that it is "heaven below" to commune with Christ; but do we do it? We profess that there is no place like the mercy-seat. How much are we at that mercy-seat? We often say that the Word of God is

53

precious — that every page of it glows with a heavenly light. Do we study it? Friends, how much time do you spend on it? I venture to say that the bulk of Christians spend more time in reading the newspaper than they do in reading the Word of God. I trust that I am too severe in this statement, but I am afraid, greatly afraid, that I am not. The last new book, perhaps the last sentimental story, will win attentive reading, when the divine, mysterious, unutterable depths of heavenly knowledge are disregarded by us.

Our Puritan forefathers were strong men because they lived on the Scriptures. None stood against them in their day, for they fed on good meat, whereas their degenerate children are far too fond of unwholesome food. The chaff of fiction and the bran of the Quarterlies are poor substitutes for the old corn of Scripture, the fine flour of spiritual truth. Alas, my brethren, too many eat the unripe fruit of the vineyards of Satan, and the fruits of the Lord's vines they utterly despise! Think of our neglect of our God, and see whether it is not true that we have treated him very badly. We have been in the shop, we have been on the exchange, we have been at the markets, we have been in the fields, we have been in the public libraries, we have been in the lecture room, we have been in the forum of debate; but our own closets and studies, our walk with God, and our fellowship with Jesus, we have far too much neglected.

Moreover, the vineyard of holy service for God we have too much left to go to ruin. I would ask you: How about the work your God has called you to do? Men are dying; are you saving them? This great city is like a seething caldron, boiling and bubbling up with infamous iniquity; are we doing anything by way of antidote to the hell-broth concocted in that caldron? Are we indeed a power working towards righteousness? How much good have we done? What have I done to pluck brands from the burning? What have I done to find the lost sheep for which my Saviour laid down his life? Come, put the questions, and answer them honestly! No, do not back out and say, "I have no ability." I fear you have more ability than you will give an account of with joy at the last great day. I remember a young man who complained that the little church over which he presided was so small. He said, "I cannot do much good. I have not above two hundred hearers." An older man replied, "Two hundred hearers are a great many to have to give an account of at the last great day." As I came in at yonder door this evening, and looked into these thousands of faces, I could not help trembling. How shall I answer for this solemn charge, for this enormous flock, in that last great day? You have all a flock of some kind, larger or smaller. You have all, as Christian people, somebody for whom you will have to answer. Have you done your Master's work in reference to those entrusted to you? O men and women, have you sought to save others from going down into the pit? You have the divine remedy: have you handed it out to these sick and dying ones? You have the heavenly word which can deliver them from destruction: have you spoken it in their ears, praying all the while that God might bless it to their souls. Might not many a man among you say to himself, "I have been a tailor", or "I have been a shop-keeper", or "I have been a mechanic", or "I have been a merchant", or "I have been a physician, and I have attended to these callings; but my own vineyard, which was my Master's, which I was bound to look to first of all, I have not kept?"

Well, now, what is the remedy for this? We need not talk of our fault any more; let us make each one his own personal confession, and then seek amendment. I believe the remedy is a very sweet one. It is not often that medicine is pleasant, but at this time I prescribe for you a charming potion. It is that you follow up the next verse to my text. Read it — "Mine own vineyard have I not kept. Tell me, O thou whom my soul loveth, where thou feedest, where thou makest thy flock to rest at noon; for why should I be as one that turneth aside by the flocks of thy companions?" Get to your Lord, and in him you will find recovery from your neglects. Ask him where he feeds his flock, and go with him. They have warm hearts who commune with Christ. They are prompt in duty who enjoy his

54

fellowship. I cannot help reminding you of what I have often spoken of, namely, our Lord's language to the church at Laodicea. That church had come to be so bad that he said, "I will spue thee out of my mouth." (Rev. 3:16) What was the remedy for that church? "Behold, I stand at the door, and knock: if any man hear my voice, and open the door, I will come in to him, and will sup with him, and he with me." (Verse 20) After supping with Christ, you will not be lukewarm. Nobody can say, "I am neither cold nor hot" when they have been in his company. Rather they will enquire, "Did not our heart burn within us, while he talked with us by the way?" If there be an angel, as John Milton sings, whose name is THE archangel Uriel, who lives in the sun, I will warrant you he is never cold; so he that lives in Christ, and walks with him, is never chill, nor slow in the divine service. Away to your Lord, then!

Hasten to your Lord, and you will soon begin to keep your vineyard; for in the Song you will see a happy change effected. The spouse began to keep her vineyard directly, and to do it in the best fashion. Within a very short time, you find her saying, "Take us the foxes, the little foxes, that spoil the vines." (Song 2:15) See, she is hunting out her sins and her follies. Farther on you find her with her Lord in the vineyard, crying, "Awake, O north wind; and come, thou south; blow upon my garden, that the spices thereof may flow out!" (Song 4:16) She is evidently keeping her garden, and asking for heavenly influences to make the spices and flowers yield their perfume. She went down to see whether the vines flourished, and the pomegranates budded. Furthermore, with her beloved, she rises early to go to the vineyard, and watch the growth of the plants. Farther on you find her talking about all manner of fruits that she has laid up for her beloved. Thus you see that to walk with Christ is the way to keep your vineyard and serve your Lord. Come and sit at his feet; lean on his bosom; rest on his arm; and make him to be the joy of your spirit. The Lord grant, dear brethren, that this gentle word, which I have spoken as much to myself as to you, may be blessed to us all!

II. Now, I turn to the congregation in general, and speak with THE MAN WHO IN ANY PLACE HAS TAKEN OTHER WORK, AND NEGLECTED HIS OWN. He can use the words of the text — "They make me the keeper of the vineyards; but mine own vineyard have I not kept."

We know many persons who are always doing a great deal, and yet do nothing; fussy people, people to the front in every movement, persons who could set the whole world right, but are not right themselves. Just before a general election there is a manifestation of most remarkable men — generally those who know everything, and a few things besides, who, if they could but be sent to Parliament, would turn the whole world upside down, and put even Pandemonium to rights. They would pay the National Debt within six months, and do any other trifle that might occur to them. Very eminent men are these! I have come across impossibly great men. None could be so great as these feel themselves to be. They are an order of very superior persons: reformers, or philosophers who know what nobody else knows, only, happily, they have not patented the secret, but are prepared to tell it out to others, and thereby illuminate us all. I suggest to our highly-gifted friends that it is possible to be looking after a great many things, and yet to be neglecting your own vineyard.

There is a vineyard that a great many neglect, and that is their own heart. It is well to have talent; it is well to have influence; but it is better to be right within yourself. It is well for a man to see to his cattle, and look well to his flocks and to his herds; but let him not forget to cultivate that little patch of ground that lies in the centre of his being. Let him educate his head, and intermeddle with all knowledge; but let him not forget that there is another plot of ground called the heart, the character which is more important still. Right principles are spiritual gold, and he that has them, and is ruled by them, is the man who truly lives.

55

He has not life, whatever else he has, who has not his heart cultivated, and made right and pure. Have you ever thought about your heart yet? Oh, I do not mean whether you have palpitations! I am no doctor. I am speaking now about the heart in its moral and spiritual aspect. What is your character, and do you seek to cultivate it? Do you ever use the hoe upon those weeds which are so plentiful in us all? Do you water those tiny plants of goodness which have begun to grow? Do you watch them to keep away the little foxes which would destroy them? Are you hopeful that yet there may be a harvest in your character which God may look upon with approval? I pray that we may all look to our hearts. "Keep your heart with all diligence; for out of it are the issues of life." (Prov. 4:23) Pray daily, "Create in me a clean heart, O God; and renew a right spirit within me" (Ps. 51:10); for if not, you will go up and down in the world, and do a great deal, and when it comes to the end you will have neglected your noblest nature, and your poor starved soul will die that second death, which is the more dreadful because it is everlasting death. How terrible for a soul to die of neglect! How can we escape who neglect this great salvation? If we pay every attention to our bodies, but none to our immortal souls, how shall we justify our folly? God save us from suicide by neglect! May we not have to moan out eternally, "They made me the keeper of the vineyards; but mine own vineyard have I not kept!"

Now, pass over that point, and think of another vineyard. Are not some people neglecting their families? Next to our hearts, our households are the vineyards which we are most bound to cultivate. I shall never forget a man whom I knew in my youth, who used to accompany me at times in my walks to the villages to preach. He was always willing to go with me any evening; but I did not need to ask him, for he asked himself, until I purposely put him off from it. He liked also to preach himself, much better than others liked to hear him; but he was a man who was sure to be somewhere to the front if he could. Even if you snuffed him out, he had a way of lighting himself up again. He was good-natured and irrepressible. He was, I believe, sincerely earnest in doing good. But two boys of his were well-known to me, and they would swear horribly. They were ready for every vice, and were under no restraint. One of them drank himself into a dying state with brandy, though he was a mere boy. I do not believe his father had ever spoken to him about the habit of intoxication, though he certainly was sober and virtuous himself. I had no fault to find with him except this grave fault — that he was seldom at home, was not master of the house, and could not control his children. Neither husband nor wife occupied any place of influence in the household; they were simply the slaves of their children: their children made themselves vile, and they did not restrain them! This brother would pray for his children at the prayer meeting, but I do not think he ever practiced family prayer. It is shocking to find men and women speaking fluently about religion, and yet their houses are a disgrace to Christianity. I suppose that none of you are as bad as that; but, if it be so, please spell this text over: "They made me the keeper of the vineyards; but mine own vineyard have I not kept." The most careful and prayerful father cannot be held accountable for having wicked sons if he has done his best to instruct them. The most anxious and tearful mother cannot be blamed if her daughter dishonours the family, provided her mother has done her best to train her up in the right way. But if the parents cannot say that they have done their best, and their children go astray, then they are blameworthy. If any of them have come to the Tabernacle tonight, and their boys and girls are — they do not know where, let them go home quickly, and look them up.

If any of my hearers exercise no parental discipline, nor seek to bring their children to Christ, I do implore them to give up every kind of public work till they have first done their work at home. Has anybody made you a minister, and you are not trying to save your own children? I tell you, sir, I do not believe that God made you a minister; for if he had, he would have begun with making you a minister to your own family. "They made me the keeper of the vineyards." "They" ought to have known better, and you ought to have known better than to accept the call. How can you be a steward in the great household of

56

the Lord when you cannot even rule your own house? A Sunday-school teacher, teaching other people's children, and never praying with her own! Is not this a sad business? A teacher of a large class of youths who has never taken a class of his own sons and daughters! Why, what will he do when he lives to see his children plunge into vice and sin, and remembers that he has utterly neglected them? This is plain dealing; but I never wear gloves when I preach. I do not know where this knife may cut; but if it wounds, I pray you do not blunt its edge. Do you say that this is "very personal"? It is meant to be personal; and if anybody is offended by it, let him be offended with himself, and mend his ways. No longer let it be true of any of us, "They made me the keeper of the vineyards; but mine own vineyard have I not kept."

Besides that, everyone who knows the Lord should feel that his vineyard lies also round about his own house. If God has saved your children, then, dear friend, try to do something for your neighbours, for your work-people, for those with whom you associate in daily labour. God has appointed you to take care of those nearest home. They say the cobbler's wife goes barefooted. Do not let it be true. Begin at home, and go on with those nearest home. Manifest Christian love to your neighbours. It is a great pity that yonder Christian man, living in a very dark part of London, comes to the Tabernacle, and does good in our societies, but never speaks a word for Jesus in the court where he lives. Poor stuff, poor stuff, is that salt which is only salt when it is in the salt-box! Throw that kind of salt away. We want a kind of salt that begins to bite into any bit of meat it touches. Put it where you like, if it is good salt, it begins to operate upon that which is nearest to it. Some people are capital salt in the box: they are also good in the cake, they are beautifully white to look at, and you can cut them into ornamental shapes; but they are never used; they are merely kept for show. If salt does not preserve anything, throw it away. Ask the farmer whether he would like it for his fields. "No", he says, "there is no goodness in it." Salt that has no saltness in it is of no use. You can make the garden path of it. It is good to be trodden under foot of men, but that is all the use to which you can put it.

O my beloved fellow-Christians, do not let it be said that you reside in a place to which you do no good whatever. I am sure if there were individual, personal work on the part of Christians in the localities where they reside, God the Holy Spirit would bless the unanimous action of his earnest, quickened church, and London would soon know that God has a people in the midst of it. If we keep away from the masses — if we cannot think of labouring in a district because it is too low or too poor — we shall have missed our vocation, and, at the last, we shall have to lament, "They made me the keeper of the vineyards; but mine own vineyard have I not kept."

You and I must cry mightily to the Holy Spirit to help us to live really and truly the lives which our professions demand of us. A day will come when all church-goings, and chapel-goings, and preachings, and singings, and sacraments, will seem fluff and useless stuff if there has not been the substance of real living for Christ in all our religiousness. Oh that we would rouse ourselves to something like a divine earnestness! Oh that we felt the grandeur of our heavenly surroundings! We are no common men! We are loved with no common love! Jesus died for us! He died for us! He died for us! And is this poor life of ours so often dull and worldly, our sole return? Behold that piece of land! He that bought it paid his life for it, watered it with bloody sweat, and sowed in it a divine seed. And what is the harvest? We naturally expect great things. Is the poor starveling life of many a professor a fit harvest for Christ's sowing his heart's blood? God the Father, God the Son, and God the Holy Spirit, all in action — what is the result? Omnipotence linking hands with love, and working out a miracle of grace! What comes of it? A half-hearted professor of religion. Is this all the result? O Lord, was there ever so small an effect from so great a cause? You might almost need a microscope to discover the result of the work of grace in some people's lives. Ought it to be so? Shall it be so? In the name of him that lives and was dead, dare you let it be so? Help us, O God, to begin to live, and keep the vineyard which you yourself have given us to keep, that we may render in our account at last with joy, and not with grief! Amen.

8. LOVE TO JESUS
NO. 338

DELIVERED ON SABBATH MORNING, SEPTEMBER 30TH, 1860
AT EXETER HALL, STRAND

"O thou whom my soul loveth." (Song of Solomon 1:7)

IF the life of a Christian may be compared with a sacrifice, then humility digs the foundation for the altar, prayer brings the unhewn stones and piles them one upon the other, penitence fills the trench round about the altar with water, obedience lays the wood in order, faith pleads the Jehovah-jireh, and places the victim upon the altar; but the sacrifice even then is incomplete, for where is the, fire? Love, love alone can consummate the sacrifice by supplying the needed fire from heaven. Whatever we lack in our piety, as it is indispensable that we should have faith in Christ, so is it absolutely necessary that we should have love for him. That heart which is devoid of an earnest love to Jesus is surely still dead in trespasses and sins. And if anyone should venture to affirm that he had faith in Christ, but had no love for him, we would at once also venture to affirm as positively that his religion was vain.

Perhaps the great lack of the religion of the times is love. Sometimes, as I look upon the world at large, and the Church which lies too much in its bosom, I am apt to think that the Church has light, but lacks fire; that she has some degree of true faith, clear knowledge, and much beside which is precious, but that she lacks to a great extent that flaming love with which she once, as a chaste virgin, walked with Christ through the fires of martyrdom, when she showed to him her undefiled, unquenchable love in the catacombs of the city, and in the caves of the rock; when the snows of the Alps might testify to the virgin purity of the love of the saints, by the purple stain which marked the shedding of blood in defense of our bleeding Lord — blood which had been shed in defence of him whom, though they had not seen his face, "unceasing they adore."

It is my pleasant task this morning to stir up your pure minds, that you, as part of Christ's Church, may feel something in your hearts today of love for him, and may be able to address him not only under the title, "Thou in whom my soul trusteth", but "Thou whom my soul loveth". Last Sabbath day, if you remember, we devoted ourselves to simple faith, and tried to preach the gospel to the ungodly; in this present hour, we devote ourselves to the pure, Spirit-born, godlike, flame of love.

On looking at my text, I shall come to regard it thus: First, we shall listen to the rhetoric of the lip as we here read in these words, "O thou whom my soul loveth". We shall then observe the logic of the heart, which would justify us in giving such a title as this to Christ, and then come in the third place to something which even surpasses rhetoric or logic, the absolute demonstration of the daily life. I pray that we may be able to prove constantly by our acts that Jesus Christ is "He whom our soul loveth".

I. First, then, the loving title of our text is to be considered as expressing the RHETORIC OF THE LIP. The text calls Christ, "Thou whom my soul loveth". Let us take this title and dissect it a little.

One of the first things that strikes us when we come to look at it is the reality of the love which is here expressed. "Reality", I say, understanding the term "real" not in contradistinction to that which is lying and fictitious, but in contrast with that which is shadowy and indistinct. Do you not notice that the spouse here speaks of Christ as of one whom she knew actually to exist, not as an abstraction, but as a Person. She speaks of

59

him as a real person, "Thou whom my soul loveth". Why, these seem to be the words of one who is pressing him to her bosom, who sees him with her eyes, who tracks him with her feet, who knows that he is, and that he will reward the love which diligently seeks him. Brothers and sisters, there is often a great deficiency in our love for Jesus. We do not realise the Person of Christ. We think about Christ, and then we love the conception that we have formed of him. But oh, how few Christians view their Lord as being as real a person as we are ourselves — very man — a man that could suffer, a man that could die, substantial flesh and blood — yet very God as real as if he were not invisible, and as truly existent as though we could compass him in our minds. We want to have a real Christ more fully preached, and more fully loved, by the church. We fail in our love, because Christ is not real to us as he was to the early Church. The early Church did not preach much doctrine; they preached Christ. They had little to say of truths about Christ; it was Christ himself — his hands, his feet, his side, his eyes, his head, his crown of thorns, the sponge, the vinegar, the nails. Oh for the Christ of Mary Magdalene, rather than the Christ of the critical theologian! Give me the wounded body of divinity rather than the soundest system of theology. Let me show you what I mean.

Suppose an infant taken away from its mother, and you should seek to foster in it a love for the parent by constantly picturing before it the idea of a mother — and attempting to give it the thought of a mother's relationship with the child. Indeed, my friends, I think you would have a difficult task to fix in that child the true and real love which it ought to bear towards her who bore it. But give that child a mother; let it hang upon that mother's real breast, let it derive its nourishment from her very heart: let it see that mother, feel that mother, put its little arms around that mother's real neck and you have no hard task to make it love its mother. So is it with the Christian. We want Christ — not an abstract, doctrinal, pictured Christ — but a real Christ. I may preach to you many a year, and try to infuse into your souls a love of Christ; but until you can feel that he is a real man and a real person, really present with you, and that you may speak to him, talk to him, and tell him of your needs, you will not readily attain to a love like that of the text, so that you can call him, "Thou whom my soul loveth". I want you to feel, Christian, that your love to Christ is not a mere pious affection; but that as you love your wife, as you love your child, as you love your parent, so you love Christ; that though your love to him is of a finer cast, and a higher mould, yet it is just as real as the more earthly passion. Let me suggest another figure. A war is raging in Italy for liberty. The very thought of liberty nerves a soldier. The thought of a hero makes a man a hero. Let me go and stand in the midst of the army, and preach to them what heroes should be, and what brave men they should be who fight for liberty. My dear friends, the most earnest eloquence might have but little power. But put into the midst of these men Garibaldi, who is heroism incarnate; place before their eyes that dignified man — who seems like some old Roman newly risen from his tomb, they see before them what liberty means, and what daring is, what courage can attempt, and what heroism can perform, There he is, and, firmed by his actual presence, their arms are strong, their swords are sharp and they dash to the battle at once; his presence ensuring victory because they realise in his presence the thought that makes men brave and strong.

So the Church needs to feel and see a real Christ in her midst. It is not the idea of disinterestedness; it is not the idea of devotion; it is not the idea of self-consecration that will ever make the Church mighty: it must be that idea incarnate, consolidated, personified in the actual existence of a realised Christ in the camp of the Lord's host. I do pray for you, and do you pray for me, that we may each one of us have a love which realises Christ, and which can address him as "Thou whom my soul loveth".

But again, look at the text and you will perceive another thing very clearly. The Church, in the expression which she uses concerning Christ, speaks not only with a realisation of his

60

presence, but with a firm assurance of her own love. Many of you, who really love Christ, seldom get further than saying, "O thou whom my soul desires to love! O thou whom I hope I love!" But this sentence does not say this at all. This title has not the shadow of a doubt or a fear upon it: "O thou whom my soul loveth!" Is it not a happy thing for a child of God when he knows that he loves Christ, when he can speak of it as a matter of consciousness? — a thing out of which he is not to be argued by all the reasonings of Satan — a thing concerning which he can put his hand on his heart, and appeal to Jesus, and say, "Lord, thou knowest all things, thou knowest that I love thee?" (Jn 21:15-17) I say, is not this a delightful frame of mind? Or, rather, I reverse the question, Is not that a sad miserable state of heart in which we have to speak of Jesus otherwise than with assured affection?

Ah, my brothers and sisters, there may be times when the most loving heart may, from the very fact that it loves intensely, and loves sincerely, doubt whether it does love at all. But then, such times will be times and seasons of great soul-searching, nights of anguish. He who truly loves Christ will never give sleep to his eyes, nor slumber to his eyelids, when he is in doubt about his heart belonging to Jesus. "No," says he, "this is a matter too precious for me to question as to whether I am the possessor of it or not; this is a thing so vital that I cannot let it be with a 'perhaps', as a matter of chance. No, I must know whether I love my Lord or not, whether I am his or not." If I am addressing any this morning who fear they do not love Christ, and yet hope they do, let me beg you, my dear friend, not to rest content in your present state of mind; never be satisfied till you know that you are standing on the rock, and until you are quite certain that you really do love Christ. Imagine for a moment one of the apostles telling Christ that he thought he loved him. Fancy for a moment your own spouse telling you that she hoped she loved you. Fancy your child upon your knee saying, "Father, I sometimes trust that I love you." What a stinging thing to say to you! You would almost as soon be said, "I hate you". Because, what is it? Shall he, over whom I watch with care, merely think he loves me? Shall she who lieth in my bosom, doubt, and make it a matter of conjecture, as to whether her heart is mine or not? Oh, God, forbid we should ever dream of such a thing in our ordinary relations of life! Then how is it that we indulge in it in our piety? Is it not sickly and maudlin piety? Is it not a diseased state of heart that ever puts us in such a place at all? Is it not even a deadly state of heart that would let us rest contented there? No, let us not be satisfied till, by the full work of the Holy Spirit, we are made sure and certain, and can say with unstammering tongue, "O thou whom my soul loveth".

Now, notice something else equally worthy of our attention. The Church, the spouse, in thus speaking of her Lord, directs our thoughts not merely to her confidence of love, but to the unity of her affections with regard to Christ. She has not two lovers, she has but one. She does not say, "O ye on whom my heart is set!" but "O thou!" She has but one after whom her heart is panting. She has gathered her affections into one bundle, she has made them but one affection, and then she has cast that bundle of myrrh and spices upon the breast of Christ. He is to her the "Altogether Lovely" (Song 5:16), the gathering up of all the loves which once strayed abroad. She has put before the sun of her heart a burning-glass, which has brought all her love to a focus, and it is all concentrated, with all its heat and vehemence, upon Christ Jesus himself. Her heart, which once seemed like a fountain sending forth many streams, has now become as a fountain which has but one channel for its waters. She has stopped up all the other issues, she has cut away the other pipes, and now the whole stream, in one strong current, runs toward him, and him alone. The Church, in the text here, is not a worshipper of God and of Baal too; she is no time-server, who has a heart for al-comers. She is not as the harlot, whose door is open for every wayfarer; but she is a chaste one, and she sees none but Christ, and she knows none whom her soul desires save her crucified Lord. The wife of a noble Persian, having been invited to be present at the wedding feast of King Cyrus, her husband asked her

61

merrily upon her return whether she did not think the bridegroom-monarch a most noble man. Her answer was, "I do not know whether he be noble or not; my husband was so before my eye that I saw none beside him, so I have seen no beauty but in him."

Thus, if you ask the Christian in our text, "Is not Such-a-one fair and lovely?" "No", she replies, "my eyes are fully fixed on Christ, my heart is so taken up with him that I cannot tell if there is beauty anywhere else, for I know that all beauty and all loveliness is summed up in him." Sir Walter Raleigh used to say that if all the histories of tyrants, the cruelty, the blood, the lust, the infamy, were all forgotten, yet all these histories might be re-written out of the life of Henry VIII. And I may say, by way of contrast, "If all the goodness, all the love, all the gentleness, all the faithfulness that ever existed could all be blotted out, they could all be re-written out of the history of Christ." To the true Church, Christ is the only one she loves; she has no divided aims, no two adored ones, but she speaks of him as of one to whom she has given her whole heart, and none have anything else beside. "Oh thou whom my soul loveth".

Come, brothers and sisters, do we love Christ after this fashion? Do we love him so that we can say, "Compared with our love to Jesus, all other loves are but as nothing." We have those sweet loves which make earth dear to us; we do love those who are our kindred according to the flesh, we were indeed beneath the beasts if we did not. But some of us can say, "We do love Christ better than husband or wife, or brother or sister." Sometimes we think we could say with St. Jerome, "If Christ should bid me go this way, and my mother hung about my neck to draw me another, and my father were in my way, bowing at my knees with tears, entreating me not to go; and my children plucking at my skirts should seek to pull me the other way, I must unclasp my mother, I must push to the very ground my father, and put aside my children, for I must follow Christ." We cannot tell whom we love the most till they have come into collision. But when we come to see that the love of mortals requires us to do this, and the love of Christ to do the reverse, then we shall see which we love best. Oh, those were hard times for the martyrs.

Take that good man for instance, Mr. Nicholas Ferrar, who was the father of some twelve children, all of them just little ones. On the road to the stake, his enemies had contrived that his wife should meet him with all the little ones, and she had set them in a row kneeling down by the roadside. His enemies expected that surely now he would recant, and, for the sake of those dear babes, would certainly seek to save his life. But no! no! He had given them all up to God, and he could trust them with his heavenly Father; but he could not do a wrong thing even for the felicity of covering these little birds with his wings and cherishing them beneath his feathers. He took them one by one to his bosom, and looked, and looked again; and it pleased God to put into the mouth of his wife and of his children words which encouraged him instead of discouraging him, and before he went from them, his very babes bid the father play the man and die boldly for Christ Jesus. Yes, soul, we must have a love like this which cannot be rivalled, which cannot be shared; which is like a flood tide — other tides may come up very high upon the shore, but this comes up to the very rocks and beats there, filling our soul to the very brim. I pray God we may know what such a love to Christ as this may mean.

Furthermore, I want to pluck you one more flower. If you look at the title before us, you will have to learn not only its reality, its assurance, its unity; but you will have to notice its constancy, "O thou whom my soul loveth". Not "did love" yesterday", or, "may begin to love tomorrow", but "thou whom my soul loveth" — "you whom I have loved ever since I knew you, and to love whom has become as necessary to me as my vital breath or my native air." The true Christian is one who loves Christ for evermore. He does not play fast and loose with Jesus, pressing him today to his bosom, and then turning aside and seeking after any old Delilah who may, with her witcheries, pollute him. No, he feels that he is a

62

Nazarite unto the Lord; he cannot, and he will not, pollute himself with sin at any time or in any place. Love for Christ in the faithful heart is as the love of the dove to its mate, when she, if her mate should die, can never be tempted to be married to another, but she sits still upon her perch and sighs out her mournful soul until she dies too.

So it is with the Christian; if he had no Christ to love he must then die, for his heart has become Christ's. And so, if Christ were gone, love could not be; then his heart would be gone too, and a man without a heart is dead. The heart, is it not the vital principle of the body? And love, is it not the vital principle of the soul? Yet, there are some who profess to love the Master, but only walk with him in fits and starts, and then go abroad like Dinah into the tents of the Shechemites. Oh, take heed, you professors, who seek to have two husbands; my Master will never be a part-husband. He is not such a one as to have half of your heart. My Master, though he is full of compassion and very tender, has too noble a spirit to allow himself to be half-proprietor of any kingdom.

Canute, the Danish king, might divide England with Edmund the Ironside because he could not win the whole country, but my Lord will have every inch of you, or none. He will reign in you from one end of the isle of man to the other, or else he will not put a foot upon the soil of your heart. He was never part-proprietor in any heart, and he will not stoop to such a thing now. What says the old Puritan? "A heart is so little a thing that it is scarce enough for a kite's breakfast, and you say it is too great a thing for Christ to have it all." No, give him the whole. It is but little when you weigh his merit, and very small when measured against his loveliness. Give him all. Let your united heart, your undivided affection, be constantly, every hour, given up to him.

Can ye cleave to your Lord?
When the many turn aside?
Can ye witness he hath the living Word,
And none upon earth beside?

And can ye endure with the Virgin band,
The lowly and pure in heart,
Who, whithersoever their Lamb doth lead,
From his footsteps ne'er depart?

Do ye answer, 'We can?'
Through his love's constraining power?'
But ah remember the flesh is weak,
And will shrink in the trial-hour?

Yet yield to his love, who round you now,
The bands of a man would cast;
The cords of his love, who was given for you,
To the altar binding you fast.

May that be your lot, constant, still to abide in him who has loved you. I will make just one more remark lest I weary you in thus trying to anatomise the rhetoric of love. In our text, you clearly perceive a vehemence of affection. The spouse says of Christ, "O thou whom my soul loveth." She means not that she loves him a little, but that she loves him with an ordinary passion, but she loves him in all the deep sense of that word. Oh, Christian men and women, I protest to you that I fear there are thousands of professors who never knew the meaning of this word "love", in relation to Christ. They have known it when it referred to mortals; they have felt its flame, they have seen how every power of the body and of the soul are carried away with it; but they have not felt it with regard to Christ. I know you

63

can preach about him, but do you love him? I know you can pray to him, but do you love him? I know you trust him — you think you do — but do you love him?

Oh, is there a love to Jesus in your heart like that of the spouse when she could say, "Let him kiss me with the kisses of his lips, for his love is better than wine." "No", you say, "that is too familiar for me." Then I fear you do not love him, for love is always familiar. Faith may stand at a distance, for her look is saving; but Love comes near, for she must kiss, she must embrace. Why, beloved, sometimes the Christian so loves his Lord that his language becomes unmeaning to the ears of others who have never been in this state. Love has a celestial tongue of her own, and I have sometimes heard her speak so that the lips of worldlings have mocked, and men have said, "That man rants and raves — he does not know what he is saying." Hence it is that Love often becomes a Mystic, and speaks in mystic language, into which the stranger cannot intrude. Oh, you should see Love when she has her heart full of her Saviour's presence, when she comes out of her chamber! Indeed, she is like a giant refreshed with new wine. I have seen her dash down difficulties, tread upon hot irons of affliction, and her feet have not been scorched. I have seen her lift up her spear against ten thousand, and she has slain them at one time. I have known her give up all she had, even to the stripping of herself, for Christ, and yet she seemed to grow richer, and to be decked with ornaments as she unarrayed herself, that she might cast her all upon her Lord, and give up all to him.

Do you know this love, Christian brothers and sisters? Some of you do, I know, for I have seen you prove it in your lives. As for the rest of you, may you learn it, and get above the low standing of the mass of Christ's Church at the present day. Get up from the bogs and fens and damp morasses of lukewarm Laodiceanism, and come up, come up higher, up to the mountain top, where you shall stand bathing your foreheads in the sunlight, seeing earth beneath you, its very tempests under your feet, its clouds and darkness rolling down below in the valley, while you talk with Christ, who speaks to you out of the cloud, and are almost caught up into the third heaven to dwell there with him.

Thus have I tried to explain the rhetoric of my text, "Thou whom my soul loveth."

II. Now let me come to THE LOGIC OF THE HEART, which lies at the bottom of the text. My heart, why should you love Christ?

With what argument will you justify yourself? Strangers stand and hear me tell of Christ, and say "Why should you love your Saviour so? My heart, you cannot answer them so as to make them see his loveliness, for they are blind, but you can at least be justified in the ears of those who have understanding; for doubtless the virgins will love him, if you will tell them why you love him. Our hearts give for their reason why they love him, first, this: We love him for his infinite loveliness. If there were no other reason, if Christ had not bought us with his blood, yet sometimes we feel if we had renewed hearts, we must love him for having died for others. I have sometimes felt in my own soul that setting aside the benefit I received from his dear cross, and his most precious passion, which, of course, must ever be the deepest motive of love, "for we love him because he first loved us" (1 |Jn. 4:19), yet setting aside that, there is such beauty in Christ's character — such loveliness in his passion — such a glory in that self-sacrifice, that one must love him. Can I look into your eyes and not be smitten with your love? Can I gaze upon your thorn-crowned head, and shall not my heart feel the thorn within it? Can I see you in the fever of death, and shall not my soul be in a fever of passionate love for you. It is impossible to see Christ and not to love him; you cannot be in his company without at once feeling that you are wedded to him. Go and kneel by his side in Gethsemane's garden, and I am persuaded that the drops of blood, as they fall upon the ground, shall each one of them be irresistible reasons why you should love him. Hear him as he cries "My God, my God, why hast thou forsaken

64

me?" (Ps. 22:1; Mat. 27:46; Mk. 15:34) Remember that he endures this out of love for others, and you must love him. If you ever read the history of Moses, you believe him to be the grandest of men, and you admire him, and look up to him as to some huge colossus, some mighty giant of the olden days. But you never feel a particle of love in your hearts towards Moses; you could not, for he is an unlovable character; there is something to admire, but nothing to win attachment. When you see Christ, you look up, but you do more, you feel drawn up; you do not admire so much as love, you do not adore so much as embrace. His character enchants, subdues, overwhelms, and, with the irresistible impulse of its own sacred attraction, it draws your spirit right up to him. Well did Dr. Watts say,

His worth, if all the nations knew,
Sure the whole earth would love him too.

But still, love has another argument why she loves Christ, namely, Christ's love for her. Did you love me Jesus, King of heaven, Lord of angels, Master of all worlds, and did you set your heart on me? What, did you love me from of old, and in eternity choose me for yourself? Did you continue to love me as the ages rolled on? Did you come from heaven to earth that you might win me to be your spouse, and do you love me so that you do not leave me alone in this poor desert world; and are you this very day preparing a house for me where I shall dwell with you forever?

A very wretch, Lord, I should prove, had I no love for you. I must love you, for it is impossible for me to resist. That thought that you love me has compelled my soul to love you. Me! me! What was there in me. Could you see beauties in me; I see none in myself; my eyes are red with weeping because of my blackness and deformity. I have said even to the sons of men, "Look not upon me, for I am black, because the sun hath looked upon me." And do you see beauties in me? What a quick eye must you have, no, rather it must be that you have made my eyes to be your looking-glass, and so you see yourself in me, and it is your image that you love. Surely you could not love me. There is that ravishing text in the Canticles, where Jesus says to the spouse, "Thou art all fair my love, there is no spot in thee." (Song 4:7) Can you imagine Christ saying that to you; and yet he has said it, "Thou art all fair my love, there is no spot in thee. He has put away your blackness, and you stand in his sight as perfect, as though you had never sinned, and as full of loveliness as though you were what you shall be when made like him at last. O brothers and sisters, some of you can say with emphasis, "Did he love me, then I must love him." I run my eye along your ranks: there sits a brother who loves Christ who, not many months ago, cursed him. There sits a drunkard — there another who was in prison for crimes — and he loved you, even you, and you could abuse the wife of your bosom because she loved the dear name, and you were never happier than when you were violating his day, and showing your disrespect to his ministers, and your hatred for his cause; yet he loved you. And me! even me! — forgetful of a mother's prayers, regardless of a father's tears, having much light, and yet sinning much, he loved me, and has proved his love. I charge you, O my heart, by the roes and by the hinds of the field (Song 2:7, 3:5), you give yourself wholly up to my Beloved, and you spend and are spent for him. Is that your charge to your heart this morning? Oh! It must be if you know Jesus, and then know that Jesus loves you.

One more reason love gives us, yet more powerful still. Love feels that she must give herself to Christ because of Christ's suffering for her.

Can I Gethsemane forget?
Or there thy conflict see,

Thine agony and bloody sweat,
And not remember thee?

Remember thee, and all thy pains,
And all thy love to me;
Yes, while a breath, a pulse remains,
Will I remember thee.

And when these failing lips grow dumb,
And mind and memory flee,
When thou shalt in thy kingdom come,
Jesus, remember me.

(James Montgomery)

My life, when it shall ebb out, may cause me to lose many mental powers, but memory will love no other name than is recorded there. The agonies of Christ have burnt his name into our hearts. You cannot stand and see him mocked by Herod's men of war, you cannot behold him made nothing of, and spit upon by menial lips, you cannot see him with the nails pierced through his hands and through his feet, you cannot mark him in the extreme agonies of his awful passion, without saying, "And did you suffer all this for me? Then I must love you, Jesus. My heart feels that no other can have such a claim upon it as you have, for none others have spent themselves for me as you have done. Others may have sought to buy my love with the silver of earthly affection, and with the gold of a zealous and affectionate character, but you have bought it with your precious blood, and you have the richest claim to it; yours shall it be, and that forever."

This is love's logic. I may well stand here and defend the believer's love for his Lord. I wish I had more to defend than I have. I dare stand here and defend the utmost extravagancies of speech, and the wildest fanaticisms of action, when they have been done for love of Christ. I say again, I only wish I had more to defend in these degenerate times. Has a man given up all for Christ? I will prove him wise if he has given up for such a one as Christ. Has a man died for Christ? I write over his epitaph that he surely was no fool who had but the wisdom to give up his heart for one who had his heart pierced for him. Let the Church try to be extravagant for once; let her break the narrow bounds of her conventional prudence, and for once arise and dare to do wonders — let the age of miracles return to us — let the Church make bare her arm, and roll up the sleeves of her formality; let her go forth with some mighty thought within her, at which the worldling will laugh and scoff. And I will stand here, and before the bar of a scoffing world, and dare to defend her.

O Church of God, you can do no extravagance for Christ. You may bring out your Marys, and they may break their alabaster boxes, but he deserves that breaking well. You may shed your perfume, and give to him rivers of oil, and ten thousands of the fat of fed beasts, but he deserves it well. I see the Church as she was in the first centuries, like an army storming a city — a city that was surrounded with a vast moat, and there was no means of reaching the ramparts except by filling up the moat with the dead bodies of the Church's own martyrs and confessors. Do you see them? A bishop has just now fallen in, and his head has been cut off with the sword. The next day at the tribunal there are twenty wishing to die that they may follow him; and on the next day twenty more; and the stream pours on till the huge moat is filled. Then, those who follow after, scale the walls and plant the blood-red standard of the cross, the trophy of their victory, upon the top.

Should the world say, "Why this expense of blood?" I answer, he is worthy for whom it was shed. The world says, "Why this waste of suffering? Why this pouring out of an energy in a cause that is at best but fanatical?" I reply, "He is worthy, he is worthy, though the whole world were put into the censer, and all men's blood were the frankincense, he is worthy to have it all sacrificed before him. Though the whole Church should be slaughtered a hecatomb, he is worthy upon whose altar it should be sacrificed. Though every one of us should lie and rot in a dungeon, though the moss should grow upon our eyelids, though our bodies should be given to the kites and the carrion crows, he is worthy to claim the sacrifice; and it were all too mean a gift for such a one as he." O Master, restore to the Church the strength of love which can hear such language, and feel it to be true!

III. Now I come to my last point, upon which I must dwell only briefly. Rhetoric is good, logic is better, but A POSITIVE DEMONSTRATION is the best.

I sought to give you rhetoric when I expounded the words of the text. I have tried to give you logic, now that I have given you the reasons for the love in the text. And now I want you to give — I cannot give it — I want you to give, each for himself, the demonstration of your love for Christ in your daily lives. Let the world see that this is not a mere label to you — a label for something that does not exist, but that Christ really is to you "him whom your soul loves". You ask me how you can do it, and I reply thus: I do not ask you to shave your crown and become a monk, or to cloister yourself, my sister, alone, and become a nun. Such a thing might even show your love to yourself rather than your love to Christ. But I ask you to go home now, and, during the days of the week, engage in your ordinary business. Go with the men of the world as you are called to do, and take the calling which Christ has given to you, and see if you cannot honour him in your calling. I, as a minister, of course, must find it to some degree less honourable work to serve Christ than you do, because my calling does, as it were, supply me with gold, and for me to make a golden image of Christ out of that is but small work, though God wotteth [knows] I find it more than my poor strength could do apart from his grace. But for you to work out the image of Christ in the iron, or clay, or common metal of your ordinary conversation — oh, this will be glorious indeed! And I think you may honour Christ in your sphere as much as I can in mine, perhaps more, for some of you may know more trouble, you may have more poverty, you may have more temptation, more enemies; and therefore you, by loving Christ under all these trials, may demonstrate more fully than ever I could, how true your love is to him, and how soul-inspiring is his love for you.

Away, I say, and look out on the morrow, and the next day, for opportunities of doing something for Christ. Speak up for his dear name if there be any that abuse him; and if you find him wounded in his members, be like Eleanor, Queen of England's king, and suck the poison out of his wounds. Be ready to have your name abused rather than he should be dishonoured; stand up always for him, and be his champion. Let him not lack a friend, for he stood as your friend when you had none beside. If you meet with any of his poor people, show them love for his sake, as David did to Mephibosheth out of love for Jonathan.

If you know any of them to be hungry, set food before them; you had as well set the dish before Jesus Christ himself. If you see them naked, clothe them; you clothe Christ when you clothe his people. No, do not only seek to do this temporal good to his children, but seek evermore to be Christ to those who are not his children as yet. Go among the wicked and among the lost and the abandoned; tell them the words of him. Tell them Jesus Christ came into the world to save sinners. Go after his lost sheep, and be a shepherd as he was a shepherd, so will you show your love. Give what you can to him, so that when you come to die, make him heir of some of your estate. I should not think I loved my friend if I did not sometimes give him a present. I should not think I love Christ if I did not give him something, some sweet cane with money, some fat of my burnt sacrifices.

I heard the other day a question asked concerning an old man who had long professed to be a Christian. They were saying that he left so much and so much, and someone said, "But did he leave Christ anything in his will?" Someone laughed and thought it ridiculous. Ah! so it would be, because men do not think of Christ as being a person; but if we had this love it would be only natural for us to give to him, to live for him, and perhaps, if we had anything at last to let him have — that so even dying we might give our friend in our dying testament a proof that we remembered him, even as he remembered us in his last testament and will. O brothers and sisters — what we want more of in the Church is more extravagant love for Christ. I want each of you to* show your love to Jesus, sometimes by doing something the like of which you have never done before.

I remember saying one Sabbath morning that the Church ought to be the place of invention as much as the world. We do not know what machine is to be discovered yet by the world, for everyman's wit is at work to find out something new. So ought the wits of the Church to be at work to find out some new plan of serving Christ. Robert Raikes founded the Sabbath-schools, John Pounds founded the Ragged-schools: but are we to be content with carrying on their inventions? No; we want something new. It was in the Surrey Hall, through that sermon, that our brethren first thought of the midnight meetings that were held — an invention suggested by the sermon I preached on the woman with the alabaster box.

But we have not come to the end yet. Is there no one that can invent some new deed for Christ? Is there no brother that can do something more for him than has been done today, or yesterday, or during the last month? Is there no one that will dare to be strange and singular and wild, and in the world's eye to be fanatical — for that is no love which is not fanatical in the eye of man. Depend upon it, that is no love that only confines itself to propriety. I would the Lord would put into your heart some thought of giving an unwonted thank-offering to him, or of doing an unusual service, that so Christ might be honoured with the best of thy lambs, and that the fat of your bullocks might be exceeding glorified by your proof of love for him.

God bless you as a congregation! I can only invoke his blessing, for oh, these lips refuse to speak of love which I trust my heart knows, and which I desire to feel more and more. Sinner, trust Christ before you seek to love him, and, trusting Christ, you will love him.

9. REST AND REFRESHMENT

A SERMON AT THE METROPOLITAN TABERNACLE

"Tell me, O thou whom my soul loveth, where thou feedest, where thou makest thy flock to rest at noon: for why should I be as one that turneth aside by the flocks of thy companions?" (Song of Solomon 1:7)

THE Spouse is speaking here. She addresses her husband under the title of "him whom her soul loves". Many earthly marriages are unhappy for lack of love, which is the very essence of the nuptial relationship. But no soul is married to Christ that does not love him. Every single instance of a spiritual union with the Lord Jesus is founded on real affection towards his blessed Person. Each and every believer can say to Jesus, "Thou whom my soul loveth." (Song 1:7, 3:1-4) The love of the Spouse, you observe, is simple, and is on him alone. She speaks as one who loved no other. As the rod of Aaron swallowed up all the other rods (Ex. 7:12), so genuine love for Jesus swallows all other loves. Affection towards our fellow-creatures remains, and so indeed it should, but it will be like tiny hillocks, scarcely worthy of notice on the chart, in comparison with that topmost Alp of love for the Lord Jesus Christ. The genuine lover of Jesus is absorbed here below with a master passion. His affections are all bound up into one, and concentrated on him who is "altogether lovely". (Song 5:16) The precept "Set not your affections upon things on earth, but on things above" (Col. 3:2), commends itself to the spiritual instinct. He is enamoured of the heavenly, so he disdains the carnal. With him, it is a soul-love — "O thou whom my soul loveth." This is superficial, as it is mere human love, the growth of the human will. It is no frenzy produced by excitement and sustained by unhealthy stimulants, but a fountain that has its spring in depths unfathomable. It is no evanescent flame [reducing, vanishing], but a fire that burns forever, for it feeds on fuel that is lasting and imperishable. "O thou whom my soul loveth." You do not love Jesus Christ at all unless the very roots of your being drink in this sacred elixir, this heavenly dew. If there are any other objects for which your heart fondly cares, they shall never lie so deep, nor be so immediately intertwined, in the roots of your nature as is your love for Christ. O my soul, you are my very soul, my inmost soul, my better self, my best self, my most real self who loves! And it must be love indeed! I think, however timid we may be, our affection will sometimes declare itself: "Tell me, O thou whom my soul loveth!" I can understand that humility which, sometimes, under a sense of our sin or infirmity makes us doubtful and anxious as to whether we really do love Jesus Christ at all; and yet, when it comes really to our appealing to him with life or death earnestness, I trust we shall never use "ifs" or "buts". Let ours then be a straight answer to his pointed question — "Lovest thou me?" (Jn. 21:15-17) Our response is surely ready — "Yea, Lord, thou knowest that I love thee." After continued and repeated self-examination, the same answer is repeated with fresh emphasis — "Yea, Lord, thou knowest that I love thee." There must be times when we can tell of this love to others, especially when, as in the case before us, there is no other ear to listen to our profession, no other person present to misunderstand our avowal. Then, we shall be able to say sincerely, as before him whose eyes are as a flame of fire (Rev. 19:12), though they are as dove's eyes (Song 1:15; 4:1), before him who searches the reins and tries the heart (Rev. 2:23) — "Yea, Lord, thou art he whom my soul loveth."

This genuine love for Christ may be attended with much ignorance. The affection may be very ardent while the intelligence is very shallow. It is, however, better to love than to know, but it is best of all when the heart kindles into a lively flame, and the mind is like a rich soil, highly cultivated. Or, contrariwise, the cloud had better darken the intelligence than the affection. Keep your heart with all diligence. (Prov. 4:23) Let no mystery that

69

puzzles your brain imperil its health. Say with fresh smiles — "Thou whom my soul loveth", though, with the next breath, you may betray some anxious enquiry.

Tell me. While confessing your ignorance, give proof of your sincerity. Though your knowledge may be limited, do not, therefore, be disheartened. Some of our young friends have had little education, and painfully lack the advantages of an early religious training. They often feel that they cannot understand the doctrines of the gospel as readily as others do. Let them not be too discouraged. Their love shall count for more than their learning. Your spiritual life is not so much to be judged by the clearness of your views as by the clinging of your tendrils. The grip of faith is good, but goodlier still the grasp of love. Genuine love thirsts for knowledge. It naturally excites in the heart a holy curiosity. The earnest prayer for instruction springs from the absorbing interest in the object of devout regard. "Tell me, O thou whom my soul loveth." From a sacred intimacy, I obtain secret information as a matter of course. My jealousy will excite my zeal to comprehend with all the saints what are "the heights and depths, and to know the love of Christ which passeth knowledge." (Eph. 3:19) Seek to be of an inquisitive frame of mind in heavenly matters. Put your questions to our Master, and blessed answers you will be given. Address them to him affectionately and earnestly, and you may expect to be amply instructed, for is it not written — "All thy children shall be taught of the Lord, and great shall be the peace of thy children"? (Is. 54:13)

Now, the special point on which the enquiry bears is the place where the Great Shepherd feeds his flock, and where he gives them rest in the noon-tide heat, when the sun's glare is oppressive. I have thought that this quest of the bride might be peculiarly appropriate to some of us who are called to fight the Lord's battles in the great public arena: we have a strong need of quiet calm, with peace breathed into our souls. And those of you, likewise, who prove it a hard struggle to earn your daily bread, and others too who are often beset and baffled with temptations and spiritual conflicts — oh, how often you must he longing to find a little arbour such as Bunyan's Pilgrim found half way up the Hill Difficulty, in which he sat down for a while, took his rest, and then went on his way! May the Lord reveal to us such quiet resting-places where we may turn into for a little refreshment, knowing that we have yet to go out again into the storm. We shall then be better fitted for the long journey that lies before us, after we have been fed, as Elijah was with the food which the angel brought him under the juniper tree. (1 Kings 19:4-5)

I. Now, observe how the soul SOUGHT FOR A PLACE WHERE SHE MIGHT OBTAIN A PRICELESS BOON, AND THAT BOON WAS REST — "Tell me, O thou whom my soul loveth, where thou feedest, where thou makest thy flock to rest at noon."

Rest! After all our labours and anxieties, it is the very thing we want, the end of all our wishes and pursuits. Some of our friends delight in the idea of heaven being a place of accumulated knowledge where they will get expanding views of the works of God in nature. I must confess such an idea of heaven has no attraction for me. I do not know why, but I never think of heaven with greater joy than when I sing that verse of Dr. Watts:

There shall I bathe my weary soul,
In seas of heavenly rest;
And not a wave of trouble roll
Across my peaceful breast.

Rest is the end for which man is ever toiling. The thirst for gold, or the ambition for fame, can never reconcile men to so severe a strain on the sinews of the body, and such exposure to anxieties of the mind, unless they were viewed as the avenues to repose and calm. Man is ever looking onward to the time when he will cast off all his cares, and enjoy

70

the haven he strives to reach. And the rest is not partial and intermittent which Jesus Christ gives to his people, but is permanent and immutable, a rest to all the powers, and all the faculties, of one's being. There is rest for the intellect in Christ. The brain is seeking after some truth which it is so certain that it can admit of no doubt. This it finds when the soul yields itself up to Christ as a disciple of his, learning from him, and following him at the same time. Faith ripens into certainty, and the heart becomes more and more steadfast in the blessed truth it has received. Then the peace is profound. It is dreadful to be tossed to and fro like a ship without an anchor. But when a man is brought to love Christ, he says "My heart is fixed (Ps. 57:7, 108:1, 112:7), and it is filled with all that its fondest affections could crave." The rootlets of the soul, like vine tendrils, have been seeking after something they could lay hold on till they come to the cross, twine themselves about it, and get perfect calm. The affections are satisfied as well as the intellect. So wishes and desires which, like horse-leaches are ever crying "Give, give" (Prov. 30:15), become content. The thirst or the believer is quenched, for he says, "Christ is all my salvation and all my desire."

All my capacious powers can wish
In thee doth richly meet;
Nor to my eyes is light so dear,
No friendship half so sweet.

Thy grace still dwells upon my heart,
And sheds its fragrance there;
The noblest balm of all its wounds,
The cordial of its care.

(Philip Doddridge)

Conscience, too, which once howled like a dog, and would not let us sleep, is as quiet as a lamb, receiving the atoning sacrifice, and acknowledging that Jesus

Bore that we might never bear
His Father's righteous ire.

In fact, all the powers within us rest tranquilly, as did the vessel on the Lake of Galilee when Jesus Christ bid the winds and waves be still. O friends, I wish you all knew what a blessed peace God has given to some of us through faith! We have had such peace and joy in believing, that severe pains or heavy losses, and painful crosses, have not broken its sacred spell. It is blessed to have this peace of God as armour for the soul, when we have to do deadly battle for the cause of Christ, or for some truth that is assailed by the adversaries. To have the Lord always before us, to know that he is at your right hand and that you shall not be moved (Ps. 16:8) — this fills a man with courage. He is not afraid to speak with the Lord's enemies in the gate (Ps. 127:5) because he has the peace which, like a river (Is. 66:12), gently glides along. So he wishes well to those he opposes; in discord, generous, and, in dissension, seeking still to make friends with those who make friends with him. Such peace the world can neither give nor take away. This peace is the proper mark of a Christian. Would that no chills or fever disturbed its equanimity! Down in the valley, under the cloud, you feel disturbed, dejected, or distracted, thinking of your dear child's illness, your husband's anxieties, or your own private distress? Possibly, your deep concern may concern your personal interest in the Lord Jesus? In every case, let your language be — "Tell me, O thou whom my soul loveth, where thou feedest, where thou makest thy flock to rest at noon; give me that rest, O my Lord!"

71

II. This craving for rest is joined with another unspeakable blessing which the Spouse seeks with ardour — she longs TO BE FED — "Tell me where thou feedest.'"

The word signifies something more than a passing meal; it implies a full supply of all the provision to be expected from the Shepherd's hand.

"Tell me where you fulfil the office of a Shepherd — guiding and guarding, providing, protecting and feeding, and leading your flock. O Lord, my wants are past reckoning, and I cannot obtain them from any other source but from the treasures of your grace. I am as weak and worthless, sorry, and sick, weary and wayward, worn and wandering, as any sheep that ever lived. Be a shepherd to me; tell me where I may find your pastoral care, and a full immunity from my pestering vexations."

Indulging, however, our fondness for our own version, let us take the word "feed" literally. "Tell me where thou feedest."

Our Lord has a habit of making his people rest and feed at the same time. "He maketh me to lie down in green pastures." (Ps. 23:2) So is it with his people. They have food a-plenty, and enjoy the place in which they partake of it. When Jesus fed the thousands, he first made them sit down on the grass — that was their rest. Then he broke the loaves, and distributed the fish; thus he gave them to eat. (Mat. 14:19) They shall be fed, and they shall lie down; they shall have both food and rest.

Now, our Lord Jesus Christ really feeds the soul. Man's body is fed on bread; man's mind is fed on knowledge; but man's spirit is fed on communion with Christ. As you rise from the lower faculty to the higher, food gets better. The food of the lower faculty, the animal, is bread, a material substance; the food of the next faculty, the mind, is thought, and knowledge; the food of the superior faculty, the spirit, is something that only the Holy Spirit can bring us — the flesh and blood of the Lord Jesus Christ himself; of which he said — "Except a man eat my flesh and drink my blood, there is no life in him, for my flesh is meat indeed, and my blood is drink indeed." (Jn. 6:51-56) When you think about the Person of Jesus that feeds your spirit, when you reflect on the work of Jesus, his incarnation, his holy life, his suffering death, his resurrection, his ascension, his intercession, and all that it guarantees, his Second Coming, and all the glory that pertains to its wonderful consummation, your happy lot it is to be led into its choicest pastures, and to be regaled with the sweetest fare.

Meditating on these things, your spirit is fed. Gathering knowledge, you foster Faith and Patience, Hope and Love, and every grace. Do you not long for such food? Are you not hungering for it? The world is a desert-waste to believers; to them, earthly joys are bladders and bubbles. You must get to your Lord, beloved, you must get to your Lord, or there is no food to your taste. Once, you could have filled your belly with the husks (Lk. 15:16), but now you turn away from them with disgust, and enquire for the bread that comes down from heaven. Away, then, with all your bread-baskets in which you sought to gather earthly comforts, and come straight away to your Lord and Master, and ask him to feed you at this hour. "Tell me where thou feedest; where thou makest thy flock to rest at noon."

III. Let us go on to observe that these two blessings of rest and food are spoken of AS BEING SEASONABLY SOUGHT AND BESTOWED. "Where thou makest thy flock to rest at noon."

Noon is the hottest time of the day. The need for rest is not felt when the dew is on the grass in the morning, and at eventide, but the sheep could not well be feeding without

72

needing to lie down. However, at noon, when the hot Eastern sun dries up the juices of the herbs, and exhales the dews, the poor sheep need to be conducted to the shadow of the rock, or under some wide-spreading oak, that they may lie down. Now, perhaps it may be like noon-tide with some of you at this very hour. You may be feeling the conditions of life to be very oppressive. Your toil fatigues you; and the stress on an over-wrought brain exhausts your spirits and injures your health. As the flock at noon-tide, therefore, you pine for rest. Or perhaps you are compassed about with troubles, and smitten with adversities, till your heart grows faint with the sultriness of the atmosphere, and you find no cheer or comfort. You are poor; the wolf is at the door; sickness has invaded your home; sighs float down from the chamber where songs once rose from the parlour; friendships, that once cheered you are exchanged for estrangements that appal you. As in the boiling heat of noon, your strength is dried up like a potsherd. (Ps. 22:15) Wearisome, dull, languid, and heavy is the air you breathe. Even as in the middle of a hot day, when you have sat with open windows, you vainly long for a gust of wind or a breath of fresh air. Fain would you get away into some deep glen in some thick wood where the dense shadows shut out every gleam of golden sunshine to relieve you from the hot burning sky. You have longed to plunge into some brook, or sit under the shadow of some great rock, for you have found it to be a weary land. (Is. 32:2) Here is the state of mind into which your spirits have fallen. Recollect, then, that Jesus Christ is not only our rest where we can rest anywhere, but our rest where we can rest nowhere. He is our food not merely when there is other food, but when there is no food; he is all in all when everywhere else there is no provision. Breathe, then, the prayer — "Tell me where thou feedest; where thou makest thy flock to rest at noon" — where you give those choicest privileges of which I am anxious to be a partaker.

IV. But notice that this is the happy lot of a favoured people — "Tell me where thou makest thy flock to rest at noon." The blessings of the covenant are not for all mankind. There is a special family, of which, dear hearer, I would have you ask if you are a member? "Thou makest" (not all the sons of men) just thy flock to rest at noon." Thy flock points to a special people. Known to God, because beloved of God the Father, and redeemed by Christ, their sins having been expiated by his atoning sacrifice. Quickened, converted, and called out by the effective calling of the Divine Spirit, they are the sheep of God's fold. They know the Shepherd's voice, he knows them, and they follow him. These enter into his rest, and none beside. My hearer, are you one of Christ's sheep? Or are you one of Satan's goats? (Mat. 25:32) Do you follow Jesus? Is he your Shepherd? Do you trust in him? I would to God that you would hear his call and obey his commandments! Rising at the sound of the gospel, come now to him and live; for the one that comes, he will in no wise cast out. (Jn. 6:37) Let this reflection, that the pasture and repose are for a special people, allure you, and not deter you from asking for the special privileges of the flock. "Lord, give me what you give your chosen! Give me the faith of your Elect that I may be partakers with them of thine inheritance. Surely, Lord, if you will only deal with me as you do to those who love your name, this is all I can desire; my soul will be satisfied." "Tell me where thou makest thy flock to rest." Oh, I rejoice to think that, when I rest in Christ, poor and insignificant though I be, I am resting where Peter and Paul rested, where Luther and Calvin rested, where Whitefield and Wesley rested, and where confessors and martyrs all rested. The same rest is for the meanest seekers as well as the mightiest of saints. Blessed be God, poor as any of you may be, and though nobody knows much about you, your Lord will not love you less, nor bestow on you fewer privileges! There are no second-class mercies; they are all first-class blessings. You shall rest where the flock rests. Oh, sweet indulgence! Seek it, brethren, and it shall be yours to realise.

V. BUT THIS PRIVILEGE COMES IN ONE WAY ONLY, and that by way of fellowship — "Tell me, O thou whom my soul loveth, where thou feedest."

Surely the food was wholesome if it came from your Master's table; but how much sweeter the relish when you partake of it at his table, and with him!

"Where thou feedest." Not where your minister feeds. Ah, poor soul, you will fare poorly if you get nothing but the scraps he brings you from the feast! He invites you to come with him to the banquet — and which the Lord himself provides. "Where thou feedest" — the commissariat shall never be lacking when communion is enjoyed. Let me be with you, my Lord; and I shall not lack any good thing. (Ps 34:10) In the same way, the rest is to be found in his presence, and nowhere else: "Where thou makest thy flock to rest at noon." Under his eye, within sound of his voice, there is sweet repose, because there is a sense of security. Worldlings may get into a dead calm or a state of drowsy indifference, but the genuine follower of Christ never can get rest, unless it is in the finished work, and full satisfaction, of the Lord Jesus Christ. He made an end of sin, and entered into his rest triumphantly. We, therefore, that believe, enter into his rest; and, by the power of the blessed and eternal Spirit, we enjoy a "peace which passeth all understanding." (Phil. 4:7) You know what it is to labour in devotion and find no rest in it. You know what it is to listen to sermons, which rather agitate than calm your troubled breasts. You retire to your room and read your Bible with little relief and no refreshment. So you still cry and groan after rest. At such times, you track the footsteps of the flock, though you fail to reach their fold. You learn, then, that rest is in his society, under his shadow, near his side.

Oh, that we might never content ourselves with anything that calms our fears, or pleases our tastes, if it stops short of this full fruition! May we scorn anything that is not true to him, and is brought home to our conscience by the still small voice of his soft whisper, and laid, like the balm of Gilead (Jer. 8:22), on our wounds by his own dear, tender, pierced hand. There is a rest that is of evil omen, a lull that is the presage of a storm. Only that rest which Jesus brings in the fulfilment of his promise — "Come unto me all ye that labour and are heavy laden, and I will give you rest" (Mat. 11:28) — only for such rest ought our souls to pant, only with such rest shall we be satisfied.

VI. ONE ONLY PLACE answers to the description — "Where thou feedest, and where thou makest thy flock to rest."

Where is the place that he feeds so peacefully and rests so securely? Instrumentally, we are fed under the Word as it is read and preached; we are fed at the table of ordinances; we are fed in our meditations; we are fed in our private prayers. We are fed by getting a meal that is not a little invigorating! But, after all, the place — pre-eminently the place of food and the place of rest — is the foot of the cross. That is the only rest for the believer, and there, the only food on which believers can flourish. Dr. Watts' paraphrase of this verse you will remember:

Where is the shadow of that rock,
Which from the sun defends thy flock?
Fain would I feed amongst thy sheep;
Among them rest, among them sleep.

The footsteps of thy flock I see;
Thy sweetest pastures here they be;
A wondrous feast thy love prepares,
Bought with thy wounds, and groans, and tears

His dearest flesh he makes me food,
And bids me drink his richest blood:
Here to these hills my soul will come,

74

Till my Beloved lead me home.

The shadow of a rock! How is it that there is such a thing as a shadow from a rock? The answer is — because the rock bears all the heat of the sun. Thus, those who are under its shadow are sheltered. It is just so with Christ. There, at that place, he bore the fierce heat of his Father's ire; on the cross he bore our sins, and "the chastisement of our peace was upon him." (Is. 53:5) There, he shelters us from the sun's burning heat; under the shadow of that cross, a cool and delicious shade which ministers peace to us; and where the blood drops, the food grows — the only food for the Lord's own chosen sheep. Ah, beloved, the best hours we ever have known were those passed nearest to the foot of the cross! God forgive the sermons and the hymns which do not lead you to the cross! Oh, that all our meditations, like roads that bend towards a centre, may lead up to this great metropolis of the Christian religion! This is the place of the atoning blood of our Lord Jesus — not to anyone or anything else, except your crucified Lord! Turn away from all your metaphysical speculations, your critical questionings, and your peculiar views of prophecy. Give no thought to arguments about God's foreknowledge and man's free-will. Let the eyes of your faith now turn with fixed gaze on the dear Lamb of God's Passover. This was, of old, the food of God's Israel on the night when they come out of Egypt. This is the food of which you shall eat and live. Oh, may you never wander from the dear enclosure of the cross! Should any of you feel afraid to come to Christ tonight lest he reject you, recollect the welcome Jesus gave to publicans and harlots when they drew near to him. There was a barrier set about Sinai; and, whoever touched that mountain must be stoned or pierced through with a dart. But there was no boundary set around the Mount where Jesus died. No, on the very summit of Calvary, there were two dying thieves, and one of them obtained mercy. Oh, come here and rest, for here rest is to be surely found! Rely more and more completely on his bleeding sacrifice, and then your spirit shall have food and rest, and I think else that thought can wish or imagination conceive. Jesus shall thus be the first and foremost in your own heart, even to the casting out of everything beside. There it is he feeds; there it is he makes the flock to rest at noon.

God bless these words to those of you who have long sighed for rest, and sighed for it in vain! Rest is to be had in Christ; and only in him. With all your schemes, and all your efforts, plans of your own and counsels of others, you will reap nothing but disappointment till you come to him. Oh that your hearts, your poor hungry hearts, might feed on Jesus! Yet know that your craving never can be appeased till you come and trust in him. May you be brought now to a simple trust in Christ crucified, and to him shall be the glory forever and ever. Amen.

10. THE CHURCH'S LOVE TO HER LOVING LORD
NO. 636

AT THE METROPOLITAN TABERNACLE, NEWINGTON

"Tell me, O thou whom my soul loveth, where thou feedest, where thou makest thy flock to rest at noon: for why should I be as one that turneth aside by the flocks of thy companions?" (Song of Solomon 1:7)

WE need to lift up our hearts to God and ask to be quickened in grace, or the precious truths in our text will not prove to us "as honey out of the rock" (Deut. 32:13; Ps. 81:16), nor the "feast of fat things…a feast of wine on the lees well refined". (Is. 25:6) We cannot appreciate the spirituality of this book unless God's Spirit shall help us. Many read these words and only see a proof of the imaginative power of an eastern mind. Some read to scoff and blaspheme, and others, even good people, neglect to read this book altogether, being unable to drink in its spirit because of their lack of that higher life of communion with the Beloved which is here so beautifully laid open to our view. Now, I am persuaded better things of you beloved. I am sure that you believe that every word of God is precious, and most certainly we say of this book, it is "more to be desired than gold, yea than much fine gold: sweeter also than honey and the honeycomb." (Ps. 19:10) This book of the Canticles is most precious to us; it is the inner court of the temple of truth. It seems to us to belong to the secret place of the tabernacle of the Most High. We see our Saviour's face in almost every page of the Bible, but here we see his heart and feel his love to us.

We shall hope this morning to speak of our own experience, as well as of the Church who is here speaking. You will perceive that she begins with a title, she expresses a desire, then she enforces it with an argument: "Tell me, O thou whom my soul loveth, where thou feedest, where thou makest thy flock to rest at noon: for why should I be as one that turneth aside by the flocks of thy companions?"

I. We commence with THE TITLE: "O thou whom my soul loveth." It is well to be able to call the Lord Jesus Christ by this name without an "if" or a "but".

A very large proportion of Christian people can only say of Christ that they hope they love him; they trust they love him; but this is a very poor and shallow experience which is content to stay here. It seems to me that no one ought to give any rest to his spirit till he feels quite sure about a matter of such vital importance. We are not content to have a hope of the love of our parents, or of our spouse, or of our children; we feel we must be certain there; and we ought not to be satisfied with a hope that Christ loves us, and with a bare trust that we love him. The old saints did not generally speak with "buts" and "ifs", and hopes, and trusts, but they spoke positively and plainly. "I know whom I have believed", says Paul (2 Tim. 1:12). "I know that my Redeemer liveth", says Job (Job 19:25). "He whom my soul loveth", says Solomon, in the song as we have it here. Learn, dear friends, to get that positive knowledge of your love to Jesus, and do not be satisfied till you can talk about your interest in him as a reality, which you have made infallibly sure by having received the witness of the Holy Spirit, and his seal upon your soul by faith, that you are born of God, and belong to Christ.

Speaking then of this title which rings the great bell of love to Jesus, let us notice first the cause, and secondly the effect of that love. If we can look into the face of him who once sweat great drops of blood, and call him, "O thou whom my soul loveth", it is interesting to consider what is the cause of our love. And here our reply is very quick. The efficient cause of our love is the Holy Spirit of God. We should never have had a spark of love to Jesus if it had not been bestowed upon us by the divine worker. Well said John: "Love is

76

of God." (1 Jn. 4:7) Certainly it is so. Our love to Christ is one beam from himself, the Sun. Certainly a man can no more naturally love Christ than a horse can fly. I grant you there is no physical disability, but there is a moral and spiritual disability which effectively disqualifies him from the high and lofty emotion of love to Jesus. Into that dead corpse, the living spirit must be breathed; for those who are dead in trespasses and sins cannot love Christ. That heart of stone must be transformed into a heart of flesh, for stones may be hurled at the Saviour, but they can never love him. That lion must become a lamb, or it can never claim Christ as its Shepherd. That raven must he turned into a dove, or it will never fly to Christ as its ark. "Except a man he born again" (Jn. 3:3, 5), we may say, he cannot see this precious sparkling jewel of the kingdom of God, love to Christ. Search yourselves then, brethren, do you love him or not, for if you love him, you have been born again; and if you do not love him, then you are still in darkness, and are not his.

And have I, Christ, no love for Thee
Nor passion for thy charms?
Nor wish my Saviour's face to see
And dwell with His arms?
Is there no spark of gratitude
In this cold heart of mine,
To Him whose generous bosom glowed
With friendship all divine?

Can I pronounce His charming name,
His acts of kindness tell,
And while I dwell upon the theme,
No sweet emotion feel?

(Samuel Stennett)

I think some of us would have to reply,

A very wretch, Lord, I should prove,
Had I no love to thee;
Sooner than not my Saviour's love,
Oh, may I cease to be!

This, then, is the efficient cause — the Holy Spirit. The rational cause, the logical reason why we love Jesus lies in himself — in his looks, in his present working, and in his Person, besides many other little founts, which all tend to swell the river — the growing, deepening river of our love to him.

Why do we love Jesus? We have the best of answers — because he first loved us. (1 Jn. 4:19) Hearken, you strangers who inquire why we should love the Saviour so.

We will give you such reasons that will satisfy you, and set your mouths watering to be partakers of the same reasons, that you may come to love him too. Why do we love him? Because or ever this round earth was fashioned between the palms of the great Creator — before he had painted the rainbow, or hung out the lights of the sun and moon, Christ's delights were with us. He foresaw us through the glass of his prescience; he knew what we should be — looked into the book in which all his "members were written, which in continuance were fashioned, when as yet there were none of them" (Ps. 139:16), and as he looked upon us, the glance was love. He delighted to sit upon the throne of glory, and to remember his dear ones who were yet to be born. It was the great prospect which his

77

mighty and infinite Spirit had — a joy that was set before him, that he should see a multitude that no man could number who should be his beloved forever.

Loved of my Christ, for him again,
With love intense I'll burn;
Chosen of Thee ere time began,
I'll choose Thee in return.

(Augustus Montague Toplady)

Oh, could you know that Jesus had loved you from before all worlds, you must love him. At least you will grant there cannot be a better reason for love than love. Love demands; no, it does not demand — it takes by almighty force, by irresistible energy, that heart captive upon whom it thus sets itself.

This Jesus loved us for no reason whatever in ourselves. We were black as the tents of Kedar; we had much deformity but no beauty, and yet he loved us; and our deformity was of such a kind that it might meritoriously have made him hate us. We kicked against him and despised him. Our language naturally was, "We will not have this man to reign over us" (Lk. 19:14), and when we heard of his loving us, we sneered at it. He was despised and rejected of men; we hid as it were, our faces from him. (Is. 53:3) He was despised and we did not esteem him. We thought his love an empty tale, a paltry trifle, and yet he loved us. No, we were his enemies. We slew him; we confess with sorrow that we were the murderers of the Prince of Life and Glory. Our hands were stained with his gore and our garments dyed with his blood, and yet he saw all this and loved us still. Shall we not love him? Sure, our heart is harder than adamant because we do not love him more. But it were hell-hardened steel if it did not love at all. Our Saviour so loved us that he stripped himself of his robes of radiance. Listen, you children of God, it is the old story over again, but it is always new to you. He stripped himself of his bright array, laid aside his sceptre and his crown, and became an infant in Bethlehem's manger amongst the horned oxen. Thirty years of poverty and shame the King of heaven spent among the sons of men, and all out of love for us. Jesus, the heavenly lover, panting to redeem his people, was content to abide here without a place in which to rest his head, that he might rescue you. See him yonder in the garden in his agony, his soul exceeding sorrowful even unto death; his forehead, no his head, his hair, his garments red with the bloody sweat. See him giving his back to the smiters, and his cheeks to them that pluck off the hair. See him as he does not hide his face from shame and spitting, dumb like a sheep before her shearers, and like a lamb that is brought to the slaughter, so he opened not his mouth, but patiently bore it all on our behalf. See him with the cross upon his mangled shoulders, staggering through Jerusalem's streets, unwept, unpitied, except by poor feeble women! See him, you that love him, and love him more as he stretches out his hands to the nail, and gives his feet to the iron. See him, as with power to deliver himself, he is made captive. Behold him as they lift up the cross with him upon it, and dash it down to its place and dislocate his bones. Hear that cry, "I am poured out like water: all my bones are out of joint, Thou hast brought me into the dust of death." (Ps. 22:14) Stand, if ye can, and view that face so full of dolour. Look till a sword shall go through your own heart as it went through his virgin mother's very soul. Oh, see him as he thirsts and has that thirst mocked with vinegar. Hear him as he prays and has that prayer parodied, "He cries for Elias, let Elias come and take him down." (Mk. 15:36) See him, as they who love him come and kiss his feet and bathe them with their tears. Will you not love him who did all that friend could do for friend; who gave his life for us? Beloved, here are a thousand crimson cords that tie us to the Saviour, and I hope we feel their constraining power. It is his vast love, the old eternal bond, the love which redeemed, which suffered in our stead, the love which pleaded our cause before

78

the eternal throne: it is this which we give as a sufficient reason why we should love the Saviour, if needs be, even unto death.

Moreover, we have another reason. I trust many here can say that they love the Saviour because of his present dealings towards them. What has he not done for us this very day? Some of you came here this morning heavy and you went away rejoicing; perhaps you have had answers to prayer this very week. You have passed through the furnace and not a smell of fire has passed upon you. You have had many sins this week, but you have felt the efficacy of his blood again and again. Some of us have known what it is during the past six days to have the ravishing delights of private communion with him. He has made us glad; our spirits have leaped for very joy, for he hath turned again the captivity of our soul. You have drunk of him as of "the brook in the way" (Ps 110:7), and you have therefore lifted up your head. Beloved, if there were nothing else which Christ had done for my soul, that which I have tasted and handled of him within the last few months would make me love him forever, and I know that you can say the same.

Nor is this all. We love the Saviour because of the excellence of his person. We are not blind to excellence anywhere, but still we can see no excellence like his.

Jesus thou fairest, dearest one,
What beauties thee adorn
Far brighter than the noonday sun,
Or star that gilds the morn.

Here let me fix my wandering eyes,
And all thy glories trace;
Till, in the world of endless joys,
I rise to thine embrace.

(Benjamin Beddome)

When Tigranes and his wife Meroe were both taken prisoners by Cyrus, Cyrus turning to Tigranes said, "What will you give for the liberation of your wife?" and the King answered, "I love my wife so that I would cheerfully give up my life if she might be delivered from servitude"; whereupon Cyrus said that if there was such love as that between them they might both go free. So when they were away, and many were talking about the beauty and generosity of Cyrus, and especially about the beauty of his person, Tigranes, turning to his wife, asked her what she thought of Cyrus, and she answered that she saw nothing anywhere but in the face of the man who had said that he would die if she might only be released from servitude. "The beauty of that man", she said, "makes me forget all others." And verily we would say the same of Jesus. We would not decry the angels, nor think ill of the saints, but the beauties of that man who gave his life for us, are so great that they have eclipsed all others, and our soul only wishes to see him and not another; for, as the stars hide their heads in the presence of the sun, so may ye all begone, ye delights, ye excellencies, when Christ Jesus, the chief delight, the chief excellence, makes his appearance. Dr. Watts says:

His worth, if all the nations knew,
Sure the whole earth would love him too.

And so it seems to us. Could you see him, you must love him. It was said of Henry VIII., that if all the portraits of tyrants, and murderers, and thieves were out of existence, they might all be painted from the one face of Henry VII; and turning that round another way,

79

we will say, that if all the excellencies, beauties, and perfections of the human race were blotted out, they might all he painted again from the face of the Lord Jesus,

All over glorious is my Lord;
Must be beloved, and yet adored.
His worth if all the nations knew,
Sure the whole earth would love Him, too.

(Isaac Watts)

These are some of the reasons why our heart loves Jesus. Before I leave those reasons, I should like to put a few questions round amongst this great crowd. O friends, would you not love Jesus if you knew something of this love as shed abroad in your hearts — something of this love as being yours? Now, remember, there is a very great promise that Christ has made, and it is this, "Him that cometh to me I will in no wise cast out." (Jn. 6:37) Now what does that refer to? Why to any "him" in all the world, that comes to Christ. Whoever you may be, if you come to Jesus —and you know that means just trusting him, leaning upon him — if you come to him, he will not cast you out; and when he has received you to his bosom, you will then know (but you cannot know till then) how much he loves you, and then, I think, you will say with us, "Yes, his name is 'Thou whom my soul loveth.'"

I shall now for a short time speak on the effects of this love, as we have dwelt on the cause of it. When a man has true love for Christ, it is sure to lead him to dedication. There is a natural desire to give something to the person whom we love, and true love for Jesus compels us to give ourselves to him. One of the earliest acts of the Christian's life is to take ourselves, and lay body, soul, and spirit upon the altar of consecration, saying, "Here I am; I give myself to thee." When the pupils of Socrates had nearly all of them given him a present, there was one of the best scholars who was extremely poor, who said to Socrates, "I have none of these things which the others have presented to you; but, O Socrates, I give you myself"; whereupon Socrates said it was the best present he had had that day. "My son, give me thy heart" (Prov. 23:26) — this is what Jesus asks for. If you love him, you must give him this.

True love next shows itself in obedience. If I love Jesus, I shall do as he bids me. He is my husband, my Lord — I call him "Master". "If ye love me" says he, "keep my commandments." (Jn. 14:15) This is his chosen proof of my love, and I am sure, if I love him, I shall keep his commandments. And yet there are some who profess to love Christ, who very seldom think of keeping some of his commandments. "This do ye in remembrance of me" (Lk. 22:19), he says, and yet some of you never come to his table. May I gently ask you, how you make this disobedience consort with genuine affection for him? "If ye love me, keep my commandments."

'Tis love that makes our willing feet
In swift obedience move.

(Isaac Watts)

We would do anything for those we love, and, if we love Jesus, no burden will be heavy, no difficulty too great: we should rather wish to do more than he asks of us, and only desire that he were a little more exacting, that we might have a better opportunity of showing forth our affection.

True love, again, is always considerate and afraid lest it should give offence. It walks very daintily. If I love Jesus, I shall watch my eye, my heart, my tongue, my hand, being so fearful lest I should wake my beloved, or make him stir until he please; and I shall be sure not to take in those bad guests, those ill-favoured guests of pride and sloth and love of the world. I shall tell them to be packing, for I have a dear one within who will not tarry long if he sees me giving sideling glances to these wicked ones. My heart shall be wholly his. He shall sit at the head of the table, he shall have the best dish there; no, I will send all others away that I may have him all to myself, and that he may have my whole heart, all that I am, and all that I have.

Again, true love to Christ will make us very jealous of his honour. As Queen Eleanor went down upon her knees to suck the poison from her husband's wound, so we shall put our lips to the wound of Christ when he has been stabbed with the dagger of calumny, or inconsistency, being willing sooner to take the poison ourselves, and to be ourselves diseased and despised than that his name, his cross, should suffer badly. Oh, what matters what becomes of us, if the King reigns? I will go home to my bed, and die in peace, if the King sits on the throne. Let me see King David once again installed in Zion's sacred halls; and my soul, in poverty and shame, shall still rejoice if the banished King Jesus shall once again come back, and have his own, and take his sceptre, and wear his crown. Beloved, I trust we can say we would not mind if Christ would make a mat of us, if he would wipe his Church's filthy sandals on us, if we might but help to make her pure. We would hold the stirrup for him to mount any day, yes, and he his horsing-block that he might mount his glorious charger, and ride forth conquering and to conquer.

Say, what matters it what we are, or where we are, if the King has his own? If we love Christ, again, we shall be desiring to promote his cause, and we shall be desiring to promote it ourselves. We shall wish to see the strength of the mighty turned at the gate that King Jesus may return triumphant. We shall not wish to sit still while our brethren go to war, but we shall want to take our portion in the fray, that, like soldiers that love their monarch, we may prove by our wounds and by our sufferings that our love is real. The apostle says, "Let us not love in word only but in deed and in truth." (1 Jn. 3:18) Actions speak louder than words, and we shall always he anxious to tell our love in deeds as well as by our lips. The true disciple asks continually, "Lord, what would you have me do?" He esteems it his highest honour to serve the Lord. "I would rather he a doorkeeper in the house of my God than dwell in the tents of wickedness." (Ps. 84:10)

**There's not a lamb in all the flock,
I would disdain to feed;
There's not a foe before whose face
I fear thy cause to plead.**

**Would not my ardent spirit vie
With angels round thy throne,
To execute thy sacred will
And make thy glory known?**

(Philip Doddridge)

Yes, indeed, we thus can sing, and mean, I trust, every word; yes, will go forth into the whole world and preach the gospel to every creature. We will tell of this love to all, and labour to win for the Master's honour a multitude which no man can number out of every nation, and kindred, and tribe, and tongue and people. I believe in an active love, a love which has hands to labour and feet to run, as well as a heart to feel, eyes to glance, and ears to listen. A mother's love is of the purest and intensest sort in the world, and it is the

81

most practical. It shows itself in deeds of untiring devotion both night and day. So also should it be with us; we should let our affections prompt us to life-long labour. The love of Christ should constrain us to live, and, if needs be, die to serve him. Heaven is the place of purest, holiest attachment to Christ; then we shall understand most about his love to us, and of all he has done to prove it; and the consequence will be that his servants shall serve him day and night in his holy temple. We are expecting a home in glory, not of idleness, but of continual activity. It is written, "His servants shall serve him" (Rev. 22:3), and we are taught to pray now that we may do his will on earth as it is done in heaven. Let us, therefore, each one, be busily engaged in the great harvest-field. The harvest is great and the labourers are few. There is room for all, and each man's place is waiting to receive him. If we truly love our Lord, we shall at once press to the front and begin the "work of faith and labour of love." (1 Thess. 1:3) Has not the Master been used to show his love to us in deeds? Look to Bethlehem, to Gabbatha, to Gethsemane, to Golgotha; yes, look to his whole life as he "went about doing good" (Acts 10:38), and see if all this will not stir you up to service. Listen to the life-story of the Lord, and you will hear a voice from each one of his deeds of love saying to you, "Go and do likewise."

And, once again, if we love Jesus, we shall be willing to suffer for him. Pain will become light; we shall sing with Madame Guyon [Jeanne Marie B. de la Mothe],

To me 'tis equal whether love ordain my life or death,
Appoint me ease, or pain.

It is a high attainment to come to, but love can make us think ourselves of such small importance that, if Christ can serve himself of us, we shall make no choice as to what, or where, we may be. We can sing once more:

Would not my heart pour forth its blood
In honour of thy name,
And challenge the cold hand of death
To damp this immortal flame?

(Philip Doddridge)

Our hearts are, I trust, so full of real devotion to Christ that we can give him everything, and endure all things for his sake.

For him I count as gain each loss,
Disgrace for him renown,
Well may I glory in his cross,
While he prepares my crown.

(John Newton)
Darkness is light about us if we can serve him there. The bitter is sweet if the cup is put to our lips in order that we may share in his sufferings, and prove ourselves to be his followers. When Ignatius was led to his martyrdom, as he contemplated the nearness of his death and suffering, he said, "Now I begin to be a Christian"; he felt that all that he had done and suffered before was not enough to entitle him to be called a follower of Christ, but now as the Master's bloody baptism was before him, he realised the truth so dear to every right-minded Christian, that he was to be like his Lord. Here we can all prove our love; we can suffer his will calmly if we are not able to do it publicly.

Weak as I am, yet through thy love,
I all things can perform;

And, smiling, triumph in thy name
Amid the raging storm.

(Philip Doddridge)

I pray God we may have such a love moreover that thirsts after Jesus, which cannot be satisfied without present communion with him.

II. This brings me to this thought, which I shall only touch upon as the swallow skims the brook with his wing, and then up and away, lest I weary you; so the second point of consideration is the DESIRE OF THE CHURCH AFTER CHRIST JESUS OUR LORD.

Having called him by his title, she now expresses her longing to be with him. "Tell me, O thou whom my soul loveth, where thou feedest, where thou makest thy flock to rest at noon." The desire of a renewed soul is to find out Christ and be with him. Stale meats left over from yesterday are very well when there is nothing else, but who does not like hot food fresh from the fire? And past communion with Christ is very well. "I remember thee from the land of the Hermonites and the hill Mizar" (Ps. 42:6), but these are only stale meats, and a loving soul wants fresh food every day from the table of Christ; and you that have once had the kisses of his mouth, though you remember the past kisses with delight, yet want daily flesh tokens of his love. He that drinks of this water will never thirst again, it is true, and for this water he will so thirst that he will be like Samuel Rutherford, who began to be out of heart with the buckets, and to want to get right to the well-head that he might lie down and drink; and then, if he could have his fill, he would drink the well quite dry. But there is no hope of that, or rather, no fear of it: the well can never be empty, for it rises as we drink.

A true loving soul, then, wants present communion with Christ; so the question is, "Tell me where you feed? Where do you get your comfort from, O Jesu? I will go there. Where do your thoughts go? To your cross? Do you look back to that? Then I will go there. Where you feed, there will I feed."

Or does this mean actively, instead of being in the passive or the neuter? Where do you feed your flock? In your house? Then I will go there, if I may find you there. In private prayer? Then I will not be slack in that. In the Word? Then I will read it night and day. Tell me where you feed, for wherever you stand as the shepherd, there will I be, for I want you. I cannot be satisfied to be apart from you. My soul hungers and thirsts to be with you. She puts it again: "Where dost thou make thy flock to rest at noon", for there is only rest in one place, where you cause your flock to rest at noon. That must be a grace-given rest, only to be found in some one chosen place. Where is the shadow of that rock? It is very hot just now here in the middle of summer, when the sun is pouring down its glorious rays like bright but sharp arrows upon us, and we that are condemned to live in this great wilderness of brown bricks and mortar, often recollect those glades where the woods grow thick, and where the waters leap from crag to crag down the hill side, and where the birds are singing among the larks. We delight to think of those leafy bowers where the sun cannot dart his rays, where, on some mossy bank, we may stretch ourselves out to rest, or have our weary limbs in some limpid stream; and this is just what the spouse is after. She feels the heat of the world's sun, and she longs to be away from its cares and troubles that have furrowed and made brown her face till she looked as if she had been a busy keeper of the vineyards. She wants to get away to hold quiet communion with her Lord, for he is the brook where the weary may lave [bathe] their wearied limbs. He is that sheltered nook, that shadow of the great rock in the weary land (Is. 32:2), where his people may lie down and be at peace.

83

Jesus, the very thought of thee,
With sweetness fills my breast;
But sweeter far thy face to see,
And in thy presence rest.

For those who find thee, find a bliss,
Nor tongue, nor pen can show
The love of Jesus, what it is,
None but his loved ones know.

(Bernard of Clairvaux)

Now, do you not want this tonight? Do not your souls want Christ tonight? My brothers, my sisters, there is something wrong with us if we can do without Christ. If we love him, we must want him.

Sun of my soul! thou Saviour dear,
It is not night, if thou be near;
Oh, may no earth-born cloud arise,
To hide thee from thy servant's eyes!

Abide with me from morn till eve,
For without thee I cannot live;
Abide with me when night is nigh,
For without thee I dare not die.

(John Keble)

Yes, we cannot do without Christ; we must have him. "Give me Christ, or else I die," is the cry of our souls. No wonder Mary Magdalene wept when she thought they had taken away her Lord, and she did not know where they had laid him. As the body suffers without food, so should we without Christ. As the fish perish out of water, so should we apart from Christ. I must quote another verse of a hymn, for really the sweet songsters of Israel have lavished all their best poesy, and very rightly so, in telling us our love-tale concerning our Beloved. I am sure that our heart's inner voice can set to sweetest music the words:

O Love divine, how sweet Thou art!
When shall I find my willing heart
All taken up by Thee?
I thirst, I faint, I die to prove
The greatness of redeeming love,
The love of Christ to me,

Oh that I could for ever sit
With Mary at the Master's feet!
Be this my happy choice:
My only care, delight, and bliss,
My joy, my heaven on earth be this —
To hear the Bridegroom's voice.

(Charles Wesley)

Yes, to be with Jesus is heaven; anywhere on earth, or in the skies, all else is wilderness and desert. It is paradise to be with him; and heaven without Christ would be no heaven to

84

me. My heart cannot rest away from him. To have no Christ would be a punishment greater than I could bear; I should wander, like another Cain, over the earth as a fugitive and a vagabond. Verily, there would be no peace for my soul. I am sure that the true wife, if her husband is called to go on a journey, longs ardently for his return. If he is gone to the wars, she dreads lest he should fall. How each letter comes perfumed to her when it tells of his love and constancy, and how she watches for the day when she shall clasp him in her arms once more. Oh, you know that when you were children, when you were sent to school, how you counted till the holidays came on. I had a little almanac, and marked out every day the night before, and so counted one day less till the time I should get home again; and so may you.

May not a captive long
His own dear land to see?
May not the prisoner seek release
From bondage to be free?"

Of course he may, and so may you, beloved, pant and sigh, as the hart panteth for the waterbrooks (Ps. 42:1) — for the comfortable enjoyment of the Lord Jesus Christ's presence.

III. THE ARGUMENT USED BY THE CHURCH.

Here is her desire. Now, to close, she backs that up with an argument. She says, "Why should I be as one that turneth aside by the flocks of thy companions?" You have plenty of companions — why should I be turned aside? Why should I not be one? Let us talk it over. Why should I lose my Lord's presence? But the devil tells me I am a great sinner. Ah, but it is all washed away, and gone forever. That cannot separate me, for it does not exist. My sin is buried,

Plunged as in a shoreless sea —
Lost as in immensity.

The devil tells me I am unworthy, and that is a reason. But I always was unworthy, and yet it was no reason why he should not love me at first, and therefore cannot be a reason why I should not have fellowship with him now. Why should I be left out? Now I am going to speak for the poorest here — I do not know where he is. I want to speak for you that have got the least faith; you that think yourselves the smallest in all Israel: you Mephibosheths that are lame in your feet, and yet sit at the king's table; you poor despised Mordecais that sit at the king's gate, yet cannot get inside the palace, I have this to say to you — Why should you be left there? Just try and reason. Why should I, Jesus, be left out in the cold when the night comes on. No, there is a cot for the little one, as well as a bed for his bigger brother. Why should I be turned aside? I am equally bought with a price. I cost him, in order to save me, as much as the noblest of the saints: he bought them with blood; he could not buy me with less. I must have been loved as much, or else, seeing that I am of so little worth, I should not have been redeemed at all. If there be any difference, perhaps I am loved somewhat better. Is there not greater, better love shown in the choice of me than of some who are more worthy than I am? Why, then, should I be left out? I know if I had a child that is deformed and decrepit, I would love it all the more: it seems as if I had a tenderer care for it. Then why should my heavenly Father be less kind to me than I should be to my offspring? Why should I he turned aside? He chose me: he cannot change in his choice. Why, then, should he cast me off. He knew what I was when he chose me; he cannot therefore find out any fresh reason for turning me aside. He foresaw I should misbehave myself, and yet he elected me. Well, then, there cannot be a reason why I should he left to fall away.

85

Again, I ask: Why should I turn aside? I am a member of his body, of his flesh, and of his bones, and though I am less than the least of all his saints, yet he has said, "I will never leave thee nor forsake thee." (Heb. 13:5) Why should I turn aside? I have a promise all to myself. Has he not said, "I will not quench the smoking flax, nor break the bruised reed"? Has he not said, "The Lord taketh pleasure in them that fear him in them that hope in his mercy"? (Ps. 147:11) If I cannot do more, I can do that. I do hope in his mercy; then why should I be turned aside? If any should think of doing so, it should not be I, for I want to be near him; I am such a poor plant that I ought to he kept in the sun: I shall never grow in the shade. My big brother, perhaps, may manage for a little time without comfort, but I cannot, for I am one of the Ready-to-Halts.

I recollect how the shepherds of Mount Clear said, "Come in, Mr. Little Faith. Come in, Mr. Feeble Mind. Come in, Mr. Ready-to-Halt. Come in, Mary". But they did not say, "Come in, Father Faithful. Come in, Matthew. Come in, Valiant-for-Truth." No, they said these might do as they liked; they were quite sure to take their own part; but they looked first to the feeblest. Then why should I he turned aside? I am the feeblest, and want his person most. I may use my very feebleness and proneness to fall as the reason why I should come to him. Why should I be turned aside? I may fall into sin. My heart may grow cold without his glorious presence; and then, what if I should perish! Why, here let me bethink myself. If I am the meanest lamb in his flock, I cannot perish without doing the God of heaven a damage. Let me say it again with reverence. If I, the least of his children, perish, I shall bring his Son dishonour, for what will the arch-fiend say? "Aha," says he, "you Surety of the Covenant, you could keep the strong, but you could not keep the weak: I have this lamb here in the pit whom you could not preserve. Here is one of you crown-jewels", says he, "and though it be none of the brightest, though it be not the most sparkling ruby in your coronet, yet it is one of your jewels, and I have it here. You have no perfect regalia: I have a part of it here." Shall that ever be, after Christ has said, "They shall never perish, neither shall any pluck them out of my hand"? (Jn. 10:28) Shall this be, when the strong arm of God is engaged for my succour, and he has said to me, "The Eternal God is thy refuge; and underneath are the everlasting arms?" (Deut. 33:27) Jesus, do not turn me aside, lest by my fall I grieve your Spirit, and lest by my fall I bring disgrace upon your name. Why should I turn aside? There is no reason why I should.

Come, my soul, there are a thousand reasons why you should not. Jesus beckons you to come. You wounded saints, you that have slipped to your falling, you that are grieved, sorrowing, and distressed, come to his cross, come to his throne again. Backsliders, if you have been such, return! return! return! A husband's heart has no door to keep out his spouse, and Jesus' heart has no power to keep out his people. Return! return! There is no divorce issued against you, for the Lord, the God of Jacob says, "He hateth putting away." (Mal. 2:16) Return! Return! Let us get to our chambers, let us seek renewed fellowship; and, oh, you that have never had it, and have never seen Christ, may you thirst after him tonight; and if you do, remember the text I gave you, "Him that cometh to me I will in no wise cast out." Whoever you may be, if you will come to Jesus, he will not cast you out.

From the cross uplifted high,
Where the Saviour deigns to die,
What melodious sounds I hear
Bursting on my ravished ear:
Love's redeeming work is done;
Come and welcome, sinner, come

Sprinkled now with blood the throne,
Why beneath thy burdens groan;

On my pierced body laid,
Justice owns the ransom paid:
Bow the knee and kiss the Son;
Come and welcome, sinner, come

(Thomas Haweis)

God bring you for Jesus' sake! Amen.

11. THE GOOD SHEPHERDESS

NO. 1115

A SERMON DELIVERED ON LORD'S-DAY MORNING,
JUNE 1ST, 1873
AT THE METROPOLITAN TABERNACLE, NEWINGTON

"Tell me, O thou whom my soul loveth, where thou feedest, where thou makest thy flock to rest at noon: for why should I be as one that turneth aside by the flocks of thy companions? If thou know not, O thou fairest among women, go thy way forth by the footsteps of the flock, and feed thy kids beside the shepherds' tents." (Song of Solomon 1:7-8)

THE bride was most unhappy and ashamed because her personal beauty had been sorely marred by the heat of the sun. The fairest among women had become swarthy as a sunburnt slave. Spiritually, it is so often with a chosen soul. The Lord's grace has made her fair to look upon, even as the lily; but she has been so busy about earthly things that the sun of worldliness has injured her beauty. The bride, with holy shamefacedness, exclaims, "Look not upon me, for I am black, because the sun hath looked upon me." She dreads alike the curiosity, the admiration, the pity, and the scorn of men, and turns herself alone to her Beloved, whose gaze she knows to be so full of love that her swarthiness will not cause her pain when most beneath his eye. This is one index of a gracious soul — that whereas the ungodly rush to and fro, and do not know where to look for consolation, the believing heart naturally flies to its well-beloved Saviour, knowing that in him is its only rest.

It would appear from the preceding verse that the bride was also in trouble about a certain charge which had been given to her, which burdened her, and in the discharge of which she had become negligent of herself. She says, "They made me the keeper of the vineyards", and she would wish to have kept them well; but she felt she had not done so, and that, moreover, she had failed in a more immediate duty — "Mine own vineyard have I not kept". Under this sense of double unworthiness and failure, feeling her omissions and her commissions to be weighing her down, she turned round to her Beloved and asked instruction at his hands. This was well. Had she not loved her Lord, she would have shunned him when her comeliness was faded, but the instincts of her affectionate heart suggested to her that he would not discard her because of her imperfections. She was, moreover, wise thus to appeal to her Lord against herself. Beloved, never let sin part you from Jesus. Under a sense of sin, do not fly from him; that is foolishness. Sin may drive you *from* Sinai; but it ought to draw you *to* Calvary. To the fountain we should fly with all the greater alacrity when we feel that we are foul; and to the dear wounds of Jesus, from whom all our life and healing must come. We should resort with the greater earnestness when we feel our soul to be sick, even though we fear that sickness to be unto death. The bride, in the present case, takes to Jesus her troubles, her distress about herself, and her confession concerning her work. She brings before him her double charge, the keeping of her own vineyard, and the keeping of the vineyards of others. I know that I shall be speaking to many this morning who are busy in serving their Lord; and it may be that they feel great anxiety because they cannot keep their own hearts near to Jesus. They do not feel themselves warm and lively in the divine service; they plod on, but they are very much in the condition of those who are described as "faint, yet pursuing". When Jesus is present, labour for him is joy, but in his absence his servants feel like workers underground, bereft of the light of the sun. They cannot give up working for Jesus; they love him too well for that, but they pine to have his company while they are working for him, and, like the young prophets who went to the wood to cut down every one a beam for

88

their new house, they say to their master, "Be content, we pray thee, and go with thy servants." (2 Kings 6:3) Our most earnest desire is that we may enjoy sweet communion with Jesus while we are actively engaged in his cause. Indeed, beloved, this is most important to all of us. I do not know of any point which Christian workers need more often to think upon than the subject of keeping their work and themselves near to the Master's hand. Our text will help us in this, under three headings. We have here, first, *a question asked*: — "Tell me, O thou whom my soul loveth, where thou feedest, where thou makest thy flock to rest at noon?" Secondly, *an argument used*: — "Why should I be as one that turneth aside by the flocks of thy companions?" And, thirdly, we have *an answer obtained*: — "If thou know not, O thou fairest among women, go thy way forth by the footsteps of the flock, and feed thy kids beside the shepherds' tents."

I. Here is A QUESTION ASKED. Every word of the enquiry is worthy of our careful meditation. You will observe, first, concerning it, that it is *asked in love*. She calls him to whom she speaks by the endearing title, "O thou whom my soul loveth".

Whatever she may feel herself to be, she knows that she loves him. She is black, and ashamed to have her face gazed upon, but still she loves her Bridegroom. She has not kept her own vineyard as she ought to have done, but still she loves him. That, she is sure of, and therefore boldly declares it. She loves him as she loves none other in all the world. He only can be called "Him whom my soul loveth". She knows none at all worthy to be compared with him, none who can rival him. He is her bosom's Lord, sole prince and monarch of all her affections. She feels also that she loves him intensely — from her inmost *soul* see loves him. The life of her existence is bound up with him: if there be any force and power and vitality in her, it is but as fuel to the great flame of her love, which burns alone for him. Mark well that it is not "O thou whom my soul believes in." That would be true, but she has passed further. It is not "O thou whom my soul honours." That is true too, but she has passed beyond that stage. Nor is it merely "O thou whom my soul trusts and obeys." She is doing that, but she has reached something warmer, more tender, more full of fire and enthusiasm, and it is "O thou whom my soul *loveth*." Now, beloved, I trust many of us can speak so to Jesus. He is to us the Well-beloved, the chief among a myriad: his mouth is every sweetness; yes, all of him is loveliness, and our soul is wrapt up in him, our heart is altogether taken up with him. We shall never serve him aright unless it is so. Before our Lord said to Peter, "Feed my lambs", and "Feed my sheep", he put the question, "Simon son of Jonas lovest thou me?" (Jn. 21:15-17), and this he repeated three times; for until that question is settled we are unfit for his service. So the bride here, having both herself and her little flock to care for, avows that she loves the spouse as if she felt that she would not dare to have a part of his flock to look after if she did not love him; as if she saw that her right to be a shepherdess at all depended upon her love for the Great Shepherd. She could not expect his help in her work, much less his fellowship in the work, unless there was first in her that all-essential fitness of love for his Person. The question, therefore, becomes instructive to us because it is addressed to Christ under a most endearing title; and I ask every worker here to take care that he always does his work in a spirit of love, and always regards the Lord Jesus not as a task-master, not as one who has given us work to do from which we would desire to escape, but as our dear Lord, whom to serve is bliss, and for whom to die is gain. "O thou whom my soul loveth" is the right name by which a worker for Jesus should address his Lord.

Now, note that the question, as it is asked in love, is also *asked of him*. "Tell me, O thou whom my soul loveth, where thou feedest." She asked him to tell her, as if she feared that none but himself would give her the correct answer; others might be mistaken, but he could not be. She asked of him because she was quite sure that he would give her the kindest answer. Others might be indifferent, and might scarcely take the trouble to reply: but if Jesus would tell her himself, with his own lips, he would mingle love with every word, and so console as well as instruct her. Perhaps she felt that nobody else could tell her as he could, for others speak to the ear, but he speaks to the heart: others speak with lower degrees of influence, we hear their speech but are not moved thereby; but Jesus speaks, and the Spirit goes with every word he utters. Therefore we hear to profit when he converses with us. I do not know how it may be with you, my brethren, but I feel this morning that if I could get half a word from Christ it would satisfy my soul for many a day. I love to hear the gospel, and to read it, and to preach it; but to hear it fresh from himself, applied by the energy of the Holy Spirit! Oh, this were refreshment! This were energy and power! Therefore, Saviour, when your workers desire to know where you feed, tell them yourself, speak to their hearts by your own Spirit, and let them feel as though it were a new revelation to their inmost nature. "Tell me, O thou whom my soul loveth." It is asked in love: it is asked of him.

Now, observe what the question is. She wishes to know how Jesus does his work, and where he does it. It appears from the eighth verse that she herself has a flock of kids to tend. She is a shepherdess, and would desire to feed her flock; hence her question: "Tell me where thou feedest?" She desires those little ones of hers to obtain rest as well as food, and she is troubled about them; therefore she says, "Tell me where thou makest thy flock to rest", for if she can see how Jesus does his work, and where he does it, and in what way, then she will be satisfied that she is doing it in the right way if she closely imitates him and abides in fellowship with him. The question seems to be just this:

"Lord, tell me what are the truths with which you feed your people's souls; tell me what are the doctrines that make the strong ones weak and the sad ones glad. Tell me what is that precious meat which you are wont to give to hungry and fainting spirits, to revive them and keep them alive; for if you tell me, then I will give my flock the same food. Tell me where the pasture is where you feed your, and straightway I will lead mine to the self-same happy fields. Then tell me how thou make your to rest. What are those promises which you apply to the consolation of their spirit, so that their cares and doubts and fears and agitations all subside? You have sweet meadows where you make your beloved flock to lie calmly down and slumber. Tell me where those meadows are, that I may go and fetch the flock committed to my charge, the mourners whom I ought to comfort, the distressed ones whom I am bound to relieve, the desponding whom I have endeavoured to encourage. Tell me, Lord, where you make your flock to lie down, for then, with your help, I will go and make my flock to lie down too. It is for myself, but yet far more for others, that I ask the question: 'Tell me where thou feedest, where thou makest them to rest at noon.'"

I have no doubt that the spouse did desire information for herself and for her own good, and I believe Dr. Watts had caught some of the spirit of the passage when he wrote:

Fain would I feed among thy sheep,
Among them rest, among them sleep.

But it does not strike me that this is all the meaning of the passage by a very long way. The bride says, "Tell me where thou feedest thy flock" as if she would wish to feed with the flock, "where thou makest thy flock to rest", as if she wanted to rest there too: but it strikes me the very gist of the thing is this, that she wished to bring her flock to feed where Christ's flock feeds, and to lead her kids to lie down where Christ's little lambs were reposing. She desired, in fact, to do her work in his company; she wanted to mix up her flock with the Lord's flock, her work with his work, and to feel that, what she was doing, she was doing for him, yes, and with him and through him. She had evidently met with a great many difficulties in what she had tried to do. She wished to feed her flock of kids, but could not find them pasture. Perhaps when she began her work as a shepherdess she

90

thought herself quite equal to the task, but now the same sun which had bronzed her face, had dried up the pasture, and so she says,

"O thou that knowest all the pastures, tell me where thou feedest, for I cannot find grass for my flock"; and she, suffering from the noontide heat, finds her little flock suffering too; and she enquires, "where dost thou make thy flock to rest at noon?" Where are cool shadows of great rocks which screen off the sultry rays when the sun is at its zenith, pouring down torrents of heat? For I cannot shade my poor flock, and give them comfort in their many trials and troubles. I wish I could. O Lord, tell me the secret art of consolation; then will I try to console my own charge by the self-same means."

We would know the groves of promise and the cool streams of peace, that we may lead others into rest. If we can follow Jesus, we can guide others, and so both we and they will find comfort and peace. That is the meaning of the request before us.

Note well that she said most particularly, "Tell *me*." "O Master, do not merely tell thy sheep where you feed, though they want to know; but tell *me* where you feed, for I desire to instruct others." She wanted to know many things, but chiefly she asks, "Tell me *where thou feedest*", for she wished to feed others. We want practical knowledge, for our desire is to be helped to bring others into rest, to be the means of speaking peace to the consciences of others, as the Lord has spoken peace to ours. Therefore, the prayer is, "Tell me". "You are my model, O Great Shepherd; you are my wisdom. If I be a shepherd to your sheep, yet am I also a sheep beneath your Shepherdry; therefore teach me that I may teach others."

I do not know whether I make myself plain to you, but I wish to put it very simply. I am preaching to myself perhaps a great deal more than to you. I am preaching to my own heart. I feel I have to come, Sabbath after Sabbath, and weekday after weekday, and tell you a great many precious things about Christ, and sometimes I enjoy them myself; and if nobody else gets blessed by them, I do, and I go home and praise the Lord for it; but my daily fear is lest I should be a handler of texts for you, and a preacher of good things for others, and yet remain unprofited in my own heart. My prayer is that the Lord Jesus will show me where he feeds his people, and let me feed with them, that then I may conduct you to the pastures where he is, and be with him myself at the same time that I bring you to him. You Sabbath-school teachers and evangelists, and others, my dear, earnest comrades, for whom I thank God at every remembrance, I feel that the main point you have to watch is that you do not lose your own spirituality while trying to make others spiritual. The great point is to live near to God. It would be a dreadful thing for you to be very busy about other men's souls and neglect your own. Appeal to the Well-beloved, and entreat him to let you feed your flock where he is feeding his people, that he would let you sit at his feet, like Mary, even while you are working in the house, like Martha. (Lk. 10:38-41)Do not do less, but rather more; but ask to do it in such communion with him that your work shall be melted into his work, and what you are doing shall be really only his working in you, and you rejoicing to pour out to others what he pours into your own soul. God grant it may be so with you all, my brethren!

II. Secondly, here is AN ARGUMENT USED. The bride says, "Why should I be as one that turneth aside by the flocks of thy companions?" If she should lead her flock into distant meadows, far away from the place where Jesus is feeding his flock, it would not be well. As a shepherdess, she would naturally be rather dependent, and would need to associate herself for protection with others. Suppose she should turn aside with other shepherds, and leave her Bridegroom, would it be right? She speaks of it as a thing most abhorrent to her mind; and well might it be. For, first, would it not look very unseemly that the bride should be associating with others than the Bridegroom? They each have a flock: there is

91

he with his great flock, and here is she with her little one. Shall they seek pastures far off from one another? Will there not be talk about this? Will not onlookers say, "This is not seemly: there must be some lack of love here, or else these two would not be so divided"? Stress may be put, if you like, upon that little word "I."

Why should I, your blood-bought spouse; I, betrothed you, or ever the earth was, I, whom you have loved — why should I turn after others and forget you? Beloved, you had better put the emphasis in your own reading of it just there. Why should I, whom the Lord has pardoned, whom the Lord has loved, whom the Lord has favoured so much — I, who have enjoyed fellowship with him for many years — I, who know that his love is better than wine — I, who have aforetime been inebriated with his sweetness. Why should I turn aside? Let others do so if they will, but it would be uncomely and unseemly for me. I pray you, brother and sister, try to feel that — that for you to work apart from Christ would have a bad look about it; that for your work to take you away from fellowship with Jesus would have a very ugly appearance: it would not be among the things that are honest and of good repute. For the bride to feed her flock in other company would look like unfaithfulness to her husband. What, shall the bride of Christ forsake her Beloved? Shall she be unchaste towards her Lord? Yet it would seem so if she makes companions of others, and forgets her Beloved? Our hearts may grow unchaste to Christ even while they are zealous in Christian work. I dread very much the tendency to do Christ's work in a cold, mechanical spirit; but above even that, I tremble lest I should be able to have warmth for Christ's work and yet should be cold towards the Lord himself. I fear that such a condition of heart is possible — that we may burn great bonfires in the streets for public display, and scarcely keep a live coal upon our hearth for Jesus to warm his hands by. When we meet in the great assembly, the good company helps to warm our hearts, and when we are working for the Lord with others, they stimulate us, and cause us to put forth all our energy and strength; and then we think, "Surely my heart is in a healthy condition towards God." But, beloved, such excitement may be a poor index of our real state. I love that quiet, holy fire which will glow in the closet, and flame forth in the chamber when I am alone; and that is the point I am more fearful about than anything else, both for myself and for you, lest we should be doing Christ's work without Christ; having much to do but not thinking much of him; cumbered about in much serving and forgetting him. Why, that would soon grow into making a Christ out of our own service, an Antichrist out of our own labours. Beware of that! Love your work, but love your Master better; love your flock, but love the great Shepherd better still, and keep ever close to him, for it will be a token of unfaithfulness if you do not.

And mark again, "Why should I be as one that turneth aside by the flocks of thy companions?" We may read this as meaning, "Why should I be so unhappy as to have to work for you, and yet be out of communion with you?" It is a very unhappy thing to lose fellowship with Jesus, yet to have to go on with religious exercises. If the wheels are taken off your chariot, it is no great matter if nobody wants to ride, but how if you are called upon to drive on? When a man's foot is lamed, he may not so much regret it if he can sit still, but if he is bound to run a race, he is greatly to be pitied. It made the spouse doubly unhappy even to suppose that she, with her flock to feed, and herself needing feeding too, should have to turn aside by the flocks of others and miss the presence of her Lord. In fact the question seems to be put in this shape:

"What reason is there why I should leave my Lord? What apology could I make, what excuse could I offer for so doing? Is there any reason why I should not abide in constant fellowship with him? Why should I be as one that turns aside? Perhaps it may be said that others turn aside, but why should I be one of them? There may be excuses for such an act in others, but there can be none for me. Your rich love, your free love, your undeserved love, your special love to me, has bound me hand and foot: so how can I turn aside? There may be some professors who owe you little, but I, once the chief of sinners, owe you so much, so how can I turn aside? There may be some with whom you have dealt hardly who may turn aside, but you have been so tender, so kind to me, how can I forget you? There may be some who know but little of you, whose experience of you is so slender that their turning aside is not to be wondered at. But how can I turn aside when you have shown me your love, and revealed your heart to me? Oh, by the banqueting house where I have feasted with you, by the Hermonites and the hill Mizar, where you have manifested your love, by the place where deep calls to deep, and then mercy calls to mercy; by those mighty storms and sweeping hurricanes in which you were the shelter of my head, by ten thousand-thousand mercies past which have been my blessed portion, why should I be as one that turns aside by the flocks of your companions?"

Let me address the members of this church, and say to you, if all the churches in Christendom were to go aside from the gospel, why should you? If in every other place the gospel should be neglected, and an uncertain sound should be given forth; if Ritualism should swallow up half the churches, and Rationalism the rest, yet why should you turn aside? You have been particularly a people of prayer; you have also followed the Lord fully in doctrine and an ordinance; and consequently you have enjoyed the divine presence, and have prospered beyond measure. We have cast ourselves upon the Holy Spirit for strength, and have not relied upon human eloquence, music, or beauties of colour, or architecture. Our only weapon has been the simple, plain, full gospel, and why should we turn aside? Have we not been favoured for these many years with unexampled success? Has not the Lord added to our numbers so abundantly that we have not had room enough to receive them? Has he not multiplied the people, and increased the joy? Hold fast to your first love, and let no one take your crown. I thank God there are churches still, a few in England and yet more in Scotland, which hold fast the doctrines of the gospel, and will not let them go. To them I would say, why should you turn aside? Should not your history, both in its troublous and its joyous chapters teach you to hold fast the form of sound words?

Above all, should we not try to live as a church, and individually also, in abiding fellowship with Jesus? For if we turn aside from him, we shall rob the truth of its aroma, yes, of its essential fragrance. If we lose fellowship with Jesus, we shall have the standard, but where will the standard-bearer be? We may retain the candlestick, but where shall the light be? We shall be shorn of our strength, our joy, our comfort, our all, if we miss fellowship with him. God grant, therefore, that we may never be as those who turn aside!

III. Thirdly, we have here AN ANSWER GIVEN by the Bridegroom to his beloved.

She asked him where he fed, where he made his flock to rest, and he answered her. Observe carefully that this answer is given in tenderness to her infirmity; not ignoring her ignorance, but dealing very gently with it. "If thou know not" — a hint that she ought to have known, but such a hint as kind lovers give when they forbear to chide. Our Lord is very tender to our ignorance. There are many things which we do not know, but ought to have known. We are children when we should be men, and have to be spoken to as unto carnal — unto babes in Christ when we should have become fathers. Is there one among us who can say, "I am not faulty in my knowledge?" I am afraid the most of us must confess that, if we had done the Lord's will better, we should have known his doctrine better; if we had lived more closely to him, we should have known more of him. Still, how very gentle the rebuke is. The Lord forgives our ignorance, and condescends to instruct it.

Note next that the answer is given in great love. He says, "O thou fairest among women". That is a blessed cordial for her distress. She said, "I am black", but he says, "O thou

93

fairest among women". I would rather trust Christ's eyes than mine. If my eyes tell me I am black, I will weep, but if he assures me I am fair I will believe him and rejoice. Some saints are more apt to remember their sinfulness, and grieve over it, than to believe in their righteousness in Christ, and triumph in it. Remember, beloved, it is quite as true today that you are all fair and without spot as that you are black, because the sun has looked upon you. It must be true because Jesus says so. Let me give you one of the sayings of the Bridegroom to his bride: "Thou art all fair, my love; there is no spot in thee." "Ah, that is a figure", you say. Well, I will give you one that is not a figure. The Lord Jesus, after he had washed his disciples' feet, said, "He that is washed needed not, except to wash his feet for he is clean every whit"; and then he added, "And ye are clean." (Jn. 13:10) If you desire an apostolic word to the same effect, let me give you this: "Who shall lay anything to the charge of God's elect?" (Rom. 8:23) — anything — any little thing, or any great thing either. Jesus has washed his people so clean that there is no spot, no wrinkle, nor any such thing upon them in the matter of justification before God:

In thy surety thou art free,
His dear hands were pierced for thee;
With his spotless vesture on,
Holy as the Holy One.

(John Kent)

How glorious is this! Jesus does not exaggerate when he thus commends his church. He speaks plain, sober truth. "O thou fairest among women", says he. My soul, do you not feel love to Christ when you remember that he thinks you beautiful? I cannot see anything in myself to love, but he does, and calls me "all fair". I think it must be that he looks into our eyes and sees himself, or else this, that he knows what we are going to be, and judges us on that scale. As the artist, looking on the block of marble, he sees in the stone the statue which he means to fetch out of it with matchless skill, so the Lord Jesus sees the perfect image of himself in us, from which he means to chip away the imperfections and the sins until it stands out in all its splendour. But still, it is gracious condescension which makes him say, "Thou art fairest among women", to one who mourned her own sunburnt countenance.

The answer contains much sacred wisdom. The bride is directed where to go, that she may find her beloved, and lead her flock to him. "Go your way forth by the footprints of the flock." If you will find Jesus, you will find him in the way the holy prophets went, in the way of the patriarchs, and the way of the apostles. And if you desire to find your flock, and to make them lie down, very well, go and feed them as other shepherds have done — Christ's own shepherds whom he has sent on other days to feed his chosen. I feel very glad, in speaking on this text, that the Lord does not give to his bride in answer to her question some singular directions of great difficulty, some novel prescriptions singular and remarkable. Just as the gospel itself is simple and homely, so is this exhortation and direction for the renewal of communion. It is easy, it is plain. You want to get to Jesus, and you want to bring those under your charge to him. Very well, then, do not seek out a new road, but simply go the way which all other saints have gone. If you want to walk with Jesus, walk where other saints have walked; and if you want to lead others into communion with him, lead them by your example where others have gone. What is that? If you want to be with Jesus, go where Abraham went in the path of separation. See how he lived as a pilgrim and a sojourner with his God. If you would see Jesus, "Come ye out from among them, be ye separate, touch not the unclean thing." (1 Cor. 6:17) You shall find Jesus when you have left the world. If you would walk with Jesus, follow the path of obedience. Saints have never had fellowship with Jesus when they have disobeyed him. Keep his statutes and observe his testimonies; be jealous over your conduct and

94

character; for the path of obedience is the path of communion. Be sure that you follow the ancient ways with regard to the Christian ordinances: do not alter them, but keep to the good old paths. Stand and enquire what apostles did, and do the same. Jesus will not bless you in using fanciful ceremonies of human invention. Keep to those which he commands, which his Spirit actions, which his apostles practiced. Above all, if you would walk with Jesus, continue in the way of holiness; persevere in the way of grace. Make the Lord Jesus your model and example; and, by treading where the footprints of the flock are to be seen, you will both save yourself and those who hear you; you will find Jesus, and they will find him too. We might have supposed that the Lord would have said, "If you want to lead your flock aright, array yourself in sumptuous apparel, or go get your music and fine anthems; by these fair things you will fascinate the Saviour into your sanctuaries." But it is not so. The incense which will please the Lord Jesus is that of holy prayer and praise, and the only Ritualism which is acceptable with him is this — "pure religion, and undefiled before God and the Father is this, to visit the fatherless and the widow, and to keep oneself unspotted from the world. (Jas. 1:27) This is all he wants. Follow that, and you will both go right, and lead others right.

Then the Spouse added, "Feed thy kids beside the shepherds' tents." Now, who are these shepherds? There are many in these days who set up as shepherds, who feed their sheep in poisonous pastures. Keep away from them; but there are others whom it is safe to follow. Let me take you to the twelve principal shepherds who came after the great Shepherd of all. You want to bless your children, to save their souls, and have fellowship with Christ in the doing of it; then teach them the truths which the apostles taught. And what were they? Take Paul as an example. "I determined not to know anything among you save Jesus Christ, and him crucified." (1 Cor. 2:2) That is feeding the kids beside the shepherds' tents, when you teach your children Christ, much of Christ, all of Christ, and nothing else but Christ. Mind you, stick to that blessed subject. And when you are teaching them Christ, teach them all about his life, his death, and his resurrection; teach them his Godhead and his manhood. You will never enjoy Christ's company if you doubt his divinity. Take care that you feed your flock upon the doctrine of the atonement. Christ will have no fellowship with a worker unless he represents him fairly, and you cannot represent Christ truthfully unless you see the ruddy hue of his atoning blood, as well as the lily purity of his life. "Feed thy kids beside the shepherds' tents"; then you will teach them the atoning sacrifice, and justification by faith, and imputed righteousness, and union with the risen Head, and the coming of the great One, when we shall receive the adoption, to wit, the redemption of the body from the grave. I speak the truth and do not lie when I say that if we want to teach a congregation so as to bless them, and keep ourselves in fellowship with Christ at the same time, we must be very particular in teaching nothing but the truth — not a part of it, but all of it. Preach that blessed doctrine of election. Oh, the depths of divine love which are contained in that blessed truth! Do not shirk it, or keep it in the background. You cannot expect Christ's presence if you do. Teach the doctrine of man's depravity. Lay the sinner low. God will not bless a ministry which exalts men. Preach the doctrine of the Holy Spirit's effective calling, for if we do not magnify the Spirit of God, we cannot expect him to make our work stand. Preach regeneration. Let it be seen how thorough the change is, that we may glorify God's work. Preach the final perseverance of the saints. Teach that the Lord is not changeable, — casting away his people, loving them today and hating them tomorrow. Preach, in fact, the doctrines of grace as you find them in the Book. Feed them beside the shepherds' tents. Aye, and feed the kids there — the little children. I begin to feel more and more that it is a mistake to divide the children from the congregation. I believe in special services for children, but I would also have them worship with us. If our preaching does not teach children, it lacks some element which it ought to possess. The kind of preaching which is best of all for grown-up people is that in which children also will take delight. I like to see the congregation made up not all of the young, nor all of the old, not all of the mature, nor all

95

of the inexperienced, but some of all sorts gathered together. If we are teaching children salvation by works, and grown-up people salvation by grace, we are pulling down in the school-room what we build up in the church, and that will never do. Feed the kids with the same gospel as the grown-up sheep, though not exactly in the same terms; let your language be appropriate for them, but let it be the same truth. God forbid that we should make our Sunday-schools the hot-beds of Arminianism, while our churches are gardens of Calvinism. We shall soon have a division in the camp if that is so. The same truth for all; and you cannot expect Christ to be with you in feeding your little flocks unless you feed them where Christ feeds us. Where does he feed us, but where the truth grows? Oh, when I read some sermons, they remind me of a piece of common by the roadside after a hungry horde of sheep has devoured every green thing; but when I read a solid gospel sermon of the Puritans, it reminds me of a field kept for hay, which a farmer is at last obliged to give up to the sheep. The grass has grown almost as high as themselves, and so they lie down in it, eating and resting too. Give me the doctrines of grace, and I am in clover. If you have to feed others, take them there. Do not conduct them to the starved pastures of modern thought and culture. Preachers are starving God's people nowadays. Oh, but they set out such beautiful China plates, such wonderful knives and forks, such marvellous vases and damask tablecloths! But as for food, the plates look as if they had been smeared with a feather; there is so little on them. The real gospel teaching is little enough. These give us nothing to learn, nothing to digest, nothing to feed upon; it is all slops, and nothing substantial. Oh for the good old corn of the kingdom; we want that, and I am persuaded that, when the churches get back to the old food again, when they begin to feed their flocks beside the shepherds' tents, and when in practical living Christian saints get back to the old Puritanic method, and follow once again the tracks of the sheep, and the sheep follow the tracks of Christ, then we shall get the church into fellowship with Jesus, and he will do wonders in our midst. But to get that, each individual must aim at winning it for himself, and if the Lord grant it to each one of us, then it will be granted to the whole, and the good times which we desire will certainly have come. My beloved, do you desire to work with Christ? Do you want to feel that Jesus is at your right hand? Then go and work in his way. Teach what he would have you teach, not what you would like to teach. Go and work for him, as he would have you work, not as your prejudices might prescribe for you. Be obedient. Follow the footsteps of the flock. Be diligent also to keep hard by the shepherds' tents, and the Lord bless you more and more, you and your children, and his shall be the glory. I have spoken only to God's people: I would there had been time to speak to the unconverted too, but to them I can only say this: may God grant you grace to know the beauties of Jesus, for then you will love him too. May he also show you the deformities of yourselves, for then you will desire to be cleansed and made lovely in Christ.

And remember, if any of you wants Christ, he wants you; and if you long for him, he longs for you. If you seek him, he is seeking you. If you now cry to him, he is already crying after you. "Whosoever will, let him come and take of the water of life freely." (Rev. 22:17)

The Lord save you for his name's sake! Amen.

12. FRAGRANT GRACES
NO. 3480

AT THE METROPOLITAN TABERNACLE, NEWINGTON

"While the king sitteth at his table, my spikenard sendeth forth the smell thereof."
(Song of Solomon 1:12)

THIS passage may be read in several ways. Literally, when Christ tabled among men, when he ate and drank with them, being found in fashion as a man, the loving spirit broke the alabaster box of precious ointment on his head while the king was sitting at his table. Three times the Church thus anointed her Lord: once his head and twice his feet, as if she remembered his threefold office, and the threefold anointing which he had received from God the Father to confirm and strengthen him. So she rendered him the threefold anointing of her grateful love, breaking the alabaster box, and pouring the precious ointment upon his head and upon his feet. (Mat. 26:7; Mk. 14:3; Lk. 7:37) Beloved, let us imitate the example of those who have gone before. What! Though we cannot, as the weeping penitent, wash his feet with our tears, and wipe them like that gracious woman, with the hairs of our head, we may reckon nothing of fair adornments, or fond endowments, if we can but serve his cause or honour his person. Let us be willing to "pour contempt on all our pride," and "nail our glory to his cross". Have you anything tonight that is dear to you? Resign it to him. Have you any costly thing like an alabaster box hidden away? Give it to the King; he is worthy, and when you have fellowship with him at his table, let your gifts be brought out. Offer to the King thanksgiving, and pay your vows to the Most High. But the King is gone from earth. He is seated at his table in heaven, eating bread in the kingdom of God. Surrounded now not by publicans and harlots, but by cherubim and seraphim, not by mocking crowds, but by adoring hosts, the King sits at his table, and entertains the glorious company of the faithful, the Church of the firstborn whose names are written in heaven. He fought before he could rest. On earth he struggled with his enemies, and it was not till he had triumphed over all that he sat down at the table on high. There sit, you King of kings, there sit until your last enemy shall be made your footstool. (Ps. 110:1) What can we do, brethren, while Christ sits at the table above? These hands cannot reach him; these eyes cannot see him; but our prayers, like sweet perfume, set burning here on earth, can rise in smoke to the place where the King sits at his table, and our spikenard can diffuse a perfume even in heaven itself. Do you want to reach Christ? Your prayers can do it. Would you now adore him; would you now set forth your love? With mingled prayer and praise, like the offering of the morning and the evening sacrifice, your incense can rise up acceptably before the Lord.

And, brethren, the day is coming when the King shall sit at his table in royal state. Lo, he comes! Lo, he comes. Let the Church never forget that. The first advent is her faith; the second advent is her hope. The first advent with the cross lays the foundation, the second advent with the crown brings forth the top stone. The former was ushered in with sighs; the latter shall be hailed with shoutings of "Grace, grace unto it". (Zech. 4:7) And when the King, manifested and recognised in his sovereignty over all lands, shall sit at his table with his Church, then, in that blessed Millennium, the graces of Christians shall give forth their odours of sweet savour.

We have thus read the text in three ways, and there is a volume in each, but now we turn over another page, for we want to read it in relation to the spiritual presence of Christ as he now reveals himself to his people. "When the King sitteth at his table" — that is, when we enjoy the presence of Christ — "my spikenard giveth forth the smell thereof." Then our graces are in active exercise, and yield a perfume agreeable to our own soul, and are acceptable before God.

In the train of reflection I shall now attempt to follow, my manner must be hurried; and should it seem feeble, brethren, I cannot help it. If you get fellowship with Christ, I care little for the merits of my sermon, or the perils of your criticism. One thing alone I crave, "Let him kiss us with the kisses of his mouth" (Song 1:2); then shall my soul be well content, and so will yours be also.

The first observation we make shall be this:

I. EVERY BELIEVER HAS GRACE IN POSSESSION AT ALL TIMES.

The text implies that when the King is not present, the spikenard yields no smell, but the spikenard is there for all that. The spouse speaks of her spikenard as though she had it, and only wanted to have the King come and sit at the table to make its presence known and felt. Ah! well, believer, there is grace in your heart, if your are a child of God, when you cannot see it yourself; when your doubts have so covered up all your hopes, that you say, "I am cast out from his presence"; yet for all that, grace may be there. When the old oak has lost its last leaf by the howling blasts of winter; when the sap is frozen up in the veins, and you cannot, though you search to the highest bough, find so much as the slightest sign of verdant existence, still, even then, the substance is in the tree when it has lost its leaves. And so with every believer, though his sap seems frozen, and his life almost dead, yet if once planted, it is there; the eternal life is there when he cannot discover it himself. Do you know — if not, I pray you may never know experimentally — that there are many things that keep a Christian's spikenard from being poured out. Alas, there is our sin. Ah, shameful, cruel sin, which robs my Master of his glory! But when we fall into sin, of course, our graces become weak and yield no fragrance to God. Ah, too, there is our unbelief, which puts a heavy stone on all our graces, and blows out the heat which was burning the frankincense, so that no altar-smoke arises towards heaven. And often, it may be, it is our bitterness of spirit, for when our mind is cast down we hang our harps on the willows, so that they give forth no sweet music to God. And, above all, if Christ is absent, if through neglect or by any other means our fellowship with him is suspended, grace is there — but oh, it cannot be seen! There is no comfort springing from it.

But, beloved, though we mention this to begin with, we rather choose to pass on and observe that:

II. GRACE IS NOT GIVEN TO A CHRISTIAN TO BE THUS HIDDEN, BUT IT IS INTENDED THAT, LIKE SPIKENARD, IT SHOULD ALWAYS BE SEEN IN THE EXERCISE.

If I understand a Christian aright, he should be a man readily discerned. You do not need to write upon a box that contains spikenard, with the lid open, the word "Spikenard". You know it is there; your nostrils tell you. If a man should fill his pockets with dust, he might walk where he would, and though he should scatter it in the air, few would notice it; but let him go into a room with his pockets full of musk, and let him drop a particle about, he is soon discovered because the musk speaks for itself. Now, true grace, like spikenard, or any other perfume, should speak for itself. You know our Saviour compares Christians to lights. There is a crowd of people standing yonder; I cannot see those who are in the shadow, but there is one man whose face I can see well, and that is the man who holds the torch. Its flames light up his face so that we can catch every feature readily. So, whoever is not discovered, the Christian should be obvious at once. "Thou also wast with

Jesus of Nazareth, for thy speech betrayeth thee." (Mat. 26:73) Not only should the Christian be perceptible, but grace has been given to him that it might be in exercise. What is faith, unless it is believing? What is love, unless it is embracing? What is patience, unless it is enduring? To what purpose is knowledge, unless it is revealing truth? What are any of those sweet graces which the Master gives us, unless they yield their perfume? I fear we do not enough gaze upon that face covered with the bloody sweat, for if we did, as sure as the King was thus in our thoughts sitting at his table, we should be more like him; we should love him better; we should live more passionately for him, and should spend and be spent, that we might promote his glory. I just note this point, and then pass on, that believers' graces, like spikenard, are meant to give forth their smell. But here is the pith of our whole subject, though we have little time to linger upon it:

III. THE ONLY WAY IN WHICH A CHRISTIAN'S GRACES CAN BE PUT INTO EXERCISE IS THAT HE MUST HAVE THE PRESENCE OF THE MASTER.

He is called "the King". I am told that the Hebrew word is very emphatic, as if it said, "the King" — the King of kings, the greatest of all Kings. He must be such to us — absolute Master of our hearts, Lord of our soul's domain, the unrivalled One in our estimation, to whom we render obedience with alacrity. We must have him as King, or we shall not have his presence to revive our graces. And when the King communes with his people, it is said to be at "his table", not ours. Especially may this apply to the Communion Table. It is not the Baptists' table; it is not my table; it is his table, because if there is anything good on it, remember, he spread it; no, there is nothing on the table unless he himself is there. There is no food to the child of God unless Christ's body be the flesh, and Christ's blood the wine. We must have Christ. It must be emphatically his table by his being present, by his spreading it, by his presiding at it, or else we do not have his presence at all. I find the Hebrew word here signifies a "round table". I do not know whether that is intended, which I understand by it — perhaps it is — it suggests to me a blessed equality with all his disciples; sitting at his round table, as if there were scarcely a head, but he was one of themselves, so close the communion he holds with them sitting at the table; so dear his fellowship, sitting like one of themselves, made like unto his brethren in all things at his round table.

Well, now, we say that when Christ comes into the ordinance of the Lord's Supper, or any other ordinance, straightway our graces are vigorous. How often have we resolved that we would live nearer to Christ! Yet, though we have resolved, and re-resolved, I fear it has all ended with resolving. Perhaps we have prayed over our resolutions, and, for a little season, we have sought it very earnestly, but our earnestness soon expired like every other fire that is of human kindling, and we made but little progress. Be not disheartened, my beloved in the Lord: I tell you, whether you are able to believe it or not, that if your heart be this night cold as the centre of an iceberg, yet if Christ shall come to you, your soul shall be as coals of juniper that have a most vehement flame. Though to your own apprehension you seem to be dead as the bones in a cemetery, yet if Jesus come to you, you shall forthwith be as full of life as the seraphs who are as flames of fire. Why do you think he will not come to you? Do you not remember how he came to melt you when first he manifested himself to your soul? You were as vile then as you are now; you were certainly as ruined then as you are now; you had no more to merit his esteem then than you have now; you were as far off from him then as you are now — I might say even further off. But lo! He came to you when you did not seek him; he came in the sovereignty of his grace and the sweetness of his mercy when you despised him. Therefore, then, should he not come to you now? Oh, breathe the prayer tenderly, and hopefully breathe the prayer, "Draw me", and you will soon find power to run, and when all your passions and powers have fled, the King will speedily bring you into his chamber. Dark as your present state may be, there are sure signs of breaking day. I want you, brethren, to

99

believe and to expect that you shall hold this night with Christ the richest, sweetest fellowship that ever mortal was privileged to enjoy, and that of a sudden. I know your cares — forget them. I know your sins — bring them to his feet. I know the wanderings of your heart — ask him to tether you to his cross with the same cords that bound him to the pillar of his flagellation [flogging]. I know your brain is perplexed, and your thoughts flying hither and thither, distracted with many cares — put on the thorn-crown, and let that be the antidote to all your manifold disquietudes. I think, Jesus is putting in his hand by the hole of the door. Are not your inward parts moved for him? Rise up and welcome him; and as the bread is broken, and the wine is passed round, come, and eat and drink of him, and do not be a stranger to him. "Do not let conscience make you linger"; do not let doubts and fears hold you back from fellowship with him who loved you or ever the earth was, but rest your unworthy head upon his blessed bosom, and talk with him, even though the only word you may be able to say is, "Lord, is it I?" Seek fellowship with him, as one who ignores every thought, feeling, or fact beside. So may it please him to manifest himself to you and to me, as he does not do to the world.

If you that have never had fellowship with Christ think I am talking nonsense, I do not marvel. But let me tell you, if you had ever known what fellowship with Christ means, you would pawn your eyes, and barter your right arms, and give your estates away as trifles for the priceless favour. Princes would sell their crowns, and peers would renounce their dignities, to have five minutes' fellowship with Christ. I will vouch for that. Why, I have had more joy in my Lord and Master in the space of the ticking of a clock than could be crammed into a lifetime of sensual delights, of the pleasures of taste, of the fascinations of literature. There is a depth, a matchless depth, in Jesus love. There is a luscious sweetness in fellowship with him. You must eat, or you will never know the flavour of it. Oh, taste and see that the Lord is good! (Ps. 34:8)

Behold! How ready he still is to welcome sinners! Trust him and live. Feed on him, and grow strong. Commune with him, and be happy. May every one of you who sit at the table have the nearest approach to Jesus that you ever had! Like two streams that, after flowing side by side, at length unite, so may Christ and our soul melt into one, even as Isis melts into the Thames, till only one life shall flow, so that the life we live in the flesh shall be no more ours, but Christ that lives in us. (Gal. 2:20) Amen.

13. A BUNDLE OF MYRRH

NO. 558

DELIVERED ON SUNDAY MORNING, MARCH 6TH, 1864
AT THE METROPOLITAN TABERNACLE, NEWINGTON

"A bundle of myrrh is my well-beloved unto me; he shall lie all night betwixt my breasts." (Song of Solomon 1:13)

CERTAIN divines have doubted the inspiration of Solomon's Song; others have conceived it to be nothing more than a specimen of ancient love songs, and some have been afraid to preach from it because of its highly poetical character. The true reason for all this avoidance of one of the most heavenly portions of God's Word lies in the fact that the spirit of this Song is not easily attained. Its music belongs to the higher spiritual life, and has no charm in it for unspiritual ears. The Song occupies a sacred enclosure into which none may enter unprepared. "Put off thy shoes from off thy feet, for the place whereon thou standest is holy ground" (Ex. 3:5) is the warning voice from its secret tabernacles.

The historical books I may compare to the outer courts of the Temple; the Gospels, the Epistles, and the Psalms bring us into the holy place or the Court of the priests; but the Song of Solomon is the most holy place: the holy of holies, before which the veil still hangs to many an untaught believer. It is not all the saints who can enter here, for they have not yet attained to the holy confidence of faith, and that exceeding familiarity of love which will permit them to commune in conjugal love with the great Bridegroom. We are told that the Jews did not permit a young student to read the Canticles — that years of full maturity were thought necessary before the man could rightly profit by this mysterious Song of loves; possibly they were wise, at any rate the prohibition foreshadowed a great truth.

The Song is, in truth, a book for full-grown Christians. Babes in grace may find their carnal and sensuous affections stirred up by it towards Jesus, whom they know, rather, "after the flesh" than in the spirit; but it needs a man of fuller growth, who has leaned his head upon the bosom of his Master, and been baptised with his baptism, to ascend the lofty mountains of love on which the spouse stands with her beloved. The Song, from the first verse to the last, will be clear to those who have received an unction from the holy One, and know all things. (1 John 2:20.) You are aware, dear friends, that there are very few commentaries on the Epistles of John. Where we find fifty commentaries on any book of St. Paul, you will hardly find one on John. Why is that? Is the book too difficult? The words are very simple; there is hardly a word of four syllables anywhere in John's Epistles. Ah, but they are so saturated through and through with the spirit of love, which also perfumes this Book of Solomon, that those who are not taught in the school of communion, cry out, "We cannot read it, for it is sealed." The Song is a golden casket, of which love is the key rather than learning. Those who have not attained to heights of affection, those who have not been educated by familiar intercourse with Jesus, cannot come near to this mine of treasure, "seeing it is hid from the eyes of all living, and kept close from the fowls of heaven." (Job 28:21) Oh for the soaring eagle wing of John and the farseeing dove's eyes of Solomon! But most of us are blind and cannot see afar off. May God be pleased to make us grow in grace, and give us so much of the Holy Spirit, that with feet like hind's feet we may stand upon the high places of Scripture, and this morning have some near and dear intercourse with Christ Jesus.

Concerning our text, let us talk very simply, remarking first that Christ is very precious to believers; secondly, that there is good reason why he should be; thirdly, that mingled with

101

this sense of preciousness, there is a joyous consciousness of possession of him; and that therefore, fourthly, there is an earnest desire for perpetual fellowship with him. If you look at the text again, you will see all these things in it.

I. First, CHRIST JESUS IS UNUTTERABLY PRECIOUS TO BELIEVERS.

The words manifestly imply this: "A bundle of myrrh is my well-beloved unto me." She calls him her "well-beloved", and so expresses her love most emphatically; it is not merely beloved, but well-beloved. Then she looks round about her to find a substance which shall be at once valuable in itself, and useful in its properties; and lighting upon myrrh, she says, "A bundle of myrrh is my well-beloved unto me." Without looking into the figure just now, we keep to the statement that Christ is precious to the believer.

Observe first, that nothing gives the believer so much joy as fellowship with Christ. Ask yourselves, you who have eaten at his table and have been made to drink of his cup, where can such sweetness be found as you have tasted in communion with Jesus? The Christian has joy as other men have in the common mercies of life. For him, there are charms in music, excellence in painting, and beauty in sculpture; for him the hills have sermons of majesty, the rocks hymns of sublimity, and the valleys lessons of love. He can look upon all things with an eye as clear and joyous as another man's; he can be glad both in God's gifts and God's works. He is not dead to the happiness of the household: around his hearth he finds happy associations, without which life would be drear indeed. His children fill his home with glee, his wife is his solace and delight, his friends are his comfort and refreshment. He accepts the comforts which soul and body can yield him according as God sees it wise to afford them unto him; but he will tell you that in all these separately, yes, and in all of them added together, he does not find such substantial delight as he does in the Person of his Lord Jesus. Brethren, there is a wine which no vineyard on earth ever yielded; there is a bread which even the cornfields of Egypt could never produce. You and I have said, when we have beheld others finding their god in earthly comforts, "You may boast in gold, and silver, and raiment, but I will rejoice in the God of my salvation." In our esteem, the joys of earth are little better than husks for swine compared with Jesus the heavenly manna. I would rather have one mouthful of Christ's love, and a sip of his fellowship, than a whole world full of carnal delights. What is the chaff to the wheat? What is the sparkling paste to the true diamond? What is a dream to the glorious reality? What is time's mirth in its best trim compared to our Lord Jesus in his most despised estate? If you know anything of the inner life, you will all of you confess that our highest, purest, and most enduring joys must be the fruit of the tree of life which is in the midst of the Paradise of God. No spring yields such sweet water as that well of God which was dug with the soldier's spear. As for the house of feasting, the joy of harvest, the mirth of marriage, the sports of youth, the recreations of maturer age, they are all as the small dust of the balance compared with the joy of Immanuel, our best beloved. As the Preacher said, so say we, "I said of laughter, It is mad: and of mirth, What doeth it?" (Eccl. 2:2) "Vanity of vanities; all is vanity." (Eccl. 1:2, 12:8) All earthly bliss is of the earth earthy, but the comforts of Christ's presence are like himself heavenly. We can review our communion with Jesus, and find no regrets of emptiness therein; there are no dregs in this wine, no dead flies in this ointment. The joy of the Lord is solid and enduring. Vanity has not looked upon it, but discretion and prudence testify that it abides the test of years, and is in time and in eternity worthy to be called "the only true delight." Where is the world with all its store?

What is the world with all its store?
'Tis but a bitter sweet;
When I attempt to pluck the rose
A pricking thorn I meet.

102

Here perfect bliss can ne'er be found,
The honey's mixed with gall;
Midst changing scenes and dying friends,
Be Thou my all in all.

(Benjamin Beddome)

We may plainly see that Christ is very precious to the believer because, to him, there is nothing good without Christ. Believer, have you not found in the midst of plenty a dire and sore famine if your Lord has been absent? The sun was shining, but Christ had hidden himself, and all the world was black to you; or it was a night of tempest, and there were many stars, but since the bright and morning star was gone on that dreary main, where you were tossed with doubts and fears, no other star could shed so much as a ray of light. Oh, what a howling wilderness is this world without my Lord! If once he grows angry, and, though it be for a moment, hides himself from me, withered are the flowers of my garden; my pleasant fruits decay; the birds suspend their songs; and black night lowers over all my hopes. Nothing can compensate for the company of the Saviour: all earth's candles cannot make daylight if the Sun of Righteousness is gone.

On the other hand, when all earthly comforts have failed you, have you not found quite enough in your Lord? Your very worst times, have they not been your best times? You must almost cry to go back to your bed of sickness, for Jesus made it as a royal throne, on which you reigned with him. Those dark nights — ah, they were not dark — your bright days since then have been darker far. Do you remember when you were poor? Oh, how near Christ was to you, and how rich he made you! You were despised and rejected by men, and no one gave you a good word! Ah, sweet was his fellowship then, and how delightful to hear him say, "Fear thou not; for I am with thee: be not dismayed; for I am thy God!" (Is. 41:10) As afflictions abound, even so consolations abound by Christ Jesus. The devil, like Nebuchadnezzar, heats the furnace seven times hotter, but who would have it less furiously blazing? No wise believer; for the more terrible the heat, the greater the glory in the fact that we were made to tread those glowing coals, and not a hair of our head was singed, nor so much as the smell of fire passed upon us, because the Son of God walked those glowing coals in our company. Yes, we can look with resignation on penury, disease, and even death; for if all comforts be taken from us, we should still be blest so long as we enjoy the presence of the Lord our Saviour.

Nor should I be straining the truth if I say that the Christian would sooner give up anything than forsake his Master. I have known some who have been afraid to look that text in the face which says, "He that loveth son or daughter more than me is not worthy of me" (Mat. 10:37), or that, "Except a man hate (or love less) his father and mother, and wife and children, he cannot be my disciple." (Lk. 14:26) Yet I have found that those have frequently proved to be the most sincere lovers of Jesus who have been most afraid that he did not have the best place in their hearts. Perhaps the best way is not to sit down calmly to weigh our love, for it is not a thing to be measured with cool judgement, but put your love to some practical test. Now, if it came to this, that you must deny Christ or give up the dearest thing you have, would you deliberate? The Lord knows I speak what I feel in my own soul — when it comes to that, I would not hesitate a second. If there were a stake and burning faggots, I might flinch from the fire, but so mighty is divine love that it would doubtless drive me to the flames sooner than let me leave Jesus. But if it comes to this, "Will thou lose your eyes or give up Christ?" I would cheerfully be blind. Or if it were asked, "Will you have your right arm withered from its socket or give up Christ?" Aye; let both arms go; let them both drop from the shoulder blades. Or if it should be, "Will you be from this day dumb, and never speak before the multitude?" Oh, better to be dumb than lose him! Indeed, when I talk of this, it seems to be an insult to my Master to put hands, and eyes, and tongue, in contrast with him.

All my capacious powers can wish
In Thee doth richly meet;
Not to mine eyes is light so dear,
Nor friendship half so sweet.

(Philip Doddridge)

If you compare life itself with Jesus, it is not to be named in the same day. If it should be said, "Will you live without Christ or die with Christ?" you would not deliberate, for to die with Christ is to live with Christ forever; but to live without Christ is to die the second death, the terrible death of the soul's eternal perdition. No, there is no choice there. I think we could go further, dear friends, and say, not only would we give up everything, but I think, when love is fervent, and the flesh is kept under, we would suffer anything with Christ. I met, in one of Samuel Rutherford's letters an extraordinary expression, where he speaks of the coals of divine wrath all falling upon the head of Christ, so that not one might fall upon his people. "And yet", says he, "if one of those coals should drop from his head upon mine, and did utterly consume me, yet if I felt it was a part of the coals that fell on him, and I was bearing it for his sake, and in communion with him, I would choose it for my heaven." That is a strong thing to say, that to suffer with Christ would be his heaven if he assuredly knew that it was for and with Christ that he was suffering. Oh, there is indeed a heavenliness about suffering for Jesus! His cross has such a majesty and mystery of delight in it that, the heavier it becomes, the more lightly does it sit upon the believer's shoulders.

One thing I know proves, beloved, that you esteem Christ to be very precious: namely, that you want others to know him too. Do you not feel a pining in your souls till others hearts are filled with the love of Christ? My eyes could weep themselves out of their sockets for some of you who are ignorant of my Master's love. Poor souls! You are sitting outside the feast when the door is wide open, and the king himself is within. You choose to be out in the highways and under the hedges sooner than come to this wedding-feast, where the oxen and fatlings are killed, and all things are ready — oh, did you know him, did you know him, you would never be able to live without him. If your eyes had ever seen him once, or if your heart had ever known the charm of his presence, you would think it to be a hell to be, for a moment, without Christ. O poor blind eyes which cannot see him, and deaf ears which cannot hear him, and hard stony hearts which cannot melt before him, and hell-besotted souls which cannot appreciate the majesty of his love, God help you! God help you! and bring you yet to know and rejoice in him. The more your love grows, beloved, the more insatiable will be your desire that others should love him, till it will come to this, that you will be like Paul "in labours more abundant" (2 Cor. 11:23), spending and being spent that you may bring the rest of Christ's elect body into union with their glorious head.

II. But, secondly, THE SOUL CLINGS TO CHRIST, AND SHE HAS GOOD REASON FOR SO DOING, for her own words are, "A bundle of myrrh is my well-beloved unto me." We will take the myrrh first, and then consider the bundle next.

1. Jesus Christ is like myrrh. Myrrh may well be the type of Christ for its preciousness. It was an exceedingly expensive drug. We know that Jacob sent some of it down into Egypt as being one of the choice products of the land. It is always spoken of in Scripture as being a rich, rare, and costly substance. But no myrrh could ever compare with Jesus Christ, for he is so precious that if heaven and earth were put together they could not buy

104

another Saviour. When God gave to the world his Son, he gave the best that heaven had. Take Christ out of heaven, and there is nothing for God to give. Christ was God's all, for is it not written, "In him dwelleth all the fullness of the Godhead bodily" (Col. 2:9). Such a precious gift of the whole of deity in the Person of Christ! How inestimably precious is that body of his which he took of the substance of the virgin! Well might angels herald the coming of this immaculate Saviour, well might they watch over his holy life, for he is precious in his birth, and precious in all his actions. How precious is he, dear friends, as myrrh in the offering of his great atonement! What a costly sacrifice that was! At what a price were you redeemed! Not with silver and gold, but with the precious blood of Christ. (1 Pet. 1:18-19) How precious is he too in his resurrection! He justifies all his people at one stroke — rising from the dead, that glorious sun scatters all the nights of all his people by one rising. How precious is he in his ascension, as he leads captivity captive, and scatters gifts among men! And how precious today in those incessant pleadings of his through which the mercies of God come down like the angels on Jacob's ladder to our needy souls! Yes, he is to the believer in every aspect like myrrh for rarity and excellence.

Myrrh, again, was pleasant. It was a pleasant thing to be in a chamber perfumed with myrrh. Through the nostrils, myrrh conveys delight to the human mind; but Christ gives delight to his people, not through one channel, but through every avenue. It is true that all his garments smell of myrrh, and aloes, and cassia (Ps. 45:8), but he has not a spiritual smell alone, the taste shall be gratified too, for we eat his flesh and drink his blood. No, our feeling is ravished when his left hand is under us, and his right hand embraces us. As for his voice, it is most sweet, and our soul's ear is charmed with its melody. Let God give him to our sight! And what can our eyes want more? Yes, he is altogether lovely. Thus every gate of the soul has commerce with Christ Jesus in the richest and rarest commodities. There is no way by which a human spirit can have communion with Jesus which does not yield to that spirit fresh and varied delights. O beloved, we cannot compare him merely to myrrh. He is everything that is good to look at, or to taste, or to handle, or to smell — all put together in one, the quintessence of all delights. As all the rivers run into the sea, so all delights centre in Christ. The sea is not full, but Jesus is full to the very brim.

Moreover, myrrh is perfuming. It is used to give a sweet smell to other things. It was mingled with the sacrifice, so that it was not only the smoke of the fat of kidneys of rams, and the flesh of fat beasts, but there was a sweet fragrance of myrrh, which went up with the sacrifice to heaven. And surely, beloved, Jesus Christ is very perfuming to his people. Does he not perfume their prayers, so that the Lord smells a sweet savour? Does he not perfume their songs, so that they become like vials full of odour sweet? Does he not perfume our ministry, for is it not written, "He causeth us to triumph in Christ, and maketh manifest the savour of his knowledge by us in every place. For we are unto God a sweet savour of Christ, in them that are saved, and in them that perish." (2 Cor 2:14-16) Our persons are perfumed with Christ. Where do we get our spikenard but from him? Where shall we go to gather camphor which will make our persons and presence acceptable before God, but to him? "For we are accepted in the beloved." (Eph. 1:6) "Ye are complete in him" (Col. 2:10) — "perfect in Christ Jesus" (Col. 1:28) — "for he hath made us kings and priests unto our God". (Rev. 1:6)

Myrrh has preserving qualities. The Egyptians used it for embalming the dead: and we find Nicodemus and the holy women bringing myrrh and aloes in which to wrap the dead body of the Saviour. It was used to prevent corruption. What is there which can preserve the soul but Christ Jesus? What is the myrrh which keeps our works, which in themselves are dead and corrupt and rotten — what, I say, keeps them from becoming a foul stench in the nostrils of God, but that Christ is in them? What we have done out of love to Christ, what we have offered through his mediation, what has been perfumed by faith in his Person, becomes acceptable. God looks upon anything we say, or anything we do, and if he sees Christ in it, he accepts it; but if there is no Christ, he puts it away as a foul thing. See to it then, beloved, that you never pray a prayer which is not sweetened with Christ. I would never preach a sermon — may the Lord forgive me if I do — which is not full to overflowing with my Master. I know one who said I was always on the old string, and he would come and hear me no more; but if I preached a sermon without Christ in it, he would come. Ah, he will never come while this tongue moves, for imagine a sermon without Christ in it — a Christless sermon! It is a brook without water; a cloud without rain; a well that mocks the traveller; a tree twice dead, plucked up by the root; a sky without a sun; a night without a star. It were a realm of death — a place of mourning for angels and laughter for devils. O Christian, we must have Christ! Do see to it that every day when you wake you get a fresh savour of Christ upon you by contemplating his Person. Live all the day, trying as much as lies in you, to season your hearts with him, and then, at night, lie down with him upon your tongue. It is said of Samuel Rutherford that he often fell asleep talking about Christ, and was often heard in his dreams saying sweet things about his Saviour. There is nothing which can preserve us and keep us from sin, and make our works holy and pure, like this "bundle of myrrh".

Myrrh, again, was used as a disinfectant. When the fever is abroad, we know people who wear little bags of camphor about their necks. They may be very good; I do not know. But the Orientals believed that in times of pest and plague, a little bag of myrrh worn between the breasts would be of essential service to whoever might carry it. And there doubtless is some power in myrrh to preserve from infectious disease. Well, brethren, certain I am; it is so with Christ. You have to go into the world which is like a great lazar-house; but if you carry Christ with you, you will never catch the world's disease. A man may be worth never so much money, he will never get worldly if he keeps Christ on his heart. A man may have to tug and toil for his livelihood, and be very poor; but he will never be discontented and murmuring if he lives close to Christ. O you who have to handle the world, see to it that you handle the Master more than the world. Some of you have to work with drunks and swearing men; others are cast into the midst of frivolities — oh take my Master with you! And sin's plagues can have no influence upon your moral nature.

But myrrh was believed by the ancient physicians to do more than this — it was a cure — it did not merely prevent, but it healed. I do not know how many diseases are said to be healed by the use of myrrh, nor do I altogether suppose that these Oriental physicians spoke from facts, for they were too much given to ascribe qualities to drugs which those drugs did not possess. However, even modern physicians believe myrrh to have many valuable medicinal properties. Certain it is that your Christ is the best medicine for the soul. His name is Jehovah Rophi — "I am the Lord that healeth thee." (Ex. 15:26) When we see Luke called "the beloved physician" (Col. 4:14), we almost grudge him the name. I will take it from him and give it to my Master, for he deserves it far more than Luke. The "beloved physician"! He touched the leper, and he was made whole. He did but look upon those who were lame, and they leaped as a hart. His voice startled the silence of Hades, and brought back the soul to the body. What cannot Christ do? He can heal anything. You who are sick this morning, sick with doubts and fears, you who are sick with temptation, you who struggle with an angry temper, or with the death-like sleep of sloth, get Christ and you are healed. Here, all things meet, and in all these things we may say, "A bundle of myrrh is my well-beloved unto me."

I have not yet done, for myrrh was used in the East as a beautifier. We read of Esther, that before she was introduced to Ahasuerus, she and the virgins were bidden to prepare themselves, and among other things, they used myrrh. (Esth. 2:12) The belief of Oriental women was that it removed wrinkles and stains from the face, and they used it constantly for the perfecting of their charms. I do not know how that may be, but I know that nothing

106

makes the believer so beautiful as being with Christ. He is beautiful in the eyes of God, of his holy angels, and of his fellow-men. I know some Christians whom it is a great mercy to speak to: if they come into your cottage, they leave behind them tokens of remembrance in the choice words they utter. To get them into the Church is a thousand mercies, and if they join the Sunday school, what value they are! Let me tell you that the best gauge of a Christian's usefulness will be found in the degree in which he has been with Jesus and learned of him. Do not tell me it is the scholar, do not say to me it is the man of eloquence, do not say it is the man of substance — well we would have all these consecrate what they have to Christ — but it is the man of God who is the strong man; it is the man who has been with Jesus who is the pillar of the Church, and a light to the world. O brethren, may the beauty of the Lord be upon us through being much with Christ!

And I must not close this point without saying that myrrh might well be used as an emblem of our Lord from its connection with sacrifice. It was one of the precious drugs used in making the holy oil with which the priests were anointed, and the frankincense which burned perpetually before God. It is this, the sacrificial character of Christ, which is at the root and bottom of all that Christ is most precious to his people. O Lamb of God our sacrifice, we must remember you!

2. Now there has been enough, surely, said about myrrh. Have patience while we just notice that he is called a bundle of myrrh, or as some translate it, a bag of myrrh, or a box of myrrh. There were three sorts of myrrh: there was the myrrh in sprigs, which, being burnt, made a sweet smell; then there was myrrh as a dried spice; and then thirdly, there was myrrh as a flowing oil. We do not know to which there is reference here. But why does it say "a bundle of myrrh?" First, for the fact that there is plenty of it. He is not a drop of it, he is a casket full. He is not a sprig or flower of it, but a whole bundle full. There is enough in Christ for my necessities. There is more in Christ than I shall ever know — perhaps more than I shall understand, even in heaven.

A bundle again, for variety; for there is in Christ not only the one thing needful, but "ye are complete in him"; there is everything needful. Take Christ in his different characters, and you will see a marvellous variety — prophet, priest, king, husband, friend, shepherd. Take him in his life, death, resurrection, ascension, and second advent. Take him in his virtue, gentleness, courage, self-denial, love, faithfulness, truth, righteousness — everywhere it is a bundle. Some of God's judgements are manifold, but all God's mercies are manifold, and Christ, being the sum of God's mercies, has in fold upon fold of goodness. He is "a bundle of myrrh" for variety.

He is a bundle of myrrh, again, for preservation — not loose myrrh to be dropped on the floor or trodden on, but myrrh tied up, as though God bound up all virtues and excellencies in his Son: not myrrh spilt on the ground, but myrrh in a box — myrrh kept in a casket. Such is Christ. The virtue and excellence which goes out of Christ is quite as strong today as in the day when the woman touched the hem of his garment and was healed. "Able to save unto the uttermost them that come unto God through him" (Heb. 7:25); is he still unto this hour.

A bundle of myrrh, again, to show how diligently we should take care of it. We must bind him up; we must keep our thoughts of him and knowledge of him as under lock and key, lest the devil should steal anything from us. We must treasure up his words, prize his ordinances, obey his precepts, tie him up and keep him ever with us as a precious bundle of myrrh.

And yet again, a bundle of myrrh for speciality, as if he were not common myrrh for everybody. No, no, no; there is distinguishing, discriminating grace — a bundle tied up for

107

his people, and labelled with their names from before the foundation of the world. No doubt there is an allusion here to the scent bottle used in every land. Jesus Christ is a bottle of myrrh, and he does not give forth his smell to everybody but to those who know how to draw out the stopper and who understand how to get into communion with him, to have close dealings with him. He is not myrrh for all who are in the house but for those who know how to put the bottle to their nostrils and receive the sweet perfume. O blessed people whom the Lord has admitted into his secrets! Oh, choice and happy people who are thus made to say, "A bottle of myrrh is my well-beloved to me."

But I am afraid I tire you, especially those of you who do not know anything about my subject. There are some here who know no more about what I am talking about than if they were Mahometans. They are listening to a new kind of religion now. The religion of Christ is as high above them as is the path of the eagle above that of the fish, and as much hidden from them as the way of the serpent on the rock from the eye of man. This is a path which the eagle's eye has not seen, nor has the lion's whelp trodden it; but I trust there are some here who know it.

III. Our third remark was to be — that with a sense of Christ's preciousness is combined A CONSCIOUSNESS OF POSSESSION. It is "*my* well-beloved".

My dear hearer, is Christ your well-beloved? *A* Saviour — that is well; but *my* Saviour — that is the best of the best. What is the use of bread if it is not mine? I could die of hunger. Of what value is gold if it is not mine? I may yet die in the workhouse. I want this preciousness to be mine. "My well-beloved!" Have you ever laid hold of Christ by the hand of faith?

Will you take him again this morning, brethren, in Jesus? I know you will. Would that those who never did take him, would take him now and say, "My Saviour". There stands his atonement, freely offered to you; may you have the grace to take it, and say, "My Saviour, my Saviour" this morning. Has your heart taken him? It is well for us to use both hands, not only the hand of faith, but the hand of love, for this is the true embrace when both arms meet around our beloved. Do you love him, O souls? Do you LOVE Christ, with an emphasis upon the word. Do not talk to me about a religion that dwells in the head and never gets into the heart. Get rid of it as quickly as you can; it will never bring you to heaven. It is not "I believe this and that" merely, but "I love". Ah, some who have been great fools in doctrine have been very wise in love! We tell our children to learn things "by heart". I think you can; you love Jesus, and if you cannot, you must confess as I do:

And have I, Christ, no love for Thee
Nor passion for thy charms?
Nor wish my Saviour's face to see
And dwell within His arms?

A very wretch, Lord, I should prove,
Had I no love to thee;
Sooner than not my Saviour love,
O may I cease to be.

(Samuel Stennett)

But that is not the only word. "A bundle of myrrh is my well-beloved *unto me*." That is not a redundant expression, that "unto me". He is not so to many. Ah, my Lord is a root out of a dry ground to multitudes! A three-volume novel suits them better than his Book. They would sooner go to a play or a dance than they would have any fellowship with him. They can see the beauties upon the cheeks of this Jezebel world, but they cannot see the perfections of my Lord and Master. Well! well! well! Let them say what they will, and let them think as they please, every creature has its own joy; but "a bundle of myrrh is my well-beloved unto me" — unto me, unto me — and if there is not another who finds him so, yet "a bundle of myrrh is my well-beloved unto me." I would it were not with others as it is — I would that others thought so also of him; but let them say what they will, they shall not drive me out of my knowledge of this — "a bundle of myrrh is my well-beloved *unto me*." The infidel says, "There is no God." The atheist would altogether laugh me to scorn. They may say what they will, but "a bundle of myrrh is my well-beloved unto me." Even bishops have been found who will take away a part of his Book, and so rend his garments, and rob him; and there are some who say his religion is out of date, and grace has lost his power; and they go after philosophy and vain conceit, and I know not what; but "a bundle of myrrh is my well-beloved unto me." They may have no nostril for him, they may have no desire after him; so let it be, but "a bundle of myrrh is my well-beloved unto me." I know there are some who say they have tried him and not found him sweet, and who have turned away from him and gone back to the beggarly elements of the world because they see nothing in Christ that they should desire him; but "a bundle of myrrh is my well-beloved unto me." Ah, Christian, this is what you want, a personal experience, a positive experience! You want to know for yourself; for there is no religion which is worth a button which is not burnt into you by personal experience; and there is no religion worth a straw which does not spring from your soul, which does not lay hold upon the very vitals of your spirit. Yes, you must say — I hope you can say as you go down those steps this morning, and enter again tomorrow into that busy, giddy world — you must say, "Let the whole world go astray, 'a bundle of myrrh is my well-beloved unto me.'"

IV. Now a practical point closes it. A SENSE OF POSSESSION AND A SENSE OF ENJOYMENT WILL ALWAYS LEAD THE CHRISTIAN TO DESIRE CONSTANT FELLOWSHIP.

"He" rather than "it" shall lie all night between my breasts.

The Church does not say, "I will put this bundle of myrrh on my shoulders" — Christ is no burden to a Christian. She does not say, "I will put this bundle of myrrh on my back" — the Church does not want to have Christ concealed from her face. She wants to have him where she can see him, and near to her heart. The bundle of myrrh shall lie all night upon my heart. The words "all night" are not in the original; I do not know how they got into the translation. He is to be always there, not only all night but all day. It would be always night if he were not there, and it cannot be night when he is there, for, as Isaac Watts writes:

My God, the Spring of all my joys,
The Life of my delights,
The Glory of my brightest days,
And Comfort of my nights.

In darkest shades if he appear,
My dawning is begun;
He is my soul's sweet morning star,
And He my rising sun.

He shall always be upon our hearts. I think that expression just means these three things. It is an expression of desire — her desire that she may have the consciousness of Christ's love continually. Do you not feel the same desire, O Christian, if you have ever been made like the chariots of Amminadib, it will go ill with you if you cannot be content to be otherwise. If you have but once tasted Christ, you will wait to feed upon him all day and all

109

night, and as long as you live. My desire is that Jesus may abide with me from morn till even, in the world and in the Church, when I awake, when I sleep, when I go out, and when I come home into the bosom of my family. Is not that your desire that he may be always with you?

But then, it is not only her desire, but it is also her confidence. She seems to say, "He will be with me thus." You may have a suspension of visible fellowship with Christ, but Christ will never really go away from people. He will be all night between your breasts; he will at all times abide faithful to you. He may close his eyes and hide his face from you, but his heart can never depart from you. He has set you as a seal upon his heart, and increasingly will make you sensible of it. Recollect that there is no suspension of Christ's union with his people, and no suspension of those saving influences which always make his people to stand complete in him.

To conclude, this is also a resolve. She desires, she believes, and she resolves it. Lord, you shall be with me, you shall be with me always. I appeal to you, brethren, will you not make this resolve in God's strength this morning to cling close to Christ. Do not go talking, as you go home, about all sorts of nonsense; do not spend this afternoon in communion with folly and vanity, but, throughout this day, let your soul keep to Christ, to nothing but Christ. This evening, we shall come to his table to eat bread and drink wine in remembrance of him. Let us try if we can, that nothing shall make us give up Christ all this day. Have you got him? Hold him, and do not let him go till you bring him to your mother's house, to the chamber of her who bore you. Then there will be the family prayer at night. Oh, seek to keep him till you put your head on the pillow. And then, on Monday morning, some of you have to go to work, and as soon as you get into the workshop or the factory, you say, "Now I must lose my Master." No, do not lose him. Hold him fast when your hand plies the hammer, and when your fingers hold the needle. Still cling to him, in the market or in the exchange, on board ship, or in the field; do not let him go. You may have him with you all day. The Mahometan usually wears a piece of the Koran round his neck, and one, when converted to Christianity, put his New Testament in a little silken bag, and always wore it there. We need not have such outward signs, but let us always have the Saviour there; let us hang him about our neck as a charm against all evil. Seek his blessed company, and place him as a star on your breast to be your honour and joy.

Well, I have done, but I must have a word with the unconverted. There are some who can say, "I will have Christ always on my tongue." Away with tongue religion! You must have him on your heart. Ah, there are some who say, "I hope I shall have Christ on my heart in all eternity." You cannot have Christ in eternity if you do not have him in time. If you despise him today — in this life — he will reject you to-morrow in the world to come; and if he call and you refuse, one day you will call and he refuse. Do not put up with desires merely, dear friends — some of you have desires, and nothing more. Do not only desire Christ, but get him. Do not stop short with saying, "I should like to have him in my heart." Give no sleep to your eyes, nor slumber to your eyelids, till, by humble faith, you have taken Christ to be your all in all. May the Lord bless these poor words, for Jesus' sake! Amen.

AN EXPOSITION, AND 22 SERMONS,

ON THE SONG OF SOLOMON, CHAPTER 2

14. AN EXPOSITION

111

1. *I am the rose of Sharon, and the lily of the valleys.*

WE have a dialogue here of love between the Lord Jesus and his people. Amongst all flowers, there is none that can be compared with him.

2. *As the lily among thorns, so is my love among the daughters.*

The child of God cannot long be mistaken for a worldling. The lily rises up above its thorny companions, but everybody knows that it is not a thorn; and chiefly do the quick eyes of the Lord Jesus discern his people wherever they may be found. You, dear friend, may perhaps come of a graceless family, or you may live in a house where God is all but unknown; yet Christ always knows his pure lilies, even if they grow among the cruel piercing thorns.

3. *As the apple tree among the trees of the wood, so is my beloved among the sons. I sat down under his shadow with great delight, and his fruit was sweet to my taste.*

You who love the Lord Jesus know what this verse means. He is a great variety of delights to you — food for your soul, a shadow for your head in the day of the sun's burning heat. When you are near to him, the sun does not smite you by day or the moon by night. There is no shadow like Christ's shadow, and no fruit like his fruit.

4. *He brought me to the banqueting house,*

That, I trust, he will again do, as he has often done before, both while we are hearing his Word and when we approach his table: "He brought me to the banqueting house",

4. *And his banner over me was love.*

Not the fiery ensign of war, but the peaceful banner of love. You have had enough of the world, beloved, during the past six days; you will again have enough of it in the six days yet to come; but just now, let love's royal banner wave over you, and give up your thoughts entirely to him who has loved you with an everlasting love, and sealed his love to you by the blood that streamed from his pierced heart.

5. *Stay me with flagons, comfort me with apples: for I am sick of love.*

The love of Christ shed abroad in our heart sometimes quite overpowers is. It is very possible to be so delighted, so full of joy with a sense of the love of Jesus, that one feels unable to bear any more of it. Oh, for more of this blessed sickness! "It is a strange thing", says Dr. Watts, "this love of Christ":

Yes! my Beloved, to my sight,
Shows a rich mixture, red and white:
All human beauties, all divine,
On my Beloved meet and shine.

For, oh! when whole, it makes me sick,
When sick, it makes me whole.
White is his soul, from blemish free,
Red with the blood he shed for me.

6- 7. *His left hand is under my head, and his right hand doth embrace me. I charge you, O ye daughters of Jerusalem, by the roes, and by the hinds of the field,*

Those lovely, but timid creatures that are so easily scared away,

7. *That ye stir not up, nor awake my love, till he please.*

O ye carking cares, keep away from us! Ye distractions that are so apt to arise in our crowded assembly, ye aches and pains that come in and make the body drag down the spirit, keep away from us for a while.

8. *The voice of my beloved!*

The spouse knows it at once, her ear is so trained that she recognises it as soon as she hears it. Jesus said that his sheep follow him, for they know his voice, and he added, "A stranger will they not follow, but will flee from him: for they know not the voice of strangers."

8. *Behold, he cometh leaping upon the mountains, skipping upon the hills.*

"I thought my sins would keep him back, for they seemed like great mountains, how could he come to me? But, 'behold,' he makes nothing of those barriers: 'he cometh leaping upon the mountains, skipping upon the hills.'"

9. *My beloved is like a roe or a young hart: behold, he standeth behind our wall, he looketh forth at the windows, shewing himself through the lattice.*

When we observe the ordinances aright, they are like latticed windows; we cannot see our Lord through them as clearly as we would, but still, we do see him, and we are thankful for these windows until we get up yonder, where we shall see him face to face.

10-13. *My beloved spake, and said unto me, Rise up, my love, my fair one, and come away. For, lo, the winter is past, the rain is over and gone; the flowers appear on the earth; the time of the singing of birds is come, and the voice of the turtle is heard in our land; the fig tree putteth forth her green figs, and the vines with the tender grape give a good smell. Arise, my love, my fair one, and come away.*

No matter what weather it is outside, it may be spring-time within. If your hearts have been frost-bound and barren, may they now begin to thaw at the approach of Jesus! Many of us have asked for his company, and believe that he will be here; and when he comes, he will make our souls rejoice. They shall be as watered gardens when the spring returns again.

14. *O my dove, that art in the clefts of the rock, in the secret places of the stairs, let me see thy countenance, let me hear thy voice; for sweet is thy voice, and thy countenance is comely.*

Christ calls you out, you hidden ones, you who are half ashamed to be seen he bids you come to him. Come away from your doubting and your fearing, your halting and your hesitating; it is Jesus who calls you, therefore come to him at once.

15. *Take us the foxes, the little foxes that spoil the vines: for our vines have tender grapes.*

Drive away every sin that would keep Christ away. Ask for his grace to subdue every wandering thought, that he may be with you in undisturbed communion.

16-17. *My beloved is mine, and I am his: he feedeth among the lilies. Until the day break, and the shadows flee away, turn, my beloved, and be thou like a roe or a young hart upon the mountains of Bether.*

[For further comments on these two verses, see Sermon No. 3185: *A Song of my Beloved.*]

15. THE INTERPRETER

Song of Solomon chapter 2

It is possible that in those golden days when Solomon walked with God, he was inspired to write the matchless book of Canticles, which is the Holy of holies of the Scriptures, standing like the tree of life in the midst of the garden of inspiration. The Song is highly allegorical, and describes Christ and his church as a bride as a bride and bridegroom who sing to each other and of each other. The passage we are about to read is a dialogue.

SOLOMON'S SONG 2

The BRIDEGROOM first speaks, and says —

1 I AM the rose of Sharon, and the lily of the valleys.

2 As the lily among thorns, so is my love among the daughters.

(*Who can this be but Jesus, in whose person the rose and lily are combined*?)

The wondering world inquires to know
Why I should love my Saviour so:
"What are his charms," say they "above
The objects of a mortal love?"

Yes! my beloved, to my sight,
Shows a sweet mixture, red and white:
All human beauties, all divine,
In my beloved meet and shine,

White is his soul, from blemish free;
Red with the blood he shed for me;
The fairest of ten thousand fairs;
A sun among ten thousand stars.

(Isaac Watts)

He paints his church as a lone lily growing amidst a wilderness of thorns, among them,
*   but not of them, her*
beauties being all the more conspicuous by contrast.

Then the BRIDE of his church exclaims —

3 As the apple tree among the trees of the wood, so is my beloved among the sons. I sat down under his shadow with great delight, and his fruit was sweet to my taste.

The golden citron excels all other trees, and Jesus is far more excellent than all others.
Shade and fruit, protection and provision are found in him. He is all in all to us who
Believe in him.

4 He brought me to the banqueting house, and his banner over me was love.

5 Stay me with flagons, comfort me with apples; for I am sick of love.

115

Love to Jesus sometimes becomes so vehement a passion that the soul cannot bear it, and the bodily frame is ready to swoon under the supreme excitement.

6 His left hand is under my head, and his right hand doth embrace me.

7, 8, 9 I charge you, O ye daughters of Jerusalem, by the roes, and by the hinds of the field, that ye stir not up, nor awake my love, nor awake my love, till he please.

The spouse now hears the voice of her husband, and rejoices to see him coming to her with all the sacred haste of omnipotent love.

The voice of my beloved! behold he cometh leaping upon the mountains, skipping upon the hills. My Beloved is like a roe or a young hart: behold he standeth behind our wall, he looketh forth at the windows, shewing himself through the lattice.

10 My beloved spake, and said unto me, Rise up, my love, my fair one, and come away.

11 For, lo, the winter is past, the rain is over and gone.

12 The flowers appear on the earth; the time of the singing of birds is come, and the voice of the turtle is heard in the land;

13 The fig tree putteth forth her green figs, and the vines with the tender grape give a good smell. Arise my love, my fair one, and come away.

When doubts and fears, trials and distresses are over and the heart is full of music, we should go forth in holy fellowship and delight ourselves with the Lord Jesus. Dark days may come, let us spend our joyful seasons in the most profitable manner, walking with out Lord in the light while the light lasts.

The Bridegroom still speaks, and calls to his beloved, saying —

14 O my dove, that art in the clefts of the rock, in the secret places of the stairs, let me see thy countenance, let me hear thy voice; for sweet is thy voice, and thy countenance is comely.

Come out from the hiding-places of fear or worldliness and own the Lord!

15 Take us the foxes, the little foxes that spoil the vines: for our vines have tender grapes.

The BRIDE, the church sings again —

16-17 My beloved is mine, and I am his: he feedeth among the lilies. Until the day break, and the shadows flee away, turn, my beloved, and be thou like a roe or a young hart upon the mountains of Bether (or, division).

If we have lost the presence of the Lord, it is our duty and our privilege to cry to him to return swiftly and triumphantly, like the fleet roe which overleaps mountains and defies all difficulties.

Yes! My Beloved to my sight
Shews a sweet mixture, red and white:
All human beauties, all divine,

In my Beloved meet and shine.

All over glorious is my Lord,
Must be beloved, and yet adored;
His worth if all the nations knew,
Sure the whole earth would love him too.

(Isaac Watts)

16. THE ROSE OF SHARON AND
THE LILY OF THE VALLEYS

From *My Sermon-Notes* (1885)

"I am the Rose of Sharon, and the Lily of the valleys."
(Song of Solomon 2:1)

Here we have the bridegroom praising himself, and this is a thing to be considered with careful attention.

This self praise is not tainted with pride: such a fault could not find a place in the lowly Jesus. His ego-ism is not egotism. He does not commend himself for his own sake, but for our sakes. He sets himself forth in glowing terms because:-

1. In condescension, he desires our love. What a poor thing for him to care about! Yet he thirsts after it.

2. In wisdom, he uses the best way to win our love.

3. In tenderness he deigns to describe himself that we may encouraged by his familiarity in praising himself to us. This is one of the most effectual proofs of lowliness.

4. Of necessity, he describes himself, for who else can describe him? "No man knoweth the Son, but the Father". (Mat. 11:27)

5. Moreover, he here states a fact which else might not be believed, seeing he makes himself so common a flower of earth, so graciously a joy for men, that all may have him.

117

We will not take up your time by trying to discover what flowers these may have been in the eastern flora: we may select those most like them in our western land, and do our Lord no wrong.

I. THE EXCEEDING DELIGHTFULNESS OF OUR LORD.

He compares himself, not only, as in other places, to needful bread, and refreshing water, but to lovely flowers. In Jesus, there are all delights, as well as all necessaries'

1. He is now all that he ever was, for his "I am" runs through all eternity in unabated force.

2. He is in himself the delight of men. He speaks not of offices, gifts, works, possessions, but of himself. "I am".

3. He is delightful to the eye of faith, even as flowers are to the bodily sight. What more beautiful than roses and lilies?

4. He is delightful to the savour which comes of him. In him is a delicious, varies, abiding fragrance.

5. In all this he is the choicest of the choice: the rose — yea, Sharon's rose: the lily — yea, the most delicious lily of the valleys. There is none like him. He is indeed "a plant of renown".

Yet blind men see no colour, and men without scent perceive no odour in the sweetest flowers, and carnal men see no delight in Jesus. Roses and lilies require eyes and light ere they can be appreciated, and to know Jesus we must have grace and gracious dispositions. He says, "I am the Rose of Sharon;" and so he is essentially; but the grace question is — "Is he this to you?" Yes or no.

II. THE SWEET VARIETY OF HIS DELIGHFULNESS.

1. Of the rose, majesty: of the lily, love.

2. Of the rose, suffering: of the lily, purity.

3. Of both, a great variety: all the roses and all the lilies, all the beauties of heaven and earth meet in Jesus.

4. Of both, the very essence. Of all the creatures, all the excellencies, virtues, and blessings, which may be found in them, come from Jesus, and abide in Jesus without limit. Many eyes are wanted to spy out the whole of Christ. No eye, nor all eyes, can see all that lies in his varied perfections.

5. Of all these, a perfect proportion, so that no one excellence destroys another. He is all a rose should be, and yet not the less perfect as a lily.

Hence, he is suitable to all the saints, the joy of all, the perfection of beauty to each one.

III. THE EXCEEDING FRESHNESS OF HIS DELIGHTFULNESS.

1. Meant to be plucked and enjoyed as roses and lilies are.

2. Abundant as a common flower. He is not as a rare orchid, but as the anemones which covered Sharon's plain, and as the lilies which abounded in all the valleys of Palestine.

118

3. Abiding in a common place, as roses of Sharon, and lilies of the valleys, where every passer-by was free to gather according to his own sweet will. No found on inaccessible steeps, or within guarded enclosures, Jesus is out in the open; a flower of the common. This is a leading idea of the text. Those who desire Christ may have him.

4. Scattering fragrance, not over a room or a house, bur far and wide, perfuming every wandering wind.

5. Yet roses and lilies fail to set forth our Beloved, for his is unfading virtue. They are soon withered, but "He dieth no more." (Rom. 6:9)

In all things, look for Jesus. See him in primroses and daisies. In Jesus, look for all things of beauty and sweetness; lilies and roses are in him.

Listen much to Jesus, for he can tell you most about himself; and, coming at first hand, it will be surely true, and come with great force and unction. Hearken, and hear him say, "I am the rose of Sharon."

OBSERVATIONS

"I am the Rose of Sharon, and the Lily of the Valleys"; words most seemly in the lips of the Lord Jesus Christ, in whom it is not robbery from others, but condescension and grace, to commend himself to the sons of men. "I am meek and lowly" (Mat. 11:29) would be the utterance of pride in Gabriel, but it is humility in Jesus, who has stooped that he might become meek and lowly. "I am the true Vine" (Jn. 15:1), "I am the good Shepherd" (Jn.10:11, 14), etc., are the expressions alike of truth and grace, and so here.

(Alexander Moody Stuart)

Not to flowers which only the rich and great can possess, but to those easily obtainable does he liken himself; for always did he stoop to the lowliest, and the common people ever heard him gladly. (Mk. 12:37) His presence on earth never failed to bring comfort to the needy, and refreshment to the downcast spirit, just as sweet odours float around roses and lilies, and minister solace to the organ of smell, while their fair forms and rich and delicate colours gratify the eye.

(Henry K. Wood, in *"The Heavenly Bridegroom and his Bride"*, *A Commentary on the Song of Solomon,* 1878)

We believe there can be little doubt that the rose is really intended by the Hebrew word. Even if in the general sense it should mean but a *flower*, we should still infer that, when applied in a particular sense it means a rose, for this would be according to the usage of the East. Thus the Persian word *gul* describes a flower in general, and the rose *par excellence*. This suffices to show the estimation in which the rose is held in the East. In the Persian language, particularly, there is perhaps no poem in which allusion to it, and comparisons drawn from it, do not recur even to repletion ,,, The extreme fragrance and beauty of the rose in some parts of Western Asia have attracted the notice of many travellers. It is also cultivated, not merely as a garden plant for pleasure, but in extensive fields, from the produce of which is prepared that valued and delicious perfume called rose-water. The size of the rose trees, and the number of the flowers, on each, far exceed in the rose-districts of Persia, anything we are here accustomed to witness.

(John Kitto, *The Pictorial Bible*, 1855)

119

17. THE BEST OF THE BEST

NO. 2472

AT THE METROPOLITAN TABERNACLE, NEWINGTON
ON THURSDAY EVENING, MAY 19TH, 1881

"I am the rose of Sharon, and the lily of the valleys."
(Song of Solomon 2:1)

THE time of flowers has come, and, as they are in some faint degree emblems of our Lord, it is well, when God thus calls, that we should seek to learn what he desires to teach us by them. If nature now spreads out her roses and her lilies, or prepares to do so, let us try not only to see them, but to see Christ as he is foreshadowed in them.

"I am the rose of Sharon, and the lily of the valleys." If these are the words of the Well-beloved — and I have no doubt that they are — then it may be suggested by some that here we have the Saviour praising himself; and it is true, but in no unworthy sense, for well may he praise himself since no one else can do it as it should be done. There is no human language that can ever set out his beauties as they deserve to be told. As good John Berridge says,

Living tongues are dumb at best,
We must die to speak of Christ,

— as he should be spoken of. He will never fully be described unless he describe himself. For certain, we should never have known God if he had not revealed himself; and every good thing that you or I know of him, he himself has told us. We make no discoveries of God except as God discloses himself to us. If, then, any cavillers [arguers] were to find fault with the Christ of God because he commends himself, I would answer: Does not God commend himself, and must not his well-beloved Son do the same? Who else is there that can possibly reveal him to us unless he unveils his own face to our admiring gaze?

Moreover, may it be always remembered that human self-praise is evil because of the motive that underlies it. We praise ourselves — and, alas, that we should be so foolish as to do so! — and do it out of pride; but when Christ praises himself, he does it out of humility. "Oh", say you, "how can you prove that to be true?" Why, in this way: he praises himself that he may win our love; but what condescension it is on his part that he should care about the love of such insignificant and undeserving people as we are! It is a wonderful stoop that the Christ of God should speak about having a bride, and that he should come to seek his bride among the sons of men. If princes were to look for consorts among beggars, that would be after all but a small stoop, for God has made of one blood all nations of men that dwell upon the face of the earth (Acts 17:26); but for Christ to forsake the thrones and glories of heaven, and the splendours of his Father's courts above, to come down to win a well-beloved one here, and, for her sake, to take upon himself her nature, and in her nature to bear the shame of death, even the death of the cross, this is stupendous condescension of which only God himself is capable. And this praising of himself is a part of that condescension, a necessary means of winning the love of the heart he has chosen. So that this is a matchless instance, not of pride, but of humility, that those dear lips of the heavenly Bridegroom should have to speak to his own commendation, and that he should say, "I am the rose of Sharon, and the lily of the valleys." O human lips, why are you silent, so that Christ must speak of himself? O human hearts, why are you so hard that you will never feel until Christ himself address you? O human eyes, why are you so blind that you will never see till Christ shows himself in his

120

own superlative light and loveliness? I think I need not defend my Master, though he used these sweet emblems to set out himself; for this is an instance not of his pride, but of his humility.

It is also an instance of the Master's wisdom, for as it is his design to win hearts to himself, he uses the best means of winning them. How are hearts won? Very often by the exhibition of beauty. Love at first sight has been begotten by the vision of a lovely countenance. Men and women, too, are struck with affection through the eyes when they perceive some beauty which charms and pleases them; so, the Saviour lifts the corner of the veil that conceals his glories, and lets us see some glimpse of his beauty in order that he may win our hearts. There are some who seem to think that they can bully men to Christ; but that is a great mistake. It is very seldom that sinners can be driven to the Saviour; his way is to draw them. He himself said, "I, if I be lifted up from the earth, will draw all men unto me. This he said, signifying what death he should die." (Jn. 12:32) And the drawings of Christ are not, as it were, with a cart rope, but with silken bonds, yes, with invisible chains, for his beauty is of such a character that it creates love; his beauty is so attractive that it draws the heart. So, in infinite wisdom, our Lord Jesus Christ sets out his own beauties, that thereby he may win our hearts. I do believe that there is no preaching like the exaltation of Christ crucified. There is nothing so likely to win the sons of men as a sight of him; and if God the Holy Spirit will but help all his ministers, and help all his people, to set out the beauties of Christ, I shall not doubt that the same Spirit will incline men's hearts to love him and trust him. Note, then, the condescension and also the wisdom which are perceptible in this self-commendation on the part of Christ: "I am the rose of Sharon, and the lily of the valleys."

I think that our Lord also speaks in this way as an encouragement to timid souls. His tender familiarity in praising himself to us is one of the most effective proofs of his lowliness. Does Christ commend himself to us? Does he say to us, for instance, "I am meek and lowly in heart"? (Mat. 11:29) What is his object in speaking this way but that we may take his yoke upon us, and learn of him, and find rest unto our souls? And if he says, "I am the rose of Sharon", what does he mean but that we may pluck him, and take him for our own? If he says, "I am the lily of the valleys", why does he take the trouble to tell us that except that he wants us to take him, and to have him for our very own? I think that it is so sweet of Christ to praise himself in order to show that he longs for us to come to him. He declares himself to be a well of living water (Jn. 4:10-11); yet why is he a well but that we may come to him, and drink? He tells us, "I am the bread which came down from heaven" (Jn. 6:35, 41), but why does he speak of himself as bread, from which if one eat, he shall never hunger? Why, is it not because he wants us to partake of him! You need not, therefore, be afraid that he will refuse you when you come to him. If a man praises his wares, it is that he may sell them. If a doctor advertises his cures, it is that other sick folk may be induced to try his medicine. When our Lord Jesus Christ praises himself, it is a kind of holy advertisement by which he would tempt us to "come, buy wine and milk without money and without price." (Is. 55:1) If he praises himself, it is that we may fall in love with him; and we need not be afraid to come and lay our poor hearts at his feet, and ask him to accept us, for he would not have wooed us by unveiling his beauties if he had meant, after all, to trample on our hearts, and say, "I care nothing for such poor love as yours." I feel most grateful, then, that I have not at this time so much to praise my Master as to let him speak his own praises, for "never man spake like this Man." (Jn. 7:46) When he commends himself, what would have been folly in others is wisdom in him. And whereas we say to our fellow-man, "Let another man praise thee, and not thine own mouth" (Prov. 27:2), I would say to Christ, "My Master, praise yourself, for you alone can do it as it ought to be done." As for your poor servant, he would try to be the echo of your voice, and that will be infinitely better than anything he can say of himself.

121

I think, also, that there is good reason for our Lord to praise himself in the fashion that he does in our text, because, after all, it is not praise. "What", say you, "and yet you have been talking all this while as if it were praise!" Well, so it is in one sense to us, but it is not so to Christ. Suppose the sun were to compare itself with a glow-worm, would that be praise? Suppose an angel were to compare himself with an emmet [ant], would that be praise? And when my Lord and Master, whose eyes outshine the sun, and who is infinitely higher than the mightiest of the angels, compares himself to a rose and a lily, is that praise? Well, it is so to you and to me, but it certainly cannot be so to him. It is a marvellous stoop for Christ, who is "over all, God blessed for ever" (Rom. 9:5), and the Light of the universe, to say, "I am a rose; I am a lily." O my blessed Lord, this is a sort of incarnation, as when the Eternal God took upon himself an infant's form! So here, the Everlasting God says, "I am" — and what comes next? — "a rose and a lily." It is an amazing stoop. I do not know how to set it out to you in human language; it is a sort of verbal rehearsal of what he did afterwards when, though he counted it not robbery to be equal with God, "he took upon himself the form of a servant, and was made in the likeness of sinful flesh, and became obedient unto death, even the death of the cross." (Phil. 2:6-8) "I am God, yet", says he, "I am the rose of Sharon, and the lily of the valleys."

What does our text mean? I think it means that our Lord Jesus Christ is exceedingly delightful; so, let us speak first, of *the exceeding delightfulness of our Lord*; and then, inasmuch as he uses two emblems — first the rose, and then the lily — surely this is to express *the sweet variety of his delightfulness*; and, inasmuch as he speaks of himself as the rose of Sharon and the lily of the valleys, I shall show you, in the last place, that this hints to us of the exceeding *freeness* of his delightfulness.

I. First, then, the text sets out THE EXCEEDING DELIGHTFULNESS OF OUR LORD.

He compares himself here, not as in other places to needful bread and refreshing water, but to lovely flowers, to roses and lilies. What is the use of roses and lilies? I know what the use of corn is; I must eat it, for it is necessary to me for food. I know why barley and rye and all sorts of roots and fruits are created; they are the necessary food of man or beast. But what do we want with roses? What do we want with lilies? They are of no use at all except for joy and delight. With their sweet form, their charming colour, and their delicious fragrance, we are comforted and pleased and delighted; but they are not necessities of life. A man can live without roses. There are millions of people, I have no doubt, that live without possessing lilies of the valley. There are all too few roses and lilies in this smoky Babylon [London] of ours; but, when we do get them, what use are they? Why, they are things of beauty, if not "a joy forever." Jesus is all that and more; he is far more than "a thing of beauty", and, to all who trust him, he will be "a joy forever." To you who are Christ's people, he is your bread, for you feed on him, and he makes you live. You could not do so without him as the sustenance of your soul. He is the living water, and your soul would pine and perish of burning thirst if you did not drink of him. But that is not all that Jesus is to you. God never intended to save his people on the scale of the workhouse, to give you just as much as you absolutely need and nothing more. No, no, no! He means you to have joy as well as have life, to look upon beauty as well as to be in safety, and to have not only a healthy atmosphere, but an atmosphere that is laden with the odour of sweet flowers. You are to find in Christ roses and lilies, as well as bread and water. You have not yet seen all his beauties, and you do not yet know all his excellence.

The exceeding delightfulness of Christ is suggested to our minds by his declaration, "I am the rose, and I am the lily."

And first, *he is in himself the delight of men*. He speaks not of offices, gifts, works, or possessions, but of himself: "I am." Our Lord Jesus is the best of all beings. The dearest,

122

sweetest, fairest, and most charming of all beings that we can think of is the Son of God, our Saviour. Come here, you poets who dream of beauty, and then try to sing its praises; but your imagination could never reach up to the matchless perfection of his Person, neither could your sweetest music ever attain to the full measure of his praise. Think of him as the God-man, God incarnate in human nature, and absolutely perfect. I was going to say something more than that, for there is not only in him all that there ought to be, but there is more than your thoughts or wishes have ever compassed. Eyes need to be trained to see beauty. No man sees half or a thousandth part of the beauty even of this poor, natural world; but the painter's eye — the eye of Turner, for example — can see much more than you or I ever saw. "Oh!" said one, when he looked on one of Turner's landscapes, "I have seen that view every day, but I never saw as much as that in it." "No", replied Turner, "don't you wish you could?" And, when the Spirit of God trains and tutors the eye, it sees in Christ what it never saw before. But, even then, as Turner's eye was not able to see all the mystery of God's beauty in nature, so neither is she a most trained and educated Christian, able to perceive all the matchless beauty that there is in Christ.

I do not think, brethren, that there is anything about Christ but what should make his people glad. There are dark truths concerning him, such as his bearing our sin; but what a joy it is to us that he bore it, and put it away for ever! It makes us weep to look at Jesus dying on the cross, but there is more real joy in the tears of repentance than there is in the smiles of worldly mirth. I would choose my heaven to be a heaven of everlasting weeping for sin sooner than have a heaven — if such a heaven could exist — consisting of perpetual laughing at the mirth of fools. There is more true pleasure in mourning before God than in dancing before the devil. Christ is, then, all beauty; even the dark parts in him are light, and the bitter parts are sweet. He has only to be seen by you, and you must perceive that, whether it be his Godhead or his manhood, whether it be his priesthood, his royalty, or his prophetic office, whether it be on the cross or on the throne, whether it be on earth or in heaven, or in the glory of his second coming, every way:

All over glorious is my Lord,
Must be beloved, and yet adored;
His worth if all the nations knew
Sure the whole earth would love him too.

(Isaac Watts)

But, next, our Lord is *exceedingly delightful to the eye of faith*. He not only tells us of what delight is in himself — "I am the rose, and I am the lily" — but he thereby tells us that there is something to see in him, for the rose is very pleasing to look at. Is there a more beautiful sight than a rose that is in bud, or even one that is full-blown? And the lily — what a charming thing it is! It seems to be more a flower of heaven than of earth. Well now, Christ is delightful to the eye of faith. I remember the first time I ever saw him; I shall never forget that sight, and I have seen him many a time since, and my grief is that I ever take my eyes off him, for it is to look away from the sun into blackness, to look away from bliss into misery. To you who look at Christ by faith, a sight of him brings such peace, such rest, such hope, as no other sight can ever afford. It so sweetens everything, so entirely takes away the bitterness of life, and brings us to anticipate the glory of the life that is to come, that I am sure you say, "Yes, yes; the figure in the text is quite correct; there is a beauty in Jesus to the eye of faith, he is indeed red as the rose and white as the lily."

And, next, the Lord Jesus Christ is *delightful in the aroma which comes from him to us*. In him is a delicious, varied, abiding fragrance which is very delightful to the spiritual nostril. Smell is, I suppose, a kind of delicate feeling. Minute particles of certain substances touch

123

sensitive membranes, and we call the sensation that is produced "smelling". It is a mysterious sense; for you can understand sight and hearing better than you can understand smelling. There is a spiritual way of perceiving the aroma of Christ. I cannot explain it to you, but there is an ineffable mysterious sweetness that proceeds from him which touches the spiritual senses, and affords supreme delight. Just as the body has its nose, and its tender nerves that can appreciate sweet odours, so the soul has its spiritual nostril by which, though Christ is at a distance, it yet can perceive the fragrant emanations that come from him, and is delightful.

What is there that comes from Christ, day to day, but his truth, his Spirit, his influence, his promises, his doctrines, his words of cheer? All these have a heavenly sweetness, and make us, with the psalmist, say to our Lord, "All thy garments smell of myrrh, and aloes, and cassia, out of the ivory palaces, whereby they have made thee glad." (Ps. 45:8) Whenever these sweet odours are wafted down to us, they make us also glad. Anything that has the savour of Christ in it is sweet to a Christian. If Christ has touched it, let me put it in my bosom and keep it there as a sweet forget-me-not until I see his face in glory. Yes, the very stones he sat on, I was about to say, the very mountains at which he looked, have become dear to us. We have no idolatrous or superstitious reverence for Palestine, or even for the garden in which he sweat great drops of blood; but for spiritual things with which he has to do, we have a never-ceasing reverence and affection. Everything that comes from him is wonderful, as the songs of the angels must have been to the shepherds of Bethlehem, and sweet to the taste, as the manna that dropped from the skies around Israel's desert camp. Yes, brothers and sisters, there is a sweet savour about the Lord Jesus Christ. Do you all perceive it?

Once more, *in all that he is, Christ is the choicest of the choice*. You notice the Bridegroom says, "I am the rose." Yes, but there were some particularly beautiful roses that grew in the valley of Sharon. "I am that rose", says he. And there were some delightful lilies in Palestine; it is a land of lilies, where there are so many of them that nobody knows which lily Christ meant, and it does not at all signify, for almost all lilies are wondrously beautiful. "But", says he, "I am the lily of the valleys", the choicest kind of lily that grew where the soil was fertile and damp with the overflow of mountain streams. "I am the lily of the valleys": that is to say, Christ is not only good, but he is the best; and he is not only the best, but he is the best of the best. He is a flower; yes, but he is a rose, which is the queen of flowers; yes, but then he is the best rose there is, the rose of Sharon. He is a Saviour, and a great one; yes, the only Saviour. He is a Husband, but what a husband! Was there ever such a Bridegroom as Christ Jesus the Lord? He is the Head; but Father Adam was a poor head compared with him. He is inexpressibly, unutterably, indescribably lovely. I might as well leave off talking about him, for I cannot hope to set him out as he deserves. If you could but see him, I would leave off, for I am sure I should be only hanging a veil before him with the choicest words that I could possibly find. Suppose you had a dear son, or husband, or friend, far away, and that I was a painter who could carry pictures in my mind's eye, and then draw them to the very life. If I stood here trying to paint your well-beloved friend, laying on my colours with all the skill I possessed, and doing my best to reproduce his features; suppose, while I was at work, that the door at the back was opened, and he came in, I would cry out, "Oh, stop, stop, stop! Let me put away my canvas, and let me pack up my brushes and my paints. Here is the loved one himself. Look at him! Look at him, not at my portrait of him!" And you would rise from your seat, and say, "It is he! It is he! You may talk as long as you like, dear sir, when he is away; but when he is himself here, your talk seems to be mere chatter." Well, I shall be quite content that you should think so, I shall be even glad if you do, provided that the reason is that you can say, "We have seen the Lord. He has manifested himself to us as he does not to the world." He is as he says, "I am the rose of Sharon, and the lily of the valleys." The best of the best, the fairest of the fair, the sweetest of the sweet, is Jesus Christ to you and to me

124

if we are indeed his people. I cannot say more about the exceeding delightfulness of my Lord; I wish I could.

II. I must pass on next, to notice THE SWEET VARIETY OF THE DELIGHFULNESS OF CHRIST.

He is not only full of joy and pleasure, and delight to our hearts, but he is full of all sorts of joy, and all sorts of pleasure, and all sorts of delights to us.

Go, worship at Immanuel's feet,
See in his face what wonders meet;
Earth is too narrow to express
His worth, his glory, or his grace.

The whole creation can afford
But some faint shadows of my Lord:
Nature to make his beauties known
Must mingle colours not her own.

(Isaac Watts)

The rose is not enough, you must have the lily also, and the two together fall far short of the glories of Christ, the true "Plant of renown." (Ezek. 34:29)

"I am the rose." That is *the emblem of majesty*. The rose is the very queen of flowers; in the judgement of all who know what to admire, it is enthroned above all the rest of the beauties of the garden. But the lily — what is that? That is *the emblem of love*. The psalmist hints at this in the title of the forty-fifth Psalm: "Upon Shoshannim, a Song of love." Shoshannim signifies lilies, so the lily-psalm is the love-song, for the lilies, with their beauty, their purity, their delicacy, are a very choice emblem of love. Are you not delighted when you put these two things together — majesty and love? A King upon a throne of love, a Prince, whose very eyes beam with love to those who put their trust in him, a real Head, united by living bonds of love to all his members — such is our dear Lord and Saviour. A rose and yet a lily; I do not know in which of the two I take the greater delight. I prefer to have the two together. When I think that my Saviour is King of kings and Lord of lords, I shout, "Hallelujah!" But when I remember that he loved me, and gave himself for me, and that still he loves me, and that he will keep on loving me forever and ever, there is such a charm in this thought that nothing can excel it. Look at the lily, and sing,

Jesu, lover of my soul,
Let me to thy bosom fly,
While the nearer waters roll,
While the tempest still is high!
Hide me, O my Saviour, hide,
Till the storm of life be past;
Safe into the haven guide;
Oh receive my soul at last.

(Charles Wesley)

Then look at the rose, and sing,

All hail the power of Jesus' name!
Let angels prostrate fall;

125

Bring forth the royal diadem,
And crown him Lord of all,

(Edward Perronet)

— then put the rose and the lily together, and let them remind you of Christ's majesty and love. The combination of these sweet flowers also suggests our Lord's *suffering and purity*.

The wondering world inquires to know
Why I should love my Jesus so:
"What are His charms", say they, "above
The objects of a mortal love?"

Yes! my Belovèd, to my sight
Shows a sweet mixture, red and white:
All human beauties, all divine,
In my Belovèd meet and shine.

White is his soul, from blemish free;
Red with the blood he shed for me;
The fairest of ten thousand fairs;
A sun among ten thousand stars.

(Isaac Watts)

The rose, with its thorn, reminds us of his suffering, his bleeding love to us, his death on our behalf, his bearing of the thorns which our sin created. Christ is a royal rose beset with thorns; but the lily shows that,

He died to atone for sins not his own;
Our debt he has paid and our work he has done
So we may receive the peace he did leave,
Who made intercession, 'My Father, forgive!'

For sinners like me he prayed on the tree;
Through his intercession the sinner goes free.
That sinner am I, who on Jesus rely,
And come for the pardon God cannot deny.

(Charles Wesley)

Jesus, when on earth, could say, "The prince of this world cometh, and hath nothing in me." (Jn. 14:30) The devil himself could not see a spot or speck in that lovely lily. Jesus Christ is perfection itself, he is all purity; so you must put the two together, the rose and the lily, to show Christ's suffering and perfection, the infinitely pure infinitely suffering. In which of the two do you take the greater delight? Surely, in neither, but in the combination of both. What would be the value of Christ's sufferings if he were not perfect? And of what avail would his perfections be if he had not died, the Just for the unjust, to bring us to God? (1 Pet. 3:18) But the two together, the rose and the lily, suffering and purity, fill us with delight.

Of both of these, there is a great variety. I wonder how many different sorts of roses there are? I should not like to have to tell you; they vary exceedingly, perhaps there are as

126

many kinds as there are days in the year. How many varieties of lilies are there? Possibly, there are as many sorts of lilies as there are of roses, for both of them are wonderfully diversified; but the joys that flow from our Lord Jesus Christ are as abundant and as varied as the roses and the lilies. Bring me which rose you please, and I will tell you that it smells sweet; bring which lily you choose, and I will say, "Yes, that also has a delicate perfume; that will do, together with the rose to serve as an emblem of Christ." Our Lord Jesus possesses every kind of beauty and fragrance. "He is all my salvation, and all my desire." All good things meet in Christ; in him all the lines of beauty are focussed. Blessed are they who truly know him!

Further, *Christ is the very essence of the sweetness both of the rose and of the lily*. When he says, "I am the rose", he means not only that he is like the rose, but that he made all the sweetness there is in the rose, and it is still in him; and all the sweetness there is in any creature comes to us from Christ, or else it is not sweetness such as we ought to love. I like to look on the bread I eat as his gift to me, and to bless his providential hand that bestows it. I like to look at all the landscape on such a fair day as this has been, and say, "Christ is in all this, giving this charming view to such a poor, unworthy creature as I am." He is in all there is that is good. He is the goodness of all the good there is. He is the very soul of the universe, whatever there is in the universe that is worthy of our soul's love. All good for our soul comes from him. Whether it be pardon of sin, or justification, or the sanctification that makes us fit for glory hereafter, Christ is the source of it all; and in the infinite variety of delights that we get from him, he is himself the essence of it all. We can become tired of most things; I suppose that we can become tired of everything earthly; but we shall never tire of Christ. I remember one who, when near his death-hour, forgot even his wife, and she was greatly grieved that he did not recognise her. They whispered in his ear the name of his favourite child, but he shook his head. His oldest friend, who had known him from his boyhood, was not recognised. At last, they asked him, "Do you know Jesus Christ?" Then he said, "Ah, yes, and I am going to him!" This ruling passion was strong in death; Christ was nearer and dearer to him than those he loved best here. All flowers will fade, even roses and lilies among them, but not this blessed Rose of Sharon, and Lily of the Valleys. Christ does not say, "I was a rose, and I was a lily", but "I am the rose, and I am the lily." He is now all that he ever was, and will be in life, in death, and throughout all eternity, to the soul that knows him, an infinite variety of everything that is delightful.

III. I must now very briefly take up the last head of my discourse, which is: THE EXCEEDING FREENESS OF OUR LORD'S DELIGHTFULNESS.

It is not very pleasant or satisfying for hungry people to stand in the street, and hear someone praising a good meal, of which they cannot get even a taste. I have often noticed boys standing outside a shop window, in which there have been all sorts of dainties; they have flattened their noses against the window-pane, but they have not been able to get anything to eat. I have been talking about my Master, and I want to show you that *he is accessible*; he is meant to be plucked and enjoyed as roses and lilies are. He says in the text, "I am the rose of Sharon." What was Sharon? It was an open plain where anybody might wander, and where even cattle roamed at their own sweet will. Jesus is not like a rose in Solomon's garden, shut up within high walls, with broken glass all along the top. Oh no", he says, "I am the rose of Sharon", everybody's rose, the flower for the common people to come and gather. "I am the lily." What lily? The lily of the palace of Shushan, enclosed and guarded from all approach? No, but, "I am the lily of the valleys", found in this glen, or the other ravine, growing here, there, and everywhere: "I am the lily of the valleys."

Then *Christ is as abundant as a common flower*. Whatever kind of rose it was, it was a common rose; whatever kind of lily it was, it was a well-known lily that grew freely in the valleys of that land. Oh, blessed be my Master's name; he has brought us a common salvation, and he is the common people's Christ! Men in general do not love him enough, or else they would have hedged him in with all sorts of restrictions; they would have made a franchise for him, and nobody would have been able to be saved except those who paid I know not how much a year in taxes. But they do not love our Lord enough to shut him in, and I am glad they have never tried to do so. There he stands, at the four-cross roads, so that everybody who comes by, and wants him, may have him. He is a fountain, bearing this inscription, "Let him that is athirst come. And whosoever will, let him take the water of life freely." (Rev. 22:17) "I am the rose of Sharon, and the lily of the valleys." Why do roses grow in Sharon? Why do lilies grow in the valleys? Why, to be plucked, of course! I like to see the children go down into the meadow when it is decked in grass, and adorned with flowers, gilded with buttercups, or white with the day's-eyes; I love to see the children pluck the flowers, and fill their pinafores with them, or make garlands, and twist them round their necks, or put them on their heads. "O children, children!" somebody might cry, "do not spoil those beautiful flowers, do not go and pick them." Oh, but they may, for nobody says they may not! They may not go into our gardens and steal the geraniums and the fuchsias; but they may get away into the meadows, or into the open fields, and pluck these common flowers to their heart's content. And now, poor soul, if you would like an apron-full of roses, come and get them. If you would like to carry away a big handful of the lilies of the valleys, come and take them, as many as you will. May the Lord give you the will! That is, after all, what is wanted. If there be that grace-given will, the Rose of Sharon and the Lily of the valleys will soon be yours. They are common flowers, growing in a common place, and there are plenty of them; will you not take them?

Even to those who do not pluck any, there is one strange thing that must not be forgotten. A man passes by a rose-bush, and says, "I cannot stop to think about roses", but as he goes along he exclaims, "Dear, dear, what a delicious perfume!" A man journeying in the East goes through a field that is full of lilies; he is in a great hurry, but, for all that, he cannot help seeing and smelling the lilies as he rushes through the field. And, do you know, the perfume of Christ has life in it? He is "a savour of life unto life." (2 Cor. 2:16) What does that mean, but that the smell of him will save? Ah, if you just glance at him, though you were so busy that you could not come in till the sermon had begun, yet a glance at this Lily will bring you joy and peace, for he is so free that, often, even when men are not asking for him, he comes to them. "What", say you, "is it so?" Yes, that it is. Such is the freeness of Christ's grace that it is written, "I am found of them that sought me not." (Is. 65:1; Rom. 10:20) He sends his sweet perfume into nostrils that never sniffed after it. He puts himself in the way of eyes that never looked for him. How I wish that someone who has never sought Christ might find him even now! You remember the story that Christ tells of the man that was ploughing the field; he was only thinking of the field, and how much corn it would take to sow it. He was ploughing up and down, when suddenly, his ploughshare hit something hard. He stopped the oxen, took his spade, and dug, and there was an old crock, and it was full of gold. Somebody had hidden it away, and left it. This man had never looked for it, for he did not even know it was there, but he had stumbled on it, as men say, by accident. What did he do? He did not tell anybody, but he went off to the man who was the owner of the field, and said, "What will you take for that field?" "Can you buy it?" "Yes, I want it; what will you take for it?" The price was so high that he had to sell the house he lived in, and his oxen, and the very clothes off his back; but he did not care about that, for he bought the field, and he bought the treasure, and then he was able to buy back his clothes, his house, and his oxen, and everything else. If you find Christ, and if you have to sell the coat off your back in order to get him, if you have to give up everything you have that you may find him, you will have such a treasure in him that, for the joy of finding him, you would count all the riches of Egypt to be

128

less than nothing and vanity. But you do not need to sell the coat off your back. Christ is to be had for nothing, only you must give him yourself. If he gives himself to you, and he becomes your Saviour, you must give yourself to him and become his servant. Trust him, I beseech you. May the Lord help you so to do, for Jesus' sake! Amen.

18. THE ROSE AND THE LILY
NO. 784

DELIVERED ON LORD'S-DAY MORNING, DECEMBER 8TH, 1867
AT THE METROPOLITAN TABERNACLE, NEWINGTON

"I am the rose of Sharon, and the lily of the valleys."
(Song of Solomon 2:1)

HERE are sweet flowers blooming serenely and this wintry weather. In the garden of the soul you may gather fragrant flowerets at all seasons of the year; and although the soul's garden, like every other, has its winter, yet, strange to say, no sooner do the roses and the lilies mentioned in the text begin to bloom, than the winter flies and the summer smiles. Outside in your garden, the summer brings the roses; but within the enclosure of the heart, the roses and lilies create the summer. I trust that we, this morning, may have grace to walk abroad in the fields of heavenly contemplation, to admire the matchless charms of him whose cheeks are as a bed of spices, as sweet flowers, whose lips are like lilies dropping sweet-smelling myrrh. May our hearts interpret the language of our text, and sing:

Is he a rose? Not Sharon yields
Such fragrancy in all her fields:
Or, if the lily he assume,
The valleys bless the rich perfume.

(Isaac Watts)

It is our Lord who speaks, "I am the rose of Sharon." How is it that he utters his own commendation, for it is an old and true adage that "self praise is no recommendation"? None but vain creatures ever praise themselves, and yet Jesus often praises himself, he says, "I am the good Shepherd"; "I am the Bread of Life"; "I am meek and lowly of heart"; and, in different speeches, he is frequently declaring his own excellence, yet Jesus is not vain. Perish the thought! Yet I said if any creature praised itself it must be vain, and that, too, is true. How then shall we solve the riddle?

Is not this the answer: that he is no creature at all, and therefore does not come under the rule? For the creature to praise itself is vain, but for the Creator to praise himself, for the Lord God to manifest and show his own glory, is becoming and proper. Hear how he extols his own wisdom and power at the end of the book of Job, and see if it is not most seemly, as the Lord himself proclaims it. Is not God constantly ruling both providence and grace for the manifestation of his own glory, and do we not all freely consent that no motive short of this would be worthy of the divine mind? So, then, because Christ talks like this of himself, since no one dare call him vainglorious, I gather an indirect proof of his deity, and bow down before him, and bless him that he gives me this incidental evidence of his not being a creature, but the uncreated One himself.

An old Scotch woman once said, "He is never so bonnie as when he is commending himself"; and we all feel it so. No words appear more suitable from his own lips than these: "I am the rose of Sharon, and the lily of the valleys." Our Lord, when he praises himself like this doubtless does so for an excellent reason; namely, that no one can possibly reveal him to the sons of men but himself. No lips can tell the love of Christ to the heart till Jesus himself speaks within. Descriptions all fall flat and tame unless the Holy Spirit fills them with life and power. Till our Immanuel reveals himself within the recesses of the heart, the soul does not see him. If you would see the sun, would you light your candles?

Would you gather together the common means of illumination, and seek in that way to behold the orb of day? No, the wise man knows that the sun must reveal itself, and only by its own blaze can that mighty lamp be seen. It is so with Christ. Unless he so manifests himself to us, as he does not to the world, we cannot behold him. He must say to us, "I am the rose of Sharon", or else all the declarations of man that he is the rose of Sharon will fall short of the mark. "Blessed art thou, Simon Barjona", said he to Peter, "for flesh and blood hath not revealed this unto thee." (Mat. 16:17) Purify flesh and blood by any educational process you may select, elevate mental faculties to the highest degree of intellectual power, yet none of these can reveal Christ. The Spirit of God must come with power, and overshadow the man with his wings, and then, in that mystic Holy of Holies, the Lord Jesus must display himself to the sanctified eye, as he does not to the purblind [partially blind] sons of men. Christ must be his own mirror; as the diamond alone can cut the diamond, so he alone can display himself.

Is it not clear enough to us all that, Jesus being God, befittingly praises himself, and we, being frail creatures, he must necessarily commend himself, or we should never be able to perceive his beauty at all? Each reason is sufficient, and both are overwhelming; it is most suitable that Jesus should preach Jesus, that love should teach us love. Beloved, happy are those men to whom our Lord familiarly unveils his beauties. He is the rose, but it is not given to all men to perceive his fragrance. He is the fairest of lilies, but few are the eyes which have gazed upon his matchless purity. He stands before the world without form or comeliness, a root out of a dry ground, rejected by the vain and despised by the proud. (Is. 53:1-2) The great mass of this blear-eyed world can see nothing of the ineffable glories of Immanuel. Only where the Spirit has touched the eye with eye-salve, quickened the heart with divine life, and educated the soul to a heavenly taste, only there is that love word of my text heard and understood: "I am the rose of Sharon, and the lily of the valleys."

"Unto you which believe he is precious" (1 Pet. 2:7), and to you he is the corner stone. To you he is the rock of your salvation, your all in all; but to others he is "a stone of stumbling, and a rock of offence, even to them which stumble at the word, being disobedient." (1 Pet. 2:8) Let it be our prayer before we advance a single foot further, that our Redeemer would now reveal himself to his own chosen people, and favour each one of us with at least a glimpse of his all-conquering charms. May the King himself draw near unto his guests this morning, and as of old, when it was winter that he walked in the Temple in Solomon's porch, so may he walk in the midst of this waiting assembly.

I. First, this morning, I shall speak with you a little, as I may be helped by the Holy Spirit, on THE MOTIVES OF OUR LORD IN THUS COMMENDING HIMSELF.

I take it that he has designs of love in this speech. He would have all his people rich in high and happy thoughts concerning his blessed Person. Jesus is not content that his brethren should think meanly of him; it is his pleasure that his espoused ones should be delighted with his beauty, and that he should be the King and Lord of their spirits. He would have us possess an adoring admiration for him, joined with most cheerful and happy thoughts towards him. We are not to count him as a bare necessary, like bread and water, but are to regard him as a luxurious delicacy, as a rare and ravishing delight, comparable with the rose and the lily. Our Lord, you observe, expresses himself here poetically: "I am the rose of Sharon."

Dr. Watts, when he had written his delightful hymns, was the subject of Dr. Samuel Johnson's criticism, and that excellent lexicographer, who wrote with great authority upon all literary matters, entirely missed his mark when he said that the themes of religion were so few and so prosaic that they were not adapted for the poet; they were not such as

131

could allow of the flight of wing which poetry requires. Alas, Dr. Johnson! How little could you have entered into the spirit of these things, for if there is any place where poetry may indulge itself to the uttermost, it is in the realm of the infinite. Jordan's streams are as pure as Helicon [mountain of central Greece, once regarded as the home of the Muses and Apollo], and Siloa's brook (Milton, which flowed past the oracle of God), as inspiring as the Castalian fount (near Delphi). Heathen Parnassus has not half the elevation of the Christian's Tabor (a mountain, see Jer. 46:18), let critics judge as they may. This book of the Song of Solomon is poetry of the very highest kind to the spiritual mind, and, throughout Scripture, the sublime and beautiful are as much at home as the eagles in their eyes of rock. Surely our Lord adopts that form of speech in this song in order to show us that the highest degree of poetical faculty should be consecrated to him, and that lofty thoughts and soaring conceptions concerning himself are no intruders, but are bound to pay homage at his cross. Jesus would have us enjoy the highest thoughts of him that the sublimest poesy can possibly convey to us; and his motives I shall labour to lay before you.

Doubtless, he commends himself because high thoughts of Christ enable us to act consistently in our relations towards him. The saved soul is espoused to Christ. Now, in the marriage estate, it is a great assistance to happiness if the wife has high ideals of her husband. In the marriage union between the soul and Christ, this is exceedingly necessary. Listen to the words of the Psalm, "He is thy Lord; and worship thou him." (Ps. 45:11) Jesus is our husband (Is. 54:5), and is no more to be called *Baal* (that is, your master), but to be called *Ishi* (your man, your husband); yet, at the same time, he is our Lord. "For the husband is the head of the wife, even as Christ is the head of the church: and he is the saviour of the body." (Eph. 5:23) When the wife despises her husband, and looks down on him, then the order of nature is broken, and the household is put out of joint. And if our soul should ever come to despise Christ, then it can no longer stand in its true relation to him; but the more loftily we see Christ enthroned, and the more lowly we are when bowing before the foot of the throne, the more truly shall we be prepared to act our part in the economy of grace towards our Lord Jesus. Brethren, your Lord Christ desires you to think well of him, that you may submit cheerfully to his authority, and so be a better spouse to this best of husbands.

Moreover, our Master knows that high thoughts of him increase our love. Men will not readily love that which they do not highly esteem. Love and esteem go together. There is a love of pity, but that would be far out of place with reference to our exalted Head. If we are to love him at all, it must be with the love of admiration; and the higher that admiration rises the more vehemently will our love flame forth. My brothers and sisters in Christ, I beseech you to think much of your Master's excellence. Study him in his primeval glory before he took upon himself your nature! Think of the mighty love which drew him from his starry throne to die upon the cross of shame! Consider well the omnipotent affection which made him stretch his hands to the nails and yield his heart to the spear! Admire him as you see him conquering in his weakness over all the powers of hell, and, by his suffering, overthrowing all the hosts of your sins so that they cannot rise against you any more forever! See him now risen, no more to die; crowned, no more to be dishonoured; glorified, no more to suffer! Bow before him, hail him in the halls of your inner nature as the Wonderful, the Counsellor, the mighty God, within your spirits, for only thus will your love to him be what it should.

A high esteem of Christ, moreover, as he well knows, is very necessary for our comfort. Beloved, when you esteem Christ very highly, the things of this world become of small account with you, and their loss is not so heavily felt. If you feel your losses and crosses to be such ponderous weights that the wings of Christ's love cannot lift you up from the dust, surely you have made too much of the world and too little of him. I see a pair of balances.

132

I see in this one the death of a child, or the loss of a beloved relative; but I perceive in the other scale the great love of Christ. Now we shall see which will weigh the most with the man: if Jesus throws the light affliction up aloft, it is well, but if the trouble outweighs Jesus, then it goes badly with us indeed. If you are so depressed by your trials that you can by no means rejoice, even though you know that your name is written in heaven, then I think you cannot love Jesus as you should. Get delightful thoughts of him and you will feel like a man who has lost a pebble but has preserved his diamond; it is like the man who has seen a few cast clouts and rotten rags consumed in the flames, but has saved his children from the conflagration [fire]. You will rejoice in your deepest distress because Christ is yours if you have a high sense of the preciousness of your Master. Do not speak of plasters that will draw out all pain from a wound! So not speak of medicines which will extirpate [eliminate] disease! The sweet love of Christ, once clapped on the deepest wound, which the soul can ever know, would heal it at once. A drop of the precious medicine of Jesus' love tasted in the soul would chase away all heart pains forever. Jesus, Jesus, Jesus, be within us, and we make no choice of situations! Put us in Nebuchadnezzar's furnace (Dan. 3:15), if you will, and walk the glowing coals as our companion, and we will fear no evil.

Further, our Lord would have us entertain great thoughts concerning himself because this will quicken all the powers of our soul. I spoke to you just now of love receiving force from an esteem of Jesus; I might say the same of faith, or patience, or humility. Wherever Christ is highly esteemed, all the faculties of the spiritual man exercise themselves with energy. I will judge your piety by this barometer: does Christ stand high or low with you? If you have thought little of Christ, if you have been content to live without his presence, if you have cared little for his honour, if you have been neglectful of his laws, then I know that your soul is sick —God grant that it may not be sick unto death! But if the first thought of your spirit has been, "How can I honour Jesus?" If the daily desire of your soul has been, "Oh that I knew where I might find him!" I tell you that you may have a thousand infirmities, and may even scarcely know whether you are a child of God at all, yet I am persuaded, beyond a doubt, that you are safe, since Jesus is great in your esteem. I do not care about your rags; it is what you think of his royal apparel? I do not care about your wounds, though they bleed in torrents. What do you think of his wounds? Are they not like glittering rubies in your esteem? I think none the less of you, even though you are lying like Lazarus on the dunghill, and the dogs are licking you (Lk. 16:20-21); I judge you not by thy poverty, but what do you think of the King in his beauty? Has he a glorious high throne in your heart? Would you set him higher if you could? Would you be willing to die if you could, but add another trumpet to the strain which proclaims his praise? Ah, then, it is well with you! Whatever you may think of yourself, if Christ is great to you, you shall be with him before long. High thoughts of Jesus set us upon high attempts for his honour. What will men not do when they are possessed with the passion of love! When once some master thought gets hold of the mind, others, who have never felt the power of it, think the man insane; they laugh at him and ridicule him. When the grand thought of love to God has gained full possession of the soul, men have been able to actually accomplish what other men have not even thought of doing. Love has laughed at impossibilities, and proved that she is not to be quenched by many waters, nor drowned by the floods. Nevertheless, impassable woods have been made a footway for the Christian missionary. Through the dense jungle, steaming with malaria, men have passed, bearing the message of truth. Into the midst of hostile and savage tribes, weak and trembling women have even forced their way to tell of Jesus. No sea has been so stormy, no mountains have been so elevated, that they could shut out the earnest spirit. No long nights of winter in Labrador or in Iceland have been able to freeze up the love of Christ in the Moravian's heart. It has not been possible for the zeal of the heir of heaven to be overcome, though all the elements have combined with the cruelty of wicked men, and with the malice of hell itself. Christ's people have been more than conquerors through him that has loved them (Rom. 8:37),

133

and when his love has been shed abroad in their hearts by the Holy Spirit (Rom. 5:5), and they have had elevated thoughts of their Lord.

I wish it were in my power to put this matter more forcibly, but I am persuaded, brethren, that our Lord, in commending himself to us this morning in the words of our text, does so with this as his motive, that by the power of his Spirit we may be led to esteem him very highly in the inmost secrecy of our heart. And shall he speak to us in vain? Shall he stand in this pulpit, this morning, as he does in spirit, and shall he say, "I am the rose of Sharon"? And shall we reply, "But we do not see your beauty"? Shall he add a double commendation, "I am the lily of the valley"? And shall our cold hearts reply, "But we do not admire your spotless purity"? I trust we are not so utterly abandoned to spiritual blindness and ingratitude. Far rather, although we confess before him that we do not admire him as we should, we will add humbly, and with the tear of repentance in our eye:

Hark, my soul! It is the Lord;
'Tis thy Saviour, hear his word.
Jesus speaks, and speaks to thee:
"Say, poor sinner, lovest thou me?"

Can a woman's tender care
Cease towards the child she bare?
Yes, she may forgetful be,
Yet will I remember thee.

Lord, it is my chief complaint
That my love is weak and faint;
Yet I love thee, and adore;
O for grace to love thee more!

(William Cowper)

II. Whatever may be the commendable motive for any statement, yet it must not be made if it is not accurate. So, therefore, in the second place, I come to observe OUR LORD'S JUSTIFICATION FOR THIS COMMENDATION, which is abundantly satisfactory to all who know him.

What our Lord says of himself is strictly true. It falls short of the mark, and it is no exaggeration. Observe each one of the words. He begins with "I am". Those two little words I would not insist upon, but it is no straining of language to say that, even here, we find a great deep. What creature can, with exact truthfulness, say, "I am"? As for man, whose breath is in his nostrils, he may rather say "I am not" than "I am". We have so short a time here, and are so quickly gone, that the ephemera, which is born and dies under the light of one day's sun, is our brother. Poor short-lived creatures, we change with every moon, and are inconstant as the wave, frail as the dust, feeble as a worm, and fickle as the wind. Jesus said, "I am", and blessed be his name, he can fairly claim the attributes of self-existence and immutability! He said, "I am" in the days of his flesh; he says, "I am" at this hour. Whatever he was and he is, whatever he has been to any of his saints at anytime, he is to us this day. Come, my soul, rejoice in your unchangeable Christ, and if you get no further than the first two words of the text, yet you have a meal to stay your hunger, like Elijah's cakes in the strength of which he went for forty days. "I am" has revealed himself to you in a more glorious manner than he did to Moses at the burning bush. (Ex. 3:13-14). This great "I AM", come in human flesh, has become your Saviour and your Lord.

"I am the rose." We understand from this that Christ is lovely. He selects one of the most charming of flowers to set out himself. All the beauties of all the creatures are to be found in Christ in greater perfection than in the creatures themselves.

White and ruddy is my Beloved,
All his heavenly beauties shine;
Nature can't produce an object,
Nor so glorious, so divine;
He hath wholly
Won my soul to realms above.

(William Williams, the "*sweet singer of* Wales")

"Whatsoever things are true, whatsoever things are honest, whatsoever things are just, whatsoever things are pure, whatsoever things are lovely, whatsoever things are of good report" (Phil. 4:8), all are to be found stored up in our Well-beloved. Whatever there may be of beauty in the material world, Jesus Christ possesses all that in the spiritual world, only in a tenfold multiplication. He is infinitely more beautiful in the garden of the soul and in the paradise of God than the rose can be in the gardens of earth, though it is the universally-acknowledged queen of flowers. But the spouse adds, "I am the rose of Sharon". This was the best and rarest of roses. Jesus is not "the rose" alone, but "the rose of Sharon", just as he calls his righteousness "gold", and then adds "the gold of Ophir" (Ps. 45:9) — the best of the best. Jesus, then, is not only positively lovely, but superlatively the loveliest, as John Berridge quaintly exclaims:

Soon as faith the Lord can see,
Bleeding on the cross for me,
Quick my idols all depart,
Jesus gets and fills my heart.

None among the sons of men,
None among the heavenly train,
Can with Jesus then compare;
None so sweet and none so fair.

The Son of David takes the first place as the fairest among ten thousand. He is the sun, and all others are stars; for in his presence all the feebler lights are hidden, and are nothing, and he is all-in-all. Blush for your deformities, you beauties of earth, when his perfection eclipses you! Away, you pageants, and you pompous triumphs of men! The King in his beauty transcends you all. Black are the heavens, and dark is the day, in comparison with him. Oh, to see him face to face! This would be a vision for which life would be a glad exchange. For a vision of his face, we could fain be blind forever to all joys beside.

Our Lord adds, "I am the lily", thus giving himself a double commendation. Indeed, Jesus Christ deserves not to be praised doubly, but sevenfold, yes, and unto seven times seven. Heap up all the metaphors that express loveliness, bring together all the adjectives which describe delight, and all human speech and all earth-born things shall fail to tell of him. The rose with all its redness is not complete till the lily adds its purity, and the two together are dim reflections of our glorious Lord. I learn from the text that, in Christ Jesus, you have a combination of contrasted excellencies. If he is red with the flush of courageous zeal, or red with triumph as he returns from Edom, he is the rose; but he is a warrior without sinful anger or cruel vengeance, he is as pure and spotless as the timid virgin who toys with the dove — he is therefore our snow-white lily. I see him red as the rose in his sacrifice:

135

See from His head, His hands, His feet,
Sorrow and love flow mingled down!
Did e'er such love and sorrow meet,
Or thorns compose so rich a crown?

(Isaac Watts)

But I see him white as the lily as he ascends on high in his perfect righteousness, clothed in his white robe of victory, to receive gifts for men. Our Beloved is a mingling of all perfections to make up one perfection, and of all manner of sweetness to compose one complete sweetness. Earth's choicest charms commingled, feebly picture his abounding preciousness.

He is the "lily of the valleys". Does he intend by that to hint to us that he is a lily in his lowliest estate, a lily of the valley? The carpenter's son, living in poverty, wearing the common garb of the poor, is he the lily of the valleys? Yes, he is a lily to you and to me, poor dwellers in the lowlands. Up yonder, he is a lily on the hill-tops, where all celestial eyes admire him; down here, in these valleys of fears and cares, he is a lily still as fair as in heaven. Our eyes can see his beauty, can see his beauty now, a lily to us this very day. Though we have not seen the King in his beauty, yet I say to you that Solomon in all his glory was not arrayed like Jesus Christ in our eyes, as we see him by faith in a glass darkly.

The words, having been opened up one by one, teach us that Christ is lovely to all our spiritual senses. The rose is delightful to the eye, but it is also refreshing to the nostrils, and the lily is the same. So is Jesus. All the senses of the soul are ravished and satisfied with him. Whether it be the taste or feeling, the hearing, the sight, or the spiritual smell, all charms are in Jesus. Often, when we have not seen the Anointed, we have perceived his presence. Travelling on Lake Lugano, one morning we heard the swell of the song of the nightingale, and the oars were stilled on the blue lake as we listened to the silver sounds. We could not see a single bird, nor do I know that we wished to see it — we were so content with the sweetness of the music. Even so it is with our Lord; we may enter a house where he is loved, and we may hear nothing concerning Christ, and yet we may perceive clearly enough that he is there. A holy influence streams through their actions, pervading the household; so that if Jesus is unseen, it is clear that he is not unknown. Go anywhere where Jesus is, and though you do not actually hear his name, yet the sweet influence which flows from his love will be plainly enough discernible.

Our Lord is so lovely that even the recollection of his love is sweet. Take the rose of Sharon, and pull it leaf from leaf, and lay by the leaves in the jar of memory, and you will find each leaf most fragrant long afterwards, filling the house with perfume; and this very day we remember times of refreshing enjoyed at the Lord's table still delightful as we reflect on them.

Jesus is lovely in the bud as well as when full blown. You admire the rose quite as much when it is just a bud as when it bursts into perfect development. And, I think, Christ to you, my beloved, in the first blush of your devotion, was not one whit less sweet than he is now. Jesus full blown, in our riper experience, has lost none of his excellence. When we see him fully blown in the garden of paradise, shall we not count it to be our highest heaven to gaze on him forever?

Christ is so lovely that he needs no beautifying. When I hear men trying to speak of him with polished sentences, which have been revised and re-revised in their manuscripts, I would ask them why they need to paint the rose of Sharon, and what they can be at in seeking to enamel the lily of the valleys? Hold up Christ crucified, and he himself is

136

beautiful enough without our paint and tinsel. Let the roughest tongue speak sincerely of him in the most broken but honest accents, and Jesus himself is such a radiant jewel that the setting will be of small consequence. He is so glorious that he is "Most adorned when unadorned the most." May we ever feel this concerning him! And if we are tempted to display our powers of oratory when we have to speak of him, let us say, "Down, busy pride, and let Christ rule, and let Christ be seen." He needs no help from you.

Again, he is so lovely that he satisfies the highest taste of the most educated spirit to the very full. The greatest amateur in perfumes is quite satisfied with the rose, and I should think that no man of taste will ever be able to criticise the lily, and argue about its form. Now, when the soul has arrived at her highest pitch of true taste, she will still be content with Christ, no, she shall be the better able to appreciate him. In the world's history, we are supposed to have arrived at an age of taste, when colour and form are much regarded. I must confess, I think it a gaudy, tasteless age, and the fashion of the day is staring, vulgar, childish, and depraved. Bright and glittering colours, and antique, grotesque forms, are much sought after; and men must needs introduce their chosen fineries and fopperies into their worship, supposing that it is comely to worship God with silks, and laces, and ribbons, and gilt, and tinsel, and I do not know what trumpery besides. Just as the harlot of Babylon arrayed herself in pearls, and fine linen, and purple, and silk, and scarlet, even so do her imitators adorn themselves. As for us, my brethren, the beauty of Christ is such that if we go into a barn to worship, we are quite as satisfied as though it were a cathedral with groined arches and glowing windows; such is the beauty of Christ in our eyes, that we are quite content to hear of him without the pealing organ and the swell of Gregorian chants. And we are even satisfied though there should be no display of taste, nothing sensuous and scenic, nothing to please the eye or charm the ear. Jesus alone affords our mind all that delightful architecture, poetry, and music could profess to give; and when our soul gets near him, she looks on all outward adornments as mere child's toys, fit to amuse the rattle-brains of this poor idiot world, and vain gewgaws to men in Christ Jesus, who, by reason of use, have had their senses exercised, and learned to delight in nobler things than those in which the swine of this earth delight themselves. God give you to know that if you want beauty, Jesus is Sharon's rose! If you want spotless charms to delight your true taste, he is the lily of the valleys.

Dwelling for another minute on this subject, let me remark that our Lord Jesus Christ deserves all that he has said of himself. Firstly, in his divine glory. The glory of Christ as God, who can write about it? The first born sons of light desire to gaze into this vision, but feel that their eyes are unable to endure the excess of light. He is over all, God blessed forever. (Rom. 9:5) Concerning Christ, I may say that the heavens are not pure in his sight, and he charged his angels with folly. Nothing is great, nothing is excellent but God, and Christ is God. O roses and lilies, where are you now? Our Lord deserves these praises, again, in his perfection of manhood. He is like ourselves, but in him was no sin. "The prince of this world cometh, but hath nothing in me." (Jn. 14:30) Throughout the whole of his biography, there is not a fault in him. Let us write as carefully as we may after the copy; we still blot and blur the pages, for in him there is no mistake. His life is so wonderfully perfect that even those who have denied his deity have been astounded at it, and they have bowed down before the majesty of his holiness. You roses of ardent love, and you lilies of purest holiness, where are you now when we compare you with this perfect man? He deserves this commendation too in his editorial qualifications. Since his blood has washed us from all our sins, we talk no further of the red roses, for what can they do to purify the soul? Since his righteousness has made us accepted in the Beloved, we will speak no more of spotless lilies, for what are these? He deserves all the praise too in his reigning glory. He has a glory which his Father has given him as a reward, in the power of which he sits down at the right hand of God forever and ever, and shall soon come to judge the world in righteousness and the people with equity. Beloved, when I think of the momentous appearance when he shall descend a second time in splendour upon the earth, I say again, you roses, your radiant beauties are utterly eclipsed, and you lilies, your snow-white purity is forgotten. I can scarcely discern you, O fair flowers of earth; you are lost in the blaze of the great white throne, and in the flames of fire that shall go before the Judge of all to prepare his way. View the Lord Jesus in any way you please; all that he himself can say concerning himself he richly deserves, and therefore glory be unto his name forever and ever, and let the whole earth say, Amen!

III. I shall now conduct you to a third consideration, namely, THE INFLUENCE OF THIS COMMENDATION UPON US.

Christ desires our loftiest thoughts of himself, and his desires are for our good. O my beloved, I wish time would stay its wing a moment or two, that I might urge on you, with all your hearts, to second the endeavours of Christ, to labour after holy elevated thoughts concerning himself, since he desires them for you. And if you ask me how you are to attain them, let me aid you a minute. Think of the ruin of this world till Christ came into it! I think I see in vision a howling wilderness, a great and terrible desert, like the Sahara. I perceive nothing in it to relieve the eye; all around I am wearied with a vision of hot and arid sand, strewn with ten thousand bleaching skeletons of wretched men who expired in anguish, having lost their way in the pitiless waste. O God, what a sight! How horrible! A sea of sand without a bound, and without an oasis, a cheerless graveyard for a race forlorn! But what is that I see? Upon a sudden, springing up from the scorching sand I see a root, a branch, a plant of renown; and, as it grows, it buds, and the bud expands — it is a rose, and at its side a lily bows its modest head; and, miracle of miracles, as the fragrance of those flowers is diffused in the desert air, I perceive that wilderness transformed into a fruitful field, and, all around it, blossoms exceedingly. The glory of Lebanon is given to it, the excellence of Carmel and Sharon. Call it not Sahara, call it Paradise. Do not speak of it any longer as the valley of death-shade, for where I saw the skeletons bleaching in the sun, I see a resurrection, and up spring the dead, a mighty army, full of life immortal — you can understand the vision.

Christ is the rose, which has changed the scene. If you would have great thoughts of Christ, think of your own ruin. Yonder, I behold you cast out an infant, unswathed, unwashed, defiled with your own blood, too foul to be looked upon except by beasts of prey. (Ezek. 16:6) And what is this that has been cast into your bosom, and which, lying there, has suddenly made you fair and lovely? A rose has been thrown into your bosom by a divine hand, and, for its sake, you have been pitied and cared for by divine providence. You are washed and cleaned from your defilement; you are adopted into heaven's family; the fair seal of love is upon your forehead, and the ring of faithfulness is on your hand — a prince unto God — though just now you were an orphan, cast away. Oh, prize the rose, the putting of which into your bosom has made you what you are!

Consider your daily need of this rose. You live in the pestilential air of this earth. Take Christ away, and you die. Christ is the daily food of your spirit. You know, believer, that you are utterly powerless without your Lord. Oh, prize him then in proportion to the necessities you have for him! As you cannot even pray or think an acceptable thought apart from his presence, I beseech you, press him to your bosom as the beloved of your soul. You are like a branch cut off and withered, thrown outside the garden gate to be burnt as are the noxious weeds, apart from him. But when you are near him, you produce fruit to the glory of God. Praise Christ, I say then, after the rate of the necessity that you have for him.

Think, beloved, of the estimation that Christ is held in beyond the skies, in the land where things are measured by the right standard, where men are no longer deceived by the

138

delusions of earth. Think how God esteems the only-begotten, his unspeakable gift to us. Consider what the angels think of him as they count it their highest honour to veil their faces at his feet. Consider what the blood-washed think of him, as day without night they sing his well-deserved praises with gladdest voices. Remember how you yourself have sometimes esteemed him. There were happy hours when you would freely have given your eyes, and felt you cared no longer for the light of earth's brightest days, for your soul's eyes would serve you well enough if you could forever be favoured with the same clear sight of Christ. Have there not been moments when the chariots of Amminadib seemed but poor dragging things compared with the wheels of your soul when Jesus ravished your heart with his celestial embrace? Estimate him to-day as you did then, for he is the same, though you are not. Think of him today as you will think of him in the hour of death, and in the day of judgement, when none but Jesus can avail to keep your soul alive.

The great King has made a banquet, and he has proclaimed to all the world that none shall enter but those who bring with them the fairest flower that blooms. The spirits of men advance to the gate by thousands, and they bring each one the flower he thinks best; but in crowds they are driven from his presence, and do not enter into the banquet. Some bear in their hand the deadly nightshade of superstition, or carry the flaunting poppies of Rome, but these are not dear to the King, and the bearers are shut out of the pearly gates. My soul, have you gathered the rose of Sharon? Do you wear the lily of the valley in your bosom constantly? If so, when you come up to the gates of heaven, you will know its value, for you have only to show this, and the porter of the gate will open; not for a moment will he deny you admission, for to that rose the porter opens ever. You shall find your way with this rose in your hand up to the throne of God himself, for heaven itself possesses nothing which excels the rose of Sharon, and, of all the flowers that bloom in paradise, there is none to rival the lily of the valleys. Get Calvary's blood-red rose into your hand by faith, and wear it; by communion, preserve it; by daily watchfulness, make it your all in all, and you will be blessed beyond all bliss, happy beyond a dream. So may it be yours forever!

IV. Lastly, I close by asking you to make CONFESSIONS SUGGESTED BY MY TEXT.

I will not make them for you, and therefore need not detain you from your homes. I will utter my own lamentation and leave you everyone apart to do the same. I stand before this text of mine to blush this morning, and to weep while I acknowledge my ungrateful behaviour.

"My Lord, I am truly ashamed to think that I have not gazed more upon you. I know, and in my heart believe, that you are the total sum of all beauty, yet must I sorrowfully lament that my eyes have been gadding about to look after other beauties; my thoughts have been deluded with imaginary excellencies in the creature, and I have meditated but little upon yourself. Alas, my Lord, I confess still further that I have not possessed and enjoyed you as I ought! When I might have been with you all the day and all the night, I have been roving hither and thither, forgetting my resting place. I have not been careful to welcome my Beloved and to retain his company. I have stirred him up by my sins, and have driven him away by my lukewarmness. I have given him cold lodgings and slender hospitality within the chambers of my heart. I have not held him fast, neither have I pressed him to abide with me as I should have done. All this, I must confess, and mourn that I am not more ashamed while confessing it. Moreover, my good Lord, although I know your great sacrifice for me, and might well have chained my heart forever to your altar (and oh that you had done so!), I must acknowledge that I have not been a living sacrifice as I should have been. I have not been so fascinated by the lustre of your beauty as I should have been. Oh that all my heart's rooms had been

139

occupied by you, and by you alone! Would God my soul were as the coals in the furnace, all on flame, and not a single particle of me left unconsumed by the delightful flames of your love. I must also confess, my Lord, that I have not spoken of you as I should have done. Although I have had many opportunities, yet I have not praised you at the rate which you deserve. I have given you at best but a poor, stammering, chilly tongue, when I should have spoken with the fiery zeal of a seraph."

These are my confessions. Brothers and sisters, what are yours? If you have none to make, if you can justly claim to have done all that you should have done for your Beloved, I envy you; but I think there is not a man here who will dare to say this. I am sure you have all had falls, and slips, and shortcomings, with regard to him. Well, then, come humbly to Jesus at once. He will forgive you readily, for he does not soon take offense at his spouse. He may sometimes speak sharp words to her because he loves her, but his heart is always true and faithful and tender. He will forgive the past, he will receive you at this moment; yes, this moment he will display himself to you. If you will but open the door to him, he will enter into immediate fellowship with you, for he says, "Behold, I stand at the door and knock: if any man hear my voice, and open the door, I will come in to him, and sup with him, and he with me." (Rev. 3:20) O Christ, our Lord, our heart is open! Come in and go out no more forever. "Whosoever believeth on the Son hath everlasting life." (Jn. 3:36) Sinner, believe and live.

19. THE LILY AMONG THORNS
NO. 1525

DELIVERED ON LORD'S-DAY MORNING,
FEBRUARY 29TH, 1880
AT THE METROPOLITAN TABERNACLE, NEWINGTON

"As the lily among thorns, so is my love among the daughters."
(Song of Solomon 2:2)

WE shall not enter into any profitless discussion this morning. We take it for granted that the Song of Solomon is a sacred marriage song between Christ and his church, and that it is the Lord Jesus who is here speaking of his church, and indeed of each individual member, saying, "As the lily among thorns, so is my love among the daughters." I will not even enter into any inquiry as to what particular flower is here intended by the word translated "lily", for it would be very difficult to select a plant from the Holy Land about which travellers and botanists agree. The lily, which we should most naturally fix on, is, as I have gathered from books of travel, not at present still found in that country, though we may not, therefore, be sure that it was never there, or may not yet be discovered. Several other fair and beautiful forms, according to the fancies of various travellers, have been preferred to occupy the place of the plant intended by the original Hebrew, but none of them quite come up to the ideal suggested to an English reader by our translation. For once, I will take the liberty of clothing the Scripture in a western dress, if need be, and venture to do what Solomon would surely have done if his Song of Songs had been written in England. I shall assume that he means one of our own lilies: either the lily of the valley, or one of those more stately beauties, matchless for whiteness, which so gloriously adorns our gardens. Either will do, and serve their turn this morning. "As the lily among the thorns, so is my love among the daughters." It is of small moment to be precise in botany so long as we get the spirit of the text. We seek practical usefulness and personal consolation, and proceed at once in their pursuit, in the hope that it may be with us as with the great Bridegroom himself, of whom the golden canticle says, "He feedeth among the lilies."

Many are taking root among us now, newly transplanted from the world, and it is well that they should be rooted in a knowledge of their calling by grace, and what it includes. They ought to know at the very commencement what a Christian is when he is truly a Christian, what he is expected to be, what the Lord means him to be, and what the Lord Jesus regards him as really being; so that they may make no mistakes, but may count the cost, and know what it is that they have ventured upon. Thinking over this subject carefully, and anxiously desiring to warn our new converts without alarming them, I could not think of any text from which I should be able, in the exposition of it, better to set out the position, condition, and character of a genuine Christian. Jesus himself knows best what his own bride is like; so let us hear him as he speaks in this matchless song. He knows best what his followers should be, and may we be well content to take the words out of his own mouth, when, in sweetest poetry, he tells us, "As the lily among thorns, so is my love among the daughters." Join me then, my brethren, at this time, in considering our Lord's lilies, and how they grow. Concerning the church of God, there are two points upon which I will enlarge: first, her relation with her Lord; and secondly, her relation with the world.

I. First, I think my text very beautifully sets out THE RELATION OF THE CHURCH, AND OF EVERY INDIVIDUAL, TO CHRIST. He styles her "my love". An exquisitely sweet name, as if his love had all gone out from him, and had become embodied in her.

The first point, then, of her relation to Christ is that she has his love. Think of it, and let the blessed truth dwell long and sweetly in your meditations. The Lord of life and glory, the Prince of the kings of the earth, has such a loving heart that he must have an object on which to lavish his affection; and his people, chosen from among men, whom he calls his church, these are they who are his "love", the object of his supreme delight. "Christ loved the church, and gave himself for it." (Eph. 5:25) He looked on his people and exclaimed, "As the Father hath loved me even so have I loved you." (Jn. 15:9) Every believer, separated from mankind, and called into the fellowship of Christ, is also the peculiar object of his love. Not in name only, but in deed and in truth, does Jesus love each one of us who have believed in him. You may each one of you say with the Apostle, "He loved me" (Gal 2:20), and you may read it in any tense you please — He loved me; he loves me; he will love me, for he gave himself for me. This shall be your song in heaven — "Unto him that loved us, and washed us from our sins in his own blood", to him be glory! (Rev. 1:5) Let your hearts saturate themselves with this honeyed thought; heaven lies hid within it; it is the quintessence of bliss — Jesus loves me. It is not in the power of words to set out the charming nature of this fact, it is a very simple proposition; but the heights and depths, the lengths and breadths of it, surpass our knowledge. That such a poor, insignificant, unworthy being as I should be the object of the eternal affection of the Son of God is an amazing wonder; yet wonderful as it is, it is a fact! To each of his people he says this morning by the Holy Spirit, "I have loved thee with an everlasting love, therefore with loving-kindness have I drawn thee." (Jer. 31:3) Each one of us may rejoice in the title under which our Lord addresses us — "My love".

This love is a distinguishing love, for in its light one special object shines as a lily, and the rest, "the daughters", are as thorns. Love has fixed on its chosen object, and compared with the favoured one, all others are as nothing. There is a love of Jesus that goes out to all mankind, for "the Lord is good to all, and his tender mercies are over all his works" (Ps. 145:9); but there is a special and peculiar love which he bears to his own. As a man loves his neighbours, but still has a special affection for his own wife, so is the church, Christ's bride, beloved above all the rest of mankind, and every individual believer is the favoured one of heaven. The saint is united to Christ in a mystical union, a spiritual marriage bond, and, above all others, Christ loves the souls espoused to him. He said once, "I pray for them. I pray not for the world, but for them which thou hast given me" (Jn. 17:9); thus indicating that there is a speciality in his intercession. We rejoice in the largeness and the width of Jesus' love, but we do not therefore doubt its speciality. The sun shines on all things, but when it is focussed on one point, ah, then there is a heat about it of which you little dreamed! The love of Jesus is focussed on those whom the Father has given him. Upon you, my brother or sister, if indeed you are a believer in Jesus Christ, the Lord's heart is set, and he speaks of you in the words of the text as "my love", loved above all the daughters, precious in his sight and honourable, so that he will give men for you and people for your life.

Observe that this is a love which he openly avows. The bridegroom speaks and says before all men, "As a lily among thorns, so is my love among the daughters." He puts it on record in that book which is more widely scattered than any other, for he is not ashamed to have it published from the housetops. The love of Christ was at first hidden in his heart, but it soon revealed itself, for even of old his delights were with the sons of men, when he bent his steps downward to this world in different forms, or ever Bethlehem's song was sung. And now, since the incarnate God has loved, and lived, and died, he has unveiled his love in the most open form, and astonished heaven and earth by it. On Calvary, he set up an open proclamation, written in his own heart's blood, that he loved his own even to the end. (Jn 13:1) He bids his ministers proclaim it to the world's end, that many waters cannot quench his love, neither can the floods drown it; and that neither life, nor death, nor things present, nor things to come, nor height, nor depth, nor any other creature, shall be

142

able to separate us from the love of God which is in Christ Jesus our Lord. (Rom. 8:38-39) He would have it known that he is not ashamed to call his people "the bride, the Lamb's wife." (Rev. 21:9) He declares it that his adversaries may know it, that he has a people in whom his heart delights, and these he will have and hold as his own when heaven and earth shall pass away.

This love, wherever it has been revealed to its object, is reciprocated. If the Lord has really spoken home to your soul and said, "I have loved you", your soul gladly answered, "This is my Beloved and this is my Friend; yea, he is altogether lovely." (Song 5:16) For what says the spouse in another place? "My Beloved is mine and I am his." (Song 2:16) I am his beloved, but he is my beloved also. By this, dear hearer, you shall know whether this text belongs to you or not. What do you say when Jesus asks you, "Lovest thou me?" (Jn. 21:15-17) Is your heart warmed at the very mention of his name? If you can truly say with Peter, "Lord, thou knowest all things, thou knowest that I love thee", then rest assured you love him because he first loved you. (1 Jn, 4:19) Do not doubt the fact, but be well assured of it, that love in your heart towards Jesus is the certain and infallible pledge of his infinite, eternal, and immutable love for you. If his name is on your heart, then be sure of this, that your name is on his breast, and written on the palms of his hands. (Is. 49:16) You are espoused to him, and the bands of the mystical wedlock shall never be snapped. This is the first point of the relation of the church with her Lord: she is the object of his love.

Next, she bears his likeness. Notice the first verse of the chapter, where the bridegroom is speaking — "I am the rose of Sharon, and the lily of the valleys." He is the lily, but his beloved is like him, for he applies his own chosen emblem to her — "As the lily among thorns, so is my love among the daughters." Notice that he is the lily, she is as the lily; that is to say, he has the beauty and she reflects it. She is comely in his comeliness which he puts upon her. If any soul has any such beauty as is described here, Christ has endowed that beloved soul with all its wealth of charms, for in ourselves we are deformed and defiled. What is the confession of this very spouse in the previous chapter? She says "I am black" — that is the opposite of a lily. If she adds "but comely", it is because her Lord has made her comely. There is no grace but the grace which has been given, and if we are graceful, it is because Christ has made us full of grace. There is no beauty in any one of us but what our Lord has wrought in us.

Note, too, that he who gave the beauty is the first to see it. While they are unknown to the world, Jesus knows his own. Long before anybody else sees any virtue or any praise in us, Jesus describes it, and is pleased with it. He is quick to say, "Behold, he is praying" or "Behold, he is repenting." He is the first to say, "I have surely heard Ephraim bemoaning himself." (Jer. 31:18) Love's eyes are quick, and her ears are open. Love covers a multitude of sins (Jas. 5:20), but it also discovers a multitude of beauties. Can it be so, O my soul, can it be so, that Christ has made you comely in his comeliness? Has he shed a beauty upon you, and does he himself look complacently on it? He whose taste is exquisite, and whose voice is the truth, who never calls that beautiful which is not beautiful, can he see beauty in your sighs and tears, in your desires after holiness, in your poor attempts to aid his cause, in your prayers and in your songs, and in your heart's love towards him — can he see a beauty in these things? Yes, assuredly he can, or he would not speak as he does in this text. Let his condescending discernment have all honour for this generous appreciation of us! Let us bless and love him because he deigns to think so highly of us who owe everything to him. "Thou art", says he, "my love, as the lily."

It is evident that the Lord Jesus takes delight in this beauty that he has put on his people. He values it at so great a rate that he counts all rival beauties to be but as thorns. He looks upon the court of an earthly monarch, and sees my lords and ladies, but makes small account of them compared with his poor saints. If in that court he spies out one who

143

loves him, one who wears a coronet and prays, he marks that one out, and counts him or her "as the lily among thorns." There is a wealthy household, honoured and famous among the old county families, but in it there is no lover of the Saviour except one, and she perhaps is a little maid whose service is among the pots; yet shall she be as the wings of a dove covered with silver. "As the lily among thorns", so she shall be. All the kingdoms of the earth are but thorn-breaks [thorn bushes] to the Lord Jesus compared with his church. Be they Roman, German, French, or English, all empires, with all their splendours, are mere gorse and furze on the common, bramble-bushes and thorn coverts, the haunts of wild and venomous creatures in the view of the King of kings; but his church, and those that make up the body of the faithful, are as lilies in his discerning eyes. He delights in them; he finds a sweet content in gazing on them. So you see, the Lord has given to his people his likeness, and that likeness he looks upon and loves.

Bringing out still further the relationship between Christ and his church, I want you to notice that her position has drawn out his love. "As the lily," says he, "among thorns, so is my love." He spied her out among the thorns. She was at first no better than a thorn herself; his grace alone made her to differ from the briars about her; but as soon as ever he had put his life and his grace into her, though she dwelt among the ungodly, she became as the lily, and he saw her. The thorn-brake could not hide his beloved. Christ's eye towards his people is so keen because it is cleared by love. There may, at this time, be in a Popish convent one truly seeking Jesus in spirit and in truth. He spies out the believer among the trusters in themselves, and calls her his love among thorns. There may be at this moment, in the most godless haunt in London, a poor, trembling heart that loves Jesus in secret: the Lord knows that heart, and it is to him as a lily among thorns. You, perhaps, are the only serious working man in the shop in which you earn your daily bread, and the whole crew holds you in derision. You may hardly know yourself whether you are really a Christian, for you are sometimes staggered about your own condition; and yet the enemies of Christ have made up their minds as to whose side you are on, and treat you as one of the disciples of the Nazarene. Be of good courage, your Lord discerns you, and knows you better than you know yourself. Such is the quickness of his eye, that your difficult and perilous position only stirs his discernment, and he regards you with more attention. The thorns cannot hide you, thickly as they cluster around you: in your loneliness you are not alone, for the Crucified is with you.

"As the lily among thorns" also carries another meaning. Dr. Thompson writes of a certain lily — "It grows among thorns, and I have sadly lacerated my hands in extricating it from them. Nothing can be in higher contrast than the luxuriant, velvety softness of this lily, and the withered, tangled hedge of thorns about it." Ah, beloved, you know who it was that in gathering your soul and mine, he lacerated not his hands only, but his feet, and his head, and his side, and his heart, yes, and his inmost soul. He spied us out, and said, "Yonder lily is mine, and I will have it"; but the thorns were a terrible barrier. Our sins were gathered round about us, and the wrath of God most sharply stopped the way. Jesus pressed through all that we might be his; and now, when he takes us to himself, he does not forget the thorns which circles his brow, and tore his flesh for our sakes. This, then, is a part of our relationship with Christ, that we cost him very dear. He saw us where we were, and he came to our deliverance; and now, even as Pharaoh's daughter called the young child's name "Moses", "because", she said, "I drew him out of the water" (Ex. 2:10), so Jesus calls his chosen "the lily among thorns", because such she was when he came to her rescue. Never will he forget Calvary and its thorns, nor should his saints allow the memory of it to fade.

Yet once more, I think many a child of God may regard himself as still being a lily among thorns because of his afflictions. Certainly the church is so, and she is there kept for Christ's own. If thorns made it hard for him to reach us for our salvation, there is another

144

kind of thorn which makes it hard for any enemy to come at us in order to harm us. Our trials and tribulations, from which we would fain escape, often act as a spiritual protection: they hedge us about, and ward off many a devouring foe. Sharp as they are, they serve as a fence and a defense. Many a time, dear child of God, you would have been an exposed lily, to be plucked by any ruthless hand, if it had not been that God had placed you in such circumstances that you may be shut up to himself. Sick saints and poor saints and persecuted saints are fair lilies, enclosed by their pains, and needs, and bonds, so that they may be for Christ alone. I see John Bunyan in prison writing his "Pilgrim's Progress", and I cannot help feeling that it was a great blessing for us all that such a lily was shut up among the thorns, that it might shed its fragrance in that famous book, and by it perfume the church for the ages following. You that are kept from roaming by sickness or by family trials need not regret these things, for perhaps they are the means of making you more completely your Lord's. How charmingly Madame [Jeanne Marie B. de la Mothe] wrote when she was immured in a dungeon. Her wing was closely bound, but her song was full of liberty, for she felt that the bolts and bars only shut her in with her Beloved, and what is that but liberty? Madame Guyon [Jeanne Marie Bouvier de la Mothe] sings beautifully:

A little bird I am,
Shut from the fields of air,
And in my cage I sit and sing
To him who placed me there;
Well pleased a prisoner to be,
Because, my God, it pleaseth thee.

Nought have I else to do,
I sing the whole day long;
And he whom most I love to please
Doth listen to my song;
He caught and bound my wandering wing;
But still he bends to hear me sing.

Thou hast an ear to hear
A heart to love and bless;
And though my notes were e'er so rude,
Thou wouldst not hear the less;
Because thou knowest as they fall,
That love, sweet love, inspires them all

My cage confines me round;
Abroad I cannot fly;
But though my wing is closely bound,
My heart's at liberty;
For prison walls cannot control
The flight, the freedom of the soul.

Oh, it is good to soar
These bolts and bars above!
To Him whose purpose I adore,
Whose providence I love;
And in Thy mighty will to find
The joy, the freedom of the mind.

"As the lily among thorns", she lived in prison shut in with her Lord, and since the world was quite shut out, she was in that respect the gainer. Oh to have one's heart made as "a

145

garden enclosed, a spring shut up, a fountain sealed"! (Song 4:12) So let my soul be — yes, so let it be — even if the enclosure can only be accomplished by a dense growth of trials and griefs. May every pain that comes, and casts us on our bed, and lays us aside from public usefulness; may every sorrow which arises out of our business, and weans us from the world; may every adversary that assails us with bitter, taunting words only thicken the thorn hedge which encases us from all the world, and constrains us to be chaste lilies set apart for the Well-beloved!

Enough on this point, I think; only do let me entreat all of you who have lately come to know the Lord to think much of your relationship with him. It is the way by which you will be supported under the responsibilities of your relationship with the world. If you know that you are his, and that he loves you, you will be strong to bear all burdens; nothing will daunt you if you are sure that he is for you, that his whole heart is true to you, and that he loves you specially, and has set you apart for himself, that you may be one with him forever. Dwell much, in your meditations, on what this text and other Scriptures teach of the relationship of the renewed heart with Christ, and know him of whom you are so well known. May the Holy Spirit teach us all this lesson, so that it may be learned by our hearts.

II. But now, secondly, our text is full of instruction as to THE RELATIONSHIP OF THE CHURCH, AND EACH INDIVIDUAL BELIEVER, WITH THE WORLD — "The lily among thorns."

First, then, she has incomparable beauty. As compared and contrasted with all else, she is as the lily to the thorn-brake. Did not our Lord say of the natural lilies — "Solomon in all his glory was not arrayed like one of these"? (Mat. 6:29; Lk. 12:27) And when I think of Christ's lilies, adorned in his own righteousness and bearing his own image, I feel that I might repeat my Master's words and say with emphasis, "Solomon in all his glory was not arrayed like one of these!" In Christ's esteem, his church bears the prize for beauty; she is the fairest among women. She is not to be compared with anything; she must be contrasted with the rest of mankind. Our Lord means that if you take worldlings at their best, and in their bravest attire, in their pomp, and glory, and parade, they are just thorns in contrast with his church. Though the church may seem to be little, and poor, and despised, yet she is better than all the princes, and kingdoms, and glories of the earth. He means that true Christians are infinitely superior to ungodly men. These ungodly men may make a fair show of virtue, and they may have much prudence and wit, and count themselves wise and great, but Jesus calls all unconverted ones "thorns", while his own believing ones he compares with "lilies". The thorns are worthless, they flourish, and spread, and cumber the ground, but they yield no fruit, and only grow to be cut down for the oven. Alas, such is man by nature, at his best! As for the lily, it is a thing of beauty and a joy forever; it grows shedding sweet perfume; and when it is gathered, its loveliness adorns the chamber to which it is taken. So does the saint bless his generation while here, and when he is taken away, he is regarded with pleasure even in heaven above as one of the flowers of God. He will, before long, be transplanted from among the thorns to the garden enclosed beyond the river, where the King delights to dwell, for such a flower is far too fair to be left for ever amid tangled briars.

There are among worldly people some who are very fair to look at in many respects: philanthropic, kind, and upright, displaying many virtues; but since these virtues have no bearing towards God, and no reference to Christ, he counts the bearers of them to be but thorns. What virtue can there be in him whose principle in life is to disregard his Maker, and disbelieve in his Saviour? He is an avowed rebel, and yet would be commended by the Lord whom he rejects. How can this be? Acts done from other motives than those of obedience to God, or love to Christ, are poor things. There may be a great inward

146

difference between actions which outwardly are the same. The apple of nature has ever the flavour of the pomegranate of grace. It may seem even to excel the fruit of grace, but it is not so. Two babes before us may appear alike as they seem to sleep side by side, but the child of nature, however finely dressed, is not the living child, and the Lord will not own the dead thing as belonging to his family. Ah, you who are struggling after holiness for Christ's sake, you who are seeking after virtue in the power of the Holy Spirit, you have the beauty of the lily, while all else are to Christ as a thicket of thorns.

Yes, and let me say what I am sorry to add — a real Christian is as superior even to a professing Christian as a lily is to thorns. I know churches in which there are many who make a profession, but, ah me, it is a pity that they should, for their life does not adorn their doctrine, and their temper is not consistent with the indwelling of the Holy Spirit! They live like worldlings, for amassing money, or to carry on business, or to enjoy good eating and drinking, or to dress and go to parties: they are as much for this world as if they were never renewed, and, it is to be feared, they never were. It will often grieve those who really love the Lord to see how mere professors pretend to do what saints labour to perform. The saints are mimicked — I almost said mocked and mimicked — by empty professors, and this is a standing source of sorrow. Their cold words often vex the zealous heart, and pierce it as with thorns. When you are full of zeal, their lack of consecration almost kindles indignation in the minds of those who are willing to give their last penny, yes, and their last breath, for their Master's honour. Do not, however, be at all astonished, for it must be so; he who is full of the grace of God will always be as the lily among thorns, even in the professing church. Do not marvel, young brother, if older professors dampen your ardour, and count your warm love to be mere fanaticism. May God give you grace to keep up your first love, and even to advance upon it, though the thorny ones wound and hinder you! May you be distinguished above your fellow-professors, for I fear that unless it is so, your life will be a poor one.

This then is the relationship of the church with the world, and of Christians to the world, that they are as much superior to the unregenerate in moral and spiritual beauty as the lily is to the thorns among which it finds itself.

Secondly, in the comparison of the saint with the lily, we remark that he has, like the lily, a surpassing excellence. I point not to its beauty just now, but to its intrinsic excellence. The thorn is a fruit of the curse: it springs up because of sin. "Thorns also and thistles shall it bring forth to thee." (Gen. 3:18) Not so the lily: it is a fair type of the blessing which make rich without the sorrow of carking [pressing] care. The thorn is a mark of wrath, and the lily is the symbol of divine providence. A true believer is a blessing, a tree whose leaves heal, and whose fruit feeds. A genuine Christian is a living gospel, an embodiment of goodwill towards men. Did not the old covenant blessing run, "In thee and in thy seed shall all the nations of the earth be blessed"? (Gen. 22:18, 26:4) I cannot refrain from quoting a metrical meditation of one who loved the Song of Solomon, and drank deep of its spirit. He says of the church. She is,

A radiant thing, where all is gloomy else,
Florescent where all else is barrenness;
A blossom in the desert, that proclaims
Man is no friendless outcast,
Hopeless, doomed
To traverse scenes of wickedness and grief;
But, pilgrim as he is, has One who plans,
Not only to protect but cheer his way.

Oh, ever testifying desert flower,

147

Still holding forth the story of God's love,
How wonderful it is that busy throngs
Pause not to look on thee! That few reflect
On the strange fact of thine existence still,
A lily among thorns — a life in death,
Distinct from, yet in contact with the world;
Burning, yet unconsumed; though cumbered, flee
With glorious liberty!

Yes, the church is a blessing, a blessing abiding, and scattering its delights in the midst of the curse; and each particular believer is, in measure, a blessing too, "as the lily among thorns."

A true Christian does not know how to harm his fellow man. He is like the lily which stings no one, and yet he lives among those who are full of sharpness. He aims to please and not provoke, and yet he lives among those whose existence is a standing menace. The thorn tears and lacerates: it is all armed from its root to its topmost branch, defying all-comers. But there stands the lily, smiling, not defying; charming, and not harming. Such is the real Christian, holy, harmless, full of love and gentleness and tenderness. In this, lies his excellence. The thorn pierces, but the lily soothes; the very sight of it gives pleasure. Who would not stop and turn aside to see a lily among thorns, and think he reads a promise from his God to comfort him amid distress? Such is a true Christian: he is a consolation in his family, a comfort in his neighbourhood, an ornament to his profession, and a benediction to his age. He is all tenderness and gentleness, and yet it may be he lives among the envious, the malicious, and the profane, a lily among thorns. The thorn says, "Keep away; no one shall touch me with impunity." The lily cries, "I come to you, I shed my soul abroad to please you."

The sweet odours of the lily of the valley are well known; perhaps no plant has so strong an aroma about it of intense and exquisite sweetness as that lily of the valley which is found in Palestine. Such is the sanctified believer. There is a secret something about him, a hallowed aroma that goes out from his life, so that his graciousness is discovered; for grace, like its Lord, "cannot be hid." (Mat. 5:14; 1 Tim. 5:25) Even if the regenerate man is not known as a professor, yet he discovers himself by the holiness of his life, when "his speech bewrayeth [betrayeth] him." (Mat. 26:73) When I was resting in the south I wandered by the side of a flowing stream, gathering handfuls of maiden-hair fern from the verdant bank — and as I walked along I was conscious of a most delicious fragrance all around me. I cast my eye downward, and I saw blue eyes looking up from among the grass at my feet. The violets had hidden themselves from sight, but they had betrayed themselves by their delicious scent. So does a Christian reveal his hidden life; his tone and temper and manners speak of his royal lineage, if indeed the Spirit of God is in him.

Such are the people of God. They court no observation, but are like that modest flower of which the poet says:

She ne'er affects
The public walk, nor gaze of midday sun;
She to no state nor dignity aspires,
But silent and alone puts on her suit,
And sheds a lasting perfume, but for which
We had not known there was a thing so sweet
Hid in the gloomy shade.

(Frederick Hulme, *Bards and Blossoms; the poetry, history, and association of flowers*)

I want you, dear Christian people, to be just like this: to have about you a surpassing wealth of blessing, and an unrivalled sweetness of influence by which you shall be known of all men. Is it so with you, or are you as rough, and stern, and repellent, as a thorn bush? Are you as selfish and as quarrelsome as the unregenerate? Or do you give yourself away in sweet odours of self-denying kindness in your families, and among your neighbours? If you do, then Jesus says of you, "As the lily among thorns, so is my love among the daughters."

The last point with regard to our relationship with the world is that the church and many individual Christians are called to endure singular trials, which make them feel "as the lily among thorns." That lovely flower seems out of place in such company, does it not? Christ said, "Behold, I send you forth as sheep among sheep — no, no, that is my mistake, "as sheep among wolves." It is a very blessed thing to be as sheep among sheep: to lie down with them under the shadow of the great rock, and feed with them in green pastures under the Shepherd's eye. This is our privilege, and we ought to value it greatly, and unite with the church, and frequent its ordinances. But even then, we shall, some of us, have to go home to an ungodly family, or go out into the world to win our bread, and then be as sheep among wolves. Grow in the church and you will be lilies in the garden; still, you cannot always live in the Tabernacle, and so you will have to go back to the ungodly world, and there you will be lilies among thorns.

The lily startles you if you find it in such a position. Often you come upon one of God's elect ones in a most unexpected way, and are as much amazed as if an angel had crossed your path. This is the wonder of the lily among thorns. You are making your way over a wild heath, and come to a tangled thorn-brake through which you must force your way. As you are driving through the dense mass, rending and tearing your garments, suddenly, you stand still as one who has seen a vision of angels, for there among the most rugged brambles a lily lifts its lovely form and smiles upon you. You feel like Moses at the back of the desert when he saw the bush which burned with fire and yet was not consumed. (Ex. 3:2) So have you met in a back slum, where blasphemy abounded, a beautiful child of God, whom all recognised as such, and you felt amazed. So have you, in a wealthy family full of worldliness and vanity, come upon a humble man or patient woman living for Christ, and you have asked how came this grace to this house? So, too, in a foreign land, where all bow down to crucifix and image, you have casually met with a confessor who has stood his ground among idolaters, protesting for his God, not by his speech so much as by his holy walk. The surprise has been great. Expect many such surprises. The Lord has a people where you are not looking for them. Do not think that all his lilies are in his garden; there are lilies among thorns, and he knows their whereabouts. Many saints reside in families where they will never be appreciated any more than the lily is appreciated by the thorns. This is painful, for the sympathy of our fellows is a great comfort. Lilies of the valley love to grow in clusters, and saints love holy company, yet in some cases it must not be; they must live alone. Nor need we think that this loneliness is unrelieved, for God goes out of the track of men, and visits those whom his own servants are passing by. The poet says,

Full many a flower is born to blush unseen,
And waste its sweetness on the desert air.

(Thomas Gray)

But the poet forgot that God is in the wilderness and the solitary place, and the sweetness of lonely flowers is his. He who planted the lily among thorns sees its beauty. It is God's flower, and does it waste its sweetness because no human nostril smells it? It is

149

blasphemous to count that wasted which is reserved for the great King. The Lord understands the incense of nature better than we do, and, as he walks abroad, he rejoices in his works. Grace struggling in loneliness is very choice in God's esteem. If man does not see you, O lonely believer, you may, nevertheless, sing, "Thou God seest me." (Gen. 16:13) The flower which blooms for God alone has a special honour put upon it, and so has the saint whose quiet life is all for Jesus. If you are unappreciated by those around you, do not, therefore, be distressed, for you are honourable in the sight of God.

The lily is altogether unassisted too by its surroundings — "the lily among thorns" borrows nothing from the growth which gathers about it. A genuine Christian is quite unhelped by ungodly men; what is worse, he is hindered by them. Yet, through divine grace, he lives and grows. You know how the good seed could not grow because of the thorns which sprang up and choked it (Mat. 13:7, 22), but here is a good seed, a choice bulb, which flourishes where you did not look for it. God can make his people live and blossom even among the thorns, where the ungodly, by their evil influences, would choke and destroy it. Happy it is when the gracious one overtops the thorn-thicket, which would check his growth, and make his influence to be known and felt above the grossness of surrounding sin.

We should not do justice to this text if we failed to see in it a reminder of the persecution to which many of the best of God's people are subjected. They live all their lives long like the lily among thorns. Some of you, dear friends, are in this condition. You can hardly speak a word but that it is picked up and made mischief of; you cannot perform an action but that it is twisted, and motives imputed to you which you disown. Nowadays, persecutors cannot drag men to the stake, but the old trial of cruel mockings is still continued; in some cases it rages even more fiercely than ever. God's people have been a persecuted people at all times, and you only fare as they fare. Bear well the burden common to all the chosen! Make no great wonder of it; this bitter trial has happened to many more before, and you may well rejoice that you are now in fellowship with apostles and prophets and honourable men in all ages. The lily among thorns should rejoice that it is a lily and not a thorn; and when it is wounded it should consider it a matter of course, and bloom on.

But why does the Lord put his lilies among thorns? It is because he works transformations, singular transformations, by their means. He can make a lily grow among thorns till the thorns grow into lilies. Remember how it is written, "The wilderness and the solitary place shall be glad for them and the desert shall rejoice and blossom as the rose." (Is. 35:1) He can put a Christian in a godless family till first one and then another shall feel the divine power, and say, "We will go with you, for we perceive that God is with you." (Zech. 8:23) It cannot happen in nature, but it does happen perpetually in grace, that the sweet perfume of the lily-believer, shed abroad on the thorn-brake of the ungodly, turns it into a lily-garden. Such holy work among ungodly people is the truest and best "FLOWER MISSION". They do well who give flowers to cheer the poor in their dreary habitations, but they do better still who are themselves flowers in the places where they live. Be lilies, my dear brethren. Preach by your actions, preach by your kindness and by your love; and I feel quite sure that your influence will be a power for good. If the Holy Spirit helps all of you to stand among your associates as lilies among the thorns, the day will come when thorns will die out, and lilies will spring up on every side: sin will be banished, and grace will abound. An Australian gentleman told me yesterday that, in his colony, the arum lily abounds as much as weeds do with us. When will this happen spiritually on our side of the globe? Ah, when! Blessed Lord, when will you remove the curse? When will you bring in better days? These are bad times, where the thorns grow thicker and sharper than ever; so protect your lilies, increase their number, preserve their snowy whiteness, and delight yourself in them. We ask this for Jesus' sake. Amen.

20. UNDER HIS SHADOW

A BRIEF SACRAMENTAL DISCOURSE

DELIVERED AT MENTONE
TO ABOUT A SCORE OF BRETHREN

PRINTED IN THE SWORD AND TROWEL, FEBRUARY 1880

Original text quoted:

"He that dwelleth in the secret place of the Most High shall abide under the shadow of the Almighty." (Psalm 91:1)

Text for the second point:

"As the apple-tree among the trees of the wood so is my beloved among the sons. I sat down under his shadow with great delight, and his fruit was sweet to my taste." (Song of Solomon 2:3)

As with sin, so with sorrow of every sort: the Lord is the rock of our refuge. No sun shall smite us, nor any heat, because we are never out of Christ. The saints know where to fly, and they use their privilege.

When troubles, like a burning sun,
Beat heavy on their head,
To Christ their mighty Rock they run,
And find a pleasing shade.

(Henry Draper, *A Collection of Psalms and Hymns*)

II. Our second picture is that of THE TREE, which is to be found in the Song of Solomon 2:3 — "As the apple-tree among the trees of the wood, so is my beloved among the sons. I sat down under his shadow with great delight, and his fruit was sweet to my taste."

Here we have not so much refuge from trouble as special *rest in times of joy*. The spouse is happily wandering through a wood, glancing at many trees, and rejoicing in the music of the birds. One tree specially charms her: the citron with its golden fruit wins her admiration, and she sits under its shadow with great delight. Such was her beloved to her, the best among the good, the fairest of the fair, the joy of her joy, and the light of her delight. Such is Jesus to the believing soul.

The sweet influences of Christ are intended to give us a happy rest, and we ought to avail ourselves of them: "I sat down under his shadow." This was Mary's better part, which Martha well-nigh missed by being "cumbered about with much serving." (Lk. 10:30) That is the good old way in which we are to walk, the way in which we find rest for our souls. Papists and papistical persons, whose religion is all ceremonies, or all working, or all groaning, or all feeling, have never come to an end. We may say of their religion as of the law, that it made nothing perfect (Heb. 7:19); but, under the gospel, there is something finished, and that something is the sum and substance of our salvation, in which, therefore, there is rest for us, and we ought to sing, "I sat down."

Dear friends, is Christ to each one of us a place of sitting down? I do not mean a rest of idleness and self-content — God deliver us from that! But there is rest in a conscious grasp of Christ, a rest of contentment with him, as our all in all. God give us to know more of this. This shadow is also meant to yield perpetual solace, for the spouse did not merely come under it, but there she sat down as one that meant to stay. Continuance of repose and joy is purchased for us by our Lord's perfected work. Under the shadow she found food; she had no need to leave it to find one single needful thing, for the tree which shaded her also yielded fruit; nor did she need even to rise from her rest, but, sitting still, she feasted on the delicious fruit. You who know the Lord Jesus know also what this means.

The spouse never wished to go beyond her Lord. She knew no higher life than that of sitting under the Well-beloved's shadow. She passed the cedar, and oak, and every other goodly tree, but the apple-tree held her, and there she sat down. "Many there are who ask, who will show us any good? (Ps. 4:6) But as for us, O Lord, our heart is fixed, our heart is fixed, resting on you. We go no further, for you are our dwelling-place; we feel at home with you, and sit down beneath your shadow. Some Christians cultivate reverence at the expense of childlike love; they kneel down, but they dare not sit down. Our divine Friend and Lover does not will that it should be so; he would not have us stand on ceremony with him, but come boldly to him.

Let us be simple with him, then,
Not backward, stiff, or cold,
As tho' our Bethlehem could be
What Sinai was of old.

(Frederick William Faber)

Let us use his sacred name as a common word, as a household word, and run to him as to a dear familiar friend. Under his shadow, we are to feel that we are at home, and then he will make himself at home with us by becoming food to our souls, and giving spiritual refreshment to us while we rest.

The spouse does not here say that she reached up to the tree to gather its fruit, but she sat down on the ground in intense delight, and the fruit came to her where she sat. It is wonderful how Christ will come down to souls that sit beneath his shadow; if we can but be at home with Christ, he will sweetly commune with us. Has he not said, "Delight thyself also in the Lord, and he shall give thee the desires of thine heart"? (Ps. 37:4)

In this second form of the sacred shadow, the sense of awe [of being in the shade of the ROCK] gives place to that of restful delight in Christ. Have you ever figured in such a scene the sitter beneath the grateful shade of the fruitful tree? Have you not only possessed security, but experienced delight in Christ? Have you sung this?

I sat down under his shadow,
Sat down with great delight;
His fruit was sweet unto my taste,
And pleasant to my sight"

(Edward Cuthbert Bairstow)

This is as necessary an experience as it is joyful: necessary for many uses. The joy of the Lord is our strength (Neh. 8:10); and it is when we delight ourselves in the Lord that we have assurance of power in prayer. Here, faith develops and hope grows bright, while love

152

sheds abroad all the fragrance of her sweet spices. Oh, get you to the apple-tree, and find out who is fairest among the fair! Make the light of heaven the delight of your heart, and then be filled with heart's-ease, and revel in complete content.

These are mere surface thoughts. The subject deserves a series of discourses. Your best course, my beloved friends, will be to enlarge on these hints by a long personal experience of abiding under the shadow. May God the Holy Spirit lead you into it, and keep you there, for Jesus' sake!

21. THE APPLE TREE IN THE WOOD
NO. 1120

A SERMON DELIVERED ON LORD'S-DAY MORNING,
JULY 6TH, 1873
AT THE METROPOLITAN TABERNACLE, NEWINGTON

"As the apple tree among the trees of the wood, so is my beloved among the sons."
(Song of Solomon 2:3)

BY "the apple tree" was probably intended by the oriental writer to refer either to the citron, or the pomegranate, or the orange. I suppose he did not refer to the apple tree of our gardens, for it would scarcely be known to him. The word would not, however, be properly rendered if we confined it to any of the three fruit trees we have mentioned, or if we excluded our own apple from it, for the term "apple" comprehends all large round fruit not enclosed in a shell; and so we may, without making any mistake, think of the apple tree of our own English orchards, and yet the metaphor will stand good, except that the shadow of our apple tree at home is hardly so excellent a retreat from the sun as the shadow of the other trees included under the term. Our own apple tree will suffice us, however, and we shall not need to enter into any minute distinctions, or carry you away to Palestine. We can sit at home in England, and say with great propriety, if we love the Lord Jesus Christ, "As the apple tree among the trees of the wood, so is my beloved among the sons." The point of the metaphor is this: there are many trees of the forest, and they all have their uses, but when one is hungry and faint and thirsty, the forest trees yield no succour, and we must look elsewhere; they yield shelter, but not refreshing nutriment. If, however, in the midst of the wood, one discovers an apple tree, he there finds the refreshment that he needs; his thirst is alleviated and his hunger removed. Even so, the church here means to say that there are many things in the world which yield us a kind of satisfaction — many men, many truths, many institutions, many earthly comforts; but there are none which yield us the full solace that the soul requires; none which can give to the heart the spiritual food for which it hungers; Jesus Christ alone supplies the needs of the sons of men. As the apple tree is the exception to the forest trees in bearing fruit, as it stands on that account in contrast with the trees of the wood, so does Jesus our Beloved contrast with all others, and transcendently excel them,

An apple tree in simple beauty stands,
And waves its juicy treasure gracefully,
Among the barren trees which eroded the wood,
Of lofty form, but destitute of fruit:
So Jesus, 'midst the failing sons of men
Bears for my use the fruits of covenant love,
And fills my heart with rare delight and rest.

Wandering, as I have been during the last few days, up and down in the New Forest — the only real forest left in our country — and finding rest in its vast solitudes, this text has often occurred to me, and thus I can do no other than speak of it to you: "As the apple tree among the trees of the wood, so is my beloved among the sons." At the outset, we shall speak of *the tree which the fainting soul most desires*. We shall then remark that *it is no small wonder that the needy one finds an apple tree in so singular a position*. And, thirdly, we shall note *her very natural conduct when she found so desirable a tree in such a position* — she sat down under its shadow with great delight, and feasted on the delicious fruit.

I. First, then, our text speaks of THE TREE WHICH THE FAINTING SOUL MOST DESIRES.

Imagine yourself, upon some sultry day in autumn, as a wanderer in the leafy lanes of a great forest, where the grand cathedral aisles reach up before you to lengths immeasurable, or huge domes of foliage rise above you like a second sky. Imagine yourself roaming amid the ferns and brakes, trampling on the briars and hollies, or sitting down on mossy banks and knolls soft with leaves of green. Suppose also that you are hungry and thirsty, and that no rippling streams offer their cooling floods, while you are so far away from human call that, hungry though you might be, even to death, there would be no eye to see you, and consequently no hand outstretched for your help. In such a plight, it needs no imagination to conceive you as glancing to the trees, your only companions, and silently appealing to them for aid. Some of them look as if their bowing branches might sympathise if they could, others grotesquely grin at you, and most of them sternly refuse you succour by their solemn silence. You ask in vain of oak, or ash, or elm. Suppose you appeal to yonder stately tree which is the greatest of them all, the king of the forest, unequalled in greatness or girth. Admire its stupendous limbs, its gnarled roots, its bossy bark, the vast area beneath its boughs. You look up at it and think what a puny creature you are, and how brief has been your life compared with its duration. You try to contemplate the storms which have swept over it, and the suns which have shone on it. Great, however, as it is, it cannot help you. If it were a thousand times higher, and its topmost boughs swept the stars, yet it could minister no aid to you. This is a fit picture of the attempt to find consolation in systems of religion which are recommended to you because they are widely followed. Here is a religion which has been patronised by kings and nobles for centuries, a religion which has the support of the great and fashionable at the present hour; will not this content you? Is it not enough to belong to the same religion as the majority, especially when that majority includes the aristocrats of the land? Is not the voice of the people the voice of God? What more do you want? Why should you be different? Alas, the great tree is not a fruit-bearing tree. The true Christian, believing in Jesus Christ with all his heart, counts it no desirable thing to be found in the broad road where many go, for he remembers that his Master spoke of it as leading to destruction: majorities are nothing to him, for he remembers that "strait is the gate and narrow is the way which leadeth unto life, and few there be that find it." (Mat. 7:13) He does not reckon that the greatness of the company will make right wrong, or overawe the judge of all, or make eternal punishment one whit the less intolerable. We do not desire the way of the multitude; the way of the Crucified we delight to follow. It is not the mightiest tree of the forest that we look to with hope, but to the Lord Jesus, our Beloved, who is the apple tree among the trees of the wood; his fruit is sweet to our taste. He is the way, the truth, and the life (Jn. 14:6) to us, his Person is most dear to us, and his teachings are the food of our spirits. Happy are you who dare to be singular with Christ. Blessed are you who have found the narrow way which leads to life eternal. Blessed are you because you are not carried away with the strong current and fashion of the age, but have heard the voice that says, "Be not conformed to this world, but be ye transformed by the renewing of your minds." (Rom. 12:2) Wisdom tells the hungry man to prefer the solitary apple tree to whole groves of the hugest oaks or beeches; and wisdom given from above has brought you, O believer in Jesus, to prefer your Redeemer to all the great ones of the earth.

Suppose that in your wanderings to and fro you come upon another tree which is said to be *the oldest* in the forest. We all of us have a veneration for age. Antiquity has many charms. I scarcely know if antiquity and novelty should run a race for popular favour, which one might win. Now-a-days, we are pestered by a class of men who would fain fascinate our nation to error by the charms of antiquity. They tell us that a certain ceremony, though no trace of it is to be found in Scripture, must be venerable because it was practiced in the fourth century; and they imagine that worship in buildings which were

155

founded by Saxons, and garnished by Normans, must be particularly acceptable with God. To be ancient, is it not a great advantage? As cleanliness is next to godliness, surely antiquity must he next to orthodoxy. Yet if there is no Scripture to warrant an ancient ceremony, it is only an ancient farce. There are some things which are so old as to be rotten, worm-eaten, and fit only to be put away. Many things called ancient are just clever counterfeits, or, where they possess some truth, they are but the bones and carcasses of that which was once good when life filled it with energy and power. There is an "old way which wicked men have trodden" (Job 22:15), as well as a good old way in which the righteous walk (Ps. 24:3-5). We cannot be certain that a thing is right because it is old, for Satan is old, and sin is old, and death is old, and hell is old; yet none of these things are right and desirable on that account. No, Jesus Christ our Lord, since the day in which we have known him by faith, has quietened our conscience, calmed our fears, and has given us joy and peace through believing. We are not to be seduced from him by all the antiquated falsehoods which may weave their spells around us. Old even to decay may be the trees in which other travellers delight, but as for us, we choose the tree off heavenly fruit — the apple tree is our choice, Jesus is our Beloved. Ritualists may glory in their fourth century doctrines, their fathers, their councils, and their ancient customs; the Bible is primitive enough for us, the cross of our Lord Jesus Christ is venerable enough for us; we are content with him and want no more. To us, the main thing is to find food for our souls, the bread that never perishes, the fruit which quenches our desperate thirst. We have found it in the Saviour, and from the Saviour we will not depart.

It may be that in the midst of the forest, while you are hungry and thirsty, you come upon a strangely *beautiful tree*: its proportions are exact, and, as you gaze at it from a distance, you exclaim — "How wonderful are the works of God!" And you begin to think of those trees of the Lord which are full of sap, the cedars of Lebanon which he has planted. (Ps. 104:16) You stand under it, and look up among the majestic boughs and spreading branches, and you again admire the beauty of nature as it comes from the hand of the Most High. But beauty can never satisfy hunger, and when a man is dying of thirst, it is vain to talk to him of symmetry and taste. He wants food. This reminds us that now-a-days there are some who try to satisfy the souls of men with beauty. Look at their processions: who would not be charmed with their varied costumes, their spangled banners, their gilded crosses, and their melodious hymns? Listen to their choir; is not the singing perfection? If you want a concert on the Sabbath day, and do not like to attend a theatre, you can find it in a cathedral and in many a parish church, and please the Lord almost as well. If you want to have your senses gratified, and cannot conscientiously attend an opera on Sunday, you can have ear and eye gratified at church, yes, and the nose as well in some places! And these amusements they mistake for religious exercises. Compared with the plainness of worship which we follow, our casting out of everything like symbols, our abhorrence of everything that would take away the mind from God himself, and fix it on secondary objects — compared with all this, their worship is enchanting indeed to the carnal mind, and we do not wonder that those who are led by taste should follow after it. But oh, if a man once hungers after the bread of heaven, his taste for finery will be reduced to a very secondary position as a governing power of his mind. If once the soul craves after God, after peace, pardon, truth, reconciliation, holiness, it will seek the Lord Jesus, the apple tree, and forget the other trees, however shapely they may be. "These bear no fruit for me", says the hungry soul. The awakened conscience listens to the chant as it is echoed among the massive pillars, and watches the smoke as it rises like a cloud among the arches of the roof, and he cries, "What are chanting and smoke to me? I want a Saviour." He sees the procession, and after he has gazed at it, he says, "What are these mummeries to me? I want washing in the blood of Christ." As the incense smokes to heaven, he says to himself, "Oh for the incense of the Saviour's merit. What are these gums of Araby to me if they should burn all day long?" He turns away, sick and faint in heart, from all the gew-gaws and outward trappings of modern Popery, and he cries, "O

156

God, you are a Spirit, and they that worship thee must worship thee in spirit and in truth. (Jn. 4:23-24) I want you, O my God; I want spiritual life within myself, that I might commune with you; and where can I find it but in my Saviour? He gives it to me; he is the only fruit-bearing tree amongst the trees of the wood."

We will pursue our investigations in the forest, and, while doing so, we will come upon some very *wonderful* trees. I have seen just lately instances in which branches are curiously interlaced with one another; the beech sends out a long drooping bough, and, lest it should not be able to support itself, another bough strikes up from below to buttress it, or descends from above and clasps it, and the boughs actually grow into one another. Strange things may be observed in the undisturbed woods, which are not to be seen in our hedgerow trees, or discerned in our gardens. Trees have odd habits of their own, and grow marvellously if left to their own sweet way. I have stood under them and said, "How can this be? This is singular indeed! How can they grow like this? What wonderful interlacings and intertwinings and gnarlings and knottings!" Yes, but if a man were hungry and thirsty, he would not be satisfied with these curiosities. So is it with some preaching that I know of. If you regard it from the standpoint of literary excellence, you confess that it is wonderful. There are great orators and deep thinkers to be found to whom I would not presume to hold a candle, whose performances are really good. I have felt, after I have heard their essays, like the Primitive Methodist who went to dinner with the squire, and then pronounced the blessing afterwards — "Lord, we thank you that we do not have such a good dinner as this every day, for it is too rich to agree with us." I have felt just like that after hearing such fine oration, though, mark you, I did not remember a bit of it after it was over, and my heart was none the better. How many sermons are published now-a-days, as well as preached, which are full of what is called thought. By the cant word "thought", is generally means contradicting the plain meaning of Scripture, and starting new notions. A man who preaches plainly what God reveals is said to be an echo of the Puritans, a dealer in platitudes, a repeater at second-hand of exploded dogmas; but to find out some new lie every week to tell your people, to shake their faith in inspiration every time you open your mouth, and make them believe that there is nothing certain, but that everything is a mere matter of opinion — that is "thought and culture" in these days; and there are in certain dissenting pulpits the most miserable specimens of this school, and in the pews a number of their silly admirers.

Brethren, some of us are always too old-fashioned to be led astray in that way, and, what is more, we have such an awful appetite. We are possessed of such a dreadful hunger, and such insatiable thirst, that we dare not go away from the apple tree because we want to be always eating; we dare not go away from Jesus Christ because we are always needing pardon, always wanting peace, always wanting fresh life; and, provided we can retain our hold on Jesus, we are not particular about the way in which some of these wonderful trees twist their boughs. We do not feel concerned about the marvels of modern thought, or the resurrection of ancient errors.

Let everlasting glories crown
Thy head, my Saviour and my Lord;
Thy hands have brought salvation down,
And writ the blessings in the word.

What if we trace the globe around,
And search from Britain to Japan,
There shall be no religion found
So just to God, so safe to man.

157

**Should all the forms that men devise,
Assault my soul with treacherous art,
I'd call them vanities and lies,
And bind the gospel to my heart.**

(Isaac Watts)

But as we are wandering in the forest and are still hungry, I hear some one saying, "Ah, here is the place for food; you need not boast of your apple tree: the ground is covered with fruit beneath this noble tree." I look up — it is autumn time — and I see a huge tree loaded with beech nuts, which fall from it like rain. "Here is the place for food." Was that a human voice I heard? No, it was the grunting of a herd of swine. See how content they are — how happy they are munching the nuts as they fall from the trees. Yonder is a grove of oaks, all shedding their acorns, and how delighted the swine are! How they fatten on the spoil! "Will you not come here?" they seem to say, as they munch in comfort. "Will you not come here? Do not tell us about trees which bear no fruit: there is fruit enough here surely." Even thus I hear a voice from the Exchange — "Here are the trees which bear us golden apples; come here and be filled." I hear it from those who cater for public amusements — "Here are the fruits that can delight the soul. Here is the place to spend a happy day." And so I hear it from the gay followers of vice — "This dalliance, this dance, this flowing bowl, this sweet-sounding viol, these are real joys!" Yes, but to you, to you, who choose them. Beech nuts and acorns are good enough for swine. To you who can find comfort, solid comfort, in the gain of merchandise, or in the pleasures of sin, or in the delights of pomp, these things are good enough; but a *man*, a God made man, a man into whom God has put a new heart — not a swine's heart, but a man's heart — which lacks apples, not acorns, wants spiritual food, food for an immortal nature; and there is no such food to be found short of the Lord Jesus Christ, for he, and he only, is the apple tree among the trees of the wood.

I might enlarge, but I will not. I will simply say what every child of God here knows, that the Lord Jesus Christ has given to us, ever since we found him, everything we have wanted. When we came to him, we were worn out with faintness; we were hungry to get rid of our sins, but we are now rid of them, every one of them. We went up to his cross, and, as we saw him hanging on it, the strings which bound our burden to our shoulders began to crack, our load rolled off into his sepulchre, and we have never seen it since. We have half fancied we have felt it again, but we never have, for, if our sins are searched for, they cannot be found, yes, they shall not be, says the Lord. You remember when you first came to that precious tree on which the Saviour died, and found that your sin was blotted out, that you were accepted in the Beloved, and were made to be from now on an heir of heaven. Oh, the lusciousness of the fruit which you gave then! Oh, the delightful quiet of that shadow under which you sat that day, blessed be his name! You had searched among the other trees, but you found no fruit there: you tried to rest in the shadow of other boughs, but you never rested till on that blood-stained tree of the cross. You saw your sin put away and your salvation secured, and then you rested and were satisfied.

But if the Lord Jesus Christ has not only satisfied us as to the past, see what he is doing for us in the present! My dear hearers, there are some of you who have never known yet what it is to be perfectly happy. I do not call it being perfectly happy to be full of excitement and laughter and apparent joy, and then go home in the evening and sit down and feel disgusted with it all. That is the froth of fancy, and not the true wine of joy.

But to be perfectly happy is to be able to think about all things on earth, and all things in heaven, and yet say, "I lack nothing; there is nothing I desire, nothing I pine after; I am saved, and I am a child of God — the eternal God is my own Father. I am on my way to

158

his glorious house, and if death should strike me now, it would be no matter, or if I am spared for another fifty years it will make no difference to me, for all is well, and could not be better. If there are crosses in my lot, they are God-sent crosses; if I have troubles, they work to my lasting good; if I lose, I am a gainer by my losses; if I have all things, I see God in all things; and if I have nothing, yet I see all things in my God: nothing more can I desire. Christ is all, and Christ is mine, and therefore I have all things." Now, that is the position of the Christian this day. He sits down under the shadow of Christ, and Christ's fruit is sweet to him. Let me ask you, can you imagine any other place where such peace of mind or such happiness can be enjoyed? Why, I know sick people who are far happier in their sickness than worldlings are in their health, and I know poor men who are infinitely more at peace, and more contented, than rich men who do not have the Saviour. Jesus Christ alone satisfies us for the past, and delights us in the present.

Then as for the future: the man who has found Christ looks forward to it not merely with complacency, not simply without dread, but with a joyful expectancy and hope. Those things that make others tremble make us glad. There is such a thing as dying: thank God, there is. Who wants to live here always? That narrow stream which separates this country from the better land must be forded by each of us. Who would have it otherwise? Instead of being afraid to cross it, we, like Dr. Watts, find no safety in any religion, unless it is:

So just to God, so safe for man,

— which will land us now in heaven.

The judgement? The Christian does not quail at the thought. Who shall lay anything to his charge? (Rom 8:33) The coming of the Lord? The believer has no fearof it, no, it is his greatest hope. Eternity, and its never-ending cycles? He does not dread it, for it is to him the climax of his joy; it is to be everlasting. O, happy people who have Christ; happy souls who rest in Jesus! They may say what none others can — "As the apple tree among the trees of the wood, so is my Beloved among the sons." Dear hearer, is he your Beloved? Can you claim him as your own? If you can, then I am sure you will bear witness, as the text does, to the satisfying power of the Saviour, and declare with Ralph Erskine:

What fool soever disagrees,
My sweet experience proves
That Jesus is the tree of trees
Among a thousand groves"

II. The spouse spoke of the tree which she most desired: THE WONDER WAS THAT SHE FOUND IT.

It was an apple tree, but it was not a fruit tree in a garden, and not in a vineyard; it was "among the trees of the wood." Who would know of so great a rarity as an apple tree in a wood if he were not first told of it? So Jesus Christ, at this present day, is not known to all mankind. It is a most unhappy thought that probably the majority of the human race has not heard of the Saviour at all, and a very large proportion has never heard of him except through misrepresentations. Only a small minority of our fellow men knows anything about the Saviour.

What millions never knew the Lord!
What millions hate him when he's known!

Even in our own country, you will not find it a difficult thing to meet with people who are totally ignorant of Christ. Try it, and you will find in country towns and in hamlets men

159

grown up who could not give you an answer to this question: "How is it that the death of Jesus saves the soul?" No, who do not even know the fact that Jesus Christ came into the world to save sinners. "Well", say you, "we know the rural districts are ignorant." Yes, but they are far superior in light to parts of London. You can readily find children in our streets, and, what is worse, artisans in our workshops, to whom the bare name of Jesus may be known, but anything like the doctrine of his substitutionary atonement is a thing of which they have not heard. Living in the light they remain in darkness, amid a thousand lamps they cannot see. One of the problems that may most surprise us is the existence of such dense ignorance in people who live in intimate connection with instructed people. If you want the grossest ignorance, probably you would not find it in Peking or Timbuctoo, but in London or New York. Where the greatest light is, there the shadows are deepest. Men nearest to the church are often furthest from God.

You cannot easily find an apple tree in a great forest. If you were put down in the middle of a forest, and told there was an apple tree there, you might wander for many a day before you discovered it, and often go over your own footsteps, lost in endless mazes; but you would not find the object of your search. Thus, though there is a Saviour, men have not found him, and there may even be souls here present who long for what Jesus is able to give, and yet have not discovered him. You know all about him in the letter of his Word, but you cannot find him spiritually, and I hear you cry, "Oh, that I knew where I might find him." (Job 23:3) I know I am speaking to some such. You have been going up and down for months with your prayers, and your tears, and your good works. You have been trying to do all you can to save yourselves, but you find your own actions to be barren trees, and you know that there is an apple tree somewhere, but you cannot find it. Ah, poor soul! You are like the Ethiopian eunuch, when he was asked if he understood what he read, he gave the answer, "How can I unless some man should guide me?" (Acts 8:31)

Do you not wonder that the spouse found her apple tree among the trees of the wood? The fact is, none ever find it unless they are led there, and none can lead a soul to that apple tree but the eternal Spirit of God. He can make use of his ministers, and he does; and therefore, brethren in the ministry, let us always be preaching about this apple tree. Let us preach Jesus Christ, let us make tracks to the tree of life. Now, whatever we do preach, let us preach Jesus Christ. I have found, wherever I have been during the last month, that though there might not be a road to this place or that, there was sure to be a London road. Now, if your sermon does not happen to have the doctrine of election or the doctrine of final perseverance in it, let it always have Christ in it. Have a road to London, a road to Christ, in every sermon. Still, the plainest preaching will require the Spirit of God to go with it, or else the soul will hear about this glorious tree, and about the sweetness of its fruit, but will never find the shadow, and will never eat the dainty apples. Have you come to Christ, dear brother and sister? Then give God the glory for it. Jesus led you, and his Spirit guided you; praise and bless his holy name!

Now, is it not a strange place for an apple tree to be found in — found in a wood? We seldom hear of such a thing; an apple tree should grow in a garden. How should it be found in a forest? And is it not a strange thing that a Saviour is found for us among men — not among angels? You shall search for a Saviour among "the helmed cherubim and worded seraphim" as long as you will, but he is not there. The Saviour is found in a manger at Bethlehem, in a carpenter's shop at Nazareth. Among the poor and needy is he seen while he sojourns amongst the sons of men. As I was turning this text over in my mind, I thought, "Ah, and what strange trees this tree grew among, for there it stands with a gallows tree on either side, and two thieves hanging on them. "He was numbered with the transgressors." (Is. 53:12; Mk. 15:28) Not among you, O you cedars, not among you, O mighty oaks, but among the bushes of the desert; among the trees accursed was Jesus found. "He made his grave with the wicked." (Is. 53:9)

160

As in some sere and unproductive wood
One lovely, fruit-producing apple-tree,
Bright contrast to the ruined thousands round;
So in this populous but vicious world
O thou Desire of nations, didst thou stand.

Now, there is something very sweet about this, because a wood is the very place where we most love to find Christ growing. If I had come the other day on an apple tree in the forest, and it had happened to be the time of ripe fruit, I should have felt no compunction of conscience in taking whatever I was able to reach, for a tree growing in the forest is free to all comers. Should there be a hungry one beneath its bough, he need not say, "May I?" when his month waters at the golden fruit: he need not say, "It would be stealing; I am unfit to take it; I am unworthy of it." Man, if there is an apple tree in the forest, no one can keep it for himself or deny your right to it, for each wanderer has a right to whatever fruit he can gather. The animals have rights of pasturage, and the birds have rights of nesting, and have rights of feeding. Pluck away, man, and eat to your fill. The shadows and the fruits of forest trees are free to all who need them. This ought to delight any seeking soul here this morning. Jesus Christ is not hedged about in the Scriptures, as some theologians would fain guard him from coming souls; the Lord has planted no protection of thorns and hollies by saying, "You must bring with you preparations for grace; you must feel that, and feel the other, and only then may you dare to come to Christ." It is a gross error to tell someone to do something, and be something, before he believes in Jesus. No, there he stands with no hedge about him, and whoever will may partake freely. If you hear the gospel call, your reply to it should be with the poet:

Just as I am, thy love unknown
Has broken every barrier down;
Now to rely on thee alone,
O Lamb of God, I come.

(Charlotte Elliott)

Christ has no barriers around him to keep you from him. If there are any, they are of your own making.

None are excluded hence but those
Who do themselves exclude.
Welcome the learned and polite,
The ignorant and rude.

Whoever comes shall be welcome to this priceless apple tree. There is some comfort, therefore, in thinking that he grows among the trees of the wood.

III. It was little wonder that when the spouse, all hungry and faint, came upon this apple tree in the forest, SHE ACTED AS SHE DID.

Straightway, she sat down under its shadow with great delight, and its fruit was sweet to her taste. She looked up at it; that was the first thing she did, and she perceived that it met her double need. The sun was hot, and there was the shadow: she was faint, and there was the fruit. Now, see how Jesus meets the needs of all who come to him. God's anger, like the hot noonday sun, falls on me, so how can I escape it? There is no escape from the anger of God except by an interposer. What is a shadow? Is it not caused by the interposition of the bough, or the rock, or whatever it may be, which comes between us

161

and the sun? If we sit under a tree in the shadow, it is because the tree receives the heat, and so we escape from it. Jesus Christ's great office is as the Interposer, the Mediator, the Substitute, the Atonement, the Sacrifice; and, when we hide beneath him, we are screened. God's wrath cannot fall on us because it has fallen on him on our behalf.

When Christ my screen is interposed
Between the sun and me
My joyful heart and lips unclosed,
Adore the glorious tree.

That is a beautiful picture in Solomon's Song where the king is said to ride in his chariot of love. He takes his spouse with him, and they ride together in his palanquin, and it has over it a canopy. Did you ever notice what it is made of? It is said, "The covering of it of purple, the midst thereof being paved with love," (Song 3:10), for truly the only interposition between us and the sun of God's wrath is the purple canopy of the atoning blood. Is it not delightful to sit down beneath the scarlet canopy of the Saviour's blood, and feel, "God cannot smite me: he has smitten his Son; payment he cannot demand the second time. If Jesus suffered in my place, how can God make me suffer again for sin? Where was the justice of the Most High in punishing an immaculate Substitute, and then punish men for whom that Substitute endured his wrath?" This is the cool, calm, holy shadow under which we abide.

But then, the spouse also found that she herself was thirsty, and that the fruit of the tree exactly met her case. Our inner life needs sustenance and food; now, in the Lord Jesus is life, and the bread of life. "He is that bread which came down from heaven, whereof if a man eat, he shall live for ever." (Jn, 6:51) Oh to get a heart full of Christ, to get a whole Christ into one's innermost soul, to have him abide in you! This is bliss! Then your soul feels, "It is enough: I have all things, for I have Jesus." Let us therefore seek at this time, and especially this afternoon in our meditations, and when we come to the communion table this evening, to abide under the shadow of Jesus, and there to be found eating the abundance of his fruit.

One thing more must be noted: the spouse, when she had begun to enjoy the provision and the shade, and had sat down under it as if she intended to say, "I never mean to leave this place; in this delicious shadow I mean to repose forever"; then she also began to tell of it to others. In the text, she describes Christ as the apple tree, and gives her reason for so calling him — "I sat down under his shadow with great delight, and his fruit was sweet to my taste." Experience must be the ground on which we found our descriptions. If a preacher wants to preach with power, let him tell what he has felt and tasted and handled. It is of little use to say Christ is precious unless you can add, "I have found him so." Therefore, the church brings in her own experience — "Sweet shade! I there sat down as one at home, and there regaled my soul with most delicious fare." She could not hold her tongue about her Beloved. She must speak out; she could not retain the secret of this apple tree, saying to herself, "Others may go to it, and so perhaps when I go another time there may be nothing left for me; but the Samaritan woman spread the news. (Jn. 429) She has it set down in black and white in the inspired volume, as an everlasting testimony, that there is an apple tree among the trees of the wood, of which she had eaten, and so others might eat of it too, and enjoy the same sweetness for themselves.

This morning, every renewed heart desires that every other heart should know the Saviour. I can speak well of my Lord and Master. I do not know that I can say anything better of him than most of his people can, for the experience of the saints is much alike; but I can say this: if there is happiness beneath the sky, Jesus can give it you; if there is peace and rest to a jaded soul, Jesus can give it you; if there is a delight, a brimming

162

delight, an overflowing delight, if there is that which can make the eyes sparkle, and the pulse beat right merrily, and the blood to leap in the veins, it is when Jesus Christ is consciously ours, and we are resting in him. I am sure, if there were an apple tree in any forest, and it were once found out, everybody would be taken to see it, for it would be such an attraction. There would be many paths to it, and everybody who had been in the forest and seen it would tell his neighbours. Now, I beseech you who have found the Saviour to be telling others what you know about him, and try to lead others to look to him.

You cannot make them feed upon him, but God can; and if you can lead them to the tree, who knows but God will give them spiritual hunger, and lead them to feed as you have fed. O you silent Christians, you silent Christians, who neither by your tongue, nor your pen, nor by any other way, ever tell about Christ, I do not know what to make of you! I wonder the seats you sit on do not push you off and speak instead of you, and that the stones of the street do not cry out against you as you pass over them. Why, what can you be made of, to be saved from going down to hell, and not want others to be saved too! Shame on you! Shame on me also whenever I am silent about such a blessed salvation, such a divine redemption. I would fain set your tongues going about this blessed apple tree among the trees of the wood. There is nothing about which you can speak so freely, without fear of exaggeration. All the world has been talking about the Shah of Persia; I wish they would talk half as much about the Christ of God. All the good you will ever get out of the great Shah you may see with your eyes shut, but the benefit that comes from the King of heaven to your own souls, and ten thousands of other souls, is unlimited. Cry the Saviour up, beloved! Set him on a high throne; give him the best of your thoughts, the best of your words, and the best of your actions. Give him of your time and your substance. He deserves to have honour above all the sons of men, for he is the best of all. As the apple tree to the hungry man excels all other trees, so does Jesus excel all other loves. Let us give him today our hearts' warmest love, and praise him forever and forever. May God grant it, for his name's sake!

22. UNDER THE APPLE TREE

NO. 3249

A COMMUNION SERMON
FOUND IN THE SWORD AND TROWEL, MAY 1879
AT THE METROPOLITAN TABERNACLE, NEWINGTON

"I sat down under his shadow with great delight, and his fruit was sweet to my taste." (Song of Solomon 2:3)

[Another Sermon by Mr. Spurgeon on the same text is No. 1120 in The Metropolitan Tabernacle Pulpit: *The Apple Tree in the Wood*]

CHRIST *known should be Christ used.* The spouse knew her Beloved to be like a fruit-bearing tree, and at once she sat down under his shadow, and fed upon his fruit. It is a pity that we know so much about Christ, and yet enjoy him so little. May our experience keep pace with our knowledge, and may that experience be composed of a practical using of our Lord. Jesus casts a shadow, let us sit under it: Jesus yields fruit, let us taste the sweetness of it. Depend upon it that the way to learn more is to use what you know, and, more over, the way to learn a truth thoroughly is to learn it experimentally. You know a doctrine beyond all fear of contradiction when you have proved it for yourself by personal test and trial. The bride in the Song as good as says, "I am certain that my Beloved casts a shadow, for I have sat under it, and I am persuaded that he bears sweet fruit, for I have tasted of it." The best way of demonstrating the power of Christ to save is to trust in him, and be yourself saved by him; and of all those who are sure of the divinity of our holy faith, there are none so certain as those who feel its divine power upon themselves. You may reason yourself into a belief of the gospel, and you may by further reasoning keep yourself orthodox; but a personal trial, and an inward knowing of the truth are incomparably to best evidences. If Jesus be as an apple the among the trees of the wood, do, not keep away from him, but sit under his shadow and taste his fruit. He is a Saviour, do not believe that fact and yet remain unsaved. As far as Christ is known to you, so far make, use of him. Is not this sound common sense? We would further remark that *we are at liberty to make every possible use of Christ.* Shadow and fruit may berth be enjoyed. Christ in his infinite condescension exists, for needy souls. Oh, let us say it over again; it is a bold word, but it is true, as Christ Jesus, our Lord existed for the benefit of his people. A Saviour only exists to save. A physician lives to heal. The good Shepherd lives, yea, dies, for his sheep. Our Lord Jesus Christ hath wrapped us about his heart; we are intimately interwoven with all his offices, with all his honours, with all his traits of character, with all that he has done, and with all that he has yet to do. The sinners' Friend lives for sinners, and sinners may have him and use him to the uttermost. He is as free to us as the air we breathe. What are fountains for but that the thirsty may drink? What is the harbour for but that storm-tossed barques may there find refuge? What is Christ for, but that poor guilty ones like ourselves may come to him, and look and live, and afterwards may have all our needs supplied out of his fullness?

We have thus the door set open for us, and we pray that the Holy Spirit may help us to enter in while we notice in the text two things which we pray that you may enjoy to the full. First, *the heart's rest in Christ:* "I sat down under his shadow with great delight;" and secondly, *the heart's refreshment in Christ:* "his fruit was set to my taste."

I. To begin with, we have here THE HEART'S REST IN CHRIST.

164

To set this out, let us notice the character of the person who uttered this sentence. She who said, "I sat down under his shadow with great delight," was *one who had known before what weary travel meant, and therefore valued rest.* The man who has never laboured knows nothing of the sweetness of repose. The loafer who has eaten bread he never earned, from whose brow there never oozed a drop of honest sweat, does not deserve rest, and knows not what it is. It is to the labouring man that rest is sweet; and when at last we come, toil worn with many miles of weary plodding, to a shaded place where we may comfortably "sit down," then are we filled with delight.

The spouse had been seeking her Beloved, and in looking for him she had asked where she was likely to find him. "Tell me," says she, "O thou whom my soul loveth, where thou feelest, where thou makest thy flock to rest at noon." He told her to go and seek him by the footsteps of the flock. She did go her way, but after while she came to this resolution; "I will *sit down* under his shadow." Many of you have been sorely wearied with going your way to find peace. Some of you tried ceremonies, and multiplied them, and the priest came to your help; but he mocked your hearts' distress. Others of you sought by various systems of thought to come to an anchorage; but, tossed from billow to billow, you found no rest upon the seething sea of speculation. More of you tried by your good works to go in rest to your consciences. You multiplied your prayers, you poured out floods of tears; you hoped, by alms-giving and by the like, that some merit might accrue to you, and that your heart might feel acceptance with God, and so have rest. You toiled and toiled, like the men that were in the vessel with Jonah, when they rowed hard to bring their ship to land, but could not, for the sea wrought and was tempestuous. There was no escape for you that way, and so you were driven to another way, even, to rest in Jesus. My heart looks back to the time when I was under a sense of sin, and sought with all my soul to find peace, but could not discover it, high or low, in any place beneath the sky; yet when I read in John Newton's hymn,

I saw One hanging on a tree,
In agony and blood,
Who fixed his languid eyes on me,
As near his cross I stood

— as the Substitute for sin, then my heart sat down under his shadow with great delight. My heart reasoned thus with herself — Did Jesus suffer in my stead? Then I shall not suffer. Did he bear my sin? Then I do not bear it. Did God accept his Son as my Substitute? Then he will never smite *me*. Was Jesus acceptable with God as my sacrifice? Then what contents the Lord may well enough content me, so, I will go no further, but "sit down under his shadow," and enjoy a delightful rest.

She who said, "I sat down under his shadow with great delight," could appreciate shade, for she had been sunburnt. This was her exclamation, "Look not upon me, because, I am black, because the sun hath looked upon me." She knew what heat meant, what the burning sun meant; and therefore shade was pleasant to her. You know nothing about the deliciousness of shade till you travel in a thoroughly hot country; then you are delighted with it. Did you ever feel the heat of divine wrath? Did the great Sun that Sun without variableness or shadow of a turning-ever dart, his hottest rays upon you — the rays of his holiness and justice? Did you cower down beneath the scorching beams of that great light, and say, "We are consumed by thine anger?" If you have ever felt *that*, you have found it a very blessed thing to come under the shadow of Christ's atoning sacrifice. A shadow, you know, is cast by a body coming between us and the light and heat, and our Lord's most blessed body has come between us and the scorching sun of divine justice, so that we sit under the shadow of his mediation with great delight.

And now, if any other sun begins to scorch us, we fly to our Lord. If domestic troubles, or business care, or satanic temptation, or inward corruption oppresses us, we hasten to Jesus' shadow, to hide under him, and there "sit down" in the cool refreshment with great delight. The interposition of our blessed Lord is the cause of our inward quiet. The sun cannot scorch *me*, for it scorched *him*. My troubles need not trouble me, for he has taken my trouble, and I have left it in his hands. "I sat down under his shadow."

Mark well these two things concerning the spouse. She knew what it was to be weary, and she knew what it was to be sunburnt; and just in proportion as you, also, know these two things, your valuation of Christ will rise. You who have never pined under the wrath of God have never prized the Saviour. Water is of small value in this land of brooks and rivers, and so you commonly sprinkle the roads with it; but I warrant you that, if you were making a day's march over burning sand, a cup of cold water would be worth a king's ransom; and so, to thirsty souls, Christ is precious, but to none beside.

Now, when the spouse was sitting down, restful and delighted, *she was overshadowed*. She says, "I sat down under his shadow." I do not know a more delightful state of mind than to feel quite overshadowed by our beloved Lord. Here is my black sin, but there is his precious blood overshadowing my sin, and hiding it for ever. Here is my condition by nature, an enemy to God; but he who reconciled me to God by his blood has overshadowed that, also, so that I forget that, I was once an enemy in the joy of being now a friend. I am very weak, but he is strong, and his strength overshadows my feebleness. I am very poor; but he hath all riches, and his riches overshadow my poverty. I am, most unworthy; but he is so worthy that, if I use his name, I shall receive as much as if I were worthy; his worthiness doth overshadow my unworthiness. It is very precious to put the truth the other way, and say,-If there be anything good in me, it is not God when I compare myself with him, for his goodness quite eclipses and overshadows it. Can I say that, I love him? So I do, but I hardly dare call it love, for his love overshadows it. Did I suppose that I served him?

So I would, but my poor service is not worth mentioning in comparison with what he has done for me. Did I think I had any degree of holiness? I must not deny what his Spirit works in me; but when I think of his immaculate life, and all his divine perfections, where am I? What am I? Have you not sometimes felt this? Have you not been so overshadowed and hidden under your Lord that you became as nothing? I knew myself what it is to feel that, if I die in a workhouse, is does not matter so long as my Lord is glorified. Mortals may cast out my name as evil, if they likes; but what matters it since his dear name shall one day be printed in stars athwart the sky? Let him overshadow me; I delight that it should be so.

The spouse tells us that, when she became quite overshadowed, then *she felt great delight*. Great "I" never has great delight, for it cannot bear to own a greater than itself, but the humble believer finds his delight in being overshadowed by his Lord. In the shade of Jesus we have more delight than in any fancied light of our own. The spouse had *great* delight. I trust that you Christian people do have great delight; and if not, you ought to ask yourselves whether you really are the people of God. I like to see a cheerful countenance; yes, and to hear of raptures in the hearts of those who are God's saints. There are people who seem to think that religion and gloom are married, and must never be divorced. Pull down the blinds on Sunday, and darken the rooms; if you have a garden or a rose in flower, try to forget that there are such beauties; are you not to serve God as dolorously as you can? Put your book under your arm, and crawl to your place of worship in as mournful a manner as if you were being marched to the whipping-post. Act thus if you will; but give me that religion which cheers my heart, fires my soul, and fills me with enthusiasm and delight, for that is likely to be the religion of heaven, and it agrees with the experience of the inspired Song.

Although I trust that we know what, delight means, I question if we have enough of it to describe ourselves as *sitting down* in the enjoyment of it. Do you give yourselves enough time to sit at Jesus' feet? *There* is the place of delight, do you abide in it? Sit down under his shadow. "I have no leisure," cries one. Try and make a little. Steal it from your sleep if you cannot get it anyhow else. Grant leisure to your heart. It would be a great pity if a man never spent five minutes with his wife, but was forced to be always hard at work. Why, that is slavery, is it not? Shall we not then have time to commune with our Best-beloved? Surely, somehow or other, we can squeeze out, a little season in which we shall have nothing else to do but to sit down under his shadow with great delight. When I take my Bible and want to feed on it for myself, I generally get thinking about, preaching upon the text, and what I should say to you from it. This will not do; I must get away from that, and forget that there is a Tabernacle, that I may sit personally at Jesus feet. And, oh, there is an intense delight in being overshadowed by him! He is near you, and you know it. His dear presence is as certainly with you as if you could see him, for his influence surrounds you. Often have I felt as if Jesus leaned over me, as a friend might look over my shoulder. Although no cool shade comes over your brow, yet you may as much feel his shadow as if it did, for your heart grows calm: and if you have been wearied with the family, or troubled with the church, or vexed with yourself, you come down from the chamber where you have seen your Lord and you feel brand for the battle of life — ready for its troubles and its temptations, because you have seen the Lord.

"I sat down," said she, "under his shadow with *great delight*." How great that delight was she could not tell, but she, sat down as one overpowered with it, needing to sit still under the load of bliss. I do not like to talk much about the secret delights of Christians, because there are always same around us who do not understand our meaning; but I will venture to say this much,-that, if worldlings could but even guess what are the secret joys of believers, they would give their eyes to share them with us. We have troubles, and we admit it, we expect to have them; but we have joys which are frequently excessive. We should not like others to be witnesses of the delight which now and then tosses our soul into a very tempest of joy. You know what it means, do you not? When you have been quite alone with the heavenly Bridegroom, you wanted to tell the angels of the sweet love of Christ to you, a poor unworthy one. You even wished to teach the golden harps fresh music, for seraphs know not the heights and depths of grace as you know them.

The spouse had great delight, and we know that she had, for this one reason, that *she did not forget it*. This verse, and the whole Song, is a remembrance of what she had enjoyed. She says, "I sat down under his shadow." It may have been a month, it may have been years ago; but she had not forgotten it. The joys of fellowship with God are written in marble. "Engraved as in eternal brass" are memories of communion with Christ Jesus. "Above fourteen years ago," says the apostle, "I knew a man." Ah, it was worth remembering all those years. He had not told his delight, but he had kept it stored up. He says, "I knew a man in Christ above fourteen years ago, whether in the body, I cannot tell; or whether out of the body, I cannot tell; God knoweth" (2 Cor. 12:2-3); so great had his delights been. When we look back, we forget birthdays, holidays, and bonfire-nights which we have spent after the manner of men, but we readily recall our times of fellowship with the Well-beloved. We have known our Tabors, our times of transfiguration-fellowship; and, like Peter, we remember when we were "with him in the holy mount." Our head has leaned upon the Master's bosom, and we can never forget the intense delight; nor will we fail to put on record for the good of others the joys with which we have been indulged.

Now I leave this first part of the subject, only noticing how beautifully natural it is. There was a tree, and she sat down under the shadow; there was nothing strained, nothing formal. So ought true piety ever to be consistent with common sense, with that which seems most fitting, most comely, most wise, and most natural. There is Christ, we may enjoy him, let us not despise the privilege.

II. The second part of our subject is THE HEART'S REFRESHMENT IN CHRIST. "His fruit was sweet to my taste."

Here, I will not enlarge, but give you thoughts in brief which you can beat out afterwards. *She did not feast upon the fruit of the tree till first she was under the shadow of it*. There is no knowing the excellent things of Christ till you trust him. Not a single sweet apple shall fall to the lot of those who are outside the shadow. Come and trust Christ, and then all that there is in Christ shall be enjoyed by you. O unbelievers, what blessings you miss? If you will but sit down under his shadow, you shall have all things; but if you will not, neither shall any good thing of Christ's be yours.

But as soon as ever she was under the shadow, then the fruit was all hers. "I sat down under his shadow," saith she, and then "his fruit was sweet to my taste." Dost thou believe in Jesus, friend? Then Jesus Christ himself is thine; and if you own the tree, you may as well eat the fruit. Since he himself becomes thine altogether, then his redemption and the pardon that comes of it, his living power, his mighty intercession, the glories of his second advent, and all that belong to him are made over to there for thy personal and present use and enjoyment. All things are yours since Christ is yours. Only mind that you imitate the spouse: *when she found that the fruit was hers, she ate it.* Copy her closely in this. It is a great fault, in many believers, that they do not appropriate the promises, and feed on them. Do not err as they do. Under the shadow you have a right to eat the fruit. Deny not yourselves the sacred entertainment.

Now it would appear, as we read the text, that *she obtained this fruit without effort*. The proverb says, "He who would gain the fruit must climb the tree." But she did not climb, for she says, "I sat down under his shadow." I suppose the fruit dropped down to her. I know that it is so with us. We no longer spend our money for that which is not bread, and our labour for that which satisfieth not; but we sit under our Lord's shadow, and we eat that which is good, and our soul delights itself in sweetness. Come, Christian, enter into the calm rest of faith by sitting down beneath the cross, and thou shalt be fed even to the full.

The spouse rested while feasting; she sat, and ate. So, O true believer, rest while you are feeding upon Christ. The spouse says, "I sat, and I ate." Had she not told us, in the former chapter, that the King *sat* at his table? See how like the Church is to her Lord, and the believer to his Saviour! We sit down also, and we eat, even as the King doth. Right royally are we entertained. His joy is in us, and his peace keeps our hearts and minds.

Further, notice that, *as the spouse fed upon this fruit, she had a relish for it*. It is not every palate that likes every fruit. Never dispute with other people about tastes of any sort, for agreement is not possible. That dainty which to one person is the most delicious is to another nauseous; and if them were a competition as to which fruit is preferable to all the rest, there would probably be almost as many opinions as there are fruits. But blessed is he who hath a relish for Christ Jesus! Dear hearer, is he sweet to you? Thou he is yours. There never was a heart that did relish Christ but what Christ belonged to that heart. If thou hast been feeding on him, and he is sweet to thee, go on feasting, for he who gave thee a relish gives thee himself to satisfy thine appetite.

What are the fruits that come from Christ? Are they not peace with God, renewal of heart, joy in the Holy Spirit, and love for the brethren? Are they not regeneration, justification, sanctification, adoption, and all the blessings of the covenant of grace? And are they not each and all sweet to our taste? As we have fed upon them, have we not said, "Yes, these things are pleasant indeed; there are none like them; let us live upon then evermore." Now, sit down, sit down and feed. It seems a strange thing that we should have to persuade people to do that, but in the spiritual world, things are very different from what they are in the natural. In the case of most men, if you put a joint of meat before them and a knife and fork, they do not need many arguments to persuade them to fall to, but I will tell you when they will not do it, and that is when they are full; and I will also tell you when they will do it, and that is when they are hungry. Even so, if thy soul is weary after Christ the Saviour, thou wilt, feed on him; but if not, it is useless for me to preach to thee, or bid thee come. However, you who are there, sitting under his shadow, you may hear him utter these words: "Eat, O friend; drink, yes, drink abundantly." You cannot have too much of these good things; the more of Christ, the better the Christian.

We know that the spouse feasted herself right heartily with this food from the tree of life; for, *in after days, she wanted more*. Will you kindly read on in the fourth verse? The verse, which contains our text describe, as it were her first love to her Lord, her country love, her rustic love. She went to the wood, and she found him there like an apple tree, and she enjoyed him as one relishes a ripe apple in the country. But she grew in grace, she learned more of her Lord, and she found that her Best-beloved was King. I should not wonder but what she learned the doctrine of the second advent, for then she began to sing, "He brought me to the banqueting house," as much as to say — He did not merely let me know him out in the fields as the Christ in his humiliation, but he brought me into the royal palace; and, since he is a King, he brought forth a banner with his own brave escutcheon, and he waved it over me while I was sitting at the table, and the motto of that banner was LOVE. (Song 2:4)

She grew very full of this. It was such a grand thing to find a great Saviour, a triumphant Saviour, an exalted Saviour; but it was too much for her, and she became sick of soul with the excessive glory of what she had learned; and do you see what her heart craves for? She longs for trial first simple joys, those countrified delights." Comfort me with apples," she says. Nothing but the old joys will revive her. Did you ever feel like that? I have been satiated with delight in the love of Christ as a glorious, exalted Saviour when I have seen him riding on his white horse, and going forth conquering and to conquer; I have been overwhelmed when I have beheld him in the midst of the throne, with all the brilliant assembly of angels and archangels adoring him; and my thought has gone forward to the day when he shall descend with all the pomp of God, and make all kings and princes shrink into nothingness before the infinite majesty of his glory. Then I have felt as though I must fall at his feet as dead at the sight of him; and I have, wanted somebody to come and tell me over again the old, old story of how he died in order that I might be saved. His throng overpowers me; let me gather fruit from his cross. Bring me apples from "the tree" again. I am awe-struck while in the palace; let me get away to the woods again. Give me an apple plucked from the tree, such as I have given out to boys and girls in his family, such an apple as this, "Come unto me, all ye that labour and are heavy laden, and I will give you rest;" or this, "This man receiveth sinners." Give me a promise from the basket of the covenant. Give me the simplicity of Christ; let me be a child and feast on apples again, if Jesus be the apple tree. I would fain go back to Christ who died on the tree in my place, Christ overshadowing me, Christ feeding me. This is the happiest state to live in. Lord, evermore give us these apples. You recollect the old story we told years ago of Jack the huckster, who used to sing,

169

I'm a poor sinner, and nothing at all,
But Jesus Christ is my All-in-all.

Those who knew him were astonished at his constant composure. They had a world of doubts and fears, and so they asked him, why he never doubted. "Well," said he, "I can't doubt but what I am a poor sinner, and nothing at all, for I know that, and feel it every day, and why should I doubt that Jesus Christ is my All-in-all, for he says he is?" "Oh!" said his questioner, "I have my ups and downs." "I don't," says Jack; "I can never go up, for I am a poor sinner, and nothing at all; and I cannot go down, for Jesus Christ is my All-in-all." He wanted to join the church, and they said he must tell his experience. He said, "All my experience is that I am a poor sinner, and nothing at all, and Jesus Christ, is my All-in-all." "Well," they said, "when you come before the church meeting, the minister may ask you questions." "I can't help it," said Jack, "all I know I will tell you; and this is all I know,

I'm a poor sinner, and nothing at all,
But Jesus Christ is my All-in-all.

He was admitted into the church, and continued with the brethren, walking in holiness; but that was still all his experience, and you could not get him beyond it. "Why," said one brother, "I sometimes feel so full of grace, I feel so advanced in sanctification, that I begin to be very happy." "I never do," said Jack; "I am a poor sinner, and nothing at all." "But then," said the other, "I go down again, and think I am not saved, because I am not as sanctified as I used to be." "But I never doubt my salvation," said Jack, "because Jesus Christ is my All-in-all, and he never alters." That simple story is grandly instructive, for it sets forth a plain man's faith in a plain salvation; it is the likeness of a soul under the apple tree resting in the shade, and feasting on the fruit.

Now, at this time, I want you to think of Jesus, not as a Prince, but as an apple tree; and when you have done this, I pray you to *sit down under his shadow*. It is not much to do. Any child, when it is hot, can sit down in a shadow. I want you, next, to feed on Jesus; any simpleton can eat apples when they are ripe upon the tree. Come and take Christ, then. You who never came before, come now; come and welcome. You who have come often, and have entered into the palace, and are reclining at the banqueting table, you lords and peers of Christianity, come to the common wood, and to the common apple tree, where poor saints are shaded and fed. You had better come under the apple tree, like poor sinners such as I am, and be once more shaded with boughs, and comforted with apples, for else you may faint beneath the palace glories. The best of saints are never better than when they eat their first fare, and are comforted with the apples which were their first gospel feast.

May the Lord himself bring out his own sweet fruit for you! Amen.

23. THE ROES AND THE HINDS
NO. 1463B

WRITTEN AT MENTONE

"By the roes, and by the hinds of the field."
(Song of Solomon 2:7)

THE spouse was in full enjoyment of fellowship with her Beloved. Her joy was so great as almost to overpower her, and yet, so nearly does fear tread upon the heels of joy, that she was filled with dread lest her bliss should come to an end. She feared lest others should disturb her Lord, for if he were grieved she would be grieved also, and if he departed, the banquet of her delight would be over. She was afraid even of her friends, the daughters of Jerusalem; she knew that the best can interrupt fellowship as well as the worst, and therefore she adjured even Zion's daughters not to sin against Zion's King. Had they aroused her Beloved, and broken his sacred peace she would not have found a recompense in their company, but would rather have regarded them with aversion for having robbed her of her chief delight. The adjuration which she used is a choice specimen of oriental poetry: she charges them, not as we should prosaically do, by everything that is sacred and true, but "by the roes, and by the hinds of the field". So far as we understand her meaning, we will endeavour to profit by it during our brief meditation. It touches one of the most mysterious points of the secret life of the believer, and we shall much need the guidance of the Holy Spirit while we endeavour to open up its meaning.

I. "The roes and the hinds of the field" are creatures of great BEAUTY.

Who can gaze upon them as they wander among the bracken without an inward admiration? Now, since nothing can be lovelier than communion with Jesus, the spouse exhorts the daughters of Jerusalem, by all the loveliest objects in nature, to refrain from disturbing it. No one would wish to drive away the gazelle, but would feast his eyes on it, and yet its graceful elegance can never be compared with that beauty of holiness, that comeliness of grace, which is to be seen in fellowship with Jesus. It is beautiful from both sides: it is a lovely display of condescension for our beloved Lord to reveal himself to us, and, on the other hand, it is a charming manifestation of every admirable virtue for a believer to enter into fellowship with his Lord. He who disturbs such mutual fellowship must be devoid of spiritual taste, and blind to all that is most worthy of admiration.

As one delights to see the red deer in the open glades of the forest, and counts them the finest ornaments of the scene, so do men, whose eyes are opened, rejoice in the saints whose high communion with heaven renders them beings of superior mould to common mortals. A soul in converse with God is the admiration of angels. Was ever a lovelier sight seen than Jesus at the table with the beloved disciple leaning on his bosom? Is not Mary sitting at the Master's feet a picture worthy of the choicest art? Do nothing, then, O you who joy in things of beauty, how can you mar the fellowship in which the rarest beauty dwells! Neither by worldly care, nor sin, nor trifling, can make even the slightest stir which might break the Beloved's repose. His restful presence is heaven below, and the best ante-past of heaven above; in it we find everything that is pure and lovely and of good report. It is good, and only good. Why, then, O daughters of Jerusalem, should ye stir up our Beloved, and cause his adorable excellence to be hidden from us? Rather join with us in preserving a joy so fair, a bliss so comely.

II. The next thought suggested "by the roes, and by the hinds of the field" is that of TENDER INNOCENCE.

171

These gentle creatures are so harmless, so defenceless, so timid, that he must have a soulless soul who would do them harm or cause them fright. By all, then, that is tender, the spouse beseeches her friends not to disturb her Beloved. He is so good, so kind, so holy, harmless, and undefiled, that the most indifferent ought to be ashamed of molesting his rest. About him, there is nothing to provoke offense, and everything to forbid it. He is a man of sorrows and acquainted with grief; he gave his back to the smiters, and his cheeks to them that plucked off the hair; he hid not his face from shame and spitting. Being reviled, he reviled not again, but in his death agonies he prayed for his enemies. Who, then, could find cause for offence in him? Do not his wounds ward off the blows which might be challenged had he been of another character? Who would wish to vex the Lamb of God? Go elsewhere, you hunters! "The hind of the morning" has already sweated great drops of blood falling to the ground. When dogs compassed him, and the assembly of the wicked enclosed him, he felt the full of grief — so will you afflict him yet again?

In fellowship with Jesus, there is a tenderness which ought to disarm all opposition, and even command respectful deference. A soul running with the Son of God challenges no enmity. The world may rise against proselytising zeal, or defiant controversy, or ostentatious ceremonialism, for these have prominence and power, and are fair game for martial spirits; but fellowship is quiet, retiring, unobtrusive, and harmless. The saints who most abound in it are of a tender spirit, fearful to offend, non-resistant, and patient — surely it would be a superfluity of cruelty to wish to deprive them of their unselfish happiness, which deprives no hearer of a drop of pleasure, and costs no eye a tear. Rather, let even those who are most indifferent to religion pay a generous respect to those who find their delight in it. Though the worldling may care nothing for the love which overpowers the believer's ravished spirit, let him tread with reverent care when he passes the closet of devotion, or hears a stray note from the song of meditative gratitude. Rough men pause when they suddenly come upon a fair gazelle grazing in a secluded spot. Charmed at the sight of such tender loveliness they have scarcely dared to move a foot lest they should alarm the gentle roe; and some such feeling may well forbid the harsh criticism or the vulgar laugh when even the infidel beholds a sincere heart in converse with its Lord. As for those of us who know the blessedness of fellowship with Jesus, it is our duty to be doubly jealous of our words and deeds, lest, in a single instance, we offend one of the Redeemer's little ones, and cause him to lose even for an hour his delight in the Lord. How often are Christians careless about this; till, at the sight of some professors, the more spiritual may well take alarm, and cry out in anguish, "I charge *you*, O ye daughters of Jerusalem, by the roes, and by the hinds of the field, that ye stir not up, nor awake my love, till he please."

III. A third thought most certainly had a place in the mind of the anxious spouse; she meant to adjure and persuade her friends to silence by everything which sets forth LOVE.

The lilies and the roes have always been sacred to love. The poet of the Canticles had elsewhere used the symbol of the text to set forth married love. "Let her be as the loving hind and pleasant roe." (Prov. 5:19) If ever there was true love in all this selfish world, it is the love of Jesus first, and next the love of his people. As for his love, it passes the love of women; many waters cannot quench it, neither can the floods drown it; and, as for the love of the church, he who knows it best says, "How fair is thy love, my sister, my spouse! How much better is thy love than wine! and the smell of thine ointment than all spices!" (Song 4:10) If love, therefore, may plead immunity from war, and ask to have its quietness respected, the spouse used a good argument when she pleaded "by the roes and by the hinds of the field", that her royal Bridegroom's rest of love might not be invaded. If you love, or are loved, or wish to be loved, have a reverent regard for those who commune with Jesus, for their souls take their fill of love, and to drive them from their bliss would be inexcusable barbarity. O you who have any heart to feel for others, do not cause the

172

bitterest of sorrow by depriving a sanctified soul of the sweetest of delights. Do not draw near this with idle tale, or loose speech, or empty mirth: the place on which you stand is holy ground, for surely God is in that place where a heart, enamoured of the altogether Lovely One, delights itself in the Lord.

Oh that all believers were so anxious to retain the enjoyment of divine love! Then they would warn off every intruder, whoever he might be. The daughters of Jerusalem were welcome to visit the spouse at fitting times; she even, on another occasion, bade them carry a message for her to her Beloved One, and gave them a full description of his surpassing charms. But when her Lord was with her at the banquet, she only asked of them that they would not come between her and the sunshine of his presence, Nor do we wonder at her jealous fear, for we have had a sip of those sweets which she had tasted, and we would sooner lose all else than lose the luxury of love divine. It is such joy as cannot be imagined by those who have never partaken of it, such joy as can never be rivalled even in the paradise above, if, in that place, there is any other joy than that which springs from divine love. Let none, then, deprive us of its continued enjoyment. By the sanctities of true love, let every friendly mind assist us to preserve the hallowed quiet so essential to communion with our Lord.

Once more, upon the very surface of the figure, there lies the idea of *delicate sensitiveness*. The roes and the hinds of the field are soon away if anything happens to disturb them. In this respect, they set out to the life the speediness with which the Beloved departs when he is annoyed by sin. He is as a roe or a young hart, for this quality, among many others, while he comes leaping upon the mountains, skipping upon the hills, he also soon withdraws himself, for the Lord our God is a jealous God. In proportion to the fire of love is the heat of jealousy, and therefore our Lord Jesus will not brook a wandering affection in those greatly beloved ones to whom he manifests himself. It needs constant watchfulness to maintain constant fellowship. Hence, the spouse entreats and beseeches those who come near her not to give umbrage to her Lord. They might do this unwittingly, hence she warns them; they might do it through carelessness, hence she "charges" them. She would have them speak softly, and move gently, lest he should be disturbed. Should we not feel a similar anxiety, that nothing in our families, or in any of our relations or connections, should be tolerated by us so as to envelope us in the wrong and grieve our Lord? Should we not specially watch every thought of our mind, desire of our heart, word of our tongue, and deed of our hand, lest any of these should give him offence, and break our rapturous communion? If we would be favoured above others, we must be more on our guard than others. He who becomes "a man greatly beloved" must needs keep his heart with sevenfold diligence, for to whom much is given, of him much will be required. (Lk. 12:48) Kings will bear from common subjects behaviour which could not be endured in favourites; that which might cause but slight pain from an enemy will sorely wound if it comes from a friend. Therefore, the favoured spouse may well use in her entreaty the name of the most tenderly susceptible of love's favourites, and plead "by the roes, and by the hinds of the field."

Dear friend, do you know what fellowship with Jesus means? If so, imitate the spouse whenever you are in the enjoyment of it. Be jealous of yourself and all around you, that the Well-beloved may not be vexed. Aim at the maintenance of life-long communion. Remember how for centuries Enoch walked with God? Our lives are but a span compared with his, so why should we not always come up from the wilderness leaning on our Beloved? The Holy Spirit has almighty power. Let us ask and receive that our joy may be full.

If you do not understand this precious secret, may the Lord reveal it to you even now. You must first receive the Lord Jesus as your Saviour, or you can never know him as your

173

Bridegroom. Faith must trust him before love can embrace him. You must be brought to be washed, or you can never be brought to be banqueted. Pant after the Redeemer as the hart panteth after the water brooks (Ps. 42:1), and, when you have drunk of the water of life, then you will be as a hind let loose. Then, too, your feet shall be like hinds' feet, and you will be set upon your high places. When this is made your own by experience, you will understand the text, and also breathe the prayer of another verse of the same song — "Make haste, my beloved, and be thou like to a roe or to a young hart upon the mountains of spices."

24. A SERMON FOR SPRING
NO. 436

A SERMON DELIVERED ON SUNDAY MORNING,
FEBRUARY 23RD, 1862
AT THE METROPOLITAN TABERNACLE, NEWINGTON

"My beloved spake, and said unto me, Rise up, my love, my fair one, and come way. For, lo, the winter is past, the rain is over and gone, the flowers appear on the earth, the time of the singing of birds is come, and the voice of the turtle is heard in our land; the fig tree putteth forth her green figs, and the vines with the tender grape give a good smell. Arise, my love, my fair one, and come away." (Song of Solomon 2:10-13)

THE things which are seen are types of the things which are not seen. The works of creation are pictures to the children of God of the secret mysteries of grace. God's truths are the apples of gold, and the visible creatures are the baskets of silver. The very seasons of the year find their parallel in the little world of man within. We have our winter — dreary howling winter — when the north wind of the law rushes out against us, when every hope is nipped, when all the seeds of joy lie buried beneath the dark clods of despair, when our soul is fast fettered like a river bound with ice, without waves of joy, or flowings of thanksgiving. Thanks be to God, when the soft south wind breathes on our soul, and at once the waters of desire are set free, the spring of love comes on, flowers of hope appear in our hearts, the trees of faith put out their young shoots, the tone of the singing of birds enters our hearts, and we have joy and peace in believing through the Lord Jesus Christ. That happy springtide is followed in the believer by a rich summer when his graces, like fragrant flowers, are in full bloom, loading the air with perfume; and the fruits of the Spirit, like citrons and pomegranates, swell to their full proportion in the genial warmth of the Sun of Righteousness. Then comes the believer's autumn, when his fruit grows ripe, and his fields are ready for the harvest. The time has come when his Lord shall gather together his "pleasant fruits", and store them in heaven. The feast of ingathering is at hand — the time when the year shall begin anew, an unchanging year, like the years of the right hand of the Most High in heaven.

Now, beloved, each particular season has its duty. The husbandman finds that there is a time to plough, a time to sow, a time to reap; there is a season for vintage, and a period for the pruning of the vine; there is a month for the planting of herbs, and for the ingathering of seeds. To everything there is a time and a purpose, and every season has its special labour. It seems from the text, that whenever it is springtide in our hearts, then Christ's voice may be heard saying, "Arise, my love, my fair one, and come away." Whenever we have been delivered from a dreary winter of temptation or affliction, or tribulation — whenever the fair spring of hope comes upon us, and our joys begin to multiply — then we should hear the Master bidding us seek after something higher and better, and we should go out in his strength to love him more, and serve him more diligently than before. This I take to be the truth taught in the text, and it will be the subject of this morning's discourse. To any with whom the time of the singing of birds has come, in whom the flowers appear, to any such I hope the Master may speak till their souls shall say, "*My* beloved spake, and said unto *me*, rise up, my love, my fair one, and come away." I shall have to use the general principle in illustration of four or five different cases.

I. First, with regard to THE UNIVERSAL CHURCH OF CHRIST.

In looking at her history, with half an eye you can plainly perceive that she has had her ebbs and flows. Often, it seemed as if her tide retired, ungodliness, heresy, and error, prevailed: but she has had her flood tide, when once again the glorious waves have rolled in, covering with their triumphant righteousness the sands of ignorance and evil. The history of Christ's Church is a varied year of many seasons. She has had her high and noble processions of victory; she has had her sorrowful congregations of mourners during times of disaster and apparent defeat.

Commencing with the life of Christ, what a smiling spring it was for the world when the Holy Spirit was poured out at *Pentecost*. Then might the saints sing in sweet accord,

The Jewish wintry state is gone,
The mists are fled, the spring comes on;
The sacred turtle dove we hear,
Proclaim the new, the joyful year;

The immortal vine of heavenly root,
Blossoms and buds and gives her fruit;
Lo, we are come to taste the wine,
Our souls rejoice and bless the vine.

And when we hear our Jesus say,
"Rise up, my love, and haste away";
Our hearts would fain outfly the wind,
And leave all earthly love behind.

(Isaac Watts)

The winter was over and past — that long season in which the Jewish state lay dead, when the frosts of Phariseeism had bound up all spiritual life. The rain was over and gone, the black clouds of wrath had emptied themselves upon the Saviour's head; thunder and tempest and storm, all dark and terrible things, were gone forever. The flowers appeared on the earth; three thousand in one day blossomed, baptised in the name of the Lord Jesus Christ. Fair promises created for beauty and delight sprang up, and, with their blest fulfilment, clothed the earth in a royal garment of many colours. The time of the singing birds was come, for they praised God day and night, eating their bread with joy and singleness of heart. The voice of the turtledove was heard, for the Spirit — that hallowed dove from heaven descended with tongues of fire upon the apostles, and the gospel was preached in every land. Then the earth had one of her joyous Sabbaths; the fig tree put out her green figs; in every land there were some converts: the dwellers in Mesopotamia, Medes, Parthians, Elamites — some of all — were converted to God, and the tender grapes of new born piety and zeal gave out a sweet smell before God. Then it was that Christ spoke in words which made the heart of his Church burn like coals of juniper: "My Fellow-friend, my Beautiful, arise and come your way."

The bride arose. Charmed by the heavenly voice of her spouse, she put on her beautiful garments, and, for some hundred years or more, she did come away; she came away from her narrowness of spirit, and preached to the Gentiles the unsearchable riches of Christ. She came away from her attachment to the State, and dared to confess that Christ's kingdom was not of this world. She came away from her earthly hopes and comforts, for they did not count their lives dear to them, that they might win Christ and be found in him. She came away from all ease and rest of body, for they laboured more and more abundantly, making themselves sacrifices for Christ. Her apostles landed on every shore; her confessors were found among people of every tongue; her martyrs kindled a light in the midst of lands afflicted with the midnight of heathen darkness. No place trodden by the foot of man was left unvisited by the heralds of God, the heroic sons of the Church. "Go ye into all the world, and preach the gospel to every creature" (Mk. 16:15) was ringing in their ears like a clarion sounding the war charge, and they obeyed it like soldiers who had been men of war from their youth.

Those were brave days of old when, with a word, the saints of God could overcome a thousand foes, that word being the faithful promise of a gracious God. Alas, alas, that season passed away! The Church grew dull and sleepy; she left her Lord, she turned aside, she leaned upon an arm of flesh, courting the endowments of earthly kingdoms. Then there came a long and dreary winter, the dark ages of the world, the darker ages of the Church. At last the time of love returned, when God again visited his people and raised up for them new apostles, new martyrs, and new confessors. Switzerland, France, Germany, Bohemia, the Low Countries, and England and Scotland, all had their men of God, who spoke with tongues as the Spirit gave them utterance. The time of Martin Luther and John Calvin, and Philipp Melanchthon, and of John Knox had come — heaven's sunny days —when once again the frost should give way to approaching summer. Then it was that men could say once again, "The winter is passed". Priestcraft has lost its power, the rain is over and gone, false doctrines shall no more be as tempests to the Church. The flowers appear on the earth — little Churches; plants of God's right hand planting are springing up everywhere. The time of the singing of birds had come. Luther's hymns were sung by ploughmen in every field; the Psalms translated were scattered among all people — carried on the wings of angels — and the Church sang aloud to God her strength, and entered into his courts with the voice of thanksgiving, in such a way as she had not hoped for during her long and weary winter's night. In every cottage, and under every rooftop, from the peasant's hut to the prince's palace, the singing of birds had come. Then peace came to the people, and joy in the Lord, for the voice of the turtle dove was heard delighting hill and valley, grove and field, with the love-notes of gospel grace. Then fruits of righteousness were produced, the Church was "an orchard of pomegranates, with pleasant fruits", camphire with spikenard, spikenard and saffron, calamus and cinnamon, with all trees of frankincense, myrrh and aloes, and with all the chief spices. A sweet savour of faith and love went up to heaven, and God rejoiced in it. Then the Master sweetly cried,

Rise up, my love, my fair one; come away,
Soar on the wings of thy victorious faith
Above the realms of darkness and of sin!

But she did not hear the voice, or she heard it only partially. Satan and his wiles prevailed; the little foxes spoiled the vines and devoured the tender grapes. Corruption, like a strong man armed, held the spouse, and she did not come at her beloved's call. In England, she would not come away; she hugged the arm of flesh; she laid hold of the protection of the State; she would not venture on the bare promise of her Lord. Oh that she had left dignities and endowments and laws to worldly corporations, and rested on her husband's love alone! Alas for our divisions at this time! What are they but the bitter result of the departure of our fathers from the chastity of simple dependence such that Jesus' loves? In other lands, she confined herself too much within her own limits, sent out a few missionaries, and did not labour for the conversion of the outcasts of Israel. She would not come away, and so the reformation never took place. It commenced, but it ceased, and the Churches, many of them, remain to this day half reformed, in a transition state somewhere between truth and error, like the Lutheran Church and the Established Church of England at the present day — too good to be rejected, too evil to be wholly received, having such a savour of godliness that they are Christ's, but having such a mixture of

177

Popery that their garments are not clean. Oh, would to God that the Church could then have heard her Master's voice, "Rise up my love, my fair one, and come away"!

And now, brethren, in these days, we have had another season of refreshing. God has been pleased to pour out his Spirit upon men again. Perhaps the late revivals have almost rivalled Pentecost — certainly in the number of souls ingathered, they may bear rigid comparison with that feast of firstfruits. I suppose that in the north of Ireland, in Wales, in America, and in many parts of our own country, there have been more conversions than took place at the descent of the Holy Spirit. The Lord's people are alive and in earnest, and all our agencies are quickened with new energy. The time of the singing of birds is come, though there are some harsh croaking ravens still left. The flowers appear on the earth though much unmelted snow still covers the pastures. Thank God, the winter is over and passed to a great extent, though there are some pulpits and churches as frost-bound as ever. We thank God that the rain is over and gone, though there are still some who laugh at the people of God, and would destroy all true doctrine. We live in happier days than those which have passed. We may speak of these times as the good old times where time is older than ever it was, and, I think, better than it has been for many a day.

And what now? Why, Jesus says, "Rise up my love, my fair one, and come away"! To each denomination of his Church he sends this message, "Come away." He seems to speak to Episcopacy, and say, "Come away; cut out of the liturgy that which is not according to my mind; leave the State, be free." He speaks to the Calvinist, and says, "Come away; be no more dead and cold as you have been; and do not let your sons hold the truth in unrighteousness." He speaks to each denomination according to its need, but to the same import: "Rise up and come away; leave deadness and coldness and wrong-doing and hardness and harshness, and bitterness of spirit; leave idleness and slothfulness and lukewarmness; rise up and come away. Come away to preach the gospel among the heathen; come away to reform the masses of this wicked city; come away from your light-heartedness and coldness of spirit. Come away; the land is before you; go up and possess it."

Thus come away. Your Master waits to aid you. Strike, for he will strike with you; build, and he will be the great master builder. Plough, and he himself shall break the clods. Arise and thresh the mountains, for he shall make you a sharp threshing instrument with teeth, and the mountains shall be beaten small until the wind scatter them like chaff, and you shall rejoice in the Lord. Rise up, people of God, in this season of revival, and come away! Why do you sleep? "Arise and pray, lest ye enter into temptation." (Mk. 14:38, Lk. 22:46)

II. I think the text has a very SPECIAL VOICE TO US AS A CHURCH.

We must use the Scripture widely, but yet personally. While we know its reference to the universal Church, we must not forget its special application to ourselves. We, too, have had a season of refreshing from the presence of the Lord. The day was with this Church in the olden times when we were diminished and brought low through oppression, affliction, and sorrow; when we could not meet more than twenty in a place, and sometimes not more than five, without a fine and persecution. Then the Church had its elders who could meet the few in private houses, and cheer their hearts, bidding them to wait in patience, waiting till better times might come. Then God sent them a pastor after his own heart, Benjamin Rider, who fed them with knowledge and understanding, and gathered together the scattered sheep during the times of peace. Then there followed him a man worthy to be pastor of this Church — one who had sat in the stocks at Aylesbury, and had seen his books burned by the common hangman before his face, and who counted not even his life dear to him that he might win Christ: that man was Benjamin Keach, the opener of the parables, and expositor of metaphors. On old Horsely Down, then a great common, a

178

large house was built where he preached the Word, and his hearers were very many. The flowers then appeared on the earth, and the time of the singing of birds came to this Church. He passed away and slept with his fathers, and was followed by Dr. John Gill, the laborious commentator; and, for some time during his sound and solid ministry, it was a good and profitable season, and the Church was multiplied and built up. But again, even under his ministry, the ranks were thinned, and the host grew small. There was doctrine in perfection, but more power from on high was needed.

Then after a space of fifty years or more of Dr. John Gill's ministry, God sent Dr. John Rippon, and once more the flowers appeared on the earth, and the Church multiplied exceedingly, producing fruit unto God. And out of her, there went many preachers who testified of the truth that was in Jesus, and were the parents of Churches which still flourish. Then the good old man, full of years and of good works, was carried to his home: and there came others who taught the Church, and ingathered many souls; but they were not to the full extent successors of the men who went before them, for they tarried for a little season. Much good they did, but they were not such builders as those were who had gone before.

Then came a time of utter deadness. The officers mourned; there was strife and division; they looked at empty pews where once there had been full congregations; they looked about them to find one who might fill the place, and bring together the scattered multitude; but they looked and looked in vain. Despondency and despair fell on some hearts with regard to this Church; but the Lord had mercy on them, and, in a very short space, through his providence and grace, the winter was passed, and the rain was over and gone. The time of singing of birds had come; there were multitudes to sing God's praises. The voice of the turtledove was heard in our land; all was peace and unity and affection and love. Then came the first ripe fruits. Many were added to the Church. Then the vines gave out a sweet smell. Converts came, till we have often said, "Who are these that fly as a cloud, and as doves to their windows?" Often has this Church asked the question, "Who has begotten me these?" And now, these eight years, we have had a season, not of spasmodic revival, but of constant progress. A glad period of abundant increase in which there has been as many converts as we could receive, till every officer of the Church has his hands full in seeing enquirers, and we have only had time to stop now and then and take breath, and say, "What hath God wrought?" (Num. 23:23) The time came when we erected this house, because no other place was large enough for us; and still God continues with us till our Church-meetings are not sufficient for the reception of converts. And we do not know how large a proportion of this assembly are believers in Christ, because time fails to hear the cases of conversion.

Well, what ought we to do? I hear the Master saying, "Rise up, my love, my fair one, and come away." I hear Jesus speaking to this Church, and saying, "Where much is given, there much shall be required." (Lk. 12:48) Do not serve the Lord as other Churches, but yet more abundantly. As he has given you showers of love, so give him your fertile fields. Let us rejoice with thanksgiving. Let this Church feel that she ought to be more dedicated to Christ than others; that her members should be more holy, loving, living nearer to God; that they should be more devoted, filled with more zeal, more fervency, doing more for Christ, praying more for sinners, labouring more for the conversion of the world. And let us be asking ourselves what we can do as a Church that is more than we have ever thought of doing: inasmuch as he feeds us with the bread of heaven, multiplies our numbers, keeps us in perfect concord and makes us a happy people. Let us be a peculiar people, zealous in good works, showing out his glory among the sons of men. It is a solemn responsibility to rest on any man's mind to be the pastor of such a Church as this, numbering very nearly two thousand in Church fellowship. I suppose such a Baptist Church has never existed before. If we are found craven [cowardly] in this day of battle,

179

woe to us! If we are unfaithful to our charge and trust, woe to us! If we sleep when we might do so much, surely the Master will say, "I will take the candlestick out of its place, and quench their light in darkness. Laodicea is neither cold nor hot, but lukewarm; I will spit her out of my mouth." And there shall come a dark day to us, with Ichabod written on the forefront of our house of prayer, and with darkness in our souls, and bitterness and remorse in our spirits, because we did not serve Christ when we might. I will cry aloud to you, and spare not to admonish and encourage you, my brethren and comrades, in the conflict for truth. Men, brethren, and fathers, young men, maidens, and mothers in Israel, shall any of us draw back *now*? O Lord, after you have so richly blessed us, shall we be ungrateful and become indifferent towards your good cause and work? Who knows but you have brought us to the kingdom for such a time as this? (Esth. 4:14) Oh, we beseech you, send down your holy fire on every heart, and the tongue of flame on every head, that every one of us may be missionaries for Christ, earnest teachers of the truth as it is in Jesus! I leave these thoughts with you. You can feel them better than I can express them; and I can better feel their might than I can make you feel it. O God, teach us what our responsibility is, and give us grace that we may discharge our duty in your sight!

III. WHEN THE TIME OF THE BRIDAL MARCH OF THE SOUL HAS ARRIVED TO EACH CONVINCED SINNER, THEN ALSO THERE ARE SPECIAL DUTIES.

Can you not remember, dearly beloved, that day of days, that best and brightest of hours, when first you saw the Lord, lost your burden, received the roll of promise, rejoiced in full salvation, and went on your way in peace? My soul can never forget that day. Dying, all but dead, diseased, pained, chained, scourged, bound in fetters of iron, in darkness and the shadow of death, Jesus appeared to me. My eyes looked to him; the disease was healed, the pains removed, chains were snapped, prison doors were opened, darkness gave place to light. What delight filled my soul! What mirth, what ecstasy, what sound of music and dancing, what soaring towards heaven, what height and depths of ineffable delight! Scarcely since then have we known joys which surpassed the rapture of that first hour. Oh, do you not remember it, dear brethren! And was it not a spring time to you? The winter had passed. It was so long, so dreary — those months of unanswered prayer, those nights of weeping, those days of watching. The rain was over and gone; the mutterings of Sinai's thunders were hushed; the flashings of its lightnings were no more perceived; God was seen as reconciled to you. The law threatened no vengeance, justice demanded no punishment. Then the flowers appeared in our heart. Hope, love, peace, patience sprang up from the sod; the snowdrop of pure holiness, the crocus of golden faith, the daffodil lily of love, all decked the garden of the soul. The time of the singing birds has come. All that is within us magnified the holy name of our forgiving God. Our soul's exclamation was,

I will praise thee every day,
Now thine anger's turned away;
Comfortable thoughts arise,
From the bleeding sacrifice.

Here in the fair gospel field,
Wells of free salvation yield
Streams of life, a plenteous store,
And my soul shall thirst no more.

Jesus is become at length,
My salvation and my strength;
And his praises shall prolong,
While I live my pleasant song.

180

(William Cowper)

Every meal seemed now to be a sacrament; our clothes were vestments; the common utensils of our trade were "holiness to the Lord." We went out into the world to see everywhere tokens for good. We went out with joy, and were led out with praise. The mountains and the hills broke forth before us into singing, and all the trees of the fields clapped their hands. (Is. 55:12) It was, indeed, a happy, a bright and a glorious season. Do I speak to some who are passing through that spring-tide now? Young convert, young believer, in the dawn of your devotion, Jesus says, "Rise up, my love, my fair one, and come away." He asks you to come out of the world and make a profession of your faith in him *now*. Do not put it off; it is the best time to profess your faith while you are young, while as yet to you the days have not come, nor the days draw near, when you will say, "I have no pleasure in them." (Ecc.12:2) Make haste, and do not delay to keep his commandments. Arise, and be baptised. Come out from among the world, and be separate, and do not touch the unclean thing. (2 Cor. 6:17) Follow Christ in this perverse generation, that you may hear him say at the last, "Of you I am not ashamed, for you were not ashamed of me in the day when I was despised and rejected by men." In this your early time, dedicate yourselves to God. If you do not draw up a form and subscribe to it by your hand, yet draw it up in your heart, and subscribe to it with your soul: "Lord, I am yours, wholly yours: all that I am, and all that I have, I devote to you. You have bought me with your blood. Lord, take me into your service. You have put away all your wrath, and given my spirit rest. Let me spend myself and be spent — in life and in death, let me be consecrated to you." Make no reserves. Come altogether away from selfishness — from anything that would divide your chaste and pure love to Christ, your soul's husband. "Rise up and come away." In this the beginning of your spiritual life, the young dawn of marvellous light, come away from your old habits; avoid the very appearance of evil; come away from old friendships which may tempt you back to the flesh pots of Egypt. Leave all these things. Come away to higher flights of spirituality than your fathers, as yet, have known. Come away to private communion. Be much alone in prayer. Come away; be diligent in the study of God's Word. Come away; shut the doors of your chamber, and talk with your Lord Jesus, and have close and intimate dealing with him. I know I speak to some young babes in grace, beginners in our Israel. Oh, take care that you begin aright by coming right away from the world, by being strictly obedient to every divine command, by making your dedication perfect, complete, unreserved, sincere, spotless.

While from your newly-sprouted vines
Whose grapes are young and tender, choice and rich,
The flavour cometh forth. Beloved one, rise!
Rise from this visible engrossing scene,
And with affections linked to things above,
Where Christ, thy treasure is, be soaring still!

IV. In the next place, our text deserves to be seen in another light. It may be that you and I have had winters of dark trouble, succeeded by soft *springs of deliverance*.

We will not enlarge much on our sorrows, but some of us have been to the gates of death, and, as we thought then, into the very jaws of hell. We have had our Gethesmanes, when our souls have been exceeding sorrowful: nothing would comfort us, we were like the fool who abhorred all manner of meat (Ps. 107:18); and nothing came with any consolation to our aching hearts. At last, the Comforter came to us, and all our troubles were dissipated. A new season came when the time of the singing of birds was once more in our hearts. We did not chatter any more like the swallow or the crane, but we began to sing like the nightingale, even with the thorn in our breast. We learned to mount to heaven like the lark, singing all the way. The great temporal affliction which crushed us was suddenly removed, and the strong temptation of Satan was taken off us. The deep depression of spirit which had threatened to drive us to insanity was, on a sudden, lifted off, and we became elastic in heart, and once again, like David, danced before the ark, singing songs of deliverance.

I address some who, this morning, are looking back to such seasons. You have just reached the realm of sunlight, and you can look back upon long leagues of shadow and cloud through which you have had to march. You have just traversed the valley of the shadow of death, and you can well remember the horrible pit and the miry clay. Hark, we can still hear the rushing as of the wings and feet of crowded, miseries, and we can still remember the terrible shadow of confusion. But we have come through it, through it all: the winter is past, the rain is over and gone, and we can rejoice now in covenant faithfulness and renewed loving-kindness. Now, have we our assurance back again; Christ is near to us, and we have fellowship with the Father and with his Son Jesus Christ. Well, then, what are we to do? Why, the Master says to us, "Rise up, and come away." Now is the time when we should mount up to be nearer to him. Now that the day dawns and the shadows flee away (Song 2:17, 4:6), let us seek our beloved amid the beds of spices, and by the lilies where he feeds. I would we had more in the Church — more in this Church — like Madame Guyon [Jeanne Marie Bouvier de la Mothe], who loved the Lord as that woman did who had much forgiven, or like Mrs. Rowe, who, in England, was what Madame Guyon was in France; or like Dr. Robert Hawker, or like Samuel Rutherford who could pray, and long, and sigh, for nearer fellowship with Christ. If there is ever a season when we ought to follow hard after the Lord, and not be content until we have embraced him, it is when we have come up from the wilderness, leaning upon our Beloved. Then should the chaste virgins sing with joyful heart concerning him to whom they are espoused:

What is this vain, this visionary scene
Of mortal things to me? My thoughts aspire
Beyond the narrow bounds of rolling spheres.
The world is crucified and dead to me,
And I am dead to all its empty shows.
But, oh! for thee unbounded wishes warm
My panting soul, and call forth all her powers
Whate'er can raise desire or give delight,
Or with full joy replenish every wish,
Is found in thee, thou infinite abyss of ecstasy and life!

(Elizabeth Singer Rowe)

Every believer should be thirsting for God, for the living God, and longing to put his lip to the well-head of eternal life — to follow the Saviour and say, "Oh, that you were as my brother, that sucked the breasts of my mother; when I should find thee without [outside], I would kiss you. (Song 8:1) Yes, I would not be despised. I would lead you and bring thee into my mother's house, who would instruct me. I would cause you to drink of spiced wine of the juice of my pomegranate. His left hand would be under my head, and his right hand would embrace me. (Song 2:6, 8:3) I charge you, O daughters of Jerusalem, that you do not stir, nor awake my love, until he please. (Song 8:4) Who is this that comes up from the wilderness, leaning upon her beloved? (Song 8:5) I raised you up under the apple tree: there your mother brought you forth; there she brought you forth who bore you."

Oh, that the believer would never be content with having drops and sips of love, but long for the full feast. Oh, my soul thirsts to drink deep of that cup which never can be drained, and to eat of all the dainties of that table which boundless love has furnished. I am

182

persuaded that you and I are content to live on pence when we might live on pounds; that we eat dry crusts when we might taste the ambrosial meat of angels, that we are content to wear rags when we might put on kings' robes; that we go out with tears on our faces when we might anoint them with fresh oil. I am satisfied that many a believer lives in the cottage of doubt when he might live in the mansion of faith. We are poor starveling things when we might be fed; we are weak when we might be mighty, feeble when we might be as giants before God, and all because we will not hear the Master say, "Rise up my love, my fair one, and come away." Now, brethren, is the time with you after your season of trouble, to renew your dedication vow to God.

Now, beloved, you should rise up from worldliness and come away — from sloth, from the love of this world, and from unbelief. What enchants you to make you sit still where you are? What delights you to make you as you now are? Come away! There is a higher life; there are better things to live for, and better ways of seeking them. Aspire! Let your high ambition be unsatisfied with what you have already learned and known; not as though you had already attained, either were already perfect. For this one thing you must do — press forward to the things that are before. (Phil. 3:14) Rise, O soul, greatly beloved, and enter into your Master's rest. I cannot get my words this morning as I would have them; but if these lips had language I would seek by every motive of gratitude for the mercies you are enjoying, by every sensation of thankfulness which your heart can experience, for grace received, to make you now say, "Jesus, I give up myself to you this day, to be filled with your love; and I renounce all other desire but the desire to be used in your service, that I may glorify thee." Then, I think, there may go out of this place this morning many young men and old men too, many youths and maidens, determined to be doing something for Christ. I well remember preaching a sermon one Sabbath morning which stirred up some brethren to the midnight meeting movement, and much good was done by it. What if some new thought should pass through some newly quickened spirit, and you should think of some fresh invention for glorifying Christ at this good hour! Is there no Mary here who has an alabaster box at home unbroken yet? Will she not today break it over the Master's head? Is there no Zacchaeus here who will today receive Christ into his house, constrained by love divine? Oh, by the darkness that has gone, and by the brightness that has come, live lovingly towards Christ! Oh, by the fears that have been hushed, by the pains that have been removed, by the joy you now experience, and by the delights which he has vouchsafed you, I beseech you, cling to him, and seek to serve him! Go into the world to bring in his lost sheep, to look after his hidden ones, to restore to him that lost piece of money for which he has lit the candle and desires you to sweep the house. O Christian men and brethren, it is an angel's work I have attempted now, and mortal lips fail; but I conjure you, if there be any bowels of mercy, if there be any consolation in Christ Jesus, "if ye then be risen with Christ, seek those things which are above, where Christ sitteth at the right hand of God." (Col. 3:1) Do not lay not up your treasure on earth, where thieves break through and steal; but lay up your treasure in heaven: for where your treasure is there shall your heart be also. (Mt. 6:21) If you love my Master, serve him: if you do not, if you owe him nothing — oh, if you owe him nothing, and have had no favour from him — then I conjure you to seek mercy. But if you have found it, and if you know it, oh, for his love's sake *love him*! This dying world needs your help; this wicked sinful world needs your aid. Up, and be doing! The battle is raging furiously. "Multitudes, multitudes in the valley of decision!" (Joel 3:14) Guards, up and at them! Do you sleep, sirs — sleep when now the shots are flying thick as hail, and the foemen are rallying for the last charge in the world's mighty Armageddon? Up! For the defiant standard of hell waves proudly in the breeze. Do you say you are feeble? He is your strength. Do you say you are few? It is not by many nor by few that God works. Do you say, "I am obscure?" God does not want the notoriety and fame of men. Up, men, women, and children in Christ! Up! Be no more at ease in Zion (Amos 6:1), but serve God while it is called today, for the war needs every

183

hand, and the conflict calls for every heart; and night is coming when no one can fight or work.

V. And now, last of all, the time is coming to us all, when we shall die upon our dying beds.

Oh, long-expected day, hasten and come! The best thing a Christian can do is to die and be with Christ, which is far better. (Phil. 1:23) Well, when we shall lie on our beds panting out our life, we shall remember that then the winter is past forever. No more now of this world's trials and troubles. "The rain is over and gone"; no more stormy doubts, no more dark days of affliction. "The flowers appear on the earth." Christ is giving to the dying saint some of the foretastes of heaven; the angels are throwing over the walls some of the flowers of Paradise. We have come to the land Beulah, where we sit down in beds of spices, and can almost see the celestial city on the hilltops, on the other side of the narrow stream of death. "The time of the singing of the birds is come"; angelic songs are heard in the sick-chamber. The heart sings too, with midnight melodies to cheer the quiet entrance of the grave. "Though I walk through the valley of the shadow of death I will fear no evil, for thou art with me." (Ps. 23:4) Those are sweet birds which sing in the groves by the side of the river Jordan. Now it is that "the voice of the turtle is heard in our land" (Song 2:12); calm, peaceful, and quiet, the soul rests in the consciousness that there is no condemnation to him that is in Christ Jesus. (Rom 8:1) Now does "the fig tree put forth her green figs"; the first fruits of heaven are plucked and eaten while we are on earth. Now, the very vines of heaven give out a smell that can be perceived by love. Look forward to your death with great joy, you that are believers in Christ. Expect it as your spring tide of life, the time when your real summer shall come, and your winter shall be over for ever.

Praise the Lord through every nation;
His holy arm hath wrought salvation;
Exalt Him on His Father's throne;
Praise your King, ye Christian legions,
Who now prepares in heavenly regions
Unfailing mansions for His own;
With voice and minstrelsy
Extol His majesty: Alleluia!
His praise shall sound all nature round,
Where'er the race of man is found.

God with God dominion sharing,
And Man with man our image bearing,
Gentile and Jew to him are given;
Praise your Saviour, ransomed sinners,
Of life, through him, immortal winners;
No longer heirs of earth, but Heaven.
O beatific light
To view his face in light; Alleluia!
And, while we see, transformed to be
From bliss to bliss eternally.

Jesus, Lord, our Captain glorious,
O'er sin, and death, and hell victorious,
Wisdom and might to thee belong:
We confess, proclaim, adore thee,
We bow the knee, we fall before thee,
Thy love henceforth shall be our song:

The cross meanwhile we bear,
The crown ere long to wear. Alleluia!
Thy reign extend world without end,
Let praise from all to thee ascend.

(James Montgomery)

May God grant that the people who fear his name may be stirred up this morning, if not by my words, yet by the words of my text, and by the influences of God's Spirit! And may you, who have never had sweet seasons from the presence of God, seek Christ, and he will be found by you. And may we all meet in the land where winters of sin and sorrow shall be all unknown.

25. THE VOICE OF THE TURTLE

SWORD AND TROWEL, MARCH 1, 1870.

"The voice of the turtle is heard in our land."
(Song of Solomon 2:12)

THERE had evidently been a previous season of discomfort when the voice of the turtle [dove] was not heard, for, preceding these words, we read, "The winter is passed, the rain is over and gone." This indicates that the spouse had previously passed through a winter of sorrow and adversity, but now was enjoying a time of joy, prosperity, and peace, fitly represented by the appearance of flowers, the singing of birds, and the voice of the turtle. Brethren, there are periods when, in the little world of our manhood, rain, and frost, and tempest, rule the cheerless day; but there are also times, especially with believers in Jesus, when all these are things of the past; for a hallowed summer reigns within, with blossoming graces, growing fruits, and sounds of tuneful praise. In the delightful calm of the heart, peace spreads her silver wings, and notes prophetic of coming bliss are heard on every side. The mountains and the hills break forth before us into singing, and all the trees of the field clap their hands. (Is. 55:12)

I. Our first remark concerning this text will be: THERE ARE SEASONS SET AND APPOINTED FOR PROSPERITY AND JOY.

The turtle was in Palestine what the cuckoo is with us. Its voice made proclamation that the rainy season was over, that spring had arrived, and that summer drew near. One of the prophets tells us "the stork in the heaven knoweth her appointed times; and the turtle and the crane and the swallow observe the time of their coming." (Jer, 8:7) These migratory birds never came at the wrong time. If their note was heard, it was a far surer indication of the weather than a day of brightness which might be but a break in the gloom. A poet of Israel might have said of the turtle dove, much the same as Michael Bruce said about the cuckoo:

Delightful visitant! with thee
I hail the time of flowers,
When heaven is filled with music sweet
Of birds among the bowers.

(Ode to the cuckoo, 1770)

Guided by the unerring wisdom of God, which, in birds, men call instinct, some-time wanderers to other lands returned to Jordan's banks and Sharon's plains as the messengers of brighter days. Our times of peace and comfort are as surely appointed as the turtle's return, and, in their in their seasonableness, we see infinite wisdom and love. Like birds of passage, our halcyon times will not visit us before the predestined hour, neither will they tarry beyond the fore-appointed moment; and they are as wisely timed as the ascent of the Pleiades or the falling of Orion. (Amos 5:8) It is most fitting that there should be a winter; it would not be good either for human health or for the earth's fertility, that vernal verdure or autumnal ripeness should run the year round. Everything that is seasonable is best. Our joys are the better because they alternate with griefs. We could not endure perpetual sunshine this side the stars; there is a needs be that we be in heaviness, an argument for every stroke of the rod, a reason for every hiding of the face of the Well-beloved. Not by chance, but by most wise and tender love, are our days of trial and of joy ordained for every one of us.

There is a set time *in which, for the first hour in our lives, we enjoy peace with God.* Seekers would certainly be finders the moment they seek. Earnest spirits, when the tears of repentance stand in their eyes, would wipe them away immediately; and truly, if Christian people were earnest in teaching the simple gospel to them, and in sympathising with them, and praying for them, the hour of comfort would not usually be far off; but, even then, there would be cases in which the clear shining would be delayed by the shower. The case of John Bunyan, who was for years in spiritual darkness, is to the point, and his flounderings in the Slough of Despond form by no means a solitary experience. Men who have afterwards become most eminent in the kingdom of God, have been long seeking the light and groping like blind men for the wall, crying out by the month together, "O that I knew where I might find him, that I might come even to his seat." (Job 23:3) Distracted with dreadful forebodings, oppressed with the weight of conscious guilt, ignorant of the way of salvation, and unable through unbelief to lay hold on eternal life, there are some who weary themselves with doleful searchings, even for years, and only at last return to their rest. One could wish that their liberation from so horrible a prison-house were more speedy, but yet we have noticed that certain of them have been the most joyful of believers when their fetters have been filed, have had little bondage during the rest of their lives, and, having lain long in Doubting Castle themselves, have been the better able to use the key of promise on behalf of the desponding.

Dear friend, if you believe in Jesus Christ now, you shall have peace; but if as yet the light does not break on your spirit, still hope on, for the morning shall soon dawn. Prisoner of hope, the day will come when HE who looses the captives shall set your feet in a large place. (2 Sam. 22:20; Ps. 18:19, 118:5) Slow breaks the light but surely. The blessedness of pardoned sin shall obliterate your woes. "Thou shalt forget the shame of thy youth, and shalt not remember the reproach of thy widowhood any more." (Is. 54:4) Before long you will sing:

The winter of my woe is gone,
The summer of my soul comes on,
The Sun of Righteousness shines forth
And scatters all the clouds of wrath.

In the same way, *our times of joy after conversion are all set and appointed.* The life of the Christian is not one of uninterrupted peace. It is often his own fault that he loses the joy of salvation; but still, it is very rarely that we meet with a Christian who always walks in the sunlight. Clouds appear to be common on most earthly skies. Do not wonder, my dear friend, if you don't always feel equally alive and happy in spiritual things. Don't be astonished if sometimes the dark side of your nature is most conspicuous; do not be surprised if you have to contend with inbred sin, rather than rejoice in the mercies of the covenant. Look abroad on nature in the wintry months, and see how the fields are white with frost, as though the earth were wrapped in a winding-sheet. Those meadows should be emerald with hope, and so they yet will be; yes, and even they will put on the beautiful array of realised enjoyment, when the kingcups shall strew them plenteously with gold, and the daisies shall look up with their sweetly simple eyes and smile because the summer has come. Bright is the hope, but it must be waited for; and meanwhile, snow, and hoar frost, and ice, and rain, must hold their carnival. Yet not one hour beyond the set time shall they riot and rule us, for the Lord has set it as his covenant for ever that summer shall not cease. (Gen. 8:22)

The voice of the turtle will soon be heard; even now, the almond hastens to put out her flowers. So is it with you. You must endure your trouble, and, it shall be followed by deliverance in due season. "It is good for a man that he both hope and quietly wait." (Lam.

187

3:26) Look at the sea — the pulsing life-blood of the world — it is not always at flood tide; at ebb it must retreat far from the shore. And yonder noble river, Father Thames, how foul his banks, how manifest the shoals in mid-river; wait till the hour comes round, and you shall see the milk white swans sailing over the sparkling waters, where you see at this moment nothing but mire and dirt. That subtle element, the air, has its appointed changes; scarcely a leaf moves on the tree to-day, and yet to-morrow hurricanes may lash the sea to fury, rending up the oaks, and dashing whole navies on the rocks. Even the solid earth has its paroxysms of disturbance when it forgets its ancient stability, and imitates the restless sea. In the nature of things, it must be so. We are in a material world, a world of changes, a world that is by-and-by to be dissolved. We are in a body subject to pains and infirmities, a body that must decay; how can we expect to find unchanging peace in a changing world and undying joy in a dying body? How can you hope to find rest where your Saviour found none, and where he has told you that you are not to find it? Do not be cast down at severe trial, as though some strange thing had happened unto you. Others beside you have heard the raven's croak, and the owl's hoot, and the bittern's cry; but, in due time, they have heard the turtle's voice again, and so will you. Your brightness shall come forth as the noonday. (Ps.37:6) The Lord shall turn your captivity as the streams in the south. (Ps.126:4) Weeping may endure for a night, but joy cometh in the morning (Ps. 30:5), and that morning is not far off; the watchful eyes of faith can catch the first gleams of it, even though darkness shadows all things visible to sense. If the vision tarries, wait for it; it will come, it will not tarry. God has appointed it, and, in due season, the voice of the turtle shall be heard in your land.

This is equally true *with regard to the future of our lives.* How fond are we of being amateur prophets! Of all callings, the most unprofitable is that of a self-ordained prophet. When we take the telescope and try to look into the nearer future, we breathe on the glass and create a haze, and then declare that we see clouds and darkness before us. We do not know what will come tomorrow, for "sufficient unto the day is the evil thereof" (Mat. 6:34); our guesses at coming disaster are foolish and wicked. Yet the vilest pretenders to necromancy and astrology are not more busy at foretelling than many of the Lord's people. One knows that in old age he will be unable to earn his living, and may be imprisoned in the workhouse; another is equally sure trade will be ruined and he will become a bankrupt; a third expects that, with her growing infirmities, she will become a weariness to all her relatives, and they will wish her dead; while a fourth is equally clear that she shall turn aside into sin, and be a castaway. These favourite theories of misery remind me of a friend who keeps pet vipers, which I earnestly recommend him to kill, or I fear they will kill him. What can be the use of indulging these fears, suspicious, and imaginings? Trials are appointed, but joys also are reserved. It is idle to paint the sun as if it were all spots, or life as if it were only sorrow. The eternal hand measures out to the heirs of heaven due portions both of affliction and prosperity, and it is a dangerous misrepresentation to talk only of the wormwood, and never of the wines on the lees. I would have you anticipate joy rather than sorrow. Remember, child of God, you are nearing heaven every hour; it should be brighter with you as you near the sun. Nearer the angels' harps, you may surely expect more music of joy. Every hour shortens the storm, and brings closer the everlasting calm. Rejoice in your prospects! You shall soon come to the land Beulah, that peaceful country which borders on the glory-land, and forms the suburbs of Jerusalem the Golden. Though your outward man is decaying, your inward man shall be renewed day by day. You shall produce forth fruit in old age to show that the Lord is upright. At eventide it shall be light.

On the margin of the river
You shall hear the turtle's voice,
Telling of the joys for ever
Bidding you e'en now rejoice.

188

One almost longs for grey hairs, for mature faith, for the deep experience, and the consummated hope, which are the portion of aged Christians. The voice of the turtle shall be heard in your land, in the halcyon days of waiting for the call to heaven. When the hour of your departure shall be actually at hand, your soul shall be at peace. 'Tis thus the Lord ordains, and thus it shall be with all the saints.

II. Secondly, THE VOICE OF THE TURTLE — WHAT DOES IT INDICATE?

There are three excellences in the sound. First, it is *the voice of peace.* The cry of the eagle tells of strife, the scream of the vulture speaks of carnage, but the soft voice of the dove proclaims peace. The dove is associated not with the laurel of war but with the olive-branch of peace. Many of us are now enjoying the purest form of peace. Believers have a right to peace. Sin, the peace-breaker, was put away by the one sacrifice of Christ; and, therefore, being justified by faith, we have peace with God through our Lord Jesus Christ. (Rom. 5:1) We have One to answer for us, whose righteousness covers all our transgressions. We rest in his love and in his finished work, and, therefore, our soul is perfectly at rest with regard to sin and the punishment of it. We have peace too as to the future. We can leave all in the hands of God. We can say, "Father, thy will be done." (Mat. 6:10; Lk. 11:2) We believe that our covenant God will never forsake us, nor will he try us above what we are able to bear. (1 Cor. 10:13) So, then, we have peace with regard to every future circumstance. Grace ruling within us puts away all anger and malice, and thus we have peace with all mankind. If any have offended us, we have from our hearts forgiven them. If we have offended any, we desire to make all restitution, to humble ourselves if needs be, and, as much as lieth in us to live peaceably with all men. (Rom. 12:18) We are in a happy state of mind when we can feel that even the new-born child is not more at peace with mankind than we are. Especially are we at peace with our fellow Christians. We would not constantly be raising discussions and controversies on vexatious and unprofitable questions. Quibbles which gender strife are not for us. We can truly say that our desire is to minister to the peace of the church, to the edification of the saints, to the unity of the body of Christ. Where this is the case, the voice of the turtle is heard in our land. Oh, may no other voice but that be heard in this church! These many years, I bless God we have been kept without division, and without internal strifes, and, by his grace, many more years shall we continue in the same condition, knit together in love, and bound together in the perfect bond of charity. So may it be in all the churches of Jesus Christ, and may the time come when, in every place, all churches and their pastors shall be able to say, "The voice of peace is heard among us; we have love one towards another, and are of one mind, striving together only for the gospel of Christ, and knowing no emulation except which shall please his brother to his good for edification."

The voice of the turtle was, next, *the voice of love.* We have always associated with the turtledove the idea of love. We have heard of it pining for its mate, and of the peculiar fondness it has for its young. The gazelle among animals, and the dove among birds, are the favourites of love. Happy is it with us when love rules in our breast. I hope, beloved, that you love the Lord Jesus Christ because he first loved you (1 Jn. 4:19); that his love constrains you, his great love with which he loved you even when you were dead in trespasses and sin (Eph. 2:1), the love which brought him to the cross to pay with his own heart's blood the price of your redemption. You can sing with the young William Featherstone,

My Jesus, I love thee, I know thou art mine,
For thee all the follies of sin I resign;
My gracious Redeemer, my Saviour art thou,
If ever I loved thee, my Jesus, 'tis now.

189

Oh, it is blessed to feel the heart knit to Christ, drawn to him, going out in lively flames of affection towards him"! As the sparks of fire seek the sun, as though they knew their origin, so should our love mount towards Christ from whom it came. May it be so! Do you feel your hearts glow with love to God? It may be that you are under his chastening hand, and you smart in your body; or it may be you have a sick one at home, or there are anxieties in your business; but, if you love the Lord intensely, you will still say, "Blessed be his name! Though he slay me, yet will trust in him." (Job 13:15) What can be more like heaven than to feel the affections going up to God with fervour? Sweet is it also to feel sincere love to all believers in Christ, so as to recognise that there is only one family, and that we, individually, are a brother or sister in that family, not in name only, but in deed and in truth. Whoever is one with Christ is one with all those who are born again. It is a blessed thing when the voice of the turtle sounds in the soul, indicating a burning love for sinners. It is well when the believer pines to see others saved. To sigh and cry before God, because the ungodly continue to reject him and despise his gospel, is a most gracious sign. Oh, that we may always continue in that same loving frame of mind, not having to ask with William Cowper,

Do I love the Lord or no?

— but feeling,

There's not a lamb among his flock
I would disdain to feed;
There's not a foe before whose face
I'd fear his cause to plead.

May our love to Christ, and to all the saints, and to the souls of men, grow exceedingly; and, in that sense, may the voice of the turtle be heard in our land, because the love of God is spread abroad in our hearts by the Holy Spirit which is given to us. (Rom 5:5)

The voice of the turtle also, in the third place, had associated with it a degree *of mournfulness.* This is not at all inconsistent with peace and love. There is a passage in Nahum in which the voice of the dove is used as an expression and illustration of deep-seated sorrow. (Nahum 2:7) There is a plaintive monotony about the notes of the dove suggestive of mourning. Now, even when the Christian is perfectly happy from one point of view, he will still feel a measure of godly sorrow, which indeed lies at the root of all spiritual joy. Just as some poets have sung the praises of a "pleasing melancholy", so there is associated with the highest joy of the Christian a sweetly serene sorrow. I will show you of what kind it is. When you live for God, and are conscious of his love, your soul is sure to say, "Oh, that I were always here! Oh, that I could always feel as I feel now!" Or else you mourn to think that you could ever have sinned against one so gracious. It is not a bitter moaning over unpardoned sin. You know you are forgiven; you are sure of that; but it is the mourning of one who laments in thinking that he should have need to be pardoned, and that he should ever have gone astray.

My sins, my sins, my Saviour!
How sad on thee they fall,
Seen through thy gentle patience,
I tenfold feel them all.

There is a great difference between the agony of remorse and the sweet sorrow of repentance. Indeed, the tear of repentance, though it is salt, is also sweet. It is acceptable to God, and must therefore be seasoned with preserving salt; but it is also sweet as honey to the soul. Rowland Hill used to say that he almost regretted he could not shed the tear of

190

repentance in heaven. He hoped to walk repenting all his life long, till he got up to the gates of Paradise, and could almost wish that he might be allowed the sweet exercise of repenting even among the angels. There is more joy in holy tears than in laughter; and when our sacred sorrows most abound, "a secret something sweetens all." In the mines of soul-sorrow, we find diamonds of the first water, such as glitter nowhere else.

Lord, let me weep for nought but sin,
And after none but thee,
And then I would — O that I might!
A constant weeper be.

It is perfectly consistent with peace and love to be sighing after more holiness, more fellowship, more usefulness, and still be lamenting deficiencies, and deploring imperfections, "Blessed are they that do hunger and thirst after righteousness." (Mat. 5:6) They are blessed, and yet they continue to hunger and thirst, and that is a part of their blessedness. May we also long to be with Jesus, and, in this sense, may we ever hear the turtle-voice in our souls: "My Saviour, when shall I come to the promised land, the land that floweth with milk and honey?"

My heart is with thee on thy throne,
And ill can brook delay;
Each moment listening for the voice,
'Rise up, and come away.'

Such pining does not break our peace. We sometimes sing with Charles Wesley —

I thirst, I faint, I die to prove
The fullness of redeeming love,
The love of Christ to me."

Such thirsting such panting, such dying, may we always experience, for thus shall we live in joy and peace.

These are the turtle's three notes. May they be ever in our souls: the note of peace, the note of love, the note of holy mourning and pining after the Saviour.

III. Now, supposing this to be the condition of our soul, WHAT THEN? This shall make our third point. There is an appointed season for all this; the season has a threefold blessedness about it: WHAT ARE ITS PARTICULAR DUTIES?

Art thou in peace to-night? Is thy love flaming like coals of juniper? Then surely thou shouldst *seek to grow in grace.* The old proverb is, "Make hay while the sun shines." The mariner takes care to hoist all sail when he has a propitious wind. Now, Christian, now is your time to make progress in the divine life. The other day you were at war with your corruptions, doubting your interest in Christ, and lamenting under the hiding of Jehovah's face. But now, it is all calm with you; therefore, arise and build up yourself on your most holy faith. The frost has gone; so lay the stones with fair colours, with windows of agates and gates of carbuncles. If the flowers do not grow in spring and summer, when will they grow? If the birds do not build their nests in propitious times, when will they? Now is your opportunity, so seize it. The Master has given you good merchandise spiritually; take care to trade much and grow rich in grace. These times are not meant for you to sleep in; depend on that. You are not blessed with this peace and quiet that you may say to your soul, "Thou hast much good laid up for many years, take thine ease." (Lk. 12:19) If you do so, it will be proof that you are naked, and poor, and miserable, and there is fear that your

191

peace is no peace, but the dangerous security of the ungodly. Now that you feel yourself so full of sacred love, and holy excitement, and divine ardour, and your spiritual pulse is quickened, and your whole spiritual nature is in health, be much at the throne of grace, and say, "Lord, help me now to push forward in my pilgrimage. Let me not grieve the Spirit, but accept his comforting and reviving influences. May I now, my Lord, spread every sail in your gracious wind, and make good headway towards my desired haven." There is such a thing as growth in grace, depend on it, though some Christians do not manifest it much. My two children have always been photographed on their birthdays, and I have had the pictures all framed in one. There are twelve of them now, and I sometimes point them out to friends, and say, "There they are in the perambulator the first year, and here they are twelve years afterwards, stout, well-grown lads", and then I ask my brethren — "Do you think that if we could have our spiritual nature photographed in this way, we would see that we had as distinctly grown as these children have?" Why, there are some Christians whom I knew twelve years ago in a spiritual perambulator, and they are in the perambulator now. They are still nothing better than babes in grace. They have not learned to walk alone in spiritual things. We still have to address them as Paul did, when he said — "I have spoken unto you as unto babes in grace." (1 Cor. 3:1) He saw that they had made no advance in the life divine. Now, a little child is a very beautiful object; in an infant there is a beauty that strikes one's eye at once, and mothers delight in their babes! But what parents would be pleased to see their children at twelve or fifteen years of age at the same size as they were when they were just one year old? Their littleness at that age would strike you with the greatest sorrow, and the wife would say to the husband, "We are the parents of a dwarf", and both would feel shocked and grieved. May you never suffer such a calamity! But is it no calamity that Christian people remain dwarfs; that year after year they make no advance, but are infants still? Such non-progress is very much the result of neglecting these appointed seasons of divine influence of which I have spoken. Because of an unhallowed indolence, professors do not arrive at the stature of men in Christ Jesus, to which it is most desirable that all saints should attain. This, then, is the duty of the season: if you have peace, and joy, and holy power within, it is a voice bidding you "to go forward."

The next duty is, *be as useful as you possibly can to others at this time.* One of the best ways to keep what God gives you is to give it away, "There is that scattereth and yet increaseth." (Prov. 11:24) It is by distribution that Christians amass grace. If we seek only our own, and not the things of others — our fellow Christians and the unconverted — we shall soon grow poor in spiritual things. He that waters others shall be watered also himself. Is it a good season with you? Tell the news to the Kings household. Has the King favoured you with a dish from his table? Deal out a portion to the hungry, and let the faint-hearted partake of your comforts. Is there no doubt about your own salvation? Why, man, now is the time to seek after the salvation of others. Have you a full assurance of your own interest in Christ? Why, then, you have nothing to distract you from spending and being spent for the increase of your Master's kingdom. Whoever constantly guards his own gates when the foe is at the door may have some excuse for not watching another man's house; but whoever has peace in his borders, and is filled with the finest of the wheat, should care for his fellow-citizens. "Whatsoever thy hand findeth to do, do it with thy might; for there is no work, nor device, nor knowledge, nor wisdom, in the grave, whither thou goest." (Eccles. 9:10) "In the morning sow thy seed, and in the evening withhold not thine hand: for thou knowest not whether shall prosper, either this or that, or whether they shall be alike good." (Eccl. 11:6)

Lastly — Are you in this happy state? *Then take care to praise God while you are in it.* Do not restrain the flow of your grateful spirits. You were icebound some time ago; now your heart is thawed, let the streams gush out according to the Master's word, for did he not say, that out of the midst of you shall flow rivers of living water? (Jn. 7:38) Praise your God with all your heart. When you lie awake in the night, and your soul is happy within you, offer your Lord "songs in the night." (Job 35:10) Praise him when you go to your labour. Worldly men have their songs; why should not the Christian sing the songs of Zion? Praise him in your silence, with your heart's music. Let your soul talk sweetly to him with gratitude and love. Speak well of his name to others. We are sometimes slow to utter the goodness of the Lord, but very seldom slow to reveal our troubles. Our griefs we pour into our fellow creatures' ears all too readily — amend this, and be eager to tell out your joys. A minister calling once on an aged woman, she began to tell him about her rheumatism and her poverty, and as he had heard that story perhaps twenty times before, he said, "My dear sister, every time I call, you tell me of your troubles, and I have no objection to hear about them, for I sympathise with you, but could you not for once tell me of your mercies?" She thanked him for reminding her of that unused string on her harp, and may I not remind some of you to dwell more frequently on the Lord's goodness to you? Let men know that the people of God are a happy people. Constrain them to enquire what it is that makes you so glad, so calm, and so patient. Compel them to desire to know Christ, if for no other reason than this, that their faces may shine with the same cheerfulness that lights up yours, I know I am bringing before you a hard duty for wintry seasons, but, when the voice of the turtle is heard, it will be easy for you — indeed, natural. You have lain among the pots, but now that you have the wings of a dove covered with silver, and your feathers with yellow gold (Ps. 68:13), mount, mount, mount; and as your spirit mounts, become like the lark which sings as it rises, and is heard where it is not seen, still pouring out a flood of song from the invisible into which it has ascended. Live near to God, but let your communion with the sons of men be cheerful and joyous. Compel them to hear your praises. This is the duty of this present season; and, if you neglect it, the voice of the turtle may not be heard in your land any longer, and you may have to sigh, and pine, and cry for the Lord to return.

O sing unto this glittering glorious King,
O praise his name, let every living thing;
Let heart and voice like bells of silver ring
The comfort that this day doth bring.

(William Henry Husk, *Songs of the Nativity*, 1868)

I would to God that this subject be the property of you all! Even in the most select congregation, there are some who have no interest in Christian peace and love, and one's heart is grieved to think of that. No turtle's voice can sound in hearts where Jesus is not trusted, where sin reigns, where spiritual death binds all the powers in iron bands. May you be led to feel your sad estate! May the rain of repentance fall, and then may the birds of faith and hope begin to sing. For then, and only then, will you understand the inward serenity of the people of God.

26. THE TENDER GRAPES

NO. 2480

AT THE METROPOLITAN TABERNACLE, NEWINGTON
ON LORD'S-DAY EVENING, AUGUST 8TH, 1880

"The vines with the tender grape give a good smell."
(Song of Solomon 2:13)

THE vine is, of all trees, the most useless unless it bears fruit. You can make hardly anything of it; you would scarcely be able to cut enough wood out of a vine to hang a pot on it; you cannot turn it into furniture, and barely could you use it in the least degree for building purposes. It must either bear fruit, or else it must be consumed in the fire. The branches of the vine that bear no fruit are necessarily cut off, and are used, as I have seen them in the South of France many a time, in little twisted bundles for kindling the fire. They burn very rapidly, so there is soon an end of them, and then they are gone.

The vine is constantly used in Scripture as a picture of the nominal Church of Christ; so, like the vine, we must either produce fruit or we shall be accounted as good for nothing. Dear friends, we must serve God, we must draw out from our very soul love for God and service to him as the fruit of our renewed nature, or else we are useless, worthless, and shall only abide our time, and then be cut down to be burned. Our end must be destruction if our life is not fruitful. This gives a very solemn importance to our lives, and it should make each of us seriously ask, "Am I producing fruit for God? Have I brought out 'fruit meet for repentance'? (Mat. 3:8) For if not, I must, by-and-by, feel the keen edge of the Vinedresser's knife, and I shall be taken away from any sort of union that I now have with the Church which is Christ's vine, and be flung over the wall as a useless thing whose end is to be burned.

Beloved, you all know that there is no possibility of producing any fruit unless we are in Christ, and unless we abide in Christ. We must bear fruit, or we shall certainly perish; and we cannot have fruit unless we have Christ, and are knit to Christ, vitally one with him, just as a branch is really, after a living fashion, one with the stem. It would be no use to tie a branch to the stem of the vine; that would not cause it to produce fruit. It must be joined to it in a living union; and so must you and I be livingly joined to Christ. Do you know, by experience, what that expression means? For, if you do not know it by experience, you do not know it at all. No one knows what life is but the One who is himself alive, and no one knows what union to Christ is but he who is himself united to Christ. We must become one with Christ by an act of faith; we must be inserted into him as the graft is placed in the incision made into the tree in which it is to be grafted. Then there must be a knitting of the two together, a vital junction, a union of life, and a flowing of the sap, or else there cannot be any bearing of fruit. Again, I say, what a serious thing this makes our life to be! How earnest should be our questioning of ourselves! "For the divisions of Reuben there were great searchings of heart" (Judg. 5:115-16); and so may there be in this matter. Let each one of us ask, "Am I bearing fruit? I am not unless I am vitally united to Christ. I have openly professed that I am in Christ, but am I producing fruit to his honour and glory?"

I think I hear someone say, "I hope I have begun to produce some fruit, but it is very little in quantity, and it is of very poor quality; and I do not suppose that the Lord Jesus will hardly stoop to notice it." Well, now, listen to what the text says; it is the Heavenly Bridegroom, it is Christ himself, who, in this Song, speaks to his spouse, and bids her come into the vineyard and look about her. For, says he, "The vines with the tender grape give a good smell." So, you see, there was some fruit, though it could only be spoken of

194

as "the tender grape." Some read the passage, "The vines in blossom give out fragrance"; others think it refers to the grape just as it begins to form. It was a poor little thing, but the Lord of the vineyard was the first to spy it out; and if there is any little fruit to God upon anyone here present, our Lord Jesus Christ can see it. Though the berry be scarcely formed, though it be only like a flower which has just begun to knit, he can see the fruit, and he delights in that fruit.

I want, as the Holy Spirit shall help me, to speak about those early fruits — those "tender grapes" — that are being produced by some who have but lately come to know the Lord.

First, we will enquire, *what are these tender grapes?* Secondly, *what is the Lord's estimate of them?* And thirdly, *what is the danger to these tender grapes?* You will learn what that is from the 15th verse: "Take us the foxes, the little foxes, that spoil the vines; for our vines have tender grapes."

I. First, then, WHAT ARE THESE TENDER GRAPES? What are these firstfruits of the Spirit of God of which our text says, "The vines with the tender grape give a good smell"? While I am preaching, I shall be going over my own experience and the experience of many of God's people; and though I shall not be specially speaking to them, it will do them good to recollect what they passed through in the early days of their Christian life. One of the first tender grapes that we spy out on the living branches of the True Vine is *a secret mourning for sin,* and very often, an open mourning, too. The man is no longer the mirthful, jovial, light-headed, dare-devil sort of fellow that he was. He has found out that his life has not been right in the sight of God; and he has become conscious that he has done much that is altogether wrong, and that he has left undone a thousand things which he ought to have done, and he feels heavy of heart, and sad in spirit. His old companions notice that there is a change in him; he does not tell them much because they would only laugh at him, but he has a wound somewhere within his heart, an arrow has pierced his conscience, and his soul bleeds inwardly. The pleasure which he once took in sin is all gone now; and, what is more, he grieves to think that he ever should have taken any pleasure in it. He hopes that God will forgive him, but he feels that he will never forgive himself. He smites upon his breast, and wishes he could smite so hard as to kill the sin which is there; but he discovers that, when he would do good, evil is present with him, and that makes him cry, "O wretched man that I am! who shall deliver me from the body of this death?" (Rom. 7:24) He used to think that to believe in Christ was a very easy thing, and that to be a Christian was almost as simple a matter as kissing his hand; but he finds it quite another thing now. He has a heavy burden to carry, and it is crushing him to the ground; he is fighting with himself, and cannot get the victory. Whenever he sees his sin, it grieves him; and he is grieved because he does not grieve more than he does. He wishes his heart would become softer, and that by some means he could weep for sin more thoroughly, for he really does hate it with all his soul. Well now, this is one of the tender grapes; and if any of you are brought into that condition, I thank God for it. This is a crop that will ripen and sweeten before long. Surely, never was there a truly gracious soul who did not produce this as one of the first fruits of the Spirit, a secret mourning for sin.

Another tender grape is *a humble faith in Jesus Christ.* The man, perhaps, has got no farther than to say,

"'Lord, I believe, help thou mine unbelief!' (Mk. 9:24) I do trust myself with you, and you said that I am saved if I do that, and therefore I conclude that I am saved. But, oh, that I had more faith! Oh, that I could trust you without a doubt! But, Lord, you know all things; you know that, humbly, tremblingly, I do accept you as my Saviour, and I am hopeful to be numbered among your people, though the meanest of them all. Though my faith is

195

but as a grain of mustard seed, I bless you that I have even that grain; and I know that it will grow, for it has within it the life you did impart."

That little trembling faith, like a freshly-lighted candle which is easily blown out, is, nevertheless, one of the tender grapes. It will grow, it will come to perfection in due time, for the least true faith has everlasting life in it. All the devils in hell could not quench a single spark of God-given faith, for it is a living thing, and it cannot be destroyed. This faith possesses immortality, and it shall defy death itself; yet, while it is so little, it is like the tender grape which gives a good smell.

Then there comes another tender grape, and that is *a genuine change of life*. The man has evidently turned right about; he is not looking the way he used to look, and he is not living as he used to live. At first, he fails, and perhaps fails a good many times, like a child who is learning to walk, and has many a tumble; but it will never walk if it does not tumble a bit. So, when men aim to live the new life, they have many slips. They thought that ugly temper of theirs would never rise again, but it does, and it grieves them very much; and some old habit, from which they thought they had clean escaped, entangles them unawares, and they say, "Surely I cannot be a child of God if I do these things again"; and there is great sorrow, and brokenness of spirit, and soul-humbling. Well, that very soul-humbling is a tender grape. That effort to do better — not in your own strength, because you have none, and you are sure to fail utterly if you attempt such a task alone — but the effort to do better in the strength of God, yet with the full consciousness of your own weakness, all that indicates a real change. I know that there are some men who have been so long steeped in evil that, to get their old habits down, is a very hard task. "Can the Ethiopian change his skin or the leopard his spots? Then may ye also do good, that are accustomed to do evil." (Jer. 13:23) Nothing but almighty power can get the blackness out of the Ethiopian's skin, or the spots out of the leopard. God can do it, and he can reverse the whole current of our lives. Yet, nevertheless, while it is being done, there is often much of painful contrition and brokenness of heart before him. See what a change it is that the Lord works in a man when he converts him from the error of his ways. There is Niagara, and see the mighty flood come roaring down. What a sight it is! But can that Niagara be made to flow up-hill? Yes, God can accomplish that marvellous feat; but while it is being done, think of the twists, and twirls, and whirlpools, and sheets of spray there will be. The vast mass of water has to stop, and then to rush up again. What roaring of waves and shaking of rocks there will be even while God is performing this great operation! So it is when there is a change of heart in one who has long been steeped in evil, one who has been an open sinner; there is a great deal of distress of heart while the work is being done. Yet, if there be a radical change in the man, it is like the tender grape, which is a sure sign of life in the vine that produces it.

Another very blessed fruit of spiritual life in the soul is *secret devotion*. The man never prayed before; he went sometimes to a place of worship, but he did not much care about it. Now, you see that he tries to get alone for private prayer as often as he can. He may not have the privilege of a room to himself, but he climbs up into a hayloft, or goes down into a sawpit, or retires behind a hedge; or, in order to be quite alone, perhaps he walks the streets of London. It is very easy to be alone in a crowded street; in busy Cheapside, there is many a man who is utterly lonely, for he does not know anybody in all the throng that rushes past him. It is a really awful loneliness that a man may have in the midst of a dense crowd, and his heart may then be talking with God as well as if he were shut up in some private room. A soul must get alone if it is really born again; it cannot live without private prayer. I like also to see the young beginners in the divine life carrying a pocket Testament, so that they may just read a short portion whenever they get a few spare moments — two or three verses to lie in their memory, like a lozenge under the tongue, to melt there, and dissolve into their inmost being. It is a grand thing to keep a man right, and

196

it is one of the tender grapes on the vine when there is a love for the Word of God, and a love for private prayer. I am sure that it is one of the tokens by which we are not very often deceived. "Behold, he prayeth" (Acts 9:11) is an indication that God has renewed his heart.

Another of these tender grapes is *an eager desire for more grace*, a longing for more of the good things of the covenant. Why, those who have just been brought to know the Lord would like us to preach seven sermons a day, and they would like to hear them all! I know that, when I was first brought to Christ, I was ravenous after the gospel. I felt like the great beast mentioned in the Book of Job, that "drinketh up a river, and trusteth that he can draw up Jordan into his mouth" (Job 20:33), so thirsty did I seem to be after the river of the water of life. I do not think that the seats felt hard to me then, or that standing in the aisle was too tiresome so long as it was but the gospel that was preached to me, for there was an eager desire after it in my soul. If anyone can tell the poor seeking one, who has just a little light, where he can get ten times the grace he has, I warrant you that he will make the journey if he may but find it, that his feeble faith may grow to full assurance, that his repentance may be deeper, that his love to God may be more intense. If his whole soul is set on attaining this object, it is manifest that these are the tender grapes that grow out of the life that is within the branches of the Vine.

There is also in such people another very precious sign of grace, and that is *a simple love for Jesus*. The heart knows little, but it loves much; the understanding is not yet fully enlightened, but the affections are all on fire. "Thy first love" is mentioned with special commendation in the Book of the Revelation (2:4); and I think that some of us, who have known the Lord for thirty years or more, can look back upon our first love with something of regret. I hope that we love Christ better now than we did then, but there was a vividness about our first love which we do not always realise in our more mature experience. It was then very much as it is when your servant lights a fire; at the first, the shavings, or the paper, or whatever it may be at the bottom of the kindling, makes a great deal more of a blaze than appears afterwards, and the fire is at its best when it all gets into one great steady ruby glow. It is to this state that the ardent love of Christians should come; but still, there is something very pleasing about that first blaze, and I could almost wish that we always blazed away as we did in the fervour of our first love. That first flame was one of the sure tokens that the fire was there, just as the tender grapes prove that the life is in the Vine-branches. If, dear friends, you are now full of love for Christ, do not let anybody quench it, or even dampen it down; but may it burn more and more, like coals of juniper, which have a most vehement flame! God grant that this love, and all the other tender grapes that I have mentioned, may be seen in everyone who has newly sought and found the Lord!

II. Now I must try to answer our second question: WHAT IS THE LORD'S ESTIMATE OF THESE TENDER GRAPES?

What does he think of that sorrow for sin, that little faith, that humble trust in his atoning sacrifice, that earnest attempt to live a changed life, that weariness of frivolity, that private prayer and study of the Scriptures, that eager desire for more grace, and that childlike love? What does the Lord think of all these?

Well, first, he thinks so much of it that *he calls his Church to come and look at it*. Look at the verses that precede our text:

"My beloved spake, and said unto me, Rise up, my love, my fair one, and come away. For, lo, the winter is past, the rain is over and gone; the flowers appear on the earth; the time of the singing of birds is come, and the voice of the turtle is heard in our land; the

197

fig tree putteth forth her green figs, and the vines with the tender grape give a good smell."

We do not usually call our friends to look at things which we do not ourselves admire; so here the Bridegroom calls his spouse to share in his joy in these tokens of the heavenly life of the Church of God. Be always on the look out for the tender grapes. I think I know some Christians who do not appreciate these early fruits as they ought. When dear children are brought to know the Lord, we cannot expect that such little shoots as they are should at first produce anything but tender grapes. There are some who do not take that view of the matter. "Ah", they say, "there is no flavour in those grapes!" Did you expect that there would be? "Oh", they cry, "they are tart and sour!" Of course they are; while they are tender grapes, they must be so. You cannot get the ripeness or the sweetness of maturity in that which is just beginning to grow. Our Lord would not have us find fault with the fruit of young converts, but rather go and look at it, and admire it, and bless God that there is at least some, and that it is as good as it is. "Ah", says one, "that young man does not know much!" Does he know that one thing, that whereas he was blind, now he can see? (Jn. 9:235) Then be thankful that he knows as much as that. "Oh", you exclaim, "but he has not much prudence!" No, my dear friend, do you suppose that this young man is to have as much prudence as you have at your age, and you are perhaps sixty or seventy? I might possibly say with truth that you have not quite so much zeal as you might have to go with your prudence. "Oh, but", you say, "we want the young man to be more mature!" Give him time, and he will get as mature as you are; but while the grapes are still tender, your Master and his calls you to look at them, and to thank him for them, for there is something very cheering in the sight of the first weak, faint tokens of the working of the Holy Spirit in the soul of a young believer.

What is Christ's estimate of these tender grapes? Well, next, *he calls them tender*. He does not call them mature, he does not speak of them as ripe; he calls them "tender". Do you know how he might have described them? He might have called them sour, but he does not; he calls them "tender." He likes to use a sweet word, you see, the softest and best word that he can use; so, when you describe a young convert, my dear brother, do not at once point out his immaturity, but call him "tender." Do not speak about his want of discretion, but call him "tender." Do not say, "Oh, well, I question whether he can be a child of God or not!" He is one of God's little ones. A little child is just as much its mother's bairn as the biggest one in the family; and no doubt that little one whose voice we heard just now is as much beloved by the mother as any of her older sons or daughters. So it should be with those who are the little children in God's great family of love; therefore, imitate your Lord, and call them "tender".

Then he says something more: "The vines with the tender grape give a good smell." Of what do they smell?

Well, first, they smell of *sincerity*. You say, "That young man does not know much, but he is very sincere." How many do I see who come to make a confession of their faith in Christ, who do not know this doctrine, or have not had that experience, but they are very sincere! I can tell that they are genuine by the way they speak; they often make such dreadful blunders theologically that I know they have not learnt it by rote, as they might get up a lesson. They talk straight out of their loving but ignorant hearts, and I like that they should do so, for it shows how true they are in what they say; and our Lord Jesus always loves sincerity. There is no smell so hateful as the smell of hypocrisy; a religious experience that is made to order, religious talk such as some indulge in which is all cant, a stench in the nostrils of God. The Lord save us from it! But these vines with the tender grape give out the sweet smell of sincerity.

Next, there is about these young believers a sweet smell of *heartiness*. Oh, how hearty they generally are, how earnest, how lively! By-and-by, some of the older folks talk about the things of God as if they were worn threadbare, and there was nothing of special interest in them; but it is not so with these new-born souls, when everything is bright and fresh, and they are lively and full of earnestness, and Jesus loves that kind of spirit. He said to the angel of the church of the Laodiceans, "I would thou wert cold or hot." (Rev. 3:15) It is lukewarmness that he cannot bear, but he approves of warm, simple heartiness; it is to him like the smell of the vines that bear the tender grapes.

There is sure to be also about these young Christians the sweet smell of *zeal*; and, whatever may be said against zeal, I will take up the cudgels for it as long as I live. In the work of God, we cannot do without fire. We Baptists like water because our Master has ordained the use of it; but we must also have fire, fire from heaven, the fire of the Holy Spirit. When I see our young men and young women full of zeal for God's glory, I say, "God bless them! Let them go ahead." Some of the old folk want to put a bit in the mouths of these fiery young steeds, and rein them in; but I trust that I shall ever be on their side, and say, "No, let them go as fast as they like. If they have zeal without knowledge, it is a good deal better than having knowledge without zeal; only wait a bit, and they will get all the knowledge they need."

These young believers have another sweet smell: they are *teachable*, ready to learn, willing to be taught from the Scriptures and from those whose instructions God blesses to their souls.

There is also another delicious smell about them, and that is, they are generally *very joyful*. While they are singing, some dear old brother, who has known the Lord for fifty years, is groaning; what is the matter with the good man? I wish that he could catch the sweet contagion of the early joy of those who have just found the Saviour. There is something delightful in all joy when it is joy in the Lord, but there is a special brightness about the delight of those who are newly converted. You see that Christ forms a correct, condescending, wise estimate of these vines with the tender grape. He calls his Church to look at them, calling them tender, and says that they have a sweet smell, and then he shows that he cares very much about them, for he says, "Take us the foxes, the little foxes, that spoil the vines: for our vines have tender grapes." He does not want even the tender grapes to be spoiled.

Some people seem to think that none but advanced Christians are worth looking after, but our Lord is not of that opinion. "Oh, it was only a lot of girls that joined the church", said somebody. "A lot of girls"? That is not the way that our Lord Jesus Christ speaks about his children. He calls them King's daughters; and let them be called so. "They were only a pack of boys and young men." Yes, but they are the material of which old men are made; and boys and young men, after all, are of much account in the Master's esteem. May we always have many such in this church!

III. So I come to my third and closing question: WHAT IS THE DANGER TO THESE TENDER GRAPES? The 15th verse says that they are in danger from foxes, and gives the command, "Take us the foxes, the little foxes, that spoil the vines: for our vines have tender grapes."

Dear young friends who have lately found Christ, there are foxes about. We try all we can to stop the gaps in the hedge that we may keep the foxes out; but they are very crafty, and they manage to get in sometimes. Foxes in the East are much smaller than ours, and they seem to be even more cunning and more ferocious than those we have in this country, and they do much mischief to the vines.

199

In the spiritual vineyard, there are foxes of many kinds. There is, first, *the hard censurer*. He will spoil the vines if he can, and especially the vines that have the tender grapes. He finds fault with everything he can see in you who are only young believers. You know that you are simply depending on Christ for salvation; but this censurer says, "You are no child of God, for you are far from being perfect." If God had no children but those who are perfect, he would have none under heaven. These censorious people find fault with this and that and the other in your life and character, and you know well enough that you have all too many imperfections, and, if they look for them, they can soon spy them out. Then they say, "We do not believe that there is any grace at all in you", though you know that by the grace of God you are what you are. (1 Cor. 15:10) It may be that there is a fault in you which they have discovered; perhaps you were taken by surprise and suddenly overcome. Possibly, they even set a trap for you, and allured you into it, provoking you to anger, and then, turning round on you, said, "You have made a profession, have you? That is your religion, is it?" and so on. May God deliver you from these cruel foxes! He will often do so by enabling you not to mind them. After all, this is only the way in which all Christians have been tried, and there is nothing strange in your experience from these censurers; they are not your judges, and you will not be condemned because they condemn you. Go and do your best in the service of your Lord; trust in Christ, and do not mind what they say, and you will be delivered from that kind of fox.

A worse fox even than that one, however, is *the flatterer*. He comes to you smiling and smirking, and he begins to express his approval of your religion, and very likely tells you what a fine fellow you are. Indeed, you are so good that he thinks you are rather too precise; you have gone a little over the line. He believes in religion, he says, though, if you watch his life, you will not think so; but he says that he does not want people to be righteous overmuch; he knows that there is a line to be drawn, and he draws it. I never could see where he drew it; but still he says he does, and he thinks that you draw the line a little too near the cross. He says, "You might be a little more worldly, you cannot get through life in your way; if you get out of society, you may as well get out of the world at once. Why do you make yourself appear so singular?" I know what he is after; he wants to get you back among the ungodly. Satan misses you, and he wants to have you again, and he is sending Mr. Flatterer to wheedle you back, if possible, into your former bondage to himself. Get away from that fox at once. The man who tells you that you are too precise ought to be precisely told that you do not want his company. There never lived a man yet who was too holy, and there never will live a man who will imitate Christ too closely, or avoid sin too rigidly. Whenever a man says that you are too puritanical, you may always smell one of these foxes. It would be better if we were all more puritanical and precise. Has not our Father said to us, "Be ye holy; for I am holy"? (Lev. 20:7; 1 Pet. 1:15-16) Did not our Lord Jesus say to his disciples, "Be ye therefore perfect, even as your Father which is in heaven is perfect"? (Mat. 5:48)

Then there comes another foul fox, *Mr. Wordly-Wiseman*. He says, "You are a Christian, but do not be a fool. Carry your religion as far as you can make it pay; but when it comes to losing anything by it, well then, don't you do it. You see, this practice is the custom of the trade; it is not right, I know; but still, other people do it, and you ought to do it. If you do not, you will never get on in business." Mr. Worldly-wiseman further says, "Never mind if you tell a lie or two, and make your advertisements say what is not true; everybody else does it as a matter of course, and why not you? Then try whether you cannot get a slice out of your customer here and a slice there when he does not know it; it is the custom of the trade. This is the way other people do, and, as it is the custom, of course you must do it." To all such talk I reply that there is another custom, a custom that God has, of turning all liars into hell; mind that you do not come under that divine rule and law. There is another custom that God has, namely, that of cutting down as hypocrites those who do not

200

walk honestly and uprightly towards their fellow-men. The plea of custom will not stand for a moment at the judgement-seat of Christ (2 Cor. 5:10); and it ought to have no weight with us here. I know that there are many young people who, unless they are watchful and careful at the very beginning of their spiritual life, will get lamed, and never will do as they ought to do because this fox has bitten them.

There is another ugly fox about, and that is, *a doubting fox*. He comes and says, "You seem very happy, and very joyful; but is it true? You appear to have become quite a different person from what you used to be; but is there, after all, such a thing as conversion?" This fox begins nibbling at every doctrine, even nibbling at your Bible, and tries to steal from you this chapter and that verse. God save you young people from all these foxes!

There are some foxes of *evil doctrine*, and they generally try to spoil our young people. I do not think anybody ever attempts now to convert me from my belief; the other day, when a man was arguing with another, I asked him, "Why don't you try me?" "Oh", he said, "I have given you up as a bad case, there is no use trying to do anything with you." It is so when we get to be thoroughly confirmed in our convictions of the truth; they give us up, and they generally say that we are such fools that we cannot learn their wisdom, which is quite correct; and so we intend to be as long as ever we live. But with some of the younger folk, they manage it thus. They say, "Now, you are a person of considerable breadth of thought, you have an enlarged mind, you are a man of culture; it is a pity that you should cling to those old-fashioned beliefs, which really are not consistent with modern progress"; and the foolish young fellow thinks that he is a wonder, and so is puffed up with conceit. When a man has to talk about his own culture, and to glory in his own advancement, it is time that we suspected the truth about him. When a man can despise others who are doing vastly more good than he ever dreamed of doing, and call such people antiquated and old-fashioned, it is time that he should get rebuked for his impudence, for that is really what it is. These clever men, as far as I know them, are simply veneered with a little learning, not sixteen-thousandth of an inch thick. There is nothing in most of them but mere presence and bluster. But there are some who hold firmly to the old gospel, who have read as much as they are ever likely to do, and are fully their equals in learning, though they do not care to boast of their acquirements. Do not any of you young people be carried away with the notion that all the learned men are heretics; it is very largely the reverse, and it is your sham, shallow philosopher who goes running after heresy. Get out of the way of that fox, or else he will do much mischief to the tender grapes.

So, brethren, I close with this remark. If you have any sign of spiritual life, if you have any tender grapes on your branches, the devil and his foxes will be sure to get at you; therefore, endeavour to get as close as ever you can to two persons who are mentioned hard by my text, namely, the King and his spouse. First, keep close to Christ, for this is your life; and next, keep close to his Church, for this is your comfort. Get among elderly Christian people, and seek to catch up with those who have long known the Lord, those who are farther on the heavenly road than you are. Pilgrims to Zion should go to heaven in company, and often, when they go in company, and they can get a Mr. Greatheart to go before them, it saves them from many a Giant Slaygood and many a Giant Grim, and they get a safe and happy journey to the Celestial City where else they might have been buffeted and worried. Keep close to God's people, whoever they may be; they are the best company for you, young believers. Some Christians may, like Bunyan's pilgrim, start on the road to heaven alone; but they miss much comfort which they might have with company, and do well to keep in company with someone of the Lord's champions, and with the rest of the army with banners who march towards the Celestial City. God bless and comfort all of you who know his name, henceforth and forever! Amen.

27. A REQUEST OF THE BELOVED

PREACHED AT THE METROPOLITAN TABERNACLE

"O my dove, that art in the clefts of the rock, in the secret places of the stairs, let me see thy countenance, let me hear thy voice; for sweet is thy voice, and thy countenance is comely." (Song of Solomon 2:14)

BELOVED, though it well becomes us as believers in Christ to pray, we must regard it as a wonderful condescension on the part of Christ that he deigns to pray to us. We feel it to be natural, and we think it is reasonable, that we should pray and present our requests to the Father. But, oh, what a strange stoop of love is this, that he should present his request, and, if I may say so, pray to us! We sometimes say to him, "Let me see thy face"; but here, in this sacred song, he actually turns round to his own people, and says to each of them, "Let me see thy face." Observe, again, that it is our duty, our privilege, and our pleasure, to praise our blessed Lord Jesus Christ. Is not this the employment of saints on earth and the enjoyment of saints in heaven? Yet, by a marvellous inversion of the usual course, we hear Christ praising us! He seems to take our part, and speak with winsome words of admiration to those who may well bow before him in adoration, saying, "Sweet is thy voice, and thy countenance is comely."

When you appeal to Christ, he hears and answers you. Believer, do you not hearken and heed when he entreats you? Then when you extol the Beloved of your soul, your praise is acceptable to him. Shall not, then, the eulogy he passes on you make your pulse race with pleasure, and swell your hearts with floods of joy? Jesus asks a favour at the hands of every one of his people, and then backs up his request with a pleasant word of matchless commendation.

We have here *a request of Christ;* but I wish you distinctly to understand that this is only addressed to God's people, to the blood-bought, the blood-washed, and to those who trust the Lord and are saved by him. To such, the Lord Jesus Christ adds a double petition. In one, he says, "Let me see thy face." The interpretation is not difficult. At least, I believe we may trace a fourfold meaning in it. Does he not here desire from his people an openness of carriage? Some of the saints go through the world as if they were half ashamed to own their love for their Lord. They wear a thick veil to hide their godliness. They make no profession, and seldom speak a word that savours of his dear name. So he calls them to put that veil away as he says, "Let me see thy face." And why, let me ask, should it not be open in the sight of all? Though the gospel never sanctions our making a parade of our religion, yet it does demand that we practise no disguise, but, before the eyes of the world, avow our faith in Jesus.

"No man, when he hath lighted a candle, putteth it in a secret place, neither under a bushel, but on a candlestick; and it giveth light unto all that are in the house. Let your light so shine before men that they may see your good works, and glorify your Father which is in heaven." (Lk. 8:16, 11:33)

We read also, "A city that is set on a hill cannot be hid" (Mat. 5:14); and Christ expressly tells you, "That which ye have spoken in the ear in closets shall be proclaimed upon the housetops." (Lk. 12:3) The Church is like the moon, with Christ as the sun. The sun shines and the moon reflects the sunlight. What should we think of the moon if she were so bashful that she would not reflect the light of the sun? Such coyness would intensify the shades of night. The shamefaced reserve of Christians leaves the world in darkness from which there is no relief. I wonder why they are ashamed of their religion. What is there to be ashamed of? Brethren, if we are professing something that is not sensible, that is not rational, something which disgusts the conscience and outrages the common sense, of mankind, by all manner of means, let us give it up. But if serving God is the truest and noblest occupation of his creatures, let us never be ashamed of it. Our Lord Jesus Christ had good reason to be ashamed of us, and yet he never is. He took up our cause and, through shame and spitting, he espoused it. Yes, "He is not ashamed to call us brethren." (Heb. 2:11) And should you and I be ashamed of him? Rather, let us be ashamed of ourselves for thinking such a thing. I beg any Christians here who have kept their religion in the background, to do so no longer, for your Lord now lovingly asks you — appeals to you by the love he published before heaven and earth and hell towards you — "Let me see thy face". Do not skulk in the corner (Acts 26:26); do not hide yourself away; but come out and say, "I am on the Lord's side." (Ex. 32:26)

And does not Christ here ask his people to have a confidence of bearing in his presence? "Let me see thy face." We are to come before God, even the Father, with covered faces. That was a sweet prayer from one who said: "O Lord, the seraphim and cherubim veil their faces with their wings whenever they come into your presence, and we have no wings with which to veil our faces; but we have something better than the wings of angels —we have the blood and righteousness of our Lord Jesus Christ." In God's presence, we must ever appear with covered faces; but, in the presence of his only begotten Son our Lord Jesus Christ, a Christian who holds down his head does not understand gospel liberty. Jesus Christ seems to say to his Church, when he sees her concealing her face, "Let *me* see thy face." Is he not "bone of our bones, and flesh of our flesh" (Gen. 2:23) — "a brother born for adversity"? (Prov. 17:17) There is no quarrel between our soul and Christ. He is our peace. (Eph. 2:14) He loved us, and gave himself for us. (Gal 2:20; Eph. 4:25) The love of Jesus Christ for his people is so high, so deep, so broad, and so pure, that they never ought to be afraid when they stand before him. You need a mediator when you come before God, but you need no mediator when you come before Christ. You think, "Were I like Peter or Paul, and I could see Christ, I should speak to him right boldly." Ah, but Peter and Paul had no righteousness to stand in except that which belongs to you as much as to them — the righteousness of Jesus Christ. And I beg you, since you are espoused, and since he loves you, and since his heart is set on you, do not distrust him, but believe in him. Well does Isaac Watts sing,

We would no longer lie
Like slaves beneath the throne.
My faith shall Abba, Father, cry,
And Thou the kindred own.

Yet many of God's people are living in abject bondage. They hope they are saved, but do not know. They hope Christ loves them, but they are afraid he doesn't; and hence they often sing,

'Tis a point I long to know.
Oft it causes anxious thought;
Do I love the Lord, or no?
Am I his, or am I not?

Could my heart so hard remain,
Prayer a task and burden prove;
Every trifle give me pain,
If I knew a Saviour's love?

When I turn my eyes within,
All is dark, and vain, and wild;
Filled with unbelief and sin,
Can I deem myself a child?

Lord, decide the doubtful case!
Thou who art thy people's sun;
Shine upon thy work of grace,
If it be indeed begun.

Let me love thee more and more,
If I love at all, I pray;
If I have not loved before,
Help me to begin today.

(John Newton)

Come, Christian! Wash your face in the divine bath of Jesus' love, and look up and let him see your face — not brazen with the impudence of self-righteousness, but clear and beautiful, with the confidence of faith in him. This, I think, is in the text —an openness of behaviour, and a confidence of conduct towards him.

Again, when he says, "Let me see thy face", does he not call for Christian courage before others? Here, I touch on the same point as before, only I take another side to the thought. Some Christians, when they have professed Christ, shrink back as if doubtful of their own propriety. I have heard of brethren whose conscience compelled them to leave the Church of England, and yet their conduct afterwards appeared to betray so much confusion that I might compare them to "Fear":

First, Fear his hand its skill to try,
Amid the chords bewildered laid;
And back recoiled, he knew not why,
E'en at the sound himself had made.

(William Collins, *Ode to the Passions: an Ode for Music*)

Surely, this is not the true spirit of a Christian. What we resolve for God we never retract. If we err in judgment, we are open to conviction; but, when we know we speak God's truth, we nail our colours to the mast and are prepared, with colours flying, to reassert it; and we shall never pull them down to please the paltry prejudice of our neighbours. Let no Christian be silent when his Master demands that he speak. There are times, dear friends, when Christ seems to lack the countenances of his people, as if their testimony would tell for something. Those that are standing in the back rank need to stand forward and say, "Here am I". (Is. 6:8) If there is someone suffering for the truth, I will suffer with him. If there is someone standing in the pillory for God's Word, I will take a share of it, and grudge him the pleasure of carrying the heavier side of the cross than I may be called on to carry. "Let me see thy face." Are any of you living in ungodly families? Let Christ see your face. Speak up for him. Do not intrude your religion unceasingly; but never hesitate and falter, or bow and cringe, as though you seek toleration for serving God. Serve your God with gladness, as one who knows he has a right to do, and who, acting with a clear conscience, asks no one else's leave. "Let me see thy face." I am afraid that many Christians get an easy berth by bridling their tongues. There is an old saw — "Speech is silvern, silence is golden" [quoted by the writer Thomas Carlyle]. I am afraid there are some who prove the proverb in a perverse sense. Do not let yours be the silence that suppresses the truth, but bear your testimony faithfully; for Christ says, "Let me see thy face."

The passage will bear one other construction, which is perhaps more likely to be the precise meaning of our text — "Let me see thy face." You know Jacob went down to Egypt to see the face of Joseph; and to hold near communion with him was doubtless his intent. (Gen. 48:11-12) Now, Christians, you have been standing so far away that I think Christ can hardly see your face; and he beckons to you — "Come near, come near; let me look you in the face." Some of my friends in the far distance I can scarcely make out their features. This, I think, I can use as a metaphor to describe the distance at which some souls live from Jesus. Peter followed afar off, and you know what came of it, for, before long, he denied his Master. Closer, closer, let us cleave to Christ. Let our prayer be Christ's prayer,

Nearer, my God, to thee,
Nearer to thee!
E'en though it be a cross
That raiseth me!
Yet all my cry shall be,
Nearer, my God, to thee,
Nearer to thee!'

(Sarah Flower Adams)

"Let me see thy face." Do you see the drift of this prayer, then, the prayer of your sweet Lord Jesus? He bows before you now. He, before whom angels bow, bows before you, and asks you — "Purchased of my blood, loved of my soul, chosen of my heart; come, let me see thy face. Come near, and let me put my hand on your, and let me kiss you with the kisses of my mouth."

In the second clause of the same request, he says, "Let me hear thy voice." This, too, seems to have a variety of meanings slumbering within. The Church has several voices. It has, that is, the voice of testimony. Throughout all ages, the true Church has been a testifying, a witness-bearing, Church. Wherever witness is borne for Christ, that voice is very sweet. She denounced the idols of Rome till her witness made the gods totter from their thrones, and images fell from their pedestals. She bore witness afterwards under priestly pretensions and Papal persecutions. In our own country, her Protestant voice was raised, and she published the Word of God, undaunted by ecclesiastical anathema or civil process. Lollards' Tower was crowded with confessors, when preachers were adjudged to the pillories, and Scripture readers were relentlessly burned in Smithfield fires. Noble was the army of her martyrs. In the same way, the Covenanting forefathers maintained their faith among the glens and craggy rocks of Scotland. In the obscure meeting-houses, and lowly places of England, it was the same. Thus did the Church bear her witness for God. And she bears her witness still by many faithful and earnest lips. In this land, her witness, I fear, is not always as clear and conspicuous as it should be; but there are countries now where persecution purifies the Church, and is a special boon to her, where her witness is as shrill as a trumpet giving a certain sound (1 Cor. 14:8), that men may marshal themselves for the battle.

Woe to the day when any church ceases to work for Christ against the sins and vices of the world! We are to be like the witnesses that were clothed in sackcloth (Rev. 11:3); slain, yet brought to life again; dying, and yet living best by death, and crying from their graves like the blood of Abel, which reaches the ear of heaven. Brethren, Christ would have his Church lift her voice now, whatever there is to testify for or against. He speaks to you, his

205

beloved ones, and he says, "Let me hear thy voice." Let it not be the minister's voice alone, but let it be your voice in your holy living. Those of you who have no faculty for public address can give testimony by a consistent piety, a strict integrity in business, and such a stern uprightness in all your conduct that it refuses to bend to the customs of other men. This will be a witness for God that even this deaf adder age (Psalm 58:4-5) must hear. Without any effort to charm, your life will draw attention.

The voice of Christian *fellowship* is, likewise, very sweet. Those who fear the Lord speak often with each other. There is much that is agreeable to Christ as well as to ourselves in Christian conversation. I hope the members of this church will never get distant and reserved towards one another. Everybody used to know everybody else at one time. I do not know that too much private intimacy among all the people is profitable. Still, there is a beauty in the fellowship of worshippers which I would not have you negligent. It grieves me to hear every now and then of those who have been attending the services at the Tabernacle for five or six months, and nobody has spoken to them. Last Thursday, I saw something which I deeply regretted. A poor man and woman, sitting in one of the pews, were turned out of their seats by a certain friend who came in late, and they had to retire to some back seats as if they were intruders. "Well", thought I, "those are just the sort of people to whom I would give the heartiest welcome, especially on a Thursday night." Those who profess to be followers of Jesus Christ should be ashamed to do honour to the affluent, and then disparage the destitute in the courts of the Lord's house. We are one, I hope, in Christ Jesus. That kind of discrimination soon strikes a death blow to all true Christian fellowship. No, those who feared the Lord of old loved to see each other's faces; and though they were not given to idle chit-chat, they delighted in talking together about the covenant grace of God. Nor were they ever long together before they found their hearts blended in sweet harmony and sacred unison. The same hope sparkled in each eye; the same songs were familiar to each tongue. Grateful remembrances of God goodness, and gladdening prospects of the glory to be revealed, drown their griefs and groans in the dark days of their discomfiture. And you know how the Lord hearkened and heard. Ah, I think I hear Jesus say to some of you that have not much Christian converse with your brothers and sisters, "Let me hear thy voice — let me hear thy voice"; for the voice of Christian converse is congenial to saints and acceptable to Christ.

And can you doubt that the voice of prayer is as sweet to the dear Saviour as the smell of the frankincense which smoked up from the censers of the priests to the Most High in days of old. We cannot all preach, but all of us, who are believers, can unite and blend our voices in prayer. Ah, does any believer here feel tempted not to pray? Jesus says, "Let me hear thy voice." I think I hear you say, "Lord, mine is a poor broken voice; I cannot pray as I should. My heart is cold, my thoughts wander, and my desires vacillate." Ah, well! Tell Jesus your troubles; only let him hear your voice. "But my voice is not worth hearing", says another. Well, let him be the best judge of that; and if he asks you to let him hear it, don't decline. I tell you, Christ loves even the cries of his children — their mewling is music to him, their tears tell the tide of their troubles or of their thanksgivings. "The tears of the penitent", says one of the early fathers, "are the wine of angels; certainly the tears of God's people are put into Christ's bottle." (Ps. 56:8) Sigh out your sorrows; tell him your griefs; let him hear you voice. I rather think that the united voice of God's people at the prayer meetings must be agreeable to Christ. If any of you are negligent, and in the habit of stopping away without good cause, let this entreaty come home to you — he who died for your redemption says, "Let me hear thy voice."

Does not this apply to the voice of *praise* also? Oh, how sweet is the voice of praise when willing hearts make melody before God! The dead music of wind and strings has little in it acceptable to him; but the living music of men's hearts and voices God loves. How glorious the swell of some noble psalm when thousands chant the praises of Jehovah-Jireh of Israel! My soul has never taken wing to mount so near to heaven as when, on certain joyful occasions, we have all united together to praise God with all our might. Sometimes, that lovely "Hallelujah, Hallelujah, Hallelujah" seems to peal out like the thunders of earth melting into the thunders of heaven. Oh, friends, let us praise Jesus, not only here but wherever we are, and as often as we find opportunity. Speak well of his name; tell others of Christ — what his arm has done, what spoils from death he has won — praise his great name alone, and say "Worthy the Lamb." An eminent saint of God, who died a martyr's death, divided the day into twenty-four parts, and, having twenty-four in his household, he always had someone, both night and day, engaged in the service of God. A very pleasant idea; at once poetical and practical! Well, if we cannot do that, at least with the dawn of the morning let our song be:

Awake, my soul, and with the sun
Thy daily stage of duty run;
Shake off dull sloth, and joyful rise
To pay thy morning sacrifice.

Wake, and lift up thyself, my heart;
And with the angels bear thy part,
Who all night long unwearied sing
High praises to the Eternal King.

(Thomas Ken)

And let us compose ourselves to sleep with some grateful sonnet like this children's hymn from John Keble:

When the soft dews of kindly sleep
My wearied eyelids gently steep,
Be my last thought, how sweet to rest
Forever on my Saviour's breast!

Let him hear your voice in praise in prayer and in testimony. I need not enlarge, except to say that the precise meaning I have no doubt about is "Let me hear thy voice in sweet communion" — talk of Christ. You will observe he does not say, "Turn your face this way or that", but "Let me see thy face"; and he doesn't say, "Let thy voice be heard", but "Let me hear thy voice." Perhaps you've come up here only to hear the minister. That will never do. Let our Lord Jesus Christ hear your voice that you may hear his. And when you are alone, do not think that religious exercises must necessarily be suspended. His presence may be known and enjoyed when you are free from the intrusion of fellow creatures. Jesus says, "Let me hear thy voice." Some of us, in the quiet retreat of our gardens, have often had reasons to thank God that, in the words of William Cowper,

Far from the world, O Lord, I flee,
From strife and tumult far;
From scenes where Satan wages still
His most successful war.

The calm retreat, the silent shade,
With prayer and praise agree;
And seem, by thy kind bounty made
For those who worship thee.

207

**There if thy Spirit touch the soul,
And grace her mean abode,
Oh, with what peace, and joy, and love,
She communes with her God!**

When, without fear of any eavesdropper, we can talk aloud to him who is invisible.

Some of us have had the richest fellowship we ever knew, when we talked with Christ as a man talks with his friend. (Song 5:16) If you cannot do it aloud, there is a way in which the soul can be lively while the lips are silent, and the verity of our communion in the daytime may be as vivid as the visions of the night, and which often leave a deeper impression on our memory. You pour out your heart before him, and he seems to pour into your soul the sweet solace of his love. Thus the secret of the Lord is with them that fear him (Ps. 25:14), and he shows them his covenant. From the cross, and from the throne, Jesus entreats all of you who love him, especially as you come to his Table — "Let me hear thy voice, and see thy face!"

And now, please notice the reasons for Jesus Christ's prayer. He says, "Sweet is thy voice, and thy countenance is comely." A strange thing to say of such creatures as you and me! What can Christ see to admire in us? Surely he knows best. But had we to judge ourselves, we should little think that there was anything in us that could give him delight. Yet we hear what he says, and we are bound to believe him.

How is it, beloved, that we may venture to inquire that there can be anything sweet and comely in the voice and countenance of believers? Well, Christ sees a sweetness and comeliness in his people because he is interested in them! He takes an interest in them as a workman does in the productions of his own skill. When the Greek ambassador came to Cyrus, the Persian monarch took him round his garden and showed him all the various fruit trees, at which Lysander expressed his delight; but Cyrus said, "You cannot, by any possibility, find such enjoyment in these gardens as I do, for", said he, "I planted and pruned all these trees myself, with my own hands, after laying out this garden entirely according to my own plans." So it is that Jesus Christ takes extraordinary delight in his people because he plants and prunes them himself. "We are his workmanship (Eph. 2:10), created anew in Christ Jesus"; and that is why he takes pleasure in us.

Then, again, you are his by purchase. What a man buys and preserves at great cost he will prize. You don't know what you're worth, but he does, for he paid for you. You cannot measure the pangs of his heart, or the woes of his spirit; but he knows it all. Down to the depths of grief, he bowed his head for you; and counted out the purple drops for your redemption. You are bought with a price. (1 Cor. 6:20, 7:23) Mark, there was a price set on you, and he knows, though you do not, the estimate that his love set on your souls; but, from his very heart, he values his purchase.

And he has an interest in you because you are his eternal choice. Before you had being, he pictured you in his own mind and loved you. Yes, not only before you had being, but before the mountains glistened with their snow-white heads in the sunlight — before the sun and moon and stars launched out in their perpetual course, he set his love on you. Dearer were you to him than all his other works, for even then he rejoiced over you with singing, where it is written, "My delights were with the sons of men." (Prov. 8:31) To think of you was his eternal solace. Do you wonder, therefore, that he should wish now to hear your voice and see your face. Besides, you are to be his everlasting reward. He looks on you as the jewels of his crown. You are to him what God has given him as his portion for the travail of his soul. (Is 53:11) He sees his Father's love

208

in you, for you are his Father's gift; and, therefore, he prizes you beyond all price, and asks you to speak to him and let him see your face. With such a loving argument, how can you deny him? I charge you, child of God, before him who died for you, do not deny him. Come, leave your family cares; cease the drudgery of your business; shake yourself free from the dust, if you can; forget awhile the cares of home; lay aside that heavy ledger, with all the losses and crosses that make your days anxious, and your nights restless. Jesus asks you to commune with him, and he uses this all-conquering argument, that he loves you, and has an interest in you. "Thy voice is sweet, and thy countenance is comely. Let me see thy face."

When Christ speaks thus, he states a fact without a tinge of sentiment, because, through the operation of his grace, the Church's face is comely, and the voice of his church is sweet. What finer sight under heaven is there than an honest, upright, sanctified, godly man? Should a prince bedeck himself with as many jewels as a Nepalese ambassador, what real worth would he be? A poor man, though covered with patched garments, if his character is full of sterling integrity, if the fear of God nestles in his heart, and love for Jesus glows in all his life, he is such a one that an angel would linger to look at. The history of our human race, how horrible it is, stained with selfishness, defiled with crime, and red with blood! Yet one silver line runs through the whole: it is the silver line of the election of grace — the sacramental host of God's elect. The only redeeming trait in the entire history of mankind is to be found in the Church of Christ. "She is clear as the sun, fair as the moon, and she yet shall be terrible, as an army with banners." (Song 6:4, 10) Her voice really is sweet. I do not mean the voice of some churches, whose pride has been obnoxious to heaven and their persecutions a pestilence on earth. Truly, the voice of Christ's Church is very sweet because it is not pretentious or discordant, but humble and harmonious. The purity of her language is drawn from the secret fountain of inspiration; she reveres the Scriptures while she renounces tradition; she speaks the truth in love (Eph. 4:15); she bears solemn witness against sin, and her voice is ever raised for righteousness and true holiness.

We have some churches whose creed is full of incongruities. Their books are so complicated that lawyers are baffled in interpreting their meaning. Revision may be prescribed, and revision of their liturgy and articles is needed, for no one who subscribes to them can interpret them, far less believe them. How can anyone believe in the whole of the Prayer Book of the Church of England? If he holds High Church views, the articles confront him with their Calvinism. If he holds Low Church views, the liturgy is Popish enough to appal him. In any case, the catechism offers him plenty to complain about. From the mitred archbishop to the meanest curate, the conscience of every member of the community is compromised. They, one and all, are fenced in with the falsehood of the system, and hazard the charge of foul hypocrisy. They do it in ignorance, and do not see that, in conforming to custom, they are committing a crime. May God open their eyes! That church's voice is never sweet which speaks in one part of her book clearly and beautifully, and in another part apocryphally and ambiguously. No, Christ wants his Church to speak plainly; and, when she finds she has made a mistake, and strayed from the straight course, she must have courage enough to retrace her steps, repeal her edicts, and return to the truth as she received it from her Lord and Master. One by one, however, I could exhort you to take care that your voice is sweet. I cannot speak too harshly of those people who, on Sunday, chatter like saints, and on Monday cheat like sinners. You may put on the garb of piety only to profane it. You may sing the praises of God never so harmoniously; but your voice is not sweet to Christ unless it is honest, healthy, and heartfelt.

Moreover, Christ loves to hear the voice and see the face of his Church because of his relationship with her. He is the Everlasting Father; and there is no one who can bear so

209

well the voice of a child as the father, unless it is the mother. Why, your children cry more sweetly than anybody else's children! When another's child is crying, you are shocked at its peevishness or passionate temper, but when your own child gives vent to its feelings, you pity the poor little thing, and are quite sure it must be suffering some kind of pain. I doubt if our Lord Jesus Christ, out of his infinite love towards his Church, can hear anything but music from her. He sees no sin in Jacob, nor iniquity in Israel, and covers their faults with the mantle of his love. ["Love covereth all sins." (Prov 10:12; 1 Pet. 4:8)] With his righteousness, he has robed his Church; with his grace, he has sanctified her; and, now he beholds her in the beauty with which she shall hereafter shine rather than in the *deshabille* of her present garb. So he says that her voice is sweet, and her countenance is comely.

While I have spoken in this way to God's people, I do not expect there has been anything to interest very many of you. Well! Well! Let me say one word to the stranger before I close. Jesus would be glad to hear your voice if it lifted up a prayer like this: "God be merciful to me a sinner. (Lk. 18:13) Lord save, or I perish!" Be it only a groan, if it is sincere, he will hear it. Standing in that aisle, or in this crowd here, if you can only, from your heart, say, "Lord, I trust you — take my sins away, and make me your servant" — know this, my brother, your voice is sweet to him, for never did a sinner cry without Christ hearing it — that is, this side of the grave, I mean. But, alas, if you do not cry now, you will cry hereafter, when the answer will be, "Because I called, and you refused, I stretched out my hand and no one paid attention; but you set aside all my counsel, and would have none of my reproof. Therefore, I will laugh at your calamity (Ps. 2:4, 37:13, 59:8), I will mock when your fear comes. (Prov. 1:26)" Do you not shudder as you listen to these threats?

May God grant you to believe in Jesus, and trust him implicitly, and prove for yourselves the faithfulness of his promises! So shall you see his face with joy, and hear his voice with unutterable delight, welcoming you into his glory. Amen.

28. LOVED AND LOVING: AMONG THE LILIES
NO. 1634B

AT MENTONE, DECEMBER, 1881

"My beloved is mine, and I am his: he feedeth among the lilies."
(Song of Solomon 2:16)

"MY BELOVED" — this is a sweet name which our love takes liberty to apply to the Lord Jesus. His inexpressible beauty has won our affection, and we cannot help loving him whatever may come of it. Whether he is ours or not, and whether he smiles upon us or frowns, we love him, and cannot do otherwise. We are carried away by the torrent of his goodness, and have no longer the control of our affections. As long as we live, we must and will love the altogether lovely One. Yes, he is that, and must be to me, "My Beloved".

But suppose — suppose for a moment — that we loved and had no right to love. Many a heart that has cried "My beloved" has been wounded even unto death because it could not come at its choice, but was doomed never to exclaim, "My beloved is mine." The beloved was longed for, but could not be grasped. This is often so in earthly love, since such love may be unlawful, or unwise, and, in every case, it is the source of grievous misery. Thank God, this is not the case with the soul enamoured of Christ Jesus, for he freely presents himself in the gospel as the object of our confidence and love. Though he is infinitely above us, yet he delights to be one with all his loving ones, and, of his own, he will give himself to us. A polluted sinner may love the perfect Saviour, for there is no word in Scripture to forbid it. Yes, if a sinner would be wedded to the Lord of glory, there is none to forbid the banns.

Suppose that our possession of Jesus were a matter of doubt, as, alas, it is with far too many! That would be a door of sorrow indeed. Life would be unhappy if it were soured by a question as to whether our Well-beloved is ours or not. To an awakened and instructed mind, it is anguish to be dubious of our hold of Christ; about this we must need to be sure, or be unhappy. All else maybe in jeopardy, but, O most blessed Lord, never allow our possession of yourself to be in dispute! It would be a poor thing to say, "My beloved may be mine", or even, "He was mine", or "Perhaps he is mine". We cannot bear any verb but one in the indicative mood, present tense — "My beloved *is* mine."

Suppose yet once again that, though we loved, and rightly loved, and actually possessed the beloved object, yet our affection was not returned. Ah, misery! To love and not be loved! Blessed be God, we cannot only sing, "My Beloved is mine", but also, "I am his". He values me, he delights in me, he loves me! It is very wonderful that Jesus should think us worth the having; but since he does, we find a matchless solace in the fact. Which is the greater miracle — that he should be mine, or that I should be his? Certainly, the second is the surer ground of safety, for I cannot keep my treasures since I am feebleness itself. But Jesus is able to preserve his own, and none can pluck them out of his hand. The truth that Jesus calls me his is enough to make a man dance and sing all the way between here and heaven. Realise the fact that we are dear to the heart of our incarnate God, and, amid the sands of this wilderness, is a fountain of overflowing joy open before us.

BUT THE TEXT IS FREE FROM ALL SUPPOSITION: it is the language of indisputable possession, the exclamation of a confidence which has made its assurance doubly sure. There are two positive verbs in the present tense, and not the smell of a doubt has passed upon them. Here is a brave positiveness which fears no controversy, "My beloved is mine and I am his", doubt it who may. No, if you must need doubt it, ask him. There he is, for

211

"he feedeth among the lilies." The spouse sees him of whom she speaks; he may be a mere myth to others, but he is a substantial, lovable, lovely, and actually beloved person to her. He stands before her, and she perceives his character so clearly that she has a comparison ready for him, and likens him to a gazelle feeding on the tender grass among the lilies. This is a very delightful state of heart. Some of us know what it is to enjoy it from year to year. Christ is ours, and we know it. Jesus is present, and by faith we see him. Our marriage union with husband or wife cannot be more clear, more sure, more matter of fact, than our oneness with Christ and our enjoyment of that oneness. Joy! joy! joy! He whom we love is ours! We can also see the other side of the golden shield, for he whom we prize beyond all the world also prizes us, and we are his. Nothing in the universe besides deserves for an instant to be compared in value with this inestimable blessing. We would not change with the cherubim: their chief places in the choirs of heaven are poor as compared with the glory which excels — the glory of knowing that I am my best Beloved's, and he is mine. A place in Christ's heart is more sweet, more honourable, more dear to us, than a throne among the angels. Not even the delights of Paradise can produce a rival to this ecstatic joy — "My Beloved is mine, and I am his."

YET THE TEXT HAS A NOTE OF CAUTION. The condition of fully assured love is as tender as it is delightful. The spouse in the seventh verse had charged her companions by all things of gentleness, delicacy, and timidity — "by the roes, and by the hinds of the field" — to refrain from offending her beloved while he deigned to abide with her. She had also compared him to a roe or a young hart, rather hiding than revealing himself; and here she likens him to the same roe, quietly pasturing in the gardens, so gently moving that he does not break or even bruise a lily, but softly insinuates himself among their delicate beauties as one of the same dainty mould. This hints in poetic imagery at the solemn and sacred truth that the dearest fellowship with Jesus can never be known by the rough and the coarse, the hard and the restless, but remains the priceless heritage of the lowly and meek; and these can only retain it by a studious care which cherishes love, and guards it from even the least intrusion. A gazelle among the lilies would start at the bark of a fox, and be gone at the voice of a stranger; and, therefore, soft whispers of inward love must say, "Take us the foxes, the little foxes", and nimble hands with noiseless fingers must draw up the lattice, that kindly eyes may look out at the windows, and may be seen by him who delights in love.

The evident intent of the language is to set out the delicacy of the highest form of holy fellowship. The Lord our God is a jealous God, and that jealousy is most seen where most of his love is displayed. The least sin, wilfully indulged in, will grieve the Holy Spirit; and slights, forgetfulness, and neglect, will cause him to turn away. If we would remain positively and joyfully assured that the Beloved is ours, and that we are his, we must use with the utmost circumspection and holy vigilance. No man gains full assurance by accident, or retains it by chance. As the gentle hind wanders in lovely spots where grow the pure white lilies, and as he shuns the places profaned by strife, and are foul with rank weeds and nettles, so does the Lord Jesus come to holy minds perfumed with devotion, and are consecrated to the Lord; and there in sacred quiet he finds solace, and abides with his saints.

May the Lord preserve us from pride, from self-seeking, from carnality, and wrath, for these things chase away our delights even as dogs drive off the hind of the morning. Both our inward and outward walk must be eagerly watched lest anything should vex the Bridegroom. A word, a glance, a thought, may break the spell and end the happy rest of the heart; and long may it be before the blessing is regained. We have some of us learned by bitter experience that it is hard to establish a settled peace, and easy enough to destroy it. The costly vase, the product of a thousand laborious processes, may be broken in a moment; and so the supreme delight of communion with the Lord Jesus, the flower of

212

ten thousand eminent delights, may be shattered by a few moments' negligence. Hence, the one lesson of our little sermon is — "I charge you, O ye daughters of Jerusalem, by the roes, and by the hinds of the field, that ye stir not up, nor awake my love, till he please."

For I am jealous of my heart
Lest it should once from him depart;
Then let my name be well impressed
As a fair signet at thy breast.
Till thou has brought me to thy home,
Where fears and doubts can never come,
Thy countenance let me often see,
And often shalt thou hear from me.

(Isaac Watts)

29. THE INTEREST OF CHRIST AND HIS PEOPLE IN EACH OTHER

NO. 374

A SERMON DELIVERED ON GOOD FRIDAY EVENING,
MARCH 29TH, 1861
AT THE METROPOLITAN TABERNACLE, NEWINGTON

"My beloved is mine, and I am his."
(Song of Solomon 2:16)

THE Church says concerning her Lord, "My beloved *is* mine and I *am* his." No "ifs", no "buts". The two sentences are solemn assertions. Not "I hope, I trust, I think", but, "my beloved *is* mine, and I *am* his." "Yes", but you will say, "the Church must then have been gazing upon her husband's face; it must have been a season of peculiar enjoyment with him when she could speak thus." No, brethren, no! The Church, when she thus spake, was in darkness, for in the very next verse she cries — "Until the day break, and the shadows flee away, turn, my beloved, and be thou like a roe or a young hart upon the mountains of Bether." I say, brethren, this solemn certainty, this double assertion of her interest in Christ and Christ's interest in her, is the utterance of the Church even in her darkness, in the cheerless season of his absence. So, then, you and I, if we believe in Christ, ought, even when we do not see his face, still to cultivate full assurance of faith, and never be satisfied unless we can say, "My beloved is mine, and I am his." When you cannot say this, my hearer, give no sleep to your eyes nor slumber to thine eyelids. Do not be happy. Take no solace, find no comfort, as long as there is any doubt about your union with the beloved — his possession of you and your possession of him.

We will now, having thus prefaced the text, come at once to it. There are two members, you perceive, in the sentence: "My beloved is mine, and I am his." These two things come in a strange order. You will say, "Surely we are first Christ's, before Christ is ours." A right thought of yours. We shall take the text, then, this evening two ways: we shall first speak of it *as it would be in order of time*. "I am my beloved's, and my beloved is mine". We shall afterwards speak *in the order of the text, which is the order of experience*. The words, as Solomon penned them, are the order of fact as far as God is concerned, but the order in which we find out God's great doings.

You know God's first things are our second things, and our second things are God's first things. For example, "Make your calling and election sure." (2 Pet. 1:10) Calling is your first thing; election is the second. But election is God's first thing, and calling is the next. You are not elected because you are called; and yet, at the same time, you will never know your election until first you have made your calling and election sure. The order of the text is the order of experience. We shall take the members of the sentence as they would be if they spoke in the order of fact.

I. To begin, then, I AM MY BELOVED'S, AND THE BELOVED IS THEREFORE MINE.

1. "*I am my beloved's.*" Glorious assertion! I am his *by his Father's gift.* Long before suns and moons were made, and stars twinkled in the midnight darkness, God, the eternal Father, had given the chosen to Christ to be his heritage and marriage dowry. If God, then, has given my soul to Christ, I am my Beloved's. Who can dispute the right of God to give, or who can take from Christ that which his Father has given to be his heritage? Fiends of hell! Legions of the pit! When God gives, can you take back the gift? If he puts the souls of the chosen into the hands of Christ, can you pluck them out from there? If *he* makes them Christ's sheep, can you pluck them out of his fold, and make them your own? God forbid we should indulge the blasphemous thought, that any can dispute the property which Christ has in his people, derived from his Father's gift.

But I am my Beloved's if I am a believer, because of *Jesus Christ purchase* of me. "Forasmuch as ye know that ye were not redeemed with corruptible things, as silver and gold, from your vain conversation received by tradition from your fathers; but with the precious blood of Christ, as of a lamb without blemish and without spot". (1 Pet. 1:18-19) Christ has an absolute right to all that he bought with blood. I do not believe in that dreamy atonement by which Christ redeems and purchases, and yet the purchase is a fiction, and the redemption a metaphor. All that Christ bought with blood he will have. If a man buy with gold and silver from an honest man, he gets his own, nor will he be content until he does; but when Christ ransoms with blood, and buys from God himself, and redeems his own people, it is not possible that he should be frustrated of his purpose, or denied the object of his death. I am my Beloved's, then, because he has paid the full price for me, and counted down the blood drops, and positively and surely has as much bought me with his money as ever Abraham of old bought flocks of sheep and oxen, or as ever of old Jacob served for Rachel and for Leah. No title deeds ever made estate more truly the property of the purchaser than did the resurrection guarantee the rights of Christ in the "purchased possession." (Eph. 1:14) "I am my Beloved's" by a double tie — by the Father's gift, and by the Son's divine purchase. These two things are not easily reconcilable in some minds; but let it be carried in your hearts as a matter of fact, that there is as much grace in the Father's giving the elect to Christ as if no price were paid, and secondly, that there was as full and true a price paid to the Father as though the Father had been justice only, and not love. The grace of God and his justice are both of them full-orbed, and never eclipsed; they are never made over to you with divided lustre, for he is as gracious as though he were not just; he is as awfully severe as though there were no grace in his nature.

But more than this, "I am my Beloved's", for I am his *by conquest*. He fought for me, and he won me; let him possess me. He went alone to that great battle. He defied all the hosts which had made me their prey; encountered first my sins, and slew them with his blood, encountered next Satan himself, and bruised the serpent's head, encountered death and slew him by "destroying him that had the power of death, that is, the devil." (Heb. 2:14) O Christ, you deserve to have those for whom you wrestled and agonised even unto blood, and who, by your strong hand, you brought out of the land of their captivity! Never could conqueror claim a subject so justly as Christ claims his people. They were not only his, eternally his, by the purchase of his blood, but they are his because he has taken them by overwhelming might, having delivered them out of the hand of him who was stronger than they. That word which he "girt" upon his thigh (Rev. 1:13) is both the right by which he claims, and the might by which he keeps his ransomed.

Besides this, every true believer can add, "I am my Beloved's" by a *gracious surrender*. With full consent I give myself to you." This is your language, brothers and sisters. It is mine. "I am my Beloved's." If I was never his before, I desire to give myself up to him now. His love shall be the fetters in which I, a happy captive, will walk at his triumphant chariot wheels. His grace shall bind me with its golden chains, so that I will be free, and yet his bondman forever. The mercies of each hour shall be fresh links, and the benefits of each day and night shall be new rivets to the chain. No Christian man would like to be his own. To be one's own is to be lost; but to be Christ's is to be saved. To be one's own is to be a wandering sheep; to be Christ's, is to return to the great shepherd and bishop and of our souls. (1 Pet. 2:25)

215

Do you not remember, many of you, the night when you first surrendered to Christ? He stood at the door and knocked; the door was overgrown with brambles, the hinges had rusted from long disuse; the key was lost; the wards of the lock were welded together with filth and rust; no, from within, the door was bolted fast. He knocked, at first a gentle knock, enough to let you know who it was. You laughed. He knocked again; you took no heed. You heard his voice as he cried, "Open to me, open to me; my hair is wet with dew, and my locks with the drops of the night." (Song 5:2) But you had a thousand frivolous excuses, and you would not open to him. Oh, do you remember when at last he put in his hand by the hole of the lock and your heart went out to him. "Jesus, Saviour! I yield, I yield. I can hold out no longer, my heart melts; my cruel soul relents. Come in! Come in! And pardon me that I have kept you out so long, resisted so long the wooing of your heavenly love." Well, *you* will say tonight, and set your solemn band and seal to it, that you are Christ's because, once again, you voluntarily and freely surrender yourself to him.

I think tonight would be a very proper occasion for each of us to renew our dedication rows. We are many of us believers; let us go to our chamber and say thus — "O God, you have best heard our prayers as a Church; we have entered your house; we have seen it filled to the full. By this, the answer which you have given to our prayers brings us to re-dedicate ourselves to you, desiring to say with the spouse more fully than heretofore, 'I am my Beloved's.'"

Let us pause here an instant. We have seen how we came to be our Beloved's; let us enquire in what sense we are so now.

We are his, first of all, by *a near affinity* that never can be sundered. Christ is the head, we are his members. There is nothing which my head possesses so truly as my hand and my heart. Your head could not say that its helmet and plume are so truly its own as the neck, the sinews, the veins, which are joined to them. The head manifestly has a distinct and peculiar property in every member. "I am my Beloved's" then, even as my hand and foot are mine. "I am my Beloved's" — if he lose me, he will be mutilated. "I am my Beloved's" — if I am cut away, or even wounded, he will feel the pain. The head *must* suffer when the members are tempted and tried. There is nothing so true and real, in the sense of property, as this. I would that you, who doubt the perseverance of the saints, would take these few words to heart. If once Christ should lose his people, he would be a head without a body, which would be a ghastly sight. No, if he lost one of his people he would be the head of a mutilated body —not a glorious sight. If you imagine the loss of one mystical member of Christ, you must suppose an imperfect Christ — one whose fullness is not full, whose glory is not glorious, whose completeness is not complete. Now, I am sure you would scotch that idea; and it will be joy for you to say, "As the members belong to the head, so am I my Beloved's."

Further than this; we are our Beloved's by a most *affectionate relationship*. He is the husband, believers are the spouse. There is nothing that a man has that is so much his property as his own wife, unless it be his very life. A man's wealth may melt away by losses, a man's estate may be sold to pay his debts, but a man's wife, as long as she lives, is his absolute property. She can say, "He is mine"; he can say, "She is mine." Now Christ says of all his people, "Ye are mine, I am married to you; I have taken you to myself, and betrothed you to me in faithfulness." What do you say! Will you deny the celestial marriage bond? God forbid! Will you not say to your Lord tonight, "Yes, I am my Beloved's?" Ah, there is no divorce court in heaven; there is no division, no separation bill possible, for he "hateth putting away"! (Mal. 2:16) If chosen, he will not reject, if once embraced, he will never cast out; his she is, and his she shall be evermore. In this sense, then, "I am my Beloved's."

216

Yet once more: "I am my Beloved's" by an *indissoluble connection*, just as a child is the property of his father. The father calls his child his own. Who can deny it? What law is so inhuman as to allow another to tear away the offspring from the parent? There is no such law among civilised men. Among the aboriginal savages of the Southern States of America, such a thing may exist; but among civilised men, there never can be any dispute but that the father's right to his child is supreme, and that no master and no owner can over-ride the rights of the parent to his son. Come, then; even so are we his. "He shall see *his* seed." (Is, 53:10) "He shall see of the travail of his soul." (Verse11) If he could lose his glories, if he could be driven from his kingdom, it he could be despoiled of his crown, if his throne could totter, if all his might could melt away as the snow-wreath melts before the summer's sun, yet at least his seed would be his own. No law, human or divine, can unchild the believing child, or unfather Christ, the everlasting Father. So then, it is a great joy to know that each believer may say, in the highest sense — "I am my Beloved's. I am his child, and he is my parent." I half wish that instead of my preaching now, we could stand up, each of us who feel the force of this sweet sentiment, and say, "'Tis true, great God, by eternal donation, by complete purchase, by a full surrender, by a mighty conquest, I am my Beloved's. He is my Head, my Husband, my Father, and my All.'"

2. The second sentence in order of time is, "My Beloved is mine." Ah, you very poor men and women, you who could not call one foot of land your own, and probably never will till you get the space where you lie down to sleep the sleep of death! If you can say, "My Beloved is mine", you have greater wealth than Croesus ever knew, or a miser ever dreamed. If my soul can claim Christ, the eternal God and the perfect man, as being my own personal property, then my soul is rich to all the intents of bliss, should the body walk in rags, or should the lips know hunger, or the mouth be parched with thirst.

But how is my Beloved mine? He is mine because *he gave himself to me of old*. Long before I knew it, or had a being, he covenanted to bestow himself on me — on all his chosen. When he said, "Lo, I come; in the volume of the Book it is written of me, I delight to do thy will, O God" (Ps. 40:7; Heb. 10:7), he did, in fact, become my substitute, giving himself to do my work and bear my sorrow. Mine he is because *that covenant has been fulfilled* in the *actual* gift. For me (I speak in the first person because I want you each to speak in the first person too), for you, my soul, he laid aside his robes of glory to become a man; for you he was swaddled in the weakness of infancy, and lay in the poverty of the manger; for you, my soul, he bore the infant body, the childish form, and human flesh and blood; for you the poverty which made him cry, "Foxes have holes, and the birds of the air have nests, but I, the Son of Man, have not where to lay mine head." (Mat. 8:20; Lk. 9:58) For you, my soul, for you that shame and spitting, that agony and bloody sweat, that cross, that crown of thorns, those expiring agonies, that dying groan. "My Beloved", in all this, "is mine." No, yours the burial, yours the resurrection and its mystic meaning, yours the ascension and its triumphant shouts, yours the session at the right hand of God. Yes, and by holy daring, we avow it, that he who sits today, "Over all, God blessed for ever", (Rom. 9:5) is ours in the splendour of his majesty, in the invincibility of his might, in the omnipresence of his power, in all the glory of his future advent. Our beloved is ours because he has given himself to us, just as he is.

But besides that, our beloved is not only ours by his own gift, which is the foundation of all, but he is ours by a *graciously completed union*. What a wonderful thing is the doctrine of union with Christ. "We are members of his body, of his flesh, and of his bones. "For this cause shall a man leave his father and mother, and shall cleave unto his wife, and they twain shall be one flesh. This is a great mystery, but I speak concerning Christ and the Church." (Eph. 5:30-31) Christ and his Church are one — one as the stones are one with the foundation; one, as the branches are one with the vine; one, as the wife is one with the husband; one, as the members are one with the head; one as the soul is one with the

217

body; no, if there can be conceived a union closer still, and there is but one, we are one with Christ, even as Christ is one with his Father. "I in them, and thou in me" (Jn. 17:23), for thus the union stands. Now, as soon as ever we are one with Christ, you see at once that Christ must be ours. There is a common property between Christ and his people. All theirs belongs to him; his belongs to them. They have not two stores, they have but one. He has cast in his wealth; they have cast in their poverty. From that day, they have common funds; they have but one purse, and have all things in common. All he is and all he has is theirs, and all they are or can be belongs to him.

I might add, but this is a high point, and needs to be experienced rather than preached upon; Christ is ours *by his indwelling*. Ignatius used to call himself the God-bearer, and when some wondered at the title he said, "I carry God about within me; our bodies are the temples of the Holy Spirit." That is an awesome text, awesome in the splendour of its meaning. Does the Holy Spirit dwell in a man? Yes, that he does. Not in this temple, "not in tabernacles made with hands"; that is to say of man's building, but within this soul, and in your soul, and in the souls of all his called ones, he dwells. "Abide in me," said he, "and I in you." (Jn. 15:4) Christ must be in you, the hope of glory (Col. 1:27); Christ must be formed in you (Gal. 4:19), as he was in Mary, or you have not yet come to know to the full the divine meaning of the spouse, when she said: "My Beloved is mine, and I am his."

Now, tonight, I wish that we could get practical good, something for our comfort, out of the thought that Christ is ours, if we are believers. Hear me, then, a moment or two, while I dilate upon that thought. Christ is surely yours. It is not a questionable property, a matter to be put into dispute with Heaven's chancery. Beyond question, Christ is the property — the rightful heritage — of every elect and called one.

Again, Christ *is* ours personally. We sometimes speak of severally and jointly. Well then, Christ is ours jointly; but, blessed be his name, he is ours severally too. Christ is as much yours tonight, however lowly you may be, as though he did not belong to another man living. The whole of Christ is yours; he is not partly mine and partly yours, and partly someone else's. He is all mine, and all yours; personally mine, personally yours. Oh that we could realise this fact!

And then, again, Christ is *always* ours. He is never more ours at one time, and less ours at another. The moment we believe in him, we may know our perfect and invariable right to Christ — a right which depends not upon the changes of the hour, or upon the temperature of our frames and feelings, but upon those two immutable things in which it is impossible for God to lie. Christ is ours tonight; and, glory be to his name for it, if we believe he is ours forever!

This sacred bond shall never break,
Though earth's old columns bow
The strong, the feeble, and the weak
Can claim their Saviour now.

(John Kent)

And this they shall do, perhaps with greater joy, but not with greater right, when they stand before the throne of God.

I cannot, tonight, in a place to which I am so accustomed, bring all my thoughts together as I would; but, I think if I could but put this truth before you, or rather, if the Spirit of God would put it so that you could feel Christ to be yours, it would make you spring from your pew with ecstasy. Why, it is enough to thrill every chord in a man; and if a man may be compared to a harp, make every string in him pour out an ocean of music. Christ is mine — myself is Christ's: there cannot be a gladder and more heavenly theme beneath the skies.

II. I have thus completed the first work of this evening, taking the sentences of the text in the order of time. I now take the text IN THE ORDER IN WHICH IT IS GIVEN TO US, WHICH IS THE ORDER OF OUR EXPERIENCE.

Do you not see, that to a man's experience God's order is reversed? We begin thus: "My Beloved is mine." I go to him, take him up in the arms of my faith, as Simeon took up the little child in the temple, and, pressing him to my heart, I say,

"Jesus you are mine. All unholy and unclean, I nevertheless obey your command. I believe you, I take you at your word. I touch the hem of your garment. I trust my soul holy with you; you are mine, and my soul can never part with you."

What next? Why then the soul afterwards says —

"Now I am yours, tell me what you would have me do. Jesus, let me abide with you. Lord, I would follow you wherever you go; put me on any service, dictate to me any commandment, tell me what you would have me do to glorify thee?"

In all my Lord's appointed ways
My journey I'll pursue;
Hinder me not! ye much loved saints,
For I must go with you.

Through floods and flames, if Jesus lead,
I'll follow where he goes;
Hinder me not! shall be my cry,
Though earth and hell oppose.

Through duty, and through trials too,
I'll go at His command;
Hinder me not! for I am bound
To my Immanuel's land.

And when my Saviour calls me home,
Still this my cry shall be,
Hinder me not! come, welcome death;
I'll gladly go with Thee!

(John Ryland)

For I am his. Christ is mine — this is faith. I am his — this is good works. Christ is mine: that is the simple way in which the soul is saved. I am Christ's: that is the equally simple method by which salvation displays itself in its practical fruits. I am afraid some of you have never carried out the last sentence, "I am Christ's." I know some, for instance, who believe (mark you, I am not speaking to those who do not) — who believe it to be the duty of every Christian to profess his faith in baptism, and are nevertheless not baptised. They say they are Baptist in principle. They are Baptists without any principle at all. They are men who know their Master's will, and do not do it, and they shall surely be beaten with many stripes. (Lk. 12:47) In others, it becomes a sin of ignorance, but with such men it is wilful. They reply, "It is a non-essential." Things non-essential to salvation are

219

nevertheless essential to obedience. As I said a few Sabbaths ago, you would not like a servant who only did what he liked, and told you that some of your commands were non-essential. I am quite certain that if a soldier did not load his gun, or stand in rank, or shoulder arms at the word of command, the court-martial would never listen for an instant to the plea of nonessential. God's commands require obedience, and it is essential that every servant be found faithful. I say, it is exceedingly essential to a Christian to do what he is told to do. Whatever Jesus bids us do, if it does not save us from anything else, at any rate, the fulfilment of it will save us from the sin of being disobedient to him.

Now, will you try, my dear friends, not in the one command only, which lies at the threshold of the house, but in all others, to feel that you are not your own? "Ah", says one man, "I am not my own, I have so much to do for my family"; another, "I am not my own, I belong to a political party"; another, "I am not my own, I belong to a firm." Just so: all these are ways in which men are kept from saying, "I am my Beloved's, and my Beloved is mine." Oh that we could, by any means whatever, feel that we were all Christ's! If I though I had a drop of blood in my veins that was not his, I would seek to have it let out; and if there were a single power I have, mental, physical, or spiritual, which could not, and would not, serve God, though it might impair my comfort, I would devoutly pray that this Jonah might be thrown into the sea, this Achan stoned with stones, this Haman hanged on the gallows. This cankered thing, it is deadly thing, this damnable thing must be cut away once for all, for "better to enter into heaven halt and maimed, than having two eyes and two arms to be cast into hell fire." (Mat. 18:9; Mk. 9:47) We must have a single eye; we must feel that we are all Christ's, and live as if we were all Christ's, We have no right to say, "My Beloved is mine" unless we can add, "And I am his." Why look, sirs, look at the great multitude of professors. How few there are that ever live as if they belonged to Christ! They act independently of *him*; they buy, they sell, on their own account. That they are stewards never penetrates their thick skulls; that all they have is not their own, but his, which never seems to have come into their heart, though they have sung it with their lips.

How can I sink with such a prop
As my eternal God,
Who bears the earth's huge pillars up,
And spreads the heavens abroad?
How can I die while Jesus lives,
Who rose and left the dead?
Pardon and grace my soul receives
From mine exalted head.

All that I am, and all I have
Shall be for ever thine,
Whate'er my duty bids me give
My cheerful hands resign.

Yet if I might make some reserve,
And duty did not call,
I love my God with zeal so great
That I should give him all.

(Isaac Watts)

Many a man has sung that, with his thumb-nail going round a coin in his purse, to find out whether it was a fourpenny or a threepenny bit. He says he would give Christ all; but then he means that the bill is to be drawn at very long credit, and he will pay when he dies. Then he will give up what he cannot take away with him, and when he leaves his rotten

220

carcass he will leave his rotten wealth. Oh that we could all feel that we were all Christ's! Why, the Church of God would not be penned and shut up within the narrow bounds of England and America long, if once we felt we were Christ's. At this very moment, China is open to Christian enterprise. The leader of the so-called "rebels" turns out to be, after all, a man who is exceedingly enlightened in the things of God. He has said to Mr. Roberts, the missionary, "I open today eighteen chapels in Nanking; write to your friends, and tell them to come over and preach, and we will be glad to hear them. I give you a passport, that no man may touch you, and anyone who will preach Christ's gospel shall go unharmed through my dominions;" and he actually issued, just a few days before the coming of the last mail, a proclamation by which all idolatry is abolished throughout his dominions, and witchcraft and fortune-telling are made crimes, and he invites and prays his brethren in England especially to send over the Word of life, that they may have it among the people.

Now, I honestly avow, if this place had not been built, and I had had nothing beyond the narrow bounds of the place in which I have lately preached, I should have felt in my conscience bound to go to learn the language and preach the Word there; but I now know what to do. I *must* abide here, for this is my place; but I would to God some were found in the Church, some in London, who have not such a gracious tie as this to keep them in their own land, to say, "Here am I, send me, I am Christ's man; there is Christ's field, let me go and reap it, for the harvest is ripe. Help me, O God, and I will seek to ingather it for your honour." "My Beloved is mine and I am his." That last "I am his" would make life cheap, and blood like water, and heroism a common thing, and daring but an everyday duty, and self-sacrifice the very spirit of the Christian life. Learn well, then, the meaning of that sentence, "*I am his*."

But will you please notice once again — (I fear lest I shall weary you, and therefore will be brief) — "My Beloved is mine", and that is my calling. He calls me to him. He gives himself to me; he is mine. I am his — that is my election. I was his before I knew him to be mine; but I learned my calling first, and my election afterwards. We have scores of people who will not come to Christ, because they cannot understand election. Meet a boy in the street, and invite him to go to a two-penny school. "No", says the boy, "I don't feel fit to go to a national school to learn to read and write; for, to tell you the truth, I don't understand the Hebrew language". You would reply, "But, my good lad, you will learn Hebrew afterwards, if you can; but that is no reason, at any rate, why you should not learn English first. Come first to the little school; you shall go afterwards to the grammar school; if you get on, you shall go to the University, take your B.A. degree and perhaps come out as a Master of Arts." But here we have poor souls that want to be M.A.'s before they have gone to the penny school. They want to read the tomes before they can read the learner's book. They are not content to spell A, B, C — "I am a sinner, Christ is a saviour" — but they long to turn over the book of decrees, and find out the deep things of God. You will find them out afterwards: you must go step by step, while the master shall say to you each time, "Friend, go up higher." (Lk. 14:10) But if you begin with election, you will have to come down again: for there will be a more honourable man than you, who will come in, and you will begin with shame to take the lowest place. I have seen plenty of high-flying Christians who began at the top of the tree; they were the men, wisdom would die with them, the judges, the dictators, the very consuls, the cardinals, the popes — they knew everything. And whenever such men are gracious men, the Lord always puts the lancet into them, and makes them grow smaller, and smaller, and smaller, till, at last, they say, "Woe is me, for I am undone!" (Is.6:5), and they cry, "My soul is even as a weaned child." (Ps. 131:2) Begin at the bottom and grow upward; but do not begin at the top and come down. That is hard work; but going up is pleasant work, joyous work. Begin by saying, "My Beloved is mine"; then you shall come to know your election by-and-bye, and say, "I am his."

221

And now I do not think I will preach any longer about my text, but just come down on my hearers for a few minutes with all my might. How many among us can dare to say this text tonight? Hundreds of you can; thousands of you can. If this were the day of judgement — if tonight you stood, fresh risen from your graves, if now you heard the trumpet sound, if now you saw the King in his beauty sitting upon the great white throne, I know that many of you would say, "My beloved is mine, and I am his." If this very day the millennial reign of Christ had begun — if the vials had been opened, the plagues poured out, and if now Christ were come, that the wicked might be driven out, and that his saints might reign, I am sure there are many of you who would say, "Welcome, welcome, Son of God; my Beloved is mine and I am his." And there are many of you, too, who, if the angel of death should pass the pew and flap his black wing in your face, and the cold air of death smite you, you would say, "Tis well, for my Beloved is mine, and I am his." You could shut your eyes and your ears to the joys and music of earth, and you could open them to the splendours and melodies of heaven. To be fearless of death should always be the mark of the Christian. Sometimes a sudden alarm may rob us of our presence of mind; but no believer is in a healthy state if he is not ready to meet death at any hour and at any moment. To walk bravely into the jaws of the dragon — to go through the iron gates and feel no terror — to be ready to shake hand with the skeleton king, to look on him as a friend, and no more a foe — this should be the habitual spirit and the constant practice of the heir of heaven. Oh, if this could be written on my soul: "My Beloved is mine, and I am his"! Come, welcome death, as Dr. Watts declares:

Come, death, and some celestial band,
I'll gladly go with you.

But — and a solemn "but" — pass the question round these galleries, and, in this area, and how many among you must say, "I never thought of that. I never thought whether I was Christ's, or Christ mine." I will not rebuke you tonight. I will not thunder at you. God's grace to me forbids that *this* should be a day of thunder. Let it be a day of feasting for everyone, and of sorrow to none. What shall I say to you, then, but this? Oh that Christ *may* be yours! When he was here on earth be chose to go among sinners — sinners of the blackest hue; and now he is in heaven up yonder, he loves sinners as much as ever he did. He is as willing to receive you tonight as to receive the thief. (Lk. 23:42-43) It will give as much joy to his heart to hear your cry tonight, as when he thanked God that these things were revealed unto babes. (Lk. 10:21) It is to his honour that you should be his; it is to his joy that he should be yours. Sinner! If you will have Christ — if now the spirit of God makes you willing — there is no bar on God's part, when the bar is taken away on your part. If you are willing, he is more willing than you are. If the gate of your heart is on the latch, the gate of heaven is open wide. If your soul but yearns after Christ, his heart has long yearned after you. If you have but a spark of love for Christ, he has a furnace of love for you. And if you have none at all — no love, no faith — oh, may you have it now! "Believe on the Lord Jesus Christ and you shall be saved." (Acts 16:31) You; yes, you!

Did you come here out of curiosity? Zacchaeus heard Christ out of curiosity; but he was saved. Did you come for a worse purpose? God bless you, anyhow, for whatever reason you came; and may he bring you to himself tonight! Trust Christ now, and you are saved. My life for yours: if you perish trusting in Christ I will perish too. Even if I should have an ear listening to me which belongs to a harlot, a thief, a murderer, yet he that believes in the Lord Jesus Christ shall be saved". And if you believe in him, and you are lost, I will be lost with you; and the whole Church of Christ must be lost too, for there is the same way to heaven for the best as for the worst — for the vilest as for the most righteous. "No man cometh unto the Father but by Christ." (Jn. 14:6) Nothing can damn a man but his own righteousness; nothing can save him but the righteousness of Christ. All your sin, your past sin, shall not destroy you; if you now believe in Jesus, it will be cast into the sea

222

forever (Mic. 7:19), and you will begin again as though you had never sinned. His grace will keep you for the future, and you will hold on your way an honour to Christ's grace, and a joy to your own soul. But if you are disobedient, and will not eat of the good of the land, then, I will say, as Isaiah said of old:

"I am sought of them that asked not for me; I am found of them that sought me not: I said, Behold me, behold me, unto a nation that was not called by my name. I have spread out my hands all the day unto a rebellious people, which walketh in a way that was not good, after their own thoughts; a people that provoketh me to anger continually to my face." (Is. 65:1-3)

God *has* stretched out his hands. Oh that you were wise, and would run into his arms tonight! I know I am speaking to some self-righteous men — some who say, "It is a shame to tell men they are depraved. *I* am not." Well, we think if their lives were written, it might be proved they were. "It is a shame", they say, "to tell men that they cannot get to heaven by their good works, because then they will be wicked." It is an odd thing, though, that the more this truth is preached, the better people are. Preaching good works as the way to heaven always produces drunkards and thieves, but preaching faith in Christ always produces the best effects.

Dr. Thomas Chalmers, who was no fanatic, says, "When I preached mere morality, I preached sobriety till they were all drunkards, I preached chastity till it was not known anywhere; I preached honesty till men grew to be thieves", but, he says, "as soon as ever I preached Christ there was such a change in the village as never was known." Well, we believe that self-righteousness will destroy you, my friend, and we therefore tell you, honestly and plainly, that you might as well hope to get to heaven by flying up in a balloon, as to get there by your good works. You may as soon sail to India in a sieve as get to glory by your own goodness. You might as well go to court in cobwebs as seek to go to heaven in your own righteousness. Away with your rags, your filthy, rotten rags! They are only a harbour for the parasites of unbelief and pride. Away with your rotten righteousness, your counterfeit gold, your forged wealth! It is of nothing worth whatever in the sight of God. Come to him, empty, poor, naked! It grates on your proud ear, does it? Better, I say, to lose your pride, than to lose your soul! Why be damned for pride's sake? Why carry your head so high that it must needs be cut off? Why feed your pride on your soul's blood? Surely, there is cheaper stuff than that for pride to drink! Why let it suck the very marrow out of your bones? Be wise! Bow, stoop, stoop to be saved. And now, in the name of Jesus of Nazareth, the man, the God, I command you, as his messenger and his servant, and at your peril reject the command, "Repent, and be baptised, every one of you." (Acts 2:38) "Believe on the Lord Jesus Christ, and thou shalt be saved" (Acts 16:31), "for he that believeth and is baptised shall be saved; he that believeth not shall be damned." (Mk. 16:16)

God add his blessing, for his name's sake! Amen.

30. "MY BELOVED IS MINE"

NO. 2442

AT THE METROPOLITAN TABERNACLE, NEWINGTON
ON LORD'S-DAY EVENING, SEPT. 11TH, 1887

"My beloved is mine, and I am his."
(Song of Solomon 2:16)

THIS is a versicle from the Song of Songs, and I do not hesitate to say that it is the soul and heart of that divine composition. The bride dressed in her richest poesy wears no jewel more precious than this diamond of full assured possession. There is poetry here which none of the sons of music can excel. It is the heart's minstrelsy at its very best. This little sonnet might be sung in heaven, and the golden harps would be well employed if every string went with the accompaniment. How I wish you could each one sing it now with a clear sweet voice!

Now I my best Beloved's am,
And he is mine.

Alas, many of the Lord's own chosen and called ones are afraid to take up this chorus and join with us! I do not condemn them, but I am eager to comfort them. What would they give? Say, rather, what would they not give — if they could but say "Christ is mine"? Yet they hesitate: the desire is strong, but the doubt is killing, and they dare not sing with us. It seems too good, too great, too glorious a claim to come from their lips. They sometimes hope, but they as often fear. They make a dash for it now and then, and trust that Christ is theirs; and then they subside into their former questioning. They are humble, modest, retiring; I fear I must add, they are, at least, in a measure, unbelieving. I want to lead these true hearts up to the table that they may feast on the dainties provided for faith. I know that even now, as they hear the text, "My Beloved is mine, and I am his," they are saying, "Happy people that can speak thus, but I cannot. I am afraid it would be presumption, and perhaps hypocrisy, on my part, if I were to use such language." And yet, dear heart, it is very possible that you have a perfect right to put in your claim; yes, and that you ought to be among the most confident and the most fully assured. What a pity it is that you should be losing so much joy! Yet some of the truest children of God walk in darkness at times, and we have provision made for them in the circumstances. "Who is among you that feareth the Lord, that obeyeth the voice of his servant, that walketh in darkness, and hath no light? Let him trust in the name of the Lord, and stay upon his God." (Is. 50:10) Oh, that I might be the means of enabling some of you to trust more bravely, and hold to your Lord in the darkness, for soon that darkness will be over!

Did I hear one mourn his faults, and lament his temptations? This need not be a hindrance. She who first sang this priceless stanza was herself warring against enemies. Read the previous verse: "Take us the foxes, the little foxes that spoil the vines: for our vines have tender grapes." Instead of letting go her Lord to hunt the foxes, she clung all the more to him, and joined him with herself in the effort to take them. "Foxes or no foxes", says she, "my Beloved is mine." Jesus belongs to us in our imperfect condition, while yet we are beset with many mischievous and cunning foes. The Song before us is found in our own Bible, which is a Book to be used on earth rather than in heaven. While yet the foxes prowl around us we may sing, "My Beloved is mine, and I am his." Indeed, it is by strength derived from such a cheering confidence that we are enabled to kill these foxes, and preserve the tender clusters till they are ripe for our Lord. Come, brethren, let us not do ourselves the serious hurt of refusing the greatest of blessings for reasons which are

224

not valid. Let us mourn our faults, but let us not, therefore, forego our privileges. I will not let my Lord go because I see a fox. No, rather, I will cling to him the more closely. If that fox should hurt my vine, yet I have a better Vine in my Lord, and one which no fox can touch. Away, you beasts of the field, you sins and doubts and fears, for my heart dares to sing, "My Beloved is mine, and I am his."

I feel that I am a bearer of a tenfold portion to the Benjamin of the family. Joseph — I mean, Jesus — has sent it, and I am eager to deliver it fresh from his dear hand. O trembling believer, it is all for you! Receive it, and eat in abundance. I am under the impression that my Master has bidden me remember that there is a Ruth here who only desires to glean, and trembles while she gathers a few scanty ears. She has not the courage to take a sheaf herself, but my Lord has said, "Let fall handfuls of purpose for her" (Ruth 2:16), and I would try to do so; but I pray that timid Ruth may have courage enough to take up what I shall gladly let fall for her, for the good Boaz, in whose field I serve, has his eye on her, and means more kindness to her than I can tell.

What I have to do tonight is to mention a few things which may help some timid one to say, "My Beloved is mine", and then do the same with regard to the second sentence in the text, "I am his."

You ask, perhaps, "May I say, 'My Beloved is mine'?" You know who that Beloved is; I have no need to tell you that. He is the chief among ten thousand, and the altogether lovely. You believe that it is he who is the ever-blessed Son of God, who became man for our sake, and, as the God-man, made atonement for our sin; and, having died, has risen from the dead and gone into his Father's within the veil, where he ever makes intercession for us. (Rom. 8:34) It is that Christ who is the light of heaven, the joy of everlasting bliss, the adored of angels. It certainly does seem a great thing to call him mine. To think that he should ever be mine, and that all he is, and all he has, and all he says, and all he does, and all he ever will be, is all mine! When a wife takes a husband to be hers, he becomes all hers, and she reckons that she has no divided possession in him; and it certainly is so with you, dear heart, if Christ is yours. He is still yours, and altogether yours, even if it does look as though you were opening your mouth very wide to be able to say it. Some of you were brought up in a school which is full of the law, and you are afraid to say what the gospel permits you to say; you have not yet dared to avail yourselves of your privileges. Some of God's heirs are often kept in the back kitchen when they have a right to sit in the parlour, and to eat of the dainties of their Lord. Some are kept from the joys to which they have a fair claim, so I am going to ask you a few questions to see whether you are one of them.

First, have you taken hold of Christ by faith? Faith is the hand with which we grasp the Lord Jesus Christ. Have you believed that Jesus is the Christ, and that God has raised him from the dead? Do you trust yourself wholly to him? I say "wholly" — with no other secret confidence. Do you lean your whole weight on him? He that hangs on two boughs, one of which is rotten, will go down. You had best trust your whole self to Christ, and let him be the top and bottom of your confidence. If you do that, then he is yours; this faith makes him yours to your joyful experience. Listen to his own words: "God so loved the world, that he gave his only begotten Son, that whosoever believeth in him should not perish, but have everlasting life." (Jn. 3:16) If you believe in Christ, you have Christ to be your everlasting life, and you may say, "My Beloved is mine."

I should hope that this is not a very difficult question for you to answer; you are either trusting in Christ, or you are not. If you are not trusting in Christ, God forbid that I should exhort you to say what would be presumptuous! But if you are resting on him who lived, and loved, and died, that he might wash us from our sins in his blood — I say, if he is all

225

your salvation and all your desire, then do not hesitate to say, "My Beloved is mine." There is no surer claim in the world than the claim of faith. God has given Christ to every believing sinner — be he who he may — God has given Christ to him by a covenant of salt (Num. 18:19), and Christ is his, and shall be his forever. Poor trembler, if you believe in him, even you may say, "My Beloved is mine."

Let me ask you another helpful question. Is he truly your Beloved, the Beloved of your soul? I remember well a dear Christian woman, who frequently said to me, "I do love Jesus, I know I do; but does he love me?" Her question used to make me smile. "Well", I said, "that is a question that I never did put to myself — 'If I love him, does he love me?' No, the question that used to puzzle me was, 'Do I love him?' When I could once settle that point, I was never again the victim of your form of doubt." If you love Christ, Christ loves you for certain, for your love to Christ is nothing more nor less than a beam out of the great sun of his love; and the grace that has created that love in your heart towards him, if you do indeed love him, proves that he loves you. Is it not so: "We love him because he first loved us"? (1 Jn. 4:19) Did love ever get into the heart by any other door than that? I am sure that it never did; so that, if you love him, you can say, "My Beloved is mine."

There are many who may love on earth, and never obtain the object of their affection. But if you love Christ, raise no question about his love for you; he is yours, and you are his. That test may help someone who, perhaps, is standing trembling behind the door, full of blushes and afraid to come in among God's people. To you, poor timid soul, we say, "Come in, you blessed of the Lord, why are you standing outside? If you love him, you are welcome to all he has."

Next, I would help you with a third question: Is Jesus dear to you above all your possessions? Perhaps you have a great deal of this world's goods. Do you set small store by all that you have as compared with Jesus? Would you see it all burn away, or melt away, or be stolen, infinitely rather than lose Christ? If you can say "Yes" to that question, then he is yours. Perhaps you have very little indeed, few earthly comforts, a narrow room, and a scant pittance to live on; but would you sooner have Christ than all the riches of the world, or would you be willing to sell Christ in order to rise in the world? Would you sell him that you might be made rich, and great, and famous? You who are sick, which would you sooner have, your sickness and Christ, or go without Christ to be made healthy and strong? According to your answer to these enquiries will be my answer to the other questions, "Are you Christ's, and is Christ yours?" I hope that many of you can say, "O sir, we would give all that we have, we would suffer all that might be suffered, we would part with the very light and our eyes too, if we could but be sure that we might each one truly say, 'My Beloved is mine.'" Well, if you love Christ beyond all earthly things, rest assured that he is yours.

Further, do you love him beyond all earthly companions? Could you part with your dearest ones for his sake? Say, are you sure of this? Oh, then, he is assuredly yours! Do you love him beyond all earthly objects? Yes, beyond the desire of learning, or honour, or position, or comfort — would you let all go for his dear sake? Many of his saints have had to do it, and they have done it very cheerfully, and said with the Apostle, "Yea doubtless, and I count all things but loss for the excellence of the knowledge of Christ Jesus my Lord: for whom I have suffered the loss of all things, and do count them but dung, that I may win Christ, and be found in him." (Phil. 3:8-9) Can you go that length? If you can, then surely he is yours.

Let me further help you with another question: Is Jesus so fully your hope and your trust that you have no other? I have often led persons into liberty through that question. They

226

have said, "I am afraid that I do not trust Christ." I have then asked, "Well, where do you trust? Everyone has a reliance of some sort; where are you trusting?" When I have pressed them closely, they have said, "Oh, we have no other trust! God forbid that we should ever have!" When I have mentioned their good works, they have said, "Good works! Why, we should be foolish indeed to talk of them!" When I have mentioned trusting in a priest, or in sacraments, they have scorned the thought; it has been loathsome to them. Then I have said, "If you have no other trust but Christ, and you are sure that you have a trust somewhere, then your trust is in Christ; and though you may question it, and doubt it, yet if you so trust in him as to trust nowhere else, he is yours, and you are his."

There is many a good and true believer who, nevertheless, is afraid that he is not a believer. When you are once on board ship, even if the vessel is tossed to and fro, and you yourself are ill, perhaps sadly sea-sick, yet as long as that ship does not go down, you will not go down, for your safety now does not depend on your health and strength, but on the ship into which you have entered. So, if you have fled to Christ away from everything else, then, though you may sigh, and cry, and fear, and tremble — for all of which I am sorry, for I would have everyone on board ship to be well and strong, and able to handle the ropes — still, if you cannot touch a rope, and if you cannot even eat your meals in your cabin, yet, if you are aboard the ship, and if that ship gets safe to land, so will you. Therefore, be of good cheer. O poor heart, if you are clean divorced from every confidence but Christ, then I believe that you are married to Christ, despite your trembling sometimes! And ask whether it is so or not. Let that thought also help you.

I would further help you in this way: If Christ is yours, your thoughts go after him. You cannot say that you love a person if you never think of him. You could not, I am sure, let another person fill your heart as Christ must fill his people's hearts, and yet never let that person occupy your thoughts. He to whom Christ belongs often thinks of him. "Well", says one, "I am so busy during the day that, often, my mind is taken up with my business, and I do not think of Christ." Do you know where those crows live that are feeding on that ploughed field? They are going up and down the furrows, picking up all the worms they can find; and as you look at them, you cannot tell where their home is, can you? No; but wait till the evening, when the day's feeding is over; then you will see which way the crows fly, and you will find out where their nests are. Do you see how quickly they are winging their way to yonder rookery? So it is with us; while we are busy in the world, picking up the worms, as it were, we have to think about those things; we cannot do our business properly without our thoughts going that way; but when the business is over, when the evening comes, which way do you go then? When you have an opportunity for thought, when your mind is going to its resting-place, which way do your thoughts fly? That shall be the true test; and if, when your thoughts are set free, they fly away to Jesus, rest assured that he is yours. That thought may help some of you poor trembling ones. We read of the apostles, "Being let go, they went to their own company." (Acts 4:23) Just so! I heard a working man who was expounding that chapter very well. He said, "If some fellows were put in prison, and they were let out, they would go to the first public-house they see, for that is where they would find their company. Just so! "Birds of a feather flock together." Now, when you are let go, when your mind gets out of the prison of your daily business, do you go to the world for your pleasure? Do you go to worldly things for your mirth, or do you fly to Christ? If you can answer, "My thoughts go naturally to Christ", then you can truly say, "My Beloved is mine."

Again, do you do more than this? Do you long for Christ's company? If "my Beloved" is indeed mine, I shall want to see him, I shall want to speak with him, I shall want him to abide with me. How is it with you? There is a great deal of religion in the world which only consists of shells or husks; the kernels are not there at all. A man goes upstairs, and kneels down for a quarter of an hour, and he says that he is praying; yet possibly he has

227

not really prayed at all. Another opens his Bible, and he reads a chapter, and he says that he has been studying the Scriptures. Perhaps it has been a mere mechanical act, and there has been no heart and soul in it. John Bradford, the famous martyr, used to say, "I have made a point of this, that I will never go from a duty till I have had communion with Christ in it." Hence, when he prayed, he prayed till he really did pray. When he praised, he praised till he truly did praise. If he was bowing in humiliation before God, he humbled himself till he was actually humbled. If he was seeking communion with Christ, he would not go away with the pleasure of merely having sought, but he kept on seeking until he found, for he felt that he had done nothing right till he had come into communion with God, and in touch with Christ.

And, once more, if your Beloved is yours, you will own it to be so. Coming into this Tabernacle, or going down to the communion table, or gathering round the family altar, what is all that if Christ is not there? It should be with you as it is with a wife whose husband is far away across the sea. "Oh", she cries, "that I could hear the music of his footstep! The rooms seem all empty now that he is away. There is his portrait on the wall, but it only makes me sigh the more for my beloved. The very dog, as he comes in, seems to know that his master is away, and makes me think of him." Is it so with you in regard to Christ? In every duty, do you sigh for him, and long for him? Holy Bernard used to say, and I believe that he could say it truly (it was in Latin, but I will give it you in English), "O my Jesus, I never went from you without you!" He meant that he never left his knees and left Christ behind him; he never went out of the house of God and left Christ behind him; but he went through the outward act of devotion with a consciousness of the presence of Christ. Now, if this is your habit, to keep up or to labour to keep up continued communion with Christ, and if you are longing for more and more of that communion, then, dear friends, you are his, and he is yours.

Further, let me help you with a still closer question: Have you ever enjoyed that communion with Christ? Did you ever speak with him? Have you ever heard his voice? I think I see you turning over the leaves of your diary; I hope you have not to go far back to read the record of your fellowship with your Lord. I hope that this morning was one instance of it, and that this evening may be another. But are there not some special days, red-letter days, in your history? I recollect that Rutherford sent this message to one of his friends who was in great sorrow: "Tell him to remember Torwood." Nobody knew what was meant except the two who had been to Torwood, where they had enjoyed such fellowship with Christ that they could never forget it all their days. That is what David meant when he said, "Therefore will I remember thee from the land of Jordan, and of the Hermonites, and the hill Mizar." (Ps. 42:6) Those were some choice spots that he recollected where the Lord had met with him. How can Christ be yours if you know nothing about communion with him? Are you married to him if he has never shown you his face, and you have never heard his voice, and never spoken with him? But if you have had Christ's company, he has manifested himself to you as he does not to the world. He would never have shown you such things as these if you were not his. Ah, have you not, sometimes, crept out of the very dungeon of despair, and seen your Lord's blessed face, and, in a moment, you have been dancing for joy? Have you not lain on the bed of sickness "weary, and worn, and sad", till his presence has made the chamber of affliction bright with the light of heaven? Have you not, sometimes, at dead of night, been weary in watching for sleep that would not come, and your Lord has come to you, and then you have been afraid to go to sleep lest you should lose the joy of his presence, and wake up without him? Oh, some of us know what that experience means — when earth has been the vestibule of heaven, and when, even in our sickness and sadness, we have been on the very verge of Jordan, and have smelt the fragrance of the spices that was wafted by the breath of the Spirit from the golden gardens on the other side of the stream. If you know anything experimentally about this matter, then you may conclude that your Beloved is indeed yours.

228

But supposing that you are not enjoying Christ's presence. I am going to put another question to you: Are you cast down when he is away? If you have grieved his Spirit, are you grieved? If Christ has gone, do you feel as if the sun itself had ceased to shine, and the candle of your existence has been snuffed out in utter darkness? Do you cry when he is away:

O for a closer walk with God,
A calm and heavenly frame;
A light to shine upon the road
That leads me to the Lamb.

Where is the blessedness I knew
When first I saw the Lord?
Where is the soul-refreshing view
Of Jesus in His Word?

What peaceful hours I then enjoyed!
How sweet their memory still!
But now I find an aching void
The world can never fill.

(William Cowper)

Oh, then, he is yours! If you cannot bear his absence, he is yours. Last Thursday night, I preached a sermon which was intended to be a very searching one, and I hope that it was. It was on the text, "Now if any man have not the Spirit of Christ, he is none of his." (Rom. 8:9) [Not recorded, but preached again on this text on Lord's-Day morning, September 21, 1873, No. 1133: *A Fatal Deficiency*, a sermon Spurgeon described as being based on one the most solemn texts in the whole Bible.]

Now see the difficulty of this poor minister. If I preach very comforting sermons, there are sure to be hypocrites who suck them down, and say, "How delightful!" But when I preach a soul-searching sermon, some dear child of God, who is as precious to her Lord as gold tried in the furnace, takes everything to herself, and begins to be very sorrowful, and to say, "That sharp knife is meant for me, for I am not one of the Lord's people." Well, after last Thursday night's sermon, a dear woman came to my vestry, broken-hearted, crying and sobbing. I hope that the discourse will be a blessing to her in the long run; but I protest that I never meant to preach to her at all. I was not aiming at her or at the sort of people to whom she belongs; it was a very different class whom I was addressing. If the preacher says anything about hypocrites, very often the hypocrites will not take it to heart, but the most sincere saint in the congregation very likely says, "Oh, I am afraid that I am a hypocrite!" If you are, you are an odd sort of hypocrite, for I never knew of a hypocrite who was afraid that he was one. He does not have grace enough for that kind of fear, but just goes on in self-conceit that all is right with him. I, for my part, feel more confidence in the broken-hearted tremblers than I do in the boasters, who never have a question about their being all right, but set it down as an undisputed fact that they are in the covenant of grace.

O beloved, I am glad if sometimes you moan like a dove, and cry in the bitterness of your spirit, "Oh, that I knew where I might find him!" It may seem to be a spot on your character, but this spot is the spot of God's children, and I am not sorry to see it on you. If Prince Immanuel has left the town of Mansoul, then there can be no marriage bells or joyous music there until he comes back again. We must invite him and entreat him to return; we must clothe ourselves in sackcloth till he does come back; if we do not act thus, then he is not ours. If you can do without Christ, you shall do without Christ; but if you cannot do without him, if you cry, "Give me Christ, or else I die", then he shall be yours. Stretch out the hand of faith and take him, and then say without hesitation, "My Beloved is mine." I am not going on to the rest of the text; but I want to say just this — if there is any man or woman here (and I know there are many), who can sit down in the pew, and quietly say, "Yes, weighing everything the preacher has said, and judging myself as severely as I can, yet I dare take Christ to be mine, and to say, 'My Beloved is mine.'" If that is your case, dear friend, then you shall get confirmatory evidence of this fact by the witness of the Spirit within your soul, which will very likely come to you in the form of perfect contentment of spirit, and perfect rest of heart. "When I can say, 'My God is mine'":

Lord, what a heaven of saving grace
Shines through the beauties of thy face,
And lights our passions to a flame!
Lord, how we love thy charming name!

When I can say, "My God is mine",
When I can feel thy glories shine,
I tread the world beneath my feet,
And all that earth calls good or great.

(Isaac Watts)

"There", says the believer, "now that my Beloved is mine, I have no other wish or want." Now will he be like Simeon when he took that blessed Babe into his arms: "Lord", said he, "now lettest thou thy servant depart in peace, according to thy Word." (Lk. 2:29) "Have you nothing more to live for, Simeon?" "No", replies the good old man, "what more can there be?" "Don't you think that, if you lived a little longer, you might have a heavy purse of gold in your hands?" "Yes", he answers, "possibly I might; but it would be a cumbrous burden. This dear Child is better than all the gold and silver in the world. If he is mine, I have enough, yes, I have all." That blessed rest of soul, which comes from a sure possession of Christ, is not to be imitated, but it is greatly to be desired. I know that some good people who, I believe, will be saved, nevertheless do not attain to this sweet rest. They keep on thinking that it is something that they may get when they are very old, or when they are about to die, but they look upon the full assurance of faith, and the personal grasping of Christ, and saying "My Beloved is mine", as something very dangerous.

I began my Christian life in this happy fashion as a boy fifteen years of age; I believed fully and without hesitation in the Lord Jesus Christ; and when I went to see a good Christian woman, I was simpleton enough to tell her that I believed in Christ, that he was mine, and that he had saved me. She said to me, "Ah, I don't like such assurance as that!" And then she added, "I trust you are believing in Christ — I hope so — but I have never got beyond a hope, or a trust, and I am an old woman." Bless the old woman, she was no example for us who know whom we have believed; we are to rise infinitely beyond that grovelling kind of life. The man who begins right, and the boy who begins right, and the girl who begins right, will begin by saying, "God has said it: 'He that believeth on him is not condemned.' (Jn. 3:18) I believe in him, therefore I am not condemned; Christ is mine."

O dear friends, do not always keep on with that miserable hoping —hoping, and hopping! Walk on both your feet, and get a good firm standing on the Rock of Ages, and say without boasting, but without doubting, "My Beloved is mine." This will bring you into the condition of the psalmist, when he said, "He maketh me to lie down in green pastures: he leadeth me beside the still waters." (Ps. 23:2) David never would have said that if he had not begun the Psalm with "The Lord is my Shepherd." If he had begun by saying,

"Perhaps the Lord is my Shepherd", he would have gone on to say, "Perhaps there may be green pastures, possibly there may be still waters; but, as yet, my soul is in a dry and thirsty land where no water is, and not a blade of grass either." Ah, David was not so stupid as that; he had his times of depression, but when he was singing that Psalm, he was in a positive, certain, frame of mind. "The Lord *is* my Shepherd." He used the indicative mood, not the subjunctive or conditional. May the Lord help you to do the same! And you may. If Christ is a satisfaction to your spirit, so that your soul is satisfied as with marrow and fatness, then do not hesitate to say, and to emphasise the utterance, "My Beloved is mine." He either is, or he is not. Which is it? Do not go to sleep tonight till you know. If Christ is yours, heaven is yours. If Christ is not yours, you are neither fit to live, nor fit to die. Remember that awful verse, "If any man love not the Lord Jesus Christ, let him be Anathema Maranatha" — "Let him be accursed, the Lord is coming!" (1 Cor. 16:22) Take heed to yourselves, therefore; if Christ is not yours, you are in terrible poverty; but if Christ is yours, you are eternally rich to all the intents of bliss. Oh, that he might be yours now by your stretching out the hand of faith, and taking him to yourself!

"I dare not take him", says someone. Well, you are a strange person; I dare not let him alone, and I challenge you to shape that "dare" into any other proper form. If he bids you take him and trust him, how dare you refuse him? Take him now, and be safe and happy forever. God bless you, for Jesus sake! Amen.

31. A SONG AMONG THE LILIES
NO. 1190

DELIVERED ON LORD'S-DAY MORNING, AUGUST 30TH, 1874
AT THE METROPOLITAN TABERNACLE, NEWINGTON

"My beloved is mine, and I am his: he feedeth among the lilies."
(Song of Solomon 2:16)

LAST Sabbath, in our morning's sermon [Metropolitan Tabernacle Pulpit, No. 1189, *The Turning Point*], we began at the beginning and described the turning point in which the sinner sets his face towards his God, and for the first time gives practical evidence of spiritual life in his soul. He stirs himself up, he goes to his Father's house, and speedily is pressed to his Father's bosom, forgiven, accepted, and rejoiced over. This morning, we are going far beyond that stage, to a position which I may call the very crown and summit of the spiritual life. We would conduct you from the door-step to the innermost chamber, from the outer court to the Holy of Holies, and we pray the Holy Spirit to enable each one of us who have entered in by Christ Jesus, to go through the door, to pass boldly into the secret place of the tabernacles of the Host High, and sing with joyful heart the words of our text, "My beloved is mine, and I am his."

For he is mine and I am his,
The God whom I adore;
My Father, Saviour, Comforter,
Now and for evermore.

The passage describes a high state of grace, and it is worthy of note that the description is full of Christ. This is instructive, for this is not an exceptional case, it is only one fulfilment of a general rule. Our estimate of Christ is the best gauge of our spiritual condition; as the thermometer rises in proportion to the increased warmth of the air, so does our estimate of Jesus rise as our spiritual life increases in vigour and fervency. Tell me what you think of Jesus and I will tell you what to think of yourself. Christ is in us, yes, more than all when we are thoroughly sanctified and filled with the Holy Spirit. When pride of self fills up the soul, there is little room for Jesus; but when Jesus is fully loved, self is subdued, and sin is driven out of the throne. If we think little of the Lord Jesus, we have very great cause to account ourselves spiritually blind, and naked, and poor, and miserable. The rebel despises his lawful sovereign, but the favoured courtier is enthusiastic in his praise. Christ crucified is the revealer of many hearts, the touchstone by which the pure gold and the counterfeit metal are discerned; his very name is as a refiner's fire and like fuller's soap; false professors cannot endure it, but true believers triumph in it. We are growing in grace when we grow in the knowledge of our Lord and Saviour Jesus Christ. Let everything else be gone and let Christ fill up the entire space of our soul; then, and only then, are we rising out of the vanity of the flesh into the real life of God.

Beloved, the grandest facts in all the world to a truly spiritual man are not the rise and fall of empires, the marches of victory, or the desolations of defeat; he cares neither for crowns nor mitres, swords nor shields; his admiring gaze is wholly fixed upon Christ and his cross and cause. To him, Jesus is the centre of history, the soul and core of providence. He desires no knowledge so much as that which concerns his Redeemer and Lord; his science deals with what Jesus is, and what he is to be, what he has done, what he is doing, and what he will do. The believer is mainly anxious as to how Jesus can be glorified, and how sinners can be brought to know him. That which concerns the honour of Jesus is our chief concern from day to day; as for other matters let the Lord do as he wills with them, only let Jesus Christ be magnified, and all the rest of the world's story has small significance for us. The Beloved is the head and front, the heart and soul of the Christian's delight when his heart is in its best state. Our text is the portrait of a heavenly-minded child of God, or rather, it is the music of his well stringed harp when love, as minstrel, touches the tenderest chords: "My beloved is mine, and I am his; he feedeth among the lilies."

We note then, first, that here is *a delighting to have Christ*; secondly, *a delighting to belong to Christ*; and thirdly, *a delighting at the very thought of Christ*.

I. First, here is A DELIGHT TO HAVE CHRIST. "*My beloved is mine.*"

The spouse makes this the first of her joy notes, the cornerstone of her peace, the fountain of her bliss, the crown of her glory. Observe here that where such an expression is truthfully used of the existence *of the Beloved is a matter of fact*. Scepticism and questioning have no place with those who thus sing. There are dreamers now-a-days who cast doubt on everything, Taking to themselves the name of philosophers, and professing to know something of science, they make statements worthy only of idiots, and demand for their self-evidently false assertions the assent of rational men. The word "philosopher" will soon come to mean a lover of ignorance, and the term "a scientific man" will be understood as meaning a fool, who has said in his heart there is no God. (Ps. 14:1, 53:1) Such attacks on the eternal verities of our holy faith can have no effect on hearts enamoured of the Son of God, for, dwelling in his immediate presence, they have passed the stage of doubt, left the region of questioning far behind, and, in this matter, have entered into rest. The power of love has convinced us. To entertain a doubt as to the reality and glory of our Well-beloved would be torment to us, and therefore love has cast it out. We use no perhapses, buts, or ifs, concerning our Beloved, but we say positively that he is, and that he is ours. We believe that we have better evidence of his being, power, Godhead, and love for us than can be given for any other fact. So far from being abashed by the cavils [arguments] of sceptics, or quailing beneath the question, "Is there such a Beloved?" we are not careful to answer in this matter, for we know that there is; our love laughs at the question, and does not condescend to answer it save by bidding those who seriously inquire to "come and see" for themselves. We have ever found, beloved, that when a time of chilling doubt has come over us — and such ague fits will come — we have only to return to meditations upon Jesus, and he becomes his own evidence by making our hearts burn within us with love of his character and Person, and then doubt is doomed. We do not slay our unbelief by reason, but we annihilate it by affection. The influence of love for Jesus on the soul is so magical — I wish I had a better word — so elevating, so ravishing, so transporting, it gives such a peace, and inspires such holy and lofty aspirations, that the effect proves the cause. That which is holy is true, and that which is true cannot rise out of that which is false. We may safely judge a tree by its fruit and a doctrine by its result: that which produces in us self-denial, purity, righteousness, and truth, cannot itself be false, and yet the love of Jesus does this beyond everything else.

There must be truth for a cause where truth is the effect; and thus love, by the savour which it spreads over the soul by contemplation of Christ, puts its foot upon the neck of doubt and triumphantly utters bold, confident declarations, which reveal the full assurance of faith. New-born love for Jesus, while yet in its cradle, like a young Hercules, it takes the serpents of doubt and strangles them. He who can say from his heart "My Beloved" is the man who is on the way to confirmed faith. Love cannot, will not, doubt; it casts away the crutches of argument and flies on the wings of conscious enjoyment, singing her nuptial hymn, "My Beloved is mine, and I *am* his."

In the case before us, *the love of the heavenly-minded one is perceived and acknowledged by herself.* "By beloved", says she. It is no latent affection; she knows that she loves him, and solemnly avows it. She does not whisper, "I hope I love the peerless one" but sings, "My beloved". There is no doubt in her soul about her passion for the altogether lovely one. Ah, dear friends, when you feel the flame of love within your soul, and give it practical expression, you will no longer inquire, "Do I love the Lord or not?" Then your inner consciousness will dispense with evidences. Those are dark days when we require evidences; well may we then fast, for the Bridegroom is not with us; but when he abides with us, enjoyment of his fellowship supersedes all evidences. I want no evidence to prove that food is sweet when it is still in my mouth; I want no evidence of the existence of the sun when I am basking in its rays, and enjoying his light, and even so we need no evidence that Jesus is precious to us when, like a bundle of myrrh, he perfumes our bosom. We are anxious doubters as to our safety, and questioners of our own condition, because we are not living with Jesus as we ought to be; but when he brings us to his banqueting house, and we walk in the light as he is in the light, we have fellowship with him and with the Father (1 Jn. 1:7), and then we believe and are sure, and our love for Jesus is indisputable, because it burns within too fervent to be denied. Why, when a Christian is in a right state, his love for Jesus is the mightiest force in his nature; it is an affection which, like Aaron's rod, swallows up all other rods; it is the mainspring of his action, and sways his whole body, soul, and spirit. As the wind sweeps over all the strings of the Aeolian harp, and causes them all to vibrate, so does the love of Jesus move every power and passion of our soul, and we feel in our entire being that our Beloved is indeed ours, and that we love him with all our hearts. Here, then, is the Beloved realised, and our love realised too.

But the pith of the text lies here: *our possession of him is proven,* we know it, and we know it on good evidence — "My beloved *is mine.*" You know it is not a very easy thing to reach this point. Have you ever thought of the fact that to claim the Lord and call him "my God" is a very wonderful thing? Who was the first man in the Old Testament who is recorded as saying "My God"? Was it not Jacob, when he slept at Bethel, and saw the ladder which reached to heaven? Even after that heavenly vision it took him great effort to reach to "My God." He said "If God will be with me and will keep me in the way that I go, and will give me bread to eat and raiment to put on, so that I come again to my father's house in peace, then shall the Lord be my God." (Gen. 28:20-21) Only after long experience of divine goodness could he climb up to the height of saying "My God." And who is the first man in the New Testament to call Jesus "My Lord and My God"? It was Thomas, and he must needs have abundant proofs before he can speak thus: "Except I see in his hands the print of the nails, and put my finger into the print of the nails, and thrust my hand into his side, I will not believe." (Jn. 20:24-29) Only when he had received such proofs could he exclaim "My Lord and my God." Blessed are they who reach it by a simpler faith, who have not seen and yet have believed.

"*My* Beloved" is a strong expression. "Beloved" is sweet, but "MY Beloved" is sweetest of all. If you think of it, it is no little thing to claim God as ours, to claim Jesus the Beloved as ours, yes, to put it in the singular, and call him *mine*; and yet, when the believer's heart is in the right condition, he makes the claim, and is warranted in so doing; for Jesus Christ is the portion of all believers. His Father gave him to us, and he has given himself to us. Jesus was made over to every believing soul as his personal possession, in the eternal covenant ordered in all things and sure. Jesus actually gave himself for us in his incarnation, becoming bone of our bone and flesh of our flesh; he has made himself ours by his passion and death, loving us and giving himself for us, to save us from our sins. He has also given us power to appropriate him by the gracious gift of faith, by which we are in very deed married to him, and enabled to call him the husband of our souls, who is ours to have and to hold, for better for worse, for life and for death, by a bond of marriage union

234

which neither death nor hell, time nor eternity, can break. Jesus is ours by the promise, the covenant, and oath of God; a thousand assurances and pledges, bonds and seals, secure him to us as our portion and everlasting heritage.

This precious possession becomes to the believer his sole treasure. "My beloved is mine" says he, and in that sentence he has summed up all his wealth. He does not say "My wife, my children, my home, my earthly comforts are mine." He is almost afraid to say so, because, while he is yet speaking, they may cease to be his: the beloved wife may sicken before his eyes, the child may need a tiny coffin, the friend may prove a traitor, and the riches may take to themselves wings. Therefore, the wise man does not care to say too positively that anything here below is his; indeed, he feels that in very truth they are not his, but only lent to him "to be returned in due time". But the Beloved is his own, and his possession of him is most firm. Neither does the believer, when his soul is in the best state, so much rejoice even in his spiritual privileges as in the Lord from whom they come. He has righteousness, wisdom, sanctification and redemption; he has both grace and glory secured for him, but he prefers rather to claim the fountain than the streams. He clearly sees that these choice mercies are only his because they are Christ's, and only his because Christ is his. Oh, what would all the treasures of the covenant be to us if it were possible to have them without Christ! Their very sap and sweetness would be gone. Having our Beloved to be ours, we have all things in him, and therefore our main treasure, yes, our sole treasure, is our Beloved.

O you saints of God, was there ever possession like this? You have your beloveds, you daughters of earth, but what are your beloveds compared with ours? He is the Son of God and the Son of Man! The darling of heaven and the delight of earth! The lily of the valley and the rose of Sharon! Perfect in his character, powerful in his atoning death, mighty in his living plea! He is such a lover that all earthly loves put together are not worthy to touch the hem of his garment, or loose the latchet of his shoes. He is so dear, so precious, that words cannot describe him nor pencil depict him; but this we say of him, he is "the chief among ten thousand, and the altogether lovely", and he is ours. Do you wonder that we glory in this fact, and count this the crowning delight of our lives, "My beloved is mine"!

The very tenure upon which we hold this priceless possession is a matter to glory in. O worldlings, you cannot hold your treasures as we hold ours. If you knew all, you would never say of anything, "It is mine", for your holding is too precarious to constitute possession. It is yours till that frail thread of life shall snap, or that bubble of time shall burst. You have only a leasehold on your treasures, terminated at the end of one frail life; whereas ours is an eternal freehold, an everlasting entail. "My beloved is mine" — I cannot lose him, nor can he be taken from me; he is mine forever, for "who shall separate us from the love of God which is in Christ Jesus our Lord? "So that, while the possession is rare, the tenure is rare also; and it the life of our life, and the light of our delight that we can sing,

Yea, thou art mine, my blessed Lord,
O my Beloved, thou art mine!
And, purchased with thy precious blood,
My God and Saviour, I am thine.

MY CHRIST! Oh, sing it in the heavens,
Let every angel lift his voice;
Sound with ten thousand harps his praise,
With me, ye heavenly hosts, rejoice.

The gift unspeakable is given,

235

The grace of God has made him mine;
And, now, before both earth and heaven,
Lord, I will own that I am thine.

(Henry Grattan Guinness)

Now, beloved friends, I cannot talk about this as I feel, I can only give you hints of that which fills me to the full with joy. I beg you to contemplate for a single moment the delight which is stored up in this fact, that the blessed Son of God, the brightness of the Father's glory, is all our own.

Whatever else we may have, or may not have, he is ours. I may not exhibit in my character all the grace I could wish, but "My beloved is mine". I may have only one talent, but "My beloved is mine". I may be very poor and very obscure, but "My beloved is mine". I may have neither health nor wealth, but "My beloved is mine". I may not be what I want to be, but "My beloved is mine." Yes, he is altogether mine, his Godhead and his manhood, his life, his death, his attributes, and prerogatives, yes, all he is, all he was, all he ever will be, all he has done, and all he ever will do, is mine. I do not possess a portion in Christ, but the whole of him. All his saints own him, but I own him as much as if there were never another saint to claim him. Child of God, do you see this? In other inheritances, if there are many heirs, there is so much the less for each, but in this great possession, everyone who has Christ has a whole Christ all to himself, from the head of much fine gold, down to his legs, which are like pillars of marble. The whole of his boundless heart of love, his whole arm of infinite might, and his whole head of matchless wisdom — all is for you, beloved. Whoever you may be, if you do indeed trust in Jesus, he is all your own.

My beloved is all mine, and absolutely mine; not mine to look at and talk about merely, but mine to trust in, to speak to, to depend on, to fly to in every troubling hour, yes, mine to feed on, for his flesh is meat indeed, and his blood is drink indeed. (Jn. 6:55) Our beloved is not ours only to use in certain ways, but ours outright, without restriction. I may draw what I will from him, and both what I take and what I leave are mine. He himself, in his ever glorious Person, is mine, and mine always; mine when I know it, and mine when I do not know it, mine when I am sure of it, and mine when I doubt it; mine by day, and mine by night; mine when I walk in holiness, yes, and mine when I sin, for "if any man sin we have an advocate with the Father, Jesus Christ the righteous." (1 Jn. 2:1) He is mine on the hill Mizar, and mine in the swellings of Jordan; mine by the grave where I bury those I love, mine when I shall be buried there myself; mine when I rise again; mine in judgement, and mine in glory; forever mine.

Note well that it is written, "My beloved is *mine*", in the singular. He is yours, and I am glad of it; but still to me it is most sweet that he is mine. It is well to bless God that others have a possession in Christ, but what would that avail if we were strangers to him ourselves? The marrow and the fatness lie in the personal pronoun singular: "*My* beloved is *mine*."

I am so glad that our Father in Heaven
Tells of his love in the Book He has given;
Wonderful things in the Bible I see,
This is the dearest, that Jesus loves me.

Oh, if there's only one song I can sing,
When in His beauty I see the great King,
This shall my song through eternity be,
"Oh, what a wonder that Jesus loves me!

236

I am so glad that Jesus loves me,
Jesus loves even me.

(Phillip Bliss)

Oh for a blessed grip with both hands on such a Christ as this! Observe well that he is ours *as our Beloved*, so that he is ours whatever our love makes of him. Our love can never praise him enough, or speak well enough of him; she thinks all descriptions fall short of his deservings. Well, then, Jesus is ours at his best; if we think him so glorious, he is ours in all that glory. Our love says that he is a fair, lovely, sweet, and precious Christ, so let us be sure that, however lovely, sweet, and precious he is, he is all ours. Our love says there is none like him, he is King of kings and Lord of lords, he is the ever blessed; well, as the King of kings and Lord of lords he is yours. You cannot think too much of him, but, when you think your best, he is yours at that best. He has not a glory so high that it is not yours, nor a lustre so brilliant that it is not yours. He is my beloved, and I would extol him, but never can I get beyond this golden circle: when I most extol him he is still mine.

Here, then, is the basis of the Christian life, the foundation on which it rests: to know that most surely Christ is altogether ours is the beginning of wisdom, the source of strength, the star of hope, and the dawn of heaven.

II. The second portion of the text deals with DELIGHTING TO BELONG TO CHRIST. "*I am his*."
This is as sweet as the former sentence. I would venture to put a question to each loving wife here present — when you were married, which was the sweetest thought to you, that you were your husband's, or that he was yours? Why, you feel that neither sentence would be sweet alone: they are necessary for each other. Ask any fond, loving heart which of these declarations could best be parted with, and they will tell you that neither can be given up. Christ is mine, but if I were not his it would be a sorry case, and if I were his and he were not mine it would be a wretched business. These two things are joined together with diamond rivets — "My beloved is mine, and I am his." Put the two together, and you have reached the summit of delight.

That we are his is a fact that may be proved — yes, it should need no proving, but be manifest to all that "I am *his*." Certainly, we are his by creation; he who made us should have us. We are his because his Father gave us to him, and we are his because he chose us. Creation, donation, election are his triple hold upon us. We are his because he bought us with his blood, his because he called us by his grace, his because he is married to us, and we are his spouse. We are his, moreover, to our own consciousness, because we have heartily, from the inmost depths of our being, given ourselves up to him, bound by love to him forever. We feel we must have Christ, and be Christ's, or die — "For me to live is Christ." (Phil. 1:21) Brothers and sisters, mind you attend to this clause, then. I am sure you will if the former one is true for you. If you can say, "My beloved is mine" you will be sure to add, "I am his, I must be his, I will be his. I am not alive unless I am his, for I count that in what I am not his, I am dead, and I only live as I live for him." My very soul is conscious that I am his.

Now *this puts very great honour upon as*. I have known the time when I could say "My beloved is mine" in a very humble, trembling way, but I did not dare to add "I am his", because I did not think I was worth his having. I dared not hope that "I am his" would ever be written in the same book side by side with "My beloved is mine." Poor sinner, first lay hold on Jesus, and then you will discover that Jesus values you. You will prize him first, and then you will find out that he prizes you, and that, though you do not feel worthy to be

237

flung on a dunghill, yet Jesus has put a value on you, saying "Since you were precious in my sight, you have been honourable, and I have loved you." It is no small joy to know that we poor sinners are worth Christ's having, and that he has even said, "They shall be mine in the day when I make up my jewels." (Mal. 3:17)

This second part of the text is true as *absolutely* as the first. "*I* am his" — not my goods only, nor my time, nor my talents, nor what I can spare, but "*I* am his." I fear that some Christians have never understood this. They give the Lord a little of their surplus, which they never miss. The poor widow who gave all her living had the true idea of her relation to her Lord. She would have put herself into the treasury if she could, for she felt "I am his." (Mk. 12:43) As for myself, I wish I could be dropped bodily through the little slot of Christ's treasure box, and be in his casket for ever, never to be heard of any more as my own, but to be wholly my Lord's. Paul desired to spend and be spent. (2 Cor. 12:15) It is not easy to do those two things distinctly with money, for when you spend a thing it is spent at one and the same time, but the Apostle meant that he would spend himself by activity, and then, when he could do no more, he would be glad to be spent by passive endurance for Christ's sake. The believer feels that he belongs to Jesus absolutely; let the Lord employ him as he may, or try him as he pleases. Let him take away all earthly friends from him or surround him with comforts; let him either depress him or exalt him, let him use him for little things or great things, or not use him at all, but lay him on the shelf; it is enough that the Lord does it, and the true heart is content, for it truthfully confesses, "I am his. I have no mortgage or lien upon myself, so that I can call a part of my being my own, but I am absolutely and unreservedly my Lord's sole property." Do you feel this, brothers and sisters? I pray God you may.

Blessed be God, this is true *evermore*! "I am his": his today in the house of worship, and his tomorrow in the house of business; his as a singer in the sanctuary, and his as a toiler in the workshop; his when I am preaching, and equally his when I am walking the streets; his while I live, his when I die; his when my soul ascends and my body lies mouldering in the grave; the whole personality of my manhood is altogether his forever and for ever.

This belonging to the Well-beloved is a matter of fact and practice, not a thing to be talked about only, but really to be acted on. I am treading on tender ground now, but I would to God that every Christian could really say this without lying: "I do live for Christ in all things, for I am his. When I rise in the morning, I wake up as his, when I sit down to a meal I eat as his, and drink as his. I eat, and drink, and sleep to the Lord, in everything giving thanks to him. It is blessed even to sleep as the Lord's beloved, to dream as his Abrahams and Jacobs do, to awake at night and sing like David, and then drop off to "sleep in Jesus." Say you, "It is a high condition." I grant it, but it is where we ought to abide. The whole of our time and energy should be consecrated by this great master principle: "*I am his*." Can you say it? Never rest till you can. And if you can, beloved, it involves great privilege. "I am his", then am I honoured by having such an owner. If a horse or a sheep is said to belong to the Queen, everyone thinks much of it. Now, you are not the Queen's, but you are the Lord's, and that is far more. Through belonging to Christ, you are safe, for he will surely keep his own. He will not lose his own sheep; he paid too dear a price for them to lose them. Against all the powers of earth and hell, the Redeemer will hold his own and keep them to the end. If you are his, he will provide for you. A good husband cares for his spouse, and even thus the Lord Jesus Christ cares for those who are betrothed to him. You will be perfected too, for whatever Christ has, he will make worthy of himself, and bring it to glory. It is because we are his that we shall get to heaven, for he has said, "Father, I will that they also whom thou hast given me be with me where I am." (Jn. 17:34) Because they are his, he would have them with him.

Now, give your thoughts licence to wonder that anyone of us should be able to say, "I am his; I who used to be so giddy and thoughtless, so sceptical, and perhaps profane. I am his." Yes, and some of you can say, "I who used to be passionate and proud, I who was a drunkard, I whose lips were black with blasphemy, I am his." Glory be to You, O Jesus Christ, for this, that you have taken up such worthless things as we are and made us yours. No longer do we belong to this present evil world; we live for the world to come. We do not even belong to the church, so as to make it our master; we are part of the flock, but, like all the rest, we belong to the Great Shepherd. We will not give ourselves up to any party, or become the slave of any denomination, for we belong to Christ. We do not belong to sin, or self, or Satan; we belong entirely, exclusively, and irrevocably to the Lord Jesus Christ. Another master waits upon us, and asks us to give our energies to his services; but our answer is, "I am already engaged." "How is that?" Paul declares, "I bear in my body the marks of the Lord Jesus, and therefore from henceforth trouble me no more." (Gal. 6:17)

"But can you not serve me in part?" "No, sir, I cannot serve two masters; I am not like a man who can do as he pleases, I have no time to call my own." "How is that?" "I belong to Christ, I am wholly his. If there is anything to be done for him, I am his man to the best of my ability; I decline no service to which he calls me, but I can serve no other Lord." Lord Jesus, help each one of us now to say:

Jesus, spotless Lamb of God,
Thou hast bought us with Thy blood;
We are Thine, and Thine alone,
This we gladly, fully own.

Help us to confess Thy name,
Bear with joy the cross and shame;
Only seek to follow Thee,
Though reproach our portion be.

When we are to glory come,
And have reached our heavenly home,
Louder then each lip shall own,
We are Thine and Thine alone.

(James George Deck)

III. To conclude: the saint feels DELIGHT IN THE VERY THOUGHT OF CHRIST. "*He feedeth among the lilies.*"

When we love someone, and we are away from home, we delight to think of her, and to remember what she is doing. You are a husband travailing in a foreign land; this morning you said to yourself, "At this time they are just getting up at home." Perhaps the time is different, for you are in another longitude, and you say to yourself, "Ah, now the dear children are just getting ready to go to Sabbath-school"; and by-and-by you think they are at dinner. So delight in the thought of Christ who made the church say, "He feedeth among the lilies." She was pleased to think of where he was and what he was doing. Now, *where is Jesus*? What are these lilies? Do not these lilies represent the pure in heart with whom Jesus dwells? The spouse used the imagery which her Lord put into her mouth. He said, "As the lily among thorns, so is my love among the daughters", and she appropriates the symbol to all the saints. A preacher who is great at spiritualising has well said on this verse,

"The straight stalk, standing up erect from the earth, its flowers as high from the ground as possible, do they not tell us of heavenly-mindedness? Do they not seem to say, 'Set your affection on things above, not on things on the earth'? (Col. 3:2) And if the spotless snow of the leaves teaches us of grace, then the gold of the anthers tells us of that crown which shall be the reward of grace."

The violet and the primrose in spring nestle close to the earth, as if in sympathy with her chilly condition, but the lily lifts up itself towards heaven in sympathy with the summer's light and splendour. The lily is frail, and such are the saints of God. Were not Jesus among them to protect them the wild beast would soon tread them down. Frail as they are, they are surpassingly lovely, and their beauty is not that which is made with hands. It is a beauty put upon them by the Lord, for "they toil not, neither do they spin, yet Solomon in all his glory was not arrayed like one of these." (Mat. 6:29; Lk. 12:27) The saints do not work for life, and spin no righteousness of their own, and yet the royal righteousness which adorns them far surpasses all that wisdom could devise or wealth procure.

Where, then, is my Lord to-day? He is up and away, among the lilies of Paradise. In imagination, I see those stately rows of milk-white lilies growing no longer among thorns: lilies which are never soiled with the dust of the earth, which forever glisten with the eternal dews of fellowship, while their roots drink in unfading life from the river of the water of life which waters the garden of the Lord. There is Jesus! Can you see him? He is fairer even than the lilies which bow their heads around him. But he is here too where we are, like lilies which have scarce opened yet, lily buds yet, but still watered by the same river, and yielding in our measure the same perfume. O you lilies of Christ's own planting, he is among you; Jesus is in this house today, the unction which has made his garments so fragrant is discerned among us.

But *what is he doing among the lilies*? It is said, "He feedeth among the lilies." He is feeding himself, not on the lilies, but *among* them. Our Lord finds solace among his people. His delights are with the sons of men. He joys to see the graces of his people, to receive their love, and to discern his own image in their faces. As he said to the woman of Samaria, "Give me to drink", so does he say to each one of his people, "Give me to drink", and is refreshed by their loving fellowship. But the text means that he is feeding his people. He feeds that part of his flock redeemed by blood of which we read that "the Lamb which is in the midst of the throne shall feed them and shall lead them unto living fountains of waters." (Rev. 7:17) Nor does he forget that part of his bock which is in the low lands of earth, but he gives them also their portion of food. He has fed us this morning, for he is the good Shepherd, and leaves none of his sheep to famish.

Then *what shall I do*? Well, I will abide among the lilies. His saints shall be my companions. Where they flourish, I will try to grow. I will be often in their assemblies. Yes, and I will be a lily too. By faith, I will neither toil nor spin in a legal fashion, but I will live by faith on the Son of God, rooted in him. I would be pure in life, and I would have the golden anther of looking to the recompense of the reward. I would lift up my soul aloft towards heaven, as the lily lifts up its flower. Jesus will come and feed by my side if I am a lily, and even I may yield him some pleasure by my humble gratitude.

Beloved, this is a choice subject, but it is sweeter, as a matter of fact, than mere hearing can make it. "He feedeth among the lilies." This is our joy, that Christ is in his church, and the pith of all I want to say is this: never think of yourself or of the church apart from Jesus. The spouse says, "My beloved is mine, and I am his"; she weaves the two into one. The cause of the church is the cause of Christ; the work of God will never be accomplished by the church apart from Christ, her power lying in his being in her midst. He feeds among the lilies, and therefore those lilies shall never be destroyed, but their sweetness shall

240

make fragrant all the earth. The church of Christ, working with her Lord, must conquer, but never if she tries to stand alone or to compass any end apart from him.

As for each one of us personally, let us not think of ourselves apart from Christ, nor of Christ apart from us. Let George Herbert's prayer be ours:

Lord, Thou art mine, and I am Thine,
If mine I am; and Thine much more
Then I or ought or can be mine.
Yet to be Thine doth me restore,
So that again I now am mine,
And with advantage mine the more,
Since this being mine brings with it Thine,
And Thou with me dost Thee restore:
If I without Thee would be mine,
I neither should be mine nor Thine.

Lord, I am Thine, and Thou art mine;
So mine Thou art, that something more
I may presume Thee mine, then Thine,
For Thou didst suffer to restore
Not Thee, but me, and to me mine;
And with advantage mine the more,
Since Thou in death wast none of Thine,
Yet then as mine didst me restore:
O, be mine still; still make me Thine,
Or rather make no Thine and Mine.

Let *mine* melt into *thine*. Oh, to have joint stock with Christ, and to trade under one name; to be married to Christ and lose our old name, and take his name, and say, "I live, yet not I, but Christ liveth in me." (Gal. 2:20) As the wife is lost in the husband, and the stone in the building, and the branch in the vine, and the member in the head, we would be so amalgamated with Christ, and have such fellowship with him that there shall be no more "mine" or "thine".

Last of all, poor sinner, you say, "There is nothing in all this for me", and I should not like to send you away without a word. You are saying, "This is a day of good tidings, but it is only for God's own people." I beg you to read through the first and second chapters of the Song, and see who it was that said, "My beloved is mine", because I should not wonder but that you are very like her. She was the one who confessed, "I am black", and so are you. Perhaps grace will, one of these days, help you to say, "I am comely". She was one with whom her mother's children were angry — perhaps you, too, are a speckled bird. She had done servile work, for they made her a keeper of the vineyards. I should not wonder but that you are doing servile work too, trying to save yourself instead of accepting the salvation which Jesus has already wrought for sinners. So it came to pass that she became very sorrowful, and passed through a winter of rain and cold. Perhaps you are there; and yet you know she came out of it when her winter was past, and the birds began to sing. She had been hidden in the secret places of the stairs, as you are now; but she was called out from the dust and cobwebs to see the face of her Lord.

One thing I wish to whisper in your ears — she was in the clefts of the rock. O soul, if you can but get there, if you can shelter in the riven side of our Beloved, that deep gash of the spear from which flowed blood and water:

241

Rock of Ages, cleft for me,
Let me hide myself in Thee;
Let the water and the blood,
From Thy riven side which flowed,
Be of sin the double cure,
Save me from its guilt and power.

(Augustus Montague Toplady)

— if you can get there, I say, though you are black and grimed with sin, and an accursed sinner only fit to be a firebrand in hell, yet you, even you, shall be able to sing with all the rapture of the liveliest saint on earth, and one day with all the transport of the brightest ones above, "My beloved is mine, and I am his: he feedeth among the lilies."

There, go your way with those silver bells ringing in your ears; they ring a marriage peal to saints, but they ring also a cheery invitation to sinners, and this is the tune they are set to — "Come and welcome! Come and welcome! Come and welcome! Sinner, come!" God bless you, for Jesus' sake! Amen.

32. "A SONG OF MY BELOVED"

NO. 3185

AT THE METROPOLITAN TABERNACLE, NEWINGTON
A SERMON FOR THE COMMUNION SERVICE

"My beloved is mine, and I am his: he feedeth among the lilies. Until the day break, and the shadows flee away, turn, my beloved, and be thou like a roe or a young hart upon the mountains of Bether." (Song of Solomon 2:16-17)

[Other Sermons by Mr. Spurgeon on parts of the same passage are: Metropolitan Tabernacle Pulpit, No. 1190: "A Song among the Lilies", No. 2,442: "My Beloved is mine"; and No. 2,478: "Darkness before the Dawn"]

IT has been well said that if there is a happy verse in the Bible, it is this one: "My beloved is mine, and I am his: he feedeth among the lilies." So peaceful, so full of assurance, so over-running with happiness and contentment is it, that it might well have been written by the same hand which penned the twenty-third Psalm: "The Lord is my shepherd; I shall not want. He maketh me to lie down in green pastures: he leadeth me beside the still waters." (Ps. 23:1-2) This passage savours of him who, just before he went to Gethsemane, said to his disciples, "Peace I leave with you, my peace I give unto you: not as the world giveth, give I unto you...In the world ye shall have tribulation: but be of good cheer; I have overcome the world." (Jn, 14:27, 16:33)

Let us ring the silver bell of this verse again, for its notes are exquisitely sweet: "My beloved is mine, and I am his: he feedeth among the lilies." Yet there is a shadow in the latter part of the text. The prospect is exceedingly fair and lovely, and earth cannot give its superior; but it is not entirely a sunlit landscape. There is a cloud in the sky which casts a shadow over the scene; it does not dim it, for everything is clear, and stands out sharply and brightly: "My beloved is mine, and I am his." That is clear enough, yet I say again that it is not altogether sunlight; there are shadows too: "Until the day break, and the shadows flee away." There is a mention also of the mountains of Bether" — the mountains of "division"; and to have anything like division is bitterness. I see here a paschal lamb, but I see bitter herbs with it. I see the lily, but I think I see it still among the thorns. I see the fair and lovely landscape of assured confidence, but a shadow, just a slight shadow, takes away something of its glory; and he who sees it has still to look for something yet beyond — "till the day break, and the shadows flee away."

The text seems to me to indicate just this state of mind; and perhaps some of you may, at this time, exemplify it. You do not doubt your salvation; you know that Christ is yours; you are certain of that, except you may not at present be enjoying the light of your Saviour's countenance. You know that he is yours, but you are not feeding on that precious fact. You realise your vital interest in Christ, so that you have no shadow of a doubt that you are his, and he is yours; but, still, his left hand is not under your head, nor doth his right hand embrace you. (Song 2:6, 8:3) A shade of sadness is cast over your heart, possibly by affliction, certainly by the temporary absence of your Lord; so even while exclaiming, "My beloved is mine, and I am his" you are forced to fall on your knees, and pray, "Until the day break, and the shadows flee away, turn, my beloved, and be thou like a roe or a young hart upon the mountains of division."

We may occupy the time profitably, if God the Holy Spirit shall enable us, in speaking on these matters. We have here, first, *a soul enjoying personal interest in the Lord Jesus Christ*, or, personal interest assured. We have, next, *a soul taking the deepest interest in*

243

Christ, and longing to know where he is, or, the deepest interest evinced, and then we have *a soul anxiously desiring present communion with Christ*, or visible fellowship, and conscious communion sought after.

I. We have here, first, PERSONAL INTEREST IN THE LORD JESUS CHRIST ASSURED.

I do not mean to try to preach tonight; I should like my text to preach. And the way in which I should like it to preach would be to see how far we can get hold of it, how we can take it word by word and drink it in. Come to each word as to a well, sit down on the brink, and drink a refreshing draught. Come to each word as to a palm tree, and eat of its fruit. The text begins with the words, "My beloved." Come, soul, can you venture to call Christ your Beloved? Only he should be beloved by you, for what has he not done for you? Favours rich and rare have been the gifts of his hand, gifts purchased by his own most precious blood. If you do not love him, my heart, you are a most ungrateful thing indeed; deceitful, rotten, loathsome above all things, and desperately wicked are you, O my head! If Jesus, being your Saviour, how is it that you do not love him? He ought to be beloved by the most of you here, for you profess to have been redeemed by his blood, and adopted into the family of God through him. You professed, when you were baptised, to be dead with him; and when you come to this communion table to-night, you profess that he is your meat and drink, your life, your soul's stay and comfort; so, if you do not love him, what shall I say to you? I will let you say to yourselves:

And have I, Christ, no love for thee
Nor passion for thy charms?
Nor wish my Saviour's face to see
And dwell within his arms?
Is there no spark of gratitude
In this cold heart of mine,
To him whose generous bosom glowed
With friendship all divine?

Can I pronounce his charming name,
His acts of kindness tell,
And while I dwell upon the theme,
No sweet emotion feel?

Such base ingratitude as this,
What heart but must detest?
Sure Christ deserves the noblest place
In every human breast.

A very wretch, Lord, I should prove,
Had I no love to thee:
Rather than not my Saviour love,
O may I cease to be!

(Samuel Stennett)

"*My beloved.*" He ought to be so, and he has been so. There was a time when you and I did not love him, but that time is over now. We recollect the happy moment when first, by faith, we saw his face, and heard him say, "I have loved thee with an everlasting love." (Jer. 31:3) Oh, the happiness of that day! You have not forgotten it. How alive and zealous some of you were then! In those first months, when you were brought into the house of mercy, and were washed and clothed, and had all your wants supplied out of the fullness

244

that is treasured up in Christ Jesus, you did indeed love him. You were not hypocrites, were you? And you used to sing with such force of voice as well as of heart:

Jesus, I love thy charming name,
'Tis music to mine ear;
Fain would I sound it out so loud
That earth and heaven should hear.

(Philip Doddridge)

Yes, we did love him, but we cannot stop at that, we *do* love him. With all our faults, and imperfections, and frailties, the Lord, who knows all things, knows that we do love him. Sometimes, brethren, it is not easy to know whether you do love Christ, or not. I have heard many remarks about the hymn containing these lines:

'Tis a point I long to know,
(Oft it causes anxious thought),
Do I love the Lord, or no?
Am I His, or am I not?

If I love, why am I thus?
Why this dull, this lifeless frame?
Hardly, sure, can they be worse,
Who have never heard his name?

(John Newton)

But I believe that every honest Christian sometimes asks these questions; and I think one good way of getting it answered is to go and hear a faithful minister. Last Sabbath morning, I sat and listened to a very simple-minded preacher in a Wesleyan Chapel; he was a most unsound Wesleyan, but a thoroughly sound Calvinistic brother; and when he began to preach about the love of Jesus Christ, the tears streamed down my cheeks. I could not help letting them fall on the sanded floor as I sat there; and I thought to myself, "Well, now, I do love the Saviour." I had thought that perhaps I did not; but when I heard of him, and the preacher began to play upon my heartstrings, the music came. When I did have Christ alone set before me that woke up my soul, if indeed it had been asleep before. When I heard of him, though only in broken accents, I could not but feel that I did love him, and love him better than life itself. I trust that it is true of many here, that Christ is our "beloved".

But the text says not only "beloved", but, "*my* beloved is mine," as if the spouse took him all to herself. It is the nature of love, you know, to monopolise. There is a remarkable passage in the third chapter of the prophecy of Hosea, which I need not quote except in outline, where the prophet is bidden to take one who had been unclean, and unchaste, and to say to her, "Thou shalt be for me, so will I also be for her." This was meant to be typical of what Christ does to his Church. Our love goes gadding about to twenty objects until Christ comes, and then he says,

"You silly thing, now you shall fly abroad no more. Come, you dove, I will give you a new heart, and my wounds shall be your dovecot, and you shall never wander away again. I will be altogether yours, and you shall be altogether mine. There shall be a monopoly between us; I will be married to you, and you shall be married to me. There shall be communion between us. I will be yours, you wandering sinner, as your husband, and you shall be mine."

245

Every heart that has been subdued by sovereign grace takes Jesus Christ to be the chief object of its love. We love our children, we love all our dear ones; God forbid that we should ever fail in loving them; but, over and above them all, we must love our Lord. There is not one among us, I think, who would make it something to question, and something to easily part with. It would be a melancholy experience to have to follow the partner of one's own in order to grow; but if it were a choice between wife and Saviour, we would not deliberate for a moment. And as for the children of our love, whom we hope to see springing up to manhood and womanhood, it would be a sorry blow for us to have them laid low, but it would not take us a second to decide whether we should lose our Isaacs or lose our Jesus. No, we should not feel that they were lost if God took them from us, but we could not afford to think for a single instant of losing him, who is our everlasting All-in-all.

The Christian, then, makes Christ his beloved beyond all beside. Let other people love what they will; but as for him, he loves his Saviour. He stands at the foot of the cross, and says, "This once-accursed tree is now the blessed bulwark of my confidence." He looks up to the Saviour, and says, "Many see no beauty in him that they should desire him, but, to me, he is the chief among ten thousand, and the altogether lovely." Let the scholar take his classics, let the warrior take his weapons of war, let the lover take his tender words and his amatory lyrics; but, as for the Christian, he takes the Saviour, he takes the Lord Jesus, to be to him Alpha and Omega, the beginning, the end, the ever-present in the midst, the All-in-All, and in him he finds his soul's solace.

Some people have thought that there is a tautology in the text when it says, "My beloved is mine." Why, of course, if he is my beloved, he is mine. What need is there to say that? Well, those who are acquainted with the Christian's experience know that all believers are subject to many doubts and fears, and they feel that they cannot make their assurance too sure, so that they like to double their expressions of assurance when they can, so each of them says, "My beloved is mine." There is no tautology; the speaker is only giving two strokes of the hammer to drive the nail home. It is put so that there can be no mistake about it, so that the spouse means what she says, and intends others also to understand it: "My beloved is mine."

But I think it may mean more than that, because we may love a thing, and yet it may not be our own. A man may call money his beloved, yet he may never get it; he may pursue it, but is not able to reach it. The lover of learning may court the love he covets in all the academies of the world, yet he may not be able to win the attainment of his desires. Men may love, and on their dying beds may have to confess that their beloved is not theirs; but every Christian has that on which his heart is set. He has Christ; he loves him, and possesses him too.

Besides, dear friends, you know that there is a time when men are not able to say that their beloved is theirs. He who has been most wealthy or most wise can take neither his wealth nor his wisdom with him to the tomb, and when the sinner who died, and was buried, wakes up in another world, Croesus will be as poor as Lazarus, and the wisest man without Christ will find himself devoid of all wisdom when he wakes up in the day of resurrection. Such may stretch out their hands, but they will only clutch emptiness, and have to cry, "Our beloved is not ours." But when we shall wake up in the image of Christ, and see him — whether we shall fall asleep or whether we shall be changed, in either case we shall be present with him — then shall each believer say, "Yes, he is mine, still mine. I have him, truly have him: 'My beloved is mine.'" I am inclined to think that, if a man can truly say this, he can say the grandest thing that ever any man said, "My beloved is mine." "Look", says the rich man, "do you see far away beyond those stately oaks yonder?

246

Do you see as far as that church spire? Well, as far as ever you can see, that is all mine." "Ah", says Death, as he lays his bony hand upon the man, "six feet of earth, *that* is yours!" "Look," says the scholar, as he points to the volumes on his shelves, "I have searched through all these, and all the learning that is there is mine." "Ah," says Death again, as he smites him with his cold hand, "who can tell the difference between the skull of the learned and the skull of the ignorant when the worm has emptied them both?" But the Christian man, when he points upwards, and says "I love my Saviour", is a possession which is surely his for ever. Death may come, and will come, even to him; but all that Death can do is open the door to admit the Christian into still fuller enjoyment of what is already his. "My beloved is mine" — so, although I may have but little, I will be satisfied with it, and though I may be so poor that the world will pass me by and never notice me, yet I will live quite content in the humblest possible obscurity because "my beloved is mine" and he is more than all the world to me. "Whom have I in heaven but thee? And there is none upon earth that I desire beside thee." (Ps. 73:25)

Now, I want to stop and see whether we have really got as far as this. How many of us have said, "My beloved is mine"? I am afraid there may be some poor Christian here who says, "Ah, I cannot say that!" Now, my dear hearer, I will ask you a question: Do you cling to Christ? Is he your only hope? If so, then he is yours. When the tide goes down, have you ever seen the limpets clinging to the rocks, or holding fast, perhaps, to the pier. Now, is that what your faith does with Christ? Do you cling to him? Is he all your trust? Do you rest on him? Well then, if you do, you do not need any other mark or sign; that one is quite enough. If you are clinging to Christ, then Christ is yours. She who did but touch the hem of his garment received the virtue which came out of him. (Lk. 5:30, 6:19) If you can cling to him, and put away every other confidence, and renounce all other trust, you can say, "Yes, if I perish, I will cling to Christ alone". Then do not let a single doubt come in to take away the comfort of your soul, for your beloved is yours.

Or perhaps, to put it another way, I may ask you, do you love Jesus? Does his name wake up the echoes of your heart? See the little child in its mother's arms. You want to hold it for a little while; but no, it will not come away from its mother. And if you still want to take it, it puts its little arms around its mother's neck, and clings there. You could pull it away, perhaps, but you do not have the heart to do it. It clings to its mother, and that is evidence to you that she is its mother. Do you cling to Christ in that way? And though you feel that the devil would pull you away from Christ if he could, you still cling to him as best you can. Do you remember what John Bunyan says about the prisoner whom Mr. Greatheart rescued from Giant Slay-good's clutches? Mr. Feeble-mind said, "When he had got me into his den, since I went not with him willingly, I believed I should come out alive again." Is that the case with you? Are you willing to have Christ, if you can have him? Are you unwilling to give him up? Then you should never give him up; he is yours. Do not think that Christ wants a high degree of faith to establish a union between himself and a sinner, for a grain of mustard-seed of faith is sufficient for salvation, though certainly not for the highest degree of comfort. If you can just trust Christ, and love Christ, then do not let Satan stop you from saying, in the words of the text, "My beloved is mine."

Well, we have got so far, but we must remember the next words: "*I am his.*" Now this is true of every Christian. I am his by Christ having made me his. I am his by choice; he elected me. I am his by his Father's gift, God gave me to him. I am his by purchase; he bought me with his blood. I am his by power, for his Spirit has won me. I am his by my own dedication, for I have vowed myself to him. I am his by profession, for I have joined with his people. I am his now by my own deliberate choice of him, moved by his grace to choose him. Every Christian here knows that this is true, Christ is yours, and you are Christ's. You are the sheep of his pasture. You are the partners of his love. You are members of his body. You are branches of his stem. You belong to him.

247

But there are some people who get to a more practical meaning of this sentence, "I am his", than others do. You know that, in the Church of Rome, they have certain orders of men and women who devote themselves to various benevolent, charitable, or superstitious work, and who come to be especially considered the servants of the Lord Jesus. Now, we have never admired these forms of brotherhoods and sisterhoods, but the spirit of the thing is just what ought to enter into the heart of every Christian man and woman. You members of Christian churches, if you are what you ought to be, you are wholly consecrated to the Saviour. "Pure religion and undefiled before God and the Father" (Jas. 1:27) should be practiced by the whole Church of Christ, not merely by certain "orders" then called "religious". Every Christian woman is "a sister of mercy". We hear of men who belong to the order of Passionists, but every believing man ought to be of the order of Palmists, moved by the passion of the Saviour to consecrate himself to the Saviour's work.

"I am his". I would like to have you take this as your motto, you professed Christians, if you have the honestly to do so. When you wake in the morning, breathe a short prayer while you are dressing, and before bowing the knee, feeling "I am Christ's, and the first thing when I wake must be a word with him, and for him." When you go about into the world, I want you to feel that you cannot trade as other men trade, that you cannot imitate their tricks and sharp practices because something whispers in your heart, "I am his! I am his! I am different from other men. They may do what they will, for their judgement is yet to come; but I am different from them, for I am Christ's man." I wish all Christians felt that the life they live is given to them that they may glorify Christ by it. Oh, if the wealth that is in the Christian Church were devoted to God's cause, there would never be any lack of the means of sustaining missions, or of building houses of prayer in the dark localities of London! If some rich men gave to the cause of Christ as some poor men and women that I know of do, there would never be any lack in the treasury. I have sometimes rejoiced over some of you; I have had to bless God that I have seen in this church apostolic piety. I have known men and women who, out of their little, have given almost all that they had, and whose one object in life has been to spend and be spent for Christ, and I have rejoiced over them. But there are others of you who have not given a tithe, no, not a fiftieth part of what you have to the cause of Christ; yet, perhaps, you stand up and sing:

I love my God with zeal so great
That I could give him all.

(Isaac Watts)

Stop that! Do not sing lies, for you know very well that you would not give him all, and do not give him all; and you also know very well that you would think it the most absurd thing in all the world if you were to give him all, or even to dream of doing so. Oh, for more consecration! We are, most of us, up to our ankles in our religion; very few of us are up to our knees. But oh for the man that swims in it, who has got off the earth altogether, and now swims in consecration, living wholly for him who loved him, and gave himself for him!

I am afraid I shall have to stop here, and ask the question, without getting any answer to it: How far can we get toward this second sentence, "My beloved is mine, and I am his." Do you feel as if you could not say that? Do you feel that you must not say it? Then let this be your prayer: "Lord, if I have not yet done all that I can, if there is anything left which I might have done for you, and which I have not done, give me grace that I may do all I can for you, and give all I can to you." There ought not to be an unconsecrated hair on a Christian's head, nor an unconsecrated drop of blood in his veins. Christ gave himself wholly for us; he deserves that we should give ourselves wholly to him. Where reserve begins, there Satan's dominion begins; for what is not Christ's is the property of the flesh, and the property of the flesh is the property of Satan. Oh, may the spiritual consecration be perfect in each one of us that, if we live, we may live for Christ, or, if we die, it may still be for him! I hope, though we may have to make many grave confessions that we can still say, "My beloved is mine, and I am his." If he stood here at this moment, if we could just clear a space, and on a sudden he should come, and stand in our midst with his wounds still visible, it would be so sweet to be able to say, "My beloved is mine, and I am his". But I am afraid that, in his presence, we should have to say, "Jesus, forgive us; we are yours, but we have not acted as if we were. We have stolen from you what was your purchase, and what you have the right to keep. From this day, may we bear in our body the marks of the Lord Jesus, and may we be wholly thine!"

II. I cannot say much upon the second part of the subject, for our time is already nearly gone. THE SOUL, BEING ASSURED OF ITS PERSONAL INTEREST IN CHRIST, LONGS TO KNOW WHERE HE IS. "Where is he?" asks the soul, and the answer comes from the text, "He feedeth among the lilies."

The worldling does not care where Christ is, but that is the Christian's one subject of thought:

Lord, Thou art mine, and I am Thine,
That I might seek and find him too.

(George Herbert)

Jesus is gone, then, among the lilies, among those snow-white saints who bloom in the garden of heaven, those golden lilies that are around the throne. He is there in that hymn of Bernard of Morlaix, translated by John Mason Neale:

Jerusalem the golden, with milk and honey blest,
Beneath thy contemplation sink heart and voice oppressed.
I know not, O I know not, what joys await us there,
What radiancy of glory, what bliss beyond compare!

— and it makes us long to be there, that we may feed with him among the lilies. But, still, there are many of his lilies here below, those virgin souls who,

Wheresoe'er the Lamb doth lead,
From his footsteps ne'er depart.

If we would find Christ, we must get into communion with his people, we must came to the ordinances with his saints; for, though he does not feed *on* the lilies, he feeds *among* them, and there, perhaps, we may meet with him. You are here tonight, dear friends, many of you members of this church, and some of you members of other churches, and you have come to the place where Christ feeds his flock. Now that he feeds among the lilies, look out for him. At the communion table, do not merely partake of the elements, but look out for him. Look through the bread and the wine to his flesh and blood, of which they are the symbols. Do not care for my poor words, but for him; and as to anything else of which you have been thinking, get beyond that to him. "He feedeth among the lilies"; so look out for him where his saints gather in his name.

249

If you would meet with him, look, too, in the blessed lily-beds of Scripture. Each Book of the Bible seems to be full of lilies; yet you must never be satisfied merely with Scripture, but must get to the Christ of Scripture, *the* Word of God, the sum and substance of the revelation of the Most High. "He feedeth among the lilies." That is where he is to be found. Lord Jesus come and feed us among the lilies tonight; come and feed our hungry souls, and we will bless your holy name.

III. I must leave that part of the subject unfinished because I want to speak of THE SOUL, ASSURED OF CHRIST'S LOVE DESIRING HIS CONSCIOUS PRESENCE: "Until the day break, and the shadows flee away, turn, my beloved, and be thou like a roe or a young hart upon the mountains of Bether."

You observe that the soul speaks here of the day breaking. All of us who love the Lord have to look for daybreak, but the sinner has a night to come. Sinner, this is your day; and when you die, that will be your long and awful night, unbroken by a single star of hope. But, Christian, this is your night, the darkest period you will ever have; but your day will break. Yes, the Lord will come in his glory, or else you sleep in him, and then your day will break. When the resurrection trumpet will sound, the day of the Lord will be darkness and not light to the sinner; but to you it will be an everlasting daybreak. Perhaps, at the present moment, your life is wrapped in shadows. You are poor, and poverty casts a shadow. You have a sick one at home, or perhaps you are yourself sickly in body; that is a shadow for you. And the reflection of your sin is another shadow. But, when the day breaks, the shadows will flee away. No poverty then; no sin then, which is better still; and,

No more fatigue, no more distress,
Nor sin nor hell shall reach the place;
No groans to mingle with the songs
Which warble from immortal tongues.

(Philip Doddridge)

Brethren, it is so sweet to know that our best things are on ahead. O sinner, you are leaving your best things behind, and you are going to your worst things; but the Christian is going to his best things. His turn is coming; he will have the best of it before long, for the shadows will flee away. No longer will he be vexed, and grieved, and troubled, but he will be eternally in the light, for the shadows *shall* flee away.

While the shadows last, you perceive that the soul asks Jesus Christ to turn, as though he had withdrawn his face from her. She says, "Have you turned away from me, my Master? Then, turn to me again. Have I grieved and vexed you by growing worldly, carnal, careless, and reckless? Then, turn to me, my Lord. Have you been angry with me? Oh, love me! Have you not said that your anger may endure for a moment, but that your love is everlasting? In a little wrath, you have hidden your face from me; but oh, now turn to me!" You know that the proper state for a Christian to be in is not a state in which Christ turns away his smiling face, but the state in which Christ's love is beaming full in his face. I know that some of you think it is best for you to be in the shade; but, beloved, do not think that. You need not have shadows forever, for you may have the presence of Christ even now to rejoice in. And I would have you ambitious to get two heavens — a heaven below and a heaven above; Christ here, and then Christ there; Christ here making you as glad as your heart can be, and the Christ for ever filling you with all the fullness of God. May we seek after that double blessing, and may we get it! Then the soul says, "Turn, my beloved, and be thou like a roe or a young hart upon the mountains of Bether." Dr. William McClure Thomson, who wrote *The Land and the Book: Pilgrimage and Mission in Palestine* (1859), tells us that he thinks he knows the mountains of Bether. It matters little whether he does

250

or does not, but he has seen the roes and the harts skipping about the precipices. Certainly, those wild creatures that are accustomed to craggy rocks will go where human footsteps would not dare to follow.

And such is the love of Jesus Christ. Our love is easily turned aside; if we are badly treated, we soon forget those who seemed to be so fond of us; but Christ is like a roe or a young hart, and he skips over the mountains of our sins, and all the dividing mountains of our unbelief, and ingratitude which might keep him away. Like a young hart, he skips over them as though they were nothing at all, and so hastens to have communion with us. There is the idea of fleetness here: the roe goes swiftly, almost like the lightning's flash, and so does the Saviour come to the soul in need. He can lift you up from the lowest state of spiritual sorrow to the highest position of spiritual joy; may he do so! Oh, cry to him, cry to him! There is nothing that can tell with a mother like the voice of her child, and there is nothing that can tell with Christ like the voice of his dear people; so come to him. Say, "Saviour, show your love to me. Dear Saviour, do not hide yourself from your own flesh. I love you; I cannot live without you; I am grieved to think that I should have driven you away. Come to me, come to me; return to me, and make me glad in your presence." Cry like this to him, and he will come to you. And you, poor sinner, who have never comfortably seen his face, remember that there is life for a look at him. (Is 45:22) God give you grace now to trust him, and may you see his face here so that you may see him hereafter with everlasting joy!

33. OVER THE MOUNTAINS
NO. 3307

AT THE METROPOLITAN TABERNACLE, NEWINGTON
A SERMON FOR THE COMMUNION SERVICE

"My beloved is mine, and I am his: he feedeth among the lilies. Until the day break, and the shadows flee away, turn, my beloved, and be thou like a roe or a young hart upon the mountains of Bether." (Song of Solomon 2:16-17)

[Other Sermons in the Metropolitan Tabernacle Pulpit by Mr. Spurgeon on the same verses are: No. 1190 *A Song Among the Lilies;* No. 2,442; *My Beloved is mine*; and No. 2477, *Darkness Before the Dawn*]

IT may be that there are saints who are always at their best, and are happy enough never to lose the light of their Father's countenance. I am not sure that there are such people, for those believers with whom I have been most intimate have had a varied experience; and those whom I have known, who have boasted of their constant perfectness, have not been the most reliable, of individuals. I hope there is a spiritual region attainable where there are no clouds to hide the Sun of our soul; but I cannot speak positively, for I have not traversed that happy land. Every year of my life has had a winter as well as a summer, and every day its night. I have, up till now, seen periods of clear shining and periods of heavy rains, and felt warm breezes and fierce winds. Speaking for many of my brethren, I confess that, though the substance is in us, as in the teil-tree and the oak, yet we do lose our leaves, and the sap within us does not flow with equal vigour at all seasons. We have our ups as well as our downs, our valleys as well as our hills. We are not always rejoicing; we are sometimes "in heaviness through manifold trials." (1 Pet. 1:6) Alas, we are grieved to confess that our fellowship with the Well-beloved is not always that of rapturous delight; but we have at times to seek him, and cry, "Oh, that I knew where I might find him!" (Job 23:3) This appears to me to have been, in a measure, the condition of the spouse when she cried, "Until the day break, and the shadows flee away, turn, my Beloved."

I. These words teach us, first, that COMMUNION MAY BE BROKEN.

The spouse had lost the company of her Bridegroom: conscious communion with him was gone, though she loved her Lord, and sighed for him. In her loneliness, she was sorrowful; but *she had by no means ceased to love him*, for she calls him her Beloved, and speaks as one who felt no doubt on that point. Love to the Lord Jesus may be quite as true, and, perhaps, quite as strong when we sit in darkness as when we walk in the light. No, *she had not lost her assurance of his love to her*, and of their mutual interest in one another, for she says, "My Beloved is mine, and I am his", and yet adds, "Turn, my Beloved." The condition of our grace does not always coincide with the state of our joys. We may be rich in faith and love, and yet have so low an esteem of ourselves as to be very depressed. It is plain from this sacred Canticle that the spouse may love and be loved, may be confident in her Lord and be fully assured of her possession of him, and yet there may, for the present, be mountains between her and him. Yes, we may even be far advanced in the divine life and yet be exiled for a while from conscious fellowship. There are nights for men as well as babes, and the strong know that the sun is hidden quite as much as do the sick and the feeble. Do not, therefore, condemn yourself, my brother, because a cloud is over you, and do not cast away your confidence; but rather, let faith burn up in the gloom, and let your love resolve to come at your Lord again whatever the barriers that divide you from him.

252

When Jesus is absent from a true heir of heaven, sorrow will follow. The healthier our condition, the sooner will that absence be perceived, and the more deeply will it be lamented. This sorrow is described in the text as a time of darkness; this is implied in the expression "until the day break." Till Christ appears, no day has dawned for us. We dwell in midnight darkness. The stars of the promises and the moon of experience yield no light of comfort till our Lord, like the sun, rises and ends the night. We must have Christ with us or we are benighted: we grope like blind men for the well, and are restless till we find it.

The spouse also speaks of shadows — "Until the day break, *and the shadows flee away*." Shadows are multiplied by the departure of the sun, and these are apt to distress the timid. We are not afraid of real enemies when Jesus is with us; but, when we miss him, we tremble at a shade. How sweet is that song, "Yea, though I walk through the valley of the shadow of death, I will fear no evil: for thou art with me; thy rod and thy staff they comfort me"! (Ps. 23:4) But we change our tune when midnight comes, and Jesus is not with us. Then we people the night with terrors: spectres, demons, hobgoblins, and things that never exist save in fancy, which are apt to swarm about us; and we are in fear where no fear exists.

The spouse's worst trouble was that *the back of her Beloved was turned towards her*, and so she cried, "Turn, my Beloved." When his face is towards her, she suns herself in his love; but if the light of his countenance is withdrawn, she is severely troubled. Our Lord turns his face from his people, though he never turns his heart from them. He may even close his eyes in sleep when the vessel is tossed by the tempest (Mat. 8:24; Mk. 4:38), but his heart is awake all the while. Still, it is painful enough to have grieved him to any degree; it cuts us to the quick to think that we have wounded his tender heart. He is jealous, but never without cause. If he turns his back on us for a while, there is doubtless a more than sufficient reason. He would not walk contrary to us if we had not walked contrary to him. Ah, it is sad work this! The presence of the Lord makes this life the preface to the life celestial, but his absence leaves us pining and fainting; neither does any comfort remain in the land of our banishment. The Scriptures and the ordinances, private devotions, and public worship are all like sundials — most excellent when the sun shines, but of small use in the dark. O Lord Jesus, nothing can compensate us for your loss! Draw near to your beloved yet again, for, without you, our night will never end.

Why is my heart so far from thee,
My God, my chief delight?
Why are my thoughts no more by day
With thee, no more by night ?

See! I repent, and vex my soul,
That I should leave thee so!
Where will those vile affections roll
That let my Saviour go?

(Isaac Watts)

When communion with Christ is broken, in all true hearts *there is a strong desire to win it back again*. The one who has known the joy of communion with Christ, if he loses it, he will never be content until it is restored. Have you ever entertained Prince Emmanuel? Has he gone elsewhere? Your chamber will be dreary till he comes back again. "Give me Christ, or else I die" is the cry of every spirit that has lost the dear companionship of Jesus. We do not part with such heavenly delights without many a pang. It is not with us a matter of "maybe he will return, and we hope he will", but it must be, or we faint and die. We cannot live without him; and this is a cheering sign, for the soul that cannot live without

253

him shall not live without him. He comes speedily where life and death hang on his coming. If you must have Christ, you shall have him.

This is just how the matter stands: we must drink of this well or die of thirst; we must feed upon Jesus or our spirit will famish.

II. We will now advance a step, and say that, when communion with Christ is broken, THERE ARE GREAT DIFFICULTIES BY WAY OF ITS RENEWAL.

It is much easier to go downhill than to climb to the same height, again. It is far easier to lose joy in God than to find the lost jewel. The spouse speaks of "mountains" dividing her from her Beloved: she means that *the difficulties were great*. They were not little hills, but mountains that closed up her way. These are Mountains of remembered sin, Alps of backsliding, dread ranges of forgetfulness, ingratitude, worldliness, coldness in prayer, frivolity, pride, and unbelief. Ah me, I cannot teach you all the dark geography of this sad experience! Giant walls had arisen before her like the towering steeps of Lebanon. How could she come to her Beloved?

The dividing (Bether) difficulties were many as well as great. She does not speak of "a mountain" but of "mountains". Alps rose on Alps, wall after wall. She was distressed to think that, in so short a time, so much could come between her and him of whom she sang just now, "His left hand is under my head, and his right hand doth embrace me." (Song 2:6) Alas, we multiply those mountains of Bether with sad rapidity! Our Lord is jealous, and we give him far too much reason for hiding his face. A fault, which seemed so small at the time we committed it, is seen in the light of its own consequences, and then it grows and swells till it towers aloft, and hides the face of the Beloved. Then has our sun gone down, and fear whispers, "Will his light ever return? Will it ever be daybreak? Will the shadows ever flee away?" It is easy to grieve away the heavenly sunlight, but ah, how hard it is to clear the skies, and regain the unclouded brightness!

Perhaps the worst thought of all to the spouse was the dread that *the dividing barrier might be permanent*. It was high, but it might break down; the walls were many, but they might fall; but, alas, they were mountains, and these stand fast for ages! She felt like the psalmist, when he cried, "My sin is ever before me." (Ps. 51:3) The pain of our Lord's absence becomes intolerable when we fear that we are hopelessly shut out from him. One night we can bear, hoping for the morning; but, what if the day should never break? And you and I, if we have wandered away from Christ, and feel that there are ranges of immovable mountains between him and us, will feel sick at heart. We try to pray, but devotion dies on our lips. We attempt to approach the Lord at the communion table, but we feel more like Judas than John. At such times, we have felt that we would give our eyes to behold once more the Bridegroom's face, and know that he delights in us, as in happier days. Still, there stand the awful mountains, black, threatening, impassable; and in the far-off land, the Life of our life is away, and grieved.

The spouse seems to have come to the conclusion that *the difficulties in her way were insurmountable by her own power*. She does not even think of herself going over the mountains to her Beloved, but she cries, "Until the day break, and the shadows flee away, turn, my Beloved, and be thou like a roe or a young hart upon the mountains of Bether." She will not try to climb the mountains, for she knows she cannot: if they had been less high, she might have attempted it, but their summits stretch to heaven. If they had been less craggy or difficult, she might have tried to climb them; but these mountains are terrible, and no foot may stand upon their long crags. Oh, for mercy in utter self-despair!

I love to see a soul driven into that close corner, and forced, therefore, to look to God alone. The end of the creature is the beginning of the Creator. Where the sinner ends, the Saviour begins. If the mountains can be climbed, we will have to climb them; but if they are quite impassable, then the soul cries out with the prophet,

"Oh that thou wouldest rend the heavens, that thou wouldest come down, that the mountains might flow down at thy presence, as when the melting fire burneth, the fire causeth the waters to boil, to make thy name known to thine adversaries, that the nations may tremble at thy presence! When thou didst terrible things which we looked not for, thou camest down, the mountains flowed down at thy presence." (Is 64:1)

Our souls are lame, so they cannot move to Christ; and lo, we turn our strong desires to him, and fix our hopes alone on him. Will he not remember us in love, and fly to us as he did to his servant of old when he rode upon a cherub, and flew, yes, he flew upon the wings of the wind? (2 Sam. 22:1; Ps. 18:10, 104:3)

III. Here comes that PRAYER OF THE TEXT WHICH FULLY MEETS THE CASE: "Turn, my Beloved, and be thou like a roe or a young hart upon the mountains of division."*

Jesus can come to us when we cannot go to him. The roe and the young hart, or, as you may read it, the gazelle and the ibex, live among the crags of the mountains, and leap across the abyss with amazing agility. For swiftness and sure-footedness, they are unrivalled. The sacred poet said, "He maketh my feet like hinds' feet, and setteth me upon my high places" (2 Sam. 22:34; Ps. 18:23; Hab 3:19), alluding to the feet of those creatures which are so fitted to stand surely on the mountain side. Our blessed Lord is called in the title of the twenty-second Psalm, "the hind of the morning"; and the spouse, in this golden Canticle, sings, "My Beloved is like a roe or a young hart; behold, he cometh leaping upon the mountains, skipping upon the hills." (Song 2:8)

Here I would remind you that this prayer is one that we may fairly offer, because it is the way of Christ to come to us when our coming to him is out of the question. "How?" say you. I answer that of old he did this; for we remember "his great love wherewith he loved us, even when we were dead in sins." (Eph. 2:4-5) His first coming into the world in human form, was it not because man could never come to God until God had come to him? I hear of no tears, or prayers, or entreaties, offered to God on the part of our first parents; but the offended Lord spontaneously gave the promise that the Seed of the woman should bruise the serpents head. (Gen, 3:15) Our Lord's coming into the world was untaught, unsought, unthought of; he came altogether of his own free will, delighting to redeem. Dr. Watts contrasts the sinner's plight with the grace of our Lord Jesus Christ:

Plunged in a gulf of dark despair
We wretched sinners lay,
Without one cheerful beam of hope,
Or spark of glimmering day.

With pitying eyes the Prince of grace
Beheld our helpless grief;
He saw, and, O amazing love!
He ran to our relief.

His incarnation was a type of the way in which he comes to us by his Spirit. He saw us cast out, polluted, shameful, perishing; and, as he passed by, his fonder lips said, "Live!" In us is fulfilled that ancient word, "I am found of them that sought me not." (Is. 65:1; Rom. 10:20) We were too averse to holiness, too much in bondage to sin, ever to have returned

255

to him if he had not turned to us. What do you think? Did he not come to us when we were enemies, and will he not visit us now that we are friends? Did he not come to us when we were dead sinners, and will he not hear us now that we are weeping saints! If Christ's coming to the earth was after this manner, and if his coming to each one of us was after this style, we may well hope that now he will come to us in the same way, like the dew which refreshes the grass, and does not wait for man, nor tarries for the sons of men.
Besides, he is coming again in person in the latter days, and mountains of sin, and error, and idolatry, and superstition, and oppression, stand in the way of his kingdom; but he will surely come, and overturn, and overturn, till he shall reign over all. He will come in the latter days, I say, though he will leap the hills to do it; and, because of that, I am sure we may comfortably conclude that he will draw near to us who mourn his absence so bitterly. Then let us bow our heads a moment, and silently present to his most excellent Majesty the petition of our text: "Turn, my Beloved, and be thou like a roe or a young hart upon the mountains of division."

Our text gives us sweet assurance that *our Lord is at home with those difficulties which are quite insurmountable to us*. Just as the roe or the young hart knows the passes of the mountains, and the stepping-places among the rugged rocks, and is void of all fear among the ravines and the precipices, so our Lord knows the heights and depths, the torrents and the caverns, of our sin and sorrow. He carried the whole of our transgression, and so became aware of the tremendous load of our guilt. He is quite at home with the infirmities of our nature; he knew temptation in the wilderness, heart-break in the garden, and desertion on the cross. He is quite at home with pain and weakness, for "himself took our infirmities, and bare our sickness." (Is. 53:4; Mat. 8:17) He is at home with despondency, for he was "a Man of sorrows, and acquainted with grief." He is at home even with death, for he gave up his Spirit, and passed through the sepulchre to the resurrection. O yawning gulfs and frowning steeps of woe, our Beloved, like hind or hart, has traversed your glooms! O my Lord, you know all that divides me from you; and you know also that I am far too feeble to climb these dividing mountains to come to you. Therefore, I pray, come over the mountains to meet my longing spirit! You know each yawning gulf and slippery steep, but none of these can stop you. Hasten to me, your servant, your beloved, and let me again live by your presence.

It is easy, too, for Christ to come over the mountains for our relief. It is easy for the gazelle to cross the mountains, for it is made for that end. So is it easy for Jesus; for this purpose was he ordained from of old, that he might come to man in his worst estate, and bring with him the Father's love. What is it that separates us from Christ? Is it a sense of sin? You have been pardoned once, but Jesus can renew most vividly a sense of full forgiveness. But you say, "Alas, I have sinned again; fresh guilt alarms me!" He can remove it in an instant, for the fountain appointed for that purpose is opened, and is still full. (Zech. 13:1) It is easy for the dear lips of redeeming love to put away the child's offences, since he has already obtained pardon for the criminal's iniquities. If with his heart's blood he won our pardon from our Judge, he can easily enough bring us the forgiveness of our Father. Oh, yes; it is easy enough for Christ to say again, "Thy sins be forgiven!" (Mat. 9:2, 5; Mk. 2:5, 9; Lk. 5:23)

"But I feel so unfit, so unable to enjoy communion." He who healed all kinds of bodily diseases can heal with a word your spiritual infirmities. Remember the man whose ankle bones received strength so that he ran and leaped (Acts 3:7); and her who was sick of a fever, and was healed at once, and arose, and ministered to her Lord. (Mk. 1:31) "My grace is sufficient for thee; for my strength is made perfect in weakness." (2 Cor. 12:9) "I have such affliction, such troubles, such sorrows, that I am weighted down, and cannot rise into joyful fellowship." Yes, but Jesus can make every burden light, and cause each yoke to be easy. Your trials can be made to aid your heavenward course instead of

256

hindering it. I know all about those heavy weights, and I perceive that you cannot lift them; but skilful engineers can adapt ropes and pulleys in such a way that heavy weights lift other weights. The Lord Jesus is great at gracious machinery, and he has the art of causing a weight of tribulation to lift from us a load of spiritual deadness, so that we ascend by that which, like a millstone, threatened to sink us down. What else hinder us? I am sure that, if it were a sheer impossibility, the Lord Jesus could remove it, for things impossible with men are possible with God.

But someone objects, "I am so unworthy of Christ. I can understand eminent saints and beloved disciples being greatly indulged, but I am a worm, and no man (Ps. 22:6), utterly below such condescension." You say that? Do you not know that the worthiness of Christ covers your unworthiness, and he is made of God unto you wisdom, and righteousness, and sanctification, and redemption? (1 Cor. 1:30) In Christ, the Father thinks not so poorly of you as you think of yourself. You are not worthy to be called his child, but he does call you so, and reckons you to be among his jewels. Listen! And you shall hear him say, "Since thou wast precious in my sight, thou hast been honourable, and I have loved thee. I gave Egypt for thy ransom; Ethiopia and Seba for thee." (Is. 43:3) Thus, then, there remains nothing which Jesus cannot overleap if he resolves to come to you, and re-establish your broken fellowship.

To conclude, *our Lord can do all this directly*. As in the twinkling of an eye, the dead shall be raised incorruptible, so in a moment can our dead affections rise to fullness of delight. He can say to this mountain, "Be thou removed hence, and be thou cast into the midst of the sea" (Mat. 21:21; Mk. 11:23), and is shall be done. In the sacred emblems now laid on this supper table, Jesus is already among us. Faith cries, "He has come!" Like John the Baptist, she gazes intently on him, and cries, "Behold the Lamb of God!" (Jn. 1:29, 36) At this table, Jesus feeds us with his body and blood. His corporeal presence we do not have, but his real spiritual presence we perceive. We are like the disciples, when none of them dare ask him, "Who art thou?" (Jn. 8:25, 21:12), knowing that it was the Lord. He is come. He looks out of these windows — I mean this bread and wine — showing himself through the lattices of this instructive and endearing ordinance. He speaks. He says, "The winter is past, the rain, is over and gone." And so it is; we feel it to be so: a heavenly spring-tide warms our frozen hearts. Like the spouse, we wonderingly cry, "Or ever I was aware, my soul made me like the chariots of Amminadib." (Song 6:12) Now, in happy fellowship, we see the Beloved, and hear his voice; our heart burns; our affections glow; we are happy, restful, brimming over with delight. The King has brought us into his banqueting-house, and his banner over us is love. (Song 2:4) It is good to be here!

Friends, we must now go our separate ways. A voice says, "Arise, let us go hence." (Jn. 14:31) O Lord of our hearts, go with us! Some will not be home without you. Life will not be life without you. Heaven itself would not be heaven if you were absent. Abide with us. The world grows dark, the glooming of time draws on. Abide with us, for it is toward evening. Our years increase, and we are near the night when dews fall cold and chill. A great future is all about us, the splendours of the last age are coming down; and, while we wait in solemn, awe-struck expectation, our heart continually cries within herself, "Until the day break, and the shadows flee away, turn, my Beloved!"

34. THE BELIEVER'S GLAD PROSPECTS
NO. 3323

AT THE METROPOLITAN TABERNACLE, NEWINGTON

"Until the day break, and the shadows flee away, turn, my beloved, and be thou like a roe or a young hart upon the mountains of Bether." (Song of Solomon 2:17)

BELOVED, without a sentence of introduction, I invite you first to see,

I. A BLESSED SEASON HERE ANTICIPATED! — a time when the day shall break, and the shadows shall flee away.

It is not every one who can count on such a time as that, for to some there is no prospect of the day breaking. They are in the shade now, and that shade will grow darker and darker with them till, in the hour of death, their sun will go down forever in a tenfold night — a night un-gladdened by a solitary star — a night that shall never have an ending — a night of gloom more terrible than imagination itself could picture. I fear that there are some in this place for whom we might utter such forebodings. The world is dark enough for them now, but they have no hope of the Lord, as though it would be brightness to them. Conscience tells them — and if conscience is not enlightened enough to do so — the Word of God tells them that the day of the Lord shall be darkness, and not light, to them. But, to every soul in this house that believes in Jesus, there is the delightful anticipation of the hour spoken of in the text, when the day breaks and the shadows flee away.

Let us take each expression and muse on it. *"Until the day break"*. In a certain sense, the Christian is now in the light, for he is a child of light, he walks in the light, and he may walk in the light as God is in the light, and so have fellowship with the Father, and feel that the blood of Jesus Christ his Son cleanses us from all sin. (1 Jn, 1:7-9) But Paul, in some passages, calls this present estate darkness. "For", he says, "the night is far spent, the day is at hand" (Rom. 13:12), meaning by this the present state of life for the believer, which is far spent, and the daylight, the glorious daylight of eternity, is close at hand.

"The daybreak." Why, this represents to the most of us, probably, the moment of death. To as many as shall be alive and remain at the coming of the Lord, it represents the coming of the Lord, and the glory of his people. "The daybreak!" *It is the hour of joy.* During the night, the earth seems sad; she has covered herself with sackcloth, her eyes are full of the drops of the night. There is silence over the plain: the woods do not send out their grateful music. There is only heard the hooting of the owl, with, perhaps, now and then, a stray note from the nightingale as though she remembered the day. Night is the time of the world's gloom, but daybreak is the time of her festival. Then is her splendour abroad. Then,

Now morn, her rosy step in the eastern clime
Advancing, sowed the earth with orient pearl ...

(John Milton, *Paradise Lost*)

Ten thousand winged songsters of the grove, waking up from their slumber, begin to pour forth incessant streams of music. Every creature, beholding the light of the sun, wakes up and is full of joy. Such will the daybreak be to us. This is not our time of fullest joy. We that are in this Tabernacle groan, being burdened. We have trials without, we have conflicts within. The daybreak is coming when we, who are not of the night, nor of darkness, though compelled to pass through it, shall emerge into our proper element, the light, and our spirits bathe themselves in all that they can desire, being satisfied with favour, and full of the blessing of the Lord. "I shall be satisfied" says David, "when I awake in thy likeness." (Ps. 17:15) We are looking for a time of ineffable delight. All the attempts that have ever been made to describe the joy and glory of heaven have necessarily been failures, and if we were to attempt again, we should fall far below that which God has revealed to us by his Spirit; for "eye hath not seen, nor ear heard, that which he hath prepared for them that love him." (1 Cor. 2:9) Thank God, our joy is drawing nearer every time the tick of a clock is heard. Behold, on flying wings it comes. Every day of winter's sorrow, summer's joy draws nearer. We said last Sunday evening, "Now is our salvation nearer than when we believed" (Rom. 13:11), and we often sing,

"Forever with the Lord!"
 Amen, so let it be!
 Life from His death is in that word
 'Tis immortality.
 Here in the body pent,
 Absent from Him I roam,
 Yet nightly pitch my moving tent
 A day's march nearer home

(James Montgomery)

This is one of the choicest consolations of the present that we are getting nearer to the daybreak.

"The daybreak!" *It is a summons to activity.* The creatures waking up prepare themselves for their day's work. All nature is astir. She was lethargic before, as it were; frostbitten under the raven wing of night, but now that the bright beams of the sun have brought the light, they have also brought restoration to vitality. Now the workman girds up his loins, and goes out to his labour. Ah, brothers and sisters, those of us who are helped to do most for God on earth are not satisfied with what we can do! This seems to be a world of trying rather than of accomplishing. We are straining to be able to serve God. I feel myself constantly, if I can imagine such an experience, like the chick within the shell — chipping it, wanting to get out of it, doing all it can; no, not do all it can — but doing something, and desiring to do more, feeling its circle to be circumscribed, and itself to be "cribbed, cabined, and confined". But what a glorious thing it will be, when the young eaglets hatch themselves, and leave the nest, and try their wings! Such the happiness we are looking forward at the daybreak; that we shall serve God day and night in his temple without any tiring, that we should serve him without any sin, that we shall adore him without any wandering thoughts, that we shall be dedicated to him without anything that can stir the jealousy of his holy mind. We shall then move forward in the path of duty with as straight a persistency, and as divine a perseverance as the thunderbolt when it is launched from the hand of the Almighty. We shall neither turn to the right hand nor to the left. (Is. 30:21) We shall be swift as seraphs, and strong as cherubs, in the course of service, and that service shall be to us the heaven of our delight. Oh, we may well long for the daybreak, because it will help his servants to serve him!

"The daybreak!" Is it not likewise *the time of clear discovery?* At night, we peep about; we spy out the forms of the mountains; we can trace by the moonbeams the course of the rivers, and may know something more or less according to the measure of our discernment, of the inferences we draw of what there is round about us. Still, the night is the time of gloom. Nor can all the tapers and lamps that men kindle turn night into day. So here; this is the time of our ignorance. We know something of the truth as God has taught

259

us, and, blessed be his name, it is such dear knowledge that we would not give it up for all the world! But still, we only see as in a glass darkly; we have not yet come to a face-to-face vision. We read like children spell at school, syllable by syllable, and we do not quite understand what we read. We are like a boy when he first begins to spell out his Latin Horace; he does not comprehend the elegance of the style, or the poetry of the language, but just spells it out, and sees something of the literal meaning, and that is all that he can get. Ah, I suppose that the greatest divine that ever lived did not know so much before he died as a child knows when he has been in heaven five minutes! All that we are able to discover here seems to be little indeed. We know in part, we prophesy in part; when that which is perfect is come, then that which is in part shall be done away. The daybreak no sooner comes to the world than you discern everything in its natural hue and its right proportion. You see colour where before everything was black; you perceive the beauty of the landscape, as the mountains rises before you; the river rolls on mightily towards the sea; even the tiny flowers challenge your notice; you mark all on earth, for, by the sun, God has painted all the world with the colours of the rainbow. And oh, what a glorious discovery our admission into the next world will bring us!

Then shall we see, and hear, and know,
All we desired or wished below
And every power find sweet employ,
In that eternal world of joy.

(Isaac Watts)

I often get confused over doctrines that puzzle me. I see this to be true, and that to be true, but, how to reconcile the two I do not know; then the thought of the daybreak comes in so comfortably. What you do not know now, you shall know hereafter. Here, it is not good for us to know all things. In some respects, it is the glory of God to conceal himself, and he may well say to us, "I have many things to say unto you, but ye cannot bear them now." (Jn. 16:12) But there it will be the glory of God to reveal himself, and it will also be to our benefit, our minds being then fortified and strengthened to receive what we could not comprehend here below.

Perhaps the glare of the divine light, if it comes to us here, even though tempered by the Mediator himself, might be too much for these poor eyes of ours. All the prophets, or nearly all of them, when they had visions from God, fell flat on their faces, and John himself, though he had leaned on Jesus' bosom, when he saw the Master in Patmos, writes these very instructive words — "When I saw him I fell at his feet as dead." (Rev. 1:17, 19:10) Now, the Lord has work for us to do, and he does not want us to be always lying at his feet as dead. Consequently, he withholds from us the full radiance of his glory. But there, we shall be able to endure much, and there we shall be privileged to enjoy much.

These eyes shall see him in that day
The God that died for me!
And all my rising bones shall say,
"Lord, who is like to thee?"

(Augustus Montague Toplady)

So, you see, we look forward to a time of perfect joy, of wonderful activity, and of full discovery.

What a blessing that we are able to look forward to this, and to talk about it as a matter of certainty! "Until the day break." Why, there are dear aged brothers and sisters here who, in the providence of God, cannot be with us very long, and how are they accustomed to speak of their departure? I hear them speak constantly with holy confidence, and not at all with any reluctance. There have been some people so foolish as not to like to be thought old, some who have seemed to regret altogether that the gray hairs are apparent on their heads. But I do not find it so among the Lord's people with whom I associate. I find them thankful that this life is not all their portion, blessing God that they do not expect to be here forever, and long for evening to undress that they may rest with God, with holy expectation anticipating the blissful moment when the day shall break. And we who are younger need not think, because we have still strength in our loins, that we shall therefore live long. Oh, how many younger than ourselves have we seen taken away during the past year! Some of our fathers will outlive us; our sires will follow us to the tomb, for youth preserves not man. Well, we too will join with the reverend *seigneurs*, and we will anticipate the daybreak, and talk with them of it tonight. The other expression of the text is instructive too — "Until the day break, *and the shadows flee away.*" What are these shadows? They are of many sorts, and they abound. This is the valley of shadows. Surely every man walks in a vain shadow, and disquiets himself in vain. Some shadows we have are precious. There are the shadows of the ordinances — Baptism and the Lord's Supper. I speak of them with the highest reverence; yet they are but shadows in themselves, and we need them because we are live in a shadowland. He that is immersed in water is not, therefore, buried with Christ: the burial with Christ is the reality, and the burial in water is but the shadow. He that eats and drinks at the table of the Master does not, therefore, eat his flesh and drink his blood: the bread and the wine, though they look substantial, are but shadows. The real flesh and blood of Jesus, these are the inner substance, and only to faith is it given to feed upon these celestial viands. These things are only intended to last until the day break, for note, "As often as ye eat this bread and drink this cup, ye do show forth the Lord's death until he come." (1 Cor. 11:26) Then when he comes, the day breaks, and the shadow, even that blessed shadow, must flee away.

Other shadows we have that we shall be very glad to lose — shadows of fearful things which haunt especially the timid, nervous, and faint-hearted people of God. Some of the Lord's people spend their lives in fighting shadows. They make troubles. They sit down and imagine disasters which cannot occur. They bind heavy burdens, and put them on their own shoulders — burdens which God never intended them to bear, and burdens which, in fact, do not exist; and some off them even create actual trouble by foolish anxiety to escape from an imaginary trouble. Well, poor trembler, poor Mr. Fearing, and you, Miss Much-afraid, and Miss Despondency, the shadows will flee away soon. Though you generally go halting to heaven, with weak hands and feeble knees, and as many sighs as breaths, and as many tears as minutes, there is an end coming to all these, and you shall be as merry as any of them by and by. You shall be as near the eternal throne as the Apostles themselves, and have as much of the divine love and enjoyment as the strongest believers in Christ ever had. Be of good courage. Strive against those fears now. They weaken you, and dishonour our Master. Repent of ever having indulged them, for they are wicked. Still, let this encourage you: that they shall all flee away at daybreak. Do not, therefore, dread dying when with that comes the daybreak. Expect it, even long for it, since then the shadows which oppress you from morn till night shall flee away.

So, too, those doubts and fears which are made of sterner stuff, the deeper shadows and heavier glooms, shall all flee away. There may be some who never have a doubt about their acceptance in Christ, but, I am afraid I cannot count myself as one of them. For the most part, I know whom I have believed, and I am persuaded that he is able to keep that which I have committed to him until that day (2 Tim. 1:12); but when it comes to close heart-work sometimes, and self-examination, I cannot give up William Cowper's hymn:

261

'Tis a point I long to know,
Oft it causes anxious thought;
Do I love the Lord or no?

If I love, why am I thus?
Why this cold and lifeless frame?
Hardly, sure, could they be worse
Who have never known his name.

Not that it is of any use having such a hymn as that in the hymnbook, for you never ought to sing it. It is not a thing to sing, but to groan out all alone before our God. I think that most of us are compelled to do that sometimes. Well, blessed be God, at the daybreak all these fears will be gone! We shall never be able then to doubt our interest in Christ, because we shall be with him where he is, and shall behold his glory. We shall never then have any fear lest after having preached to others we ourselves should be cast away. (1 Cor. 9:27) We shall not be afraid lest we be shipwrecked, for though it may be but on boards and broken pieces, yet we shall then have come safe to land: all these fears will vanish forever.

May not these shadows represent to some of us *that daily sense of sin* which comes on us, and drives us to the cross? Oh, the sombre shade which a tender conscience feels under a sense of sin! Some men have not any such tenderness; they can make a profession, and be easy in living inconsistent lives. Not so a heart that lives near to Christ; the more pure it is, the more it mourns over its spots. If you are in the dark, you will not see the mire on your garments, but the brighter the light the more you will see every spot, and the more you will mourn over it. I believe that the more sanctified a man becomes by the work of the Holy Spirit within, the more heavy the burden of sin becomes to him. It is not that he has more sin, but that he feels what he has more; and in the light of the love of Christ, which he enjoys in the secret places of communion, he sees more of the abomination of sin, and hence is more humbled under it. Oh, but it shall all flee away presently! They are without fault before the throne of God. He shall present us, not having spot, or wrinkle, or any such thing. (Eph. 5:27) Oh, what a blessed presentation! At the daybreak, truly, the shadows will flee away. Do you not think that the text might have a still more extensive meaning, and take in *everything here below?* Things terrestrial, after all, are but shadows. The things which are seen are temporal; only the things which are not seen are eternal. The things which are seen, all these things which are round about us, are but shadowy things; they are passing before us, and they will soon be gone, like the dissolving view on the screen. But the eternal things, what men think so shadowy and dreamy, these are the only realities, since they will last for ever. Well, the shadows will flee away: that means this poor flesh and blood body, full of sickness, which declines as the shadow; that house, those lands. Oh, you rich men! Your shadows will all flee away. If you are believers, you will not be sorry for that. And, oh, you poor people! Your one room, cold and cheerless, the toil of every day, the needle, the stitching long for little reward — all shadows, and very dark shadows, and they seem very real to you now — well, they will be over soon — so soon! They will flee away, and all be gone, and,

Leaving all you loved below,
Up to your Father you will go.

We will not tarry longer on these two causes, "Until the day break" — we expect a daybreak — "and the shadow flee away" — we expect that shadows will flee away. We know they will, we rejoice that they will. Here we sit, looking out into the future, not

262

knowing what may befall us, but singing to our souls this song — "Until the day break, and the shadows flee away."

But while the season of joyful release is anticipated, there is also,

II. A PRAYER PRESENTED. "Until the day break, and the shadows flee away, turn, my beloved, and be thou like a roe or a young hart upon the mountains of Bether."

Till heaven shall come to us, and we to heaven, sweet Lord Jesus be with us. Let us have your company. But a difficulty arises. There is so much between us and Christ to keep him away. Hence the prayer, "Come, Lord; be like some hart or roe like the chamois off the Alps, that leaps from crag to crag — come over all these mountains of division (Bether), and come to us when we cannot come to you."

Remember, beloved, that our sins were once like these mountain of Bether. Christ has come over them. Our daily sins sometimes seem to our unbelief to be mountains of separation. Christ will come over these. He will bring us again to the cleansing fountain; he will give us the kiss of reconciliation; he will imprint the seal of peace upon our foreheads. He will kiss us with the kisses of his lips, and he will send us away rejoicing that he has come over the mountains.

One great mountain that separates us from our Lord is *our lack of sight of him.* You know it is not easy to love one you never saw, to love one you have heard of but have not seen at all. But faith gets over this difficulty with regard to Christ, for faith has pictorial power, and it pictures Christ; faith has a realising power, and it grasps Christ; faith has an appropriating power, and it claims Christ; faith has a power of wing that takes the spirit right away to Christ in holy imagination and sacred fancy and blessed meditation, and so it overcomes the difficulty. But still it is a difficulty, and hence the delightful power and force of the expression of the Apostle — Whom, having not seen, we love; in whom, though now we see him not, yet believing, we rejoice with joy unspeakable and full of glory." (1 Pet, 1:7-8) The prayer is, then, "Oh, Saviour, not only come over my sin, but come over this great difficulty, that I never saw you, never heard your voice, and never touched your hand. Yet come to me over these separating mountains, and make yourself real to my spirit everyday I live."

Ah, brothers and sisters, there are many mountains. I shall not mention them all, but I will name one more, and that is the mountain of *our natural coldness, lethargy, and indifference,* and, piled on the top of these, are our cares and our worldliness. I wish I could keep my heart red hot for Christ, but everything seems chilled. You cannot even live in God's service as I do, but what, in serving Christ, himself, you become as Martha did, cumbered with much serving. (Lk. 10:40) Oh, that the heart were always on the mountain with Christ — no, I won't say that — were it even in the garden, so long as it were but with him, in Gethsemane, or in Tabor; it would matter little so long as we could keep with him. But we have many things to do, and many beings to think of, more often than we need, and then we get away from Christ, and then we cannot get back again as quickly as we want, and so we have to sing with Dr. Watts,

Our souls can neither fly, nor go
To reach eternal joys.

Well, then, he comes to us. He kindles a flame of sacred love, and that kindles ours. Oh, our great Lord, until the day break, often comes in this way to us; until the shadows flee away! Oh, come to our hearts again and again, overleaping the mountains, and revealing you to us.

263

Here is a blessed thing to think of all the year round. Do not ask the Lord to take away the shadows; do not ask that you may feel this world to be a bright place to your hearts; but turn your thoughts to this — "Lord, whether it be bright or not to my soul, come to me. Oh, come to me; be near to me; let me walk in the conscious enjoyment of your daily presence. To your will, I leave everything else; only keep near to me. "Do you ask, now, when this prayer may be used? I think it is a very delightful prayer every night when we go to bed. "Lord, until the day break, and the shadows flee away literally in the morning, come and tarry with me."

O may my soul on thee repose!
And may sweet sleep mine eyelids close,
Sleep that may me more vigorous make
To serve my God when I awake.

If in the night I wakeful lie,
My soul with heavenly thoughts supply.
Let no ill dreams disturb my rest,
No powers of darkness me molest.

(Charles Wesley)

If I toss to and fro on my bed, may I have to say, as thy Spouse did, "By night, upon my bed, I sought him whom my soul loveth." (Song 3:3) May I cry with the Psalmist, "When I awake I am still with thee." (Ps. 139:18) I think you may put your head on the pillow each night very delightfully with that as your prayer. Then you may pray this prayer *whenever any trouble has come upon you.* Now you may say, "Lord, I see the day has not broke with me yet; the shadows have not fled away; there is this heavy loss in business; there is that dear child ill; there is the wife sickening; there is this disease in my own body. But, Lord, until this trouble is removed, come near, come near, and nearer still." If there is one child in the family the mother cares most about, it is the one that is the most sickly. You are sitting here tonight, and you are thinking about one of your children, but it is not about the one that is one-and-twenty, and grown up, it is the little one you have in the cradle. The more helpless it is, the more thought you give it, and so does God consider you, poor helpless, troubled ones. Pray, then, as you are entering into the cloud, "Lord Jesus, abide with me in the thick and dark night, till the day break, and the shadows flee away."

This prayer will do whenever the affairs of the Church of God, or of the nation, seem to be in a bad state. There are times with every church when it does not prosper as we desire. There are times in this nation when we see error very rife and true religion at a discount. Well, then, Christian, instead of your fretting yourself about the ark of the Lord, which you can no more keep right than Uzzah could, say, "Lord, I would walk with thee". I will say as Joshua did, "As for me and my house, we will serve the Lord." (Josh. 24:15, 21) "Only come, be near to my heart, and keep my heart close to you."

And what a blessed petition this would be when we are coming to die. We feel within ourselves that the machinery of life must come to a stop. There are certain indications which mark that the last mortal strife is drawing near. Oh, now to bend the knee at the bedside, or, if unable through weakness or faintness, to do that, to stay one's self upon the bed and say, "Until the day break, so near now to these poor failing eyes, till the shadows flee away, and this poor, crumbling body is changed for glory and immortality, come, my beloved, be like a roe or a young hart upon the mountains of Bether." It is blessed to fall asleep in Jesus with that prayer upon one's lips! Well, you are sure to die with it on your lips if you always live with it on your lips. If it is always in your heart, it will be in your heart at the last. So I commend it to you for daily use and for every special crisis. May the Lord make it to be a blessing to your souls!

Only, again I say, I wish with all my heart — it is my heart's desire and prayer — that all of you may have a day break to look forward to. It is so sad a thing that so many live as if they were to live here always. They live as if they were to die like dogs, and there would be as much an end of them as of the bullock that is struck with the pole-axe in the shambles. But, as you will live for ever, I must again remind you that there remains for you nothing but a fearful looking for of judgement and fiery indignation. (Heb. 10:27) Would you have a day break? Jesus Christ is the sun. Trust him. He has told us that he who believes and is baptised shall be saved. (Mk. 16:16) To believe is to trust. Now, leaving all your sins — 'tis time you left them; now, abhorring all those things in which you once took delight, and you may well abhor them, for they are damnable; they are serpents; fair are their scales but deadly are their fangs — leaving all these, come to Jesus. He died for sinners, for the very worst of sinners, and whoever trusts him shall have everlasting life. Oh, that you just now might end your service of the devil, and forthwith commence your service for the Lord Jesus. May the Master grant it by the power of his Holy Spirit, and his shall be the praise!

265

35. DARKNESS BEFORE THE DAWN
NO. 2478

AT THE METROPOLITAN TABERNACLE, NEWINGTON

ON LORD'S-DAY EVENING, AUGUST 1ST, 1886

"Until the day break, and the shadows flee away, turn, my beloved, and be thou like a roe or a young hart upon the mountains of Bether." (Song of Solomon 2:17)

THE spouse sings, "Until the day break, and the shadows flee away"; so the beloved of the Lord may be in the dark. It may be night with her who has a place in the heart of the Well-beloved. A child of God, who is a child of light, may be for a while in darkness; firstly, darkness comparatively, as compared with the light he has some times enjoyed, for days are not always equally bright. Some days are bright with a clear sunshine, other days may be overcast. So the child of God may one day walk, with full assurance of faith, in close fellowship with the Father and with his Son Jesus Christ. At another time, he may be questioning his interest in the covenant of grace, and may be rather sighing than singing, rather mourning than rejoicing. The child of God may be, then, in comparative darkness.

Yes, and he may be in positive darkness. It may be very black with him, and he may be obliged to cry, "I see no signs of returning day." Sometimes, neither sun nor moon appears for a long season to cheer the believer in the dark. This may arise partly through sickness of body. There are sicknesses of the body which, in a very peculiar way, touch the soul. Yet exquisite pain may be attended with great brightness and joy. But there are certain other illnesses which influence us in another way. Terrible depression comes over us; we walk in darkness, and see no light. I should not like to guess how heavy a true heart may sometimes become; there is a needs-be that we are in heaviness through manifold trials. There is not only a needs-be for the trials, but also for the heaviness which comes out of them. It is not always that a man can gather himself together, and defy the fierce blasts, and walk through fire and water with heavenly equanimity. No, brethren, "a wounded spirit who can bear?" (Prov 18:14) And that wounded spirit may be the portion of some of the very fairest of the sons of God; indeed, the Lord has some weakly, sickly sons who, nevertheless, are the very pick of his family. It is not always the strong ones by whom he sets the most store, but, sometimes, those that seem to be driven into a corner, whose days are spent in mourning, are among the most precious in his sight. Yes, the darkness of the child of God may be comparative darkness, and it may be to a great extent positive darkness.

But yet it can only be temporary darkness. The same text that suggests night promises dawn: "Until the day break, and the shadows flee away", says the song of the spouse. Perhaps no text is more frequently on my lips than is this one; I do not think that any passage of Scripture more often recurs in my heart when I am alone, for just now I feel that there is a gathering gloom over the church and over the world. It seems as if night were coming on, and such a night as makes one sigh and cry, "Until the day break, and the shadows flee away."

I am going to speak upon three things which are in our text. The first will be: *our prospect*. We have a prospect that the day will break, and the shadows flee away. Secondly, *our posture* "until the day break, and the shadows flee away." Thirdly, *our petition*: "Turn, my Beloved, and be thou like a roe or a young hart upon the mountains of division." We are content to wait for him to come to us; if gladdened with his presence, the night will seem short, and we can well endure all that it brings. Let the prayer of our text be put up by any of you who are waiting in the darkness, and may it be speedily answered in your happy experience!

I. First of all, let us consider OUR PROSPECT. Our prospect is that the day will break, and that the shadows will flee away. We may read this passage in many ways, and apply it to different cases.

Think first of *the child of God, who is full of doubt*. He is afraid that, after all, his supposed conversion was not a true one, and that he has proved it to be false by his own misbehaviour. He is afraid, I scarcely know of what, for so many fears crowd in upon him. He is crying to God to remove his doubts, and to let him once again,

When I can read my title clear to mansions in the skies,
I bid farewell to every fear, and wipe my weeping eyes.

(Isaac Watts)

His eyes are looking toward the cross, and, somehow, he has a hope, if not quite a persuasion, that he will find light in Christ, where so many others have found it. I would encourage that hope till it becomes a firm conviction and a full expectation. The day will break for you, dear mourner, the shadows will yet flee away. While I say that, I feel able to speak with great confidence, for my eye, as it looks round on this congregation, detects many brothers and sisters with whom I have conversed in the cloudy and dark days. We have prayed together, dear friends, have we not? I have repeated in your hearing those precious promises which are the pillows of our hope; yet, at the time, it seemed as if you would never be cheered or comforted. Friends who live with you grieved much to see you so sad; they could not understand how such as you, who have lived so scrupulously as you believed to be right, should, nevertheless, come into sadness and despondency. Well, you have come out of that state, have you not? I can almost catch the bright expression in your eye as you flash back the response, "It is so, sir; we can sing among the loudest now, we can leap as a hart, and the tongue that once was dumb can now sing praises to the Lord who delivered us." The reason for this great change is that you did still cling to Christ even when it seemed to be no use to cling. You had a venturesome faith; when it seemed a risky thing even to believe, you did believe, and you kept on believing, and now the day has dawned for you, and the shadows have fled away. Well, so shall it be to all who are in a like case, if they will but trust in the Lord, and stay themselves on our God. Though they walk in darkness, and see no light, yet, by-and-by, the day shall break for them also.

This expression is equally applicable when we come into some *personal sorrow not exactly of a spiritual kind*. I know that God's children are not long without tribulation. As long as the wheat is on the threshing-floor, it must expect to feel the flail. Perhaps you have had a bereavement, or you may have had losses in business, or crosses in your family, or you have been sorely afflicted in your own body, and now you are crying to God for deliverance out of your temporal trouble. That deliverance will surely come. "Trust in the Lord, and do good; so shalt thou dwell in the land, and verily thou shalt be fed." (Ps. 37:3) "I have been young", said David, "and now am old; yet have I not seen the righteous forsaken." (Ps. 37:25) The Lord will yet relight your candle, and surround your path with brightness. Only patiently hope, and quietly wait, and you will yet see the salvation of the Lord. "Many are the afflictions of the righteous." (Ps. 34:19) Listen to that! You know that part of the verse is true, and so is the rest of it: "...but the Lord delivereth him out of them all." Clutch at that, for it is equally true. "In the world ye shall have tribulation." (Jn. 16:33) You know that is true. "Be of good cheer", says Christ, "I have overcome the world." Therefore, expect that you also will overcome it through your conquering Lord. Yes, in the

267

darkest of all human sorrows there is the glad prospect that the day will break, and the shadows will flee away.

This is the case again, I believe, on a grander scale with reference *to the depression of religion at the present time*. Some of us are obliged to go sorrowing when we look at the state of the church and the world. We are not accustomed to take gloomy views of things, but we cannot help grieving over what we see. More and more it forces itself upon us that the old-fashioned gospel is being either neglected or trampled in the dust. The old spirit, the old fire that once burned in the midst of the saints of God, is there still, but it burns very low at present. We want — I cannot say how much we want — a revival of pure and undefiled religion in this our day. Will it come? Why should it not come? If we long for it, if we pray for it, if we believe in it, if we work for it, and prepare for it, it will certainly come. The day will break, and the shadows will flee away. The mockers think that they have buried our Lord Jesus Christ. So, perhaps, they have; but he will have a resurrection. The cry is, "Who will roll us away the stone?" The stone will be rolled away, and he, even the Christ in whom our fathers trusted, the Christ of Martin Luther and of John Calvin, of George Whitefield and of John Wesley, that same Christ will be among us yet in the fullness and the glory of his power, by the working of the Holy Spirit in the hearts of myriads of men. Let us never despair; but, on the contrary, let us brush the tears from our eyes and begin to look for the light of the morning, for "the morning cometh", and the day will break, and the shadows will flee away.

Let me encourage any friends who have been labouring for Christ in any district which has seemed strikingly barren, where the stones of the field have seemed to break the ploughshare. Still believe on, beloved; that soil which appears most unfruitful will perhaps repay us after a while with a hundred-fold harvest. The prospect may be dark; perhaps, dear friends, it is to be darker yet with us. We may have worked, and seemed to work in vain; possibly the vanity of all our working is yet to appear still more; but, for all that, "the morning cometh." "They that sow in tears shall reap in joy." (Ps. 126:5) We must not be in the least afraid, even in the densest darkness; but, on the contrary, look for the coming blessing.

I believe that this is to be the case also *in this whole world*. It is still the time of darkness; it is still the hour of shadows. I am no prophet, nor the son of a prophet, and I cannot foretell what is yet to happen in the earth; it may be that the darkness will deepen still more, and that the shadows will multiply and increase; but the Lord will come. When he went up from Olivet, he sent two of his angels down to say, "Ye men of Galilee, why stand ye gazing up into heaven? This same Jesus, which is taken up from you into heaven, shall so come in like manner as ye have seen him go into heaven." (Acts 1:11) He is surely coming; and though the date of his return is hidden from our sight, all the signs of the times look as if he might come very speedily. I was reading, the other day what old Master William Bridge says on this subject: "If our Lord is coming at midnight, he certainly will come very soon, for it cannot be darker than it now is." That was written two hundred years ago, but our Lord has not yet come, and I might say much the same as Master Bridge did. Do not doubt as to Christ's coming because it is delayed. A person lies dying, and the report concerning him is, "Well, it does not look as if he could live many hours." You call again, and they say, "Well, he still survives, but it seems as if he could scarcely get through the night." Do you go away and say, "Oh, he will not die; for I have expected, for several days, to hear that he has passed away"? Oh, no, but each time you hear the report, you feel, "Well, it is so much nearer the end." And so is our Master's coming; it is getting nearer every hour, so let us keep on expecting it. That glorious advent shall end our weary waiting days, it shall end our conflicts with infidelity and priestcraft, it shall put an end to all our futile endeavours; and when the great Shepherd appears in his glory, then shall every faithful under-shepherd and all his flock appear with him; and then shall the day break, and the shadows flee away.

As to the shadows fleeing, what are those shadows that are to flee at his approach? The types and shadows of the ceremonial law were all finished when Christ appeared the first time; but many shadows still remain: the shadows of our doubts, the grim mysterious shadows of our fears, the shadows of sin, so black, so dense, the shadows of abounding unbelief — ten thousand shadows. When he comes, these shall all flee away; and with them shall go heaven and earth — the heaven and earth that now is, for what are these but shadows? All things that are unsubstantial shall pass away when he appears; when the day breaks, then shall everything but that which is eternal and invisible pass away. We are glad that it will be so; and we pray that soon the day may break, and the shadows flee away. This, then, is our prospect.

II. Now I want to occupy a few minutes of your time in considering OUR POSTURE. We are here, like soldiers on guard, waiting for the dawn. It is night, and the night is deepening; how shall we occupy ourselves until the day break, and the shadows flee away?

Well, first, we will wait in the darkness with *patient endurance* as long as God appoints. Whatever of shadow is yet to come, whatever of cold damp air and dews of the night is yet to fall upon us, we will bear it. Soldiers of the cross, you must not wish to avoid these shadows. He who has called you to this service knew that it would be night time, and he called you to night duty; and being put upon the night watch, keep at your post. It is not for any of us to say, "We will desert because it is so dark." Has not the thought sometimes crossed your mind, "I am not succeeding; I will run away"? Have you not often felt, like Jonah, that you would go to Tarshish that you might escape from delivering your Master's message in Nineveh? Oh, do not so! The day will break, and the shadows flee away; and until then, watch through the night, and do not fear the shadows. Play the man, remembering through what a sevenfold night your Master passed, when, in Gethsemane, he endured even a bloody sweat for you. When, on the cross, even his mid-day was midnight, what must have been the darkness over his spirit? He bore it; then you bear it too. Let no thought of fear pass over your mind; or, if it does, do not let your heart be troubled, but rise above your fear until the day break, and the shadows flee away. Be of good courage, soldiers of Christ, and still wait on in patient endurance.

What next are we to do until the day break? Why, let there be *hopeful watching*. Keep your eyes towards the East, and look for the first grey sign of the coming morning. "Watch!" Oh, how little is done of this kind of work! We scarcely watch as we ought against the devil; but how little do we watch for the coming of our Master! Look for every sign of his appearing, and be ever listening for the sound of his chariot wheels. Keep the candle burning in the window to let him see that you are awake. Keep the door on the latch, that when he comes you may quickly open to him. Watch hopefully until the day break, and the shadows flee away.

Then, further, dear friends, while we maintain patient endurance and hopeful watching, let us give each other mutual encouragement. Men who have been shipwrecked will give each other a hand, and say, "Brother, maybe we shall escape after all." Now that it is midnight all around, let every Christian give his fellow-soldier a grip of his hand. Courage, brothers, the Lord has not forgotten us. We are in the dark, and cannot see him; but he can see us, and he knows all about us, and maybe he will come walking on the stormy waters in the middle watch of the night when our little bark seems ready to sink beneath the waves by the boisterous wind. I seem just now as though I were a soldier in this great guard-room, and as if we were sitting in these shadows, and perhaps in the darkness, and

269

seemed very much dispirited; and I would say to you my comrades, "Come, brothers, let us cheer up! The Lord has appeared to one and another of us. He has given to some of us the light of his countenance, and he is coming back to welcome us all to himself. Let us not be dismayed; our glorious Leader does not forget the weakest and feeblest of us, neither is any part of the battle-field beyond the reach of the great Captain's eye. He sees which way the struggle is going, and he has innumerable reserves, which he will bring up at the right time. I seem to hear the music of his horse's hoofs even now. He is coming who shall tip the scales at the worst moment of the conflict, for the battle is the Lord's, and he will deliver the enemy into our hand. Let no man's heart fail him because of yonder Goliath; the God who raised up men to slay the lion and the bear will yet find a David and a smooth stone to kill this mighty giant. Therefore, brothers, be of good courage."

What further should we do in the dark? Well, one of the best things to do is *to stand still and keep our place*. "Until the day break and the shadows flee away", let us keep our place, and firmly maintain our position. A brother who sat at the back of me, twenty years ago, dropped in again recently to hear me preach; and he said to me, after the service, that he had been away in America, and come over here again after twenty years. He added, "It is the same old story, Spurgeon, as when I was here before; you are sticking to the same old gospel." I replied, "Yes, and if you come in twenty years' time, if God spares me, I shall still be sticking to the same old gospel, for I have nailed my colours to the mast, and I do not mean to have anything to do with this new-fangled progressive theology." To me, the gospel came to perfection long ago in the Person of the Lord Jesus Christ, and it can never go beyond that perfection. We preach nothing but that gospel which has saved our own souls, and saved the souls of the myriads who have gone to their eternal rest, and we do not intend preaching anything else until somebody can find us something better, and that will not be tomorrow nor the day after, not as long as the world stands. It is dark, very dark, so we just stop where we are, in steadfast confidence in the Lord who has placed us where we are. We are not going to plunge on in a reckless manner, for we mean to look before we leap; and as it is too dark to look, we will not leap, but will just abide here hard by the cross, battling with every adversary of the truth as long as we have a right hand to move in the name of the Almighty God, "until the day break, and the shadows flee away."

What else ought we to do? Keep up a careful separation from the works of darkness that are going on all around us. If it seems dark to you, gather up your skirts, and gird up your loins. The more sin abounds in the world, the more ought the Church of God to seek after the strictest holiness. If ever there was an age that wanted back again the sternest form of Puritanism, it is this age. If ever there was a time when we needed the old original stamp of Methodists, we need them now — a people separated to God, a people that have nothing to do but to please God and save souls, a people that will not in any way bow themselves to the fashions of the time. For my part, I would like to see a George Fox come back among us, yes, Quaker that he was, to bear such a testimony as he did in the power of the Spirit of God against the evils of his time. God make us to feel that now, in the dark, we cannot be even as lenient as we might have been in brighter days towards the sin that surrounds us! Are any of you tempted into "society" so-called, and into the ways of that society? Every now and then, those who read the papers get some little idea of what is going on in "society." The stench that comes from "society" tells us what it must be like, and makes us wish to keep clear of it. The awful revelations that were once before made, which caused us to be sick with shame and sorrow, might be made again; for there is just the same foulness and filthiness beneath the surface of the supposed greater decency. O Christian people, if you could but know, as the most of you ought not to know, how bad this world is, you would not begin to talk about its wonderful improvements, or to question the doctrine of human depravity! We are going on, according to some teachers, by "evolution" into something; if I might prognosticate what it is, I should say that it is into devils that many men are being evolved. They are going down, down, down, save where eternal grace is begetting in the heart of men a higher and better and nobler nature, which must bear its protest against the ignorance or hypocrisy which this day talks about the improvements of our civilisation, and the progress that we are making towards God. "Until the day break, and the shadows flee away" — keep yourselves for your Lord, and hear this voice sounding through the darkness, the voice of a wisdom that sees more than you see: "Come out from among them, and be ye separate, saith the Lord, and touch not the unclean thing; and I will receive you, and will be a Father unto you, and ye shall be my sons and daughters, said the Lord Almighty." (2 Cor. 6:17-18) "Until the day break, and the shadows flee away" — lift your hands to heaven, and pledge yourselves to walk a separated pilgrim life until he comes, before whose face heaven and earth shall flee away.

III. Now, I close by noticing OUR PETITION: "Until the day break, and the shadows flee away, turn, my Beloved, and be thou like a roe or a young hart upon the mountains of Bether."

I am not going to preach upon that part of our text, but only just urge you to turn it into a prayer. We have to wait, brothers and sisters; we have to wait in the darkness, cheered here and there with the light from a golden lamp that glows with the light of God. The world lies in darkness, but we are of God, little children. Therefore, this must be our prayer to our Well-beloved, "*Come to us.*"

"Turn to me, O my Beloved, for you have turned away from me, or from your Church. Turn again, I beseech you. Pardon my lukewarmness, forgive my indifference. Turn to me again, my Beloved. O you Husband of my soul, if I have grieved you, and you have hidden your face from me, turn again to me! Smile again at me, for then shall the day break, and the shadows flee away. Come to me, my Lord, visit me once again."

Send up that prayer, beloved.

The prayer of the spouse is in this poetic form: "*Come over the mountains of division.*" As we look out into the darkness, what little light appears to reveal to us Alp upon Alp, mountain upon mountain, and our Beloved seems divided from us by all these hills. Now, our prayer is that he would come over the top of them, for we cannot go over the top of them to him, but he can come over the top of them to us, if he thinks fit to do so. Like the hinds' feet, this blessed Hind of the morning can come skipping over the hills with utmost speed to visit and deliver us. Make this your prayer:

"Great Master, sweetly-beloved One, come over the mountains of division, and come quickly, like a roe or a young hart. Come easily, come unexpectedly. As roes and harts, let no one know when they will come, so come to me."

I wish that, even while we are sitting here, our Divine Lord would come to our spirits with all his ravishing charms, so that we might cry, "Or ever I was aware, my soul made me like the chariots of Amminadib." Have you never felt an influence steal over you which has lifted you out of yourself, and made you go as on burning wheels, with axles hot with speed, where before you had been sluggish and dull? Our Well-beloved can come and visit us, all on a sudden, without any trouble to himself. It cost him his life's blood to come to earth to save us; it will cost him nothing to come just now to bless us. Remember what he has already done; for, having done so much, he will not deny you the lesser blessing of coming to you. Are you saved by his grace? Then do not think that he will refuse you fellowship with himself. Pray for it now. Before we come to the communion table, pray for it, and while you are sitting there, let this be your cry, "Come to me, my Beloved, over the hills of division; come as a roe or a young hart"; and he will come to you. Put up your prayer in the sweet words we sang just now:

When wilt thou come unto me, Lord?
O come, my Lord most dear!
Come near, come nearer, nearer still,
I'm blest when thou art near.

When wilt thou come unto me, Lord?
Until thou dost appear,
I count each moment for a day,
Each minute for a year.

(Thomas Shepherd)

Oh that this might be one of those happy seasons when you shall not be fed by the preacher's talk, but by the Master revealing himself to you! May God graciously grant it!

I may be addressing some who long to find the Saviour. This morning, I got from a friend who came in to see me an illustration which I will give to you. He told me — and oh, how he made my heart rejoice! — that six years ago, he was, as the Apostle says, "going about to establish his own righteousness." (Rom 10:3) He is a man of reputation, and when a friend sent him some of my sermons to read, he thought to himself, "What do I want these sermons for? I am as good as any man can be." But he did read them, and the friend asked him, "Have you read those sermons of Mr. Spurgeon's that I sent you?" "Yes", he replied, "I have; but I have not got any out of them." "Why not?" "Why", he said, "he has spoiled me; he has dashed my hopes to the ground, he has taken away my comfort and my joy; I thought myself as good as anybody living, and he has made me feel as if I were rotten right through." "Oh", said his friend, "that medicine is working well; you must take some more of it." But the more of the sermons he read, the more unhappy he became, and the more he saw the hollowness of all his former hopes; and he came into a great darkness, and the day did not break, and the shadows did not flee away. But, on a sudden, he was brought out into the light. As he told me the story this morning, his eyes were wet, and so were mine. This is how the Lord led him into peace. I wish the telling of it might bring the same blessing to some of you. He continued, "I went with my friend to fish for salmon in Loch Awe. I threw a fly, and as I did, a fish leaped up and took it in a moment." "There", said the friend to him, "that is what you have to do with Christ, just what that fish did with your fly." I am sure I do not know whether the fly took the fish, or the fish took the fly; it was both, for the bait took the fish, and the fish took the bait. Do just that with Christ, and do not ask any questions. Leap up at him, take him in, lay hold of him." The man did, and at once he was saved. I wish that somebody else would do the came. I will never ask you to answer the question whether it is Christ who takes you or you who take Christ, for both things will happen at the same moment. Will you have him? Will you have him? If you will have him, he has you. If you are willing to have Christ, Christ has already made you willing in the day of his power. (Ps. 110:3) Throw yourself on Christ, as the salmon opened his mouth, and took in the bait; so you take Christ into your very soul. Writing to the Romans, Paul says, "The word is nigh thee, even in thy mouth, and in thy heart: that is, the word of faith, which we preach." (Rom 10:8) What is the thing to do with what is in your mouth when you want to keep it? Why, swallow it, of course! Do so with Christ; let him go right down into your soul. I put him into your mouth, as it were, while I am preaching. Accept him, receive him, and he is yours directly. Then shall the day break, and the shadows flee away, and your Beloved shall have come to you over the mountains of division, never to leave you again, but to abide with you for ever. God bless you! Amen.

SEVEN SERMONS ON THE SONG OF SOLOMON

CHAPTER 3

36. I FOUND HIM WHOM MY SOUL LOVETH

"It was but a little that I passed from them, but I found him whom my soul loveth: I held him, and would not let him go, until I had brought him into my mother's house, and into the chamber of her that conceived me." (Song of Solomon 3:4)

The first position is, "*I passed from them.*" We must go beyond the fellowship of the best of men, and commune with him whom our soul loveth. Our love must lead to action, "*I sought him.*" Those who love Jesus seek his presence with an agony of desire.

After this seeking, we read at first, "*I found him not.*" Sad, but needful disappointment. But this lasts not forever; we soon come into the region of our text, where everything is bright with sunlight. Three flashes of delight follow each other: "*I found him*"; "*I held him*"; "*I brought him*". May these be our joyous experience! To that end, let us muse upon them, and pray the Holy Spirit to help us.

I. "I FOUND HIM": or, love in fellowship.

1. I was enquiring for him.

2. I had got beyond all men and means, and could not be content with any but himself.

3. I beheld his person. He drew near in his Word and ordinances. I perceived him by the Spirit. Faith saw him clearly.

4. I was assured of his presence. My heart felt peculiar influences operating upon it. It was a time of love.

5. I knew him to be mine. There were not doubts and fears. He was "my Beloved", and I was all his own.

6. I was filled with content. I looked for no one else, for in finding him I had found my all for earth and heaven.

Do we know what this blessed finding means?
If not, never let us rest till we do.

II. "I HELD HIM"; or love in possession.

1. By my heart's resolve, determining never to lose him again.

2. By my tearful pleas, entreating him not to make me wretched by withdrawing. I pleaded —

My joy in his society.
My need of his gracious protection.
My love to him, which made me hunger for him.
His love to me, which surely would not let him leave me.

3. By making him my all in all. He stays where he is prized, and I set him on a high throne in my spirit.

4. By renouncing all other loves, sin, idols, etc. He is jealous, and I kept myself altogether for him.

5. By a simple faith: for he is pleased with trust; and dwells where he is rested in.

6. By his own power. "I would not let him go" because I held him by his promise, and by the power which it gave me.

If you have Jesus, hold him.
He is willing to be constrained. See how often in his life on earth, "they constrained him" (Lk. 24:29) and he yielded to their will.

III. "I brought him"; or love in communication

The love of Jesus creates in our hearts love to our fellow believers for their Redeemer's sake.
The Church of God is our mother (Gal. 4:26): the holy assembly is her chamber, where we were born unto God, and nurtured in his fear. We are to labour to promote communion with Christ among those who are our brethren, taking Jesus with us whensoever we go up to the gatherings of the faithful.

This we should do —

1. By our own spirit: communing with Jesus before we go to public worship, and going there with him in our company. We shall always find him in the church if we take him in our hearts to its hallowed services.

2. By our words: we should so speak as to set forth Jesus, and promote fellowship with him. Alas, how many speak controversially, or without savour, or with carnal oratory wherein is no room for the Beloved! Oh, for a crucified style of speech!

3. By our prayer, we should bring him into the assembly; aye, bring him into society where hitherto he has been unknown. The world also was once our mother. Oh, that we could introduce the Lord Jesus into her chambers, that he might reign and rule there! "Thy kingdom come". By loving violence (Mat. 11:12), we will constrain him to come with us in his presence and power.

See what the church needs! — Christ in her midst.
See how he is likely to come — he must be brought.
See what must first be done — he must be held.
See who alone can do this — those who have found him.
Yet see also, who may find him — all who love him, and seek him.

Are we among the number?

FURTHER SUGGESTIONS

Hold him by not offending him. First by sloth. When the soul turns sleepy or careless, Christ goes away. Secondly, by idols. You cannot hold two objects. Thirdly, by being unwilling to be sanctified. Fourthly, by an unholy house. "I brought him into my mother's house". Remember to take Christ home with you, and let him rule in your house. If you walk with Christ abroad, but never take him home, you will soon part company forever.

(Robert Murray McCheyne)

275

"*I found him*": I, a man, found the Lord of Glory; I, a slave, found the great Deliverer; I, the child of darkness, found the Light of life; I, the uttermost of the lost, found my Saviour and my God; I, widowed and desolate, found my Friend, my Beloved, my Husband. Go and do likewise, sons and daughters of Zion, and he will be found of you; for "then shall ye find when you search with all your heart."

Bu we have another mother, and other brethren, in the human family from which we are sprung. The Church has the first, not the only claim on our affections; the perishing world has its right to a large share of our pity and our prayers. Comparatively, it is not hard for us to bring Jesus into the Church, which is his mother's house, as well as ours. But the world hates Christ, has nothing in common with him, is aware that he rightfully claims the dominion, is sensitively jealous of the claim, and lives with its doors barred against him night and day. No criminal keeps so vigilant a watch against the officers of justice, no lonely widow makes her gates so fast against the midnight robber, no miser spurns so haughtily the beggar from his door, as the unrenewed heart keeps watch and ward against the entrance of Jesus, and scornfully sends him away when he asks for a lodging in the soul. To introduce him, therefore, into this house of our mother is a work demanding effort, watchfulness, patience. There is much to provoke him to turn away; we must plead with him, and not let him go; and with our mother's children we must also plead with "the soft tongue that breaketh the bone" (Proverbs 25:15), for they are offended with us a well as with him. So sought and prevailed the Bride of the Lamb, till she brought her own Beloved into the midst of her mother's children, by whom she had been herself so hardly entreated, requiting evil with good. Have you attempted with? Are you engaged in the effort now? If not, rise and commence such a work of faith and labour of love on behalf of the lost.

(Alexander Moody Stuart)

37. THE DISCONSOLATE LOVER
NO. 3485

AT THE METROPOLITAN TABERNACLE, NEWINGTON

"By night on my bed I sought him whom my soul loveth: I sought him, but I found him not. I will rise now, and go about the city in the streets and in the broad ways I will seek him whom my soul loveth: I sought him but I found him not. The watchmen that go about the city found me: to whom I said, Saw ye him whom my soul loveth? It was but a little that I passed from them, but I found him whom my soul loveth: I held him, and would not let him go, until I had brought him into my mother's house, and into the chamber of her that conceived me." (Song of Solomon 3:1-4)

HOW exquisitely pleasant is communion with our Lord Jesus Christ! And how supremely favoured are those who enjoy it! Holy Scripture exhausts every earthly figure to delineate its sacred charms, its ineffable delights: yes, inspiration itself exhausts its metaphors without compassing its mystery, because it is impossible for human language to express the sweetness of his grace or the solace of our acquaintance with him. In just so much as it is sweet to know that fellowship, so it is sad not to know or to experience it. But alas, how frequently is this communion unfelt and unproved!

I. THE BRIDEGROOM WAS MISSED.

In addressing this large assembly, I can but think a considerable number of the Lord's people are in the condition of the spouse. You do not at present enjoy access to Christ, or fellowship with him. It may do you good to consider the things that remain to you, though this fellowship be suspended, for remember that it is not upon communion with Christ our life depends. Our salvation stands in the knowledge of him, not in communion with him. We are made safe by what he has done, not by what we feel. Not our enjoyments, but his sufferings we must lay as the solid foundation of our hope.

There remains for us, dear friends (for I confess to be sometimes in the same state) — though there be no privileged token of our love to Christ, nor any palpable enjoyment of his love to us — there remains at this hour the positive conviction and the open confession that we love him. Four times, I think, does this benighted spouse cry, "Him whom my soul loveth." She cannot see him, but she cherishes a tender affection for him. She does not enjoy his presence just now, but her heart cleaves to him and appreciates his excellence. What though she may have been idle and slothful, or though her spirit may be heavy and hazy, one thing she knows, she does love her Lord; about that there can be no mistake. Publicly in the streets, in the hearing of the watchmen, before the ministers and messengers of the gospel, she does not blush to say, "Him whom my soul loveth." So it was with Peter. When he had much to regret, much to reprove himself for, he could say, "Lord, thou knowest all things, thou knowest that I love thee." (Jn. 21:15-17) In like manner, can you not vouch for your sincerity when there is reason enough to challenge your propriety? You feel guilty of carelessness or cowardice, something that might reflect on your gratitude, but you cannot admit a wantonness or a wilfulness that could extinguish your love. My faithless heart, you would tell him, has merited your rebuke, but your infinite discernment can bear witness to the kindling of my desires. Do not believe my actions but believe my innermost soul. Do not judge me by the utterances of my recent lips; rather look upon the throbbing of my penitent heart. You, O Jesus Christ, are he whom my soul loves.

277

Though the spouse does not just now enjoy communion with Christ, she knows its sweetness, and she feels uneasy until she partakes of it again. As the compass needle cannot stop until it points to the pole, so she trembles until her soul rests in personal communion with Jesus. Next best to present fellowship is to hunger and thirst after it. And you note, too, in this case, and all the cases of every true believer in Jesus, not only is love constant, and desire after Christ earnest, but there remains sufficient strength resolutely to seek for him. You may not as yet have your desire accomplished, yet your heart is buoyed up with hope, and you are saying, "I must seek him." You are not like the traveller across the desert who, at last, loses all heart, gives up all effort, and perishes on the sand for lack of water. But you feel an inward impulse stronger than any outward discouragements, and, though faint, you are still pursuing. What if you have sought him and not found him, yet will you seek him again till you do find him, for divine grace stimulates you and urges you forward. As the spark flies upwards towards the sun, so the newborn nature of the Christian seeks and soars after Christ. It is not simply unhappy without him, but is restless and resolute to discover him. It would break through every law of nature to establish this law of grace. The new nature seeks the source from which it came; it pines and pants to meet with him and talk to him in whom are all its life and strength and joy. Do you not feel this desire after Jesus, though you are complaining of dullness and deadness, and worldliness? Is there not some such indescribable yearning in your breast for a communion which you well understand, but do not now enjoy? I do not know how you lost the fellowship, my brother, which you so grievously miss. There are many ways in which this may come about. You and I often lose the sweetness of communion with Christ, I do not doubt, through unbelief. We think so lightly of unbelief as though it were an infirmity and not a sin, whereas, of all evils, it is the chief.

What can be more displeasing to the tender heart of Jesus than ungenerous thoughts concerning him? When last you were repining and reflecting that he had forgotten you, you quickly lost that hallowed calm, and that sweet confidence which once you knew. Could you wonder at it? How could he walk with you while you were casting into his ear a foul suspicion against his truthfulness and his love? Faith is the hand which holds the Saviour and will not let him go; unbelief opens the door and bids him go. How shall he tarry when we will not believe in him? If you tell him to his face that he is not true and trustworthy, you cannot expect to lean your head upon his bosom? How can you expect this? Perhaps, my dear brother, you have been too busy with the world, and yet I know some with their hands full of business, and their heads full off enterprise, who have constant communion with Christ. But perhaps you have let the world steal into your heart. All the water in the sea, as I have often told you, does not frighten the mariner, but that little drop of water in the hold, which betokens a leak in the ship, gives him great distress. You might have an empire to govern, and yet never lose fellowship with Jesus, but with nothing more than your little family to manage, you may lose him if you let the cravings and the covetousness of the world, its fashions or its ambitions, get inside your heart. Keep that chamber clear for Christ. Let your heart be the marriage-bed, and keep it chaste for him who is your husband and your Lord, or possibly, dear brother, you have been negligent in the use of private prayer, and what can shut the windows through which Jesus looks as soon as laxness or slackness appears in supplication? Unless you are much upon your knees, you cannot expect to have your head much upon his bosom. The appointed place of audience is the mercy-seat. If you refuse to resort there, how can you look for Christ to grant you another audience-chamber? Is it reasonable that he should alter his fixed institutions to suit your foolish negligence? Go then, dear brother, if you would renew your fellowship, go again to your closet, and there pray to the Lord your God, and make your supplication to him.

In many other ways, the Christian may lose his fellowship with Christ. Specially by the indulgence of some known sin: by harbouring resentment or cherishing a bitter spirit

278

against a brother, by averting the eye to some gospel truth, by dissembling convictions in deference to the company you keep or the society in which you move, by not coming out from the world, or mingling too much with the ungodly. It may suffice to refer to these evils without enlarging upon them. When you miss the fellowship, there is little comfort in accounting for the way you lost it. Your heart is rather craving its restoration. Tell me how I may find him whom my soul loves, for I desire to renew my fellowship with him.

Come then, beloved, with hearts humbled on account of past sin, and yet encouraged with the assurance that he who received us at the first is willing to receive us still; and let us go to him anew. We were all over foul and vile then; if we find it the same now, we will return to him; if it be in as bad a plight, yet let it be with as good a plea. Come to Jesus, as once you came to him, though, perhaps, you have known the Master, lo, these many years. The same words will suit your case,

Just as I am without one plea,
But that thy blood was shed for me,
And that thou bidd'st me come to thee,
Oh! Lamb of God, I come.

(Charlotte Elliott)

While our text conducts us onward to the successful restoration of communion, it glances also at,

II. UNSUCCESSFUL ATTEMPTS TO FIND THE BELOVED ONE.

Of how many of us might it be said that with a lazy attitude and a listless wish, we have yawned after a boon for which we might have vehemently yearned. "By night on my bed I sought him whom my soul loveth." As it were on her bed of sloth and idleness, she dreamed of a happiness she was far from enjoying. But we shall never get the privilege of close communion with Christ by merely wishing for it. What though now and then, with a hectic flush upon our cheek, we exclaim, "Would to God I were like Christ; oh that I lived nearer to him! I am not satisfied with what I know, I desire to know more!" This is no symptom of health. Does the idler ever prosper? He who lies in bed and will not sow by reason of the cold, where is his harvest? What pearls come into the hand of the merchantman who says, "A little more sleep and a little more slumber"? And do you think the pearl of pearls, the pearl none other in the universe can compare with, the highest privilege which the King Eternal ever bestowed on his own courtiers — do you think that this, the most distinguished favour he ever confers upon the darlings of his heart, this intimate fellowship with Jesus — do you think he will communicate that to you whiles you are tossing on your bed in indolence which is the bane of virtue and the nurse of folly? It was not because she sought him by night that she did not find him, for Jesus is often found by his people in the dark. When no rays of light, no gleams of comfort, can steal over our senses, if we seek Jesus with our whole heart, though to our own apprehension we grope about like blind men, we shall find him, to the joy of our spirits. It was not the night that prevented her finding him; it was the bed — her supineness, her languor, and her sloth. Shake yourself from the dust and believe! George Turberville cautions,

Eschew the idle life!
Flee, flee from doing nought!
For never was there idle brain
But bred an idle thought.

No longer give into the insidious temptation which is so apt to beset us all. May the Lord deliver us from the lukewarmness of the Church of Laodicea, lest he should spue us out of his mouth. When she sought him thus, she could not find him; no marvel you will think, for your own experience has taught you that such disappointment is the invariable rule.

With no better success did she seek him when afterwards she went about in a self-sufficient spirit. I may be wrong in my conjecture, but to me the words, "I will rise now," sound a little like dependence on her own exertions. "I will rise now" has not half so grateful a ring about it, nor is it half so graceful, as "Draw me, we will run after thee." This confiding rather than that confidence seems to be the impression which becomes the saint when, cold and crushed, he keenly feels how desolate he is. Arise, did I say, shake off dull sloth? Ah, then, 'tis easier said than done. "Awake, my soul" is a poor invocation compared with "O Sun of righteousness, arise!" or "Make haste, my Beloved" or "Come, Lord Jesus, quickly come." Beware, my brethren, of seeking after Christ in a legal spirit. Beware of going to Calvary as though you were going to Sinai. In coming to Christ, no merit of your own could recommend you; so in longing for him to appear to you again, no strivings of your own can avail you. Let his rich grace be your poor plea. Your best way of suing is to declare,

Oh! for this no strength have I,
My strength is at thy feet to lie.

(Augustus Montague Toplady)

Once again, in trusting in the scrupulous using of the mean, the bride seems to have thoroughly relied upon attaining her end. Lest I should seem too censorious of her conduct, allow me to say that my criticism of the text is bent on taking and applying the rebukes to ourselves. Do you not notice, however, how sure she seems of finding him if she goes about the city, in the streets and in the broadways, and if she meets the watchmen and inquires of them? But it does not appear that the fitness of the places to seek, or the people to enquire of, were of much help. She went down one street, and another, as we may resort to the street of private prayer, a narrow and little-frequented way, and she said, "I shall find him there"; but after she had walked through it she said, "He is not here; my chamber is not a palace as it used to be; no more is it the privy-closet of the King of Kings, the audience-chamber royal" So she saw a wider way, and she said, "I will walk down here," as we may go to the prayer-meeting. "What blessed hours I have oft enjoyed there," said she; "I shall find him in that highway I feel sure", but, after traversing all its length, she said,

I go where Athena goes,
But find not Jesus there.

Then, says she, "I will go into the broad places where the preaching of the gospel is to be heard. I will go with the throng; where God speaks through his servants I will be", but service after service, and sermon after sermon, were like clouds without rain, and wells without water. Others were refreshed, but she, trusting in the means, came away without a blessing. So, brethren, you may traverse every street in the city, you may even come to that street paved with gold, the ordinance of the Lord's Supper, or you may go down Waterstreet, where in the ordinance of baptism, the Lord often reveals his death and burial to his people, but after having traversed both these streets you will be compelled to say, "Though I love the means, they are a weariness to me when Jesus is not revealed to me in them." What a difference there is between our preaching at one time and our preaching at another! How often do I bless God in the evening for that which I groaned over in the morning, when my spirit was bowed, my tongue tied, and I could not preach as I would! It

280

is a grand thing for the minister to be humbled in the sight of his hearers, when you discern that it is not the man in whom the power is vested, but it is his God whose might you cannot resist. My fear often is that your smiles may provoke his frowns; and he may withhold his blessing from me because you attribute to some genius of mine an influence which his Spirit alone could exert. When I was only a lad, a stripling fresh from the country, you said when there were conversions, "How God helps him!" I am jealous of you now, lest you should not say the same still. God will take away his blessing when you refrain from offering him the praise. If you once ascribe what is done in any degree whatever to the creature, or to any power that he has, you will excite the jealousy of his Lord. Remember the lessons that the spouse was taught. Means and ordinances are just what God likes to make them. Even divine institutions are beggarly elements when he forsakes them. They can be nothing better than matters of duty, and they may be very far from being matters of privilege. When he wills, he can make his ministers do exploits. The least of all his servants shall be mighty as David was, when he slew the giant Goliath with only the sling and stone. We are nothing of ourselves. The hand that moves the instrument is everything. If you would come to Christ, or seek after Christ, looking too much to the means, you will have to return again with the mournful cry, "I sought him, but I found him not." Such, then, are the unsuccessful efforts to regain communion with Christ.

III. WE FIND THE SUCCESSFUL HERE SET SIDE – BY - SIDE WITH THE UNSUCCESSFUL.

We shall now hold her up as an example which you will do well to imitate. With what constancy she sought this communion. She began at dead of night, as indeed it is never too late to seek renewed fellowship. Yet she sought on. The streets were lonely, and it was a strange place for a woman to be at such a strange time, but she was too earnest in seeking to be abashed by such circumstances.

The watchmen met her, and they were astonished, as well they might, how she came to be there at that hour. But she sought on; she would never rest until she had found him. Believer, if you would have fellowship with Christ, you must be in continual quest after it. They soul must get a craving for the one thing, and that such a craving nothing else can satisfy. I would my own soul were like Anacreon's harp, only in a better sense. You know he says, though he wished to sing of Cadmus, his harp would sing of love alone. Oh that we might sing of the love of Jesus and of his love alone, then it would not be long before our fellowship with him would be renewed!

And as she sought Jesus continually, she neglected no means that seemed to her right and promising. Though I have warned you against trusting in what are called the means of grace, I had not the slightest intention of undervaluing, much less of disclaiming, them. We cannot rationally expect the Lord to reveal himself other than in the way of his own appointment. He may sometimes do so, and he likes to surprise us with his grace, but we have no right to expect it. Abraham's servant closely followed his master's injunctions. And when he blessed the Lord God of his master Abraham, who had not left his master destitute of his mercy and his truth, he testified, "I being in the way, the Lord led me to the house of my master's brethren." It is in the way appointed that God most commonly deigns to meet with us. I do not expect that those of you who, every time there is half a shower of rain, stop at home will be very well fed, nor those of you who neglect the Monday prayer-meeting on any trivial excuse. There are a goodly number of you who do so; you cannot expect that you will grow in grace if you forsake the assembling of yourselves together. Those of you who, when the brethren join together in earnest prayer, cannot be present, must not marvel, if, like Thomas, you are not there when Jesus appears. You have good cause to be full of doubts and fears, when your fellow disciples are full of joy and love. Use the means; use all the means, I entreat you. Who knows how

281

great and rich a blessing obedience in even the least of the Lord's commands may bring to our souls! It is a blessed thing to walk tenderly and observe scrupulously the statutes of the Lord; to be afraid of leaving anything undone which is commanded, or of doing anything that is forbidden, lest in the omission or the commission we should by some means or other vex a jealous God, and provoke him to keep back from us much that we might have enjoyed through the means of his own appointment.

But the chief beauty of the whole story is that the spouse did not stop with the means of grace. She applied to the watchmen on the walls, but, better still for her, the watchmen found her. The expression is remarkable, because it is expressive of much that we have often proved. You know, sometimes, what it is to be found by the watchmen on the walls. You come here with a trouble of which nobody knows anything, and the watchman discovers you. In the description of your case he finds you out. It often happens that the very thing you were talking of by the way, the watchman relates to you. You perceive that you cannot be hidden. How strange it seems to you. Is not this a token of the Father's love that he guides the watchman to discover you in your midnight wanderings where you are unknown to any but your God, and thought you would be unrecognised by anyone? Yes, but even then you know, I hope, how to pass by the watchman. She asked, "Saw ye him, whom my soul loveth?" Why did they not answer? Perhaps because they were blind and never did see for themselves. Alas, that some watchmen on the walls have need to watch for their own souls rather than for the souls of others! Still, not the best of the watchmen there could console her with a smile of Jesus' face. We can tell you what we have felt and proved of his love. We can sometimes, when the Lord helps us, tell you how his people are ravished with his smiles, but a smile of his face; it is for him to give, and none but he can bestow it. It were not possible for him to send that second-hand. You must go direct to him. Yet see what honour God puts upon his servants, because she says it was but a little she had gone. You must go beyond the minister a little, but only a little. The Lord helps his servants to bring you to the verge of fellowship. We know it is all of the Lord, to him be all the glory! Still, he chooses in the use of means to make it but a little between the earnest, spiritual exercise of outward means, and the supply of the inward spiritual grace. "It was but a little that I passed from them, ere I found him whom my soul loveth."

Thus far, beloved brothers and sisters, have I led you on. Now I want you to go a little further. Away beyond the Church, away in advance of the bread and wine spread out for our mutual repast, a little beyond all these. It is not these that will satisfy your craving. A feast of bread and wine will never gratify this longing of your spirit. You want Jesus. The minister cannot suffice you; you want Jesus. You have got to this point of desire. You want Christ and nothing but Christ. Go on then, dear brother, and to attain your object I can propose nothing better than the simple method I proposed to you just now. Go to him as you did at first. Forget the past, except to remember with penitence your sin, and anticipate in the future the grace that welcomed you as a stranger. You know the love and mercy that are in his heart, unworthy as you are; so cast yourself at his feet, and you may have the love of your espousals given back to you. You may once again cross the Jordan of doubt and fear, and enter into the Canaan of your blest inheritance, enjoying rapt and rich fellowship with him.

If you do see him, be sure you lay hold of him. He himself loves to be embraced. Let your love lay hold of his love, for his love is laying hold of you. Hold him fast. Dismiss all ungrateful thoughts, for they will fill your hands so that you cannot hold him. Divest yourself of all cares for a while, and now with an empty hand just lay hold of his righteousness and strength.

And when you get the boon you long for, I charge you tell your brothers and sisters. Bring him to your mother's house. There are some in your mother's house sore sick with weary

282

apprehensions and dreary misgivings; tell them that you have seen your beloved, and it will cheer their spirits. Tell them the same news that made good old Jacob's eyes overflow with tears of joy; tell them Jesus is still alive; tell them that Jesus yet sits upon the throne; that he is still full of love for his chosen ones; and I think their despondent souls will straightaway revive, and they with you will feast on free grace and dying love.

Well, dear friends, I shall occupy no more time in talking to you, for we want to devote the rest of our time at the communion table to calm and quiet musings. I have conducted you as far as I can. Surely there is no need to excite Christians to that which is sweet to them; yet I beseech you, let no sense of unworthiness keep you back, for you always were unworthy; as such Christ loved you at first. Neither let any consciousness of backsliding keep you back. "As a wife treacherously departeth from her husband, so do ye depart from me" (Jer. 3:20), says the Lord by the mouth of his servant; and yet he says, "Return, return." (Song 6:13) I do not know of any figure more striking, none that involves more bitter reproach, yet for all that he bids her come back. Though you are thus guilty, and have been unfaithful to your loving husband, still he bids you come back, and assures you of a welcome. That hymn may suit the backsliders as well as the unconverted sinners.

Come, ye sinners, poor and wretched,
Weak and wounded, sick and sore;
Jesus ready stands to save you,
Full of pity joined with power;
He is able,
He is willing; doubt no more!

Let not conscience make you linger,
Nor of fitness fondly dream;
All the fitness he requireth,
Is to feel your need of him.
This he gives you;
'Tis the Spirit's rising beam!

(Joseph Hart)

Oh, how sad it makes my heart when I think of some of you to whom this is all an idle tale. All this discourse is arrant nonsense in the judgement of some of you. Our faith must seem to you strangely credulous. Our views must seem to you altogether visionary. Howbeit, there is a land that you have never seen, a life that you have never felt, a truth that has never dawned on your understanding. These things that are so real to us are strange to you; still, it is more strange and more strangely sad to me that you should be without God, without Christ, without hope in the world. We are pleased to greet you in this sanctuary; though we can well imagine that the sight and sound are foreign to you as would be the other side of a sea you have never crossed. You may be led to ask, "What is it? What does it mean? Is there another and a better life? Are there other and brighter joys than we have ever tasted? Do these Christians have comforts that I do not know? Have they a love which I do not have? I would that I knew the same!" A, thoughtless, heedless sinner! Be you a high caste or a low caste sinner, know this, that Jesus Christ, the Son of God, bled on the cross and died for such as you. Whoever believes in him shall never perish, but have everlasting life. Trust in him, and you are saved. This is the love that won our hearts. Oh, may it win yours! The things of which we have been speaking spring from that simple fact, that he loved us and gave himself for us.

The way in which we learned the mystery of his love is as open to you as it was to us. This was the way. We put our trust in him; we knew we were not worthy of him, but we did trust

283

him. Through his grace, without introduction or preparation, we draw near to him, and cast ourselves on his mercy. May you do the same! Let there not be an hour's delay, for the days are flying — the years are flying. Your grave is very close; within a few days you may be borne away. Fly at once to him who bids you trust him. God help you to do this, for Jesus Christ's sake! Amen.

38. LOVE'S VIGILANCE REWARDED
NO. 2485

AT THE METROPOLITAN TABERNACLE, NEWINGTON
ON LORD'S-DAY EVENING, OCT. 7TH, 1877

"It was but a little that I passed from them, but I found him whom my soul loveth: I held him, and would not let him go, until I had brought him into my mother's house and into the chamber of her that conceived me." (Song of Solomon 3:4)

WHEN I look upon this great assembly of people, I think to myself there will be many here to whom these chapters we have read from the Song of Solomon will seem very strange. Of course they will, for they are meant for the inner circle of believers in the Lord Jesus Christ. This sacred Canticle is almost the central Book of the Bible; it seems to stand like the tree of life in the midst of the Garden of Eden, in the very centre of the Paradise of God. (Rev. 2:7) You must know Christ, and love Christ, or else many of the expressions in this Book will seem to you as an idle tale.

The subject on which I am about to speak will be very much of the same character. Outsiders will not be able to follow me; but then we are coming to the communion table, so I must, for a while forget, the unsaved among my hearers, and think only of those who know the secret of the Lord which is with those who fear him. To my mind, it is a very melancholy thought that there should be any who do not know the sweetest thing in all the world, the best and happiest thing beneath the stars, the joy of having Christ in their heart as the hope of glory. While I may seem to forget you, dear friends, for a while, I cannot really help remembering you all the time; and it is the earnest desire of my heart that while I am speaking of some of those delights which are enjoyed only by the people of God, you may begin to long for them; and I remind you that, when you truly long for them, you may rest assured that you will have them. Around the garden of the Lord there is no wall so high as to keep out one real seeking and trusting soul; and in the wall itself there is a gate that ever stands ajar, no, that is ever wide open to the earnest seeker.

I am not going to try so much to preach a sermon as to talk out freely from my heart some of those delightful experiences which belong to the children of God. I want this service to be a time, not of carving meat, but of eating it; not of spreading tables, but of sitting at them, and feasting to the full on the bounteous provisions that our Lord has prepared for us.

I. First, before we actually come to our text, we may notice THREE PRELIMINARY STEPS IN THE SPOUSE'S PROGRESS.

The first one is implied in the words, *"I love him."* She refers to her Beloved under the title of "Him whom my soul loveth." Can you, dear friend, give the Lord Jesus that title? If he were to come here just now as he came to the Lake of Galilee, and pass along these crowded ranks, and say to each one of us, "Lovest thou me?" (Jn. 21:15-17), what would your answer be? I am glad that I speak to many whose answer would be, "Lord, thou knowest all things; thou knowest that I love thee." I can at this moment think of many reasons why I should love the Christ of Calvary, but I cannot think of one reason why I should not love him. If I turn to what I read about him in this blessed Book, it all makes me love him. If I recall what I have experienced of his grace in my heart, it all makes me love him. When I think of what he is, and what he did, and what he is doing, and what he will yet do, it all makes me love him. I am inclined to say to my heart, "Never beat again if you do not beat true to him." It were better for me that I had never been born, than that I

285

should not love one who is in himself so inconceivably lovely, who is, indeed, perfection itself.

Yet there is one reason that rises above all others why you and I should love the Lord Jesus Christ; it is this, "He loved me, and gave himself for me." (Gal. 2:20) It used to be said by the old metaphysicians that it was impossible for love not to be returned in some measure or other. I do not think that statement is universally true; but I hope it is true concerning our Lord's love for us and our heart's love for him. If he has loved us with an everlasting love, if he loved us even when we were his enemies, and loved us so as to take upon himself our nature — if this dear Son of God loved us so much that he became man for our sakes, and, being found in fashion as a man, humbled himself, and became obedient unto death, even the death of the cross (Phil 2:6-7) — oh then, we must love him in return! We would be worse than the beasts that perish if, conscious of such love as this, we did not feel that it melted us, and that, being melted, our soul did not bow out in love to him alone! Can you stand at the foot of the cross and not kiss the feet of him who was wounded for your transgressions? Can you see him dead and taken down from the cross, and not wish to wrap him in your fine linen, and bring your sweet spices to embalm his precious body? Can you see him risen from the grave and not call him "Rabboni" (Jn. 20:16), and long, as Mary did, to hold him by the feet? Can you, by faith, see him in our assemblies, saying, "Peace be unto you" (Jn. 20:19, 21, 26) and not feel that you delight in him in your innermost soul? It cannot be; surely, it cannot be! We must and will say, and we feel that we may appeal to the Searcher of all hearts while we say it — "I love him, I do love him because he first loved me." (1 Jn. 4:19)

Then, in the spouse's progress, there came another step: "*I sought him.*" Notice how the chapter begins: "By night on my bed I sought him whom my soul loveth", for love cannot bear to be at a distance from the loved one; love longs for communion; love will do anything to get at the object of its affection. Where there is true love to Jesus Christ, we cannot bear to be away from him; and since we must be so in personal presence for a while, till the day break, and the shadows flee away (Song 2:7, 4:6), we long to be with him in heart, and to feel that he also is with us in spirit according to his promise, "Lo, I am with you alway, even unto the end of the world." (Mat. 28:20)

"*I sought him.*" Can you put your finger on that sentence and say, "That is true, too"? Have you been seeking him this Sabbath day? Are you coming to his table tonight seeking him? Were you at the Saturday night prayer meeting, or at this morning's early gathering, seeking him with his people? Or, in your private devotions, did you make a point of crying, "Lord, let me meet with you, let me find you"? If not, begin now; seek him with your whole heart, let your soul breathe out its burning desires after him. "I sought him." He is not far from anyone of us. You sought him once when you were burdened with your sin, and then you found him. He cast that sin of yours into the depths of the sea. Come and seek him again, and your fears, your doubts, your distresses of mind, shall be buried in the same deep grave. So the spouse sings of her Beloved: "I sought him."

Then comes a little minor or mournful music, for the next clause is, "I sought him, *but I found him not.*" The spouse is so sad about it that she tells out her woe twice, "I sought him, but I found him not." Do you know that experience? I hope you are not realising it at this time; but many of us have known what it is. If we have been indulging in any sin, of course we could not find him then. If we have been gold-hearted, like the spouse who sought him on her bed, like her, we have not found him. We have had to rise, we have had to stir up ourselves to lay hold of him, or else we have not found him. You have known what it is to go to the public service of the sanctuary where others have been fed, yet you have had to come away, and say, "There has not been a morsel for me." Have you not even turned to the Bible, and to private prayer, and still you have had to say, "I sought him, but I found him not"? This is a very sad experience; but if it makes you sad, it will be good for you. Our Lord Jesus Christ would not have us think little of his company; and, sometimes, it is only as we miss it that we begin to appreciate the sweetness of it. If we always had high days and holidays, we might not be so thankful when our gala days come round. I have even known some of Christ's people get so pleased with the joy of his company that they have almost forgotten him in the joy! If a husband gave his wife gold rings and ornaments, and she was so gratified with the presents that she took but little note of him, but only prized the jewels that he gave her, I can well understand what would be the jealousy of his heart. It may be that this is why your Lord hides his face, for you never know his value so much as when the darkness deepens, and the Star of Bethlehem does not shine.

When real soul-hunger comes on, and the Bread of heaven is not there, when you feel the pangs of the thirst of the spirit, and you are like Hagar in the wilderness, and cannot find the well of water, then will your Lord teach you his true value. And when you really know him, and know him better than you formerly knew him, then you shall no longer have to sigh, "I sought him, but I found him not", but you shall change your dolorous ditty for the cheerful language of the text: "It was but a little that I passed from them, but I found him whom my soul loveth."

So I have brought you back to the text: these are the three steps by which we have ascended to the holy gate — first, "I love him"; next, "I sought him"' and then, "I found him not."

II. Secondly, inside the text there are THREE FURTHER STEPS: "I found him", "I held him", "I brought him into my mother's house, and into the chamber of her that conceived me."

This is the first of the second series of steps: "*I found him.*" I do not wish to stand here and speak for myself alone; but I want, beloved, that you should each one of you also say, "I love him", "I sought him", and now, "I have found *him*." Notice what the spouse said: "I found him." She was not satisfied with finding anything else: "I found him." If she had found her nearest and dearest friend, if the mother of whom she speaks had met her, it would not have sufficed. She said, "I love him, I sought him", and she must be able to add, "I found him." Nothing but Christ consciously enjoyed can satisfy the craving of a loving heart which once sets out to seek the King in his beauty.

The city watchmen found the spouse, and she spoke to them; she enquired of them, "Saw ye him whom my soul loveth?" She did not sit down and say to anyone of them, "O watchman of the night, your company cheers me! The streets are lonely and dangerous; but if you are near, I feel perfectly safe, and I will be content to stay awhile with you." No, but she leaves the watchmen, and still goes along the streets until she finds *him* whom her soul loves. I have known some who love the Lord, and are very happy while the preacher is proclaiming the truth to them; but they have stopped with the preacher, and have gone no further. This will never do, dear friends; do not be content to abide with us, who are only watchmen, but go beyond us, and seek till you find our Master. I should groan in heart, indeed, if any of you believed simply because of my word, as if it were my word alone that led you to believe, or if you should look merely to me for anything you need for your soul. In myself, I am nothing, and I have nothing; I only watch that, if I can, I may lead you to my Lord, whose shoe-ratchets I am not worthy to unloose. O you who love Christ, go beyond the means of grace! Go beyond ordinances, go beyond preachers, go beyond even the Bible itself, into an actual possession of the living Christ. Labour after a conscious enjoyment of Jesus himself till you can say with the spouse, "I found him whom my soul loveth." It is good to find sound doctrine, for it is very scarce nowadays. It is good to learn the practical precepts of the gospel; it is good to be in the society of the saints; but if you put any of these in the place of communion with your Lord himself, you do badly. Never be content till you can say, "I found *him*." Dear souls, did you ever find him? Have you yet found him? If you have not, keep on seeking, keep on praying, till at last you can say, "Eureka! I have found him whom my soul loves. Jesus is indeed mine."

What is meant by the words, "I found him"? Well, I think a soul may say, "I found him", in the sense employed in the text, when first of all it has a clear view of his Person. My Beloved is divine and human, the Son of God and yet the Son of man. My Beloved died, yet he is alive again. My Beloved was on earth, but he is now in heaven, and he will shortly come again. I want thus to find him myself, and I want each one of you to do the same. Picture him on Calvary, and see him risen from the dead. Try, if you can, not so much by imagination as by faith, to behold him as he now sits at the right hand of the Majesty on high, where harps unnumbered tune his praise. Yet even there he bears the wounds he received for us here below. How resplendent are the nail-prints! The marks of his death on earth are the glory of his Person above.

This is the Man, the exalted Man,
Whom we unseen adore;
But when our eyes behold his face,
Our hearts shall love him more.

(Isaac Watts)

Let your soul picture him so plainly that you can seem to see him, for this will be a part of your finding him.

But that will not be enough; you must then get to know that he is present with you. We cannot see him, but yet he who walks amid the seven golden candlesticks (Rev. 1:12, 20, 2:1) is, in spirit, in this house of prayer at this moment.

"My Master, you are here. There is no empty seat at the table left to be filled by you, nor do we expect to see you walking among us in your calm majesty, clothed with your seamless garment down to your feet; and we do not want to see you. Our faith realises you quite as well as sight could do, and we bless you that you hear us as we speak to you. You are invisible, yet assuredly present; you are looking into our faces; you are delighting in us as objects of your redeeming love. You especially remember that you died for us; and, as a mother gazes upon the babe for whom she has endured so much, or as a shepherd looks upon the sheep that he has brought back from its long wanderings, so are you now looking upon each one of your loved ones."

If, dear friends, you can get that thought fully into your minds, that Christ is really here in our midst, you can then each one begin to say, "I have found him."

But you want more than that, namely, to feel that he loves you, loves you as if there were nobody else for him to love, loves you even as the Father loves him. That is a daring thing to say, and I should never have said it if he had not first uttered it; but he says, "As the Father hath loved me, so have I loved you." (Jn. 15:9) Can you comprehend how each one of the blessed Trinity loves each of the others, and especially how the Father loves the Son? Even so does Jesus Christ love you, my believing brother, my believing sister. Note that he *loves* you; it is not only that he loved you, and died for you, but he still loves you. He says to you, individually, "I have graven thee upon the palms of my hands." (Is. 49:16) Look at the nail-print; that is his memorial, his forget-me-not, and by it he says,

Forget thee I will not, I cannot, thy name
Engraved on my heart doth for ever remain:
The palms of my hands whilst I look on I see
The wounds I received when suffering for thee.

(Isaac Watts)

Now have you not found him? If you have pictured him to your mind's eye, if you are certain of his presence with you, and then, above all, if you are fully assured of his love, you can say, "I have found him."

If you can in truth say that, I hope there will come with it this one other thing, namely, an exceeding great joy. I cannot speak to you as I would wish; my words cannot express the joy of heart which I feel in knowing that I have found him, that he is with me, and that he has loved me with an everlasting love. I shall never understand, even in heaven, why the Lord Jesus should ever have loved me. I can say to Jesus what David said in his lamentation over Jonathan, "Thy love to me was wonderful, passing the love of women." (2 Sam. 1:26) There is no love like it, and why was it fixed upon me? Have you never felt that you could go in, like David, and sit before the Lord and say, "Who am I, O Lord God? And what is my house that thou hast brought me hitherto?" (2 Sam. 7:18) Yet wonderful as it is, it is true; for Jesus loves you, loves you now at this very moment. Do you not rejoice in it? I assure you that, in the least drop of the love of Christ when it is consciously realised, there is more sweetness than there would be in all heaven without it. Talk of bursting barns, overflowing wine-vats, and riches treasured up; these give but a poor solace to the heart. But the love of Jesus, this is another word for heaven; and it is a marvel that even while we are here below we should be permitted to enjoy a bliss beyond what the angels know, for,

Never did angels taste above
Redeeming grace and dying love,

(Isaac Watts)

— but that joy is ours if we can truly say, "I have found him."

If you have come as far as that — and if you have not, may God help you to this point right speedily — come to the table of your Lord. You are indeed his children, so you have a right to come. Hear the King's invitation, "Eat, O friends; drink, yea, drink abundantly, O beloved." (Song 5:1) These joys are not merely for some of the Lord's people but for all his saints; then, do not stand back, but come and feast on the rich provision of love divine.

Now we come to the second step. The spouse says, "*I held him.*" This is a deeper experience than the former one. "I held him" means more than "I found him". Sometimes, Jesus comes to his children and manifests himself very sweetly to them; but they behave towards him in an unseemly manner, and soon he is gone. I have known him reveal himself to his people most delightfully, but they have grown cold and wayward and foolish, and he has been obliged to go away from them. When you get to the top of the mountain, it needs great grace to keep you there. I do not find it difficult to get into communion with Christ, but I confess that I do not find it so easy to maintain that communion. So, if you have found him, do as the spouse says that she did: "I held him."

How are we to hold Christ? Well, first, let us hold him by our heart's resolve. If now we have him near us, let us lovingly look him in the face and say, "My Lord, my sweet, blessed Lord, how can I let you go? My all in all, my heart's Lord and King, how can I let you go? Abide with me, do not go from me." Hold him by your love's resolve, and it shall be as chains of gold to fasten him to you. Say to him,

"My Lord, will you go away from me? See how happy you have made me. A glimpse of your love has made me so blest that I do not envy the angels before your throne. Will you take that joy away from me by taking yourself away? Why did you give me a taste of your love if you did not mean to give me more? This little has but put me out of liking for all things else; you have spoilt me now for all my former joy. O tarry with me, my Master, else am I unhappy indeed!"

Further, say to him,

"Lord, if you go, your chosen one will be unsafe. There is a wolf prowling about; what will your poor lamb do without you, O mighty Shepherd? There are cruel adversaries all around seeking to harm me; how can I live without you? Will you deliver your turtle-dove over to the cruel fowler who seeks to slay her? Be that far from you, O Lord! Therefore, abide with me."

Tell him how you will sorrow if he goes away,

My God, my life, my love!
To thee, to thee I call;
I cannot live if thou remove,
For thou art all in all,
Thy shining grace can cheer
This dungeon where I dwell:
'Tis paradise if thou art here,
If thou depart, 'tis hell.

(Isaac Watts)

"Nothing can revive my spirit if you are gone from me. Oh, stay with me, stay with me, I beseech you, most blessed Lord!" As long as you can find arguments for his staying, Christ does not want to go from you. His delights are with the sons of men, and he is happy in the society of those whom he has purchased with his precious blood. Keep on giving your reasons why he should remain with you, and so hold him; be bold enough even to say to him, "I will not let thee go except thou bless me." (Gen. 32:26) Get you to Jacob's boldness when he said to the Angel of the covenant, "I will not let thee go except thou bless me", but go even beyond that; do not put in any "except" at all, but say, "I will not let you go, for I cannot be blest if you have gone from me."

Further, brethren, hold him by making him your all-in-all. He will never go away if you treat him as he should be treated. Yield up everything to him, be obedient to him, be willing to suffer for him, do not grieve His Holy Spirit, crown him, extol him, magnify him, keep on singing his praises, for so will you hold him. Renounce all else for him, for he sees that you truly love him when you count all things but dross for his dear sake. He says, "I remember thee, the kindness of thy youth, the love of thine espousals, when thou wentest after me in the wilderness." (Jer. 2:2) Those were the days when some of you could brook a father's frown for the sake of Christ's love, when you could have given up your situation and all your prospects in life to follow Jesus. It was then that he delighted in you; and in proportion as you break your idols, put away your sins; and keep your heart chaste and pure for him alone, you shall abide in his love. Yes, and you shall get deeper and deeper into it till what was a stream up to your ankles shall soon be breast-deep, and, by-and-by, shall be waters to swim in. (Ezek. 47:5) Christ and you cannot fully agree unless you walk as he would have you walk, in careful holiness and earnest service for him. "Can two walk together, except they be agreed?" (Amos 3:3) And is there anything in this vile world that is fit to stand in rivalry with him? Is there any gain, is there any joy? Is there any beauty that can be compared with his gain, his joy, his beauty? Let each of us cry, "Christ for me! Go, harlot-world; do not come near even the outside of my door. Go away, for my heart is with my Lord, and he is my soul's chief treasure." If you talk like that, you will hold him fast till you have your heart's desire, and bring him to your mother's house.

Hold him, too, with a simple faith. That is a wonderful hold-fast. Say to him, "My Lord, I have found you now, and I rejoice in you; but still, if you hide your face from me, I will still believe in you. If I never see a smile from you again till I see you on your throne, yet I will not doubt you, for my heart is fixed, not so much upon the realisation of your presence, as upon yourself and your finished work. Though thou slay me, yet will I trust in thee" (Job 13:15) Ah, then he will not go away from you. You can hold him in that way; but if you begin to put your trust in enjoyments of his presence instead of in himself alone, it may be that he will take himself away from you in order to bring you back to your old moorings, so that, as a sinner, you may trust the sinner's Saviour, and trust in him alone.

One word more before we leave this point. The only way to hold Christ is to hold him by his own power. I smiled to myself as I read my text, and tried to make it all my own: "I held him, and would not let him go." I thought to myself, the spouse said of her Bridegroom that she would not let him go; and shall I ever say to my Lord that I will not let him go? He is the King of kings, the omnipotent Jehovah; can I hold him? He is the mighty God, and yet a poor puny worm like myself says, "I would not let him go." Can it really be so? Well, the Holy Spirit says that it is, for he guided the pen of the writer of this Song when he wrote, "I held him, and would not let him go." Think of poor Jacob, who, when the angel just touched him, felt his sinews shrink directly; yet he said, "I will not let thee go." And I, a poor trembling creature, may hold the Omnipotent himself, and say to him, "I will not let thee go." How is that wonder to be accomplished? I will tell you. If Omnipotence helps you to hold Omnipotence, why, then, the deed is done! If Christ, and not you alone, holds Christ, then Christ is held indeed, for shall he vanquish his own self? No; Master, you could slay death, and break the old serpent's head, but you cannot conquer your own self. And if you are in me, I can hold you, for it is not I, but Christ in me that holds Christ, and will not let him go. This is the power which enables us, with the apostle, to say, "I am persuaded that neither death, nor life, nor angels, nor principalities, nor powers, nor things present, nor things to come, nor height, nor depth, nor any other creature, shall be able to separate us from the love of God, which is in Christ Jesus our Lord." (Rom. 8:38-39)

The next step is described in the words "*I brought him*." With this we finish. "I brought him into my mother's house, and into the chamber of her that conceived me." And where, I pray you, beloved, is our mother's house? I do not believe in any reverence for mere material buildings; but I have great reverence for the true Church of the Living God. The Church is the house of God and the mother of our souls. It was under the ministry of the Word that most of us were born to God; it was in the assembly of the saints that we heard the message which first of all quickened us into newness of life; and we may well be content to call the Church of Christ our mother, since our elder Brother — you know his name — when one said to him, "Behold, thy mother and thy brethren stand without, desiring to speak with thee" (Mat. 12:47), pointing to his disciples, he answered, "Behold, my mother, and my brethren. For whosoever shall do the will of my Father which is in heaven, the same is my brother, and sister, and mother." (Mat. 12:49-50) Surely, where Jesus chooses to call the assembly of the faithful by the sacred name of mother, we may rightly do the same.

And we love the Church, which is our mother. (Gal. 4:26) I do hope that all the members of this church love the whole Church of God, and also have a special affection for that particular part of it in which they were born again for God. It would be unnatural — and grace is never unnatural, though it is supernatural — it would be unnatural not to love the place where we were born into the heavenly family. I do not know, and never shall know on earth, the man who was the means of my conversion. I may know him when I get to heaven; but if he is still living anywhere in this world, God bless him! And I know that many of you would say the same of the outward instrumentality which was used as the means of blessing to you; and you will say the same, will you not, of all the brotherhood of which some of us are but the spokesmen and representatives? We love the Church of God. Well, then, whenever we find our Beloved, we have to hold him, and not let him go, and then to bring him down to the house of our mother, and to the chamber of her that conceived us.

How can you bring Christ to his Church? Partly, you can bring him by your spirit. There is a wonderful power about a man's spirit, even though he does not speak a word. Silent worshippers can contribute very greatly to the communion of saints. I know some brethren — I will not say that any of them are here now — but I have known some brethren whose very faces dishearten and discourage one, whose every movement seems to make one feel anything but spiritual. But I know others of whom I can truly say that it is always pleasant to me to get a shake of their hands, and to have a look from their eyes. I know that they have been with Jesus, for there is the very air of saintliness about them; I do not mean sanctimoniousness; that is a very different thing. In the old pictures, the painters used to put a halo round the head of a saint — a most absurd idea; but I do believe that there is a real spiritual halo continually surrounding the man who walks with God.

If you, dear friend, have really found Christ, and bring him with you into the assembly, you will not be the one who will criticise, and find fault, and quarrel with your neighbour because he does not give you enough room in the pew. You will not be the person to pick holes in other people's coats; but you will be very considerate to others. As for yourself, anything will do for you, and anywhere will do for you, for you have seen the Beloved. You want other people to get as much good as they can. You are no longer selfish; how can you be, when you have found him whom your soul loves? And now, your poor brother need not be very choice in the selection of his words; if he will only talk about Jesus, you will be quite satisfied. If his accent should be a little broken, you will not mind that. So long as you feel that he wishes to extol your Lord; and that will be enough for you. So, in this manner, in spirit, you will bring the Beloved to your mother's house, to the chamber of her that conceived you.

But, dear friend, it will also be a happy thing if you are able to talk about your Lord, for then you can bring him to the Church with your words. Those of us who are called to preach the Word often have to cry to the Lord to help us to bring Christ into the assembly by our words — though, indeed, the words of any human language are but a poor conveyance for the Christ of God. Oh, let the King, my blessed Master, ride in the chariot of angelic song, and not in the lumbering wagon of my poor sermons! I long to see him flying on the wings of the wind, and not in the car of my feeble language; yet he has come to you many a time that way, and you have been glad. Let him come as he will, if he will but come; it is our delight to bring him into our mother's house, into the chamber of her that conceived us. Therefore, dear friends, each one of you in turn, as you are able, talk to your brother and to your sister, and say, "I have found him whom my soul loveth." You know that when Samson killed the lion, he said nothing about it; it would have been a great feat for anyone else to boast of, but Samson could kill a lion any day, so he did not think much of doing that; but when he afterwards found a swarm of bees and honey in the carcase of the lion, he took some of it and began to eat, and carried a portion of it to his father and mother. (Judges 14:8-14) If ever you find sweetness and preciousness in Christ, the true strong One, be sure that you carry a handful of honey to your friends, and give portions to those for whom otherwise nothing might be prepared.

Therefore, hold Christ fast, and bring him to your mother's house by your spirit and by your words.

But if, alas, you feel that you cannot speak for Christ, then, beloved, bring him by your prayers. Do pray, especially at these communion seasons, that the King himself will come near and feast his saints today. Ask him not only to bless you, but to bless all his saints, for you are persuaded that they all love him better than you do, and that they all want him as much as you do, and that they will all praise him even more than you do, if he will but come and manifest himself to them. In this way, each one of you, as you some to the house of prayer, and to the place of fellowship, will be a real accession to our spiritual force, and we shall seem to get nearer and nearer to our Master as the house fills with loving worshippers who have found him, and held him, and brought him here.

Now may we find all this to be especially true as we gather around the table! The Lord be with you all, for his dear name's sake! Amen.

39. THE REAL PRESENCE, THE GREAT NEED OF THE CHURCH

NO. 1035

A SERMON DELIVERED ON LORD'S DAY MORNING
FEBRUARY 11TH, 1872
AT THE METROPOLITAN TABERNACLE, NEWINGTON

"It was but a little that I passed from them, but I found him whom my soul loveth: I held him, and would not let him go, until I had brought him into my mother's house, and into the chamber of her that conceived me. I charge you, O ye daughters of Jerusalem, by the roes, and by the hinds of the field, that ye stir not up, nor awake my love, till he please." (Song of Solomon 3:4-5)

IS it necessary to say that the Lord Jesus Christ is no longer corporeally present in his church? It ought not to be needful to assert so evident a truth; and yet it is important to do so since there are some who teach this in what they are pleased to call "the Holy Sacrament", with Christ actually present in his flesh and blood. Such people unwittingly deny the real humanity of our Lord Jesus Christ, for if he has indeed assumed our humanity, and is in all points made "like unto his brethren" (Heb. 2:17), his flesh and blood cannot be in two places at any time. Our bodily humanity cannot be present in more places than one at any time, and if Christ's humanity is like ours, it cannot be in an unlimited number of places at the same time; in fact, it could only be in one place. Where that place is we know from Scripture, for he sits at the right hand of God, expecting till his enemies to be made his footstool. (Ps. 110:1) Unless you are to suppose that the humanity of Christ is something altogether different from ours, it cannot be here and there and everywhere; but to suppose that it is a different humanity from ours is to deny that he is Incarnate in our nature. Our Lord Jesus told his disciples that he would go away, and he has gone away. He ascended into heaven, bearing humanity up to the throne of God. "He is not here, for he is risen." (Mat. 28:6) Remember, also, that because the Lord Jesus is absent corporeally, the Holy Spirit the Comforter is with us, for he especially said, "If I go not away, the Comforter will not come unto you: but if I depart, I will send him unto you." (Jn. 16:7) Those who believe that Christ's flesh and blood is, or can be, present on earth deny the presence of the Holy Spirit; for the Scripture is plain enough on that point — that the bodily absence of our Lord is the cause and condition of the presence of the Comforter. If Jesus still dwells corporeally on the earth, then the Spirit of God is not on the earth. Many other most serious errors follow from the supposition that the humanity of the Redeemer is present anywhere except at the right hand of God, even the Father; yet it is imagination which lies at the basis of the sacramental system, and thousands are greatly enamoured of it.

No word of mine this morning is intended to have the remotest connection with any sacramental presence of the corporeal nature of our Lord; our mind has a far greater matter before it. Let us, therefore, having guarded ourselves so as not to be misunderstood, proceed to speak of another presence of our blessed Lord. The fact is that Christ Jesus, the Lord, is present in his church by the Holy Spirit. The Holy Spirit is this day the representative of Christ in the midst of the church, and it is in the power and the energy of the Holy Spirit that Christ is with us always, and will be even to the end of the world. As God, Jesus is everywhere; as man, he is only in heaven; as God and man in one person, Mediator and Head of the Church, he is present with us by the Holy Spirit, the Comforter, whom the Father has sent in his name. It is by the working of the Spirit of God that Christ's presence in the church is manifested; and we are to expect no other presence than that: we have the spiritual divine presence of the second person of the blessed Trinity, and the presence of Christ Jesus also in the power of his representative on earth, the Holy Spirit. This presence, not a bodily, but a spiritual presence, is the glory of the church of God. When she is without it, she is shorn of her strength; when she possesses it, all good things follow. Brethren, if a church is without the Spirit of God in it, it may have a name to live, but it is dead, and, you know, that after death there follows corruption, corruption which breeds foulness and disease. Hence, those churches which have turned aside to error have not only lost all power to do good, but have become obnoxious, and the cause of great evil in the midst of the world. If any professing church does not abide in Christ, it is cast out as a branch and is withered; and while it is decaying, it is injurious, and there is need for the world's welfare that it may not be utterly destroyed. We must have Christ in the church, or the body which was meant to be the medium of the greatest good becomes the source of the grossest evil. Let the Spirit of God be in the church, then there is power given to all her ministries, whether they be ministries of public testimony in the preaching of the Word, or ministries of holy love amongst the brethren, or ministries of individual earnestness to the outside world, they will all be clothed with energy, in the fullness of the power of the Lord Jesus. Then her ordinances become truly profitable, then baptism is burial with the Lord, and the sacred supper is a feast of love; then the communion of the brethren in their solemn prayer and praise becomes deep and joyful, and their whole life and walk are bright with the glow of heaven. In the presence of the Lord, the graces of the saints are developed; the church grows rich in all spiritual gifts; and her warfare becomes victorious, and her continual worship sweet as the incense of the golden censor. What the moon is to the night, or the sun to the day, or the Nile to Egypt, or the dew to the tender herb, or the soul to the human frame, so is the presence of Jesus to his church. Give us the Spirit of God, and we will ask no endowments from the State, nor sigh for the prestige of princely patronage. Endow us, O God, with the Holy Spirit, and we have all we need. The poverty of the members, their lack of learning, their lack of rank, all these shall be as nothing. The Holy Spirit can make amends for all deficiencies, and clothe his poor and obscure people with an energy at which the world shall tremble. This made the apostolic church mighty, when she had the Holy Spirit outpoured upon her. The lack of this made the medieval ages dark as midnight, for men contended about words and letters but forgot the Spirit. The return of this inestimable blessing has given us every true revival: the working of the eternal Spirit, the presence of Christ in the midst of his people who is the Sun of Righteousness arising with healing in his wings. (Mal. 4:2) This has been our confidence, as a church, these eighteen years, and if we are yet to see greater and better things, we must still rely on this same strength, the divine presence of Jesus Christ by the wonder-working Spirit. "Not by might, nor by power, but by my Spirit, saith the Lord." (Zech. 4:6)

It becomes, then, the great desire of every earnest Christian who loves the church of God that Christ should be in the church, and that by his Spirit he should work wonders there, and I selected this text with the view of stirring up the spiritual-minded among you to seek so great a blessing. Let me endeavour, in opening up this blessed text, to show the means and the course of action necessary if we would see the church revived by her Lord's presence.

I. First, we learn from the text that before ever we can bring the Well-Beloved into our mother's house (the church), WE MUST FIND HIM PERSONALLY FOR OURSELVES.

We begin with that. "It was but a little that I passed from them, but I found him whom my soul loveth." How can we bring into the chamber of the church him whom we have not yet met within ourselves? How can we communicate grace to others instrumentally unless, first of all, we have received it into our own hearts? I am not now about to speak of the need of conversion; we all know that no spiritual act can be performed until we become spiritual men; but I am now speaking about something higher than bare conversion. If we would bless the church, we must ourselves occupy a higher platform than that of being merely saved; we must be believers, walking in fellowship with Christ, and having, in that respect, found him whom our soul loves. There are many believers who have only just enough grace to enable us to hope that they are alive; they have no strength with which to work for God's cause, they have not an arm to lend to the help of others, neither can they even see that which would comfort others, for they are blind, and cannot see afar off, lacking in all their sight, and all their strength, for themselves. Those who are to bring the Well-Beloved into our mother's house must be of another kind. They must get beyond the feebleness which is full of doubting and fearing into the assurance which grasps the Saviour, and the fellowship which lives in daily communion with him. I know there are some such in this church, and I would single them out, and speak to them thus: "Brother, if you would bring Christ into the church which you love, then, first of all, your innermost soul must so love Christ that you cannot live without his company. This must be your cry: "Saw ye him whom my soul loveth?" And this must be the goal of your aspirations: "I have found him whom my soul loveth." It must not be talk, it must be soul-love; it must not be a profession of affection for Jesus, but the innermost part of our being must be moved by his name. The words are very strong: "…him whom my soul loveth"; as if though the spouse might love the daughters of Jerusalem, might love the watchmen of the city, might love them all in their place; yet her soul's love, the essence of her love, her deepest, fondest, purest, and most real love, was all for him. Are there not such hearts here, virgin minds in whom Christ is first, last, middle, chief, and all in all? Oh, if there are, you are the men, you are the women, who, finding your Beloved, can bring him into the church. May God multiply your number, and may each of you have compassion on the languishing church of this chill age, and labour to restore to her the glory which has faded from her brow. Pray for Laodicea in her lukewarmness, and Sardis in her spiritual death; but you will only prevail in proportion as your innermost soul loves the Redeemer and abides in his love.

These ardent lovers of Jesus must diligently seek him. The chapter before us says that the spouse sought him, sought him on her bed, sought him in the streets, sought him in the broadways, sought him at last at the lips of the watchmen, sought him everywhere where he was likely to be found. We must enjoy the perpetual fellowship of Jesus. We who love him in our souls cannot rest until we know that he is with us. I fear that with some of us our sins have grieved him, and he has taken himself off to the far-off "mountain of myrrh and hill of frankincense." (Song 4:6) It may be our lax living, our neglect of prayer, or some other fault, that has taken from us the light of his countenance. Let us resolve this morning that there shall be no rest in our souls until once again he has returned to us in the fullness of his manifested love, and abide in our hearts. Seek him, brother, seek him, sister. He is not far from any of you; but do seek him with an intense longing for him; for, until you do, you are not the man to bring him into the assembly of the brethren. Labour to bring Jesus into the chambers of the church, but first be sure that you have him yourself, or your zeal will be hypocrisy.

In seeking our Lord, we must use all ministries. The spouse enquired of the watchmen. We are not to despise God's servants, for he is usually pleased to bless us through them, and it would be ungrateful both to him and to them to pass them by as useless. But, while we use the ministries, we must go beyond them. The spouse did not find her Lord through the watchmen; but she says, "…it was but a little that I passed from them, that I found him whom my soul loveth." I charge you, my dear hearers, never rest content with listening to me. Do not imagine that hearing the truth preached simply and earnestly will, of itself, be a blessing to your souls. Far, far beyond the servant, pass to the Master. Be this the longing of each heart every Sabbath-day: "Lord, give me fellowship with yourself." True, we are led to see Jesus sometimes, and I hope often, through listening to the truth proclaimed, but, O Lord, it is no outer court worship that will satisfy us; we want to come into the holy of holies and stand at the mercy-seat itself. It is not seeing you afar off and hearing about you that will content our spirits. We must draw near to you, and behold thee as the world cannot. Like Simeon, we must take thee into our arms or we cannot say that we have seen God's salvation. Like John, we must lean our heads upon the bosom or we cannot rest. Your apostles are well enough, your prophets well enough, your evangelists are well enough. But oh, we feel constrained to go beyond them all, for we thirst after fellowship with you, our Saviour! Those who feel thus will bless the church, but only in this way.

Note that we must search to the very utmost till we find our Beloved. The Christian must leave no stone unturned till he gets back his fellowship with Christ. If any sin obstructs the way, it must be rigorously given up; if there is any neglected duty, it must be earnestly discharged, if there is to be any higher walk of grace, which is necessary to continuous fellowship. We must ascend it, fearing no hill of difficulty. We must not say, "There is a lion in the way" — if there are lions we must slay them; if the way is rough, we must tread it; we must go on hands and knees if we cannot run; but we must reach for fellowship with Jesus; and we must have Christ or pine till we do. Sacrifices we must make and penalties we must endure, but to Christ we must come, for we are feeble when we are absent from him, and quite incapable of rendering any great service to the church till once for all we can say, "I found him, I held him, and I would not let him go." O dear brothers and sisters, I know there are some of you who can enter into what I mean; but I would to God there were many more to whom the first thought of life was Christ Jesus. Oh, for more Enochs, men who walk with God, whose habitual spirit is that of close communion with Jesus, meditating upon him, yes, more than that, sympathising with him, drinking into his spirit, changed into his likeness, living over again his life, because he is in them the monarch of their souls! Oh that we had a chosen band of elect spirits of this race, for surely the whole church would be revived through their influence; God, even our own God, would bless us; and we should see bright, halcyon [happy] days dawning for the bride of Christ. Here, then, is the first point: we must find the Lord Jesus for ourselves, or we cannot bring him into our mother's house.

I would beg every believer here to ask himself a few questions, such as these: "Am I walking in constant fellowship with Christ? If I am not, why not? Is it that I am worldly? Is it that I am proud, or indolent, or envious, or careless? Am I indulging myself in any sin? Is there anything whatever that divides me from Christ my Lord?" Let this be the resolution of every one of the Lord's people: "From this time on, I will seek the Lord my Saviour, and I will not be satisfied until I can say, 'I am coming up from the wilderness leaning upon the Beloved.'"

II. This brings us to the second point of the subject. If we would be a blessing to the church, and have already found Christ, WE MUST TAKE CARE TO RETAIN HIM. "I found him whom my soul loveth; I held him, and I would not let him go."

From this, I learn that in order to be of great use to the church of God, it is needful for those who commune with Christ to continue in that communion. How comparatively easy it is to climb to the top of Pisgah! It needs but a little effort; many bold and gracious spirits are fully equal to it. But to keep there, to abide in that mountain, this is the difficulty. To come to Christ, and to sit down at his feet, is a simple enough thing for believers, and many of us have attained to it; but to sit day after day at the Master's feet is quite another matter. Oh, could I always be as I sometimes am! Could I not only rise above, but remain there! But, alas, our spiritual nature is too much like this weather — it is balmy today; one would think that spring or summer had come; but, perhaps, tonight we may be chilled with frost and tomorrow drenched with rain. Ah, how fickle are our spirits! We are walking with Christ, rejoicing, leaping for joy; and then the cold frosts of worldliness come over us, and we depart from him. You will never be strong to impart great blessings to others till you cease to wander, and learn the meaning of that text: "Abide in me." (Jn. 15:4) Note well, it

297

is not "Look at me", nor "Come near to me, and then go away from me", but "Abide in me". The branch does not leave the vine and then leap back again to the stock; you never saw a living branch of the vine roaming into the corners of the vineyard, or rambling over the wall; it abides in connection with the parent stem at all times, and thus should it be with the Christian.

Mark this, that according to the text, it is very apparent that Jesus will go away if he is not held. "I held him and I would not let him go", as if he would have gone if he had not been firmly retained. When he met with Jacob that night at the Jabbok, he said, "Let me go." (Gen. 32:26) He would not go without Jacob's letting him, but he would have gone if Jacob had loosed his hold. The patriarch replied, "I will not let thee go, except thou bless me." This is one of Christ's ways and manners; it is one of the peculiarities of his character. When he walked to Emmaus with the two disciples, "he made as if he would have gone further" (Lk. 24:28). They might have known it was none other than the Angel of the Covenant by that very habit. He would have gone further, but they constrained him, saying, "Abide with us for the day is far spent." If you are willing to lose Christ's company, he is never intrusive; he will go away from you, and leave you till you know his value and begin to pine for him. "I will go", says he, "and return to my place, till they acknowledge their offence, and seek my face: in their affliction they will seek me early." He will go unless you hold him.

But note, next, he is very willing to be held. Who could hold him if he were not? He is the omnipotent Saviour, and if he willed to withdraw he could do so. Let us hold him as we might. But, mark his condescension. When his spouse said, "I held him, and I would not let him go"; he did not go, he could not go, for his love held him as well as her hands. Christ is willing to be held. He loves that sacred violence which takes him by force, that holy diligence which does not leave a gap open by which he may escape, but shuts every door, bars every bolt, and says, "I have you now, and I will take care that, if I lose you, it shall be through no fault of mine." Jesus is willing enough to be retained by hearts which are full of his love.

And, brethren, whenever you have Christ, please remember that you are able to hold him. She who held him in the Song was no stronger than you are; she was but a feeble woman, poorly fed under the Old Testament dispensation; but you have drunk the new wine of the new covenant, and you are stronger than she. You can hold him, and he will not be able to go from you. "How", say you, "shall I be able to hold him?" Oh, have you grasped him? Is he with you? Now, then, hold him fast by your faith; trust him implicitly, rest in him for everyday's cares, for every moment. Walk by faith and he will walk with you. Hold him also with the grasp of love. Let your whole heart go out towards him. Embrace him with the arms of mighty affection, and enchain him with ardent admiration. Lay hold of him by faith, and clasp him with love. Be also much in prayer. Prayer casts a chain about him, for never leaves the heart that prays. There is a sweet perfume about prayer that always attracts the Lord; wherever he perceives it rising up to heaven, there will he be. Hold him, too, by your obedience to him. Never quarrel with him. Let him have his way. He will stop in any house where he can be master; he will stay nowhere where some other will lords it over his own. Watch his words; be careful to obey them all. Be very tender in your conduct, so that nothing will grieve him. Show him that you are ready to suffer for his sake. I believe that where there is a prayerful, careful, holy, loving, believing walk towards Jesus, the fellowship of the saint with his Lord will not be broken, and may continue for months and years. There is no reason, except in ourselves, why fellowship with Jesus should not continue throughout an entire lifetime, and oh, if it did, it would make earth into heaven! It would lift us up to the condition of angels, if not beyond them, and we should be the ones who would bring Christ into the church, and, through the church, into the world.

298

The church would be blest, and God would be glorified, and souls would be saved, if there were some among us who thus held him, and would not let him go.

I want to call your attention to one thought before I leave this, and that is, when the spouse says, "I held him." Now, a great many people in the world are holding to their creed, and if it is a correct one I hope they will hold it; but that has become the main business of their religious life; they do nothing else but hold this doctrine or that. Hold it, brother, hold it: it would be a pity you should let it go if it is the truth, but still it is more important to hold your Lord. Certain others are engrossed in holding scriptural ordinances and saying, "I hold this and I hold that." Well, hold it brother; if it is God's ordinance, do not let it go. But, after all, if there is anything I hold above all else, I hold him. Is not that the best grip a soul ever gets, when it lays hold of Christ? "I held him and I would not let him go." Ah, Lord, I may be mistaken about doctrine, but I am not mistaken about you. I may, perhaps, be staggered in my belief of some dogma which I thought was truth, but I am not staggered about you. You, the Son of God made flesh for me, you are all my salvation and all my desire: I rest on you only, without a shadow or mixture of any other hope, and I love you supremely, desiring to honour you and obey you in life and till death. I hold you, you Covenant Angel, and I will not let you go.

Dear friends, make this the benchmark of your life, that you hold him and will not let him go. You will be the kind of men to bless the church by leading the Well-Beloved into her chambers, if you know how to abide in him yourselves.

III. It appears from the text that, after the spouse had thus found Christ for herself and held him, SHE BROUGHT HIM INTO THE CHURCH — "I brought him to my mother's house."

We ought lovingly to remember the church of God. By the Holy Spirit, we were begotten unto newness of life, but it was in the church, and through the preaching of the Word there that we were brought into the light of life. We owe our conversion, most of us, to some earnest teacher of the truth in the church of God, or to some of those godly works which were written by Christian men. Through the church's instrumentality, the Bible itself has been preserved for us, and by her the gospel has been preached to every age. She is our mother, and we love her. I know that many of you, dear friends, the members of this church, love the church, and you can say, "If I forget thee, let my right hand forget her cunning." (Ps. 137:5) When you are away from this place, and cannot mix in our solemn assemblies, your heart mourns like one in banishment. Have I not heard you cry, "Zion, Zion, our holy and beautiful house, where we have worshipped our God, the house which is built of living stones, among whom Christ himself is the corner-stone, even your church, O Jesus! Would God I were in her midst again, and could once more unite my praises with those that dwell within her." Yes, and because we love our mother's house, and the chamber of her that conceived us, we desire to bring Christ into the church more and more. Did I hear a harsh but honest voice exclaim, "But, I find much fault with the church?" Brother, if you love her, you will go backward and cast a mantle over all. But, suppose your candour is compelled to see faults in her; then there is so much the more need of her Lord's presence in her to cure those faults. The more sickly she is, the more she wants him to be her strength and her physician. I say, therefore, to you, dear friend, above all things, seek to bring Christ into an imperfect church, and a weak church, and an erring church, that she may become strong in the Lord and in the power of his might. I have shown you by whom it must he — by those who have found him, and who hold him.

Now we will mention the methods by which our blessed Lord can be brought into his church. The saints can bring him in by their testimony. I hope that often Christ is here when I have borne testimony to you of his power to save, of his atoning blood, of his exaltation in heaven, of the perfection of his character, and of his willingness to save.

Many a Sabbath day his name has been like ointment poured out in this place. Is there any subject that so delights you as that which touches upon Christ? Is not that the rarest string in all the harp of scriptural truth? Well, every true minister, by bearing witness for Christ, helps to bring him into the church.

But, others can do it by their prayers. There is a mysterious efficacy in the prayers of men who dwell near to God. Even if they were compelled to keep to their beds, and do nothing but pray, they would pour benedictions upon the church. We want our dear sick friends to get well and come among us at once in full health. But I do not know, I do not know; they may be of more service to the church where they are. "You that make mention of the Lord, do not keep silent, and give him no rest day or night, till he establish and make Jerusalem a praise in the earth." (Is. 62:7) Now, were there not some saints kept awake at night by sickness to pray, we should not so fully realise that word, "Give him no rest day or night." Some of those dear ones, whose faces we miss from among us, keep up the perpetual ministry of intercession. Their incense of prayer goes up at all hours. When most of us are rightly enough asleep, they are compelled to wake, and therefore are led still to pray. How many blessings come down on the church of God through the prayers of his feeble saints it is not possible for us to say; but I believe if all of us were to set apart a special time for praying and pleading with Christ, he would come into his church, and it would not be long before we saw a wonderful effect resulting from those pleadings. Wrestling prayers bring Christ into the innermost chambers of the church of God. Let us try the power of prayer.

And, there is no doubt, dear brethren, that Christ is often brought into the church by the example of those eminent saints who abide in Christ. You know what I mean. There is a very manner and air about some Christians which honours Christ, and benefits his people. They may not be gifted in speech, but their very spirit speaks — they are so gentle, loving, tender, earnest, truthful, upright, and gracious. Their paths, like the paths of God himself, drop fatness. They are the anointed of the Lord, and you perceive it. Perhaps you could not say that this virtue or that is very prominent, but it is there altogether. It is their life at home, their life in public, their church life, their private life, their entire conduct, which makes you see that the Holy Spirit is in them; and when they come into the church, they bring the Spirit of God with them, and are thus a great means of blessing to all with whom they associate. I do pray, brethren, that in some way or other, each one of us may try to bring Jesus Christ into the midst of his own people. I am afraid there are some who, on the contrary, are driving him away — church members that, instead of blessing the church, are a curse to it. I see a great heap before me — a vast heap that God has gathered through my instrumentality; but the winnowing fan is going, and the chaff is flying. Are you, dear friends, among the chaff or the wheat? Are you seed for the sower or fuel for the flame unquenchable? Oh, live near to Christ, live in Christ! May Christ live in you; then you will enrich the church of God; but if you do not, but only make a profession of love with your lips, what can I say to you? I mourn over you. Take heed of living a weak life — a life without God in it, a life without Christ in it, a life which a Pharisee might live. Seek to live the life of a trueborn child of God lest you hinder the church's usefulness, and deprive her of her Lord's presence.

IV. This leads me to the last point, which is this, to CHARGE THE CHURCH THAT SHE BE CAREFUL NOT TO DISTURB THE LORD'S REPOSE.

May we be enabled by divine grace to bring the Lord into the chambers of our mother's house. "I charge you, O ye daughters of Jerusalem, by the roes and by the hinds of the field, that ye stir not up, nor awake my love, till he please."

Observe, then, that the Lord Jesus in his church is not indifferent to the conduct of his people. We are not to suppose that because the sin of all God's elect is pardoned, therefore it is of small consequence how they live. By no manner of means! The Master of this great house is not blind or deaf, neither is he a Person who is utterly careless as to how the house is managed. On the contrary, as God is a jealous God, so is Christ a jealous husband to his church. He will not tolerate in her what he would tolerate in the world. She lies near his heart, and she must be chaste for him. What a solemn work the Lord did in the early church. That story of Ananias and Sapphira — it is often used most properly to illustrate the danger of lying (Acts 5:1-5); but that is not the point of the narrative. Ananias and Sapphira were members of the church at Jerusalem, and they did not lie to men, which would have been sin enough, but, in lying to the church officers, they lied to God, and the result was their sudden death. (Acts 5:1-5) Now, you are not to suppose that this was a solitary case. Wherever there is a true church of God, the judgements of God are always falling on it. I speak now not only what I have read, but what I have known and seen with my own eyes, what I am as sure of as I am sure of any fact in history. The Apostle Paul, speaking of the same in his day, said that in a certain church there was so much sin that many were weak and sickly among them, and many slept (1 Cor. 11:30); that is to say, there was great sickness in the church, and many died. Judgements are begun in the house of God and are always going on there. I have seen men in the church who have walked at a distance from God, who have been visited with severe chastisements; others who have been of a hot and proud spirit have been terribly humbled; and some who have arrogantly touched God's ark, and the doom of Uzzah has fallen upon them. (2 Sam. 6:6-7) I have seen it and I know it. And so it always will be. The Lord Jesus Christ, looking around his church, if he sees anything evil in it, will do one of two things: either he will go right away from his church because the evil is tolerated there, or he will leave that church to become like Laodicea, which went on from bad to worse till it becomes no church at all; or else he will come, and he will trim the lamp, or to use the figure of the fifteenth chapter of John, he will prune the vine-branch, and, with his knife, will cut off this member or the other, and cast them into the fire, while, as for the rest, he will cut them till they bleed again, because they are fruit-bearing members, but they have too much wood, and he wants them to bring forth more fruit. It is not a trifling matter to be in the church of God. God's fire is in Zion, and his furnace in Jerusalem. "His fan is in his hand, and he shall thoroughly purge" — what, the world? Oh no, "his floor", the church. (Mat. 3:3, 7) And then, again, "He shall sit as a refiner and purifier of silver, and he shall purify" (Mal. 3:3) — purify what? The heathen nations? No, "the sons of Levi" — his own people. So Christ is not indifferent to what is going on in the church, and it is needful that when he comes to the church to take his repose, and solace himself there, we should not stir him up nor awake him till he please.

Many things drive our Lord away, and these shall be our closing words. Dear fellow members of this church, may we, each one, be more watchful lest the Bridegroom should withdraw from us. He will go away if we grow proud. If we are boastful, and say, "There is some reason why God should bless us", and should begin to speak critically of weaker brethren, the Lord will let us know that "not unto us, O Lord, not unto us, but unto thy name shall be all the glory." (Ps. 115:1)

Again, if there is a lack of love among us, the Lord of love will be offended. The holy dove does not love scenes of strife; he frequents the calm still waters of brotherly love. There the Lord commanded the blessing, even life for evermore, where brethren dwelt together in unity. (Ps. 133:1) If any of you have half a hard thought towards another, get rid of it. If there is the beginnings of anything like jealousy, quench the sparks. "Leave off strife," says Solomon, "before it be meddled with" (Prov. 17:14), as if he said, "End it before you begin it", which, though it seems strangely paradoxical, is most wise advice. "Little children love one another." (1 Jn. 4:7) "Walk in love as Christ also has loved us." (Eph 5:2) May discord be far from us!

Notice the beautiful imagery of the text. "I charge you by the roes and the hinds of the field..." In ancient times, gazelles were often tamed, and became the favourite companions of Eastern ladies. The gazelle might be standing near its mistress, fixing its loving eyes upon her, but if a stranger clapped his hand, it would hasten away. The roes and hinds "of the field" are even yet more jealous things, for a sound will startle them; even the breath of the hunter tainting the gale puts them to speedy flight. Even thus is it with Jesus. A little thing, a very little thing, will drive him from us, and it may be many a day before our repentance will be able to find him again. He has suffered so much from sin that he cannot endure the approach of it. His pure and holy soul abhors the least taint of iniquity.

Let us gather from the text that there are some things in the true church which give our Lord rest. He is represented here as though he slept in the church: "That ye stir not up nor awake my love till he please." Wherever he sees true repentance, real faith, holy consecration, purity of life, chastity of love, there Christ rests. I believe he finds no sweeter happiness even in heaven than the happiness of accepting his people's prayers and praises. Our love is very sweet to him; our deeds of gratitude are very precious, the broken alabaster boxes of self-sacrifices done for him are very fair in his esteem. He finds no rest in the world, he never did; but he finds sweet rest on the bosoms of his faithful ones. He loves to come into a pure church, and there to say, "I am at home. I will declare thy name unto my brethren: in the midst of the congregation will I praise thee." (Ps. 22:22)

Let us be very watchful, too, against all impurity. Anything like uncleanness in a Christian soon send the Master away from the church. You know what it was that brought the evil upon the house of Eli? It was because his sons made themselves vile even at the tabernacle door. (1 Sam. 3:3) The young people in that case were the immediate cause of the mischief, but it was the fault of the older ones that they did not restrain them. Watch against all evil passions and corrupt desires. "Be ye perfect (holy) even as your Father which is in heaven is perfect." (Mat. 5:48)

And then again, a lack of prayer will send him away. There are members of some churches who never come to the prayer-meetings, and I am afraid that their private prayers cannot be any too earnest. Of course, we are not speaking of those who have good excuse; but there are some who habitually and wilfully neglect the assembling of themselves together; these are worthy of condemnation. Oh, let us continue as a prayerful church, as we have hitherto been, otherwise the Master may say, "They do not value the blessing, for they will not even ask for it; they evidently do not care about my Spirit, for they will not meet together and cry for him." Do not grieve him by any such negligence of prayer.

So, too, we may grieve the Spirit by worldliness. If any of you who are rich get to imitate the fashions of the world, and act as worldlings do, you cannot expect the Lord to bless us. You are Achans in the camp (Josh. 7:18-20), if such is the case. And if you who are poor get to be envious of others, and speak harshly of those to whom God has given more substance than to you, that again will grieve the Lord. You know how the children of Israel in the wilderness provoked him, and their provocation mostly took the form of murmuring; they complained of this and of that: if they had the manna they wanted flesh, and if they had water gushing from the rock they must needs have more. I pray you by the bowels of mercies that are in Christ Jesus, by all the compassion he has manifested towards us, by the high love he deserves of us, since he laid down his life for us, by our allegiance to him as our King, by our trust in him as our Saviour, by our love to him as the Bridegroom of our souls, "...stir not up nor awake my love till he please."

Let me ask you to be more in prayer; let me beg you to live nearer to him; let me entreat you for the church's sake, and for the world's sake, to be more thoroughly Christ's than you ever have been, and may the power of the Holy Spirit enable you in this. I do not fear lest I should lose that which I have wrought, for God will establish the work of our hands among us, but yet I send up to him daily the prayer that this church may not be found in years to come to be a building of wood and hay and stubble, that will be consumed in the fire of heresy or discord, or some other testing flame which God may allow to come upon it. But oh, may you, my beloved brothers and sisters, be gold, and silver, and precious stones, that the workman at the last, may be saved, and not have to suffer loss, nor the Master be dishonoured in the eyes of men. May you stand as a sparkling pile of precious gems, inhabited by the eternal Spirit, to the praise and the glory of his grace, in which he has made us accepted in the Beloved! Amen.

40. THE INTERPRETER

Song of Solomon 3:6-11

That the practical nature of the Song of Solomon may be more clearly seen, we have now before us a passage in which the original form of the Canticle is preserved, and its meaning made more clear by an improved translation,

The first speakers are the DAUGHTERS OF JERUSALEM.

6 What is this coming up from the wilderness,
   As if it were pillars of smoke,
   Odorous of myrrh and frankincense,
   With all the fragrant dust of the merchant?

The FRIENDS OF THE BRIDEGROOM then reply.

7 Behold his Chariot,
   It is Solomon's;
   Sixty valiant men around it
   Of the valiant of Israel!

8 All of them graspers of the sword,
   Trained unto battle;
   Every man his sword by his side
   Against alarm by night.

9 The chariot made him King Solomon,
   Of the trees of Lebanon;

10 Its pillars made him silveren,
   The seat thereof golden,
   Its coverings of crimson,
   The midst thereof inlaid with LOVE
   For the daughters of Jerusalem.

11 Go forth and look, ye daughters of Zion,
   On King Solomon
   In the diadem
   Wherewithal his mother crowned him,
   Upon the day of his espousal,
   And the day of the gladness of his soul.

Then follows a song of THE KING, in which he extols the beauty of his bride.

[See Song chapter 4]

41. THE ROYAL PAIR IN THEIR GLORIOUS CHARIOT

A SERMON DELIVERED ON SUNDAY MORNING,
NOVEMBER 30TH, 1862
AT THE METROPOLITAN TABERNACLE, NEWINGTON

"Who is this that cometh out of the wilderness like pillars of smoke, perfumed with myrrh and frankincense, with all powders of the merchant? Behold his bed, which is Solomon's; threescore valiant men are about it, of the valiant of Israel. They all hold swords, being expert in war: every man hath his sword upon his thigh because of fear in the night. King Solomon made himself a chariot of the wood of Lebanon. He made the pillars thereof of silver, the bottom thereof of gold, the covering of it of purple, the midst thereof being paved with love, for the daughters of Jerusalem. Go forth, O ye daughters of Zion, and behold King Solomon with the crown wherewith his mother crowned him in the day of his espousals, and in the day of the gladness of his heart." (Song of Solomon 3:6-11)

GREAT princes in the east were in the habit of travelling in splendid palanquins, which are, at the same time, chariots and beds. The person reclines within, screened by curtains from public view; a body-guard protects the equipage from robbers, and blazing torches light up the path along which the travellers proceed. King Solomon, in this Song, describes the Church of Christ, and Christ himself, as travelling through the world in such a palanquin. The day is coming when both our divine Lord and his chosen bride shall be revealed in glory before the eyes of all men. The present age is the period of concealment — the mystical Solomon and his beloved Solyma [Jerusalem, Zion] are both on earth, but they are unseen by men; like the ark of old, they dwell within curtains; only the anointed priests of God can discern their beauties, and even these gaze rather by faith than by sight. "Lo I am with you alway, even unto the end of the world" (Mat. 28:20) is certainly true, for Jesus is here; but equally correct is that word of Peter, "Whom having not seen, ye love; in whom, though now ye see him not, yet believing, ye rejoice with joy unspeakable and full of glory." (1 Pet. 1:8) He is here in the reality, power, and influence of his presence, but he is not here as to the visibility of his kingdom and Person, for we wait with our loins girt about, and with patience of hope, until the revelation of Jesus Christ. The portion of the blessed canticle now before us is, we think, descriptive of the progress of the hidden Christ through the world. He has been borne along, in very truth, but he himself has been so little perceived by men that they even ask the question, "Who is this that cometh out of the wilderness?" (6) He is not now manifested openly to men. If any should say, "Lo here!" or "Lo there! this is Christ!" (Mat. 24:23), do not believe them, for Christ is not as yet seen. When he comes, he shall be as perceptible as the lightning's flash, which every man's eye discerns without the need of an instructor. So, like his true Church. She also is hidden like her Lord, and though her hand, her foot, or her face may be sometimes seen, yet the whole elect body has never yet been beheld. If any say, "Lo, here is the Church of Christ!" or "Lo there!", do not believe them, for it is a fact that there is no corporation of men of which we can say exclusively or even universally, "Lo, this is the Church of Christ." There are tares growing with the wheat in the best guarded field, and, on the other hand, no one enclosure contains all the wheat. The true Church of Christ is scattered here and there; it is found among all denominations, and there is not one denomination of which you can say, "This only is the Church of Christ, or all its members belong to the body of Christ's spouse." Just now, the mystical bride is in a certain sense as invisible as her husband. Behold, then, the betrothed ones carried through the world in the sumptuous chariot of which we have to speak this morning.

I must now claim your attention while I notice, first, the glory of the progress of Christ through the world, as described in the sixth verse; secondly, the security of Christ's cause, as represented in the seventh and eighth verses; thirdly, the superlative excellence of it, as described in the ninth and tenth verses; and lastly, our joyful duties with regard to it, as openly declared in the eleventh verse.

I. First, then, THE MAGNIFICENT PROGRESS, THE GLORIOUS ON-GOING OF THE CHURCH AND HER LORD THROUGH THE WORLD. "Who is this that cometh out of the wilderness like pillars of smoke, perfumed with myrrh and frankincense, with all powders of the merchant?"

The equipage excites the attention of the onlooker; his curiosity is raised, and he asks, "*Who is this*?" Now, in the first progress of the Christian Church, in her very earliest days, there were people who marvelled greatly; and though they set down the wonders of the day of Pentecost to drunkenness, yet "they were all amazed, and were in doubt, saying one to another, What meaneth this?" (Acts 2:12) In after years, many a heathen philosopher said, "What is this new power which is breaking the idols in pieces, changing old customs, making even thrones unsafe — what is this?" By-and-by, in the age of the Reformation, there were cowled monks, cardinals in their red hats, and bishops, and princes, and emperors, who all said, "What is this? What strange doctrine has come to light?" In the times of the modern reformation, a century ago, when God was pleased to revive his Church through the instrumentality of George Whitefield and his brethren, there were many who said, "What is this new enthusiasm, this Methodism? Where did it come from, and what power is this that it wields?" And, doubtless, whenever God shall be pleased to bring forth his Church in power, and to make her mighty among the sons of men, the ignorance of men will be discovered breaking out yonder, for they will say, "Who is this?" Spiritual religion is as much a novelty now as in the day when Grecian sages scoffed at it on Mars' Hill. (Acts 17:10-31) The true Church of God is a stranger and pilgrim still, an alien and a foreigner in every land, a speckled bird, a dove in the midst of ravens, a lily among thorns.

The ignorance of men concerning spiritual things is not, however, caused by the darkness of the things themselves, for Christ and his Church are *the great lights of the world*. When great persons travelled in their palanquins, and more especially on marriage processions, they were attended by a number of people who, at night, carried high up in the air burning cressets which gave out a blaze of light. Sometimes these lights were simply torches carried in the hands of running footmen; at other times they were a sort of iron basket lifted high into the air on poles, from which went up a pillar of smoke and flame. Our text says "Who is this that cometh out of the wilderness like pillars of smoke?" — a beautiful illustration of the fact that wherever Christ and his cause are carried, light is a sure accompaniment. Into whatever region the gospel may journey, her every herald is a flash of light, her every minister a flaming fire. God makes his Churches the golden candlesticks, and says to his children, "Ye are the light of the world" (Mat. 5:14), which is certainly as ever God said, "Let there be light" and there was light over the old creation (Gen.1:3), so does he say, whenever his Church advances, "Let there be light", and there is light. Dens of darkness, where the bats of superstition have folded their wings and hung themselves up for perpetual ease, have been disturbed by the glare of these divine flaming torches. The innermost caverns of superstition and sin, once black with a darkness which might be felt, have been visited with a light above the brightness of the sun. "The people which sat in darkness have seen a great light, and to them which sat in the region and shadow of death light has sprung up." (Mat. 4:16) Thus says the Lord to the nation where his kingdom comes — "Arise, shine, for thy light is come, and the glory of the Lord hath risen upon thee!" (Is. 60:1) Bear the Church of Christ to the South Seas; carry Christ and his spouse in his palanquin to the Caffir, the Hottentot, or the Esquimo, and everywhere the night of death is ended, and the morning with its glorious dawn has come. Lift high your lamps, you servants of our Lord. Lift high, lift up the cross of the Redeemer; for in him is light, and the light in the life of men.

But you will tell me that our text rather speaks of "*pillars of smoke*" than of sparkling lamps. Brethren, the smoke is but the effect of the flame, and even the pillar of smoke is luminous. What is the smoke that has attended the Church? What but the deaths of her martyrs, the sufferings of her confessors, the patient endurance of her valiant sons? Wherever she goes, the thick smoke of her suffering goes up to heaven. "We are always delivered unto death" (2 Cor. 4:11), said the Apostle. The cause of truth involves a perpetual sacrifice; her smoke ascends forever. Black smoke, I say, is in the eye of man; but to God it is a sweet-smelling savour. Never did fat of rams, or the fat of kidneys of fed beasts, smell so sweetly before the Most High as the faith, the love, the courage, which has ascended up to heaven from the dauntless heroes of the Church in past ages, when, at the stake, they have been faithful even unto death. Suffering and grief and woe are the lot of the spouse of the despised and rejected Saviour, but all these are as nothing if she may scatter that terrible blackness which blinds the face of man, and makes him a stranger to his God.

It often happens that oriental monarchs of immense possessions are not content with burning common coals in these cressets, but frequently consume sandal-wood and other woods which give out a delightful smell; or else, if they use ordinary coals, they sprinkle upon them frankincense and myrrh, so that a delicious perfume is spread on all sides. In the olden times, they also went to great expense in obtaining drugs, which the merchants collected from all parts of the earth, and these were carefully compounded into the renowned "*powders of the merchants*", which yielded a delicious variety of delicate perfumes, not to be produced by any one aromatic essence. Our inspired poet describes the travelling procession of the royal pair, and does not fail to dwell on the delightful perfume of myrrh and frankincense, with all the powders of the merchant, which make the wilderness smell as a garden of roses. Wherever the Church of Christ proceeds, though her pathway is a desert, though she marches through a howling wilderness, she scatters the richest perfume. The pages of history were only worthy to be blotted in oblivion were it not for the sweet odours which the Church has left upon it. Look at all past ages, and the track of the Church is still redolent with all the richest fragrance of human virtue and divine grace. Wherever the Church advances, she makes manifest the savour of the knowledge of Christ in every place! Men believe in Jesus, and to the Lord faith has all the fragrance of myrrh. They love Jesus; and love in the esteem of heaven is better than frankincense. Loving Christ, they endeavour to be like him, till patience, humility, brotherly-kindness, truthfulness, and all things that are honest, lovely, and of good repute, like "powders of the merchant", are spread abroad throughout the whole earth. Tell me where the Church is not, and I will tell you where sin reigns; tell me where Christ and his Church are carried, and I will tell you where you will find every virtue that can adorn humanity, and every excellence that can magnify the excellence of the grace of God. If you would find an antidote for the deadly exhalations which lurk among this world's deserts of sin, if you would destroy the foul pestilence which reigns in the darkness of heathenism, of Popery, and of infidelity, cry to the Mighty One, "Arise, you unknown traveller, arise, and bid your servants carry you into the midst of all this misery and death! The light of your flaming torches shall scatter the darkness, and the burning of your precious perfumes shall say to evil, 'Fold your wings!', and to the pestilence of sin, 'Get back unto your den!'"

Among the ten wonders which Jewish tradition ascribes to the Temple, we find that the rain never extinguished the fire of the wood which was laid in order upon the altar, nor did the wind ever conquer the pillar of smoke so as to disperse or bend it. Truly it is so with the Church of God, as she comes out of the wilderness; for who shall quench her flaming lamp, or stay the incense of her golden censers? Ride on, Great Prince, and bear your spouse with you in your majestic chariot, till you have lit the world with your divine light, and have made it a temple filled with a cloud of incense of sweet smell to the nostrils of Jehovah!

II. We have, secondly, to notice THE SECURITY OF CHRIST'S CHURCH AT ALL TIMES.

Of course when travelling through a wilderness, a royal procession was always in danger of attack. Arabs prowled around; wandering Bedouins were always prepared to fall upon the caravan; and, more especially, was this the case with a marriage procession, because then the robbers might expect to obtain many jewels, or, if not, a heavy ransom for the redemption of the bride or bridegroom by their friends. What shall I say of the attacks which have been made upon the Church of Christ, and upon Christ himself? They have been incessant. When one form of evil has been routed, another has presented itself. Evil teems with children. The frogs and lice of Egypt were not more numerous than the enemies of the Lord's anointed and his bride. Every day produces new battles. These attacks arise from all quarters; sometimes from the world, and sometimes, alas, from even professed members of the Church. Adversaries lurk everywhere, and, until the Church and her Lord shall be revealed in the splendour of the Millennium, having left the wilderness forever, we must expect to find her molested on every side. My dear brethren, we know that Christ's cause in the world is always safe because of divine protection, and because the legions of God's angels keep watch and ward over the saints. But we have something more tangible than this. Our gracious God has been pleased to commit to *men* the ministry of Christ. "For unto the angels hath he not put in subjection the world to come, whereof we speak." (Heb. 2:5) The Lord has ordained that chosen men should be the protectors of his Church; not that they have any power of themselves to do anything, but He girds the weak with strength, and makes the feeble mighty. So then, men, even the sons of men, stand in array around the travelling palanquin of Christ to guard both the bridegroom and the bride.

Read the 7th and 8th verses carefully, and you will notice that *there are enough swordsmen* — "Threescore valiant men are about it." There are always enough men chosen by God to guard the Church. Poor Unbelief holds up her hands and cries — "Ah, the good men are all dead; Zion is under a cloud; the Lord has taken away the great men; we have no valiant defenders of the faith, none such as this crisis may require!" Ah! Unbelief, let the Lord say to you, as he did to Elias — "Yet have I left me seven-thousand in Israel, all the knees which have not bowed unto Baal." (1 Kings 19:18) There shall be just as many warriors as the crisis requires. We do not know where the men are to come from, but the Lord will provide. There may be sitting in the Sunday school today a child who shall one day shake this nation from one end to the other; there may be even here, unknown, obscure, and unobserved, the man whom God will make strong to rebuke the infamous infidelity of our age. We do not know where the anointing rests. We, in our folly, would anoint Eliab or Abinadab, but God has chosen David, the shepherd's boy, and he will bring him forward and teach him how to hurl the stone at Goliath's brow. Do not tremble, neither be afraid; for God who makes man, and makes his mouth, will find the sixty men when the sixty is needed. "The Lord gave the word; great was the company of them that published it." (Ps. 68:11) "The glory of the Lord shall be revealed, and all flesh shall see it together, for the mouth of the Lord hath spoken it." (Is. 40:5)

Observe that these warriors *are men of the right mettle*. "Yes", says poor trembling Little-Faith, "we have hosts of men, but they are not like the great-hearts of old; they do not have the qualifications which the age requires." Ah! but remember, around the bed of Solomon there are "threescore *valiant* men"; and glory be to my Master, that while I may not flatter the ministry, I must not dishonour him by believing that he has left his Church without *valiant* defenders. There are Luthers still living who bid defiance to all adversaries,

308

men who can say, "We count not our lives dear to us that we may finish our course with joy, and fulfil the ministry which the Lord has delivered to us." Do not fear; you may not at present know the valour of the Lord's body-guard, but when the Church's battle grows hotter than just now, suddenly there shall be seen a champion stalking to the front of the battle, and men shall say, "Who is this? How he wields that battle-axe! How he splits the armour of his foes! See how he piles them heaps on heaps, and mounts that hill of slaughtered enemies to smite a greater foe! Who is this?" And the answer shall be, "This is a man whom God has found; the world did not know him, but God has trained him in the camps of Dan, and now the Spirit moves him to smite the Philistines."

"Ah!" I think I hear you say, "But though there may be so many men, and men of the right sort, I am afraid *they are not in the right place*." Look again at the text. It is written — "Threescore valiant men are ABOUT IT"; that is, there are some on that side, and some on this side, some before, and some behind; they are all round the travelling chariot of Christ". "I wish there might be one in our parish", says someone. Pray for him, and he who has promised to send you all good things may yet send him to you. "Pray ye the Lord of the harvest that he may send forth labourers into his harvest." (Mat. 9:38) It is singular how God sometimes raises a mighty man in this denomination, then in that, and then in the other. Suppose any body of Christians should try to monopolise all the valiant men themselves; why, they could not do it, because every side of the royal bed must be guarded, and in his own place each man is set for the defense of the gospel! The Church is compassed about with mighties who are under God to do great exploits. If the Lord guides the flight of sparrows, surely he knows how to dispose his ministers; and let the Church be well content to let them occupy their posts until the wilderness is past, and the glory shall be revealed. The Church often makes mistakes, and thinks she can make ministers, or at least choose their position. She can do no such thing. God sends the valiant man; and all you can do is to recognise his valour, and accept him as your champion. Beyond that, you cannot go; this is God's work, not man's. A minister made by men, made valiant by human strength, had better take himself at once ignominiously to his tent, for his disgrace will be certain. God, who sends the men, knows where to put them, so that they may stand round about the bed, and leave no corner unprotected.

Notice that these men *are all well armed*. The text says expressly, "They all hold swords". What swords are these? Every valiant man in Christ's Israel holds "the sword of the Spirit, which is the Word of God." (Eph. 6:17) A man who is a good textuary will usually be a good divine; he who draws from the treasury of the written Word will find his spoken word to be fruitful in profiting the people of God. If we use worldly reason, if we rely upon refinement, argument, eloquence, or any other form of the wisdom of man, we shall soon find our enemies will defeat us; but to ply the Word right and left, to give gospel cuts and strokes such as the devil himself cannot parry, this is to overcome the world through the Word of God. Besides this, and here is an opportunity for you all to carry swords — every valiant man in God's Israel carries the sword of prayer, which is comparable to those huge two-handed swords of the olden times, which the soldier lifted up and brought down with such tremendous force as to cleave a man in half. Prayer is a weapon which no man can effectively resist. If you know how to use prayer, bring it down on your foeman's head, and woe to him! I would to God that in this Church there were found many of these valiant men of Israel! Indeed to God, may all the Lord's servants be prophets, that it might be said of all of you that you are holding swords. Your holy lives can be swords with which to smite your enemies. The tongues with which you speak of Christ lovingly, tenderly, persuasively — these may be weapons against our common enemy. Oh, that when we hear the muster roll at last, it may be said of every Church-member that he held a sword! Do not tremble, you timid ones, for the ark of the Lord; neither let your fears promote your unbelief. God knows full well how to give the right weapons to the right men, and his Church shall be secure even to the end.

309

Further, my brethren, these men are not only well armed, *but they are well trained*. They are all expert in war: men who have endured temptations themselves; men whose souls have been exercised; men who have slain both the lion and the bear, and are men of war from their youth. Christian ministers especially should be no novices, but both in the school of temptation, and in some school of the prophets, they should be disciplined for the fight. May there be such found here! I look out daily for such among you as are taught by God, and much of my time is spent with our college, with men, and means, and above all with his Spirit. Fools are not the men for this age. We want a sound knowledge of doctrine, practical power in preaching, and a thorough insight into the human heart; and where these by earnest prayer can be found in a man and further developed by careful teaching, so we are bound to give our aid. Such men should be looked after, and no pains should be spared to bring them out. In fact, dear friends, you ought to think it a high honour to be allowed to help in putting such men into working order. Oh, how I groan to get my friends to feel the importance of sending out trained young ministers! I give my time and my substance cheerfully, but when will the Christian Church help in this matter as it should?

Furthermore, these men were not only well-trained, but you will see *that they were always ready*. Each man has his sword upon his thigh, ready to be drawn out. I know some nominal ministers who seem to me to carry no sword at all. They keep a sheath, a very handsome sheath, with a hilt at the top and a stick inside. What is the good of such men? We want men to have *swords* in their sheaths, men who can speak with power, and have the demonstration of the Spirit and its power resting on them. Such men should wear their swords where they are to be got at, so that, when the adversary comes, they may dash at him at once. Rejoice, O daughter of Zion, your Lord has not left you, even at this day, without some such men! Observe also that these men were *watchful*, for "they had their sword on their thigh because of fear *in the night*." They never sleep, but watch out always for the Church's interest. Pray that the Lord may raise up many such, who, night and day with tears, will watch for the souls of men, and against the enemies of our Israel.

Dear friends, some of you may, at times, be alarmed when you hear of attacks made on the Bible. At one time, it was thought that ethnology would prove that the human race could not be one; and Moses was terribly abused by some who said it was not possible that all of us could have come from one pair. That battle was fought, but you hear nothing of it now. It is over; learning and argument in the hand of God has routed those antagonists. Then they pelted us with shells, and bones of lizards. Geology threatened to dig our graves; but we have lived all through that struggle, and we have found geology to be a great blessing, for it has shed new light on the first chapter of Genesis, and made us understand a great deal better what it meant. Another Amalekite advances to the combat; this time it is with figures and numbers. We are to be speared with arithmetic, and slain with algebra! And what will be the result of it? Why, it will do the Bible a world of good, for we shall understand it better. I thank God whenever the Bible is attacked; for all those who know the times and seasons, begin to study just that part of Scripture more carefully, and then we get a clearer light shed on it, and we find ourselves more confirmed than ever that this is the very truth, and that God has revealed it to us. "Well, but who will take this matter up?" I do not know, and I do not particularly care, but I know my Master has his threescore valiant men round about his bed, and that each man has his sword on his thigh because of fear in the night, and never mind what the battle may be. The end of it will be for God's glory, and there shall be progress with the chariot of Christ through that which seemed as if it must overthrow it. Cast aside your fears; rejoice, and be glad, O daughter of Zion! Your Lord is with you in the travelling chariot, and the threescore valiant men are watching out against your foes.

III. Meanwhile, reposing in peace, let us notice THE EXCELLENCE OF THIS CHARIOT IN WHICH JESUS RIDES.

It is not difficult to convey to people mostly unacquainted with Eastern manners and customs an idea of what this palanquin is. It is a sort of large sedan in which one or two people may recline with ease. Of course, this palanquin could not be made of gold or silver because then it would be too heavy for carriage; it must be made of wood. Hence, King Solomon made a bed, or chariot, or palanquin, from the wood of Lebanon. Then there needed four pillars supporting the covering and the curtains; the pillars are of silver. The bottom of it should be something massive, in order to sustain the weight of the person; so its bottom is of gold. The canopy on the top is a covering of purple. Since to lie on gold would be very unpleasant, it is covered with delicate, daintily wrought carpets; and so we have its bottom "paved", or rather carpeted, with love for the daughters of Jerusalem. Some delicate devices of needlework adorn the bottom of this bed-chariot in which the king and his spouse recline during their journey. The doctrines of the gospel are comparable for their antiquity, and for their sweet fragrance, for their incorruptibility is as the wood of Lebanon. The gospel of Christ never decays; Jesus Christ is "the same yesterday, today, and for ever". (Heb. 13:8) Not one single truth bears any sign of rot. And to those souls that are enlightened from above, the gospel gives out a fragrance far richer than the wood of Lebanon.

No beams of cedar or of fir,
Can with thy courts on earth compare;
And here we wait, until thy love,
Raise up to nobler seats above.

And when we hear our Jesus say,
"Rise up, my love, make haste away!"
Our hearts would fain outfly the wind,
And leave all earthly loves behind.

(Isaac Watts)

I rejoice to know concerning you as a Church that the more you understand the doctrines of grace the better you love them. You are confirmed in the present faith, and well you may be, for our doctrine is worthy of your confidence. We are not afraid that any truth which Christ has uttered should be tried by the most stringent criticism, for not one single stone of all the bulwarks of Gospel doctrine can ever be removed out of its place. When cedars of Lebanon have yielded to the worm, even then shall the truth as it is in Jesus will remain the same. As for the silver pillars which bear up the canopy, to what should I liken them but to *the attributes of God* which support and guarantee the efficiency of the great atonement of Christ, beneath which we are sheltered? There is the silver pillar of God's *justice*. He cannot, he will not, smite the soul that hides beneath the cross of Christ. If Christ has paid the debt, how is it possible that God should visit again a second time the iniquity of his people, first on their Surety, and then again on themselves? Then stands the next, the solid pillar of his *power*. "They shall never perish, neither shall any pluck them out of my hand; my Father which gave them me is greater than all, and none is able to pluck them out of my Father's hand." (Jn. 10:28) Then on the other side is the pillar of his *love*, a silver pillar indeed, bright and sparkling to the eye — love unchanging and eternal, strong as the power of, and fast as, the justice which bear up the canopy on the other side. And here, on this side, stands *immutability*, another column upon which the atonement rests. If God could change, then might he cast away his blood-bought; but "because I am God and do not change, therefore you sons of Jacob rejoice." As for the *covering of the chariot*, it is of purple. I need not tell you where it was dyed. No Tyrian

311

hues are mingled here. Look up, Christian, and delight yourself in that blood-red canopy which shelters you from the sun by day, and from the moon by night! From hell and heaven, from time and from eternity, you are secured by this covering which is of purple. Oh, tempting theme to dilate upon the precious and glorious doctrine of atonement! Whenever our adversaries assail the Church, whatever may be the apparent object of their animosity, their real one is always the same — a desperate hatred for the great truth that "God was in Christ reconciling the world unto himself, not imputing their trespasses unto them". (2 Cor. 5:19) Well, as they hate it, let us love it; and in it let us take our greatest delight.

As for the *bottom of this palanquin*, which is of gold — may not this represent the eternal purpose and counsel of God, that purpose which he formed in himself or ever the earth was? Pure was the decree of God, holy, wise, just, for his own glory, and most true; and as the precious things of the Temple were all of gold, well may the basis of eternal love, an immutable and unchangeable decree, be compared to much fine gold. I do not know, brethren, how it is with you, but I find it most pleasant to have as the basis of my hope, the firm decree of God. Atonement covers me, I know, but still on this I must rest, for Jehovah wills it. God decrees it, he has said it, and it must be done; he has commanded and it stands fast. Oh, that golden sovereignty, on which is written — "I will have mercy on whom I will have mercy; it is not of him that willeth, nor of him that runneth." (Rom. 9:16) Dear brethren, the Apostle plainly tells us that this is the basis on which even the silver pillars rest, "for he hath blessed us with all spiritual blessings in Christ Jesus, according as he hath chosen us in him from before the foundation of the world." (Eph. 1:3-4) Then, to make this all soft and pleasant to recline upon, here is a "paving" of needlework, soft cushions of love on which to rest. There is a double meaning here, for both the bride and bridegroom find rest in love. Our Lord finds rest in the love of his people. "Here will I dwell for ever." As it were, they make these carpets of needlework in their love and affection for him, and in their trust and confidence in him; and here he rests. On the other hand, our Beloved spent his life to work for us as our bed of rest, so that we must translate it "love *of*," as well as love *for*, the daughters of Jerusalem." *We* rest in Christ's love; *he* rests in our love. Come, I need not explain further, brothers and sisters. Take your rest now to the full. You are married to Christ; you are one with him; betrothed to him in faithfulness, embraced in the arms of his affection. Do not fear the noise of archers; the "threescore valiant men" protect you, and the king himself embraces you. Now solace yourself with him; take your fill of his sweet society, and say to him from the bottom of your heart, "Let him kiss me with the kisses of his mouth, for his love is better than wine." (Song 1:2) Leave fighting for the proofs to the valiant men who can do it. As for you, you daughters of Jerusalem, rest upon your Lord's bosom. Leave conflict to the men ordained to fight, the men expert in war. As for you, be expert in communion; understand the motions of Jesus' heart; look to the lustre of his loving eyes; behold his beauties; be ravished with his divine affection to you; and now let your soul be satisfied with favour, and be full of the loving-kindness of the Lord!

IV. We close, then, by noticing THE DUTY OF EVERY BELIEVING HEART newest in connection with the subject.

Let every believer, while he recognises himself as part of the Church inside the palanquin, yet look upon himself personally as one of the daughters of Zion, and let us each *go forth* this morning to meet King Solomon. It is not King David; for King David is the type of Christ up to the time of his crucifixion — "despised and rejected of men, a man of sorrows and acquainted with grief" (Is. 53:3), and yet King of the Jews. King Solomon is the type of Christ ever since the day when,

They brought his chariot from above,

312

To bear him to his throne.

(James Fanch)

Then stands the next, the solid pillar of his *power*, and, with sound of trumpet, conducted him to his Father's presence-chamber above. Now we read of King Solomon; King Solomon for wealth, for wisdom, for dignity, for honour, for peace. But "a greater than Solomon is here". (Mat. 12:42; Lk. 11:31) He is the "Wonderful, the Counsellor, the Mighty God, the Everlasting Father, the Prince of Peace" (Is. 9:6), and therefore he is King Solomon going forth. Get up from your beds of sloth; rise from your chambers of ease; go forth, go forth to pray, to labour, to suffer; go forth to live in purity, leaving Babylon behind; go forth to walk with him alone, leaving even your kinsfolk and acquaintance if they will not follow with you. Therefore, why do you tarry at home when the King is abroad? "Behold the Bridegroom cometh, come ye forth to meet him" (Mat. 25:6), *and behold King Solomon*. Today, let your eye rest upon him. Let your eye behold the head that today is crowned with glory, wearing many crowns.

Behold, you too, his hands which once were pierced, but are now grasping the sceptre. Look to his girdle where swing the keys of heaven and death and hell. Look to his feet, once pierced with iron, but now set upon the dragon's head. Behold his legs, like fine brass, as if they glowed in a furnace. Look at his heart, and that bosom which heaves with love for you; and when you have surveyed him from head to foot, exclaim, "Yea, he is the chief among ten thousand, and altogether lovely". (Song 5:16) Does sin prevail? Behold King Solomon. Have doubts and fears arisen? Behold King Jesus. Are you troubled, and does your enemy annoy you? Look up to him; behold King Solomon. I pray you to remember the light in which you are to behold him. Do not think that Christ has lost his former power. Behold him as he was at Pentecost, *with the crown with which his mother crowned him in the day of his espousals*. Oh, how glorious was our Lord when the Church crowned him with her zeal, and the arrows went abroad, and three thousand fell slain by his right hand to be made alive by the breath of his mouth! Oh, how these early saints crowned him when they brought of their substance and laid it at the apostle's feet, neither did any man count that anything he had was his own! They crowned him with their heart's purest love; the Church had on her brow her bridal-wreath, and her husband wore his nuptial crown. Behold him today as wearing that crown still, for he is the same Christ, and go forth to meet him, and labour for him, and love him as the first saints did.

Do not forget that his mother is to crown him soon in the day of his espousals. He is our brother as well as our husband, and the Church is *his* mother as well as ours. Oh, she is to crown him soon! The day of his espousals draws near. Hark! I hear the trumpet sound! Jesus comes, and his feet stand on Mount Olivet; kings and princes lick the dust before him; he gathers sheaves of sceptres beneath his arm even as the mower gathers wheat with the sickle. He treads on principalities and powers, the young lion and the dragon he tramples under foot. And now his saints cry, "Hosanna, blessed is he that cometh in the name of the Lord." (Mk. 11:9) The long expected one is come, and his mother crowns him in the day of his espousals! Courage, poor heart, courage! Go forth and see King Solomon today as he is to us, and remember:

Behold what wondrous grace
The Father hath bestowed
On sinners of a mortal race
To call them Sons of God!

Nor doth it yet appear
How great we must be made;

But when we see our Saviour here,
We shall be like our Head.

We would no longer lie
Like slaves beneath the throne;
My faith shall Abba, Father, cry,
And Thou the kindred own.

(Isaac Watts)

When we look on *Him*, let us rejoice that this is to be our glory. We are to put off this sackcloth and put on scarlet and fine linen. The dust is to be wiped from our brow, and the sweat from our face; the shackles are to be taken from our wrist, and the gyves [fetters] from our legs; and we are to be emancipated, ennobled, glorified, made partners with Christ in all his splendour, and taught to reign with him, world without end.

But there are some here that I can hardly call the daughters of Jerusalem, yet they are always round about Zion's gate. Oh, there are many of you who are always listening to our voice and joining in our hymns, and yet you have not seen our Master yet! Go forth; leave your sinful pleasures, and leave your self-righteousness too; go forth and behold King Solomon. Look to Jesus, sinner, bleeding on the cross, and as you look, love and trust; and I know that as soon as you have seen him and trusted him, you will have a crown to put on his head. It will be the day of your espousal to him, and you will crown him with such a crown. You will decorate that crown with jewels dug from the secret mine of your deepest heart, and, having made this crown, you will put it on his head, and fall down before him, and sing,

All hail the power of Jesu's name,
Let angels prostrate fall;
Bring forth the royal diadem,
And crown him Lord of all.

(Edward Perronet)

Well, then, we will lay aside every fear, and continue all day gazing on our matchless Christ, adoring him, exalting him, and having fellowship with him. For all is well; his travelling chariot is always safe, and soon he will step out of it with his bride at his right hand, and the world will be astonished to behold the beauties of the royal pair when he is exalted, and those that are with him, before the presence of his Father and all the holy angels!

42. PAVED WITH LOVE

NO. 1134

A SERMON DELIVERED ON LORD'S-DAY MORNING,
SEPTEMBER 28TH, 1873
AT THE METROPOLITAN TABERNACLE, NEWINGTON

"...the midst thereof being paved with love, for the daughters of Jerusalem."
(Song of Solomon 3:10)

THIS portion of the Song describes the royal bridegroom as travelling up from the wilderness in an eastern palanquin, attended by his bodyguard, and by those who bear torches and burn perfumes. We have a description of the sumptuous chariot-bed in which this great monarch travelled, describing it as being made of cedar-wood, with pillars of silver, a base of gold, curtains of purple, and then, within it, a tessellated floor, with a pavement, not of precious stones, but of priceless love. Metaphor is suddenly dropped in this last item, and the result is a complicated, but very expressive, form of speech. Some regard the expression as signifying a pavement of stone, engraved with hieroglyphic emblems of love, which made up the floor of this travelling chariot; but this would surely be very uncomfortable and unusual, and therefore others have explained the passage as referring to choice embroidery and dainty carpets, woven with cost and care, with which the interior of the travelling-chair was lined. Into such embroidery, sentences of love poetry may have been worked. Needlework was probably the material of which it was composed; skilful fingers would there set out emblems and symbols of love. As the spouse in the second chapter sings, "His banner over me was love" (Song 2:4), probably alluding to some love word upon the banner. Thus, probably, tokens of love were carved or embroidered, as the case may have been, upon the interior of the chariot, so that "the midst thereof was paved with love, for the daughters of Jerusalem." We need not, however, tarry long over the metaphor, but endeavour to profit by its teaching.

This palanquin (or travelling chariot) in which the king is carried represents the covenant of grace, the plan of salvation, and, in fact, the whole system by which the Lord Jesus comes down in mercy among men, and by which he bears his people along with himself through the wilderness of this world, onward to the rest which he has prepared for them. It is, in a word, the mediatorial work of Jesus. The ark was carried through the wilderness preceded by the pillar of cloud and fire, as a symbol of the divine presence in mercy, and here we have a somewhat similar representation of the great King of grace, borne in regal splendour through the world, and bearing his elect spouse with him. May it be ours to be made to ride like Jeshurun upon the high places of the earth in happy fellowship with him whose goings forth were of old, even from everlasting. (Mi9c. 5:2)

I. I beg you first, to notice, this morning, THE GROWTH WHICH IS INDICATED HERE AS TO OUR VIEWS OF THE COVENANT OF GRACE.

The description advances step by step, each sentence mentioning an additional and far-enhanced preciousness. Thus do those who study the work of salvation prize it more and more. At first glance, the sweet singer who speaks in this song perceived that the chariot was made of cedar, a costly wood; a closer view revealed "the silver pillars, beauteous to behold": further observation showed "the basis all of burnished gold." From cedar to silver, and from silver to gold, we have a clear advance as to the precious material. On looking again, the observer remarks "the top of princely purple", which is yet more precious as a type of imperial dignity, and a token of that effectual atonement which was wrought out by the ensanguined stream of Calvary. The blood which dyed that purple canopy is much

315

more precious than gold that perishes, though it is tried with fire. And then, though one would think there could be no advance beyond the precious blood, the song proceeds yet one step further, for we find that "the midst thereof was paved with love, for the daughters of Jerusalem."

Beloved, the whole way of salvation was devised by the Lord Jesus Christ. It is all his planning, and all his own carrying out. Hence the Song says, "King Solomon made himself a chariot of the wood of Lebanon." (Song 3:9) Jesus is the sole author and finisher of our faith; salvation is his from first to last; every part of the covenant reveals his master-hand. This is the glory of the whole, and this the believing eye perceives at very first glance, and is thereby made glad. But further knowledge reveals other bright and glorious facts, and, as the matter is considered, wonder and gratitude increase. Let us, then, take a brief survey of this glorious gospel chariot, such a wondrous thing — Jehovah's covenant of grace. The first item is, that it is made of "the wood of Lebanon". The finest wood on the earth was that of the cedar, and the finest cedars were those that grew on the Lebanon range. The Lebanon cedars, indeed, appear to have possessed qualities not found in the common cedar with which we are acquainted. That which was reckoned the best wood is used as the token of the super-excellence of the covenant of grace. Cedar, moreover, was not only the most costly wood, and the most esteemed, but is one of the most lasting. London says that it is particularly valued for its durability, fit type of that "everlasting covenant ordered in all things and sure" (2 Sam. 23:5), of which not one jot or tittle shall ever fail. Heaven and earth shall pass away, but the word on which we trust shall abide for ever. In addition to its other excellencies, cedar-wood exhales a sweet perfume, so that a chariot of cedar would not only be very lasting but very delightful to ride in, even as at this day we joy in God's salvation, and are filled with peace through believing. When we look at the covenant of salvation, at the very first glimpse of it we see that there is none like it: many schemes have been imagined and preached up as ways of salvation. But not one of them can be likened to the method of atonement by blood, reconciliation through a substitutionary sacrifice, redemption by the incarnate God, salvation all of grace from first to last. When this is compared with a chariot, no timber less noble than the sweet-scented fir, cut from the monarch of Israel's royal forest, could worthily set it forth. Lies and vanity make up all other plans, but this is royal truth. Other ways of salvation have been tried, but they have soon proved to be failures: the worm of human depravity has eaten into the choicest wood that was ever felled in the forests of human merit; decay has seized on all the goodly oaks of unaided human endeavours; and rottenness has devoured all fleshly boastings. But the cedar-wood of our hope in Jesus has shown no sign of crumbling to decay, and it never will. There is in the atonement made by Christ a perpetuity of prevalence; it has availed for sin, and will avail to the very end of time, so that whoever confides in it has a hope which will not deceive him. I dare await the test of a long and afflicted life, or of a sudden and painful death, for the ground of my hope is undisturbed by outward circumstances; like the cedar, it is adapted to abide all weathers. As surely as the body of the Lord saw no corruption, so surely shall my hope never turn to despair, and, even if it be buried, it shall rise again. What consolation such a hope affords us! And for this reason, as perfume comes forth from cedar-wood, so fragrant comforts come pouring forth from the salvation which Jesus Christ has wrought for us. It is a pleasant, as well as a safe thing, to rest in what Christ has done. Our joy is greatest when our faith in him is most simple; the bare cedar-wood is most fragrant. We derive from every part of his work some joy: every part of it smells most sweetly; he is all happiness, all consolation, all bliss to us; and when our spirit casts itself on him in perfect simplicity, it breathes a perfumed atmosphere, delicious and reviving. If such is the first and lowest item in the description of the chariot, what will the richer portions be?

We now look more closely at the royal chariot, and note well the four pillars which support the canopy; and, as we gaze, we find that they are of silver — something more precious than cedar-wood, for the salvation of Jesus grows on us, and to us, who believe he is more and more precious. There are some pictures so well painted that you may examine them with a magnifying glass, and, instead of detecting defects, you will perceive yet greater beauties. So may you examine the work of our blessed Lord microscopically, if you choose; the more you look the more you will marvel, for he is so really glorious, so intrinsically precious, so infinitely to be admired. And what are these pillars, do you think, which support the canopy, and add such beauty to the chariot? What are they but divine holiness and infinite purity? Silver is constantly used in Scripture as a type of that which is precious and pure — "As silver tried in a furnace of earth, purified seven times." (Ps. 12:6) And, O beloved, how holy the gospel is; the Lord's Word is very pure in itself, and very improving to those who receive it. Wherever the true gospel is preached, it promotes holiness, and, in so doing, acts according to its nature, creating its like. There is not a doctrine of the gospel which is not according to godliness, none of its blessings making provision for the flesh, none of its precepts encouraging sin, none of its promises winking at iniquity. The spirit of the gospel is the spirit of holiness always; it wages determined war against the lusting of the flesh, and consequently the gospel is abhorred by the unclean. It lays the axe at the root of sin, and, like a fire, devours all evil. As for the Lord Jesus Christ himself, is he not immaculate holiness? If you would see holiness embodied, where can you look but to the Person of our well-beloved Master? Where are his imperfections? Can you find a flaw either in his language or in his actions, in himself or in the spirit that moved him? Is he not altogether perfect? Look, then, at the gospel, the way of salvation, and the covenant of grace, and you will see holiness conspicuous everywhere, but especially when you come to deal with the centre of the gospel, the great atoning sacrifice.

Four silver pillars hold up this crimson canopy. The blood red propitiation covers us from the wrath of God, and the holiness of God holds up this interposing medium. He is not unrighteous to forget the blood of the atonement. Because he is a just God he is now the Saviour of those who are sheltered beneath the reconciling blood of Calvary. The Lord could not forgive sin till first the honour of his law had been vindicated; but that being done, the selfsame honour requires that the atonement should be respected and the believing sinner saved. When we see Christ on the cross, we learn how God's inflexible justice, like unbending pillars of pure silver, holds up aloft the crimson shelter of vicarious death, beneath which the saints are secure. Even to save his own elect, Jehovah would not mar his integrity, nor suffer his great white throne to be stained with injustice. He is no respecter of persons, and, when sitting on the throne of judgement, even his own chosen whom he loves with everlasting love must be treated with the same impartiality as his enemies. This he has effected by accepting his Son in their place, and exacting from him those penalties which were due from them, but might be justly received at the hands of their federal Head. There is no injustice in the salvation of the believer, there is not even an abatement of the claims of just retribution; all is done openly, and so as to challenge the severest examination. Conspicuously before the eyes of all, the silver pillars of purity bear up the sacred atonement. Is not this a matter for superlative delight?

But we look more closely, and discern what would not have been perceived at a distance, "the bottom" of the chariot-bed "is of gold", the most precious metal of all. This is to indicate that the foundations of salvation are imperishable, and unchangeably precious. The basis of grace is laid in the immutable purpose and unchanging decree of God, and in the everlasting, undiminished, unchangeable love of God towards his dear Son, and to those who are in him. Blessed be God for a salvation which will not yield under pressure, or fail us in our hour of peril! It is no base metal, but gold tried in the fire. I cannot understand those who think that God loves his people one day and hates them the next; that though he knew what they would be, and knew that they would fall into sin, yet he resolved to take them to himself as his children for a little while, and then afterwards to disinherit them. God forbid I should ever understand a doctrine so dishonouring to the

Lord, who does not change. My own love for my children makes me feel that they must be my children as long as *they* live and *I* live; and surely God's children must, and shall be, his children while God himself shall live and his people shall exist. Beloved, the basis on which we rest as saved sinners is not the shifting foundation of our own feelings, doings, prayings, and resolvings. If our salvation depended on our good behaviour, we might as well build on the clouds, and pile up bubbles as our cornerstones. Yes, and if it rested on our own unaided faith, if there were no guarantee of grace to keep that faith alive, but all rested on the exercise of faith by us, it were better never to have had a hope of salvation at all than to have had such a wretched, unsubstantial mockery, certain to end before long in fatal disappointment. You and I have not so learned Christ. We have left the miry clay for the solid rock. (Ps. 40:2) God has made an eternal purpose concerning his people, and that will never be changed. Infinite love ordained their salvation, and will never reverse its decree, though day and night should cease. Infinite power guarantees the fulfilment of the divine purpose, and what can stand against omnipotence? A complete atonement has been made already, and it will never lose its efficacy; therefore those for whom it was wrought must be saved. There is, moreover, an indwelling Spirit who has come into God's people, to abide with them forever according to the covenant promise, "I will dwell in them, and I will walk in them. I will be their God, and they shall be my people." (2 Cor. 6:16) Our spiritual life does not hang on a thread, as it would do if it were in our own keeping, but it depends on Jesus; for has he not said, "Because I live ye shall live also"? (Jn. 14:19) Nothing can be more secure than the salvation of the soul that believes in Jesus, for it rests in God alone. Of the chariot of salvation, we may say with quaint Ralph Erskine,

Its bottom is a groundwork sure
Of pure and solid gold,
From bankrupt beggary to secure,
From falling through to uphold.

Let us view the royal canopy of the chariot: "the covering thereof is of purple." As the king and his bride travelled, they needed to be screened from the sun's baleful rays; and lo, over the head of the spouse hangs a regal covering of purple. Look up, my soul, and see what interposes between your God and you! He must smite you, for you are a sinner; but you are covered and sheltered, and are living happily. What is it that shields you? What, indeed, but the atoning blood!

Ah, who can view that purple covering
And turn away unmoved, insensible?
Who can discern it, and forget that day
When impious greetings shouted forth disdain,
When, crowned with thorns, the Man of sorrows stood
In purple robes of cruel mockery;
Despised, rejected, yet a king indeed,
Whom they shall see hereafter on his throne.

The atonement shelters us: never was a soul injured by the rays of God's justice when hidden beneath this purple; and never shall there be. There is no repose for the conscience anywhere else, but there is perfect repose here. I often hear theories about what Christ did, which reminds me of Dr. Duncan's description of Robertson of Brighton: "Robertson believed that Christ did something or other, which somehow or other had some connection or other with salvation." This may suit others, but is of no use to me. I feel that if Christ did not actually and literally die as my Substitute, the just for the unjust, I am not saved, and never can be at rest in my heart again. I renounce all preaching whatever if substitution is not the leading feature of my theme, for there is nothing worth preaching when that is gone. I regard that doctrine as the fundamental truth of the gospel,

318

which, denied, you have slain the gospel, and which, cast into the background, you have covered the gospel with a cloud. That Jesus Christ was made sin for us that we might be made the righteousness of God in him; that though he was just, he was treated as a sinner, and, in our room and place and stead, suffered the wrath of God due to us; this is the kernel and vital heart of the gospel. Conscience tells everyone that God must punish sin; its voice, more or less loudly, always proclaims that sin must be punished. This is no arbitrary arrangement, it is inevitable; sin and suffering have a natural relationship. If God is just, sin must bring evil consequences upon the man who commits it; and until conscience understands that this evil was borne by Christ, that he suffered what ought to have been suffered by the sinner, and that he was justly a substitute because he was the head and Adam of those for whom he died — until, I say, the conscience knows this, it cannot find rest. Get under the blood-red canopy, and then you are at peace, but not till then. Hence, you find that whenever God revealed himself to his people, the most apparent thing was always the blood: Abel must bring a bleeding lamb, and Noah a slaughtered beast. When the Lord feasted with his chosen in Egypt, the blood adorned the lintel and the two side-posts of every house in which he revealed his saving power. When he marched through the wilderness, one of the coverings of his tabernacle was made of rams' skins dyed red; and all within and around the holy courts themselves were perpetual sprinklings of blood, for almost all things were, under the law, purified by blood (Heb. 9:21); the voice of the law always proclaiming what the gospel proclaims too, that "without shedding of blood there is no remission of sin." (Heb. 9:22) Our Saviour's life must end in blood upon the tree; and before that closing scene, his last feast of love, his communion with his disciples, had for its most conspicuous provision the cup of red wine in which his blood was symbolised. Every time he sets out visibly his communion with his people here below, the wine must be poured out. God cannot, and will not, reveal himself to man except through the medium of the perfect satisfaction by the pouring out of the life of *he Substitute in the place of the sinner.

"*The covering thereof is of purple*." Oh, it is not for these lips to tell how precious that purple is! It is not possible even for this heart to know how precious is the blood of the Son of God, the vital blood which, out of love for us, he poured out freely for our redemption. Sit at your ease, my brothers and sisters in salvation, rejoicing as you look upward, and let no doubts nor fears, mistrusts nor suspicions, vex you, for beneath the blood-red canopy you are secure.

There is yet one more step — we rise from the blood to the love which caused it to flow, and we read of the royal chariot — "The midst thereof was paved with love, for the daughters of Jerusalem", not merely the bottom covered with it, but, as in a carriage, the whole vehicle lined with something soft to sit on, and lean against. So the whole covenant of grace is, within, garnished and beautified, and made delightful to the believer's soul, by the sweet love of God in Christ. The covenant is love in its secret places, all love, unalloyed love, invisible love, and nothing else but love. When one comes to know most of the covenant, and admires the wisdom, the power, the purity, the eternity of all that God has done, yet the most striking characteristic of it to the advanced Christian is the love, the mighty love of God, by which he is brought by Jesus Christ into eternal salvation. You have crowned me with loving kindness; you have loved my soul out of the pit; you have loved me, and given yourself for me. Your love has redeemed me with a price most precious; your love has made me what I am; your love carries on the work, and your love will complete it, and present me to you in its own perfect image; for "the midst of it is paved with love, for the daughters of Jerusalem."

The point we have proved is this, that everything in the study of the gospel grows on you. I earnestly exhort you, therefore, to meditate much in the Scriptures, to consider much the Person and character of your Lord, to meditate full and often on his beauties, and on all

319

the work he has done on your behalf. Do not be satisfied with a superficial survey, as many Christians are. These are not the days of contemplation as the old Puritan times were, for we are too apt to be superficial; but do remember that while there are nuggets of gold on the very surface of Scripture, yet the most valuable mines of gold are far down, and you must dig into them. Pray God that you may be well taught in the things of Christ! There are some sciences in which you can master all that is worth knowing in a short time, and the further you go in the study the more you perceive that nothing is very certain, and you soon get weary of it. But the science of Christ crucified grows on you; you get more assured of the facts of it, and more intensely delighted in them. I exhort you, therefore, to sit constantly at the Master's feet with Mary, and I pray that each one of us may know, by following on to know the Lord, what is "the breadth, and length, and depth, and height; and to know the love of Christ, which passeth knowledge" (Eph. 3:18-19)

II. We shall now NOTE THE POSITION FROM WHICH THE LOVE MENTIONED IN OUR TEXT IS BEST SEEN. "The midst thereof is paved with love."

It is not, therefore, to be seen from the outside. The mere outsider understands nothing of the love of God to his people as displayed in the covenant of grace. I am certain that there are many of you here present who have heard the gospel for years, and yet no more know the sweetness of it than the floor I am standing on. A man may pass the door of the London Tavern or the Mansion House for years, and yet have no notion of the banquets within, for these are indoors, and you must enter to partake of them. Savoury vapours floating from the festive board may awaken a transient imagination, but no more. The cock on the dunghill turned over the diamond, and, according to the fable, remarked that he cared very little for it, for he would sooner have found a grain of barley! So many hear of the sweetness of true religion, but they do not have the taste or the ability to perceive its sweetness. O unregenerate hearer, you will never know how sweet the gospel is! It is impossible you should while you remain in the state you are now in. But I tell you, if you could get half a glimpse of the joy which even the poorest Christian has, you would never rest content until you have enjoyed it too. If men said concerning Naples, "See Naples and die" because of its beauty, I might say to you, it was worthwhile dying a thousand deaths to get a glimpse of Christ. When once your faith has perceived his beauty, you will wonder how you could have been satisfied to be blinded so long. What must it be to be forgiven all your sins and to know it? What must it be never to be afraid of death, to be able to look forward to departing from this world as a thing longed for, and not dreaded? What must it be to be able to look up and say, "God is my Father, and I feel that I am his child"? "What must be the joy and bliss of having familiar fellowship with God, so that you are called his friend, as Abraham was of old? (Ex. 33:11) I wish I could start your mouths watering after these things. If you had but a little taste of them, you would long for more; but until the Lord grant you that taste, all we can say of the love of Christ will hold no charm for you. The love which lines the chariot of salvation is not to be known by those who remain outside; "the secret of the Lord is with them that fear him, and he will show them his covenant." (Ps. 25:14)

And so note next, when the Christian himself stands apart from his Lord, and judges by outward appearances, he cannot perceive, as once he did, the loving kindness of the Lord. Providence grows dark as a winter's day. The tried believer cries, "My wife has been taken from me; my property is melting away; my business fades; I am sick in body and weary in soul; I cannot see a trace of the love of God to me in all this." Brother, the description in the Song does not say that the chariot is plated with love on the outside, but is paved with love *within*, "in the midst of it." Oh that you had faith to believe that the heart and real core of every providence is love! The exterior of it may be as a thorn hedge, but sweet fruit ripens within. "Oh", says you, "but I have looked at the Bible lately, and as I have glanced over its once-cheering promises, they appear to smile at me no more. Some of the words grate very harshly on my ear, and almost condemn me." I do not wonder, for although I can, at this moment, see love in the very outside of Scripture, yet there are times when I cannot, when I can only, feel as if every text thundered at me, and out of God's own mouth come heavy sentences against me. Beloved, it does not say — I repeat it — that the exterior part of this palanquin was adorned with self-apparent love, but that love was in the midst. If you stand examining the exterior of providence, and the mere letter of the Word, and begin to judge and try your God, I should not wonder if little enough of love should be conspicuous to you. Look into the heart of God and read what he has written there. When faith takes a step up, and mounts to the inside of the chariot of grace, she finds that it is paved with love for the daughters of Jerusalem.

Come and sit side-by-side with Jesus in his chariot of grace, his bed of rest. Come and recline with him in hallowed fellowship. There is room enough for you, and strength enough to bear your weight. Come now, and be carried with him who carried all your cross. Sit down with him who, in his hands and in his side, bears the memorials of his dying love for you. What company you have, and what royal accommodation is provided for you! I think I sit in the chariot with the Beloved now, and I begin to look around me. I catch a glimpse of the purple above my head, and remember the unspeakable love which bled and died for sinners. I look at the silver pillars which support the covering, and how infinite holiness stands fast, and, in love for me, secures my perfection. I place my foot on the golden bottom of the chariot and know that divine power is pledged by love to preserve and bear me through. I see above me, and around me, and beneath me, nothing but love — the free, unbounded love of God.

Now, beloved, indulge yourselves with a glance around you for a minute. Look back to old eternity; let your eyes peer through the mists which hide that ancient age before the ages began! What do you see there but love, "according to his eternal purpose which he purposed in Christ Jesus or ever the earth was"? Look a little closer; see the Garden of Eden and the fall — what strikes your eye there but love? The seed of the woman shall bruise the serpent's head. Look to the cross, and at God incarnate here below; behold Jesus living in suffering, and dying in shame! Here love comes to her climax, and lays bare all her matchless charms. Look to the time of your own life. Was not love present at your birth, perfuming your first breath? Were you not nursed in love, cradled in love, and wrapped in love? Have you not since then, even in your sinfulness, been loved with an exceeding great and wondrous love? Did not love turn your heart of stone into flesh? Has not love dwelt in you since then even to this day? Have not even your trials been sent in love? Blind unbelief calls it severity; look now, as Jesus sits at your side, and say, was it not the wisest form of love that smote you, and made you cry out in bitterness? Oh, I do remember this day nothing in the dealings of God with me but love. I sat down last night, as this text charmed my spirit, and tried to think over my whole life, if perhaps I might light upon some unkindness of my God to me. But my solemn witness is that, from the first day my life began to beat, from the first hour I knew anything of the Lord whatever, all his dealings have been love, love, love, love, love, love alone — nothing else but love. Of my life, I can and must say, "The midst thereof has been paved with love."

Look at the tessellated pavement of love beneath your feet for a moment. Do you not see the Father's love? — that golden mass of uncreated love, for the Father himself loves you. Look at Jesus' love, another diamond pavement beneath your foot. Jesus loved you to the death with a love that many waters could not quench or floods drown. Look at the love of the Spirit, too: equally precious is the tender affection of the loving Comforter. Think how the Holy Spirit has borne with you, has striven with you, and endured your bad manners in the wilderness, and blessed you still. Look at those delightful embroideries from the divine needle — the precious promises. A thousand promises there are, but they are all love. Look down and see how all the attributes of God are engaged for you, but they are all in

321

league with love. Look, then, at all the providences of God towards you, at all the exercises of his grace in your heart, and you will see many and strange colours of varied beauty, all blending in one wondrous pattern of deep, unsearchable love. I cannot speak this morning, my tongue fails me; but I feel the love of Jesus in my own soul, and I pray that you may feel it in yours. Of this one thing be assured: that as it was in the beginning, it is now, and ever shall be, love, love, love, right on, forever and forever. The Lord who has begun to love you will never cease from doing so. The midst of the covenant of grace is paved with love for the daughters of Jerusalem.

III. I want you to notice THE PECULIAR POSITION OF THE PAVEMENT OF LOVE DESCRIBED IN THE TEXT. It is "in the midst" of the chariot, and only from its midst can it be seen.

It is in the midst of it; and therefore Jesus rides upon it, and his espoused ones ride upon it. It is a very simple thought, but it richly deserves to be beaten out a little. Jesus is represented here as the King in the chariot, and as the chariot is lined with love, we are taught that Jesus dwells in love. Where is he now? Among the thrones and principalities above, but he abides still in love. Love brought him down from heaven to earth; love conducted him in all his weary journeys over the acres of Palestine; love led him to the garden, the death-sweat, and the cross; and equally at this hour love attends him. He loves in heaven as he loved below. Whatever he is doing, whatever he is feeling, whatever he is saying, we know this one thing about him, he dwells in love for us. He is in his chariot, and all around him in that chariot is love.

The chariot was a royal one, and, as the king rode along, he was reigning, but he was reigning in love, and it is so with Jesus. All things are in his hands, and he governs all things in love for his people. Heavenly principalities serve him, and angels are his willing messengers; but there is no power which Jesus has that he does not wield in love for us. Has his power seemed sometimes to be exercised harshly? It is not so; it cannot be so. He reigns in love. Our Joseph is lord over all Egypt, and since Joseph loves his brothers, the good of all the land of Egypt is theirs. Jesus rules all the world for his people's benefit; all things are theirs, whether things present or things to come, all are theirs. Jesus reigns in love.

And Jesus rests in love. This chariot was a place for the traveller to rest in; he reclined as he was carried along. Nothing gives Jesus such rest as his love in his people. It is his solace and his joy. It is almost inconceivable by us that Jesus should derive joy from the fact that he loves us, but so it is. That text we read on Thursday evening comes again to our recollection — "He will rest in his love, he will joy over thee with singing." (Zeph. 3:17). [Sermon 2720, delivered earlier in 1859] It is a joy for Christ to love his people. His own heart finds a joy in their joy, a heaven in their heaven. To see them saved is bliss to him. Oh, how glad we ought to be of this! Jesus rests in love.

But as the traveller rested, he also proceeded on his way; the bearers carried the palanquin from place to place, and the traveller made progress, but always with the same surroundings within his curtained bed. So Jesus, in all his glorious marchings, in everything he does or is yet to do, still marches on in love. Read the Book of Revelation, and think of the trumpets, and the falling stars, and the opened vials full of judgements, and you may well tremble; but then fall back on the doctrine of the Scriptures, and say, "These are the goings forth of my Lord the King, but he always rides in a chariot which is paved with love for the daughters of Jerusalem." So let him come with earthquake and with flame, if he so chooses. Let him come. Let him even loose destroying angels to smite the earth; and let the whole world before his coming rock and reel, and all men's hopes depart like visions in the night, I will not fear, for sure am I that he cannot come except in love to me. No judgement can bring wrath to his people, no overturning can overturn their hopes, no rod of iron can shatter their bliss. This is surely a thought which should make your spirit glad.

Now, notice that as Jesus rides in this chariot, so do you, O believer, and at this moment your standing is upon love. You stand up in this palanquin on love. You are accepted in the Beloved; you are not judged according to the law, but you are judged according to grace; you are not estimated at the judgement seat by what you have done, but according to his abounding mercy. Recline this morning in the love of God. Ah, take your rest in it! As the rich man tries to find solace in his riches, and the strong man in his strength, and the great man in his fame, so stretch yourselves, and lie at ease on this glorious bed of almighty love.

And, beloved, take care that when you labour to make progress, you still make it in the power and energy of his love. Do not strive after virtue and grace by the law, for you will never get them. The chariot in which you rest is also the chariot in which you are to be carried forward towards perfection. Grow in grace, but keep to the cross. Cling still to the love of God in Christ Jesus, for that always keeps you safe. You sleep in it, you wake in it, you eat and you drink in it. Wherever you are, love surrounds you. It is in the atmosphere you breathe; it is to be found in every place wherever you roam. You are never out of the love which is in the midst of the chariot.

These are things not to be talked of so much as to be thought over. Carry them home, and if you have leisure this afternoon, try to mark, learn, and inwardly digest this precious truth — "The midst thereof is paved with love for the daughters of Jerusalem."

IV. To close, DWELL ON THAT LOVE itself just for a moment.

Remember, it is a special love: it is not love for all men. There is some consolation in universal benevolence, but here we go deeper, and rejoice in love for the daughters of Jerusalem. There is an electing, discriminating, distinguishing love, which is settled upon a chosen people — a love which goes forth to none beside, but only to them; and it is this love which is the true resting place of the saint.

It is love undeserved, for what daughter of Jerusalem ever deserved that our glorious King should fall in love with her? It is a love, therefore, which is a theme for eternal wonder. Why did you love me, Redeemer? Why did you make a covenant of grace with me, and line that covenant with immutable love? This love is everlasting and eternal. It never had a beginning, and it never will have an end. Simply as I have stated the truth, it is a nut with heaven for its kernel. You were always loved, O believer, and you always shall be, come what may.

It is love unrivalled, for never was there such affection as that which Christ has for his chosen, love unexampled, to which none of us shall ever reach. We should seek to love as God has loved us, but to the infinite, the boundless degree, we shall never arrive. There is no love like the love of God in Christ. It is love which to us has become, this day, our brightest thought, our truest comfort, and our most potent incentive. Law rules the slaves of this world, but love rules the freemen of the world to come. The ungodly, if they do right after a fashion, do it from fear of punishment or hope of reward; but the true-born children of God find in the love of Christ their sole motive: they are obedient not because they are afraid of being lost — they know they never will be: not because they hope to get to heaven by their good works — they have heaven already by the works of another, guaranteed to them by the promise of God. They serve God out of pure gratitude for what they have received, rejoicing as they work in the service of one they love so well.

323

Beloved, may the love of God be shed abroad in your hearts by the Holy Spirit this morning, and all the days of your lives, and oh that many who have never tasted of that love may be made to long for it, that they may be made alive by it, and to God shall be glory! Amen and Amen.

TEN SERMONS ON THE SONG OF SOLOMON

CHAPTER 4

43. THE INTERPRETER

Song of Solomon 4:1-7

(Song of THE KING)

1 Lo thou fair one,
  My companion.
  Lo thou fair one!
  Thy Eyes are doves within thy locks;
  Thy Hair like a flock of the goats,
  That hang adown Mount Gilead.

2 Thy Teeth like a flock of sheep even shorn,
  That had come up from the washing,
  That are all of them twin-bearing,
  And bereft not one among them.

3 Like a line of scarlet are thy Lips,
  And thy speaking beauteous;
  Like to a pomegranate cloven
  Are thy Temples through thy locks.

4 Like the Tower of David is thy Neck,
  Builded for an armoury,
  With a thousand shields hung upon it,
  All bucklers of the mighty;

5 Twain breasts of thine like a pair of fawns,
  Twinlings of the roe,
  That are feeding among the lilies.

6 Until breathe the day,
  And flee away the shadows,
  I will go my way
  To the Hill of Frankincense —
  Thou art all fair,
  My Love, and no spot in Thee.

In the first Song (chapter 3), the king is seen in his travelling palanquin or chariot-bed, coming up from the wilderness. We may expound the picture as representing our Lord and King going up into his glory from this wilderness world. Mark the sweet odours of his merits, and the smoke of his sacrifice, observe also the attendant angels, as Milton calls them, "the helmed cherubim and the sworded seraphim," who, having kept watch, around him in the wilderness, now attend him to swell the pomp of his ascension. Thus will Jesus come a second time, and his church shall go forth and gaze upon him. That glorious chariot of love, whose purple canopy well sets forth the atoning blood, is his salvation in which in which the church rides and rests with her Lord. Happy those who are in the faith!

The song in which the king extols his bride will be understood by those who know that the imputed righteousness of the Lord Jesus puts upon the saints a perfect comeliness, so that they are "all fair" in the sight of God. Every single line has its meaning, and spiritual minds will find great delight in reading the works of such writers as John Gill, or James Durham, or Alexander Moody Stuart, upon this priceless book.

44. FRAGRANT SPICES FROM THE MOUNTAINS OF MYRRH:
THE FIRST BUNDLE

A COMMUNION ADDRESS AT MENTONE

PRINTED IN SWORD AND TROWEL, JUNE 1865

"Thou art all fair, my love; there is no spot in thee."
(Song of Solomon 4:7)

HOW marvellous are these words! "Thou art all fair, my love; there is no spot in thee." The glorious Bridegroom is charmed with His spouse, and sings soft canticles of admiration. When the bride extols her Lord, that is no wonder, for He deserves it well, and in Him there is room for praise without possibility of flattery. But does He who is wiser than Solomon condescend to praise this sunburnt Shulamite? 'Tis even so, for these are His own words, and were uttered by His own sweet lips. No, do not doubt, O young believer, for we have more wonders to reveal! There are greater depths in heavenly things than you have, at present, dared to hope. The Church not only is all fair in the eyes of her Beloved, but in one sense she always was.

In God's decree, her form he viewed;
All beauteous in his eyes she stood,
Presented by the eternal name,
Betrothed in love, and free from blame.

Not as she stood in Adam's fall,
When guilt and ruin covered all;
But as she'll stand another day,
Fairer than sun's meridian ray.

Then justice on sweet mercy smiled,
And truth with peace was reconciled;
The scene so vast, each one amazed,
They kissed and, lost in wonder, gazed.

O glorious grace, mysterious plan,
Too great for angel mind to scan!
Our thoughts are lost, our numbers fail,
All hail, redeeming love! All hail!

(Augustus Montague Toplady)

He delighted in her before she had either a natural or a spiritual being, and, from the beginning, could say, "My delights were with the sons of men." (Prov. 8:31) Having covenanted to be the Surety of the elect, and having determined to fulfil every stipulation of that covenant, he, from all eternity, delighted to survey the purchase of His blood, and rejoiced to view his Church in the purpose and decree, as already by him delivered from sin, and exalted to glory and happiness.

Oh, glorious grace, mysterious plan
Too great for angel-mind to scan,
Our thoughts are lost, our numbers fail;
All hail, redeeming love, all hail!

328

(John Kent)

Now, with joy and gladness, let us approach the subject of Christ's delight in his Church, as declared by him whom the Spirit has sealed in our hearts as the faithful and true Witness. (Rev. 3:14)

Our first bundle of myrrh lies in the open hand of the text.

I. CHRIST HAS A HIGH ESTEEM FOR HIS CHURCH.

He does not blindly admire her faults, or even conceal them from himself. He is acquainted with her sin in all its heinousness of guilt, and deserving of punishment. That sin he does not shun to reprove. His own words are, "As many as I love, I rebuke and chasten." (Rev. 3:19.) He abhors sin in her as much as in the ungodly world, no, even more so, for he sees in her an evil which is not to be found in the transgressions of others — sin against love and grace. She is black in her own sight (Song 1:5-6). How much more so in the eyes of her Omniscient Lord! Yet there it stands, written by the inspiration of the Holy Spirit, and flowing from the lips of the Bridegroom, "Thou art all fair, my love; there is no spot in thee." How then is this? Is it a mere exaggeration of love, an enthusiastic canticle, which the sober hand of truth must strip of its glowing fables? Oh, no! The King is full of love, but he is not so overcome with it as to forget his reason. The words are true, and He means us to understand them as the honest expression of his unbiased judgement, after having patiently examined her in every part. He would not have us diminish anything, but estimate the gold of his opinions by the bright glittering of his expressions; and, therefore, in order that there may be no mistake, *he states it positively:* "Thou art all fair, m love", *confirming it by a negative:* "there is no spot in thee." When He speaks *positively,* how complete his admiration! She is "fair", but that is not a full description; he styles her "all fair." He views her in himself, washed in his sin-atoning blood, and clothed in his meritorious righteousness, and considers her to be full of comeliness and beauty. No wonder that such is the case, since it is but his own perfect excellence that he admires, seeing that the holiness, glory, and perfection of his Church are his own garments on the back of his own well-beloved spouse, and she is "bone of his bone, and flesh of his flesh." (Gen. 2:23) She is not simply pure, or well-proportioned; she is positively lovely and fair! She has actual merit! Her deformities of sin are removed; but more, she has, through her Lord, obtained a meritorious righteousness by which an actual beauty is conferred upon her. Believers have a positive righteousness given to them when they become "accepted in the Beloved." (Eph. 1:6.)

Nor is the Church barely lovely; she is *superlatively so.* Her Lord styles her, "Thou fairest among women." (Song 1:8.) She has real worth and excellence which cannot be rivalled by all the nobility and royalty of the world. If Jesus could exchange his elect bride for all the queens and empresses of earth, or even for the angels in heaven, he would not, for he puts her first and foremost — "fairest among women." Nor is this an opinion he is ashamed of, for He invites all men to hear it. He puts a "behold" before it, a special note of exclamation, inviting and arresting attention. "*Behold*, thou art fair, my love; *behold*, thou art fair." (Song 4:1.) His opinion, he publishes abroad even now, and, one day from the throne of his glory, he will avow the truth of it before the assembled universe. "Come, ye blessed of My Father" (Mat. 25:34) will be his solemn affirmation of the loveliness of His elect.

Let us mark well *the repeated sentences of his approbation*.

329

Lo, thou art fair! lo, thou art fair!
Twice fair thou art, I say;
My righteousness and graces are
Thy double bright array.

But since thy faith can hardly own
My beauty put on thee;
Behold! behold! twice be it known
Thou art all fair to Me!

(Ralph Erskine)

He turns again to the subject, and a second time looks into those doves' eyes of hers, and listens to her honey-dropping lips. It is not enough to say, "Behold, thou art fair, my love". He rings that golden bell again, and sings again, and again, "Behold, thou art fair."

After having surveyed her whole person with rapturous delight, he cannot be satisfied until he takes a second gaze, and, afresh, recounts her beauties. Making but little difference between his first description and the last, he adds extraordinary expressions of love to manifest his increased delight.

"Thou art beautiful, O My love, as Tirzah, comely as Jerusalem, terrible as an army with banners. Turn away thine eyes from me, for they have overcome me: thy hair is as a flock of goats that appear from Gilead. Thy teeth are as a flock of sheep which go up from the washing, whereof every one beareth twins, and there is not one barren among them. As a piece of a pomegranate are thy temples within thy locks…My dove, my undefiled is but one; she is the only one of her mother, she is the choice one of her that bare her." (Song 5:4-7, 9.)

The beauty which He admires is *universal*. He is as much enchanted with her temples as with her breasts. All her offices, all her pure devotions, all her earnest labours, all her constant sufferings, are precious to his heart. She is "all fair." Her ministry, her psalmody, her intercessions, her alms, her watching, all are admirable to him, when performed in the Spirit. Her faith, her love, her patience, and her zeal, are alike in esteem as "rows of jewels" and "chains of gold." (Song 1:10) He loves and admires her everywhere. In the house of bondage, or in the land of Canaan, she is ever fair. On the top of Lebanon, his heart is ravished with one of her eyes, and in the fields and villages he joyfully receives her loves. He values her above gold and silver in the days of his gracious manifestations, but he has an equal appreciation of her when he withdraws himself, for it is immediately after he said, "Until the day break, and the shadows flee away, I will get me to the mountain of myrrh, and to the hill of frankincense" (Song 4:6), that he exclaims, in the words of our text, "Thou art all fair, my love." At all seasons, believers are very near the heart of the Lord Jesus, always as the apple of His eye and the jewel of His crown. Our name is still on his breastplate, and our persons are still in his gracious remembrance. He never thinks lightly of his people; and certainly, in all the compass of His Word, there is not one syllable that looks like contempt of them. They are the choice treasure and peculiar portion of the Lord of hosts; and what king will undervalue his own inheritance? What loving husband will despise his own wife? Let others call the Church what they may, but Jesus does not waver in his love to her, and does not differ in his judgement of her, for he still exclaims, "How fair and how pleasant art thou, O love, for delights!" (Song 7:6.)

Let us remember that he who pronounces the Church and each individual believer to be "all fair" is none other than the glorious Son of God, who is "very God of very God." Hence, his declaration is decisive, since infallibility has uttered it. There can be no mistake

330

where the all-seeing Jehovah is the Judge. If He has pronounced her to be incomparably fair, she is so beyond a doubt; and, though hard for our poor puny faith to receive, it is nevertheless as divine a verity [truth] as any of the undoubted doctrines of revelation.

Having thus pronounced her *positively* full of beauty, he now confirms his praise by *a precious negative*: "There is no spot in thee." As if the thought occurred to the Bridegroom that the carping world would insinuate that he had only mentioned her comely parts, and had purposely omitted those features which were deformed or defiled, He sums all up by declaring her universally and entirely fair, and utterly devoid of stain. A spot may soon be removed, and is the very least thing that can disfigure beauty, but even from this little blemish, the Church is delivered in her Lord's sight. If He had said there is no hideous scar, no horrible deformity, no filthy ulcer, we might even then have marvelled; but when he testifies that she is free from the slightest spot, all these things are included, and the depth of wonder increased. If he had but promised to remove all spots, we should have had eternal reason for joy; but when he speaks of it as already done, who can restrain the most intense emotions of satisfaction and delight? O my soul, here is marrow and fatness for you; eat your full, and be abundantly glad of it! Christ Jesus has no quarrel with his spouse. She often wanders from him, and grieves his Holy Spirit, but He does not allow her faults to affect his love. He sometimes chides, but it is always in the tenderest manner, and with the kindest intentions — it is "My love" even then. There is no remembrance of our follies, he does not cherish bad thoughts about us, but pardons and loves as well after the offence as before it. It is well for us it is so, for if Jesus were as mindful of injuries as we are, how could he commune with us? Many a time, a believer will put himself out of humour with the Lord for some slight turn in providence, but our precious Husband knows our silly hearts too well to take any offence at our bad manners.

If He were as easily provoked as we are, who among us could hope for a comfortable look or a kind salutation? But he is "ready to pardon...slow to anger." (Neh. 9:17) He is like Noah's sons, when he goes backward, and throws a cloak over our nakedness; or we may compare him with Apelles, who, when he painted Alexander, put his finger over the scar on the cheek, that it might not be seen in the picture. "He has not beheld iniquity in Jacob, neither has he seen perverseness in Israel" (Num. 23:21); and, hence, he is able to commune with the erring sons of men.

But the question returns — How is it so? Can it be explained so as not to clash with the most evident fact that sin remains even in the hearts of the regenerate? Can our own daily bewailings of sin allow anything like perfection as a present attainment? The Lord Jesus says it, and, therefore, it must be true; but in what sense is it to be understood? How are we "all fair" though we ourselves feel that we are black, because the sun has looked upon us? (Song 1:6.) The answer is ready, if we consider the analogy of faith.

1. In the matter of justification, the saints are complete and without sin. As [James] Durham says, these words are spoken "in respect of the imputation of Christ's righteousness wherewith they are adorned, and which they have put on, which makes them very glorious and lovely, so that they are beautiful beyond all others, through His comeliness put upon them."

And Dr. John Gill expresses excellently the same idea, when he writes, "...though all sin is seen by God, *in articulo providentiae* (in the matter of providence) where nothing escapes his all-seeing eye, yet *in articula iustificationis* (in the matter of justification), he sees no sin in his people, so as to reckon it to them, or condemn them for it; for they all stand 'holy and unblameable and unreproveable in His sight.'" (Col. 1:22) The blood of Jesus removes all stain, and His righteousness confers perfect beauty; therefore, in the Beloved, the true believer is at this hour as much accepted and approved in the sight of God as

331

Christ is when He stands before the throne in heaven. The beauty of justification is at its fullness the moment a soul is, by faith, received into the Lord Jesus. This is righteousness so transcendent that no one can exaggerate its glorious merit. Since this righteousness is that of Jesus, the Son of God, it is therefore divine, and is, indeed, the holiness of God. Hence, John Kent was not too daring when, in a bold flight of rapture, he sang,

In thy Surety thou art free,
His dear hands were pierced for thee;
With His spotless vesture on,
Holy as the Holy One.

Oh, the heights and depths of grace,
Shining with meridian blaze;
Here the sacred records show
Sinners black, but comely too!

2. But perhaps it is best to understand this as relating to the design of Christ concerning them. It is His purpose to present them "without spot, or wrinkle, or any such thing." (Eph. 5:27.) They shall be holy and unblameable and unreproveable in the sight of the Omniscient God. In prospect of this, the Church is viewed as being virtually what she is soon to be, actually. Nor is this a frivolous antedating of her excellence; for be it ever remembered that the Representative, in whom she is accepted, is actually complete in all perfections and glories at this very moment. As the Head of the body is already without sin, being none other than the Lord from heaven, it is in keeping that the whole body should be pronounced comely and fair through the glory of the Head. The fact of her future perfection is so certain that it is spoken of as if it were already accomplished, and indeed it is so in the mind of him to whom a thousand years are but as one day. (2 Pet. 3:8) Durham says, "Christ often expounds an honest believer, from His own heart, purpose, and design, in which respect, they get many titles, otherwise unsuitable for their present condition." Let us magnify the name of our Jesus, who loves us so well that he will overleap the dividing years of our pilgrimage, that He may give us even now the praise which seems to be only fitting for the perfection of Paradise. As Ralph Erskine sings:

My love, thou seemest a loathsome worm:
Yet such thy beauties be,
I spoke but half thy comely form;
Thou art wholly fair to Me.

Whole justified, in perfect dress;
Nor justice, nor the law
Can in thy robe of righteousness
Discern the smallest flaw.

Yea, sanctified in every part,
Thou art perfect in design:
And I judge thee by what thou art
In thy intent and Mine.

Fair love, by grace complete in Me,
Beyond all beauteous brides;
Each spot that ever sullied thee
My purple vesture hides.

II. OUR LORD'S ADMIRATION IS SWEETENED BY LOVE.

He addresses the spouse as "My love". The virgins called her "the fairest among women". They saw and admired, but it was reserved for her Lord to love her. Who can fully tell the excellence of His love? Oh, how his heart goes out after his redeemed! As comparing the love of David and Jonathan, it is far exceeded in Christ. No tender husband was ever so fond as he. No figures can completely set out his heart's affection, for it surpasses all the love that man or woman has heard or thought of. Our blessed Lord himself, when he would declare the greatness of it all, was compelled to compare one inconceivable thing with another to express his own thoughts. "As the Father hath loved me, so have I loved you." (John 15:9) All the eternity, fervency, immutability, and infinity which are found in the love of Jehovah the Father towards Jehovah-Jesus the Son, are copied to the letter in the love of the Lord Jesus towards his chosen ones. Before the foundation of the world, he loved his people; in all their wanderings, he loved them; and, to the end, he will abide in his love. (Jn. 13:1) He has given them the best proof of his affection, in that he gave himself to die for their sins, and has revealed to them complete pardon as the result of His death. The willing nature of his death is further confirmation of his boundless love. How Christ delighted in the work of our redemption! "Lo, I come: in the volume of the book it is written of Me, I delight to do Thy will, O my God." (Ps. 40:7-8) When he came into the world to sacrifice his life for us, it was a freewill offering. "I have a baptism to be baptised with." (Lk. 12:50) Christ was to be, as it were, baptised in His own blood, and how he thirsted for that time! "How am I straitened till it be accomplished." There was no hesitation, no desire to be rid of his engagement. He went to his crucifixion without once halting by the way to deliberate whether he should complete his sacrifice. The stupendous mass of our fearful debt he paid at once, asking neither delay nor diminution. From the moment when he said, "Not My will, but Thine, be done" (Lk. 22:42), his course was swift and unswerving; as if he had been hastening to a crown rather than to a cross. The fullness of time was His only remembrancer. He was not driven by bailiffs to discharge the obligations of his Church, but joyfully, even when full of sorrow, he met the law, answered its demands, and cried, "It is finished." (Jn. 19:30)

How hard it is to talk of love so as to convey the meaning with it! How often have our eyes been full of tears when we realised the thought that Jesus loves us! How has our spirit been melted within us at the assurance that he thinks of us and bears us on His heart! But we cannot kindle the same emotion in others, nor can we give, by word of mouth, so much as a faint idea of the bliss that is found in that exclamation, "Oh, how he loves!" (Jn. 11:36) Come, reader, can you say of yourself, "He loved me"? (Gal. 2:20) Then look down into this sea of love, and endeavour to guess its depth. Does it not stagger your faith that he should love *you?* Or, if you have strong confidence, say, does it not enfold your spirit in a flame of admiring and adoring gratitude? O you angels, such love as this you never knew! Jesus does not bear your names in his hands, or call you His bride. No! This highest fellowship he reserves for worms, whose only return is tearful, hearty thanksgiving and love.

III. LET US NOTE THAT CHRIST DELIGHTS TO THINK ON HIS CHURCH, AND LOOK UPON HER BEAUTY.

As the bird returns often to its nest, and as the wayfarer hastens to his home, so does the mind continually pursue the object of its choice. We cannot look too often on that face which we love; we desire always to have our precious things in our sight. It is even so with our Lord Jesus. From all eternity, "His delights were with the sons of men" (Prov. 8:31) His thoughts rolled onward to the time when his elect should be born into the world, viewing them in the mirror of his fore-knowledge. "In thy book", he says, "all my members were written, which in continuance were fashioned, when as yet there was none of them." (Ps.

333

139:16) When the world was set upon its pillars, he was there, and set the bounds of the people according to the number of the children of Israel. Many a time, before his incarnation, he descended to this earth in the likeness of a man. On the plains of Mamre (Gen. 18), by the brook of Jabbok (Gen. 32:24-30), beneath the walls of Jericho (Josh. 5:13), and in the fiery furnace of Babylon (Dan. 3:19-25), the Son of man visited his people. Because his soul delighted in them, he could not rest away from them, for his heart longed after them. Never were they absent from his heart, for he had written their names on his hands, and graved them on his heart. (Is. 49:16) As the breast-plate containing the names of the tribes of Israel was the most brilliant ornament worn by the high priest, so the names of Christ's elect were his most precious jewels, which He ever hung nearest his heart. We may often forget to meditate on the perfections of our Lord, but he never ceases to remember us. He does not care one half so much for any of His most glorious works as he does for his children. Although his eye sees everything that has beauty and excellence in it, he never fixes his gaze anywhere with that admiration and delight he spends on his purchased ones. He charges his angels concerning them, and calls upon those holy beings to rejoice with him over His lost sheep. (Lk. 15:4-7) He spoke of them to himself, and, even on the tree of doom, he did not cease to soliloquize concerning them. He saw of the travail of his soul, and he was abundantly satisfied. (Is. 53:11)

That day acute of ignominious woe,
Was, notwithstanding, in a perfect sense,
"The day of his heart's gladness", for the joy
That his redeemed should be brought home at last
(Made ready as in robes of bridal white),
Was set before him vividly — he looked —
And for that happiness anticipate,
Endurance of all torture, all disgrace,
Seemed light infliction to his heart of love.

Like a fond mother, Christ Jesus, our thrice-blessed Lord, sees every dawning of excellence, and every bud of goodness in us, making much of our growth, and rejoicing over the beginnings of our graces. As he is to be our endless song, so we are his perpetual prayer. When he is absent, he thinks of us, and, in the black darkness, he has a window through which he looks upon us. When the sun sets in one part of the earth, it rises in another place beyond our visible horizon; and even so Jesus, our Sun of Righteousness, is only pouring light upon his people in a different way, when, to our apprehension, he seems to have set in darkness. His eye is ever upon the vineyard, which is his Church: "I the Lord do keep it; I will water it every moment: lest any hurt it, I will keep it night and day." (Is. 27:3) He will not trust his angels to do it, for it is his delight to do all with his own hands. Zion is in the centre of his heart, and he cannot forget her, for every day his thoughts are set upon her. When the bride, by her neglect of him has hidden herself from his sight, he cannot be quiet until, again, he looks upon her. He calls her out with the most wooing of words: "O My dove, that art in the clefts of the rock, in the secret places of the stairs, let me see thy countenance; let me hear thy voice; for sweet is thy voice, and thy countenance is comely." (Song 2:14) She thinks herself unfit to keep company with such a Prince, but he entices her from her lurking-place, and, inasmuch, as she comes out trembling, and bashfully hides her face with her veil, he bids her uncover her face, and let her Husband gaze at her. She is ashamed to do so, for she is black in her own esteem, and therefore he urges that she is comely to him.

Nor is he content with looking, for he must feed his ears as well as his eyes, and, therefore, he commends her speech, and entreats her to let him hear her voice. See how truly our Lord rejoices in us! Is not this unparalleled love? We have heard of princes who

334

have been smitten by the beauty of a peasant's daughter, but what of that? Here is the Son of God doting on a worm, looking with eyes of admiration on a poor child of Adam, and listening with joy to the lisping of poor flesh and blood. Ought we not to be exceedingly charmed by such matchless condescension? And should not our hearts as much delight in him as he does in us? O surprising truth! Christ Jesus rejoices over His poor, tempted, tried, and erring people.

IV. IT IS NOT TO BE FORGOTTEN THAT SOMETIMES THE LORD JESUS TELLS HIS PEOPLE HIS LOVE THOUGHTS.

He does not think it enough, behind her back, to tell it, but in her very presence, He says, "Thou art all fair, my love." It is true, this is not his ordinary method; he is a wise lover who knows when to keep back the intimation of love, and when to let it out. But there are times when he makes no secret of it; times when he will put it beyond all dispute in the souls of His people.

The Holy Spirit is often pleased in a most gracious manner to witness with our spirits of the love of Jesus. He takes of the things of Christ, and reveals them to us. No voice is heard from the clouds, and no vision is seen in the night, but we have a testimony surer than either of these. If an angel should fly from heaven, and inform the saint personally of the Saviour's love for him, the evidence would not be one whit more satisfactory than that which is borne in the heart by the Holy Spirit. Ask those of the Lord's people who have lived the nearest to the gates of heaven, and they will tell you that they have had seasons when the love of Christ towards them was a fact so clear and sure that they could no more doubt it than they could question their own existence.

Yes, beloved believer, you and I have had times of refreshing from the presence of the Lord, and then our faith mounted to the topmost heights of assurance. We have had confidence to lean our heads on the bosom of our Lord, and we have had no more question about our Master's affection than John had when in that blessed posture (Jn, 13:25); no, nor so much; for the dark question, "Lord, is it I that shall betray Thee?" (Mat. 26:22) has been put far from us. He has kissed us with the kisses of His love (Song 1:2), and killed our doubts by the closeness of his embrace. His love has been sweeter than wine to our souls. We felt that we could sing, "His left hand is under my head, and his right hand doth embrace me." (Song 8:3) Then all earthly troubles were light as the chaff of the threshing-floor, and the pleasures of the world as tasteless as the white of an egg. We would have welcomed death as the messenger who would introduce us to our Lord, to whom we were in haste to be gone; for His love stirred us to desire more of him, even his immediate and glorious presence. I have, sometimes, when the Lord has assured me of His love, felt as if I could not contain more joy and delight. My eyes ran down with tears of gratitude. I fell on my knees to bless him, but rose again in haste, feeling as if I had nothing more to ask for. But I must stand up and praise him. Then I lifted my hands to heaven, longing to fill my arms with him, panting to talk with him as a man talks with his friend, and to see him in his own Person, that I might tell him how happy he had made his unworthy servant, and might fall on my face and kiss his feet in unutterable thankfulness and love. Such a banquet have I had with one word from my Beloved — "*thou art Mine*" — that I wished, like Peter, to build tabernacles in that mount, and dwell there forever. But, alas, we have not, all of us, yet learned how to preserve that blessed assurance. We stir up our Beloved and awaken him; then He leaves our unquiet chamber, and we grope after him, and make many a weary journey trying to find Him.

If we were wiser and more careful, we might preserve the fragrance of Christ's words far longer; for they are not like the ordinary manna which soon rotted, but are comparable to that omer of it which was put in the golden pot, and preserved for many generations. The sweet Lord Jesus has been known to write his love-thoughts on the heart of his people in so clear and deep a manner that they have for months, and even for years, enjoyed an abiding sense of his affection. A few doubts have flitted across their minds like thin clouds before a summer's sun, but the warmth of their assurance has remained the same for many a gladsome day. Their path has been a smooth one; they have fed in the green pastures beside the still waters, for his rod and staff comforted them (Ps. 23:4), and his right hand led them. (Song 2:6; 8:3) I am inclined to think that there is more of this in the Church than some men would allow. We have a goodly number who dwell in the hills, and behold the light of the sun. There are giants in these days, though the times are not such as to allow them much room to display their gigantic strength. In many a humble cottage, in many a crowded workshop, in many a village manse, there are to be found men of the house of David, men after God's own heart, anointed with the holy oil. It is, however, a mournful truth, that whole ranks in the army of our Lord are composed of dwarfish Littlefaiths. The men of fearful mind and desponding heart are everywhere to be seen. Why is this? Is it the Master's fault or ours? Surely he can't be blamed! Is it not then a matter of enquiry in our own souls: "Can I not grow stronger?" "Must I be a mourner all my days?" "How can I get rid of my doubts?" The answer must be: yes, you can be comforted, but only the mouth of the Lord can do it, for anything less than this will prove unsatisfactory.

I do not doubt that there are means, by the use of which those who are now weak and trembling may attain to boldness in faith and confidence in hope. But I cannot see how this can be done unless the Lord Jesus Christ manifests his love to them, and tells them of their union with him. This he will do, if we seek it from him. The importunate pleader shall not lack his reward. Hasten to him, O timid one, and tell him that nothing will content you but a smile from his own face, and a word from His own lips! Speak to him and say:

"O my Lord Jesus, I cannot rest unless I know that you love me! I desire to have proof of your love under your own hand and seal. I cannot live on guesses and surmises; nothing but certainty will satisfy my trembling heart. Lord, look upon me, if, indeed, you love me; and though I be less than the least of all saints, say to my soul, 'I am thy salvation.'" (Ps. 35:3)

When this prayer is heard, the castle of despair must totter; there is not one stone of it which can remain on another, if Christ whispers his love to you. Even Despondency and Much-afraid will dance, and Ready-to-Halt will leap on his crutches.

Oh, for more of these Bethel visits, with more frequent visitations from the God of Israel! Oh, how sweet to hear him say to us, as He did to Abraham, "Fear not, Abram, I am thy shield, and thy exceeding great reward." (Gen. 15:1) To be addressed as Daniel was of old, "O man greatly beloved" (Dan. 10:19), is worth a thousand ages of this world's joy. What more can a creature want this side of heaven to make him peaceful and happy than a plain avowal of love from his Lord's own lips? Let me ever hear you speak in mercy to my soul, and, O my Lord, I ask no more while here I dwell in the land of my pilgrimage! Brethren, let us labour to obtain a confident assurance of the Lord's delight in us for this, as it enables him to commune with us, and will be one of the readiest ways to produce a like feeling in our hearts towards him. Christ is well pleased with us; let us approach him with holy familiarity; let us unbosom our thoughts to him, for his delight in us will secure us an audience. The child may stay away from the father when he is conscious that he has aroused his father's displeasure, but why should we keep at a distance when Christ Jesus is smiling on us? No, since his smiles attract us, let us enter his courts, and touch his golden sceptre. O Holy Spirit, help us to live in happy fellowship with him whose soul is knit to us!

O Jesus! Let eternal blessings dwell
On Thy transporting name.
Let me be wholly Thine from this blest hour.
Let Thy loved image be for ever present;
Of Thee be all my thoughts, and let my tongue
Be sanctified with the celestial theme.
Dwell on my lips, Thou dearest, sweetest name!
Dwell on my lips, 'till the last parting breath!
Then let me die, and bear the charming sound
In triumph to the skies. In other strains,
In language all divine, I'll praise Thee then;
While all the Godhead opens in the view
Of a Redeemer's love. Here let me gaze,
For ever gaze; the bright variety
Will endless joy and admiration yield.
Let me be wholly Thine from this blest hour.
Fly from my soul all images of sense,
Leave me in silence to possess my Lord:
My life, my pleasures, flow from Him alone,
My strength, my great salvation, and my hope.
Thy name is all my trust; O name divine!
Be Thou engraven on my inmost soul,
And let me own Thee with my latest breath,
Confess Thee in the face of every horror,
That threatening death or envious hell can raise;
Till all their strength subdued, my parting soul
Shall give a challenge to infernal rage,
And sing salvation to the Lamb for ever.

(Elizabeth Singer Rowe)

45. FRAGRANT SPICES FROM THE MOUNTAINS OF MYRRH: THE SECOND BUNDLE

PRINTED IN SWORD AND TROWEL, JULY 1865

"Thou art all fair, my love; there is no spot in thee." (Song of Solomon 4:7)

[We return to the delightful topic with which we opened last month's number of our Magazine.]

Our Lord's admiration is sweetened by love. He addresses the spouse as "My love". The virgins called her "the fairest among women"; they saw and admired, but it was reserved for her Lord to love her. Who can fully tell the excellence of his love? Oh, how his heart goes out after his redeemed! As for the love of David and Jonathan (1 Sam. 1:26), it is far exceeded in Christ. No tender husband was ever so fond as he. No figures can completely set his heart's affection forth, for it surpasses all the love that man or woman has heard or thought of. Our blessed Lord, himself, when he would declare the greatness of it, was compelled to compare one inconceivable thing with another, in order to express his own thoughts. "As the Father hath loved me, so have I loved you." (Jn. 15:9) All the eternity, fervency, immutability, and infinity, which are to be found in the love of Jehovah the Father towards Jehovah-Jesus the Son, are copied to the letter in the love of the Lord Jesus towards his chosen ones. Before the foundation of the world, he loved his people; in all their wanderings he loved them, and "unto the end he will abide in his love." (Jn. 13:1)

He has given them the best proof of his affection, in that he gave himself to die for their sins, and has revealed to them complete pardon as the result of his death. The willing manner of his death is further confirmation of his boundless love. How Christ delighted in the work of our redemption! "Lo, I come: in the volume of the book it is written of me, I delight to do thy will, O my God." (Ps. 11:7-8) When he came into the world to sacrifice his life for us, it was a freewill offering. "I have a baptism to be baptised with." (Lk. 12:50) Christ was to be, as it were, baptised in his own blood, and how he thirsted for that time! "How am I straitened till it be accomplished." (Lk. 12:50) There was no hesitation, no desire to be quit of his engagement; he went to his crucifixion without once halting by the way to deliberate whether he should complete his sacrifice. The stupendous mass of our fearful debt he paid at once, asking neither delay nor diminution. From the moment he said, "Not my will, but thine, be done," (Lk. 22:42), his course was swift and unswerving, as if he had been hastening to a crown rather than to a cross. The fullness of time was his only remembrancer; he was not driven by bailiffs to discharge the obligations of his Church, but joyously, even when full of sorrow, he met the law, answered its demands, and cried, "It is finished." (Jn. 19:30)

How hard it is to talk of love so as to convey our meaning with it! How often have our eyes been full of tears when we have realised the thought that Jesus loves us! How has our spirit been melted within us at the assurance that he thinks of us and bears us on his heart! But we cannot kindle the same emotion in others, nor can we give, by word of mouth, so much as a faint idea of the bliss which coucheth in that exclamation, "O how he loved!" (Jn. 11:36) Come, reader, can you say of yourself, "He loved me?" (Gal. 2:20.) Then look down into this sea of his love, and endeavour to guess its depth. Does it not stagger your faith, that he should love *you?* Or, if you have strong confidence, say, does it not enfold your spirit in a flame of admiring and adoring gratitude? O you angels, such love as this you never knew! Jesus does not bear your names on his hands, or call you his bride. No, this highest fellowship he reserves for worms, whose only return is tearful, hearty thanksgiving and love.

338

Let us note that Christ delights to think about his Church, and to look upon her beauty. As the bird returns often to its nest, and as the wayfarer hastens to his home, so does the mind continually pursue the object of its choice. We cannot look too often on that face which we love; we desire always to have our precious things in our sight. It is even so with our Lord Jesus. From all eternity, "his delights were with the sons of men" (Prov. 8:31), and his thoughts rolled onward to the time when his elect should be born into the world, viewing them in the mirror of his foreknowledge. "In thy book he says all my members were written, which in continuance were fashioned, when as yet there was none of them." (Ps. 139:16.)

When the world was set up on its pillars, he was there, and he set the bounds of the people according to the number of the children of Israel. Many a time before his incarnation, he descended to this lower earth in the similitude of a man: on the plains of Mamre, (Genesis 18) by the brook of Jabbok, (Gen. 32:24-30,) beneath the walls of Jericho, (Joshua 5:13,) and in the fiery furnace of Babylon. (Dan. 19-25) The Son of man visited his people. Because his soul delighted in them, he could not stay away from them, for his heart longed after them. Never were they absent from his heart, for he had written their names on his hands, and graved them on his side. As the breast-plate containing the names of the tribes of Israel was the most brilliant ornament worn by the high priest, so the names of Christ's elect are his most precious jewels, which he ever hands nearest his heart. We may often forget to meditate on the perfections of our Lord, but he never ceases to remember us. He cares not one half so much for any of his most glorious works, as he does for his children. Although his eye sees everything that has beauty and excellence in it, he never fixes his gaze anywhere with that admiration and delight which he spends on his purchased ones. He charges his angels concerning them, and calls upon those holy beings to rejoice with him over his lost sheep. (Lk. 15:4-7) He talked of them to himself, and, even on the tree of doom, he did not cease to soliloquise concerning them.

That day acute of ignominious woe,
Was, notwithstanding, in a perfect sense,
The day of his heart's gladness, for the joy
That his redeem'd should be brought home at last,
(Made ready as in robes of bridal white,)
Was set before him vividly, — he look'd; —
And for that happiness anticipate,
Endurance of all torture, all disgrace,
Seem'd light infliction to his heart of love.

(*Meditations*)

Like a fond mother, Christ Jesus, our thrice-blessed Lord, sees every dawning of excellence, and every bud of goodness in us, making much of our littlest, and rejoicing over the beginnings of our graces. As he is to be our endless song, so we are his perpetual prayer. When he is absent, he thinks of us; and, in the black darkness, he has a window through which he looks upon us. When the sun sets in one part of the earth, it rises in another place beyond our visible horizon; and even so Jesus, our Sun of Righteousness, is only pouring light upon his people in a different way, when, to our apprehension, he seems to have set in darkness. His eye is ever on the congregation of the righteous. "I the Lord do keep it; I will water it every moment: lest any hurt it, I will keep it night and day?' (Is. 27:3)

He will not trust to his angels to do it, for it is his delight to do all with his own hands. Zion is in the centre of his heart, and he cannot forget, for every day his thoughts are set upon

339

her. When the bride, by her neglect of him, has hidden herself from his sight, he cannot be quiet until again he looks upon her. He calls her forward with the most wooing words: "O my dove, that art in the clefts of the rock, in the secret places of the stairs, let me see thy countenance, let me hear thy voice; for sweet is thy voice, and thy countenance is comely." (Song 2:14)

She thinks herself unfit to have company with such a prince, but he entices her from her lurking place, and, inasmuch as she comes forward trembling, and bashfully hides her face with her veil, he bids her uncover her face and let her husband gaze upon her. She is ashamed to do so, for she is black in her own esteem, and, therefore, he urges that she is comely to him, nor is he content with looking, for he must feed his ears as well as his eyes, and therefore commends her speech, and entreats her to let him hear her voice. See how truly our Lord rejoices in us! Is not this unparalleled love! We have heard of princes who have been smitten by the beauty of a peasant's daughter, but what of this? Here is the Son of God doting on a worm, looking with eyes of admiration on a poor child of Adam, and listening with joy to the lispings of poor flesh and blood. Ought we not to be exceedingly charmed by such matchless condescension? And should not our hearts as much delight in him, as he does in us? O surprising truth! Christ Jesus rejoices over his poor, tempted, tried, and erring people.

It is not to be forgotten that sometimes the Lord Jesus tells his people his love thoughts. "He does not think it enough to tell it behind her back; but, in her very presence, he says, 'Thou art all fair my love.' It is true, this is not his ordinary method; he is a wise lover, who knows when to keep back the intimation of love and when to let it out; but there are times when he will make no secret of it, times when he will put it beyond all dispute in the souls of his people." (Ralph Erskine's Sermons) The Holy Spirit is often pleased in a most gracious manner to witness with our spirits of the love of Jesus. He takes of the things of Christ and reveals them to us. No voice is heard from the clouds and no vision is seen in the night, but we have a testimony surer than either of these. If an angel should fly from heaven and inform the saint personally of the Saviour's love for him, the evidence would not be one whit more satisfactory than that which is born in the heart by the Holy Spirit. Ask those of the Lord's people who have lived the nearest to the gates of heaven, and they will tell you that they have had seasons when the love of Christ towards them has been a fact so clear and sure that they could no more doubt it than they could question their own existence. Yes, beloved believer, you and I have had times of refreshing from the presence of the Lord, and then our faith has mounted to the topmost heights of assurance. We have had confidence to lean our heads on the bosom of our Lord, and we have had no more question about our Master's affection than John had when, in that blessed posture, no, nor so much; for the dark question, "Lord is it I that shall betray thee" (Mat. 26:22) has been put far from us. He has kissed us with the kisses of his love (Song 1:2), and killed our doubts by the closeness of his embrace. His love has been sweeter than wine to our souls. We felt that we could sing, "His left hand is under my head and his right hand doth embrace me." (Song 8:3.)

Then all earthly troubles were light as the chaff of the threshing-floor, and the pleasures of the world as tasteless as the white of an egg. We would have welcomed death as the messenger who would introduce us to our Lord to whom we were in haste to be gone; for his love had stirred us to desire more of him, even his immediate and glorious presence. I have sometimes, when the Lord has assured me of his love, felt as if I could not contain more joy and delight. My eyes ran down with tears of gratitude. I fell upon my knees to bless him, but rose again in haste, feeling as if I had nothing more to ask for, but must stand up and praise him; then have I lifted my hands to heaven longing to fill my arms with him; panting to talk with him, as a man talks with his friend, and to see him in his own Person, that I might tell him how happy he had made his unworthy servant, and might fall on my face and kiss his feet in unutterable thankfulness and love. Such a banquet have I had on one word of my beloved — *"thou art mine"* that I wished, like Peter, to build tabernacles in that mount and dwell forever. (Matthew 17:4; Mark 9:5; Luke 9:33) But alas, we, who are young saints, have not yet learned how to preserve such assurance! We stir up our beloved, and awake him, and then he leaves our unquiet chamber, and we grope after him in the night and make many a weary journey after him. If we were wiser and more careful, we might preserve the fragrance of Christ's words far longer; for they are not like the ordinary manna which soon rotted, but are comparable to that omer of it which was put in the golden pot and preserved for many generations.

The sweet Lord Jesus has been known to write his love thoughts on the hearts of his people in so clear and deep a manner that they have, for months, and even years, enjoyed an abiding sense of his affection. A few doubts have flitted across their minds like thin clouds before a summer's sun, but the warmth of their assurance has remained the same for many a gladsome day. Their path has been a smooth one, they have fed in the green pastures beside the still waters, for his rod and staff have comforted them, and his right hand hath led them. I am inclined to think, that there is more of this in the Church than some would allow. We have a goodly number who dwell on the hills and behold the light of the sun. There are giants in these days, though the times are not such as to allow them room to display their gigantic strength; in many a humble cottage, in many a crowded workshop, in many a village manse, there are to be found men of the house of David, men after God's own heart, anointed with the holy oil. It is, however, a mournful truth, that whole ranks in the army of our Lord are composed of dwarfish little faiths. The men of fearful mind and desponding heart are everywhere to be seen. Why is this? Is it the Master's fault, or ours? Surely he cannot be blamed! Is it not then a matter of inquiry in our own souls. Can I not grow stronger? Must I be a mourner all my days? How can I get rid of my doubts? The answer must be: yes, you can be comforted, but only the mouth of the Lord can do it, for anything less than this will be unsatisfactory. I do not doubt that there are means, by the use of which, those who are now weak and trembling, may attain to boldness in faith and confidence in hope; but I don't see how this can be done unless the Lord Jesus Christ manifest his love to them, and tell them of their union with him. This he will do, if we seek it of him. The importunate pleader shall not lack his reward. Hasten towards him, O timid one, and tell him that nothing will content you but a smile from his own face, and a word from his own lips. Speak to him and say:

"O, my Lord Jesus, I cannot rest unless I know that thou lovest me. I desire to have proof of thy love under thine own hand and seal. I cannot live upon guesses and surmises; nothing but certainty will satisfy my trembling heart. Lord, look upon me, if, indeed, thou lovest me, and though I am less than the least of all saints, say unto my soul, 'I am thy salvation.'"

When this prayer is heard, the castle of despair must totter, for there is not one stone of it which can remain upon another if Christ whispers out of his love. Even Despondency and Much-afraid will dance, and Ready-to-Halt leap upon his crutches.

Oh, for more of these Bethel visits, more frequent visitations from the God of Israel! Oh, how sweet to hear him say to us, as he did to Abraham, "Fear not Abram, I am thy shield, thine exceeding great reward." (Gen. 15:1)

To be addressed as Daniel was of old, "Oh man, greatly beloved", (Dan. 10:19) is worth a thousand ages of this world's joy. What more can a creature want this side of heaven to make him peaceful and happy than a plain avowal of love from his Lord's own lips? Let me ever hear you speak in mercy to my soul; and oh, my Lord, I ask no more while here I dwell in the land of my pilgrimage. Brethren, let us labour to obtain a confident assurance

341

of the Lord's delight in us, for this, as it enables him to commune with us, will be one of the readiest ways to produce a like feeling in our heart's towards him. Christ is well-pleased with us; let us approach him with holy familiarity; let us unbosom our thoughts to him, for his delight in us will secure us an audience. The child may stay away from the father, when he is conscious that he has aroused his father's displeasure, but why should we keep at a distance when Christ Jesus is smiling on us. No, since his smiles attract us, let us enter into his courts, and touch his golden sceptre. O Holy Spirit, help us to live in happy fellowship with him whose soul is knit to us.

O Jesus! let eternal blessings dwell
On thy transporting name.
Let me be wholly thine from this blest hour.
Let thy lov'd image be for ever present;
Of thee be all my thoughts, and let my tongue
Be sanctified with the celestial theme.
Dwell on my lips, thou dearest, sweetest name!
Dwell on my lips, 'till the last parting breath!
Then let me die, and bear the charming sound
In triumph to the skies In other strains,
In language all divine, I'll praise thee then;
While all the Godhead opens in the view
Of a redeemer's love. Here let me gaze,
For ever gaze; the bright variety
Will endless joy and admiration yield.
Let me be wholly thine from this blest hour.
Fly from my soul all images of sense,
Leave me in silence to possess my Lord:
My life, my pleasures, flow from him alone,
My strength, my great salvation, and my hope.
Thy name is all my trust; O name divine!
Be thou engraven on my inmost soul,
And let me own thee with my latest breath,
Confess thee in the face of ev'ry horror,
That threat'ning death or envious hell can raise;
Till all their strength subdu'd, my parting soul
Shall give a challenge to infernal rage,
And sing salvation to the Lamb for ever.

(Elizabeth Singer Rowe)

This huge round earth is sustained in its orbit, without prop or pillar, by the unseen power of the Almighty God. Turning round upon its own axis with marvellous regularity, and moving through space with inconceivable rapidity, it performs all its movements without band or wheel; the hand which causes its revolutions is not to be discerned by mortal eye. Everywhere in the great, and in the little, the same rule holds good; the Mighty Worker is himself unseen, yet manifest and majestic is his presence. We are not to see, nor to expect to see, the Divine hand with human senses; but faith discerns it, and admires its doings.

It were well if anxious inquirers could be brought to remember this, for they too often look for signs and wonders, and cannot be persuaded of the power of divine grace unless they see or hear some strange thing. Now the facts of salvation are these: God has accepted Christ Jesus his own dear and only Son, in his living and dying righteousness as the substitute for his chosen people. As their substitute, Christ has finished all that the divine law required, and so saved his people; and the Lord has revealed to us in his Word that those who believe in his Son Jesus Christ are the objects of his choice and heirs of all the boons purchased by the Saviour's blood. The one question is, Have *I faith?* Can I trust Jesus? Can I give up seeing my own works and prayers, and believe that Jesus' blood and righteousness can save me? Do I now rest on an unseen Redeemer, and whether I feel better, or do not feel better, whether I see an improvement in myself or do not see a single hopeful sign, do I heartily and entirely rely upon the work of God's appointed and accepted Saviour?

The world is safe though it hangs on nothing but God's Word, and equally secure will that soul be which can dare to have done with feeling and doing, and lay hold on the unseen energy of God's love, working through the cross of Christ. The clouds do not fall, though no great chains uphold them; and the firmament does not crack, though its arch is without a pillar. It is a mighty secret, to live upon God alone. Friend, I pray the Lord teach it to you this day at Calvary's foot, for his own name's sake. Amen.

46. THE INTERPRETER

Song of Solomon 4:8-16, 5:1

Our last two readings (Song 3:6-11, and Song 4:1-7) gave us two parts of a delightful Canticle: we will now read the third portion, in which the King is the chief speaker, and rejoice to extol his bride, even as the Lord Jesus rejoiceth over his church.

THE KING thus speaks —

8 Along with me from Lebanon, my Bride,
   Along with me from Lebanon come;
   Look from off the top of Amana,
   From the top of Shenir and Hermon,
   From the dwellings of the lions,
   From the mountains of the leopards:

Jesus would have us look above the highest earthly delight, and leave all earthly loves for his sake. Shall he say, "Come with me," and shall we refuse to follow? Hear how he sets forth his love his love to us, his joy over us.

9 Thou hast taken my heart, my Sister, my Spouse,
   Thou hast taken my heart with one
   Of thy eyes, with a single chain of thy neck;

Though but one grace be seen in us, Jesus spies it out, and is charmed with it; such is his condescending love.

10 How pleasant is thy love, my Sister, my Spouse,
   How good is thy love above wine,
   And the odour of thine ointments above all perfumes!

11 Honey from the comb dropping are thy lips, my Spouse,
   Honey and milk are under thy tongue,
   And the scent of thy garments like the scent of Lebanon.

In the esteem of Jesus, the love, the spirit, the words, and the outward conduct of his people are all acceptable.

12 A garden enclosed,
   My Sister, my Bride,
   A spring shut up,
   A fountain sealed;
   Thy plants a Paradise
   Of granate-apple trees,
   Along with fruits most choice;
   Of henna-plants with nards,

14 The spikenard and the saffron,
   The sweet cane and cinnamon,
   With all trees of frankincense;
   With myrrh and the lign aloes,
   With all the chief of spices:

15 A fountain for the gardens,
   A well of living waters,
   And streams out of Lebanon.

Jesus thus extols his beloved Church, but having done so, he intercedes for her, that the Holy Spirit may visit her, for what would she be without him? Listen to the Redeemer's prayer.

16 Awake, O North wind;
   And come, thou South;
   Breathe upon my garden,
   Flow its odours forth.

Moved by the love of her Lord, and influenced by the Spirit, the Church begs the Lord to come nearer to her.

   Come, let my Loved One into his garden,
   And let him eat his pleasant fruit.

To her he answers lovingly.

Song 5:1

1 I am coming into my garden,
   My Sister, my Bride;
   I have gathered my myrrh
   Along with my balm;
   I have eaten my honey
   With my honey-comb;
   I have drunk my wine
   Together with my milk;
   Eat, O friends, drink and quaff ye,
   O well-beloved.

Jesus accepts us and our fruit; let us therefore rejoice in him and feast upon him.

He calls me from the lion's den,
From this wild world of beasts and men,
To Zion, where his glories are —
Not Lebanon is half so fair;

Nor dens of prey, nor flowery plains,
No earthly joys, nor earthly pains,
Shall hold my feet, or force my stay,
When Christ invites my soul away.

(Isaac Watts)

345

47. A CALL TO COMMUNION

AT THE METROPOLITAN TABERNACLE

"Come with me from Lebanon, my spouse, with me from Lebanon: look from the top of Amana, from the top of Shenir and Hermon, from the lions' dens, from the mountains of the leopards."
(Song of Solomon 4:8)

IN the verses which immediately precede our text Christ has been raising his Church. He tells her that she possesses all sorts of beauties, and he concludes his description by saying, `Thou art all fair, my love; there is no spot in thee.' Observe, dear brethren, that such beauty belongs to no one by nature. Are we not in ourselves black as the tents of Kedar? (Song 1:5) So defiled, polluted and worthy of detestation, as we feel and know ourselves to be, what right can we have to a smile from Jesus' face? But see how he deals with us. He finds us in our loathsomeness and deformity, and, having first washed us in his blood, he next puts his own beauty on us, hangs his own jewels on our necks, clothes us with his own spotless righteousness, and then, though it is his beauty and not our own, yet he admires us for that very beauty with which he has arrayed us. At first, Jesus loves us only because he will love us. (Deut. 7:7-8) While we are yet dead in trespasses and sins his heart goes after us; and when our sins break out in our face like leprosy, yet still his heart clings to us with a force that is stronger than death and mightier than the grave. But after he has fairly got a hold of us with the strong hand of grace, and made new creatures of us, then, though he still continues to love in sovereignty, yet now there is the springing up of a love of complacency towards us on account of what he has made us to be. When he finds us as sinners, he can take no such delight in us, though he regards us even then with benevolence; but, when he has converted the sinner into a saint, and cast all his sins behind his back, and covered him with his immaculate righteousness, he loves that saint with a pure appreciation of comeliness of the character of which he is possessed, being conformed to his own image, and endowed with the best gifts and the choicest graces. Then, as true love always begets a desire for the company of those we love, so the Lord feels a longing towards his people. If the Lord has looked on you, beloved, and made you a new creature; if he has made you white by his washing, and glorious by the imputation of his righteousness, then he longs after your company. He loves you with a vehemence that cannot be satisfied without your society on earth, and he will never be completely satisfied until he has that same society in heaven. He will not be contented until you sit on his throne, and wear his crown, and share his joy.

Our text contains the longing of a gracious Saviour after a gracious soul. He has given that soul the beauty of God; and has given it, in himself, perfection; and now he longs and pants to have communion with that soul. Let us take the words and meditate on them now, as a loving invitation addressed to us as we sit around the Table to commemorate the Lord's death; and afterwards, if time permits, as a divine summons to meet every one of the Lord's people by-and-by. Yet a little while, the hireling's day will be over, and the good Shepherd shall say to each of us, "Come with me; come with me."

What a sweet invitation this is from Christ to our souls, to his spouse, to every believer here! "Come with me from Lebanon, my spouse, with me from Lebanon: from the top of

346

Amana, from the top of Shenir and Hermon, from the lions'. ..
dens, from the mountains of the leopards."

I shall attempt to show you that the Saviour calls his people away from everything else to himself. He lures them, and draws them away, from all earthly enjoyments! "Come with me, my spouse, with me from Lebanon." Lebanon was a place for enjoyment. There, in the forest, King Solomon built his summer palace, the resort of those who wished for pleasure. It was covered, we are told, with odoriferous herbs, so that all the air was laden with a sweet perfume. On the top of Lebanon stood the glorious cedars, and these also yielded a fragrance. It was a place of delight and of retirement. A man who could not enjoy himself there would surely be miserable everywhere else, Lebanon was to the Jewish mind the very picture of a terrestrial Paradise. If a man would choose where he would go and refresh himself, he would go to the cool snowy hills of Lebanon in the midst of the summer. Well, brethren, even on earth we have some gratification! I do not like the sad complaint of those who are always saying,

Oh, what a wretched land is this, which yields us no supplies!

(*The Englishman's Brief On Behalf Of His National Church*, 1880)

This world is not a fit home for a Christian; he can never find that in it which satisfies his loftier aspirations. But still, there are many mercies that spring up along the pilgrim's path, and not a few joys which are both lawful and refreshing. What shall we say to those of you whom God has planted in families, and on the parental hearth, that rallying-place of the affections? We have sometimes been told that the old Saxon words are the best in our English language. Such words as "mother" and "father", "home" and "heaven" — how they touch our softer feelings! Is there not sweet music at the mention of "home"? What happy thoughts it awakens! And can we speak of our parents without kindling precious memories? Then we turn to our children with fondest love as the gems of our house. Yes, and all the members of the social circle — be they husband or wife, brothers or sisters, cousins or friends. Do they not supply us with a Lebanon in which we are not ashamed to take much delight? Then beyond the pale of such familiar society, there is an outer world which must yield us some sort of comfort. The very losses that, at times, we usually groan over are set against gains that at other times made us glad. The struggles we have are not without successes, or else we should not so willingly engage in them. Weary toil gets its wages. And most of us like talking about our trials when we have come out of them with a little triumph. Rest is peculiarly refreshing to those who labour and are heavy laden. (Mat. 11:28) Whatever our condition in life, there is little decency in being perpetually discontented. The Christian, beyond all other men, ought to be alive to the fruits that are luscious to the taste, and the flowers that please us with their colour and their fragrance. There is no virtue in the Pharisaic spirit which forges prohibitions, and imposes abstinence from those bounties of Providence freely bestowed on us by God. In vain, they deliver to us precepts that have no divine authority. Such a species of asceticism Jesus Christ neither practised nor enjoined on his disciples. If anyone has a fair title to those temperate enjoyments of this present life that involve no sin, it is the true heir of life eternal.

How vast the treasure we possess!
How rich thy bounty, King of grace!
This world is ours, and worlds to come;
Earth is our lodge, and heaven our home.

All things are ours: the gifts of God;
The purchase of a Saviour's blood;
While the good Spirit shows us how

347

To use, and to improve them too.

If peace and plenty crown my days,
They help me, Lord, to speak thy praise;
If bread of sorrows be my food,
Those sorrows work my lasting good.

I would not change my blest estate
For all the world calls good or great;
And while my faith can keep her hold,
I envy not the sinner's gold.

Father, I wait thy daily will;
Thou shalt divide my portion still;
Grant me on earth what seems thee best,
Till death and heaven reveal the rest.

(Isaac Watts)

Who are so free in a father's house as his children? For them, are not the good things brought out in their season, stored up, and afterwards spread out — for strangers or for his own sons and daughters? Friends, we say it with gratitude, and let those who choose to murmur — there are joys beneath the skies, wells of water in the waste howling wilderness, and pleasant palm-trees in the dreary desert! But here comes the point: the Saviour cries, "Come with me from Lebanon, my spouse, with me from Lebanon." Beloved, you are called on tonight to forget all the earthly joys of which you are now partaking, or have ever known, to indulge in that spiritual repast which the well-beloved Lord of our souls has provided for those who love him. Tear yourselves away from these inferior delights which you only relish because you are creatures made in the image of the first Adam, and tuck into those heavenly viands which are delicious to your taste, because you are now made in the image of the second Adam; for they better suit your new-born nature. As you think of the joys you have felt on earth, let them only be as stepping-stones, as rungs in a divine ladder to raise you up to a more spiritual state of mind.

Let a father's love remind you of the love of him who gave his Son for you. Let the joys of friendship only help you to understand the affection of the "friend that sticketh closer than a brother." (Prov. 18:24) Let even your marriage ties here below teach you to think of the tender regard of him who is more closely allied to you than your earthly spouse ever can be, for he is yours and you are his, and by eternal union one. You have been drinking of the nether springs, perhaps, this afternoon in your households. "Come with me", says Jesus, "and drink of the upper streams where the river flows more sweet, more pure, more deep." You have slaked your earthly thirst with sweet cordials, your mouth has been satisfied with good things, and your youth has been renewed like the eagle's. (Is. 40:32) Come now, and wait on the Lord, and quench your spiritual thirst with the wine, and the milk, and the dainties that he offers you. Now let your souls feed on heavenly bread, and drink of the water which flows from the Rock of Ages. It is not always easy, particularly when these joys of sense are in prospect rather than in retrospect, to banish them from memory. Christian, you may be anticipating something in the week that is coming; there is a joy that is flitting before your imagination, and you are beginning to seek it. I beseech you, hear the voice of Jesus as he says:

"Come with me from Lebanon, my spouse, with me from Lebanon." Do not linger so much on the scenes that are about to open up, which dazzle you for an hour and then pass away; but

348

come and enjoy my society, and commune with me. Oh, put those other cups aside, and drink of my chalice! Lay aside all other food to come and feast on this heavenly manna which is better than angels' food. What, can you not leave a while that greed of earthly cheer? Can you not, at least for this sacred hour, forego the common propensities of men? 'Tis Jesus speaking."

Oh, I pray you by his wounds and by his love, regard what he is saying." 'Tis he, his name is written on your heart. 'Tis he, his heart was broken for your sake. 'Tis he, his head is wet

with dew, and his locks with the drops of the night. (Song 5:2) 'Tis he, who knocks at the door of your heart, and says:

> "Let me come in to you; come now, commune with me; come away from all those allurements that would entice you. Cut the cords that bind you; lift yourself up from the dust; shake yourself and arise; put on your beautiful garments of contemplation and adoration, and come with me from Lebanon, my spouse, with me, from Lebanon, come with me even from earthly delights and from human joys."

Cannot we do that tonight? Oh, if the Spirit of God enables us, we can, my brothers, my sisters! Oh, if the Holy Spirit will give us wings, we shall mount like eagles, and leave the world like a speck behind as we soar upward with our face towards the sun, and our eyes fixed on him! Picture him now, and this may help you. Bring your imagination into play. Portray before your eyes the Sufferer. He is despised and rejected. (Is 53:3) He gave his back to the smiters, and his cheeks to those who plucked out the hair. He does not hide his face from shame and spitting. He hangs on yonder tree. The passers-by wag their heads; the scoffers thrust out the tongue; the multitude reviles; and he dies in grief. Will you not think now of what he did for you? Must he ask you twice? Will not your willing heart say rather, "Yes, Jesus, martyred, murdered for my sake, I will come with you from every earthly joy"? Or, if that picture doesn't draw you, see him yonder. He has led captivity captive (Eph. Ps. 68:16; Eph. 4:8), and dragged your foes at his triumphal chariot wheels. There he sits — Prophet, Priest, and King — on the eternal throne.

Jesus, that King of Glory, reigns
On Zion's heavenly hill,
Looks like a Lamb that has been slain,
And wears His Priesthood still.

He ever lives to intercede
Before His Father's face:
Give Him, my soul, your cause to plead,
Nor doubt the Father's grace.

(Isaac Watts)

More glorious far is he than all the kings of earth, casting into the shade even those principalities and powers whose radiance is said to be brighter the sun. Will not this enchant you? Will not your hearts fly upward towards his throne? If you will not respond to his voice, certainly you will not be his. But oh, Spirit of God, come and make us obedient to the loving request! — "Come with me from Lebanon, my spouse, with me from Lebanon."

But, to pass on, Jesus invites us to come with him even from spiritual enjoyments, for at least two of the three mountains mentioned here indicate the spiritual mirth of a believer than his temporal happiness. "Come with me from Amana" The name *Amana* signifies "firmness" or "steadfastness". And when he says, "Come with me from Hermon, know how Hermon is the place where the dew of God drops, and, in the Scripture, is like those who dwell together in unity. (Ps. 133:1-3) Well, now, some of you and I have sweet enjoyment — standing, as it

349

were, on the summit of Amana — contemplating the steadfastness of the purposes and decrees of God. I know of no mountain which is more delightful to visit, unless it is Mount Calvary. Behold and see how, in days of old, or ever he had laid the foundation of the earth, Jehovah resolved in himself that he would have a people who would show forth his praise; and how, before the day-star's lamp was lit, he elected those people to be his in the sovereignty of his infinite love. However, since then, the purpose of his heart has stood like a mountain of brass, firm to all the seed. Not one of his chosen has he cast away, not one of his beloved has he cast away, not one of his beloved has he given over to the sword, and not one of his darlings has he cast to the power of the dogs. There is a divine felicity in discerning the everlasting love of God, and, in tracking it through the course of time, watching the flow of that river of infinite unfailing love. It is Nathanael Parker Willis who remarks concerning winter:

It is a season for the quiet thought,
And the still reckoning with thyself. The year
Gives back the spirits of its dead, and time
Whispers the history of its vanished hours;
And the heart, calling its affections up,
Counteth its wasted ingots. Life stands still
And settles like a fountain, and the eye
Sees clearly through its depths, and noteth all
That stirred its troubled waters. It is well
That Winter with the dying year should come!

The haze hangs thick over all that is changing; but that which is permanent and unchanging stands out in peerless beauty before our vision. Still, as we gaze, Christ seems dearer and heaven seems nearer, and our confidence grows stronger that he who loved us at the beginning will love us even to the end. Oh, how sweet to know that nothing from the heart of Christ can sever one of the blood-bought! To think that our Redeemer entered heaven as our forerunner, and that you and I are certain to be with him there. We are as sure to be glorified with him as he is to be glorified with his Father. Why, we are one with him, and we were chosen in him from before the foundation of the world" (Eph. 1:4) Yet when you stand on the top of Amana, it is well to look to your feet, for sometimes high doctrines and weak heads do not agree. When you are on the top of Amana, tarry there as long as you like, but mind that you look from Amana to Golgotha. Oh, I love to hear the doctrine of election preached with the preacher's eye always fixed upon Christ! In the hands of some men, predestination is as hard as a piece of granite. The points of Calvinism with some are like so many halberds [axe with spikes] which they are forever pushing at coming sinners to keep them back from Christ, or else they thrust them into the heart of their brethren in malice and in envy. Let us never so misuse the doctrines of grace. I would have them preached as Dr. [Robert] Hawker did. Such was his loyalty and love for the divine Master that the doctrines of grace, as he taught them, distilled like the dew. You might be saturated with a sense of the divine sovereignty, but, instead of revolting against the absolute claims of the Almighty on your allegiance, you would find yourself refreshed by the sweet influence of his authority. All honour to our most precious Christ, whether he be preached out of contention or goodwill. The sun is bright anyhow, but never as bright when Jesus shines on the crystal of truth, and the crystal reflects the rays of the sun. Brethren, cherish sound doctrine; but, as in the first chapter of the Ephesians, let the *in him,* and the in *whom,* and *in the Beloved,* prove that Jesus Christ himself is the focus of your faith. Let your enjoyment of the infinite privileges and inviolable safety of his chosen people be based and bottomed on the fact that you are one with him. Your heart can only be steadfast as you abide in him; you cannot live without him; therefore, you must wait for the fullness of joy when you shall be with him forever. So look from the top of Amana.

350

Here, too, another mountain is mentioned. Climb to the summit of Mount Hermon, for there is much spiritual strength to be derived from brotherly love. Some churches really are an atrocious scandal to our sacred profession. We have received into our fellowship many Christians who tell us they have been members of six, seven, or eight churches in a very short career — paltry Baptist communities with a building up some court or gateway — which consisted of a lot of quarrelsome people who can hear no preacher to their edification. Discontent drew them together, and it is only a little while before they begin to wrangle with one another, and split up again. Such places may be of some little service to other churches as conduits to a common sewer carrying off the refuse of faithless, factious folk who are always fomenting feuds. But, sorry am to say it, many Christians have been so disgusted with the entire order of church fellowship by their example that they have said, "I will never join a church again." Thank God this has not been our experience. The Lord has given us, notwithstanding the thousand faults that mar our beauty, something like love for one another. I do think that sometimes when we meet together for solemn prayer and sacred praise our sighs and songs have gone up to heaven in sweet concert, and we have been almost as happy as we could be this side of the pearly gates. Down in the Lecture Hall, where we have been breaking bread every Lord's-day, the few hundreds of us who meet there have found the communion of saints passing sweet, and we have been inclined to sing that familiar ditty,

Mid scenes of confusion and creature complaints,
How sweet to my soul is communion with saints!

(David Denham)

A quarrelsome church — what a hell on earth it is! A happy church — a united church — what a blissful scene! My soul would always dwell on Hermon, for there the Lord commanded the blessing, even life for evermore. (Ps. 133:3) But remember, Christian, when you are on Hermon, you must still look to Christ as the centre and sum of all bliss and blessedness. If we seek for all our solace in the brotherhood of saints, apart from the Saviour, of whom the whole family in heaven and earth is named, we shall soon lose the savour of fellowship. Unless we have communion with Christ, we become a mere club of odd fellows holding common opinions. Let the members of the church be all dear to you beyond any creature qualities that may commend them, but love the Head most, for he is Lord of all. Love the brethren, but oh, love Christ! Cherish a full recognition of the unity of the flock amid all the diversity of folds in which the sheep are penned, but cleave close to the good Shepherd. Let your union with Christ be indisputable, and, when sweetest frames and tenderest feelings steal over you in fellowship with Christian brethren, still hear the voice of the Elder Brother saying — "Look from the top of Amana, from the top of Shenir and Hermon.'

So, then, in our highest spiritual enjoyments, whether solitary or with our companions, the enjoyments of the bedroom or of the sanctuary, the Lord's Table or baptism, the hearing of the Word, or the singing of praise, the core of our happiness should be Christ. We must still point to him as the centre of the target. Though the visible church, and the vital doctrines of the gospel, may be, as it were, the proper circumference, yet let him be the centre at which we aim — "Looking unto Jesus, the author and finisher of our faith." (Heb. 12:2)

Our time flies very rapidly, so let us note again that this invitation bids us come away as much from the entanglements and trials as from the enjoyments of life. You see it concludes in this way — "From the lions' dens; from the mountains of the leopards." You do not want much explanation here. You who mingle with the world know that there are many "lions' dens" in it, and you who are constantly toiling and struggling for your livelihood will not fail to interpret the meaning of "the mountains of the leopards." Where is there not a lions' den? In what region is there perfect safety for a Christian? We certainly cannot say of the common walks of life — "No lion shall be there, neither shall any ravenous beast come up thereon." (Is 35:9) True, in the secret path of fellowship with Jesus, there is safety, perfect safety, where the redeemed walk. But while we are men, and among men, we must still be subjected to these beasts of prey, and especially to that roaring lion that goes about seeking whom he may devour. (1 Pet. 5:8) But a sweet voice says — "Come with me from the lions' dens and from the mountains of the leopards." Sister, forget the sickness of your household. Brother, put aside the thought of your poverty for a moment. Merchant, dismiss your calculations, and cast your care on him who cares for you. (1 Pet. 5:7) You who are vexed with many doubts, rock them to rest awhile; and you who are distressed with temptations, don't think about them. Hearken to the voice of Jesus. He is speaking to you. Are not his words sufficient to draw you away from the strife and clamour of your circumstances, and give you strength and confidence to come to him? "Come with me from Lebanon, my spouse, with me from Lebanon." Come away from every earthly care, and away from anxieties, and apprehensions, and despondencies. Flee, you doves, when the hawk pursues you, flee to the clefts of the divine rock, the wounds of Jesus, and hide yourselves there. Oh, that the Spirit of God might enable every one of us to feel as if the whole world with its joys and its sorrows were dead tonight, and as if we were alone with Christ, talking and communing with him! Do not deny your Master the gratification that he asks of you. He asks it because you are his spouse. He loves you; he knows that you love him; he is married to you; you are married to him. You are to live with him forever; you are to be a partner of his glory; you are soon to dwell in his own house, never to be separated from him. Is it not natural that he should want you to come with him now? Can you refuse him? Shall not the sweet love which has made you what you are, and which has bound you to him by such silken chains, shall not this draw you to him now? He wants you to come to him for your good as well as for his own delight. It will make you like him to be with him. Being with you, he will be like a bundle of myrrh (Song 1:13) and will perfume your character. He knows it will charm your grief away. What if you were to depart from the world, were he with you, death would be swallowed up in victory. (1 Cor. 15:54) He knows what there is on this earth to hinder you, and he knows that you will be sanctified by his presence. He knows it will make your faith strong and your love burn vigorously. He knows you need his presence; he understands your emptiness and your weakness without him; and, like as a father pitieth his children (Ps. 103:13), so he pities you, and prescribes this as a remedy for all your ills and all your diseases — "Come with me from Lebanon, my spouse, with me from Lebanon." I will take as my motto at the table tonight — WITH JESUS. Let it be yours as well as mine. With Jesus! Let us try to get every thought with Jesus, every wish with Jesus, every single reflection that looks back, and every hope that looks forward — let it all be with Jesus, and let us sing with Robert Cleaver Chapman, [described by Spurgeon as "the saintliest man I ever knew"]:

The cords that bound my heart to earth
Are broken by His hand ;
Before His cross I found myself
A stranger in the land.

My heart is with Him on His throne,
And ill can brook delay,
Each moment listening for the voice,
" Rise up, and come away !"

With hope deferred oft sick and faint,
"Why tarries He?" I cry ;

Let not the Saviour chide my haste,
For then would I reply :

May not an exile, Lord, desire
His own sweet land to see?
May not a captive seek release,
A prisoner, to be free?

In a very short time, we shall have this message sent to every one of us personally concerning our departure from this world.

"Come with me from Lebanon, my spouse, with me from Lebanon." You will have to go up to your bed as Moses went up to the top of Nebo. (Deut. 34:1) Your brief sojourn below will be left behind you as a panorama that has passed before your eyes. The curtain falls. The busy, boisterous scenes are succeeded by a blank. No longer are you able to attend to the ordinary duties that have usually engaged your attention. Common cares and special trials recede into the background. On that sick bed, you shall feel a strange solitude. To the top of Amana, and to the top of Hermon, you go up, leaving the world far below you, its joys and griefs alike dwindling and growing smaller and smaller. Another world begins to dawn on your nearer sense as you draw close to the verge of time. High up on those lofty peaks another voice will greet your ears, saying — "Come with me, come with me." Then you will leave the poor body, the weak flesh, to become food for worms, and you will mount upwards to be with Jesus. He will come and meet you, and your soul shall spread her wings in haste to go to him. You shall fly undismayed through death's iron gate, nor fear the terror as you pass.

You will go up with Jesus through the fields of ether to the glorious place of his regal abode. There you shall behold his face, and abide in his presence forever, embosomed in his affection, and partakers of his glory.

What joy, what beauty must be there,
In soul and sense — beyond whate'er
Beauty, or joy we call;
Where in his glory shines the King,
Where flows of bliss th' unsullied spring,
Source, centre, end of all!

(Thomas Grinfield)

And yet we do not find it very pleasant to think of death. There are gloomy surroundings that indispose us to sing the *Nunc dimittis*! ["Now dismiss" = Simeon, Lk. 2:29] When languor and disease invade our mortal frame, we start and stand aghast. The graveyard may be so cultivated that it is fair to look on as a garden of flowers. But we shrink at the sight of that cold wet tomb, and those heavy clods as they fall so drearily on the coffin-lid. Who likes to think of lying there in that narrow bed — a mouldering mass of corruption! Ah, but it is all a mistake; we are not our very selves going to be tenants of that house at all! It is merely the body that must be committed to the tomb, there to be refined. We do not go there; *we*, the true *we*, conscious of life, and tenacious of existence — we mount to heaven. We who believe in Jesus, and are preserved by Jesus, we go to be with Jesus. He is not dead, he left the tomb, and we shall go to dwell with him. Our doom is not among the dead, but our destiny is to live where he ever lives. Is it not infinitely sweeter to paint the rapture of the soul in its flight to glory, quitting the domain of sin and sorrow, than to depict those dismal bugbears that haunt our sickly

353

dreams? Blessed death! Blessed death! Were there no dying, we might weep to die. Henry Vaughan's poem on death is a poem of light:

They are all gone into the world of light!
And I alone sit lingering here;
*Their very memory is fair and bright,
And my sad thoughts doth clear.
I see them walking in an air of glory,
Whose light doth trample on my days:
My days, which are at best but dull and hoary,
Mere glimmering and decays.

Dear, beauteous death! the jewel of the just,
Shining nowhere but in the dark;
What mysteries do lie beyond thy dust,
Could man outlook that mark!

He that hath found some fledged bird's nest may know
At first sight, if the bird be flown;
But what fair well or grove he sings in now,
That is to him unknown.

O Father of eternal life, and all
Created glories under thee!
Resume thy spirit from this world of thrall
Into true liberty!

Must we always be shut up in this dreary prison? Like the caged lion, we might run and rage round the bars of our cage. Oh, how the Christian must long to break through the barriers of mortality, and breathe the air of liberty and brightness of an immortal spirit. Our gracious Christ, I think, has crowned death with garlands. Welcome shall be the hour of our departure on the pathway to the realms of the blessed, unless it be granted to us, which were better still, to be caught up together with the Lord in the air. (1 Thess. 4:17) How we shall hail the call of Jesus, "Come with me", though a pale angel bear the message! (Rev. 6:8) The portals close: our brief day is past; but now the gates of Paradise are opened wide to let us in and enjoy the charming wonders of the celestial city. Well now, you have not yet heard this summons, but you may hear it before the labours of this day are over, and your tired limbs lie down to sleep. Here is a sweet thought to some concerning a sudden release from all their cares and sorrows, if perhaps, change should come in the twinkling of an eye. We are never sure to be here long as prisoners in this world. Why, when I think how near death may be to some of us, the stone walls of our dungeon seem to be but mere cardboard. Glistenings of the eternal state gleam through the fence and fort of this mortal nature when we remember that we may be in heaven in a minute. I say, there is just one pulse to stop, the heart to cease its usual beating, and, before the clock next ticks, we may be gone, and you and I may know even as we are known. The land is not very far off; the King in his beauty is only screened from our view by a cloud. Wait his pleasure, and, before long, the angelic messenger shall have the golden token to bring you, the silver cord shall be loosed, the pitcher shall be broken at the fountain, and the wheel broken at the cistern (Eccl. 12:6); then shall the dust return to the earth as it was, and the spirit shall return to God who gave it (verse 7), so shall you will be blessed forever.

354

Ah, dear friends, I would that all in this congregation could understand me! Alas, then, that I should have been talking riddles to so many of you. The sweet voice of the Shepherd, who says "Come with me", will sound strange to you who are not of his sheep. You do not know him. Oh, what you are missing! What can compensate a soul for the lack of that consolation which is in Christ? To be sheltered from the wrath to come; to be forgiven all your sins; to be delivered from the fear of death; to be given a good hope through grace — this is a cause of unspeakable gratitude. Do I hear you say, "Oh, that I had satisfaction like that? I would give all earthly pleasures for such celestial cheer." Soul, you can have it for the seeking. You need not distract your heart with doubts. "Seek, and ye shall find." (Mat. 7:7; Lk. 11:9) If you believe in Jesus, he will befriend you. "And what is it to believe?" you ask. It is to trust him. My Lord Jesus asks nothing of you. You might come into this house with a heart as hard as adamant, but, with a glance of his gracious eye, he can melt it. Black as your character may be, he can brighten it. He has the happy art of turning foes into friends. Oh, that these lips of mine might utter his love to the lowly, saying — "Look unto me, and be ye saved, all ye ends of the earth." (Is. 45:22) Look and you will be lightened.

There is life for a look at the Crucified One;
There is life at this moment for thee;
Then look sinner, look unto him and be saved,
Unto him who was nailed to the tree.

(Amelia Matilda Hull)

Look to him as the substitute for your sins. If you trust him, your trust will be the evidence that he has loved you, and given himself for you.

God grant that you may look to him now. Your look may interpret to you his love. My text shall then be a test of truth to your conscience. He who bought you with his blood shall say to you, "Come with me from Lebanon, my spouse, with me from Lebanon: look from the top of Amana, from the top of Shenir and Hermon, from the lions' dens, and the mountains of the leopards." It will be a happy crisis in your life-story, one and all of you, if you listen and respond to such a call.

355

48. CHRIST'S ESTIMATE OF HIS PEOPLE
NO. 282

DELIVERED ON SABBATH MORNING, JANUARY 23rd, 1859
AT NEW PARK STREET CHAPEL, SOUTHWARK

"How fair is thy love, my sister, my spouse! how much better is thy love than wine! and the smell of thine ointments than all spices! Thy lips, O my spouse, drop as the honeycomb: honey and milk are under thy tongue, and the smell of thy garments is like the smell of Lebanon." (Song of Solomon 4:10-11)

I SHALL not, this evening, attempt to prove that the Song of Solomon has a spiritual meaning. I am sure it has. It has been frequently said, and, I believe, has commonly been thought, that this song was originally written by Solomon upon his marriage with Pharaoh's daughter. Now I am as sure as I am of my own existence, that this is one of the grossest mistakes that ever were committed. There is nothing about Pharaoh's daughter in it. It is, first of all, improbable that it was written of her; and, in the next place, I will go further and affirm that it is impossible that it could have been written by Solomon in honour of her. If you look all through the song, you will find that this is so. In the first beginning, she is compared with a shepherdess. Now, all shepherds are abominations to the Egyptians; do you think, therefore, that Solomon would compare an Egyptian princess with the very thing she abominated. In the next place, all the scenery is in the land of Canaan, none of it in Egypt; and, besides that, all the places that Solomon speaks of, such as Engedi, Lebanon, Amana, and Damascus were all out of the way. Not one of them would have been passed in coming out of Egypt to Jerusalem, and very probably the Egyptian princess did not even know there were such places at all, so that if Solomon had wished to praise her, he would not have compared her eyes with the fish-ponds of Heshbon, but would have spoken of the sweet waters of the Nile. Besides, it could never have been Pharaoh's daughter. Did Pharaoh's daughter ever keep sheep? Yet the person who is represented here did. Did the watchman ever follow her about the streets, and try to take away her veil from her? Solomon would have shown them something if they had! Therefore, that is impossible. In one place, Solomon compares her with a company of horses in Pharaoh's chariot. Now, horses were, among the Israelites, common things; and what would Pharaoh's daughter have said if Solomon had compared her with a company of horses? She might well have looked him in the face and said, "Have you not some better comparison for me than my father's horses?" It is very unlikely that Solomon perpetrated that folly. It is improbable, therefore, and we may almost say impossible, that it could be Pharaoh's daughter. She never came from Lebanon and from the top of Amana; most probably she never heard of those places, or, if she had, she could not have come from them, for she came from Egypt. The fact is, that this book has been a puzzle to many men for the simple reason that it was not written for them at all. Learned men and wise men find this a stone on which they are broken to powder, just because it was not written for them. Men who are disposed to laugh at Scripture find here an opportunity to exercise their profane wit, just because the book is not written for them. This book was called by the Jews, "the Holiest of Holies". They never allowed anyone to read it till he was thirty years of age; it was thought to be such a sacred book. Many a Christian who reads it cannot understand it. And as good Joseph Irons says, "This dwarfish age is not likely to esteem this book as it ought to be esteemed; only those who have lived near to Jesus have drunk out of his cup, have eaten his flesh and drunk his blood, only those who know the fullness of the word 'communion' can sit down to this book with delight and pleasure. And to such men, these words are as wafers made with honey, manna, angels' food: every sentence is like gold, and every word is like much fine gold."

The true believer who has lived near to his Master will find this book to be a mass, not of gold merely, for all God's Word is this, but a mass of diamonds sparkling with brightness, and all things you can conceive are not to be compared with it for its matchless worth. If I must prefer one book above another, I would prefer some books of the Bible for doctrine, some for experience, some for example, some for teaching; but let me prefer this book above all others for fellowship and communion. When the Christian is nearest to heaven, this is the book he takes with him. There are times when he would leave even the Psalms behind. When standing on the borders of Canaan, when he is in the land of Beulah, and is just crossing the stream, and can almost see his Beloved through the rifts of the storm cloud, then it is that he can begin to sing the Song of Solomon. This is about the only book he could sing in heaven; but, for the most part, he could sing this through, the one still praising him who is his everlasting lover and friend.

With these preliminary remarks, let us go at once to the text. I have said that this is Jesus speaking to his Church. How, when the Church praises Jesus, you do not wonder, for he deserves all she can say of him, and ten thousand times more. When she uses such large expressions concerning his loveliness, you feel that she falls far short of her mighty theme; that she does but demean him by her comparisons, for she can only compare the greater with the lesser, and the beautiful and the eternal with that which is mutable and transient. But to hear Christ turn round upon his Church, and seem to say to her,

"You have praised me, I will praise you; you think much of me, I think quite as much of you; you use great expressions of me, I will use just the same to you. You say my love is better than wine, so is yours to me; you tell me all my garments smell of myrrh, so do yours; you say my word is sweeter than honey to your lips, so is yours to mine. All that you can say of me I say it back to you; I see myself in your eyes, I can see my own beauty in you; and, whatever belongs to me, belongs to you. Therefore, O my love, I will sing back the song! You have sung it to your beloved, and I will sing it to my beloved; you have sung it to your Ishi (Hos. 2:16), I will sing it to my Hephzibah (Is. 62:4); you have sung it to your husband, I will sing it to my sister, my spouse."

Now note how sweetly the Lord Jesus sings to his spouse, First, he praises her love: "How fair is thy love, my sister, my spouse! How much better is thy love than wine!" Next, he praises her graces: "The smell of thy ointments is much better than all spices." Then he praises her words: "Thy lips, O my spouse, drop as the honeycomb." Then he praises her thoughts, the things that do not come out of her mouth, but lie under her tongue: "Honey and milk are under thy tongue." Then he finishes by praising her works: "The smell of thy garments is like the smell of Lebanon."

I. Beginning at the beginning, then, Christ first PRAISES HIS PEOPLE'S LOVE.

Do you love God, my hearer? Do you love Jesus? If not, stand away! These things have nothing to do with you, for if you do not follow Christ, you have neither part nor lot in the matter. You are in the gall of bitterness, and in the bond of iniquity. (Acts 8:23) But can you say as Peter did, when his Master asked him thrice, "Simon, son of Jonas, lovest thou me?" Can you say, "Lord, thou knowest all things, thou knowest that I love thee." (Jn. 21:15-17) And do you know, O my Lord, that my grief is that I do not love you more. I pant to have my little love increased that my heart may be eaten up with love, that zeal of love for you may completely consume me?" Hearken then, to what the Lord Jesus says to you tonight, by his Holy Spirit, from this song! Your love, poor, feeble, and cold though it be, is very precious to the Lord Jesus; in fact it is so precious that he himself cannot tell how precious it is. He does not say how precious, but he says, "How fair." This is an expression that men use when they do not know how to describe anything. They lift up

357

their hands, they put in a note of exclamation, and say, "How fair! How precious! How much better is thy love than wine!" The fact is that Jesus values our love at such a price that the Holy Spirit, when he dictated this Song of Solomon, could not see any word in all human language that was large enough to set out Christ's estimation of our love.

Have you ever thought of Christ's love to you till your heart has been melted, while your beloved spoke to you till the tears ran down your eyes, and you believed you could do as Mary Magdalene did, and kiss his feet, and wash them with your tears, and wipe them with the hairs of your head? Now, can you believe it? Just what you think of Christ's love, Christ thinks of yours. You value his love, and you are right in doing so; but I am afraid that you still undervalue it. He even values your love; if I may so speak, he sets a far higher estimate upon it than you do. He thinks very much of little, estimating it not by its strength, but by its sincerity. "Ah", he says, "he does love me, he does love me, I know he does; he sins, he disobeys me, but still I know he loves me. His heart is true, he does not love me as I deserve, but still he loves me." Jesus Christ is delighted with the thought that his people love him, which cheers and gladdens him. Just as the thought of his love gladdens us, so the thought of our love gladdens him. Notice how he puts it when he says, "How much better is thy love than wine!" Now, wine when used in Scripture, frequently signifies two things: a great luxury, and a great refreshment. Wine is a luxury, especially so in this country, and even in the East, where there was more of it, good wine was still a dainty thing. Now, Jesus Christ looks upon his people's love as being a luxury to him; and I will show you that he does. When he sat at the feast of Simon the Pharisee, I have no doubt there were sparkling wine cups on the table, and many rich dainties were there, but Jesus Christ did not care for the wine or for the banquet. What did he care for then? That poor woman's love was much better to him than wine. He could say to Simon the Pharisee, if he had chosen, "Simon, put away your wine cups, and take away your dainties; this is my feast, the feast of my people's love."

I told you also that wine was used as an emblem of refreshment. Now, our Saviour has often been refreshed by his people's love. "No", says one, "that cannot be." Yes! You remember once he was weary and thirsty, and sat on the well of Samaria. He needed wine then indeed to refresh him, but he could not get so much as a drop of water. He spoke to a woman (whom he had loved from before all worlds), and put new life into her, and she at once desired to give him drink; but she ran away first to tell the Samaritans what she had heard. Now, the Saviour was so delighted at her wishing to do good, that when his disciples came, they expected to find him fainting, for he had walked many a weary mile that day, so they said, "Whence hath he meat?" and he said, "I have meat to eat that ye know not of." (Jn. 4:32) It was that woman's love that had fed him. He had broken her heart, he had won her to himself, and when he saw the tear roll from her eye, and knew that her heart was set upon him, his spirits all revived, and his poor flagging strength grew strong. It was this that encouraged him.

No, I will go farther. When Christ went to his cross, there was one thing that cheered him even in the agonies of death; it was the thought of his people's love. Are we not told by the Apostle Paul in the Epistle to the Hebrews that our blessed and divine husband, the Lord Jesus, "...for the joy that was set before him, endured the cross, despising the shame?" What was that joy? Why, the joy that he should see his seed, and that seed would love him, and that he would have his love written in their hearts in remembrance of his dying pains and agonies. Jesus was cheered, even in his death agonies, by the thought of the love of his people, when the bulls of Bashan roared at him, and the dogs bayed at him, when the sun was put out in darkness, when his Father's hand was heavy upon him, when the legions of hell compassed him, when the pangs of body, and the tortures of spirit, all beset him; it was this that cheered him. "My people, they are dear to me, for them I stretch these bleeding hands; for them shall this heart be pierced and oh, how they will love me,

358

how they will love me on earth! How they will love me spiritually in Paradise!" This was the wine the Saviour had to drink; this was the cup of his delightful joy that made him bear all these pains without a murmur, and this was the meaning of these words of Jesus — "How much better is thy love than wine!"

Pause here, my soul, to contemplate a moment, and let your joy wait awhile. Jesus Christ has banquets in heaven such as we have never yet tasted, and yet he does not feed there. He has wines in heaven richer far than all the grapes of Eshcol could produce, but where does he seek his wines? In our hearts, my friends, in our hearts. Not all the love of angels, nor all the joys of Paradise, are so dear to him as the love of his poor people, sprinkled with sin, and compassed with infirmity. Is that not a thought! I may preach about it, but I can only speak it to you. Read it, mark it, learn it, and inwardly digest it. And oh, if you saw him standing here tonight, looking into your eyes, and saying to you personally, "You love me, I know that you love me, your love is to me better far than wine", would you not fall at his feet and say, "Lord, is my love so sweet to you? Then shame upon me that I should give you so little of it." And then you would break out into the Song we sang this morning [Our Own Hymnbook 377, Krishna Pal, translated from Bengali by Joshua Marshman]:

O thou, my soul, forget no more
The Friend who all thy sorrows bore;
Let every idol be forgot;
But, O my soul, forget him not.

Jesus for thee a body takes,
The guilt assumes, thy fetters breaks,
Discharging all they dreadful debt:
And canst thou ere such love forget?

Renounce thy works and ways with grief,
And fly to this most sure relief;
Nor him forget who left his throne,
And for thy life gave up His own.

Infinite truth and mercy shine
In him, and he himself is thine:
And canst thou then, with sin beset,
Such charms, such matchless charms forget?

Ah, no; when all things else depart,
His name shall cheer and warm my heart;
And lisping this, from earth I'll rise,
And join the chorus of the skies.

Ah, no: when all things else expire,
And perish in the endless fire,
This name all others shall survive,
And through eternity shall live.

This is the first point: the love of the believer is sweet to Christ.

II. Do not imagine, however, that Christ despises our faith, or our hope, or our patience, or our humility. All these GRACES are precious, to him, and they are described in the next sentence under the title of ointment, and the working of these graces, their exercise and development, are compared with the smell of ointment.

Now, both wine and ointment were used in the sacrifices of the Jews; sweet smelling myrrh and spices were used in meat offerings and drink offerings before the Lord. "But", says Jesus Christ to his church, "all these offerings of wine, and all that burning of incense, is nothing to me compared with your graces. Your love is my wine, and your virtues are my sweet smelling ointments." For now you have a little faith, but oh, how little it is! You seem to have got just faith enough to know how unbelieving you are; you have got love, but somehow you have only got love enough to let you know how little you love him. You have some humility, but you have only enough to discover you are very proud. You have some zeal for Christ, but you have only enough to make you chide yourself that you are so cold. You have some hope, but you have only hope enough to lead you to see how despairing and desponding you often are. You have some patience, but you have only patience enough to teach you how often you murmur when you ought not to. "I confess", say you, "that all my graces are a stench in my own nostrils, and all the good things I trust I have, I cannot look on them with any pride or self-congratulation. I must bury myself in dust and ashes; and even those things, I can but weep over them, for they are so marred by my own evil nature." But now then, the very things that you and I very properly weep over, Christ delights in. He loves all these: the smell may seem to be but very faint and feeble, yet Jesus observes it, Jesus smells it, Jesus loves it, and Jesus approves it. Yes, believer, when you are on your sick bed and are suffering with patience; when you go about your humble way to do good by stealth; when you distribute your alms to the poor; when you lift up your thankful eye to heaven; when you draw near to God with humble prayer, and make confession of your sin to him; all these acts are like the smell of ointment to him, the smell of a sweet savour, and he is gratified and pleased. O Jesus, this is condescension indeed, to be pleased with such poor things as we display. Oh, this is love, as it proves your love to us, that you can make so much out of so little, and esteem so highly that which is of such little worth! Have you never known a little child, when he feels love in his heart, go into the garden or the field and bring you a little flower. It may be but a little buttercup or a daisy, a great thing to him, perhaps, but a trifle to you — worthless in fact — yet you took it and smiled and felt happy because it was a token of your child's love?

So Jesus esteems your graces, for they are his gift to you. Mark, first of all, they are very poor things in themselves, till he esteems them as tokens of your love, and rejoices in them, and declares they are as sweet to him as all the spices of Araby, and all the rich odours of the merchants. This is the second thing.

III. Now we come to the third: "Thy lips, O my spouse, drop as the honeycomb."

Christ's people are not a dumb people. They were once, but they TALK now. I do not believe a Christian can keep the secret that God gives him if he were to try; it would burst his lips open to get it out. When God puts grace into your heart, you may try to hide it, but hide it you cannot. It will be like fire in the bones, and will be sure to find its way out. Now, the church is a talking church, a preaching church, and a praising church; she has got lips, and every believer will find he must use his lips in the service of Christ. Now, it is but a poor, poor matter that any of us can speak. When we are most eloquent in our Master's praise, how far our praises fall beneath his worth! When we are most earnest in prayer, how powerless is our wrestling compared with the great blessing that we seek to obtain! When our song is loudest, and begins to be something akin to the chorus of the angels, even then, how marred it is with the discord of our unbelief and our worldliness! But Jesus Christ does not find any fault in what the Church speaks. He says, "No, 'Thy lips, O my spouse, drop us the honeycomb.'" You know the honey that drops out of the honeycomb

360

is the best — it is called the life-honey. So the words that drop from the Christian's lips are the very words of his life, his life-honey, and they ought to be sweet to everyone. They are as sweet to the taste of the Lord Jesus as the drops of the honeycomb.

Here is a little caution to some of you that talk too much. Some of you do not let your words drop as the honeycomb; they gush out as a great stream that sweeps everything before it, so that others cannot thrust in a word edgeways; no, not if it were squeezed together and sharpened at one end could it be got in. They must talk, their tongue seems set on a hinge like a pendulum, forever going on, swing! swing! swing! Now, Christ does not admire that. He says of his church in his commendation, her lips "drop as the honeycomb." Now a honeycomb, when it drops, does not drop so much as the drops that fall from the eaves of houses; for the honey is thick and rich, and therefore it takes some time. One drop hangs for a time; then comes another, and then another, and does not all come in quick succession. Now, when people are often talking a great deal, it is poor and thin, and good for nothing; but when they have something good to say, it drops by slow degrees like the honey from the honeycomb. Mark, I do not want you to say one good word less. There are those other words, those awkward ones. Oh that we could leave them out! I am as guilty of this myself, I fear, as many others. If we could talk half as much, it would be, perhaps, twice as good; and if we were to say only a tenth of what we do, perhaps we should be ten times better, for he is a wise man that knows how to speak well, but he is a great deal wiser a man who knows how to hold his tongue. The lips of the true church, the lips of the true believer, drop like the honeycomb, with rich words, rich thoughts, rich prayers, rich praises. "Oh", says one, "but I am sure my lips do not drop like that when in prayer. Sometimes even I cannot get on at all, and when I am singing, I cannot put my heart into it, and when I am trying to instruct others, I feel I am so ignorant that I know nothing myself." That is your estimate. I am glad you are so humble as to think that. But Christ does not think so. "Ah", he says, "that man would preach if he could; that man would honour me better if he could." And he does not measure what we do, but what we want to do. And so it is that he reckons our lips drop like the honeycomb. What is sweeter in the world than honey from the honeycomb? But whatever may be the sweetest thing to the world, the words of the Christian are the sweetest things to Christ. Sometimes believers are privileged to sit down together, and begin to talk about what he said, and what he suffered for them here below. They begin to speak of his exceeding glories and his boundless and matchless love; they begin to tell one another what they have tasted and handled of the good word of life, and their hearts begin to burn within them when they speak of these things by the way. Do you know that Jesus is in that room, smiling Jesus is there, and he is saying to his own soul, "It is good to be here, the lips of these my brethren drop as the honeycomb, and their words are sweet to me." At another time the Christian is alone in his chamber, and he talks with his God in a few broken words, and with many sighs, many tears, and many groans, and little does he think that Jesus Christ is there, saying to such a one, "Thy lips, O my beloved, drop with honey like the honeycomb."

And now, Christians, will you not talk much about Jesus? Will you not speak often of him? Will you not give your tongue more continually to prayer and praise, and speech that ministers to edifying, when you have such a listener as this, such an auditor who stoops from heaven to hear you, and who values every word you speak for him? Oh, it is a sweet thing to preach when the people listen to catch every word! I would give in if I had to preach to an inattentive audience. And yet I do not know. Plato, we are told, was once listening to an orator, and when all the people had gone away but Plato, the orator went on with all his might. Being asked why he proceeded, he replied that Plato was sufficient audience for any man. And surely if in preaching, or in praying, all the world should find fault, and all the world should run from it, Jesus is enough to be the hearer for anyone. And if he is satisfied, if he says our words are sweeter than the honeycomb, we will not stop; all the devils in hell shall not stop us. We could continue to preach, and praise, and

361

pray, while immortality endures. If this be honey, then the honey shall drop. If Christ prizes it, we set his opinion against all the opinions of the world; he knows better than any others; he is the best judge, for he is the last and final judge — we will go on talking of him, while he goes on to say that our lips drop as the honeycomb. "But", says one, "if I were to try to talk about Jesus Christ, I do not know what to say." If you wanted any honey, and nobody would bring it to you, I suppose the best way, if you were in the country, would be to keep some bees, would it not? It would be very well for you Christian people if you kept bees. "Well", says one, "I suppose our thoughts are to be the bees. We are always to be looking about for good thoughts, and flying on to the flowers where they are to be found. By reading, by meditation and by prayer, we are to send bees out of the hive." Certainly, if you do not read your Bibles, you will have no honey, because you have no bees. But when you read your Bibles, and study those precious texts, it is like bees settling on flowers and sucking the sweetness out of them. There are many other books, though the Bible is the chief one that you may read with great advantage; over which your thoughts may be as busy as bees among flowers. And then you must attend the means of grace continually. You must listen often to the preaching of the Word; and if you hear a minister who is a plant of the Lord's right hand planting, and you take in what you hear, you will be like the bees sucking sweetness out of flowers, and your lips will be like the honeycomb. But some people have nothing in their heads, and they are never likely to have, for they are so wise that they cannot learn, and they are such fools that they will never teach. Some waste the time they have. Now, I would have my people read much the Word of God, and study it, and then read such books that illustrate it. I will tell you where I have been sipping a bit just lately, and I have often sipped much from — it is this book of the Song of Solomon. It is a favourite book of mine. And there is a sweet little book by Joseph Irons called *Nymphas, Bride and Bridegroom Communing. A Periphrastic Exposition of the Song of Solomon in blank verse*. If any of you have that little book, set your bees to work on it, and if you do not suck honey out of it, I am very much mistaken. Then let the bees bring the honey to the hive of your memory, and let it be added to the stores of your mind, and in this way you will get rich in precious things, so that when you speak, the saints will be edified, your prayers will be full of marrow and fatness, and your praises will have something in them, because you have sent your bees well abroad, and therefore your lips will drop as the honeycomb.

IV. This brings us to the next topic — "Honey and milk are under thy tongue."

I find it necessary, when I preach, to keep a good stock of words under my tongue as well as those that are on it. It is a curious operation of the mind in the man who continually preaches. It sometimes happens while I am speaking to you that I am thinking about what I am going to say at the close of my sermon, and when I am thinking about people downstairs or in the gallery, and how I shall hit Mr. So-and-so, I am still talking right on, speaking with all my heart on the subject on which I am addressing you. It is because, by continually preaching, we get into the habit of keeping words under our tongue as well as those that are on the top, and sometimes we find it necessary to keep those words under our tongue altogether and not let them come further. Very often, I have got a simile just ready to come out, and I have thought, "Ah, that is one of your laughable similes, take that back!" I am obliged to change it for something else. If I did that a little oftener perhaps, it would be better, but I cannot do it. I have sometimes a whole host of them under my tongue, and I am obliged to keep them back. "Honey and milk are under thy tongue." That is not the only meaning. The Christian is to have words ready to come out by-and-by. You know, the hypocrite has words on his tongue. We speak about solemn sounds on a thoughtless tongue, but the Christian has his words first under the tongue. There they lie. They come from his heart; they do not come from the top of his tongue — they are not superficial service work, but they come from under the tongue — deep down — things that he feels, and matters that he knows. Nor is this the only meaning. The things that are

362

under the tongue are thoughts that have never yet been expressed; they do not get to the top of the tongue, but lie there half formed and are ready to come out; but either because they cannot come out, or we have no time to let them out, there they remain, and never come into actual words. Now Jesus Christ thinks very much even of these; he says, "Honey and milk are under thy tongue"; and Christian meditation and Christian contemplation are to Christ like honey for sweetness, and like milk for nourishment. Honey and milk are two things with which the land of Canaan was said to flow; and so the heart of a Christian flows with milk and honey, like the land which God gave to his ancient people. "Well", says one, "I cannot find that my heart is like that. If I sit down and think of Jesus, my thoughts turn upon the glories of his Person and the excellence of his office. But oh, sir, my thoughts are such dull, cold, useless things; they do not feed me or delight me!" Ah, but, you see, Christ does not estimate them as you do; he feeds on them, they are like honey to him, and though you think little of your own thoughts, and are right in doing so, yet, oh, remember, such is the love of Jesus, such is his abundant condescension and compassion, that the very least things that you have he values at a great price. The words you are not speaking, the words you cannot utter, the groans you cannot bring out — these the Holy Spirit utters for you; and these Jesus treasures up as choice and peculiarly precious things. "Honey and milk are under thy tongue."

V. And then, last of all, "the smell of thy garments is like the smell of Lebanon."

The odoriferous herbs that grew on the side of Lebanon delighted the traveller, and, perhaps, here is an allusion to the peculiarly sweet smell of the cedar wood. Now, the garments of a Christian are twofold — the garment of imputed righteousness, and the garment of inwrought sanctification. I think the allusion here is to the second. The garments of a Christian are his EVERY DAY ACTIONS — the things that he wears upon him wherever he goes. Now, these smell very sweet to the Lord Jesus. And let us speak to some of you here present, who manifestly are not God's children, for you smell of the garlic of Egypt rather than of the cedar of Lebanon; and there are some professors, and, perhaps, some now present, whose smell is anything but like that of Lebanon. Take heed, you that do not live up to your profession. You have sad evidences within that you do not have not possession. If you can dishonour Christ's holy gospel by living in sin, tremble, lest when he shall come in the terror of judgement, he should cry, "Depart, ye cursed; I never knew you!" But if you are lovers of Christ, and really have your hearts set upon him, your daily actions are observed by him, and the smell of it is to him as sweet as the smell of Lebanon. What should you think if Jesus should meet you at the close of the day and say to you, "I am pleased with the works of today?" I know you would reply, "Lord, I have done nothing for you." You would say, like those at the last day, "Lord when saw we thee hungry and fed thee? When saw we thee thirsty and gave thee drink?" (Mat. 25:35-39) You would begin to deny that you had done any good thing. He would say,

"Ah, when you were under the fig tree I saw you (Jn. 1:48, 50); when you were at your bedside in prayer, I heard you. I saw you when the tempter came, and you said, 'Get thee hence, Satan'; I saw you give your alms to one of my poor sick children; I heard you speak a good word to the little child, and teach him the name of Jesus; I heard you groan when swearing polluted your ears; I heard you sigh when you saw the iniquity of this great city; I saw when your hands were busy; I saw that you were not an eye-servant or a man-pleaser, but that in singleness of purpose you served God in doing your daily business; I saw you, when the day was ended, give yourself to God again; I marked you mourning over the sins you have committed, and I tell you I am pleased with you."

"The smell of thy garments is like the smell of Lebanon." And, again, I hear you say, "But, Lord, I was angry, I was proud", and he says, "But I have covered this over, I have cast it

363

into the depths of the sea; I have blotted it all out with my blood. I can see nothing bad in you; you are all fair, my love, there is no spot in you." What would you do then? Would you not at once fall down at his feet and say, "Lord, I never knew love like this: I have heard that love covers a multitude of sins, but I never knew a love so broad as to cover all mine. And then declare that you can see no sin in me at all — ah, that is love!" It may melt our heart, and make us seek to be holy, that we might not grieve Christ, make us labour to be diligent in his service, that we might not dishonour him.

I dare say some of you think when ministers preach or go about doing their pastoral duty, that of course Christ is very much pleased with them. "Ah", says Mary, "I am only a poor servant girl; I have to get up in the morning and light the fire, lay out the breakfast things, dust the parlour, make the pies and puddings for dinner, and clear away the things again, and wash them up — I have to do everything there is to do in the house — Christ cannot be pleased with this." Why Mary, you can serve Christ as much in making beds as I can in making sermons; and you can be as much a true servant of Christ in dusting a room as I can in administering discipline in a church. Do not think for a single moment that you cannot serve Christ. Our religion is to be an everyday religion — a religion for the kitchen as well as for the parlour, a religion for the rolling pin, and the jack-towel, quite as much as for the pulpit stairs and the Bible — a religion that we can take with us wherever we go. And there is such a thing as glorifying Christ in all the common actions of life. Servants, be obedient to your masters, not only to those who are good and gentle, but to the difficult. (1 Pet. 2:18)

You men of business, you need not think that when you are measuring your ribbons, or weighing out your pounds of sugar, or when you are selling, or buying, or going to market, and such like, that you cannot be serving Christ. Why a builder can serve Christ in putting his bricks together, and you can serve Christ in whatever you are called to do with your hands, if you do it as unto the Lord, and not unto men. I remember Mr. Jay once said that if a shoeblack were a Christian, he could serve Christ in blacking shoes. He ought to black them, he said, better than anyone else in the parish; and then people would say, "Ah, this Christian shoeblack, he is conscientious; he won't send the boots away with the heels half done, but will do them thoroughly." And so ought you. You can say of every article you sell, and of everything you do, "I turned that out of my hands in such a way that it shall defy competition. The man has got his money's worth; he cannot say I am a rogue or a cheat. There are tricks in many trades, but I will not have anything to do with them; many get money fast by adulteration in trade, but I will not do it, I would sooner be poor than do it." Why, the world says, "There is a sermon in that grocer's window — look, you don't see him telling lies to puff his goods: there is a sermon there." People say, as they pass by, "It is a godly man that keeps that shop; he cannot bring his conscience down to do what others do. If you go there, you will be well treated, and you will come out of his shop and say, I have spent my money well, and I am glad that I have dealt with a Christian man." Depend on it! You will be as good preachers in your shops as I shall be in my pulpit, if you do that. Depend on it, there is a way of serving Christ in this way; and this is to comfort you and cheer you. Upon all the actions of your daily life, the Lord Jesus looks down from heaven and says, "The smell of thy garments is like the smell of Lebanon." I know you can hardly believe that Jesus Christ takes notice of such little things as that, but be does. You say, "Oh, but they are too trifling." But don't you know that the God who wings an angel guides a sparrow? Don't you know that "the very hairs of your head are all numbered?" (Mat. 10:30) God not only wings the whirlwind, and gives an edge to the lightning flash, but he guides the chaff from the hand of the winnower, and steers the grain of dust in the evening gale. Do not think anything too little for you. He observes the mighty orbs as they whirl through space, but he notices you too, as you go about your business. And those little cups of cold water you give to his people — those little services you do for his church, those self-denials that you make for his honour, and those conscientious scruples which you foster, and which will not allow you to act as the world does, all these he observes, and he says, "The smell of thy garments is like the smell of Lebanon."

And now to conclude, what shall we say to this? I was reading sometime ago an article in a newspaper, very much in my praise; and you know, it makes me sad, so sad, that I could cry, if ever I see anything praising me; it breaks my heart. I feel I do not deserve it; and then I say, "Now I must try and be better so that I may deserve it. If the world abuses me, I am a match for that, I begin to like it. It may fire all its big guns at me, but I will not return a solitary shot, just store them up, and grow rich upon the old iron. All the abuse it likes to heap upon me I can stand; but when a man praises me, I feel it is a poor thing I have done, sad that he praises me for what I do not deserve. This crushes me down, and I say I must set to work and deserve this. I must preach better. I must be more earnest, more diligent in my Master's service.

Now, will not this text produce just the same effect in you? When the Lord comes to you, and begins saying, "You are not so humble, nor so prayerful, nor so believing, as you ought to be", you say, "I do not care about this whipping." But when he comes and begins to praise you, and tells you, "your lips drop as the honeycomb, that all your actions smell of myrrh, and that your love is better than wine, and that the thoughts under your tongue are better to him than wine and milk", what will you say? Oh, Lord, I cannot say you are mistaken, for you are infallible; but if I might say such a thing, if I dared so think you are mistaken, I should say, "You are mistaken in me." But Lord, I cannot think you are mistaken, so it must be true. Still, Lord, I do not deserve it; I am conscious I do not, and I never can deserve it. Still, if you will help me, I will strive to be worthy of your praise in some feeble measure. I will seek to live up to those high encomiums which you have passed upon me. If you say, "My love is better than wine", Lord, I will seek to love you better, that the wine may be richer and stronger. If you say, "My graces are like the smell of ointment", Lord, I will try to increase them, so as to have many great pots filled with them. And if my words drop as the honeycomb, Lord, there shall be more of them, and I will try to make them better, so that you may think more of such honey; and if you declare that the thoughts under my tongue are to you like honey and milk, then, Lord, I will seek to have more of those divine thoughts. And if my daily actions are to you as the smell of Lebanon, Lord, I will seek to be more holy, to live nearer to you; I will ask for grace, that my actions may be really what you say they are.

You that do not love God, I could weep over you, for you have nothing to do with this text. It is a frightful thing that you should be shut out of such praise as this — may Christ bring you in! You must first be brought to feel you are nothing; you must then be led to feel that Christ is everything, and then, after that, you will understand this text, and these words will speak to you.

49. THE LORD'S OWN VIEW OF HIS CHURCH AND PEOPLE

NO. 1957

AT THE METROPOLITAN TABERNACLE, NEWINGTON

"A garden inclosed is my sister, my spouse; a spring shut up, a fountain sealed."
(Song of Solomon 4:12)

WE understand this sacred love song to be a Canticle of Communion between the Lord Jesus Christ and his church. He is the bridegroom, and she the bride. Solomon furnishes the figure, as some think, as his Solyma [Jerusalem, Zion] is with him; but the type is dimly seen, it being the antitype which shines forth as the sun to the view of all spiritual minds.

At the very outset of the present discourse, it is needful, for the sake of the less instructed, to say what the church is. A church is a congregation of the faithful — that is to say, of believers in the Lord Jesus, in whom the Holy Spirit has created faith in Christ, and the new nature of which faith is the sure index. The one church of Jesus Christ is made up of all believers throughout all time. Just as any one church is made up of faithful men, so the one church of Christ is made up of all faithful churches in all lands and of all faithful men in all ages.

The church was viewed as one in the purpose of God before the world was. The Eternal Father chose for himself a people, and gave them over to his SON, that they might be his portion forever and ever. This is the church of which we read — "Christ loved the church, and gave himself for it." (Eph. 5:25) This is "the church of God, which he hath purchased with his own blood." (Acts 20:28) This is the church with which the marriage supper will be celebrated when the Well-beloved will come to take his own to himself forever. While we, at this time, speak of the church as a whole, it will be quite correct for each individual believer to take home to himself any truth, whether doctrinal, experimental, or practical, which we deal with as the heritage of the church. Each saint may say, "This belongs to me." That which belongs to the redeemed family belongs to each member of that family. That which is true of light is true of each light-beam; that which is true of water is true of each drop; and that which is true of the church as a whole is true of each member of that mystical body.

The love of the Lord Jesus is for his church as a body, and it is the same for each believer as a member of that body. That which is true of the whole number is true of the units which make it up. He who invites a company to a feast virtually invites each person of that company. Jesus loves each one of his people with that same love with which he loves the whole of his people; insofar that, if you, my brethren, are Christ's beloved, and if you were the only people that were ever born into the world, and all his love were yours, he would not then love you one atom more than he loves you now. The love of Jesus is dispersed, but not divided; it flows to all with the same force with which it flows to one. To redeem a single soul our Ransom must have laid down his life, and he loves each one with such a love that he laid down his life for each one, as much as if there had not been another to redeem. We shall not be presumptuous if we enjoy all the love of Jesus of which we are capable, enjoying and appropriating the words of love to ourselves as if they were meant for us alone. The invitation of the bridegroom in this Song gives a permit to the largest faith and to the most daring enjoyment. "Eat, O friends; yea, drink abundantly, O beloved." (Song 5:1)

I shall call your attention to four things, with as much brevity and earnestness as possible. Come, gracious Spirit, and lead us into the sweetness of them!

I. The first is, THE NEARNESS OF KIN OF THE CHURCH TO CHRIST, AND CHRIST TO THE CHURCH. He calls her in the text, "My sister, my spouse."

As if he could not express his near and dear relationship to her by any one term, he employs two. "My sister" — that is, one by birth, partaker of the same nature. "My spouse" — that is, one in love, joined by the sacred ties of affection that can never be snapped. "My sister" is by birth, "My spouse" is by choice. "My sister" in communion, "My spouse" in absolute union with myself. Now, I want you who love the Saviour to get a full hold of this thought of near and dear kinship under this head. Oh, how near akin Christ is to all his people!

But first, *do try to realise the Person of Christ*. I am not going to speak to you at this time of a doctrine, or a mere historical fact that has vanished into the dim past, No, we speak of a real Person. Jesus Christ *is*. As Man and as God in the perfection of his nature he still exists. He dwells at the right hand of God at this moment, and though he cannot be here in his corporeal person, yet he is everywhere by his spiritual presence, which is more real still. Do not spirit him away. Believe that he truly is, and that he truly is here — as much here, and as really here, as he was in Jerusalem, when he sat at the head of the table and entertained the twelve at the last supper. Jesus is a real Man, a real Christ — recollect that.

Then let this further truth be equally well realised, that *he has so taken upon himself our human nature that he may correctly call his church his sister*. He has become so truly man in his incarnation that he is not ashamed to call us brethren. He calls us so because we are so. No; he is not a deified man any more than he is a humanised God. He is perfectly God, but he is also perfectly man; and a man such as we are, touched with the feeling, not only of our attainments, but of our infirmities; not only trusting in all points as we do, but tempted in all points like as we are, though without sin. (Heb. 4:15) When he was here, he was evidently a man and eminently a man; and he now so remembers all that he passed through while here below that he remains in perfect sympathy with us at this very moment. Change of place has made no change of heart in him. He in his glory is the same Jesus as in his humiliation.

No man is so fully a man as Jesus Christ. If you speak of any other man, something or other narrows his manhood. You think of Milton as a poet and an Englishman rather than as a man. You think of Oliver Cromwell rather as of a warrior than as a man. Either his office, his work, his nationality, or his peculiar character, strikes you in many a man rather than his manhood; but Jesus is *the* Man, the model Man: in all his deeds and words man to the fullness of manhood, in its purest and truest state. The second Adam is, *par excellence*, man. We may not think of him as one among a vast number who may be distantly akin to us, as all men are akin to one another by descent; but *the Lord comes near to each individual*. He takes each one of his believing people by the hand, and says, "My brother!" In our text, he salutes the whole church as "My sister!" He says this with tender emphasis. The love between brothers, if those brothers are what they should be, is very strong, and particularly disinterested and admirable. A brother is born for adversity. A true brother is one upon whom you can rely in time of need. One heart in two bodies is the realisation of true brotherhood. Such is emphatically the relationship of the Redeeming Lord to each believer. He is your brother. "The man is next of kin to us." You may have the joy of saying, "I know that my near Kinsman liveth, and that he shall stand at the latter day upon the earth: and though after my skin worms destroy this body, yet in my flesh shall I

367

see God." (Job 19:25) Happy the man who, without presumption, can feel the ties of kinship with the Son of Man, and can sing with the poet of the sanctuary,

Jesus, our Kinsman and our God,
Arrayed in majesty and blood,
Thou art our life; our souls in thee
Possess a full felicity.

(Isaac Watts)

As we have already observed, the first term "*sister*" implies kinship of nature, but the second term *"my spouse"* indicates another kinship, dearer, and, in some respects, nearer: a kinship undertaken of choice, but, once undertaken, is irrevocable and everlasting. This kinship amounts to unity, insofar that the spouse loses her name, loses her identity, and, to a high degree, is merged in the greater personality to which she is united.

Such is our union with Christ, if indeed we are his, that nothing can so well illustrate it as the marriage union. He loves us so much that he has taken us up into himself by the absorption of love. We may henceforth forego our name, for "this is the name wherewith she shall be called, The Lord our righteousness." (Jer. 23:6, 33:16) Wonderful that the very name which belongs to our Lord Jesus, and one of the most majestic of his names, should yet be used as the name of his church! The Lord Jesus Christ's name is now named upon her, and she is permitted to make use of his name whenever she draws near to the throne of the heavenly grace in prayer. "In his name" — this is to be her great plea whenever she intercedes with heaven. She speaks in the name which is above every name, the name at which angels bow.

The Bridegroom calls his church "my sister, my spouse." Now come, renewed heart, you who have learned to trust your Saviour, see how near, how dear, you are to him! If he says, "My sister, my spouse", answer to him, "My Brother, my Husband." If he is not strange to you, oh, do not be cold to him! Do not think of him as of some great one to whom you may not approach. Do you hold in your memory that great text, "It shall be at that day, saith the Lord, that thou shalt call me Ishi (my Husband), and shalt call me no more Baali, (my Lord). For I will take away the names of Baalim out of her mouth, and they shall no more be remembered by their name." (Hos. 2:17) We feel no dreadful lordship now. Though he is Master and Lord, yet it is such a loving lordship which he exercises towards us that we rejoice in it. We hear a voice full of music, saying, "He is thy Lord, and worship thou him" (Ps. 45:11); but his commandments are not grievous. His yoke is easy, and his burden is light. (Mat. 11:30) When we bow before him, it is not because we fear with servile trembling, but because we rejoice and love. We rejoice in his rule and reign. Perfect love has cast out fear. (1 Jn. 4:18) We live in such joyful fellowship with him as a sister has with a brother, or a wife with her husband. Do not be backward towards your own Betrothed. Do not be stiff and cold. Do not set a boundary around the mount, for it is not Sinai: there are no bounds to the hill of Zion. Do not hang up a curtain, for he has rent the veil. Do not think of him as though he were far divided from you, when he is exceeding near to you, and has taken you up unto himself to be one with him forever.

Lost in astonishment I see
Jesus, thy boundless love to me:
With angels I thy grace adore,
And long to love and praise thee more.

Since thou wilt take me for thy bride,
Oh, keep me, Saviour, near thy side!
I fain would give thee all my heart,
Nor ever from my Lord depart.

(John Fawcett)

I do not know how to preach on this subject. Who can? Is it a subject for exposition in a mixed assembly? If it were, who could compass it? I beg you, O believers, to sit in your pews, and let holy thoughts occupy you. Let this choice subject saturate your willing minds. If you are true believers, if you have been born again, if you are really looking to Christ alone for salvation, he has brought you into a condition of the utmost conceivable nearness with himself. He has participated in *your* nature, and he has made you a partaker of *his* nature, and, in so many words, he says, "I will betroth thee unto me for ever; yea, I will betroth thee unto me in righteousness, and in judgement, and in loving-kindness, and in mercies. I will even betroth thee unto me in faithfulness: and thou shalt know the Lord." (Hos. 20:19-20) Can you grasp it? It will make your heart dance for joy if you can. Never did a more joyful thought illuminate a human mind. One with Jesus! By eternal union, one with Jesus! Is not this heavenly? There can be no divorce between Christ and his church, for thus it is written, "The Lord, the God of Israel, saith that he hateth putting away." (Mal. 2:16) He will have nothing to do with putting away. Having espoused us, he declares the thing done. "I am married unto you, saith the Lord." (Jer. 3:14) He has taken our nature, and made us "partakers of the divine nature" (1 Pet. 1:4); and after he has done that, who shall separate us from the love of God which is in Christ Jesus our Lord? (Rom. 8:35, 39) Neither height, nor depth, nor angels, nor principalities, nor powers, nor things present, nor things to come, shall ever be able to effect a break up of this most complete, perfect, mystical union between Christ and his people. Again, I pray the Holy Spirit to make every believer feel this, and then we shall go home from this house glad in spirit. My heart will be as a wedding-feast, and the joy-bells of my soul will ring out with the words of William Williams, the "sweet singer of Wales":

White and ruddy is my Beloved
All his heavenly beauties shine;
Nature can't produce an object,
Nor so glorious, so divine;
He hath wholly
Won my soul to realms above.

Such as find thee find such sweetness
Deep, mysterious, and unknown;
Far above all worldly pleasures,
If they were to meet in one;
My Beloved,
O'er the mountains haste away.

II. To a second thought, I would call your attention. See in the text THE SECURITY OF THE PEOPLE OF GOD IN CONSEQUENCE OF BEING WHAT THEY ARE. "A garden inclosed is my sister, my spouse; a spring shut up, a fountain sealed."

We are not only like a garden, but a garden enclosed. If the garden were not enclosed, the wild boar out of the wood would strip the vines and uproot the flowers; but infinite mercy has made the church of God an enclosure into which no invader may dare to come. "For I, saith the Lord, will be unto her a wall of fire round about, and will be the glory in the midst

369

of her." (Zech. 2:5) Is she a spring? Are her secret thoughts and loves and desires like cool streams of water? Then the bridegroom calls her "a spring shut up." Otherwise, every beast that passed by might foul her waters, and every stranger might quaff her streams. She is a spring shut up, a fountain sealed, like some choice cool spring in Solomon's private garden around the house of the forest of Lebanon — a fountain which he reserved for his own drinking by placing the royal seal upon it, and locking it up by secret means known only to himself. Legend has it that there were fountains which no one knew about but Solomon, and he had so shut them up that, with his ring, he touched a secret spring, a door opened, and living waters leaped out to fill his jewelled cup. No one knew except Solomon the secret charm by which he set flowing the pent-up stream from which no lips drank but his own. Now, God's people are as much shut up, and preserved, and kept from danger by the care of Christ, as the springs in Solomon's garden were reserved expressly for himself.

Beloved, this is a cheering thought for all believers, that the Lord has set apart him that is godly for himself. (Ps. 4:3) He has taken measures to preserve all his chosen from all those who would defile and destroy them. He walled them round about with his divine decree of old, saying, "This people have I chosen for myself." He then issued his command that none should injure them, saying, "Touch not mine anointed, and do my prophets no harm." (1 Chron, 16:22; Ps. 105:15) He sets a hedge about them in providence, so that nothing shall by any means harm them. He has shut them up from the enemy, and sealed them up for perpetual preservation. The wandering Bedouins in the East plundered the open fields; but a king's garden, enclosed and protected, is safe from their ravages. So are the saints enclosed from all invading powers. Especially has the Lord walled them about with grace. While angels keep watch and ward around this sacred garden to drive off the powers of darkness, the invincible grace of God is ever like a wall about the plants of the Lord's right hand planting, so that neither sin nor the world shall be able to uproot them. You are a garden, and a garden is a tender thing, soon destroyed; but the Lord who planted you has seen to your protection and provision. A garden in the East is a very needy place. One day's burning sun might suffice to wither all its verdure; but then the Lord has declared of his church, "The sun shall not smite thee by day, nor the moon by night" (Ps. 121:6), and "I the Lord do keep it; I will water it every moment; lest any hurt it, I will keep it night and day." (Is 27:3) A garden is a dependent thing, requiring perpetual care from the husbandman; and that care the church of God shall have, for it is written, "He careth for you." (1 Pet. 5:7) Jesus says, "My Father is the husbandman" (Jn. 15:1); and surely that is enough.

In a garden, weeds spring up; and, alas, in the church, and in our hearts, the weeds of sin are plentiful! But there is One who will take care to pluck up evil growths, and cut away all rank shoots, that none of the precious plants may be choked or overgrown. In all ways, every single plant, however feeble, shall be tended with all-sufficient skill.

It is very precious to see how the Lord lays himself out to preserve his own beloved. We are too dear to him to let us perish. Yet, O tender plant, you are often fearful! Did you say the other day that he had left you? How can this be? Do you know at what a price he bought you? Leave you? Will the husband forget his beloved spouse, and will the Husband of your soul forget you? Do not let the thought tarry with you for a moment, for it is dishonouring to your Lord's love. "Can a woman forget her sucking child, that she should not have compassion on the son of her womb? Yes, they may forget, yet will I not forget thee." (Is. 49:15) You are as safe as Jesus, for on his heart he bears your name. You are as safe as he is, for on the arm of his strength he wears your name, as the high priest wore the names of the tribes on his shoulder, as well as on his breastplate. "I give unto my sheep", says he, "eternal life; and they shall never perish, neither shall any man pluck them out of my hand." (Jn. 10:28) I want you to enjoy a sense of this security. I will not preach upon it much, but I ask you to believe it, and rejoice in it. Are you really in Christ? If so, who is to pluck you out? Are you really trusting him? How can he fail you? Have you not been begotten again into the divine family? How can that new life be quenched? Do not let anything drive from your mind a sense of your security in Christ. I hear someone say that this might lead men to carnal security. Far from it: the security of the Spirit is a death-blow to the security of the flesh. I tell you, sirs, that it is most needful that you should not believe in Jesus Christ halfway, as some do that trust the Lord to put away the sin of the past, but cannot trust him for the future. I believe in him to put away all my sins that ever shall be, as well as all the sins that have been. To believe in him only to obliterate the years of former sin is but a limping half-way faith. Believe in him for all the years that shall be. What does he say? "The water that I shall give him shall be in him a well of water springing up into everlasting life." (Jn. 4:14) Do you believe in him to give you life for a little time, so that you venture to take a quarter's ticket of membership? I am glad that you believe even so much; but why limit his power? Believe in the Lord Jesus for the whole of life, yes, for eternity. "According to your faith be it unto you!" (Mat. 9:29) Do you believe in him to give you a sip of the living water to stay your thirst for a while? Believe in him a great deal more than that, and accept him as quenching your thirst forever. For "ye are complete in him." (Col. 2:10) "He that believeth in him hath everlasting life." (Jn. 6:47)

I look upon this sense of security in a Christian as being the mainspring of unselfish virtue. What is that perpetual anxiety to save yourself? What is that daily hungering and perpetual thirsting? It is only a spiritualised selfishness. Only when a man is saved does he forget self. When I know that I am saved, I am able to glorify God. The thought of saving myself by anything that I can do, or be, or feel, I hurl to the winds, for I am already saved as a believer in Christ. Now is there scope for virtue. Now is there an opportunity to love God, and to love one's fellow-men from a pure, unselfish motive. A man is drowning, the ship is going down from under him; he is not a likely man to be looking after the interests of those about him. Once let him grasp an oar in the lifeboat, and he is the man to be the saviour of others. I want you to be out of the wreck, and into the lifeboat, that you may be a hearty worker for the salvation of the perishing. I want you to get out of that "if", "perhaps", "peradventure", "may be" into certainty and full assurance, for then your undivided zeal will go for the glory of God. "We know that we have passed from death unto life" (1 Jn. 3:14), says the Apostle, speaking in the name of the saints in his day; and when you once know this, then you will rejoice to proclaim life to those around you. When you are assured that you are not only a garden, but a garden enclosed, not only a spring, but a spring shut up, and a fountain sealed against all adversaries — then you will give all your strength to him who has thus secured you. A happy and holy security in Christ will put spirit into you, and cause you to do exploits. For the love you bear his name, you will be ready to live to this sole end — to magnify and glorify the Lord Jesus, whose you are, and whom you serve.

I leave this thought, but I pray the Holy Spirit to breathe over his people a delicious sense of perfect security in Christ Jesus.

III. Thirdly, THE MOST STRIKING IDEA OF THE TEXT IS THAT OF SEPARATION: "A garden inclosed is my sister, my spouse; a spring shut up, a fountain sealed."

A garden is a plot of ground separated from the common waste for a special purpose: such is the church. The church is a separate and distinct thing from the world. I suppose there is such a thing as "the Christian world"; but I do not know what it is, or where it can be found. It must be a singular mixture! I know what is meant by a worldly Christian; so I suppose the Christian world must be an aggregate of worldly Christians. But the church of Christ is not of the world. "You are not of the world", says Christ, "even as I am not of the world." (Jn. 17:14) Great attempts have been made of late to make the church receive the

371

world, and, wherever it has succeeded, it has come to this result, the world has swallowed up the church. It must be so. The greater is sure to swamp the lesser. They say, "Do not let us draw any hard and fast lines. A great many good people attend our services who may not be quite decided, but still, their opinion should be consulted, and their vote should be taken upon the choice of a minister, and there should be entertainments and amusements, in which they can assist." The theory seems to be, that it is well to have a broad gangway from the church to the world. When this is carried out, the result will be that the nominal church will use that gangway to go over to the world, but it will not be used in the other direction. It is thought by some that it would perhaps be better to have no distinct church at all. If the world will not come up to the church, let the church go down to the world: that seems to be the theory. Let the Israelites dwell with the Canaanites, and become one happy family. Such a blending does not appear to have been anticipated by our Lord in the chapter which we read just now: I mean the fifteenth chapter of John. Read verses eighteen and nineteen: "If the world hate you, ye know that it hated me before it hated you. If ye were of the world, the world would love his own: but because ye are not of the world, but I have chosen you out of the world, therefore the world hateth you." Did he ever say — "Try to make an alliance with the world, and in all things be conformed to its ways"? Nothing could have been further from our Lord's mind. Oh, that we could see more of holy separation, more dissent from ungodliness, more nonconformity to the world! This is "the dissidence of Dissent" that I care for, far more than I do for party names, and the political strife which is engendered by them.

Let us, however, take heed that our separation from the world is of the same kind as our Lord's. We are not to adopt a peculiar dress, or a singular mode of speech, or shut ourselves out of society. He did not do so; for he was a man of the people, mixing with them for their good. He was seen at a wedding-feast aiding the festivities; he even ate bread in a Pharisee's house, among captious enemies. He neither wore phylacteries, nor enlarged the borders of his garments, nor sought a secluded cell, nor exhibited any eccentricity of manner. He was separate from sinners only because he was holy and harmless, and they were not. He dwelt among us, for he was of us. No man was more a man than he; and yet, he was not of the world, neither would you count him among them. He was neither Pharisee, nor Sadducee, nor Scribe; and, at the same time, none could justly confound him with publicans and sinners. Those who reviled him for consorting with these last did, by their very reviling, admit that he was a very different person from those among whom he went. We want all members of the church of Christ to be, manifestly and obviously, distinct people, as much as if they were of a separate race, even when they are seen mingling with the people around them. We are not to cut ourselves of from our neighbours by affectation and contempt. God forbid! Our very avoiding of affectation, our naturalness, simplicity, sincerity, and amiability of character, should constitute a distinction. Through Christians being what they seem to be, they should become remarkable in an age of pretenders. Their care for the welfare of others, their anxiety to do good, their forgiveness of injuries, their gentleness of manner — all these things should distinguish them far more than they could be distinguished by a livery, or by any outward signs. I long to see Christian people become more distinct from the world than ever because I am persuaded that, until they are so, the church will never become such a power for blessing men as her Lord intended her to be. It is for the world's good that there should be no alliance between the church and the world by way of compromise, even to a shade. See what came to pass when the church and the world became one in Noah's day: when "the sons of God saw the daughters of men that they were fair" (Gen. 6:2) and were joined with them. Then came the deluge. Another deluge, more desolating even than the former, will come, if ever the church forgets her high calling, and enters into confederacy with the world.

The church is to be a garden, walled, taken out of the common, and made a separate and select plot of ground. She is to be a spring shut up, and a fountain sealed, no longer open to the fowls of the air and the beasts of the field. Saints are to be separate from the rest of men, even as Abraham was when he said to the sons of Seth, "I am a stranger and a sojourner with you." (Gen. 23:4)

Come now, my dear friends, are you of this sort? Are you foreigners in a country not your own? You are no Christians, remember, if you are not so. "Come out from among them, and be ye separate, saith the Lord, and touch not the unclean thing." (2 Cor. 6:17) That is the Lord's own word to you. Did not he himself suffer outside the gate that you might go forth unto him outside the camp? (Heb. 13:13) Are you at one with the rest of mankind? Could anybody live with you, and never see that any alteration had taken place in you? Would they think that you were just the same as any other man? Then, by your fruits you shall be known. If there is no difference of life between you and the world, the text does not address you as the "sister" and the "spouse" of Christ. Those who are such are enclosed from the world, and shut up for Christ. "I wish I were more so", cries one. So do I, my friend, and may you and I practically prove the sincerity of that desire by a growing separation from the world!

IV. Lastly, I think THE TEXT BEARS EVEN MORE FORCIBLY ANOTHER IDEA, NAMELY, THAT OF RESERVATION. The church of God is "a garden enclosed."

What for, then? Why, that nobody may come into that garden to eat its fruit, but the Lord himself. It is "a spring shut up", that no one may drink of the stream but the Lord Jesus. I beg you to consider this for a few minutes; and then practically to remember it all your life. A church exists only for the Lord Jesus to accomplish his ends and purposes among the sons of men. May this never be forgotten! May the Spirit of God daily sanctify us to the Lord, to be a peculiar people! I am persuaded that if any church desires to be much honoured by the Lord in these days, both as to internal happiness and external usefulness, it will find that the nearest way to its desire is to be wholly consecrated to the Lord. The church is not formed to be a social club, to produce a society for itself; not to be a political association, and to be a power in politics; nor even to be a religious confederacy, promoting its own opinions. It is a body created by the Lord to answer his own ends and purposes, and it exists for nothing else. The heavenly bridegroom says to his church, "Forget also thine own people, and thy father's house; so shall the king greatly desire thy beauty: for he is thy Lord; and worship thou him." (Ps. 45:10-11) Churches which fail of their high vocation shall be cast out as salt that has lost its savour. If we do not live for the Lord, we are dead while we live. If we do not bring glory to his name, we cannot justify our existence. If we are not as a garden enclosed for Jesus, we are mere bits of waste land. If we are not fountains sealed for Jesus, we are mere brooks in the valley, and shall soon run dry.

"But", cries one, "are we not to seek the good of our fellow-men?" Assuredly we are to do so for Christ's sake. "Are we not to seek to help on sanitary, educational, and purifying processes, and the like?" Yes, so far as all can be done for his sake. We are to be the Lord's servants for the blessing of the world, and we may do anything which he would have done. In such a garden as the text speaks of, every plant bears flowers for its owner, and every tree yields fruit for him. I pray God that this church, whether it carries on its Orphan-houses, or its College, or its Colportage, or whatever else it does, may do it all for Christ. Keep this thought to the front as a church and people. You are not to bear fruit for the markets, but fruit for the Master's table. You are not to do good that you may have honour as an industrious and energetic community, but that glory may be given to Jesus, to whom you belong. "All for Jesus" is to be our motto. Not one among us may dare to live to himself, even in the refined way in which many are doing it, who even try to win souls

373

that they may have the credit of being zealous and successful. We may so far degenerate as even to attempt to glorify Christ that we may have the credit of glorifying him. It will not do. We must be truly, thoroughly, really living for Jesus: we must be a garden enclosed, reserved, shut up for him. O brother, your life is to be a stream that flows for the refreshment of him who poured out his life for you! You are to let him drink of the deep fountains of your heart, but no one else may rival Jesus there. You are a spring shut up, a fountain sealed for Jesus, for Jesus only, and that altogether, and always. Should self come forward, or personal advantage, you are to bid them be gone. They must have no admission here. This garden is strictly private. Trespassers beware! Should the world, the flesh, or the devil leap over the wall, and stoop down to drink of the crystal fountain of your being, you are to chase them away, lest their leprous lips should defile this spring, and prevent the King from drinking there again. Our whole being is to be a fountain sealed for Jesus Christ alone. All for Jesus: body for Jesus, mind for Jesus, spirit for Jesus, eyes for Jesus, mouth for Jesus, hands for Jesus, feet for Jesus, all for Jesus. The wall must wholly enclose the garden, for a gap anywhere will admit an intruder. If one part of our being is left under the dominion of sin, it will show its power everywhere. The spring must be sealed at the very source that every drop may be for Jesus throughout the whole of its course. Our first thoughts, desires, and wishes must be his, and then all our words and deeds.

I long to prize God's matchless worth
Above the passing things of earth;
Wholly reserved for Christ that died,
Surrendered to the Crucified.

(Augustus Montague Toplady)

Brethren, do we belong to Jesus? Does he know the walks of our garden and the secret springs of our nature? Here is evidence by which you may judge whether Jesus fully possesses you. Is there anything, my brethren, that ever stirs you like the name of Jesus? I recollect, some years ago, when I was very weary, faint, and heart-sore, I was vexed with the question as to whether all was right between my Lord and my heart. I went into an obscure country meetinghouse, where a brother who preached did me a great service. There was not much in the preaching, in and of itself, but it was all about Jesus Christ, and I found myself within a few minutes weeping freely. The gospel had found out the secret fountains of my being, and set them flowing. The name of Jesus acted on me like a charm. Aye, I thought, my Lord knows how to get at my heart as nobody else does; depend upon it, he must have been there before! I was quite sure that my Lord had the key that could open the sealed fount of my being, for I was stirred to the innermost depth of my soul. Then I knew that he was no stranger to me. There is a secret drawer inside my soul that nobody can ever open except himself. He made that drawer, and knows the secret spring which shuts and opens it. My Lord — and my Lord only — can play upon the strings of my heart as a minstrel on his harp; and therefore I know that I belong to him. Beloved, I am sure that many of you can thus assure yourselves of your interest in Christ. He holds the clue to the maze of your soul, and can enter the sacred chamber of your spirit. Can he not? Do you ever feel so happy as when he is near? Why, you love the very place where his honour dwells. It happens at times that you are sick and sorry, and begin to doubt your interest in Christ; but if anybody begins extolling the Saviour, you are ready to cry out with delight. Oh, how I love to hear him praised! It sets my heart a-dancing. I cry with Herbert, "Oh, for a well-tuned harp!" for I want to make music too. When Jesus is set out in all his glories and beauties, you can hardly contain yourself, and you want to be singing his high praises. No wonder that the Methodist cries, "Bless the Lord!" You, who are very proper and quiet, half wish that you had courage enough to shout "Hallelujah!" You may freely do so if you like. Well now, if the Lord Jesus Christ holds the reins of your soul at that rate, I feel persuaded that you are his. If his name awakes the echoes of your whole being as nothing else can, then it must be because there are certain secrets between you and him which no one else can know. My heart is often like the captive king who sat pining in a lonely tower, with nothing to relieve his sadness, as he remembered his native land, and his vacant palace, and the malice of the enemy who kept him in exile. Nothing roused him from his dreamy melancholy. Many were the voices within and without the castle, but they were nothing to him. The serenade of troubadours only mocked his misery. But on a certain day a tender voice thrilled him. He listened to the verse of a song. It was even as life from the dead. None knew the next verse but himself. See what effect that sonnet had on the monarch! His eyes, how they sparkle! His whole frame, how it is re-animated! He sings in response. With what rapture he pours forth the lay! He is a fine singer, surely! We did not know that the King had such a voice. How charmed he is as a third stanza is sung by the minstrel below! And why? Because it is his friend Blondel, who has at last found him out and thus salutes him. They knew, and nobody else in the world knew that song. Even thus, the secret of the Lord is with them that fear him. (Ps. 25:14) My Lord knows what it is that moves me, and my heart melts when he speaks. My heart has a song which it sings to her Beloved, and he has a song for me. I feel that I must be his, for nobody stirs my soul as he does.

Dear friends, if you know that this is so, be happy in his love. See to it that you live wholly to him, and for him. As you have a good hope that he is altogether yours, be altogether his. Honour him in your families, and honour him in the outside world. Serve the Lord wherever you are, whether you are most found in the kitchen, the parlour, the workshop, the street, or the field. Make it your delight that you are reserved for him. Acknowledge that the vows of the Lord are upon you. You are his sister and his spouse — give him love in both forms: find in him a brother and a bridegroom. You are his garden enclosed, his spring shut up, his fountain sealed — then yield your all to him, both of fruit and flow, of work of hand and warmth of heart. Be yours the honour, the bliss, of being altogether your Lord's.

50. A SECRET AND YET NO SECRET
NO. 431

A SERMON DELIVERED ON SUNDAY MORNING,
JANUARY 26TH, 1862
AT THE METROPOLITAN TABERNACLE, NEWINGTON

"A garden enclosed is my sister, my spouse; a spring shut up, a fountain sealed…a fountain of gardens, a well of living waters, and streams from Lebanon." (Song of Solomon 4:12, 15)

OBSERVE the sweet titles with which Christ, the husband, addresses his Church, the bride. *My sister*, one near to me by ties of nature, my next of kin, born of the same mother, partaker of the same sympathies. Then *my spouse*, nearest and dearest, united to me by the tenderest bands of love; my sweet companion, part of my own *self. My sister*, by my Incarnation which makes me bone of your bone and flesh of your flesh; *my spouse*, by heavenly betrothal in which I have espoused you to myself in righteousness. *My sister*, whom I knew of old, and over whom I watched from her earliest infancy; *my spouse*, taken from among the daughters, embraced by arms of love, and affianced to me forever. See, my brethren, how true it is that our royal kinsman is not ashamed of us, for he dwells with manifest delight upon this twofold relationship. Do not, O Beloved, slow to return the hallowed flame of his love! We have the word "my" twice in our version, as if Christ dwelt with rapture on his possession of his Church. "His delights were with the sons of men" (Prov. 8:31) because those sons of men were his. He, the Shepherd, sought the sheep because they were *his* sheep; he lit the candle and swept the house, because it was *his* money that was lost; he has gone about "to seek and to save that which was lost" (Lk. 19:10) because that which was lost was *his* long before it was lost to itself or lost to him. The Church is the exclusive portion of her Lord; none else may claim a partnership, or pretend to share her love. Jesus, your Church delights to have it so! Let every believing soul drink solace from these wells. O soul! Christ is near to you in ties of relationship; Christ is dear to you in the bonds of marriage union, and you are dear to him. Behold, he grasps both of your hands with both of his, saying, "*My* sister, *my* spouse." Mark the two sacred holdfasts by which thy Lord gets such a double hold of you that he neither can nor will ever let you go. Do you say in your heart this morning, "My brother, my husband?" Seek to be near him in nature — to be like your brother, a son of God; and to be near to him in fellowship — to have near and dear intimacy with your husband, that you may know him, and have fellowship with him, being conformable unto his death. (Phil. 3:10)

Leaving this porch of cedar, let us enter the palace. Observe the contrast which the two verses present to us. I think that the Spirit of God intends that the verses should be understood, as we intend to use them this morning; but even if we should be mistaken as to the precise interpretation of the passage in its context, we shall not err in enlisting so beautiful a string of metaphors in the service of the truth. You know, beloved, there are two works of the Holy Spirit within us. The first is when he puts into us the living waters; the next is when he enables us to pour out streams of the same living waters in our daily life. Our blessed Lord expressed what we mean when, on that great day of the feast, he cried, saying, "If any man thirst let him come unto me and drink. He that believeth on me, as the Scripture hath said, out of his belly shall flow rivers of living water. This spake he of the Spirit, which they that believe on him should receive." (Jn. 7:37-38) The Spirit of God first implants in us the new nature. This is his work — to regenerate us, to put into us the new principle, the life of God in Christ. Then next, he gives us power to send out that stream in gracious emanations of holiness of life, of devoutness of communion with God, of likeness to Christ, of conformity to his image. The streams are as much of the Holy

376

Spirit as the fountain itself. He digs the well, and he afterwards, with heavenly rain, fills the pools. He first of all makes the stream in the desert to flow from the flinty rock, and, afterwards, out of his infinite supplies, he feeds the stream and bids it follow us all our days.

I was pleased to meet a quotation the other day from one of the early fathers, which just contains in it views I have frequently expressed to you: "The true believer is composed of body, soul, and the Holy Spirit." After the greatest research, eminent mental philosophers have given up all idea of a third principle which they can discover in man, as man. They can find nothing but the body and the soul. But, rest assured that, as there is a certain something in the vegetable which we call vegetable life, as there is a sensitive substance which makes animal life, as there is a mysterious subsistence developed as mental life, so there is some real, substantial, divine principle forming spiritual life. The believer has three principles, the body, the soul, and the indwelling spirit, which is none other than the Holy Spirit of God, who abides in the faithful continually. Just such a relationship as the soul bears to the body, does the spirit bear to the soul; for as the body without the soul is dead, so the soul without the spirit is dead in trespasses and sins; as the body without the soul is dead naturally, so the soul without the spirit is dead spiritually. And, contrary to the general teaching of modern theologians, we declare that the Spirit of God not only renovates the faculties which were there already, but does actually implant a new principle — that he does not merely set to rights a machinery which had before gone awry, but implants a new life which could not have been there. It is not a waking up of dormant faculties — it is the infusion of a supernatural spirit to which the natural heart is an utter stranger.

Now, we think the first verse, to a great extent, sets out the secret and mysterious work of the Holy Spirit in the creation of the new man in the soul. Into this secret, no eye of man can look. The inner life in the Christian may well be compared to an enclosed garden — to a spring shut up — to a fountain sealed. But the second verse sets out the manifest effects of grace, for no sooner is that life given than it begins to show itself. No sooner is the mystery of righteousness in the heart, than, like the mystery of iniquity, it "doth already work." (2 Thess. 2:7) It cannot lie still; it cannot be idle; it must not rest; but, as God is ever active, so this God-like principle is active too; thus you have a picture of the outer life proceeding from the inner. "A fountain of gardens, a well of living waters, and streams from Lebanon." (15) The first is what the Christian is before God; the next is what the Christian will become before men. The first is the blessedness which he receives in himself; the next is the blessedness which he diffuses to others. We will begin, then, where God the Holy Spirit begins with us, when he enters the recesses of the heart and breathes the secret life.

I. With regard to the first text, you will clearly perceive that in each of the three metaphors you have very plainly the idea of *secrecy*.

There is a *garden*. A garden is a place where trees have been planted by a skilful hand; where they are nurtured and tended with care, and where fruit is expected by its owner. Such is the Church; such is each renewed soul. But it is a garden *enclosed*, and so enclosed that one cannot see over its walls, so shut out from the world's wilderness that the passerby must not enter it — so protected from all intrusion that it is a guarded Paradise — as secret as was that inner place, the holy of holies, within the tabernacle of old.

The Church — and mark, when I say the Church, the same is true of each individual Christian — is set out next as a *spring*. "A spring" the mother of sweet draughts of refreshing water, reaching down into some impenetrable caverns, and bubbling up with perennial supplies from the great depths. Not a mere cistern, which *contains* only, but a fresh spring, which, through an inward principle within, begets, continues, and overflows. But then, it is a spring *shut up*, just as there were springs in the East, over which an edifice was built, so that none could reach the springs except those who knew the secret entrance. So is the heart of a believer when it is renewed by grace; there is a mysterious life within which no human skill can touch.

And then, it is said to be a *fountain*; but it is a fountain *sealed*. The outward stones may be discovered, but the door is sealed, so that no one can get into the hidden springs; they are altogether hidden, and hidden too by a royal will and decree of which the seal is the emblem.

I said the idea is very much that of secrecy. Now, such is the inner life of the Christian. It is a secret which no one else knows, no, which the very man who is the possessor of it cannot tell to his neighbour. "The wind bloweth where it listeth, and thou hearest the sound thereof, but canst not tell whence it cometh or whither it goeth; so is every one that is born of the Spirit." (Jn. 3:8) There are mysteries in nature so profound that we only label them with some hard name, and leave them, and all the knowledge that we have about them is that they are beyond the reach of man; but what they are, what are those mysterious impulses which link distant worlds with one another, what is the real essence of that power which flashes along the electric wire, what is the very substance of that awful force which rives the oak, or splits the spire, we do not know. These are mysteries; but even if we could enter these caverns of knowledge, if we could penetrate the secret chamber of nature, if we could climb the lofty tree of knowledge till we found the nest where the callow principles of nature as yet unfledged are lying, yet even then we could not find out where that hidden life is. It is a something — as certain a something as the natural life of man. It is a reality — not a dream, not a delusion. It is as real (though far more divine) as that "vital spark" which we say is "of heavenly flame." But though real, it is not in itself perceptible by human senses. It is so hidden from the eyes of those who do not possess it, that they do not believe in its existence. "Oh", say they, "there is no difference between a Christian and another man. There may sometimes be a little difference in his outward acts, but as to his being the possessor of another life, the idea is vain." As to the regenerate being men of a distinct race of being, as much above man naturally as man is above the brute beasts, carnal men would scorn to acknowledge. They cannot make this out. How can they? It is a spring shut up, it is a fountain sealed. No, and the Christian himself, though he feels the throbbings of the great life-force within, though he feels the perpetual bubblings up of the ever-living fountain, yet he does not know what it is. It is a mystery to him. He knows it came there once upon a time; perhaps he knows the instrumentality by which it came; but what it was he cannot tell. "One thing I know, whereas I was blind, now I see; whereas I once loved sin, I now hate it; whereas I had no thoughts after God and Christ, now my heart is wholly set upon divine things." This he can say. But how it was he does not know. Only God did it — did it in some mysterious way, by an agency which it is utterly impossible for him to detect.

No, there are times when the Christian finds this well so shut up that he cannot see it himself, and he is led to doubt about it. "Oh", says he, "I question whether the life of God is in me at all." I know some have scouted the idea of a Christian's being alive, and, at the same time, doubting his spiritual existence. But however great a paradox it may seem, it is, nevertheless, a mournful truth in our experience. That spring, I say, is sometimes shut up even to ourselves, and that fountain is so fast sealed that, although it is as really there as when we could drink of it, and the garden is as truly there as when we refreshed ourselves among its spicy beds, yet we cannot find any solace there. There have been times when, if we could have the world for it, we could not discover a spark of love in our hearts towards God — no, not a grain of faith. Yet he could see our love when our blind

378

eyes could not, and he could honour our faith even when we feared we had none. There have been moments when, if heaven and hell depended on our possession of full assurance, we certainly must have been lost, for not only had we no full assurance, but we had scarcely any faith. Children of light walk in darkness: there are times when they do not see their signs, when, for three days, neither sun nor moon appears. There are periods when their only cry is, "My God, my God, why hast thou forsaken me?" (Mk. 15:34) There is little wonder about this when we see how secret, how impalpable, how indiscernible by eye, or touch, or human intellect, is the Spirit of God within us. It is little wonder that sometimes flesh and blood should fail to know whether the life of God is in us at all. "A garden enclosed, a spring shut up, a fountain sealed."

A second thought is written upon the surface of the text. Here you see not only secrecy, but *separation*. That also runs through the three figures. It is a garden, but it is a garden enclosed — altogether shut out from the surrounding heaths and commons, enclosed with briars and hedged with thorns, which are impassable by the wild beasts. There is a gate through which the great husbandman himself can come; but there is also a gate which shuts out all those who would only rob the keeper of the vineyard of his rightful fruit. There is separation in the spring also. It is not the common spring, from which every passer-by may drink; it is one so kept and preserved distinct from men that no lip may touch, no eye may even see, its secret. It is a something which the stranger does not intermeddle with; it is a life which the world cannot give and cannot take away. All through, you see, there is a separateness, a distinctiveness. If it is ranged with springs, still it is a spring specially shut up; if it is served with fountains, still it is a fountain bearing a particular mark — a king's royal seal, so that all can perceive that this is not a general fountain, but a fountain that has a proprietor, and stands specially by itself alone. So it is with the spiritual life. It is a separate thing.

The chosen of God, we know, were separated in the eternal decree. Their names were written in a different book from the rest of men; the Book of Life records their names, and none but theirs. They were separated by God in the day of redemption, when Christ redeemed them from among men out of every kindred, and nation and tribe. They are separated day by day by divine providence, for the fiery pillar gives light to them, while it is darkness to the Egyptians. But their separation, so far as they can most clearly see it, must be a separation caused by the possession of the life which others do not have. I fear there are some professed Christians who have never realised this. They are a garden. One could hardly speak badly of their character, for their carriage is excellent, their deportment amiable; their good works commend them before men, but still they are not separate from sinners; in vital essential distinction they have little manifest share. Their speech may be half of Canaan, but the other half is of Ashdod; they may bring to God thank-offerings, but there is a niche in their house for Baal too. They have not yet heard the cry, "Come ye out of here, my people, that ye be not partakers of her plagues." (Rev. 18:4) Not yet has the mandate of the prophet rung in their ears, "Depart ye, depart ye, go ye out from hence, be ye clean that bear the vessels of the Lord." (Is. 52:11)

They are a garden, but they are not a garden walled round. Oh, how many we have in this day of this kind! They come to church, they go to the world, they talk as God's people talk, and they murmur as the rebellious murmur. They understand well the gift of prayer, but they understand little of the secret of the inner life of devotion. Brethren, if you and I have ever received that third, that noble, that divine principle, the life of God, into our souls, it will be utterly impossible for us to feel at home with the men of the world. No, we shall say, "without [outside] the camp" must be my place, bearing his reproach. Sometimes, indeed, we shall not feel at home with the professing Church; we shall be constrained to come out even from her if we would follow the Lord fully. Aye, and there are sacred seasons when we shall be so enclosed that we shall not be at ease in any society, however select, for

379

our souls will pine for sweet solitude, secret communion, hidden embraces; we shall be compelled to walk alone with Christ. The garden will be shut up even from other gardens, distinct even from other places where Christ walks. Oh, there will be periods with your soul, if it is renewed, when you must be alone, when the face of man will disturb you, and when only the face of Jesus can be company for you! I would not give a farthing for that man's spiritual life, who can live altogether with others, if you do not sometimes feel that you must be a garden enclosed, that you must enter into your closet and shut the door. If you do not feel seasons when the society of your dearest friend is an impediment, and when the face of your sweetest relation would but be a cloud between you and Christ, then I cannot understand you. O you children of Christ, be as chaste virgins, kept alone for Christ. Do not gad about, O my heart, but stay at home with Jesus, your lover, your Lord, your all. Shut up your gates, O my heart, to all company but his. O my sweet wellspring of delights, be shut up to every lip but his, and O fountain of the issues of my heart, be sealed only for him, that he may come and drink, and drink again, and take sweet solace in you, your soul being his, and his alone.

In the third place, it is worthy of a more distinct remark, that you have in the text the idea of *sacredness*. The garden enclosed is walled up that it may be sacred to its owner; the spring shut up is preserved for the use of some special person; and the fountain sealed more eminently still bears the mark of being sacred to some distinguished person. Travellers have said that they have discovered gardens of Solomon which were of old enclosed where the king privately walked, and they have also found wells of most deliciously cold water, which have been carefully covered, so that no one unacquainted with the stone in the wall, which might revolve, or might be removed, could have found the entrance to the spring. At the foot of some lofty range of mountains, a reservoir received the cooling streams which flow from melted snows. This reservoir was carefully guarded, and shut out from all common entrance, in order that the king alone might enter there and refresh himself during the scorching heat. Now such is the Christian's heart. It is a spring kept for Christ. Oh, I would that it were always so! Oh, how often we pollute the Lord's altar! How frequently, my soul, do you let in intruders! Alas, how common it is for us to be feasting other friends and shutting the door against *him*! How often do we keep him waiting in the street, while we are entertaining some barbarian who is passing by, who offers us his kiss, but is meanwhile stabbing us with his right hand? Christian men and women, I appeal to your experience now. Have you not to mourn frequently, that you are not so much for Christ as you could wish to be? Though you recognise the truth of the text, "Ye are not your own, but are bought with a price" (1 Cor 6:20), do you feel its force as you ought to do in the actions you perform for Christ? Are they all wholly for him? Could you take for your motto, "All for Jesus?" Could you feel that, whether you buy or sell, whether you read or pray, whether you go out in the world or come back to your home, that Jesus only is the one object on whom your heart is set, and for whom your life is spent? Blessed are they, those virgin souls, who, wherever the Lamb leads them, from his footsteps ne'er depart! Thrice happy are they who wear the white robe unsoiled by contact with the world! Thrice blessed are they who can say, "Let him kiss me with the kisses of his lips, for his love is better than wine!" (Song 1:2) Every Christian should feel that he is God's man — that he has God's stamp on him — and he should be able to say with Paul, "From henceforth let no man trouble me, for I bear in my body the marks of the Lord Jesus." (Gal. 6:17)

But I think there is another idea prominent here, and it is that of *security* — security to the inner life. "A garden enclosed." The wild boar out of the wood shall not break in there, neither shall the little foxes spoil the vines. "A fountain shut up." The bulls of Bashan shall not muddy her streams with their furious feet, neither shall the wild beast of Lebanon come there to drink. "A fountain sealed." No putrid streams shall foul *her* springs; her water shall be kept clear and living; her fountains shall never be filled up with stones. Oh, how sure and safe is the inner life of the believer. Satan does not know where it is, for "our life is hid with Christ." (Col. 3:3) The world cannot touch it; it seeks to overthrow it with troubles, and trials, and persecutions, but we are covered with the Eternal wings, and are safe from fear of evil. How can earthly trials reach the spirit? As well might a man try to strike a soul with a stone as to destroy a spirit with afflictions. Surely in the floods of great waters they shall not come nigh unto him; he has placed us in the secret place of the tabernacles of the Most High; in his pavilion hath he hidden us, and in a high rock has he secured us. As a castle preserves the besieged, and as the ramparts keep those who find refuge behind them, even so munitions of stupendous rock will be your dwelling place. "Who is he that shall harm you" (1 Pet. 3:13) when God is your protector? "No weapon that is formed against thee shall prosper, and every tongue that riseth against thee in judgement shalt thou condemn." (Is. 54:17) No temptation shall be able to destroy the purity of the life within; no crushing weights of doubts shall be able to take away the vital principle from that new source of strength. If all the powers of earth and hell could combine, and in their utmost fury assault the spirit in its weakest hour, that immortal principle must still exist — it would boldly defy them all, and triumph over every one of them; for he who gave it pledged his life for its preservation. The Spirit in the Christian is a spark of the Godhead, and, till the Godhead dies, the Christian's inner life can never expire. We are immortal, even though we are mortal. Within this outward crust that perishes there is a soul which endures, and within that soul which endures there is a something which might outlast even the soul itself — a part of the being of God, the indwelling Holy One of Israel, who is himself most surely divine. God dwells in us, and we in him. We are one with Christ, even as Christ is one with the Father; and are therefore as imperishable through Christ's life as Christ himself. Truly may we rejoice in the fact that because he lives we shall live also.

Once more only. I think in looking at the text you get the thought of unity. You notice, it is but one garden — "a garden enclosed." It is but *one* spring, and that is shut up; it is but *one* fountain. So the inner life of the Christian is but one. There is the old life which still survives — that old death rather, the body of sin and death, struggling against the law of life which God has put into his members, but this has no kinship with the life divine. It is alone, and knows no relationship with earth. There is but one life for all Christians; either we have it or we are dead. There are degrees of operation, but it is the same God. There are differences of administration, but it is the same Spirit who quickens. We may not all of us have "one Lord, one faith, and one baptism." (Eph. 4:5) I wish we had. I would that the two baptisms would cease, and that once again the Church would recognise and practice the baptism of believers. But we do have one Spirit, otherwise we are not Christians. I may dissent myself as much as I please from another man who is in Christ — I cannot do that, however, without sin; but dissociate myself as I may, I must be one with him, for the life that is in him is in me. The same life which quickens me, if I am in Christ, dwells also in him. When I hear strict communion talked of, it reminds me of a little finger which was washed very clean, and therefore thought the rest of the body too filthy to have fellowship with it; so it took a piece of red tape and bound it tightly round itself, that the life-blood might not flow from itself into the rest of the body. What do you think of that, brethren? Why, as long as that little finger was itself alive, the pulsations and the motions of the blood went from it to all the rest of the body, and that little piece of red tape there was just a ridiculous sham. It did not affect anything; it had no influence; it only enabled the little finger boastfully to glory, and perhaps to earn for itself the sad distinction — "These are they that separate themselves"; but the blood flowed on unimpeded, and the nerves and sinews felt the common life-throb still. They forgot, when they denied fellowship in the outward act of eating bread and drinking wine, that the essential spirit of communion was far too spiritual to be thus restrained; it had overleaped their boundary and was gone. The only way in which a Christian can leave off communing with all other Christians is by leaving off being a Christian. Thus can the finger leave off communing with the rest of the body — by rotting away, and not how else, as long as it is alive. Communion is the lifeblood of the soul. The Holy Spirit is the Spirit that quickens the body of the Church, and that same Holy Spirit will go into every member, and you may try to check him by Church decrees, or stop him by your trust-deeds and your ordinances, that such-and-such a Church shall never be loosed from the bands of ancestral bigotry; but the Church's life will beat freely through all the members of the Church's fellowship, and communion *will* go to all who are in Christ. There is but one garden, but one spring, but one sealed fountain; and if you have it in your heart, and I have it in mine, there is a relationship between you and me that is as near as if you and I had the same soul, for you and I have the same Spirit. If you could imagine two bodies quickened by the very same mind, what a close connection that would be! But here are hundreds of bodies, hundreds of souls, quickened by the selfsame Spirit. Brethren, indeed not only ought we to love one another, but "the love of Christ constraineth us" (2 Cor. 5:14), so that we cannot resist the impulse; we do love each other in Christ Jesus.

II. I shall now need your attention, while, with brevity, I try to open the second text, which presents a decided contrast, because it deals not so much with the inner life as with the active life that goes abroad into all the deeds of the Christian in the world, and is the natural outgoing of the life within.

First, notice that in contradistinction to our first thought of secrecy, you have in the text *manifestation*. "*A fountain of gardens*." Everybody can see a fountain which runs streaming through many gardens, making deserts fertile. "*A well of living waters*." Whatever the traveller does not see, when he is riding along on a thirsty day, he is sure to see the fountain; if there is one anywhere, he is certain to observe it. "*And streams from Lebanon*." So that any passer-by in the valley, looking up the side of the mountain, will see by the clusters of trees which skirt the stream where the stream is; or, if it is a smaller brook, just as sometimes in Cumberland and Westmoreland, on a rainy day you see the mountain suddenly marked with streaks of silver all down its brown sides, where the brooks are rippling, so the Christian become like the streams leaping down Lebanon's steep sides, clearly perceived even from a distance, manifest to the most casual observer. Now, brethren, this is what you and I ought to be. No man ought to court publicity for his virtue or notoriety for his zeal; but, at the same time, it is a sin to be always seeking to hide what God has bestowed on us for the good of others. A Christian is not to be a city in a valley — he is to be a city set upon a hill. (Mat. 5:14) He is not to be a candle put under a bushel, but a candle in a candlestick, giving light to all. Retirement may be lovely in the eyes of some, and the hiding of oneself is doubtless a blessed thing, but the hiding of Christ in us can never be justified, and the keeping back of truth which is precious to us, is a sin against our kind, and an offence against God. Those of you who are of a nervous disposition, and of retiring habits of life, must take care that you do not too much indulge your natural propensity, lest you should be useless to the Church. Seek in the name of him who was not ashamed of you to do some little violence to your feelings, and tell others what Christ has told you. Do not keep it secret — it is too precious — it too much concerns the vital interests of man.

Speak! If thou cannot with trumpet tongue, yet speak with a still small voice. If the pulpit must not be your tribune, if the press may not carry on its wings your words, yet say, as Peter and John did, "Silver and gold have I none, but such as I have give I unto thee." (Acts 3:6) And speak, too, as you as gently as you can to ones, if not loudly to twenties; quietly to twos, if not publicly to scores. By Sychar's well, talk to the Samaritan woman, if you cannot on the mountain preach the sermon; in the house, if not in the temple, in the field, if not upon the exchange; in the midst of your own household, if you cannot in the midst of the great family of man. At any rate, do not hide your talent, and do not wrap it up. "It is but one", you say. So much the more reason why you should make the greater use of that one. Do not conceal it; bring it out; trade with it; and so you will multiply the talent, and you will bring in good interest to your Lord and Master. The inner life is secret, so mind that you have this inner mystery; but out of the secret comes the manifest. Darkness becomes the mother of light; from the dark mines comes the blazing coal. Oh, see to it that from all that is hidden and secret and mysterious, there comes out the plain and the manifest, that men may see the holiness, truthfulness, and zeal of God in your life!

But clearly enough, again, we have in this second text, in opposition to the separation of the first, *diffusiveness*. The garden was enclosed before; now it is "a fountain of gardens". The well was shut up, now it is a well of living waters; before, we had the fountain sealed, now we have streams dashing down the sides of Lebanon. So a Christian is to be separate in his inner life; but in the outer manifestation of that inner life, he is to mingle for good among his fellow-men. It was usual in Romish countries for women who wished to be especially holy to make recluses of themselves; and in the Church of St. Roche, in Paris, there was a small building erected on the side of the Church. The only opening was a little grating, through which the necessaries of life were passed. Within this narrow cell, there lived for eighty years, and died, I think, at the age of ninety-six, a woman doubtless devout, but certainly superstitious. There she passed her life. The only sound she heard was the tramp of the worshippers on the Church pavement, and the chant of the daily service; but she lived there, thinking she was serving God by being separate from others. That is not the separation of the New Testament. We are to be separate from sinners, as Christ was, and whoever went among them more than he did? We are to be healthy, and by that health separate from the leper; we are to be clean, and, by that cleanness, separate from the filthy. But we are to go among them; we are to visit; we are to distribute ourselves what Christ has given to us. If we keep ourselves altogether apart, we shall be useless to our fellow-men; we shall be like stagnant pools, we shall grow putrid by degrees. We must let the streams flow abroad; we must seek to give to others what Christ has given to us. Now, some of you who keep yourselves separate in that sense, I beg you to see if there is no mission of mercy for you? Go out among them as physicians in the midst of the sick, as torchbearers in the midst of darkness. Go out as looseners of the bonds among the captives; as openers of prison doors among those that are bound. And he who has given you the true principle within, which is and must be shut up, will bless the outgoings of your zeal, both in the morning and in the evening, and cause that, watering others, your own soul shall be watered too.

Briefly, we are obliged to speak on each of these points; but notice, thirdly, that in opposition to the sacredness of the first text we have in the second verse an unlimited *freeness*, especially in that last expression — "*streams from Lebanon.*" What can be freer than the brook, which leaps along the mountain side? There, the bird wets its wings; there the red deer comes to drink, and even that wild beast of Lebanon, of which we read in the Book of the Kings, comes there, and without let or hindrance slakes its thirst. What can be freer than the rivulet singing with liquid notes adown the glen? It belongs to no one; it is free to all. Whoever passes by, be he peer or peasant, may stoop there and refresh himself from the mountain stream. So be it with you, Christian. Carry about with you a piety which you do not wish to keep for yourself. A light loses none of its own lustre when others are lit at its flame. Remember, you shall earn riches by giving riches, and, in this sense, giving away shall be an increase of your wealth. I know some who are in a bad sense, like fountains shut up. They love the doctrine of election, but there is one doctrine they love better, and that is, the doctrine of exclusion. They love to think they are shut in, but they feel quite as much delight that others are shut out. Their conversation is always flavoured with the thought of shutting others out. They are told that in such-and-such a Church there has been a large increase. Well, they hope they are genuine; by which they mean that they do not believe they are. A young believer begins to tell them something of his joys. Well, they don't like to be too fast in pronouncing an opinion; by which they mean, they would not like one more to get in than should, and they are half afraid that perhaps some may overstep the bounds of election and get saved who should not be. Well, brethren, I love the doctrine of election, I love to think that the garden is enclosed, but I do love in my own life to exemplify the equally precious truth of the freeness of the gospel, so that if I speak to anyone, it will not be to discourage them, but to encourage them not to say, "Get you gone!" but "Come and welcome!" Depart, you cursed" is nothing to do with me; my business is to say, "Come, you blessed." I would rather go to the door and say, "Come in, you blessed of the Lord, why are you standing outside?" than slam it in a sinner's face with "What have you to do here?" No, we must be shut up in the inner life; but let every wall be broken down as to the outer life. We must be hidden springs within, but let us be sweetly flowing rivulets without, giving drink to every passer by.

And not to detain you long, you will notice that, while we had in the other text the idea of security, in connection with that we have here in this text the idea of *approach*. The garden was shut up — that was to keep it. There are no walls here, so that all may come to it. The streams were shut up before; here it is an open well. The fountain was sealed in the first verse; here it is a flowing stream, which is to teach us this — that the way God keeps his people in security is not by shutting out their enemies from attacking them, but, while laying them open to temptation and attack, he yet sustains them. It is not much to preserve oneself behind a wall which cannot be scaled, but to stand where arrows are flying thick as hail, where lances are being pushed with fury, where the sword-cuts are falling on every part, to stand, I say, invulnerable, invincible, immortal; this is to wear a divine life which cannot be conquered by human power. Such is the Christian. We *are* to pray, "Lead us not into temptation", but indeed, we often are tempted, notwithstanding our prayer. God will put us where we must be tempted — put us where we must be tried, because, if we are not tried, there is no honour to him; and if we are not tempted, then where is the glory to the grace that delivers us out of temptations? The Lord does not put his plants into a hot-house, as some gardeners do; no, he puts them out in the open air, and if the frost is coming, he says, "Ah, but no frost can kill them, and they will be all the sturdier in the summer for the cold in the winter!" He does not shelter them either from the heat of the sun, or from the cold by night, for in this world we must have tribulation, and we must have much of it too, for it is through much tribulation that we inherit the kingdom. But what God does to his people is this: he keeps them *in* tribulation, preserves them in temptation, and brings them joyfully out of all their trials. So, Christian, you may rejoice in your security; but you must not think that you are not to be attacked. You are a stream from Lebanon, to be dashed down many a cascade, to be broken over many a rough rock, to be stopped up with many a huge stone, to be impeded by many a fallen tree; but you are to dash forward with the irresistible force of God, sweeping everything away, till you find at last the place where shall be your perfect rest.

And last of all, in opposition to the unity of which I spoke, we have in our second text great *diversity*. You have "a fountain", not of a garden, but "of gardens"; you have a well, but it is a well of living waters; you do not have a stream, but streams — streams from Lebanon. So a Christian is to do good in all sorts of ways, and his fruit are to be of many kinds; he is to be like the trees of Paradise, which bear twelve kinds of fruits. (Rev. 22:2) The Christian is to have all sorts of graces: "Whatsoever things are pure, whatsoever things are lovely, whatsoever things are of good repute". (Phil. 4:8) He is to have all these. It is an old proverb that a man may have too many irons in the fire; but it depends on what fire it is; for if it is God's fire, put all the irons into it. A man may attempt too much they say — but not for Christ. If you should attempt great things, and have great faith, you shall succeed in all that you attempt. There seems to be a fear among some Christians, either of doing too much themselves, or else letting other people do too much; and I know some to whom that text might *almost* be applied, "They have the key of the kingdom of heaven, but they neither enter themselves, and they that would they hinder." Not content to refuse the

384

burden for themselves, they will not even touch it with one of their little fingers; but they are afraid that others will carry the burden instead. Well, we are not afraid as these are. Blessed be God, if there is a trench to be filled up, let us struggle which shall lead the way; if there is a rampart to be climbed, if there is no other to throw the irons over with the scaling-ladder, let your minister attempt the deed, and lead the van, for he is well assured that there are many here who would jostle with him, and say, "Let me come first; let me serve my Master; let me live or let me die, if I may but glorify him." What, bring forth for Christ a little shrivelled cluster upon the topmost bough — a cluster which the very birds of heaven will not deign to touch because it is too little even for their appetites? No, rather let us have every bough weighed down with clusters, like those of Eshcol, which will take two ordinary men to carry, but which we can bear in rich profusion, because the life of the Spirit of God is in us. We are a race of little doers, of little givers, of little thinkers, of little believers. O God, raise us up again giants in these days! Give us again the consecrated men who will stand upon the sword like the old Roman, and say, "For God I devote myself; to Christ I give body, soul, and spirit, and if I am offered up on the sacrifice of your faith, I joy and rejoice with you all." Oh, if the fountain, the secret fountain, were better seen to, I think there would be more of these outward streams! And if the sealed well were better guarded, we should see more of these rapid streams from Lebanon, which would make glad the people of God, and the world at large.

And now, how many of you have the secret spring within you? If your soul is not renewed by grace, you cannot do good. "Except a man be born again, he cannot *see* the kingdom of God." (Jn, 3:3) No one enters fully into discipleship with Christ till the water as well as the Spirit has been reverently received. "Except a man be born of water and of the Spirit ye cannot *enter* the kingdom of heaven." But these two things being done, being born of water and of the Spirit, go out to show to others the mystery, the *fellowship* of the mystery — to make all men know that God has appeared to us in Christ Jesus, reconciling the world to himself, not imputing their iniquities. (2 Cor. 5:19) Preach of Christ when you know Christ, but not till then. Let the streams flow out where you have the inner fountain, but not till then. Sad reflection! There are some of you that do not have it. Oh, if you do not have it, you will perish! You cannot get it of yourselves. He alone can give it. You are in his hands to give it to you. Oh, may your longings end in groanings today, and may you groan to God, "Lord, renew me! Lord, cause me to be born again!" And those groanings will be proofs that he has begun the good work, and those longings shall be evidence that there is a well in you, though it is a well shut up — a well shut up even from yourself. God grant that you may seek and find it through Jesus Christ; and to him be glory, forever and ever! Amen.

51. GRACE FOR COMMUNION

NO. 1941

ON LORD'S-DAY AFTERNOON COMMUNION SERVICE,
JAN. 2ND, 1887

Awake, O north wind; and come, thou south; blow upon my garden, that the spices thereof may flow out. Let my beloved come into his garden, and eat his pleasant fruits." (Song of Solomon 4:16)

THE soul of the believer is the garden of the Lord. Within it are rare plants, such as yield "spices" and "pleasant fruits". Once it was a wilderness, overgrown with thorns and briars; but now it is "a garden enclosed", an "orchard of pomegranates".

At times within that garden, everything is very still and quiet; indeed, more still than might be wished. Flowers are in bloom, but they seem scentless, for there are no breezes to waft the perfume. Spices abound, but one may walk in the garden and not perceive them, for no gales bear their fragrance on their wings. I do not know that, in itself, this is an evil condition: it may be that "...he giveth his beloved sleep." To those who are worn with labour, rest is sweet. Blessed are they who enjoy a Sabbath of the soul! The loved one in the text desired the company of her Lord, and felt that an inactive condition was not altogether suitable for his coming. Her prayer is first about her garden, that it may be made ready for her Beloved; and then to the bridegroom himself, that he would come into his garden, and eat its pleasant fruits. She pleads for the *breath of heaven*, and for *the Lord of heaven*.

First, she cries for THE BREATH OF HEAVEN to break the dead calm which broods over her heart.

She cannot unlock the caskets of spice, nor cause the sweet odours to flow forth: her own breath would not avail for such an end. She looks away from herself to an unseen and mysterious power. She breathes this earnest prayer, "Awake, O north wind; and come, thou south; blow upon my garden!"

In this prayer, there is an evident sense of *inward sleep*. She does not mean that the north wind is asleep: it is her poetical way of confessing that she herself needs to be awakened. She has a sense of *absent-mindedness*, too, for she cries, "Come, thou south." If the south wind would come, the forgetful perfumes would come to themselves and sweeten all the air. The fault, whatever it is, cannot lie in the winds; it lies within us.

Her appeal, as we have already said, is to that great Spirit who operates according to his own will, even as the wind blows where it wills. She does not try to "raise the wind" — that is an earthly expression relating to worldly matters; but, alas, it might fitly be applied to many imitations of spirituality! Have we not heard of "getting up revivals"? Indeed, we can no more command the Holy Spirit than we can compel the wind to blow east or west. Our strength lies in prayer. The spouse prays, "Awake, O north wind; and come, thou south!" She thus owns her entire dependence upon the free Spirit. Although she veiled her faith in a divine Worker under the imagery of her song, yet she spoke as to a person. We believe in the personality of the Holy Spirit, so that we ask *him* to "Awake" and "Come". We believe that we may pray to him; and we are impelled to do so.

Notice that the spouse does not mind what form the divine visitation takes so long as she feels its power. "Awake, O north wind"; though the blast be cold and cutting, it may be that

386

it will effectively fetch forth the perfume of the soul in the form of repentance and self-humiliation. Some precious graces, like rare spices, naturally flow in the form of tears; and others are only seen in hours of sorrow, like the gums which exude from wounded trees. The rough north wind has done much for some of us in the way of arousing our best graces. Yet it may be that the Lord will send something more tender and cheering; and if so, we would cry, "Come, thou south." Divine love warming the heart has a wonderful power to develop the best part of a man's nature. Many of our precious things are brought out by the sun of holy joy.

Either movement of the Spirit will sufficiently bestir our inner life; but the spouse desires both. Although in nature you cannot have the north wind and the south blowing at the same time, yet in grace you can. The Holy Spirit may be at one and the same time working grief and gladness, causing humiliation and delight. I have often been conscious of the two winds blowing at once; so that, while I have been ready to die to self, I have been made to live unto God. "Awake, O north wind; and come, thou south!" When all the forms of spiritual energy are felt, no grace will be dormant. No flower can keep asleep when both rough and gentle winds arouse it.

The prayer is — "blow", and the result is — "flow". Lord, if you blow, my heart will flow out to you! "Draw me, we will run after you." We know full well what it is to have grace in our souls, and yet to feel no movement of it. We may have much faith in existence, yet none in exercise, for no occasion summons it into action. We may have much repentance, yet no conscious repenting; much fire of love, yet no love flaming forth; and much patience in the heart, though at the moment we do not display it. Apart from the occurrences of providence, which arouse our inward emotions one way and another, the only plan by which our graces can be set in active exercise is by the Holy Spirit breathing on us. He has the power to quicken, arouse, and bestir our faculties and graces, so that holy fruit within us becomes perceptible to ourselves, and to others who have spiritual discernment. There are states of the atmosphere in which the fragrance of flowers is much more diffused than at other times. The rose owes much to the zephyr which wafts its perfume. How sweet is even a field of beans after a shower! We may have much spice of piety, and yet yield small fragrance, unless the living power of the Holy Spirit moves upon us. In a wood, there may be many a partridge, or gay pheasant, and yet we may not see so much as one of them until a passing foot tramples down the underwood, and causes the birds to rise up on the wing. The Lord can thus discover our graces by many a messenger; but the more choice and spiritual virtues need an agent as mysterious and all-pervading as the wind — need, in fact, the Spirit of the Lord to arouse them. Holy Spirit, you can come to us when we cannot come to you! From any and every quarter, you can reach us, taking us on our warm or cold side. Our heart, which is our garden, lies open at every point to you. The wall which encloses it does not shut you out. We wait for a visitation. We feel glad at the very thought of it. That gladness is the beginning of the stir; the spices are already flowing out.

The second half of the prayer expresses our central desire: we long for THE LORD OF HEAVEN to visit us.

The bride does not seek that the spices of her garden may become perceptible for her own enjoyment, nor for the delight of strangers, nor even for the pleasure of the daughters of Jerusalem, but for her Beloved's sake. *He* is to come into his garden, and eat his pleasant fruits. We are a garden for his delight. Our highest wish is that Jesus may have joy in us. I fear that we often come to the communion table with the idea of enjoying ourselves; or, rather, of enjoying our Lord; but we do not rise to the thought of giving *him* joy. Possibly that might even seem presumptuous. Yet, he says, "My delights were with the sons of men." (Prov. 8:31) See how joyfully he cries in the next chapter: "I am come into my garden, my sister, my spouse: I have gathered my myrrh with my spice; I have eaten my honeycomb with my honey; I have drunk my wine with my milk." (Song 5:1) Our heavenly bridegroom rests in his love, and rejoices over us with singing. Often he takes more delight in us than we do in him. We have not even known that he was present, but have been praying him to come; and all the while he has been near us.

Note well the address of the spouse to her Beloved in the words before us. *She calls him hers* — "My Beloved". When we are sure that he is ours, we desire him to come to us as ours, and to reveal himself as ours. Those words "My Beloved" are a prose poem: there is more music in them than in all the laureate's sonnets. However slumbering my graces may be, Jesus is mine. It is as mine that he will make me live, and cause me to pour out my heart's fragrance.

While he is hers, she owns that *she is wholly his*, and all that she has belongs to him. In the first clause, she says, "Awake, O north wind; and come, thou south; blow upon *my* garden"; but now she prays, "Let my Beloved come into *his* garden". She had spoken just before of her fruit, but now they are his fruit. She was not wrong when she first spoke; but she is more accurate now. We are not our own. We do not produce fruit of ourselves. The Lord says, "From me is thy fruit found." (Hos. 14:8) The garden is of our Lord's purchasing, enclosing, planting, and watering; and all its fruit belongs to him. This is a powerful reason for his visiting us. Should not a man come into his own garden, and eat his own fruit? Oh, that the Holy Spirit may put us into a fit condition to entertain our Lord!

The prayer of the spouse is — "*Let my Beloved come*." Do we not say, "Amen, let him come"? If he does not come in the glory of his Second Advent at this moment, as, perhaps, he may not, yet let him come. If not to his judgement-seat, yet let him come into his garden. If he will not come to gather before him all nations, yet let him come to gather the fruit of his redemption in us. Let him come into our little circle; let him come into each heart. "Let my Beloved come." Stand back, you that would hinder him! O my Beloved, let not my sinful, sluggish, wandering thoughts prevent you from coming! You visited the disciples, "the doors being shut"; will you not come where every opened door speaks of your welcome? Where should you come but to your garden? Surely my heart has great need of you. Many a plant within it needs your care. Welcome, welcome, welcome! Heaven cannot welcome you more heartily, O my Beloved, than my heart now does! Heaven does not need you so much as I do. Heaven has the abiding presence of the Lord God Omnipotent; but if you do not dwell within my soul, it is empty, and void, and waste. Come, then, to me, I beseech you, O my Beloved!

The spouse further cries — "*Let him eat his pleasant fruits*." I have often felt myself overcome with the bare idea that anything I have ever done should give my Lord pleasure. Can it be that any offering I ever gave him should be thought worthy of his acceptance; or that anything I ever felt or said should be a joy to him? Can he perceive any perfume in my spices, or taste any flavour in my fruit? This is a joy worth worlds. It is one of the highest tokens of his condescension. It is wonderful that the King from the far country should come from the glory land, where all choice fruits are at their best, and enter this poor enclosure in the wilderness, and there eat such fruit as ours, and call them pleasant, too! O Lord Jesus, come into our hearts now! O Holy Spirit, blow upon our hearts at this moment! Let faith, and love, and hope, and joy, and patience, and every grace be now like violets which betray themselves by their perfume, or like roses which load the air with their fragrance!

Though we are not content with ourselves, yet may our Lord be pleased with us! Do come to us, O Lord! That you are our Beloved is a greater wonder than that you should come to us. That you have made us your garden is a greater favour than that you should eat our

388

fruit. Fulfil to us that gracious promise, "I will sup with him, and he with me" (Rev. 3:20), for we do open to you. You said to the woman of Samaria, "Give me to drink", and will you not now accept a draught of love from us? She had no husband, but you are our Husband; will you not drink from the cup which we now hold up to you? Receive our love, our trust, our consecration. Delight yourself also in us, as we now delight ourselves in you. We are asking a great thing of you, but your love warrants large requests. We will now come to your table, where you shall be our meat and drink. But suffer our spices to be the perfume of the feast, and let us each say, "While the King sitteth at his table my spikenard sendeth forth the smell thereof." Fulfil this wish of our soul, divine Lord and Master! Amen.

52. "MY GARDEN" — "HIS GARDEN"

NO. 2475

AT THE METROPOLITAN TABERNACLE, NEWINGTON
ON THURSDAY EVENING, JULY 20TH, 1882

"Awake, O north wind, and come, thou south; blow, upon my garden, that the spices thereof may flow out. Let my beloved come into his garden, and eat his pleasant fruits." (Song of Solomon 4:16)

WHAT a difference there is between what the believer was by nature, and what the grace of God has made him! Naturally, we were like the waste howling wilderness, like the desert which yields no healthy plant or verdure. It seemed as if we were given over to be like a salt land, which is not inhabited; no good thing was in us, or could spring out of us. But now, as many of us as have known the Lord are transformed into gardens; our wilderness is made like Eden, our desert is changed into the garden of the Lord. "I will turn unto you", said the Lord to the mountains of Israel, when they were bleak and bare, "I will turn unto you, and ye shall be tilled and sown" (Ezek. 36:9); and this is exactly what he said to the barrenness of our nature. We have been enclosed by grace, we have been tilled and sown, we have experienced all the operations of the divine husbandry. Our Lord Jesus said to his disciples, "My Father is the husbandman", and he has made us to be fruitful unto his praise, full of sweetness where once there was no fruit, and nothing that could give him delight.

We are a garden, then, and in a garden there are flowers and fruits, and, in every Christian's heart, you will find the same evidences of culture and care; not in all alike, for even gardens and fields vary in productiveness. In the good ground mentioned by our Lord in the parable of the sower (Mat. 7:24-27), the good seed did not all produce a hundredfold, or even sixty-fold; there were some parts of the field where the harvest was as low as thirty-fold, and I fear that there are some of the Lord's gardens which yield even less than that. Still, there is the fruit, and there are the flowers, in a measure; there is a good beginning made wherever the grace of God has undertaken the culture of our nature.

I. Now, coming to our text, and thinking of Christians as the Lord's garden, I want you to observe, first, that THERE ARE SWEET SPICES IN BELIEVERS.

The text assumes that, when it says, "Blow upon my garden, that the spices thereof may flow out". There are in the Lord's garden sweet flowers that drip with honey, and all manner of delightful perfumes. There are such sweet spices within the believer's heart; let us think of them for a few minutes.

First, let me remind you of *the names of these sweet spices.* For instance, there is faith. Is there anything out of heaven sweeter than faith — a faith which trusts and clings, which believes and hopes, and declares that, though God shall slay it, yet will it trust in him? In the Lord's esteem, faith is full of fragrance. He never delighted in the burning of bulls and the fat of fed beasts (Is. 1:11), but he always delighted in the faith which brought these things as types of the one great sacrifice for sin. FAITH is very dear to him. Then comes love; and again I must ask — Is there to be found anywhere a sweeter spice than this — the love which loves God because he first loved us, the love which flows out to all the brotherhood, the love which knows no circle within which it can be bounded, but which loves the whole race of mankind, and seeks to do them good? It is exceedingly pleasing to God to see Love growing where once all was hate, and to see faith springing up in that

390

very soul which was formerly choked with the thorns and briers of doubt and unbelief. And there is also HOPE, which is indeed an excellent grace, a far-seeing grace by which we behold heaven and eternal bliss. There is such a fragrance about a God-given hope that this poor sin-stricken world seems to be cured by it. Wherever this living, lively hope comes, there men lift up their drooping heads and begin to rejoice in God their Saviour. You do not need me to go over all the list of Christian graces, and mention meekness, brotherly kindness, courage, uprightness, or the patience which endures so much from the hand of God. But whatever grace I might mention, it would not be difficult at once to convince you that there is a sweetness and a perfume about all grace in the esteem of him who created it, and it delights him that it should flourish where once its opposite alone was found growing in the heart of man. These, then, are some of the saints' sweet spices.

Next notice, that *these sweet spices are delightful to God*. It is very wonderful that we should have within us anything in which God can take delight; yet when we think of all the other wonders of his grace, we need not marvel at all. The God who gave us faith may well be pleased with faith. The God who created love in such unlovely hearts as ours may well be delighted at his own creation. He will not despise the work of his own hands; rather, he will be delighted with it, and find sweet complacency in it. What an exaltation it is to us worms of the earth that there should ever be anything in us well-pleasing to God! Well did the psalmist say, "What is man, that thou art mindful of him? and the son of man, that thou visitest him?" (Ps. 8:4) But God is mindful of us, and he does visit us. Of old, before Christ came into this world in human form, his delights were with the sons of men; much more is it so now that he has taken their nature into heaven itself, and given to those sons of men his own Spirit to dwell within them. Let it ravish your heart with intense delight that, though often you can take no complacency in yourself, and go about with your head bowed down, like a bulrush, and cry, "Woe is me!" Yet in that very cry of yours, God hears a note that is sweet and musical to his ears. Blessed be repentance, with the tear-drops in her eyes, sparkling like diamonds. God takes delight even in our longings after holiness, and in our loathing of our own imperfections. Just as the father delights to see his child anxious to be on the best and most loving terms with him, so God delights in us when we are crying after that which we have not yet reached, a perfection which shall make us to be fully like himself. O beloved, I do not know anything that fills my soul with such feelings of joy as the reflection that I, even I, may yet be, and do something, that will give delight to the heart of God himself! He has joy over one sinner that repents, though repentance is but an initial grace. And when we go on from that to other graces, and take yet higher steps in the divine life, we may be sure that his joy is in us, and therefore our joy may well be full.

These spices of ours are not only delightful to God, but *they are healthful to man*. Every particle of faith that there is in the world is a sort of purifier; wherever it comes, it has a tendency to kill what is evil. In the spiritual sanitary arrangements which God made for this poor world, he put men of faith, and the faith of these men, into the midst of all this corruption, to help keep other men's souls alive, even as our Lord Jesus said to his disciples, "Ye are the salt of the earth." (Mat. 5:13) The sweet perfumes that flow out from the flowers which God cultivates in the garden of his Church are scattering spiritual health and sanity all around. It is a blessed thing that the Lord has provided these sweet spices to overpower and counteract the unhealthy odours that float on every breeze. Think, then, dear friends, of the importance of being God's fragrant flowers, which may yield perfumes that are delightful to him, and are blessed and healthful to our fellowmen. A man of faith and love in a church sweetens all his brethren. Give us but a few such in our midst, and there shall be no broken spiritual unity, there shall be no coldness and spiritual death. But all will go well where these men of God are among us as a mighty influence for good. And, as for the ungodly around us, the continued existence in the earth of the Church of Christ is the hope of the world. The world that hates the Church does not know what it is doing,

391

for it is hating its best friend. The spices with which God is conserving this present evil age, lest his anger should destroy it because of the growing corruption, can be found in the flowers which he has planted in the garden of his Church.

It sometimes happens that *these sweet odours within God's people lie quiet and still*. There is a stillness in the air, something like that which the poet Coleridge makes "The Ancient Mariner" speak of in his graphic description of a calm within the tropics. Do you, dear friends, never get into that becalmed condition? I recollect, when I was young, reading an expression — I think of Ralph Erskine's — in which he says that he likes a roaring devil better than a sleeping devil. It struck me then that, if I could keep the devil always asleep, it would be the best thing that could possibly happen for me; but now I am not so sure that I was right. At all events, I know this, when the old dog of hell barks very loudly, he keeps me awake; and when he howls at me, he drives me to the mercy-seat for protection; but when he goes to sleep, and lies very quiet, I am very apt to go to sleep, too, and then the graces that are within my soul seem to be absolutely hidden.

Mark you, hidden grace, which in no way reveals itself by its blessed odours, is all the same as if there were none to those that watch from the outside, and sometimes to the believer himself. What is wanted, in order that he may know that he has these sweet perfumes, is something outside himself. You cannot stir your own graces, you cannot make them more, and you cannot cause their fragrance to flow out. True, by prayer, you may help to this end; but then, that very prayer is put into you by the Holy Spirit, and when it has been offered to the Lord, it comes back to you laden with blessings. But often, something more is needed, some movement of God's providence, and much more, some mighty working of his grace, to come and shake the flower bells in his garden, and make them shed their fragrance on the air. Alas! on a hot and drowsy day, when everything has fallen into a deep slumber, even God's saints, though they may be wise virgins, go as soundly asleep as the foolish virgins, and they forget that "the Bridegroom cometh". (Mat. 25:6) "While the Bridegroom tarried, they all slumbered and slept"; and, sometimes, you and I must catch ourselves nodding when we ought to be wide awake. We are going through a part of that enchanted ground which John Bunyan describes, and we do not know what to do to keep ourselves awake.

At such times, a Christian is very apt to ask, *"Am I indeed planted in God's garden? Am I really a child of God?"* Now, I will say what some of you may think a strong thing, but I do not believe that he is a child of God who never raised that question.

He has no hope who never had a fear;
And he who never doubted of his state,
He may, perhaps — perhaps he may — too late."
I have sung, and I expect that I may have to sing again —
'Tis a point I long to know;
Oft it causes anxious thought;
Do I love the Lord or no?
Am I his, or am I not?

(William Cowper)

I can't bear to get into that condition, and I cannot bear to keep in it when I am in it; but still, there must be anxious thoughts about this all-important matter. Because you happened to be excited on a certain occasion, and thought you were converted, and were sure of heaven, you had better look well to the evidence on which you are relying. You may have been mistaken after all; and while I would not preach up little faith, I would preach down great presumption. No one can have a faith too strong, and no assurance can be too full, if it comes truly from God the Holy Spirit; but if it comes merely from your fancying that it is so, and, therefore, you will not examine yourself whether you be in the faith (2 Cor. 13:5), I begin to make up my mind that it is not so, because you are afraid to look into the matter. "I know that I am getting rich", says a merchant. "I never keep any books, and I do not want any books, but I know that I am getting on well in my business." If, my dear sir, I do not soon see your name in the *Gazette*, I shall be rather surprised.

Whenever a man is so very good that he does not want to enquire at all into his position before God, I suspect that he is afraid of introspection, and self-examination, and that he dare not look into his own heart. This I know: as I watch the many people of God committed to my care here, I see some run on for ten years or more serving God with holy joy, and having no doubt or fear. They are not generally remarkable for any great depth of experience, but when God means to make mighty men of them, he digs about them, and soon they come to me crying, and craving a little comfort, telling me what doubts they have, because they are not what they want to be. I am glad when this is the case; I rejoice because I know that they will be spiritually better off afterwards. They have reached a higher standard than they had previously attained, and they have a better knowledge now of what they ought to be. It may be that, before, their ideal was a low one, and they thought that they had reached it. Now God has revealed to them greater heights, which they have to climb; and they may as well gird up the loins of their mind to do so with divine help. As they get higher, they perhaps think, "Now we are at the top of the mountain", when they are really only on one of the lower spurs of it. Up they go, climbing again. "If once I can reach that point, I shall soon be at the summit", you think. Yes, and when you have at length got there, you see the mountain still towering far above you. How deceptive is the height of the Alps to those who have not seen them before! I said to a friend once, "It will take you about thirteen hours to get to the top of that mountain." He replied, "Why, I can run up in half-an-hour." I let him have a try, and he had not gone far before he had to sit down to pant and rest. So you think of a certain height of grace, "Oh, I can easily reach that!" Yes, just so; but you do not know how high it is; and those who think that they have reached the top do not know anything about the top; for he who knows how high is the holiness to which the believer can attain will go on clambering and climbing, often on his hands and knees, and when he has reached that point which he thought was the summit, he will sit down and say, "I thought I had reached the top, but now I find that I have only begun the ascent." Or he might say with Job, "I have heard of thee by the hearing of the ear" (and then I did not know much of thee, or of myself either) "but now mine eye seeth thee. Wherefore I abhor myself, and repent in dust and ashes." (Job 42:5-6)
You see, then, that there are sweet spices lying in Christians, like hidden honey and locked-up perfume within the flowers on a hot day.

II. What is wanted is that THOSE SWEET ODOURS SHOULD BE DIFFUSED. That is to be our second head. Read the text again: "Awake, O north wind; and come, thou south; blow upon my garden that the spices thereof may flow out."

Observe, first, that *until our graces are diffused, it is the same as if they were not there*. You may go through a wood, and it may be abounding in game, yet you may scarcely see a hare or notice a pheasant anywhere. There they lie all quiet and undisturbed; but, by-and-by, the beaters go through the wood making a great noise, and away the pheasants fly, and you may see the timid hares run like hinds let loose, because they are disturbed and woken up. That is what we sometimes need, to be aroused and stirred from slumber. We may not know that we have any faith till there comes a trial, and then our faith starts boldly up. We can hardly know how much we love our Lord till there come a test of our love, and then we so behave ourselves that we know that we do love him. Often, as I have already reminded you, something is needed from without to stir the life that lies hidden within. It is so with these sweet flowers in the Beloved's garden; they need either the north wind or the south wind to blow on them that they may shed abroad their sweet odours.

Notice next, that *it is very painful to a Christian to be in such a condition that his graces are not stirring.* He cannot endure it. We who love the Lord were not born again to waste our time in sinful slumber; our watchword is, "Let us not sleep, as do others." (1 Thess. 5:6) We were not born to inaction; every power that God has put within us was meant to be used in working, and striving, and serving the Lord. So, when our graces are slumbering, we ourselves are in an unhappy state. Then we long for any agency that would set those graces moving. The north wind? Oh, but if it should blow, then we shall have snow! Well, then, let the snow come, for we must have our graces set in motion, for we cannot bear that they should continue to lie quiet and still. "Awake, O north wind!" — a heavy trial, a bleak adversity, a fierce temptation — anything, so long as we just begin to diffuse our graces. Or if the north wind is dreaded, we say, "Come, thou south!" Let prosperity be granted to us; let sweet fellowship with our brethren rouse us, and holy meditations, full of delight, stir our souls. Let a sense of the divine life, like a soft south wind, come to our spirit. We are not particular which it is; let the Lord send whatever he pleases, or both together, as the text seems to imply, only let us be aroused. "Quicken thou me, O Lord, according to thy Word" (Ps. 119:25) — whichever Word you choose to apply — only quicken your servant, and do not let the graces within me be as if they were dead!

Remember, however, that *the best Quickener is always the Holy Spirit;* and that blessed Spirit can come as the north wind, convincing us of sin, and tearing away every rag of our self-confidence, or he may come as the soft south wind, all full of love, revealing Christ, and the covenant of grace, and all the blessings treasured for us there. Come, Holy Spirit! Come as the Heavenly Dove, or as the rushing mighty wind; but come! Drop from above, as gently as the dew, or come like rattling hail; but come, blest Spirit of God! We feel that we must be moved, we must be stirred, our heart's emotions must once again throb to prove that the life of God is really in us; and if we do not realise this quickening and stirring, we are utterly unhappy.

You see also, dear friends, from this text, that *when a child of God sees that his graces are not diffused abroad, then is the time that he should take to prayer.* Let not one of us ever think of saying, "I do not feel as if I could pray, and therefore I will not pray." On the contrary, then is the time when you ought to pray more earnestly than ever. When the heart is disinclined from prayer, take that as a danger-signal, and at once go to the Lord with this resolve, as did Charlotte Elliott,

I will approach thee — I will force
My way through obstacles to thee:
To thee for strength will have recourse
To thee for consolation flee!

Oh cast me, cast me not away,
From thy dear presence gracious Lord!
My burden at thy feet I lay:
My soul reposes on thy word.

Then you seem to yourself to have little faith, and little love, and little joy, then cry to the Lord all the more, "Cry aloud, and spare not." Say,

"O my Father, I cannot endure this miserable existence! You have made me to be a flower, to shed abroad my perfume, yet I am not doing it. Oh, by some means, stir my

394

flagging spirit till I shall be full of earnest industry, full of holy anxiety to promote your glory, O my Lord and Master!"

While you are thus crying, you must still believe, however, that God the Holy Spirit can stir your spirit, and make you full of life again. Never permit a doubt about that fact linger in your bosom, else will you be unnecessarily sad. You, who are the true children of God, cannot ever come into a condition out of which the Holy Spirit cannot uplift you. You know the notable case of Laodicea, which was neither cold nor hot, and therefore so nauseous to the great Lord that he threatened to spit her out of his mouth; yet what is the message to the angel of that church?" Behold, I stand at the door, and knock." (Rev. 3:20) This is not said to sinners, it is addressed to the angel of the church of the Laodiceans: "Behold, I stand at the door, and knock: if any man hear my voice, and open the door, I will come in to him, and will sup with him, and he with me." Oh, matchless grace! He is sick of these lukewarm professors, yet he promises to sup with them, and they shall sup with him. That is the only cure for lukewarmness and decline, to renew heart-fellowship with Christ; and he stands and offers it to all his people now. "Only open the door, and I will sup with you, and you shall sup with me." O you whose graces are lying so sinfully dormant, who have to mourn and cry because of "the body of this death" (Rom. 7:24) — for death in you seems to have taken to itself a body, and to have become a substantial thing, no mere skeleton now, but a heavy, cumbrous form that bows you down — cry still to him who is able to deliver you from this lukewarm and sinful state! Let everyone of us send up the prayer of our text, "Awake, O north wind; and come, thou south; and blow upon my garden, that the spices thereof may flow out."

III. Our third and closing head will help to explain the remaining portion of our text: "Let my Beloved come into his garden, and eat his pleasant fruits." These words speak of THE COMPANY OF CHRIST, AND THE ACCEPTANCE OF OUR FRUIT BY CHRIST.

I want you, dear friends, to notice specially one expression which is used here. While the spouse was, as it were, shut up and frozen, and the spices of the Lord's garden were not blowing out, she cried to the winds, "Blow upon *my* garden." She hardly dared to call it her Lord's garden; but now, notice the alteration in the phraseology: "Let my Beloved come into *his* garden, and eat his pleasant fruits." The wind has blown through the garden, and made the sweet odours flow out. Now it is no longer "my garden" but "his garden". It is wonderful how an increase of grace transfers our properties. While we have but little grace, we cry, "*my*", but when we get great grace, we cry "*his*". Whenever you are sinful and infirm, brother, that is yours, you rightly call it "*my*"; but when you become strong, and joyful, and full of faith, that is not yours, brother, and you rightly call it "*his*". Let him have all the glory of the change, while you take all the shame and confusion of face to yourself, that ever you should have been so destitute of grace. As the spouse says, "Let my Beloved come into his garden. Here are all the sweet perfumes flowing out; he will enjoy them, let him come and feel himself at home amongst them. He planted every flower, and gave to each its fragrance; let him come into his garden and see what wonders his grace has wrought."

Do you not feel, beloved, that *the one thing you need to stir your whole soul is that Christ's should come into it?* Have you lost his company lately? Oh, do not try to do without it! The true child of God ought not to be willing to bear broken communion for even five minutes, but should be sighing and crying for its renewal. Our business is to seek to "walk in the light as God is in the light" (1 Jn. 1:7), fully enjoying communion with Christ our Lord; and when that fellowship is broken, then the heart feels that it has cast all its happiness away, and must robe itself in sackcloth and sorrowfully fast. If the presence of the Bridegroom shall be taken away from you, then indeed you have cause to fast and be sad. The best condition a heart can be in, if it has lost fellowship with Christ, is to resolve

395

that it will give God no rest till it gets back to communion with him, and to give itself no rest till once more it finds the Well-beloved.

Next, observe that when the Beloved comes into his garden, the heart's humble but earnest entreaty is, *"Let him eat his pleasant fruits."* Would you keep back anything from Christ? I know you could not if he were to come into his garden. The best things that you have, you would first present to him, and then everything that you have, you would bring to him, and leave all at his dear feet. We do not ask him to come to the garden that we may lay up our fruit, and put them by, and store them up for ourselves; we ask him to come and eat them. The greatest joy of a Christian is to give joy to Christ. I do not know whether heaven itself can overmatch this pearl of giving joy to the heart of Jesus Christ on earth. It can match it, but not overmatch it, for it is a superlative joy to give joy to him — the Man of sorrows, who was emptied of joy for our sakes, and who now is filled up again with joy as each one of us come and bring his share, and cause the heart of Christ to receive a new and fresh delight. Did you ever reclaim a poor girl from the streets? Did you ever rescue a poor thief who had been in prison? Then I know that, as you have heard of the holy chastity of the one, or of the sacred honesty of the other of those lives that you have been the means of restoring, you said, "Oh, this is delightful! There is no joy equal to it. The effort cost me money, it cost me time, it cost me thought, it cost me prayer, but I am repaid a thousand times." Then, as you see them growing up so bright, so transparent, so holy, so useful, you say, "This work is worth living for, it is a delight beyond measure." Often, people come to me, and tell me of souls that were saved through my ministry twenty years ago. I heard, the other day, of one that was brought to Christ by a sermon of mine nearly thirty years ago, and I said to the friend who told me, "Thank you, thank you; you could not tell me anything that would give my heart such joy as this good news that God made me the instrument of a soul's conversion." But what must be the joy of Christ who does all the work of salvation, who redeems us from sin, and death, and hell, when he sees such creatures as we, made to be like him, and knows the divine possibilities of glory and immortality that lie within us?

What are we going to be, brothers and sisters, we who are in Christ? We have no idea of what holiness, and glory, and bliss, shall yet be ours. "It doth not yet appear what we shall be." (1 Jn. 3:2) We may rise even while on earth to great heights of holiness — and the higher the better; but there is something better for us than mortal eye has ever seen, or mortal ear has ever heard. There is more grace to be in the saints than we have ever seen in them before. The saintliest saint on earth was never such a saint as they are yonder before the throne of the Most High; and I do not know but that, even when they get there, there will be a something still beyond for them, and that through the eternal ages they will still take as their motto, "Onward and upward!" In heaven, there will be no "Finis". We shall still continue to develop, and become something more than we have ever been before; not fuller, but yet capable of holding more, ever growing in the possibility of reflecting Christ, and being filled with his love; and all the while our Lord Jesus Christ will be charmed and delighted with us. As he hears our lofty songs of praise, as he sees the bliss which will ever be flashing from each one of us, as he perceives the divine ecstasy which shall be ours forever, he will take supreme delight in it all. "My redeemed", he will say, "the sheep of my pasture, the purchase of my blood, borne on my shoulders, my very heart pierced for them, oh, how I delight to see them in the heavenly fold! These, my redeemed people are joint-heirs with me in the boundless heritage that shall be theirs forever; oh, how I delight in them!"

"Wherefore, comfort one another with these words", beloved, and cry mightily that, on this church, and on all the churches, God's Spirit may blow to make the spices flow. Pray, dear friends, all of you, for the churches to which you belong; and if you, my brother, are a pastor, go on asking especially for this divine wind to blow through the garden which you have to cultivate, as I also pray for this portion of the garden of the Lord: "Let my Beloved come into his garden, and eat his pleasant fruits." The Lord be with each one of you, beloved, for his dear name's sake! Amen.

FOURTEEN SERMONS ON THE SONG OF SOLOMON

CHAPTER 5

53. LOVE JOINING IN LOVE
NO. 1943

A SHORT ADDRESS TO A FEW FRIENDS AT MENTONE
AT THE BREAKING OF BREAD
ON LORD'S-DAY AFTERNOON, JAN. 9TH, 1887

"I am come into my garden, my sister, my spouse: I have gathered my myrrh with my spice; I have eaten my honeycomb with my honey; I have drunk my wine with my milk: eat, O friends; drink, yea, drink abundantly, O beloved." (Song of Solomon 5:1)

NO sooner does the spouse say, "Let my Beloved come into his garden", than her Lord answers, "I am come into my garden." "Before they call, I will answer; and while they are yet speaking, I will hear." (Is. 65:24) When we desire our Lord Jesus to come to us, he has already come in a measure; our desire is the result of his coming. He meets us in all our desires, for he waits to be gracious. Our "come" is no sooner uttered than it is lost in his "Behold, I come quickly!" (Rev. 3:11, 22:7, 12)

When we perceive that the Bridegroom has come, we see also that he has done exactly what he was asked to do. How cheering to find that our mind is in harmony with his mind! Our heart says, "Let my Beloved come into his garden, and eat his pleasant fruits." His heart replies, "I have gathered my myrrh with my spice; I have eaten my honeycomb with my honey; I have drunk my wine with my milk." "Delight thyself also in the Lord; and he shall give thee the desires of thine heart." (Ps. 37:4) The Lord Jesus makes the desires of his saints to be the foreshadowings of his own actions: "The secret of the Lord is with them that fear him." (Ps.25:14) His secret counsel is made known in the believing soul by desires inspired of the Holy Spirit.

Note well that the bridegroom kindly takes to himself as his own all that is in the garden. His spouse speaks of "his pleasant fruits", and he acknowledges the least and most homely of them to be his own. He repeats the possessive particle — "my": *my* myrrh, *my* spice, *my* honeycomb, *my* honey, *my* wine, *my* milk. He disdains nothing which the garden of his bride produces. He is fond of the notion of joint-heirship, even as in another place he says, "My Father, and your Father, my God, and your God." (Jn. 20:17) Let us also value the personal possessive pronouns: the sweetness of the promises lies in them. These are our arms with which we embrace the promises. Beloved brethren in Christ Jesus, is it not charming to see our Lord appropriating us, and all that we are, and all that we have, and all that grows within us, and all the varied forms of his grace which are the outcome of his own work within our hearts? Within us, certain things are bitter but wholesome; and he says "my myrrh." Some things are sweet, though homely; and he says "my honey." Some things are of a rarer sort, and he says "my spice"; while others are common-place enough, and he says "my milk." Our Lord makes no exception to any one of the true growths of the garden, whether it is myrrh or milk; and he asks for nothing more than that the garden may be expected to yield. He is content without the butter of kine, or the flesh of fed beasts, and satisfies himself with honey fresh from the hive.

I note with much delight that matters, which seem inconsistent with perfection, are not refused by the heavenly bridegroom. As the Lord did not refuse as an offering the leavened cakes of the first-fruits, so, in this instance, he says, "I have eaten my honeycomb with my honey." The honey would be purer without the comb; but as it is incident to it, he takes the one with the other. He graciously accepts not only our heart's desire, but the very mode in which our weakness works towards that desire. It is as if he

399

delights in the words of our prayers as well as in the essence of our prayers, and prizes the notes of our songs as well as the meaning of them. Yes, I believe our Lord puts our tears as well as our sorrows into his bottle (Ps. 56:8), and hears our groanings as well as our desires. The honeycomb which contains the honey is precious to him. After he had risen from the grave, he ate a piece of a honeycomb (Lk. 24:42), and I do not doubt that he had a reason for choosing that food: sweet gathered from sweets, yet not without wax. Our Lord accepts our services without nicely noting, and critically rejecting, the infirmity that goes with them.

Note also that he himself gathers what he enjoys: "I have gathered my myrrh with my spice." Many a holy thing, which we have not in detail offered to him in set form, he knows to have been given in the gross; and so he takes with his own hand what he knows we have by a comprehensive covenant made over to him. How sweetly he fills up our blanks, and believes in our consecration, even when we do not repeat the form of it! Moreover, he makes mixtures out of our fruit, for he gathers myrrh with balsam, and drinks wine with milk, thus taking the rarer with the more common. He knows how to make holy compounds out of the graces of his people, thus increasing their excellence. He is the best judge of what is admirable, and is the best fashioner and compounder of character; and he is using his skill on us. Often, by our mingled experiences, he accomplishes an increase of virtue in us. Some graces are the result of work and wisdom, as wine which must be trodden from the grapes; others are natural, like milk which flows from living fountains without the art of man: but the Lord accepts them both, and so combines them so that they are pleasant to him to a high degree. Simple faith and experimental prudence make up a sacred milk and wine; and the like may be seen in rapturous love and calm patience, which blend most deliciously. The Lord loves us and makes the most of us. He is pleased with all that is the true product of his grace, and finds no faults with it; on the contrary, he says, "I have eaten my honeycomb with my honey."

Having made these observations on the Lord fulfilling the prayer of the spouse, I should like to deliver the following remarks on the text.

It is evident that *the Lord Jesus is made happy by us*. These poetical sentences must mean that he values the graces and works of his people. He gathers their myrrh and spice because he values them; he eats and drinks the honey and the milk because they are pleasant to him. It is a wonderful thought that the Lord Jesus Christ has joy in us. We cost him anguish, even to death, and now he finds a reward in us. This may seem a small thing to an unloving mind, but it may well ravish the heart that adores the Well-beloved. Can it be true that we bring joy to the Son of God, Prince Emmanuel? The King has been held in the galleries, but he has been charmed by us. Our first repentance made him call together his friends and his neighbours. (Lk. 15:6, 9) The first gleam of faith he ever saw in us made his heart rejoice; and all that he has seen in us ever since of his own image, wrought by his grace, has caused him to see of the travail of his soul. (Is. 53:11) Never has a husbandman taken such pleasure in the growth of his choice plants as our Lord has in us. "The Lord taketh pleasure in them that fear him in those that hope in his mercy." (Ps. 147:11, 149:4) That is a thought to be rolled under the tongue like a sweet morsel. Yes, the Lord's church is his Hephzibah, for, says he, "my delight is in her." (Is. 62:4)

The second thought is that *the Lord Jesus will not, and cannot, be happy by himself: he would have us share with him*. Note how the words run — "I have eaten"; "Eat, O friends!" "I have drunk"; "Drink, yea, drink abundantly, O beloved." His union with his people is so close that his joy is in them that their joy may be full. He cannot be alone in his joy. These verses of our quaint hymn by Joseph Denham Smith are always true:

My God I have found the thrice blessed ground,
Where life and where joy and true comfort abound.

'Tis found in the blood of him who once stood
My refuge and safety, my Surety with God.

Accepted I am in the once-offered Lamb;
It was God who himself had devisèd the plan.

And though here below, 'mid sorrow and woe,
My place is in heaven with Jesus, I know.

And this I shall find, for such is his mind,
He'll not be in glory and leave me behind.

For soon he will come and take me safe home,
And make me to sit with himself on his throne.

He will not be happy anywhere without us. He will not eat without our eating, and he will not drink without our drinking. Does he not say this in other words in the Revelation — "If any man hear my voice, and open the door, I will come in to him, and will sup with him, and he with me"? (Rev. 3:20) The inter-communion is complete: the enjoyment is for both. To make our Lord Jesus happy, we must be happy also. How can the Bridegroom rejoice if his bride is sad? How can the Head be content if the members pine? At this table of fellowship, his chief concern is that we eat and drink. "Take, eat" said he (Mat. 26:26; Mk. 14:22; 1 Cor. 11:24); and again, "Drink ye all of it." (Mat. 26:27) I think I hear him now say — "I have eaten, and I have drunk; and although I will drink no more of the fruit of the vine until that day that I drink it new in the kingdom of God (Mk. 14:25), yet eat, O friends: drink, yes, drink abundantly, O beloved!" Thus we have seen, first, that Christ is made happy by us; and, secondly, that he insists on our sharing his joy with him.

If we have already enjoyed happy fellowship with him, *the Lord Jesus calls on us to be happier still.* Though we may say that we have eaten, he will again say, "Eat, O friends!" He presses us to renew, repeat, and increase our participation with him. It is true we have drunk out of the chalice of his love; but he invites us again, saying, "Drink, yes, drink abundantly, O beloved!" Of other wines, it would be bad to say, "Drink abundantly"; but, of this wine, the Lord says with emphasis, "Drink abundantly, O beloved!" Oh, for grace to renew all former enjoyments with greater zest, and deeper intensity! It has been sweet even to taste and sip; what must it be like to eat and drink abundantly? Must it not mean that, though we know the Lord Jesus, we should try to know more of him, yes, to know all that can be known of that love which passes all understanding? (Phil. 4:7) Should we not labour to realise more of HIM, taking in the whole truth concerning his Person and love by meditation, contemplation, understanding, and reverent simplicity? Let nothing lie alone: let us eat and drink all the stores of the banquet of love.

As the mouth with which we eat is faith, does not the Saviour seem to cry, "Believe in me; trust in me; confide in me abundantly"? Eat and drink with a large appetite by receiving into your heart's belief all that can be received. Oh, for grace to appropriate a whole Christ, and all the love, the grace, the glory that is laid up in him!

Does it not also mean, have greater enjoyment in divine things? Partake of them without stint. Do not restrict yourself as though you could go too far in feeding on the Lord Jesus. Do not be afraid of being too happy in the Lord, or of being too sure of his salvation, or of having too much assurance, or too much devout emotion. Do not dread the excitements that come from fellowship with Christ. Do not believe that the love of Jesus can be too powerfully felt in the soul. Permit the full sweep and current of holy joy in the Lord to carry you away: it will be safe to yield to it. "Rejoice in the Lord alway: and again, I say, Rejoice." (Phil. 4:4)

Beloved, let us now take our fill of Christ. Since we believe, let us believe more unreservedly: if we enjoy, let us enjoy more thoroughly; if we have life, let us have it more abundantly. In this case, we may eat, and our soul shall live; we may drink, and not only forget our misery but drink again, and enter into bliss. Our Lord beckons us from the shore to the sea: he calls us from the lower seat to come up higher. He would have us gladder, stronger, fuller, and holier. He presses the provisions of his love on us, like a host whose joy lies in seeing all the guests feasting. Do not hold back. Do not be satisfied with a little believing, and scant enjoying, and cool feeling: but let us enter fully into the joy of our Lord.

True, we are unworthy, but he invites us. We would be wise to yield to his loving pressure. We may not have such another feast just yet, and possibly, we may have to go for forty days in the wilderness on the strength of this meal. Therefore, let us keep the feast heartily. Our Lord, in this invitation, challenges our friendship and our love. He says, "Eat, O *friends*!" Prove yourselves friends by being free at his Table. "Drink, yea, drink abundantly, O *beloved*!" If this is his way of testing us, let us not be slow to accept it. Let us show our love by joying in him as he joys in us. Amen.

54. THE KING FEASTING IN HIS GARDEN
NO. 919

DELIVERED ON LORD'S-DAY MORNING, MARCH 6TH, 1870
AT THE METROPOLITAN TABERNACLE, NEWINGTON

"I am come into my garden, my sister, my spouse: I have gathered my myrrh with my spice; I have eaten my honeycomb with my honey; I have drunk my wine with my milk: eat, O friends; drink, yea, drink abundantly, O beloved." (Song of Solomon 5:1)

I BELIEVE this text to be appropriate to the spiritual condition of our church. If I am not very sadly mistaken, the Lord of Hosts is with us in a very remarkable way. Our meetings for prayer have been distinguished by an earnest and fervent spirit; our meetings with enquirers have been remarkably powerful; in a quiet manner, without any outward outcries, souls have been smitten down with conviction of sin, and have been comforted as they have received Christ by faith. We are not a deserted church, we are not left with broken hedges, with the wild boar of the wood committing devastations; but the Lord has sent a gracious rain which has quickened the seed, and he has watered the plants of his garden, and made our souls rejoice in his presence. Now, if the text is appropriate, as I believe it is, the duty to which it especially calls us should have our earnest attention. The workers for Christ must remember that, even if they have to care for the garden, their chief business must be to commune with the Lord and Master of that garden, since he himself this morning calls them to do so. "Eat O friends; drink, yea, drink abundantly, O beloved." In happy and auspicious times, when the Spirit of God is working, it is very natural to say, "We must now work more abundantly than ever", and God forbid that we should hinder such zeal, but the more spiritual privilege is not to be put in second place. Let us commune as well as work; for there we will find strength for service, and our service will be done the better, and become more acceptable, and ensure the larger blessing. If, while we serve like Martha, at the same time we commune like Mary, we shall not then become cumbered with much serving; we shall serve and not be cumbered, and shall feel no fretfulness against others whose only faculty may be that of sitting at the Master's feet. (Lk. 10:40)

The text divides itself readily into three parts. First, we have the presence of the heavenly Bridegroom — "I am come into my garden, my sister, my spouse"; we have, secondly, the satisfaction which he finds in his church — "I have gathered my myrrh with my spice, I have eaten my honeycomb with my honey, I have drunk my wine with my milk"; and thirdly, we have the invitation which he gives to his loving people — "Eat, O friends; drink, yea, drink abundantly, O beloved."

I. The voice of the Master himself calls us to consider HIS PRESENCE: "I am come."

He tells us he has come. What? Could he come without our perceiving it? Is it possible? May we be like those whose eyes were held so that they did not know him? (Lk. 24:16) Is it possible for us to be like Mary Magdalene, seeking Christ while he is standing very near us? Yes, and we may even be like the disciples who, when they saw him walking on the water, were afraid, thought he was a spirit, and cried out, and had need for him to say, "It is I, be not afraid" (Mat. 14:27) before they knew who it was! Here is our ignorance, but here is his tenderness. He may come, and yet we may not recognise him; but here, when he comes, he takes care to advertise the blessed fact, and calls us to observe and consider, and to delight in it. He would, for our own comfort, prevent it being said of us, "He came unto his own, and his own received him not." (Jn. 1:11)

Let us then observe first, this coming was in answer to prayer. Our translators, in dividing the Bible into chapters, seem to have been utterly regardless of the connection or the sense, so that they brought down their guillotine between two verses which must not be divided. The church had said, "Awake, O north wind; and come, thou south; blow upon my garden" (Song 4:16). She also added, "Let my beloved come into his garden, and eat his pleasant fruits." In answer to that prayer, the Beloved replies, "I am come into my garden." Prayer is always heard, and the prayer of faithful souls finds an echo in Jesus' heart. How quickly the spouse was heard! Scarcely had the words died away — "Let my Beloved come" — before she heard him say, "I am come!" "Before they call, I will answer; and while they are yet speaking, I will hear." (Is. 65:24) He is very near his people, and hence, he very speedily answers their request. And how fully does he answer it too! You will perhaps say, "But she had asked for the Holy Spirit; she had said, 'Awake, O north wind; and come, thou south'; and yet there is no mention of the heavenly wind as blowing through the garden." The answer is that the Beloved's coming means all that. His visit brings both north and south wind; all benign influences are sure to follow when he leads the way. Spices always flow out from the heart when Christ's sweet love flows in; and, where he is, Christians have all things in him. There was a full answer to her prayer, and there was more than an answer, for she had just said, "Let him come and eat." But, lo, he gathers myrrh and spice, and drinks of wine and milk. He does exceeding abundantly above what she had even asked or even thought (Eph. 3:20), after the right royal manner of the Son of God, who does not answer us according to the poverty of our expressions, and the leanness of our desires, but according to his riches in glory, giving us grace upon grace out of his own inexhaustible fullness.

Brethren, this church has had a full reward for all her prayers. We have waited on God often; all day long there has been prayer in this house, and, during this last mouth, there has scarcely been an hour in which supplication has been suspended; and the answer has already come. We are so apt to overlook the answer to prayer. Let it not be so! Let us praise the Lord that prayer has not been a vain service; it has brought down his presence, the chief of all blessings, and that for which we most interceded at his throne. Let us exalt him! We can hear him say now, "I have come into your meetings, I am blessing you, I am saving souls, I am elevating some of you into nearness of fellowship with myself, I am chastening some of your spirits with sadness to think you have lived in such grovelling an estate. I am with you, I have heard your prayers, and I have come to abide with you as a people." Now, if this is the case, let us next observe what an unspeakable blessing this is! If the voice had said, "I have sent my angel", that would have been a precious boon; but it does not say so; the word is, "I am come." What, does he, before whom angels adoringly bow their heads, he before whom perfect spirits cast their crowns, does he condescend to come into the church? Yes, it is even so. There is the personal presence of Christ in the midst of his people. Where two or three are met together in his name, there is he in the midst of them. (Mat. 18:20) His corporeal presence is in heaven, but his spiritual presence, which is all we want — all it is expedient for him as yet to grant — is assuredly in our midst. He is with us truly and really when we meet together in our solemn assemblies, and with us too when we separate and go our ways in private to fight the battles of the Lord.

Brethren, for us to enjoy his presence as a church is a privilege whose value is only to be measured by the melancholy results of big absence. Where Jesus Christ is not in the garden, the plants wither, and produce untimely figs; and the fruit falls from the trees. Blossoms do not appear, or, if they do, they do, they disappoint when Jesus is not there to knit and fructify them. But when he comes, even the driest boughs in the garden become like Aaron's rod that budded. (Heb. 9:4) Yes, our older brethren in the church remember times of trouble, times when the ministry was not with power, when the gatherings on the

Lord's-day were joyless, when the voice of wailing saddened the courts of Zion; but now we rejoice, yes, and will rejoice. The contrast between the past and the joyous present should increase our gratitude, till we praise the Lord on the high-sounding cymbals with jubilant exaltation.

Remember, too, that if he had dealt with us according to our sins, and rewarded us after our iniquities, we should never have heard the footfall of the Beloved traversing the garden. How many have grieved the Holy Spirit by careless living and backsliding! How have most of us followed him afar off instead of keeping step with him in service and fellowship! Alas, my Lord, if you had regarded only the sins of the pastor of the church, you had long ago left this flock; but you have not dealt with us severely; but according to your love and mercy, you have blotted out our sins like a cloud, and, like a thick cloud, our transgressions (Is. 44:22), and still you condescend to come into your garden.

If you take each word of this remarkable sentence, you will find a meaning. "I am come." There is the personal presence of Christ who often said, "I am come." (Jn. 5:43, 10:10, 12:46) There is the certainty that it is so. It is no delusion, no dream, and no supposition. "I am truly come." Blessed be the name of the Lord; at this present time it is assuredly so. Many of his saints can bear testimony that they have seen his face and felt the kisses of his lips, and have proved even this day that his love is better than wine. Note the next word, "I am come into my garden." How near is the approach of Christ to his church! He does not come to the garden door, nor look over the wall, nor in at the gate and out again; but into his garden. Down every walk, amidst the green alleys, among the beds of spices, he walks, watching each flower, pruning the superfluous foliage of every fruit-bearing plant, and plucking up by the roots what his heavenly Father has not planted. His delights are with the sons of men. His fellowship with his chosen is most familiar; so that the spouse may sing, "My beloved is gone down into his garden, to the beds of spices, to feed in the gardens, and to gather lilies." (Song 6:2) Jesus Christ the Lord does not forget his church, but fulfils the promise: "I the Lord do keep it, I will water it every moment; lest any hurt it, I will keep it night and day." (Is 27:3) Brethren, this is a solemn, as well as a pleasant, fact. You, who are members of this church, recollect that Jesus has come into the church, that he is now going his rounds among you, and marking your feelings towards him. He knows today who is in fellowship with him and who is not; he discerns between the precious and the vile.

He never comes without his winnowing fan when he visits his threshing floor; beware if you are the chaff. He has come into his garden. O you that have not enjoyed much of his gracious company, pray him to spare a look towards you, and be like the sunflower, which turns its face to the sun to refresh itself with its beams. Oh, pant and long for his presence! If your soul is as dark as the dead of night, call out to him, for he hears the faintest sigh of any of his chosen.

"I am come into my garden" says he. Note here the possession which Christ claims in the church. If it were not his garden, he would not come into it. A church that is not Christ's church shall have none of his presence, and a soul that is not Christ's has no fellowship with him. If he reveals himself at all, it is to his own people, his blood-bought people, the people that are his by purchase and by power, and by the surrendering of themselves to him. When I think of this church as committed to my care, I am overawed, and well may my fellow-officers be cast down under the weight of our responsibility; but, after all, we may say, "Master, this garden is not ours; it is your garden. We have not begotten all this people, neither can we carry them in our bosoms; but you, great Shepherd of the sheep, you will guard the fold." Since the garden is his own, he will not allow even the least plant to perish. My brethren who work for Christ, do not be downcast if certain portions of the work should not seem to succeed. He will attend to it. "The pleasure of the Lord shall prosper in his hand." (Is. 53:10) It is more his work than ours, and souls are more his responsibility than ours. So let us hope and be confident, for the Master will surely smile upon his "vineyard of red wine."

The next word denotes cultivation. "I am come into my garden." The church is a cultivated spot; it did not spring up by chance, but was arranged by himself. It has been tended by himself, and the fruit belong to him. Thankful are we if we can truly know that, as a church,

We are a garden walled around,
Chosen and made peculiar ground;
A little spot enclosed by grace
Out of the world's wide wilderness

(Isaac Watts)

Christ, the Great Cultivator, exercises care and skill in training his people, and delights to see his own handiwork in them.

And then there are the two choice words at the close, in which he speaks of his church herself, rather than of her work. As if he would draw the attention of his people to themselves and to himself, rather than to their work, he says, "My sister, my spouse." There is one name for the garden, but there are two names for her. The work is his work, the garden is his garden; but see, he wants communion not so much with the work as with the worker; thus he speaks to the church herself. He calls her, "My sister, my spouse." "Spouse" has something in it of dearness. That is not the first word, for what can be dearer to the husband than the bride? But then, there was a time when the spouse was not dear to the bridegroom. There was a period perhaps when he did not know her, when there was no relationship between them both. Though they are made one flesh by marriage, yet they were of different families; and, for this cause, he adds the dear name of "sister" to show an ancient relationship to her, a closeness and a nearness by blood and by birth, as well as by betrothal and wedlock. The two words, put together, make up a confection of such inexpressible sweetness that, instead of seeking to expound them to you, I will leave them to your meditations. And may he who calls the church "Sister" and "Spouse" open up their richness to your souls!

Here, then, is the gist of the whole matter. The Master's presence is in his church in a very remarkable way. Beloved, I pray that none of you may be like Adam, who fled among the trees to hide himself from God when he walked in the garden. (Gen. 3:8) May it be that your business is not act like an overshadowing thicket to conceal you from fellowship! He calls you, O backslider; he calls you as once he called Adam — "Where art thou?" He calls, "Come, beloved, come and commune with your Lord; come away from those carking [troubling] cares and anxieties which, like gloomy groves of cypress, conceal you from your Lord, or rather, your Lord from you." Do you not hear not his call: "O my dove, that art in the clefts of the rock, in the secret places of the stairs, let me see thy countenance, let me hear thy voice; for sweet is thy voice, and thy countenance is comely." (Song 2:14) Let none of us be like the disciples in another garden when their Lord was there, and he was in agony, but they were sleeping. Up, you sleepers, for Christ has come! If the midnight cry, "Behold, the Bridegroom cometh" (Mat. 25:6) awoke the virgins, shall not "I am come" awaken you? It is his own voice; it is not "He cometh", but "I am come." Start up, you slumberers; and now, with heart and soul, seek fellowship with him. It would be a sad thing if, while Christ is with us, any were slumbering, and then should wake up to say, "Surely God was in this place and I knew it not." (Gen. 28:16) Rather, may you invite him to come into your souls to abide with you until the day break and the shadows flee away, and you behold him face to face! (Song 2:17, 4:6)

406

II. Thus much on the first point. Now may his Holy Spirit help us to view OUR LORD IN HIS CHURCH!

The beautiful expressions of the text are capable of many holy meanings, and it is not possible that any expositions of mine could fully unveil their treasures; but let me observe, first, that Christ is delighted with the offerings of his people. He says, "I have gathered my myrrh with my spice." Let us consider myrrh and spice — sweet perfumes — offered by way of incense to God, and as being indicative of the offerings which his people bring to him. What if I say that prayer is like sweet smelling myrrh, and that the Beloved has been gathering the myrrh of holy prayer, the bitter myrrh of repenting sighs and cries, in the midst of his church, lo, these many months! You perhaps thought that poor wordless prayer of yours was never heard, but Jesus gathered it, and called it spice; and when some brother was praying aloud, and, in silence, your tears fell thick and fast for perishing sinners, for you could not bear that they should die, nor endure that Christ's name should be blasphemed, the Beloved gathered up the precious drops, and counted them as costly oil of sweetest smell. Was it not said in the Psalm, "Prayer also shall be made for him continually, and daily shall he be praised"? (Ps. 72:15) And you prayed for him, that his name might be as ointment poured out (Song 1:3), and that he might gird his sword upon his thigh (Song 3:8) and ride out prosperously. Jesus observed, and delighted in your heart's offering. Others did not know that you were praying; perhaps you thought that you were hardly praying; but he gathered his myrrh with his spice from you. No faithful prayer is ever lost. The groanings of his people are not forgotten; he gathers them as men gather precious products from a garden which they have tilled with much labour and expense.

And then, may not spice represent our praises? These, as well as prayer, come up as incense before his throne. Last Thursday night, when my brother [James, his assistant] spoke to you, if you felt as I did, I, am sure your heart sent up praise as a smoke of incense from the warm coals of a censer, as he cast on them handfuls of frankincense in the form of various motives for gratitude and reasons for praise. Oh, it was good to sing God's praises as we then did by the hour together. It was delightful, too, to come to his Table and make that ordinance in very deed a Eucharistic [thankful] service of praise to God. Praise is pleasant and comely, and most of all because Jesus accepts it, and says, "Whoever offers praise glorifies me."

When the Lord, in another place, speaks of offering sweet cane bought with money (Is. 43:24), is he not referring to other offerings which his people bring, in addition to their prayers and praises, when they give to him the first fruits of all their increase, and present thank-offerings to his name. He has said, "None of you shall appear before me empty" (Ex. 23:15, 34:20), and I hope none of you have been content to do so. The contributions given for the spread of his cause, for the feeding of his poor, and clothing of his naked ones, are given by true hearts directly to him. Though they may be but as two mites that make a farthing [one-quarter of an old penny], yet are offered in his name, are they not also included in this word, "I have gathered my myrrh with my spice"?

The Saviour's satisfaction is found, in the next place, in his people's love — "I have eaten my honeycomb with my honey." Am I wrong if I believe that this sweetness refers to Christian love, for this is the richest of all the graces, and sweetens all the rest. Jesus Christ finds delightful solace in his people's love, both in the inward love which is like the honey, and in the outward manifestation of it, which is like the honeycomb. He rejoices in the love that drips in all its preciousness from the heart, and in the honeycomb of organisation, in which it is, for order's sake, stored up and put in his hand. Or, what if it should mean that Christ overlooks the imperfections of his people? The honeycomb is not good eating, but he takes that as well as the honey. "I have eaten my honeycomb with my

407

For more resources go to CharlesSpurgeonBooks.com

honey." As he looks at his people, and sees what he has done for them, his loving heart rejoices in what his grace has accomplished. As a benevolent man, who might take a child from the street and educate it, would be pleased see it growing up, prospering, happy, well-informed, talented, so, when Jesus Christ, remembering what his people used to be like, sees in them displays of grace, desires after holiness, self-denials, communion with God, and such like, this is to him like honey. He takes an intense satisfaction in our sweet fruits, which he himself has caused us to produce; despite every imperfection, he accepts our love, and says, "I have eaten my honeycomb with my honey."

Turning again to our precious text, we observe that our Lord's satisfaction is compared with drinking as well as eating, and that drinking is of a twofold character. "I have drunk my wine." Does he intend by this his joy, which is fulfilled in us when our joy is full? Does he mean that, as men go to feasts to gladden their hearts with wine, so he comes to his people to see their joy, and is filled with exultation? Does he mean this? Surely he does. And the milk — may not that mean the Christian's common, ordinary life? As milk contains all the constituents of our nourishment, may he not mean by this the general life of the Christian? Our Lord takes delight in the graces of our lives. Someone has said that wine may represent those actions resulting from well-considered dedication and deep spiritual thought; for wine must be pressed from the grape with labour, and preserved with care. There must be skill, and work, and forethought, spent on it; but milk is a natural product, flowing freely, plentifully, spontaneously; it is a more common and ordinary, yet precious, thing. So the Lord delights that his people should give to him those elaborate works which they have to tend with long care, and watch over with much anxiety, before they are produced.

This is the wine; but he would have them give him the simple outgushings of their souls, the outflowings that go out without labour, the little deeds of love which need no forethought, the everyday outgoings of their inner life — these are milk, and are equally acceptable to him. Well, if it is so, certain it is that Christ finds great pleasure is his people, and, in their various forms of piety, he drinks his wine with his milk.

Permit me now to call your attention to those many great little words which are yet but one — I refer to the word "my". Observe that it is repeated eight or nine times. Here is the reason for the solace which the bridegroom finds in his church. Does he walk in the church as men do in a garden for pleasure? Then he says, "I am come into my garden." Does he talk with his beloved? It is because he calls her "my sister, my spouse." Does he love her prayers and praises? It is because they never would be prayed or praised if he had not created these fruits of the lips. He says not, "I have gathered your myrrh with your spice." Oh, no! Viewed as ours, these are poor things, but viewed as his they are most acceptable, "I have gathered my myrrh with my spice." So if he finds any honey in his people, any true love in them, he first put it there. "I have eaten my honeycomb with my honey." Yes, and if there is any joy and life in them to make his heart glad, he calls it "my wine", and "my milk". As I read these words, and thought of our Lord being fed by us, I almost cried out, "'Lord, when saw we thee an hungered, and fed thee? Or thirsty, and gave thee drink?" (Mat. 25:37, 44) Do you find any satisfaction in us? Surely, our goodness does not extend to you! How shall we give you something to eat?" Yet he declares it, and we may blushingly believe him, and praise his name, for surely if he found it so, it is because he made it so. If he has got anything out of us, he must first have put it in us; if he sees of the travail of our soul, it is because the travail came first.

Note well, lovers of Jesus, that our Lord in this heavenly verse is fed first. "I have eaten", says he, and then he turns to us and says, "Eat, O friends." If any of you seek friendship with the Well-beloved, you must commence by preparing him a feast. Remember our Lord's own parable: "Which of you, having a servant ploughing or feeding cattle, will say

408

unto him by-and-by, when he is come from the field, 'Go and sit down to meat?' And will not rather say unto him, 'Make ready wherewith I may sup, and gird thyself, and serve me, till I have eaten and drunken; and afterward thou shalt eat and drink?'" (Lk. 17:7-8) Even if your poverty compels you to say, "As the Lord liveth, I have not a cake, but a handful of meal in a barrel, and a little oil in a cruse" (1 Kings 17:12), listen to him as he answers, "Fear not, make me thereof a little cake first." (13) Be assured that, after you have done that, your barrel of meal shall not waste, neither shall the cruse of oil fail. The way for believers to be fed by Christ is to seek to feed him; look to his being satisfied, and he will assuredly look to you. "Ye shall eat neither bread, nor parched corn, nor green ears, until the selfsame day that ye have brought an offering unto your God." (Lev. 23:14.) "Bring ye all the tithes into the storehouse, that there may be meat in mine house, and prove me now herewith, saith the, Lord of hosts, if I will not open you the windows of heaven, and pour you out a blessing, that there shall not be room enough to receive it." (Mal. 3:10) See, my brethren, you must find food for your Lord, and then, but not till then, there will be food for you.

In the feast, it is remarkable how complete the entertainment is. There is the sweetest food, and the most nourishing and exhilarating drink, and then, over and above, there is the rarest perfume, not counted to be needful in ordinary entertainments, but crowning all, and making up a right royal feast. How marvellous that our Beloved should find within his church all that his soul desires! Having given himself over to her, he delights in her, rests in his love, and rejoices over her with singing. For the "joy that was set before him, he endured the cross, despising the shame, and this day he continues to be filled with the, selfsame delight. (Heb. 12:2)

III. I would fain linger, but time forbids. We must now remember, in the third place, that the text contains an INVITATION.

The Beloved says, "Eat, O friends; drink, yea, drink abundantly, O beloved." In the invitation, we see the character of the invited guests; they are spoken of as "friends". We were once aliens, but now we are more. You shall be like the Lord from whom the love proceeds. O you who stand shivering in the cold shallows of the river of life, why do you tarry there? Descend into the greater depths, the warmer waves, and let the mighty stream lave you breast-high; yes, go farther, and plunge where you can find no bottom, for it is blessed and safe swimming in the stream of Christ's everlasting love; and he is inviting you to it now. When you are at the big banquet-table, do not pick here and there a crumb, do not sip now and then a drop: he says "eat", and adds "drink abundantly". The invitation to receive abundantly applies to all refreshment. Your eating and drinking may be without stint. You cannot impoverish the Most High God, possessor of heaven and earth. When you are satiated [filled] with his love, his table will still be loaded. Your cups may run over, but his flagons will still be full to the brim. If you are in difficulty at all, you are not in difficulty in him; you are in difficulty in yourselves. But now let me say to my brethren, and especially to my fellow workers in the kingdom of Christ, it is for us just now, while our Lord is walking in his garden, while he is finding satisfaction in his work and in his people, to beware of taking any satisfaction in the work ourselves, and equally to beware that we do not neglect the appropriate duty of the occasion, namely, that of feasting our souls with our Lord's gracious provisions. You are caring for others, it is well; you are rejoicing over others, it is well; still watch well yourselves, and rejoice in the Lord in your hearts. What did he say to the twelve when they came back glorying that even the devils were subject to them? Did he not reply, "Nevertheless rejoice not in this, but rather rejoice that your names are written in heaven"? (Lk. 10:20) It is your personal interest in Christ, you being yourselves saved, Christ being present with you, that is your main joy. Enjoy the feast for yourselves, or you will not be strong in handing out the living bread to others. See that you are first partakers of the fruit, or you will not labour aright as God's husbandmen.

The more of personal enjoyment you allow yourselves in connection with your Lord, the more strong you will be for his service, and the more out of an experimental sense of his preciousness you will be able to say with true eloquence, "O taste and see that the Lord is good." (Ps. 34:8) You will tell others what you have tasted and handled; you will say, "This poor man cried, and the Lord heard him, and delivered him from all his fears." (Ps. 34:6) I put this before you with much earnestness, and I pray that none of you may think it safe so to work as to forget to commune, or else seek the good of others and so miss personal fellowship with the Redeemer. I might now conclude, but it strikes me that there may be some among us who are, in their own apprehension, outside the garden of Christ's church, and are therefore mourning over this sermon, saying, "Alas, that is not for me. Christ has come into his garden, but I am a piece of waste ground. He is fed and satisfied in his church, but he finds nothing in me. Surely I shall perish from the way when his wrath is kindled but a little!" I know how apt poor hearts are to write bitter things against themselves, even when God has never written a single word against them; so let me see, if by turning over this text, we may not find thoughts of consolation for the trembling ones who are brought near. We were once enemies, now we are made servants; but we have advanced from the grade of service (though servants still) into that of friends, "henceforth he calls us not servants but friends, for the servant knoweth not what his Lord doeth, but all things that he has seen of his Father he has made known unto us." (Jn. 15:15) The friendship between Christ and his people is not in name only, but in deed and in truth. Having laid down his life for his friends, having brought them to know his friendship in times of trial and of difficulty, he, at all times, proves his friendship by telling his secrets to them, and exhibiting an intense sympathy with them in all their secret bitterness. David and Jonathan were not more closely friends than Christ and the believer, when the believer lives near his Lord. Never seek the friendship of the world, nor allow your love for the creature overshadow your friendship with Christ.

He next calls his people "beloved" as well as "friends". He multiplies titles, but all his words do not express the full love of his heart. "Beloved." Oh, to have this word addressed to us by Christ! It is music! There is no music in the rarest sounds compared with these three syllables, which drop from the Redeemer's lips like sweet smelling myrrh. "Beloved!" If he had directed but that one word to any one of us, it might create a heaven within our soul, which neither sickness nor death could mar. Let me sound the note again: "BELOVED!" Does Jesus love me? Does he own his love? Does he seal the fact by declaring it with his own lips? Then I will not stipulate anything for promises, nor make demands of him. If he love, he must act towards me with loving-kindness; he will not smite his beloved unless love dictates the blow; he will not forsake his chosen, for he never changes. Oh, the inexpressible, the heaped-up blessedness which belong to the man who feels in his soul that Christ has called him beloved!

Here, then, you have the character in the text of those who are invited to commune with Christ; he calls them his friends and his beloved. The provisions presented to them are of two kinds: they are bidden to eat and to drink. You, who are spiritual, know what the food is, and what the drink is, for you eat his flesh and drink his blood. The incarnation of the Son of God, and the death of Jesus the Saviour, these are the two sacred viands on which faith is sustained. To feed on the very Christ of God is what is needed, nothing but this can satisfy the hunger of the spirit; but whoever feeds on him shall know no lack. "Eat," says he, "and drink." You ask, "Where are the provisions? I answer, they are contained in the first words of the text, "I am come." If he has come, then eat; if he has come, then drink; there is food, there is drink for you in him.

Note that delightful word "abundantly". Some dainties satiate, and even nauseate when we have too much of them, but no soul ever had too much of the dear love of Christ, no heart ever did complain that his sweetness cloyed. That can never be. Some things, if you have too much of them, may harm you; they are good to a certain point, beyond that, evil; but even the smallest child of grace shall never over-feast himself with Jesus' love. No, the more you have, the more you shall enjoy, the more blessed you are, the more you shall know. There may be a soft breath in the text which will fan the smoking flax, a tender hand that will bind up the bruised reed. (Is. 42:3; Mat. 12:20)

I will briefly indicate two or three comfortable thoughts.

Seeking soul, should it not console you to think that Jesus is near? The kingdom of God has come near you, for he is come into his garden. He was in our last meeting for anxious souls, for many found him there. You are not, then, living in a region where Christ is absent, maybe, when he passes by, he will look on you. Can you not put out your finger and touch the hem of his garment, for Jesus of Nazareth is passing by? Even if you have not touched him, yet it should give you some good cheer to know that he is within reach and within call. Though you are like the poor withered lily in the garden, or, worse still, like a noxious weed, yet, if he is in the garden, he may observe you and take pity on you.

Notice, too, that although the text speaks of a garden, it never was a garden till he made it so. Men do not find gardens in the wilderness. In the wilds of Australia or the backwoods of America men never stumble upon a garden where human foot has never been — it is all forest, or prairie, or mountain. So, mark you, soul, if the church is a garden, Christ made it so. Why cannot he make you so? Why not, indeed? Has he not said, "Instead of the thorn shall come up the fir tree, and instead of the brier shall come up the myrtle tree: and it shall be to the Lord for a name, for an everlasting sign that shall not be cut off"? (Is. 55:13) This garden-making gives God a name, and Jesus receives honour by ploughing up the wastes, extracting the briers, and planting firs and myrtles there. See, then, there is hope for you yet, you barren heart. He may yet come and make your wilderness like Eden, and you desert like the garden of the Lord; joy and gladness shall be found therein, thanksgiving, and the voice of melody." (Is. 51:3)

Note, too, that the Bridegroom gathered myrrh, and fed on milk and wine and honey. Yes, I know you thought, "He will find no honey in me; he will find no milk and wine in me." Ah, but then the text did not say he found them in the church; it says, "I have eaten my honeycomb with my honey; I have drunk my wine with my milk." And if he put those things into his church, and then took comfort in them, why not put them into you, and take comfort in you too? Be of good cheer; arise, he is calling you this morning.

Another word perhaps may help you. Did you notice, poor hungry soul, how Jesus says, "Drink abundantly"? "Ah", you say, "he did not say that to me!" I know it. He said that to his friends and to his beloved, and you dare not put yourselves among them yet; but do you not see how generous he is to his friends, and how he stints at nothing? He evidently does not mean to lock anything up in the store-room, for he tells them to eat and drink abundantly. Now, surely, where there is such a festival, though you dare not come and sit at the table with the guests, you might say with the Syro-phoenician woman, "Yet the dogs under the table eat of the children's crumbs." (Mat. 15:27) It is good knocking at a door where they are keeping open house, and where the feast reveals a lavish hospitality. Knock now and try it. If it were a poor man's dinner, with a dry crust and a poor herring, or if it might be a miser's meal spread most begrudgingly, I would not advise you to knock; but where there is wine and milk in rivers, and the good man of the house bids his guests eat and drink abundantly, I say knock, for God says it shall be opened. (Mat. 7:7-8)

Another thought. Jesus finds meat and drink in his church, and you are afraid he would find neither in you — I want to tell you a truth which, perhaps, you have forgotten. There was a woman who was a sinner; she had had five husbands, and he with whom she was then living was not her husband. She was an adulteress and a Samaritan; but Christ said, after he had conversed with her, that he had found meat to eat that his disciples knew nothing about. Where did he get it from? If he had drunk that day, he did not get it from Jacob's well; for he had nothing to draw with, and the well was deep. He found large refreshment in that poor woman, to whom he said, "Give me to drink." The Samaritan harlot refreshed the soul of Jesus when she believed in him, and owned him as the Christ. (John 4) Have you never read that word of his, "My meat and my drink is to do the will of him that sent me and to finish his work"? And what was the will of him that sent him? Well, I will tell you what it was not. "It is not the will of your Father that is in heaven, that one of these little ones should perish." (Mat. 18:14) The will of God and the will of Christ is this: to save sinners; for this purpose, Jesus born was and sent into the world. He came into the world to seek and to save that which was lost. See, then, poor lost one, in saving you Christ will find both meat and drink. I trust, therefore, that you will look to him and cry to him, and cast yourself on him, and you will never, as long as you live, have any cause for regretting it.

Finally, the text represents the Lord as saying, "I am come into my garden." It may imply that he is not always in his garden. Sometimes, his church grieves him, and his open presence departs; but listen, O sinner, there is a precious thought for you: he is not always in his garden, but he is always on the throne of grace. He does not always say, "I am come into my garden", but he always says, "Come unto me, all ye that labour and are heavy-laden, and I will give you rest." (Mat. 11:28) He never leaves the mercy-seat; he never ceases to intercede for sinners. Come, and welcome, then. If you have not seen the Beloved's face, come and bow at his feet. Though you have never heard him say, "Thy sins are forgiven thee" (Lk. 5:20), yet come now with a broken and a contrite heart and seek absolution at his hands. Come, and welcome! Come, and welcome! May the sweet bridegroom with cords of love draw you, and may this morning be a time of love. And as he passes by, if he sees you weltering in your blood (Ezek. 16:6), may he say to you, "Live!"

May the Lord grant it; and on his head shall be many crowns! Amen.

55. THE INTERPRETER

Song of Solomon 5:2-16

We will again read in the Song, giving the language in its correct form. The bride hears the Bridegroom knocking at her door, but she excuses herself from rising to admit him and acts as unkindly to him, as alas, we too often have done to our Lord Jesus. The whole story is rehearsed in choicest song.

THE BRIDE

2 I am asleep, but my heart is waiting;
   The voice of my Well-beloved knocking;
   "Open unto me, my Sister,
   My friend, my dove, my innocent,
   For my head is filled with the dew,
   My locks with the drops of the night."

Observe her indolent excuses. How cruel she is to her friend! How selfish! How self-indulgent! Have we not cause to blush, as in her conduct we see our own?

3 I have put off my coat,
   How shall I put it on?
   I have washed my feet,
   How shall I soil them?

4 My Well-beloved thrust his hand
   Through the wicket of the door,
   And my heart was troubled for him.

5 I arose, to open to my Beloved One,
   And my hands were dropping myrrh,
   And my fingers myrrh the purest,
   On the handles of the bar.

6 I opened,
   I unto my Well-beloved had withdrawn,
   He was gone!
   My soul swooned away for his word;
   I sought him, but I found him not;
   Called him but he answered not!

7 Find me did the watchers,
   That walk round the city;
   They smote me, wounded me,
   Strip my veil from off me
   Did the keepers of the walls.

8 I lay a charge upon you,
   O daughters of Jerusalem;
   If ye find my Well-beloved,
   What are ye to tell him —
   That sick of love am I.

Although the spouse has been sadly negligent, and so had grieved her Lord, and made him hide his face from her, yet she still loved him, and therefore was intensely earnest to find him again. She hoped that perhaps her Lord would listen to others, even if he closed his ear a while for her, the therefore she begged the daughters of Jerusalem to speak to him on her behalf. When we are in darkness, the prayers of our brethren may be a great service to us.

The song represents the DAUGHTERS OF JERUSALEM as saying —

9 What is thy Beloved more than any beloved,
   O thou Fair One among women?
   What is thy Beloved more than any beloved,
   That is this wise thou chargest us?

To this enquiry THE BRIDE replies —

10 My Beloved is white and red,
   The chief among a myriad.

11 His head is a mass of gold most fine;
   His locks are branches clustering,
   Black as the raven-down.

12 His eyes are like the doves,
   By the brooks of waters,
   Washing themselves with milk,
   Sitting within the floods.

13. His cheeks like beds of balsams,
    Flowers of sweetest smell;
    His lips the scarlet lilies
    Dropping purest myrrh.

14 His hands have rings of gold
   Inset with beryl stones;
   His body is bright ivory,
   Overlaid with sapphires;

15 His legs pillars of marble,
   Set in golden sockets.
   His look is like to Lebanon,
   Noble as the cedars;

16 His mouth is every sweetness;
   Yes, all of him loveliness.

   This is my Beloved One,
   And this is my Companion,
   O daughters of Jerusalem.

56. ASLEEP AND YET AWAKE: A RIDDLE
NO. 1561

DELIVERED ON LORD'S-DAY MORNING, OCTOBER 10TH, 1880
AT THE METROPOLITAN TABERNACLE, NEWINGTON

"I sleep, but my heart waketh: it is the voice of my beloved that knocketh."
(Song of Solomon 5:2)

WE are glad to perceive in this Song the varied experience of the bride. She was the well-beloved of the heavenly Bridegroom, but she was not without her faults. Though the "fairest among women", she was human, and, therefore, she had not reached angelic perfection. She was not perfect to begin with, for, at the outset, she confessed, "I am black, because the sun hath looked upon me: they made me the keeper of the vineyards; but mine own vineyard have I not kept." (Song 1:5-6) She was not perfect even in the exhibition of her love for him who had chosen her, for she had to acknowledge, as on the occasion before us, that she treated him in an unworthy manner. She kept him waiting at her door in the chilly night, and grieved him so that he withdrew. She was not perfect even to the end of the chapter, for she could not hear her Lord's voice as clearly as certain of her companions, and she cried in the last chapter of her song, "Cause me to hear it." (Song 8:13)

Brethren, we shall not be able to claim entire perfection as long as we are this side the hills of division. Till the day break, and the shadows flee away, our Lord will have to sanctify and cleanse his spouse "with the washing of water by the word, that he might present it to himself a glorious church, not having spot, or wrinkle, or any such thing; but that it should be holy and without blemish." (Eph. 5:46-47) We are glad, I say, to have the experience of the spouse — that is, of the church as a whole — because we know that, as is the church, such are the members, and the rule that holds good for the whole will be found in its measure and proportion to be fulfilled in all its parts. We, too, have to say, "I am black, because the sun hath looked upon me", and, at times, we have to ask, "Why should I be as one that turneth aside by the flocks of thy companions?" (Song 1:7) We have had mournfully to cry, "I sought him, but I could not find him; I called him, but he gave me no answer" (Song 5:6), while the watchmen have justly smitten us and wounded us for our neglect of our Lord. Let us bless God, that, in the book of revealed truth, he has not merely given us the ideal standard after which we are to seek, but he has also preserved for us the humbler patterns of those who have striven to reach to the utmost height, and who have climbed a good way towards it, but who, nevertheless, have proved that, though they were the best of men, they were just men at the best. Thus our Lord has saved us from despair by making us to know that we may be sincere, and true, and accepted, though we, too, fall short, as yet, of the holiness which we pant after with our whole hearts.

Nor are we alone favoured with the poetic story of the bride; we have also in the Word of God the biographies of the saints, and the memoirs of the godly, and these are exceedingly useful to us. I fear we should not, brethren, at certain times, know whether we are God's people at all if we were not able to compare ourselves with others of the family. We may lose our way sometimes, as poor sheep have often done, and then, through the greatest comfort derived from seeing the footprints of the Shepherd, in no small measure of consolation gained through marking the footsteps of the flock. The sight of human footsteps on the sandy waste has caused us to take heart again. We have exclaimed, "Here one has been who was surely a child of God, and, though I am here, I may be a child of God too. I have similar failings and weaknesses, and I chide myself for them; but I will not utterly condemn myself and say I cannot be a believer, for I perceive that these spots were on others of God's children too." The perception of our likeness to others who were truly saints has often afforded us a spark of hope when we were in a maze, and dared scarcely hope that we were right towards God.

Frequently, the experience of others will help us to thread our way when it winds and twists, and we cannot see an inch in front us. The young man thinks that he understands himself, but no old man does. Ask the man who is best acquainted with himself, and he will tell you that he is increasingly a riddle, and that his experience becomes an enigma profounder every day. The believer feels that he needs the help of the Divine Teacher to enable him to trace the thread of his spiritual life through all the tangle of the skein. It needs a grace-taught man to make himself out, and to comprehend, what he is, and where he is, and what is the very truth of his life's paradox. At times, I ask myself,

"Am I all sin, or is there yet a spark of grace?" Soon grace shines like the sun, and then I almost dream that sin is extinct. We are driven to read ourselves in others. We look at the saints of Holy Scripture, and, as we mark their lives, we say, "I can understand this man better than I can myself, for lookers-on see more than players; and now, by understanding him, I begin also to comprehend my own position. I calculate my latitude and longitude by observing a star; I estimate the contending influences that rage within me by seeing how others drifted, or stemmed, the torrent. I see the strange convolutions of my inter-twisted soul in others, and, as in a glass, I discern myself."

But, my brethren, we must take care that we do not wrongly use the memoirs of saints as recorded in Scripture: they are not all for our imitation, but many of them for our warning. You may not do all that a good man has done. If you were to copy certain of the actions of the most gracious men, you would soon find yourself faultier than they; for you would be sure to throw the emphasis on their errors, but their graces you would probably miss: you would copy their faults and aggravate them. Follow no man where he does not follow Christ. Above all, the lives of the saints may never be used as an excuse for our faults. We shall not be justified in following afar off because Peter did so (Mat. 26:58; Mk. 14:54; Lk. 22:54), nor in calling fire from heaven on our enemies because James and John wished to do so (Lk. 9:54), nor in quarrelling because Paul and Barnabas fell into sore contention. (Acts 15:2) We may wisely quote David as an encouragement to a penitent, that God will forgive his sin; but not as an apology for ourselves should we be tempted to commit the sin. We must often use even the saints of God rather as beacons than as harbour-lights, as lighthouses set upon rocky coasts to advise us of the dangers into which they fell. Take care that Holy Scripture are used for holy ends, and that holy men are viewed as helps to holiness, and not as excuses for imperfection. Let us learn from their virtues by imitation, from their faults by warning, and from both instruction. Judgement is profitable to direct us. "Follow the Lamb whithersoever he goeth" (Rev. 14:4); but there is not a sheep of his flock to whom you may do the same. Do whatever Jesus does; copy the example of Christ in all its touches, so far as it is imitable, but do not do the same even towards the beloved John, though his head comes fresh from his Master's bosom; no, not towards Paul, though he is not a whit behind the very chief of the apostles. Let us come, then, dear friends, to use the example of our text, with those due limitations which we have thus set out!

We have in this text, first, slumber confessed, "I sleep"; but over against this, wakefulness is claimed — "...but my heart waketh." Very soon, we have the mystery solved — how is it that the heart still keeps awake? — "...it is the voice of my beloved that knocketh." Before we close, we shall try, fourthly, to have a lesson learned from the text. May the Holy Spirit make the whole subject profitable to us and practically influential on our lives!

I. First, then, here is SLUMBER CONFESSED. The spouse laments her state, and sighs, "I sleep."

It strikes us at once that her sleep is a state recognised. We are astonished that she should say, "I sleep", and we conclude that it is not so profound a sleep as it might be; for when a man can say "I sleep," he is not altogether steeped in slumber. When children of God perceive their own imperfections and mourn over them, there is evidently a root of virtue in them; when they perceive the decay of their grace there is some grace left undecayed with which they are bemoaning their decline. I would not give you encouragement, dear brother, if you are asleep at all to continue in it; but yet I would say this, that if you mourn over your sluggishness, you are not altogether a sluggard, if you feel uneasy in your dullness you are not altogether given over to spiritual stupidity, if you are anxious to be aroused out of your slumber, it is certain that you are not given over to sleep yourself in the sepulchre of insensibility. God be thanked that you cannot enjoy pleasant dreams on the bed of carelessness. You do not sleep as others do; you are evidently not steeped in that fatal slumber of spiritual death in which the dead world is slumbering all around. Infinite mercy has had some dealings with you, and has made you so far to be spiritually awake, that you can feel that you sleep, and mournfully confess it. When a man detects pride within him, but has grace enough to long to be humble, when a man feels hardness of heart but groans about it and wishes to be softened, when a man laments the stubbornness of his will and cries to God to give him full submission, when a man mourns a sluggishness of heart and strives after quickening — then he has marks and signs of spiritual life, and of an inward energy which will, by God's grace, cast out his disease and bring him spiritual health. There is life where there is pain; there is growth where there is a yearning of desire. The holy fire still lingers in the breast, though it is so smothered by the ashes that only a little smoke can be discerned; it will revive again, it will rekindle and burn up, for it is of God's creating. He who can mournfully say, "I sleep" will one day be wide awake. Be very thankful, therefore, when you have a tender conscience. Cultivate a quick perception, and when you are aware of the slightest defalcation (spiritual embezzlement] or decline. Confess at once to God that you begin to sleep. Furthermore, as this sleep is a matter recognised, so is it a matter complained of. The spouse is not pleased to sleep: she says, "I sleep", but she does not mention it as a matter for congratulation. She is not pleased with her condition. Here again, I would remark that it is well for saints, when they perceive that they are in the least degree backsliding, that they should mourn before God, and accuse themselves before him. "Judge yourselves, that ye be not judged" (Mat. 7:1) to adapt a verse. Before another person can hint that you are careless, find it out yourself, and mourn over it. Before another can complain of your dullness, and say, as the shipmen did to Jonah, "What meanest thou, O sleeper?" (Jon. 1:6) Complain of yourself. Act tenderly to others, but severely towards yourself. So all prudent men will do if God keeps them prudent.

This sleepiness is not a thing to be indulged in but to be abhorred. To say the least of it, it is a low state of enjoyment. Sleep is peaceful and quiet, but it cannot enjoy the sweets of the senses, and the delights which the mind can receive there. Sleep is cousin to death, and he that slumbers lies at the door of the sepulchre. The image of death is set on the sleeper's face, and it is a miracle, and a sort of foretaste of the resurrection, that any one wakes again after he has fallen into a deep slumber. It is not, therefore, good spiritually for us to be asleep, for then we cannot taste the honey of the Word, or enjoy the fragrance of the ordinances, or see the beauties of Christ; nor will any of the spiritual passions be delighted, or our spirit be carried away with holy joy. Therefore, when we come into God's house, and hear the old familiar story of the cross, and it does not charm us, let us mournfully say, "I sleep". When others are ready to dance before the Lord with exultation while singing the solemn psalm, if we ourselves feel no devout gratitude, let us cry self-

417

complainingly, "I perceive that I sleep"; and when at the Table the chosen emblems of the bread and wine do not bring the Master near to us, and we go away as hungry as we came because we have not fed on his body and his blood, then let us say again, "Alas, I sleep, I sleep; for these things would be most sweet and nourishing to me if my spiritual faculties were as they ought to be." If we fail to enjoy the banquets of our Bridegroom's love, it must be because a deadness is stealing over us, and we are not so thoroughly alive and awake as we were in days gone by; and this is a condition to be deplored as soon as it is perceived.

We ought to complain of ourselves if we sleep, because it is a state of danger. While men slept, the enemy came and sowed tares among the wheat. (Mat. 13:25) It is bad, then, to have a drowsy minister and drowsy church officers, for these will not watch the fields for God. He who sleeps is in danger of the thief or the murderer. While Saul lay stretched on the plain, Abishai lifted up his spear and said, "Let me smite him but this once." (1 Sam. 26:8) He who sleeps may lose his all, yes, lose himself. Let us, therefore, dread this perilous state; and if we feel it creeping over us, let us shake ourselves, and say, "I sleep, but I will not give way to slumber, Lord, arouse me." Sleep is a state of inaction. A man cannot do his daily business while his eyes are closed in slumber. There is a somnambulism [sleep walking, for example] which can do much; but I know of no spiritual somnambulism. You cannot walk the road to heaven asleep, nor preach the gospel as you should, nor serve God and your generation aright, if you are in a spiritual slumber. I know a great many who are so; alive, I hope, but very sleepy. They do very little; they are too sluggish to attempt much. "The slothful man saith, 'There is a lion in the way; a lion is in the streets.'" (Prov. 26:13) This was his argument for keeping in the chimney-corner. In truth, the lion is about as real as the monster which has been described lately as prowling over this county of Surrey, devouring women and children all the way from Banstead Downs to Clapham Common. Solomon seems to have been very familiar with this fable of the sluggard's lion, for, in another proverb, he makes the idler cry, "There is a lion without. I shall be slain in the streets." (Prov.22:13) These poor creatures are so dreamy in spirit that they see a lion everywhere, threatening them if they try to do good in any form; they must needs sit quiet and still, and try to enjoy themselves as best their sleep will allow them to do, for they cannot venture out to work because of the lion. They cannot teach a little Sunday-school class, for there is a lion there! Nor will they go out to speak to a dozen people in a village: a furious lion is roaring there! In fact, they will be devoured if they leave their easy retirement, and put their heads out of doors. God help us to escape this lazy condition! May we live while we live! Let not our souls merely act as salt to keep our carcasses from rottenness, but let them be the seed-plot and hotbed of holy actions, out of which shall yet spring glory to God and blessing to our fellow men. If you do not feel active and energetic, make it a matter of self-complaint, and utter the shame-faced confession, "I sleep." Yet again, this slumber should not only be a matter of complaint as an ill to be dreaded, but be regarded as a fault to be ashamed of. A Christian man should not say, "I feel dull, careless, and inactive", and make the confession as if he almost deserved to be pitied for a misfortune which was no fault of his. My brother, you may be pitied, but you are also to be blamed, perhaps blamed far more than pitied.

An apparent spiritual slumber may creep over us because the body is very weak and sickly, and here pity is allowable, yes, justly due. Certain states and conditions of the flesh no doubt will overcome the spirit, as when even the choicest of the apostles slept in the garden. The Master at first said, "What, could ye not watch with me one hour?" (Mat. 26:40), but afterwards, he made a generous excuse for them and said, "The spirit truly is willing, but the flesh is weak." (Mat. 26:41; Mk. 14:38) Make excuses for others, and let your Lord make excuses for you, but do not frame apologies on your own account. David writes in his Psalm (77:10), "I said, 'This is my infirmity.'" Quite right, David! I dare say it was so; but the other day I said the same concerning myself, and, before long, I answered

418

to my conscience for it, for conscience asked, "Is it not your sin as well as your infirmity?" I was compelled to divide the statement, no, at last to withdraw the first part of me altogether and cry, "God, be merciful to me a sinner." May we not be too ready to lay the blame of our impatience, our unbelief, or our hastiness, on the body when we ought to take all blame to ourselves. It is always safest to blame ourselves, and it is frequently dangerous to admit an excuse. Still, sometimes dullness may be an infirmity. When a man is weary with a hard day's work, or with business that has cost him much care, and he kneels by his bedside at a very late hour to pray, and finds himself going to sleep, I do not think that his fault is a very grievous one. It is certainly not that dreadful sin which shall never be forgiven, either in this world or in that which is to come. (Mat. 12:32) When a man is brought very low by weakness of the body, and he cannot, on the Sabbath-day, feel himself up to the mark in all respects, I do not think we should hold a church-meeting and turn him out; nor do I think that he should excommunicate himself. When a widowed spirit is broken with bereavement, when the husband is dead, when children or brothers have died, when parents have been snatched away, and the heart is very heavy, if the heart cannot rejoice in the Lord, it is a pity that it cannot, but there is a measure of infirmity as well as fault in the heaviness of the soul. In such cases, good people may guardedly say with David, "This is my infirmity." May God help us when we feel such infirmities, that we may speedily rise above them, being made strong in weakness, and being taught to glory in infirmities because the power of Christ rests upon us.

Again, I repeat it: for others, we may put in the gentle word even as the Master did for his disciples, "The spirit truly is willing, but the flesh is weak", but for ourselves, we should rather use heart-searching and self-condemnation that we may make the bed of slumber thorny to our idle flesh. Brethren, when a Christian man's soul is heavy with slumber, he ought to be ashamed. Think of who it is that loves us, even Jesus, the eternal son of God. Has he loved us and can we ever be cold towards him? Then blush, and let the scarlet abide in your face!

Think of what Jesus has done for us, and what love he has manifested towards us. O Gethsemane! O Calvary! Are we thus redeemed; and after this, does our love decline into slumber? Break, my heart! Break with indignation at yourself, that such should be the case! And what is this time in which we live? A time when all the powers of darkness are on the alert, raging to do evil and mischief. Are we sleeping now, when the adversary is daily making an attack on us? When men are dying, and are perishing by millions, can it be that we slumber still? And such as we are, who do little enough when we are wide awake, and have little enough of power and ability, how is it that we can slumber? If we are lethargic, should we not bow ourselves in the dust before God and beseech him to have mercy on us?

Furthermore, it is an evil to be fought against. When a man is obliged to say, "I sleep", let him not content himself with sleeping on. Now is the time for much prayer: let him wrestle with this deadly foe till he is fully aroused. Falling into indifference on the road to heaven is something like sleeping on the vast plains of snow, where, if a man gives way to the natural inclination to slumber which comes on through intense cold, he might lie down and never rise again. Oh, take care, you that are looking for glory and eternal life that you do not yield to sleep, for your Master is coming, and it may be that within another hour you may hear the midnight cry. Let us whip ourselves with a strong resolve that we will not sleep. Let us say to our soul, "Come, wake up! My spirit, you shall not sleep! This cannot be. I must not have it, I will not, I dare not. I will goad you, I will crucify you to the cross, for you will not slay yourself with suicidal slumber." With this resolve, let us seek out means of waking ourselves up. Sometimes we may do well to seek for a better ministry than we have attended. Alas, there are ministries which are as cradles to rock babes to sleep in. There are preachers who charm most wisely if their intention is to send the universe to

419

sleep. Beware of preaching which comforts you in idleness, and increases your spiritual insensibility. There are certain preachers who mar the gospel, and tell their tale so heartlessly that, I think, if all heaven rocked and reeled with tempest, a man might yet sleep on so long as such soothing voices lulled his ears. We cannot afford to waste our Sabbaths in listening to another gospel, or in hearing lullabies that make us duller than we are. But if you cannot reach a rousing ministry, read good books: turn to solid gospel treatises such as the Puritans bequeathed us. Search the Scriptures and the works of godly men, whose words are all on fire; these, thrown upon your soul like burning coals, may set it on fire. Christian converse, too, is another useful means of keeping us awake. John Bunyan mentions that, in going over the Enchanted Ground, the pilgrims, to prevent drowsiness, fell into good discourse. Here is his quaint rhyme about it:

When saints do sleepy grow, let them come hither
And hear how these two pilgrims talk together:
Yea, let them learn of them in any wise,
Thus to keep open their drowsy, slumbering eyes,
Saints' fellowship, if it be managed well,
Keeps them awake, and that in spite of hell.

Imitate this example, but if discourse does not avail, get to work for Christ. This is a very effective way of keeping yourself awake, God the Holy Spirit blessing you in it. In looking after the souls of others your own soul will receive a watering. I do not think that soul-slumber so often visits the active as it does those who have little to do in the Master's service. If active service does not suffice, then cry mightily to God, "I sleep, my Saviour; awake me, I pray you!" You are half awake already if you can cry in that fashion. Cry again, "I sleep, my Lord. Use even a rod upon me to wake me rather than I should slumber." You are not asleep, brother, you are already awakened: the bitter anguish of the soul in its horror of its own slumber has already been blessed of God to its arousing. Anyhow, this sleep is an evil which must be overcome. Come and make up your minds to-day, members of this church, so that you will not yield to drowsiness. I hope none of you are inclined to say, "Well, I may get to heaven in this sleepy way, and so what matters? My fellow members would put me in the ambulance and carry me along like a wounded soldier, and this will be easier than marching at the double day after day." No, no, my brother, we have enough of the invalid and wounded already. We have as many as we can carry of the non-effectives. We need no more. Ask the blessed Physician to make you strong, that you may tug at the guns with the rest of us, or charge the enemy at bayonet point when the trumpet sounds. I said years ago I would sooner lead a dozen real live earnest Christians than a dozen hundred of the half-and-half sort, and this feeling grows with me. I would almost as soon not be a Christian as be like some Christians are: they have enough religion to make them uncomfortable, but not enough to make them useful. They drink such shallow draughts that they increase their responsibility rather than their energy. Oh, for a deep draught of grace that will fill us with all the fullness of God, and make us men in Christ to the utmost capacity of our sanctified manhood. Cold meat may be pleasant, but cold religion is a bad dish to serve to Christ or to ourselves either. God make us like those creatures that are said to live in the fire! May he fill us with his own Spirit, and make us burn and blaze with an unquenchable heat of love towards him of whom it is said that the zeal of God's house was eating him up. (Ps. 69:9; Jn. 2:17) He poured out his soul to death that he might redeem us for himself, so let us see to it that we are altogether his own. With this, I leave the sleeping for another theme.

II. We reach the point of the paradox: here is WATCHFULNESS CLAIMED by one who confessed to sleep. "My heart waketh", says the Bride, "I sleep, but my heart waketh."

It may seem an odd thing to sleep and yet be awake, but I commenced by saying that the Christian is a great puzzle. Ralph Erskine's *Gospel Canticles, Part 4: The Believer's Riddle, or the Mystery of Faith* (1720) is a remarkable production, but every word of it may be justified by experience and by Scripture. A man is a mass of contradictions, but a man in Christ is far more so. Ralph Erskine rightly says,

I'm in my own and others' eyes,
A labyrinth of mysteries.

We are asleep and awake at the same time. As Ralph Erskine rhymes it,

Both sleeping flesh I have, that rests
In sloth unto my shame,
And waking grace, that still protests
Against this lazy frame.

There is an inner life within every Christian which can never die, and there is about him an inward death which can never rise to life. Jesus said, "The water that I shall give him shall be in him a well of water springing up into everlasting life" (Jn. 4:14); hence this divine life, though it may grow weak and feeble and slumbering, yet never passes into the condition of absolute death, or even of complete insensibility. Something of heaven is about the man of God when the earth encompasses him most. "Sin shall not have dominion over you" (Rom. 6:14): God has the throne still, even when Satan rages most. This inward life shows itself usually in the uneasiness of the declining heart. When a believer feels that he is not what he ought to be, nor what he wants to be, he cannot be happy. He cannot rest and be content. There was a time when such a condition would have satisfied him, but now he is distressed beyond measure, and, like Noah's dove, finds no rest for the sole of his foot. Hear him sing in the minor key,

Where is the blessedness I knew
When first I saw the Lord?
Where is the soul-refreshing view
Of Jesus and his word?

What peaceful hours I then enjoyed!
How sweet their memory still!
But they have left an aching void
The world can never fill.

(William Cowper)

He sleeps, but his heart beats, sighs, and palpitates, with dire unrest. The inner life shows itself, too, in desire, for the heart is the centre of desire, and it leads the man to say "I am not what I would be. I live at a poor dying rate: Christ's love is so great to me, and mine for him so chill. Lord, lift me out of this frozen state; I cannot bear this grave of lethargy. Lord, bring my soul out of prison! Give me more grace; give me to love Jesus better and be more like him. Poor as I am, I long to be enriched by your love and mercy. Oh, visit me with your salvation!" Such a pleading heart is still awake, though the mind may be dull. The Lord judges us by our earnest desires more than by our accomplishments. An old writer says that if you send a man on horseback for the doctor, if the horse is a sorry jade that cannot move quickly, you praise the man when you see him whipping and spurring and doing his best to hasten on. You do not blame him for something that is beyond his power. So says he — oftentimes when our desires whip and spur our languid spirits, God sees what a rate we would go at if we could, and he takes the will for the deed. Often our

421

desires are so aroused that we would harness the lightning and bit the tempest if we could, and spur both to a swifter speed. Desires prove wakefulness — "I sleep, but my heart waketh."

The spouse gave another proof of her wakefulness by her discernment. She says, "It is the voice of my beloved that knocketh." Even when half asleep, she knew her Lord's voice. You may catch a true believer at his worst, but he still discerns the gospel from anything else, and can detect another gospel in a moment. You can come out with all your eloquence, your poetry, and sweet concocted phrases, with a something that is not the gospel of the blessed God, and you shall, for a moment, please the ear of the Christian because of the literary excellence of your address, but he soon detects you. It is true of all Christ's sheep — "A stranger will they not follow, for they know not the voice of strangers." (Jn 10:5) The awakening believer perceives that the most musical voice of a stranger has not the charm in it which is found in the voice of his Lord. Yes, he soon closes his ear to it in disgust, and in holy trembling lest he should be deceived. His resolve is, "I will hear what God the Lord will speak." (Ps. 85:8) He determines to be deaf to other voices, but to his Redeemer he says, "Speak, Lord, for thy servant heareth." (1 Sam. 3:9-10) Blessed is he who, in his dullest state, can still discern and discriminate and cry, "It is the voice of my beloved."

This wakefulness of heart shows itself often in the soul chiding itself. "I sleep", says she. She would not have blamed herself, as I have tried to describe her doing, if she had not been, in some measure, awake. This blessed, living wakefulness within the heart will, by-and-by, display itself in action. The heart will wake up all that is within us, and we shall hasten to our Beloved. It is wonderful how a true Christian flies back to God as soon as the Spirit of the Lord sets him free from the net. "Whom have I in heaven but thee, and there is none upon earth that I desire beside thee." (Ps. 73:25) Brethren, you and I cannot rest anywhere short of Christ. When we were ravens, we could rest on our own wings, or on the carrion of this world, but now that we have been made doves, we must seek our Noah and his ark. A friend at the back of this Tabernacle furnished me with some pigeons just a little while ago. They were taken home to Norwood, and shut up for a few days, and well fed, in the hope that they would stay with us; but no sooner were they set at liberty than they soared aloft, made three circles in the sky, and then flew direct for this spot. How I wished on my sick bed that I had their wings, and could hasten here too. It is so with believers. The devil may put us in captivity and shut us up a while; but give us the opportunity, and our heart knows the way back to Jesus. The spouse has "dove's eyes" (Song 1:15, 4:1), and she sees from afar: she makes short work of it, and is back again with all the speed of the chariots of Amminadib.

This puzzle of "I sleep, but my heart waketh" has been experienced by thousands. I quote no solitary instances; there are hundreds of them. I lately met with a little poem by Thomas Vaughan which touched my heart, because it so aptly described my state. I will read it to show you that the paradox of a believer's life is no fiction of mine, but is the frequent experience of God's people. In a little out-of-the way poem, which perhaps not one of you has ever seen, Henry Vaughan quaintly sings:

My sweetest Jesus! 'twas thy voice, 'If I
Be lifted up I'll draw all to the sky.'
Yet I am here: I'm stifled in the clay,
Shut up from thee, and the fresh East of day.
I know thy hand's not short; but I'm unfit,
A foul, unclean thing! to take hold of it.
I am all dirt: nor can I hope to please
Unless in mercy thou lovest a disease.

422

Diseases may be cured, but who'll reprieve
Him that is dead? Tell me, my God, I live.
'Tis true, I live: but I so sleep withal
I cannot move, scarce hear when thou dost call,
Sin's lullabies charm me when I would come,
But draw me after thee, and I will run.
Thou knowest I'm sick: let me not feasted be,
But keep a diet, all prescribed by thee.
Should I carve for myself, I would exceed
To surfeit soon, and by self-murder bleed.
I ask for stones and scorpions, but still crest
And all for love: shouldest thou grant I were lost.
Dear Lord, deny me still: and never sign
My will, but when that will agrees with thine.
And when this conflict's past, and I appear
To answer, what a patient I was here,
How I did weep when thou didst woo: repine
At thy best sweets, and in a childish whine
Refuse thy proffered love; yet cry and call,
For rattles of my own to play withal:
Look on thy cross and let thy blood come in
When mine shall blush as guilty of my sin.
Then shall I live, being rescued in my fall.
A text of mercy to thy creatures all.
Who having seen the worst of sins in me,
Must needs confess, the best of love's in thee.

Does not this writer dip his pen into your soul's sorrows?

III. Spare me a minute or two while I dwell on the heading of MYSTERY SOLVED. "I sleep, but my heart waketh."

How does her heart wake up? It is because the voice and knock of her Beloved are heard. Every child of God has a wondrous union with Christ. "Because I live", says Christ, "ye shall live also." (Jn. 14:19) Ask yourself why you are alive in such a body of death and grave of sin, as your poor nature is? You live because Christ lives; and you cannot die till he does. This is why you cannot sleep as others do, because he does not sleep. "He that keepeth Israel shall neither slumber nor sleep," (Ps. 121:4), and till Christ's spiritual life shall altogether slumber out into forgetfulness and inaction, yours never shall. The mystic union between yourselves and him secures you from destruction, which, apart from him, would sweep you away as with a besom [broom]. This is why, dear friends, when you get where you should not be, you cannot be happy because Jesus is not happy when you are there. He groans over your follies; they cost him wounds, and bloody sweat, and death, and they must cost you something, too, if you indulge them. That field all tangled with the brambles tore the shepherd when he sought you out, and the briars will tear you also if you wander there. The reason why you are awake at all is because Jesus calls you. His voice rings in your ears through his Word both heard and read. He more than calls; he knocks at your heart by affliction, by mercy, by warning, by comfort. He will do more with you yet if you are his; he will put in his hand by the hole of the door, and then you shall open to him and he will come and sup with you and you with him. (Rev. 3:20) The mystery is all solved: the saint would be a sinner if it were not that he is one with the sinner's Saviour. The living believer would be a lump of death and corruption if it were not that he is one with him who is the resurrection and the life, who has said, "Whosoever believeth in me shall never die", and again, "…though he were dead yet shall he live." (Jn. 11:25)

423

What a blessing is this vital union with the ever-blessed Head, immortal and unslumbering!

IV. Now for THE LESSON LEARNED.

It is this: be very careful when you possess great joys, for in this instance the spouse had been with the Beloved in choice fellowship, and yet was soon drowsy. He had given her to drink abundantly, and he had feasted with her, but, no sooner had the sun set, than she said, "I sleep." We are singular creatures. Our very perfect brethren, although they do not see it, generally exhibit some glaring imperfection if you let them talk for five minutes. When you knock at the door to see if Mr. Pride is at home, you need not praise him long before he will show his full-length portrait. We are thankful for these brethren so far as they are saints, for good people are scarce; but I wish they would not tell us so much about their saintliness, for I have noticed that great cry often goes with little wool, and the noisiest thing that goes down the street is the dust-cart. He who makes most noise about his own perfection has the least of it. Let us be careful whenever we rise to the summit of the hill, be careful to keep up, be careful that we so act when we are up that we do not come down with a run. Whenever the Lord visits you, entertain him right heartily. Be careful that nothing grieves him, lest he depart. High joys may produce slumber; the chosen three upon Mount Tabor were soon overcome with heaviness. At the too transporting sight of the transfigured Saviour, darkness covered them. (Lk. 9:7, 35) Mind what you do when on the Mount; be careful to carry a full cup with a steady hand.

Next, when you are blaming yourselves for your own work, do not forget the work of the Spirit in you. "I sleep": smite your heart for that, but do not forget to add if it is true, "My heart waketh." Bless God for any grace you have, even if it is only little. What if I am not sanctified as I wish to be, and shall be, yet I am perfectly justified! What if I do not exhibit my Father's likeness so completely as I hope to do, yet I am his child! What if, as yet, I do not produce all the fruits of the Spirit, yet I have the germs of them, the buds and blossoms, and soon shall have the ripe fruit! In Aaron's rod, we see that the same power that could put the buds and blossoms on a dry stick could put the almonds there too. (Num. 17:8)

Lastly, make sure above all things that you have that true faith which knows the voice of Jesus. The spouse would not have awaked if it had not been for the charm of Jesus' voice which affected even her drowsy faculties. Some people can be more easily awakened by the voices of those they love than by any other means. The charm of memory, the charm of intimate affection, the charm of delight, gives music to some tongues: let your ear find all its music in the voice of Jesus. Know his voice. He says, "Incline your ear, and come unto me: hear, and your soul shall live." (Is. 55:3) "My sheep hear my voice, and I know them, and they follow me" (Jn 10:27), "and I give unto them eternal life." (28) God bless you, dear friends, with a faith that trusts Jesus, knows his voice, and follows him, and may we be aroused out of all our sleepiness (if we are at all drowsy) into a holy wakefulness, so as to serve the Lord our God with all our heart and soul and strength while we live. Come, Holy Spirit, and give us this privilege, for Jesus' sake. Amen.

57. WARNING AND ENCOURAGEMENT
NO. 3013

AT THE METROPOLITAN TABERNACLE, NEWINGTON
ON LORD'S-DAY EVENING, IN THE YEAR 1864

"I sleep, but my heart waketh: it is the voice of my beloved that knocketh, saying, 'Open to me, my sister, my love, my Love, my undefiled: for my head is filled with dew, and my locks with the drops of the night.'" (Song of Solomon 5:2)

HOW changeable is the creature! In the verse preceding our text, we find the spouse in a happy, healthy, heavenly frame of mind, for her Beloved was with her, and she was in the enjoyment of the closest communion with him. We find him saying, "I am come into my garden, my sister, my spouse: I have gathered my myrrh with my spice; I have eaten my honeycomb with my honey; I have drunk my wine with my milk; eat, friends; drink, yea, drink abundantly, O beloved." (Song 5:1) Yet, from the height of this glorious fellowship, how soon the spouse comes down to the depths of such a cry as this, "I sleep, but my heart waketh"! Truly, the weather of our isle is not more variable than the feelings of believers. One day, the sun shines hot and strong, the next day comes a black cloud, accompanied with the lightning-flash and the voice of thunder; then comes the rattling drops of hail; and before long, in a few more hours, it is hot again, or perhaps the chilly North wind begins to blow. Have you not been on Mount Tabor at one moment, and at another in the Vale of Achor? Have you not been at one time like the chariots of Amminadib, driving so fast that the axles were hot with speed, and, soon after, you have been like Pharaoh's chariots when the wheels cane off, so that you crave heavily. Now you mount as on eagle's wings, and then you sink as in deep mire, where there is no standing. At one moment, you are delighting in God's goodness and mercy, and the next, crying, "All thy waves and thy billows have gone over me." (Ps. 42:7) Lord, what a changeable creature is man! When you have taken him up to his highest altitude, how speedily he comes down by the force of your hand to the very depths! How soon do you bring him down from his highest eminence even to the very dust!

Christian, when the Lord favours you, and your soul walks in close fellowship with him, remember that there is a devil within you and a devil without you. Be careful of your footsteps; even when you are on the top of the mountain, even when Jesus is sitting by you and whispering in your ear that you are his, watch yourself with the greatest, possible care, for never will you lose your corruption. Your communion may be transient, but your corruption is perpetual. To be with Christ is but a thing of a moment with you, but to be with your corruption is a thing of every hour of the day. I pray you, keep this in mind; and whenever you are in your best frame, then be doubly careful, lest you should lose your Beloved, and have to cry once again, "I sleep, but my heart waketh." Dr. Ives, who used to live on the road to Tyburn at the time when prisoners were always carried in a cart to be hanged there, would frequently say, when he had any friends with him, and when he saw the criminals riding by, "There goes Dr. Ives"; and when they asked him what he meant, he replied, "Such crimes as that felon has committed I should have committed but for the grace of God." That is true even of you who live nearest to God; you, who have the most familiarity with Christ, and enjoy the most holy fellowship with him, would soon become the very leaders of the hosts of Satan if your Lord withdraws his grace. David's eyes go astray, and the sweet psalmist of Israel becomes the shameless adulterer who robs Uriah of his wife. (2 Sam. 11:3) Samson one day slays a thousand of his enemies with the might of his arm and the valour of his heart; another day his honour is betrayed, his locks are shorn, and his eyes are put out by a strumpet's treacherous wiles. (Judg. 16:13-18) How soon are the mighty fallen! Behold Solomon, the wisest of men, yet the greatest fool that

425

ever lived. Even Job fails in patience, and Abraham staggers as to his faith. "Let him that thinketh he standeth take heed lest he fall." (1 Cor. 10:12) These observations seem to come at once to our minds when we consider such passages as abound in this "Song of songs, which is Solomon's." We find, at one moment, that the spouse is so happy that she cries out, "Stay me with flagons, comfort me with apples; for I am sick of love" (Song 2:5), and, at another moment, she is searching for her Beloved, and cannot find him, and is mourning because of the darkness, and of the cruelty of "the watchmen that go about the city". (Song 3:3)

The text very readily suggests three subjects for meditation: first, *a lamentable state:* "I sleep"; secondly, *a hopeful sign:* "but my heart waketh"; and, thirdly, *a potent remedy:* "It is the voice of my Beloved."

Nothing can waken a believer out of his sleep like the voice of his Beloved.

I. First, here is A LAMENTABLE STATE: "I sleep".

I think I can describe this state pretty well because I experience it too often, and am afraid many of you could also describe it with some degree of accuracy, for frequently you too fall into it. What is it for a Christian to sleep? Well, thank God, there is a sleep which the believer never knows. He can never again sleep that deadly sleep in which Christ found him while he was in his sinful state. He shall never sleep the judicial sleep into which some were cast as the result of sin. He shall not sleep, as others do, to his eternal ruin: yet he may sleep dangerously and sinfully; and this is the state in which the Christian is found when he is thus sleeping — *in a state of inaction.* You are doing something for God, but you are rather doing it as a matter of custom than as a matter of loving earnestness. You pray; you go up to the house of God; you teach in the Sabbath-school; but you do these things mechanically, as a man walks who is sound asleep. You are in a sort of spiritual somnambulism. The work that you are called upon to perform, you do after a fashion; but there is none of the power of God in the work, and no earnestness thrown into it. It is done, and that is an end of it; but your heart has been absent from it.

Coupled with this, there is *a lack of vigour in everything to which such a one sets his hand.* If he preaches, there is no force or burning energy, no boiling, scalding periods; he just takes his text, and speaks on it. Perhaps God's people are edified, perhaps sinners are saved; but that preacher has no enjoyment in his work during the whole time he performs it thus sluggishly. A man, to enjoy the work of the Lord, must throw his whole strength into it. It is the same when you come to prayer. You pray after a sort; but it is not that wrestling with the angel that gets the blessing from him. (Gen. 32:23-30) You knock at the door, but not with that force which causes it to open. You have forgotten your former vigour. Whereas, once your place of prayer was the witness of groans and tears, now you can go into it and come out of it without so much as a single sob. And it is just the same when you read the Scriptures. Once, the page sparkled with promises, and your soul was satisfied with marrow and fatness; but when you read it now, it is very dull, and you no longer derive refreshing consolation from it. Like the Temple from which God has removed himself, you walk through it: there are the pillars where stand all the symbols of worship; the altar is there, but God, the King, has gone; and a voice has been heard to say, "Arise, let us go hence". (Jn. 14:31) And so you go through the sacred edifice, and find nothing there. In this same sleepy state, we go up to the house of God to listen to his Word; and if our sleep has got a strong hold on us, we cannot get any comfort. We begin to rail at the minister because we are not edified as we used to be, and we think that a change has come over him. That is possible; but it is just as likely, and more so that our lack of enjoyment of God's Word is owing to ourselves. We sit and hear as God's people hear, and we sing as God's people sing, and pray as they pray, after the outward form; but we

426

For more resources go to CharlesSpurgeonBooks.com

go out as a man rises from his bed on which he has tossed all night, and we feel that we are not a whit refreshed; and the Sabbath, that was once a joy and delight to us, has perhaps become a weariness and a burden.

There is no enjoyment while a man is asleep; and, as there is no enjoyment, there is no consciousness of pain. Ah, beloved, I have known seasons when I would almost have given my right arm to be able to shed tears of repentance — where I wished that I might again have a broken heart — when I have longed to make my soul feel even the pains of hell rather than not feel anything at all; for this is one of the worst states a Christian can be in — to go nodding on through life, slumbering over eternal realities, dreaming over heaven, and nodding his head, and continuing still to sleep, when he is in the presence of the Most High God, and should have gathered up all his powers, and strung them to the highest pitch of intensity. Have not you been in such a state? If you have not, what a happy man you are! There are most holy men, some of the giant servants of God, who have fallen into this state, and have been compelled to cry out, "I sleep", finding themselves happy indeed if they could add, "I sleep, but my heart waketh."

Such a state as this is very sinful. Is it not sinful, O my soul, to be trifling with the eternal state, and playing at prayer? Can you be so dull and heavy about eternal things, when worldlings are so thoroughly awake about their silver and gold and commercial pursuits? When souls are being hurried to eternity, how is it that I can still be indifferent? While time is speeding on, and eternity is so near, how can I still take myself to my slothful couch, and cry, "A little sleep, a little slumber, a little folding of thy hands to sleep?" (Prov. 6:10, 24:33) Chosen in Christ, redeemed with his precious blood, quickened by the Divine Spirit, and made partakers of the divine nature, how can it be consistent with our position and condition to sleep as others do? The light of God's grace has shone upon us; is this a time to slumber? Let the world sleep if it will, for its object and aims are not worthy of the Christian's high ambition. But should you and I sleep, when heaven is before us, and hell behind us, when there is temptation everywhere surrounding us, and angels beckon us to heaven, while a glorious company of saints holds us in full survey? Come, my brethren, we must feel that such a state as this is sinful to the highest degree. And how dangerous it is, too! A man who sleeps in his enemy's camp is exposed to imminent peril. There lies Sisera asleep in Jael's tent. Little do you know, O silly dreamer, when that woman's hand lifts up the mallet to drive the nail through thy brain! (Judg. 4:18-21) If you desire sleep, Christian, wait till you get home; there you shall have rest enough for ever in your Father's house; but to sleep here is to sleep in the dragon's jaw, to sleep on the top of the mast when the ship is driving before the storm. No, wait and think of your position and condition, and sleep no longer. O God, have mercy on your people who have long prospered!

There is the pinnacle of the Temple; and blessed is the man whose feet do not slip when he stands here. I do not think we sleep so much spiritually when we have bodily affliction, though bodily pains frequently make a Christian long for his rest; nor do I think we have slumbering times when we are losing our friends. Men cannot easily sleep when the funeral knell is tolling in their ears, and when they are following dear departed ones to the grave. Nor do I think we sleep much when we are the subjects of very violent temptations, and have a great many doubts and fears. But when we are in our vessel, when the day is fine, and the sail is spread, and the wind blows softly, and the ship goes on steadily without motion, gliding as o'er a sea of glass, then it is that the mariner, perhaps, forgets the rock and the shoal. The poet Robert Stuart de Courcy Laffan was right, when John Gadsby included his poem in his hymn collection, and called it *The Christian's Spiritual Voyage*:

Jesus, at thy command
 I launch into the deep;
And leave my native land,
Where sin lulls all asleep;
For thee I would the world resign,
And sail to heaven with thee and thine.

Thou art my Pilot wise;
My compass is thy word;
My soul each storm defies,
While I have such a Lord;
I trust thy faithfulness and power,
To save me in the trying hour.

By faith I see the land –
The port of endless rest;
My soul, thy sails expand,
And fly to Jesus' breast!
O may I reach the heavenly shore
Where winds and waves distress no more.

Whene'er becalmed I lie;
And storms forbear to toss;
Be thou, dear Lord, still nigh,
Lest I should suffer loss;
For more the treacherous calm I dread,
Than tempests bursting o'er my head.

Come, Holy Ghost, and blow
A prosperous gale of grace;
Waft me from all below
To heaven, my destined place,
Then, in full sail, my port I'll find,
And leave the world and sin behind.

I do not like trouble, and pray God to deliver me from it. I cannot well endure bodily pain; I find myself impatient under tribulation. But I am able to say this, that if I had my choice between the severest affliction and a state of sinful slumbering, I would prefer to have the affliction. "There is no devil", said someone, "like having no devil"; that is to say, there is no temptation like the temptation of not being tempted. The worst form of danger is when a man is left to himself, when he is not much tossed about, when he is quiet and easy. It ought not to be so. The greater our prosperity, the better should we love God; and the more our spirit is at ease, the more we should serve him with both our hands, and render him hearty thanks for his favour towards us. It should be so, but it is not so. In these smooth waters, we are sure to meet with mischief; and, therefore, may the Lord in his mercy watch over us when we are in much prosperity!

Do I hear somebody ask, "How may I know when I am asleep?" If you are a true Christian, you will soon know it by a sort of instinct, when an unutterable sense of misery comes over you. The sleep of a sinner I may compare to the sleep produced by opium, which gives its victim dreams of the most magnificent character, carrying the soul up to heaven, and then, later, dashing it down to the depths. All sorts of fantastic imaginations are the offspring of that deadly drug; yet the man enjoys himself while under its influence; and though it causes some happiness in the use of it, it will bring him to hell as surely as

428

murder itself. The sleep of a Christian, when he falls into this state, is rather like the sleep produced by henbane [stinking nightshade]: it produces a kind of uneasy, short, disturbed, unreeling rest. It does a man little harm compared with the other, and his constitution recovers from the shock much more readily. Such, I say, is the Christian's sleep: there is no pleasure in it as there is in the sinner's sleep; but his sleep is uneasy, his conscience pricks him, his heart wakes, and he finds no peace in it. It lasts but for a little time, and it does him much damage; but, still, not the deadly damage that the world's sleep of sin brings to its votaries [devout adherents]. God save you from it! May he ever keep you from falling into that kind of sleep!

I think many of you will not need me to warn you of this. Still, if you want to know, let me ask you to compare yourself with what you used to be. Are you as lively in divine things as you once were? Is prayer as fervent and refreshing to your souls as it once was? Do you find that willingness to pray that you once had? Do you find that you have to find yourself into your closet, and, when you get there, you offer up your prayers and desires with coldness which once you were wont to offer with loving fervour? Do you still continue to have the blessedness you had when first you knew the Lord? If not, that is a symptom of sleep. Then, compare yourself with what you ought to be. Think how you ought to have grown during the years you have been a believer. Are you what you ought to have been? Then, if you are not, you must be asleep, or else you would have made better progress. Compare yourself with what others have been, and you will see cause for shame; and if so, my brethren, you are asleep. You are in a dangerous condition, and I pray the living God, by the demand for watchfulness when the prince of this world comes, by the agonies of Christ in Gethsemane, yes, by the blood of him who poured out his soul to death, that you arouse yourselves from this deadly sleep; for it is a state that will lead to some great and grievous sin, some black and terrible fall, unless God prevent it by his grace. First you sleep, then you slumber, then you sin, then you sin again, then you go deeper still, and so you continue unless God, in his grace, steps in to deliver you from the consequences of this dreadful sleep.

II. Yet, secondly, there is, in the text, A HOPEFUL SIGN.

I think that most of us, though we sleep, can say as the spouse does, "my heart waketh." Beloved, it is a blessed sign that *the spouse knows her state, and truly confesses it*. She does not say, mark you, "I am a little tired; my eyes are heavy"; no, but with honesty of heart she says, "I sleep."

Ah, it is a good sign when you and I know our state, and are willing to confess it before God. I heard of a believer in Christ who, on one occasion, was intoxicated, and was expelled from the church as the result of it. But he was visited by many Christian brethren, and among the rest, by one who prayed with him. They prayed together to God, but he could not get any peace. "No", said his friend, "and you never will until you come to the point, and confess your sin as it really is." When the man said in his prayer, "Lord, you know that I have disgraced myself; I have been drunk", it was then that he obtained peace. He directed the lances to the wound; and he put before God the right state of the case; and this is what we must do, beloved, if we would have restoring and renewing grace — we must tell the Lord what our sin really is. As the spouse did, we must confess, "I sleep."

But you will observe that *the spouse is as bold in saying,* "as my heart waketh", *as she was in saying,* "I sleep." What does this mean, "my heart waketh?" Why, just this. "My conscience tells me that this sleepy state is not a proper one for me to be in; and my heart cries that I must get out of it. I cannot find any rest while I slumber. At a distance from God, I cannot be happy." Peter may follow afar off, but he cannot be happy afar off; he

429

may sit and warm his hands with the servants in Pilate's hall, but he cannot warm his heart. Sinners may say, "Why make all this fuss about a little sleep? There is no great sin in it." Ah, but little sins trouble believers far more than great sins trouble sinners. If a Christian's soul is but a little away from God, it is sufficient to mar his joy and make him unhappy. A man clad in armour may go walking through a wood and never feel the thorns; but another man, who has had his armour taken off, will be scratched and torn there. Sinners clad in the armour of sin do not feel the thorn of Christ's desertion; but saints who have thrown this armour aside, and are tender of heart, feel even his slightest frown.

My dear hearer, perhaps you are slumbering this evening, and are content to be so; then you are no child of God; but if you are slumbering, and there is some power, something within you, that keeps crying out, "O God, I would be delivered!" though this voice be never so feeble, though this cruel sleep of yours may almost have gagged it, yet still, if it continues to rebel against this state, and cries out, "Lord, I would be changed, I would be different; turn to me, and I shall to turned; revive me, and I shall be revived"; if there be such a longing as this in you, you are still a child of God, and well may you exclaim, "I sleep, but my heart waketh."

"Lord, I would live near to you if I could. I am like a man that rides a sorry jade of a horse; the horse will not go, but he spurs him, hacks at the bit, and strikes him again and again, for the man would go if he could; and so it is with me. 'The spirit indeed is willing, but the flesh is weak', (Mat. 26:41; Mk. 14:38), and 'when I would do good, evil is present with me' (Rom. 7:21), and 'how to perform, that which is good I find not.' (Rom. 7:18) Lord, help your servants, and let them not sleep any longer!"

III. Now, thirdly, here is A POTENT REMEDY: "the voice of my Beloved."

Some Christians try to get themselves into a healthy state of heart by looking to the law, by self-examination, and by a thousand other remedies; but, after all, *the true cure for every disease in the Christian is in Christ himself.* You may try to chasten yourselves for your sins, but you will continue to sin if that is all that you do. Beloved, I know that the heart has a great objection to coming to Christ after being in a sleepy state. Old Legality whispers in our ears that "You cannot go and trust Christ as you did, for see how badly you have behaved; you must not go to the fountain filled with blood now, as you did at first, for see, you have played the harlot, and you cannot go with the same confidence as you went at first." "Ah, Old Loyalty, I can, and I will." The law never did bring us out of our state of nature, and will it bring us now out of our state of lethargy? If the law had first of all quickened us, then it would do well to look for restoration by the law; but inasmuch as we found our first life by simply believing in Christ, the only way to renew that life is by believing in Jesus Christ again. I will listen, then, not to the voice of the curse, not to the condemnation of Moses, but to the voice of my Beloved, for no music is like his, and nothing can so wake my soul as hearing him speak to me.

Hear, then, the voice of you Beloved in the gospel; he is your Beloved still, though you are asleep. But he does not sleep; and he calls to you, "Come to my bosom; come, my beloved; open the doors of your heart to me. Come, my affianced and precious one, I have not put you away, though you have grieved me, and opened my wounds afresh. I have loved you with an everlasting love. Open the doors of your heart to me, and let me come into communion with you." It is the voice of Jesus speaking to you through your minister, and he cries to you, "Come to me now; trust me once again; and your spiritual strength will be renewed."

Then *turn to this precious Book, and you will hear the voice of your Beloved there.* In words like these, he speaks to you: "Turn, backsliding children, says the Lord; for I am

430

married to you." Hear him as he cries to you, "I will be as the dew unto Israel: he shall grow as the lily, and cast forth his roots as Lebanon." (Hos. 14:5) Hear him as he cries to you, ungodly ones, "Let the wicked forsake his way, and the unrighteous man his thoughts; and let him return unto the Lord, and he will have mercy upon him; and to our God, for he will abundantly pardon." (Is. 55:7)

Hear, then, your Beloved's voice; and mark, dear brethren, *if you do not hear the voice of your Beloved in the days of prosperity, you will be likely enough to hear it in affliction.* If nothing else will keep you awake, the rod will. If you sleep in prosperity, you will have adversity; and sooner than you should be lost, you may lose everything. If, my brethren, God sees that we cannot stand our present peace and prosperity, he will send his servant Death into our families; he will take away our possessions; he will place us in adversity; he will wither all our fair flowers, and break all our idols and dash in pieces everything that stands between our soul and him. Oh, that we were wise, and would hear his gentle voice! "Be not as the horse, or as the mule, which have no understanding: whose mouth must be held in with bit and bridle" (Ps. 32:9), but hear what the Lord says to you from the watchtower of his ministry, and from the witness box of his Word, and then you shall escape the rod.

And perhaps, my brethren, *the Beloved may speak to you without the ministry, and without the Word.* If he does so, I pray you to catch his words. It may be, while you are sitting here, or when you are walking home, or perhaps at the Lord's Table where some of us hope to meet directly; you will hear him whisper some kind, assuring word that will sink your fears again. I have known what it is to preach, on a Sunday here, sometimes, and I have felt like a butcher, who stands in his shop cutting out joints of meat for others, They are fed, but he himself has nothing; or as a cook, who prepares and sends up dinners, but cannot so much as get a taste himself. Then I have gone downstairs to the Lord's Table with a dull heart, and, perhaps, in a second, as though a strange miracle had been wrought, my soul was as full of devout joy and holy mirth as ever spirit was out of heaven. And if you ask me how that has been caused, I would say it was caused by some kindly look of my Beloved, some loving glancing of his eye, or some sweet word from his mouth, and my soul rejoiced with joy unspeakable. Why should it not be so with you tonight? That is the best thing to waken you up. If your heart is dull and heavy, as soon as your Beloved speaks, you will at once awake to spirit and to life.

My time has gone, but I want to say this to you: I am sometimes — no, I am often — haunted with the fear lest we, as a church, should fall asleep. Oh, how greatly has the Lord blessed us these many years! And what favour seems to rest upon every agency! The preaching of the Word has been very successful, but still it is open to the conversion of many. In our classes, how God is honoured! Ah, you little know, some of you, what others of us see; and even we do not see one-tenth of what God is doing in the class conducted by one of our sisters here; and our Sabbath-schools may very well be a delight, for the Lord is working a great work in them; but I am always jealous over you, lest you should slumber. How easy it is to fall asleep! I often fear that my voice, which was once like a trumpet to you, will become like sleep music; that you will become so accustomed to it, and I, perhaps, become so dull and heavy, that the life of God will almost die out among us. My soul weeps and cries to God over this matter. My Master knows that I would cheerfully resign, that another voice might speak to you if that would keep alive your zeal and enthusiasm. If it is, however, not my fault, even a changed ministry would not suffice. When churches grow to a great size, people think they must always continue so, and that God will always bless them as he has done. Why, sirs, as our first blessings came in, as an answer to prayers, all future blessings must come in the same way.

431

I remember well, when we used to meet together in Park Street to have holy communion with the Lord, how we used to wrestle with him in prayer, so much so, that I had scarcely been able to pronounce the benediction, much less give any address, because we all seemed to be carried away in the mighty majesty of wrestling prayer. We have now, sometimes, very choice seasons; but I am afraid not altogether such as we had once. At any rate, if there is any falling off, I thank God it is very little indeed; it is scarcely perceptible as yet; but how soon may that be, unless we watch and be jealous with a holy jealousy? Let us work with Christian earnestness in prayer. O you who have done little for Christ of late, I pray you, do more for him. You who think your time of service is over, and that you might retire like pensioners, and no more fight, I want you to enlist again, put on the colours once more, as if you were raw recruits. You, who once could defy persecution, and stand up in the street to preach Christ, and laugh at all your fears, gather up your courage once again. Oh, that you would wake up, as a church, and put on your beautiful array of past times, when you were despised and persecuted, and the minister's name was a byword and a proverb, and you yourselves, because you were linked with him, were thought to be fools and the off-scouring of all things! But now I tremble lest we should grow respectable and great, and men should think we are respectable, and depart from us. My soul begs and beseeches you to renew your prayers for me that I may preach with greater vigour. What if my ministry should become as dull and stupid as the ministry of one-half of my brethren? What if it should become as useless and as unprofitable as the ministry of nine out of ten who occupy the pulpit? I had sooner die than live to be such a being, as many who stand up in the pulpit wholly to waste people's time, and not win souls. My spirit pants to have the consuming zeal of Richard Baxter, and the earnest, passionate enthusiasm of George Whitefield; but I cannot get it except through your prayers; or getting it, it cannot be maintained without your vehement cries and entreaties before the Lord.

Perhaps we, as a church, have been brought to our present state for a great purpose which has never dawned on us. We have done something for God already: we are filling the pulpits of our village churches with men sound in the faith, and earnest for God; we are erecting a great barrier against the every-day increasing encroachment of heresy and infidelity; but we want to do something more, and something is looming upon us in the future — I scarcely know what — some high and holy purpose which this church has been brought up to this point to accomplish. Shall we draw back? Men of Ephraim, will you draw back in the day of battle? Will you be condemned for not coming to the help of the Lord against the mighty? Shall the angel pronounce over you the sentence, "Ichabod, for the glory of the Lord has departed from you" (Sam.4:21) because of your declining to continue earnest in zeal?" If that is so to any extent, let us return to the Lord; let us take to Christ words of repentance and faith; and let us beseech him to make this church again his buckler and two-edged sword, and make his minister once more a captain in the midst of the Lord's hosts; for the day of the Lord is mighty, and the battle of the Lord is terrible; and every man must take his place, and every soldier draw his weapon from his thigh, for the day of the Lord is drawing near, and the battle of God is to be fought now, even now. Let us arise, my brethren; let us rush like lions to the prey, like swift eagles to the chase; and God will help us, God will help us, and that right early. (Ps. 46:5) This church cries tonight, "I sleep", but she can also say, "My heart waketh." The heart of the church is awake still. I think my voice to you to-night is an echo of the voice of your Beloved.

Sisters, brothers, bestir yourselves: let us cry mightily to God; let us labour for the winning of souls; let us pant and pray for a great increase to our membership; and God will save sinners in answer to our prayer, and his name shall be glorified forever and ever. Amen.

58. NEARER AND DEARER

NO. 793

DELIVERED ON LORD'S-DAY MORNING, FEBRUARY 2ND, 1868
AT THE METROPOLITAN TABERNACLE, NEWINGTON

"I sleep, but my heart waketh: it is the voice of my beloved that knocketh, saying, Open to me, my sister, my love, my dove, my undefiled: for my head is filled with dew, and my locks with the drops of the night. I have ye put off my coat; how shall I put it on? I have washed my feet; how shall I defile them? My beloved put in his hand by the hole of the door, and my bowels were moved for him. I rose up to open to my beloved; and my hands dropped with myrrh, and my fingers with sweet smelling myrrh, upon the handles of the lock. I opened to my beloved; but my beloved had withdrawn himself, and was gone: my soul failed when he spake: I sought him, but I could not find him; I called him, but he gave me no answer. The watchmen that want about the city found me, they smote me, they wounded me; the keepers of the way has took away my veil from me. I charge you, O daughters of Jerusalem, if ye find my beloved, that ye tell him, that I am sick of love." (Song of Solomon 5:2-8)

THE healthiest state for a Christian is that of unbroken and intimate fellowship with the Lord Jesus Christ. From such a state of heart, he should never decline. "Abide in me, and I in you" (Jn 15:4) is the loving precept of our ever-loving Lord. But, alas, my brethren, as in this world our bodies are subject to many sicknesses, so our souls also, by reason of the body of this death with which we are encompassed, are often sorely afflicted with sin, sickness, and an evil heart of unbelief in departing from the Lord. We are not what we might be, we are not what we should be, we are not what we shall be, and we are not what we wish to be. I fear that many of us are not walking in the light of God's countenance, are not resting with our heads upon the Saviour's bosom, nor sitting with Mary at the Master's feet; we dwell in Kedar rather than Zion, and sojourn in Mesech rather than Jerusalem. Spiritual sickness is very common in the church of God, and the root of the mischief lies in distance from Jesus, following Christ afar off, and yielding to a drowsy temperament. Away from Jesus, we are away from joy. Without the sun, the flowers pine; without Jesus, our hearts faint. My object, this morning, is to put myself into the hands of the Holy Spirit, that he may now come, and, like a physician, prescribe for you, that if any of you in your hearts have become like the spouse in this part of the Song, you may as fully imitate her in that which is good as in that which is blameworthy. If you do not soon find your Beloved to your soul's joy, may you at least, like the spouse, declare that you are "sick of love", and continue to follow his track until you overtake him.

I. Commencing where the text begins, we observe that the spouse confesses A VERY COMMON SIN: she cries, "I sleep."

She had no right to be asleep, for her Beloved knew no rest. He was standing outside in the cold street, with his head wet with dew, and his locks with the drops of the night; so why should she be at ease? He was anxiously seeking her; how was it that she could be so cruel as to yield to slumber! It is a most unseasonable thing, my brothers and sisters, for any of us to be indolent and indifferent, for we profess to have gone out to meet the Bridegroom, and it is shameful for us to sleep because, for a little while, he tarries. The world is perishing. We are sent into the world instrumentally to be its saviours — how dishonourable, that with such necessities for activity, and with such noble ends to be served by industry, we should fold our arms and delight ourselves in indolence! Nothing can be more inexcusable than for us to sleep, seeing that we are not of the night or of

433

darkness. If we had been the children of the night, it might seem according to our nature for us to be sluggards; but we have avowed that the light of the glory of God in the face of Jesus Christ has shone into our eyes; so let us not, therefore, sleep as do others, but let us watch and be sober, (1 Thess 5:6) for they that sleep, sleep in the night; and since the night is past to us, it is highly indecent and improper that we should still continue to toss upon the bed of sloth. No time for slumber, it seems to me, can be more unseasonable to the Christian than the present one, for the world is reeking with wickedness and superstitions like the frogs of Egypt are covering the land. Everyone who is but so much as half awake can see the enemy industriously sowing tares among the wheat. (Mat. 13:39) Shall the watchmen of Zion continue to slumber on their watchtowers when the foe is undermining the bulwarks? Shall the shepherds sleep when the wolf has broken into the fold? Shall the seamen sleep when the gale is furiously driving the vessel on the rocks? So far as our own hearts are concerned, we have no private reasons for slumbering, for our daily cares require watchfulness. The temptations that assail us every hour demand of us that we should stand with our loins girt; and our abounding enemies all warn us that our danger is extreme unless we are always fully equipped in our celestial armour. (Eph.6:11, 13) If we must sleep, let it be in a less dangerous position than these hostile lands through which we march today; there will be rest enough on the other side of Jordan, where the drawn sword is exchanged for the well-tuned harp. But to be careless now is to sleep in the midst of a bloody conflict, to dream upon the verge of a precipice, and to sport in the jaws of death. From our beds, let the Master's voice arouse us, for he cries aloud, "What I say unto you I say unto all, Watch." (Mk. 13:27)

Do you not find, my brethren, that almost unconsciously to yourselves, a spirit of indifference is stealing over you? You do not give up private prayer, but alas, it becomes a mere mechanical operation. You do not forsake the assembling of yourselves together, but still your bodily presence is all that is given, and you derive no refreshment from the unspiritual exercise. Have you not sat at the Lord's Table spiritually asleep? Has not the heavenly watcher detected your soul nodding when the sacred emblems have been spread before you, or even in your mouth? Have you not been content with the bare symbols, which spells barrenness, while the spiritual essence, which is marrow and fatness, you have not tasted? I find from the very fact that I am always engaged in the Master's service from the early morning till far into the night, that I become dull and carnal, being cumbered with much serving (Lk. 10:40), so that I have to question the vitality of my religion because its freshness and vigour are flagging. It is grievous to go on like a clock which is wound up, not because you rejoice in the work, but because you must. My soul shudders at the thought of routine religion, formal service, dead devotion, mechanical godliness. What a mercy to reach the fresh springs, to feel a daily renewed youth, an anointing with fresh oil! For this, I pine and pant. One gets driving on in the dark, as coachmen sometimes do when they are asleep on the box: dangerous work, this! I know that I am safe in Christ, but I could fain suffer anything rather than become habitually with a slumbering heart. Better smart under the long whip of affliction, or feel the stings of conscience, or even the darts of the devil, than lie down in carnal security's lap to be shorn of one's locks by the Philistines (Jdg. 16:19); yet I fear this has been my case. I do not know how far my confession may be echoed by my brethren today, but I am shrewdly suspicious that the more wakeful you are, the more heartily you will acknowledge a terrible tendency in the other direction. Again, let me remind you that to sleep now is an evil thing, dangerous to yourselves, a cruel thing to others, an ungrateful act towards Christ, and dishonourable to his cause. Shall such a King be served by lie-abed soldiers? Shall his midnight pleadings be repaid by our daylight sleepiness? Shall an agony of bloody sweat be recompensed by heavy eyelids and yawning mouths? Away, for ever away, O you who are redeemed by the Well-beloved, with this detestable slumber of which I fear you must honestly confess yourselves to have been guilty!

II. The song before us reminds us of A HOPEFUL SIGN: "My heart waketh."

What a riddle the believer is! He is asleep, and yet he is awake. His true self, the I, the veritable Ego of the man is asleep; yet his heart, his truest self, his affections, are awake. The believer is a standing paradox; he cannot even understand himself. The wakefulness of the heart, does it not mean just this? "I sleep, but I am not content to be asleep"? The true believer is not satisfied to slumber. Time was when, if he could have pacified his conscience, he would have been extremely thankful, however deadly might have been the drug which caused the slumber, but now the man starts, shivers, tosses to and fro in his sleep, is unrested by his rest, dreams horribly, and cries to be awakened. The saved man cannot be happy in a false and rotten peace. The divine life within struggles against the monstrous serpent of sin, which tries to twist its folds of sleep around it. No renewed heart can enjoy perfect rest while conscious of being an idler in the vineyard, and a loiterer in the race. Backsliding believer, does your heart wake? If so, you will know it, for it will smite you, it will upbraid you, and demand of you whoever you are that you should thus behave yourself? Elect of God, yet asleep while Jesus is dishonoured! Redeemed by blood, yet misspending time which belongs to your Redeemer! Married to Christ, and yet absent from your Husband, and content without a smile from his dear face! How can this be? Be ashamed and be confounded, and never show your face anymore, for this is ingratitude of the deepest dye.

It is a hopeful sign when someone can conscientiously say as much as the spouse in this case, but remember it is not much to say. Do not pride yourself on it. Be ashamed that you are asleep at all. Do not congratulate yourself that your heart is awake. Be thankful that infinite love affords you grace enough to keep your heart alive, but be ashamed that you have no more, when more may be had, and should be had. Mere longings and moanings are so small a work of grace that they should alarm rather than console. It will be a foul temptation of Satan it you are led to say, "I am content to sleep so long as my heart does but wake." Firm resolves of amendment are needful, and something more than resolves. Alas, I need to add those few words, because most of our resolutions vanish in thin air! We get as far as this: "I am not quite content to be in such a lukewarm state of mind, so I will, therefore, by-and-by, endeavour to arouse myself, and renounce this downy bed of sloth." This is not much to say, for it is no more than we ought to do; it is all the less because we so seldom keep the vow, but, like the disturbed sluggard, we turn over to the other side and mutter sullenly, "A little more folding of the hands to sleep." (Prov. 6:10, 24:33) I myself fear that there are thousands of God's children who are enough awake to know that they are asleep, enough convinced of their wrong to know that they are wrong, and to hope that they will one day be better; but alas, they continue in the same unhallowed condition! May I invite every believer to make a strict examination of his own spiritual state. My brother, you may be sleeping through great worldly prosperity, for nothing tends to slumber more surely than a gentle rocking in the cradle of luxury. On the other hand, you may be sleeping because of overwhelming sorrow, even as the Twelve fell asleep when our Lord was in the garden. Some make a downy pillow of their wealth, but others fall asleep in their poverty, like Jacob with a stone for his pillow. (Gen. 28:18) To be surrounded with constant worldly occupation, to be oppressed with many cares in business, this is to pass through the enchanted ground, and happy is the man who has grace enough to overcome the influence of his position. Now, if your heart today is sufficiently awake to tell you that you are not living as near to God as you were some years ago, that you have not the love for him you once had, that your warmth and zeal for Christ has departed from you, I beseech you, hear the voice of Jesus Christ: "As many as I love, I rebuke and chasten: be zealous therefore, and repent." (Rev. 3:19) "Repent and do the first works." (Rev. 2:5) Turn to your Saviour now, that this very day, before the sun goes down, you may exclaim with rejoicing, "I found him whom my soul loveth: I hear him, and will not let him go." (Song 3:4)

III. The third thing in the text is A LOVING CALL.

Asleep as the spouse was, she knew her Husband's voice, for this is an abiding mark of God's people. "My sheep hear my voice." A half sleeping saint still has enough spiritual discernment to know when Jesus speaks. At first, the Beloved one simply knocked. His object was to enter into fellowship with his church, to reveal himself to her, to unveil his beauties, to solace her with his presence. Such is the object of our blessed Lord, this morning, in bringing us to this house. I hope this sermon will be a knock: I trust my discourse may give many knocks on the door of every backsliding believer here. Jesus cries, "Open to me! Open to me!" Will you not admit your Saviour? You love him. He gave himself for you, and he pleads for you: let him into your soul and commune with him this morning. When you turn to read his Word, every promise is a knock. He says, "Come and enjoy this promise with me, for it is yea and amen in me." Every threat is a knock. Every precept is a knock. In outward providences, every boon we receive through our Mediator's intercession is a gentle knock from his pierced hand, saying, "Take this mercy, but open to me! It comes to you through me; open to me!" Every affliction is a knock at our door: that wasting sickness, that broken bone, that consumptive daughter, that rebellious child, that burning house, that shipwrecked vessel, and dishonoured bill — all these are Christ's knocks, saying, "These things are not your joys; these worldly things can afford no rest for the sole of your foot; open to me, open to me! These idols I am breaking, these joys I am removing; open to me, and find in me a solace for all your woes."

Knocking, alas, seems to be of little use to us. We are so stubborn and so ungenerous towards our heavenly bridegroom that he, the crucified, the immortal lover of our souls, may stand and knock, and knock, and knock again, and the preacher and adversity may be his double hammer; yet the door of the heart will not yield.

Then the Bridegroom tried his voice. If knocking would not do, he speaks in plain and plaintive words, "Open to me, my sister, my love, my dove, my undefiled." The Lord Jesus Christ has a sweet way of making the Word come home to the conscience; I mean, not now that effective and irresistible power of which we shall speak by-and-by, but that lesser force which the heart may resist, but which renders it very guilty for so doing. Some of you who are the Lord's people, have heard soft and sweet whispers in your heart, saying, "You are saved; now, my beloved, live in the light of your salvation. You are a member of my mystical body; draw near and enjoy fellowship with me, such as a member ought to have with its Head." Do you not see the Lord Jesus beckoning to you with gentle finger, and saying, "Come with me oftener into the closet of secret prayer; get oftener alone to muse on things divine; acquire the habit of walking with me in your business. Abide in me, and I in you"? Do not these admonitions visit you like angels' whispers, and have you too often resisted them? Have you not been thoughtful for them for the moment, and recorded them in your diary, and then forgotten them and lived as frigidly as you did before, though the Sun of Righteousness was waiting to rise on you with healing in his wings? (Mal. 4:2)

Now, beloved, observe the appeals which the Beloved here makes. He says, "Open to me", and his plea is the love the spouse has for him, or professes to have, the love he has for her, and the relationship which exists between them. "Open to me, my sister", next of kin to me, bone of my bone, flesh of my flesh, born of the same mother"; for Jesus is "the seed of the woman" even as we are. One with us in our humanity, he takes each human heart that believes him to be his mother, and sister and brother. "Open to me, my sister." If you are so nearly related to Jesus, why do you act so coldly towards him? If, indeed, he is your closest kinsman, how is it that you live so far remote, and do not come to visit him, neither open the doors of your heart to entertain him? "My dove", my gentle one, my favourite, my innocent." Oh, if you are indeed his dove, how can you stay away from the

436

dovecote? How can you be satisfied without your mate? One turtledove pines without the other; how is it you do not pine to have fellowship with the dear Husband of your soul? "My love" — Jesus calls us what we profess to be. We say we love him; yes, and unless we have been dreadfully deceived, we do love him. It brings the water to my eyes to think of it, that I should so often be indifferent to him, and yet I can say it as before him, "Thou knowest all things, thou knowest that I love thee." (Jn. 21:17) Men and brethren, if we love him, let us crave his presence in our souls. How miserable must it be to live as some do, day after day, without a real soul-stirring, heaven-moving, prayer! Are there not some who continue week after week without searching the Word, and without rejoicing in the Lord? Oh, wretched life of banishment from bliss! Dear hearer, can you be satisfied to go out into the world, and to be so occupied with it that you never have a desire towards heaven? If so, mourn over such backsliding, since it exiles you from your best Beloved's bosom.

The Bridegroom adds another title, "My undefiled." There is a spiritual chastity which every believer must maintain; our heart belongs to no one but Christ. All other lovers must be gone; he fills the throne. He has bought us; no other has paid a part of the price; so he shall have us altogether. He has taken us into personal union with himself; of his mystical body, we make up a part; we ought, therefore, to hold ourselves as chaste virgins to Christ, undefiled with the pollution's of the flesh and the rivalries of earthly loves. To the undefiled, Jesus says, "Open to me." Oh, I am ashamed, this morning, to be preaching from such a text, ashamed of myself most of all, that I should need to have such a text applied to my own soul! Why, beloved, if Christ deigns to enter such a poor miserable cottage as our nature, ought we not to entertain the King with the best we have, and feel that the first seat at our table is all too poor and too mean for him? What if, in the midst of this dark night, our Beloved comes to us who profess to love him, shall he have to knock and speak and plead by every sweet and endearing title? Yet shall we refuse to arise and give him the fellowship he craves? Did you notice that powerful argument with which the heavenly lover closed his cry? He said, "My head is filled with dew, and my locks with the drops of the night." Ah, sorrowful remembrances, for those drops were not the ordinary dew that fall on the houseless traveller's unprotected head; his head was wet with scarlet dew, and his locks with crimson drops of a tenfold night of God's desertion, when he "sweat as it were great drops of blood falling down to the ground." (Lk. 22:44) My heart, how vile you are, for you shut out the Crucified! Behold the Man, thorn-crowned and scourged, with traces of the spittle of the soldiery, can you close the door on him? Will you despise the One who is "despised and rejected of men"? Will you grieve the "Man of sorrows, and acquainted with grief"? (Is. 53:3) Are you forgetting that he suffered all this for you, for you, when you deserve nothing at his hands? After all this, will you give him no recompense, not even the poor return of admission to your loving communing? I am afraid some of you believers think it a very small thing to live a day or two without fellowship with God in prayer. Probably you have fallen into such a sleepy state that you can read your Bible without enjoyment, and yet you do not feel it to be any very remarkable thing that it is so. You come to and fro to the Tabernacle and listen to the gospel, and it does not come home to you with the power it once had, yet you do not feel at all alarmed about it. My Master does not treat your state of mind with the same indifference that you do, for it causes him pain, and, though as Mediator, his expiatory grief's are finished once for all, yet he has anguish still over your indifference and coldness of heart; these sorrows are the drops that bedew his head, they are the dewdrops that hang about his raven locks. Oh, will you grieve him? Will you open all his wounds and crucify him afresh, and put him to an open shame? Doors of the heart, fly open! Though rusting on your hinges, open at the coming of the sorrowful Lover who was smitten of God and afflicted. Surely the argument of his grief should prevail instantly with every honest heart: he whose head is wet with dew, and his locks with the drops of the night, must not be kept standing in the street. It behoves that he be entertained with our warmest love; it is imperative that he be housed at once.

437

IV. Yet the spouse did not hasten to open the door, and I am afraid the like delay may be charged on some of us. Our shame deepens as we pursue our theme, and think how well our own character is photographed here by the wise man; for notice, in the fourth place, that after the knocking and the pleading, the spouse made A MOST UNGENEROUS EXCUSE.

She sat like a queen, and knew no sorrow. She had put off her garments and washed her feet as travellers do in the East before they go to rest. She was taking her ease in full security, and therefore she said to her Beloved, "I have put off my tunic, I cannot robe myself again. As for my feet, I have washed them, and to tread the floor to open the door would defile them. Therefore, I pray, have me excused." A bad excuse was, in this case, far worse than none because it was making one sin an apology for another. Why did she put off her coat? The bridegroom had not come; she should have stood with her loins girt about, and her lamp trimmed. Why had she washed her feet? It was right to do so if the emblem had indicated purity, but it indicated carnal ease. She had left holy labour for carnal rest. Why did she? She thus makes her wicked slumber and inaction to be an excuse for barring her Husband. My dear brothers and sisters, there is a temptation which is very cunning on the part of Satan, and perhaps he will exercise that on some of you this morning. While I have been preaching, you have said, "Well, that is just like me. The text fully opens up my experience", and the devil will then say, "Be satisfied; you see you are just in the same condition as the spouse, therefore it is all right." Oh, damnable temptation! What can be viler than this, that because another has sinned against the Beloved, I am to be content to sin in the same way! Perhaps you will turn this sad course of conduct in the ancient spouse into an excuse for your own negligence. Shall I publish the excuse she made? It is this: "O Lord, I know that if I am to enter into much fellowship with you, I must pray very differently from what I have done of late, but it is too much trouble; I cannot stir myself to so much energy. My time is so taken up with my business, I am so constantly engaged that I could not afford even a quarter of an hour for retirement. I have to cut my prayers so short." Is this the miserable excuse in part? Shall I go on? Shall I tell out more of this dishonourable apology? It is this: "I do not want to begin an examination of myself; it may reveal so many unpleasant truths. I sleep, and it is very comfortable to sleep; I do not want to be driven out of my comforts. Perhaps, if I were to live nearer to Christ, I should have to give up some of these things which I so much enjoy. I have become conformed to the world of late; I am very fond of having Mr. So-and-so to spend an hour with me in the evening, and his talk is anything but that which my Master would approve, but I cannot give him up. I have taken to read religious novels. I could not expect to have the Lord Jesus Christ's company when I am poring over such trash as that, but still I prefer it to my Bible; I would sooner read a fool's tale than I would read of Jesus' love." How ashamed I feel this morning to have to put it into words like these, the sins of some of you, but my words are literal truth. Do not many of you live as if you had a name to live, and were dead? (Rev. 3:1) Jesus Christ comes and knocks this morning, and reminds you that the happiest life is living near to him, that the holiest, purest, sweetest hours you ever had were those in which you threw yourselves on him, and gave up all beside. He reminds you of your better days. Oh, do not, I pray you, offer him excuses frivolous and vexatious. Oh, do not despise your Lord who died for you, in whose name you live, with whom you hope to reign forever, who is to wrap you about with glory in the day of his appearing. Let it not be said that he is pushed into a corner and his love despised, while the vile painted-faced world takes up the love of your life. It should not be so; it is baseness itself on our part when it is so.

Still, as a wonder of wonders, although shamefully and cruelly treated, the beloved Husband did not go away. We are told that he "put in his hand by the hole of the door", and then the heart of his spouse was moved for him. In the Eastern door, there is generally a place near the lock into which a man may put his hand, and there is a pin inside which, if removed, unfastens the door. Each one of these locks is different from another, so that no one usually understands how to open the door except the master. So the Master in this case did not actually open the door — you notice the spouse did that, but he pulled out the pin so that she could see his hand. She could see that the doer was not fast closed now he had removed the bar. "My Beloved put in his hand by the hole of the door." Does not this picture THE WORK OF EFFECTIVE GRACE, when the truth does not appeal to the ear alone, but comes to the heart, when it is no longer a thing thought of and discussed and forgotten, but an arrow which has penetrated into the reins, and sticks fast in the loins to our wounding, and ultimately to our spiritual healing? No hand is like Christ's hand. When he puts his hand to the work, it is well done. He "put in his hand", not his hand on me to smite me, but his hand in me to comfort me, to sanctify me. He put in his hand, and straightway his beloved began to pity him and to lament her unkindness. She thought, as she looked at that hand pierced with the nail mark, "O Jesus, have I no love for you? Have you done all this for me, and have I been a transparent hypocrite after all, and locked you out when I ought to have admitted you? I have used no other friend so badly. I should have been ashamed to have thought of such conduct, even to a foe. But you, O you who have due more for me than mother, brother, husband, friend, could have done, to you I have been an ingrate most base and wilful." Her heart was moved with repentance; her eyes gushed with tears; and she rose to let him in.

As she arose, she first buckled on her garments, and then she searched for the alabaster box of precious ointment that she might anoint his weary feet and dewy locks. No sooner did she reach the door than see the love of God for her! Her "hands dropped with myrrh, and her fingers with sweet smelling myrrh." Here is the Holy Spirit come to help our infirmities. She begins to pray, and the Holy Spirit helps her. She begins already to enjoy the sweetness, not of communion, but of the very desire after communion. For, beloved, when our tears begin to flow because we are far from Christ, those holy drops have myrrh in them. When we begin to pray for grace, there is even a blessedness about our yearning, and longing, and sighing and panting and pining; our fingers drop with sweet smelling myrrh upon the handles of the lock. An unction from the Holy One descends upon the soul when it is earnestly seeking for its Beloved. But that ought never to satisfy us. Behold, another temptation of the devil, when he says to you, "On this very morning, you felt some sweetness in hearing about Christ; your hands have evidently dropped with myrrh on the handles of the lock." Yes, but still it is not the myrrh that will content the loving heart, it is Christ she wants; and if not only hands, but lips and feet. And had her whole frame dropped with myrrh, this would never have contented her until she could get the Lord himself. I pray you, beloved, if the life of Jesus is in you of a truth, do not rest satisfied with all the graces and promises and doctrines and gifts of the Spirit of God, but seek after this most excellent gift, to know Christ, and to be found in him; to say of him, "He loved me, and gave himself for me" (Gal. 2:20); and, yet more, "His left hand is under my head, and his right hand doth embrace me." (Song 2:6) It was that effectively putting in of the hand that moved her. O Lord, grant the like to us!

VI. But now, in the sixth place, observe THE DESERVED CHASTISEMENT the Bridegroom inflicted.

When her spouse was willing to commune, she was not; and now that she is willing, and even anxious, what happens? I wish to describe this to you because some of you may have felt it, and others of you who never have, but, preserving your intimacy with Christ up till now, you may be warned by it. The newly awakened one went to the door and opened it to her Beloved, for though he was gone, she did not doubt of her love, or his love for her. "I opened to my Beloved, but..." it says in Hebrew, "He had gone, he had gone." Here is the voice of lamentation, the reduplicated cry of one that is in bitter distress. There must have been a sad relief about it to her sinful heart, for she must have felt afraid to look her dear one in the face after such heartless conduct; but sad it would have been to face him, it was infinitely sadder to say, "He is gone! He is gone!" Now she begins to use the means of grace in order to find him. "I sought him", she says, "and I found him not. I went up to the house of God; the sermon was sweet, but it was not sweet to me, for he was not there. I went to the communion table, and the ordinance was a feast of fat things to others, but not to me, for he was not there. I sought him, but I could not find him." Then she took herself to prayer. She had neglected that before, but now she supplicated in real earnest: "I called him; I said to him, 'Come, my Beloved, my heart wakes for you. Jesus, reveal yourself to me as you do not to the world.

O love divine, how sweet thou art!
When shall I find my willing heart
All taken up by thee?
I thirst, I faint, I die to prove
The greatness of redeeming love,
The love of Christ to me.

Stronger His love than death or hell;
Its reaches are unsearchable;
The first born sons of light
Desire in vain its depths to see;
They cannot reach the mystery
The length, and breadth, and height.

Thy only love do I require,
Nothing on earth beneath desire,
Nothing in heaven above;
Let earth, and heaven, and all things go,
Give me Thy only love to know,
Give me only Thy love.

(Charles Wesley)

Her prayers were many; she kept them up day and night. "I called him, but he gave me no answer." She was not a lost soul; do not mistake that. Christ loved her just as much then as before; no, loved her a great deal more. If there can be any change in Christ's love, he must have much more approved of her when she was seeking him in sorrow than when she was reclining upon the couch and neglecting him. But he was gone, and all her calling could not bring him back. What did she do then? Why, she went to his ministers, she went to those who were the watchmen of the night, and what did they say to her? Did they cheer her? Perhaps they had never passed through her experience; perhaps they were mere hirelings. However, it might be that they smote her. Sometimes, the truthful preaching of the gospel will smite a child of God when he gets out of his walk with God; and it is right it should be so. But they did more than smite, they "wounded" her until she began to bleed from the wounds given by the very men whom she hoped would have comforted her. "Surely", she might have said, "you know where the city's King is, for you are the city's guards!" But she received no comfort. When a poor soul in this case flies to an unsympathising minister, he will say, "Well, you say you have lost the presence of Christ; you should bestir yourself to find it." "Yes", says the spouse, "I rose up and opened to him." "You should use the means." "But I have used the means; I sought him, but I did not find him." "You should pray." "I did pray; I called him, but he gave me no answer." "Well then", perhaps they will add, "you should wait patiently for him." "Oh, but" she says, "I cannot, for I must have him; I am sick of love." And then perhaps the minister will be

440

sharp, and say, "I fear you are not a child of God." Now what is that? Why, it is taking away the veil from the mourning seeker; plucking away the ensign of sincerity from the benighted seeker. No woman went into the streets of Jerusalem without her veil, unless she was of the baser sort, and the watchmen seemed to say to this woman, "You are of ill name, or you would not be here at this time of night crying out for one you have lost." Oh, cruel work to pull off her veil and expose her, when she was already wretched enough! Sometimes a sharp sentence from a true minister may put a poor soul in the stocks which rather ought to have been comforted. I hope these hands will never pull away the veil from any of you poor mourning lovers of Christ. Far rather would these lips tell him when I speak with him, that you are sick of love. But it cannot be helped at all times, for when we are dealing with the hypocrite, the tender child of God thinks we mean him; when we are speaking against the formalist, as we must do, the genuine believer writes bitter things against himself. When the fan is in our hand, and we are seeking thoroughly to purge the floor, it sometimes happens that some of the lighter wheat gets blown a little away with the chaff, and so distress is brought to weak but real children of God.

If so, recollect it is not our fault, for we would not grieve you; but it is your fault for having lost your Beloved; for if you had not lost him, you would not have been saying, "Tell me where I shall find him!" But you would have been rejoicing in him, and no watchmen would have smitten you, and no keepers of the walls would have taken away your veil from you, for Jesus would have been your Protector and your Friend.

VII. Now, to close. As the poor spouse did not then find Christ, but was repulsed in all ways, she adopted A LAST EXPEDIENT. She knew that there were some who had daily fellowship with the King, daughters of Jerusalem who often saw him, and, therefore, she sent a message by them, "If ye see my Beloved, tell him that I am sick of love."

Enlist your brother saints to pray for you. Go with them to their gatherings for prayer. Their company will not satisfy you without Jesus, but their company may help you to find Jesus. Follow the footsteps of the flock, and you may, by-and-by, discover the Shepherd. And what a message it is to send to Christ! Do not send it by other people's lips only; send it by your own. Tell him, "I am sick of love." This is of all things the most painful, and the most happy thing in all the world. This is a sickness that I should like to die of, but I should like to feel it in rather a different shape from this. There are two lovesicknesses in the Song of Solomon. The one is when the spouse longs for the presence of her Lord, and the second is, when she gets that presence, he is so glorious to her that she is ready to die with excess of joy, and exclaims, "Stay me with flagons, comfort me with apples: for I am sick of love." If you cannot get the second, recollect that the first is the clear way to it. Resolve in your heart, my brother and sister, that you never will be happy till you win the face of Christ. Settle it in your soul that there shall he no end to your cries and tears till you can say with all your heart, "My Beloved is near by; I can speak to him; I am in the enjoyment of his love." If you can be content without it, you shall go without it, but if you must have it, you shall have it. If your hunger breaks through stone walls to reach your Lord, no stone walls will keep him from you. If you are insatiable after Christ, he will feed you with himself. If you bid goodbye to all the dainties of the world, and all its sweet draughts and delicacies, and must have Christ, and Christ alone, then no hungering soul shall long be kept without him. He must come to you. There are cords that draw him to you at this hour. His love draws you to him, but your love draws him close to you. Do not be afraid, for your soul shall be like the chariots of Amminadib, perhaps even this morning, and you shall go on your way rejoicing. The Lord grant it may be so for his love's sake! Amen.

59. THE SOUL'S DESERTION
NO. 3552

AT THE METROPOLITAN TABERNACLE, NEWINGTON

"My beloved had withdrawn himself, and was gone."
(Song of Solomon 5:6)

The happiest condition of a Christian out of heaven is to live in the conscious enjoyment of the presence of the Lord Jesus. When the love of Christ is shed abroad in the heart by the Holy Spirit (Rom. 5:5), the believer need not envy any angel with his harp of gold. It does not matter what may be his outward trial; the Holy Spirit is able to make the heart live above all surrounding circumstances, so that we can have summer in the middle of winter, and pluck our ripest fruits when there are neither leaves nor fruits on the tree. But the Christian is unhappy, unhappy to the utmost degree, whenever he loses his sense of the presence of his Lord. Then the pillars of his house are made to tremble; his fresh springs are dried up; the sun is hid from his eyes; and the sky is so dark overhead that he walks in, rather, wanders about, a world which cannot render to his soul any substantial comfort. Were he a worldling, he could live in the world, but, having been taught by grace to aspire after something nobler and better, the loss of that is exceedingly grievous to his spirit. I question whether most Christians do not sometimes lose the enjoyment of the Lord's company. I question yet further whether there are not very many professors who live contentedly under that loss; nor can I account for this, except on the supposition that they can have known but little of that presence as their best estate. Otherwise, they must be in a most sickly and slumbering condition of soul, gradually becoming worse and worse; or else they never could bear to have things as they are with them. It seems to me that a real believer, in a sound state of health, no sooner loses the presence of his Lord than he begins to cry for him. Where has Christ gone? Why have I lost sight of him? The sounds of his footsteps still linger in the ear. The believer wakens and starts, and asks himself, "How is this? Where has my Beloved gone? What is it that has chased him from me? I cannot live if he is removed; therefore, let me speedily seek him, and never rest until once more I am restored to full communion with him." Let me, then, talk a little with such believers who have lost for a while the comfortable presence of their Lord.

The first question shall be:

I. WHY WAS THE BELOVED GONE?

According to the text, he was gone. Read the preceding verses, or perhaps you have them in your memories. The spouse had been asleep. This was the beginning of the mischief. "I sleep, but my heart waketh." (Song 5:2) If we begin to fall asleep, we must not wonder if we miss the quickening and comforting influences of our Lord's presence. Jesus Christ did not put us in his Church that we might sleep away our time on earth. Do not fancy that such an active spirit as that which burned and blazed in our Saviour's flesh can be content to hold communion with lazy sluggards who toss upon their beds, and say, "Yet a little more sleep and a little more folding of the arms to slumber." It is the active Christian who keeps pace with Christ. Christ is a quick walker; if you crawl along the path of duty, he will soon leave you behind, until you begin to enquire, "Whither is he gone", and quicken your pace to overtake him. Are there any here who have missed Christ's presence, and who may trace it to the fact that they have been drowsy in prayer of late, heavy in all the exercises of study and duty, and, in fact, sleepy altogether? Have they been without care for the conversion of others, having scarcely any concern even for their own children; perhaps indifferent to the welfare of Christ's Church; feeding little upon the

442

Word; and resorting but little to the assemblies of the saints? Do not marvel if the Beloved withdraws himself when his spouse does nothing but nod and sleep, instead of keeping company with him in active service!

After the spouse had fallen asleep, her Beloved came and knocked at the door, saying, "Open to me, my sister, my love, my dove, my undefiled; for my head is filled with dew, and my locks with the drops of the night." (Song 5:2) Yet she refused to open the door to him. Surely this is another sin which drives Christ away. When admonished for falling into a drowsy state, we pay no regard to it. Depend upon it; there is extreme peril to a soul that does not accept the warning. Awful as it is to sin, when unwarned, it is still more horrible to persevere in sin in the teeth of rebuke, and after gentle, loving expostulations [dissuasions]. What, did conscience prick me, and will I not be scrupulous? After having seen my fault, and smarted for it, do I still persist in it? Have I been lukewarm and indifferent? Does the Holy Spirit visit me, remonstrate with me, and make me feel that I am gradually backsliding, and little by little declining? Have I vowed and resolved that I would seek spiritual recovery, and am I still as dull, careless, and unconcerned as ever? This argues badly for my soul! The Beloved will not put up with these rebuffs forever. Out of love for us, he will hide his face; if we grieve him, he will go; if we walk disobediently towards him, he will soon walk obstinately towards us. These are God-provoking sins; it is a defying of his Spirit when you spurn his gentle admonitions.

Note further, that the spouse, when her Beloved knocked at the door, made idle excuses that she had put off her cloak, and her sandals, and could not put them on. She was taking her rest on her couch, and could not bring herself to come to the door to let him in. Ah, how often self-indulgence lies at the bottom of the sin that drives Christ away! A believer cannot let his lower nature get the uppermost, and yet find that he is walking agreeably to the Lord's mind. Your spiritual nature ought to keep your mental nature under control, and your mental nature ought to keep your bodily or animal nature entirely in check. A man who is a thinker and a philosopher will scorn to let mere passions govern him, but a true Christian, having a yet higher spirit within him than the mere mind, having that new living seed within himself which comes from God, and leads him to God, should not, and must not, allow his baser nature to reign supreme. If we indulge the flesh, depend on it, Christ will not be with us. He does not come to dwell with swine, but with men; and not with men of the earth earthy, except in order to renew them and make them like himself who is the second man, the Lord from heaven (1 Cor. 15:47), in order to make them heavenly. If your conversation is to be with Christ, it must be in heaven. If you would enjoy the sunlight, you must not bow your face down to the earth. If you seek to be enriched in the things of God, you must not be for ever groping among the dark pits and bogs and morasses of earth. Oh, soul, are you indulging yourself, and taking things easy? Carnal security is one of your worst enemies. Do I hear anyone say, "It is enough, my soul; you have much spiritual goods laid up for many years; take your ease"? Do you think that there is no need for you to watch? You have become so experienced that there is no occasion for you to be much in prayer, for a word with you is like an hour with some; that there is no reason for you to be continually striving against your besetting sin, for you have got such complete mastery over these infirmities. Oh, when we talk so, we betray the darkness in which we are living, the self-deception we are fostering, the corruption we are degenerating into, and the desertion we are provoking. Such backsliding as this will soon make Jesus hide his face from us.

Beloved, the simple reason for Christ's conscious absence from our souls is, in most cases, sin. I say "in most cases", for sometimes Christ may hide himself in absolute sovereignty, but I am always jealous lest we should charge God foolishly. You are so apt to put too many saddles on that stalking horse. There are such multitudes of professors who would even excuse their sins on the plea of divine sovereignty which exposed them to temptation, but I scarcely like to mention it. I believe that God does not afflict willingly or arbitrarily, the children of men. Neither does Christ hide his face from his people for nothing; but "your iniquities have separated between you and your God, and your sins have hid his face from you that he will not hear." (Is. 59:2) He chastises us, not as silly parents may do, out of mere spleen or caprice, or to please themselves, as the Apostle seemed to think some fathers did in his day; for he says, "They verily chastened us after their own pleasure." (Heb. 12:10) But when God chastens us, it is for our profit. Our good is his aim, and his end in using the rod of correction. He makes us smart for the sin which seemed sweet. He nauseates our palate with the bitter fruits of disobedience, that we may afterwards relish the peaceable fruit of righteousness. (Verse 11)

Now, beloved, in each individual case, the hiding of the Lord's face may be occasioned by a different sin. It is very probable that my Lord thinks it to be a high sin in me which he would take little notice of in you. It is equally possible that he may think something peculiarly offensive in you that he would not visit in my case with stripes, for according to our constitution, our office, our experience, our light, and our several circumstances, may our transgressions be estimated. You are not provoked, perhaps, by a good deal of noise from one of your children, but half that noise from another infant would vex you exceedingly. Because the one happens to be of a quick, impetuous temperament, you put it down to natural disposition; but the other being of gentler habit and quieter mood, you reprove him for his excitement, as if it were of evil propensity, intended to aggravate and annoy. So you may have a confidential servant in your family, from whom you may reasonably expect more care, thoughtfulness, and circumspection than you look for in any of the other servants. The more trust you repose, the more scrupulousness you require.

Let us, then, each one according to his position, seek grace to walk uprightly, carefully, and tenderly. It has been well said that what an ordinary subject might do or say, one of the Cabinet Council must not even think. The favourite of kings has a dangerous path to walk, and though it is a blessed privilege to be a favourite of heaven, it involves a very solemn responsibility. "You only have I known of all the inhabitants of the earth; therefore, I will punish you for your iniquities." (Amos 3:2) You can see defilement on a white slab which you would not have noticed on the common soil; so there are sins which spoil the character of saints that would hardly be observed in ordinary society. The presence of Christ can only be preserved with incessant watchfulness and inviolate fidelity. The sacred Dove is soon disturbed. The Beloved is soon woken up and made to stir. Hence it should be our cry, "I charge you by the roes and by the hinds of the field, that ye stir not up, nor awake, my love until he please." (Song 2:7, 3:5)

Having thus considered the reason why the Beloved is gone, let us enquire:

II. WHAT FOLLOWS AFTER THE WITHDRAWAL OF HIS PRESENCE?

Great mistakes have been made on this subject. Some suppose that believers suddenly cease to be followers of Christ, go back into the world, apostatise, and perish. But the Lord does not desert his people in this way. He has not cast away his people whom he foreknew, and he never will. Once he has put his hand to the work of their salvation, he will not turn away from them. When he turns away, it is always with a gracious motive; hence the consequences, though often very sad, are not fatal. The withdrawal of his conscious presence is not intended to slay us, though it brings us very low, and would leave us a prey to destruction were it not that he stays his hand in time, and gives grace to keep the soul alive in its desertion.

As soon as ever Christ has gone, there is a suspension of those influences that once made the Christian happy and strong. The Holy Spirit no longer comforts the soul. The

444

Word does not enliven or invigorate. The sweetest sermons fail to cheer the heart. Even the promises of God's Holy Book are like lanterns without candles, bringing no light. When Christ hides his face from a disciple, his spirits flag, and he feels a general depression. He cannot pray as it was his wont to do, and he cannot preach as he once did. The holy duties to which he tenaciously clings become rather a burden than a pleasure. Instead of those delightful walks he had alone, when his soul went up to God in quiet meditation, he finds his thoughts have all dissipated, scattered here and there. Nor can he by any means concentrate them, far less making them soar and mount towards Christ. He goes to his Bible — not as often as he did, nor yet as solemnly as he did — but the book does not speak to him. God answers him neither by Urim nor by Thummim, nor by open voice. And now he does not seem to have the illuminations of God's Spirit. He does not dive into the meaning of the Word as once he did. Providence, again, seems dark. The secret of the Lord does not appear to be with him as it was formerly. He has no enjoyment. The soul follows after God after a fashion; but, alas, he has to cry, "Why art thou cast down, O my soul, and why art thou disquieted within met?" (Ps. 42:5, 11, 43:5) Thus divine influences are, for a while, suspended.

Then it follows that he loses much of his assurance. He used to know he was a Christian. Now, he begins to sing,

'Tis a point I long to know,
Oft it causes anxious thought;
Do I love the Lord, or no?
Am I his, or am I not?

(John Newton)

So he has to furbish up his old evidences, and eat some of the stale meat that he used to care little for when he was living on a daily portion from the King, even a portion from the King's table. He sits down in the ashes and is glad to sit there. Sometimes, he mourns because he cannot mourn, and frets because he cannot fret. While he sees his sin, he is afraid he has not a true feeling for it. Though he still looks to the cross of Christ, and to the precious blood of atonement, he does not seem to have the power of looking that he once had, nor derive that comfort that comes from casting himself on the finished work, which previously he did when Jesus Christ was manifestly with him.

The parable of the deserted house

Perhaps it will aid you in realising the dark features of this desertion if I use a little parable. You see often enough a house that is left by its former tenant, and is shut up. Jesus Christ never altogether leaves a heart of which he has once taken possession. There is one room in a believer's soul which the Holy Spirit never quits. Where he comes, he comes to abide, and abide forever. Still, that room is so secret that, while he resides there, the whole house may look as if it were deserted. Compare that empty house with a cheerful home. What a contrast between its previous and present condition! Why, the joy has gone from it. The blinds are drawn down — or, maybe the windows stare at you in their desolation. The house looks unfurnished. It is no longer an ornament to the street. Its decorations have vanished since its inhabitants fled. The house is there, with all its capacities, but the home, with all its vivacities, is a-wanting. The life and the loveliness have gone from it. And so it is a child of God soon loses all his joy and comfort when the tenant of his soul is withdrawn. No sparkling of the eye, no singing of the great hallelujahs, no sounding of the cymbals, even the high-sounding cymbals. (Ps. 150:5) He would be glad enough to get a note out of the sackbut now. He cannot get up to those glorious

445

songs which once made his spirit keep tune with the angels because the joys of heaven had come down to earth.

Then the house, being empty, is sure to get into a filthy state. There is nobody to clean or dust; all sorts of spiders and foul things get into the corners and crannies, and, the longer the house is shut up, the more these creatures multiply. Down in the cellar, there is a little vegetation — long yellow stalks and roots trying to live — left there by some old inhabitant. But there is nothing fair or beautiful; all is uncomfortable. So it gets to be in our hearts; all sorts of evils spring up. Evils we little suspected, which would have been kept in check by the presence of Christ, begin to multiply and increase in us, and the little good that is there seems be an unhealthy sprout, producing nothing to perfection.

A house with nobody in it decays. How the metal rusts! How the paint gets stained! How the wood begins to rot! How the whole thing has a damp kind of smell! It is all going to ruin. Why, ten years of habitation would not do so much mischief as these twelve months of being shut up. When Jesus Christ has gone, everything is amiss — love nearly expires, hope scarcely glimmers, faith is well-nigh paralysed, no grace is in lively exercise. Without the life of God in the soul, there is a total collapse, and a chill strikes right through the spirit. Has the house been long empty? The boys outside are pretty sure to mark it for their sport, and break the windows. In fact, it stands exposed to all sorts of outward damage. So, too, with malice and mischief, the devil comes upon a man when he knows that he has lost the light of God's countenance. What a horrid old coward he is! When the child of God is rejoicing in the company of Christ, he has not often to encounter Satan. The accuser of the brethren well knows how to time his tactics and his temptations. But when he sees that the Lord has departed, then Satan takes courage, and attacks the child of God to his serious damage and hurt.

I heard the other day of a good country ploughman who told a story of victory over temptation in his own simple style. He was a man who feared God above his neighbours, and seemed to live above the world in spiritual things. A minister asked him if he did not get tempted and worried sometimes by Satan. "Yes", he said; "I have known much about being tempted by Satan in my time. Why, sir, ten years ago I was threshing in this barn here, and the devil came upon me with a strong temptation. It plagued and worried me so much that I could not get rid of it; till at length I put down my flail, and got away into a corner, just beyond the wheat there, and I wrestled with God against him until I gained such a victory that I came back to my place rejoicing. Many a time since then", said the old man, "he has lurked about my path; but I never stop to parley. I repeat the promise by which I found a way of escape that day in this barn, and I feel myself made strong by the remembrance of that victory." Yes, and just so when we can remember some of those occasions when we seemed to overcome temptation by private communion with God; it was then we got strong, but,

But if the Lord be once withdrawn,
And we attempt the work alone,
When new temptations spring and rise,
We find how great our weakness is.

(Isaac Watts)

Like Samson (which Dr. Watts mentions in the next verse), when his hair was shorn, we think we will defeat Satan as at other times, but we,

...make our limbs with vain surprise,
Make feeble fight, and shut our eyes.

446

When houses have long been left without tenants, and look deserted, some get up a rumour that they are haunted. And sure I am that, when a heart has been left by Christ, and there have been no comfortable enjoyments of his presence, our souls are haunted with strange, mysterious doubts and fears, vexations and forebodings which you cannot grapple with; horrors that do not take any shape; troubles that ought not to be distressing; alarms that are made up of shadows; dangers that have not any real existence. Oh, that Christ were there! As phantoms all vanish in the sunlight, so all these dreary doubts and dismal dilemmas are chased away if Christ returned. Oh, that our poor empty house could once more have its gates flung open wide, and that the King could come to dwell in his own palace, and make it all bright and lustrous with his presence! Master, see how sick we are without you! Come, blessed Physician! Jesus, see what wretched beings we are if you withdraw! Come, our Beloved, come to us! Let the sad effects of your departure quicken your footsteps, and bring you over the mountains of Bether (division) to the longing spirits of your fainting children.

Passing on, let us enquire:

III. WHAT COMFORT THERE IS FOR A SOUL WHEN THE BELOVED HAS WITHDRAWN HIMSELF AND HAS GONE!

Let me reply, there is no comfort at all that will be of any service to you unless you get him back. Ah, but if a wife loves her husband, and he has gone away, we may quote the old song:

There is nae luck about the house
When the gude man's awa'.
There's little pleasure in the house
When my gude-man's awa'.

(The Mariner's Wife, 1776)

The dear man, the joy of her heart, being gone, she could not make anything go well. And so, where the loving heart has lost its Beloved, its best Beloved, there seems to be no joy anywhere. Nothing can make up to a regenerate soul for the loss of the society of her Lord. And yet some considerations may help stay us while we are seeking for it. Though he has gone, he is our Beloved still. Though we cannot see him, yet we love him; and, if we cannot enjoy him, we thirst after him, and that is some consolation, though a poor consolation, thinking it has not quite lost all its life, for it has got life enough to smart, and life enough to be in pain, and life enough to feel itself in exile until Christ's return. I think, too, there is some comfort in this, that though he has gone, he has gone out of love. Was it in a tiff of anger? Yet it was rather a rebuke of our sins than a rejection of our person. Christ withdraws because he wants to bring us to our senses, and draw us more closely to himself. He knows that if we were to have enjoyments, and yet walk in sin, this would be highly dangerous; therefore, these enjoyments must be withheld till the heart is broken, and the soul abhors itself in dust and ashes. (Job 42:6)

It is some comfort also that, though he has gone, he has not gone out of earshot. Jesus Christ can still hear the cry of his people. No, he has not gone beyond the reach of his eyesight. He is looking upon his poor deserted one to see what the effect of his hiding himself is.

And there is this to be said, that he is not so far gone but what, at any moment, he can return, and his return can at once make our souls like the chariots of Aminnadib. He can

447

rise is our darkness, and that in the next instant if it so pressed him. He has gone, but not altogether gone. He has not taken his love from us, nor shall his loving-kindness utterly fail. Still on his hands, he bears the marks of his passion for our salvation. Still on his breast plate, glitter the jewels that bear our names. He cannot forget us, though he hides himself. He may be asleep, but it is in the same vessel with us, and near the helm. He may appear to have utterly deserted us, but "can a woman forget her sucking child that she should not have compassion on the son of her womb." (Is. 49:15) Yes, she may forget, but Christ will never forget his saints.

Now, lastly:

IV. WHAT IS OUR DUTY IN SUCH A PLIGHT?

If he has gone, what then? I answer: our duty is to repent of what drove him away. We must institute a search at once. Bunyan describes the citizens of Mansoul as searching for the reason why Prince Immanuel had withdrawn himself; and they took Master Carnal-Security and burned his house, and hanged him on a gallows on the site where the house stood, for it was through feasting with him that the Prince was angered, and his subjects lost his presence. Search yourselves if you are not as happy as you once were; if you are not living as near heaven-gate as you used to be, see to it yourselves. And having so done, and found out the evil, ask grace to purge it. Oh, you will fall into that evil again if you trust in your own strength, but, in reliance on the Holy Spirit's power, you can overcome it. You can put your foot on the neck of this evil, and so destroy it, that it shall not molest you again.

And then, beloved, let me earnestly entreat you — and I am speaking more to myself, perhaps, than I am to any of you — to stir up your whole soul to recover lost ground. Be ashamed that there is any lost ground to recover. Oh, it is easier to lose Christ than it is to find him after we have lost him! It is easier to go straight on in the strength of grace than it is, like the Pilgrim, to have to go back to find your roll which you have lost under the settle in the arbour of ease, and then, after going back, to go over the same ground again. When you have got the wings of an eagle, what blessed work it is to soar, and to pass over long tracks of country! But when the eagle-wing is gone, and you have to limp painfully along like David, with broken bones, it is hard work. But, beloved, if you have slipped at all, ask grace to recover now. For my own part, I feel I have so little grace that I have none to lose. As for falling back — oh, what should we be if we fell at all back; for we are back enough now! We are nowhere at all in comparison with the saints of God in the olden days. We are but beginners and babes, but where, where, where, shall we be if we are to go farther back still? No, no, sovereign grace will prevent so dreadful a catastrophe! Press forward. And, brethren, will it not be a great thing, and a right thing, for us to endeavour to set apart much time for special prayer that we may have lost grace restored? Should we not set ourselves to this one thing, that we must get back by the simplicity of faith to the cross-foot, and, by the earnestness of love, to the bosom of the Master once more; and then we will not be satisfied with preaching, and praying, and going to places of worship, or with ordinances, or with anything, until we get Christ back again? Oh, my soul, I charge you to be content with nothing till you get your Lord again. Say, with the good housewife I spoke of just now, whose husband was away from home, "Yes, this room must be decorated, and every part of the house cleaned; but, ah, the joy of my heart to see him return, and, until he comes, the house cannot be cheerful and joyful." It is so with our souls. We must have the King back, and back soon. But when he does come back, we must hold him fast and not let him go. Charge your souls to be more careful in the future, lest you again provoke him to jealousy.

Alas for those who never knew my Lord! Oh, may they seek him early, and find him speedily! If it is sad to lose his presence for a while, what must it be to live and die without Christ? Oh, that is a black word for anyone to have written on his brow, "Without Christ"! If you are in this condition, dear hearer, may divine grace bring you to Christ and Christ to you, that you may enjoy the fellowship of his love! Amen.

60. HEAVENLY LOVE-SICKNESS!

NO. 539

A SERMON DELIVERED ON SUNDAY MORNING,
NOVEMBER 8TH, 1863
AT THE METROPOLITAN TABERNACLE, NEWINGTON

"I charge you, O daughters of Jerusalem, if ye find my beloved, that ye tell him that I am sick of love." (Song of Solomon 5:8)

SICK! That is a sad thing; it moves your pity. Sick of love — love-sick! Something that stirs up other emotions which we shall presently attempt to explain. No doubt certain sicknesses are peculiar to the saints: the ungodly are never visited with them. Strange to say, these sicknesses, to which the refined sensibilities of the children of God render them peculiarly liable, are signs of vigorous health. Who but the beloved of the Lord ever experience that *sin-sickness* in which the soul loathes the very name of transgression, is unmoved by the enchantments of the tempter, finds no sweetness in its besetting sins, but turns with detestation and abhorrence from the very thought of iniquity? Not less is it for these, and these alone, to feel that *self-sickness* whereby the heart revolts from all creature-confidence and strength, having been made sick of self, self-seeking, self-exalting, self reliance, and self of every sort. The Lord afflicts us more and more with such self-sickness till we are dead to self, its puny conceits, its lofty aims, and its unsanctified desires. Then there is a *twofold love-sickness*. Of the one kind is that love-sickness which comes upon the Christian when he is transported with the full enjoyment of Jesus, even as the bride elated by the favour, melted by the tenderness of her Lord, says in the fifth verse of the second chapter of the Song, "Stay me with flagons, comfort me with apples: for I am sick of love." The soul overjoyed with the divine communications of happiness and bliss which came from Christ, the body scarcely able to bear the excessive delirium of delight which the soul possessed, she was so glad to be in the embraces of her Lord, that she needed to be stayed under her overpowering weight of joy. Another kind of love-sickness widely different from the first, is that in which the soul is sick, not because it has too much of Christ's love, but because it has not enough present consciousness of it; sick, not of the enjoyment, but of the longing for it; sick, not because of excess of delight, but because of sorrow for an absent lover. It is to this sickness we call your attention this morning. Their love-sickness breaks out in two ways, and may be viewed in two lights. It is, first of all, the soul *longing for a view of Jesus Christ in grace*; and then again, it is the same soul *possessing the view of grace, and longing for a sight of Jesus Christ in glory*. In both these senses we, us accurately as the spouse, may adopt the languishing words, "If ye find my beloved, tell him that I am sick of love."

I. First, then, let us consider our text as the language of a soul LONGING FOR THE VIEW OF JESUS CHRIST IN GRACE.

1. Do ye ask me concerning *the sickness itself*: What is it? It is the sickness of a soul panting after communion with Christ. The man is a believer; he is not longing after salvation as a penitent sinner under conviction, for he is saved. Moreover, he has love to Christ, and knows it; he does not doubt his evidence as to the reality of his affection for his Lord, for you see the word used is "*My* beloved," which would not be applicable if the person speaking had any doubt about her interest; nor did she doubt her love, for she calls the spouse, "My *beloved*." It is the longing of a soul, then, not for salvation, and not even for the certainty of salvation, but for the enjoyment of present fellowship with him who is her soul's life, her soul's all. The heart is panting to be brought once more under the apple tree; to feel once again his "left hand under her head, while his right hand doth embrace her." She has known, in days past, what it is to be brought into his banqueting house, and to see the banner of love waved over her, and she therefore cries to have love visits renewed. It is a panting after communion. Gracious hours, my dear friends, are never perfectly at ease except they are in a state of nearness to Christ; for mark you, when they are not near to Christ, they lose *their* peace. The nearer to Jesus, the nearer to the perfect calm of heaven; and the further from Jesus, the nearer to that troubled sea which images the continual unrest of the wicked. There is no peace to the man who doth not dwell constantly under the shadow of the cross; for Jesus is our peace, and if he be absent, our peace is absent too. I know that being justified, we have peace with God, but it is "through our Lord Jesus Christ." So that the justified man himself cannot reap the fruit of justification, except by abiding in Christ Jesus, who is the Lord and Giver of peace. The Christian without fellowship with Christ loses all his *life* and energy; he is like a dead thing. Though saved, he lies like a lumpish log:

Come, Holy Spirit, heavenly Dove,
With all thy quickening powers;
Kindle a flame of sacred love,
In these cold hearts of ours,

Look how we grovel here below,
Fond of these earthly toys;
Our souls can neither fly nor go
To reach eternal joys.

(Isaac Watts)

He is without vivacity, yes, more, he is without animation till Jesus comes; but when the Lord sensibly sheds abroad his love in our hearts, then *his* love kindles ours; then our blood leaps in our veins for joy, like the Baptist in the womb of Elizabeth. The heart when near to Jesus has strong pulsations, for since Jesus is in that heart, it is full of life, of vigour, and of strength. Peace, liveliness, vigour — all depend upon the constant enjoyment of communion with Christ Jesus. The soul of a Christian never knows what *joy* means in its true solidity, except when she sits like Mary at Jesus' feet. Beloved, all the joys of life are nothing to us; we have melted them all down in our crucible, and found them to be dross. You and I have tried earth's vanities, and they cannot satisfy us; nay, they do not give a morsel of meat to satiate our hunger. Being in a state of dissatisfaction with all mortal things, we have learned through divine grace, that none but Jesus, none but Jesus can make our souls glad. "Philosophers are happy without music" said one of old. So Christians are happy without the world's goods. Christians, with the world's good, are sure to bemoan themselves as naked, poor, and miserable, unless their Saviour is with them. You that have ever tasted communion with Christ will soon know why it is that a soul longs after him. What the sun is to the day, what the moon is to the night, what the dew is to the flower, such is Jesus Christ to us. What bread is to the hungry, clothes to the naked, the shadow of a great rock to the traveller in a weary land, such is Jesus Christ to us. What the turtle is to her mate, what the husband is to his spouse, what the head is to the body, such is Jesus Christ to us; and therefore, if we have him not, nay, if we are not conscious of having him; if we are not one with him, nay, if we are not consciously one with him, little marvel if our spirit cries in the words of the Song, "I charge you, O ye daughters of Jerusalem, if ye find my beloved, tell him that I am sick of love." Such is the character of this love-sickness.

We may say of it, however, before we leave that point, that it is *a sickness which has a blessing attending it*: "Blessed are they that do hunger and thirst after righteousness;" and therefore, supremely blessed are they who thirst after the Righteous One — after him,

451

who in the highest perfection embodies pure, immaculate, spotless righteousness. Blessed is that hunger, for it comes from God! It bears a blessing within it; for if I may not have the blessedness in full bloom of being filled, the next best thing is the same blessedness in sweet bud of being empty till I am filled with Christ. If I may not feed on Jesus, it shall be next door to heaven to be allowed to hunger and thirst after him. There is a hallowedness about that hunger, since it sparkles among the beatitudes of our Lord. Yet it is a sickness, dear friends, which, despite the blessing, *causes much pain*. The man who is sick after Jesus, will be dissatisfied with everything else; he will find that dainties have lost their sweetness, and music its melody, and light its brightness, and life itself will be darkened with the shadow of death to him, till he finds his Lord, and can rejoice in him. Beloved, ye shall find that this thirsting, this sickness, if it ever gets hold upon you, is *attended with great vehemence*. The desire is vehement, as coals of juniper. Ye have heard of hunger that it breaks through stone walls: but stone walls are no prison to a soul that desires Christ. Stone walls, no, the strongest natural barriers, cannot keep a lovesick heart from Jesus. I will venture to say that the temptation of heaven itself, if it could be offered to the believer without his Christ, would be as less than nothing; and the pains of hell, if they could be endured, would be gladly ventured upon by a love-sick soul, if he might but find Christ. As lovers sometimes talk of doing impossibilities for their fair ones, so certainly a spirit that is set on Christ will laugh at impossibility, and say, "It shall be done." It will venture upon the hardest task, go cheerfully to prison and joyfully to death if it may, but find the beloved, and have its love-sickness satisfied with his presence. Perhaps this may suffice for a description of the sickness here intended.

2. You may enquire concerning the cause of this love-sickness. What maketh a man's soul so sick after Christ? Understand that it is the *absence* of Christ which makes this sickness in a mind that really understands the preciousness of his presence. The spouse had been very wilful and wayward, she had taken off her garments, had gone to her rest, her sluggish slothful rest, when her beloved knocked at the door. He said "Open to me, my beloved; for my head is filled with dew, and my locks with the drops of the night." She was too slothful to wake up to let him in. She urged excuses — "I have put off my coat; how shall I put it on? I have washed my feet: how shall I defile them?" The beloved stood waiting, but since she opened not he put in his hand by the hole of the lock, and then her heart was moved towards him. She went to the door to open it, and to her surprise, her hands dropped with myrrh, and her fingers with sweet smelling myrrh upon the handles of the lock. There was the token that he had been there, but he was gone. Now she began to bestir herself, and seek after him. She sought him through the city, but she found him not. Her soul failed her; she called after him, but he gave her no answer, and the watchman, who ought to have helped her in the search, smote her, and took away her veil from her. Therefore it is that now she is seeking, because she has lost her beloved. She should have held him fast, and not have permitted him to go. He is absent, and she is sick till she finds him.

Mingled with the sense of absence is *a consciousness of wrong doing*. Something in her seemed to say, "How couldst thou drive him away? That heavenly bridegroom who knocked and pleaded hard, how couldst thou keep him longer there amidst the cold dews of night? O unkind heart! What if thy feet had been made to bleed by thy rising? What if all thy body had seen chilled by the cold wind, when thou wast treading the floor? What had it been, compared with his love to you?" And so she is sick to see him, that she may weep out her love and tell him how vexed she is with herself that she should have held to him so loosely, and permitted him so readily to depart. So, too, mixed with this, was *great wretchedness* because he was gone. She had been for a little time easy in his absence. That downy bed, that warm coverlet, had given her a peace, a false, cruel, and a wicked peace, but she has risen now, the watchmen have smitten her, her veil is gone, and, without a friend, the princess, deserted in the midst of Jerusalem's streets, has her soul

452

melted for heaviness, and she pours out her heart within her as she pines after her lord. "No love but my love, no lord but my lord," saith she, with sobbing tongue and weeping eyes; for none else can gratify her heart or appease her anxiety. Beloved, have you never been in such a state, when your faith has begun to droop, and your heart and spirits have fled from you? Even then it was your soul was sick for him. You could do without him when Mr. Carnal-security was in the house, and feasted you, but when he and his house have both been burned with fire, the old love-sickness came back, and you wanted Christ, nor could ye be satisfied till ye found him once again. There was *true love* in all this, and this is the very pith of all love-sickness. Had not she loved, absence would not have made her sick, nor would her repentance have made her grieve. Had she not loved, there would have been no pain because of absence, and no sinking of spirits, but she did love, thence all this sickness. It is a delightful thing to be able to know when we have lost Christ's company, that we do love him — "'Yea, Lord, thou knowest all things; thou knowest that I love thee.' I did deny thee, yea, in the moment of thy sorrow, I said, 'I know not the man.' I did curse and swear that men might think I was no follower of thine, but still thou knowest all things; thou knowest that I love thee." When you can feel this, dear friends, the consciousness that you love will soon work in you a *heart-burning*, so that your soul will not be satisfied till you can tell out that love in the Master's presence, and he shall say unto you, as a token of forgiveness, "Feed my sheep." I do not doubt that in this sickness there had been *some degree of fear*. Sorrowful woman! She was half afraid she might never find him again. She had been about the city — where could he be? She had sought him on the walls and on the ramparts, but he was not there. In every ordinance, in every means of grace, in secret and in public prayer, in the Lord's Supper, and in the reading of the Word, she had looked after him, but he was not there; and now she was half afraid that though he might give his presence to others, yet never to her, and when she speaks, you notice there is half a fear in it. She would not have asked others to tell him if she had any assuring hope that she should meet him herself — "If ye find him," she seems to say, "O ye true converts, you that are the real grace-born daughters of Jerusalem; if he reveals himself to you, though he never may to me, do me this kindness, tell him that I am sick of love." There is half a fear here, and yet there is *some hope*. She feels that he must love her still, or else why send a message at all? She would surely never send this sweet message to a flinty, adamantine heart, "Tell him I am sick of love," but she remembered when the "glancings of her eyes had ravished him; she remembered when a motion from her hand had made his heart melt, and when one tear of her eyes had opened all his wounds afresh. She thinks, "Perhaps, he loves me still as he loved me then, and my moanings will enchain him; my groans will constrain him and lead him to my help." So she sends the message to him — "Tell him, tell him I am sick of love." To gather up the causes of this love-sickness in a few words, does not the whole matter spring from *relationship?* She is his spouse; can the spouse be happy without her beloved lord? It springs from union; she is part of himself. Can the hand be happy and healthy if the life-floods stream not from the heart and from the head? Fondly realising her *dependence*, she feels that she owes all to him, and gets her all from him. If then the fountain be cut off, if the streams be dried, if the great source of all be taken from her, how can she but be sick? And there is besides this, *a life and a nature* in her which makes her sick. There is a life like the life of Christ, nay, her life is in Christ, it is hid with Christ in God; her nature is a part of the divine nature; she is a partaker of the divine nature. Moreover she is in *union* with Jesus, and this piece divided, as it were, from the body, wriggles, like a worm cut asunder, and pants to get back to where it came from. These are the causes of it. You will not understand my sermon this morning but think me raving, unless you are spiritual men. "But the spiritual judgeth all things, yet he himself is judged of no man."

3. *What endeavours such love-sick souls make!* Those who are sick for Christ will first send their *desires* to him. Men use pigeons sometimes to send their messages. Why, what sort of carrier pigeons do they use? The pigeon is of no use to send anywhere but to the place from which it came, and my desires after Christ came from him, and so they will always go back to the place from which they came, they know the way to their own dovecot, so I will send him my sighs and my groans, my tears and my moans. Go, go, sweet doves, with swift and clipping wings, and tell him I am sick of love. Then she would send her *prayers*. Ah, I think she would say of her desires, "They will never reach him; they know the way but their wings are broken, and they will fall to the ground and never reach him." Yet she will send them whether they reach him or not. As for her prayers, they are like arrows. Sometimes messages have been sent into besieged towns bound to an arrow, so she binds her desires upon the arrow of her prayers, and then shoots them forth from the bow of her faith. She is afraid they will never reach him, for her bow is slack, and she knoweth not how to draw it with her feeble hands which hang down. So what does she do? She has traversed the streets; she has used *the means*; she has done everything; she has sighed her heart out, and emptied her soul out in prayers. She is all wounds till he heals her; she is all a hungry mouth till he fills her; she is all an empty brook till he replenishes her once again, and so now she *goeth to her companions*, and she saith, "If ye find my beloved, tell him I am sick of love." This is using the intercession of the saints. It is unbelief that makes her use it, and yet there is a little faith mixed in her unbelief. It was unbelief, but not a misbelief. There is efficacy in the intercession of saints. Not of dead saints — they have enough to do to be singing God's praises in heaven without praying for us — but saints on earth can take up our case. The king has his favourites; he has his cup-bearers; he has some that are admitted into great familiarity with him: give me a share in a good man's prayers. I attribute under God the success the Lord has given me, to the number of souls in every quarter of the earth who pray for me — not you alone, but in every land there are some that forget me not when they draw near in their supplications. Oh! we are so rich when we have the prayers of saints. When it is well with thee, speak for me to the Captain of the host, and if he should say to thee, "What was his message?" I have no other message but that of the spouse, "Tell him I am sick of love." Any of you who have close familiarity with Jesus, be the messengers, be the heavenly tale-bearers between love-sick souls and their divine Lord. Tell him, tell him, we are sick of love. And you that cannot thus go to him, seek the help and aid of others. But after all, as I have said this is unbelief though it is not misbelief, for how much better it would have been for her to *tell him herself*. "But," you say, "she could not find him." Nay, but if she had had faith she would have known that her prayers could; for our prayers know where Christ is when we do not know, or rather, Christ knows where our prayers are, and when we cannot see him they reach him nevertheless. A man who fires a cannon is not expected to see all the way which the shot goes. If he has his cannon rightly sighted and fires it, there may come on a thick fog, but the shot will reach the place; and if you have your hearts sighted by divine grace after Christ, you may depend upon it, however thick the fog, the hot-shot of your prayer will reach the gates of heaven though ye cannot tell how or where. Be satisfied to go to a Christ yourself. If your brethren will go, well and good, but I think their proper answer to your question would be in the language of the women in the sixth chapter, the first verse, "Whither is thy beloved gone, O thou fairest among women? Whither is thy beloved turned aside, that we may seek him with thee?" They will not seek him *for* us they say, but they can seek him *with* us. Sometimes, when there are six pair of eyes, they will see better than one; and so, if five or six Christians seek the Lord in company, in the prayer-meeting, or at his table, they are more likely to find him. "We will seek him with thee."

4. Blessed love-sickness! We have seen its character and its cause, and the endeavour of the soul under it; let us just notice *the comforts which belong to such a state as this*. Briefly they are these — *you shall be filled*. It is impossible for Christ to set you longing after him without intending to give himself to you. It is as when a great man doth make a feast. He first puts plates upon the table, and then afterwards there cometh the meat. Your longings and desirings are the empty plates to hold the meat. Is it likely that he means to mock you? Would he have put the dishes there if he did not intend to fill them with his oxen and with his fatlings? He makes you long: he will certainly satisfy your longings. Remember, again, that he will give you himself *all the sooner for the bitterness of your longings*. The more pained your heart is at his absence the shorter will the absence be. If you have a grain of contentment without Christ, that will keep you longer tarrying but when your soul is sick till your heart is ready to break, till you cry, "Why does he tarry? Why are his chariots so long in coming?" when your soul faints until your beloved speaks unto you, and you are ready to die from your youth up, then in no long space he will lift the veil from his dear face, and your sun shall rise with healing beneath his wings. Let that console you. Then, again, when he does come, as come he will, oh, *how sweet it will be!* I think I have the flavour in my mouth now, and the fullness of the feast is yet to come. There is such a delight about the very thought that he will come, that the thought itself is the prelude, the foretaste, the antepast of the happy greeting. What! Will he once again speak comfortably to me? Shall I again walk the bed of spices with him?

Shall I ramble with him amongst the groves while the flowers give forth their sweet perfume: I shall! I shall! And even now, my spirit feels his presence by anticipation: "Or ever I was aware, my soul made me like the chariots of Amminadib." You know how sweet it was in the past. Beloved, what times we have had, some of us. Oh, whether in the body or out of the body, we cannot tell — God knoweth. What mountings! Talking of eagles' wings — they are earthly pinions, and may not be compared with the wings with which he carried us up from earth. Speak of mounting beyond clouds and stars! — they were left far, far behind. We entered into the unseen, beheld the invisible, lived in the immortal, drank in the ineffable, and were blessed with the fullness of God in Christ Jesus, being made to sit together in heavenly places in him. Well, all this is to come again, "I will see you again, and your heart shall rejoice." "A little while, and ye shall not see me: and again, a little while, and ye shall see me." "In a little wrath I hid my face from thee for a moment; but with everlasting kindness will I have mercy on thee, saith the Lord thy Redeemer." Think of this. Why, we have comfort even in this sickness of love. Our heart, though sick, is still whole, while we are panting and pining after the Lord Jesus.

O love divine, how sweet thou art!
When shall I find my willing heart
All taken up by thee?
I thirst, I faint, I die to prove
The fullness of redeeming love,
The love of Christ to me!

(Charles Wesley)

II. And now, secondly, with as great brevity as we can. This love-sickness may be seen in A SOUL-LONGING FOR A VIEW OF JESUS IN HIS GLORY.

1. And here we will consider *the complaint* itself for a moment. This ailment is not merely a longing after communion with Christ on earth — that has been enjoyed, and generally this sickness follows that:

Since I have tasted of the grapes,
I ofttimes long to go
Where my dear Lord the vineyard keeps
And all the clusters grow.

Upon the true and living vine
My famished soul will feast,

455

And banquet on the fruit divine,
An everlasting guest

It is the enjoyment of Eshcol's first fruits which makes us desire to sit under our own vine and our own fig tree before the throne of God in the blessed land.

Beloved, this sickness is characterised by certain marked symptoms; I will tell you what they are. There is a loving and a longing, a loathing and a languishing. O happy soul that understands these things by experience. There is *a loving* in which the heart cleaves to Jesus:

Do not I love thee from my soul?
Then let me nothing love:
Dead be my heart to every joy
When Jesus cannot move.

(Philip Doddridge)

A sense of his beauty! An admiration of his charms! A consciousness of his infinite perfection! Yes, greatness, goodness, and loveliness, in one resplendent ray combine to enchant the soul till it is so ravished after him that it cries with the spouse, "Yea, he is altogether lovely. This is my beloved, and this is my friend, O ye daughters of Jerusalem." Sweet loving this — a love which binds the heart with chains of more than silken softness, and yet than adamant more firm.

Then there is *a longing*. She loves him so that she cannot endure to be absent from him; she pants and pines. You know it has been so with saints in all ages; whenever they have begun to love they have always begun to long after Christ. John, the most loving of spirits, is the author of those words which he so frequently uses — "Come quickly, even so, come quickly." "Come quickly" is sure to be the fruit of earnest love. See how the spouse puts it — "O that thou wert as my brother, that sucked the breasts of my mother! When I should find thee without, I would kiss thee; yea, I should not be despised." She longs to get hold of him; she cannot conclude her song without saying, "Make haste, my beloved, and be thou like to a roe or to a young hart upon the mountains of spices." There is a longing to be with Christ. I would not give much for your religion if you do not long to be with the object of your heart's affections.

Then comes *a loathing*. When a man is sick with the first lovesickness, then he does not loathe — it is, "Stay me with flagons, comfort me with apples." When a man has Christ, he can enjoy other things; but when a man is longing after Christ and seeking after Christ, he loathes everything else — he cannot bear anything besides. Here is my message to Jesus: "Tell him — "what? Do I want crowns and diadems? Crowns and diadems are nothing to me. Do I want wealth, and health, and strength? They are all very well in their way. No — "Tell him, tell the beloved of my soul that I grieve after himself — his gifts are good — I ought to be more grateful for them than I am, but let me see his face; let me hear his voice. I am sick of love, and nothing but that can satisfy me, everything else is distasteful to me." And then there is a *languishing*. Since she cannot get the society of Christ, cannot as yet behold him on his throne nor worship him face to face, she is sick until she can. For a heart so set on Christ will walk about traversing highway and by-way, resting nowhere till it finds him. As the needle once magnetised will never be easy until it finds the pole, so the heart once Christianised never will be satisfied until it rests on Christ — rests on him, too, in the fullness of the beatific vision before the throne. This is the character of the love-sickness.

2. *As to its object* — what is that? "Tell him that I am sick of love;" but what is the sickness for? Brethren, when you and I want to go to heaven I hope it is the true love-sickness. I catch myself sometimes wanting to die and be in heaven for the sake of rest; but is not that a lazy desire? There is a sluggish wish that makes me long for rest. Perhaps, we long for the happiness of heaven — the harps and crowns. There is a little selfishness in that, is there not? Allowable, I grant you; but is not there a little like selfishness? Perhaps, we long to see dear children, beloved friends that have gone before; but there is a little of the earthy there. The soul may be as sick as it will, without rebuke, when it is sick to be with Jesus. You may indulge this carry it to its utmost extent without either sin or folly. What am I sick with love for? For the pearly gates? No; but for the pearls that are in his wounds. What am I sick for? For the streets of gold? No; but for his head which is as much fine gold. For the melody of the harps and angelic songs? No, but for the melodious notes that come from his dear mouth. What am I sick for? For the nectar that angels drink? No; but for the kisses of his lips. For the manna on which heavenly souls feed? No; but for himself, who is the meat and drink of his saints himself; himself — my soul pines to see him. Oh, what a heaven to gaze upon! What bliss to talk with the man, the God, crucified for me; to weep my heart out before him; to tell him how I love him, for he loved me and gave himself for me; to read my name written on his hands and on his side — yes, and to let him see that his name is written on my heart in indelible lines; to embrace him, oh! what an embrace when the creature shall embrace his God — to be for ever so close to him, that not a doubt, nor a fear, nor a wandering thought can come between my soul and him forever:

Oh! how the thought that I shall know
The man that suffered here below,
To manifest his favour,
For me, and those whom most I love,
Or here, or with himself above,
Does my delighted passion move,
At that sweet word "for ever".
For ever to behold him shine,
For evermore to call him mine,
And see him still before me.
For ever on his face to gaze,
And meet his full assembled rays,
While all the Father he displays,
To all the saints for ever.

(Joseph Swain)

What else can there be that our spirit longeth for? This seems an empty thing to worldlings, but to the Christian this is heaven summed up in a word — "To be with Christ, which is far better" than all the joys of earth. This is the object, then, of this love-sickness.

3. Ask yet again what are *the excitements of this sickness?* What is it makes the Christian long to be at home with Jesus? There are many things. There are sometimes some very little things that set a Christian longing to be at home. You know the old story of Swiss soldiers, that when they have enlisted into foreign service they never will permit the band to play the "*Ranz des Vaches*" (The Song of the Cows), because as soon as ever the Swiss hears the Song of the Cows, he thinks of his own dear Alps, and the bells upon the cows necks, and the strange calls of the herd-boys, as they sing to one another from the mountains' peaks; and he grows sick and ill with home-sickness. So if you were banished, if you were taken prisoner or a slave, why, to hear some note of one of old England's

457

songs would set your spirit a-pining for home, and I confess, when I hear you sing sometimes:

Jerusalem! my happy home!
Name ever dear to me;
When shall my labours have an end,
In joy, and peace, and thee?
Jerusalem, my happy home!
My soul still pants for thee;
Then shall my labours have an end,
When I thy joys shall see.

O Christ do thou my soul prepare
For that bright home of love;
That I may see thee and adore,
With all Thy saints above.

(Joseph Bromehead)

It makes me say, "Ye daughters of Jerusalem, if ye find my beloved, tell him, that I am sick of love." It is the home-song that brings the homesickness. When we remember what he used to be to us, what sweet visits we have had from him, then we get sick to be always with him, and, best of all, when we are in his presence, when our soul is overjoyed with his delights, when the great deep sea of his love has rolled over the mast-head of our highest thoughts, and the ship of our spirit has gone right down, foundering at sea in the midst of an ocean of delights, ah, then its highest, its deepest thought is, "O that I may always be with him, in him, where he is, that I might behold his glory — the glory which his Father gave him, and which he has given me, that I may be one with him, world without end." I do believe, brethren, that all the bitters and all the sweets make a Christian, when he is in a healthy state, sick after Christ: the sweets make his mouth water for more sweets, and the bitters make him pant for the time when the last dregs of bitterness shall be over. Wearying temptations, as well as rapt enjoyments, all set the spirit on the wing after Jesus.

4. Well now, friends, *what is the cure of this love-sickness?* Is it a sickness for which there is any specific remedy? There is only one cure that I know of, but there are some palliatives. A man that is sick after Christ longs to be with him, and pants for the better land, singing as we did just now,

Father, I long, I faint to see
The place of thine abode.

(Isaac Watts)

He must have the desire realised, before the thirst of his fever will be assuaged. There are some palliatives, and I will recommend them to you. Such for example is a strong faith that realizes the day of the Lord and the presence of Christ, as Moses beheld the promised land and the goodly heritage, when he stood on the top of Pisgah. If you do not get heaven when you want it, you may attain to that which is next door to heaven, and this may bear you up for a little season. If you cannot get to behold Christ face to face, it is a blessed make-shift for the time to see him in the Scriptures, and to look at him through the glass of the Word. These are palliatives, but I warn you, I warn you of them. I do not mean to keep you from them, use them as much as ever you can, but I warn you from expecting that it will cure that love-sickness. It will give you ease but it will make you more sick still, for he that lives on Christ gets more hungry after Christ. As for a man being satisfied and wanting no more when he gets Christ — why he wants nothing but Christ it is true, in that sense he will never thirst; but he wants more, and more, and more, and more of Christ.

To live on Christ is like drinking seawater; the more you drink, the thirstier you get. There is something very satisfying in Christ's flesh, you will never hunger except for that, but the more you eat of it, the more you may; and he that is the heartiest feaster, and hath eaten the most, hath the best appetite for more. Oh, strange is this, but so it is; that which we would think would remove the lovesickness, and is the best stay to the soul under it, is just that which brings it on more and more. But there is a cure, there is a cure, and you shall have it soon — a black draught, and in it a pearl: — a black draught called Death. Ye shall drink it, but ye shall not know it is bitter, for ye shall swallow it up in victory. There is a pearl, too, in it — melted in it. Jesus died as well as you, and as you drink it, that pearl shall take away all ill effect from the tremendous draught. You shall say, "O death, where is thy sting? O grave, where is thy victory?" When you have once drunk that black draught, you are secure against that love-sickness for ever. For where are you? No pilgrimage, no weary flight through cold ether, thou art with him in paradise. Dost thou hear that, soul? Thou art with him in paradise, never to be separated, not for an instant; never to have a wandering thought, not one; never to find thy love waning or growing cold again; never to doubt his love to thee any more; never more to be vexed and tempted by sighing after what thou canst not view. Thou shalt be with him, where he is:

The everlasting doors
Shall soon the saints receive,
Above you angel powers
In glorious joy to live;
Far from a world of grief and sin,
With God eternally shut in.

(Charles Wesley)

Till then, beloved, let us strive to live near the cross. Those two mountains, Calvary and Zion, stand right opposite one another. The eye of faith can sometimes almost span the interval. And the loving heart, by some deep mystery of which we can offer you no solution, will often have its sweetest rapture of joy in the fellowship of his griefs. So have I found a satisfaction in the wounds of a crucified Jesus, which can only be excelled by the satisfaction I have yet to find in the sparkling eyes of the same Jesus glorified. Yes; the same Jesus! Well spake the angels on Mount Olivet — "*This same Jesus*, which is taken up from you into heaven, shall so come in like manner as ye have seen him go into heaven." "This same Jesus"! My soul coats on the words; my lips are fond of repeating them. This same Jesus!

And am I blessed with Jesus' love,
And shall I dwell with him above,
And will the joyful period come
When I shall call the heavens my home?

And does the happy hour draw near
When Christ will in the clouds appear,
And I without a vail shall see
The Man, the Christ, who bled for me?

If in my soul such joy abounds,
While weeping faith explores his wounds,

459

How glorious will those tears appear,
When perfect bliss forbids a tear!

Think, O my soul, if 'tis so sweet
On earth to sit at Jesus' feet,
What must it be to wear a crown
And sit with him upon his throne?

Would to God you all had this love-sickness! I am afraid many of you have it not. May he give it you! But oh, if there is a soul here that wants Jesus, he is welcome! If there is one heart here that says, "Give me Christ," you shall have your desire. Trust Jesus Christ, and he is thine; rely upon him, thou art his. God save thee and make thee sick *of* vanities, sick *after* verities; pining even unto sickness for Jesus Christ, the beloved of my soul, the sum of all my hope, the sinners only refuge, and the praise of all his saints; to whom be everlasting glory! Amen.

61. THE INCOMPARABLE BRIDEGROOM AND HIS BRIDE

NO. 2469

AT THE METROPOLITAN TABERNACLE, NEWINGTON
ON LORD'S-DAY EVENING, JUNE 10TH, 1866

"What is the beloved more than another beloved, O thou fairest among women? What is thy beloved more than another beloved, that thou dost so charge us?" (Song of Solomon 5:9)

THIS morning [see Metropolitan Tabernacle Pulpit, No. 694: *Sin Laid on Jesus*], we had the great privilege of preaching the doctrine of substitution, and of directing the minds of God's people to the solid rock of the meritorious sacrifice of Christ on which all their hopes of heaven must be built. What we have to say tonight is less doctrinal, and more practical; therefore, let us guard ourselves at the outset. If we should, with very much earnestness, urge believers to good works, let nobody suppose that, therefore, we might imagine that men are saved by works. Let no one for a moment dream that, in urging the believer to produce fruit unto righteousness, we are at all teaching that salvation is the work of man. I have no doubt that all of us who know anything of true religion are of the same opinion as that celebrated Scotch divine, old David Dickson, who was asked, when dying, what was the principal subject on which his thoughts were engaged, and he answered, "I am gathering up all my good works, and all my bad works, tying them into one bundle, and throwing them all alike down at the foot of the cross, and am resting alone on the finished work of Jesus." It is related of that mighty master in Israel, James Durham, that his experience at the last was very much akin to that of his friend, for he said, "Notwithstanding all my preaching, and all my spiritual experiences, I do not know that I have anything to hang upon excepting this one sentence spoken by Christ, 'Him that cometh to me I will in no wise cast out.'" (Jn 6:37) "Ah", replied someone who stood by Mr. Durham at the time, "you might well hazard a thousand souls, if you had them, on the strength of that one precious text."

Having said so much by way of caution, I want to address some earnest words to the people of God on certain practical truths that arise from our text; and the first thing I have to say is this, that the daughters of Jerusalem recognised in the spouse an exceeding beauty, which dazzled and charmed them, so that they could not help calling her the "fairest among women." This was not her estimate of herself for she had said, "I am black, but comely." (Song 1:5) Nor was it the estimate of her enemies, for they had smitten her, and wounded her. It was the estimate of fair, candid, and impartial onlookers.

I. This leads me to remark, firstly, that OUR CHARACTER SHOULD GIVE WEIGHT TO OUR PROFESSION OF RELIGION.

You will observe that it was in consequence of thinking her the "fairest among women" that they asked the spouse, "What is thy Beloved more than another beloved?" They thought that one so fair might well have her choice of a Bridegroom, and that one so lovely herself would be likely to have an eye to loveliness in her Husband. Consequently, they considered her judgement to be worth some attention, and they put to her the question why her Beloved was more than another beloved. Take it for granted, dear friends, as a truth which your own observation and experience make everyday clearer and clearer, that your power to spread religion in the world must mainly depend on your own personal character — of course, in absolute reliance upon the Holy Spirit. I suppose it is the earnest wish of every Christian to win for Christ some new converts, and bring some fresh

461

province under the dominion of the King of kings. I will tell you how this may be accomplished.

Your power to achieve this noble purpose must largely depend on your own *personal consistency*. It little avails what I say if I do the reverse. The world will not care about my testimony with the lip, unless there is also a testimony in my daily life for God, for truth, for holiness, for everything that is honest, lovely, pure, and of good report. (Phil. 4:8) There is that in a Christian's character which the world, though it may persecute the man himself, learns to value. It is called consistency — that is, the making of the life stand together, not being one thing in one place and another in another, or one thing at one time and quite different on another occasion. It is not consistency to be devout on Sunday and to be dishonest on Monday. It is not consistency to sing the songs of Zion today, and shout the songs of lustful mirth tomorrow. It is not consistency to occasionally wear the yoke of Christ and yet frequently to make yourself the serf of Satan. But to make your life all of a piece is to make it powerful, and when God the Holy Spirit enables you to do this, then your testimony will tell upon those among whom you live. It would be ludicrous — if it were not so sorrowful a thing — to be spoken of even with weeping, that there should be professed Christians who are, through inconsistency, among the worst enemies of the cross of Christ. I heard the other day, a story which made me laugh. A poor creature, in a lunatic asylum, had got it into his head that he was some great one, and addressed a person who was visiting the asylum in the following words: "I am Sir William Wallace; give me some tobacco!" What a ridiculous contrast between his proud assertion and his poor request! Who but a lunatic would say such a thing? Yet alas, we know people who say, by their actions if not their words, "I am a Christian, but I will take advantage of you when I can. I am one of the blood-royal of heaven; my life is hid with Christ in God (Col. 3:3), and my conversation is in heaven (Phil. 3:20), but — but — I like worldliness, and sensual pleasure, and carnal mirth quite as much as other men!" I say again, that this kind of thing would be superlatively ludicrous if it were not ineffably sorrowful, and it is, anyhow, utterly contemptible. If your life is not all of a piece, the world will soon learn how to estimate your testimony, and count you to be either a fool or a knave, and perhaps both.

But it is not enough to be barely consistent; what the world expects in Christians is real holiness as well as consistency. Holiness is something more than virtue. Virtue is like goodness frozen in ice, hard and cold; but holiness is that same goodness when it is thawed into a clear, running, sparkling stream. Virtue is the best thing that philosophy can produce, but holiness is the true fruit of the gospel of Jesus Christ, and of that alone. There must be about us an unworldliness, a something out of the common and ordinary way, or else, mark you, that uncommon gospel, that heavenly gospel, which we hold, will not seem to be producing its legitimate fruit. If you are just barely honest, and no more, if you are barely moral, and no more, it is of no service that you should try to speak of Christ; the world will not reckon you as the fairest among women, and it will not enquire anything about your Well-beloved.

But, brothers and sisters, I feel as if, instead of exhorting you like this, I might better turn to confession myself, and ask you to join me in confessing how far short we come of being anything like the fairest among women in character. We hope that we have something Christ-like about us; but oh, how little it is! How many imperfections there are! How much there is of the old Adam, and how little of the new creature in Christ Jesus! Archbishop Usher was once asked to write a treatise on Sanctification, and this he promised to do; but six months rolled by, and the good Archbishop had not written a sentence. He said to a friend, "I have not begun the treatise, yet I cannot confess to a breach of my promise, for, to tell you the truth, I have done my best to write on the subject; but when I came to look into my own heart, I saw so little of sanctification there, and found that so much which I could have written would have been merely by rote like a parrot might talk, that I had not

462

the face to write it." Yet, if ever there was a man renowned for holiness, it was Archbishop Usher; if ever there was a saintly man who seemed to be one of the seraphic spirits permitted to stray beyond the companionship of his kind among poor earth-worms here, it was James Usher; yet this is the confession he made concerning himself! Where, then, shall we hide our diminished heads? I am sure we may all say with good Mr. John William Fletcher of Madeley, who was another bright example of seraphic holiness, that what we want is more grace. He wrote a pamphlet on some political matter, and Lord North wrote to know what he could give him in return. His answer was, "I want what your lordship cannot give me — more grace." That is also true of us; we want more grace. It is to be had; and if we had it, and it transformed us into what we should be, oh, what lives of happiness and of holiness we might lead here below, and what mighty workers should we be for our Lord Jesus Christ! How would his dear name be made to sound to the utmost ends of the earth! On my part, I fear it is but a dream; but just conceive that all of you, the members of this church, were made to be truly saintly, saints of the first water, saints who had cast off the sloth of worldliness, and had come out in the full glory of newness of life in Christ Jesus, oh, what a power might this church become in London, and what a power felt the wide world over! Let us seek it, let us strive after it, recollecting that it is a truth never to be denied, that only in proportion to the sanctity and spirituality of our character will be our influence for good amongst the sons of men.

II. Advancing now a step, our second remark will be, that WE SHOULD CHARGE OTHERS CONCERNING CHRIST. "What is thy Beloved more than another beloved, that thou dost so charge us?"

The "fairest among women" was asked why she had spoken thus: "I charge you, O daughters of Jerusalem, if ye find my Beloved, that ye tell him, that I am sick of love." By this "charge" is meant, I suppose, that the spouse adjured them, and spoke solemnly to them about her Beloved. *Christians, be troublesome to the world!* O house of Israel, be like a burdensome stone to the world! You are not sent here to be recognised as honourable citizens of this world, to be petted and well-treated. Even Christ himself, the peaceable One, said, "I am come to send fire on the earth; and what will I, if it be already kindled?" (Lk. 12:49) What I mean is this: we are not to be quiet about our religion. The world says to us, "Hold your tongue about religion, or at least talk about it at fit times; but do not introduce it at all seasons so as to become a pest and a nuisance." I say again, and you know in what sense I mean it, be a nuisance to the world; be such a man that worldlings will be compelled to feel that there is a Christian in their midst. An officer was walking out of the royal presence on one occasion, when he tripped over his sword. The king said to him, "Your sword is rather a nuisance." "Yes", was the officer's reply, "your majesty's enemies have often said so." May you be a nuisance to the world in that sense, troublesome to the enemies of the King of kings! While your conduct should be courteous, and everything to be desired as between man and man, yet let your testimony for Christ be given without any flinching, and without any mincing of the matter.

This afternoon, I was reading a sermon by a certain divine, whose subject of discourse was, why the working-classes do not go to a place of worship, and the preacher seems to have made up his mind that, whatever is preached in this Tabernacle, is especially obnoxious to labouring men and women. The reason he gives why the working-classes do not attend places of worship is that we preach such dreadful doctrines. It is very remarkable that places where these truths are preached are crowded, while places where the opposite things are proclaimed are often empty! It is curious, if the doctrine of the gospel is such a very horrible thing that it drives people away, that, at the places where it is preached, there are more people than can get in, whereas where some of the modern doctrines are declared, you may see more spiders than people! Here is a singular circumstance, certainly, yet one for which we can easily account. A Socinian minister was

463

once asked by one who preached Evangelical truth, "If I, who proclaim doctrines which you say are obnoxious to common reason, have my place full, and you, who preach such pretty, reasonable doctrines, can get nobody to listen to you, do you not think it is because the people have an idea that what I teach is true, and that what you preach, though it is very pleasant and palatable, is not true, and therefore they do not care to hear it?" It is not by altering our testimony that we are to hope to win an audience, and it is not by hiding the light of the gospel under a bushel that you or I shall discharge our obligations to our Lord. We must speak up for Christ, and so speak up for Him that men will be moved to ask us the question: "What is thy Beloved more than another beloved that thou dost so charge us?"

I have read that Mr. Gilpin of Exeter had every pew in his chapel where he preached sketched out on a plan, and the names of all the occupants of the pews written on it so that he might *pray for every one, and, if possible, speak to everyone.* Such a plan might not be practicable in so large a building as this, but it is an excellent method; and if we cannot adopt it, let this place be mapped out in your own mind, and let every believer, wherever he sits, consider that there is a little district allotted to him, and let him seek to have a word of courteous Christian conversation about divine things with all who sit near him. I suggest this as a very excellent mode of beginning to "charge" others about Christ; and then, in your daily business, in the workshop, at fit times and seasons, at periods when Christian prudence and Christian zeal would give their voice together, introduce Christ, and begin to talk of him, and hold him up as the great cure-all for human diseases, the great staff and support for human weakness. We shall never see as much blessing as we might until the work of the Church becomes far more general than it is at present. There is something which every believer can do for his Lord. He must be able to tell of what he has tasted and handled of the Word of Life (1 Jn. 1:1), and if he has not tasted and handled it, then he is not a child of God at all. The best teaching in the world is experimental; nothing wins men like personal witnessing, not merely teaching the doctrine as we find it in the Book, but as we have felt it in its living power in our own hearts. When we begin to tell of its effect on ourselves, it is wonderful what power there is on others in that testimony. A person talks to me about a certain medicine, how it is compounded, what it looks like, how many drops must be taken at a dose, and so on. Well, I do not care to hear all that, and I soon forget it; but he tells me that for many months he was bed-ridden, in sore distress and great pain, and likely to die; and, looking at him as he stands before me in perfect health, I am delighted with the change, and he says that it was that medicine which restored him. If I am a sick man in the same state as he was, I would say to him, "Give me the name and address, for I must try that medicine for myself." I believe that the simple witness of converted boys and girls, converted lads and lasses, especially the witness of converted fathers and mothers and friends beloved, the witness that comes from the grey head that is backed up by years of godly living, has a wonderful power for the spread of the gospel, and we cannot expect that God will give us any very large blessing until the whole of us shall be at work for our Lord. We need not all climb up the pulpit stairs, but each one of us can proclaim Christ according to our ability, and according to the circumstances in which he has placed us. When we shall do that, then we may expect to see "greater things than these." (Jn. 1:50) Days that shall make us laugh for very joy of heart, and well nigh make us dance like David did before the ark, will come when all the rank and file of the army, and even those who halt on their crutches, shall march unanimously against the foe.

III. Thirdly, it is important for us to MAKE ALL WHO COME IN CONTACT WITH US FEEL THAT CHRIST JESUS IS FIRST AND FOREMOST IN OUR LIVES.

You perceive that the question of the text is not, "What is thy Beloved that he should be equal to others?" It is, "What is thy Beloved more than another beloved?" The idols of the

464

heathen are all made to stand in the Pantheon face to face, and there is no quarrelling among them; but as soon as you introduce Christ there, they must all go down, or he will not stay. The principle of the toleration of every form of doctrine — I mean not, of course, civil toleration, which we hold to be always necessary and right, but I mean mental toleration — the principle of the mental toleration of all forms of doctrine, and all forms and shades of action, is heathenish, for where Christ comes he comes to reign; and when once he enters the soul of a man, it is down, down, down with everything else.

There is a text which is often misunderstood. I heard it read only last Sunday: "No man can serve two masters." (Lk. 6:24, 16:13) I very much question whether he cannot; I believe he could serve, not only two, but twenty. That is not the meaning of the text; the true reading of it is, "No man can serve two *masters*." They cannot both be masters; if two of them are equal, then neither of them is really the master. It is not possible for the soul to be subject to two master-passions. If a man says, "I love Christ", that is well; but if he says, "I love Christ, and I love money, and I love them both supremely", that man is a liar, for the thing is not possible. There is only one that can be the master-passion; and where Jesus enters the soul, love for him must be the master-passion of the heart.

It strikes me that a Christian, living fully up to his privileges, would be such a man as this — if he had, on one side, the opportunity to enjoy pleasure, and, on the other, a painful opportunity of honouring Christ, he would prefer to honour Christ rather than to enjoy himself. If, on the one hand, there were gain, even lawfully to be had, and on the other hand, Christ could be honoured in a way that would bring no monetary gain, the man would prefer the glorifying of his Master to the obtaining of the advantage in cash which was held out to him. And if it comes to this, that by soft speeches he may get himself into good repute, and that by sternly speaking out and rebuking error he may honour his Master but bring much contempt on himself, if he is a genuine Christian, he will always take the latter course. The first question he will ask will be, "How can I most honour my Lord? How can I best glorify him?"

It is clear that *Christ is not first in every nominal Christian's heart*. No, alas, he is not first, and he is not even second, he is very far down in the scale! Look at them — good honest trades people, perhaps, but from the first dawn of Monday morning to the putting up of the shutters on Saturday night, what is the main business of their life? It is only, "What shall we eat? Or what shall we drink? Or wherewithal shall we be clothed?" (Mat. 6:31) Now, where is Christ in such a case as that? Look at others; with them the question is, "Where shall I invest such-and-such an amount of spare cash? How shall I best lay by such-and-such a sum? What field shall I buy next? What house shall I add to my estate?" As for the Lord Jesus, he is put off with the cheese-parings and the candle-ends; he gets a little now and then dropped into the offering-box, but it is only a mere trifle compared with what he ought to receive. The man's words are nine hundred and ninety-nine for himself, and perhaps not much more than half a one for Christ; almost all his time goes to the world, and not to his Lord; his whole self goes to himself, and not to the Saviour to whom he professes to belong. This is not the case with *the truly Christ-like man*. With him, Christ is first, Christ is last, Christ is middle, Christ is all in all; and when he speaks about anything connected with Christ, his words come with such a solemn earnestness, that men are impressed with what he says, and turn round to him, and ask, as the daughters of Jerusalem enquired of the spouse, "What is thy Beloved more than another beloved, that thou dost so charge us?"

IV. Our last thought is this: if ever, through the grace of God, we should possess such a character, and bear such a testimony as we have been talking about, so that men ask us the question of the text, and IT WILL BE WELL FOR US TO BE PREPARED TO ANSWER IT.

This is an age in which the world asks many questions, and, from some Christians, it cannot give an answer. I will say one thing which some of you may not like to hear, perhaps, but I cannot help that. There are some of you who are Baptists; but why? Well, I suppose, because I happen to be one, and you have followed me without carefully studying the teaching of the New Testament on the question. I fear it is so with some of you, and there are others of you who are Wesleyans, or Independents, or Church people, but the only reason you can give for being so is that your grandmother, or your mother, happened to be of that denomination. This is an age in which people do not estimate truth as they should. A good earnest controversy seems to me to be a very healthy thing, because it turns men's attention somewhat more than usual to divine things; but you know how it is, even with many professing Christian people. They think it would be wicked to read a novel; but if it is written upon a religious subject, it is a very proper thing then. There is hardly a weekly newspaper, nowadays, or even a penny magazine, that can prosper without having a novel in it; and there must be a market for all this rubbish or it would not be supplied so plentifully. Why, sirs, in Puritan times, men read solid books like John Owen *On the Mortification of Sin*; they studied such works as Richard Gilpin *On Satan's Temptations*, or Stephen Charnock on *The Divine Attributes*; but, in these days, people who ought to read these solid books, so as to be able to give a reason for the hope that is in them, are often wasting their time over poor stuff which only addles the brain, and does the soul no good. I would to God that we could again see a race of sturdy believers who would hold to nothing but what they have tested by the Word of God! They will receive nothing merely because it was taught by their minister, or by their parents, or by any human authority, but who would accept with unquestioning faith everything that is revealed in the Inspired Book. Our motto should still be, "To the law and to the testimony: if they speak not according to this word, it is because there is no light in them." (Is. 8:20) We want to raise again — and oh, may God give us grace to do so! — a race of men who shall be rooted and grounded in the faith, and who, when they are asked for a reason of the hope that is in them (1 Pet. 3:15), shall be able to give it, not with fear and trembling and hesitation, but with holy boldness and determination, because they have tested and tried the matter for themselves.

See how the spouse does; she does not pause a minute before she gives her reply. She is asked, "What is thy Beloved more than another beloved?" and she has the answer, as we say, at her finger-ends, and why is this? Why, because she had it in her heart. So she says, "My Beloved is white and ruddy, the chiefest among ten thousand." She does not say, "Stop a bit, I must read up on that question; I must get myself well-instructed about it." It is such a vital point, that she had one so dear to her, as it touched the Person of her Lord, and at once, "Is my Beloved better than any other beloved? Certainly he is, and here are the reasons." She puts them together one after another without a pause, so that the daughters of Jerusalem must be convinced. I commend her example to you also, my beloved in Christ Jesus, Do study the Word, that your faith may not stand in the wisdom of men, but in the power of God. I beseech you, if I have taught you anything that is not revealed in the Scriptures, or if you have received anything only on my authority, give it up till you have tested and tried it by the Word of the Lord. I am not afraid what the result will be, for if I have erred in anything, I pray the Lord to teach me, and also teach you, so that we may grow together in the unity of the Spirit in the bonds of the faith. (Eph. 4:3) Do let us all seek to be taught by God; and then, with a holy life added to this divine instruction, and a clear testimony for Jesus Christ constantly borne by us, our witnessing must tell upon the age in which we live.

Oh, that the Lord would send us times of true revival once again! Run your finger down the page of history till you come to the Reformation; what was there in Luther, in Calvin, in Zwingli, that they should have been able to shake the world any more than there is in men who live nowadays? Nothing but this: that they believed what they did believe, and they spoke with an awful earnestness, like men who meant what they said. And straightway there arose a noble race of men, men who felt the power of faith, and lived it out, and the world was made to feel that "there were giants in the earth in those days." (Gen. 6:4) Then, again, in later times, when the Church had fallen into a fatal slumber, there came the age of Whitefield and Wesley. What was the power of the early Methodists? Why, simply the power of true sincerity combined with holiness! What if I say that it was the power of intruding religion on men, of forcing men to hear God's voice, of compelling a sleeping world to wake out of its slumbers? As I sat, last week, in the hall of the Free Church Assembly in Edinburgh, just beneath the Castle, I started in my seat, when I thought the whole hall was going to fall, for, at one o'clock, the gun on the Castle was fired from Greenwich by electricity. It startled every one of us, and I noticed that nearly everybody took out his watch to see whether it was right by the gun. I thought to myself, "That is just what the Christian Church ought to do. It ought, at the proper time, to give a loud, clear, thundering testimony for God and for truth, so that every one might examine his own conscience, and get himself put right where he is wrong." Our testimony for Christ ought not to be like the ticking of an ordinary clock, or as sounding brass or a tinkling cymbal (1 Cor. 13:1), but a mighty booming noise that commands and demands a hearing.

Let our soul be but linked with heaven, let the Spirit of the Lord flash the message along the wires, and our life may be just as accurate and just as startling as that time-gun at Edinburgh. So, when men ask us, "What is thy Beloved more than another beloved that thou dost so charge us?" we shall have an answer ready for them, which, we pray, God will bless to them, for Christ's sake! Amen.

62. CHRIST'S PERFECTION AND PRECEDENCE.
NO. 2478

AT THE METROPOLITAN TABERNACLE, NEWINGTON
ON LORD'S-DAY EVENING, AUGUST 1ST, 1869

"My beloved is white and ruddy, the chiefest among ten thousand."
(Song of Solomon 5:10)

THE spouse in this verse styles her Lord "my Beloved", from which it is easy for us to gather that it is of the utmost importance that our heart's affection should be really and truly set on Christ Jesus our Lord. We must trust him, and we must love him. Christ on the cross saves us when he becomes to us Christ in the heart. It is of small service for us to know of Christ if we do not really trust and love him. It will be of little avail for us to talk of him unless our heart is really welded and knit to him. Let us, therefore, dear friends, commence this evening's meditation with a solemn enquiry made by each one for himself or herself: "Can I call the Lord Jesus Christ, who was crucified on Calvary, but who now reigns at the right hand of the Father, can I truly call him 'my Beloved'?" There may be a question raised in your soul by a natural anxiety, lest you should presume, but do not be content until you have solemnly and seriously searched your hearts to know, whether in very deed and truth, an ardent affection burns within your spirit towards the Lord Jesus. It would better for you that you had never been born than that you should live and die without love for Christ. Remember that startling sentence of the Apostle Paul, which is so solemn that I can scarcely quote it without tears: "If any man love not the Lord Jesus Christ, let him be Anathema Maranatha" (1 Cor 16:22); that is, let him be accursed at the coming of the Lord. It will be so with you, dear friends, however shining your moral attributes may have been. However you may have carved your name on the rock of history, you must go down to endless misery and shame unless your heart has in it a vital sense of true religion, a sincere love for the crucified Christ of Calvary.

If this important personal enquiry has had its due weight on our minds, it may lead us to another consideration, namely, that it is a blessed thing, if we do love Christ, to be able to speak about our affection for him as a matter of course, and a matter of fact; not as a thing that hangs trembling in the balance, but as an ascertained truth and certainty. The spouse does not speak of "Him whom I hope to love by-and-by", or of "Him whom I trust I shall one day know", but she calls him, without question or qualification, "my Beloved." She is quite sure about this blessed relationship; she raises no doubts, and she has no fears concerning it. I do not say that, if any man has a doubt about his love for Christ, he need, therefore, necessarily condemn himself; but I do say that he must never be content to continue in such a state. Perhaps, those who love the Master best are the very people who will be the most likely to have such a high opinion of the love which he deserves, that they will often chide themselves that they do not love him at all, when they see how little their love is compared with that perfection of affection which he deserves. We must not affirm that the question of anxiety is sinful; it is painful, and anxious, and, if it is not divinely removed, it will become sinful; but the anxiety is not so in itself. Yet, beloved, I beseech you to press on beyond this stage of your pilgrim journey. Do not be content to live on hopes, and fears, and peradventures, and surmises. You would not like to think that perhaps you loved your child, or your husband, or your friend. You would not care to say, "I hope I love virtue, I hope I love honesty"; but it is a baser thing still for us to allow a question to exist as to whether we love him who is dearer than our own family, and who is better than any one moral excellence, seeing that he is the combination of all excellences. O beloved, seek to reach the blessed heights of full assurance, that each one of you may be able to say of Christ, "This is my Beloved, and this is my Friend." (Song 5:16) I would as soon doubt my own existence as doubt the love that burns within my heart towards him who has bought me with his precious blood." Therefore, sing, as we have often done, the words of young William Featherstone:

My Jesus, I love thee, I know thou art mine,
For thee all the follies of sin I resign;
My gracious Redeemer, my Saviour art thou,
If ever I loved thee, my Jesus, 'tis now.

If we have reached that stage in our journey heavenwards, it would be well if we go on a step further. Loving our Lord and Saviour in our heart, and being assured of that love in our inmost conscience after earnest heart-searching, it would be well if we have the courage never to hesitate in the avowal of that love. Our love for Christ is so sacred a passion that it is not to be talked of in all company. We must not cast our pearls before swine. (Mat. 7:6) But, on the other hand, it is so ennobling a passion that we need never blush to own it in any company. If we ever are ashamed of loving Christ, we have good reason to be ashamed of such shameful shame. When you have heard his dear name reviled, did you ever start for fear lest you should be called on to share his reproach? Did you ever sit silent when you ought to have spoken up because Christ was being blasphemed? Did you ever try to make it out to yourself that it was a prudent retirement that shunned the conflict when, in very truth, it was hateful cowardice that turned its back on the Crucified in the hour of his need? I fear that the charge might be brought against most of us; if so, let us humbly confess it on our knees alone, and blush before the presence of our blessed Master. Remember what we sang just now:

Jesus and shall it ever be?
A mortal man ashamed of thee!
Ashamed of thee, whom angels praise,
Whose glories shine thro' endless days.

Ashamed of Jesus! sooner far
Let evening blush to own a star;
He sheds the beams of light divine
O'er this benighted soul of mine.

Ashamed of Jesus! just as soon
Let midnight be ashamed of noon:
'Tis midnight with my soul, till he,
Bright Morning Star, bid darkness flee.

Ashamed of Jesus! that dear Friend
On whom my hopes of heaven depend!
No; when I blush, be this my shame,
That I no more revere his name.

(Joseph Grigg)

What can there be to be ashamed of in loving him whom angels love, whom God loves, whom all holy spirits love? What! Not love him? If he were not in himself God, yet he has been so good to me that I must love him. It is an old proverb, that we must speak of friends as we find them, and praise the bridge that carries us over the stream. Here is one in whom we have found such goodness, such kindness, such gentleness, and such disinterested affection, one who has done such wonders for us that, if we do not love him, and boldly declare that we love him, we have good reason to be ashamed of ourselves,

469

and hide our heads in confusion forever and ever! Young people, you who have lately come to love Christ, do not begin as some of your fathers did, in that half-hearted fashion which has continued with them until this day. Alas, there are some professing Christians who have grown grey, and yet have scarcely ever dared to speak the name of Christ in company. Yes, some of them have even been ashamed up to this moment to be baptised and come to the Lord's Table. They say that they love Christ, and I hope they do; yet, up to this hour, baptism has been a cross too heavy for them to bear, and the Lord's Supper has seemed to them to be an ordeal instead of a means of blessing. Play the man, young Christian! Do not be ashamed to avow your Lord! If ever there was unfurled in this world a banner that deserved the utmost allegiance of human hearts, it is the blood-stained banner of the cross; and if ever there was a Leader who deserved that men should not speak his praises, as Shakespeare did,

With 'bated breath, and whispering humbleness,

— but with manly enthusiasm, that Leader is the Christ of God who loved you, and gave himself for you. Yes, utter it in the face of a scoffing world, stand to it in the teeth of a ribald infidel generation, declare it before the crowd of gainsayers who mock you to scorn as you pronounce it: "This is my Beloved — the Christ that died, the Christ that ever lives at the right hand of God — this is my Beloved, and I am not ashamed to avow him."

Suppose that we have come as far as this — and I believe that many of us have come so far — it is our bounden duty to go a step further. Loving Jesus, knowing that we love him, and boldly confessing our love for him, let us next so study his Person and his character that we shall be able to give a reason for the love that is in us to any who makes the enquiry: "What is thy Beloved more than another beloved?" You observe that the spouse not only calls him, "my Beloved", but she describes the complexion of his countenance, and the details relating to his whole Person. She has a word of praise for all his features and all his members. She knows him so well that she speaks of him with a tongue like the pen of a ready writer. (Ps. 45:1) So, beloved, let us study Christ as we come again to this communion table. You, who love and fear him, do not neglect your Bibles; do not neglect that fellowship which, like the light of a candle, shines on the pages of the Bible. Some of you are studying earthly sciences; perhaps you give your minds to the classics, or you delight to master the mysteries of mathematics; but oh, take care that this most excellent science, the science of Christ crucified, is not made to take second place with you. Always put this science first; try to understand the glory of your Lord's Person without beginning of days or end of years. Search into the purity of his character in all that he was here below from his birth to his death. Be conversant with Christ in all his sacred offices; think much of his precious blood, and of all the holy mysteries that cluster around his cross. Trace him from Bethlehem to Gabbatha, and then, from Gabbatha, follow him in his resurrection and ascension along the star-bespangled way up to the throne of his glory, and let your soul linger hopefully in the full belief of his second coming, and in all the glory that shall surely follow the day of his august appearing. Study Christ, study Christ, so as to be able to tell others of him, and do not be not slow in communicating to those of an enquiring mind what you have yourself heard, and seen, and handled, of the Word of life, for so the spouse does in the chapter before us.

This much must suffice by way of introduction, or rather, by way of practical exhortation to those of you who are enlisted beneath Christ's royal banner of love.

Now, let us proceed to consider the general description of the Bridegroom given by his spouse in this verse. First, she says, "My Beloved is white and ruddy." These words set out *his charming complexion*. Secondly, the spouse calls her Beloved "the chiefest among ten thousand", and so she describes *his personal precedence*.

470

I. First, then, the spouse says, "My Beloved is white and ruddy", and so she sees HIS CHARMING COMPLEXION.

It seems to me that the spouse intends by these words to call attention to two chief characteristics of her Lord's most blessed Person. Had not Solomon often seen the snow-white lambs — the emblems of purity, — brought up to the temple to be offered in sacrifice? "So", says she, "my Beloved is white." Had he not also seen the uplifted knife in the priest's hand, and then seen the ruby stream as it flowed down to the foot of the altar till the white lamb was stained crimson in its own blood? So he puts the two together: the white, the immaculate purity, the red, the sacrificial blood-shedding; and these two things, whether they are meant in the text or not, are certainly the two essentials of the Christian faith concerning the Person of Christ. He is no Christian, and, indeed, cannot be a Christian, who has not learned well, and joyfully received the two truths Our Lord is, first of all, in himself white; that is, *he has immaculate perfection of character*. God in him is light and no darkness at all — perfect purity without a trace of sin. He is very God of very God, the Holy One of Israel. In his Godhead, Jesus Christ is perfection itself. As to his manhood, the term whiteness well describes him who was born without natural corruption, or taint of hereditary depravity — "that holy thing" (Lk. 1:35), the Christ of God, who became incarnate, yet without sin. (Heb. 4:15) Does not this word "white" describe him also in his actual life? There was never any sin in Christ. You may challenge every word of his, and you will find it pure. You may thrust it into the furnace heated seven times hotter than it was used to be heated, yet it will come out as it went in, for no dross will be found in it. As for Christ's actions, they are matchless and perfect in every respect; the two great objects of his life were the glory of God and the good of man. So pure, indeed, is the character of Christ that, even those who hate his religion, and have read the writings of the four Evangelists with no design but to find some ground for cavilling [argument], have, nonetheless, been cowed before the majesty of the perfect life of Christ. In fact, it is today as it was of old, when the officers were sent to take him prisoner; they went back without him for they said, "Never man spake like this Man." (Jn. 7:46) There is no spot in him; he is the Lamb of God without blemish, the perfect Christ, and hence it is that we love him. We love those who possess true excellence, and, therefore, we must love Christ, for he has every excellence in perfection. If there were no atonement, if we did not regard our Lord Jesus as our Saviour, yet still every true heart ought to love him, and to be won over to him. There are such charms in his character that, if our souls were not besotted by the love of sin, we must worship and adore this glorious Son of God, who is the brightness of the Father's glory, and the express image of his person. (Heb. 1:3) He is so white and pure that we ought to love him.

But, next, we come to the blood-shedding, *the sacrificial character of Christ*. Alas, that this glorious doctrine of the atoning sacrifice should ever be cast into the background as it so often is, for the blood-shedding of Christ is the very essence of Christianity. In the fullness of time, Jesus Christ, born of a woman, came into this world as the Substitute for sinners. The vengeance of God against sin was poured out on him; he suffered death that those who trust him might not die; the Lamb of God was slain in their room, and place, and stead, that he might render satisfaction to the injured honour, sadly broken law of God. This is the chief reason, after all, why Christ's people love him, because, in his precious blood, they see the pardon of all their sins, they see the lifting of themselves up into the life of God, they see the open way of access unto the Father, they see the gates of heaven opened to all believers. Beloved, there are some in these days who cry up the glorified Christ, and I will cry him up with them, nor shall they find a word too strong for his praise; yet they would have men trust in the glorified Christ. They preach the doctrine of the second advent as though it were the chief teaching of Holy Scripture, and they seem to look to the second coming of Christ rather than to the first; but let Paul's words be always our motto: "We preach Christ crucified, unto the Jews a stumbling-block, and unto

471

the Greeks foolishness, but unto them which are called, both Jews and Greeks, Christ the power of God, and the wisdom of God." (1 Cor. 1:23-24) With that same Apostle, let us cry, "God forbid that I should glory, save in the cross of our Lord Jesus Christ." (Gal 6:14) His throne is glorious, and his glory speaks for itself; but the despised and crucified Christ is the source of the sinner's salvation, and this truth is ever to be preached and held up as the first and cardinal doctrine of our holy faith.

Brethren, let us thus look to Jesus, "white" in his spotless innocence, "ruddy" in his sacrificial suffering. Let us view him as the one sinless Being, and also as the chief of martyrs, the One in whom was no sin, yet upon whom the Lord causes to meet the iniquity of all his people with all the suffering it deserved, and all the vengeance and wrath of Almighty God that was rightly due to transgressors. I must not detain you longer upon this part of the subject, but I cannot pass from it without asking the question: Do we all love this precious One in whom there is all excellence, and in whom there is also this matchless suffering, this sin-atoning grief? Oh, if your heart is truly set on Christ, you have a portion so rich that you need not envy even the angels; for,

Never did angels taste above,
Redeeming grace and dying love.

(Isaac Watts)

If this is your lot, you are happy, thrice happy, though poor, and sick, and unknown. If Christ is indeed your Beloved, you are married to One who is the equal of the Eternal God. If your heart embraces Christ, and Christ is really yours, you have more than the world can ever compass, you have more than heaven itself could give if Christ were withdrawn from its courts of glory. Be happy then, be joyful in your Lord, let your heart go up to him, and rest in him; and when you come to the communion table, let it be with your eye and your heart fixed on your Beloved, who is "white and ruddy."

But, my dear hearer, if you do not have Christ, oh, how I wish you did, and you may have him this very night. Many of you are strangers to me. At this time of the year, when so many of our regular hearers take their vacation at the seaside or in the country, there is room for more strangers. Well, dear friends, we are strangers to one another, but I hope many of you are not strangers to the Master; or if you are, possibly the Lord brought you here that you might meet with him, and that he might meet with you. It would be a blessed Sabbath indeed to your soul if now you could say, "This perfect Man, I must love him; this suffering Substitute, I must trust him. God has laid him in Zion as a foundation and a chief cornerstone. I will come and build all my hopes for time and for eternity on him and his great atoning sacrifice." You are black, poor sinner, but then he is white; and his white shall stand in the place of thy black. You are black, but then he is ruddy, and his crimson blood shall wash away every speck and stain of your sin. All you have to do is simply to look to him by faith, for there is life in a look at him. Only trust him, trembler; only trust him, guilty sinner; only trust him, and that simple trust shall bring you life, health, perfection, heaven, God himself. God grant that it may be so!

II. Now, passing on to the remaining words of the text, notice that the spouse says of her Beloved that he is "the chiefest among ten thousand." These words set out HIS PERSONAL PRECEDENCE.

"The chiefest among ten thousand" — is it not incorrect to say, "*the* chiefest"? I do not care if it is; and I would not like to see the word altered into "chief". Human words at best are such poor things that they stagger under the mighty burden of the perfections of Christ. We seem to need some of those huge pillars and pedestals we sometimes see

472

outside massive piles of architecture, that we may bear up the ponderous truth of our text. We must have such words as "chiefest", for common language does not suffice in such a high case as this. I suppose that in heaven they have done with our poor imperfect speech, and know how to speak of Christ as he deserves. Anyhow, we believe with good John Berridge,

Living tongues are dumb at best,
We must die to speak of Christ.

He is the chiefest among ten thousand, and, it so happens, that this word "chiefest" may mean any one of three or four things. First, take it as it stands — "chiefest" — that is to say, *Christ is higher, better, lovelier, more excellent, than any who are round about him*. If you bring ten thousand angels, he is the chiefest Angel, the Messenger of the covenant. If you bring ten thousand friends, he is the chiefest Friend, the "Friend that sticketh closer than a brother." (Prov. 18:24) If you bring ten thousand physicians, he is the best Physician, for he heals all diseases. If you find ten thousand shepherds, he is the Good Shepherd, the Great Shepherd, the Chief Shepherd. If you find one, two, a hundred, a thousand, ten thousand, all excellent, they must all give way when he appears, as the stars are forgotten when the sun arises in its strength. Christ is the chiefest, the best, the highest of all beings; whatever excellences there may be in others, they are all eclipsed by the surpassing excellences that are found in him.

Christ is the chiefest among ten thousand; that is to say, *he is the Head, the Ruler, the Prince, the King, the Lord over all*. There he stands, with his feet like most fine gold, and, all around him, are the chariots of God with twenty thousand, even thousands of angels, and there is not one who lifts his head as high even as his Lord's feet, and amongst all the cherubic and seraphic host there is not one who would not count it his highest heaven to fly at Christ's command to the meanest cottage, or even to a dunghill where Lazarus is lying with the dogs licking his sores. (Lk. 16:20-21) Christ is King of all the angels, and here below, too, there are ten thousand forces and powers continually at work, for God has possession of his hosts and armaments on earth as well as in heaven. But Christ is Lord High Admiral of all the seas, the great Commander-in-chief of all the battalions, the mighty King who rules over all; and when he comes into his Church, we know that he is Chief there. Who dares look at him and claim equality with him? I tremble at the thought of that dreadful blasphemy which might well have condemned England to the lowest hell for daring to call an earthly monarch "the head of the Church". It cannot be, it is sheer impiety, for man or angel ever to dare to steal that title off Christ. He alone is King in the midst of Zion; he is the one and only Head of the Church. It was a brave deed of Cameron and his comrades to lift up their voices against this infamy when first it sought to spread itself in Scotland; and it is ill on our part that we have not lifted up our voices more loudly against it in this our land. A man or a woman, head of the Church? No, never! Let Christ, and Christ alone, wear the crown he bought with his own blood; he alone is King, and let him ever be so proclaimed and acknowledged. In matters of religion, we need no Caesar's favour, and we do not fear Caesar's frown. Christ is the one Head of his Church, and his true Church is free both from the control and the patronage of the State, and so she shall be wherever true hearts beat loyally to Christ, and wherever true lips speak his praises. He is "the chiefest among ten thousand." There may be ten thousand bishops, but he is the Bishop of souls. If there are ten thousand fathers, he is "the Everlasting Father." If there are ten thousand teachers, yet shall they not be called Rabbis, for One is our Teacher and Rabbi, even Christ, and at his feet the reverent Church adoringly bows, hailing him — and him alone — as Head and Master, "the chiefest among ten thousand."

According to the Septuagint, the text has another meaning. In Scripture, our Lord is called the chosen One, the prophet of God. As the psalmist puts it, speaking by prophecy, "I

473

have exalted One chosen out of the people." (Ps. 89:19) Christ is chosen out of ten thousand as the Mediator to stand between God and men. Whoever else might have been employed by God for this service — and we are not able to think of any other — yet first of all was Christ chosen of God; and today we may call him the chosen One because he is the chosen of his Church. If the question were put to us, and a poll were demanded upon it — "Of all the Church of Christ, who shall be Head and Lord? Who shall be Master? Who shall be the Teacher? Who shall be the Beloved?" — would not all of us hold up our hands for him — yes, hands and hearts as well, and we would even lay down our heads on the block if it were necessary to secure his election. Every one of us would, with a burst of acclamation, unconstrained except by his own charms, elect him to be the Head and Lord in the midst of Zion. I put to you, dear hearer, an even more personal question — Have you chosen him? If not, will you, by his grace, put your hand on your heart now, and say, "Now have I chosen him because he has first chosen me"? I pray you at once to make a choice of him; for if you do, you will never regret it. I have stood by a great many death-beds; but there is one scene I never saw, and never expect to see, and that is a child of God repenting that he ever loved Christ Jesus. Say what we have often sung:

O happy day that fixed my choice
On Thee, my Saviour and my God!
Well may this glowing heart rejoice,
And tell its raptures all abroad.

'Tis done! the great transaction's done;
I am my Lord's, and he is mine;
He drew me, and I followed on,
Charmed to confess the voice divine.

High heaven, that heard the solemn vow,
That vow renewed shall daily hear;
Till in life's latest hour I bow,
And bless in death a bond so dear.

(Philip Doddridge)

May Christ be the chosen of your heart! God grant that no soul here may refuse admission to the Prince of Peace!

Lastly, according to the margin of our Bible, the text bears this meaning, and probably should be thus read: "*He is the Standard-bearer among ten thousand.*" The "ten thousand" we may consider to be the warriors of God, enlisted to fight his battles against error and sin. Who is the Standard-bearer of God's militant host below? The only answer is that "Christ is the Standard-bearer among ten thousand." For a standard-bearer, there was need of a select man, with good strong arms, who could firmly grasp the pole that held aloft the standard — a man resolute of heart who, having once taken charge of the flag, would sooner die than loose his hold of the colours. It needed for a standard-bearer one who was courageous, one who would not be alarmed by the din and strife of battle and turn his back, but who would go at the head of the host, carrying the banner into the very thick of the fray, to lead on the militant band till they had put all their foes to rout. The standard-bearer should be a stronger man than all the rest of the host, for,

If the standard-bearer fall,
As fall full well he may,
For never saw I promise yet,
Of such a deadly fray.

474

(Thomas Babbington Macaulay)

— what mischief would come to the host, and what confusion to the hearts of all the warriors! Now, our Lord Jesus Christ has come into this world, and set up a standard because of the truth (Ps. 60:4), and well does he handle it, firmly does he grasp it. When on the cross, the battle thickened round him; all the hosts of hell, and all the bands of cruel ones on earth, sought to smite him, and to seize the standard, too, but he bore it still aloft through all the dreadful fray; and this day, though he is now in heaven, yet by his blessed Spirit that standard is still unfurled to the breeze. In the order of his providence, it seems to me that Christ is always bearing that standard a little farther and a little farther on, and if Christians would but keep nearer to Christ, and be more like him, the victories of his Church would be daily fresh and new. We should soon see this world conquered for Christ if we kept step with the Divine Standard-bearer. He is bearing that standard in front of some of you into that alley at the back of the house where you live; dare you follow him, and go and win some spoil for him? Christ's banner is uplifted in many parts of London tonight; dare you follow it? Dare you stand in the streets, and in the by-ways, to tell of heaven's accomplished salvation, and of Christ's finished work that saves from death and hell? The nations of the earth need the gospel; and Christ is opening the gates of brass to our missionaries. Are there no young men here who will follow Christ's banner as it gleams afar? Have I no young John Williams here? Is there no young man here who will be a Robert Moffat or a William Knibb? But there is the Standard-bearer; Christ is not in the background. Oh, why should we be so slow to follow him? We are not straitened in him but in ourselves. God give us to be worthy followers of so glorious a Standard-bearer as Christ Jesus our Lord!

Lift up your eyes to heaven, and see him there bearing the standard at the right hand of God, and the troops are marshalling, and the bugle sounds for some of us. Grey-heads, are you ready? Young men and maidens, are you ready? If the trumpet sounds in your ears tonight, are you ready to rally round that standard, and sing the praises of him who has called you? He is coming soon, and then, when the Standard-bearer is here, shall we not have a share in his triumph? Shall we rise to shame and confusion of face, or shall we rise to participate in the splendour of his universal reign? God grant that we may all love and trust the Divine Standard-bearer, and may all be found among his faithful soldiers for evermore! The Lord be with you, beloved, for his dear Son's sake! Amen.

63. SPICES, FLOWERS, LILIES, AND MYRRH
NO. 2479

AT THE METROPOLITAN TABERNACLE, NEWINGTON
ON THURSDAY EVENING, AUGUST 5TH, 1880

"His cheeks are as a bed of spices, as sweet flowers: his lips like lilies, dropping sweet smelling myrrh." (Song of Solomon 5:13)

IN this chapter, the spouse describes in detail the person of her Beloved. She is not satisfied with saying, "He is altogether lovely"; but she delights to talk of the charms of each part of his sacred person, and to picture the beauties of his divine form and features, so that by it, she may, perhaps, win some other heart first to admire and then to love him.

Dear friends, there are some things about which you would be wise not to go into detail. You had better speak in general terms of half the things on earth; for if you once describe them in detail, you will have to confess that they are marred by a thousand imperfections. You may be content to give merely a surface glance at them; for if you dive beneath the surface, you will soon discover much that will alter your opinion of the thing that, at first sight, looked so lovely. But it is not so with Jesus, our Well-beloved. You may talk of him as long as ever you please, and praise him as much as ever you can, yet you will never discover that you have exaggerated his excellences. You may go into detail about him, and dwell with much minuteness on everything relating to his character, his offices, his words, and his deeds, and you shall be made to wonder at the perfection of each one of them. You may apply the microscope to Christ; you may examine his little things, if, indeed, anything can be little that refers to him; you may look into the deep things of Christ, the hidden things of Christ and his secrets. The more closely you look, the more you will be amazed, and astonished, and filled with delight.

It is of Christ, the Heavenly Bridegroom, that we perceive the spouse to be speaking, and mentioning in detail at least ten particulars, dwelling with delight on the beauties of his head and his locks, his eyes and his cheeks, his lips and his hands, and every part of him. Beloved friends, I think it shows true love to Christ when we want to speak at length about everything that concerns him. The general hearer says, "Oh, yes, yes! Of course, Christ is the Son of God, and he is also perfect man, I believe that", but he does not want you to go into minute particulars concerning your Lord. It is not so with those who truly love the Saviour; they want to know all that can be known about him. True love likes to become familiar with the object of its affection; its heart is set on that object, it studies it, and can never know it too well or too closely. True love for Christ thinks of him from morning till night. It is glad to be released from other thoughts, that it may follow only its one darling pursuit. True love for Christ seeks to get to him, to live with him, to live upon him, and thus to know him so intimately that things which were unobserved and passed over at first, stand out in clear light to the increased joy and delight of the contemplative mind. I wish, dear friends, that we had many more of those people about, who study Christ from head to foot that they may learn all that can be learned about him, those who would be able, with the spouse, to talk of his charms and beauties in detail, and describe them as she does with rapturous delight.

You know how very unacquainted many people are with the Song of Solomon; they shut up this Book of Canticles in despair and say that they cannot understand its meaning. You will find that it is just the same with every truly spiritual thing. If you put into the hands of any one of them a deeply spiritual book, he will say, "I cannot comprehend what the writer means; the man seems to be in a rapture, and I cannot make out what he is aiming at by such writing." Just so; unspiritual people are all at sea in spiritual things, and even some of God's children, who know Christ so as to be saved by him, seem to be altogether out of their depth when we begin to speak of the things we have made touching the King, or dilate upon those special truths which only experience and fellowship with Christ can reveal to the soul. In speaking on our text, I am sure that I shall not say too much in praise of my Lord and Master; my fear is that I shall not say a thousandth part as much as he deserves — and yet, maybe, it shall seem but trivial talk to some who, as yet, do not know that one hair of his head is worth more than the whole world, and that one drop of his precious blood has an eternal efficacy about it. On the other hand, I know that I shall not speak too enthusiastically enough for those whose hearts are warm with love for Christ. May the Lord, in his great mercy, make us all to have such hearts, and he shall have all the praise!

There are two things I shall speak of as I am helped by the Holy Spirit. First, *Christ looked upon is very lovely:* "His cheeks are as a bed of spices, as sweet flowers." Secondly, *Christ listened to is very precious:* "His lips like lilies, dropping sweet smelling myrrh." There is an important distinction between the two heads of my discourse that I want you to notice before I proceed further; for there is a considerable difference between Christ looked upon and Christ listened to. There are some who listen to Christ's gospel, and they do well; but those who also look with eyes of love upon his sacred person, those who contemplate not only what he says but what he is, those who delight to know not only what he taught but what he is who taught it, these are they who have penetrated yet further into the mysteries of Christ.

I. With these we begin, as we consider our first point — CHRIST LOOKED UPON IS VERY LOVELY.

Note that these saints first see their Lord's loveliness, and then they say concerning him, "His cheeks are as a bed of spices, as sweet flowers." But why do they mention his cheeks?

I suppose, first, because *every part of Christ is inexpressibly delightful.* Take any portion of his countenance that you may, and it has surpassing beauty about it. The spouse had already spoken of her Beloved's head, and locks, and eyes, and now she mentions his cheeks. Any sight of Christ is delightful; a single passing glimpse of him is a foretaste of heaven, the beginning of paradise. Though you see but little of Christ, yet if it be Christ whom you really see, that sight will save you. Though you see Christ, as it were, with just one eye, and though that eye is dim, and though that dim eye is filled with tears, yet, if you do but see him at all, that sight will save you; and just in proportion as you are able to see him, your delight will increase. But a sight of him in any capacity, and under any form, has great richness of sweetness in it.

Think for a moment what is meant by a sight of "his cheeks". Though you may not yet see the majesty of his brow as King of kings and Lord of lords; though you may not perceive the brightness of the lightning flashes of his eyes, which are as a flame of fire; though you may scarcely be able to imagine at present what will be the glory of his second advent; yet, if you can but see the cheeks that he gave to the smiters, if you know something of him as the suffering Saviour, you shall find that there is inexpressible delight in him, and with the spouse you will say, "His cheeks are as a bed of spices." To a believing soul, then, there is great delight in every part of the Lord Jesus Christ.

But, I think, the saints see *great loveliness in those parts of Christ which have been most despised.* Just now, I mentioned the cheek as one of those parts of Christ's blessed body that were exposed to special shame, as Isaiah foretold, using by inspiration the very words of the Messiah in his agony: "I gave my back to the smiters, and my cheeks to them that plucked off the hair: I hid not my face from shame and spitting." (Is. 50:6) Oh, if we could but see him now, if we could but gaze on his face as it is in glory, what a subject of meditation it would be! To think that ever the spittle of cruel mockers ran a-down those blessed cheeks — that infinite loveliness was insulted with inconceivable contempt — the holy face of the Incarnate Son of God distained with the accursed spittle of brutal men. [See Metropolitan Tabernacle Pulpit, No. 2473: *"An Awful Contrast"*] O my soul, how low your Lord has stooped! Can you really believe it possible that it should have been so? Yes, you know that it was so; yet, is it not sad to think that his dear face, which is like the sun shining in its strength, which is indeed the very heaven of heavens, the light of the temple of God above, is it not sad to think that his face should have been spit upon for your sake, and, because of your sin, and your iniquity? Alas, that each of us had a part in that shameful deed! It was Alfonso Michael de Liguori who asked some very difficult questions in this regard:

My Jesus! say what wretch has dared
Thy sacred hands to bind?
And who has dared to buffet so
Thy face so meek and kind?

'Tis I have thus ungrateful been,
Yet, Jesus, pity take!
Oh, spare and pardon me, my Lord,
For Thy sweet mercy's sake!

My Jesus! who with spittle vile
Profaned thy sacred brow?
Or whose unpitying scourge has made
Thy precious blood to flow?

My Jesus! whose the hand that wove
That cruel thorny crown?
Who made that hard and heavy cross
That weighs Thy shoulders down?

My Jesus! who has mocked thy thirst
With vinegar and gall?
Who held the nails that pierced thy hands,
And made the hammer fall?

My Jesus! say, who dared to nail
Those tender feet of thine:
And whose the arm that raised the lance
To pierce that heart divine?

And Father! who has murdered thus
Thy loved and only One?
Canst thou forgive the blood-stained hand
That robbed thee of thy Son?

"It was I, with my vain and idle talk, with my false and proud speech, that spat into that dear face." How sad that he should ever have been made to suffer so! O glorious love that he should be willing even to stoop to this terrible depth of ignominy that he might lift us up to dwell with him on high! So, I say again, every part of Christ is lovely, but that which has been most despised and most subjected to suffering and shame for us is the peculiar subject of our delightful contemplation.

Next, my brethren, *those parts of Christ in which we do not immediately see any special office or use* are, nevertheless, particularly lovely to the saints. I can gaze by faith on the brow of him who plans for me, and admire his infinite wisdom. I can think of the eye of him who looks in love on me, and bless him for his care. I can praise the lips that speak for me in heaven, and speak to me on earth, and I can bless the matchless eloquence that never ceases to plead for me and with me. But as for the cheeks of Christ, what do they do for me? What peculiar function have they to perform? I fear that we are all too apt to ask concerning Christ, "How is this to work to our advantage, and how is that to turn out for our profit?" Has it come to this — that we are never to love Christ except when we see when we are profited by him? If there is an abstruse doctrine, as we think it, that does not appear to have a practical application, are we, therefore, never to think of it? If we cannot see that we derive comfort, or profit, or sanctification, from some teaching which may be high, mysterious, sublime, so that we do not see where it leads, yet, beloved, are we to refuse to think of it? Until the question "*Cui bono?*" (To whose good?) is answered, will we seal up that sacred page, and never read it? Do you care only for the lips that speak to you? Have you no love for the cheeks that are silent? Do you care for nothing but for the eyes that are watching over you? If there comes to you nothing from those cheeks of your Lord, yet shall they not be to you "as a bed of spices, as sweet flowers"? The fact is, we are not to judge concerning Christ in any such fashion as this; on the contrary, if there is any duty which Christ has commanded, but which, instead of seeming to be easy and profitable to us, is hard, and requires that we should give so much that Judas will cry out, "To what purpose is this waste?" (Mat. 26:8), let us never mind him, but break our alabaster boxes, and pour out the sweet perfume on our dear Master.

Let the cheeks that seem to have no special office to fulfil, let that part of Christ, or of Christianity, that seems to serve no end that we can see, be, nevertheless, precious to us! These are *his* cheeks, therefore they are precious to me; this duty is a command from him, therefore I must perform it; and this doctrine, of which I do not see a practical purpose, is, nevertheless, a doctrine of his teaching, therefore I accept it with delight.

But further, beloved children of God, the followers of Christ have an intense admiration, an almost infinite love, for *that part of Christ by which they are able to commune with him*, and perhaps that is one reason why his cheeks are here especially mentioned. The cheek is the place of fellowship where we exchange tokens of love. What a blessing it is that Christ should have a cheek for the lips of love to approach, and to kiss! What a privilege it is that ever it should be possible for a loving heart to express its affection for Christ! If he had accepted us, and then put us right away from him, and said, "There, you may love me, but you must never tell me of it"; if we were conscious that, when we talked of our love for Christ, he never knew it, for he was far away, and high above us, and did not care for such poor love as ours. In such a case, he would not be half such a Christ as he now is to us. If he had taken himself away to the ivory palaces, and had shut the door, and if, when we tried to gaze up at him there, he only looked down on us with his countenance "as Lebanon, excellent as the cedars" (Song 5:15), but never stooped to where we were that he might commune with us, and that we might tell out to him the story of our love, he would not be half so sweet to us as he is now.

Many of you know what it is to pray right into his very ear in the time of your sorrow, and you also know what it is to speak right into his ear in the hour of your joy; and, sometimes, when you have been alone with him (now I am talking of the deep things of Christ, of the pearls which are not to be cast before swine) you know that he has heard what you have said to him. You have been as certainly assured that he has been listening to your declaration as if, like Peter, you had heard him ask, "Lovest thou me?" and you had answered, "Lord, thou knowest all things; thou knowest that I love thee." (Jn. 21:15-16), and you were delighted with the thought that he knew that you loved him, and that you might tell him that it was so. You rejoiced also that you could go out into the world and do something that he would see you do, something that you did not do for the sake of the church, much less for your own sake, but which you did all for him, just as you would give him the kisses of love upon his own cheeks, which are "as a bed of spices, as sweet flowers." Those of you who have ever been in communion with Christ know what I mean, and you know that anything by which you come into close contact with Christ is very, very delightful to you.

How greatly we rejoice to think of Christ's humanity, because we feel that it brings him very near to us! He is our Brother, he feels what we feel, and, through his humanity, this wondrous Man is next of kin to us. He who is truly God is also our near Kinsman, bone of our bone, and flesh of our flesh. How the blessed doctrine of the union of the saints with Christ delights us, as we remember that we are members of his body, of his flesh, and of his bones! How the wondrous truth of the indwelling of the Holy Spirit charms us, because the same Spirit that rested upon him rests also upon us, and the holy oil that was first poured upon him who is the Head descends even to us who are as the hem of the garment that reaches even to the ground! It is the same Spirit upon him that is upon us, and so again we are one with him. Does not this truth also make prayer very sweet as the means of getting to Christ, and does it not make praise very sweet as another means of communicating with Christ? And oh, though some put the sacred table of the Lord out of its proper place, yet is the communion of the body of Christ a dear and blessed ordinance. Often, we know him in the breaking of bread when we have not recognised him before, even though he talked with us by the way. So, you see, the saints delight in those truths concerning Christ which enable them to have fellowship with him, and thus they realise what the spouse meant when she said, "His cheeks are as a bed of spices, as sweet flowers."

I have tried to show you that the saints see great beauty in Christ when they look upon him; but now I have to remind you that saints also labour to tell others of the loveliness of Christ when they look upon him. In this blessed service, however, they must, in part, labour in vain, for, as we have often sung in Linguori's hymn:

Oh, spare and pardon me, my Lord,
We must die to speak of Christ.

I suppose that even he who has seen Christ in heaven could not fully tell us of his beauties. Paul has not told us much of what he heard in paradise, though he told all he could tell after he had been caught up to the third heaven. He "heard unspeakable words, which it is not lawful (or possible) for a man to utter." (2 Cor. 12:4) Oh, how one longs for just a moment's sight of Christ in glory! One might be content to have only a dry crust, and lie in an underground dungeon for the rest of one's life, if one might but gaze on his blessed face for once, and hear him say, "I have loved thee with an everlasting love." (Jer. 31:3) Perhaps you think you would have a deal to tell if that were your blessed experience; but, beloved, you might not have anything to tell; you would only feel less able to speak than ever you were before. You would be so dazzled, so astonished, so amazed, at the glory of Christ that, perhaps, you might never be able to speak at all.

The spouse, however, in our text tries to speak of the loveliness of Christ by making comparisons. If she cannot do it with one emblem, she must have two even concerning his cheeks; they are "as a bed of spices", and "as sweet flowers."

Notice, in the metaphors used by the spouse, that there is *a blending of sweetness and beauty:* "as a bed of spices" — there is sweetness; and then "as sweet flowers" — there is beauty. There is sweetness to the nostrils and beauty to the eye, spice for its fragrance and flowers for their loveliness. In Christ, there is something for every spiritual sense, and for every spiritual sense there is a complete satisfaction and delight in him. Look at him, and he is to your sight as sweet flowers.

Get a spiritual taste of him, and then he is as honey and the honeycomb. Take, as it were, a spiritual smell of him, and you shall find that he is "as a bed of spices." Touch him, or hear him, and it shall be just the same; you shall find the daintiest, the highest, the most harmonious feelings your spirit ever knew when you but approach him with any spiritual sense in full exercise. Our blessed Master may be viewed from every side, and yet he is perfect from every aspect. We have seen him far above us. There are few things that look well when set up aloft, and gaze at from below; but he does. We shall one day see him side by side, and, I warrant you, that we shall count him lovely then even as we reckon him lovely now. Angels have looked down on him from above, gazing on him when he was here on earth, and he was infinitely lovely to their vision then. Seen by daylight or by moonlight, seen in the crowd or seen in solitude, seen in our days of sorrow or seen in our times of joy, our Lord Jesus possesses all kinds of loveliness compacted into one perfect loveliness, all perfections blended to make one perfection, every sweet concocted and distilled to make one perfect sweetness. Well, therefore, may his spouse pile up the metaphors, and blend sweet spices with fragrant flowers in trying to describe his charms.

Notice that, when the spouse is speaking even of the cheeks of her Beloved, she brings in the idea of *abundance*. Spices, yes, "a bed of spices"; flowers — not one or two, but, according to the Hebrew, "towers of perfume", which I understand to mean those raised beds which we delight to have in our gardens, where there are many flowers set in order, forming charming banks of beauty. No doubt Solomon had some of those in his garden, for "there is no new thing under the sun" (Eccl. 1:9); and those raised beds of dainty flowers are fit emblems of the beautiful cheek of Christ, with its delicate tints of white and red. So, in Christ, there is infinite abundance.

There is also in Christ infinite variety; there is in him all you can want of any one thing, and there is more than all you can want of everything. There is all that your soul could take in of any one thing, and more than your soul could take in if it were multiplied a million times, and could take in a million precious things at once. There is all that you have ever wanted, and all that you ever will want. Did I say "want"? There is in Christ all you can desire, for that is one of his names, "He is all desires." (Ps. 37:4) When you get to heaven, and have a larger heart than you possess at present, when your soul shall be spacious as the sea, if it could be as vast as the universe itself, still he would be able to fill it, and still to be himself overflowing with blessing. There is in him abundance, and there is variety. Oh, what a Christ he is! "As a bed of spices, and as sweet flowers."

The spouse's metaphors seem to me also to suggest *use and delight*. She speaks of spices, for which there is practical use in surgery and in medicine, for preservation and for perfume; and she also mentions sweet flowers, for which there may not be any particular use, but which are charming for ornament and for the delectation [delight] of taste. So, dear friends, in Christ Jesus there is all that we want; but there is a great deal more. There is something beside and beyond our actual necessities, for there are many spiritual luxuries. I like, at the Lord's Table, to think to myself, "Here is bread, that is the staff of life; but what is that in the cup? Wine! Ah! Why not water? Here is more than I need, for I can live without wine, but the Lord says that I shall not do so. He will not only give his people the best of things, but the best of the best; when our Lord keeps house, he does not allow us just so many ounces of bread, and so many ounces of meat, as they do in the workhouse, but he says, "Eat ye that which is good, and let your soul delight itself in fatness." (Is. 55:2) The Bridegroom cries, "Eat, O friends; drink, yes, drink abundantly, O beloved" (Song 5:1), and he does not merely bring out wine, but you know how it is described — "wines on the lees well-refined." (Is. 25:6) Christianity is not the bondslave's starvation allowance that some people make it out to be — duty, and doing, and serving, to win Christ, and to keep up your position, and I know not what else beside! It is heirship with Christ, the possession in him of everything, and the privilege of living up to our royal income — oh, that we could attain to that high life style! "All things are yours" (1 Cor. 3:21) then, so claim them as your own. God has given you his dear Son, and given you himself, for he said, "I will be their God." (2 Cor. 6:16) Then, live with the joy that a man ought to have who has Jehovah to be his God, and Jesus Christ to be his Saviour. The Lord has given us everything; then let us live at the rate of joy that we ought to have, who possess everything. God bring us to that happy state!

"His cheeks" — those features of the Beloved which do not at first seem likely to yield us anything —"are as a bed of spices, as sweet flowers", inexpressibly precious, yielding to us both what we need and what will delight and overflow our souls. You see, beloved, what saints think of Christ; let each one of us ask himself or herself, "Do I think of him in this way? Do I thus admire him? Is he everything to me?" These are sure marks of a true Christian that he does love his Master, and he does praise him. There is many a poor child of God who is half afraid that he is not among the number of God's people; but he says, "I do love Jesus. Oh, I would do anything to glorify him!" My dear friend, do not ever get the idea that you love him without his loving you. You may be quite sure that the reason why you love him is because he first loved you; and if you love him very much, you may rest assured that he loves you a great deal more. If you have but a spark of love for him in your heart, he has a furnace of love for you in his heart. If your love for him is but as a single grain, his love for you is abundant as the richest harvest. His love for you is as much above your love for him as the heavens are higher than the earth.

Oh, that we may think more highly of Christ! Perhaps it will help us to do so if we consider how worthy he is of that love, and how wondrously his thoughts of us exceed our thoughts of him. I sometimes feel very sad when I think about some who profess to be the Lord's people. Ah, me, there are many who, I hope, may prove to be his people; but they do not reflect much credit upon him! Some of God's children are a very queer lot; if we had such sons and daughters as God has, some of us would never be able to bear with them at all; for we should be impatient with them, and turn them out of doors to get on as best they can by themselves. When you get sick, and sad, and weary of God's people, turn your thoughts to God himself; and if ever you see any spots in the Church, Christ's bride, look at her glorious Husband, and you will only love him the more as you think of his wonderful condescension in having loved such a poor thing as his Church, even at her best. Think how bright he is, how glorious, how surpassing are his charms, even when seen through the defects and imperfections of his redeemed ones. We may well marvel that ever such love as his could have been lavished upon such unworthy beings as his people. Do not get depressed and distressed, dear friends, because of your own imperfections, or the imperfections of others; or if you do, quickly rise again to fight against sin under the blessed conviction that there are no imperfections in him, that he is altogether lovely, altogether sweet, and that the day must come when we, who are one with him even now, shall be like him, for we shall see him as he is. (1 Jn. 3:2) Complete sanctification is the lot of every redeemed soul. If we have known the Lord, and already have something of his likeness, we shall go on to know him till we are perfected in that likeness. Let that blessed consummation be the subject of our constant prayer, and our confident expectation.

II. Now, secondly, but briefly, let us turn to the other part of our text — "His lips like lilies, dropping sweet smelling myrrh." These words teach us that CHRIST LISTENED TO IS

VERY PRECIOUS. When he is silent, and we only look at him, he is lovely to our eyes; but when he speaks, we can see "His lips like lilies, dropping sweet smelling myrrh."

Notice, first, that it is well, whenever we hear the voice of Jesus Christ, *to try to see the blessed Person who is speaking.* The gospel is very precious to those of us who know its power; but, beyond all question, Christ himself is even more precious than his gospel. It is delightful to read any promise of the Scriptures, but it is more delightful to come into communion with the faithful Promiser. The time when I most enjoy a promise from the Word of God is when it seems to me as if it must have been written only yesterday on purpose to meet my case, or if I could see the eternal pen writing every one of the strokes, and making them all for me. Whenever you hear one of the Lord's promises, think of the divine lips that spoke it and you will love the promise all the better because you have thought of the lips that uttered it. The spouse does not say in our text, "His words are sweet" but she speaks of "his lips like lilies, dropping sweet smelling myrrh." Why should we not believe more in a personal Christ, and why should we not always see the connection between the mercy and the hand that gives it, and between the promise and the lips that speak it?

Some of you may remember William Huntington's story that I have sometimes quoted to you about an old farmer, who, when one of his daughters was married, gave her a thousand pounds as a wedding present. There was another daughter, and her father did not give her a thousand pounds when she was married, but he gave her something as a wedding present, and then he kept on pretty nearly every day in the week sending her what he called "the hand-basket portion, with father's love"; and so, in the long run, she received a great deal more than her sister. It was not given in one lump sum, and then was over and done with, but it kept on coming — now a sack of flour, and then this, and that, and the other, always "with father's love", so she had far more than the thousand pounds, and also had far more of his love. I do like, when I get a mercy, to have it come to me with my Heavenly Father's love, just as my daily portion as I need it; not given as a lump sum, so that I might go away with it into a far country, as we are sure to do if we had all our mercy at once, but given day by day, as the manna fell, with our Heavenly Father's love every time, a fresh token of infinite grace and infinite love. So, you see, the mercy leads you to think of the hand that gives it, and of the Father who sends it, as in the text it is not the words of the Beloved, but his lips which the spouse says are "like lilies, dropping sweet smelling myrrh."

Notice the comparison in the text — *lilies*; not white lilies, of course, but red lilies, crimson lilies, lilies of such a colour as are frequently to be seen, which would be a suitable emblem of the Beloved's lips. Christ's lips are peculiarly delightful to us for *it is with them that he speaks to us, and intercedes with the Father for us.* When he pleads as the Intercessor on behalf of a poor soul like me, his lips are indeed in God's sight like lovely lilies. The Father looks at his dear Son's lips, and is charmed with them, and blesses us because of Christ's intercession. And whenever Christ turns round, and speaks to us, shall we not listen at once, with eyes and ears wide open, as we say, "I like to watch his lips as he is speaking, for his lips are to me as lilies"?

I suppose this comparison means that Christ's lips are very pure, as the lily is the purest of flowers; and that they are very gentle, for we always associate the lily with everything that is tender, and soft, and kind. There is not a thorn about it as there is with the rose. We do not speak of it as George Herbert does of the rose:

Sweet rose, whose hue angry and brave
Bids the rash gazer wipe his eye:
Thy root is ever in its grave
And thou must die.

Sweet spring, full of sweet days and roses,
A box where sweets compacted lie;
My music shows ye have your closes,
And all must die.

It is not so; the lily is all tenderness, and is without a thorn, though often it may be found growing among thorns. The lily also is inconceivably beautiful, and so is Christ in speaking to his people. "Never man spake like this Man." (Jn, 7:46) The very words of Christ are the loftiest poetry and the sweetest music. Though they sometimes make us weep, great joy lies deeply hidden beneath the grief he causes our spirits. "His lips are like lilies."

But, dear friends, the spouse's comparison fails, for she said, "...his lips like lilies, dropping sweet smelling myrrh." These lilies do not do it, but Christ does. He is more than a lily, or he is a lily of such a sort as never bloomed on earth except once. He was the only lily that ever dropped sweet smelling myrrh. The spouse says that his lips do that. What does it mean? Does it not mean that his Word is often full of a very sweet, mysterious, blessed influence? You have come here often, and it is not because I have spoken that there has been a blessing to your souls; but when I have set out Christ to you — and I have no other theme but him — there have often come to you mysterious droppings; you have had singular feelings in your spirit caused by the secret exudations [emissions] of the Word, the outflowings from the Word, and inflowings into your spirit, causing you to say, "What a change has come over me! I went into God's house very heavy, but I came away quite relieved. I went in there perplexed and worried, and I came away knowing clearly what I ought to do. I went in there cold and chilly, and feeling myself at a distance from God; and I came out ready to dance with the sense of his realised presence." Ah, that change has been caused by some of the sweet smelling myrrh that has dropped from the lips of Christ.

There are many people who meet with us on the Sabbath who do not care to come out to the week-night services. I take the week-night attendance as something of a test of piety; any hypocrite can come out on a Sunday, but it is not every hypocrite who will come out on a Thursday night, though some do, I dare say. But still, most of them are for Sunday religion only, but a week-day religion they do not want. That is to say, they feed on the Word after a fashion, and worship God after a fashion, when most other people do, but give me that religion that loves to creep out on a week-night and is willing to take a back seat if it may give them a bit of spiritual food. Give me that man who says, "My soul must be fed. I have been tearing about all this week, almost worn out with fatigue, and perplexed with a great many cares. It is a delightful thing to be able to get into the house of prayer, to hear about Christ, and to feed on him." Oh, you who eat your morsels in secret behind the door, I believe more in you than in those who sit openly at the table, but who never have a secret feast at all!

"Oh, but", says one, "I do not hear the Word with profit." No, of course you don't. You see, you are looking to the lips of a man; but if you look to the lips of the Master, you will find that "His lips are as lilies, dropping sweet smelling myrrh." You may have heard the story of the lady who was present when Mr. Ebenezer Erskine preached at a Scotch communion service; she thought she had never heard such a man in all her life, for he preached Christ so sweetly that she was charmed. She enquired where he was to preach the next Sabbath, and she left her own place of worship to go to hear Mr. Ralph Erskine again; but it was a dreadfully dry discourse, she said, and she was foolish enough to go into the vestry, and to say to the preacher, "My dear sir, I have been bitterly disappointed in hearing you this morning. I heard you last Sabbath, and you so extolled Christ that I enjoyed the service above measure, and I thought I would come again to hear you, and now I have got nothing." "No, madam", replied the good man, "last Sabbath you went to worship God, and to feed on Christ, so you received the blessing you sought; today, you came to hear Mr. Erskine, and you have heard me, but you have missed the blessing." Oh, dear friends, beware of going to places of worship merely to hear men! Of course, you must hear a man speaking; but go with this view, that those lips which are as lilies, dropping sweet smelling myrrh, should be the lips to which you really are listening, and to whom you are praying all the time, "Lord, speak to me through the minister, speak to me through the hymn, speak to me through the prayer, speak to me through any part of the service — yes, speak through the speaker's not speaking if you will, — only you speak to me, when those dear lips of yours drop sweet smelling myrrh into my soul!" Pray thus, and you will not be disappointed, you can be sure of that. This blessing is what you and I must seek after day by day, for we need this myrrh for the healing of the wounds that sin has made. We need this myrrh in our spiritual worship that we may offer it up to God. We need this myrrh to perfume us, and make our lives fragrant in the midst of our daily cares. We need this myrrh to kill the contagion that abounds in this wicked world, and we shall get it through the Word when it comes fresh from the lips of Christ. O God, bring us all into this blessed state!

I close by saying that, if there are any here present who do not prize the Word of God, which do not care to listen to the lips of Christ. I pray God that they may speedily be converted; for if they are not, they will hear him speak when his lips shall be not as lilies, but as a flaming fire, and his Word shall be spoken then that shall burn as an oven, and his enemies shall be consumed by it. God give grace to such as have not believed in Jesus to look to him and listen to him now! "Incline your ear" says he, "and come unto me: hear, and your soul shall live, and I will make an everlasting covenant with you, even the sure mercies of David." (Is. 55:3) Yes, he says, "Look unto me, and be ye saved, all the ends of the earth: for I am God, and there is none else." (Is 45:22)

May God add his blessing to these words, for our Lord Jesus Christ's sake! Amen.

64. ALTOGETHER LOVELY
NO. 1001

A SERMON DELIVERED ON LORD'S-DAY MORNING,
JULY 23RD, 1871
AT THE METROPOLITAN TABERNACLE, NEWINGTON

"Yea, he is altogether lovely."
(Song of Solomon 5:16)

WHEN the old Puritan minister had delivered his discourse, and dwelt upon firstly, and secondly, and thirdly, and perhaps upon twenty-fifthly (!) before he sat down, he usually gave a comprehensive summary of all that he had said. Everyone who carefully noted the summary would carry away the essence of the sermon. The summary was always looked upon by the Puritan hearer as one of the most valuable helps to memory, and, consequently, a most important part of the discourse. In these five words, the spouse here gives you her summary. She had delivered a tenfold discourse concerning her Lord; she had described in detail all his various beauties, and, when she had surveyed him from head to foot, she gathered up all her commendations in this sentence: "Yea, he is altogether lovely." Remember these words, and know their meaning, and you will possess the quintessence of the spouse's portion of the Song of Songs.

Now, as in this allegorical song, the bride sums up her witness in these words, so may I say that all the patriarchs, all the prophets, all the apostles, all the confessors, yes, and the entire body of the church, have left us no other testimony. They all spoke of Christ, and they all commended him. Whatever the type, or symbol, or obscure oracle, or open word in which they bore witness, that witness all amounts to this: "Yea, He is altogether lovely." Yes, and I will add that, since the canon of inspiration has closed, the testimony of all saints, on earth and in heaven, has continued to confirm the declaration made of old. The verdict of each particular saint and of the whole elect host as a body still is this, "Yea, he is altogether lovely." From the sighs and the songs which mingle on the dying beds of saints, I hear this note supreme above all others, "He is altogether lovely"; and from the songs unmingled with groans, which perpetually peal out from immortal tongues before the presence of the Most High, I hear this one master note: "Yea, he is altogether lovely." If the whole church desired to say with the apostle, "Now of the things which we have spoken this is the sum", she need not wait for a brief and comprehensive summary, for it lies before her in this golden sentence: "Yea, he is altogether lovely."

Looking at my text in this light, I feel much humbling of spirit, and I hesitate to preach on it, for I say in my heart, "It is high, I cannot attain unto it." (Ps. 139:6) These deep texts show us the shortness of our plumb-line; these ocean verses are so exceeding broad that our skiffs are apt to be driven far out of sight of land where our timid spirits tremble to spread the sail. Then I comfort myself by the thought that, though I could not comprehend this text in a measure, nor weigh its mountains in scales, or its hills in a balance, yet it is all mine, by the gift of divine grace, and, therefore, I need not fear to enter on the meditation of it. If I cannot grasp the ocean in my span, yet may I bathe in it with sweet content! If I cannot describe the king in his beauty, yet may I gaze upon him, since the old proverb says, "A beggar may look at a prince." Though I differ to preach from such a heavenly word as that before us, and spread before you all its marrow and fatness, yet may I gather up a few crumbs which fall from its table. Poor men are glad of crumbs, and crumbs from such a feast are better than loaves from the tables of the world. Better to have a glimpse of Jesus than to see all the glory of the earth, and all the days of our life. If we fail in this subject, we may do better than if we succeeded with another; so we will pluck up courage, seek divine help, and draw near to this wondrous text, with our shoes off our feet like Moses, when he saw the bush aglow with God. (Ex. 3:1-5)

This verse has been translated in another way: "He is all desires"; and so indeed Jesus is. He was the desire of the ancients; he is the desire of all nations still. (Hag. 2:7) To his own people, he is their all in all; they are complete in him; they are filled out of his fullness. Philip Doddridge writes with delight:

Jesus, I love thy charming name,
'Tis music to my ear;
Fain would I sound it out so loud,
That earth and heaven might hear.

Yes, thou art precious to my soul,
My transport and my trust;
Jewels to thee are gaudy toys,
And gold but sordid dust.
All my capacious powers can wish
In thee doth richly meet;
Nor to my eyes is light so dear.
Nor friendship half so sweet.

Thy grace shall dwell upon my heart.
And shed its fragrance there;
The noblest balm of all its wounds,
The cordial of its care.

I'll speak the honours of thy name
With my last labouring breath ;
And, dying, triumph in thy cross,
The antidote of death.

He is the delight of his servants, and fills their expectations to the full. But we will not dispute about translations, for, after all, with such a text, so full of unutterable spiritual sweetness, everyone must be his own translator; and into his own soul must the power of the message come by the enforcement of the Holy Spirit. Such a test as this is very like the manna which fell in the wilderness, of which the rabbis said it tasted after each man's liking. If the flavour in a man's mouth was very sweetness, the angel's food which fell around the camp was luscious as any dainty he had conceived. Whatever he might be, the manna was to him as he liked. So shall this text be. To you, with low ideas of Christ, the words will but glide over your ears, and be meaningless; but if your spirit is ravished with the precious love of Jesus, there will be songs of angels, and, more than that, the voice of God's own Spirit to your soul in this short sentence, "Yea, he is altogether lovely."

I am an engraver this morning, and I seek something on which I may engrave this heavenly line. Shall I take to me ivory or silver? Shall I borrow crystal or gold? These are too common to bear this unique inscription, and I set them all aside. Shall I spell my text in gems, with an emerald, a sapphire, a ruby, a diamond, or a pearl for each single letter? No, these are poor perishable things, things all of which we put away. I need an immortal spirit to be the tablet for my writing. No, I must lay aside my graving tool, and ask the Spirit of God to take it. I want a heart prepared by the Holy Spirit, upon whose fleshy tablets there shall be written this morning no other sentence than this, and this shall suffice for a right royal motto to adorn it well: "Yea, he is altogether lovely." Spirit of God, find out the prepared heart, and, with your sacred hand, write in eternal characters the love of Christ, and all his inimitable perfections.

In handling our text this morning, we will note three points of character, and then we will show three uses to which we may profitably turn it.

I. We shall consider THREE POINTS OF CHARACTER which are very noticeable in these words, and the first of which suggests itself is this: the words are evidently uttered by one who is under the influence of *overwhelming emotion*.

The words are rather a veil to the heart than a glass through which we see its emotions. The sentence labours to express the inexpressible; it pants to utter the unutterable. The person writing these words evidently feels a great deal more than any language can possibly convey to us. The spouse begins somewhat calmly in her description: "My beloved is white and ruddy." She proceeds in due order, commencing at the head, and proceeding with the different parts of the person of the Beloved, but she warms, she glows, she flames, and, at last, the heat which had for a while been repressed is like fire within her bones, and she bursts out in flaming words. Here is the live coal from off the altar of her heart: "Yea, he is altogether lovely." It is the utterance of a soul that is altogether overcome with admiration, and therefore feels that, in attempting to describe the Well-beloved, it has undertaken a task beyond its power. Lost in adoring wonder, the gracious mind desists from description, and cries with rapture, "Yea, he is altogether lovely." It has often been thus with true saints; they feel the love of Jesus to be overpowering and inebriating.

Believers are not always cool and calm in their thoughts towards their Lord: there are seasons with them when they pass into a state of rapture, their hearts burn within them, they are in ecstasy, they mount up with wings as eagles, their souls become like the chariots of Amminadib, they feel what they could not tell, they experience what they could not express, though the tongues of men and of angels were perfectly at their command. Favoured believers are altogether enraptured with the sight they have of their all-beautiful Lord. It is to be feared that such raptures are not frequent with all Christians, though I should gravely question his saintship who has never experienced any degree of holy rapture: but there are some saints to whom a state of overwhelming adoration of their Lord has been, by no means, an unusual thing. Communion with Jesus has not only entranced them now and then, but it has perfumed all their life with holiness; and if it has not caused their faces literally to shine like the face of Moses (Ex. 34:29-30), it has made the spiritual glory to flash from their countenances, and elevated them among their fellow Christians to be leaders of the host of God, whereas others have admired and wondered. Perhaps I am speaking to children of God who know very little of what I mean by the overwhelming emotions created by a sight of our Lord; they have not so seen the Lord as to have felt their souls melting within them while the Beloved spoke with them, To those I shall speak with sorrowful sympathy, being, alas, too much like them; but my prayer shall go up all the while: "Lord, reveal yourself to us, that we also may be compelled to say, 'Yea, he is altogether lovely.' Show us your hands and your side, till we exclaim with Thomas, 'My Lord and my God.'" (Jn. 20:28)

1. Shall I tell you why it is, my brethren, that many of you only seldom enjoy the exceeding bliss of Jesus' presence? The cause may lie partly in what is, alas, something too common among Christians, *a great degree of ignorance of the person of the Lord Jesus*. Every soul that sees Jesus by faith is saved by faith. If I look to Christ with a bleary eye, that is ever so weak and clouded with tears, and if I only catch a glimpse of him through clouds and mists, yet the sight saves me. But who can remain content with such a poor gleam of his glory as that? Who wishes to see only "through a glass, darkly"? (1 Cor.

13:12) No, let my eyes be cleansed till they become as doves by the rivers of waters Song 5:12), and I can see my Lord as he is seen by his bosom friends, and sing of those beauties which are the light and crown of heaven itself. If you do but touch the hem of Jesus' garment, you shall be made whole; but will this always satisfy you? Will you not desire to get beyond the hem and beyond the garment, to himself, and to his heart, and there forever take up your abode? Who desires to be forever a babe in grace, with a half awakened dreamy twilight consciousness by the Redeemer? Brethren, be diligent in the school of the cross, where there is enduring wisdom. Study your Saviour much. The science of Christ crucified is the most excellent of all sciences; and to know him and the power of his resurrection is to know what is best worth knowing. Ignorance of Jesus deprives many saints of those divine raptures which carry others out of themselves; therefore, let us be among those children of Zion who are taught by the Lord.

Next to this, you will find the *lack of meditation* to be a very serious robber of the wealth of renewed hearts. To believe a thing is, as it were, to see the cool crystal sparkling in the cup; but to meditate upon it is to drink it up. Reading gathers the clusters, while contemplation squeezes out their generous juice. Meditation is of all things the most soul-fattening when combined with prayer. The spouse had meditated much in this chapter, for otherwise she would not have been able to speak in detail concerning her Lord. O saintly hearts, imitate her example! Think, my brethren, of our Lord Jesus: he is God, the Eternal, the Infinite, the ever blessed, yet he became man for us — man of the substance of his mother, like ourselves. Meditate on his spotless character; review the sufferings he endured on Calvary; follow him into the grave, and from the grave to the resurrection, and from the resurrection up the starry way to his triumphant throne. Let your souls dwell on each of his offices, as prophet, priest, and king; pore over each one of his characteristics, and every scriptural title; pause and consider every phase of him, and, when you have done this, begin again and yet again. It is good to chew the cud by meditation, then shall the sweetness and fatness of divine truth come to your soul, and you will burst out with such rapturous expressions as that of the text, "Yea, he is altogether lovely." Most of you are too busy, you have too much to do in the world; but; what is it all about? Scraping together dust, loading yourselves with thick clay. Oh, that you were busy after the true riches, and could step aside awhile to enrich yourselves in solitude, and make your hearts vigorous by feeding upon the Person and work of your ever blessed Lord! You miss a heaven below by a too eager pursuit of earth. You cannot know these joyful raptures if meditation is pushed into a corner.

Another reason why little of the Lord's beauty is discerned is *the low state of spiritual life in many a Christian*. Many a believer is just alive, and no more. Do you not know such starving souls? May you not be one of such yourself! His eyes are not delighted with the beauties of Christ, he is purblind [partly blind], and cannot see afar off; he does not walk with Jesus in the garden of pomegranates, for he is too feeble to rise from the couch of weakness. He cannot feed on Christ for his appetite is gone — a sure sign of terrible decline. For him there are no climbings to the top of Amana, no leaping for joy in the temple, no dancing before the ark with David; no, if he is carried to the feet of Jesus in an ambulance like the sick man borne of four (Mk. 2:3-12); it is as much as he has yet received. To be strong in the Lord, and in the power of his might (Eph. 6:10), to have the wings of eagles with which to mount above the clouds of earth (Is. 40:31), to this, many are strangers. But beloved, there are noble spirits, and better taught, who know something of the life of heaven even while here below. The Lord strengthen us with grace in our inner man, and then shall we drink deeper draughts of the wines on the lees well refined (Is. 25:6), and then also, our eyes being open, we shall see Jesus more clearly, and bear fuller witness that he is "fairer than the children of men." (Ps. 45:2)

I am afraid that *the visits of Christ to our souls have been un-esteemed, and the loss of those visits has not caused us corresponding sorrow*. We did not sufficiently delight in the beauty of the Bridegroom when he came to us. When our hearts were somewhat lifted up with his love, we grew cold and idle, and then he withdrew his conscious presence; but, alas, we were not grieved, but wickedly tried to live without him. It is wretched work for a believer to try and live without his Saviour. Perhaps, dear brethren, some of you have tried it until, at last, you almost succeeded. You were wont to mourn like doves if you had no word from our Master in the morning, and, without a love-token before you, you went to rest, tossing uneasily on your bed. But now you are carnal, and worldly, and careless, and quite content to have it so. Jesus hides his face, the sun is set, and yet it is not night with you. Oh, may God be pleased to rouse you from this lethargy, and make you mourn your sad estate! Even if an affliction should be needful to bring you back from your backsliding, it would be a cheap price to pay. Awake, O north wind, with all your cutting force, if your bleak breath may but stir the lethargic heart! May the Lord grant us grace so to love Christ that, if we have not our fill of him, we may be ready to die with hungering and thirsting after him. May we never be able to find a place to build our nest on while our wing wanders away from the tree of life! Like the dove of Noah, may we drop into the water and be drowned sooner than find rest for the sole of our foot except on the ark, Christ Jesus, our Saviour.

Beloved, if none of these suggestions hits the mark, and reveals the cause why so little is known of rapturous love for Christ, let me suggest another. Very often, *professors' hearts are vain and frivolous*; they are taken up during the week with their business. This might plead some excuse; but when they have little spaces and intervals, these are filled up with very vanity. Now, if the soul has come to look at the mere trifles of this world as all-important, is it any wonder that it should be unable to perceive the exceeding preciousness of Christ Jesus? Who will care for the wheat when he dotes on the chaff? And with this, it will often happen that the professor's mind has grown proud as well as vain; he does not remember his natural poverty and meanness, and consequently does not value the riches of Christ Jesus. He has come to think himself an established, experienced Christian; he fancies that he is not like those foolish beginners who are so volatile, and so readily led astray; he has acquired the wisdom of years and the stability of experience. O soul, if you are great, Christ will be little; you can never see him on the throne until you have been on the dunghill yourself. If you are anything, so much the less is Christ; for if he is all in all, then there is no room for anything else, and if are something, you have stolen just so much from the glory of thy Lord Jesus. Lie low in the dust; it is the place for you.

**The more thy glories strike my eyes,
The humbler I shall lie.**

(Isaac Watts)

The humbler I am in myself, the more will I be capable of seeing the enchanting beauties of Christ.

Let me just say these two or three words. I believe those are the happiest saints who are most overwhelmed with a sense of the greatness, goodness, and preciousness of Christ. I believe these to be the most useful saints, also, and are in the Christian church as a tower of strength. I pray that you and I, walking with God by faith, may, nevertheless, often have our festival days, our notable seasons, when he will specially bless us with the kisses of his love, and we shall drink larger draughts of his love, which is better than wine. Oh, to be carried right away with the divine manifestation of the chief among ten thousand, so that our souls shall cry out in rapture, "Yea, he is altogether lovely." This is one characteristic of the text: may it be transferred to us.

2. A second characteristic is this, and very manifest it is on the surface of the verse — here is *undivided affection*. "He is altogether lovely." Note that these words have a world of meaning in them, but chiefly they tell us this, that Jesus is to the true saint the only lovely one in the world. "He is altogether lovely", and there is no loveliness anywhere else. It is as though the spouse felt that Christ had engrossed all the beauty and all the loveworthiness in the entire universe. Who among us will say that he erred? Is not Jesus worthy of all the admiration and love of all intelligent beings? But may we not love our friends and kinsfolk? Yes, but in him, and in subservience to him; so, and so only, is it safe to love them. Did not our Lord himself say, "If any man love father or mother more than me, he is not worthy of me"? (Mat. 10:37) Yes, and in another place he put it more strongly still, for he said, "Except a man hate father and mother" (Lk. 14:26) — or love them not at all in comparison with me — "he is not worthy of me." Except these are put on a lower stage than Jesus, we cannot be his disciples. Christ must be monarch in our breast. Our dear ones may sit at his footstool, and we may love them for his sake, but he alone must fill the throne of our hearts. I may see excellent things in my Christian brethren, but I must not forget that there would be none in them if they were not derived from him; that their loveliness is only a part of his loveliness, for he wrought it in them by his own Spirit. I am to acknowledge that Jesus is the monopoliser of all loveliness, the engrosser of all that is admirable, in the entire universe; and I am, therefore, to give him all my love, for "he is altogether lovely." Our text means, again, that in Jesus, loveliness of all kinds is to be found. If there is anything that is worthy of the love of an immortal spirit, it is to be seen in abundance in the Lord Jesus. Whatsoever things are true, whatsoever things are honest, whatsoever things are just, whatsoever things are pure, whatsoever things are lovely, whatsoever things are of good report; if there be any virtue, and if there be any praise (Phil. 4:8), all can be found without measure in Christ Jesus. As all the rivers meet in the sea, so all beauties unite in the Redeemer. Take the character of any gracious man, and you shall find a measure of loveliness, but it has its bounds and its mixtures. Peter had many virtues, but he had not a few failings. John, too, excels, but in certain points he is deficient; but in this, our Lord transcends all his saints, for all human virtues, all divine, are harmoniously blended in him. He is not this flower or that, but he is the Paradise of perfection. He is not a star here or a constellation there, he is the whole heaven of stars, no, he is the heaven of heavens; he is all that is fair and lovely condensed in one.

When the text says again that Jesus "is altogether lovely", it declares that he is lovely in all views of him. It generally happens that, to the noblest building, there is an unhappy point of view from which the architecture appears at a disadvantage. The choicest piece of workmanship may not be equally complete in all directions. The best human character is deformed by one flaw, if not with more; but with our Lord all is lovely, regard him as you will. You can contemplate him from all points, and only find new confirmation of the statement that "he is altogether lovely." As the everlasting God, before the world was made, angels loved him and adored; as the babe at Bethlehem, or as the man at Bethany; as walking the sea or as nailed to the cross; in his grave, dead, and buried, or on his throne triumphant; rising as forerunner, or descending a second time to judge the world in righteousness; in his shame, despised and spit upon, or in his glory, adored and beloved; with the thorns about his brow and the nails piercing his hands, or with the keys of death and hell swinging at his girdle; view him as you will, and where you will, and when you will, he remains "altogether lovely." Under all aspects, and in all offices and in relations, at all times and all seasons, under all circumstances and conditions, anywhere, everywhere, "he is altogether lovely."

Nor is he to any degree unlovely; the commendation forbids any idea that he is less than "altogether lovely." Where could you find room for deformity? When Apelles painted Alexander, he laid the monarch's finger on an unsightly scar; but there are no scars to conceal when you portray the countenance of Prince Immanuel. We say of our country — and who among us will not say it? — "With all her faults, we love her still"; but we love Jesus, and find no strain put on our heart, for trace of fault he has none. There is no need of apologies for Jesus; no excuses are required for him. But what is that I see on his shoulder? It is a hard rough cross; and if I follow him, I must carry that cross for his sake. Is not that cross unsightly? Oh, no! He is altogether lovely, cross and all. Whatever it may involve to be a Christian, we count even the reproach of Christ to be greater riches than the treasures of Egypt. The world will honour a half Christ, but a whole Christ it will not acknowledge. The bat-eyed Socinian says, "I admire the man Christ, but I will not adore Jesus as God." To him, the eternal word is but half lovely, if lovely at all. Some will have Christ the exemplar, but they will not accept him as the vicarious sacrifice for sin, the substitute for sinners. Many will have Christ in silver slippers — my lord archbishop's religion — but they would not listen to the gospel from a poor gracious Methodist, or think it worth their while to join the unlettered throng whose devout songs rise from the village green. Alas, how much we see of crosses of gold and ivory, but how little do men love the lowly cross of Jesus! Brethren, we think Jesus "altogether lovely" even in poverty, or when hanging naked on the cross, deserted and condemned. We see unspeakable beauty in Jesus in the grave, all fair with the pallor of death. Jesus bruised as to his heel by the old serpent is yet comely. His love to us makes him evermore "white and ruddy" to our eye. We adore him anywhere and everywhere, and in any place, for we know that this same Christ whose heel is bruised breaks also the serpent's head, and he who was naked for our sakes is now arrayed in glory. We know that the "despised and rejected" is also King of kings, and Lord of lords, the "Wonderful, Counsellor, The Mighty God, The Everlasting Father, the Prince of Peace." (Is. 9:6) "Yea, he is altogether lovely." There are no flaws in him.

The text intends us to know that Jesus is lovely to the highest degree: not lovely positively, and then failing comparatively, but lovely superlatively, in the highest possible sense. But I leave this for your hearts to enlarge on. I will close this point by saying, every child of God acknowledges that Christ Jesus is lovely altogether to the whole of himself. He is lovely to my judgement; but many things are so, and yet are not lovely to my affections; I know them to be right, and yet they are not pleasant. But Jesus is as lovely to my heart as to my head, as dear as he is good. He is lovely to my hopes: are they not all in him? Is not this my expectation — to see him as he is? But he is lovely to my memory too: did he not pluck me out of the net? He is lovely to all my powers and all my passions, my faculties and feelings. As David puts it, "My heart and my flesh crieth out for the living God" (Ps. 84:2) — the whole of the man seeking after the whole of the Saviour; the whole Saviour sweet and inexpressibly precious to the man's entire being. May it be so with you and with me! But is it so? Do you not set up idols in your hearts?

Men of God, do you not need to take the scourge of small cords, and purge the temple of your souls this morning? Are there not buyers and sellers where Christ alone ought to be? Oh, to love him wholly, and to love him only, so that we have no eyes for other beauty, no heart for other loveliness, since he fills our souls, and is to us "altogether lovely."

3. The third characteristic of the text is that to which I desire to draw the most attention, and that is *ardent devotion*. I called the text a live coal from off the altar, and surely it is so. If it should drop into our hearts to set them on fire, it would be an unspeakable mercy. Ardent devotion flames from this sentence. It is the language of one who feels that no emotion is too deep when Jesus moves the heart. Some may chide you, and say you think too much of your religion? It cannot be, it cannot be! If the zeal of God's house should eat us up until we have no existence except for the Lord's glory, we should not have gone too far. If there is corresponding knowledge to balance it, there cannot be too much of zeal for God. The utterance is that of one whose heart is like a furnace, of which love is the fire. "He is altogether lovely" — it is the exclamation of one who feels that no language is too strong to commend the Lord. The spouse looked through the Hebrew tongue to find an intense expression, and our translators ransacked the English language for a forcible word, they have put it in the most weighty way — "He is altogether lovely." There is no fear of exaggeration when you speak of Christ; hyperboles are only sober truth when we depict his excellences. We have heard of a portrait painter who owed his popularity to the fact that he never painted truthfully, but always added a flattering touch or two. Here is one who would defy his art, for it is impossible to flatter Jesus. Lay on, you men of eloquence, spare no colours, you shall never depict him too bravely. Bring out your harps, you seraphs; sing aloud, you blood-washed ones; all your praises fall short of the glory which is due to him.

It is the language of one who feels that no service would be too great to render to the Lord. I wish we felt as the apostles and martyrs and holy men of old did, that Jesus Christ ought to be served at the highest and richest rate. We do little, very little. What if I had said we do next to nothing for our dear Lord and Master nowadays? The love of Christ does not constrain us as it should. But those of old bore poverty, and dared reproach, and marched weary leagues, and passed tempestuous seas, and bore perils of robbers and of cruel men, to plant the cross in lands where, as yet, Jesus was not known — labours that nowadays could not be expected of men — were performed as daily matters of commonplace by the Christians of the earliest times. Is Christ less lovely, or is his church less loyal? Would God she estimated him at his right rate, for then she would return to her former mode of service!

Brethren, we want to feel, and we shall feel, if this text is deeply engraven on our hearts, that no gift is too great for Christ, though we give him all we have, and consecrate to him all our time and ability, and sacrifice our very lives for him. No suffering is too great to bear for the sake of the Crucified, and it is a great joy to be reproached for Christ's sake. "He is altogether lovely." Then, my soul, I charge you, think nothing hard to which he calls you, nothing sharp which he bids you endure. As the knight of the olden times consecrated himself to the Crusade, and wore the red cross on his arm, fearing not to meet death at the hands of the Infidel if he might be thought a soldier of the Lord, so we too would face all foes for Jesus' sake. We want — only refined and purified, and delivered from its earthly grossness — we want the chivalrous spirit once again in the church of God. A new crusade would I preach: had I the tongue of such a one as the old hermit to move all Christendom, I would say, "This day Christ, the altogether lovely one, is dishonoured: can you endure it? This day, idols stand where he should be, and men adore them. Lovers of Jesus, can ye bear it? This day, Juggernaut rides through the streets on his bloody way; this day, God's Christ is still unknown to millions, and the precious blood does not cleanse the nations. How long will you have it so? We, in England, with ten thousand Christian hearts, and as many tongues endowed with eloquence, and purses weighted with gold, shall we refuse our gifts, withhold our witness, and suffer the Lord to be dishonoured? The church is doing next to nothing for her great Lord; she falls short both in her duty and in the grim need of a perishing world. Oh, for a flash of the celestial fire! Oh, when shall the Spirit's energy visit us again! When shall men put down their selfishness and seek only Christ? When shall they leave their strifes about trifles to rally round his cross! When shall we end the glorification of ourselves, and begin to make him glorious, even to the world's end? God help us in this matter, and kindle in our hearts the old consuming heart-inflaming fire, which shall make men see that Jesus is all in all to us!

II. Thus I have shown you the characteristics of the text, and now I desire to USE IT IN THREE WAYS FOR PRACTICAL PURPOSES. As time flies, we must treat it briefly. The first word is to you, Christians. Here is very *sweet instruction*.

The Lord Jesus "is altogether lovely." Then if I want to be lovely, I must be like him, and the model for me as a Christian is Christ. Have you ever noticed how badly boys write at the bottom of the pages in their copy-books? There is the copy at the top; and in the first line they look at that; in the second line, they copy their own imitation; in the third line, they copy their imitation of their imitation, and so the writing gets worse and worse as it descends the page. Now, the apostles followed Christ; the first fathers imitated the apostles; the next fathers copied the first fathers, and so the standard of holiness fell dreadfully; and now we are too apt to follow the very lees and dregs of Christianity, and we think if we are about as good as our poor, imperfect ministers or leaders in the church, we shall do well and deserve praise. But now, my brethren, cover up the mere copies and imitations, and live by the first line. Copy Jesus; "he is altogether lovely"; and if you can write by the first line, you will write by the truest and best model in the world. We want to have Christ's zeal, but we must balance it with his prudence and discretion; we must seek to have Christ's love for God, and we must feel his love to men, his forgiveness of injury, his gentleness of speech, his incorruptible truthfulness, his meekness and lowliness, his utter unselfishness, his entire consecration to his Father's business. Oh, that we had all this, for, depend on it, whatever other pattern we select, we have made a mistake; we are not following the true classic model of the Christian artist. Our master model is the "altogether lovely" One. How sweet it is to think of our Lord in the double aspect as our exemplar and our Saviour! The laver which stood in the temple was made of brass: in this the priests washed their feet whenever they offered sacrifices; so does Christ purify us from sin. But the tradition is that this laver was made of very bright brass, and acted as a mirror, so that as often as the priests came to it they could see their own spots in it. Oh, when I come to my Lord Jesus, not only do I get rid of my sins as to their guilt, but I see my spots in the light of his perfect character, and I am humbled, and taught to follow after holiness.

The second use to which we would put the verse is this: here is a very *gentle rebuke* to some of you. Though very gentle, I beseech you to let it sink deep into your hearts. You do not see the lowliness of Christ, yet "he is altogether lovely." Now, I will not say one hard word! But I will tell you sorrowfully what pitiable creatures you are. I hear enchanting music, which seems more a thing of heaven than of earth: it is one of Handel's half-inspired oratorios. Yonder sits a man who says, "I hear nothing to commend it." He has not the power to perceive the linked sweetnesses, the delicious harmonies of sounds. Do you blame him? No, but you who have an ear for music, say, "How I pity him: he misses half the joy of life!" Here, again, is a glorious landscape, hills and valleys, and flowing rivers, expansive lakes and undulating meadows. I consider the point of view of a friend, whom I would gratify, and I say to him, "Is not that a charming scene?" Turning his head to me, he says, "I see nothing." I perceive that he cannot enjoy what is so delightful to me; he has such little sight, but he sees only what is very near, and he is blind to all beyond. Now, do I blame him? Or if he proceeds to argue with me, and say, "You are very foolish to be so enthusiastic about a non-existent landscape, it is merely your excitement", shall I argue with him? Shall I be angry with him? No, but I shed a tear, and whisper to myself, "Great are the losses of the blind."

Now, you who have never heard music in the name of Jesus, you are to be greatly pitied, for your loss is heavy. You who never saw beauty in Jesus, and who never will forever, you need all our tears. It is hell enough not to love Christ! It is the lowest abyss of Tartarus, and its fiercest flame, not to be enamoured of the Christ of God. There is no heaven that is more heaven than to love Christ and to be like him, and there is no hell that is more hell than to be unlike Christ, and not to want to be like him, but is to be averse to the infinite perfections of the "altogether lovely." May the Lord open those blind eyes of yours, and unstop those deaf ears, and give you the new and spiritual life! And then you will join in saying, "Yea, he is altogether lovely."

The last use of the text is that of *tender attractiveness*. "Yea, he is altogether lovely." Where are you this morning, you who are convinced of sin and want a Saviour, where have you crept to? Are you hidden away where my eyes cannot reach you? At any rate, let this sweet thought reach you. You need not be afraid to come to Jesus, for "he is altogether lovely." It does not say he is altogether terrible — that is your misconception of him; it does not say he is somewhat lovely, and sometimes willing to receive a certain sort of sinner. But "he is altogether lovely" and, therefore, is always ready to welcome to himself the vilest of the vile. Think of his name. It is Jesus, the Saviour. Is not this lovely? Think of his work. He has come to seek and to save that which was lost. (Lk. 15:4) This is his occupation. Is not that lovely? Think of what he has done. He has redeemed our souls with blood. Is not that lovely? Think of what he is doing. He is pleading before the throne of God for sinners. Think of what he is giving at this moment — he is exalted on high to give repentance and remission of sins. Is not this lovely? Under every aspect, Christ Jesus is attractive to sinners who need him. Come, then, come and welcome, there is nothing to keep you away, there is everything to bid you come. May this very Sabbath day in which I have preached Christ, and lifted him up, be the day in which you shall be drawn to him, never again to leave him, but to be his forever and forever! Amen.

65. THE WELL-BELOVED

A COMMUNION ADDRESS AT MENTONE

"Yea, he is altogether lovely."
(Song of Solomon 5:16)

THE soul that is familiar with the Lord worships him in the outer court of nature, where it admires his *works*, and is charmed by every thought of what he must be who made them all. When that soul enters the nearer circle of inspiration, and reads the wonderful *words* of God, it is still more enraptured, and its admiration is heightened. In revelation, we see the same all-glorious Lord as in creation, but the vision is clearer, and the consequent love is more intense.

The Word is an inner court to the Creation; but there is yet an innermost sanctuary, and blessed are those who enter it, and have fellowship with the Lord himself. We come to Christ, and, in coming to him, we come to God; for Jesus says, "He that hath seen me hath seen the Father." (Jn. 14:9) When we know the Lord Jesus, we stand before the mercy-seat where the glory of Jehovah shines out. I like to think of the text as belonging to those who are as priests unto God, and stand in the Holy of holies, while they say, "Yea, He is altogether lovely." His works are marvellous, his words are full of majesty, but he himself is altogether lovely.

Can we come into this inner circle? All do not enter here. Alas, many are far off from him, and are blind to his beauties! "He was despised and rejected of men" (Is. 53:3), and he is so still. They do not see God in his works, but dream that these wonders were evolved, and not created by the Great Primal Cause. As for his words, they seem to them as idle tales, or, at best, as inspired only in the same sense as the language of Shakespeare or Spenser. They do not see the Lord in the stately aisles of Holy Scripture, and have no vision of *himself*. May he, who opens the eyes of the blind, have pity on them!

Certain others are in a somewhat happier position, for they are enquirers after Christ. They are like those who, in the ninth verse of the chapter, asked, "What is thy Beloved more than another beloved, O thou fairest among women? What is thy Beloved more than another beloved that thou dost so charge us?" They want to know who this Jesus is. But they have not seen him yet, and cannot join with the spouse in saying, "He is altogether lovely."

If we enter this sacred inner circle, we must become witnesses, as she does who speaks of Christ, "Yea, He is altogether lovely." She knows what he is, for she has seen him. The verses which precede the text are a description of every feature of the heavenly Bridegroom; all his members are there set out with the richness of Oriental imagery. The spouse speaks what she knows. Have we, also, seen the Lord? Are we his familiar acquaintances? If so, may the Lord help us to understand our text!

If we are to know the full joy of this verse, we must come to our Lord as his intimates. He permits us this high honour, since, in this ordinance, he makes us his table-companions. He says, "Henceforth I call you not servants; but I have called you friends." (Jn. 15:15) He calls on us to eat bread with him; yes, to partake of him by eating his flesh and drinking his blood. (Jn. 6:54, 56) Oh, that we may pass beyond the outward signs into the closest intimacy with *himself*! Perhaps, when you are at home, you will examine the spouse's description of her Lord. It is a wonderful piece of tapestry. She has wrought into its warp and woof all things charming, sweet, and precious. In him, she sees all lovely colours —

"My Beloved is white and ruddy." In comparison with him, all others fail, for he is "chiefest among ten thousand" chieftains. (Song 5:10) She cannot think of him as comparable with anything less valuable than "fine gold." (Song 5:11, 15) She sees, soaring in the air, birds of different wing; and these must aid her, whether it be the raven or the dove. The rivers of waters, and the beds of spices and myrrh-dropping lilies, must come into the picture, with sweet flowers and goodly cedars. All kinds of treasured things are in him; for he is like gold rings set with beryl, and bright ivory overlaid with sapphires, and pillars of marble set on sockets of fine gold. She labours to describe his beauty and his excellence, and strains all comparisons with their utmost use, and somewhat more. Yet she is conscious of failure, and therefore sums up all with the pithy sentence, "Yea, He is altogether lovely."

If the Holy Spirit will help me, I should like to lift the veil, that we may, in sacred contemplation, look on our Beloved.

I. We would do so, first, WITH REVERENT EMOTIONS. In the words before us, "Yea, He is altogether lovely", two emotions are displayed: namely, admiration and affection.

It is *admiration* which speaks of Him as "altogether lovely" or beautiful. This admiration rises to the highest degree. The spouse would fain show that her Beloved is more than any other beloved; therefore she cries, "He is altogether lovely." Surely no one else has reached that point. Many are lovely, but no one save Jesus is "altogether lovely." We see something that is lovely in one, and another point is lovely in another; but all loveliness meets in Him. Our soul knows nothing which can rival Him: He is the gathering up of all sorts of loveliness to make up one perfect loveliness. He is the climax of beauty; the crown of glory; the uttermost of excellence.

Our admiration of Him, also, is unrestrained. The spouse dared to say, even in the presence of the daughters of Jerusalem, who were somewhat envious, "Yea, He is altogether lovely." They knew not, as yet, His perfections; they even asked, "What is thy Beloved more than another beloved?" But she was not to be blinded by their want of sympathy, neither did she withhold her testimony from fear of their criticism. To her, He was "altogether lovely" and she could say no less. Our admiration of Christ is such that we would tell the kings of the earth that they have no majesty in his presence; and tell the wise men that he alone is wisdom; and tell the great and mighty that he is the blessed and only Potentate, King of kings, and Lord of lords. (Rev, 19:16)

Our admiration for our Lord is inexpressible. We can never tell all we know of our Lord; yet all our knowledge is little. All that we know is that his love passes knowledge (Eph 3:19), that his excellence baffles understanding, that his glory is unutterable. We can embrace him by our love, but we can scarcely touch him with our intellect, He is so high, so glorious. As for describing him, we cry, with Mr. Berridge:

Then my tongue would fain express
All His love and loveliness;
But I lisp, and falter forth
Broken words, not half His worth.

Vexed, I try and try again,
Still my efforts all are vain:
Living tongues are dumb at best,
We must die to speak of Christ.

"He is altogether lovely." Do we not feel an inexpressible admiration for Him? There is none like unto you, O Son of God!

Still, our paramount emotion is not admiration, but *affection*. "He is altogether" — not beautiful, nor admirable — but "lovely." All His beauties are loving beauties towards us, beauties which draw our hearts towards him in humble love. He charms us, not by a cold comeliness, but by a living loveliness, which wins our hearts. His is an approachable beauty, which not only overpowers us with its glory, but holds us captive by its charms. We love Him: we cannot do otherwise, for "He is altogether lovely." He has within himself an unquenchable flame of love which sets our soul on fire. He is all love, and all the love in the world is less than his. Put together all the loves of husbands, wives, parents, children, brothers, sisters, and they only make a drop [in the ocean] compared with his great deeps of love, unexplored and unexplorable. This love of his has a wonderful power to beget love in unlovely hearts, and to nourish it into a mighty force. "It is a torrent which sweeps all before it when its founts break forth within the soul." It is a Gulf Stream in which all icebergs melt. When our heart is full of love for Jesus, his loveliness becomes the passion of the soul, and sin and self are swept away. May we feel it now!

There he stands: we know him by the thorn-crown, and the wounds, and the visage more marred than that of any man! (Is. 52:14) He suffered all this for us. O Son of man! O Son of God! With the spouse, we feel, in the inmost depths of our soul, that you are "altogether lovely."

II. Now would I lift the veil a second time with deep solemnity, not so much to suggest emotions as to secure your intelligent assurance of the fact that "He is altogether lovely." We say this WITH ABSOLUTE CERTAINTY.

The spouse places a "Yea" before her enthusiastic declaration, because she is sure of it. She sees her Beloved, and sees him to be altogether lovely. This is no fiction, no dream, no freak of imagination, no outburst of partiality. The highest love for Christ does not make us speak more than the truth. We are as reasonable when we are filled with love for him as ever we were in our lives; no, never are we more reasonable than when we are carried clean away by a clear perception of his superlative excellence.

Let us meditate on the proof of our assertion. "He is altogether lovely" — *in his Person*. He is God. The glory of Godhead I must leave in lowly silence. Yet is our Jesus also man, more emphatically man, than anyone here present this afternoon, for we are English, American, French, German, Dutch, Russian; but Christ is man, the second Adam, the Head of the race: as truly as he is very God of very God, so is he man, of the substance of his mother. What a marvellous union! The miracle of miracles! In his incomparable personality, he is altogether lovely; for, in him, we see how God comes down to man in condescension, and how man goes up to God in close relationship. There is no other such as he, in all respects, even in heaven itself: in his personality he must ever stand alone, in the eyes of both God and man, he is "altogether lovely."

As for *His character*, time would fail us to enter into that vast subject; but the more we know of the character of our Lord, and the more we grow like him, the more lovely will it appear to us. In all aspects, it is lovely; in all its minutiae and details, it is perfect; and, as a whole, it is perfection's model. Take any one action of his, look into its mode, its spirit, its motive, and all else that can be revealed by a microscopic examination, and it is "altogether lovely." Consider his life as a whole, in reference to God, to man, to his friends, to his foes, to those around him, and to the ages yet to be, and you will find it absolutely perfect.

More than that: there is such a thing as a cold perfection, with which one can find no fault, and yet it commands no love; but in Christ, our Well-beloved, every part of His character attracts. To a true heart, the life of Christ is as much an object of love as of reverence — "He is altogether lovely." We must *love* that which we see in him: admiration is not the word. When cold critics commend him, their praise is half an insult: what know [the attitude] of frozen hearts to our Beloved? As for a word against him, it wounds us to the soul. Even an omission of his praise is a torture to us. If we hear a sermon which has no Christ in it, we weary of it. If we read a book that contains a slighting syllable of him, we abhor it. He, himself, has become everything to us now, and, only in the atmosphere of fervent love for him, can we feel at home.

Passing from his character to *his sacrifice*, there, especially, "He is altogether lovely." You may have read "Rutherford's Letters"; I hope you have. How wonderfully he writes, when he describes his Lord in garments red from his sweat of blood, and with hands bejewelled with His wounds! When we view his body taken down from the cross, all pale and deathly, and wrapped in the cerements [burial garments] of the grave, we see a strange beauty in him. He is to us never lovelier than when we read in our Beloved's white and red that his Sacrifice is accomplished, and he has been obedient to death for us. In him, as the sacrifice once offered, we see our pardon, our life, our heaven, our all. So lovely is Christ in His sacrifice, that he is for ever most pleasing to the great Judge of all; yes, so lovely to his Father, that he makes us also lovely to God the Father, and we are "accepted in the Beloved." (Eph. 1:6) His sacrifice has such merit and beauty in the sight of heaven, that in him God is well pleased, and guilty men become in him pleasant to the Lord. Is not his sacrifice most sweet to us? Here, our guilty conscience finds peace; here, we see ourselves made comely in his comeliness. We cannot stand at Calvary and see the Saviour die, and hear him cry, "It is finished!" (Jn. 19:30), without feeling that "He is altogether lovely." Forgive me that I speak so coolly! I dare not enter fully into a theme which would pull up the sluices of my heart. Remember what he was when He rose from the grave on the third day. Oh, to have seen him in the freshness of *his resurrection beauty*! And what will he be in *his glory*, when He comes again the second time, and all His holy angels with Him, when He shall sit on the throne of his glory, and heaven and earth shall flee away before his face? To His people, he will then be "altogether lovely." Angels will adore him, saints made perfect will fall on their faces before him; and we ourselves will feel that, at last, our heaven is complete. We shall see him, and, being like him, we shall be satisfied.

Every feature of our Lord is lovely. You cannot think of anything that has to do with him which is unworthy of our praise. All-over glorious is our Lord! The spouse speaks of his head, his locks, his eyes, his cheeks, his lips, his hands, his legs, his countenance, his mouth; and when she has mentioned them all, she sums up with reference to it all by saying, "Yea, He is altogether lovely."

There is *nothing unlovely about him*. Certain people would be beautiful were it not for a wound or a bruise, but our Beloved is all the more lovely for his wounds; the marring of his countenance has enhanced its charms. His scars are, for glory and for beauty, the jewels of our King. To us, he is lovely even from that side which others dread: his very frown has comfort in it to his saints, since he only frowns on evil. Even his feet, which are "like unto fine brass, as if they burned in a furnace" (Rev. 1:15, 2:18) are lovely to us for his sake. These are his poor saints who are sorely tried, but are able to endure the fire. Everything of Christ, everything that partakes of Christ, everything that has a flavour or savour of Christ, is lovely to us.

There is *nothing lacking about his loveliness*. Some would be very lovely were there a brightness in their eyes, or a colour in their countenances: but something is away. The absence of a tooth or of an eyebrow may spoil a countenance, but in Christ Jesus there is no omission of excellence. Everything that should be in him is in him; everything that is conceivable in perfection is present to perfection in him.

In Him is nothing excessive. Many a face has one feature in it which is overdone; but, in our Lord's character, everything is balanced and proportionate. You never find his kindness lessening his holiness, nor his holiness eclipsing his wisdom, nor his wisdom abating his courage, nor his courage injuring his meekness. Everything is in our Lord that should be there, and everything in due measure. Like rare spices, mixed after the manner of the apothecary [chemist], our Lord's whole Person, and character, and sacrifice, are as incense sweet to the Lord.

Neither is there anything in our Lord which is incongruous with the rest. In each one of us, there is, at least, a little that is out of place. We could not be fully described without the use of a "but". If we could all look within, and see ourselves as God sees us, we should note a thousand matters which, if we could now permit, which we should never allow again. But, in the Well-beloved, all is of a piece, all is lovely; and when the sum of the whole is added up, it comes to an absolute perfection of loveliness — "Yea, He is altogether lovely."

We are sure that the Lord Jesus must be himself exceedingly lovely since *he gives loveliness to his people*. Many saints are lovely in their lives. One reads biographies of good men and women that make us wish to grow like them; yet all the loveliness of all the most holy among men has come from Jesus their Lord, and is a copy of his perfect beauty. Those who write well do so because he sets the copy.

What is stranger and more wonderful still, *our Lord Jesus makes sinners lovely.* In their natural state, men are deformed and hideous to the eye of God; and as they have no love to God, so he has no delight in them. He is weary of them, and is grieved that he made men on the earth. The Lord is angry with the wicked every day. (Ps. 7:11) Yet, when our Lord Jesus comes in, and covers these sinful ones with his righteousness, and, at the same time, infuses into them his life, the Lord is well pleased with them for his Son's sake. Even in heaven, the infinite Jehovah sees nothing which pleases him like his Son. The Father from eternity loved his Only-begotten, and, again and again, he has said of him, "This is my beloved Son, in whom I am well pleased." (Mat. 3:17, 17:5; Mk. 1:11; 2 Peter 1:17) What higher encomium [praise] can be passed on Him?

If we had time to think over this subject, we should say of our Lord that *he is lovely in every office.* He is the most admirable Priest, and King, and Prophet that ever yet exercised the office. He is a lovely Shepherd of a chosen flock, a lovely Friend, lovely Husband, a lovely Brother: he is admirable in every position that he occupies for our sakes.

Our Lord's loveliness appears in every condition: in the manger, or in the temple; by the well, or on the sea; in the garden, or on the cross; in the tomb, or in the resurrection; in his first, or in his second coming. He is not as the herb, which flowers only at one season; or as the tree, which loses its leaves in winter; or as the moon, which waxes and wanes; or as the sea, which ebbs and flows. In every condition, and at every time, "He is altogether lovely."

He is lovely, whichever way we look at him. If we view Him as in the past, entering into a covenant of peace on our behalf; or, in the present, yielding himself to us as Intercessor, Representative, and Forerunner; or, in the future, coming, reigning, and glorifying his people; "He is altogether lovely." Behold him from heaven, view him from the gates of hell, regard him as he goes before, look up to him as he sits above; he is as beautiful from one point of view as from another; "Yea, He is altogether lovely." Wherever we may be, he is the same in his perfection. How lovely he was to my eyes when I was sinking in despair! To see him suffering for my sin the tree was as the opening of the gates of the morning to my darkened soul. How lovely he is to us when we are sick, and the hours of the night seem lengthened into days! "He giveth songs in the night." (Job 35:10) How lovely has he been to us when the world has frowned, and friends have forsaken, and worldly goods have been scant! To see "the King in his beauty" (Is. 33:17) is a sight sufficient, even if we never saw another ray of comfort. How blessed, when we lie dying, to hear Him say, "I am the resurrection and the life"! (Jn. 11:25) Mark that word; he doe not say, "I will give you resurrection and life," but, "I am the resurrection and the life." Blessed are the eyes which can see that in Jesus it is really him. When we think of seeing him as he is, and being like him, how heaven approaches us! We shall soon behold the beatific vision, of which he will be the centre and the sun. At the thought of it, our soul takes wing, and our imagination soars aloft, while our faith, with eagle eye, beholds the glory. As we think of that glad period, when we shall be with our Beloved forever, we are ready to swoon away with delight. It is near, far nearer than we think.

III. The little time which we can give to this meditation has run out, and therefore I hasten to a close. I have bid you look at our Lord as "altogether lovely" with reverent emotions, and with absolute certainty. Now, to conclude, think of Him WITH PRACTICAL RESULTS. "He is altogether lovely." What shall we do for this chiefest among ten thousand?

First, *we will tell others of him*. For that cause was our text spoken. The daughters of Jerusalem asked the spouse, "What is thy Beloved more than another beloved?" (Verse 9) Her answer is here: "He is altogether lovely." It is a great joy to praise our Lord to enquiring minds. We, who are preachers, have a glorious time of it when we extol our Lord. If we had nothing to do but preach Christ, and had no discipline to administer, no sin to battle with, no doubts to drive away, we should have a heavenly service. For my part, I wish I could be bound over to play only on this one string. Paul did well when he turned ignoramus, and determined to know nothing among the Corinthians save Jesus Christ, and him crucified. (1 Cor. 2:2) As the harp of Anacreon would resound love alone, so would I have but one sole subject for my ministry — the love and loveliness of my Lord. Then to speak would be its own reward; and to study and prepare discourses would be only a phase of rest. Fain would I make my whole ministry to speak of Christ and His surpassing loveliness!

You who are not preachers cannot do better than speak much of Jesus as opportunity offers. Make *him* the theme of conversation. People talk about ministers; but we beg you to talk of our Master. Our undecided neighbours are always talking of hypocrites and inconsistent professors; but we would say to them, "Never mind about his followers: talk about the Master himself." His followers, by themselves considered, never were worth your words; but what a theme is this — "He is altogether lovely"! Our Lord's people are far worthier than the world thinks them to be; for my part, I rejoice in the many gracious and beautiful characters with which I meet. But even if all the bad reports we hear were true, this would not detract from the loveliness of our Lord, who is infinitely beyond all praise.

The next practical result of viewing the loveliness of our blessed Lord is that *we appropriate him to ourselves*, grasping him with our two hands of faith and love, and making the rest of the verse to be our own: "This is my Beloved, and this is my Friend, O daughters of Jerusalem!" (Song 5:16) Since he is so amiable, he must be "my Beloved"; my heart clings to him. Since he is admirable, I rejoice that he is "my Friend"; my soul trusts in him. The heart that most appreciates Jesus is the most eager to appropriate him. Whoever beholds Jesus as "altogether lovely "will never rest till he is altogether sure that Jesus is altogether his own. I think I may also add that appreciation is in great measure the seal of appropriation, for the soul that values Christ most is the soul that has most surely taken possession of Christ. Sometimes a heart prizes the Lord very highly, and tremblingly longs for him; but it is my conviction that the very fact of prizing him argues a measure of possession of him. Jesus never wins a heart to which he refuses his love. If you love him, he loves you: be sure of that. No soul ever cries "Yea, He is altogether lovely" without sooner or later adding, "This is my Beloved, and this is my Friend."

Do not rest, any one of you, till you know of a surety that Jesus is yours. Do not be content with a hope, but struggle after the full assurance of faith. This is to be had, and you ought not to be content without it. It may be your lifelong song, "My Beloved is mine, and I am His." (Song 2:16, 6:3) You need not pine in the shade: the sun is shining, so "walk in the light." (Is. 2:5) Away with the idea that we cannot know whether we are condemned or forgiven, in Christ or out of him! We may know, we must know; and, as we appreciate our Lord, we shall know. Either Jesus is ours, or he is not. If he is, let us rejoice in the priceless possession. If he is not ours, let us at once lay hold of him by faith; for, the moment we trust in him, he is ours. The enjoyment of religion lies in assurance: a mere hope is scant diet.

Once more, it is a fair fruit of our delight in our Lord that *our valuation of him becomes a bond of union between us and others*. The spouse cries, "This is my Beloved, and this is my Friend, O daughters of Jerusalem!" and they reply, "Whither is thy Beloved gone, O thou fairest among women? Whither is thy Beloved turned aside, that we may seek him with thee?" (Song 6:1) Thus, you see, they institute a companionship through the Well-beloved. Few of us in this room would ever have known each other had it not been for our common admiration of the Lord Jesus. We should have gone on walking past each other by the sea to this day, and we should have missed much cheering fellowship. Our Lord has become our centre; we meet in him, and feel that in him we are partakers of one life. We seek our Well-beloved together, and around his Table we find him together; and finding him, we have found one another, and the lost jewel of Christian love glitters on every bosom. We have differing views on certain parts of divine truth; and I do not know that it is wrong for us to differ where the Holy Spirit has left truth without rigidly defining it. We are bound each one devoutly to use his judgment in the interpretation of the Sacred Word; but we all agree in this one clear judgment: "Yea, He is altogether lovely." This is the point of union. Those who enthusiastically love the same Person are on the way to loving each other. This is growingly our case; and it is the same with all spiritual people. Professors quarrel, but possessors are at one. We hear much discourse upon "the Unity of the Church" as a thing to be desired, and we may heartily agree with it; but it would be well also to remember that in the true Church of Christ real union already exists. Our Lord prayed for those whom the Father had given him that they might be one (Jn. 17:21-22), and the Father granted the prayer: the Lord's own people are one. In this room, we have an example of how closely we are united in Christ. Some of you are more at home in this assembly, taken out of all churches, than you are in the churches to which you nominally belong. Our union in one body as Episcopalians, Baptists, Presbyterians, or Independents, is not the thing our Lord prayed for; but our union is *in himself*. That union, at this moment, we enjoy; and therefore we eat of one bread, and drink of one cup, and are baptised into one Spirit (1 Cor. 11:14), at his feet who is to each one of us, and so to all of us, ALTOGETHER LOVELY.

William Williams wrote this hymn with a completely dedicated spirit:

White and ruddy is my Beloved
All His heavenly beauties shine;
Nature can't produce an object,
Nor so glorious, so divine;

He hath wholly
Won my soul to realms above.

Farewell, all ye meaner creatures,
For in Him is every store;
Wealth, or friends, or darling beauty,
Shall not draw me any more;
In my Saviour
I have found a glorious whole.

Such as find thee find such sweetness
Deep, mysterious, and unknown;
Far above all worldly pleasures,
If they were to meet in one;
My Belovèd,
O'er the mountains haste away.

66. THE BEST BELOVED

"Yea, he is altogether lovely."
(Song of Solomon 5:16)

NO words can ever express the gratitude we owe to him who loved us, even when we were dead in trespasses and sins; the love of Jesus is unutterably precious and worthy of daily praise. No songs can ever fitly celebrate the triumphs of that salvation which he wrought single-handed on our behalf. The work of Jesus is glorious beyond compare, and all the harps of angels fall short of its worthy honour. Yet I do believe, and my heart prompts me to say so, that the highest praise of a ransomed soul, and of the entire Christian church, should be offered to the blessed Person of Jesus Christ, our adorable Lord. The love of the redeemed heart is excelled by the heart which exhibited that love, and the wonders of his hand are outdone by the hand of the Sender himself which wrought those godlike miracles of grace. We ought to bless him for what he has done for us as Mediator in the place of humble service under the law, and for what he suffered for us as Substitute on the altar of sacrifice from before the foundation of the world; and for what he is doing for us as Advocate in the place of highest honour at the right hand of the Majesty on high. But still, the best thing about Christ is Christ himself. We prize his work, but we worship him. His gifts are valued, but he himself is adored. While we contemplate, with mingled feelings of awe, admiration, and thankfulness, his atonement, his resurrection, his glory in heaven, and his second coming, still, it is Christ himself, stupendous in his dignity as the Son of God, and superbly beautiful as the Son of man, who sheds an incomparable charm on all those wonderful achievements, in which his might and his merit, his goodness and his grace, appear so conspicuous. For him, let our choicest spices be reserved, and to him let our sweetest anthems be raised. Our choicest ointment must be poured on his head, and for his own self alone our most costly alabaster boxes must be broken.

"He is altogether lovely." Not only is his teaching attractive, his doctrine persuasive, his life irreproachable, his character enchanting, and his work a self-denying labour for the common good of all his people, but he himself is "altogether lovely". I suppose, at first, we shall always begin to love him because he first loved us (1 Jn 4:19), and, even to the last, his love for us will always be the strongest motive of our affection towards him. Still, there ought to be added to this another reason less connected with ourselves, and more entirely arising out of his own superlative excellence; we ought to love him because he is "lovely" and deserves to he loved. The time will come, and with some of us it has come, when we can heartily say, "We love him because we cannot help it, for his all-conquering loveliness has quite ravished our hearts." Surely it is but an unripe fruit to love him merely for the benefits which we have received at his hand. It is a fruit of grace, but it is not of the ripest flavour; at least, there are other fruits, both new and old, which we have laid up for you, O our beloved, and some of them have a daintier taste. There is a sweet and mellow fruit which can only be produced by the summer sun of fellowship-love because of the Redeemer's intrinsic goodness and personal sweetness. Oh, that we might love our Lord for his own sake, love him because he is so supremely beautiful that a glimpse of him has won our hearts, and made him dearer to our eyes than light! Oh, that all true and faithful disciples of our beloved Lord would press forward towards that state of affection, and never rest till they reach it! If any of you have not reached it, you need not, therefore, doubt your own safety, for whatever the reason why you love Jesus — if you love him at all — it is a sure pledge and token that he loves you, and that you are saved in him with an everlasting salvation. Still covet earnestly the best gifts (1 Cor. 12:31), and rise to the highest degree of devotion. Love as the purest of the saints have loved; love as John the Apostle loved, for still your Lord exceeds all the loving homage you can pay to him. Love his Person, love him for himself; for he is better than all that he has done or given; and as from him all blessings flow, so back to him should all love return.

Our text tells us that Christ is "altogether lovely". What a wealth of thought and feeling is contained in that exclamation! I am embarrassed to know how to preach on such a subject, and am half inclined to wish it had not been laid so much on my heart. What, I pray you, what is loveliness? To discern it is one thing, but it is quite another to describe it. There is not one among us but knows how to appreciate beauty, and is enamoured of its attractions, but how many here could tell us what it is?

Stand up, my brother, and define it. Perhaps, while you were sitting down, you thought you could easily tell the tale, but now you are on your feet you find that it is not quite so easy to clothe in words the thoughts which floated through your brain. What is beauty? Cold-blooded word-mongers answer, fitness. And certainly there is fitness in all loveliness. But do not tell me that beauty is mere fitness, for I have seen a world of fitness in this world which, nevertheless, seemed to me to be inexpressibly ugly and unlovable. A wise man tells me that beauty is proportion; but neither is this a full description by many a league. No doubt it is desirable that the features should be well balanced; the eyes should be fitly set; not one feature should be exaggerated, and none should be dwarfed.

In nature what affects our hearts,
Is not the exactness of peculiar parts:
'Tis not a lip nor eye we beauty call,
But the joint force and full result of all.

(Alexander Pope)

Harmony is beauty. Yet I have seen the chiselled marble, fashioned with skilful art into a well-nigh perfect form, which did not, could not, impress me with a sense of loveliness. There stands in one of the halls of the Vatican a statue of Antinoüs, beloved of the Emperor Hadrian. Every feature in that statue is perfection in itself, and is in complete harmony with all the rest. You could not find the slightest fault with eye or nose or mouth. It is, indeed, as much the ideal of male beauty as the Venus is of female charms; yet no one could ever have been enchanted with the statue, or have felt affection for the form which it represents. There is no expression whatever in the features. Everything is so adjusted and proportioned that you need a divergence to relieve you. The material is so carefully measured out that there lacks a stir, a break in the harmony, to give at least some semblance of a soul. Beauty, then, consists not in mere harmony, nor in balancing the features. Loveliness, surely, is attractiveness. Yes, but that is another way of saying you do not know what it is. It is a something that attracts you, and constrains you to exclaim:

Nought under heaven so strongly doth allure.

(Robert Burton)

We feel its power, we become its slaves; but we cannot write with pen of cold steel, nor could we write even with a pen of lightning, a description of what it is. How, then, can I, enamoured, entranced, enraptured as I am with him "whom my soul loveth" (Song 1:7, 3:1-3) — how can I speak of him? He is altogether lovely? Where shall I find words, terms, expressions that fitly set him apart? Unless the Eternal Spirit shall upraise me out of myself I must forever be incapable of setting out the Well-beloved.

Besides, were I baffled by nothing else, there is this, that the beauty of Christ is mysterious. It surpasses all the comeliness of human form. He may have had great beauty according to the flesh. That I cannot tell; but I should imagine that such a perfect soul as his must have inhabited a perfectly moulded body. Never yet did you or I gaze with satisfaction on the work of any painter who has tried to picture our Lord Jesus Christ. We have not blamed the great masters, but we feel that the effort surpassed their powers. How could they photograph the sun? The loftiest conceptions of great artists in this case fall far short of the mark. When the brightness of the Father's glory is the subject, the canvas glows in vain. Art sits at her easel and produces diligently many a draft of the sacred features; but they are all failures, and they must be. Who can ever depict Emmanuel, God-with-us? (Mat. 1:23) I suppose that, by-and-by, when our Lord had entered into his active life, and encountered its struggles his youthful beauty was marred with lines of sadness and sorrow. Still, his courage so overshadowed his cares, the mercy he showed so surpassed the misery he shared, and the grace he dispensed so exceeded the griefs that he carried, that a halo of real glory must ever have shone around his brow. His countenance must still have been lovely even when surrounded with the clouds of care and grief. How can we describe even the marred visage? It is a great mystery, but a sure fact that, in our Lord's marred countenance, his beauty is best seen. Anguish gave him a loveliness which else he would not have reached. His passion put the finishing touch on his unrivalled loveliness.

But, brethren, I am not about to speak of Christ's loveliness after the flesh, for now, after the flesh, know we him no more. (2 Cor. 5:16) It is his moral and spiritual beauty, of which the spouse in the song most sweetly says, "Yea, he is altogether lovely." The loveliness which the eye dotes on is mere varnish when compared with that which dwells in virtue and holiness. The worm devours the loveliness of skin and flesh, but a lovely character endures forever.

I. THIS IS RARE PRAISE. Let that be our first head. This is rare praise.

What if I say it is unique? For of no other being could it be said, "Yea, he is altogether lovely." It means, firstly, that all that is in him is lovely, perfectly lovely. There is no point in our Lord Jesus that you could improve. To paint the rose were to spoil its ruddy hue. To tint the lily, for he is lily as well as rose, were to mar its whiteness. Each virtue in our Lord is there in a state of absolute perfection: it could not be more fully developed. If you were able to conceive of each virtue at its ripest stage, it would be found in him. In the matter of transparent ingenuousness and sterling honesty, did ever man speak or act as truthfully as he? Ask, on the other hand, for sympathising tenderness and love; was ever any so gentle as Jesus? Do you want reverence for God? How he bows before the Father. Do you want boldness before men? How he beards the Pharisees. You could not better anything that you find in Jesus. Wherever you cast your eye, it rests with satisfaction, for the best of the best of the best is to be seen in him. [See in this Collection, Metropolitan Tabernacle Pulpit No. 2472: *The Best of the Best*] He is altogether lovely at every separate point so that the spouse, when she began with his head, descended to his feet, and then, lifting her eyes upward again upon a return voyage of delight, she looked into his countenance, and summed up all that she had seen in this one sentence, "He is altogether lovely." This is rare praise.

And he is all that is lovely. In each one of his people, you will find something that is lovely — in one there is faith, in another abounding love; in one tenderness, in another courage, but you do not find all good things in any one saint — at least not all of them in full perfection — but you find all virtues in Jesus, and each one of them at its best. If you would take the best quality of one saint, and the best quality of another — yes, the best out of each, and all the myriads of his people — you would find no grace or goodness among them all which Jesus does not possess in the fullest degree and to the highest perfection. He combines all the virtues, and gives them all a sweetness over and beyond themselves. In flowers, you have a separate beauty belonging to each, when no one flower is just like another, but each one blushes with its own loveliness. But in our Lord, these separate and distinct beauties are found united in one. Christ is the posy in which all the beauties of the garden of perfection are bound up. Each gem has its own radiance: the diamond is not like the ruby, nor the ruby like the emerald; but Christ is that ring in which you have sapphire, ruby, diamond, emerald set in choice order, so that each one heightens the other's brilliance. Do not look for anything lovely out of Jesus, for he is all the loveliness. All perfections are in him, making up one consummate perfection; and all the loveliness which is to be seen elsewhere is but a reflection of his own unrivalled charms.

In Jesus Christ — this, moreover, is rare praise again — there is nothing that is unlovely. You have a friend whom you greatly admire and fondly esteem, of whom, nonetheless, I do not doubt you have often said to yourself in an undertone, "I wish I could take away a little of the rough edge of his manners here and there." You never think that of Christ. You have observed of one man that he is so bold as to be sometimes rude; and of another that he is so bland and amiable that he is apt to be effeminate. You have said, "That sweetness of his is exceedingly good, but I wish that it were qualified with sterner virtues." But there is nothing to tone down or alter in our divine Lord. He is "altogether lovely". Have you not sometimes, in describing a friend, been obliged to forget or omit some rather prominent characteristic when you wished to make a favourable impression? You have to paint him as the artist once painted Oliver Cromwell; the great wart over the eyebrow was purposely left out of the portrait. Cromwell, you know, said, "Paint me as I am, warts and all." We have, however, often felt that it was kind to leave out the warts when we were talking of those we esteemed, and to whom we would pay a graceful tribute. But there is nothing to leave out in Christ, nothing to hold back, or to guard, or to extenuate. In him is nothing redundant, nothing overgrown. He is "altogether lovely". You never need put the finger over the scar in his case, as Apelles did when he painted his hero Alexander. No; tell it all out. Display the details of his private life and secret thoughts; they need no concealment. Lay bare the very heart of Christ, for that is the essence of love and loveliness. Speak of his death-wounds, for, in his scars, there is more beauty than in the uninjured comeliness of another. Even when he lies dead in the tomb, he is more comely than the immortal angels of God at their best estate. Nothing about our Lord needs to be concealed; even his cross, at which his enemies stumble, is to be daily proclaimed, and it will be seen to be one of his choicest beauties.

Frequently, too, in commending a friend whom you highly appreciate, you have been prone to ask for consideration of his position, and make excuse for blemishes which you would fain persuade us are less actual than apparent. You have remarked how admirably he acts considering his surroundings. Conscious that someone would hint at an imperfection, you have anticipated the current of conversation by alluding to the circumstances which rendered it so hard for your friend to act commendably. You felt the need of showing that others influenced him, or that infirmity restrained him. Did you ever feel inclined to apologise for Christ? Did he not always stand unbending beneath life's pressure, upright and unmoved amid the storms and tempests of an evil world? The vilest calumnies [lies] have been uttered against him in the age just past which produced creatures similar to Thomas Paine, but they never required an answer; and as for the more refined attacks of our modern scepticism, they are for the most part unworthy even of contempt. They fall beneath the glance of truth, withered by the glance of the eye of honesty. We never feel concerned to vindicate the character of Jesus; we know it to be safe against all-comers. No one has been able to conjure up an accusation against Jesus.

They seek false witnesses, but their testimony does not agree together. The sharp arrows of slander fall blunted from the shield of his perfection. Oh, no; he is altogether lovely in this sense — that there is nothing whatever in him that is not lovely. You may look, and look, and look again, but there is nothing in him that will not bear scrutiny, world without end. Taking the Lord Jesus Christ as a whole — this is what our text intends to tell us, he is inexpressibly lovely, altogether lovely. The words are packed as tightly as they can be, but the meaning is greater than the words. Some translate the passage "He is all desires", and it is a good translation too, and contains a great truth. Christ is so lovely that all you can desire of loveliness is in him; and even if you were to sit down and task your imagination, and burden your understanding, to contrive, to invent, to fashion the ideal of something that should be inimitable — yes (to utter a paradox), if you could labour to conceive something which is inconceivably lovely, yet still you would not reach to the perfection of Christ Jesus. He is above, not only all we think, but all we dream of. Do you all believe this? Dear hearers, do you think of Jesus in this way? We speak that we do know, and testify that we have seen. (Jn. 3:11) But no one among you will receive our witness until he can say, "I also have seen him, and having seen him, I set to my seal that he is altogether lovely."

II. And now, secondly, as this is rare praise, so likewise IT IS PERPETUAL PRAISE.

You may say of Christ whenever you look at him, "Yea, he is altogether lovely." He always was so. As God over all, he is blessed for ever, Amen! When in addition to his godhead, he assumed our mortal clay, was he not inimitably lovely then? The babe in Bethlehem was the most beautiful sight that ever the world beheld. No fairer flower ever bloomed in the garden of creation than the mind of that child of Nazareth gradually unfolding as he "grew, and waxed strong in spirit, filled with wisdom: and the grace of God was upon him." (Lk. 2:40) All the while he lived on earth, what moral perfections, what noble qualities, what spiritual charms were about his sacred Person! His life among men was a succession of charming pictures.

And he was lovely in his bitter passion, when, as the thick darkness overshadowed his soul, he prayed in an agony of desire, "Not my will, but thine, be done." (Lk. 22:42) The bloody sweat did not disfigure, but adorn him. And oh, was he not lovely when he died? Without resentment, he interceded for his murderers. (Lk. 23:34) His patience, his self-possession, his piety, as God's faithful martyr, have fixed as the meridian of time, the hour when he said, "It is finished" and " bowed his head". (Jn. 19:29-30), and "cried with a loud voice, Father, into thy hands I commend my spirit." (Lk. 23:46) He is lovely in his resurrection from the dead; beyond description lovely. Not a word of accusation did he utter against his cruel persecutors, though he had risen clothed with all power in heaven and in earth. (Mat. 28:18) With such tender sympathy did he make himself known to his sorrowing disciples that, despite the waywardness of their unbelief, their hearts' instinct told them it was "the same Jesus." (Acts 1:11, 2:36) He is "altogether lovely".

He will be lovely when he comes with solemn pomp, and sound of the trumpet, and his escort of mighty angels, and brings all his saints who have departed with him, and calls up those that are alive and remain on the earth till his advent, to meet him in the air. 1 Thess. 4:17) Oh, how lovely he will appear to the two throngs, who will presently join in one company! How admirable will his appearance be! How eyes, ears, hearts and voices will greet him! With what unanimity the host redeemed by blood will account their highest acclamations as a trivial tribute to his honour and glory! "He is altogether lovely." Yes, and he shall he lovely forever and ever when your eyes and mine shall eternally find their heaven in beholding him. "Jesus Christ, the same yesterday, today, and for ever" (Heb. 13:6) is always worthy of this word of praise — "altogether lovely."

Let us retrace our steps for a minute. The more we study the four Gospels, the more charmed we are with the gospel; for as a modern author has well said, "The Gospels, like the gospel, are most divine because they are most human." As followers of Jesus, rank yourselves with those men who accompanied him all the time that he went in and out among them (Acts 1:21); and you will find him lovely in all conditions. Lovely, when he talks to a leper and touches and heals him; lovely, by the bedside when he takes the fever-stricken patient by the hand and heals her; lovely, by the wayside when he greets the blind beggar, puts his finger on his eyes and bids him see; lovely, when he stands on the sinking vessel and rebukes the waves; lovely, when he meets the bier and rekindles the life that had expired; lovely, when he visits the mourners and goes with the sisters of Bethany to the new-made grave, and weeps, and groans, and majestically lovely when he bids the dead come out. (Jn. 11:43) Lovely is he when he rides through the streets of Jerusalem on a colt, the foal of an ass. Oh, had we been there, we would have plucked the palm branches, and taken off our garments to strew the way. Hosanna, lovely Prince of Peace! (Zech. 9:9; Mat. 21:5) But he was just as lovely when he came from the garden with his face all besmeared with bloody sweat; just as lovely when they said, "Crucify him, crucify him"; just as lovely, and, if possible, more so, when down those sacred cheeks there dripped the cursed spittle from the rough soldiers' mouths; yes, and loveliest, to my eyes loveliest of all, when mangled, wounded, fainting, bruised, dying, when he said, "My God, my God, why hast thou forsaken me?" (Mat. 27:46; Mk. 15:34) uttering a plaintive cry of utmost grief from the felon's gibbet on which he died. Yes, view him where you will, in any place whatever, is he not — I speak to you who know him, and not to those who never saw him with the eye of faith — is he not, in the night and in the day, on the sea and on the land, on earth and in heaven, altogether lovely?

He is lovely in all his offices. What an entrancing sight to see the king in his beauty, with his diadem on his head, as he now sits in yonder world of brightness! How charming to view him as a priest with the Urim and Thummim, wearing the names of his people bejewelled on his breastplate! And what a vision of simple beauty, to see him as a prophet, teaching his people in touching parables of homely interest, of whom they said, "Never man spake like this man"! (Jn. 7:46) The very tones of his voice, and the glance of his eyes, made his eloquence so supreme that it enthralled men's hearts. Yes, he is lovely, altogether lovely in any and every characteristic. We do not know which best beseems him, in the highest or the lowliest positions. Let him be what he may — Lamb or Shepherd, Brother or King, Saviour or Master, Foot-washer or Lord — in every relation, he is "altogether lovely".

Get a view of him, my brethren, from any point, and see whether he is not lovely. Do you recollect the first sight you ever had of him? It was on a day when your eyes were red with weeping over sin, and you expected to see the Lord dressed in anger coming out to destroy you. Oh, it was the happiest sight I ever saw when I beheld my sins rolling into his sepulchre, and, when looking up, I beheld him as my substitute bleeding on the tree. Altogether lovely was he that day. Since then, providence has given us a varied experience, and taken us to different points of view, that we might look at Christ, and see him under many aspects. We look at statues from several standpoints as we criticise them. A great many in London are hideous from all points of view; others are very well if you look at them this way, but if you go over yonder and look from another viewpoint, the artist appears to have utterly failed. Now, beloved, look at Jesus from any viewpoint you like, and he is at his best from each and every corner. You have been in prosperity: God multiplied your children, and blessed your basket and your store — was not Jesus lovely then? Assuredly he was the light of your delights. Nothing he had given you vied with himself. He rose in your hearts superior to his own best gifts. But you tell me that you have been very sick, and you have lost one after another of your dear ones; your means have been reduced; you have come down in the world. Say then, is Jesus lovely now? I know that you will reply "Yes, more than ever is Christ delightful in mine eyes." Well, you have had very happy times, and you have been on the mount of hallowed friendship.

The other Sunday morning, many of us were up there, and thought, like Peter, that we should like to stay there forever; and is not Jesus lovely when he is transfigured and we are with him? Yes, but at another time, you are down in the depths with Jonah, at the bottom of the sea. Is Christ lovely then? Yes, even there, he hears our prayer out of his holy temple, and brings us again from the deep abyss. We shall soon lie dying. Oh, my brethren, what brave talk God's people have often given us about their Lord when they have been on the edge of the grave! That seems to be a time when the Well-beloved takes the veil off his face altogether, and sits by the bedside, and lets his children look into his face and see him as he is. I warrant you, the saints forget the ghastliness of death when their hearts are ravished with the loveliness of Christ.

Yes, hitherto, up to this point, Jesus has been lovely; and now let us add that he will always be so. You know there are people whom you account beautiful when you are young, but when you grow older in years, riper in judgement, and more refined in taste, you meet with others who look far more beautiful. Now, what to you think of your Lord? Have you met with anyone, in fact or fable, more beautiful than he? You thought him charming when you were but a babe in grace. What do you think of him now? Taste, you know, grows, and develops with education: an article of *vertu* which fascinated you years ago has no longer any charms for you because your taste is raised. Has your spiritual taste outgrown your Lord's beauties? Come, brothers, does Christ go down as you learn truth more exactly, and acquaint yourself more fully with him? Oh no! You prize him a thousand times more today than you did when the first impression of his goodness was formed in your mind. Some things which look very lovely at a distance lose their loveliness when you get near them: but is it not true (I am sure it is) that the nearer you get to Christ, the lovelier he is? Some things are only beautiful in your eyes for their novelty: you admire them when you see them once; if you were to see them a dozen times, you would not care much for them. What do you say about my Master? Is it not true that the oftener you see him, the more you know him, and the more familiar your fellowship with him, the more he rises in your esteem? I know it is so; and well, therefore, did the spouse say, "He is altogether lovely."

Christ is altogether lovely in this respect — that, when men reproach him and rail at him, he is often all the lovelier in his people's eyes. I warrant you, Christ has been better known by the burn-side in Scotland by his covenanting people than ever he has been seen under the fretted roof of cathedral architecture. Away there in lonely glens, amid the mosses and the hills, where Covenanters met for fear of Claverhouse and his dragoons, the Lord Jesus shone out like the sun in his strength. We have, nowadays, to be satisfied with his moonlight face, but, in persecuting days, his children have seen his sun face, and oh, how glad they have been! Hear how the saints sing in prison! Listen to their charming notes, even on the rack, when the glory of his presence fills their souls with heaven on earth, and makes them defy the torments of the flesh. The Lord Jesus is more lovely to the soul which can bear reproach for him than he is to any other. Put the cross on his back if you will, but we love him all the better for that. Nail up his hands, but we love him all the better for that. Now fasten his feet; yes, but our soul melts with love for him, and she feels new reasons for loving him when she beholds the nails. Now stand around the cross, you worldlings, and mock him if ye will. Taunt and jest, and jeer and jibe — these only make us love the better the great and glorious One, who "made himself of no reputation, and took upon him the form of a servant, and being found in fashion as a man, humbled himself and became obedient unto death, even the death of the cross." (Phil. 2:5-8)

Beloved, keep on looking at Christ from all these points of view till you get to heaven, and, each time, you will be more enamoured of him. When you reach the celestial city and see him face to face, then you shall say, "The half has not been told us" (2 Chron 9:6); but even here below, Christ is altogether lovely to his people.

III. I leave that head just to notice, in the third place, that though this praise is rare praise, and perpetual praise, yet also IT IS TOTALLY INSUFFICIENT PRAISE.

Do you say that he is altogether lovely? It is not enough. It is not a thousandth part enough. No tongue of man, no tongue of angel, can ever set out his unutterable beauties. "Oh", say you, "but it is a great word, though short; very full of meaning though soon spoken — altogether lovely." I tell you, it is a poor word. It is a word of despair. It is a word which the spouse uttered because she had been trying to describe her Lord, and she could not do it, and so she set this down in very desperation, as much as to say, "There, the task is too great for me. I will end it. This is all I can say — 'Yea, he is altogether lovely.'" I am sure John Berridge was right when he said,

Living tongues are dumb at best,
We must die to speak of Christ.

Brethren, the praise of the text is insufficient. I know, because it is praise given by one who had never seen him in his glory. It is Old Testament praise, this, that he is altogether lovely; praise uttered in report rather than upon actual view of him. Truly, I do not know how to bring better, but I shall know one day. Till then, I will speak his praise as best I can, though it falls far short of his infinite excellence. Our text is a cloth of gold, but it is not fit for our Beloved to put the sole of his foot on. He deserves better than this, for it is only the praise of a church that had not seen him die, and had not seen him rise, and had not seen him in the splendour at the divine right hand. "Well" say you, "try if you can do better!" No, I will not, because, if I did praise him better, the style would not last long, for he is coming quickly, and the best thing the best speaker could ever say of him will be out of date by the majesty of his appearing. His chariot is waiting at his door now, and he may soon come out of his secret chambers and be among us, and oh, the glory! Oh, the glory! Paul, you know, stole a glance through the lattice one day when he was caught up into the third heaven. Somebody said to me, "I wonder Paul did not tell us what he saw." Yes, but what he saw he might not tell, and the words he heard were words which it were not lawful for a man to utter, and yet live among this evil generation. (2 Cor. 12:2-4) We shall hear those words ourselves soon, and see those sights not many days hence, so let it stand as it does: "He is altogether lovely." But when you have thus summed up all that our poor tongues can express, you must not say, "Now we have described him." Oh no, sirs, you have but held a candle to this glorious sun, for he is such a One as thoughts cannot compass, much less language describe.

I leave this point with the reflection that God intends to describe him, and send him out one day. He is waiting patiently, for longsuffering is part of Christ's character; and God is setting out the longsuffering of Christ in the patient waiting of these eighteen hundred years. But the day will presently dawn, and usher in the everlasting age when Christ shall be better seen, for every eye shall see him, and every tongue confess that he is Lord. (Phil. 2:11)

The whole earth will one day be sweet with the praise of Jesus. Earth, did I say? This alabaster box of Christ's sweetness has too much fragrance in it for the world to keep it all to itself; the sweetness of our Lord's Person will rise above the stars, and perfume worlds unknown. It will fill heaven itself. Eternity shall be occupied with declaring the praises of Jesus. Seraphs shall sing of it; angels shall harp it; the redeemed shall declare it. He is "altogether lovely! The cycles of eternity as they revolve shall only confirm the statement of the blood-redeemed that he is altogether lovely. Oh, that the day had come when we shall bow with them, and sing with them! Wait a little while and are not weary and you shall be at home, and then you shall know that I spoke the truth when I said that this was insufficient praise. Earth is too narrow to contain him, heaven is too little to hold him, eternity itself too short for the utterance of all his praises.

IV. So I close with this last thought, which may God bless for practical uses. This praise is VERY SUGGESTIVE.

If Christ is altogether lovely, it suggests a question. Suppose I never saw his loveliness. Suppose that in this house there should be souls that never saw anything in Christ to make them love him. If you were to go to some remote island where beauty consisted in having one eye and a twisted mouth, and a sea-green complexion, you would say, "Those people are strange beings." Such are the people of this world. Spiritual beauty is not appreciated by them. This world appreciates the man who makes money, however reckless he may be in the welfare of others while scheming to heap up riches for himself. As for the man who slays his fellow-creatures by thousands, they mount him on a bronze horse, put him on an arch, or they pile up a column, and set him as near heaven as they can. He slew his thousands: he died blood-red; he was an emperor, a tyrant, a conqueror; the world felt his power and paid its homage. As for this Jesus, he only gave his life for men; he was only pure and perfect, the mirror of disinterested love. The vain world cannot see in him a virtue to admire. It is a blind world, a fool world, a world that lies in the hand of the wicked one. Not to discern the beauties of Jesus is an evidence of terrible depravity. Have you, my dear friend, frankly to confess that you were never enamoured of him who was holy, harmless, and undefiled, and went about doing good? (Acts 10:38) Then let this come home to you — that the question is not as to whether Christ is lovely or not, the mistake is here —that you have not a spiritually enlightened eye, a fine moral perception, nor even a well-regulated conscience, or you would see his loveliness at once. You are dark and blind. God help you to feel this!

Do you not love Christ? Then let me ask you why you do not? There was never a man yet who knew Christ, that could give a reason for not loving him, neither is there such a reason to be discovered. He is altogether lovely. In nothing is he unlovable. Oh, I wish the good Spirit of God would whisper in your heart, and incline you to say, "I will see about this Christ. I will read of him. I will look at the four portraits of him painted by the evangelists, and, if he be indeed thus lovely, no doubt he will win my heart, as he appears to have won the hearts of others." I pray he may. But do not I beg you continue to deny Christ your love. It is all you can give him. It is a poor thing, but he values it. He would sooner have your heart than all the gold in Europe. He would sooner have the heart of a poor servant girl, or of a poor humble labourer of the soil, than the queen's diadem. He loves love. Love is his gem, his jewel. He delights to win it, and if he is indeed altogether lovely, let him have your love. You have known people, I dare say, whom you could not help loving. They never had to say to you, "Love me", for you were captivated at once by the very sight of them. In the same way, many and many have only received one beam of light from the Holy Spirit, and have there seen who Jesus was, and they have at once said of him, "Thou hast ravished my heart with one of thine eyes" (Song 4:9); and so it has been that, all their life long, they have loved their Lord. Now, the praise is suggestive still further. "Is Christ altogether lovely? Then I do love him? As a child of God, do I love him as much as I ought? I do love him. Yes, blessed be his name, I do love him! But what a poor, cold, chilly love it is. How few are the sacrifices I make for him. How few are the offerings that I present to him. How little is the fellowship I maintain with him." Brother, is there a rival in your heart? Do you allow anyone to come in between you and the "altogether lovely"? If so, chase out the intruder. Christ must have all your heart; and let me tell you, the more we love him the more bliss we shall have. A soul that is altogether given up to the love of Christ lives above care and sorrow. It has care and sorrow, but the love of Christ kills all the bitterness by its inexpressible sweetness. I cannot tell you how near a man may live to heaven, but I am persuaded that a very large proportion of the bliss of heaven may be enjoyed before we go there. There is one conduit pipe through which heavenly joy will flow, and, if you draw from it, you may have as much as you will. "Abide in me", says Christ; and if you abide in his love, you shall have his joy fulfilled in yourselves that your joy may be full. You will have more capacious vessels in heaven, but even now the little vessel that you have can be filled up to the brim by knowing the inexpressible loveliness of Jesus and surrendering your hearts to it.

Oh, that I could rise to something better than myself. I often feel like a chick in the egg; I am picking my way out, and I cannot get clear of my prison. Oh, would I chip the shell, come forth to freedom, develop wings, and soar heavenward, singing on the road! Would God that were our portion! If anything can help us to get out of the shell, and begin to rise and sing, it must be a full and clear perception that Jesus is altogether lovely. Come, let us be married to him afresh tonight. Come, believing hearts, yield again to his charms; again, surrender yourselves to the supremacy of his affection. Let us have the love of our espousals renewed. As you come to his Table, think you of the lips of Christ, of which the spouse had been speaking before she uttered my text — "His mouth is most sweet." There are three things about Christ's mouth that are very sweet. The first is his word: you have heard that. The second is his breath. Come, Holy Spirit, make your people feel that. And the third is his kiss. May every believing soul have that sweet token of his eternal love!

Forgive my ramblings. May God bless to all his people the word that has been spoken. May some that never knew my Master ask to know him tonight! Go home and seek him. Read the Word to find him. Cry to him in prayer and he will be found by you. He is so lovely that I should not live without loving him; and I shall deeply regret if any one of you shall spend another four-and-twenty hours without having had a sight of his divine face by faith.

SEVEN SERMONS ON THE SONG OF SOLOMON

CHAPTER 6

67. MORNING, NOON AND NIGHT
OR, THREE COURSES AT THE BANQUET
OF MEDITATION: NOON

SWORD AND TROWEL, NOVEMBER 1866

"I am my beloved's, and my beloved is mine."
(Song of Solomon 6:3)

OH for grace to remember in the midst of this day that I am my Beloved's. Blessed be the name of my adorable Lord, for he is the *beloved* of my soul! I dare not deny that my heart is enamoured of his beauties, and enchanted by his glories. He is better to me than all things in the world beside. Father, mother, wife or husband, children and friends, all these are dear, but Jesus is dearer far than these. He is my best beloved, the chief one of my heart. How precious is that little word *my*: how delightful to repeat it with the confidence which the gracious Spirit hath fostered in my soul! Yes, he is mine, by his own loving gift. "He loved me, and gave himself for me." (Gal. 2:20) And I have taken him to be mine, my hope, my trust, my aim, my strength, my comfort, my heaven, and my all. Thou art *my beloved*, O lovely Jesus, and as such, my heart cleaves fast to you.

The text reminds me, that not only is he mine but I am his; and to this truth I give my hearty assent. I am his by his father's gift, by his own bloody purchase, by his triumphant conquest of my heart, and by my own surrender to him. Remember, my soul, the solemn dedication which you made, for you publicly avowed yourself to be the Lord's. Look back to the solemn hour when you gave yourself unreservedly to him, and confess now how badly you have fulfilled your promise and covenant. Adored be the grace which has had patience with an unworthy servant, whose false heart has so continually violated the most solemn engagements, and forgotten the most pressing obligations! And now, let me remind myself of the purpose of my vow, or rather, the measure of my duty. I am to be Christ *wholly* without any reserve. All that I am, and all I have, belong only to my Lord Jesus. I must not rob him of his righteous due, or defraud the king's exchequer of the little reverence it claims from me. Then again, I am Christ's *alone*. No one else can share with him; he is the sole owner of my entire being. Rivals he will not endure; let me therefore beware of setting up any idol in my heart, and let me daily pray that! Let me be preserved as a chaste virgin, having neither love nor look for any but my espoused Husband, Emmanuel, *my Beloved.* It will, under the divine influence of the Holy Spirit, be very useful for me to recollect that I am *always* the rightful property of my Redeemer. I pray that this day I may acknowledge this truth in the shop, the market, the counting-house, the family, or wherever providence may call me. Yet my dedication must not end here; I must carry it further than my chamber and my closet. Whatever I do, whether I eat or drink, I must do all to his glory. (1 Cor. 10:31) Have grace to acknowledge one more fact: I am his *absolutely,* without conditions or limitations? Whatever he pleases to do with me, I must not murmur, for I am so entirely his that, if he slay me (Job 13:15), he has a right to do whatever he wills with his own.

Oh, that I may henceforth live out these weighty truths, etc, especially let me seek to do so during the remainder of this day! What shall I do for him to prove my love? How much can I afford to offer to him of my substance before the sun goes down? I will, at this time, pay a quit-rent-to my liege Lord as an acknowledgment that all my stock belongs to him and not to myself. If he is pleased to take away some of my treasures before, I must endeavour to be resigned, for he is only taking of his own, what he has graciously lent to his servant. Yes, if he removes all my comforts from me, it is my business to yield without a murmuring word, for only by so doing can I prove that I am my Beloved's. My soul, is this painful for you? Then chide thyself, and remember who it is to whom you resign yourself. Does a wife weep because she is her husband's? Is it not her joy and delight! Surely, when the Spirit enables me to feel aright, I can say, "Jesus, I am yours, and it is my honour to be so. I would not be my own if I could, for my heart's highest ambition is to be yours, entirely yours, forever.

68. THE CHURCH AS SHE SHOULD BE
NO. 984

AT THE METROPOLITAN TABERNACLE, NEWINGTON

"Thou art beautiful, O my love as Tirzah, comely as Jerusalem, terrible as an army with banners." (Song of Solomon 6:4)

THERE are various estimates of the Christian church. Some think everything of her; some think nothing of her; and probably neither opinion is worth the breath that utters it. Neither Ritualists who idolise their church, nor sceptics who vilify all churches, have any good knowledge of the true spiritual church of Jesus Christ as to be entitled to give an opinion. The king's daughter is all glorious within, with a beauty they are quite unable to appreciate. What is usually the most correct character that is obtainable of a woman? Shall we be guided by the praises of those neighbours who are on good terms with her, or by the scandal of those who make her the subject of ill-natured gossip? No; the most accurate judgement we are likely to get is that of her husband. Solomon says so in his Proverbs concerning the virtuous woman: "Her husband also [riseth up), and he praiseth her." (Prov. 31:28) Of that fairest among women, the church of Christ, the same observation may be made. It is to her of small consequence to be judged by man's judgement, but it is her honour and joy to stand well in the love and esteem of her royal spouse, Prince Emmanuel. Though the words before us are allegorical, and the whole song is crowded with metaphor and parable, yet the teaching is plain enough in this instance; it is evident that the Divine Bridegroom gives his bride a high place in his heart, and to him, whatever she may be to others, she is fair, lovely, comely, beautiful, and, in the eyes of his love, without a spot. (Eph 5:27) Moreover, even to him there is not only a beauty of a soft and gentle kind in her, but a majesty, a dignity in her holiness, in her earnestness, in her consecration, which makes even him say of her that she is "terrible as an army with banners", "fearful as a bannered army." She is every inch a queen: her aspect in the sight of her beloved is majestic. Take, then, the words of our text as an encomium [flowing praise] on Christ's church, pronounced by him who knows her best, and is best able to judge concerning her; and you learn that, to his discerning eye, she is not weak, dishonourable, and despicable, but bears herself as one of highest rank, consciously, joyously strong, in her Lord's strength.

I. On this occasion, let us note, first of all, WHY IT IS THAT THE CHURCH OF GOD IS SAID TO BE AN ARMY WITH BANNERS.

That she is *an army* is true enough, for the church is one, but many, consisting of men who march in order under a common leader with one design in view, and that design a conflict and a victory. She is the church militant here below, and both in suffering, and in service, she is made to prove that she is in an enemy's country. She is contending for the truth against error, for the light against darkness: till the day break and the shadows flee away, she must maintain her sentinels and kindle her watch fires; for all around her there is cause to guard against the enemy, and to defend the royal treasure of gospel truth against its deadly foes. But why an army *with banners*? Is not this, first of all, for *distinction*? How shall we know to which king an army belongs unless we can see the royal standard? In times of war, the nationality of troops is often declared by their distinguishing regimentals. The grey coats of the Russians were well known in the Crimea; the white livery of the Austrians was a constant eyesore in bygone days to the natives of Lombardy. No one mistook the Black Brunswickers for French Guards, or our own Hussars for Garibaldians. Quite as effectively, armies have been distinguished by the banners which they carried. As the old knights of old were recognised by their plume and helmet and escutcheon, so an army is known by its standard and the national colours. The tricolor of the French readily marked their troops as they fled before the terrible black and white of the German army. The church of Christ displays its banners for distinction's sake. It desires not to be associated with other armies, or to be mistaken for them, for it is not of this world, and its weapons and warfare are far other than those of the nations. God forbid that followers of Jesus should be mistaken for political partisans or ambitious adventurers. The church unfurls her ensign to the breeze that all may know whose she is and whom she serves. This is of the utmost importance at this present time, when crafty men are endeavouring to palm off their inventions. Every Christian church should know what it believes, and publicly avow what it maintains. It is our duty to make a clear and distinct declaration of our principles, that our members may know to what intent they have come together, and that the world also may know what we mean. Far be it from us to join with the Broad Church cry, and furl the banners on which our distinctive colours are displaced. We hear on all sides great outcries against creeds. Are these clamours justifiable? It seems to me that, when properly analysed, most of the protests are not against creeds, but against truth, for every one who believes anything must have a creed, whether he writes it down and print it or not; or if there is someone who believes nothing, or anything, or everything by turns, he is not fit to be set up as a model. Attacks are often made against creeds because they are a short, handy form by which the Christian mind gives expression to its belief, and those who hate creeds do so because they find them to be weapons as inconvenient as bayonets in the hands of British soldiers have been to our enemies. They are weapons so destructive to theology that it protests against them. For this reason, let us be slow to part with them. Let us lay hold of God's truth with iron grip, and never let it go. After all, there is a Protestantism still worth contending for; there is a Calvinism still worth proclaiming, and a gospel worth dying for. There is a Christianity distinctive and distinguished from Ritualism, Rationalism, and Legalism, and let us make it known that we believe in it. Up with your banners, soldiers of the cross! This is not the time to be frightened by the cries against conscientious convictions, which are nowadays nicknamed sectarianism and bigotry. Believe in your hearts what you profess to believe; proclaim openly and zealously what you know to be the truth. Do not be ashamed to say such-and-such things are true, and let men draw the inference that the opposite is false. Whatever the doctrines of the gospel may be to the rest of mankind, let them be your glory and boast. Display your banners, and let those banners be such as the church of old carried. Unfurl the old primitive standard, the all-victorious standard, of the cross of Christ. In very deed and truth — *in hoc signo vinces* (in this sign, conquer) — the atonement is the conquering truth. Let others believe as they may, or deny as they will, for you, the truth as it is in Jesus is the one thing that has won your heart and made you a soldier of the cross.

Banners were carried not merely for distinctiveness, but also to serve the purposes of *discipline*. Hence, an army with banners had one banner as a central standard, and then each regiment or battalion displayed its own particular flag. The host of God, which so gloriously marched through the wilderness, had their central standard. I suppose it was the very pole upon which Moses lifted up the brazen serpent (at any rate, our brazen serpent is the central ensign of the church); and then, besides that, each of the twelve tribes had its own particular banners. With these uplifted in the camp, the tribes marched in order so that there was no confusion on the march, and in time of battle there was no difficulty in marshalling the armed men. It was believed by the later Jews that "the standard of the camp of Judah represented a lion; that of Reuben, a man; that of Joseph, an ox, and that of Dan, an eagle. The Targumists, however, believe that the banners were distinguished by their colours, the colour for each tribe being analogous to that of the precious stone for that tribe in the breastplate of the high priest; and that the great standard of each of the four camps combined the three colours of the tribes which composed it." So, brethren, in the church of God there must be discipline — the discipline not only of admission and of dismission, in receiving the converts and rejecting the hypocrites, but the discipline of marshalling the troops to the service of Christ in the holy war in which we are engaged. Every soldier should have his orders, every officer his troop, every troop its fixed position in the army, and the whole army a regularity such as is prescribed in the rule: "Let all things be done decently and in order." (1 Cor. 14:40) As in the ranks each man has his place, and each rank has its particular phase in the battalion, so in every rightly constituted church each may, each woman, will have, for himself or herself, his or her own particular form of service, and each form of service will link in with every other, and the whole combined will constitute a force which cannot be broken. A church is not a load of bricks, remember. It is a house builded together. (Eph. 2:2) A church is not a bundle of cuttings in the gardener's hand: it is a vine, of which we are the branches. The true church is an organised whole; and life, true spiritual life, wherever it is paramount in the church, without rules and rubrics, it is quite sure to create order and arrangement. Order without life reminds us of the rows of graves in a cemetery, all numbered and entered in the register: order with life reminds us of the long lines of fruit trees in Italy, festooned with fruitful vines. Sunday-school teachers, bear the banner of the folded lamb; sick visitors, follow the ensign of the open hand; preachers, rally to the token of the uplifted brazen serpent; and all of you, according to your sacred calling, gather to the name of Jesus, armed for the war.

An army with banners may also be taken to represent *activity*. When an army holds up its colours the fight is over. Little is being done in military circles when the banners are put away; the troops are on furlough, or are resting in barracks. An army with banners is exercising, or marching, or fighting; probably it is in the middle of a campaign, and is marshalled for offense and defense, and there will be rough work before long. It is to be feared that some churches have hung up their flags to rot in state, or have encased them in dull propriety. They do not fool us into not expecting great things or seeing great things. They do not expect many conversions; if many did happen, they would be alarmed and suspicious. They do not expect their pastor's ministry to be with power; and, if it were attended with manifest effect, they would be greatly disturbed, and perhaps would complain that he created too much excitement. The worst of it is that do-nothing churches are usually very jealous lest any should encroach on their domain. Our churches sometime ago appeared to imagine that a whole district of this teeming city belonged to them to cultivate or neglect, as their monopolising decree might be. If anybody attempted to raise a new interest, or even to build a preaching station, within half a mile of them, they resented it as a most pernicious poachings on their manor. They did nothing themselves, and were very much afraid lest anybody should supplant them. Like the lawyers of old, who took away the key of knowledge, they did not enter into it themselves, and those who were entering in they hindered. That day, it is to be hoped, has gone once for all; yet too much of the old spirit lingers in certain quarters. It is high time that each church should feel that, if it does not work, the sole reason for its existence is gone. The reason for a church being a church dies without mutual edification and the conversion of sinners; and if these two ends are not really answered by a church, it becomes a mere name, a hindrance, an evil, a nuisance; like the salt which has lost its savour, it is neither fit for the land nor yet for the dunghill. (Lk. 14:35)

May we all in our church fellowship be active in the energy of the Spirit of God! May none of us be dead members of the living body, mere impediments to the royal host, baggage to be dragged about rather than warriors pushing on the war! May we, everyone of us, be soldiers filled with vigour to the fullness of our manhood, by the eternal power of the Holy Spirit; and may we be resolved that any portion of the church which does not uplift its banner of service shall not long number us among its adherents. Be it ours to determine that, whether others will or will not serve God, and extend the kingdom of his dear Son, we will, in his name and strength, contend even to death. Unsheathe your swords, you soldiers of the cross, arise from your slumbers, you careless ones; gird on your swords and prepare for the war. The Lord has redeemed you by his blood not that you might sleep, but that you might fight for the glory of his name.

Does not the description "an army with banners" imply a degree of *confidence*? It is not an army retiring from the foe, and willing enough to hide its colours to complete its escape. An army that is afraid to venture out into the open keeps its banners out of the gleam of the sun. Banners uplifted are the sign of a fearlessness which rather courts than declines the conflict. Ho, you warriors of the cross! Unfurl the gospel's ancient standard to the breeze; we will teach the foeman what strength there is in hands and hearts that rally to the Christ of God. Up with the standard, you brave men at arms; let all eyes see it; and on it the foemen glare like lions. We will call upon the Lion of the tribe of Judah (Rev. 5:5) to lead the van, and we will follow with his Word like a two-edged sword in our hands:

Stand up! stand up for Jesus!
Ye soldiers of the cross!
Lift high hits royal banner;
It must not suffer loss:
From victory unto victory
His army shall he lead
Till every foe is vanquished
And Christ is Lord indeed.

(George Duffield)

We cannot place too much reliance in the gospel; our weakness is that we are so diffident and so apt to look somewhere else for strength. We do not believe in the gospel as to its power over the sons of men as we should believe in it. Too often we preach it with a coward's voice. Have I not heard sermons commencing with abject apologies for the preacher daring to open his mouth, apologies for his youthfulness, for his assertions, for his venturing to intrude upon men's consciences, and I do not know what else? Can God own ambassadors of this cowardly cringing breed, who mistake fear of men for humility! Will our Captain honour such carpet-knights who apologise for bearing arms? I have heard that, of old, the ambassadors of Holland, and some other states, when introduced to his celestial majesty, the brother of the son and cousin of the moon — the Emperor of China — were expected to come crawling on their hands and knees up to the throne; but when our ambassadors went to that flowery land, they declined to pay such humiliating homage to his impertinent majesty, and informed him that they would stand upright in his presence as free men should, or else they would decline all dealings with him, and, in all probability, his majesty would hear from a cannon's mouth far less gentle notes than he would care for. Even thus, though we may well humble ourselves as men, yet, as ambassadors of God, we cannot crouch to the sons of men to ask them what message would suit them best. It must not, shall not, be that we shall smooth our tongues and tone our doctrines to the taste of the age. The gospel that we preach, although the worldly-wise despise it, is God's gospel for all that. "Ah", says he, "there is nothing in it: science has overthrown it." "And", says another, "this gospel is but so much platitude; we have heard it over and over again." Ah, sir, and though it be platitude to you, and you decree it to be contemptible, you shall hear it or nothing else from us, "For it is the power of God, and the wisdom of God." (1 Cor. 1:24) In its simplicity lies its majesty and its power. "We are not ashamed of the gospel of Christ." (Rom. 1:16) "God forbid that we should glory, save in the cross of our Lord Jesus Christ." (Gal 6:14) We will proclaim it again with confidence. We will bring out once more the selfsame truth as of old; and as the loaf barley bread smote the tent of Midian, so that it lay along (Judg. 7:13), so shall the gospel overturn its adversaries. The broken pitcher, and the flaming torches, and the old war cry, "The sword of the Lord and of Gideon" (Judg. 7:18, 20) shall yet fill the foeman with dismay. Let us but be bold for Jesus, and we shall see what his arm can do.

The gospel is the voice of the eternal God, and has in it the same power as that which brought the world out of nothing, and which will raise the dead from their graves at the coming of the Son of Man. The gospel, the word of God, can no more return to him void than can the snow go back to heaven, or the rain-drops climb again the path by which they descended from the clouds. Have faith in God's Word, faith in the presence of the Holy Spirit, faith in the reigning Saviour, faith in the fulfilment of the everlasting purposes, and you will be full of confidence, like an army with banners.

Once more, an army with banners may signify *constancy and perseverance* in holding the truth. We see before us not an army that has lost its banners, that has suffered its colours to be torn away from it, but an army which bears aloft its ancient standard, and swears by it still. Let us be very earnest to maintain the faith once delivered to the saints! Let us not give up this doctrine or that, at the dictates of policy or fashion! But whatever Jesus says to us, let us receive it as the word of life. Great injury may be done to a church before it knows it, if it tolerates error here and there; for false doctrine, like the little leaven, soon leavens the whole lump. If the church is taught by the Spirit to know the voice of the Good Shepherd, it will not follow a stranger, for it does not know the voice of strangers. (Jn 10:5) This is part of the education Christ gives to his people: "All thy people shall be taught of the Lord." (Is. 54:13) "They shall know the truth, and the truth shall make them free." (Jn. 8:32) May we, as a church, hold fast to the things which we have learned, and have been taught by God; and may we be preserved from the philosophies and refinings of these last days! If we give up the things which are verily believed among us, we shall lose our empower, and the enemy alone will be pleased; but, if we maintain them, the maintenance of the old faith by the Spirit of God shall make us strong in the Lord and in the power of his might. Wrap the colours around you, you standard bearers, in the day of danger, and die sooner than give them up. Life is little compared with God's loving-kindness, and that is the sure heritage of the brave defender of the faith. Thus resolute for truth, the church becomes an army with banners.

II. Secondly, the church is said to be TERRIBLE.

To whom is she terrible? She should be amiable, and she is. May God grant that our church may never be terrible to young converts by being morose and uncharitable! Whenever I hear of candidates being alarmed at coming before our elders, or seeing the pastor, or making confession of faith before the church, I wish I could say to them: "Dismiss your fears, beloved ones; we shall be glad to see you, and you will find your fellowship with us a pleasure rather than a trial." So far from wishing to repel you, if you really do love the Saviour, we shall be glad enough to welcome you. If we cannot see in you the evidence of a great change, we shall kindly point out to you our fears, and shall be thrice happy to point you to the Saviour; but be sure of this, if you have really believed in Jesus you will not find the church terrible to you. Harsh judgements are contrary to the spirit of Christ and the nature of the gospel; where they are the rule, the church is despicable rather than terrible. Being bigoted and uncharitable are indications of weakness, not of strength.

To what and to whom is the church terrible? I answer, firstly, in a certain sense she is terrible *to all the ungodly*. A true church in her holiness and testimony is very terrible to sinners. The ungodly do not care to rush about a mock church, nor about sham Christians, but a really earnest Christian abashes the ungodly. We have known some who could not use the foul language which they were accustomed to when they were in the presence of godly men and women, though these persons had no authority or position or rank. Even in the most ribald company, when a Christian of known consistency of character has wisely spoken a word of reproof, a solemn bashfulness comes over the majority of those present; their consciences bear witness against them, and they feel how awful goodness is. Not that we are ever to try and impress others with any dread of us; such an attempt would be ridiculed, and end in deserved failure; but the influence we describe flows naturally out of a godly light. Majesty of character never lies in affectation of demeanour but in solidity of virtue. If there is real goodness in us — if we really, fervently, zealously, love the right, and hate the evil — the outflow of our life almost without a word will judge the ungodly — it will condemn them in their heart of hearts. Holy living is the weightiest condemnation of sin. We have heard of an ungodly son who could not bear to dive in the house where his departed father had, in his lifetime, so devoutly prayed; every room and every piece of furniture reproved him for forsaking his father's God. We have read of others who were wont to dread the sight of certain godly men whose holy lives held them more in check than the laws of the land. The bad part of this is that the terror of the ungodly suggests to them an unhallowed retort upon their reprovers, and becomes the root out of which persecution springs. Those whom the ungodly fear because they condemn them by their character they try to put out of the world if they can, or bespatter them with slander if they cannot smite them with the hand of cruelty. The martyrdom of saints is the result of the darkness hating the light because the light makes manifest its evil deeds. There will be always in proportion to real holiness, earnestness, and Christ-likeness in a church something terrible in it to the perverse generation in which it is placed; it will dread it as it does the all-revealing day of judgement.

Also, there is something terrible in a living church to all *errorists*. Just now, two armies have encamped against the host of God, opposed to each other, confederates against the church of God. For example, there is Ritualism, with its superstition, its priestcraft, its sacramental efficacy, and its hatred of the doctrines of grace; and, on the other side, there is Rationalism, with its sneering unbelief and absurd speculations. These, like Herod and Pilate, agree in nothing but in opposition to Christ; they have one common dread, although they may not confess it. They do not dread those platform speeches in which they are so furiously denounced at public meetings, nor those philosophical discussions in which they are overthrown by argument; but they hate, but they fear, and therefore abuse and pretend to despise the prayerful, zealous, plain simple preaching of the truth as it is in Jesus. This is a weapon against which they cannot stand — the weapon of the old gospel. In the days of Martin Luther, it did marvels; it wrought wonders in the days of George Whitfield and John Wesley. It has often restored the ark of the Lord to our land, and it will again. It has lost none of its ancient power, and therefore is the terror of the adversaries of Christ. Ralph Erskine writes:

Thine aspect's awful majesty
Doth strike thy foes with fear;
As armies do when banners fly,
And martial flags appear.
How does thine armour, glittering bright,
Their frighted spirits quell!
The weapons of thy warlike might
Defy the gates of hell.

Even *to Satan himself* the church of God is terrible. He might, he thinks, deal with individuals, but when these individuals strengthen each other by mutual converse and prayer, when they are bound to each other in holy love, and make a temple in which Christ dwells, then is Satan hard put to it. O brothers and sisters, it is not every church that is terrible like this; its tent is a church of God in which there is the life of God and the love of God; a church in which there is the uplifted banner, the banner of the cross, held high amid those various banners of truthful doctrine and spiritual grace, of which I have just now spoken.

III. We will take a third point, and that is: WHY IS THE CHURCH OF CHRIST TERRIBLE AS AN ARMY WITH BANNERS?

Why is it terrible because of its banners? The whole passage seems to say that the church is terrible as an army, but that to the fullest degree she owes her terribleness to her banners — "Terrible as an army with banners." I believe the great banner of the Christian church is the uplifted Saviour. "I, if I be lifted up from the earth, will draw all men unto me." (Jn. 12:32) Around him then we gather. "Unto him shall the gathering of the people be." (Gen. 49:10) As the brazen serpent in the midst of the camp in the wilderness, so is the Saviour lifted high, our banner. The atoning sacrifice of Christ is the great central standard of all really regenerate men, and this is the main source of dismay to Israel's foes.

But we shall take the thoughts in order. The church herself is terrible, and then terrible because of her banners. Brethren, the army itself is terrible. Why?

Firstly, because it consists of elect people. Remember how Haman's wife enquired concerning Mordecai whether he belonged to the seed of the Jews; for if he did, then she foretold that her husband's scheme would prove a failure — "If Mordecai be of the Seed of the Jews, before whom thou hast begun to fall, thou shalt not prevail against him, but shalt surely fall before him." (Esth. 6:13) Now, the church of God as made up of men and women is nothing more than any other organisation. Look at its exterior, and you see in it few people of great education, and a great many of no education. Here and there we may find a wealthy and powerful person, but hundreds who are poor and despised. It does not possess in itself, naturally, the elements of strength according to ordinary reckoning. Indeed, its own confession is that, in itself, it is perfect weakness, a flock of sheep among wolves. But here lies its strength: that each of the true members of the church are of the royal seed; they are God's chosen ones, the seed of the woman ordained of old to break the head of Satan and all his serpent seed. (Gen. 3:15) They are the weakness of God, but they are stronger than men; he has determined with the things that are not to bring to nought the things that are. (1 Cor. 1:28) As the Canaanites feared the chosen race of Israel because the rumour of them had gone out among the people, and the terror of Jehovah was upon them, so it is with the hosts of evil. They have dreamed their dreams, as the Midianites did, and valiant men like Gideon could hear them telling it; when the barley cake shall fall upon the royal tent of Gideon and smite it till it lies along. Then shall the sword of the Lord, and of Gideon, rout the foe. The elect shall overcome through the blood of the Lamb, and none shall say them nay. You are a royal priesthood, a peculiar people, a chosen generation (1 Pet. 2:9); and in you, the living God will gloriously declare his sovereign grace.

The church, again, consists of a *praying people*. Now, prayer is that which links weakness with infinite strength. A people who can pray can never be overcome because their reserve forces are never exhausted. Go into battle, my brother; and if you are vanquished with the strength you have, prayer shall call up another legion. Yes, twenty legions of angels, and the foe shall marvel to see undefeated adversaries still holding the field. If ten thousand saints were burned tomorrow, their dying prayers would make the church rise like a phoenix from its ashes. Who, therefore, can stand against a people whose prayers enlist God in their quarrel? "The Lord of hosts is with us; the God of Jacob is our refuge." (Ps. 46:7, 11) We cry to the Lord, and he hears us; he breaks through the ranks of the foe; he gives us triumph in the day of battle. Therefore, terrible as an army with banners are those who wield the weapon of all-prayer.

Again, a true church is *based on eternal truth*. I need not quote to you the old Latin proverb which says that truth is mighty and must prevail. Truth is, and truth shall be. It alone is substance, and must outlast the lapse of ages. Falsehoods are soon swollen to their perfection of development, like the bubbles with rainbow hues which children blow, but they are dispersed as easily as they are fashioned; they are children of the hour, while truth is the offspring and heir of eternity. Falsehood dies, pierced through the heart by the arrows of time, but truth, in her impenetrable mail, bids defiance to all foes. Men who love the truth are building gold and silver and precious stones (1 Cor. 3:12); and though their architecture may progress only slowly, it is built for eternity. Ramparts of truth may often be assailed, but they will never be carried by the foe. Establish a power among men of the most ostentatious and apparently stable kind, but rest assured that, if untruth be at the root of it, it must perish sooner or later; only truth is invincible, eternal, and supreme. The fear of the true church, and the dread of her, falls on the enemy because they have wit enough left to know that truth has an abiding and indestructible power. I was very much amused the other day to read a criticism by an eminent infidel, whose name would be well known if I were to mention it, in which he speaks very highly of the exceeding great skill and wisdom and common sense always exhibited in the arrangements of the Roman Catholic Church in opposition to Infidelity, and of the imbecility and childishness manifested by Christian ministers in assailing Rationalism with their dogmatism, etc. I was very glad to receive information so valuable, and I thought: "I see, my friend, what kind of warfare you like best. You admire the Roman Catholic kind of fighting, but you do not admire that which evangelical ministers have adopted. It is no aim of ours to please our enemies in our mode of warfare, just the reverse; and if we have discovered a weapon which galls you, we will use that same arm more freely than ever." There is a story of an officer who was rather awkward in his manners, and, upon some great occasion, almost fell over his sword in his haste. His majesty remarked, "Your sword seems to be very much in the way." "So your majesty's enemies have very often felt", was the reply. So, when the enemies of the truth are finding fault with our procedure, we accept their verdict when we have turned it the other way upwards. If they do not admire our mode of warfare, we think it is in all probability about the best method we could adopt. We would still, God granting us help, continue preaching the "foolishness" of the gospel, and deliver again and again the old truth that "God was in Christ reconciling the world unto himself, not imputing their trespasses unto them." (2 Cor. 5:19) Instead of lifting up a new banner (which would better please our adversaries), it shall be the old banner still — "None but Christ." "By grace are ye saved through faith; and that not of yourselves: it is the gift of God." (Eph. 2:10) Salvation is by free favour, through the expiatory sacrifice of Jesus Christ our Lord.

We are now to observe that the chief glory and majesty of the church lies mainly in the banner which she carries. What cause for terror is there in the banner? We reply: the enemies of Christ dread the cross because they know what the cross has done. Wherever the crucified Jesus has been preached, false systems have tottered to their downfall. Dagon has always fallen before the ark of the Lord. Rage the most violent is excited by the doctrine of the atonement, a rage in which the first cause for wrath is fear. The terribleness of the church lies in her banners because those banners put strength into her. Drawing near to the standard of the cross, the weakest soldier becomes strong: he who might have played the coward becomes a hero when the precious blood of Jesus is felt with power in his soul. Martyrs are born and nurtured at the cross. It is the blood of Jesus which is the life-blood of self-denial; we can die because our Saviour died. The presence of Alexander made the Greeks more than giants: the presence of our Redeemer makes believers swifter than eagles, and stronger than lions.

Moreover, the powers of evil tremble at the old standard because they have a presentiment of its future complete triumph. It is decreed by God, and fixed by his predestinating purpose, that all flesh shall see the salvation of God. Jesus must reign; the crucified One must conquer. The hands nailed to the wood must sway the sceptre of all kingdoms. Like potters' vessels dashed to pieces must all the might and majesty of men be that would oppose the crown and sceptre of Christ's kingdom. In Christ preached, lies the battle-axe and weapons of war, with which the Lord will work out his everlasting decrees. The church, with the name of Immanuel emblazoned on her banner, which it is her duty to keep well displayed, and lifted high, is sure to be terrible to all the powers of darkness.

We will close with one or two reflections. Will each one here say to himself: "An army, a company of warriors; am I one of them? Am I a soldier? I have entered the church; I made a profession; but am I really a soldier? Do I fight? Do I endure hardness? Am I a mere carpet-knight, a mere lie-a-bed soldier, one of those who are pleased to put on regimentals in order to adorn myself with a profession without ever going to the war?"

Am I a soldier of the cross,
A follower of the Lamb?
And shall I fear to own His cause,
Or blush to speak His Name?

Must I be carried to the skies
On flowery beds of ease,
While others fought to win the prize,
And sailed through bloody seas?

Are there no foes for me to face?
Must I not stem the flood?
Is this vile world a friend to grace,
To help me on to God?

Sure I must fight if I would reign;
Increase my courage, Lord.
I'll bear the toil, endure the pain,
Supported by thy Word.

(Isaac Watts)

Pass the question round, my dear brothers and sisters: Are you soldiers who engage in actual fighting for Jesus, under his banner? Do you rally round it? Do you know the standard? Do you love it? Could you die in defense of it? Is the person of Jesus dearest of all things to you? Do you value the doctrine of the atoning substitution? Do you feel your own energy and power awakened in the defence of that, and for the love of that? Let not one go away without facing the searching question.

And then "terrible". Am I in any way terrible through being Christian? Is there any power in my life that would condemn a sinner? My holiness about me should make a wicked man feel ill at ease in my company? Is there enough of Christ about my life to make me like a light in the midst of the darkness? Or is it very likely that, if I were to live in a house, the inhabitants would never see any difference between me and the ungodly? Oh, how many Christians there are who need to wear a label round their necks! You would never know they were Christians without it! They make long prayers and great pretences, but they are Christians in nothing but the name. May your life and mine never be so despicable, but may we convince gainsayers that there is power in the gospel of Jesus Christ, and make them confess that they, not having it, are losing a great blessing!

One other thought. If I am not a soldier, if I am not a servant of Christ in very truth, and yet I come to the place of worship where Christians meet, and where Christ is preached, the day will come when the church of God will be very terrible to me. I will suppose that there is a person listening to this sermon who has been hearing the preaching of the Word in this place now for many years. Imagine that the last day has come. You are brought before the great judgement-seat, and this is the question: "Did this sinner hear the gospel faithfully preached? He is ungodly, he has rejected Christ: does he deserve to be cast away? Did he really hear the gospel, and did he reject it?" If I am asked to provide my witness, I must say, "To the best of my ability, I tried to tell him the gospel of Jesus Christ." "Was this sinner prayed for by the church?" There are many of the members of this church who would feel bound to declare "Yes, Lord, we did pray for him." Yes, and all of us should say, "If we did not pray for him by name, we included him in the general company of those who attend the means of grace, for whom we made a constant intercession." Is there any member of the church who would be able to make an apology for being a rejecter of Christ? He has wilfully rejected the Saviour, he knowingly continues in sin. Will anybody be an advocate for him? Not one tongue would be able to excuse you at the judgement, or argue against the righteous sentence of God. When the great Judge condemns the sinner to be taken away to execution, the whole church with whom that sinner has worshipped, and in whose presence that sinner has rejected Christ, will become "terrible as an army with banners"; for all its voices will say, "Amen, Amen, Amen! Thou art righteous, O Lord." (Rev. 16:5, 19:4

This is no picture drawn from fancy. Do you not know that the saints shall judge the world? (1 Cor. 6:2) They shall sit as co-assessors with the Son of God at the last great assize, and shall say "Amen!" to every verdict which proceeds from his mouth. Oh that the thought of this might be blessed of God's Spirit so as to lead many of you to be reconciled to God!

Jesus is still the loving Mediator, and a full surrender of yourselves to him will assuredly save you. Whoever believes in him is not condemned; and this is what it means to believe in him — that you trust in him, and know that God has given us eternal life — and this life is in his Son who suffered in the place of sinners, that whoever believes in him might not perish, but have everlasting life. (Jn. 3:16) May the Lord bless you, for the Lord Jesus' sake! Amen.

69. TURN AWAY THINE EYES FROM ME

MY SERMON NOTES (1889)

"Turn away thine eyes from me, for they have overcome me."
(Song 6:5)

Much of our life's business consists in overcoming evil, but here we have to deal with overcoming him who is perfect good.

It is not to be supposed that there is any opposition in the heavenly Bridegroom, nor any unwillingness to be overcome by his bride: no, it is in the loving heart of Jesus which is readily overcome by the love of his chosen one.

Let us learn from this most remarkable exclamation —

I. THAT LOOKING UPON HIS CHURCH HAS OVERCOME THE HEART OF THE LORD JESUS.

1. He left heaven to be one with her. He could not bear to see her ruin, but left his Father that he might share her lot.

2. He died to redeem her: "found guilty of excess of love."

3. His delight is in her now; she is lovely in her sight.

4. His eternal joy is to spring from her: he will see in her the result of his death-agony: "he will rest in his love."

Jesus is so overcome that he still gives all that he is, and has, yea, and his own self, to his beloved.

II. THAT THE EYES OF HIS CHOSEN STILL OVERCOME THE LORD JESUS.

Because his eyes are full of love. Therefore is he overcome by our eyes when we are —

1. Looking up in deep repentance.

   — At first seeking for pardon.
   — At times when we pine for restoration from backsliding.
   — Whenever we are struggling to maintain fellowship, and mourning our breaches of it.
   — Whenever we groan under inbred sin, and would be free from it.

2. Looking at him by faith for salvation.

   — At first, by a desperate act, daring to glance with feeble hope.
   — Afterwards, in simplicity, day by day gazing at his wounds.
   — In deep distress still hoping on, and never removing our eyes.

3. Looking for all things to his love alone.

   — When in sore trouble, patiently submitting.

— When in humble hope, quietly waiting.
— When under severe tests, firmly believing.
— When in full assurance, joyfully expecting.

4. Looking in prayer.

— In personal trouble, like Jacob, pleading the promise, and saying, "I will not let thee go, except thou bless me." (Gen. 32:26) The Lord says, "Let me go."
— In holy compassion pleading for others, like Moses, to whom the Lord said, "Let me alone." (Ex. 32:10; Deut. 9:14)

5. Looking in rapturous, restful love.

— He is altogether lovely, and all mine: my eyes swim with tears of delight as they gaze on him, and thus they overcome him.
— My heart burns with love to him, and I adore him; and this wins everything from him.

6. Looking in sacred longing for his appearing.

— Pining for a personal revelation of himself to me by his Spirit.
— Most of all, sighing for his speedy coming in the glory of the Second Advent. He replies, "Behold, I come quickly!" (Rev. 3:11, 22:7, 12)

Oh, the power of a spiritual man with Jesus!
Oh, the power of a church with heaven! The Lord will deny nothing to the prayer of his elect.

III. THAT IF THE CHURCH WOULD BUT LOOK TO HER LORD MORE, SHE WOULD OVERCOME THE WORLD MORE.

To overcome the Lord is the greater thing, and, when this is done, the church may well go forth conquering and to conquer all that is less than the Lord. The eyes of the church should be set on Jesus, and then she would overcome. If we were —

1. Weeping for dishonour done to him, he would see this, and retrieve our defeat.

2. Depending on him for our strength, our faith would give us victory through Jesu's love.

3. Obediently following his commands, he would then feel it right to give honour to his own truth, and to reward obedience to his own precepts.

4. Confidently expectant of victory, Jesus would make bare his arm for us. Faith's eyes calmly watching, or flashing with exultant expectancy, would be as flames of fire to the foe.

5. Eagerly pleading for his interposition, our tearful earnest eyes would soon succeed with our gracious God.

See the secret of strength. Look to Jesus, and overcome.
Let us lament our infrequent use of this conquering weapon.
Now for a long and loving look at the Bridegroom of our souls.

Help us, O Holy Spirit, to whom our eyes owe their sight!

HINTS

Who has not felt the power of the eye? The beggar looked so imploringly that we gave him alms; the child's eye so darkened with disappointment that we indulged his desire; the sick man gazed so sadly at our departure that we turned back, and lengthened our visit. But the eyes of those we love master us. Does a tear begin to form? We yield at once. We cannot endure that the beloved eyes should weep. Our Lord uses this figure to most encouraging purpose. The weeping eyes of prayer move the loving heart of Jesus. Matthew Henry says, "Christ is pleased to borrow these expressions of a passionate lover to express the tenderness of a compassionate Redeemer, and the delight he takes in his redeemed, and in the workings of his own grace in them."

We read in Matthew 15:28 that the Lord Jesus said to the Canaanitish woman, "O woman, great is thy faith; be it unto thee as thou wilt." He seems to surrender at discretion, conquered by that faith which he had himself put into her heart. Now, faith is the eye of the soul, and here is an instance of the eyes overcoming the Lord. We cannot vanquish him with the works of our hands, or the eloquence of our lips; but we can win the victory b y the pleading of our eyes — these eyes which are as the eyes of doves, seeing afar — the eyes of true faith.

Some devout persons find it a profitable exercise to bow the knees, and to look up. Using few words, they commune through a long upward pleading glance. One only cried, "My God" (Ps. 7:1), and at another time "God be merciful to me a sinner" (Ps. 57:1; Lk. 18:13); and yet he came forth from his closet as one who had bathed in heaven.

"Have you a glimpse of Christ now that you are dying?" was the question asked of an old Scottish saint, who, raising himself, made the emphatic reply, "I'll have none of your glimpses now that I am dying, since that I have had a full look at Christ these forty years gane."

(Frances Anne Budge, *Annals of the Early Friends*, 1877)

70. THE OVERCOMING CHRIST
NO. 2486

AT THE METROPOLITAN TABERNACLE, NEWINGTON
ON LORD'S-DAY EVENING, OCT. 8TH, 1876

"Turn away thine eyes from me, for they have overcome me."
(Song of Solomon 6:5)

THIS is the language of the Heavenly Bridegroom towards his spouse. In great condescension, he speaks to her, and bids her take note that her eyes have overcome him. This morning (See Metropolitan Tabernacle Pulpit, No. 1317: *Overcome Evil with Good*), our subject was: overcoming evil with good. We have a very different subject this evening; for we are to talk about overcoming him who is goodness itself, the perfection of everything that is excellent. Saints first learn the art of overcoming evil, and then they learn the way to overcome goodness, too. But how different, dear friends, are the weapons employed in these two warfares; for while, this morning, as we spoke of overcoming evil, we saw that there was much for us to do and think, and we all felt it was more than we could do or think apart from divine grace. Yet here, there is nothing to be done but just to give a look. The Heavenly Bridegroom confesses himself to be overcome by the very look of the eyes of his spouse; she has but to gaze steadily at him, and his heart is vanquished by the glances of her eyes.

Now, it must not be supposed, because of the language of the text, that there is any opposition between Christ and his people which has to be overcome. He loves his bride far too well to allow any division of feeling to separate them in heart from one another. Nor is it to be imagined that the spouse had to gain some blessing from an unwilling hand, and therefore pleaded with her eyes as well as with her lips. Oh, no! There is a holy discipline in Christ's house that sometimes withholds the coveted blessing till we have learned to pray in downright earnest; but the power that wins the victory in prayer has its real basis in the love of Christ himself. It is because he loves us so much that he permits our prayers to conquer him. It is not so much because we love him as because he loves us, that he permits the look of our eyes to overcome his heart.

This, then, is the subject for our meditation now — the way in which God's people overcome the heart of Jesus Christ, and make him say, "Turn away thine eyes from me, for they have overcome me."

I. First, dear friends, let us notice that LOOKING ON HIS CHURCH HAS ALREADY OVERCOME THE HEART OF OUR HEAVENLY BRIDEGROOM.

It was so *in the far-distant past*, not when she looked at him, but when he looked at her, that she overcame him. Ages upon ages ago, or ever the earth was, Christ conceived in his heart the purpose to redeem from among men a people that would be precious in his sight forever and ever. Through the glass of divine foreknowledge, he looked at his people, and recognised the person of every one of them. He saw them all ruined in the Fall, all stained with sin, all contaminated in nature by our first parents' disobedience and rebellion. As he looked at them, he had a steady resolve that he would rescue them, and perfect them, and lift them up to a level with himself, and make them into a race that would praise God forever in heaven with "hallelujahs" and "hosannas" beyond all the harmonies of angels. His heart was so moved towards them that he longed for the time when he should enter upon the great work of their redemption. Long ago, he said, "My delights were with the sons of men." (Prov. 8:31) His heart was always projecting itself forward in anticipation of that happy yet dreadful day when he should be called upon to redeem his people. Every time he thought of them, he was overcome with the very recollection of his great love towards them; and when the long-expected day did at last come,

Down from the shining seats above
With joyful haste He fled,
Entered the grave in mortal flesh,
And dwelt among the dead.

He spoiled the powers of darkness thus,
And brake our iron chains;
Jesus hath freed our captive souls
From everlasting pains.

(Isaac Watts)

He was found as a babe in Bethlehem's manger, lying among the horned oxen feeding in the stable of the village inn. Oh, marvellous mystery! That he, whom the heaven of heavens could not contain, was not satisfied to be over all, God blessed for ever (Rom. 9:5), but, for our sakes, he must also become man. He was so overcome by the love he had for his chosen, that he left his Father's throne of light to become one flesh with his people, and to be made a man like ourselves, and might be next of kin to us. Ah, gracious Saviour, your church's eyes did indeed overcome you when they drew you from amid the royalties of heaven down to the sins and sorrows of earth!

You know, too, *when he lived down here among men*, how often his inmost heart was stirred as he looked on the people whom he loved. And specially, do you recollect the scene on that last night when their redemption-price was about to be paid. He took the cup that he was to drink, and sipped at it; but his holy soul revolted from it, and, with the bloody sweat on his face, he cried, "O my Father, if it be possible, let this cup pass from me." (Mat. 26:39) Then he turned, and looked upon his people. Truly, there was not much to see in them. He had taken three specially privileged apostles to be the representatives of all his chosen, and those three were asleep when he was in his terrible agony. Yet somehow, the sight of them seemed to strengthen him for the fearful ordeal he was enduring. Backward and forward three times he ran to gaze upon them, and they so overcame him that he turned back, and said to his Father, "Nevertheless not as I will, but as thou wilt", and went through with that tremendous work of laying down his life for his people, and drinking the cup of wrath that was their due. They overcome him as he had looked at them.

And, beloved, now that *our Lord is risen from the dead*, he still feels the power of the sight of his redeemed. The great joy of Christ at this moment is found in gazing at his redeemed ones. Look at him as a man, if you will; and what a wonderful Man he is! But remember also that God has highly exalted him, and given him a name which is above every name (Phil. 2:9). And what does the glorified and exalted Christ think as he looks upon the myriads in heaven, all of whom would have been in hell but for him? Then he looks down to the saints on earth and sees the myriads who are all trusting in him, all conquering sin by his might, and all spared from going down to the pit by the merit of his precious blood. And he seems again to say, "Turn away thine eyes from me, for they have overcome me", as if Christ felt that a silence for his people brought almost too much joy for him. What a day will that be when he will descend from heaven with a shout, with the voice of the archangel, and with the trump of God (1 Thess 4:16); when all his people, raised from the dead, or changed in the twinkling of an eye, shall admire him, and he shall be admired in them! (1 Cor. 15:52)

And what will be the joy of his heart when the "great multitude, which no man could number, of all nations, and kindreds, and people, and tongues" (Rev. 7:9), all redeemed by his blood, shall be gathered to Christ, and be the delight of his heart forever and ever! That will be a joy sufficient even for the immensity of his infinite heart, as he sees in them the reward of his awful agonies, the rich return for the shedding of his precious blood. His benevolence — which was the great mainspring of all that he has done — will be gratified and satisfied as he looks on each one of his redeemed, and sees the fruit of his travail in every individual child of his grace, in each sinner reclaimed, in each saint preserved and perfected. I can well conceive of him saying in that day, "Turn away thine eyes from me, for they have overcome me." The joy that Christ will feel in his own sight of his people, and in the glances of the multitudes that he has saved, must be a delight beyond anything we can ever imagine.

II. Now I must pass to a second point, which is this: that THE EYES OF CHRIST'S CHOSEN ONES STILL OVERCOME HIM.

This is a practical point upon which we may profitably spend some little time: the eyes of Christ's chosen ones still overcome him.

And firstly, the eyes of his chosen overcome him when they look up in deep repentance, glancing at him hopefully through their tears. Let me try to give you a picture of such a case. Here is a poor soul, conscious of having sinned, and sinned deeply. Once, sin was thought to be only a trifle; now, it is seen to be a horrible evil, to be trembled at and hated. Once, God was judged to be too severe in sending men to hell, but now, the convinced one has nothing to say against God's justice, for he is all taken up with speaking against himself and his sin. There stands this poor soul, with red and weeping eyes, saying, "O God, I have sinned, and I am still sinning; and if you cast me into the abyss, I dare not challenge your justice. Yet have pity on me, O Lord! God, be merciful to me a sinner!" (Lk. 18:13) When those tear-filled eyes are turned to the Lord Jesus, and sin is confessed again and again with deep contrition and childlike repentance, it is not possible for him long to refuse to grant the pardon we seek. He seems to say to the poor penitent, "Turn away thine eyes from me, for they have overcome me." I cannot bear to see you weeping and sorrowing so. Your sins, which are many, are all forgiven you, for I have loved you with an everlasting love. Go, and sin no more." (Jn. 8:11) There is a wonderful power in the penitent eye, in the full confession that makes a clean breast of every sin before the face of the Lord Jesus Christ.

Remember, brethren, that when we have once repented, we do not leave off repenting, for penitence is a grace that is as long-lived as faith; and as long as we are capable of believing, we shall also necessarily need to repent, for we shall always be sinning. So, *whenever the child of God feels that he has gone astray in any way*, even though he was living near to God, he has gone back and grown cold in heart; he has only to come to Christ again, and cry after him, and confess his folly in having left him, and his ingratitude in having been so indifferent to him, and Christ will indeed receive him back again. You cannot long mourn his absence, and seek to return to him, and feel that you will die, if you do not get back the realisation of his sweet love again — you cannot be long in that state before he will be vanquished by your weeping eyes, and say to you "Turn away thine eyes from me, for they have overcome me." And if a child of God, who has not lost fellowship with his Lord, is, nevertheless, jealous lest he should do so — let his morning prayer be, "O my Lord, keep me from everything that would take me away from your love"; and, at night, he looks back over his conduct during the day, and says, "Cleanse thou me from every secret fault" (Ps. 19:12), for,

For I am jealous of my heart
Lest it should once from him depart;
Then should I lose my best delight
Should my Belovèd take to flight

— if there is kept up this delightful tenderness of conscience towards Christ, so that our eyes, with weeping for very fear of sin, still look after him, then we will hold him spellbound, and the deep sorrow of our loving hearts shall vanquish him, and he will bestow the blessing which our soul is seeking.

Another kind of glance that has great power with the Lord Jesus is *when the soul looks to Christ for salvation*. Then it is that the eyes vanquish the Saviour. It is hard at first to look to Christ and believe that he can save you. I suppose some of you, dear friends, have a distinct recollection of the first faith-glance you ever took at Christ. I well remember mine. It seemed so strangely simple, and yet so sublime and wonderful, that I could scarcely think it true that there was life in a look at him. I did but glance half furtively at first, as if I thought it could not mean that such a sinner as I would receive mercy from Christ simply by looking at him. Did he really mean me when he said, "Look unto me, and be ye saved, all the ends of the earth"? (Is. 45:22) I had long sought him, and I had prayed to him; but I could not conquer him, nor win mercy from him by my seeking and my praying. But oh, when my eyes, already red with weeping, looked at him with a steady glance that seemed to say:

I do believe, I will believe,
That Jesus died for me,
And by his blood, his precious blood,
From sin has set me free.

(A *refrain* added to William Cowper's hymn, *Alas and did my Saviour bleed*)

Then he cried, "Turn away thine eyes from me, for they have overcome me", (Song 6:5) "I have blotted out, as a thick cloud, thy transgressions, and, as a cloud, thy sins". (Is. 44:22)

Many times since then, you and I have looked to Jesus Christ *when a sense of sin has been very heavy on us*. I suppose all of you who are really children of God sometimes get into that state in which you begin to ask, "Was I ever really converted? Did my sin really roll from my shoulders and disappear in the tomb of Christ?" When these questions arise in your heart, go and stand once more at the foot of the cross, and look at your suffering Lord. I have looked, and looked, and looked again, until I have seemed to look him all over, and, at last, I have begun to sing,

Oh, 'tis sweet to view the flowing
Of my Saviour's precious blood,
With divine assurance knowing,
He has made my peace with God.

While the eyes of faith are resting upon Jesus, he is overcome by them, and he darts inexpressible joy into our hearts as he says to us, "Turn away thine eyes from me, for they have overcome me." His heart is carried by storm by the faith-looks of his children.

We also give another overcoming glance *when we look to the Lord Jesus Christ for all things*. Worldlings do not understand the terms on which we are linked with Christ. To them, Christ is someone who lived eighteen hundred years ago and then died; but to us, he is alive, he is our familiar Friend, we are intimately acquainted with him, we are in the habit of taking all our troubles to him, and asking him for all that we need. And he removes our sorrows, and grants us the desires of our hearts. There are times with all of us when we get into trouble of one sort or another; and, blessed be his name, he has taught us, when we are in trouble, to lift up our eyes to "the hills from whence cometh our help". (Ps. 121:1) Now, perhaps, dear brother, you have for a while been looking to Christ and saying, "Lord, I believe you will help me. Did you die to save me from hell, and will you not supply me with bread and water while I am in the wilderness? Have you covered me with the robe of your perfect righteousness, and will you not find me clothes to cover my nakedness, and shield me from the weather? Have you done the greater, and will you not do the less?"

When another trouble comes, you keep on looking to him still. You will not believe that he can be unkind. You give him credit for loving you, and caring for you, so you look to him, and, as you look, you submit to his will, and say, "I will never distrust you, my Lord." If he sends yet another rough providence, you continue looking to him, and only say,

"Show me that in which you contend with me. 'Though thou slay me, yet will I trust in thee.' (Job 13:15) I have known you too long to doubt you now, my blessed Lord. You have done too much for me in the past for me to turn away, and say, "I will not trust you. My Lord and Master, you cannot make me believe that you do not love me, for I know you better. My inmost soul is assured that you love me, so I look to you still, and watch the movement of you countenance; and as I look, my heart says, "My Lord, I cannot tell why you have smitten your servant again and again; yet, if it be your love that makes you smite, smite on. Whatever is most for your glory, do with me as you will."

When yours eyes are like that, full of submission, full of hope, full of trust, it cannot be long before the Lord will, somehow or other, deliver you; for he will say,

"I cannot hold out against you any longer. 'Turn away thine eyes from me, for they have overcome me.' 'I will deliver thee, and thou shalt glorify me.' (Ps. 50:15) I will bring you out of the furnace, for I only sit there as Refiner till I see my own image in you. And when I see my eyes in your eyes, and my heart in your heart, and my character in your character, then will I bring you out of the furnace as gold seven times purified."

Blessed Spirit, give us such eyes as these, which will overcome even the heart of Christ!

Again, there are the eyes of prayer which often overcome the Lord Jesus Christ, and this victory comes, sometimes, *when we are praying for ourselves*. You know what it is in prayer to come to him and say,

"Lord, I am in great straits, and you have yourself brought me there. It has not been through my folly, but it is by your own act and deed that I am where I am. Now, Lord, you promised that in six troubles you will deliver us, and in seven there no evil shall touch us. (Job 5:19) You said, 'Thy shoes shall be iron and brass; and as thy days, so shall thy strength be." (Deut. 33:25) Now, Lord, you are God, and you cannot lie; therefore will you not keep your promise? Here, Lord, you see my difficulty and my trial, and your inspired Apostle has said that all things work together for good to them that love God, to them who are the called according to his purpose. (Rom 8:28) Your servant David declared that 'many are the afflictions of the righteous: but the Lord delivereth him out of them all'. (Ps. 34:19) Now, Lord, I look to you to do this for me."

It is one of the greatest things in all the world when a godly man, with the simplicity of a child, just believes God, and fully trusts him for everything. It has come to be a matter of marvel, in this evil age, that a man can say that God grants him many mercies in answer to prayer. People hold up their hands and say, "Dear, dear, what a wonder!" A wonder that God hears prayer? It would be a greater wonder if he did not hear it. Beloved, to me, prayer is a matter of fact; for me to go and take a promise to God, and ask him to fulfil it, and to get it fulfilled, is as common, and as usual, and as much a matter of fact, as it is for you who are in business to take cheques, pass them across the counter at the bank, and receive the cash for them. [See Spurgeon's *Chequebook of the bank of* faith] Do you think that God is a fiction? If he is, then all our religion is a farce; but if God is real, then prayer is real, too. Many of us know that it is real, for we have tried it, and still try it every day we live. In every time of trouble, we bring it to God's feet, and say, "Dear Lord, as you are true and faithful, you will help us through it"; and we find that he does help us through it. We speak what we do know, and testify what we have seen many a time. When a child of God, in deep distress, believes in his Father, and steadily looks to him for deliverance, those eyes of his have mighty power, and God seems to say to him, "Turn away thine eyes from me, for they have overcome me." You cannot look steadily at God and say, "Lord, I am sure about your faithfulness, I am sure about your promise, and I cannot, and will not, doubt it." But before long, you shall see the hand of the Lord made bare for your deliverance, and you also shall be among the happy number who must bear witness that, truly, there is a God in Israel. Thus prayer prevails with God when we present it for ourselves.

So does it also overcome him *when we pray on behalf of others*. Moses, you know, prayed for others and prevailed. Do you, dear children of God, know what it is to wrestle with the Lord for the souls of others? I am sure that many of you do; there are your dear children, kinsfolk, friends, and neighbours, whom you bring before the Lord. I will tell you when you will win the day, mother, when, with tears, you say, "O God, you have given me these children; now give them to me according to the spirit as well as according to the flesh." You will overcome the Lord, dear father, when you spread out your suit before him and say, "Deny my children what you will, but do save them; let them all be yours in the day when you make up your jewels." (Mal. 3:17) You will succeed when, rising from your knees, you set those children a Christian example; and, having pleaded with God for them, you go and plead with them for God, and feel as if your heart would break if you did not see your boys and girls converted. When, like Hannah, you even come to be a woman of a sorrowful spirit because you feel that you must have your children brought to God, then the Lord Jesus will look at you till he says to himself, "I cannot let that poor soul cry and sigh in vain; it is not in my heart — the heart of one who was born of a woman — to let that pleading woman's prayer go without an answer." To you, he will say, "Turn away thine eyes from me, for they have overcome me. Be it unto you even as you will." (Mat. 9:29) And you, dear child of God, who are teaching in the Sunday-school class, or you who are preaching in some small village station, when you get to feel inward grief of heart over those with whom you have to deal, when that grief increases till it comes to be a perfect agony, and you cannot help crying out in anguish of soul when you feel as if you must have them saved, as if you would give everything you had if they might be brought to Christ, when you even wake at night to pray for them, and, in the midst of your business cares, you get distracted with the thought that some whom you love are perishing, at such times as that your powerful eyes in prayer shall move the heart of Christ, and overcome him, and he shall give you those souls for your hire.

Brethren, if we do not pray for sinners, for whom shall we pray? Sisters, if we do not plead for the abandoned, if we do not offer supplication for those who are perverse in heart, we have omitted to pray for the very persons who most need our intercession. Let us bring these hardened hearts beneath the almighty hammer. Let us, by prayer, bring these lepers beneath the healing touch of him who, despite their loathsomeness, can say to them, "Be clean." Let no degree of natural or inherited depravity, or of depravity that has come from long continuance in sin, hinder us from praying for all the unsaved that we know, "O God, have mercy upon these guilty ones!"

I will not further enlarge on this point, for it is settled beyond all question that those who love the souls of men will not be hindered from prayer for them on any account whatever. I conjure you, who have prayed for husbands or children, or friends, do not leave off pleading for them. If you have prayed for twenty years, and they are not converted, pray twenty years more; and if they have grown more wicked while you have pleaded, still pray on; and if heaven and earth and hell seem to combine together to bid you cease your supplications, still pray on. As long as you live, make intercession for transgressors; and as long as they live, let your cries go up to God on their behalf. So shall you "overcome heaven by prayer" as you plead for the ungodly.

Once again, there is another time when the eyes of the believer seem to overcome the heart of Christ, and that is, *when we have turned right away from the world, and looked to him alone.* I have known it so again and again; have not you beloved? In this world, at present, our Lord is somewhat concealed; he does not fully reveal himself to his people. Here, he says to us as he said to Mary, "Do not touch me." (Jn. 20:17) He lets us wait till the veil is drawn up, and then we shall see him face to face, and be like him. Here, we have to live by faith rather than by sight, and it is expectation rather than enjoyment that makes up much of our present bliss. Yet, at times, I have known my Lord come wonderfully near to his servants, and lay bare his inmost heart to them. It seemed as if he could not help it. It has been at some such gathering as this, when we have gone right away from the world, and have forgotten its cares and pleasures for a while, and we have sat down to think only of him. Our soul has surveyed him in his Godhead and in his manhood, as our Prophet, Priest, King, and near Kinsman, living, dying, risen, ascended, soon to come. We have looked him over, and there has not been any part of his character which we have not admired, nor one office in which we have not trusted him, nor one deed for which we have not blessed him. We have come to think, "He is altogether lovely" (Song 5:16), and, while we have been admiring him in a perfect rapture, there has been added to it this sweet thought: He is all goodness, and he is all mine, from the crown of his head to the sole of his foot. "My Beloved is mine, and I am his." (Song 2:16, 6:3) We have not said much, and we could not have said much just then. We have been quite quiet and alone with our Lord, and we have felt that silence was the only eloquence we could use as we looked at him again, and again, and again. At such seasons, my soul has felt ready to swoon away in his presence. You remember how John, in Patmos, when Jesus appeared to him, said, "When I saw him, I fell at his feet as dead" (Rev, 1:17, 19:10), and well he might, for he had a brighter vision of his Lord than you and I can have at present. But even faith's view of him is enough to transport us straight away into heaven itself. Well, brethren, whenever we are thus happily engaged in contemplation of our Lord, not only is he very near us, but he is greatly moved by our love, and he says to us, "Turn away thine eyes from me, for they have overcome me." And, meanwhile, to prove how overcome he is, he begins to reveal himself more fully to us.

You may perhaps have read, in the life of holy Mr. Flavel the extraordinary instance he records of the love of Christ being poured into his soul. He says that he was riding on a horse, going to some engagement, and he had such a sense of the love of Christ that he completely lost himself for several hours; and when he came to himself again, he found his horse standing quite still, and discovered that he had been sitting on horseback all those hours, utterly lost to everything but a special revelation of the wonderful love of Jesus. You may also have heard of Mr. Tennant, the mighty American preacher, and friend of George Whitefield, who was found, lost and absorbed, in a wood, to which he had retired, and his friends had to call him back, as it were, from the sweet fellowship he had been enjoying with Christ. You may remember, too, John Welsh, the famous Scotch preacher, who had to cry out, "Hold, Lord, hold! I am but an earthen vessel, and if I feel more of thy glorious love, I must soon die; so stay thy hand a while." There are such experiences as these, I will not enquire whether you have ever known them; but if you have, I will tell you one thing. All the infidels in the world, and all the devils in hell, will never make you doubt the truth of the Scriptures if you have once been face to face with Christ, and have spoken with your Master as a man speaks with his friend. Such things have happened to those whose cloud-piercing eyes have been so fixed on Christ that he, at last, has felt the mighty fascination of their loving and believing glances, and has revealed himself in still greater measure to them, and made them even more blest than they were before.

Last of all, sometimes the eyes of Christians have great power in overcoming Christ *when they long for his appearing*. Have you never seen the saints lie dying with such language as this on their lips: "Why are his chariots so long in coming? Why does he tarry?

Haste, my Beloved, fetch my soul
Up to thy blessed abode:
Fly, for my spirit longs to see
My Saviour and my God.

There where my blessèd Jesus reigns,
In heaven's unmeasured space,
I'll spend a long eternity
In pleasure and in praise.

Millions of years my wandering eyes
Shall all thy beauties rove,
And endless ages I'll adore
The glories of thy love.

(Isaac Watts)

I have heard them say, with evident regret, "I thought to have been in heaven long before now." I have seen them almost grieve when the doctor has said that they were better, and that there was hope that they might last another month or two. They seemed to say,

"Why should my banishment continue? Why should my release be postponed? These chains of clay which seem so hard to shake off, these fetters of brass, will they never drop from me? Must I still linger in this world of pain, and sorrow, and sin, and suffering? Why not let me go?"

They have been like a poor thrush which I have sometimes seen a boy try to keep on a little bit of turf; it longed for the broad fields, and beat itself against the wires of its cage. So is it with our dear suffering friends, at times; yet they have learned patiently to wait till their change came. But often, their eyes have been so fixed on their Lord that they have said to him, "Will you never come?" And, at last, Christ has looked out of heaven so sweetly on those sick ones, and said, "Your eyes have overcome me, come up higher"; and they have leaped out of their body into his bosom, and the pierced hands have received their blood-washed spirits, and they have been "for ever with the Lord." (1 Thess. 4:17) I am looking forward, and I trust we who are believers in the Lord Jesus Christ, are all looking forward to that day when God will let us languish in life, when we shall see the bars of the prison opened once for all, and we pass through them, and leave this dying world behind, to go to the land of the living, the land of the hereafter, where we, too, shall be "for ever with the Lord." Keep your hearts always longing for that blest hour! Keep you eyes ever looking upward, beloved! Set small store by anything here, and be ever ready to depart; and so, full often, shall Jesus say to you, as though he could no longer bear that you should gaze upon him, though indeed he loves it all the while, "Turn away thine eyes from me, for they have overcome me."

God bless you all, beloved, for Christ's sake! Amen.

71. THE CHARIOTS OF AMMINADIB

NO. 1155

AT THE METROPOLITAN TABERNACLE, NEWINGTON

"Or ever I was aware, my soul made me like the chariots of Amminadib."
(Song of Solomon 6:12)

WE cannot be quite sure at this date what these chariots of Amminadib were to which the inspired poet refers here. Some suppose that he may be alluding to a person of that name, who was renowned, like Jehu of old, for his furious driving. Hence it might have been familiar at the time, and afterwards have become proverbial to speak in metaphor of the chariots of Amminadib. The conjecture seems harmless; still it is only a conjecture and cannot be verified. It is quite possible, however, that our translators may have retained as a proper name a conjunction of two words, which, taken separately, are capable of being interpreted. You remember the word "Ammi" as it occurs in the prophet Hosea. "Say unto your brethren, Ammi", which signifies "ye are my people" (Hos. 2:1), even as earlier he had said, "Call his name Loammi, for ye are not my people." (Hos. 1:9) The word Ammi, thus stands for "people", and the other word, "Nadib" means "willing"; so that the two united might be rendered "willing people" — "like the chariots of a willing people." Or the words may be read, I think, more correctly, "The chariots of the princely people" — the princely chariots, the chariots of the prince. Some have understood them to mean the chariots of God, of the people that surround the Great Prince himself; that is to say, the chariots of the angels, according as we read, "The chariots of God are twenty thousand, even thousands of angels." (Ps. 68:17) In this case, the figure would be a very striking one — "Or ever I was aware, my soul made me like the chariots of the attendants upon the Great King. I was like the cherubim themselves, all aglow with consecrated fire." (Song 6:12) In whatever way the critical point is deciphered, the practical solution appears to be this: the writer's soul was quickened because he was full of life, full of energy, full of might, full of spirit, and full of princely dignity too; and not only stimulated to a high degree, but also elevated, lifted up from dullness, indifference, and apathy — "Or ever I was aware, my soul made me like the chariots of Amminadib."

To whom does this text refer? Probably those of us who would never raise a doubt about the Song being a dialogue between Christ and the spouse — a matter we have no intention of canvassing just now, as we take it for granted — which might find no small difficulty in determining to which of the two sacred personages this speech belongs, whether to Solomon or to the Shulamite (the masculine or the feminine variety of the same name) — the prince the husband, or the princess the spouse — whether, in a word, it was Christ or the church. There is very much to be said for it being Christ himself who is speaking. You will notice in this chapter that, from the fourth verse, he has been referring to his church. "Thou art beautiful, O my love, as Tirzah, comely as Jerusalem, terrible as an army with banners. Turn away thine eyes from me, for they have overcome me", and so on. He is speaking of his church to the tenth verse. "Who is she that looketh forth as the morning, fair as the moon, clear as the sun, and terrible as an army with banners?" Then the eleventh verse goes on, "I went down into the garden of nuts to see the fruits of the valley, and to see whether the vine nourished, and the pomegranates budded. Or ever I was aware, my soul made me like the chariots of Amminadib." May it not be the Lord himself who is speaking here? We may entertain the question for a moment without absolutely fixing on this as its proper solution. If it refers to Christ, it means just this: that he had been for a while away from his people. They had grieved him, and he had hidden his face from them. Out of very love and faithfulness, he felt bound to chasten them by hiding from them the brightness of his countenance. But he began to think tenderly of his people, and his heart turned towards his church; and while he was thinking of her, he saw such beauties in her that his soul was melted with her charms. Oh, what an extraordinary thing that he should see loveliness in his poor imperfect church! But he saw such loveliness about her that, as her image rose up before his face he said, "Thou hast ravished my heart, my sister, my spouse; thou hast ravished my heart with one of thine eyes." "Turn away thine eyes from me, for they have overcome me." And then, musing upon her still, and coming into her garden, and seeing the various graces like plants and flowers in their different stages of development, his heart began to grow warm again towards her and all that concerned her. It had never really been cold; it only seemed so in the deviation of his usual manner, but, like Joseph before his brethren, he could not refrain any longer. When he saw some of his people budding with desires, others bursting into the realisation of those desires, when he saw some like ripe and mellow fruit on the bough, ready for heaven, others just commencing the divine life, He was charmed to be in the garden of nuts; or ever he was aware, he found he must be with his people; and he must return in the fullness of his love to his church. Not her beauties only, but the kindling of his own soul began to stir him. His free grace sought free scope; his infinite love became more than a match for the temporary prudence that had made him hide his face, and, swift as the chariots of Amminadib, he sped back to his people to let them see him again, and let them enjoy fellowship again. There are other Scripture passages where the Saviour is spoken of as being like a roe or a young hart upon the mountains of Bether (or division) (Song 2:17), because he is so willing to come to his people, so willing to make matters up with them, and end the days in which they mourn, because the bridegroom is absent. When he has hidden his face for a while out of love for them, and out of desire to reveal to them their faults, I say again, he is so willing to blot out their faults once more, and to return to them again with mercies, that his return is compared with swiftness and irresistibility to the motions of the chariots of Amminadib.

It is a delightful thought that if communion between our souls and Jesus is suspended, it is not because he takes pleasure in it. His delights are with the sons of men. A thousand times he invites his chosen to abide in him, to continue in his love, and to remain in his company. In this Song, he cries, "Come with me, my spouse." (Song 4:8) This should encourage us to seek him for renewed love-tokens, however serious may have been our departures from him, and however dark our prospects in the hiding of his face. If he, who is the aggrieved party, is eager to be reconciled, the matter is easy, and we may at once rise to the blessed condition from which our sin has cast us down. Jesus longs to embrace us, his arms are opened wide; do not our hearts warm at the sight? Do we not at once rush to his bosom and find a new heaven in a fresh sense of his boundless love? Why hesitate? What possible cause can there be for abiding in darkness? Lord, we fall upon your bosom, and our joy returns. Not that I intend to adopt that view as the groundwork of our present examination. It appears to me that without, in the slightest degree, wresting the passage, or deviating from an honest interpretation, we may understand that this is the language of the church concerning Christ. If so, Christ's words conclude at the end of the tenth verse, and it is the church that speaks at the eleventh. There is not an instance in the whole Song, so far as I can remember, of the Prince himself speaking in the first person singular. Either, therefore, this would be a solitary exception, or else, following the current plan, where the same pronoun is used, the church is speaking to Christ, and telling him of herself. "I went down into the garden of nuts, to see the fruits of the valley, and to see whether the vine flourished and the pomegranates budded. Or ever I was aware, my soul made me like the chariots of Amminadib."

Taking the text, then, as referring to the church in particular, and, more generally, to the Lord's people, there will be *four observations* which we would pointedly make, and prayerfully meditate. May God bless us now in fulfilling this purpose!

I. Our first observation is this: what is most wanted in all religious exercises is THE MOTION, THE EXERCISE OF THE SOUL. "Or ever I was aware, my soul made me" — or, my soul became — "like the chariots of Amminadib."

Soul-worship is the soul of worship, and if you take away the soul from the worship, you have killed the worship; it becomes dead and barren from then on. Let us turn over that well known thought. It may benefit us if we look at the many sides of it.

There are professors in this world who are perfectly content if they have gone through the mechanical part of public devotion. If they have occupied their seats, joined in the hymns and the prayers, and listened to the preaching, they go away quite content and easy. They would not like to be absent from the solemn assembly, and their conscience would prick them if they neglected the outward ordinances; but, having gone through them, and complied with the usual form, they are perfectly content with themselves, and think they have done what is lawful and right, comely and excellent. Now, it is never so with the child of God. If his soul is awakened from the torpor of death, and his sensibilities quickened into the vigour of life, he will feel that, unless in the song he has really praised God in strains of gratitude with emotions of thankfulness, he has rather mocked his heavenly Father than acceptably adored him. He knows that prayer, if it is not the soul that speaks with God, becomes just the carcase of prayer, destitute alike of the sweet savour which can find acceptance with God, and of the sweet satisfaction that can bring refreshment to one's own breast. When he hears the Word preached, he longs to feel it penetrate his heart, even as the rain soaks into the soil; and if he cannot so receive the truth of the gospel when it breaks upon his ear as the engrafted Word that saves his soul, and so feed on it as the bread of life which nourishes his soul, he goes away sad at heart, deploring that, while others were feasting at the banquet, he was there without appetite, and had not the pleasure or the profit which they derived.

Beloved, in our public services, we ought to account nothing truly and rightly done which is not done with the heart. That is one reason why, in this Tabernacle, we have tried to lay aside everything of outward show or external form, which might distract the thoughts or disturb the simplicity of waiting on the Lord. As far as I can, I try to avoid the use of all symbols, except the two which Scripture has ordained, lest the symbol should tempt you to rest satisfied with itself, as I believe it generally does, and so prevent you reaching the Lord with your heart. We try to lay aside everything that would at all touch your senses in the worship, anything which appeals to the ear in the way of sweet music, anything of the aesthetic that would appeal to the eye. If you do not worship God with your souls, I hope you will get tired of our fellowship. Yet, be it confessed, I painfully feel that it is almost as easy not to worship God with the bald plainness of Quakerism as it is not to worship God with the studied pomp of Ritualism. In any form, or without any form of worship, the amount of real devotion must be measured by the quantity of soul that is in it, provided the quality is pure, sincere, and guileless. If the soul is there, in the full exercise of its powers and passions, knowing what is revealed, and feeling what is inspired, I believe God is gracious to pity and forgive a thousand mistakes in outward fashion and skill of execution. The preacher's modulation may be faulty, and the people's singing may be ill-timed to barbarous tunes, without peril of the unpardonable sin. But if the soul is lacking, though you should have tried to worship according to the pattern given in the Mount, and have never had a word uttered, or a sound made, but such as in itself would be accredited by men and acceptable with God had it been quickened by the Spirit, yet without that divine Spirit which alone gives force and fervour to the human soul, it is all null and void. I think every genuine Christian knows it is so, and feels it is so. He says, "My heart crieth out for God, for the living God." (Ps. 84:2) Nor can he be satisfied unless he finds God, and draws near before him.

As in public worship, it is precisely the same in our own private and personal transactions with the Most High. The religious worldling will say a prayer when he wakes in the morning, and perhaps, unless he is out late, or too sleepy at home, he will have a bit of prayer at night again, in the way of the repetition of some collect, or something he has learnt by rote. And very likely, he has family prayer too. It is not so much a custom as it was, but there are some who think they cannot go through the day unless they have what they call "Prayers". But mark how the Christian prizes private prayers above everything that has to do with the ordering of his daily habits. And see how he esteems family prayer to be a necessity in every Christian household! At the same time, he is not content because he prays for a few minutes, but must draw near to the Lord. He is not satisfied because he gathered his children together, and read the Scriptures, and prayed with them, if, on adding up the sum total of the day, he is compelled to say, "It was heartless worship. When I awoke it was heartless worship, when I gathered my children and my servants it was the same, and it was sleepy, heartless worship when I knelt by my bed-side and professed to seek the Lord at nightfall." If it is heartless, it is unacceptable; God cannot receive it. If we have not thrown our heart into it, depend upon it, God will never take it to his heart and be pleased with it. Only that prayer which comes from our heart can get to God's heart; if we pray only from the lips, or from the throat, and not low down from the very bowels of our nature, we shall never reach the bowels of our Father who is in heaven. Oh, that we may be more and more scrupulous and watchful in these things! In the diary of Oliver Heywood, one of the ejected ministers, he often says, "God helped me in prayer in my chamber and in the family." And once he writes this — "In my chamber this morning I met with more than ordinary incomings of grace and outgoings of heart to God." I am afraid we may get satisfied with ourselves, especially if we are regular in private Scripture reading, private prayer, family prayer, and public prayer, while instead of being satisfied with these exercises we ought to be weeping over them and deploring the formal and heartless way in which we are prone to discharge them. Be it always recollected that we do not pray at all unless the soul is drawn out in pleading and beseeching the Lord. *Si nil curarem, nil orarem*, said Melanchthon ("Were I without cares, I should be without prayers.") Now, perhaps you may know a friend of yours who thinks himself a poet. He can make poetry at any time, all the year round. Just pull him by the sleeve, and he will make you very soon a verse or two on the spur of the moment to show the readiness of his wit and the versatility of his talent. Yet I dare say, you think that he is about as far off from being a poet as a sparrow is from being an eagle. You know if he were a poet, he would not be able to command the glow of imagination at one time, and at another time he would hardly be able to control it. He would sometimes have a divine ablates [removal by melting] upon him, as some call it, and then noble thoughts in appropriate words would flow from his pen. Otherwise he would be just as dull and insipid as ordinary mortals. He would tell you indignantly that he could not write verses to order like those who scribble rhyme to advertise tailor's wares. Unless the inspiration comes on me, he would say, I cannot compose a line. In the same way, a man cannot always pray, and the man who pretends he can only utters jargon. He never prays at all as the other never makes poetry at all. Prayer is a divine art. It is a thing that needs the inspiration not of the muses, but of the Spirit of God himself; and it is when the Spirit comes upon us with divine force, and makes our soul like the chariots of Amminadib, that we can pray; and at other times, when that Spirit is not with us, we cannot pray as we did before. Every living child of God knows this. We must measure our prayers by the state of soul we were in.

Take another illustration from the painter. A person who thinks himself a painter can paint any day you like, and anything you ask him — a mountain, a river, a horse, an insect, or a flower — it is all the same to him. He takes a brush, and soon produces something which ordinary people might think to be a picture; but send that daub of his to the Royal Academy, and they will tell you that it may do for a tea tray, but not for the walls of a gallery. But the man that *can* paint, how does he mix his colours? The great painter will tell you that he mixes his brains with his colours; and when he takes his brush and dips it into the paint, he lays it on with his soul. In a great picture, such as sometimes we have seen with a Titian or a Raphael, it is not the colour but the man's heart that has got out on to the canvas. Somehow, he has managed to drop his brush into his soul. That is real painting. And so it is with prayer. The humblest man that prays to God with his soul understands the fine art of prayer; but the man who chants a pompous liturgy, or repeats an extemporaneous effusion [outpouring], has not prayed. He has dashed off what he thinks to be a picture, but it is not a picture, it is not a prayer. Had it been a prayer, it would have had a palpable [evident] inspiration in its light and shade. A painting consist of few lines, but you will see the painter's hand in it; and a prayer may consist of only half a dozen words, but you can see the hand of God in it. The formality repels you in the one case, the vitality attracts you in the other.

So, we come back to the proposition with which we started. We can only pray according to the proportion in which our soul puts out its force and feeling, and it is the same with praise. We have praised God up to the amount of soul that was in the sense as well as in the sound, be it with an organ or without an organ, with good music or with groanings that cannot be uttered. (Rom. 8:26) We may have praised God either way, but only if our soul has been in full swell. With every kind of religious exercise, the soul is the standard of the whole compass of worship.

II. We proceed to a second remark: SOMETIMES IT HAPPENS THAT THE HEART IS NOT IN THE BEST STATE FOR DEVOTION.

If religion is a matter of soul, it cannot always be attended to with equal pleasure and advantage.

You can always grind a barrel-organ; it will invariably give you the same discordant noise, which people call music, but the human voice will not admit of being wound up in the same fashion, nor will it, for the most part, discharge the same monotonous functions. The great singer finds that his voice changes, and that he cannot always use it with the same freedom. If the voice is a delicate organ, how much more delicate is the soul! The soul is continually the subject of changes. Ah, how often it changes because of its contact with the body! If we could be disembodied, oh, how we would praise God and pray to him! "The spirit truly is willing, but the flesh is weak." (Mat. 26:41; Mk. 14:38) I sat among some brethren the other day who were devout, and I tried to be, but I had a splitting headache. I do not know whether you could pray under so grievous a disability; let me confess to you that I could not. At another time, not long ago, I was one of a solemn assembly, when various disturbances occurred in the room — somebody getting up, and others coming in late, as some of you do — and I could not get into a right frame as I ought to have done. Little things affect little minds, and our minds, many of them, are little. In that case, I could not pray because my mind was being distracted and my attention was being taken away. Such distractions frequently happen, and bitterly they remind us of our infirmities. The apostles themselves fell to sleeping when they ought to have been praying; and under Paul's preaching, Eutychus went to sleep, and Paul never blamed him. He died as the result of it, but he got raised again from the dead; so I suppose there was no fault in him. We may sometimes, without any wilfulness on our part, as a necessary result of the weakness of our nature, or the stress of our toil and care, bring ourselves into a condition in which we cannot feel like the chariots of Amminadib, and it is no use for us to attempt it. The body does affect the soul materially; and a thousand outside agencies will tell on our mental susceptibilities. I have known people come into this Tabernacle who have, perhaps, been annoyed with somebody in their pew, or somebody outside. It ought not to be so, but it is so. A little fly buzzing about one's face — as small a thing as that — will disturb one's devotion, so that you cannot pray as you would and as you desire.

And then, alas, our sins are a much more serious hindrance to our devotion. A sense of guilt puts us into such a state that we cannot be bold in our faith, and childlike in our confidence, when we appear before God. Perhaps we have been angry. How can we come before the Lord calmly when our spirit has been just now tossed with tempest? Probably, we have been seeking the world, and going after it with all our might. How can we suddenly pull up, and put all our strength into a vigorous seeking of the kingdom of God and his righteousness in a moment? It is possible, too, that there is a sick child at home, or a wife lying suffering, or serious losses and crosses about business and domestic affairs. Perhaps one has a very heavy heart to bring before the Lord. Now, God's grace can help us to overcome all these things, and can even make our souls like the chariots of Amminadib. We do want grace for such emergencies. The soul, in its different phases and states, has need of help from the sanctuary to which it repairs. "Well", perhaps one here will say, "I always do what I think right every Sunday in much the same manner. I always pray the same, and I don't know but what I can always sing God's praises the same." Yes, let me answer our good friend. I have a doubt about your thorough sameness, or of your habitual self-content. If you were to ask one of the statues in St. Paul's Cathedral how it felt, I have no doubt it would say that it always felt the same, because it never had any feeling. Appeal to anything destitute of life, you will find that it has no change. But where there is life, and that which is intensely delicate — spiritual life, and where it is placed in circumstances so hostile to it as the circumstances which surround us here — you will find that not only the revolutions of the seasons, but the variations of the temperature, affect it. And every one who has this life in him experiences such changes. We have read of those who have no changes, and therefore have no fear of God. The fact that a believer cannot at all times draw near to God as his spirit would desire, becomes accordingly the key which interprets to him the grace and goodness by which he sometimes gains access after a manner that surprises and delights his spirit.

III. This leads cheerfully to our third observation: THERE ARE SEASONS WHEN OUR HEART IS SWEETLY MOVED TOWARDS GOD. "Or ever I was aware, my soul made me like the chariots of Amminadib."

Have you not proved welcome opportunities when all your thoughts were quickened, enlivened, and stimulated to activity in the highest degree about your highest interests? We have ceased to moan,

Look how we grovel here below,
Fond of these earthly toys;
Our souls, how heavily they go
To reach eternal joys,

(Isaac Watts)

— and we have been all wings, and could soar and mount aloft. Like David, we could have danced before the ark of God for very joy (2 Sam. 6:14), and if any had said to us that we might ourselves fall by our enthusiasm while we seemed vile by our hilarity, we should have replied that we purposed to be viler still. All within us was awake; there was not a slumbering faculty. Our memory told us of the goodness of the Lord in days gone by; and our hopes were regaled by the mercy we had not yet tasted, but which was made sure to us by promise, and brought near to us by faith. Our faith was active and bright of eye. Our love especially sheds a clear light over all our prospects. Oh, we have had blessed times when our soul has been light and rapid as the chariots of Amminadib. And at such times we were conscious of great elevation. The chariots of Amminadib were those of a prince. And oh, we were no more mean, and low, and beggarly, and grovelling, but we saw Christ, and were made kings and princes and priests with him. Then we longed to crown his head. Then we could have performed martyrs' deeds. Then we were no cowards, we were afraid of no foes, we sat down at the feet of Jesus, and thought everything little compared with him; sufferings for his sake would have been a gain, and reproach would have been an honour. We had princely thoughts then, large, liberal, generous, capacious thoughts concerning Christ and his people, his cause, and his conquests: our souls were like the chariots of Amminadib. At the time, they were full of power; for, when the chariots of Amminadib went out, who could stop them? Who could lay his hand on the reins and turn the coursers as they went onward in their mighty tramping?

Such was our spirit. We laughed at thoughts of death, and poured contempt on the trials of life. We were "strong in the Lord and in the power of his might." (Eph. 6:10) Oh, what splendid times we have had when God has been with us. Do you remember when you had them? I recollect, when newly converted, how full my spirit was of love and holy triumph, like the chariots of Amminadib. Yours, no doubt, were much like mine. The love of your espousals was upon you. With what pleasing rapture you embraced your Lord and said, "I will never let him go." Stronger is love than death or hell. You felt it to be so. You flamed and burned and glowed, and though in yourself you were like low brushwood, yet you were like the bush in the desert that burned with fire because God was in your soul. Do you remember that? Well, now, since then, in private prayer sometimes, you have had gracious access, and meditation has been added to prayer, and the love of Christ has come in on you like a great flood tide, and drowned everything in your soul except itself. There have been periods when a sense of the eternal, immutable, never-ending love of God, his electing sovereign favour, that love of God, the love of God, in giving his Son for you, has told on your spirit with a mighty influence, laying you prostrate for very joy, when you could not speak, because words were too poor to express the emotions of your soul. You had to feel the force of James Thomson's hymn of the seasons,

Come, then, expressive silence, muse his praise,

— for you could not speak it. You know it has been so with you sometimes, and has not it been so sometimes under the Word, when you have been ready to stand up and clap your hands for joy? Have not I seen gratitude and exultation reflected on your faces sometimes when the Lord has been present in the preaching of the gospel, and the truth has come to you like marrow and fatness from the King's own hands. Dr. Watts has proved to be a faithful interpreter of the very scene and circumstance that ravished your heart:

The King himself draws near
And feasts his saints today;
Here we may sit and see him here,
And love, and praise, and pray.

Oh, yes! In God's house you have known the days of heaven upon earth. If I might speak for the rest of you, I should pronounce the choicest periods of fellowship those we have found at the Lord's Table. When the bread has been broken, and the wine poured out, down in the Lecture Hall, he has been with us in the breaking of bread. If ever we have come near to Christ, surely it has been in that blessed communion. There are windows of agate and gates of carbuncle through which Christ comes to his people in the ordinances he has ordained. We will never slight them. We cannot. The Master puts such reality and fullness of joy into them. Apart from him, they are idols; but with him, when he is there, when we have the *real presence* — not the superstitious presence some speak of — but the *real* presence which his own Spirit imparts, and our waiting souls participate. Ah, then we said,

No beams of cedar or of fir
Can with his courts on earth compare,
As myrrh new bleeding from the tree,
Such is a dying Christ to me.

(Isaac Watts)

Not infrequently, too, have I known that the Lord has appeared to his people and warmed their hearts when they have been working for him. Some idle, indolent, sluggish professors, who have used the ordinances, have not found benefit in the ordinances because the Lord has intended to rebuke their sloth; but when they have got up and gone out among the poor, when they have gone out to visit the sick, the sorrowful, and the dying, they have heard such delightful expressions from the lips of holy, suffering men and women, or felt their hearts so kindled by a sight of divine compassion in the midst of desperate poverty and gracious pardon for grievous sin, that a quickening has come over them; and whereas they did not seem to care before whether souls were lost or saved, they have gone out into the world with zeal to win fresh trophies for the Messiah, their hearts have become like the chariots of Amminadib, through the benefits they have received from Christian service. A great many Christian people will never be happy, and will never be fully alive to the destinies that wait on their Redeemer, till they get something to do to give them an interest in those mighty issues. The rule of the Christian life is: "If any would not work, neither should he eat." (2 Thess. 3:10) If you will not serve God as Christians, you shall not feed upon the sweet things of the kingdom to your own soul's comfort. A little more service and your soul would become like the chariots of Amminadib. Beloved, there is no need for me to go farther; I merely say this to bring up your grateful memories that you may thank God for what he has done; for remember, whatever he has done in the past, he will do again in the future. When the Lord has come once to his people, he says, "I will see you again, I will come to you again, and your hearts shall rejoice." Of everything he has ever given you, he has got as much in store, and he is quite as able to give it to you now as he was before. You have never gone so high in joy, but you may go higher yet; you have never drunk such draughts from the well of Bethlehem as left the well empty; you shall drink again of it. Do not say, "I had those sweet times when I was young, I shall never have them again." You shall have precious times again. Get back to your first love, dear brother, dear sister; get forward to a higher love than ever you had, for God will help you. You might say, "I look back and think this,

What peaceful hours I once enjoyed!
How sweet their memory still!
But they have left an aching void
The world can never fill.

(William Cowper)

Thank God for that ache! Bless God for the aching void. If your soul aches for God, he will come to your relief before long. Whenever a soul puts up a flag of distress at the masthead, he may be sure that Christ is on the look-out for just such a soul. He has thrown up the windows of heaven, and wherever he sees a soul that does what is right, and longs to find joy and reconciliation with God, he will come to it, and, before long, it will be better for you than even the chariots of Amminadib, and more desirable.

IV. Our last observation is this: SOMETIMES THE SWEET SEASONS COME TO US WHEN WE DO NOT EXPECT THEM. "Or ever I was aware, my soul made me like the chariots of Amminadib."

Some poor hearts do not reckon ever to have these joys again. They say, "No, no, they are all gone; the last leaf has blown from the tree; the last bower [arbour] has faded in the garden. My summer is past. It is all over with me! "That is the bitter complaint and hollow murmuring of unbelief. But the Lord for whom you wait can suddenly appear, and while you are saying hard things of yourself he will refute them with the beams of his countenance. Even at this very moment, you may stand like Hannah, a woman of sorrowful spirit, feeling as if you would be sent away empty; yes, and God's servant himself may address you with rough words as Eli did her, and may even tell you that you are drunk, when it is deep grief that enfeebles your steps and chokes your voice (1 Sam. 1:9-17); and, all the while, the Lord may have in store for you such a blessing that you have never dreamed of. And he may say to you, "Go your way, my daughter; I have heard your petition, and your soul shall have its desire." Or ever I was aware, while my unbelief led me to think such a thing impossible, you have made me like the chariots of Amminadib. "Or ever I was aware" — as if it came on me almost without my own consent. Glad enough I was when it did come, but it took me by surprise; it led me captive. Now, is not that the way the Lord dealt with you when you were not aware of it, when you had no reason to expect him, when you found and felt yourself to be utterly lost, ruined, and undone? Did he not surprise you with his mercy, and embrace you with his loving-kindness?

Again, you are diminished and brought low through oppression, affliction, and sorrow. There is nothing that leads you to expect a season of joy; you are just as empty and unworthy as you can well be. You feel as if your heart were of stone, and you cannot stir it, and you are saying, "I only wish I could enjoy the freedom that my companions have, and keep the solemn feasts with their holy gladness: but, alas for me! I am afraid I have got to be a mere mechanical Christian, without the lively instincts and lofty inspirations of spiritual worship." Thus you write bitter things against yourself. Oh, beloved, the Lord is looking down upon you now as his son or daughter, as his own dear child, and is about to surprise you with his infinite love!

Let me give you one text to put into your mouth and take home with you. The Lord has said, concerning every one of his people, "Thou art all fair, my love; there is no spot in thee." (Song 4:7) "Why, now, I am all covered over with spots and blemishes", you say, "and no beauty"; but the Lord Jesus Christ has washed you with his blood, and covered you with his righteousness. Do you think he can see any imperfection in that? You are members of his body, united with him. In Christ, you are without spot or wrinkle or any such thing. (Eph. 5:27) You are all spots in yourself, but he sees you as he intends to make you before he has done with you, and he can discern unspeakable beauties in you. You say,

"Oh, does he think that? Surely then I see unspeakable beauties in him! His love to me opens my eyes to see how dear a one he must be. Is he enamoured of me? Has he given his whole heart to me? Did he prove his love to me by bleeding on the cross? Oh, then, I must love him, if he will but let me! Shall such a poor worm as I love infinite perfection? Oh, yes, I must, since infinite perfection deigns to love me, and since the Sun of Righteousness in all his glory deigns to shine on my soul!

"You are beginning to warm already, I see you are. Or ever you are aware, your soul is making you like the chariots of Amminadib. And if you keep on with those holy contemplations, you will leave off all misgivings about your love for him, so deeply absorbed will you be in musing on his love for you. You will forget all the while about your sin, while you recollect the blood that has put that sin away, the perfect righteousness that has made you accepted in the Beloved, and the everlasting covenant which, through, grace has put your feet on a rock, and saved your eyes from tears and your feet from falling. Engaged in such sweet soliloquies, or ever you are aware, your soul will make you like the chariots of Amminadib. May the Lord make it so! God grant that surprising grace may come in the same way even to sinners, lead them to Jesus, and constrain them to look to him. Then, while looking, faith will breathe in their spirit, so that they will sing with the author John Stocker,

**Thy mercy is more than a match for my heart,
Which wonders to feel its own hardness depart;
Dissolved by thy goodness, I fall to the ground,
And weep to the praise of the glory I've found.**

72. INWARD CONFLICTS

NO. 593

DELIVERED ON SUNDAY MORNING, OCTOBER 9TH, 1864
AT THE METROPOLITAN TABERNACLE, NEWINGTON

"Return, return, O Shulamite; return, return, that we may look upon thee. What will ye see in the Shulamite? As it were the company of two armies." (Song of Solomon 6:13)

THIS verse is not addressed to the Church in her doubting state, nor while seeking her absent Lord, but refers to her in her very best condition, when she has lately come from the enjoyment of fellowship with her divine spouse, and when her soul, in consequence, is like the chariots of Amminadib. Read the context, and you will perceive that believers who are rejoicing in the Lord may look upon this text as their own. Observe the title of the person addressed — it is a marriage name. She has been espoused to Solomon, and taken his name and become Solyma, for such is the best rendering of the word rendered "Shulamite". This name is appropriate to souls who are united with Christ, to those whom Christ has betrothed to himself in righteousness, who live in union with their Lord.

You who abide in the Lord Jesus are, by a mysterious bond, made one with Christ; and he has conferred on you his own name — he is Solomon, and you are Solyma [Jerusalem, Zion, at peace]. That is a remarkable expression in the book of Jeremiah: "This is her name wherewith she shall be called, The Lord our Righteousness." (Jer. 33:16)

One would have thought that such a title was incommunicable; but yet so close is the union between Christ and his people that the Holy Spirit actually transfers that dignified expression "The Lord our Righteousness" to his Israel, his beloved. The title Solyma also signifies both perfection and peace. There is perfection in every child of God, but not perfection in the flesh. We are perfect in Christ Jesus; complete in him; spotless, by being washed in his blood; glorious, by being robed in his righteousness. Every child of God is right sumptuously arrayed in the wedding dress of the Saviour's righteousness. We may truly say that "Solomon in all his glory was not arrayed like one of these." (Mat. 6:29; Lk. 12:27) Every believer stands in Christ perfectly accepted. (Eph. 1:6) The sweet name "Solyma", means also peace — "Therefore being justified by faith, we have peace with God through Jesus Christ our Lord." (Rom. 5:1) The true heir of heaven is not at enmity with God, nor at war with his own conscience. The silver trumpet has proclaimed an everlasting peace; God's sword has been sheathed in the Saviour's heart, and divine justice is on the side of the chosen people.

The request of the text next demands a moment's consideration. It is repeated four times: "Return, return, O Solyma; return, return, that we may look upon thee." Does not this request proceed from the daughters of Jerusalem who desire to behold her beauty? Souls that are anxious about their own state may well desire to understand the experience of the true child of God. You want to know whether you also are a Christian, therefore you would know how Christians feel, how they think of Christ, how they are moved by his Spirit, what is their appearance when his love is shed abroad in their hearts. You anxiously desire to see the true Christian, that you may measure yourselves, and see whether there is the life of God in you. These daughters of Jerusalem also desire to look upon her for their own delight; for, as to gaze upon beauty is exceedingly pleasant, so is it specially delightful to the pure in heart to have fellowship with the pure in heart — to see the fruit which the Spirit has brought forth — to behold the cleanness of the believer's walk, and to know the savour of the believer's conversation. No beauty equals the beauty of holiness; nothing is so comely as uprightness; and therefore we do not wonder that four times the request to return is made. Perhaps, too, these daughters wanted to look at her as an example to themselves. Saints look on the beauty of others that they may be enabled to emulate [copy] their excellence. Let us read with affectionate attention the biographies of holy men, that they may be a stimulus to ourselves, exciting us to exert ourselves in the Redeemer's cause, and may afford us some hope that the highest Christian attainments are not altogether beyond our reach. I think this is the reason why the daughters of Jerusalem said, "Return, return, O Solyma": they would comfort themselves by seeing whether they are like her; they would delight themselves by beholding her perfections; they would also stir up their own souls by seeing her example.

The rest of the text, you will observe, may be considered two ways: either the spouse asks the question, which is the most probable — she says, "What shall you see in Solyma?" She thinks that there is no beauty in her, nothing in her that anyone should delight in her, or fix his eyes upon her, or derive any profit from regarding her. "Why", says she, "all that you see in me is a company of two armies — a conflict between good and evil. If you look on me, you see nothing but good and evil fighting together, darkness and light contending. I am not worth your looking at." So she would fain veil her face and go away, if it were not for the earnest request which seems to hold her fast — or, as some think, this question is asked by bystanders, and is answered by the daughters of Jerusalem: "What shall you see in the Shulamite?" the giddy crowd enquires; and instructed believers cry, "We shall see in her the concurrence of two triumphant armies returning as choristers, with music and dancing, from the field of battle. We shall see in her the King immortal, invisible, with all his hosts of grace; we shall see in her the purified soul co-working with the glorious Saviour; we shall see in the Christian Church the activity of sanctified manhood, combined with the majestic power of deity residing within." This is what she might not say of herself; but what they would see in her.

Observe, then, the two meanings, and let us dismiss the second for another occasion. There is in every Christian a sweet composition of Christ's power and of the activity of his own soul; there is the power of God, and there is the creature himself made willing in the day of God's power. (Ps.110:3) There is in the Christian, God working in him to will and to do of his own good pleasure, and the man himself working out his own salvation with fear and trembling. (2:12-13) In the Christian Church, you find man working for God and God working in man; and all this in such a joyful manner as to be rather resembling the triumph of returning conquerors than the going forth to fight of those who make war. What do we see in Solyma? We see the blessed confluence of the two great armies of sanctified humanity and of God made flesh. But we are now coming to take the text in the first sense — the Church blushingly declares that there is nothing to he seen in her except conflict, turmoil, the wrestling of two great powers — two mighty armies contending for the mastery. Upon this point, may God give us light for the comfort of many who are passing through this stage of Christian experience.

I. At the outset, we shall, this morning, first call upon you who know the Lord, to OBSERVE THE FACT OF THE TWO ARMIES IN EVERY CHRISTIAN.

This is very evident; but to aid your reflections, let me remind you, throughout this very book you see traces of it. This Canticle is a marriage song — it therefore speaks less of the battle-field than some other portions of Scripture, for, at the marriage feast, allusions to trial and to warfare ought to be but few. Yet, that the Church is not altogether sanctified is clear if you note such passages as the fifth verse of the first chapter: "I am black", says she, "but comely, O ye daughters of Jerusalem, as the tents of Kedar, as the curtains of Solomon." She is black: here is her natural state — here we have the manifestation of her continued depravity of heart. "I am black, but comely" — here is her spiritual condition —

the Spirit of God has clothed her with beautiful graces; Christ has washed her and made her fair in his sight. "I am like the tents of Kedar" says she; the smoke-dried curtains of those Arab wanderers who dwelt in this country set out her sinfulness; and yet, in Christ, she compares herself with those embroidered curtains, heavy with gold and silver threads, which hang around the throne of Solomon. In the third chapter, she plainly proves that she is not always enjoying fellowship, but is in a mixed condition.

"By night on my bed", here is her slothfulness; "I sought him whom my soul loveth", here is her activity; "I sought him", here is her desire; "but I found him not", here is her sad experience of his absence. Then in the fifth chapter, the second verse, there is a singular co-mixture: "I sleep", I am sluggish, cold, dead, lethargic; "but my heart waketh", the inward principle is still vital, still panting after something better. We find her in the third verse making vain excuses for not opening to her Lord; but, before long, you come to the fifth verse, and you find her opening to her beloved, though her beloved has withdrawn: refusing but soon complying; the two natures battling; the one fast closing the door, and the other opening it and seeking the beloved with tearful complaint. Throughout the song there is always this mixture. But, as I said, we cannot expect to find much of this in a nuptial ode. Turn, therefore, to the great book of battle songs, the book of Psalms, and here you have in almost every psalm indications of the complexity of the Christian character. So strange are some of the Psalms that it has been well said they might have been written rather by two people than one. David begins out of the very depths calling to God, and then ending with all the jubilant notes of a conqueror, leading captivity captive. I shall not have time to refer to many passages, but the forty-second Psalm will strike you, where the one David seems to be reasoning with another David: "Why art thou cast down, O my soul? and why art thou disquieted within me? Hope thou in God: for I shall yet praise him." And the next Psalm 43 is much to the same effect. Perhaps, however, the most eminent and striking paradox of the whole is the seventy-third Psalm, the twenty-second verse. There he says of himself, "So foolish was I, and ignorant: I was as a beast before thee." He could not go further than that surely in a description of himself. "Nevertheless, I am continually with thee: thou hast holden me by my right hand. Thou shalt guide me with thy counsel, and afterward receive me to glory. Whom have I in heaven but thee? and there is none upon earth that I desire beside thee." Heavy as a stone, he lies stuck in the mire, and yet, on a sudden, he takes to himself wings and outstrips the eagle's flight as he loses himself in the splendour of the Sun of Righteousness, mounting so high as to be entirely lost to all but God. David's experience, as we find it pictured for us in the Psalms, is but our own written out in large capital characters; and here we see what strange incongruities, what marvellous paradoxes are found in men.

If we need still further instruction on this matter, let me refer you to the epistles of our Apostle Paul. I read in your hearing just now that extraordinary passage in the seventh chapter of Romans. How could there have been more graphically described than we have there, the war and the contention which is always going on between the baser nature and the divine life which God has implanted within us? To the like effect is the seventeenth verse of the fifth chapter of the Galatians, where he says, "For the flesh lusteth against the Spirit, and the Spirit against the flesh: and these are contrary the one to the other: so that ye cannot do the things that ye would." We are carnal and yet spiritual; lost in self yet saved in Christ; all imperfections and yet perfect; incomplete in all things and yet complete in everything. Strange contradictions, but yet most strangely true!

Another evidence of this matter is the concurrent experience of saved souls. I thought of just taking down at random biographies from my library shelves and writing out passages, but I had scarcely time for that; in truth you have only to read the truthful life of any Christian man, and you soon find that he is not all Spirit but also flesh; not all renewed nature but still compassed with infirmity. We have whole volumes on this subject. There is

Bunyan's *Holy War*, describing God's conquest of the town of Mansoul, and its subsequent attacks by sins lurking within and foes storming without. Sibbe's book, *The Soul's Conflict* contains a mass of experimental knowledge. But you will perhaps feel more pleased if I give you, instead of word prose, one or two expressions in the form of rhyme, which show you that our hymn-writers — they should be among the more joyous of the Christian Church — have been compelled sometimes to sing paradoxes concerning themselves. Ralph Erskine has left us that strange work, *The Believer's Riddle*, the greatest riddle that was ever written, a perfect maze to all but those who have the clue within. He says,

My heart's a mirror, dim and bright,
A compound strange of day and night,
Of dung and diamonds, dross and gold,
Of summer's heat and winter's cold.

Joseph Hart, whose hymns come indeed from the heart — rightly named was he! — in his hymn called *The Paradox*, writes,

How strange is the course that a Christian must steer,
How perplexed is the path he must tread;
The hope of his happiness rises from fear,
And his life he receives from the dead.
His fairest pretentions must wholly be waved,
And his best resolutions be crossed;
Nor can he expect to be perfectly saved
Till he finds himself utterly lost.
When all this is done and his heart is assured,
Of the total remission of sins;
When his pardon is signed and his peace is procured,
From that moment his conflict begins.

We have that hymn of John Newton's, which you will find in your Rippon's Selection [No. 309]:

I would, but cannot sing,
I would, but cannot pray
For Satan meets me when I try,
And frights my soul away,

— and so on. Still more remarkable is that hymn

I asked the Lord that I might grow
In faith, and love, and every grace;
Might more of his salvation know,
And seek more earnestly his face.

(John Newton)

But I need not continue because you have it in your hymn book. You will there find that, instead of God's working in the way in which he expected, the singer was made to feel the hidden evils of his heart, and so he was humbled and brought in true penitence nearer to God. William Cowper thus sings of himself in a hymn that is also in your book,

The Lord will happiness divine
On contrite hearts bestow;
Then tell me, gracious God, is mine
A contrite heart or no?

I sometimes think myself inclined
To love thee, if I could;
But often feel another mind,
Averse to all that's good.

My best desires are faint and few,
I fain would strive for more!
But, when I cry, 'My strength renew'
Seem weaker than before.

Oh make this heart rejoice or ache!
Decide this doubt for me;
And, if it be not broken, break,
And heal it, if it be.

Thus, if time did not fail us, we might go through all those men who have at any time served the Church of God, and say of them all that they have experienced, felt, and confessed — a struggle and a conflict between what God has implanted and what nature has left in them. Nor do I think, dear friends, that we ought at all to wonder at this. It sounds strange in the worldly ear, but we ought not to marvel, for this is only according to the analogy of nature. If you look around, everywhere you will discern contending forces, and, out of these contending forces, the rule of nature comes. See yonder orbs; moved by a mysterious impulse, they seek to fly off into space, but the sun holds them by invisible bands. The force of the sun's attraction would draw them at once into his heat, but, on the other hand, the centrifugal force would drive them far away into distant space; between these two they keep the circular orbit which God has at present appointed. So we have a corrupt nature within us which would drive us to sin, and on the other hand the divine power within would draw us into perfect conformity and union with Christ. Between those two forces, the Christian life becomes much what it is.

Observe how in this word, death and life are contending together. Death crowds his graves, but life wins the victory; death may toll the knell, and this is his note of triumph, but every cry of every new-born infant is another shout of the battle of life in which life claims still to be victorious. Look at your own persons, and, in your own bodies, you see this duplex action. You breathe, but the same lungs which receive the fresh, pure air, give out the noxious vapour. There is scarcely an organ of the body which is without an apparatus for the secretion of an injurious substance and its expulsion. The brightest eye that ever swam in light casts out some defilement; the skin, if it is healthy, has a part of its functions to throw off from us what would certainly breed disease. There is going on in every human body a strange conflict between life and death; and, every moment, our life stands, as it were, in the centre of two great armies which are contending whether we should be the prey of the worm, or should still continue to breathe.

Do you wonder, therefore, if the whole world of nature is, or has, fallen into this state, that man, the little world, should be the same? Wonder or not, certain it is that it is so; and let those who have been staggered because they have felt a battle within, from this time on, rather rejoice, because this is the path which all the people of God have trodden before.

II. Now concerning THE ORIGIN OF THIS CONFLICT.

There is but a slight battle in an unrenewed man. There is a sort of conflict of a minor kind between conscience and his grosser passions. Even Ovid could speak of this, and several heathen writers confess a war within; but there is no conflict to any high degree in the ungodly man because, while the strong man armed keeps his house, his goods are at peace. While there is one master, a man may cheerfully serve him; but in the moment of regeneration, a new master comes into the house — a stronger than he has come, and he will bind the strong man, and, after many conflicts, cast him out for ever, and get that house into his own possession. (Mat. 12:29; Mk. 3:27; Lk. 11:21) The new nature which God implants in his people is directly the opposite of the old one. As the old nature comes from Satan, being defiled and depraved by the Fall, so the new nature comes direct from heaven, pure and without spot.

As the old nature is sin, is essentially sin, so the new nature is essentially grace — it is a living and incorruptible seed which lives and abides forever, a seed which cannot sin, because it is born of God. When these two, therefore, come into conflict, it is as when fire and water meet — either the one or the other must die. There can be no truce, no parley; the two are deadly foes; the life of the one is the death of the other; the strength of the one the weakness of the other. Now, the old nature has been there beforehand; it is like a tree well rooted — it has been there twenty, thirty, forty, fifty, or sixty years, according to the date of conversion, and it is not easily to tear it up by its roots. Even when grace comes into the heart and makes sin to fall like Dagon did before the ark of God (1 Sam. 5:4), yet it is true of sin as it was of Dagon, the stump, however, is left, and there is still enough vitality in that old stump to breed pain and confusion without limit. The reigning power of sin falls dead the moment a man is converted, but the struggling power of sin does not die until the man dies. Bunyan said that unbelief had as many lives as a cat, and sin has the same vitality. Until we are wrapped in our winding-sheets, we shall never have that black thread of depravity drawn out of us; it will, it must, continue to be there till God shall sanctify us, spirit, soul, and body, and take us home. When you remember how pure is the new life which God has given you — it is from God himself; an emanation from his Spirit; as pure as deity — and think how sinful, on the other hand, is your corrupt nature. Can it be possible that these two should be at peace? Can two walk together except they be agreed? (Amos 3:3) Can these two principles, which are entirely opposed to one another, by any chance patch up a league? It cannot be, and even if it could be, there are allies abroad that will never be quiet: there is Satan, who will never rest from stirring up our corruptions, and on the other hand there is the Holy Spirit, who will never pause in the putting out his divine power till all evil is cast up, root and branch. Since these two must fight — the Spirit of God and the spirit of evil — so the two principles within which are their children, must continue in conflict till our dying day. Here, then, is the source of this conflict.

Oh my dear hearers, some of you do not know anything about this. Remember, you are in the gall of bitterness (Acts 8:23) if you do not. If you are all one way, then you are all the wrong way. If there is in you no conflict, it is because there is no divine power come there to drive the evil one out. The more of these wars and fightings you feel, the more you have cause to thank God and take courage. "The battle is not yours, but God's." (2 Chron. 20:15) You do not go to war at in own charges. You shall overcome, as thousands have done before you, through the blood of the Lamb.

III. This brings us to a third reflection. Let us for a moment consider THE REALITY OF THIS CONFLICT.

The warfare in the Christian mind is not a thing of imagination; it is most true and real. If you want proof of it, you must pass through it. Did you ever kneel down in an agony of spirit, resisting some furious temptation from within? Some of us know what it is to feel the cold sweat running down our brows when we have to fight against ourselves in fearful struggles against the black thoughts of unbelief. Perhaps it may be that the base heart within has even doubted the existence of a God, and dared to prompt us to defy the deity; and we have loathed that thought, and hated it so much that our whole spirit was put to the utmost stretch of tension in order to win a victory over ourselves. You must, if you are at all subject to strong emotions, have felt that this struggle was a terrible fact; to you there could be no doubt about it, for your whole soul felt it — your heart was like a field which is torn up and soaked with blood in the fury of battle. There is a frightful reality in this conflict when we remember how some Christians fall during it, and sin gets the mastery. Recollect, sin may win a battle, though it cannot win the campaign. What, were there no corruptions in David, do you think, that made him sin with Bathsheba? Was there no corrupt heart left in Noah when he was naked to his shame? Was there no corruption in Lot when he sinned in the cave? Why, those black things, which have stained the character of these holy men throughout all time, prove to us how dreadful must be the power of sin, and how mighty must be the power which keeps sin down. Remember what the joy of a Christian is when he feels that he has triumphed over sin. Ah, there is something real here! If the daughters of Jerusalem praised David when he came back with Goliath's head, so do all our powers bless and praise God when he gives us the neck of our spiritual enemies. Like the songstress of old, Deborah, we sing, "O my soul, thou hast trodden down strength." (Judg. 5:21) These are no fictions, imaginations of a poetic and fevered brain — he that has once been along the road to heaven knows that, above all things, the traveller has need to be on the watch against himself.

IV. In the fourth place, let us notice THE CHANGES WHICH TAKE PLACE IN THIS WARFARE.

The conflict in a Christian is not always carried on with the same fury. There is always war, but there is not always battle; the flesh always hates the Spirit, and the Spirit is always the opponent of the flesh; but they are not always fighting, and, when they fight, it is not always with the same fury. You ask me why? Well, sometimes the flesh is not so powerful as at other times. There are moments when, if sin were in the Christian's way, the flesh would not choose it. I may not be able to tell you exactly why, but certain it is that, partly from changes of body, and also from certain phenomena of mind, there are seasons when the propensities to do evil, though still as evil, are not so vigorous as they were: their strength is fearful, but it sleeps. The young lion is ever a lion, but its claws are concealed, and it plays like a lamb. The raging sea is not always in tempest, yet tempests sleep in its waves. Perhaps there is more to be dreaded in the quietness of our depravity than in the raging of it, for sometimes it is the treacherous calm which the Christian ought more to fear than the storm.

Again, it is quite certain that the Spirit's work within us is not always equally active. The Spirit of God is always in a Christian: he dwells in the believer as in a temple. "My loving-kindness will I not utterly take from him" (Ps. 89:33) is true for every saint; but yet you must know that your faith is often weak, that your love is not always like a flame of fire. You cannot pray at all times as you would, Ah, brethren, we can sometimes dash along in service like the chariots of Amminadib, but at other times the wheels are fallen off, and we drag the chariots heavily, like Pharaoh in the midst of the Red Sea! A change then in the flesh, or a change in the spirit, may produce a diversity in the present form of the conflict; it is always there, but not always the same. I suppose that when it is most furious, the reason for its fury may be sought in the strength of both sides. I do not think that when the flesh is strong and the spirit is weak that there is much conflict, then rather there is a speedy defeat; but when the Spirit of God is gloriously at work in our souls, when faith is vigorous, when hope is bright, when love is flaming, and when, at the same time the corrupt powers put out all their might, then it is that the conflict is stern. Some Christians do not enter into this state of strong conflict because of two reasons: they are men of weak passions, and grace in them is at low ebb. But when a believer is endowed with a strong mental nature, and the Spirit is also vigorous within him, then there will go on a contest something like the combat of two Samsons fighting and struggling together as to who shall get the victory.

Ah, brethren, these things may change as I have said, but the war is never over! Do not any of you say, "I shall never be tempted again." Grey-headed brethren, do not think that the old man is ever dead. If professors fall into grave sin, and dishonour the Church, they are as often old men as young men; no, I think I may say that they are more often older men than younger ones. It is sad it should be so, but it is so; and there is many a professor who has stood well for forty years, but makes a fool of himself at the last; and though he has been honoured in God's Church, yet he leaves a blot on his name, and the godly say in a whisper, "No doubt he was a child of God, but it is best that he should be dead, for, in his dotage, he fell into sin." No, we shall never be out of gunshot of the devil till we have crossed the river of death. Our carnal minds are like a powder magazine, only wanting a spark; and ah, what an explosion there would be with any of us! May the Lord keep the sparks away! Let us be very vigilant and very careful; there is an enemy behind every hedge; there is a foe waiting for us at every step; and before this Sabbath's hallowed hours be over, you and I may have slipped and fallen into sin, to our own perpetual harm and hindrance, unless almighty grace shall supervene.

V. A few words now on THE EFFECTS OF THIS CONFLICT.

Some say, "But why does God not remove out of the Christian the old nature?" Some uninstructed Christians even think that, in conversion, the Lord turns the old nature into a new one, which is very far from the fact. The old nature remains in the Christian; it has received a blow which will ultimately be its death, but it still lives, and the new nature in the Christian comes to struggle with it for the mastery. But why is this? Well, I cannot tell you. Such a question reminds me of the Negro's enquiry to the minister: "You say that God is omnipotent, and therefore he is greater than Satan?" "Yes." "Then why doesn't God kill the devil and have done with him?" We believe God to be as morally omnipotent as he is physically omnipotent; and if he willed it, we do not doubt but that evil of every form and shape might disappear out of the universe. Why then does he permit it? Ah, why? But there we leave it. Be amazed at the mystery if you will, but do not question God, nor cast the blame of sin upon his holy character. There it is; he allows sin to remain in the universe, and after all we can say, we observe the fact, but the reason we cannot tell. Still, I think we may, in some respects, see how sin is overruled in the Christian. Sin remaining in the believer drives him humbly to confess his own nothingness, excluding all boasting from his tongue, compelling him to trust in his God, taking away from him his propensity to trust in himself, leading him to value the precious blood which cleanses him, and prizing the Holy Spirit who sanctifies him, and rejoicing in the faithfulness, and patience, and longsuffering of God who still continues to be gracious to him. And oh, what songs will the man of God sing when he gets to heaven! How much sweeter will be the music, because of the conflict! How much more glorious the victory because of the warfare! If I could be totally delivered from sin, root and branch, I certainly would; but yet I am conscious that no Christian would glorify God so much in heaven as he does now, if there were not sin to be contended with. A creature that could not sin, could scarcely show much of the praise of God by its holiness; but that the creature can sin, no, that there is a strong drawing towards sin, and yet the divine grace keeps a man from it, and sanctifies him even to perfection, why, this will make the song come swelling up of "Hallelujah! hallelujah! hallelujah!" If no adversaries had been tolerated, then no victories could have been won. If there were no temptations for us to struggle with, then there would be no elbow-room for our faith, no power for the display of the bare arm of God. Doubtless, it is best as it is, and when the winding up of the chapter comes, perhaps we shall see that our sins committed have been made the means of saving us from other sins which might have been our ruin. Many believers would have grown too proud to be borne with, if some infirmity had not plucked the plume from their helmets, and made them mourn with brokenness of heart before God. God can bring good out of evil by his overruling grace while on the other hand, our good works have often been the greatest curse we ever had. Good works have puffed us up, and so have led us into pride; while our sins, though pulling us down, have, through almighty grace, led us to make men work for eternity.

VI. I want your attention on this last point, which is: THE CONCLUSION OF IT ALL.

This contest, is it forever to continue? Shall we forever tremble in the balance? Will there be no valley of decision where our souls may take their rest? Yes, brethren, the fight will soon be over, and the victory is guaranteed and glorious. Yes, even at the present day, the Christian is making progress. I do not admire the term "progressive sanctification", for it is unwarranted in Scripture; but it is certain that the Christian does grow in grace, and, though his conflict may be as severe in the last day of his life as in the first moment of conversion, yet he does advance in grace, and all his imperfections and conflicts within cannot prove that he has made no progress. Let me show you this. You know that at certain periods in your children's history they pass through diseases incidental to childhood. Here is your babe of a month old, and there is your child of three or four years; this child of three or four years of age is suffering from some of those complaints incidental to infancy; it is not in such good health as your child of a month old; it is far weaker, and its life seems far more in danger. Yet you will not say that there is no progress, for this child of three years old has passed through three years of its difficulties and hazards, which this little one newly-born has yet to encounter. We all know that there are certain growing pains which the lad feels when he is verging out into his manhood, but these pains do not prove a lack of strength, but the very reverse: the muscles are being braced and the sinews are being strengthened.

Stand by the seashore when the tide is coming up. There rolls up a big wave. Just mark the place in the sand. For the next few minutes, there is no wave coming up as high as that — no, some waves that suck back the rest, and you might even think the sea was still retiring. Is there, therefore, no progress made? Why, friend, you will see in a moment, if you will just wait, when another great wave comes sweeping up, far outstripping the one that we marked just now; and when you shall come back in an hour's time, and the sea has come to the fullness of its strength, you will see that the receding of any one individual wave is no mark of its retrogression. You have just to mark the whole sea, and take time in which to examine it, and then you discover there has been progress, and that progress has been effected by alternate advance and retreat. Along the coast of Essex, the sea is greatly encroaching on the land, and, every time we go to some of the watering-places, we perceive that the cliff has fallen, hundreds or thousands of tons have been carried away; and yet it you are there at a tide which has gone far out. You will often think, "Why, surely the land is gaining on the sea! I never walked out so far as this before; I never saw these rocks exposed and dry before." Well, it is a strangely low tide, but at the same time, ask the old fisherman who has lived there all his days, and he will tell you that his mother was married out in a Church which stood where that ship is floating, far out to sea, and that all the intervening soil has been washed away. He recollects when this place, which is now a footpath on the cliff's brink, was a quarter of a mile inland; and then you understand that though, on any one occasion, the land may apparently have gained; yet, on the whole, there has been a progress in the sea.

And so it is with spiritual life. There are times when it seems as if sin has gained on you, and you are going back in spiritual things; there is cause for alarm, but not despair; cause for watchfulness, but not for terror. Go to the Lord, and pray to him to send a mightier wave of his irresistible grace, that your soul may be filled with all the fullness of God. The day is often gloomy at eleven o'clock, but that is no proof that you are not getting towards noon. Many a cold wind howls in the days of March and April, colder than there might have been at Christmas, but that is no proof that you are not getting on to summer. There may come a frosty night in May, nipping the flowers, but that is no proof that the frost is all coming back again. So you may feel within yourself such things as cause you to bow your head in sorrow, and to cry out to God in grief, but even these things shall but speed you on your way towards your desired haven. The battle will certainly end right. Just anticipate for a moment the glory of the victory. You shall be free from sin one day; you shall be perfect, even as your Father who is in heaven is perfect (Mat. 5:48); you shall wave the palm branch, and wave it the more joyously because you had to contend with flesh and blood, and with spiritual wickedness; you shall join the eternal song, and it shall roll up to the throne all the more gloriously,

Give me the wings of faith to rise
Within the veil, and see
The saints above, how great their joys,
How bright their glories be!

Once they were mourning here below,
With sighing and with tears,
They wrestled hard as we do now,
With sins, and doubts, and fears.

(Isaac Watts)

Come, anticipate that triumph, and pluck up courage! Go out, all you servants of God, as Barak went against Sisera; and the day shall come when your foes shall be swept away. That river of death shall do for your enemies what the Kishon did for Jabin — it shall sweep them away for ever. Standing by the Red Sea of the atoning sacrifice, you shall sing to the Lord who has triumphed gloriously, and cast the horse and the rider into the depths of the sea.

I have preached this morning especially for the comfort of those who are thus exercised, and who say, "If it be so, why am I thus?" You will now see that, instead of having cause for distress in all these conflicts, you have only a reason to come to Christ again. Come to Jesus again; look up to him once more, and take him today to be your Saviour and your all. Put your case into his hands, trust him, and you shall be more than conquerors through him who loved you. (Rom. 8:37) Trust him, trust him now, and we will meet in heaven at last to sing his praise forever. Amen.

73. "RETURN, RETURN, O SHULAMITE; RETURN, RETURN!"

NO. 1794

A SERMON DELIVERED ON LORD'S-DAY MORNING, AUGUST 10TH, 1884 AT THE METROPOLITAN TABERNACLE, NEWINGTON

"Return, return, O Shulamite; return, return, that we may look upon thee. What will ye see in the Shulamite? As it were the company of two armies." (Song of Solomon 6:13)

THE translation of the word "Shulamite" is unhappy: it is unmusical, and misses the meaning. The Hebrew word is feminine from "Solomon." "Solomon" may stand for the bridegroom's name, and then the well-beloved bride takes her husband's name in its feminine form, which is Shulamith, Salome, or perhaps better "Solyma." The King has put his name on her, and as Caius has his Caiia, so Solomon has his Solyma. He is the Prince of Peace, and she is the Daughter of Peace. Earlier, she was called "the fairest among women", but now she is espoused unto her Lord, and has a fullness of peace. Therefore she is called the Peace-laden, or the Peace-crowned. You know how true it is so with the justified in Christ Jesus. Because the sound is sweeter, and the sense is clearer, permit me to read the text this way — "Return, return, O Solyma: return, return, that we may look upon thee. What will ye see in Solyma? As it were the company of two armies." May the Holy Spirit, like a dove, rest on us while we linger among the verses of this Song of Loves.

A soul redeemed by blood, and brought by the Holy Spirit into loving, living, lasting union with the Well-Beloved, cannot remain unnoticed. Solomon was known all over the world; Solomon was sought after for his wisdom, and, therefore, Solyma will shine with something of his brightness, and will be enquired after too. In the Church of God, no one lives to himself, or travels through the world unwatched. If you are interested in Christ, heaven and earth and hell will be interested in you. Some are but as a chip in the porridge; they have no savour in themselves, and none comes from them; but the believing man, the Christ-communing man, is full of influences both repellent and attractive, and he may be sure that, where he comes, he will be known and read. As the house of Israel is among the nations like a burning torch in dry stubble, so also is spiritual Israel. Voices will cry after the bride of Christ, "Return! Return! Return! Return!" A pilgrim bound for the Celestial City cannot go through the world, even through the worst part of it such as Vanity Fair, without being noticed and questioned and sought after, and, if possible, ensnared. Do not think, you who have been made a living man by the quickening of the Holy Spirit, that you can glide through this world as the spiritually dead do, for they may be quietly borne along to the place of corruption: the life within you is too strange, too operative, to be overlooked. You are a wonder to many, and you may well be so, for God has wrought great marvels in you and for you. Beloved, you are the Lord's witnesses, and witnesses must not skulk away in the background or stay dumb. When they bear their honest witness, it is in open court, where they will be heard and regarded by all who are concerned in the suit, whether *pro* or *con* (for or against). Oh, saints of God, you are never unobserved, you are compassed about with a great cloud of witnesses, and none of these witnesses are indifferent to you! They all watch you with steady gaze to see how you are running your race. The good are intent that you should so run as to obtain; but there are evil ones who long for your defeat. Solyma is addressed by urgent voices, who plead with her to return to them. For good or evil, multitudes of tongues cry to her, "Return, return, O Solyma, return, return."

Will you kindly notice from the connection of my text what state Solyma [Zion, Jerusalem] was in when these calls came to her? She was in her glory and beauty. In admiration, the question is asked, "Who is she that looketh forth as the morning, fair as the moon, clear as the sun, and terrible as an army with banners?" (Song 6:10) A church or an individual Christian in a low state of grace may escape observation. Who cares about a dead church? Who fights with a lukewarm people? But if Jesus Christ is in the church, or in the heart, he will soon be seen. The evangelist tells us, "He could not be hid." (Mk. 7:24) You may slip down the street in the night without a candle, and, like a thief, you may pass by unobserved, but if the Lord has lit your candle, and you bear it with you, the watchmen will notice you, the dogs will bark at you, and others will spy you out. As fire reveals itself, so also does grace. A bundle of lavender may proclaim its own whereabouts by its fragrance, and so does the life of God in the soul. You may be sure that if the Lord of Hosts is with you, and in you, you will assuredly arouse the animosity of some and the admiration of others. I pray that you and I may be in a bright, clear, forceful condition, as the bride was in this part of the Canticle; for then shall we be sought after, and enquired about.

It appears that the church in her beauty had gone down to attend to her work. "I went down into the garden of nuts to see the fruits of the valley, and to see whether the vine flourished, and the pomegranates budded." (Song 6:11) She did not sit down in the house to admire herself, nor go into the street to show herself: she went down into her Lord's garden to attend to her proper work, and then it was that they cried, "Return, return." Neither the world nor Christ himself will call much after us if we go out to make displays of our own excellence. "Come, see my zeal for the Lord of Hosts" is a wretched piece of self-consciousness, which disgusts more than it attracts. A diligent life is an attractive life. Do you, like an ant, work in your season, carrying your due burden upon the ant-hill? And if you do this for love of Jesus, you do nobly. Plod on without courting approbation, and rest content to do your utmost for the common good. In fellowship with your Lord, humbly do your day's work in your day. Do not seek great things for yourself. (Jer. 45:5) Do not ask to rule in the court, but be willing to work in the field; do not seek to recline on the couch, but take your pruning-knife, and go out among the vines to fulfil your office; and, in that self-forgetting service, your beauty shall be manifested, and voices shall salute you, crying, "Return, return."

It appears, too, that while she was thus engaged, she was the subject of a great stir and emotion of heart. Perhaps she had felt dull and dreary till she entered on her work, but, while she was busy with her pomegranates and her nuts, she cries, "Or ever I was aware, my soul made me like the chariots of Amminadib." She felt that she could hasten like the chariots of a willing people, who rush to the fight from love of their Prince. She felt as if she could run after her Beloved: that she could leap, she could fly. Like a chariot that is drawn by Pharaoh's swiftest coursers, her spirit left all behind. Thus vigorous and active, she was watched by many eyes, and soon she heard voices coming from the four quarters of the universe, crying, "Return, return, O Shulamith; return, return." Dear friends, I would that all Christians were what they should be. I am told, but I would not judge, that large numbers of professing people are only half alive, and are altogether asleep. If that is so, I do not wonder that they are so inconsiderable in their influence. If they are neither diligent in their Master's business, nor fervent in spirit towards him, they are justly despised by those about them. If it be so with you, my brethren, you are losing the joy of the Christian life when you might be filled with delight; you are poverty-stricken, where you might be rich; you are as beggars in the city where you are entitled to take up an honourable burgess-ship. May the Lord revive you! May he forgive your coldness, and set your souls on fire with love for Jesus! If you have life, may you now have it more abundantly! Does not your Master desire that the feeblest of you may be as David, and David as the angel of the Lord?

I speak to you who are the beloved of the Lord, to you who labour in holy service, to you who are quickened with a high degree of spiritual life, and feel your souls within you stirred with sacred enthusiasm. You are worth addressing: may the Holy Spirit make my address worthy of your attention!

Let us use our text in two ways; and may each be profitable!

First, *she hears the lower voices that cry, "Return, return, O Solyma return, return"*, and she answers them with most conclusive negatives. Read the text another way, and in the second place, *she hears voices from above, which cry, "Return, return, O Solyma: return, return,"* and she answers them by her actions as well as by her words.

I. Let us listen for a minute or two, but only with our ears, not with our hearts, to THE LOWER VOICES.

Where do these voices come from? There are voices from the vasty deep of sin and hell, voices from the tombs which we have quitted, voices from the Egypt from which we have fled. They are crying evermore, like unquiet Spirits, "Return, return." Especially they call to young souls, who are newly wedded to Jesus, in the hope that they have not as yet forgotten their own kindred and their father's house. When we have gone a long way in the divine life, the world feels dubious of our return, and almost gives us up, preferring rather to accuse than to invite. After many years of faithful service, and of resolute nonconformity to the world, many temptations which assaulted our youth are unknown to our maturity. The devil is not altogether a fool, although he is great in that direction; and therefore he does not continue forever to use nets which have failed to entangle the birds. If he finds that cajolery will not ensnare us, he leaves his old tactics and tries other methods. When "Return, return" will not woo us, he puts on his lion form, and roars till the mountains shake. Upon young believer, he very commonly uses very powerful inducements to go back. In the hope that he is dealing with Mr. Pliable, he exhibits the hardness of godliness and the pleasantness of sin, and draws the moral that they had better retrace their steps. To them, he calls as sweetly as his cruel voice can tune itself, "Return, return, O Shulamith: return, return."

By *old companions*, he does this. They say, "You have left us all, we do not know why. You have turned fanatic; you have joined with gloomy Christian people, and you are not half the good fellow you used to be. Are you not getting a little tired of those dreary ways? Are not the rules of Christ too precise and puritanical? Are not the ways of God too self-denying? Is not godliness too holy and too heavenly for poor fallible beings like yourselves? If so, the door is open: we will welcome you back. It is true you rent yourself away, and said that you need to go on a pilgrimage to the Celestial City, but we will not throw this in your teeth if you will give up such nonsense. Come, be a good fellow with us once more. We have not drunk up all the wine, nor broken all the viols. We are care-for-nothings still, and shall be glad to make you as light-hearted as ourselves. You were a jolly fellow before you took these blues, and turned so squeamish. Come, shake it off, and be yourself again." How winningly they put it! How cleverly they mimic the tones of true friendship! One would think they sought our good, and were anxious to be our guardian angels.

Sometimes, the desires of nature come to their help, and tender passion is enlisted on the side of evil. Bright eyes and gentle lips speak to the natural heart, and plead with it to return. The tender love of women has thus played the temptress, and so has the strong affection of men. Courtesy and amiability cry, "Why do you fight so shy of us? You know what happy times we used to have together. Come, you have tried these Christian people and their faith; you must have found it very moping and melancholy: return and be merry once more. See how much more free we are than they, so do not live by rule and order; return to the liberty of sin." Thus do her former comrades cry, "Return, return, O Solyma."

The *old joys* sometimes, in moments of weakness which come upon us, revive at the memory, and attempt to mislead us. I have known the young Christian remember what he once thought were joys, and though he had clean left them, and hated them, yet, in the distance which lends enchantment, he did not notice so much of their shallowness, baseness, and brevity, and thought to himself, "In those days, I laughed away the hours right merrily; life was light as a feather; in its froth and foam I saw rainbows of delight. Shall I try these things again? Was I not too hasty in renouncing them?" All the while the voices cry enchantingly, like the songs of the Sirens, "Return, return, O Solyma; return, return." They bring out their most melodious music, and omit all discordant passages from the sonnet of life. They would have us hark back to what was once their joy. Oh, brothers, 'tis a wretched temptation, and yet some fall for it.

Do you not know how the world will even call us back to our *old cares?* We used to fret and worry until, by God's grace, we were led to try walking by faith, and then the Lord helped us to rest in his love and wait patiently for him. Now, perhaps, for years we have had no burdens, for we have cast them on the Lord: we have gone to him in the morning, and told him the fears of the day, and at night we have had little else to do but bless him for the mercy which has averted all those fears. We have lived in sweet contentment, rich in joyful expectation, and not poor even in present felicity [happiness]; and now, perhaps, the world says, "You have spent too much of your money on religion; why did you not save it? You wasted a mint of your time in furthering a kingdom which is imaginary. Oh, if you had given up those energies to the world, and stuck to your business, how much richer you might have been! Come now, quit those dreams! Shall those prayer meetings, leaving that tiresome office in the Sunday-school, giving up philanthropic speculations, and following after your personal interests, act like a sensible man, and you may get on then. If you mind the main chance, you may rise in the social scale."

There are times when steady, sober people, for whom the temptations of gaiety and vice have no charm at all, stand spellbound by these more solid but equally degrading offers. Madame Bubble, as you know, offers to the pilgrim her person, and there are many who turn with loathing from so vile an offer; but then, she also offers her purse, and there are men like Mr. Standfast, who are as poor as an owlet, to whom that offer comes with dangerous force. Her voice has a shrill metallic ring, as she cries, "Return, return, O Solyma; return, return. Return from generosity to selfishness, from holy zeal to worldliness and prudence. Seek what all the nations of the world seek after, what you can see with your eyes, and enjoy with your mouth." Many are these calls. I need not go into details, but you will hear them soon enough. The Sirens are a numerous and ensnaring sisterhood.

When do these voices come? Their sound is heard often — "Return, return, return, return" — four times over, the text has it. They come so often that the word in the Epistle to the Hebrews is more than justified — "And truly, if they had been mindful of that country from whence they came out, they might have had opportunity to have returned." (Heb. 11:15) These opportunities come into our way everywhere, and at all times. If you wish to leave off being a Christian, if you wish to follow the world in its pleasures or in its labours, the doors are always open. It is a wonderfully forgiving world if you will but quit your protest against it. If we run away from our old master, and wish to return to his service, his yoke is always ready for our neck. He will never deny us employment, even though it is to feed swine. Only too glad is the devil to pardon runaways. He is not ashamed to return with seven others to the house which he aforetime quitted. (Mat. 12:45; Lk. 11:26) Often, often the child of God in his early days hears the entreaties of destroyers, as with all subtlety they plead, "Return, return, O Bride of Solomon; return, return."

At times, these voices come from quarters to which our hearts lie open. Many a man has been wooed from the ways of holiness by her that lay in his bosom. For example, Samson had his Delilah. Oftener still, the professing Christian woman has been solicited to forsake her Lord by him who should have helped her in her noblest aspirations. Children have been misled by parents, friends by friends, for Satan has many servants, and many to do his bidding almost unwittingly. It is a fight to reach to heaven, and few there be to help us in it, but the path to hell is downward, and multitudes thrust out their hands to urge us to the infernal deeps. These cries are borne to us by every gale, in tones both loud and gentle, "Return, return, return, return."

Dear brethren, we will find that they solicit us in our best moments. I cannot fully account for the fact, but so it is, that I am most liable to speak unadvisedly with my lips when I have just enjoyed the raptures of high fellowship with God. Yonder shines the Mountain of Transfiguration in its unrivalled splendour, but lo, at the very foot of it the devil rages in the lunatic child! (Mat. 17:14-18; Mk. 9:17-19; Lk. 9:38-42) Our highest graces are not to be trusted, for, as the most venomous serpents lurk among the brightest flowers, so are temptations most abundant hard by our most spiritual and heavenly joys. Do not trust yourself, O child of God, when you have seen the invisible, when you have stood within the circle of fire, and spoken with God as only his favourites may! Do not think yourself secure when you come down into your worldly business, though you have bathed your forehead in the serene light of communion. As pirates distinctly aim to attack the most heavily-laden galleons, so Satan assails you when your vessel has just left the Gold Coast of meditation and prayer. Therefore, watch, and pray evermore. That detestable voice, which dared ask the Master himself to fall down and worship Satan (Mat. 4:9), will come to you when you are most bright and shining with the glory of hallowed fellowship, and will whisper to you, "Return, return. Come down from the mount, and break the commandments to shivers at its foot." The fiend will call you Solyma, quoting your heavenly name — the name of peace and love — and yet he will dare to say, "Return, return." He will flatter us for our virtues, yet tempt us to the worst of vices." Get behind me, Satan. Avaunt [archaic, go away], foul fiend!" Even when repulsed, he will return to the charge, crouch at our feet, and whine out still, "Return, return." The treasures of Egypt, and the pleasures of sin, are his bait and bribe. We cannot, and will not, return at his bidding, yet his frequent solicitation puts us to make a stand, and makes us cry for help.

Notice that our text goes on to say *why they wish us to return*. "Return, return, that we may look upon you." And is that all? Am I to be a traitor to my Lord, and quit his holy ways, and forfeit heaven, to be made a show of by you, O Satan, or by you, O world? Is this a full reward for treachery — "that we may look upon thee?" Why, their looks are daggers. As the eyes of basilisks are the eyes of the ungodly world, so they are malignant stars that blast the soul. Whenever you long for ungodly men to see your piety, your piety will wither at their glance. Remember how that expression of looking upon Zion is sometimes used in Scripture. In Micah 4:11 we find it — "Now also many nations are gathered against thee that say, 'Let her be defiled, and let our eye look upon Zion.'" They wished to spy out her sorrows and weaknesses that they might jest at her, and grieve her. These enemies will do the same with you if you give them the opportunity. Trust a wolf at your throat sooner than worldly men in religious matters. They cannot mean you good, nor do you good, should they say so. They will draw you out, and then expose you. They will entice you into sin and then report your faults. When the world loves the holy man, it is the love of the vulture for the sick lamb. Fear the worldling, even when he comes bearing you gifts.

Now hear *Solyma's wise answer to her tempters*. She says, "What will you see in Solyma?" Do you ask me, O world, to come back and show myself to be your friend? Do you promise me approbation? Do you vow to look upon me, and admire me, and take me as an example? What is there in me that thou canst approve of? What wilt thou see in Solyma? What can the world see in a believer? The world does not know us because it did not know Christ. A blind man wants to see me: I need not go far to oblige him, for he will get but little out of it if I yield to his request. What a vain reason — "That we may look upon thee"! They are so blind they cannot even see themselves, nor know that they are blind. What have you and me to do with them? No, let us walk in the light, and have fellowship with God, and then our life shall be hid with Christ in God (Col. 3:3), only to be manifested when our Lord is manifested; and we are well content to have it so. Listen, O blind world, while we tell you what you would see if we did come to you! "What will you see in Solyma?" You would see — we grieve to say it — a conflict in us: "As it were the company of two armies." You would see two things in us; and yet neither would give you satisfaction. There is sin in us, but inasmuch as it grieves us to have it there, we will not show it to you. We do not wish to make mirth for the daughter of Babylon; and when her children ask us to make music for them by singing one of the songs of Zion, we answer, "How shall we sing the Lord's song in a strange land?" (Ps. 137:4) If we must tell you what you would see in us, we will confess to our faults, but warn you that, out of this, you would get but little joy. You would see two armies, it is true, but neither of them will yield to you. You would see in us a nature like your own; but it is mortified, kept under, and laid under condemnation. It would give you no great pleasure to see it, for we reckon it to be dead. The dead make poor company.

There is in us, it is true, a capacity for all your worldly joys; but the world is crucified to us, and we are crucified to the world. (Gal. 6:14) There is in us a capacity for all your merriment, but, if we were forced to be with you, we should be dreadful killjoys! You would wonder that we did not laugh when you laugh at sin, and that we should not be as ready as you are to run into an excess of riot. We should soon weary you, for the Lord has said, "I will make Jerusalem a burdensome stone for all people." (Zech. 12:3) You would say by and by, "Let these slow souls begone: they hinder our mirth." If we came among you as we are, it would happen with us before long as it did with Israel, for "Egypt was glad when they departed." (Ps. 105:38) Our nature that is like your nature is under restraint, and dies daily, and its expiring groans would be sorry music in your ears.

Then, do you know we have another army in us? That is, there is a new life in us, which life is the indwelling Spirit of God, as it is written, "I will dwell in them, and walk in them." (2 Cor 6:16) If we did return at your request, if we came in the fullness of the blessing of the gospel of Christ, with the Holy Spirit indwelling our bodies, and making them his temples, you would not know what to make of us, and, consequently, you would scoff at us, as Ishmael did at Isaac (Gen 21:9), or envy us as his brethren envied Joseph (Gen. 37:11). You would be sure to ridicule us, for you would not understand us, and, therefore, you would count us hypocrites and sanctimonious fools. As well might oxen commune with men as the wicked with the godly! We have a life beyond you and above you, into which you cannot enter. We are sorry for you that you will not receive the heavenly life which is in Christ Jesus, but as you do not have it, we cannot make you our confidantes or associates. You would grieve us, and we should provoke you; therefore, we are best apart. You say, "Return, return, O Solyma; return, return, that we may look upon thee", and our only answer must be, "What would ye see in Solyma?" Nothing but that which would rebuke and anger you: you would see a company of two armies, both fighting against you.

Come, young brothers and sisters, you who have been tempted to go back, you cannot even tolerate the thought. You have burned your boats behind you, and must conquer or die. Like one of old, you say, "I have opened my mouth unto the Lord, and I cannot go back." (Judg. 11:35) To go back were to give the lie to the Word of God, to make God himself false, to tell the worldling that there are, after all, no pleasures in Christ like the pleasures of the world. It would be to spit in your Saviour's face, to play the Judas, to sell Christ for pieces of money, or for the filthy lusts of this present evil world. "Go back!" It were to renounce heaven and all its glories; it were to choose a terrible death-bed, with a guilty conscience ringing the knell of your soul; it were to choose eternal banishment from the presence of God and from the glory of his power. You cannot return; you cannot even look back. If you are a true Shulamith, you will not even deliberate for a moment about it, but, flinging yourself into the Beloved's arms, you cry, "Lord, to whom should I go? Thou hast the words of eternal life." (Jn. 6:68) God help you so to do, for Jesus' sake!

That is the first part of our subject.

II. Now we turn to listen, not with our ears only, but with our hearts too, to the call of THE HIGHER VOICES which cry, "Return, return."

Brethren, to go to heaven, to go to Christ, to go towards holiness, is a return to God's people: for God's people are originally his children. Though they are prodigals, and have gone into a far country (Lk. 15:13), they always were his children; even when they spent their substance in riotous living they were still his sons, and each of them can speak of "My Father's house." To come to Christ, and holiness, and hear him, is to return. Besides, all God's people have a new life put into them. Where did that new life come from, but from heaven and God? Therefore, to go towards God is, for the quickened ones, to return. All God's, people are bound for heaven; it is in their charter — an agreement that they should sail for heaven; thus to heaven they must go. When the Israelites came out of Egypt to go to Canaan, they were not going to a strange land; they were returning to what had always been their inheritance according to the covenant. They were going out of the house of bondage, and were returning to the land that flowed with milk and honey, where their fathers had sojourned before them.

Now, today, as a child of God, I can hear voices out of the yet beyond, ringing out of the glory, and crying to me, "Return, return." My Father is in heaven, my Saviour is on the throne, many brethren have gone before; all my heart is with my treasure, therefore I hear the shining ones crying to me every day, "Return, return, O Solyma; return, return!" Every harp in the heavenly choir is ringing out an invitation to all the Lord's beloved, every palm-bearing hand is beckoning to us; every glorified lip is calling us to come up higher.

To "return", I think, means this — come nearer to Christ, nearer to God, nearer to holiness. You are saved; seek to be like your Saviour. You enjoyed splendid days at first, in the love of your espousals: return to them; walk always in the light as God is in the light. You were once in the banqueting-house, and the banner over you was love (Song 2:4): return to that house of fellowship. Everyday, seek to lose yourself more in Christ, to live more completely in him, by him, for him, and with him. Return, return, to greater heights of holiness, to deeper self-denial, to braver service, to intenser love, to more burning zeal, to more of the Godlike and the Christlike. "Return, return." The holiest and the best call us that way. Every saint in heaven cries, "Return"; every child of God on earth who is full of the inner life entreats us to return; and chiefly, that dear voice, which once for us cried, "My God, my God, why hast thou forsaken me?" (Mat. 27:46; Mk. 15:34) is always calling to us, "Return, return." Oh, how sweetly he uses the name he himself gave us, our marriage name! Hear him beseech us, "O Solyma, my best beloved, return, return, and come to me!" These are the higher voices. Notice that, in the text, the word "return" appears four times over. Is it not because it is of the highest importance that every child of God should keep returning, and coming nearer to the Father's house? Is it not because it is our highest joy, our strongest security, our best enrichment, to be always coming to Christ as to a living stone (1 Pet. 2:4), and getting into closer fellowship with him? As he calls four times, is it not a hint that we are slow in coming?

We ought to come to Jesus not only at his first call, but even at the glances of his eyes, when he looks as though he longed for our love. It ought to be our rapture to think only of him, and live wholly for him; but as we fail to answer first pleas, he cries four times, "Return, return, O Solyma; return, return. Come to your own Husband, your own loving Lord." He never ceases to entreat until we do return. Are not the reduplications of this call hint at his strong desire after us, his condescending love for us? It does seem so wonderful to me that Christ should want our fellowship, but he does. He cannot be happy without us. Still he sits down on the well when he is thirsty, and, looking across to Samaria's fallen daughter, he says to her, "Give me to drink." (Jn. 4:7, 10) His people are his fullness; he cannot be filled if they are away. I dared not have said this if the Holy Spirit had not declared it, but it is true. Without his people, Jesus would be a Head without a body, and that is a ghastly sight; a King without subjects, and that would have been a wretched parody of royalty, a Shepherd without sheep, and that would have been a dolorous [sad] office, having many pains but no reward. Jesus must have us, or he is a Bridegroom without a bride, bereaved and barren. Oh, how he loves us! How he longs for communion with us! Shall he stand and cry, "Return, return", and will we not come to him at once? Hear him again in another way. He knocks at our door and cries, "Open to me, my sister, my love, my dove, my undefiled: for my head is filled with dew, and my locks with the drops of the night." (Song 5:2) Will we not admit him? If he seeks our company, and therefore calls us to return, our spirit bursts her fetters, for she is ashamed of the bonds that hold her on the right and on the left. She cries "Let me go; I must be with my Lord; his voice compels me. My soul would leap out of the body rather than not come to him who cries, 'Return, return, return, return.'"

I have shown you why the call is so often repeated. Do you not think it is a very instructive call? Permit me to put it in this way: "Return" — that is, to your first simple faith. If you have risen to greatness of conceit and pride of knowledge, return to your humble thoughts. Shrink to nothing again in the presence of your God. Come to the cross as you came at first, saying,

Jesus, thou for me hast died,
And thou in me shalt live,
I shall feel thy death applied,
I shall thy life receive;
Yet, when melted in the flame
Of love, this shall be all my plea,
I the chief of sinners am,
But Jesus died for me.

(Charles Wesley)

Return to your first loving fellowship with Christ, for then the days were only bright with his presence, and the night watches were not weary while you communed with him. Return to the happy love of your espousals, when you went after him into the wilderness; for those were halcyon [happy, peaceful] days. Return, return, to your first ardour in service. Nothing was too hot or too heavy for you then; you were impetuous to be engaged in seeking his redeemed. You have grown lazy now, and you think service for God too severe a strain on you. Return to your first diligence in joyous service. Return also to your eagerness for holy growth. Then, you desired to have the best that God could give you: in those days you resolved to be a thorough Christian, not barely to live, but to live to God in the highest degree. Return to that, and aspire after more. If you have left the best form of consecration, return to it. Oh, sea, rise once more to high-water mark, if you have turned to ebb! Oh, soul, come back to the highest you have ever attained or longed for! As the eagle cries "higher"; as the river cries "fuller"; as the day cries "brighter"; so let it be with you. You are married to him whose blood has bought you, and he cannot, will not, be in heaven without you. Therefore, hasten to obey while he says to you, "Return, return!"

I beg you to observe what the spouse has to say to this when she is thus called upon to return to the Lord. The Lord said to her, "Return, return, that we may look upon thee." Is not that a reason for coming back? The Lord says — "that I may look upon thee." He desires your society, and seems gently to hint that you have kept aloof from him. He seems to say, "You have not been much with me alone lately; you have neglected the reading of the Word, and the hearing of it; I have scarcely seen your face. Therefore return, that I may look upon you." Cover your face and say,

"Lord, why should you look upon me? I am full of sin, but then draw near to him, that his look of love may bring you to repentance, and cause your sin to pass away. Remember, he has power in his eyes to look you into purity and beauty. Come and say, 'Look upon me, Lord; search me, try me, and know my ways.' (Ps. 139:23) Return, that with infinite pity your Beloved may see what ails you, and then, with his dear pierced hand, may perform divine surgery on you, and make you well again.

"Return, that we may look upon thee." I think I may use the phrase to express also that intense satisfaction Jesus has in every believer. With what pleasure the mother looks upon her child! She remembers no more the travail for joy that a man is born into the world (Jn. 16:21), but, with infinitely greater satisfaction, Christ sees of the travail of his soul in every believer. You ought to show yourselves to Jesus, you have cost him so much, and he has loved you even to the death, and loves you still; you ought to abide with him. Return to him that he may look upon you.

And I think, too, when we live near to him, and get into fellowship with him, Jesus feels a sweet complacency towards us. O dear parents, you know the pleasure you take in your loving children! If they have been away from you for years, what a satisfaction it is to see them again within your doors. There is no sight like it! Your Lord loves you so much that it gives him profound pleasure; it swells his heaven to the brim to see you living in his love. What must be his grief when you go fussing about the world, and have no time to talk with him, when you go out sporting and mixing with his enemies, and say that you have no leisure to commune with him! You bring delight to him who is Immanuel, God with us, when you frequently approach him, or constantly abide with him. You make him glad with your secret devotion, your heart's affection, your holy boldness, your all-absorbing zeal. Oh, do come to your Lord that he may look upon you!

Did I hear you bashfully say, "What do you see in Solyma? If Jesus looks on such a dead dog as I am, what will he see in me? I am so full of evil." He will see in you what delights him. He will see his own work there; yes, he will see himself there. Did you never see the sun reflected in a little splinter of glass? The mirror was scarcely an inch in diameter, yet you saw the heavens in it. Have you never looked at a bubble blown by a schoolboy's pipe, and seen a thousand rainbows in it? When the Lord looks on his people, he sees the reflection of himself: he can see himself in our eyes, and therefore those eyes charm him so that he cries, "Thou hast ravished my heart, my sister, my spouse; thou hast ravished my heart with one of thine eyes, with one chain of thy neck." (Song 4:9) The infinite love there is between Christ and ourselves makes him see no sin in Jacob, neither iniquity in Israel; but he looks until he exclaims, "Thou art all fair, my love, there is no spot in thee." (Song 4:7) Do not be ashamed to return to your Lord, for he lovingly urges you to do so.

Let your heart and your flesh, like two armies, welcome him; let all your inward conflict aim at coming nearer to him. Take no rest till, like Jacob's two bands, you are altogether under the blessing of the angel of the covenant.

I will now turn my text about a little, and give you another rendering, which will suit the heart that is welcoming its Lord. Our Mahanaim, our meeting of hosts, shall not be for war, now that the Lord invites us, like Jacob to return to the land of milk and honey; but the companies shall be as musical as they are martial. There are within our experiences companies of singing soldiers, and choirs of camps. This song exhibits the warring soul triumphant in her Lord, and meeting him with timbrel and harp.

Spouse of Christ, in arms contending
O'er each clime beneath the sun,
Blend with prayers for help ascending
Notes of praise for triumphs won.

Ever praising, ever praying,
Help ye thus your brethren here,
That the will of God obeying
We in peace may persevere.

So may we, with hearts devoted,
Serve our God in holiness;
So may we, by God promoted,
Share that heaven which ye possess.

(William Palmer's translation from the Latin of Jean de Contes)

Oh, if my Lord will come and meet me, he shall see in me whole choirs of songsters! My heart, like Miriam, shall take a timbrel, and all my powers, like the daughters of Israel, shall follow, dancing and singing with glad accord. (Ex. 15:20) On the high-sounding cymbals, my heart shall play, singing, "His own right hand and his holy arm have gotten him the victory." (Ps. 98:1) Glory! Glory! Where he comes, glory dwells. When shall I come into his presence and behold my God, my exceeding joy? Then will I praise him with body and soul, with heart and with voice. His coming with all his perfections, and my coming with all my desires, shall make a Mahanaim, and the two hosts, once met, shall encamp together, guarding the King's pavilion, which glitters in the midst. Then shall the warriors become minstrels, and the soldiers shall be singers, as in the valley of Berachah, where all the people triumphed, and they returned to Jerusalem playing their harps and psalteries and trumpets.

Here I leave you in the joyful presence of the King. We cannot cease speaking at any higher point. May the Lord keep us in his presence, for his love's sake! Amen.

TWO SERMONS ON THE SONG OF SOLOMON

CHAPTER 7

74. A CALL FOR REVIVAL
NO. 1066

A SERMON DELIVERED ON LORD'S DAY MORNING,
AUGUST 18TH, 1872
AT THE METROPOLITAN TABERNACLE, NEWINGTON

"Come my beloved, let us go forth into the field, let us lodge in the villages. Let us get up early to the vineyards; let us see if the vine flourish, whether the tender grape appear, and the pomegranates bud forth: there will I give thee my loves. The mandrakes give a smell, and at our gates are all manner of pleasant fruits, new and old, which I have laid up for thee, O my beloved."
(Song of Solomon 7:1-11)

I REMEMBER having heard it said that, when a church is in a right condition, all that it wants on the Sabbath day is that the sermon should be like the orders given by a commanding-officer to his troops. It need not be rhetorical or eloquent, it only needs to be clear and plain — a word of direction for the Lord's servants. If the soldiers are prepared for action, they will not look to be regaled with oratory, but, having heard the words of command, they will, with all their hearts, go about to obey them. Assuredly, the church needs instructing, consoling, and edifying, as well as directing; but this morning I feel that I have a word from the Captain of our salvation, addressed first to this particular regiment, and next to those other portions of the Grand Army which are represented here this morning. I speak as unto wise men; judge what I say.

Travelling along our island just now, you see everywhere the sickle, or the reaping machine, in full work. Harvest whitens the plains; everywhere the loaded wagons are bearing home the precious fruits of the earth. My spirit is stirred within me, and my soul is on fire, for I see everywhere a harvest except in the church of Christ. Reapers are busy everywhere except in the fields of our divine Boaz. All fields are ripe, except those of Bethlehem; all barns are filling except those of the Great Husbandman. Christ Jesus has scarcely a sheaf ingathered of late; we hear of very few results from the sacred sowing of the Word. Here and there, the church, like Ruth, gathers an ear — a very precious ear it is true — for who shall estimate the value of a single soul; but we have no wave-sheaves as in the days of Pentecost, or, if we have them, they are few and far between; and as for the harvest home which we have so long expected, our eyes fail in looking for it in vain. As a church, constituting a part of the Master's field, we have had for years one continued harvest, but still, never such a one as has satisfied our spirits, for our idea of our king is such that the largest increase to his church would not content us; we should still feel that our Lord Jesus deserved far more. As he has not yet seen of the travail of his soul so as to be satisfied, so neither are we his servants content on his behalf, but we long, and cry, and pray for a larger harvest as his reward for the dread sowings of Gethsemane and Golgotha, in bloody sweat and streams of vital blood.

The time when our churches can operate extensively with the greatest convenience will soon be upon us. We do not usually look for any great things during the summer, when congregations are scattered at the seaside, and workpeople are busy for many hours in the day. The summer of nature is the winter of the Church, and the earth's winter is our harvest. These warm days will soon be gone, and the long evenings will come, and, with them, abounding opportunities of doing good. Therefore, it seemed to me to be a seasonable thing to give the rallying cry this morning, and bid our friends remember that the harvest of the church comes on apace. I would urge you all to sharpen your sickles, and, with good hope and prayerful confidence, prepare for the appointed weeks of our harvest. May God, by his Holy Spirit, inspire you with zeal for the work that awaits you, and cause you to walk in fellowship with Jesus in all that you do.

I. We shall, this morning, first of all, call your attention to the fact which is implied in the words of our text, that LOVE IS THE GREAT MOTIVE FOR ACTION IN THE CAUSE OF CHRIST.

All through these verses, the spouse acts with reference to her beloved. It is for him that she goes out into the field; and, for the sake of his company, and the quiet enjoyment of his love, she would lodge in the villages. All manner of pleasant fruits, new and old, which are stored within her gates, she declares to be laid up for her beloved. Love, then, is the fittest and most powerful motive to holy service. "The love of Christ constraineth us." (2 Cor. 5:14) This love has about it certain marked peculiarities. It is first of all a love which realises the person of the Beloved. In the text, the spouse speaks of "my beloved" as of a real personage, whom she sees, upon whom she leans, and with whom she talks. Christ Jesus is to his church no fiction, no myth, no imaginary hero. Throughout the song, both the personages are most real to each other, so real that they both enter into graphic descriptions of each other's beauties, and present us with portraits drawn by the pencil of admiring love.

Now, a church will always be strong when the Lord Jesus is real to her; by this, indeed, may her power be estimated. Jesus must be to us no historical person who was once on earth, but is now dead and powerless; he must be an actual person, living still in our midst. Imagine, my brethren, with what enthusiasm the present audience would be stirred if I should retire, and in my place there should come forward the very Christ who was nailed to the cross of Calvary. You would know him by his hands and by his feet, the sacred marks of his passion. Oh, how the sight of him would stir your souls! You would be bowing your heads in adoration, but grudgingly closing your eyes even for a second in prayer, for you would desire, without a pause, to drink in the blessed vision. And if the crucified One should stand here and say, "My brethren, my blood-bought ones, for whom I laid down my life, there is yet much to be done to extend my kingdom. There are precious souls, brothers and sisters of yours, who do not know my name, who must be brought in. There are ignorant ones to be taught and sinful ones to be restored." And suppose he should then point with his hand to one of you, and say, "I send you there", and to another, "I send you there." Why, you would feel at once anointed to the appointed work, and go out to do it with much earnestness, carefulness and joy. You would be right pleased to receive a commission from those dear honey-dripping lips.

My brethren, have you forgotten that you walk by faith, and will you permit it to be thought that sight would have more power over you than faith? I trust you will not have it so. Then, remember, by faith you may realise, and ought to realise, this morning that Jesus walks among the golden candlesticks, and is in his church now, saying to every one of his people, "Go and serve me! Seek my blood bought ones! Help my feeble ones! Feed my sheep and my lambs!" I pray you, let your faith this morning sweeten your duties by the knowledge that they arise out of your Beloved's personal commands. Execute his holy commands as if you had received them, as in very deed you have, directly from himself. Let your heart go with mine, while I say, "Jesus, my beloved, though I do not see you, and must be content to behold you by faith alone, yet my faith shall be more influential than my sight. I know that you are here; and what you bid me do, my soul shall perform with all her might, because you have said it.

Note next, that the love here spoken of was well assured of the affection of its Beloved. Note the verse that precedes our text: "I am my beloved's, and his desire is towards me." A Christian is never strong for service when he does not know whether Christ loves him or not. If that is a question, you have put out the fire by which, alone, the force can be generated which must work the machinery of your spirit. You must know beyond question that Jesus loves you, and gave himself for you. You must feel that he is loving you now, and that his heart is looking out through those dear eyes which once wept over Jerusalem, and that the meaning of his loving glance is, "Soul, I love you; I loved you so that I gave myself for you, and I have not repented of the gift. I love you still as much as I loved you on Calvary's bloody tree." It is strengthening to feel that still "his desire is toward me." Oh, when you feel, "Jesus loves me, and Jesus wants me to show my love for him. At this moment, Jesus thinks of me and takes a delight in me." This will make you strong as a giant in the cause of your beloved. Between the very jaws of death, a man would venture who felt that the love of Christ was set upon him. Love for Jesus is the fountain of courage, the mother of self-denial, and the nurse of constancy. Strive, then, for a well-assured sense of the Saviour's love. Do not be content till you possess it, for it will be health to your spirit and marrow to your bones. It will be a girdle of strength to your loins, and a chain of honour about your neck.

Observe that the love of the spouse was lived in fellowship with the Well-beloved. "Come, my beloved, let us go, let us lodge, let us get up, let us see, "There will I give thee my loves." True love to Jesus grows stronger and stronger in proportion as it abides in him. We are cold in our love because we live at a distance from him. The angel who dwells in the sun has never to complain of an ice-bound heart; and he who lives in Christ and abides in him will blaze and glow with a warmth of love comparable to that of Christ himself. I do not think that the numbers of a church have so much to do with the work it accomplishes; that depends more upon the degree of love, than upon the length of the church roll. A small church inflamed with ardent affection for the divine Lord will do more for him than a great host eaten up by worldliness. Love burns its way by its own vehement flames. Coals of juniper are soon felt. The Enochs are the men — they walk with God, and hence, they have power over their times. The Johns are the men, for they lean on Jesus' bosom, and, when they come out to tell of what they have seen and heard, they speak (1Jn. 1:1-2) with authority as sent by the Most High. The Lord give us, as members of his church, to abide in habitual fellowship with Jesus; not to have occasional spasms of delight in God, but one unbroken rest in him. We do not now and again look through the windows of agates, and behold the king in his beauty, but we would continue "looking unto Jesus." (Heb. 12:2) We would have his praise continually in our mouths, and his love burning like the quenchless altar fire of the temple, forever within our hearts. This is the one thing needful to promote and sustain a revival in a church. If we have abounding love for Jesus, we can prosper under disadvantages, but, if we do not have it, we have lost the great secret of success. Love for Jesus teaches our hands to war and our fingers to fight. It sets us side by side with the conquering Immanuel, and makes us share in his victories. It yokes us with the strong Son of God, and so makes our infirmities to be but opportunities for the display of his power.

This love leads the church to hold all things in joint possession with Christ. Observe that word "at our gates are all manner of pleasant fruits." Love for Jesus constrains us to make over all that we hold to him, while faith appropriates all that Jesus has to itself. Love will not stand to have divided properties. Such was the love of Jesus that he gave all that he had to us. He could not bear to have anything, not even his throne itself, that should be altogether his alone. He stripped himself to his last rag to clothe us, and then gave us his breath to be our life, and his blood to be our health; and now today, if we love him as we should, we are saying,

If I might make some reserve,
And duty did not call;
I love my God with zeal so great,

That I would give Him all.

(Isaac Watts)

I like to think in church matters especially, that we are all Christ's, that if we have any ability, it is Christ's ability — to be laid at his feet; if we have any substance, it is Christ's money — to be used in spreading his church. Our Sunday School is Christ's nursery, and the little ones are Christ's lambs. Our work out of doors in preaching at the corners of the streets is Christ's mission; it is his trumpet, which is blown when the gospel is preached; and every form of agency is not ours — it is Christ's, or if ours, it is only because it is his. Oh, to have more and more all things common with our Lord, and no longer to speak of mine or yours! Beloved, we are joint-heirs with him; all that we have is his, and all that he has is ours. When the church believes and acts on this, the hour of her success is close at hand.

Consider once more the love which is the great motive for Christian action, a love which looks to Jesus for united operation. It is, "Come, my beloved, let us go forth into the field, let us get up early to the vineyard." Oh, it is glorious when Christ comes with the preacher, not the servant alone, but the master looking through his servant's eyes, and speaking with his servant's tongue, and pleading with his servant's heart. Oh, it is good teaching in your Sabbath school when Jesus sits there amongst the boys and girls and speaks to their hearts. It is good going into lodging-houses or calling, at the people's doors to tell them of the Saviour, when Jesus knocks as well as you, and the crucified goes with you among the fallen, the infidel and the profane. All is well when the Redeemer leads the way. Do not be afraid, beloved, for you go in good company. Who among us will be afraid to do anything, or go anywhere, when Jesus says, "I will go with you"? "Lo, I am with you alway". (Mat. 28:20) Such was the prayer the spouse sent up, and doubtless she was led to pray for that which God will grant.

Let us pray with her as she prayed.

Come, Saviour, come up with us to whatever we attempt for you! If there are any brethren here who are working away for you in dark places in London, dear Saviour, carry the lantern with them, and be their light! If they are digging for you, and quarrying amid granite rocks which refuse to yield to their strokes, come Almighty One, wield your hammer, and straightway the stone shall be broken. Come with us, Lord. This is the fellowship we desire of you, the fellowship of labour and of soul-winning. We would not only sit at your feet to learn, but we would take up our cross and follow you. We would go with you wherever you go; we would fight, or labour, or suffer, or live, or die, at your bidding. Be this the fellowship you will bestow upon us!

II. Secondly, LOVE LEADS US TO GO AFIELD IN THE SERVICE OF JESUS. "Come, my beloved, let us go forth into the field."

A loving church spontaneously puts herself out to widened service. She has a large heart towards her Lord, and longs to see him reign over all mankind. She does not wait to hear again and again the Macedonian's cry, "Come over and help us" (Acts 16:9), but she is prompt in mission enterprise. She does not tarry till she is forced by persecution to go abroad, preaching the Word everywhere, but she sends out her champions far and wide. As sure as ever she loves her Lord, she asks herself this question: "What more can I do for him?" When she looks over the plot of ground she has been tilling, she says, "It is not large enough: the harvest I can get out of this will not be sufficient for my dear Lord"; and she says to him, "Let me go to the regions beyond, to break up the fallow ground, and cause the wilderness to blossom." (2 Cor. 10:16) Now, beloved members of this church, do you not feel some such desire this morning? It is upon my heart that we should be undertaking larger things for Christ. Keep up the old agencies by all manner of means; quicken them, strengthen them; but does not love suggest that, as increasing years add increasing indebtedness to Christ as we are always receiving fresh mercies, so we should make new and larger returns to our best friend? If by us, as a church, nothing new may be ventured, yet cannot each individual have his own plan, and branch out afresh? Will not each say in his heart, "What can I do for Jesus today, over and above what I should have done if things had gone on in the ordinary course? Enquire of him concerning your love, and, if your hearts are with him, it will not be long before you will discover what he would have you do.

The spouse, when she said, "Let us go forth into the field", knew that the proposal would please her Lord; for the nature of Christ is a large and loving one, and, therefore, he will bless the far off ones. His is no narrow heart; his thoughts of love are far reaching; and when the church says, "Let us go forth into the field", truly her Lord is not backward to accept the invitation. The spouse does not guess at this, nor does she merely infer it from her Bridegroom's nature, but she has it as an express command from his own lips, "Go ye into all the world and preach the gospel to every creature." (Mk. 16:15) There stand the orders, and when our largest enterprises have been fulfilled we shall not have exceeded them. There is no exclusion put on any tribe or clan, no classes are laid under ban, no individuals are exempted. Therefore, Church of Christ, by the love you bear to your crucified Master, by his wounds and death for you, and by his living love to you, seek out the lost and gather together the outcasts. You fishers of men, launch out into the deep and let down your nets for a draught. (Lk. 5:4) You sowers of holy seed, go out and sow the untrodden wastes. You consecrated builders, break away from the old foundations, and lay fresh groundwork for a larger temple for your God and King. Surely the Spirit of love in a church will suggest this.

Note that the spouse is evidently prepared for any discomfort that may come as the result of her labour. She must necessarily leave the fair palaces of her royal husband and lodge in rustic cottages. Poor lodging there for Solomon's fair spouse! But what cares she? Any roof that covers her from the evening dew, and shields her from the drops of the night, shall be quite sufficient for her; yes, if he is there, the tents of Kedar shall be as fair as the curtains of Solomon, for his sake. Brothers and sisters, if you serve the Lord Christ in breaking up fresh ground, you may have to meet difficulties and make sacrifices, but they will be as nothing to you; you will welcome them for his dear sake. Am I stirring no heart now? Has my finger touched no responsive string? I think I feel in my own soul that some of you are responding. Some brother, some sister, is here — I do not know to whom the prophetic word is coming — who is saying, "Lord, I am your spouse; I will go out with you into the field, and I will lodge with you in the villages, if there I may but glorify your name."

Observe, too, that the spouse is quite ready to continue in this uncomfortable service. She says, "I will lodge in the villages" — there she will abide awhile, not paying a flying, visit, but stopping until the good work is done for which her Lord and she went forth. Oh, get out, you Christians, into the distant fields of labour. Many of you — how often have I said it! — sit here Sunday after Sunday, and hear many sermons, when I believe you would be better engaged if you were preaching yourselves, and winning souls for the Redeemer. I have often been glad to miss some of my dearest brethren from our assemblies. Your presence gives me great pleasure, but when I know you have been away seeking after Christ's blood-bought souls, I have taken pleasure in your absence. Go, and the Lord go with you; go, more of you; yes, I say, go, more of you. Your empty seats will be occupied by sinners whom God will save, while you, dear comrades, if you are fighting for my Master somewhere else, you will do my Master much more service than you could have done by listening to me. We must not allow a single talent to lie idle; we must not waste an hour of these blessed Sabbaths; we must get away among the ignorant ones, and carry them the light; we must hunt for precious souls. For our master's sake, and in his strength and company, we must compass sea and land for his redeemed ones. Only, if any of you go, do not try to go alone. Stop until you breathe the prayer, "My beloved, let us go." You go in vain when you do not go with the Master, but when you have secured his company, then go and welcome, for you "shall doubtless come again rejoicing, bringing your sheaves with you." (Ps. 126:6)

Observe how the spouse says, "There will I give thee my loves." It is as much as to say, if Jesus will therefore go with us into active service, then we will reveal to him the love of our hearts. I suppose there may have been times in the Church when a hermit's life would suitably reveal the heart's love to Jesus, but I am certain it is not so now. If there are any here who love contemplation, and desire to spend their whole lives in quiet retirement, I am persuaded that such a course would be injurious to their generation, and to the cause of truth. Of course, there may be exceptions, and if you have no gifts but such as could be serviceable to Christ in solitude, use them in solitude; but, from most of us, the times demand activity. So dark is the world, we cannot afford to lose a glow-worm's spark. Men are perishing; can we let them perish? Would we suffer a soul to be lost even though it was given to us in exchange to enjoy the highest fellowship with Christ? Behold, this day the sheep have gone astray, and the wolves are howling after them; not even to enjoy the great Shepherds's company, can we, the under-shepherds, dare to leave the wanderers to perish. The Church today has her vocation, which is not so much to eat the fat and drink the sweet, as to light her candle and sweep her house, and seek diligently till she find her lost piece of money. (Lk. 15:8) Do not think that active service prevents fellowship; no, it is but another form of sitting at his feet, another shape of fellowship quite as true, and, because more called for at this era, even more acceptable. I know I have had as great fellowship with Christ in his service as ever I have had in quiet contemplation. When I have met with a poor soul who has rejected the Lord, I felt my heart breaking over him like the heart of Christ over obstinate Jerusalem. When I have seen the tears flowing from a penitent's eyes who could not, as yet, find the Saviour, I felt sympathy with Jesus when he looked on the same, and had compassion on them. And when I have seen the glow of joy, when the sun of Christ's countenance has shone at last on the troubled heart, I entered into the joy of the Lord when he rejoices over one sinner that repenteth. (Lk. 15:7, 10) Laziness never yet had communion with Christ. Those who walk with Christ must walk swiftly. Jesus is no idler or loiterer; he is about his father's business, and you must march with quick step if you would keep pace with him. As vinegar to the teeth, and as smoke to the eyes, are sluggards to active persons. (Prov. 10:26) Those who have much to do have no fellowship with gossips who drop in to while away the hours with chat.

Jesus has no fellowship with you who do not care for souls that are perishing. He is incessantly active, and so must you be if you would know his love. There is a fierce, furnace-heat beating on everything today: men are toiling hard to hold their own, and Jesus must not be served by slothful hearts. I am sure I am not straying from his mind, when I say to you, beloved, if you would know the Beloved fully you must get up early, and go afield with him to work with him. Your joy shall be in spending and being spent for him.

III. Thirdly, LOVE LABOURS ALSO AT HOME. Nearer the palace there were vineyards, and the spouse said, "Let us get up early to the vineyards."

Note, then, that the Church does her work at home as well as abroad. When she loves her Lord, she works with zeal, getting up early. All in Holy Scripture who loved God much rose early to worship him. We never read of one saint engaged in sacred service who rose late. Abraham rose early, David rose early, Job rose early, and so did they all. It is put here as a very type and symbol of an earnest, vigorous service of Christ. Dear brethren, there is such a thing, you know, as keeping the Sunday-school going, and keeping the Tract Society going, and keeping the Evangelists' Society going, and yet nobody is up early, but, after a fashion, everybody is nodding. I know these warm Sunday mornings; it is not a very difficult thing for some of you, if you try hard, to go to sleep during a sermon. Well, that is a visible slumber, and is soon got over, but there is an invisible sleep which will come on Sunday afternoon when you are teaching, which is neither so soon discovered nor so easily cured. You are talking, talking, addressing your class, or speaking to your men and women, or whatever else may be your calling, and, all the while, your soul is nodding. Anybody can wake you up with a poke in your side if only your body is sleeping, but, when the soul is slumbering, it is not so easy. I fear greatly that a large proportion of Christian workers are usually asleep. What a difference there is between what a man teaches when he is asleep and what he teaches when he is awake. You can see it in a minute. I could not describe the difference, but it is apparent in tone and manner, and in every other way. The man may say and do the self-same thing, but still it is a different thing. The children soon perceive it if it is in your class; your hearers soon perceive it if it is in your pulpit. Oh, that God would wake up this Church! I do not believe that success so much depends on what the Church does as on how she does it. You may take your hammer, and go tinkering about, and not fasten a tin-tack, but if your arm has muscle in it, you will soon be driving the nails home to the very head, and clinching them. May the Lord's love so come upon you all, my brethren, that what you do, you may do with all your might, plunging your whole soul into his service, and never sparing force in anything.

Notice that God's people, when they are awake, first look well to the Church. "Let us see if the vine flourish." The Church is Christ's vine; let us take stock of it. Beloved, we ought to be, each one of us, in a measure, pastors of the Church. In so large a Church as this, the pastoral office cannot be vested in one, or even in twenty. Each must look after his brother, and thus you must be pastors of one another. Watch over one another, pray for one another. How wonderful is the power of prayer. We do not know what blessings come from our prayers. Ten thousand darts might long ago have pierced the Lord's elect, were it not that the prayers of the saints are a shield over their heads, defending the holy host from harm. Then the Church looks after the little ones. "Let us see if the vine flourish, whether the tender grape appear." No earnest Church forgets the children of her Sabbath school, and every other agency for the young will be sure to be well minded. An active church seeks to bring Jesus among the children, to see if the tender grapes appear. She pays her visits and performs her services, but ever in his dear company. Helpers in the Sabbath school, and workers for Christ, I salute you. May the Lord be with you! May the Lord give you to see many tender grapes appearing, and may this Church have joy of you as hundreds are converted to God by your instrumentality.

Then the church also takes notice of all enquiries. "Let us see whether the pomegranates bud forth." If a church is alive, there will be always many to observe where the first tear of repentance is glistening. Into this congregation, every Sabbath day, thank God, come people who are pricked in the heart. Watch them, brethren. Those of you who occupy your seats, and do not go a-field, can do the cause great service by watching at home. There is no need to leave those seats in order to be useful. Around you, there are unconverted people. Each Sabbath morning and evening there come in here strangers, and it may be the Lord will deal with them, only you be on the alert; speak with them, and try if you can to use the shorthanded claymore, that if my longer bladed sword may not have reached them, you who are near at hand may send a deadly wound into the very heart of their sins. O my brethren, words fail me to set before you the ways in which you might show your love for Jesus in the Church itself, but I am certain that there is no need for me to speak further. Love herself will teach you. Mothers somehow bring up their children, though there are no colleges for mothers. Love with its instincts makes them wise, and so will Christians with their love for Jesus, becoming wise to serve. I do believe the less rule and human direction there is in the church, the better. I do not want to say, "Brother, do this, and do that." If you love Christ, you will know what to do better than anybody else can tell you. You will find your own places; the Lord will lead you to them. I might put a square man into a round hole if I had the placing of you, but love always puts the man into the right position, telling him what suits his qualification, It puts him to his work, and, what is more, it keeps him at it. I shall measure your love for Jesus, and measure my own, not by the way in which we can talk, or the way in which we can criticise other workers, but by the way in which we shall henceforth labour for the Lord.

IV. The last point is this, that LOVE IN A CHURCH BRINGS OUT ALL ITS STORES FOR THE BELOVED.

The church of God has in herself, through the rich love of her husband, all manner of pleasant fruits. This church is a large one, but the same truth holds good for the smallest church. The Lord never leaves his church without a suitable measure of gifts and graces. If our spiritual nostril and eye could act this morning, we should discern all the fruits of the Paradise of God in this church, and we should smell the sweet savour of all pleasant things; for some brethren here have the apples of faith, others bear the delicious pomegranates of love, and others yield the charming clusters of hope and joy. There are all manner of pleasant fruits among us. One has one, another another, and, in some hearts, there are many fruits united. A church of God, if well cultivated, is rich in multiform displays of the fruit of the Spirit of God. Some of these fruits are new, and oh, how full of savour they are! Our new converts, thank God for them, what a freshness and power there is about their love! Certain mouldy old professors have lost their taste all together; they have passed beyond the time in which they were sweet; they have got into the sleepy pear state, and are going rotten. They are chips in the porridge, for the taste has gone out of them, if they ever had any. Alas, some have acquired a nauseous flavour, and are very naughty figs indeed. The new fruits may be sharp, and have more pungency than mellowness about them; but, for all that, they are choice to the Lord Jesus, whose soul desires the first ripe fruits. I thank God for youthful zeal; it might with advantage have a little more knowledge mingled with it, yet the zeal is good, and the fervency is good. May we never be without new-born souls!

Then there are old fruits, the experience of believers who are ripening for heaven, the well-developed confidence which has been tried in a thousand battles, and the faith which has braved a lifetime of difficulties. These old fruits — the deep love of the matron to Christ, the firm assurance of the veteran believer — there is a mellowness about them which the Lord delights in.

All these choice things ought to be laid up. Every good thing in a church is meant to be stored up, not to be despised and forgotten; and the point of this is that all in the church ought to be laid up for our Beloved. And now is the time when I earnestly ask, in the name of the Lord Jesus, by the roes and by the hinds of the field, yes by each sacred token of the love you bear your Master, that each one of you should bring out his pleasant fruits, whether they are new or whether they are old. We do not bring them out to buy his love, we know better; for though we should give all the substance of our house for love, it would be utterly despised. We do not bring out these fruits to secure his love for the future; we know it is an everlasting love that never can be taken away from us. We do not bring them out because we want to commend ourselves. Ah, no; any beauty we have does not lie in the fruits of our storehouses, but in what he has put upon us, and in what his love sees in us! Neither do we bring out these pleasant fruits to feed on them ourselves. Old experiences are mouldy things; old manna breeds worms and stinks; and as for any fruits which we have brought forth, we take no satisfaction in them ourselves. All we have belongs to him, and to him alone, and at his feet we would lay the whole. I beseech you, brethren, if you have any love, pour it out on him; if you have any faith, exercise it for him; if you have any courage, be bold for him; if you have any endurance, endure hardness for him; if you have any grace, any virtue, any gift of his Spirit, anything that is lovely and of good repute, use it for him. Now is the day, now is the hour, now his love puts in her claim and serves you with her sacred writs. By the espousals which you have not forgotten, by the covenant which you have often repeated with him, by the seals of his table, by your burial with him in baptism in days gone by, I beseech you now, bring out all your pleasant things for your Beloved; none for anyone else, but all for him.

I fear we often forget to do all for him. I know if I preach a sermon, and have any recollection that such and such a passage might please a learned or wealthy hearer, I have failed to please God. If I have any consideration in my mind as to whether I shall gain esteem for excellence of speech, I am weak directly; but if I preach for Jesus only, then, whoever finds fault, my work is sweet to him. And if you pray in the prayer meeting, or teach in the class, or give your contribution to the Lord's work; if you feel you have done it for him, oh, then you know you have done rightly because that is the point which sweetens all. I believe that many have stolen up to the offering-box and dropped in what they could give for the Lords sake, and none has known it, and therefore Christ has accepted it; while others may have given large sums ostentatiously because others of their standing were giving as much, and, therefore, they were not accepted. I want your aid for the College and the Orphanage, but do not give for my sake, but for my Lord's sake. Put what you give into the pierced hand; make that your treasury. Jesus is your Master. No one else has bought you, no one else has died for you, no one else will receive you until his fond embrace at the last, no one else is preparing heaven for you, no one else can say, "Well done good and faithful servant." (Mat. 25:21, 23) Serve him, then, with both your hands, with all your heart, with every drop of blood in your veins, and every breath in your lungs. Give him yourself, your whole self, from the sole of your foot to the crown of your head, and when you have done that, if he spare you for another half century, you will find that you have spent the best life for yourself, though that must not enter into your thoughts.

I have thus spoken to my own dear friends and brethren in Christ, but let me remind those who are not in Christ that nothing of this has anything to do with them. I don't bid you do anything for Christ. I cannot. Christ does not want his enemies to work in his vineyard. I do not ask you either to give to Jesus or to work for him? Why should you? Till you love him, your service would be a mockery of him. I hold up no standard to enlist under it men whose hearts are disloyal toward our Captain. Ah, no; but if your service is rejected, and you feel grieved at heart that it is so, let me whisper this word in your ear — your heart may yet be made right. You may yet come and serve him. Here is his message to you: "Come now and let us reason together, saith the Lord; though your sins be as scarlet they shall be as white as snow; though they be red like crimson they shall be as wool." (Is. 1:18) "He that believeth and is baptised shall be saved." (Mk. 16:16) There is the point for you, good friend. You must begin with being yourself saved, and then, when you are saved, thou canst serve Christ. Christ will have no one work for him with the view of saving himself; you must first be saved, and then you do not have your own salvation to look to. When you have left that with Christ, you can then labour for him. A rich English merchant was requested by Queen Elizabeth to take up certain affairs of hers. "Your Majesty", said he, "I am willing enough, but if I do your bidding my business will be ruined." "Sir," said the Queen, "You attend to my business, and I will attend to yours."

Now then, give the business of your soul's salvation up to Christ. Let him save you; and when that is done, you can make it your business to serve him, and he will be glad of such a servant. May the Lord bless you, for Jesus' sake! Amen.

75. GOOD WORKS IN GOOD COMPANY
NO. 605

DELIVERED ON SUNDAY MORNING, DECEMBER 18TH, 1864
AT THE METROPOLITAN TABERNACLE, NEWINGTON

"Come, my beloved, let us go forth into the field; let us lodge in the villages. Let us get up early to the vineyards; let us see if the vine flourish, whether the tender grape appear, and the pomegranates bud forth: there will I give thee my loves. The mandrakes give a smell, and at our gates are all manner of pleasant fruits, new and old, which I have laid up for thee, O my beloved."
(Song of Solomon 7:11-13)

THE daughters of Jerusalem had been praising the Church as the fairest among women. They spoke of her with admiring appreciation, extolling her from head to foot. She wisely perceived that it was not easy to bear praise; and therefore she turned aside from the virgins to her Lord, making her boast not of her own comeliness, but of being affianced to her beloved: "I am my beloved's, and his desire is toward me." (Song 6:3, 7:10) Solomon said in his Book of Proverbs, "As the fining pot for silver, and the furnace for gold; so is a man to his praise" (Prov. 27:21), meaning to teach us that praise is a serious ordeal. Very many men can bear censure and abuse, for their spirit rises so superior to it all that they are even profited by it; but to be flattered, or even duly honoured, is not so easy a thing to endure. The sun's warm beams made the traveller undo his coat, when the wind made him wrap it the more closely about him, The warmth of praise may make us relax our integrity, unless we remain very watchful. How many have been foolish enough, when standing on a pinnacle, to look down and admire their own elevation, and then their brain reeled, and they might have fallen to their own shameful ruin. If we must at any time listen to the praises of our virtues, if we served God so that the Church recognises and rewards our usefulness, it is well for us to listen just as long as we are obliged to do, but no longer; and then let us turn aside at once to something more practical and more healthy for our spirits.

The spouse seems abruptly to break off from listening to the song of the virgins, and turns to her own husband-Lord, communion with whom is ever blessed and ever profitable, and says to him, "Come, my beloved, let us go forth into the field; let us lodge in the villages." In communion with Christ is a certain cure for every ill. Whether it is the bitterness of woe, or the cloying surfeit of earthly delight, close fellowship with the Lord Jesus will take the gall from the one and the satiety [full beyond satisfaction] from the other. Live near to Jesus, Christian, and it is matter of secondary importance whether you live on the mountain of honour, or in the valley of humiliation. Live near to Jesus, and the glowing coals of the furnace cannot consume you, nor the chill blasts of wintry affliction destroy you. Living near to Jesus, you are covered with the wings of God, and underneath you are the everlasting arms. (Deut. 33:27) If you read the three verses before us with attention, you will see that the Church all through anxiously desires fellowship with her Lord. It is "Come with me" — "let us". She will do nothing unless she is near to her beloved, and in the enjoyment of his company.

I think she desires three things by her words: first, she desires to practice self-examination; she would go and see whether the vine flourishes, and whether the tender grape appears; but it is self-examination with him. She desires next to go into active service: it is to this end that she would lodge in the villages and go among the tender plants, that she may labour there, but it is with him — "Let us go!" "Come with me!" In the third place, she has a store of fruit laid up for him. Some things done and some things doing, things old and new, but they are all for him, and she will not mention them except for him, much less bring them out for them to be enjoyed by a rival. "They are laid up for thee, O my beloved." Let us try to make a personal matter of the text this morning, and may God hear the desire of our hearts, that we may have true fellowship with his own dear Son.

I. First, then, IN THE MATTER OF SELF-EXAMINATION.

This is a most desirable and important business, but every believer should desire to have communion with Christ while he is attending to it. Self-examination is of the utmost importance. No trader who wishes to succeed would neglect to keep his books. No husbandman who wishes to prosper would be careless as to the state of his fields. No flock-master who would see his herds abundantly increase would leave to his servants the care of them, and fail to tend them with a watchful eye. If you would have your business prosper, see to it carefully yourself. In soul-business, it is of no use taking anything for granted where there are so many temptations to self-deception in our own hearts; where so many around us are deceived, and are willing to help us to be deceived too; and where Satan sedulously [zealously] and craftily seeks to cry to us, "Peace, peace; when there is no peace." (Jer. 6:14) It is of the first and last importance that we should search ourselves whether we are in the faith (2 Cor. 13:5), and whether, being in the faith, our graces are growing, our faith increasing, and our love deepening. Well does the spouse suggest that she should see whether the vine flourished, whether the tender grape appeared, and the pomegranates budded forth; for our spiritual vineyard needs perpetual watchfulness. While you are attending to this important business, see to it at the same time that you keep up your communion with Christ, for you will never know so well the importance of self-examination as when you see him. Mark him there! See him fastened to the accursed tree, wearing the thorn-crown all set with ruby drops of his own blood. Look at his griefs, if repenting tears do not blind you. Behold his awful agonies, and gaze into that visage more marred than that of any man, and stay awhile and listen to the heartrending shriek, "Eloi! Eloi! Lama sabachthani?" (Mk. 15:34) And did Christ suffer all this that souls might be saved? Then surely, my soul, it should be your chief business, to see that you have an interest in him. What! Shall I miss that which is purchased with such a price? When such a crimson stream from Christ's own heart flows to cleanse away sin, shall I think it a matter of no account whether I am cleansed or not? When that head, which once was reverenced by angels, is now crowned with the thorns of mockery and cruelty, should I not use all the thoughts of my head and brain to find out whether I am one with Christ, and a partaker of his passion? That cannot be a little heritage which Christ has purchased with such agonies: let me fear lest I should lose it. That cannot be a slight evil which cost my Saviour such griefs: let me search myself to see whether I myself am delivered from it. I am sure, beloved, that you cannot have a better candle to look into the secret recesses of your soul than a candle lit at the fire of Jesus' love. Know his love for you, and all his griefs on your behalf, and you will charge your own heart after this fashion — "See to it that you make sure work as to your interest in Jesus, that you are really one with him, that your faith in him is genuine, and that you shall be found in him in peace at the day of his appearing."

Self-examination, however, is very laborious work: the text hints at it. It does not say, "Let us go", but "Let us get up". Self-examination is ever uphill work. It is by no means a pleasant task; it is one from which the flesh recoils, for the flesh cries, "Let well alone; you are easy and comfortable; you have a hope which affords you much solace; do not dig too deep, the house stands well enough just now; do not be too anxious about the foundations; rest assured that it is all right; you would not have all these joys and present comforts if you had built upon the sand." We need to school ourselves to perform a duty so irksome. But, beloved, if we attempt to examine this, feeling that Christ is with us, and that we are having communion with him, we will forget all the labour of the deed. There I see him in the garden, sweating great drops of blood in prayer! (Lk. 22:44) Can I view him prostrate on that cold winter's night (when the ground was hard with frost), so burning with his soul's travail that huge gouts of blood-red gore are falling upon the frozen earth! And shall I think any toil too great to make sure of my interest in him? Does he, when the cup is put to him, say, "Not as I will, but as thou wilt" (Mat. 26:39), and drink it up with resignation? And shall the far less bitter cup of self-examination, which is so much for my good, be refused by me? No, Saviour of the world, I have not yet resisted unto blood, striving against sin (Heb. 12:4); but if it must be, if all my powers and members must be made to bleed, if my poor heart must be brayed as in a mortar, then let it be, so that I may but be found one with you, washed in you blood and covered with your righteousness. Keep close to the Saviour, and the difficulties of self-examination will vanish, and the labour become light. Self-examination should always be very earnest work. The text says, "Let us get up early." It has been well observed that all men in Scripture that have done earnest work rose up early to do it. The dew of the morning, before the smoke and dust of the world's business have tainted the atmosphere, is a choice and special season for all holy work. In this passage, getting up early signifies that the Church felt she must give her best hour to this necessary work; and as the work might be long, she gets up early that she may have a long day before her; that before the sun goes down, she may have examined every vine, and looked to every pomegranate, and examined all the mandrakes of the garden. So we must set to work earnestly with self-examination. This is but child's-play. If you would find out the trickery of your deceitful heart, you must be very careful and watchful. If you would know on what foundation your hope is built, it is a labourer's work to dig out the rubbish, and to find out where the foundation is laid. Whoever has to prove the title-deeds of his estate, does not always find it an easy business: there are many manuscripts through which he must wade, and numerous title-deeds to be read, verified, and collated, before the case is clear. And so it must be with you. The great matter, "Do I believe in Jesus", needs no hours of deliberation, for if I do not, I will now begin again; but to know the growing state of one's graces is not so easy. After all, you may be deceived; therefore come at it with a soul all glowing with zeal, saying, in earnest prayer, "Search me, O God, and know my heart: try me, and know my thoughts: and see if there be any wicked way in me, and lead me in the way everlasting." (Ps. 139:23) Now, I think, there is nothing that can make you do this earnest work so well as to say to your Master and your Lord, "Lord, come with me." "While we examine ourselves, abide with us to help us in the work." I cannot be careless when I hear Christ say, "My meat and my drink is to do the will of him that sent me." (Jn. 4:34) I cannot be careless in my own Christian career when I see him straining every nerve that he may run the race and win the crown for me. When I see him sitting yonder, above all principalities and powers, pleading for my soul with never-ceasing intercession, I cannot be dull and sluggish. Wake up, you drowsy powers; be stirred up, you sleeping passions, to examine yourselves anxiously and carefully, since for Zion's sake Christ does not hold his peace, and for Jerusalem's sake does not rest.

Yet again, self-examination, it seems to me (I may be wrong), is not the simple work that some people think, but is beset with difficulties. I do believe that most self-examinations go on a wrong principle. You take Moses with you when you examine yourself, and consequently you fall into despair. He who looks at his own character and position from a legal point of view, will not only despair when he comes to the end of his reckoning, but he will be a wise man if he does not despair at the beginning; for if we are to be judged on the footing of the law, no flesh living shall be justified. The very brightest members of Christ's family, those who bear the most of the Saviour's image, and honour him best among men, may well shrink from the place where even Moses did "exceedingly fear and quake." (Heb. 12:21)

O brethren, remember to take Jesus with you, and not Moses, lest you dishonour the grace of God, and harbour suspicion against the faithfulness of God, when you ought rather to have suspected yourself. If I take Jesus with me, see on what different principles the examination is carried on! I do not ask, "Am I perfect?" That question Moses would suggest — "Am I perfect in myself?" but I ask, "Am I perfect in Christ Jesus?" That is a very different matter. I do not put it this way: "Am I without sin naturally?" but like this: "Have I been washed in the fountain opened for sin and for uncleanness?" (Zech. 12:1) It is not, "Am I in myself well-pleasing to God?" but, "Am I accepted in the beloved?" The Christian man sometimes looks at his evidences, and grows ashamed of them, and alarmed concerning his own salvation. "Why", says he, "my faith has unbelief in it, for it is not able to save me." Suppose he had looked at the object of his faith instead of his faith, then he would have said, "There is no failure in him, and therefore I am safe." He looks at his hope: "Why" says he, "my very hope is marred and dimmed by an anxious carefulness about present things; how can I be accepted?" Yes, but if he had looked at the ground of his hope, he would have seen that "the foundation of God standeth sure" (2 Tim. 2:19), and that whatever our hope may be, that promise never fails. Then he looks at his love: "Oh!" says he, "surely I am condemned, for my love is so cold"; but if he had looked at Christ's love, he would have said "No, never shall I be condemned; for many waters cannot quench his love, neither can the floods drown it, and, loving me as he does, he will never condemn me, nor cast me away." I do not want you to look at Christ so as to think less of your sin, but to think more of it; for you can never see sin to be so black as when you see the suffering which Christ endured on its behalf.

But I do desire you, dear friends, never to look at sin apart from the Saviour. If you gaze at the disease and forget the remedy, you will be driven to despair. If you look at the gathering gangrene and forget the all-gracious Surgeon who is able to remove it, you may well lie down and die. If you see your own emptiness and poverty, and forget his fullness, you will never glorify his name. If you are lost in a sense of your own corruptions, and forget the eternal glory which belongs to you in Christ, so that you are even now raised up together, and "made us sit together in heavenly places in him". (Eph. 2:6) I say, if you forget this grace-given brightness, and only remember your native blackness, your spirit will turn aside from the path of faith, and you will hang your harp on the willows, and fail to glorify your God.

Examine yourselves, but let it be in the light of Calvary, not by the blazing fires of Sinai's lightnings, but by the milder radiance of the Saviour's griefs. Am I resting on you, you Son of God? Are your wounds my hiding place? Have your nails nailed me to your cross? Has your spear pierced my heart, and broken it with grief for sin; and am I now crucified with you to the world, buried with you as to the power of sin, risen with you to newness of life, and, like yourself, waiting for the day of manifestation, when sin, death, and hell, shall be trodden under foot, and Jesus shall be all in all?

Come, let us look to the vines and the pomegranates, but let us make sure that our crucified Lord accompanies us; or else we shall do the work amiss. It appears, from the words of the spouse, that the work of self-examination should be carried on in detail, if it is to be of real service. It is written, "Let us see if the vine flourish, the tender grape appear and the pomegranates bud forth." We must not take a general view of the garden, but particularise, and give special attention to each point. If a candle is guarded on all sides, if there is but one place left open, the wind will find it out, and blow out the light. So in self-examination; if we find ourselves right in many points, it is not enough: we must seek to be right in all points. The main thing is your faith. Is that faith simple? Does it depend on Jesus only? Is it real? Is it an active living faith? Does it work by love? Does it purify the soul? But when you have examined faith, you may possibly make a mistake; therefore go on to see what your love is. Do you love the Saviour? Can you truly say, "The very thought of you with rapture fills my breast?" Can you hear the music of his name without feeling your blood leap in your veins? Oh, you can, dear friend, if you have reason for grave questioning. Try your active graces; go from one to the other, and search them all out. The worm may be at the root just in that part of the soil where you have not upturned the sod. One leak may sink a ship, therefore search the vessel well before you launch her upon the stormy deep. It is little by little that backsliders fall; even Judas did not at first betray his Master with a kiss. Men are schooled in the downward road. Let us be particularly anxious, therefore, that we do not fall little by little; and let us watch that we do not suffer small sins to get force and head, till, like little sparks, they kindle a great fire?

If you wish to be exact in prying into every part and corner, you cannot do better than take Jesus with you. "Tempted in all points like as we are" (Heb. 4:15), he will know all the points in which we are tempted; and, while we are earnestly examining, his gracious finger will point out the spots where our weakness lie, and we shall thus fulfil the prayer we have often prayed: "Search me, O God, and know my heart: try me, and know my thoughts: and see if there be any wicked way in me, and lead me in the way everlasting." (Ps. 139:23-24) When children are at school, and have to learn to write, every schoolteacher knows that, at the first line, they keep their eye on the copy at the top; the next line they look at their own writing, and their penmanship is not quite so good, and the next line they probably look at the last they have written, and so their writing gets worse and worse as they reach the bottom of the page, because they have been imitating themselves, and copying their own writing. It is well for the Christian, if he does not fall into this mistake. He must keep his eye on his great Exemplar, not on himself. He will be far more likely to see his own faults by looking to Christ, than by looking at any of his own attainments. What a delightfully white thing snow is! When it has newly fallen, take the whitest linen you may have ever seen, put it down, and you will find it looks positively yellow by the side of it. Take the fairest sheet of paper that ever came from the mill, and compare it with the snow; it does not look white at all. There is no whiteness that I know of which can at all emulate the heavenly whiteness of the snow. So, if I put my character side by side with another man's, I may say of it, "It bears comparison!" But if I put it by the side of Christ's perfections, since his whole life is like the pure and spotless snow, I discover at once my own failures and spots. Oh, to have our great pattern ever before our eyes! Jesus should not be a friend who calls upon us now and then, but one with whom we walk evermore. You have a difficult road to travel. See, O traveller to heaven, that you do not go without your guide.

You have to pass through the fiery furnace: do not enter it unless, like Shadrach, Meshach, and Abednego, there is a fourth with you, like unto the Son of Man. (Dan. 3:24-25) You have to storm the Jericho of your own deceptions: do not attempt scaling until like Joshua, you have seen the Captain of the Lord's host with his sword drawn in his hand. You have to meet the Esau of your many temptations: do not meet him until, at Jabbok's brook, you have laid hold of the angel, and wrestled with him, and prevailed. (Gen. 32:24-28) In every case, in every condition, you need Jesus; but most of all, when you come to deal with your own heart's eternal interests. Oh, keep close to him, lean your head upon his bosom, ask to be refreshed with the spiced wine of his pomegranate, and then there shall be no fear but that you shall be found by him at the last, without spot, wrinkle, or any such thing. (Eph. 5:27) Seeing you have lived with him, and lived in him here, you shall live with him forever.

II. THE CHURCH WAS ABOUT TO ENGAGE IN EARNEST LABOUR, and desired her Lord's company.

It is the business of God's people to be trimmers of God's vines. Like our first parents, we are put into the garden of the Lord for usefulness. Observe that the Church, when she is in her right mind, in all her many labours, desires to retain and cheerfully to enjoy communion with Christ.

Some people imagine that one cannot serve Christ actively and yet have fellowship with him. I think they are very much mistaken. I confess it is very easy to get into Martha's position, and to be "cumbered with much serving". (Lk. 10:40) You may have to preach here and there so many times a week, to attend committees, to visit sick people, and to do so many other things that you may really, unless you are careful, fritter away your own inward life in outward exercises. You may have to complain with the spouse, "The keeper of the vineyards; but mine own vineyard have I not kept." (Song 1:6) I do not think, however, that there is any reason why this should be the case except through our own folly. Certain it is that a person may do nothing at all, and yet grow quite as lifeless in spiritual things as those who are most busy. Mary was not praised for sitting still; no, but for sitting still at Jesus' feet. And so, Christians are not to be praised if they neglect duties, merely because they live in retirement, and keep much at home. It is not sitting, I say, but sitting at Jesus' feet. Had Martha been sitting still, or had Mary been sitting anywhere else, I do not doubt that the Master would have given a word of rebuke; he would never have said that mere sitting still was choosing the good part. Indeed, I know some of you who are none the better for doing nothing, but a great deal the worse; for those who do nothing grow sour, and are always willing to find fault with the way in which others serve Christ. Do not think, therefore, that mere activity is in itself an evil; I believe it is a blessing. Taking a survey of Christ's Church, you will find that those who have most fellowship with Christ are not the ones who are recluses or hermits, who have much time to spend with themselves, but are the useful indefatigable labourers who are toiling for Jesus, and who, in their toil, have him side by side with them, so that they are workers together with God.

Let me, then, try and press this lesson home to you, that when we, as a Church, and each of us as individuals, have anything to do for Christ, we must do it in communion with him. We come up to his house, and what do we come for? It is said that, among Church people, the prayers are the main thing, and among Dissenters the sermon. I believe that in both cases this would be a fault. Praying should not eclipse preaching, for to preach or to listen to preaching, is as true an act of worship as to pray. We never worship God better than when we hear his Word, reverently receive it, and are moved by it to love and gratitude. To hear preaching is, in a sense, praying; since the true effect of all preaching that is worth listening to draws us into a spirit of devotion, and makes us ready for prayer, and every other form of worship. But what do we come here for? I am afraid there are some who come merely because it is the time to come, because the hour of worship has come round; and others come only because a certain preacher happens to stand on the platform. Ah, this is not how God's own beloved ones come up to his house! They desire to meet with him. Their prayer as they tread the hallowed courts of God's house will be, "My heart and my flesh crieth out for the living God." (Ps. 84:2) There is no hymn sung so well as when we really praise Jesus in it. No prayer is as true as that prayer which really comes to the mercy-seat, and spreads itself before the all-seeing eye. There is no preaching like that which is full of Christ, which gives out a savour of his good ointments. Worship is not to be commended because of the glorious swell of a Gregorian chant, or because of the equally majestic volume of sound which this great assembly may send up from that sweet instrument, the human voice. A service is not to be commended because of the eloquence of the preacher, or because of the display of learning which he is able to make in expounding his discourse. No, to the Christian it is, "Was the Master there?" The question one Sunday morning was, "What think ye, that he will not come to the feast?" (Jn. 11:56) Coming to the Lord's Table, the child of God's business is not so much with the bread and the wine, as with his blood and with his flesh. May I feed on him? May I see him? And if I get to him, then it is well with me. If I have, then, to serve God in the public engagements of his house, let me say, "Come, my beloved, let us get up to the vineyards."

You have other service to do, dear friends. This afternoon, many of you will be occupied in your Sunday-school classes. There will be a knot of lads or girls around you. You will, perhaps, be conducting classes of hundreds of young men and young women. This evening, again, many will be occupied in preaching, or you will be engaged at home with your own children. Oh, how blessed it is to go to the classes, or into the pulpit, having the Master with you! It sometimes happens to the preacher that he is like the butcher at the block; he has a cleaver in his hand, and cuts off large pieces of meat as food for those present, but he himself gets none. But it is otherwise with him when he has his Master with him. Then, whether the rest of the assembly are fed or not, certainly he himself is satisfied as with marrow and with fatness. After all, what a blessed sort the teacher is who can teach when the love of God is shed abroad in his heart! You will bear with the rudeness of those boys; you will put up with the inattention of those girls; you will not get angry at the folly of that youth; you will not forget to be in earnest with that poor wanderer, when Jesus Christ stands by your side. A vision of the Crucified, my brethren, is what we want. When we are toiling in his harvest-field, and sit down to wipe the sweat from our brow, we grow very weary; the harvest is plenteous, but the labourers are few (Mat. 9:37; Lk. 10:2) We feel that the edge of our sickle is growing very, very blunt, and we wish we could lie down under the spreading tree from the heat of the sun, and toil no longer; but, just then, we see the Crucified One coming forward with his mighty sickle; and as we mark the blood-drops streaming from his brow, and see the nail-print in the hand with which he grasps the sickle, when we see how he toils, and how he labours, and with what an awful love he sacrifices himself, he has stripped off his very garments, and in all the nakedness of self-denial, gives himself up that he may save others while himself he cannot save. Then we pluck up our heart again, and take our sickle in the hand which once hung down, saying, "Jesus, I will never be weary, for you were not weary; and when I am faint awhile, I will see you, whose meat and drink it was to do his Father's will (Jn. 4:34), and I will make it my meat and my drink to serve you." Surely you cannot do God's work as well as when you have Jesus Christ with you.

But it is possible, dear friends, that some of you may be engaged in the service of winning for God some soul. I know those who have one soul laid on their heart. Perhaps it is the most solemn work under heaven to have to pray for one soul. I have so many to look after that I cannot but feel I may rightly excuse myself from any very sedulous [persevering] attention to one; but there are some of you who have only one person to look after — one child, one friend, one soul. You tried to talk to that one person the other day: you burst into tears when you heard the answer you received. You have been praying for months, but instead of seeing any answer to your prayer, the person prayed for is growing worse. You are sure that he is never more vile than when you are most earnest. Friend, I should not wonder if Satan should whisper to you, "Give it up!" But let me, I pray you, urge you never to do so. And if you want something that will make you never to give up praying for that soul, see yonder, the eternal Son of God, who came into this world to save such a sinner as you yourself are, and you wilt never think you are doing anything too hard, when trying to save your fellow-man from destruction. Oh, for a vision of the Saviour's face covered with the spittle! See him marred and bruised by the rough Roman soldiers! Behold him as his back smarts beneath the thongs of the cruel whips! See him as Pilate brings him out, and cries, "Ecce homo!" (Behold, the man!) Mark him as he treads the Via Dolorosa! (The way of sorrows) See him while they lift him up on high and dislocate his bones! Why, what is all that you can endure compared with this? When your soul swells with fearful grief, you do not feel such grief as this; you are just sipping at the cup which the Saviour drained to the dregs. You but feel a scratch from those nails which went right through his hands; you do not have but for a moment a flesh wound from that spear which pierced his heart.

Courage, you solitary labourer; let Christ's griefs solace you. Come with me, my Beloved; come with me, my Lord; and my toil will be easy.

There are some Christians engaged in works of heroism, works of peculiar daring for Christ. I should not like to be misunderstood, but I really think that, amid the gross darkness of the Popish Church, there have been some who have caught the true idea of the Christian life far better than most of us. Let me tell you to what I refer. There have been some who have denied themselves all the comforts of life, and have lived in suffering and poverty out of love for Jesus, and from a sincere desire to benefit their fellow-men. There have been produced in that Church men whose passionate love no labour or persecution could extinguish, who have fed the poor and nourished the sick. There are women who have gone into the hospitals, among diseases the most contagious, and have risked life and lost life for the sake of nursing the sick. There are those living at this present moment on the tops of such mountain-passes as St. Bernard and the Simplon, spending the prime of their life in seclusion in inhospitable frost, where somebody must live and work, but where nobody would ever live if it were not for the sake of religion, simply that they may serve the poor weary traveller when he comes wading through the snow, or is likely to be lost in the snow-storm, No one shall take precedence of me in my abhorrence of the thrice accursed doctrines of the harlot of Rome; but from our enemies it is right to learn; and I learn, and would teach this, that self-denial and consecration are among the highest of the Christian virtues. I would to God that our people had the spirit of self-consecration in proportion to the light they enjoy! I would to God we had true Sisters of Mercy who devote themselves going from house to house among the sick. We have some, but we want more; some who would be hospital nurses, and who would count it but a small sacrifice even if they gave up themselves for the good of others. Missionaries we want who will face the malaria and deadly fever; our societies cry out for such, but very few come forward. We want men of substance, who would take their substance and go out with it to a foreign land to evangelise; men who, having prospered in business, would now count it an honour to spend the rest of their days in some new and special work of charity or piety.

Oh, when I see the Saviour in all his agonies doing so much for us, I cannot but think that we as a Christian people do next to nothing for him! There are no stakes of Smithfield now, thank God; there are no dungeons in the Lollard's Tower; no crowns of martyrdom for suffering brows; but there are still special spheres of labour where we could make the name of Christ illustrious. Let me hold up for your imitation some in modern times, who by works of faith and labours of love, have made us feel that the old spirit of Christianity is not dead. Our beloved friend, Mr. George Muller, of Bristol, for instance. There burns a holy devotion, an intensity of faith, a fervour of perseverance, which I would to God we all possessed. May we have more of this, and so, by keeping close to Jesus, we shall produce better fruit, richer clusters and more luscious grapes than are commonly produced on those vines which are in a less happy part of the vineyard.

III. And now let me close by remarking that, according to the text, THE CHURCH DESIRES TO GIVE TO CHRIST ALL THAT SHE PRODUCES. She has "all manner of pleasant fruits", both "new and old", and they are laid up for her beloved.

We have some new fruit. This morning, I hope, we feel new life, new joy, new gratitude: we wish to make new resolves and carry them out by new labours. Our heart goes up in new prayers, and our soul is pledging herself to new efforts. But we have some old things too. There is our first love: a choice fruit that one, and Christ, delights in it! There is our first faith: that simple faith by which, having nothing, we became possessors of all things. There is our joy when first we knew the Lord; let us revive it. How happy we were then, when the candle of the Lord shone round about us! Old things! Why, we have the old remembrance of the promises. How faithful God has been! In that sickness of ours, how softly makes our bed! In those deep waters, how placidly he buoyed us up! In that flaming furnace, how graciously he delivered us, so that not even the smell of fire passed upon us. Old fruits, indeed! We have many of them, for his mercies have been more than the hairs of our head. Old sins we most regret, but then we have had repentances which he has given us, by which we have wept our way to the cross, and learned the merit of his blood. We have fruit, this morning, both new and old; but here is the point — they are all to be for Christ.

Do you not, after doing good service, detect yourself whispering, "I have done that well?" You intended that nobody should know it; you tried to do it as a secret act of devotion; you were half inclined to tell somebody when it was done; and though it came out, you say it was by accident; but you had a finger in that accident, and you did not altogether regret that you had something of the honour of it. Do you not find, when you are really serving your Master, that if somebody does not pat you on the back, you grow cold? I know some Sunday-school teachers who, if they are looked after and encouraged, can do well, but who, if they have no encouragement, could not keep on in their work. Oh, it is so easy for us to preach when there are many souls being fed under us, and the Master honours us in the eyes of men. Would it be quite as easy to serve him without honour? I have known brethren who have met with a little bad feeling among their people, and perhaps they have not always been able to keep their own temper, and they have run away from their charge, left the sheep in the wilderness, because, in their inmost heart they were serving themselves, at least to a degree.

Truly, beloved, those are the best and most acceptable services in which Christ is the solitary aim of the soul, and his glory without any admixture whatever, the end of all our efforts. Let your many fruits be laid up only for your beloved: bring them out when he is with you: bless his name for them. Put jewels into his crown, but never say, "Unto me be honour, and to my name be praise," but "Sing unto Jesus, and to Jesus only be glory, while heaven endures."

Oh, that strangers to Jesus would believe our testimony concerning him! We are asked sometimes for proofs of our religion. There is one proof we defy anyone to contradict, and that is the intense joy which the love of Christ gives to us. We are not fools, and I may add, we are not dishonest, and our witness is that there is a joy in love for Christ, and in the enjoyment of his presence, which could not possibly have come to us from any but a divine source. We do not speak because we have not tried other joys; some of us have had our fill of them. We can say of some that their sweet is soon lost in bitterness, of others, that they cloy upon our taste. But communion with Christ has no after-bitterness in it. It never cloys; it is a sun without spots; it is a moon which never wanes; it is an ocean which never ebbs; it is a river which flows on forever — it is all heaven and all bliss.

Oh, if you only knew it, you would never doubt again! Your soul would rest implicitly on Christ, whom God set out to be a propitiation for sin. And, remember, if you rest on him and trust in him, you are saved, and will be with him where he is, beholding his glory evermore. May God bless these words for Jesus' sake! Amen.

NINE SERMONS ON THE SONG OF SOLOMON

CHAPTER 8

76. THE SPICED WINE OF MY POMEGRANATE
OR, THE COMMUNION OF COMMUNICATION

PREACHED AT A COMMUNION SERVICE AT MENTONE

PRINTED IN SWORD AND TROWEL, NOVEMBER 1865

"I would cause Thee to drink of spiced wine of the juice of my pomegranates."
(Song of Solomon 8:2)

THE immovable basis of communion having been laid of old in the eternal union that subsisted between Christ and his elect, it only needed a fitting occasion to manifest itself in active development. The Lord Jesus had forever delighted himself with the sons of men, and he ever stood prepared to reveal and communicate that delight to His people. But they were incapable of returning his affection, or enjoying his fellowship, having fallen into a state so base and degraded that they were dead to him, and careless concerning him. It was therefore needful that something should be done for them and in them before they could hold converse with Jesus, or feel concord with him. This preparation being a work of grace, and a result of previous union, Jesus determined that, even in the preparation for communion, there should be communion. If they must be washed before they could fully converse with him, he would commune with them in the washing; and if they must be enriched by gifts before they could have full access to him, he would commune with them in the giving. He has therefore established a fellowship in imparting his grace, and in the partaking of it.

This order of fellowship we have called "The Communion of Communication", and we think that a few remarks will prove that we are not running beyond the warranty of Scripture.

The word *koinonia*, or communion, is frequently employed by inspired writers in the sense of communication or contribution. When, in our English version, we read, "For it hath pleased them of Macedonia and Achaia to make *a certain contribution* for the poor saints which are at Jerusalem" (Rom. 15:26), it is interesting to know that the word *koinonia* is used here, as if to show that the generous gifts of the Church in Achaia to its sister Church at Jerusalem was a communion. John Calvin would have us notice this, because, says he, "The word here employed well expresses the feeling by which it behoves us to succour the needs of our brethren, even because there is to be a common and mutual regard on account of the union of the body." He would not have strained the text if he had said that there was in the contribution the very essence of communion. John Gill, in his commentary on the above verse, most pertinently remarks: "Contribution, or communion, as the word signifies, it being one part of the communion of churches and of saints to relieve their poor by communicating to them." The same word is employed in Hebrews 13:16, and is there translated by the word *communicate* — "But to do good and to communicate, forget not: for with such sacrifices God is well pleased." It occurs again in 2 Corinthians 9:13 — "And for your liberal *distribution* unto them, and unto all men"; and, in numerous other passages, the careful student will observe the word in various forms representing the ministering of the saints to one another as an act of fellowship. Indeed, at the Lord's Supper, which is the embodiment of communion, we have ever been in the habit of make a special contribution for the poor of the flock, and we believe that in the collection there is as true and real an element of communion as in the partaking of the bread and wine. The giver holds fellowship with the receiver when he bestows his benefaction for the Lord's sake, and because of the brotherhood existing between him and his needy friends. The teacher holds communion with his young disciple when he labours to instruct him in the faith, being moved to do it in a spirit of Christian love. The one that intercedes for a saint because he desires his well-being as a member of the one family enters into fellowship with his brother in the offering of prayer. The loving and mutual service of church-members is fellowship of a high degree. And let us remember that the recipient communes with the benefactor: the communion is not confined to the giver, but the heart, overflowing with liberality, is met by the heart brimming with gratitude, and the love manifested in the bestowal, is reciprocated in the acceptance. When the hand feeds the mouth, or supports the head, the different members feel their unity, and sympathise with one another; and so is it with the various portions of the body of Christ, for they commune in mutual acts of love.

Now, this meaning of the word communion furnishes us with much instruction, since it indicates the manner in which recognised fellowship with Jesus is commenced and maintained, namely, by giving and receiving, by *communication* and reception. The Lord's Supper is the divinely-ordained exhibition of communion, and, therefore, in it, there is the breaking of bread and the pouring out of wine, to picture the free gift of the Saviour's body and blood to us; and there is also the eating of the one and the drinking of the other to represent the reception of these priceless gifts by us. As without bread and wine there could be no Lord's Supper, so without the gracious bequests of Jesus to us there would be no communion between him and our souls: and as participation is necessary before the elements really represent the meaning of the Lord's ordinance, so is it needful that we should receive his bounties, and feed upon his Person, before we can commune with Him.

It is one branch of this mutual communication we have selected as the subject of this address. "Looking unto Jesus" (Heb 12:2), who has delivered us from our state of enmity, and brought us into fellowship with him, we also pray for the rich assistance of the Holy Spirit, that we may be refreshed in spirit, and encouraged to draw more largely from the covenant storehouse of Christ Jesus the Lord.

We shall add another text, and proceed at once to our delightful task. "*And of His fullness have all we received, and grace for grace*." (John 1:16) As the life of grace is first begotten in us by the Lord Jesus, so is it constantly sustained by him. We are always drawing from this sacred fountain, always deriving sap from this divine root; and, as Jesus communes with us in the bestowing of mercies, it is our privilege to hold fellowship with him in the receiving of them.

There is this difference between Christ and ourselves, in that he never gives without manifesting fellowship, but we often receive in so poor a way that communion is not reciprocated, and we then miss the heavenly opportunity of its enjoyment. We frequently receive grace insensibly; that is to say, the sacred oil runs through the pipe, and maintains our lamp (Zech. 4:12), while we are unmindful of its secret influence. We may also be the partakers of many mercies which, through our dullness, we do not perceive to be mercies at all; and, at other times, well-known blessings are recognized as such, but we are backward in tracing them to their source in the covenant made with Christ Jesus.

Following out the suggestion of our explanatory preface, we can well believe that when poor saints received the contribution of their brethren, many of them, in earnest, acknowledged the fellowship that was illustrated in the generous offering; but it is probable that some of them merely looked on the material of the gift, and failed to see the spirit moving behind it. Sensual thoughts in some of the receivers might possibly, at the season when the contribution was distributed, have mischievously injured the exercise of spirituality, for it is possible that, after a period of poverty, they would be apt to give greater prominence to the fact that their need was met than to the sentiment of fellowship with their sympathising brethren. They would rather rejoice over famine averted than concerning fellowship manifested. We do not doubt that, in many instances, the mutual benefactions of the Church fail to reveal our fellowship with our poor brethren, and produce in them no feelings of communion with the givers.

Now, this sad fact is an illustration of the yet more lamentable statement we have made. We again assert that, as many of the partakers of the alms of the Church are not alive to the communion contained in the act, so the Lord's people are never sufficiently attentive to fellowship with Jesus in receiving his gifts; but many of them are entirely forgetful of their privilege, and all of them are too little aware of it. No, worse than this, how often does the believer pervert the gifts of Jesus into food for his own sin and depravity! (1 Cor. 11:20-22) We are not free of the fickleness of ancient Israel, and well might our Lord address us in the same language:

"Now when I passed by thee, and looked upon thee, behold, thy time was the time of love; and I spread my skirt over thee, and covered thy nakedness: yea, I sware unto thee, and entered into a covenant with Thee, saith the Lord God, and thou becamest mine. Then washed I thee with water; yea, I throughly washed away thy blood from thee, and I anointed thee with oil. I clothed thee also with broidered work, and shod thee with badgers' skin, and I girded thee about with fine linen, and I covered thee with silk. I decked thee also with ornaments, and I put bracelets upon thy hands, and a chain on thy neck. And I put a jewel on thy forehead, and earrings in thine ears, and a beautiful crown upon thine head. Thus wast thou decked with gold and silver; and thy raiment was of fine linen, and silk, and broidered work; thou didst eat fine flour, and honey, and oil: and thou wast exceeding beautiful, and thou didst prosper into a kingdom. And thy renown went forth among the heathen for thy beauty: for it was perfect through my comeliness, which I had put upon thee, saith the Lord God. But thou didst trust in thine own beauty, and playedst the harlot because of thy renown." (Ezek. 16:8-16.)

Ought not the mass of professors confess the truth of this accusation? Have not the bulk of us most sadly departed from the purity of our love? We rejoice, however, to observe a remnant of choice spirits, who live near the Lord, and know the sweetness of fellowship. These receive the promise and the blessing, and so digest them so that they become good blood in their veins. Thus they feed on their Lord and grow up into him. Let us imitate those elevated minds, and obtain also their high delights. There is no reason why the meanest of us should not be as David, and David as the servant of the Lord. We may now be dwarfs, but growth is possible; let us, therefore, aim at a higher stature. When the following advice is followed, and the Holy Spirit helping us, we shall attain it.

Make every time of need a time of embracing your Lord. Do not leave the mercy-seat until you have clasped him in your arms. In every time of need, he has promised to give you grace to help, and what is stopping you from obtaining sweet fellowship as a precious addition to the promised assistance? Do not be like the beggar who is content with the alms, however grudgingly it may be cast to him; but, since you are a near kinsman, seek a smile and a kiss with every benison [ancient word for blessing] he gives you. Is he not better than his mercies? What are they without him? Cry aloud to him, and let your petition reach his ears:

"O my Lord, it is not enough to be a partaker of your bounties, I must have you also. If you do not give me yourself with your favours, they are of little use to me! O smile on me, when you bless me, or else I am still unblessed! You put perfume into all the flowers of your garden, and fragrance into your spices; if you withdraw yourself, they are no more pleasant to me. Come, then, my Lord, and give me your love with your grace."

Take good heed, Christian, that your own heart is in tune, that when the fingers of mercy touch the strings, they may resound with full notes of communion. How sad is it to partake of favour without rejoicing in it! Yet such is often the believer's case. The Lord casts his lavish bounties down at our doors, and we, like churls [Anglo-Saxon for a lower class freeman], scarcely look out to thank him. Our ungrateful hearts and unthankful tongues mar our fellowship by causing us to miss a thousand opportunities for exercising it.

If you would enjoy communion with the Lord Jesus in the reception of his grace, *endeavour to be always sensibly drawing supplies from him*. Make your needs public in the streets of your heart, and, when the supply is granted, let all the powers of your soul be present at the reception of it. Let no mercy come into your house unsung. Note in your memory the list of your Master's benefits. Therefore, should the Lord's bounties be hurried away into the dark, or buried in forgetfulness?

Keep the gates of thy soul ever open, and sit by the wayside to watch the treasures of grace, which God the Spirit hourly conveys into your heart from Jehovah-Jesus your Lord.

Never let an hour pass without drawing on the bank of heaven. If all your needs seem satisfied, look steadfastly till the next moment brings another need, and then do not delay, but, with this warrant of necessity, hasten to your treasury again. Your necessities are so numerous that you will never lack a reason for applying to the fullness of Jesus; but, if ever such an occasion should arise, enlarge your heart, and then there will be need of more love to fill the wider space. Do not allow any supposed riches of your own suspend your daily receivings from the Lord Jesus. You have a constant need of him. You need his intercession, his upholding, and his sanctification. You need him to work in you all your works, that he should preserve you up to the day of his appearing. There is not one moment of your life in which you can do without Christ. Therefore, be always at his door, and the needs you bemoan shall be remembrances to turn your heart to your Saviour. Thirst makes the heart pant for the waterbrooks (Ps. 42:1), and pain reminds us that we need a physician. Let your needs conduct you to Jesus, and may the blessed Spirit reveal him to you while he lovingly affords you the rich supplies of His love! Go, poor saint, let your poverty be the cord to draw you to your rich Brother. Rejoice in the infirmity that makes room for grace to rest upon you, and be glad that you have constant needs to compel you perpetually to have fellowship with your adorable Redeemer.

Study yourself, and seek out your necessities, as the housewife searches for chambers where she may store her summer fruit. Regard your needs as rooms to be filled with more of the grace of Jesus, and allow no corner to be unoccupied. Pant after more of Jesus. Be covetous of him. Let all the past incite you to seek greater things. Sing the song of the enlarged heart:

All this is not enough: methinks I grow
More greedy by fruition; what I get
Serves but to set
An edge upon my appetite;
And all Thy gifts invite
My prayers for more.

(Christopher Harvey)

Cry out to the Lord Jesus to fill the dry beds of your rivers until they overflow, and then empty the channels which have, hitherto, been filled with your own self-sufficiency, and beseech him to fill these also with his superabundant grace. If your heavy trials sink you deeper in the flood of his consolations, be glad of them; and if your vessel is sinking up to its very bulwarks, do not be afraid. I would be glad to feel the mast-head of my soul twenty fathoms beneath the surface of such an ocean; for, as Rutherford said, "Oh, to be over the ears in this well! I would not have Christ's love entering into me unless I would enter into it, and be swallowed up by that love." Cultivate an insatiable hunger, and a quenchless thirst, for this communion with Jesus through his communications. Let your heart cry forever, "Give, give" until it is filled in Paradise. From *Nymphas*, by Joseph Irons, we read:

O'ercome with Jesu's condescending love,
Brought into fellowship with Him and His,
And feasting with Him in His house of wine,
I'm sick of love — and yet I pant for more
Communications from my loving Lord.
Stay me with flagons full of choicest wine,
Pressed from His heart upon Mount Calvary,
To cheer and comfort my love-conquered soul.
Thyself I crave!
Thy presence is my life, my joy, my heaven,
And all, without Thyself, is dead to me.
Stay me with flagons, Saviour, hear my cry,
Let promises, like apples, comfort me;
Apply atoning blood, and covenant love,
Until I see Thy face among the guests
Who in Thy Father's kingdom feast.

This is the only covetousness allowed: but this is not merely beyond rebuke, it is worthy of commendation. O saints, do not be straitened in your own soul, but enlarge your desires, and so receive more of your Saviour's measureless fullness! I charge you, O soul, to hold continual fellowship with your Lord, since he invites and commands you thus to partake of his riches.

Rejoice in benefits received. Let the satisfaction of your spirit overflow into streams of joy. When the believer reposes all his confidence in Christ, and delights himself in him, there is an exercise of communion. If he forgets his psalm-book, and, instead of singing, is found lamenting, the mercies of the day will bring no communion. Awake, O music! Stir yourself up, O my soul! Be glad in the Lord, and rejoice exceedingly! (Phil. 4:4) Behold his favours, rich, free, and continual! Shall they be buried in unthankfulness? Shall they be covered with a winding-sheet of ingratitude? No, I will praise him! I must extol him. Sweet Lord Jesus, let me kiss the dust of your feet, let me lose myself in thankfulness, for your thoughts to me are precious (Ps. 94:19, 139:17), and how great is the sum of them! Lo, I embrace you in the arms of joy and gratitude, and here it is that I find my soul drawn to you! This is a blessed method of fellowship. It is kissing the divine lip of benediction with the sanctified lip of affection. Oh, for more rejoicing grace, more of the songs of the heart, more of the melody of the soul!

Seek to recognise the source of your mercies as lying alone in him who is our Head. Imitate the chicken, which, every time it drinks from the brook, lifts up its head to heaven, as if it would return thanks for every drop. If we have anything that is commendable and gracious, it must come from the Holy Spirit, and that Spirit was first bestowed on Jesus, and then, through him, on us. The oil was first poured on the head of Aaron, and, from there, it ran down on his garments. (Ps. 133:2) Look on the drops of grace, and remember that they distil from the Head, Christ Jesus. All your rays are begotten by this Sun of Righteousness (Mal. 4:2), all your showers are poured from this heaven, and all your fountains spring from this great and immeasurable depth.

Oh, for grace to see the hand of Jesus in every favour! So will communion be constantly and firmly exercised. May the great Teacher perpetually direct us to Jesus by making the mercies of the covenant the hand-posts on the road which leads to him! Happy is the believer who knows how to find the secret abode of his Beloved by tracking the footsteps of his loving providence. In this is wisdom, which the casual observer of mere second causes can never reach. Labour, O Christian, to follow up every clue which your Master's grace affords you!

Labour to maintain a sense of your entire dependence upon his good will and pleasure for the continuance of your richest enjoyments. Never try to live on the old manna, nor seek to find help in Egypt. All must come from Jesus, or you are undone forever. Old anointings will not suffice to impart unction [power] to our spirit; your head must have fresh oil poured on it from the golden horn of the sanctuary, or it will cease from its glory. Today, you may be on the summit of the mount of God; but he who has put you there must keep you there, or you will sink far more speedily than you dream. Your mountain only stands firm when he settles it in place. If he hides his face, you will soon be troubled. If the Saviour should see fit, there is not a window through which you see the light of heaven which he could not darken in an instant. Joshua bade the sun stand still (Josh. 10:12-13), but Jesus can shroud it in total darkness. He can withdraw the joy of your heart, the light of your eyes, and the strength of your life. In his hand your comforts lie, and at his will they can depart from you. Oh, how rich the grace which supplies us so continually, and does not refrain itself because of our ingratitude! O Lord Jesus, we bow at your feet, conscious of our utter inability to do anything without you, and, in every favour we are privileged to receive, we would adore your blessed name, and acknowledge your inexhaustible love!

When you have received much, admire the all-sufficiency which still remains undiminished; thus shall you commune with Christ, not only in what you obtain from him, but also in the superabundance which remains treasured up in him. Let us always remember that giving does not impoverish our Lord. When the clouds, those wandering cisterns of the skies, pour floods on the dry ground, there remains an abundance in the storehouse of the rain; so in Christ there is always an unbounded supply, though most liberal showers of grace have fallen ever since the foundation of the earth. The sun is as bright as ever after all its shining, and the sea remains quite as full after all the clouds have been formed from it: so is our Lord Jesus always the same overflowing fountain of fullness. All this is ours, and we may make it the subject of rejoicing fellowship. Come, believer, walk through the length and breadth of the land, for as far as the eye can see, the land is yours. And far beyond the utmost range of your observation, it is yours also, the gracious gift of your gracious Redeemer and Friend. Is there not ample space for fellowship *here?*

Regard every spiritual mercy as an assurance of the Lord's communion with you. When the young man gives jewels to the virgin to whom he is affianced, she regards them as tokens of his delight in her. Believer, do the same with the precious presents of your Lord. The common bounties of providence are shared by all men, for the good Householder provides water for his swine as well as for his children. Such things, therefore, are no proof of divine complacency. But you have richer food to eat. "The children's bread" (Mat. 15:26) is in your wallet, and the heritage of the righteous is reserved for you. Look, then, on every motion of grace in your heart as a pledge and sign of the moving of your Saviour's heart towards you. There is his whole heart in every mercy he sends you. He has impressed a kiss of love on each gift, and he would have you believe that every jewel of mercy is a token of his boundless love. Look on your adoption, justification, and preservation, as sweet enticements to fellowship. Let every note of the promise sound in your ears like the ringing of the bells of the house of your Lord, inviting you to come to the banquets of his love. Joseph sent to his father asses laden with the good things of Egypt (Gen. 45:23), and good old Jacob doubtless regarded them as pledges of the love of his son's heart. Be sure not to think less of the kindnesses of Jesus.

Study to know the value of his favours. They are no ordinary things, no paste jewels, no mosaic gold; they are every one of them so costly, that, had all heaven been drained of treasure, apart from the precious offering of the Redeemer, it could not have purchased so much as the least of his benefits. When you see your pardon, consider how great a boon is contained in it! Ponder that hell would have been your eternal portion unless Christ had plucked you from the burning! (Zech. 3:2) When you are enabled to see yourself as clothed in the imputed righteousness of Jesus, admire the profusion of precious things of which your robe is made. Think how many times the Man of sorrows (Is. 53:3) wearied himself at that loom of obedience where he wove that matchless garment; and reckon, if you can, how many worlds of merit were cast into the fabric at every throw of the shuttle! Remember that all the angels in heaven could not have afforded him a single thread rich enough to weave into the texture of his perfect righteousness. Consider the cost of your maintenance for an hour; remember that your needs are so great that all the granaries of grace that all the saints could fill, could not feed you for a minute.

What an expensive dependent you are! King Solomon made marvellous provision for his household (1 Kings 4:22), but all his beeves and fine flour would be as a drop in the bucket compared with your daily needs. Rivers of oil and ten thousand rams or fed beasts would not provide enough to supply the necessities of your hungering soul. Thy least spiritual need demands infinity to satisfy it, and what must be the amazing aggregate of your perpetually repeated draughts on thy Lord! Arise, then, and bless your loving Prince Immanuel for the invaluable riches with which he has endowed you. See what a dowry your Bridegroom has brought to his poor, penniless spouse. He knows the value of the blessings he brings you, for he paid for them out of his heart's richest blood; so do not be so ungenerous as to pass them over as if they were of little worth. Poor men know more of the value of money than those who have always revelled in abundance of wealth. Ought not you former poverty teach you the preciousness of the grace that Jesus gives you? For remember, there was a time when you would have given a thousand worlds, if they had been yours, in order to procure the very least of his abundant mercies.

Remember how impossible it would have been for you to receive a single spiritual blessing unless you had been in Jesus. On none of Adam's race is the love of God fixed, unless they are seen to be in union with his Son. No exception has ever been made to the universal curse on those of the first Adam's seed who have no interest in the second Adam. Christ is the only Zoar in which God's Lots can find a shelter from the destruction of Sodom. (Gen. 19:22) Out of him, the withering blast of the fiery furnace of God's wrath consumes every green herb, and it is only in him that the soul can live. As when the prairie is on fire, men see the heavens wrapped in sheets of flame, and, in hot haste, they fly before the devouring element. They have just one hope. There is in the distance a lake of water. They reach it, they plunge into it, and are safe. Although the skies are melted with the heat, the sun darkened with the smoke, and the earth utterly consumed in the fire, they know that they are secure while the cooling flood embraces them. Christ Jesus is the only escape for a sinner pursued by the fiery wrath of God, and we would have the believer remember this. Our own works could never shelter us, for they have proved but refuges of lies. Had they been a thousand times more and better, they would have been just as a spider's web, too frail to hang eternal interests on. There was just one name, one sacrifice, one blood, by which we could escape. All other attempts at salvation were a grievous failure. For, though a man could scourge out of his body rivers of blood, and in neglect of himself could outlast Moses or Elias; though he could wear out his knees with prayer, and had his eyes nailed on heaven; though he could build hospitals for all the poor on earth, and exhaust the mines of India in alms; though he could walk like an angel of light, and, with the glittering of an outward holiness, dazzle the eyes of all beholders; no (if it were possible to be conceived), though he should live for a thousand years in a perfect and perpetual observation of the whole law of God, if the only exception to his perfection were the very least deviation from the law (Jas. 2:10), yet such a man as this could no more appear before the tribunal of God's justice than stumble before a consuming fire. How, then, with your innumerable sins, could you escape the damnation of hell, much less become the recipient of bounties so rich and large? Blessed window of heaven, sweet Lord Jesus, let your Church for ever adore you as the only channel by which mercies can flow to her. My soul, give him continual praise, for, without him, you would have been poorer than a beggar!

Be mindful, O heir of heaven, that you could not have had one ray of hope, or one word of comfort, if you had not been in union with Christ Jesus! The crumbs which fall from your table are more than grace itself would have given you, had you not been in Jesus, beloved and approved. All you have, you have in him: in him chosen, in him redeemed, in him justified, and in him accepted. You have risen in him, but, without him, you would have died the second death. (Rev. 2:11, 20:6, 14, 21:8) You are in him raised up to the heavenly places (Eph. 1:3, 20, 2:6, 3:10), but, out of him, you would have been damned eternally. Bless him, then! Ask the angels to bless him. Rouse all ages to a harmony of praise for his condescending love in taking poor guilty nothings into oneness with his all-adorable Person. This is a blessed means of promoting communion, if the sacred Comforter is pleased to take of the things of Christ, and reveal them to us as ours, but only ours as we are in him. Thrice-blessed Jesus, let us never forget that we are members of your mystical body, and that it is for this reason that we are blessed and preserved.

Meditate upon the gracious acts which procured your blessings. Consider the ponderous labours which thy Lord endured for you, and the stupendous sufferings by which he purchased the mercies which he bestows. What human tongue can speak of the unutterable misery of his heart, or describe so much as one of the agonies which crowded upon His soul? How much less shall any finite comprehension arrive at an idea of the vast total of His woe! But all his sorrows were necessary for your benefit, and, without them, not one of your unnumbered mercies could have been bestowed. Do not be unmindful of the words of Dr. Watts:

How condescending and how kind
Was God's eternal Son!
Our misery reached his heavenly mind,
And pity brought him down.

He sunk beneath our heavy woes,
To raise us to his throne;
There's ne'er a gift his hand bestows,
But cost his heart a groan.

This was compassion like a God,
That when the Saviour knew
The price of pardon was his blood,
His pity ne'er withdrew.

Look upon the frozen ground of Gethsemane, and behold the bloody sweat which stained the soil! Turn to the hall of Gabbatha, and see the victim of justice pursued by his clamouring foes! Enter the guard-room of the Praetorians, and view the spitting, and the plucking of the hair! Then conclude your review on Golgotha, the mount of doom, where death consummated his tortures; and if, by divine assistance, you are enabled to enter, in some humble measure, into the depths of your Lord's sufferings, you will be the better prepared to hold fellowship with him when next you receive his priceless gifts. In proportion to your sense of their costliness will be your capacity for enjoying the love which is centred in them.

Above all, and chief of all, never forget that Christ is yours. Amid the profusion of his gifts, never forget that the chief gift is himself, and don't forget that, after all, his gifts are but himself. He clothes you, but it is with himself, with his own spotless righteousness and character. He washes you, but his innermost self, his own heart's blood, is the stream with which the fountain overflows. He feeds you with the bread of heaven, but do not forget that the bread is himself, his own body, which he gives to be the food of the soul. Never be satisfied with a less communication than a whole Christ. A wife will not be put off with maintenance, jewels, and attire; all these are nothing to her unless she can call her husband's heart and person her own. It was the Paschal lamb on which the ancient Israelite feasted that exodus night, never to be forgotten.

So feast on Jesus, and on nothing less than Jesus, for less than this will be food too light for your soul's satisfaction. Oh, be careful to eat his flesh and drink his blood, and so receive him into yourself in a real and spiritual way! For nothing short of this will be an evidence of eternal life in your soul!

What more shall we add to the rules which we have here delivered? There remains but one great exhortation, which must not be omitted. Seek the abundant assistance of the Holy Spirit to enable you to put into practice the things which we have said, for without his aid, all that we have spoken will be tantalising the lame with rules to walk, or the dying with regulations for the preservation of health. O Divine Spirit, while we enjoy the grace of Jesus, lead us into the secret abode of our Lord that we may sup with him, and he with us! (Rev. 3:20) And grant to us hourly grace that we may continue in the company of our Lord from the rising to the setting of the sun! Amen.

77. LEANING ON OUR BELOVED
NO. 877

DELIVERED ON SUNDAY MORNING, JUNE 20TH, 1869
AT THE METROPOLITAN TABERNACLE, NEWINGTON

"Who is this that cometh up from the wilderness, leaning upon her beloved?"
(Song of Solomon 8:5)

CAREFUL Bible readers will have noticed that, in the verses which precede my text, the spouse was particularly anxious that her communion with her Lord might not be disturbed. Her language is intensely earnest: "I charge you, O daughters of Jerusalem, that ye stir not up, nor awake my love until he please." She valued much the fellowship with which her beloved solaced her; she was jealously alarmed lest she should endanger the continuance of it, lest any sin on her part, or on the part of her companions, should cause the Beloved to withdraw himself in anger. Now, it is a very striking fact that, immediately after we read a verse so full of solicitous care concerning the maintenance of communion, we immediately come upon another verse in which the upward progress of that selfsame spouse is the theme of admiration. She who would not have her beloved disturbed is the selfsame bride who comes up from the wilderness, herself leaning upon him; from which it is clear that there is a most intimate connection between communion with Christ and progress in grace; therefore, the more careful we are to maintain fellowship with our Lord, the more successful will we be in going from strength to strength in all those holy graces which are landmarks on the road to glory. The well-head and fountain of growth in grace is well-sustained communion and manifest oneness with Christ. We may strive after moral virtue if we will, but we shall be like those foolish children who pluck flowers and thrust them into their little gardens without roots; but if we strive after increasing faith in Jesus, we shall be as wise men, who plant choice bulbs and living seeds, from which, in due time, shall up the golden cups or the azure bells of lovely flowers, emblems of things that are lovely and of good repute. To live near Christ is the one thing needful; to keep up that nearness, and never to suffer our fellowship to be interrupted, should be our one great business here below; and all other things, this being sought after in the first place, will be added to us. We shall come up from the wilderness when we are anxious that our beloved's fellowship with us shall not be disturbed.

That preface strikes the key-note of this morning's discourse. Our real theme, whatever may be the form our meditation takes, will be communion with Christ as the source of spiritual progress.

I. We shall, without further remark, come at once to the consideration of the text, and we notice THE HEAVENLY PILGRIM AND HER DEAR COMPANION. "Who is this that cometh up from the wilderness, leaning upon her beloved"?

Every soul that journeys towards heaven has Christ for its associate. Jesus suffers no pilgrim to the New Jerusalem to travel unattended. He is with us in sympathy. He has trodden every step of the way before us. Whatever our temptations, he has been so tempted; whatever our afflictions, he has been so afflicted. He is touched with the feeling of our infirmities, having been tempted in all points like as we are. (Heb. 4:15) Nor is Jesus near us in sympathy alone; he is with us to render practical assistance. When we least perceive him, he is often closest to us. When the howling tempest drowns his voice, and the darkness of the night hides his Person, he is still there, and we need not be afraid. It is no fiction, no dream, no piece of imagination that Christ is really with his people. "Lo, I am with you *alway*, even to the end of the world" (Mat. 28:20) is true for all his saints; and,

"Fear thou not; for I am with thee: he not dismayed; for I am thy God" (Is. 41:10) is no meaningless assertion, but to be understood as a certain verity and a practical truth. In every step of this pilgrimage, from the wicket-gate of repentance up to the pearly gate which admits the perfected into paradise, Jesus Christ, in sympathy of heart, and in actual presence of help, is very near to his people. Let this be the pilgrim's encouragement this morning. Dear friends, who among us would not undertake a journey in such company? If he were here today and said, "My child, I call you to go on pilgrimage", perhaps you would start back with dark forebodings on the way; but if he added, "But I will be with you wherever you go", we should each one reply, "Through floods, or flames, if you lead, we will follow you wherever you go. Lead the van, O Crucified, and we will follow you. Let us but see your footprints in the road, and, whether the path winds up the hill of difficulty or descends into the valley of humiliation, it shall be the best road that ever mortal footsteps trod, if it is marked with the tokens of your most blessed presence." Courage, then, you wayfarers traversing the vale of tears! You come up from the wilderness in dear company, for one like the Son of God is at your side.

Note the title that is given to the companion of the spouse. "*Her beloved*" Indeed, he of whom the song here speaks is beloved above all others. He was the Beloved of his Father or ever the earth was; he was declared to be the Lord's Beloved, in the waters of Jordan, and at other times, when out of the excellent glory there came the voice, "This is my beloved Son in whom I am well pleased." (Mat. 17:5; Mk. 1:1; Lk. 3:22; 2 Pet. 1:17) Beloved of his Father now, our Jesus sits forever glorious at God's right hand. Jesus is the Beloved of every angel, and of all the bright seraphic spirits that crowd around the throne of his august majesty, casting their crowns before his feet, and lifting up their ceaseless hymns. They are not merely servants who obey because they must, but reverent admirers who serve because they love. He is the Beloved of every being of pure heart and holy mind. The hosts triumphant, who have washed their robes and made them white in the blood of the Lamb (Rev. 7:14), sing that word "Beloved" with an emphasis our colder hearts as yet have failed to reach; but still is he Beloved of the militant band this side of the Jordan. Yes, Lord, with all that we have to confess of hardness and indifference, we do love you, and you know it.

Would not our heart pour forth its blood,
In honour of thy name,
And challenge the cold hand of death
To damp the immortal flame?

Thou knowest I love Thee, dearest Lord,
But O, I long to soar
Far from the sphere of mortal joys,
And learn to love Thee more!

(Philip Doddridge)

The adamant is softer than our hearts by nature, and yet the love we bear you, O divine Redeemer, stimulated by the love which you have shown to us, has made our souls melt in your presence.

Lord, it is my chief complaint
That my love is weak and faint;
Yet I love Thee, and adore:
O for grace to love Thee more!

(William Cowper)

Note well that the sweetest phrase of the text is "leaning on her beloved." That Jesus is beloved is most true, for is he not my beloved? Ah, if this is true, there is a heaven wrapped up in it. I say to you who are listening to the word this morning, is Jesus your beloved? Do you love him? Can you put out the finger of your timid faith and touch the hem of his garment, and receive the virtue which goes out from him? Do you dare say, "He is all my salvation, and all my desire. Other refuge have I none; my soul hangs in her utter helplessness entirely on him." Then he is your beloved; and the more you can foster the well-grounded belief that Jesus is yours, the more you can roll that truth under your tongue as a sweet morsel, the happier and holier you will be. Realise this fact that Jesus is as actually and truly yours as your husband, your wife, your child, your mother, or your own self, then will peace and love reign within your spirit. The spouse could not have leaned on Jesus as the Beloved; she could only find rest in him as her beloved. Till you get a sense of his being yours you do not dare to lean; but when you come to know that Christ is yours by an act of appropriating faith, then comes the after-result of faith in the consecrated repose which the soul feels in the power and love of him on whom she relies.

Thus, O pilgrim to the skies, you are reminded that you have with you a companion whose name to you is "my beloved." Pause awhile, and look about you! Do you not see him? Can you not perceive the marks of his presence? Then rejoice that you are found in such company, and take care to enjoy the honours and privileges which such society secures you.

II. We now pass on to something deeper. We have said that the pilgrim has a dear companion, but that much of the blessedness found in the text lies in HER POSTURE TOWARDS HIM. "Who is this that cometh up from the wilderness leaning upon her beloved?"

Her posture, then, is that of "leaning." His relation to her is that of a divine supporter. What does this leaning mean? Why, first of all, there can be no leaning on another unless we believe in the other's presence and nearness. A man does not lean on a staff which is not in his hand, or on a friend of whose presence he is not aware. The instincts that lead us to preserve our uprightness will not permit us to lean on a shadow or on a nothing. It behoves you then, O Christian, if you would be like this wondrous woman in the text, seek to be conscious of the presence of Christ. It is true your senses cannot perceive him, but your senses are less to be relied on than your faith, for senses may be mistaken, but the faith of God's elect does not err. God makes that which faith depends on to be more real than anything that the senses can perceive. Christ Jesus is with you; though you do not hear his voice and see his face, he is with you. Try to grasp that truth, and realise it clearly, for you will never lean until you do.

Leaning also implies nearness. We cannot lean on what is far off and unapproachable. Now, it is a delightful help to us in believing repose if we can understand that Christ is not only with us, but to an intense degree near us. I love that hymn we sang just now [No. 784 in Our Own Hymn Book] concerning our Lord's coming near us, and making his name a common word among us. The Christ of a great many professors is only fit to occupy a niche on the church wall, as a dead, inactive, but revered person. Jesus is not a real Christ to many; he is not a Christ who can really befriend them in their hour of grief, nor a brother born for adversity, nor a condescending companion. But the Christ of the well-taught Christian is one who lives, and was dead and is alive for evermore, a sympathising, practical friend, who is actually near, entering into our sorrows, sharing in our crosses, and taking a part with us in all the battle of life. Come, child of God, see that it is so with you. Realise Christ first, and then believe that he is nearer to you than friend or kinsman can be, for he pours his counsels right into your heart, being so near that, at times when your secret trouble cannot be shared by any mortal, it is shared by him; so near that when your heart's inmost recesses must necessarily be locked up to all other sympathy, those recesses are all open to his tenderness; so near to you that you live in him, and he abides in you, and you abide in him. A sacred unity exists between you and him, so that you may drink of his cup, and be baptised with his baptism, and, in all your sorrows and afflictions, he himself takes his share.

These two things being attended to, leaning now becomes easy. To lean implies the throwing of one's weight from oneself on to another, and this is the Christian's life. The first act that made him a Christian at all was when the whole weight of his sin was laid on Christ. When, by faith, the sinner ceased to carry his own burden, but laid it on the great Substitute's shoulder, it was that leaning which made him a Christian. In proportion as he learns this lesson of casting all his burden upon his Lord (Ps. 55:22), he will be more and more a Christian; and when he shall have completely unloaded himself, and cast all his matters on his God, and live in the power and strength of God and not in his own, then he shall have attained to the fullness of the stature of a perfect man in Christ Jesus. (Eph. 4:13) To lean, I say, is to throw your weight off from yourself onto another — being fatigued, to make another fatigued if he can be; being wearied, to make another take your weariness, and so to proceed with your load transferred onto a substitute. Yes, I repeat it: this is the true Christian life — to leave everything that troubles me with him who loves me better than I love myself; to leave all that depresses me with him whose wisdom and whose power are more than a match for all emergencies. Here is wisdom, never to try to stand alone in my own strength, never to trust to creatures, for they will fail me if I rest on them, but to make my ever-blessed Lord Christ, in his manhood and in his Godhead, the leaning place of my whole soul, casting every burden upon him who is able to bear it. This is what I think is meant in the text by leaning.

One would imagine that there must have been of latter years a society for the improvement of texts of Scripture; and, if so, I cannot congratulate that honourable company upon its success. This text has been a favourite object of the society's care, for I think I never heard it quoted correctly in my life. It is generally quoted, "Who is this that cometh up from the wilderness, leaning upon the *arm* of her beloved?" But it is not in the text at all. There is no distinct reference to an arm at all. There is an arm here undoubtedly, but there is a great deal more — there is a whole Person; and the text speaks of leaning upon the whole Person of "her beloved." Observe, then, that the Christian leans on Christ in his personality and completeness, not merely on the arm of his strength, as that altered text would have it, but on the whole Christ. The leaning place of a Christian is, first of all, Christ's Person. We depend on the Lord Jesus as God and as man. As God, he must be able to fulfil every promise, and achieve every covenant engagement. We lean on that divinity which bears up the pillars of the universe. Our dependence is on the Almighty God, incarnate in human form, by whom all things were created, and in whom all things consist. We lean also on Christ as man; we depend upon his generous human sympathies. Of a woman born, he is partaker of our flesh; he enters into our sicknesses and infirmities with a pitiful compassion which he could not have felt if he had not been the Son of man. We depend on the love of his humanity as well as on the potency of his deity. We lean on our beloved as God and man. Ah, I have known times when I have felt that none but God could bear me up! There are other seasons when, under a sense of sin, I have started back from God, and felt that none but the Man Christ Jesus could minister peace to my anguished heart. Taking Christ in the double nature as God and man, he thus becomes a suitable leaning place for our spirit, whatever may happen to be the state in which our mind is found. Beloved, we lean upon Christ himself in all his offices. We lean upon him as priest, for we expect our offerings and our praises and our prayers to be received, because they are presented through him. Our leaning for acceptance is on him. We also lean on him as our prophet. We do not profess to know, or to be able to discover, truth by ourselves, but we sit at his feet, and, what he teaches, that we receive as certainty. We lean on him as our King. He will fight our battles for us, and manage all the affairs of our heavenly citizenship. We have no hope of victory except in the strength of him who is the Son of David and the King of kings. We lean upon Christ in all his attributes. Sometimes it is his wisdom — in our dilemmas he directs us; at other times it is his faithfulness — in our strong temptations he remains the same. At one time, his power gleams out like a golden pillar, and we rest on it, and, at another moment, his tenderness becomes conspicuous, and we lean on that. There is not a trait of his character, there is not a mark of his Person, whether human or divine, but what we feel it safe to lean on, because he is a whole Christ, perfection's own self, lovely and excellent beyond all description. We lean our entire weight on HIM, not on his arm, not on any part of his Person, but it is on himself that we depend.

Beloved, there is no part of the pilgrimage of a saint in which he can afford to walk in any other way but in the way of leaning. He comes up at the first, and he comes up at the last, still leaning, still leaning on Christ Jesus; yes, and leaning more and more heavily on Christ the older he grows. The stronger the believer becomes, the more conscious he is of his personal weaknesses; and, therefore, the more fully does he cast himself on his Lord, and lean with greater force on him. Beloved, it is a blessed thing to keep to this posture in all we do. Oh, it is good preaching when you lean on the Beloved as you preach and feel that "he will help me, he will give me thoughts and words, he will bless the message, he will fill the hungry with good things, and make the Sabbath to be a delight to his people." Oh, it is blessed praying when you lean on the Beloved; you feel then that you cannot be denied; you have come into the King's court, brought your Advocate with you, and you lay your prayer at the foot of the throne, the Prince himself putting his own sign, manual, and seal and stamp of love on your desires. This is the sweet way to endure and suffer with content. Who would not suffer when Jesus makes the bed of our sickness, and stays us up, and gives us tokens of his love? This is the divine method of working. Believe me, no sacred work can long be continued with energy except in this spirit, for flesh flags, and even the spirit languishes unless there is a constant leaning on the Beloved. As for you, men of business, you with your families, and with your shops, and with your fields, and your enterprises, you will find it poor living unless you evermore lean on your beloved in all things. If you can bring your daily cares, your domestic troubles, your family sicknesses, your personal infirmities, your losses and your crosses, if you can bring all things to Jesus, it will be easy and happy living. Even the furnace itself, when the coals glow most, is cool and comfortable as a royal chamber spread for banqueting with the king when the soul reclines on the bosom of divine love. O you saints, strive after more of this! We are such lovers of caring for ourselves, we so want to set up on our own account; we pine to run alone while our legs are too weak; we aspire to stand alone when the only result can be a fall. Oh, to give up this wilfulness which is our weakness, and, like a babe, lie in the mother's bosom, conscious that our strength is not in ourselves but in that dear bosom which bears us up!

I would encourage the heir of heaven, who is in trouble, to lean. I can encourage you from experience. The Lord has laid on me many burdens in connection with much serving in his church, and I sometimes grow very weary; but whenever I bring myself — or rather the Holy Spirit brings me to this pass — to be clear that I cannot do anything of myself, and, do not mean to try, but will just be God's obedient servant and ready instrument, and leave every care with him, then it is that peace returns, thought becomes free and vigorous, and the soul once more, having cast aside its burden, runs without weariness and walks without fainting. I am sure, my dear fellow servants, life will break you down, this London life especially, unless you learn the habit of leaning on Jesus. Do not be afraid to lean too much. There was never yet a saint blamed for possessing too much faith; there was never such a thing known as a child of God who was scolded by the Divine Father for having placed too implicit reliance on his promise. The Lord has said, "As thy days so shall thy strength be." (Deut. 33:25) He has promised "I will never leave thee, nor forsake thee." (Heb. 13:5) He has told you that the birds of the air neither sow nor reap, nor gather into barns, and yet are fed. (Lk. 12:24) He has assured you that the lilies of the field do not toil, neither do they spin, and yet your heavenly Father makes them more beautiful than Solomon in all his glory. (Mat. 6:28-29) Why do you not cast your care on him who cares for ravens and for flowers of the field? Why are you not assured that he will also care for you?

Thus much upon the leaning. "Who is this that cometh up from the wilderness leaning upon her beloved?"

III. Our third point shall be: HER REASONS FOR LEANING.

She was a pilgrim, and she leaned on her beloved. Was she justified in such leaning? Not every confidence is wise. There are refuges of lies, and helpers of no value. Ahithophels are a numerous race. "He that eateth bread with us doth lift up his heel against us." (Ps. 41:9; Jn. 13:18) Friends who seemed to be strong and faithful turn out to be as broken reeds, or as sharp spears to pierce us to our harm. Did she do well, then, in leaning on her beloved? What were her reasons? She was right, and some of her reasons were as follows. She leaned on her beloved because she was weak. Strength will not lean, conscious strength scorns dependence. My soul, do you know anything of your weakness? It is a sorrowful lesson to learn; but oh, it is a blessed and profitable lesson, which not only must be learned, but which it were well for you to pray to learn more and more, for there is no leaning on Christ except in proportion as you feel you must! I do believe that, as long as we have a grain of self-sufficiency, we never trust in the All-sufficient. While there is anything of self left, we prefer to feed on it; and only when at last the mouldy bread becomes too sour for eating, and even the husks that the swine eat are such as cannot fill our belly, it is only then that we humbly ask for the bread of heaven to satisfy us. My soul, learn to hate every thought of self-sufficiency. Brethren, you find yourselves tempted at times, especially if you have had a happy week, and have been free from trials, to think, "Now, really I am better than a great many. I think I am now growing to be an old experienced saint. I have now escaped the power of ordinary temptations, and have become so advanced in grace that there is no likelihood of my sinning in those directions where new converts show their weakness." There is your weak point, brother. Set a double guard where you think you are strongest. Just when you are most afraid, and say to yourself, "Oh, that I might be kept from such a sin — I know that is my besetment, and I am afraid I shall be led into it", you are less likely to sin there than anywhere. Your weakness is your strength, and your strength is your weakness. Be nothing, for only so can you be anything. Be poor in spirit, for only so can you be rich towards God. The spouse leaned because she was weak. Brother, sister, is not this a good argument for you? For me? Are we not also weak? Come then, let us lean wholly on him who is not weak, and to whom all power belongs, to bear all his people safely through.

She leaned, again, on her beloved, because *the way was long.* She had been going through the wilderness. It was a lengthy journey, and she began to flag, and so she leaned. The way is long with us; we have been converted to God now some of us these twenty years, others forty, and there are some in this house who have known the Lord more than sixty years, and this is a long time in which to be tempted and tried, for sin is mighty and the flesh is weak. If one good spurt would win the race, most of us would strain every nerve; but to tug on in our weariness year after year when the novelty has gone, and when there comes, besides, another sort of novelty, fresh temptations, new allurements which we did not know about before, O soul, to win the crown by pressing on, and on, and on, till we hear the Master's plaudit, this is no mean labour. If we can lean, we can hold on, not else. Faith, casting herself upon the power of her Lord, never grows exhausted. She is like the eagle when it renews its youth. She drinks from the fountain head of all vitality, and her lost vigour comes back to her; such a soul would be strong evermore though she had to live the life of a Methuselah; myriads of years would not exhaust her, for she has learned to cast that which exhausts upon him who is inexhaustible, and therefore keeps on the even tenor of her way. She leaned because the road was long. Aged friends, here is a good argument for you; and young men and maidens, who have lately set out on the pilgrimage, since the way may be long to you, here also is a good reason for your leaning at the beginning, and leaning on to the end.

She leaned again because *the road was perilous*. Did you notice that she came up from the *wilderness*! The wilderness is not at all a safe place for a pilgrim. Here it is that the lion prowls, and the howl of the wolf is heard; but she leaned on her beloved, and she was safe. If the sheep fears the wolf, they had better keep close to the shepherd, for then the shepherd's rod and staff will drive the wolf away. There is no safety for us except in close communion with Christ. Every step you get away from Jesus, your danger doubles; and when you have lost the sense of his sacred presence, your peril is at its maximum. Come back, come back, O wanderer, and get close to your Great Helper, and then you will laugh to scorn the fiends of hell, the temptations of life, and even the pangs of death — for he is blessedly safe who leans all on Christ. The careful are not safe, the fretful are not safe, the anxious are not safe; they are tossed to and fro in a frail bark, on a sea whose waves are too strong for them; but those who leave their cares to the great caring One, those who cast their anxieties upon him who never forgets, these are always safe. "Trust in the Lord, and do good; so shalt thou dwell in the land, and verily thou shalt be fed." (Ps.37:3) "The young lions do lack, and suffer hunger: but they that seek the Lord shall not want any good thing." (Ps. 34:10) There may arise a famine, despite all your industry; you may rise up weary and stay up late, and eat the bread of carefulness, and yet have no prosperity. You may keep the city, and the watchman may pass along the walls each hour of the night, and yet it may be taken by assault, But blessed is he that trusteth in the Lord, for neither shall his city be destroyed, nor shall famine come to his land; or, if so it be, in famine he shall be fed, and, in the days of peril, the angels shall keep watch and ward about him. Lean, then, on the Beloved because the way is perilous. This is good reasoning for all of us, for we are in danger; tempted on all sides — liable to sin for a thousand causes. O my brethren, in this age of temptation, lean on the Beloved, for it is your only safety!

Again, she leaned on the Beloved because *her route was ascending*. Did you notice it? "Coming *up*." The Christian's way is up — never content with past attainments, but up; not satisfied with graces to which he has reached, but up. He is not good who does not desire to be better; he is not gracious who would not be more gracious. You do not know the light if you do not desire more light. The heavenly way is upward, upward, upward, upward! This is the way to heaven. The tendency of man's nature is downward. How soon we descend, and how prone is our soul, from her most elevated condition to sink back into the dull dead level of her natural estate! If we are to go up, we must lean. Christ is higher than we are; if we lean, we shall rise the more readily to his elevation. He comes down to us that we, leaning on him, may go up to him. The more we lean, the more truly we cast the weight of our spiritual wrestling, spiritual struggling, spiritual growth, on him, then the more surely shall we gain the wrestling, the struggling, and the growth. Depend as much for growth in grace on Christ as for the pardon of sin. He is made of God unto you sanctification as well as redemption. (1 Cor. 1:30) Look for sanctification through the blood, for it is a purifier as well as a pardoner. The same blood which puts away the guilt of sin is, by the Holy Spirit, applied as the blood of sprinkling to put away from us the reigning power of sin. Oh that we knew more about this, this going up! But I am afraid we do not go up because we do not lean. If there is here this morning a poor child of God who cries, "I the chief of sinners am, and my only hope is in my blessed Lord. I do not feel that I grow in the least; I sometimes think I get worse and worse. But one thing I do know, I trust him more than ever I did, and feel my need of him more." Dear heart, you are the very one who is going up. I know you are, for you are leaning. But if there is another who boasts, "I believe I have made distinct advances in the divine life, and I feel that I am growing strong and vigorous, and I believe that one of these days I shall reach perfection", I think it is very likely that this brother is going down; at any rate, I would recommend to him this prayer: "Hold me up, and I shall be safe", with this caution, "Let him that thinketh he standeth take heed lest he fall." (1 Cor. 10:12)

Yet I must detain you another moment to observe that the spouse leaned on her beloved because *her walk was daily separating her more and more from the whole host of her other companions.* The church is in the wilderness, but this traveller was coming up from the wilderness. She was getting away from the band marching through the desert, getting more and more alone. It is so, and you will find it is so; the nearer you get to Christ, the lonelier you must necessarily be in certain respects. The sinner is in the broad way where thousands walk, the Christian is in the narrow way — there are fewer in this latter; but if the believer keeps to the centre of the narrow way, and if he presses on with vigour, he will find his companions to be fewer and fewer; I mean the companions of his own stature, those of his own size and attainments. If he continues in rapid advance, he will, at last, get to such a position that he will see no one except Jesus only, and then he will be sure to lean more heavily than ever, since he will discover that all men are vanity, and all confidence in the arm of flesh are but lies and deceit.

The spouse leaned upon her beloved because *she felt sure that he was strong enough to bear her weight.* The One on whom she leaned was none other than God over all, blessed for ever, who cannot fail or be discouraged. She leaned yet again, *because he was her beloved.* She would have felt it unwise to lean if he were not mighty; she would have been afraid to lean if he had not been dear to her. So is it; the more you love the more you trust, and the more you trust the more you love. These twin graces of faith and hope live and flourish together. In proportion as that dear crucified Saviour reigns in your soul, and his beauties ravish your heart, in that proportion you feel that all is safe because everything is in his hands, then, on the other hand, in proportion as you trust all to him, and have not a suspicion or a doubt, in that proportion your soul will be knit to him in affection.

I appeal to any here who are the servants of Christ, but have fallen out of the habit of leaning, whether it would not be as well to return to it! Was not it better with you when you leaned than it is now?

Before you set up for yourselves, were you not happier and better than now? Before you let that wicked pride of yours get the upper hand, you were wont to take every daily trouble and burden to your Lord, but, at last, you thought you were wise enough to manage for yourselves. I ask you, have you not from that very day met with many sorrows and defeats and down-castings? And there is this pang about all untrustful living, if a man gets into any troubles through his own wisdom, then he has to blame himself for it; but if any trial comes upon us direct from God, then we feel we cannot blame ourselves, for it belongs to our God to do as he wills; and since he cannot err, we expect that he will justify his own proceedings. It is better to trust in the Lord than to put confidence in man; it is better to trust in the Lord than to put confidence in princes. Wait only on God, and let your expectations be from him, and he will bring out your judgement as the light, and your righteousness as the noonday (Ps. 37:6); and in the day when the wicked shall be confounded, and those that trusted in themselves shall be melted away as the fat of rams, you shall shine forth as the sun in the kingdom of your Father. (Mat. 14:43)

IV. Now let us close. The last point is this: THE PERSON AND THE PEDIGREE of her who was leaning on her beloved.

The text says, "Who is this?" What made them enquire," Who is this?" It was because they were so astonished to see her looking so happy and so little wearied. Nothing amazes worldlings more than genuine Christian joy. Holy peace in disturbing times is a puzzle to the ungodly. When they hear the righteous sing:

> "God is our refuge and strength, a very present help in trouble. Therefore will not we fear, though the earth be removed, and though the mountains be carried into the midst of the sea; though the waters thereof roar and be troubled, though the mountains shake with the swelling thereof. There is a river, the streams whereof shall make glad the city of God, the holy place of the tabernacles of the most High. God is in the midst of her; she shall not be moved: God shall help her, and that right early." (Ps. 46:1-4)

They say one to another, "Where did these men learn that song? They are men of like passions with ourselves, how is it they have learned to bear trial?" Therefore, they enquire, "Who is this? Who is this?" How fine a thing it would be if we all so leaned on Christ in all respects as to enjoy unbroken serenity, so that our kinsfolk and neighbours should be led to enquire, "Who is this?" For then might we have an opportunity of telling them concerning our Well beloved, who is the stay of our peace and the source of our comfort.

Who then is this that leans on her beloved? I will tell you. Her name was once called "outcast", after whom no one seeks, but, according to this old book, her name is now Hephzibah, for the Lord *delights* in her. The name of the soul that trusts in God, and finds peace in so doing, was, by nature, a name of shame and sin. We were afar off from God even as others; and if any soul is brought to trust in Christ, it is not from any natural goodness in it, or any innate propensity towards such trusting; it is because grace has brought a wonderful transformation, and God the Holy Spirit has made those who were not a people to be called the people of God. (1 Pet. 2:10) Good news this, for any of you who feel your guilt this morning! You have been hitherto serving Satan, but mercy can yet bring you to lean upon the Beloved; grace can bring you up from the wilderness instead of permitting you to go down into the pit. She, who today joyfully trusts in her God, was once a weeping Hannah, a woman of a sorrowful spirit, but now her soul rejoices in the Lord, for he has remembered her low estate. (1 Sam. 1:1-18) She was once a sinful Rahab, dwelling in a city doomed to destruction, but she has hung the scarlet line of faith in the precious blood in her window; and if all others perish, she shall be secure in the day of destruction. (Josh. 2:1-17, 6:17-25) She who is here spoken of is a Ruth. She came from afar as an idolatress; she left the land of her nativity, and she has entered into union with the Lord and his people. Her cry is, "Where thou dwellest I will dwell. Thy people shall be my people, thy God shall be my God." She was once a stranger, but she is now an Israelite indeed; she was once accursed, but she is now blessed; once foul, but now washed; once lost, but now found again. (Ruth 16-18) In a word, the soul that leans on Christ habitually every day, and casts her care on him, is one of a princely race; she has been begotten into the family of God; the blood imperial flows in her veins, and, in the day when the crowns of princes and emperors shall melt into the common dust to which they belong, the crown jewels and the diadems of these believing souls shall glitter with immortal splendour in the kingdom of God.

My dear hearer, do you trust Jesus? Does the Holy Spirit move you to begin to trust him today? If so, though your journey may be in a wilderness of trouble, you shall come up out of it to a paradise of bliss; and your peace and comfort shall all spring from leaning on the

Well-beloved. May the Lord bless us, and teach us that sacred art of dependence on the Beloved for Christ's sake! Amen.

78. LOVE AND JEALOUSY

NO. 3516

AT THE METROPOLITAN TABERNACLE, NEWINGTON

"Love is strong as death; jealousy is cruel as the grave."
(Song of Solomon 8:6)

TAKEN in its most natural sense, this is certainly true of creature love. It is a mighty, all-constraining, irresistible passion. Even the love of friendship has proved itself occasionally to be "strong as death." "Greater love hath no man than this, that he lay down his life for his friends." (Jn. 15:13) There have been those who were willing to sacrifice their lives for their friends. Filial affection has sometimes proved to be more than a match for the terrors of the grave. Some pleasing instances are on record, worthy to be written among the golden deeds of manhood, in which brothers and sisters have seemed to contend with each other which should die first, if by chance a brother's precious life might, by such a sacrifice, be preserved. What a mighty instinct of love glows in a mother's heart! You recollect that famous story of the mother whose child was taken from her by a Jesuit missionary, to be trained separate and apart from its parents; how she swam through rivers, and passed through what seemed to be impenetrable forests, guided only by the midnight star, till she arrived at the place where her offspring was — braving death in a thousand shapes — from wild beasts and venomous serpents, from floods and jungles, from fierce men and relentless persecutors — that she might reach her child. Have there not been instances where, in the stormy blasts of winter, a mother has wrapped her garments about her infant, and, exposing herself to the fury of the elements, has sacrificed her own life that the little one might live?

Love has indeed often proved itself to be "strong as death". When merely the common passion, which burns in the breast of ordinary men and women towards each other, it has asserted its strength in a fond devotion which reckoned on no consequences, spared itself no pain, and fixed no limit to endurance, not counting life itself too dear to be parted with in so high a service. Nor do we lack painful proofs of the converse proposition, as it is stated in the second clause of our text. Jealousy has often proved itself "cruel as the grave". You have only to recall the most appalling murders that have been committed within your memory, or, if you please, those that you have read about in the history of nations, and you will find that jealousy has instigated those that were most vindictive and relentless. When jealousy begins to turn its sharp tooth on a man's heart, his reason fails him. Madness takes possession of his faculties. A determined purpose, which he would not have dared to contemplate under the influence of a well-balanced judgement, prompts, plans, and performs, almost without premeditation, an atrocious crime, when jealousy rules the cruel hour. We believe it, and we deplore it. No revenge has ever been found too bitter, too malicious, too lawless for jealousy to inflict. Relentless as the grave, it does not spare youth or beauty, respects fame or fortune, but accounts all comers as its prey. Not that these things, a phenomenon of nature, much concern the Christian minister. He has to handle these themes because they concern you as men. It is to men he speaks. He has to tell them of the salvation of Jesus Christ. It is rather the business of the mental philosopher than the faithful evangelist to take up these phenomena of the human mind. Our business is to understand these things spiritually. This Song of Songs is spiritual, or else it has no claim on our attention; for its very inspiration is incredible. We cannot imagine the Holy Spirit giving us this song merely for the purpose of entertaining us with the figures and metaphors of eastern allegory. There must be a deep and hidden meaning in it.

Now, we believe it will be fair to say that there are two high spiritual forms of love and jealousy, and that our text is lucid in its description of both — first; the love and jealousy of the saints with regard to Christ; and secondly, the love and jealousy of Christ with regard to his saints. We begin with:

I. THE LOVE AND JEALOUSY OF THE SAINTS WITH REGARD TO CHRIST.

The saints love their Lord and Master, or else they could not be saints. Love is the fountain of their saintship. They are sanctified by love. It is the love of Jesus Christ which constrains them to hate sin, leading them forward in the path of holiness. The Holy Spirit uses the same passion of love to work in us the purging of ourselves from every unhallowed thing, and to inflame our desire after everything that is agreeable to the mind of Christ. The saints have received, by the Holy Spirit, a love for Christ which is "strong as death." And how strong is death? Think for a moment how strong death is! It is so strong that the armies which lay encamped upon the field just now, and could tread an empire beneath their feet, yield to his imperial sway, and are themselves trodden beneath the feet of death. Xerxes, as he sat on his golden throne, wept at the thought that death should so soon mow down the myriads of his Persian hosts. Over all the multitudes which have been born into the world, with but two exceptions, death has swayed his sceptre. So strong is he that he has hitherto reigned as a Universal Monarch. Nor will he ever resign his sceptre until he shall come, whose kingdom shall have no end? He is indeed "the death of death, and hell's destruction." The monarchy of death is not only universal, but its commands are imperious, and instantaneously obeyed. When, at God's command, death seizes the body, it finds no power to resist. The vital energy at once ceases; the tongue of music is dumb, and the hand of skill is motionless forever. Then shall the dust return to the earth as it was, and the spirit shall return to God who gave it. (Eccl. 12:7) In vain the physician's skill; it cannot avert the stroke of death. No long siege is necessary; it requires not years, nor months, nor weeks, to scale the ramparts of a man's citadel of bodily strength. As death knocks at the door, it flies open. The arrest must be made. Willing or unwilling, the prisoner must go with the officer. The demand is peremptory, and the obedience passive. Seems it not as if nature has no parallel for this strong irresistible force of death?

Behold the love of our Lord Jesus Christ! Mark you, it is as strong as death! It can, and it does, overcome all adversaries; yes, even death itself. My brothers and sisters, it may, perhaps, strengthen your courage if I remind you that some of your comrades have tried their love in competition with death. They have "resisted unto blood, striving against sin." (Heb. 12:4) They have met with death in the cruellest forms. They were stoned, they were sawn in half, they were burned at the stake, and they were dragged at the heels of wild horses. Think of Marcus of Arethusa, stung to death by wasps, or of holy Mr. Samuel, starved to death in his dungeon with but a mouthful of bread and a drop of water given him each day, only just enough to continue his lingering existence. And yet these people who thus met death with no downy pillow to rest their head on, and with no voice of friendship to comfort them, never wavered in their attachment to their Master. They suffered persecution, and nakedness, and peril, and the sword; but nothing could separate them from the love of God, which was in Christ Jesus the Lord. (Rom. 8:38-39) Some of them met with death in the gloomiest forms, as well as in the cruellest shapes. They were cast into lonely dungeons, where it was almost literally true that "the moss grew upon their eyelids." Think of our brethren in Holland, persecuted alike by Protestants and Romanists. They have been despised of all men, and have suffered death in deep desertion. They have been thrown into dungeons, and left there till the slimy snails crawled over them, till the toads gathered rounds them, till their emaciated frames absolutely rotted and decayed in the nauseous places of their confinement. Not that they desired to escape, or sought liberty at the expense of conscience; rather, they counted it a joy that they had fallen into different trials for the sake of Christ. With none to cheer them, with no brother's voice to help them raise a tune, with no hymn to chant them on their way to public martyrdom, without an eye to look upon them except the eye of their Master, their love truly proved itself to have been "strong as death".

Still worse, I think, to bear: some of them met death in the most lingering manner. Many a man could stand on the burning faggot, endure with heroism his hour of torture, and then ascend in the chariot of Elijah up to heaven; but to be roasted before a slow fire, to be starved by a low regimen, to be breathing in a toxic atmosphere, for the martyrdom to extend over a week, a month, or a year — how could this be endured? The supernatural grace of God has made a bed of spikes into a bed of roses to some of the martyrs. Amid the flames, they even leaped and sung for very joy. That was a grand saying of one of the martyrs of Mary's age, who, when he was told by Bonner that his life would be spared if he would recant, said, "Look you here, Bishop; if I had as many lives as I have hairs on my body, I would burn as many times as that before I would bend myself down before the superstitions of Rome." Another of the martyrs, when his finger was put into the candle flame that he might feel what kind of peril he was about to encounter, told his persecutors that, if be had as much agony in all his body as he then had in his finger, he would not give up the faith which he had received from God, to adopt any of the traditions of men. Death has thus come piecemeal to a man; he has had to "die daily" (1 Cor. 15:31), in deaths often like the Apostle Paul, continually having to face the grim fiend.

The love Jesus Christ has kindled in the souls of his people has been undiminished in quantity, and undimmed in brightness. In fact, I think that the love which Christians have for Christ seems to flame the more vehemently the more troubles they have to endure. Have you never seen a chemist, when illustrating a lecture, take a small piece of solid matter [sodium], put it on some water, and the moment it touches the water it began to burn? In ordinary cases, contact with water extinguishes fire; but this substance touches the water and burns there, as it burns nowhere else. So it seems to be with the Christian. The best and most brilliant part of the Christian's love comes out under some overwhelming trouble. He triumphed, when the opportunity arose to put him to the test. "Love is strong as death."

Although you and I are not born in an age in which we are likely to attain to the distinguished honour of wearing the ruby crown of martyrdom, their example may excite our emulation. Have you, dear young friend, been subjected to, a little jeering and sneering in the workshop, or to a little harsh treatment at home? Maybe you are beginning to falter and flag. Consider yourself, then. What part do you have in that love which is strong as death if it cannot bear this? If any of you have been sorely tempted to do an unholy thing to get you out of your pecuniary embarrassments, ask yourselves, where is the love which is strong in death, and will you dare to stoop? If you do not maintain your integrity, you have not a drop of martyr's blood in you, and if you do not have the spirit of Christ, you are none of his. (Rom 8:9) When I see professors turn pale at a laugh of the thoughtless, or look terrified when some article in a newspaper or a magazine thrusts hard against their principles, I wonder how they would have behaved themselves in the great old times of Luther; or had they belonged to the school of which Calvin was the great exponent, or might it have been their chance to encounter the struggles, political and social, with which such bold reformers as John Wickliffe and Hugh Latimer were mixed up. Let not worthy sons of valiant sires pander to craven fears. Rather, let that love which is as strong as death brace your nerves, and replenish you with a divine inspiration. Doubtless, brethren, we shall have an opportunity of testing this love, though not at the ignominious stake perhaps, nor yet in the desolate prison. The average trials and troubles of life, the peculiar contingencies of each individual's career, the special besetments and temptations that pertain to a child of God — all these make it momentous to live; to live as becomes godliness. And what do you think? Can it be child's play to die? To finish one's course and to know that alterations and emendations cannot be made. Our flesh creeps at the prospect of the grave; but our soul trembles at the outlook and the judgement.

Our faith must be firm, and our fellowship unwavering; then our love will be tenacious, yes, as strong as death. You should not lose your confidence when you lose your health. The animal spirits may sink, but you are not dependent upon anything as contingent as they are in the atmosphere. The spirit that sustains you is divine. With decay comes depression; they are both the fruit of disease or of infirmity. Faith can survive, and love can triumph over both.

Jesus can make a dying bed
Feel soft as downy pillows are;
While on his breast you lean your head
And breathe your life out softly there.

(Isaac Watts)

This is what Christ can do. Do you ask what he will do? If you live to his praise, and rest in his love, you shall find that that love is strong as death. Instead of it growing cooler and weaker when the outward man decays, that love of yours will get you to the land of Beulah, and you shall sit on the banks of Jordan, expecting the coming of the Master, and singing happy canticles and blessed love-songs, even in the prospect of your departure. Love is strong as death.

I wish every Christian would think it over in his own mind whether his love for Christ is not very poor and flat compared with what it should be? It seems to me that there is a notion abroad that a Christian man may be expected to betray weakness on other points. Is it not a fact that evangelical or orthodox books are by far written in a feeble style? How many devout ministers preach a sound gospel like simple twaddle? If you want strong common-sense, you often get more of it in secular, than in religious, periodicals. The ready pen and the forcible tongue are frequently employed on the wrong side. I think the idea prevails among pious people that everything we do for Christ ought to he done in a quiet, gentle, soft, milk-sop fashion — that we must pray in a very smooth tone of voice, speak in a whisper, and sing so as not to shock anybody's nerves! This seems to me to be totally inconsistent, and utterly alien, to the spirit of genuine Christianity. When you espouse godliness, you need not renounce manliness. If anything is fitted to develop all the energies of a man's nature, and draw out all the powers and faculties of his being, it should be his enlisting on the side of King Jesus. My Master calls you to serve him, not with a timid, vacillating, fitful service, but he demands that you be bold and brave, valiant and venturesome, in his service. He provides you with strength, and may well require your diligence. 'Tis meet that you serve him with all your powers of body, soul, and spirit. The love we bear for Christ should not be a mere complacency, bland and gentle, a matter for well-bred reticence rather than for blind avowal. No; let it be a mighty, all-constraining potion that gets hold of a man like a whirlwind, and carries him along. Ah, I think this love of Jesus should be dearer to the heart than light to the eye; it should throb with every pulse of life; it should warm one's blood as it circulates through the veins; it should inflame the heart with zeal, and mould the constitution of one's soul. The gold phlegmatic man, or the supine lukewarm man, is alike unfit to engage in our Master's service. Should not the love of disciples to their Lord be stronger than the love of the husband to the wife, of the mother to her child, or of friend to friend; a love compared with which there is no love on earth to he found; a love that is strong as death? Connected with this love, and as a result of it, jealousy is brought to our notice. "Jealousy is cruel as the grave."

Whenever love absorbs the heart, jealousy will guard the object of affection. Only let a provocation occur, something of jealousy is sure to appear. Your love for Christ especially lacks the genuine stamp if it is never roused to jealousy by the malice of foes, and the faithlessness of professed friends of our Lord. Many Christians, nowadays, have a kind of love which is too fond of ease, and too full of compromise to kindle any jealousy in their breasts. The saints of olden times, how sensitive they were; how quickly their hot indignation was kindled! When Baal, the abomination of Moab, was worshipped in Israel, Moses said to the judges, "Slay ye every one his men that were joined unto Baalpeor." (Num. 25:5) So, too, at the time that the golden calf was made in the wilderness, you will remember that Moses' anger grew hot, and he stood in the gate of the camp and said, "Who is on the Lord's side, let him come unto me" (Ex. 32:26), and all the sons of Levi gathered themselves to him. At his bidding, by the word of the Lord, they took every man his sword, and went in and out from gate to gate to slay every man, his brother, his companion, and his neighbour. There fell of the people that day about three thousand men. Their love for Jehovah gave them a jealousy which was cruel as the grave in avenging idolatry. You remember how it was accounted to Phinehas, the son of Eleazar, for righteousness, that he rose against a man of Israel, a prince among the Simeonites, and thrust him through with a javelin when he was caught in sin with a Midianitish woman. (Num. 25:7-8) Such jealousy was as cruel as the grave. Men like Elijah did not say, in gentle accents, "Comprehensive charity is better than covenant truth. Give us full liberty to worship Jehovah, and you shall have perfect liberty to worship Baal." Indeed not! He contested the question with the idolatrous priests. The verdict came by fire from heaven. The frightened multitude saw it, and cried out, "Jehovah, he is the God." Then said Elijah, "Take the prophets of Baal; let not one of them escape." (1 Kings 18:39-40) This was the voice of a man who loved the Lord, who was jealous for his name, and in whom was excited in him a holy anger and a righteous enmity against the worshippers of idols. Now, under the Christian dispensation, we can have no such anger against individuals. Our Lord has taught us, by his example, that they are rather to be pitied than hated by us.

But, on the other hand, in zeal for the Lord of Hosts, and in hatred of every false way, a Christian, walking in the light of the gospel, should excel the most devout Jew under the old dispensation. Persecution is unprincipled. It violates the law of love to which we owe a supreme allegiance. But true faith never can hold fellowship with infidelity. Vital godliness must be at hostility with all the unrighteousness of men. Do we seem to speak bitterly? I suppose it never will be a very sweet thing to tell people of their faults. We should like to know whether Luther did not speak bitterly. What kind of honey did he use? Did Calvin declaim in soft and silvery tones? Did Hugh Latimer, when he encountered Popery, line his mouth with velvet, and deliver himself in delicate phrases?

What do you think, men and brethren? Did ever patriot stand upon maudlin civilities when he saw conspirators plotting against his country? Did any noble-minded philanthropist cringe with misgivings, or apologise for interfering with the miscreant libertines who defile the youth and beauty, or debauch the homes of the people? And can it be possible that any lover of God, and valiant defender of the faith ever did, or ever shall, buckle to those damnable heresies which are alike insulting to the Lord, who bought us, and destructive to the souls of men whose redemption is inestimably precious in his sight? No, but they only cared to clear themselves of the blood of souls against the last great day. What I long to see in every church is not a breach of charity between man and man, but the utter destruction of that pseudo charity which is now the curse of the Christian Church. If you have a partiality towards what Christ hates, pity for Agag, whom God abhorred, a wish to tolerate that which exalts human pride, though it be utterly derogatory to your Master; truly then, you are a traitor, however unintentionally to your Master. You do not show any wise and discriminating love for him, for if your love were vehement, you would be jealous of his crown jewels, and you would not suffer any other to be recognised as the head of the

Church but your Lord. If you love him, you will be jealous of his atonement, and you will not allow anything else to cleanse from sin but that blood he shed for our remission. If you love him, you will become jealous of his spirit, and you will not be willing that the new birth, which comes from his operations, should be set down to any mere ceremony. If you love Jesus Christ, you will be jealous of his Deity, and you will not be party to bits of bread and drops of wine being adored as the body and blood of Christ when you know that he is in the body up above, dwelling before the eternal throne. You will feel that error instead of being stared at as an object of scientific interest, like a thing to be shuddered at as a malignant disease, and to be guarded against as an epidemic. With Jezebel, you can have no peace while she loves her vicious unions. You will contend against every faction that conspires to tarnish the Redeemer's glory, and cast him down from his excellence. "Jealousy is cruel as the grave." "Hard" is the word. "Jealousy is hard as the grave." Truly, the grave is hard. It has not the slightest compunction. It holds fast the prey that Is taken by its Master. As Christians, we are, and we must be, lovers of mankind. Men we love; men we would at all times help and serve. No clime nor caste, no geographical line or national character, can define the boundary of our heart's yearning for the welfare of humanity, while we act on the commission to preach the gospel to every creature. But error we must scout, and cry out against it, and rest not day or night till the arm of God has torn it up root and branch. This seems to me to be a natural consequence of loving Christ much. If you love Christ just a little, you will hate error but little. If you do not love the truth at all, you will not hate error at all. You will say, "Oh, what does it matter? It is a mere theological dispute; let it be left to the schools to wrangle over." Not so; when you once get to think, "Such and such a truth is precious to me as my life; it is identified with any being and my well-being." From that very moment, you will be filled with a jealousy which is hard as the grave.

Turning now from our love and jealousy for our Saviour, let us speak a little about —

II. THE SAVIOUR'S LOVE AND JEALOUSY TOWARDS US.

Our Lord Jesus Christ, we know, has a love for us that passes all understanding; and, however it may seem to grate on the ear, it is equally true that he has a jealousy over his people which watches them with incessant care. I need not prove to you that the love of Jesus Christ for us is as strong as death; he verified that when he tasted death in all its bitterness — forsaken, not only by men, but, worst of all, forsaken of his God. "*Eli, Eli, lama, sabachthani*" (Mat. 27:46) was the concentration of all griefs. Such was his cry on the accursed tree. Death never made him flinch. He faced and felt its agonies extremely, and loved us then as he loved us before, and as he loves us still with infinite tenacity. The fact that his love is strong as death admits of no question. But here is the point I am coming to; his jealousy is cruel, or hard as the grave. He is never cruel towards his people, but is very hard on foe or rival that would come between his people and him — yes, hard is the grave!

Consider this, my beloved friends. You and I once cherished a self-righteousness that stood in the way of our receiving Christ. We would not look to him, nor trust him, but we loved our own works. We thought ourselves at least as good as others, and we rested there. Now, how relentless the Lord was in cutting down that self-righteousness of ours! He never gave it any quarter. How he denounced it, doomed it, and utterly destroyed it! We thought so much of it that we would have harboured it, but he would not tolerate a vestige of it. He turned our beauty into ashes and our glory into confusion of face; for he loathed our self-righteousness more than we ever loathed our uncleanness and impiety. He counted it fit neither for the land nor yet for the dunghill. How he dealt with us in severity then! What cuts and wounds we had! We were killed, some of us, by his law. We cried out of the depths to him, but still he had no pity and no mercy, apparently. We seemed to sink deeper and deeper into the mire, till, as we read the Book of Job, and the Lamentations of Jeremiah, we felt that the expressions we found there had been written on purpose for us. We tried to pray, but our prayers came back from the brazen sky, reverberating in our ears in notes of despair. We went to the house of God, but we found no comfort there. We turned to the Bible, but not a promise cheered us, for the Lord Jesus was jealous of our self-righteousness, and he would not give us a comfortable word, nor so much as one kind look till that self-righteousness was wholly gone. When that was turned out of us, oh, the love-passages, the blessed revelations of his divine grace that he then gave us! But he would not give us so much as a glance of kindness, or a sentence of cheer, until first, he had got rid of the unholy thing that provoked his jealousy.

Since then, we have had many visits from him, yet he has not, ceased to be jealous. I held interviews today with a goodly number of those who have lately found Christ, and, I observed among them, many who were brought to seek his face by the death of a husband, or a child, land in some cases, it was not only the loss of one child, but of another and another. I have frequently met with instances where a woman has been bereaved both of her child and of her husband before she yielded up her heart to Jesus. He has had to be "cruel as the grave" before he got rid of the object of his jealousy. She was wrapped up in the affections of earth; she had given herself up wholly to earthly things; and so one gourd must wither, and then another, till there was nothing earthly left to shelter her (see Jonah 4:6-10), and then the poor weeping eye was turned to the Cross, and then came consolation. Christ's jealousy is thus "cruel", but, oh, what a blessed cruelty it is! It is better to enter into life halt and maimed, and having only one hand, than having two eyes and all our friends and kinsfolk about us, to be cast into hell-fire. It is better that we should suffer from cruel providences here, than that we should be permitted to go wafting along streams of pleasure down to the gulf of everlasting ruin. Blessed cruelty that makes us love the Saviour by revealing the Saviour's inextinguishable love for us!

And since the day of our conversion, how many times you and I have cherished tastes and habits which we preferred before Christ, and the walk of faith with him! It is so easy to let the creature come in, and usurp the place of the Beloved — thus to live half for God and half for our friends. But that will not do, for God will have us all love and serve him with all our heart, and soul, and strength. Our dearest friends, the partners of our every joy and sorrow, every hope and fear of our mortal lives, if they take away our hearts from Christ, will either prove a bane to us, or else they will be taken away from us. I recollect the story of a Christian woman who had made a great idol of her child. He was her only son, and she lost him. Nothing then would console her, till at length, one day, she went into a Quaker meeting. She sat there a long time, and not a word was spoken. Presently, one of the members rose up and simply said, "Verily I perceive thy children are idols." Not another word was uttered during the whole of the meeting. That word, however, was sent by the providence of God, and fastened like a nail in the right place. It had done its work; the mother's heart was comforted; she saw the reason for her loss, and submitted her soul to the discipline. Now it is not children only of which we make idols. There are twenty other things. Twenty, did I say? Why, the world is swarming with idols! Man is such an idolater that, if he cannot idolise anything else, he will idolise himself, and set himself up, and bow down and worship himself. But the Lord Jesus will never tolerate idolatry in any heart that belongs to him. If he did not love you, you might do as you liked; but if he loves you, and has chosen you, and your heart then goes after idols, he will chasten you, vindicating his affection, as well as his authority, with the rod. What would it matter to me what your children did, in comparison with the responsibility I feel for my own? Whatever mischief they might do in the street, I might not feel called on to interfere. You and I alike feel that we are each accountable to punish our own children when they are naughty. And so is it with God. If you were not his children, you might live as you wish, and enjoy a measure of immunity for a while. But if you are his people, you are not your own masters, and you will have a cross, if not a curse, come into your house. The spell of the idol will spoil your blessing. "Jealousy is cruel as the grave."

Yet, let me say it again, this is blessed cruelty. We are very apt to think that a surgeon must have a hard heart and a cruel nature when we take a shallow view of the operations he performs, and the nerve with which he performs them. A better judgement might convince you that the surgeon's knife is dictated by necessity, wielded with skill, careful to spare pain, and designed to restore health. "Oh", you say, "only amputation will save life; my child's leg must be taken off, it is festering; it is mortifying; I could not touch it, I could not do it, it cannot be done." And when you hear that the surgeon has cut through the flesh and bone, you are apt to think, "What a cold heart he must have!" Ah, but which is the more profitable, that love of yours that would let the child die rather than do violence to its feeling, or that which would cut off its leg, in spite of all entreaties, to save its life? Oh, thank God for the surgeon! His deep incisions are tender mercies; his misgiving would be our undoing. And has not our God thus to deal with us when he takes those things from us which tend to fatal issues, and might otherwise prove our destruction? A fable has been sometimes told of a little plant which grew under a big tree, and was shielded by it from the storm, and kept tranquil and happy. The little plant prayed that it might grow into a tree, and its prayer was heard. The woodman came along and cut down the tree. Then the poor plant was exposed to the shower, and the wind, and the snow, and the frost, and it said, "Alas for me! I am left in a pitiful condition." But the angel of the tree told it that was the only way by which it could ever grow into a tree. So, dear friends, when you lost your property, when the bank broke, when you lost your friend, when your mother died, when you lost, perhaps, your reputation through a slander which went abroad, it was only the taking down of the tree that the plant might grow, which could not have grown in any other way. The discipline of nature is harsh and cruel, you may think. Ah well, the Lord lets you think as you like, misjudge him if you please, for he knows that time will soon correct your judgement, and then you will think very differently as you see the end from the beginning. You will judge more wisely now when your faith is brought into active exercise. You yourself will then begin to abhor idolatry as Christ does, and will marvel as much with thankfulness as thoughtfulness that it is taken away. I have been reminded by this of what Rutherford said to Lady Erskine when she lost her husband. "Well, your ladyship", he said, "the Lord Jesus Christ sets great store by your love, for it is clear that he will have it all; he has taken away those who might have had a part of it, and he said, 'I will have it all! I have bought it, and I will have it.'" Perhaps the Master has been doing the same, or will do the same, with some of us, so that he may get all our hearts to himself.

Now for our practical conclusion. Let our jealousy towards Christ now be cruel as the grave. Is there anything which keeps our heart from perfectly loving Christ? Let us have done with it at once. Have you got into any habit which keeps you from living near to Jesus? Is there any favourite sin which mars your communion with him? Have you any little practice which, in itself, may be excusable, but which, in its tendency, may be injurious? Give it all up. Whoever is poor for Christ's sake is richer than the richest of men, and whoever gives up a pleasure for the sake of Christ has more enjoyment in so doing than he would ever have had in the pleasure itself. It may be that you have been for some time trifling with a conviction which you have embraced as a truth, only it would have involved a sacrifice; therefore, you have halted and wittingly overlooked it. I know there are very many Christians just now who are in a position which they cannot justify, but they say they cannot see their way out of it. They apologise for themselves with questioning like this: "How am I to get right? What shall I do?" Now, dear friends, ask yourselves, does not the Lord Jesus Christ deserve to have from you simple, absolute, unhesitating obedience? "Yes", say you. Then yield it to him, and ask grace, that from this day on you may look with holy jealousy on the most pleasant things that in, any form or disguise, come between you and your Lord and Master. Oh, what a happy life, what a blessed life you would lead! Yours will be a path of separation. You may have to journey over a rough road. Nevertheless, let your love be strong as death, and your jealousy cruel as the grave, and you will enjoy a communion with Christ dearer than life, and a Sabbath of peace that is like the days of heaven on earth. Well, my dear hearers, there are some of you who have no part nor lot in the inheritance that we esteem beyond all other possessions. May God give you a share in it!

Oh, if you have no love for Christ in this life, what can there be for you in the next but a fearful looking for judgement and fiery indignation! (Heb. 10:27) But trust in Jesus, trust in Jesus, and you will be saved. Being saved, you will love him, and, loving him, you will be jealous of everything that comes in the way to divide you from him. You will be with him at last in the land where doubts and fears can never enter, and where jealousy can no longer intrude. Thus you shall be forever with the Lord. Amen.

79. THE SHULAMITE'S CHOICE PRAYER
NO. 364

DELIVERED ON SUNDAY EVENING, FEBRUARY 24TH, 1861
AT NEW PARK STREET, SOUTHWARK

"Set me as a seal upon thine heart, as a seal upon thine arm: for love is strong as death; jealousy is cruel as the grave: the coals thereof are coals of fire, which hath a most vehement flame. Many waters cannot quench love, neither can the floods drown it." (Song of Solomon 8:6-7)

THIS is the prayer of one who has the present enjoyment of fellowship with Christ, but, being apprehensive lest this communion should be interrupted, she avails herself of the opportunity now afforded her to plead for something which shall act as the abiding token of a covenant between her and her beloved, when his visible presence is withdrawn.

You will notice that this is not the cry of a soul that is longing for fellowship, for that cry is — "Tell me O thou whom my soul loveth, where thou feedest." (Song 1:7) It is not even the cry of the soul that has some fellowship and needs more, for then it would say, "Oh that thou wert as my brother!" (Song 8:1) Nor is it the cry of a soul that has had fellowship, but has lost it for that is, "Saw ye him, whom my soul loveth?" (Song 3:3) And she goes "about the streets and in the broad ways" saying, "I will seek him." (Song 3:2) But this is the prayer of the spouse when she has been coming up from the wilderness, leaning upon his bosom. The thought strikes her that he that has sustained her is about to go from her, to depart and leave her for a season, because it is expedient and more useful for her; and she prays that, since he is no more in the earth, but has entered into the ivory palaces where her God dwells, that he would be pleased to make a covenant with her never to forget her, and that he would give here some sign and mark by which she might be well assured that she is very near to his heart, and still written on his arm. I take it to be the prayer of the Church at the present day, now that Christ is before the Father's throne. The Bridegroom is not with us; he has left us, gone to prepare a place for us, and is coming again. We are longing for his coming; we are saying in the language of the last verse of this Song of Songs, "Make haste, my beloved, and be thou like to a roe or to a young hart upon the mountains of spices." Yet before he went, it seemed as if his Church prayed to him, "Set me as a seal upon thine heart, as a seal upon thine arm." (Song 8:6) And this is the cry of the Church to-night, and I trust your cry too, that while he is not present but is absent from you, you may be near to him, and have a sweet consciousness of that blessed fact.

Now, without preface, let me first notice *the prayer*, and secondly, *the reasoning with which the spouse argues her suit*. The prayer is, "Set me as a seal upon thine heart, as a seal upon thine arm." The argument is four-fold: she pleads in this way — "Love is strong as death;" she gets bolder — "Jealousy is cruel as the grave"; she wrestles again — "The coals thereof are coals of fire, which hath a most vehement flame"; and yet once again, she brings out her choice words: "Set me as a seal upon thine heart, for many waters cannot quench thy love, neither can the floods drown it."

I. THE PRAYER, you will notice, is two-fold, although it is really and essentially one — "Set me as a seal upon thine heart, as a seal upon thine arm."

Now I think I can perhaps explain this text best by a reference to the high priest of old. You know that when he put on his holy garments — those robes of glory and beauty — he wore the breast-plate of cunning work in which four rows of precious stones were set. If you will turn to Exodus, chapter thirty-nine, and verse fourteen, you read, "And the stones were according to the names of the children of Israel, twelve, according to their names, like the engravings of a signet, every one with his name, according to the twelve tribes." How suggestive of this prayer! — "Set me as a seal or as an engraved signet, as a precious stone that has been carved — set my name upon thy breast." Let it be always glittering there! But beside this breast-plate, there was the ephod, and we are told that "they made shoulder-pieces for it, to couple it together; by the two edges was it coupled together." Then, in the sixth verse, we read: "And they wrought onyx stones inclosed in ouches of gold, graven, as signets are graven, with the names of the children of Israel; and he put them on the shoulders of the ephod, that they should be stones for a memorial to the children of Israel; as the Lord commanded Moses." So it was set as a signet on his shoulder, or on his arm, as well as on his heart. I think these were to indicate that the high priest loved the people, for he bore them on his heart; and that he served the people as a consequence of that love, therefore he bore them on his shoulders. And I think the prayer of the spouse is just this — she would know once for all that Christ's heart is entirely hers, and that he loved her with the intensity and the very vitality of his being; that his inmost heart, the life-spring of his soul, belonged to her. And she would also know that that love moved his arm. She longed to see herself as supported, sustained, strengthened, defended, preserved, and kept by that same strong arm which put Orion in its place in the sky (Amos 5:8), and holds the Pleiades (Job 38:31), that they should give their light for evermore. She longed that she may know the love of his heart, and that she may experience the power of his arm. Can we not, each of us, join the spouse in this prayer to night?

Oh, Lord, let me know that my name is engraved on your heart; not only let it be there, but let me know it! Write my name not only in your heart, but may it be as a signet on your heart that I may see it. Doubtless, there are the names of very many written on Christ's heart, who have not yet been able to see their names there; they are there but not written as on a signet. Christ has loved them from all eternity. His heart has been set on them from everlasting, but as yet they have never seen the signet. They have never had the seal of the Spirit to witness within that they are born of God. While their names may be in his heart, they have not seen them there as a seal on his heart. And, no doubt, there are multitudes for whom Christ has fought and conquered, and whom he daily keeps and preserves, who have never seen their names written as a seal on his arm. Their prayer is that they may see Christ's love visibly, that they may discover it in their experience, and that it may be beyond question and no more a matter of doubt, that his hand and his heart are engaged for their eternal salvation. I repeat it, you can all join in this prayer you people of God; it is a cry that you should put up now, and continue to put up till it is fully answered. Oh, let me know, my Lord, that I am yours, bound to your heart, and let me know that I am yours, protected and preserved by your arm. This is the prayer, then; I shall say no more about it because I wish to speak more at length on the arguments with which it is here pleaded.

II. The spouse argues with her Lord like this: It is to my advantage that you should thus write my name on your hand and heart, for I know this concerning your love, that it is *strong*, that it is firm, that it maintains a wonderful intensity, and that it has a sure and unquenchable eternity.

With these four pleas, she backs up her suit.

1. She pleads that he would show her his love because of the *strength* of it. "Thy love is strong as death." Some expositors think that this refers to the Church's love. Others say, "No, it means the love of Christ to his Church." I am not sure how to determine which it means, for they are extremely like each other. Christ's love to his Church is the magnificent image; the affection which his people bear to him is the beautiful miniature. They are not alike in degree and measure, for the Church never loves Christ as much as Christ loves her, but, they are as much alike as the father in his strength is to the babe in weakness; there is the same image and superscription. The love of the Church to Christ is the child of Christ's love for the Church, and, consequently, there is something of the same attribute in both; and while it is true that Christ's love for us is so strong that he defied and endured death for us, it is true also that the love of the Church for him is as strong as death. Her chosen sons and daughters have endured the pangs of the rack and the pains of the sword, and have gone through a thousand deaths sooner than be turned aside from their chaste fidelity to their Lord. I shall, however, keep to the first idea that this is the love of Christ, and shall use it in this way as being the plea of his Church that, because his love is strong, she desires to be certified of her interest in it, and to see most visibly the signet and seal of her being really in his heart. "Love is strong as death." What a well-chosen emblem this is! What beside love is as strong as death! With steadfast foot, Death marches over the world. No mountains can restrain the invasion of this all-conquering king. There is no chalet on a mountain Alp so high that his foot cannot climb to hunt the inhabitant. There is no valley so fair that he does not intrude and stalk, as a grim skeleton across the plain. Everywhere, and in every place beneath the moon, do you hold sway, O death! The lordly lion bows his neck to you. Leviathan yields up his course which floats many a rood [an old measurement] on the briny waves. (Is 27:1) You are the great fisher. You have put your hook into his jaw and dragged him from the sea. Master of all you are! You have dominion given to you. You wear an iron crown, and dash in pieces as though they were just potter's vessels, the strongest of the sons of men. None among the sons of Adam can withstand Death's insidious advances.

When his hour has come, none can bid death a delay. The most clamorous prayers cannot move the flinty heart of Death. Insatiable, and not to be appeased, he ever devours and devours. That scythe is never blunted, that hour-glass never ceases to flow. Mightiest among the mighty are you, O Death. But Christ's love is "strong as death". It too can climb the mountain and lay hold on the mountaineer, far removed from the sound of the ministration of the gospel. It too can march into the valley, and though Popery, with all its clouds of darkness, should cover it, yet the love of Christ can will its glorious way. What can stand against it? The stoutest must yield to it, and adamantine hearts are dashed to shivers by one blow of its golden hammer. As the sun dissolves the chains of frost, and bids the will rush on in freedom, though once bound, as if it were stone, so does this love of Christ. Wherever it comes, it give life and joy, and liberty, and snaps the bonds, and has its way, never being retarded, never being hindered, because it is written "I will have mercy on whom I will have mercy and I will have compassion on whom I will have compassion." (Rom. 9:15)

Who can measure the strength of Christ's love? Men have defied it, but their defiance has been overcome. They have resisted long, but they have been compelled to throw down their weapons. They have crossed it, but they have found it hard to kick against the pricks. (Acts 9:5, 26:14) They have gone on caring for none of these things, but thus the eternal counsel has decreed it — Christ must, he shall have, that redeemed man, and he has had him. Jesus Christ's love is strong as death. Sooner might a man live, after God's will had decreed that he should die, than a sinner remain impenitent one hour after God's love had decreed to melt his heart. Sooner might you defy the grave, and hurl back on his haunches the pale horse of Death (Rev. 6:8), than turn back the Holy Spirit when he comes in his divine omnipotence to lay hold on the heart and soul of man. As all the owls and bats with all their hootings could not scare back the sun when once its hour to rise has come, so all the sins, and fears, and troubles of man, cannot turn back the light of love when God decrees that it should shine on the heart. "Stronger than death" his love is found to be.

Death is but weakness itself when compared with the love of Christ. What a sweet reason why I should have a share in it! What a blessed argument for me to use before the throne of God! Lord, if your love is so strong, and my heart so hard, and myself so powerless to break it, oh, let me know your love, that it may overcome me, that it may enchain me with its sure but soft fetters, and that I may be your willing captive evermore!

But let me notice here that, when the spouse says that Christ's love is strong as death, you must remember that she may, in faith, have foreseen that it would one day be tried which was the strongest. You know, do you not, that these two once entered into the lists to try their strength; and it was a struggle, sure, upon which angels gazed. Jesus — I mean incarnate love — at the first, seemed to shrink before death. "He sweat as it were, great drops of blood falling to the ground." (Lk. 22:44) You cannot see the brow of his antagonist, but could you have perceived it? Death — then invaded — was trembling more than Christ — the invader. Christ had the prophecy of victory, but Death — the fates were against it. Well do you remember that story of how the Saviour's back was ploughed, his hands pierced, and his side opened? Death — I think I see the flush that crossed his pale face as he thought that he had gained the victory, but Jesus triumphed. Love reigned, while Death lays prostrate at his feet. Strong as Death indeed was Jesu's love, for he swallowed up Death in victory; not merely overcame it, but seemed to devour it, to make nothing of it, and put it away once and for all. "O Death," said Love, "I will be your plague! O grave, I will be your destruction!" And Love has kept its word, and proved itself to be "strong as Death."

Well, beloved, we may add to these few remarks this word. Rest assured that as Death will not give up its prey, so neither will Love. How hard and firm does Death hold its captives! Till that resurrection trump shall set loose their bonds, none shall go free. Their ashes he preserves as carefully as a king keeps the jewels of his crown. He will not allow one of them to escape, as Israel did out of the land of Pharaoh. In the house of bondage, there they must lie. And is not Christ's love as strong as this? He shall keep his own. Those who are his, he never will let go. No, when the archangel's trump shall dissolve the grasp of death, then shall be heard the cry, "Father, I will that they also whom thou hast given me be with me where I am." (Jn. 17:24) And when Death itself is dead, Love shall prove its eternal strength by taking its captives home. Love then, is strong as Death. Lord Jesus, let me feel that love; let me see your arm nerved with it, and your heart affected by this strong love, which all my enemies cannot defeat, which all my sins cannot overturn, which all my weakness cannot defy. I think this is a most sweet and powerful argument to lead you to pray the prayer, and one you will use when you are pleading before God.

2. Let us now turn to the second plea — "Jealousy is cruel as the grave." Friedrich Krummacher, in a sermon on this passage, following the translation of Martin Luther, quotes it as though it ran like this — "Jealousy is firm as hell"; and I believe that such is the proper translation, at least quite as correct as the present one — "Jealousy is firm as hell." Those of you who have Bibles with the margins in them (and the margins are generally like fine gold) will perceive the words in the corner, "Hebrew, *hard*" — "Jealousy is hard as the grave", which is just the idea of firmness; it is as firm as the grave. *Sheol*, I believe the word is here for *grave*, otherwise we translate it "Hades" — the place of separated souls without reference to good or evil — or, as Luther translates it — "hell". "Jealousy is hard as hell." The idea is just this, that the love of Christ, in the form of jealousy, is as hard and as sternly relentless as is the grave and hell. Now, hell never looses one of its bond-slaves. Once let the iron gate be shut upon the soul, there is no escape. When the ring of fire has once girdled the immortal spirit, none can dash through the flaming battlements. The dungeon is locked. The key is dashed into the abyss of destiny, and never can be found.

Fixed is their everlasting state,
Could they repent 'tis now too late.

(Joseph Hart)

"Escape for thy life, look not behind thee" (Gen. 19:7) is a cry that may be uttered on earth, but which can never be heard in hell. Those who are once there are there forever and forever. That modern doctrine of the restoration of damned souls has no foundation in the Word of God. It is a dream, and they shall find it so who once enter that place. "Where their worm dieth not, and where their fire is not quenched" (Mk. 9:44, 46, 48) — a more perfect picture of an unrelenting seizure could not be found anywhere. The firmness and hardness of the grave and hell are without abatement. When once they have got their hands on their prey, they hold it with a tenacity that defies resistance. Well, but such also is the love of Christ. If just now we had to speak of its strength, we have now to speak of its tenacity, its hardness, its attachment to those whom it has chosen. You may sooner unlock Hades and let out the spirits that are in prison there, than you could ever snatch one from the right hand of Christ. You may sooner rob death of its prey than Jesus of his purchased ones. You may spoil the lion's den, but shall the lion of the tribe of Judah be so spoken of? Shall the prey be taken from the mighty, and the lawful captive delivered? Before one child of God shall be lost, you shall go first and make death relax its grasp, and then, next, you shall make hell, with all its fury, give up its prey. As soon as ever it can be proved that one child of God perishes, it can be proved that the fires of hell can be put out; but, until then, there shall never be a shadow of a fear of that. As certainly as ever lost souls are lost, so certainly believing souls are saved.

Oh, little do they know the love of Christ who think that he loves today and hates tomorrow! He is no such lover as that. Even earthly worms would despise such affection. Is Christ's affection a play of fast and loose? Does he choose, and then refuse; does he justify, and then condemn? Does he press to his bosom, and afterwards reject with distaste? It is not so. If you have seen Niagara in its tremendous strength, leaping from its rock into the depths beneath, you might conceive some hand bidding it leap back, or staying it in its mid-flight. Some mighty imagination might conceive that stream staying in its course, and made to ascend and climb the hills, instead of leaping downwards in its strength; but even then, no imagination can conceive the love of Christ retracing its eternal pathway. The divine fury which is in it drives it on and on; it must go as it has begun. The love of Christ is like an arrow which has been shot from the bow of destiny; it flies, it flies, and heaven itself cannot change its course. Christ has decreed it: such men shall be his, and his they shall be; nor will he turn one of them away, or make a new election, or plan a new redemption, or bring those to heaven whom he never intended to bring, or lose those whom he ordained to save. He has said it, and he will do it. He has commanded his covenant forever, and it shall stand fast. He will have compassion on whom he will have compassion, and he will have mercy on whom he will have mercy.

You have then, here, another reason why you should pray that your name may be on Christ and on his arm — once there, it is there forever. So surely there, so jealously there, so hardly there, so fixedly there, it can never be removed, come what may. Christ is jealous of his people; he will not let another have his spouse. He will not sit still and see the prince of darkness walking off with her whom he espoused to himself in the eternal ages. The supposition is absurd! That cruel jealousy of his would make him start up from his heavenly repose to snatch his chosen spouse from him who would seek to lead her to the hellish altar. She shall not be divorced from him; she must not be married to another.

O love divine, how sweet Thou art!
When shall I find my willing heart
All taken up by Thee?
I thirst, I faint, I die to prove
The greatness of redeeming love,
The love of Christ to me.

Stronger His love than death or hell;
Its riches are unsearchable;
The first-born sons of light
Desire in vain its depths to see;
They cannot reach the mystery,
The length, and breadth, and height.

God only knows the love of God;
O that it now were shed abroad
In this poor stony heart!
For love I sign, for love I pine;
This only portion, Lord, be mine,
Be mine this better part!

O that I could forever sit
With Mary at the Master's feet!
Be this my happy choice:
My only care, delight, and bliss,
My joy, my heaven on earth, be this –
To hear the Bridegroom's voice!

(Charles Wesley)

3. If the love of Christ is strong as death, if it be such that it can never be moved from its object, yet the question arises, may not the love itself die out? Even should it abide the same in its purpose, yet may not its intensity be diminished? "No", says the Shulamite, "it is an attribute of Christ's love that its coals are coals of fire which have a most vehement flame." More forcible is the language of the original — "The coals thereof are the coals of God" — a Hebrew idiom to express the most glowing of all flames — the coals of God! — as though it were no earthly flame, but something far superior to the most vehement affection among men. Some who look carefully at it think there is an allusion in this sentence to the fire which always burnt at the altar, and which never went out. You remember, there were coals of fire which were always kept burning under the Levitical dispensation. The flame was originally kindled by fire from heaven, and it was the business of the priest perpetually to feed it with the sacred fuel. You will remember, too, that one of the cherubim flew and took a live coal from off this very altar, and said to Isaiah, "Lo, this hath touched thy lips." (Is. 6:7) Now, the love of Christ is like the coals on the altar which never went out. But the spouse has brought out a fuller idea than this. She seems to say, "Its vehemence never decreases; it is always burning to its utmost intensity." Nebuchadnezzar's furnace was heated seven times hotter, but no doubt it grew cool; Christ's love is like the furnace, but it is always at the seven-fold heat, and always has within it its own fuel. It is not like fire merely, but like coals of fire, always having that within itself which supports it.

Why did Christ love the spouse? What lit the fire at first? He kindled it himself. There was no reason whatever why Christ should love any of us, except the love of his own heart. And what is the fuel that feeds the fire? Your works and mine? No, brethren, no, no, a thousand times no! All the fuel comes from the same place; it is all from his heart. Now, if the flame of Christ's love depends on anything we did, if it were fed with our fuel, it would either die out, or else it would sometimes dwindle as the smoking flax, and then again it might kindle to a vehement heat. But since it depends on itself, and has the pure attributes of divinity, it is a self-existent love, absolute and independent of the creature. Well, then, may we understand that it never shall grow less, but always be as a vehement flame.

Now, I do not want to preach about this, but I wish you would think of it a little. Christian, turn it over in your mind — Christ loves you, not a little, not a little as a man may love his friend, not even as a mother may love her child, for she may forget the infant of her womb. He loves you with the highest degree of love that is possible; and what more can I say, except I add, he loves you with a degree of love that is utterly impossible for man. No finite mind could, if it should seek to measure it, get any idea whatever of the love of Christ towards us. You know, when we come to measure a drop with an ocean, there is a comparison. A comparison I say there is, though we should hardly be able to get at it; but when you attempt to measure our love with Christ's, the finite with the infinite, there is no comparison at all. Though we love Christ ten thousand times as well as we do, there would even then be no comparison between our love for him and his love to us. Can you believe this now — "Jesus, loves *me*?" Why, to be loved by others here often brings a tear to one's eye; it is sweet to have the affection of one's fellow. But to be loved by God, and to be loved to an intense degree — so loved that you have to leave it as a mystery that the soul cannot fathom — you cannot tell how much! Be silent, O my soul! Be silent too before your God, and lift up your soul in prayer in this way — "Jesus, take me into this sea of love, and let me be ravished by a sweet and heavenly contentment, in a sure confidence that you have loved me, and given yourself for me."

4. We shall now turn to the last argument of this choice prayer, which is equally precious. It is the *unquenchable eternity of this love*. There is that in its very essence which defies any opposite quality to extinguish it. The argument seems to me to run thus — "Yes, but if Christ's love does not die out of itself — if it has such intensity that it never would of itself fail, yet may not you and I put it out?" No, says the text, "Many waters cannot quench love, neither can the floods drown it." Christ has endured many waters already — the waters of bodily affliction, the waters of soul travail, the waters of spiritual desertion. Christ was in this world like Noah's ark; the depths came up from beneath, hell troubled him; the great water-floods came from above; it pleased the Father to bruise him. The cataracts leaped on him from either side; he was betrayed by his friends, and he was hunted by his foes. But the many waters could no more destroy his love than it could drown the ark of gopher wood. Just as that ark mounted higher, and higher, and higher, the more the floods prevailed; so then, that love of Christ seemed to rise higher, and higher, and higher, just in proportion to the floods of agony that sought to put it out. Fixed and resolved to bring his ransomed home, the captain of our salvation becomes perfect through suffering, plunges into the thick of the battle, and comes out of it more than conqueror. And oh, since then, my beloved, what floods has Christ's love endured! There have been the floods of our sins, and the many waters of our blasphemy and ungodliness. Since conversion, there have been the many waters of our backslidings, and the floods of our unbelief. What crime on crime, what transgression on transgression, have we been guilty of! Yet he has never failed us up to this moment. "By the grace of God, we are what we are. And we are persuaded that neither life, nor death, nor things present, nor things to come, nor angels, nor principalities, nor powers, nor height, nor depth nor any other creature shall be able to separate us from the love of God which is in Christ Jesus our Lord." What if we should be tried in circumstances? "Neither famine, nor persecution, nor nakedness, nor peril, nor sword, shall be able to separate from the love of Christ." (Rom. 8:39) What if we backslide and wander from his ways? "Though we believe not, he abideth faithful." (2 Tim. 2:13) And what if in the last black hour we should have bitter sufferings on the dying bed? Still he shall be with us in the last moment, for it is written, "The last enemy that shall be destroyed is death." (1 Cor. 15:26) So you see Death is to be destroyed, and we are to be victors over him. Gather up, then, all the thoughts of how we have tried, and how are shall try, the Master, and let us set to our seal tonight our own solemn "Yea and Amen" to this most precious declaration of the Shulamite. "Many waters cannot quench love neither can the floods drown it." Then, Lord, write my name on your heart, engrave my name as a signet on tour arm that I may have a share in this unfailing and undying affection, and be yours now, and shine forever.

Poor sinner! I know you have been saying, while I have been preaching thus, — "I wish I had a share in that love." Well, this prayer you may pray tonight:

"Set me — it is a black name — set me as a seal on your heart, as a seal on your arm. Love me, Lord. Help me, Lord. Let your heart move towards me; let your arm move for me, too. Think of me, Lord, and set me on your heart. Work for me, Lord; set me on your arm. Lord. I long to have your love, for I hear it is as strong as death, and you know I am chained by Satan, and am his bond-slave. Come and deliver me: you are more than a match for my cruel tyrant. Come with your strong love, and set me free. I hear that your love is firm too, as hell itself. Lord, that is the love I want! Though I know I shall vex you, and wander from you, come and love me with a love that is firm and everlasting. O Lord, I feel there is nothing in me that can make you love me. Come and love me, then, with that love which finds its own fuel. Love me with those coals of fire which have a 'vehement flame'. And since many waters cannot quench your love, prove that in me; for there are many waters of sin in me, but Lord, help me to believe that your love is not quenched by them; there are many corruptions in me, but, Lord, love me with that love which my corruptions cannot quench. Here, Lord, I give myself away; take me; make me what you would have me to be; and keep and preserve me even to the end."

May the Lord help you to pray that prayer, and then may he answer it for his mercy's sake!

80. UNPURCHASABLE LOVE

NO. 2466

AT THE METROPOLITAN TABERNACLE, NEWINGTON,
ON THURSDAY EVENING, JUNE 6TH, 1872

"If a man would give all the substance of his house for love, it would utterly be contemned." (Song of Solomon 8:7)

THAT is a general truth, applying to all forms of real love; for you cannot purchase love. If it is true love, it will not run on rails of gold. Many a marriage would have been a very happy one if there had been a tithe as much love as there was wealth; and, sometimes, love will come in at the cottage door, and make the home bright and blest, when it refuses to recline on the downy pillows of the palace. Men may give all the substance of their house, and form a marriage bond; the bond may be there, but not that which will make it sweet to wear. "If a man would give all the substance of his house for love, it would utterly be contemned." Who, for instance, could purchase a mother's love? She loves her own child specially because it is her own; she watches over it with sedulous [careful] care, she denies herself the necessary sleep at night if her babe goes sick, and she would be ready to part with her own life sooner than it should die. Bring her someone else's child, and endow her with wealth to induce her to love it, and you will find that it is not in her power to transfer her affection to the son or daughter of a stranger. Her own child is exceedingly precious to her, and another infant, that to an unprejudiced eye might be thought to be a far more comely babe, shall receive tenderness from her, for the woman is compassionate, but it can never receive the love that belongs to her own offspring.

Take again, even the love of friends. I only instance that just to show how true our text is in relation to all forms of love. Damon loved Pythias; the two friends were so bound together that their names became household words, and their conduct towards one another grew into a proverb. Yet Damon never purchased the heart of Pythias, neither did Pythias think to pay a yearly stipend for the love of Damon. The introduction of the question of cost would have spoilt it all; the very thought of anything mercenary, anything like payment on one side, or receipt on the other, would have been a death-blow to their friendship No; if a man should give all the substance of his house even for human love, for the common love that exists between man and man, it would utterly be despised.

Rest assured that this is pre-eminently true when we get into higher regions, when we come to think of the love of Jesus, and when we think of that love which springs up in the human breast towards Jesus whenever the Spirit of God has renewed the heart, and shed abroad the love of God within the soul. (Rom. 5:5) Neither Christ's love for us nor our love for him can be purchased; neither of those could be bartered for gold, or rubies, or diamonds, or the most precious crystals. If a man should offer to give all the substance of his house for either of these forms of love, it would be utterly despised.

I. We will begin at the highest manifestation of love, and commune together with it. So let me say, firstly, that THE LOVE OF OUR LORD JESUS CHRIST IS ALTOGETHER UNPURCHASABLE.

This fact will be clear to us if we give it a moment's careful thought. Indeed, so clear is it that I scarcely like to multiply words on it, and I do so only that you may dive the deeper into this glorious truth. It must be quite impossible to purchase the love of Christ, because *it is inconceivable that he could ever be mercenary.* It would be profane, surely, it would amount to blasphemy, and a very high degree of it, to suppose that the love of his heart could be bought with gold, or silver, or earthly stores. No, if he loves, it must be all free, like his own royal self. If he deigns to cast his eye so far downward as to view the creatures of an hour, and set his love on them so that his delight is with the sons of men. It is not possible that he could gain anything from them. No, were we angels, we could not think that he could love us because of some service we render, or some price we pay to him. The bare idea runs cross-counter to all we know of Jesus; it is a flat contradiction of all our beliefs and all our knowledge concerning him. He loves us because he pities us, but not because there is a fee when he comes to us as the great Physician.

He instructs us because he grieves over our ignorance, and because he knows the sorrow of it, and would have us learn of him; but his instructions are not given in order that we may each one bring our school pence to him. He labours, it is true; but none can say that he labours for hire; though if he asked all worlds for his hire, he might well claim them for such labours as those which he has performed. The feats attributed to Hercules are nothing compared with the wonders wrought by Christ. He has cleansed stables far more filthy than the Augean, and slain monsters far more terrible than the hydra-headed demons of the ancient fables. True, "He *shall* see of the travail of his soul, and shall be satisfied" (Is. 53:11). There was a joy that was set before him, for which he endured the cross, despising the shame (Heb. 12:2); yet the love that lay at the bottom of it all was love unsought, and love unsought, and love in which not so much as a single atom of anything like selfishness could ever be discovered. The pure stream of his love leaps like a crystal rill [small stream], and there is no sediment that can be found in it; it is altogether unmixed love for us.

Besides, brethren, there is another point that renders this idea of purchasing Christ's love as impossible as the first thought shows it to be incredible; *for all things are already Christ's*. Therefore, what can be given to him with which to purchase his love? If he were poor, we might enrich him; but all things are his. "He was rich", (2 Cor. 8:9) says the Apostle; "he is rich" we may also reply. He could say to us, at this moment, if we were so foolish as to attempt to bribe him to win the love of his heart, "I will take no bullock out of thy house, nor he-goats out of thy folds. For every beast of the forest is mine, and the cattle upon a thousand hills. I know all the fowls of the mountain: and the wild beasts of the field are mine. If I were hungry, I would not tell thee: for the world is mine, and the fullness thereof." (Ps. 50:9-10) All things are Christ's, not only on this speck of a world, but throughout the universe. The things that are seen by us are as nothing compared with the things that we have not seen; yet all belong to Christ, and he has the power to create ten thousand times more than ever yet have been formed by him. There is nothing which he conceives in his infinite mind but he could at once fashion by his almighty power; there is nothing he might desire but he could, in an instant, command it to appear before him. "Let it be", he might say, and it would be even as he had said. With what, then, could you bribe him, and where is the substance of your houses that you would give in exchange for his divine love? O you who dwell in houses of clay, where is the substance which you could bring to him who is Lord of heaven and earth? Our substance? It is but a shadow. Our wealth? It is a child's plaything in his sight; it is nothing compared with his boundless riches.

Let us also note that, if Christ's love could be won by us by something we could bring to him, or do for him, it would suppose that there was something of ours that was of equal merit and of equal value with his love, or, at any rate, *something which he was willing to accept as bearing some proportion to his love*. But, indeed, there is nothing of the sort. Gold and silver — I scarcely like to mention them in the same connection with the love of Christ — I am sure that our poet Philip Doddridge was right when he said,

Yes, thou art precious to my soul,
My transport, and my trust;
Jewels to thee are gaudy toys,
And gold is sordid dust.

Think of the difference between gold and the love of Christ in the hour of pain, in the hour of depression of spirit; what can the strong boxes of the merchants do for him then? But one drop of the love of Christ helps him to bear up, however fast the heart may palpitate, or however much the spirits may have been cast down. What is the use of earthly riches when one comes to die? One laid his money bags close to his heart to see if they could make a plaster that would give him rest, but they were hard and cold. But the love of Jesus, like the touch of the king's hand in the old superstition, heals even the disease of death itself, and makes it no longer death to die. There is nothing, then, by way of treasure that could be compared with the love of Christ. I will say it, and every believer here will agree with me, that there is no emotion we have ever felt in our most sanctified moments, there is no holy desire that has ever flashed through our soul in our most hallowed times, there is no seraphic longing that has ever been begotten in us when the Spirit of God has been most operative in our hearts, that we should dare to put side by side with the love of Christ, and say that it was at all fit to be reckoned as a fair price for it. Our best is not one-thousandth part as good as Christ's worst. Our gold is not equal to his clay. There is nothing that can be found in us, or that ever will be in us, that we should dare to say could, for a moment, stand in comparison with his love.

Well, then, since there is no coin of metal, or emotion of mental condition, or power of spiritual grace, that could be counted out or weighed as the purchase price of Christ's love, we will not dream of having anything of the kind; for there comes, at the back of this thought, the consciousness that, even if we do possess anything that is really valuable, if there is something about us now that is commendable, and pure, and acceptable, *it all belongs to Christ already*. We have nothing with which we can buy anything from him, because all we have belongs to him. Under the righteous law of God, all the good of which we are capable is already due to our Creator. His command is, "Thou shalt love the Lord thy God with all thine heart, and with all thy soul, and with all thy might." (Deut. 6:5; Mat. 22:37; Mk. 12:30; Lk. 10:27) Very comprehensive, very sweeping, are the demands of the law of the Lord. You must not imagine that there is the slightest truth in the idea that man may come to do more for Christ than it is his duty to do; this cannot be, for all that is possible for us to do is already Christ's. "Ye are not your own" (1 Cor. 6:19), and yet you talk about giving yourself to him. You belong to him now, you Christians, doubly so; and all men are under obligation to Christ even for the temporal favours he has bestowed upon them. You, believer, cannot say, "Now I am going to do for Christ something more than; I think, something that might absolutely be claimed by him." Why, if you are really what you claim to be, you are his already, body, soul, and spirit! All your time, all your money, all your faculties, all the possibilities that are in you, are all his now; and therefore, how can you come to purchase his love? No, it cannot be purchased; that is certain for many other reasons besides these that I have given you.

But what a blessing it is that *we have the love of Christ, though we could not purchase it!* The Son of God has loved us; he has bestowed on us what he never would have sold us; and he has given it to us freely, "without money and without price." (Is. 55:1) And, beloved, this love is no new thing. He loved us long before we were born. When his foreknowledge sketched us in his mind's eye, he beheld us in love. He proved his love, too. It was not merely contemplative love, but it was practical love, for he died for us before we knew anything about him, or were even here to learn about him. His love is of such a wonderful kind that he always will love us. When heaven and earth have passed away, and, like a scroll, the universe is rolled up, or is put away like a worn-out vesture, he will still love us as he loved us at the first. The greatest wonder to me is that this unpurchasable love, this unending love, is mine; and you, my brothers and sisters, can always say to each other if you have been regenerated, "This love is mine; the Lord Jesus Christ loves me with a love I never could have purchased."

Perhaps someone is saying just now, "I wish I could say that." Do you really wish it? Then, let the text serve to guide you as to the way by which you may yet know Christ's love for you. Do not try to purchase it; abandon that idea at once. Perhaps you say, "I never thought of buying it with money." Possibly not, but the mass of mankind thinks of purchasing it in some way or other. They hear from their priests of certain ceremonies, and they attach great importance to them, and offer them as a bribe to Christ; but these things will never buy his love. They then resort to prayer — not prayers from the heart, but prayers said as a sort of punishment; and it is thought by many that surely these will procure his love, but they never will. We have even known some who have punished themselves, tortured themselves, thinking they would get Christ's love in that fashion. Now, if I knew anybody who tried to win my love by making himself miserable, I should say to him, "My good fellow, you will never make me love you in that way; be as happy as you can, that method is a great deal more likely to touch my heart than the other." I don't believe that penance and mortification afford any pleasure to God; I think he would be more likely to say, "Poor silly creatures; when I make gnats, I teach them to dance in the summer sunshine; when I make the fish of the sea, they leap up from the waves with intense delight; and when I make birds, I show them how to sing." God has no delight in the miseries of his creatures, and the flagellations [floggings] that fools give to themselves they deserve for their folly, but they certainly bring no pleasure to the heart of God. It is vain to think of purchasing the love of Christ in such a way.

"But surely, surely, we can do something. We will give up this vice, we will renounce that bad habit, we will be strict in our religion, and we will be attentive to all moral duties." So you should; but when you have done all, do you think you have done enough to win his love? Is the servant, who has only done what he ought to have done, entitled to the love of his master's heart because of that? You will not win Christ's love so; if you have his love shed abroad in your heart, you have infinitely more than you have ever earned. Suppose any person here were to say, "I feel so resolved to be saved that I will give all I have in this world to some good cause, and then I will give myself to go abroad into foreign lands to some fever-stricken place, to die in the service of God." Ah! Should you do all that, you would utterly be contemned if you thought thus to purchase the love of God. Will he be bartered with? Will he put up his heart to be sold in the market, he whose very temple was defiled by the presence of buyers and sellers? It cannot be. Go, and chatter, and bid, and barter with your fellow-men; even they will disdain you if you think that love is to be procured in this way, but do not dream that you are thus to deal with your God. I say again, it cannot be. The text does not merely say that the price would be refused, but "it would utterly be contemned." Love would open her bright eyes and look at the man, and then she would frown, and say, "How can you insult me so? Take back your gold, and begone"; and God's great love, even when his pity was in the ascendant, would but weep a tear, and then reply, "I pity you, for you do not know what you are doing; and I despise the price you bring to me. How could you think that I was such a one as yourself, and that my love could be purchased with paltry pelf [booty] that you can bring?"

We cannot spare more time for that point, but it is one that you may think over for many a day, that your heart may be charmed with it till you love and bless your Saviour with all your heart, and mind, and soul, and strength.

II. My second remark is: IN OUR CASE, NOTHING CAN EVER SERVE AS A SUBSTITUTE FOR LOVE.

If Christ has loved us, or if we desire to realise that he has done so, *the one thing needful and essential is that we have true love for him*. God's demand of each one who professes to be his child is, "My son, give me thine heart." (Prov. 23:26) There are many who would like to be thought as his sons, and, therefore, every morning they wickedly say, "Our Father which art in heaven" though God is not their Father. If they were to say, "Our father" to him who is their father, they would pray to the devil, for God is no father of theirs. Alas, there are many who want to be thought as God's children, and they will come and bring to him anything but love. A sad, sorrowful truth!

If God would but say to men, "I will accept *unspiritual service*", he might be the God of the whole earth at once; or rather, let me more truly say that he would be the demon of the whole earth, for men do not care what the religion is externally, so long as it does not trouble their hearts. The last thing some people will do is to think. "Give you a guinea? Oh, certainly." Excellent is the charity for which you are pleading. A guinea for the hospital? Certainly. Five guineas for a new place of worship? Certainly. When I have money, I am always glad to give it; but don't you come and bother me with any of your doctrines, for I don't want to hear about them. You religious people are so divided into sects and parties, and you are always controverting and contradicting one another, so I do not want to think about these things." That is a very poor excuse, is it not? Because this seems to be a matter which requires a great deal of thought, therefore this person will not give it any consideration at all; and because those who do think about it do not exactly agree on all points, therefore this man says, "I shall not think of it at all." Because all the charts of an intricate portion of the ocean may not happen to be exactly alike, therefore this man will not even study that part of the sea over which his own vessel must go, although there all the charts do agree! He makes an excuse on some trivial matter to neglect altogether the steering of his vessel. He will strike on a rock one day, and he will have no one to blame for it but himself.

"Oh!" says another person, "I don't mind saying prayers; or I will go to church and listen to the reading of prayers. I don't mind hearing sermons, but don't come and tell me that *I have to repent of my sins*. I cannot do that; I do not understand what you mean. I join in *The General Confession* every Sunday; I say that I am a miserable sinner though I don't know that I am particularly miserable, and I don't know that I am particularly a sinner either; but still, I always say that, and I don't mind saying it. Yet if you come to me, saying, 'Repent,' I can't do that." Men will offer to God anything but that which has to do with the heart. You may call upon them to torment their bodies, as the priests of false religions have done; and they will not object to that. The fakir in Hindustan will pierce himself with knives, or lie on a bed of nails, or swing himself up by a hook in his back, and hang there by the hour together in all but mortal agony. A man will do almost anything except bow his heart before his God. He will not confess that Jehovah is Lord of all, and that he himself is a poor sinful creature who deserves to be punished; he will not obey a law that is spiritual, and demands the allegiance of the secret thoughts and intents of his heart; and he will not accept a faith which is so superlatively pure that it demands that sin be given up, and tells him that even when given up it must be washed out in the precious blood of Jesus, and that a man must exercise repentance towards God and faith in the Saviour or he cannot be saved.

The most unpopular truth in the world is this sentence that fell from the lips of Christ, *"Ye must be born again"* (Jn.3:3), and, consequently, there are all sorts of inventions to get the truth out of those words. "Oh, yes!" say some, "you must be born again, but that means the application of aqueous fluid to an infant's brow." As God is true, that teaching is a lie; there is no grain or shade of truth in it. "Except a man be born again" (that is, from above), "he cannot see the kingdom of God." No operation that can be performed by man can ever regenerate the soul; it is the work alone of God the Holy Spirit, who creates us anew in Christ Jesus. Men do not like that truth; the spiritual still displeases the natural man. They will profess to worship God in Jerusalem or at Gerizim, and fight about the place where he ought to be worshipped to show how little good their religion has done them! They will not speak to each other; the Jew will have no dealings with the Samaritan to prove how unlike he is to the God who makes his sun to shine both on the just and on the unjust. (Mat. 5:45) But when you utter this message: "God is a Spirit, and they that worship him must worship him in spirit and in truth" (Jn 4:23-24), they are offended, and sadly turn away.

The truth holds good, still, whatever men think of it. If you do not give God your heart, you have given him nothing. If you do not give God your soul, if you do not love him, if you serve him not because you love him, if you do not come to him, and surrender to him your inner self, if you may have been baptised — immersed or sprinkled — if you may have come to the communion table, if you may have bowed your knees till they have grown horny, if you may have prayed till you are hoarse, and if you have wept till the fountains of your eye are dry, if you may have given all your gold, and lacerated every member of your body with mortification, and starved yourself to a skeleton, you have truly done nothing towards obtaining love from Christ. The substance of your house is utterly contemned if you offer it to the Lord in the place of the love of your heart.

Love he must have. This is his lawful demand. His people delight to render it; and if you do not, then you are none of his.

III. This takes us to a third truth, which is, that THE SAINTS' LOVE IS NOT PURCHASED BY CHRIST'S GIFTS.

The love of saints for their Lord is not given to Christ because of his gifts to them. I must explain what I mean, lest, at the very outset, I am mistaken or misunderstood. We love our Lord, and we love him all the more because of the many gifts he bestows on us; but *his gifts do not win our love*. I will show you why. All that he has given me today, he gave me many years ago. The covenant of grace was always mine. I heard the preacher tell about it. He told how Christ had died for me, that he loved me, and gave himself for me. Truly, he had done so, for he had poured out his blood for my redemption. I would not believe it to be so, or, believing it, I did not think it was of any consequence. Then the preacher spread out the rare gifts of Christ before me, and I saw that he had given these to those that believed in him; but I did not think them worth examining, and I turned away from them. I should never have loved him if he had not given me much more than the substance of his house. I needed his blessed Spirit to show me the value of the substance of his house, and, above all, to show me that for which this day I love my Saviour best of all, namely, *himself*, HIMSELF.

Oh, it is "Jesus Christ himself" who wins the love of our hearts! *If he had not given us himself, we should never have given ourselves to him.* All else that may be supposed to be of the substance of his house would not have won his people's hearts until, at last, they learnt this truth, and the Spirit of God made them feel the force of it: "He loved me, and gave himself for me." (Gal. 2:20)

"My Beloved is mine, and I am his" is now one of the sweetest stanzas in love's canticle. (Song 2:16) The spouse does not say, "His crown is mine, his throne is mine, his breastplate is mine, his crook is mine", delighting in everything that Christ has as a King, and a Priest, and a Shepherd; but, above all else, that which wins and charms her heart is this, "He himself is mine, and I am his."

But I mean, mainly, to say, under this head, that *there are some of Christ's gifts that do not win our hearts*; that is to say, our hearts do not depend on them. And they are, first, his temporal gifts. I am very thankful, and I trust that all God's people are also, for health and strength. I have lost these sometimes, but I did not love my Lord any the less then; neither do I love Christ this day because I am free from pain. If I were not free from pain, I would still love him. Christ has given to some of you a competence, you have all you want for this world; but is that why you love Christ? Oh, no, beloved! If he were to take all this away, I know that you would love him in your poverty. The devil was a liar when he said of Job,

"Doth Job fear God for nought? Hast not thou made a hedge about him, and about his house, and about all that he hath on every side? You have blessed the work of his hands, and his substance is increased in the land. But put forth thine hand now, and touch all that he hath, and he will curse thee to thy face." (Job 1:9-10)

We do not love God altogether for what he gives us in this world; ours is not such poor cupboard-love as that. We love him because he first loved us, and we do not pretend to have climbed to that high state of disinterested love in which there is no gratitude mingled with it. We must always be grateful to him, and love him for that reason; but still, temporal things never win our heart's love to God. There are numbers of you who have health and wealth, and many other things that so many desire, but they will never make you love God; they never will. You love them, and make idols of them very readily, but they do not lead you to love the Lord. The children of God who love their dear Saviour can tell you that they do not love him because of what he gives them, for if he takes from them, they would love him all the same. With Job, they say, "The Lord gave, and the Lord hath taken away; blessed be the name of the Lord." (Job 1:21) They do not love him simply because he caresses them, for if he chastens them, they love him still, and kiss the rod with which he smites them.

I mean also to say that *we do not love Christ because of his temporary indulgence of us in spiritual things*. You know, beloved, our Saviour very frequently favours us with manifestations of his presence. We are overjoyed when he comes very near to us, and permits us to put our fingers into the prints of the nails. We have our high days and festivals when the Bridegroom is with us, definitely with us. He takes all the clouds out of our sky, and gives us the bright shining of the sun; or he opens the lattices, and shows us himself in a way only second to that in which we shall see him when we behold him face to face. And oh, how we love him then! But, thank God, when he draws the lattice back again, and hides his face, we do not leave off loving him because of that. Our love for our Lord does not depend on the weather. True, our love is not manifested to him so sweetly when we are in the dark as when he cheers us with his smile, but still, it is there all the while. We could not let him go. "Though he slay me" — he who loves me, though he turn to be my enemy, and slay me — "yet will I trust in him." We will hold to him still, and love him still, not because of the substance of his house, but because of what he is in himself. There are times when we are half inclined to say with the elder brother, "These many years have I been with thee, privileged to serve thee, and yet thou hast not given me so much as a kid that I might make merry with my friends." (Lk. 15:29) Perhaps we have been long without the light of his countenance, and have had no love-tokens from him; but, for all that, we remain in his service, and abide in his house; and even if our Father should answer us roughly, we will tell him that he is still our Father. We do not love him merely for the substance of his house, but for himself, and because his Spirit has made love for him to be an instinct of our new nature, and he has put within us such a principle that we cannot help loving him. Even if we should be called to pass through terrible trials and adversities, and have to walk a long time in clouds and darkness, yet still would we love him and rejoice in him.

IV. The last observation I have to make on our text is this: THE LOVE OF SAINTS CANNOT BE BOUGHT OFF FROM CHRIST AT ANY PRICE.

The love of some people to religion is very cheaply bought and very speedily sold. It is very lamentable to notice the great number of people who are quite content to go and worship God with Christian brethren, and to hear the gospel preached, while they are themselves poor, or in middling circumstances, but who find, as soon as they have accumulated a little wealth, *that the world has a church of its own*, and they must go there, "Because, you see, everybody goes there; and if you are cut off from Society, where are you?" I have been asked that question, sometimes, and I have replied, "Where are you? Why, where Christ would have you be — 'without the camp, bearing his reproach.'" (Heb. 13:13) But that place of separation, "without the camp", is a position which is not always taken up cheerfully by professedly Christian people. It is very sorrowful to see how, because God has entrusted them with wealth, they get drawn away from the gospel, and from the Church of God. And though they are troubled a little at first, they soon get rid of one scruple after another, and subside altogether into worldliness.

Well, now, I am not altogether sorry that there is this test in the world. Every good husbandman keeps a winnowing fan. Of course, he that is foolish, when he sees a great heap lying on the barn floor, says, "All this is my wheat that I have brought in." He does not want to have it diminished, for it is the result of his labour; but if he is a wise husbandman, and says, "Though I have brought in a great heap, I know that there is chaff with it", and he is glad to have the winnowing fan used, and the corn tossed up that the fresh breeze may blow through it. If the mere professors go, let them go. "They went out from us, but they were not of us; for if they had been of us, they would no doubt have continued with us." (1 Jn. 2:19)

There are some who go away from Christ's people, and renounce religion and love to Christ, because of business. *It will pay better in certain lines not to be religious*; and therefore, as the main thing with them is to get money — religiously if they can, but irreligiously if need be — therefore, by-and-by, they are offended, and they sell Christ Jesus. I am pained to see the numbers of people who go and live in the suburbs of London, and make that an opportunity for selling their religion, such as it is. It is not long ago that I stood at a dying bed, and a part of what I heard there was, "O sir, ten years ago, we used to be members of such and such a church; we came to live out here, but there was no place of worship handy; so we have not been anywhere." That person was dying without hope, after selling Christ for love of a little country air. That was about all it was, and little more was to be gained by it.

"Oh, but", asks someone, "do saints sell Christ like that?" No, not they; these are only the professors who have mingled with the saints. These are like the mixed multitude that came out of Egypt with the children of Israel; howbeit they are not all Israel that are of Israel. (Rom. 9:6) The saints sell Christ? No, they are too much like their Master to do that. You recollect how Satan took the Master to the top of a high mountain, and showed him all the kingdoms of the world, and the glory of them, and said, "All these things will I give thee, if thou wilt fall down and worship me." (Mat. 4:9) Wicked thief! It was not his to give; yet he tempted Christ in that way. But Jesus answered, "Get thee hence, Satan: for it is written, 'Thou shalt worship the Lord thy God, and him only shalt thou serve.'" (Mat. 4:10) If any of Christ's followers are tempted in the same fashion, let them give the same reply. All the substance of the devil's house could not win the love of anyone who has set his affection on Jesus. "Who shall separate us from the love of Christ?" The cruel Romanists have taken the martyrs into the lone dungeon of the Inquisition, and tormented them there in such a way that it pains us even to read or hear of what they suffered. But did they give up Christ? No, not they! They never would. At other times, they have taken Christians into a palace, and said, "We will clothe you in scarlet and fine linen; you shall fare sumptuously every day; but you must give up Christ." Yet they would not. All the substance of this world has been laid at the feet of holy men, and they have rejected the price with scorn. I know men today, and rejoice to know them, who have sacrificed honour and position among men, who have borne abuse and scorn, and have been glad to bear it, and counted it their privilege that they were not only permitted to have Christ as their Saviour, but also that they were allowed to suffer for his sake.

O brothers and sisters, may the Lord so clothe us with the whole armour of righteousness that no temptation may ever be able to wound our love for Jesus! Let us feel, "We can let all else go, but we can never let him go."

O Thou from whom all goodness flows!
I lift my soul to Thee;
In all my sorrows, conflicts, woes,
Good Lord, remember me.

When on my groaning, burdened heart,
My sins lie heavily,
Thy pardon speak, new peace impart;
In love, remember me.
When trials sore obstruct my way
And ills I cannot flee,
Oh, give me strength, Lord as my day:
For good, remember me.

Distressed with pain, disease, and grief,
This feeble body see:
Grant patience, rest, and kind relief;
Hear and remember me.

If on my face for thy dear name,
Shame and reproaches be,
All hail reproach, and welcome shame,
If thou remember me!

This hour is near, consigned to death
I own the just decree,
Saviour, with my last parting breath
I'll cry, "Remember me."

And when before thy throne I stand,
And lift my soul to thee,
Then with the saints at thy right hand,
Dear Lord, remember me.

(Thomas Haweis)

There let them be for his sake. Give me but a vision of the Crucified, let me see that thorn-crowned brow, let me but gaze into his dear languid eyes, so full of love for me, and I will then say, "My Master, through floods or flames, if you lead, I'll follow where you go. When many turn aside, I will still cling to you, and witness that you have the living Word, and that there is none on earth that I desire beside you. I will give up the treasures of Egypt, for I have respect to the recompense of the reward. I will let the ingots of gold go, every one of them; I will cast them into the sea without regret. But if you will abide in the vessel, my soul shall be content. Bind me to your altar, for I am but flesh and blood, and may start aside in the trial-hour. Cast the links of thy love about me; chain me to yourself; yes, crucify me; nail me to your cross, and let me be dead to the world, for then the world will leave off tempting a corpse. Let me be dead with you, for then the world that cast you out may cast me out, too, and have done with me; and it were well, then, to be counted as the off-scouring of all things for your dear sake, my Lord!" If a man should give all the substance of his house to bribe the saints to sell their Lord, it would utterly be contemned. By this test, shall we prove you, O professors! By this trial, shall it be known whether you can stand firm in the evil day. God grant that you may, for our Lord Jesus Christ's sake! Amen.

81. CHRIST'S LOVE FOR HIS VINEYARD
NO. 2785

AT NEW PARK STREET CHAPEL, SOUTHWARK
ON A THURSDAY EVENING, IN THE SUMMER OF 1860

"My vineyard, which is mine, is before me: thou, O Solomon, must have a thousand, and those that keep the fruit thereof two hundred." (Song of Solomon 8:12)

YOU are aware that these Canticles are responsive songs — that one sentence is uttered by Solomon, and the next by Solyma [Jerusalem, Zion], his spouse. We believe that, in this "Song of Songs, which is Solomon's", we also hear Christ speaking to his Church, his bride, and the Church responding to his words of love in tones which his love suggested to her. The fact that it is a responsive song sometimes renders it the more difficult to understand, because it is not easy, in every case, to discover whether it is Solomon or Solyma — Christ or his Church — that is speaking. The first sentence in our text is just of that character; it may be Christ who says, "My vineyard, which is mine, is before me", or it may be his Church which is saying, "My vineyard, which is mine, is before me." With regard to the latter part of the verse, we have no difficulty, for we can see on the very face of it, that it is addressed by the spouse, the bride, to her Divine Bridegroom, to whom she say; "Thou, O Solomon, must have a thousand."

I. Let us look at the first sentence: "My vineyard, which is mine, is before me."

We have no difficulty in understanding that this vineyard is Christ's Church. She is not compared to a grove of trees — even of fruit-bearing trees — because there are many trees which are valuable, not only for their fruit, but also for their timber; and should they produce no fruit, they would still be of some value. Not so is it with the members of Christ's Church; they are like the vine, for the vine, if it produces no fruit, is fit for nothing, it cumbers the ground. The Lord said to the prophet Ezekiel,

"What is the vine tree more than any tree, or than a branch which is among the trees of the forest? Shall wood be taken thereof to do any work? Or will men take a pin of it to hang any vessel thereon? Behold, it is cast into the fire for fuel: the fire devours both ends of it, and the midst of it is burned. Is it meet for any work?" (Ezek. 15:2-4)

No, if it is fruitless, unless. It must bear fruit, or it is of no value whatever. Hence, the Church is always compared with a vineyard because, if she does not produce fruit to the Lord Jesus Christ, she is less useful even than an ordinary mercantile and commercial community. That mercantile community, or body corporate, instituted for wise purposes, may further some useful design; but the Church is of no use whatever unless she produces the fruits of holiness and of gratitude to her Lord, her Divine Husbandman. Better that she should be not called a church at all than that she should pretend to be the Church of Christ, and yet produce no fruit to his praise.

So we have no difficulty in understanding that the vineyard mentioned in the text is Christ's Church, because it is so significant a symbol of the body of believers banded together in love for their Saviour, and known by the name of "the Church of the Lord Jesus Christ." We must, therefore, consider the opening sentence of our text as being, first, THE WORDS OF THE LORD JESUS CHRIST; and here you see at once two things — first, that Christ claims a special property in his Church; and, secondly, that he has special regard and care for her: "My vineyard, which is mine, is before me."

The Master here, then, claims a special property in his Church. Twice he mentions that claim: "My vineyard, which is mine", as if he meant to assert his rights, and to maintain them against all comers, being ready to defend them in Heaven's High Court of Chancery, or before all the hosts of his enemies which might seek to snatch his inheritance from him. "Whatever is not mine", says the Divine Lover, "my Church is." She is so mine that, if I gave up Lebanon, if I should renounce Bashan, and give up all the rest of my possessions, I must retain Zion, my vineyard, my best-beloved." We know that the Church is Christ's by special bonds — not simply by creation. It is true that the Lord Jesus has created all his people, but then he does not claim them merely on that ground, because all men are his by creation; no, the very devils in hell are his in that sense; and, therefore, he does not claim his Church simply by right of being her Creator. Nor does he claim her merely by the prerogatives of providence; for, in that sense, the cattle on a thousand hills are his, and the lions of the forest, and the young ravens which cry to him, for he supplies all their needs. All things are his by providence, from the stars of heaven down to the midge in the summer's air, or the worm that conceals itself in the grass at eventide.

But our Lord Jesus claims his Church by a far higher title than that of creation or providence. Nor is the Church his merely by right of conquest. It is true that he has fought for his people, and that they may be considered as the spoils that he has taken in war. He has rescued his people from the hand of him that was stronger than they; all of them, as he takes them with him into heaven, may be looked on as signs and wonders, trophies of what his strong arm has done in delivering them from their mighty and malignant foes. But, beloved, Christ claims his Church by a better title even than this.

First, he claims the Church as his own by his Father's gift. You know that the Church is the property of all three Persons of the holy and blessed Trinity. She is the Father's property by election; she is the Son's property by donation, passing from the hand of the Father to that of the Mediator; and, then, the Church is the Spirit's by his indwelling and inhabitation; so that all three of the Divine Persons have a right to the Church for some special office which they exercise towards her. So Christ claims his Church as his Father's gift, a love-token, a reward, a sign of the Father's favour and regard towards him. He looks on his people as being dear, not only for their own sakes, but for the sake of him who gave them to his Son, to be his forever and ever. They are his, then, by donation; and, as such, since the Father gave them to him, they are very, very precious in his sight.

Next, Christ's Church is his by purchase. There are some who say that all men are Christ's by purchase. But, beloved, you and I do not believe in a sham redemption which does not redeem. We do not believe in a universal redemption which extends even to those who were in hell before the Saviour died, and which includes the fallen angels as well as unrepentant men. We believe in an effective redemption, and can never agree with those who would teach us that Christ's blood was shed in vain. The good Shepherd laid down his life for his sheep. Christ loved his Church, and gave himself for it. He bought his own people with his blood. He purchased, not the world's wide wilderness, but the "spot enclosed by grace", the vineyard which his own right hand has planted. Dear, then, to the heart of Jesus is every vine, and every cluster of grapes in this vineyard, because he bought the whole of it with his blood. As Naboth, when asked to sell his vineyard to Ahab, answered the king, "The Lord forbid it me, that I should give the inheritance of my fathers unto thee" (1 Kings 21:3), and kept it even at the cost of his life. Do you think that our Lord Jesus will ever part with his vineyard, which is not only his by inheritance from his Father, but also his by purchase, "not with corruptible things, as silver and gold" (1 Pet. 1:18), but with his own most precious blood? On every leaf in that vineyard, his blood has fallen. The red juice that flows so freely from the clusters, when pressed, is but his blood in another form. If the soil of the vineyard is rich, it is because he has enriched it with his blood. If the vines produce forth plenteously, it is because of the care he takes with them.

More than this, the Church is Christ's by one other tie, which, perhaps, makes it dearer still to him. She is his bride, his spouse. Now, whatever a man may not have a right to, he certainly has a right to his own espoused wife. Whatever legal quibbles may be raised about a piece of earth, about a man's title to his freehold property, to his own wife he certainly has a clear right and title. And Jesus looks into the eyes of his spouse, when he has redeemed her out of the hand of the enemy, and taken her to himself — when he placed the jewels of his grace about her neck, and in her ears, and on her hands, when he adorned her with the robe of his own righteousness, and made her beautiful in his beauty. He looks at her and says, "You are mine; you are mine; and no one else can claim you. My spouse, you are no harlot; you shall not play the part of an adulteress with many lovers, for you are mine, and no one but myself can claim you. None but myself shall partake of your embraces, none but myself shall receive of the love of your heart."

By these three ties, then, O Church of Christ, you are his special property, and by each of these you are endeared to him! Jesus sees on you, O Church of God, the mark of his Father's love-gift! He sees, too, the evidence of his own loving purchase, and his espousal of you to himself, to be his forever and ever.

But we must pass on to notice that, in the first sentence of our text, we are not only told about Christ's special right to his Church, but also about his special care and observation of her: "My vineyard, which is mine, is before me."

The Church is "before" Christ in the sense that, he so loves her, that he never has her out of his presence. The vineyard is so dear to the Husbandman that he never leaves it. He may sometimes hide himself among the vines, but he is always close at hand, watching how they progress, and delighting himself with their fragrance and fruitfulness. The Bridegroom is never absent from his spouse, for he loves her too much to be separated from her. Is it not a sweet thought that believers are ever under the eye of Christ? He will not be happy unless he had them continually before him. His Church may be willing to endure his absence for a while, but he loves her so much that he cannot bear to be away from her. She may grow so cold towards him that his absence may seem to her to be but a small matter; but the decay of her love is not a little matter to him. His love is as strong as death, and his jealousy is cruel as the grave; so he cannot bear to have her out of his sight even for a minute. He will always pour upon her the beams of his love, and ever fix on her the affection of his whole heart.

The expression, "My vineyard, which is mine, is before me" may also mean that Jesus is always caring for it, as well as always loving it. There is never a moment when Christ ceases to care for his vineyard. He himself said, "I the Lord do keep it; I will water it every moment: lest any hurt it, I will keep it night and day." (Is. 27:3) What! Water it every moment? Keep it night and day? Yes, he will never neglect it. His word to his Church is, "Lo, I am with you alway" (Mat 28:20) — not me rely for half a day, or for an hour in the day, leaving his ministers to care for them at other times — but, "Lo, I am with you alway, even unto the end of the world." Jesus still walks among the golden candlesticks (Rev. 2:1); he does not light the candles and then leave them to burn by themselves, but he walks among them, and keeps them from going out. "My vineyard, which is mine, is before me." Christ is always in his Church, always caring for his Church, always bidding his providence assist her agencies, always upholding her in her hours of trial, leading her into all truth, instructing her sons and daughters, and making all her members "meet to be partakers of the inheritance of the saints in light." (Col. 1:12)

There is also, in this expression, not only a sense of love and care, but also of knowledge: "My vineyard, which is mine, is before me." Christ knows every vine in the vineyard, and he knows all the fruit that is on each vine, and how much there was last year and how much there will be in years to come. Before there was a vine in that vineyard, Christ knew how many plants would be planted, where they would be put, of what sort they would be, and how much fruit they would produce. He did not find out by degrees what his inheritance was to be; he knew all about it long before the worlds were formed. There is nothing in his Church that is new to him; he foreknew, and foresaw, and foreordained every single particle of mould that lies in that vineyard, and every stone that is in its walls, and every vine growing within them. Yes, and every leaf, yes, and every particle of blight or mildew that falls upon a leaf. All was settled and ordained, or foreknown, and prepared for, by the great Proprietor.

"My vineyard, which is mine, is before me." There is a sweet thought here for all who love the Saviour. You, as his Church, and each one of you who are his people, are specially preserved by him. Then, "Why sayest thou, O Jacob, and speakest, O Israel, 'My way is hid from the Lord, and my judgement is passed over from my God?'" (Is. 40:27) I tell you soul, that he sees you as much as if there were no others for his eye to look at; and he cares for you as infinitely, and with as undivided a heart, as if you were the only soul that he ever bought with his blood. If you were his only elect one, his only redeemed one, his only loved one, he could not deal with you more tenderly and more lovingly than he is dealing with you now. If you are Christ's, you are never behind his back, you are ever before him. He can always see you, though you cannot always see him. When the eye of your faith is dim, the eye of his care is not. When your heart seems dead and cold, his heart is still hot with infinite affection; and when you say, "My God has ceased to be gracious", you make him tell a lie, and slander him. He is really manifesting his graciousness in another way. He has changed the manifestation of his purpose of love and mercy; but his purpose is the same as ever — to drench you with floods of mercy, to wash you with streams of grace, and to fertilise you till you shall be like that of Eshcol, a "branch with one cluster of grapes" which was so large and weighty that "they bare it between two upon a staff" (Num. 13:23) — no more, till the great Husbandman shall make of you such a vine as earth has scarcely seen as yet, and shall, therefore, have to transplant you to a better vineyard, even to the hill-top of glory.

I think, then, if we regard the first sentence as the language of Christ, it is very sweet to hear him say, "My vineyard, which is mine, is before me." My brethren, the deacons and elders of the church, must always take comfort from this thought. If there is anything in the church that grieves us, we must feel "It is his vineyard, not ours; it is before him, so he will know what to do with it." I am sure, dear brethren, we should lay down our tasks if we did not have our Master with us. I should not dare to be a minister, and you would not dare to be church-officers, unless we felt that it was before him. In your different districts, let the sick, the sorrowful, the backsliding, all be carried before your God; and let all the members feel that, although we are but feeble creatures to be the leaders of so great a host, yet that the church may grow and increase until we are not only fifteen hundred, but fifteen thousand, if the Lord will, and that the church would then be just as carefully looked after as it is now, for it would still be before him. He who is the Husbandman is just as able to care for his vines when they are most numerous as if there were only one, and that one had the whole of his attention.

II. Now, very briefly, I want you to regard this first sentence of our text as THE LANGUAGE OF THE CHURCH ITSELF.

According to the eleventh verse, "Solomon had a vineyard at Baalhamon; he let out the vineyard to keepers. Every one for the fruit thereof was to bring a thousand pieces of silver." So, dear brethren, everyone of us whom the Lord has brought to himself, has a part of his vineyard to keep for him. We can't sing with Charles Wesley:

A charge to keep I have,
A God to glorify,
A never-dying soul to save,
And fit it for the sky,

— because we do not believe anything of the sort. We leave the work of saving our souls in higher hands than our own; but after our souls are saved, then we have a charge to keep, and that charge is to publish the name and fame of Jesus to the utmost of our power, and seek to bring others under the sound of the gospel, and tell them what they must do to be saved.

There are a great many people who seem to forget that they have a vineyard of their own to keep; or else, if they remember it, they cannot say, "My vineyard, which is mine, is before me", for they go about gazing at other people's vineyards, instead of keeping their eye fixed on their own. They say, "Look at So-and-so's vineyard; I don't think he trims his vines in the new style." I usually notice that those people who have such wonderful plans of their own, and who are always finding fault with other people's plans, never do anything except find fault. I like the deacons and elders of the church, and the teachers in the Sunday-school, to have no other plan than this — to do all the good they can, and to do it in the name of the Lord Jesus. When they are doing that, let other people not interfere with them, but they themselves do all the good that they can. It is always well when a man has his work before him, knows what he is going to do, and then goes straight at it. There are far too many people gadding about to see what others are doing, and to find out their plans and methods of working. Let me tell you, brethren, that the best way to succeed is to have no plan but this: "Whatsoever thy hand findeth to do, do it with thy might." (Eccles. 9:10) When I see the members of a church laying down a multiplicity of rules, I know that they are getting themselves into a multiplicity of troubles. If they will but leave rules and regulations to come up when they are needed, they will find them when they want them. Let everyone who has the Spirit of God within him set about the work which he is called to do. Let him attend to the portion of the vineyard which is before him, and try to get his thousand pieces of silver out of his own portion, and not from another's. There is always a set of grumblers about who think they could preach better, and manage Sunday-schools better than anybody else. They are the people who generally do nothing at all.

I sometimes receive anonymous letters, asking me to amend my style in this way or the other. I know where they come from — they are either from people who are very idle, to whom the penny post gives occupation for their idle hours, or from those who think they can bring themselves to our notice by their communications. I usually thrust all such letters into the fire. Now, if these people, instead of wasting their time in that way, would write a letter with good sound gospel teaching in it to some poor sinner who wants to know the way of salvation; or if, instead of wasting their pennies on me — for I think I can do better without their advice than with it — they would bestow them upon some poor crossing-sweeper, they would do more good. It is always the grumbling souls who are the idle souls; but the men who get the thousand pieces of silver out of their vineyard, have their own work so constantly before them that they have no leisure to look on the work of other people with a view of finding fault with it. They know well that they have no right to interfere between other men and their Master; and that, to their own Master, each one must stand or fall.

I pray that this church, and every member of it, may ever be able to say, in the words of our text, "My vineyard, which is mine, is before me." I am not responsible for my brother, but I am responsible for myself. I will always keep my own work before my eye; I will go about it, and do what I have to do, just as if there were nobody else in the world to do anything. I will work as hard as if I were the only Christian alive. At the same time, I will always comfort myself with the thought that my feeble labours are not all that are being rendered to the Master, but that there are more than seventy thousand who have not bowed the knee to Baal, and who are serving the one living and true God. I will, while I am working, wish to every other worker greater success than I have myself. If I see any prospering more than I am myself, I will bless God for it; but I will still say, "My vineyard, which is mine, is before me." However well my neighbour is getting on, that is no reason why I should slacken my efforts; and however badly another may succeed, that is no reason why I should neglect my own duty in order to chide him, "My vineyard, which is mine, is before me."

The next time you are tempted to complain of some brother or sister, check yourself and say, "It is my vineyard which is before me. There are some ugly thistles in it, and some great nettles over there in the corner. I have not trimmed my vines this summer; I have not taken the little foxes which spoil the vines; but, henceforward, I will attend more diligently to "my vineyard, which is mine." A blessed way of keeping from finding fault with other people is to look well to your own vineyard.

III. I now turn to the second part of our text, which is THE LANGUAGE OF THE CHURCH TO HER GREAT PROPRIETOR LORD: "Thou, O Solomon, must have a thousand" — "must have a thousand."

Whatever others have, our Lord must have Solomon's portion; "and those that keep the fruit thereof two hundred." So, then, in the first place, the fruit of the vineyard belongs to Christ; but, in the second place, both Christ and his Church agree to reward the keepers of the vineyard, and to let them have their two hundred.

First, then, all the fruit of the vineyard belongs to Christ, and he must have it. Dwell on that word "must", and let each one of you feel its blessed necessity. There are some churches where, if they have any fruit, they keep it to themselves. The Word has free course, and is glorified; sinners are saved, saints are comforted, and then they take the honour and glory to themselves. There are other churches which give all the glory to the minister. The work is succeeding well, everything prospers, and then the keeper of the vineyard has the thousand pieces of silver. There are other churches which give all the glory to the rich people in their midst. "Everything will go well", say they, "while the squire attends with us, while Mr. So-and-so is one of our deacons, and Mr. So-and-so is so generous a subscriber to our funds." So that there, also, the thousand pieces of silver are given to man. Ah, but that must not be, brethren! Stand back, you intruders! We dare not give you so much as a farthing's worth of the fruit of this vineyard. The vineyard is Christ's, he purchased it with his own life's blood; so the fruit is all his, and he must have it all; none of it must be given to anyone else. Open wide your hand, O thief, and give up the fruit you have taken to yourself! We demand it from you imperatively; give it all up, sir, for Jesus Christ must have it all, even as Solomon had the thousand pieces of silver. But, brothers and sisters, it sometimes happens that, in a church, there is no glory at all. The church is so badly off, the congregation is so small, there is such an absence of zeal, and very feeble has the spirit of prayer become that there is no glory to be given to anyone. What shall we say to such a church as that? "Brethren, do not rest satisfied with such a state of things as that; do not say, 'Solomon must be content with a hundred.' No, he must have his thousand." I want all the members of this church to feel that our Solomon, our Lord Jesus Christ, must have his thousand pieces of silver. We must not allow one year to go below the mark of the previous one. If Christ received glory through us last year, he must have as much or more glory through us this year. If we had a revival in years gone by, we must have a revival now. If Solomon had a thousand pieces of silver from us once, we must never let our tribute to him be any less. Souls must still be brought to the Saviour, should, even, as Dr. Watts writes, consider carefully:

Where Satan reigned in shades of night
The gospel strikes a heavenly light;
Our lusts its wondrous power controls,
And calms the rage of angry souls.

Lions and beasts of savage name
Put on the nature of the lamb;
While the wide world esteem it strange,
Gaze and admire, and hate the change.

May but this grace my soul renew,
Let sinner gaze and hate me too!
The word that saves me does engage
A sure defence from all their rage.

The ministry must still be powerful, the prayer-meetings continuing to be full of faith and fervour, where the members must keep on striving together in love for the extension of Christ's kingdom, his kingdom must come, and his will must be done on earth as it is in heaven. We will not put in an "if" or a "perhaps"; it must be so, and we will not be satisfied unless it is. "Thou, O Solomon, must have a thousand."

Suppose, my brethren, in looking back upon the past year, we find that we have not had so much of the Master's presence, and have not done so much for him, as in years gone by; shall we say that we will make it up next year? Oh, no, that will not do! Our Solomon must have his thousand this year. Shall he have less than the stipulated rent for his vineyard? Shall I contribute less, today, to my Lord's honour, than I did yesterday? Shall I be less zealous, less useful, less laborious? Shall the minister preach less than he did? Shall the elders visit less than they used to do? Will you, church members, pray less, and serve Christ less? If you love him less, you will do so. But, brethren, I trust that you do not love him less; and I am sure that you owe him more, for you are plunging every day deeper and deeper into debt to him. He is continually revealing to you more and more of the heights and depths, and lengths and breadths, of his love, which passes knowledge; he is ever leading you further, and yet further still, into the mysteries of his kingdom, and teaching you to know him, which is much more than knowing mere doctrine. So I ask you — Can you love him less than you did in years gone by? Will you pray to him less earnestly, and praise him less fervently? No, brothers and sisters, I think that, as Christians, we should unanimously cry, "As we come nearer to yourself, O Lord, make us the more fruitful! And as the years increase upon us, let it not be said that we do less for our Master at fifty than we did at five-and-twenty!" Let not people be able to say concerning anyone of us, "He ran well; what was hindering him?" Let not the Spirit of God have to chide anyone of us, and say, "Thou hast left thy first love." (Rev, 2:4) Let us insist on it that, as we began, so we will continue; or, rather, that we will not simply go on as we began, but that we will seek to go "from strength to strength" (Ps. 84:7) until every one of us shall appear in Zion before our God. I charge you, O you daughters of Jerusalem, by the undiminished beauty and the undivided love of your Lord, that you love him no less than you did in the day of your espousal to him! O you keepers of the vineyard, my brethren in the ministry, and you who go out from this church to preach the Word, if you gave him glory last year, if you loved the souls of men, if you knew how to wrestle with the Angel of the covenant in months gone by, you must do the same now! You must not do less than you used to do, you must not preach less earnestly, you must not pray less fervently; but you must, rather, love him more, and serve him better. May the Spirit of God enable you so to do!

But, alas, there are some of you who never give our King Solomon anything! Perhaps you are the people of God; at least, you profess to be so; but what are you doing for him? I don't think there are many members of my own church of whom I have cause to complain, but there may be some. Perhaps you have been converted for years, yet you do not know that you were ever the means of bringing a soul to Jesus. You say that you love the Saviour, but what are you doing for him? It is not doing anything for him merely to come here, on Sabbath-days or week-nights, to listen to his Word. There are other and better ways of showing your love for the Saviour than by simply coming to hear another man talk to you about him. Oh, if I have one idle member in the church who talks of loving Christ, but does nothing for him, I would look that member in the face if I knew which one it was, and I would say that faith without works is dead (Jas. 2:20, 26), that the love which does not show itself in practical piety is a pretended love, a painted flame, and not the gift of heaven!

I feel that I must also say that, if we are all doing something for Christ, we are none of us doing enough for him. I feel, sometimes, brethren, as if I wished that I had a thousand tongues with which to tell the story of his grace; and as if I longed that each day were a year, and each year a century, in which I could keep on telling of his love. Often, when the sermon is over, I chide myself because I seem to have spoken so coldly of the theme that demands a tongue of fire; I have painted so badly that lovely face, which, if you could but see, would so captivate your hearts that you would never want to see anything else beside. Yet I can honestly say, from my very heart, that I desire to give my Lord and Master his thousand pieces of silver.

I'll praise my Maker with my breath,
And when my voice is lost in death,
Praise shall employ my nobler powers.

(Isaac Watts)

I cannot stop preaching, brethren, and you cannot cease praying; we cannot, any of us, if we truly love our Lord, give up working for him. I am sure that, if we should live to be so very old, and so very feeble, that we could hardly get outside our own door, we would still try to serve him to the very last; we would find some means of praising him even on our dying bed.

Now, I conclude with a few remarks on the last words of the text — "…and those that keep the fruit thereof two hundred", which means that the keepers of the vineyard are to receive a reward. Christ's ministers are to receive the love and regard and esteem of his people for his sake. Joseph Irons put this thought very prettily; I forget his exact words, but they are to the effect that Christ's ministers really do get their two hundred. [Possibly Spurgeon was thinking of Joseph Iron's words]:

Made faithful to their trust,
They cannot, will not, spare,
Their King is holy, true and just,
To recompense their care.

They have one hundred while they are preaching, in their own enjoyment of the sweetness of the mystery which they open up to others; and then they have another hundred in the success of their ministry — in the joy of seeing sinners saved, harlots reclaimed, and drunkards converted. Our Lord is a blessed Paymaster, for he pays us while we are doing his work, in the work itself. He pays us when the work is done, and then he says that he has only begun to pay us; for, when the whole of our work here is over, we shall enter into his joy, and receive the fullness of our reward.

I may, perhaps, have some members of country churches present who are not kind to their minister. I can speak plainly on this point because my people are almost too kind to me. But I say to members of other churches — Take care of your minister, for you will never get a blessing unless you are kind to him whom God has set over you. If your minister does not have his two hundred, — that is, if he does not have your love and respect, and if you do not give him sufficient to keep him above need, you cannot expect the Spirit of God to work with you. I believe there are scores of churches in which no good is ever done for this very reason. God says, "You starve my minister, so I will starve you. You find fault with him, and quarrel with him; then I will find fault with you, and quarrel with you. There will be no blessing on you; you will be like Gilboa, for there will be neither dew nor rain on you." (2 Sam. 1:21) I sometimes hear sad stories of what is done to the minister of Christ in some churches; he is looked upon as the drudge and slave of the community. Some self-important, pompous man lords it over both pastor and people; and that poor man, even when he is preaching the everlasting gospel, often has to wonder how he will get his next coat in which he is to appear in the pulpit. The one he has is nearly out at the elbows; but, if he were to hint that another is needed, he would receive notice to go elsewhere. They would tell him that he was a mere hireling, looking for loaves and fishes — as if there were either loaves or fishes to be got out of such people as they are. I have often heard it remarked that the minister has a certain sum paid to him; but the great mass of the people never think, "He is our pastor, we must try to cheer his heart, and make glad his spirit." This state of things ought to be altered; and, until it is, the Lord will have a quarrel with those who act like this.

I will say no more on that point, but repeat that our great Solomon must have his thousand. The minister will cry, even though he is himself starving, "Solomon must have his thousand." I was once travelling through Hertfordshire, and stayed the night at a certain place [Tring], and the minister said to me, "Will you preach here this evening, sir?" "Yes", I replied, "I should like an opportunity of talking to your people if you will give them notice." I went into the minister's house, and I found that they only gave him thirteen shillings a week, and I saw that his coat was threadbare. When I went into the pulpit, I thought", I will just give these people something", and I did, too, I can assure you. And after that, I gave him something, and they gave him something, and we just managed to contribute together enough to get him a "new suit of livery", as he called it; and I don't think that brother was quite as low down in the depths of poverty as he was then. There are scores of places in the country where ministers are treated as that poor man was, but it ought not to be. The minister of Christ must have some regard, some esteem, some honour in his church; but, after all, our Lord Jesus Christ must have his thousand. My own people may take home to themselves the first part of my discourse, but you big farmer deacons must take the latter part to yourselves. Don't you go to sleep tonight until you have thought, "What can we do for that poor dear man who is to preach for us next Sunday'?"

As for my own members, you can think about the first part. Let it be your joy to know that the vineyard is Christ's vineyard, and that it ever lies before him; and let each one of you seek to give to Jesus his thousand pieces of silver — all the honour, and the glory, and the praise, and the love, and the service that you can render to him from the beginning of the year to its end.

82. THE BRIDEGROOM'S PARTING WORD
NO. 1716

DELIVERED ON LORD'S-DAY MORNING, APRIL 15TH, 1883
AT THE METROPOLITAN TABERNACLE, NEWINGTON

"Thou that dwellest in the gardens, the companions hearken to thy voice: cause me to hear it." (Song of Solomon 8:13)

THE Song is almost ended: the bride and bridegroom have come to their last stanzas, and they are about to part for a while. They utter their *adieux*, and the bridegroom says to his beloved, "Thou that dwellest in the gardens, the companions hearken to thy voice: cause me to hear it." In other words, when I am far away from you, fill this garden with my name, and let your heart commune with me. She promptly replies — and it is her last word till he comes — "Make haste, my beloved, and be thou like to a roe or to a young hart upon the mountains of spices." These farewell words of the Well-beloved are very precious to his chosen bride. Last words are always taken note of: the last words of those who loved us dearly are much valued; the last words of one who loved us to the death are worthy of a deathless memory. The last words of the Lord in this canticle remind me of the commission the Master gave to his disciples or ever he was taken up, when he said to them, "Go ye into all the world, and preach the gospel to every creature." (Mk. 16:15) Then, scattering benedictions with both his hands, he ascended into the glory, and "a cloud received him out of their sight." (Acts 1:9) As the sermon progresses, you will see why I say this, and you will detect a striking likeness between the commission connected with the ascension and the present *adieu*, when the spiritual Solomon says to his espoused Solyma [Jerusalem, Zion], "Thou that dwellest in the gardens, the companions hearken to thy voice: cause me to hear it."

I. We will get to our text at once, without further preface, and we notice in it, first of all, AN APPOINTED RESIDENCE. The bridegroom, speaking of his bride, says, "Thou that dwellest in the gardens."

The Hebrew is in the feminine, and hence we are bound to regard it as the word of the Bridegroom to his bride. It is the mystical word of the church's Lord to his elect one. He calls her an *inhabitress* of the gardens — that's the word. So then, dear friends, we who make up the church of God are here addressed this morning under that term, "Thou that inhabitest the gardens." This title is given to believers here on earth, first by way of distinction from the Lord himself, as he whom we love dwells in the ivory palaces, in which they make him glad (Ps. 45:8). He has gone up to his Father's throne, and has left these gardens down below. He came down awhile that he might look upon his garden, that he might see how the vines flourished, and gather lilies, but he has now returned to his Father and our Father. (Jn. 20:17) He watered the soil of his garden with his bloody sweat in Gethsemane, and made it bear fruit to life by being himself laid to sleep in the tomb of Joseph of Arimathea (Mat. 27:60); but all this lowly work is over now. He does not dwell in the gardens as to his corporeal presence; his dwelling-place is on the throne. Jesus has not taken us up with him, for he will come another time to do that; but now he leaves us among the seeds and flowers and growing plants to do the King's work until he comes. He was a visitor here, and the visit cost him dear; but he has gone back to the place from where he came, having finished the work which his Father gave him: our life-work is not finished, and hence we must tarry awhile below, and be known as inhabitants of the gardens.

It is expedient that we should be here, even as it is expedient that he should not be here. God's glory is to come of our sojourn here else he would have taken us away long ago. He said to his Father, "I pray not that thou shouldest take them out of the world, but that thou shouldest keep them from the evil." (Jn. 17:15) He himself is an inhabitant of the palaces, for there he best accomplishes the eternal purposes of love; but his church is the inhabitress of the gardens, for there she best fulfils the decrees of the Most High. Here she must abide awhile until all the will of the Lord shall be accomplished in her and by her, and then she also shall be taken up, and dwell with her Lord above. The title is given by way of distinction, and marks the difference between her condition and that of her Lord.

Next, it is given by way of enjoyment. She dwells in the gardens, which are places of delight. Once you and I pined in the wilderness, and sighed after God from a barren land. We trusted in man, and made flesh our arm, and then we were like the heath in the desert, which "shall not see when good cometh." (Jer. 17:6) All around us was the wilderness of this world, a howling wilderness of danger and need and disorder. We said of the world at its very best, "Vanity of vanities, all is vanity." (Eccl. 1:2, 12:8) Do you remember how you roamed, seeking rest and finding none? Your way was the path of darkness, which leads to death. Then you were poor and needy, and sought water, and there was none, and your tongue cleaved unto the roof of your mouth for thirst. (Job 29:10) Then came the Lord that bought you, and he sought you until he brought you into the gardens of his love, where he satisfied you with the river of the water of life, and filled you with the fruit of his Spirit, and now you dwell in a goodly land. "The fountain of Jacob shall be upon a land of corn and wine; also his heavens shall drop down dew." (Deut. 33:28)

Your portion is with the Lord's saints, yes, with himself; and what can be a better portion? Is it not as the garden of the Lord? (Gen. 13:10) You dwell where the great Husbandman lavishes his care on you, and takes pleasure in you. You dwell where the infinite skill and tenderness and wisdom of God manifest themselves in the training of the plants which his own right hand has planted; you dwell in the church of God, which is laid out in due order, and hedged about and guarded by heavenly power; and you are, therefore, most fitly said to dwell in the gardens. Be thankful, it is a place of enjoyment for you: awake and sing, for the lines have fallen unto you in pleasant places; yea, I have a goodly heritage. (Ps.16:6) Just as Adam was put into the Garden of Eden for his own happiness, so you are put into the garden of the church for your comfort. It is not a perfect paradise of bliss, but it has many points of likeness to paradise: for God himself walks there, the river of God waters, and the tree of life is there unguarded by the flaming sword. Is it not written, "I the Lord do keep it: I will water it every moment; lest any hurt it, I will keep it night and day"? (Is. 27:3) See, beloved, although you are distinguished from your Lord by being here while he is there, yet you are made partakers of his joy, and are not as those who are banished into a salt land to die in desolation. (See Jer. 17:6) The Lord's joy is in his people, and you are made to have a joy in them also: the excellent of the earth, in whom is all your delight, are made to be the comrades of your sojourning.

The title is also used by way of employment as well as enjoyment. Adam was not put into the garden that he might simply walk through its borders and admire its flowers and taste its fruits; he was placed there to keep it and dress it. There was sufficient to be done to prevent his stagnating from want of occupation. He had not to toil sufficiently to make him wipe the sweat from his brow, for that came from the curse: "In the sweat of thy face shalt thou eat bread" (Gen. 3:19): but still he was not permitted to be idle, for that might have been a worse curse. Even for a perfect man, unbroken leisure would not be a blessing. It is essential even to an unfallen creature that he should have work to do — fit work and honourable, seeing it is done by the creature for the great Benefactor who created him. If we didn't have our daily tasks to fulfil, we would corrode into rust, and recreation would soon gender corruption. You and I are set in the garden of the church because there is work for us to do, which will be beneficial to others and to ourselves also. Some have to take the broad axe and hew down mighty trees of error; others of a feebler sort can, with a child's hand, train the tendrils of a climbing plant, or drop into its place a tiny seed. One may plant and another may water: one may sow and another gather fruit. One may cut up weeds and another prune vines. God has work in his church for us all to do, and he has left us here to do it. Our Lord Jesus would not keep a single saint out of heaven if there were not a needs-be for his being here in the lowlands, trimming these gardens of herbs, and watching these beds of spices. Would he deny his well beloved the palm branch and the crown if it were not better for us to be holding the pruning-hook and the spade? A schoolbook with which to teach the little children may be, for a while, more to our true advantage than a golden harp. To turn over the pages of Scripture with which to instruct the people of God may be more profitable to us than to hear the song of the seraphim. I say, the Master's love for his own, which prompts him to pray, "I will that they also whom thou hast given me be with me where I am, that they may behold my glory" (Jn. 17:24), would long ago have drawn all the blood-bought up to himself above, had it not been the fact that it is in infinite wisdom seen to be better that they should abide in the flesh. You are the salt of the earth, you are the light of the world (Mat. 5:13-14): shall the salt and the light be at once withdrawn? You are to be as dew from the Lord in this dry and thirsty land (Ps. 63:1); would you be at once withdrawn? Brothers, have you found out what you have to do in these gardens? Sisters, have you found out the plants for which you are to care? If not, rouse yourselves, and do not let a moment pass till you have discovered your duty and your place. Speak to him who is the Lord of all true servants, and say to him, "Show me what you would have me do. Point out, I pray you, the place where I may serve you." Would you have it said of you that you were a wicked and slothful servant? (Mat. 25:26) Shall it be told that you dwelt in the gardens, and allowed the grass to grow up to your ankles, and allowed the thorns and the thistles to multiply until your land became as the sluggard's vineyard, pointed at us as a disgrace, and a warning to all that passed by? "O thou that dwellest in the gardens!" The title sets out employment constant and engrossing.

Dear friends, it means also eminence. I know many Christian people who do not feel that they dwell in the gardens. They reside in a certain town or village where the gospel may he preached, but not in demonstration of the Spirit and in power. (1 Cor 2:4) A little gospel is made to go a long way with some preachers. In some ministries, there is no life or power, no unction or savour. The people that meet under such preaching are cold of heart and dull in spirit; the prayer meetings are forgotten; the communion of saints has well nigh died out; and there is a general deadness as to Christian effort. Believe me, it is a dreadful thing when Christian people have almost to dread their Sabbath days; and I have known this to be the case. When you are called to hard toil through the six days of the week, you want a good spiritual meal on the Sabbath, and if you get it, you find in it a blessed compensation and refreshment. Is it not a heavenly joy to sit still on the one day of rest, and be fed with the finest of the wheat? I have known men made capable of bearing great trials —personal, relative, pecuniary, and such like, because they have looked backward on one Sabbatical feast, and then forward to another. They have said in their hour of trouble, "Patience, my heart! The Lord's day is coming when I shall drink and forget my misery. I shall go and sit with God's people, and I shall have fellowship with the Father and with the Son, and my soul shall be satisfied as with marrow and fatness, till I praise the Lord with joyful lips." But what a sorry case to dread Sunday, and mutter, "I shall get nothing next Sunday any more than I did last Sunday except some dry philosophical essay, or a heap of the childish toys and fireworks of oratory, or the same dull mumbling of mechanical orthodoxy." Oh, brothers and sisters, my text is scarcely meant for those who dwell in such deserts, but it speaks with emphasis to those who dwell where sweet spiritual fruit is plentiful, where odours and perfumes load the air, where the land flows with milk and honey. If any of you happen to dwell where Christ is set out evidently crucified among you, and where your hearts leap for very joy because the King himself comes near to feast his saints and make them glad in his presence, then it is to you that my text has a voice and a call: "Thou that dwellest in the gardens, in the choicest places of all Immanuel's laud, let me hear your voice."

Yet one more word. The title here employed is not only for eminence but for permanence. "O thou that dwellest in the gardens." If you are only permitted to enjoy sound gospel teaching now and again, and then are forced to cry, "It may be another twelve months before I shall be again fed on royal dainties", then you are in a trying case, and you need to cry to God for help. But blessed are those who dwell in the good land, and daily fill their homers with heavenly manna. "Blessed are they that dwell in thy house: they will be still praising thee." (Ps. 84:4) No spot on earth is as dear to the Christian as that where he meets his Lord. I can understand why the Jew asked of a certain town that was recommended to him as good for business. "Is there a synagogue there?" Being a devout man, and finding that there was no synagogue, he said he would rather remain where trade was dull, but where he could go with his brethren to worship. Is it not so with us? How my heart longs for these blessed assemblies! Give me a crust and a full gospel rather than all riches and a barren ministry. The profitable bearing of the Word is the greatest enjoyment on earth to godly men. It would be banishment to go where every week's business turned into a mint of money if one were also compelled to be a member of an unhappy, quarrelsome, or inactive church. Our greatest joy is in you, O Jerusalem! Let our tongue cleave to the roof of our mouth if we do not prefer you above our greatest joy!

How charming is the place
Where my Redeemer God
Unveils the beauties of his face,
And sheds his love abroad!

Not the fair palaces,
To which the great resort,
Are once to be compared with this,
Where Jesus holds his court.

(Samuel Stennett)

Beloved, if you dwell in the gardens you have a double privilege, not only of being found in a fat and fertile place, but in living there continually. You might well forego a thousand comforts for the sake of this one delight, for under the gospel your soul is made to drink of wines on the lees well refined. (Is. 25:6)

This, then, is my first head — appointed residence — "Thou that dwellest in the gardens." Is not this a choice abode for the Lord's beloved? I leave you to judge how far this describes yourselves. If it is your case, then listen to what the Bridegroom has to say to you.

II. Secondly, let us note the RECORDED CONVERSE — "Thou that dwellest in the gardens, the companions hearken to thy voice."

She was in the gardens, but she was not quiet there, and why should she be? God gave us tongues on purpose that they should be used. As he made birds to sing, and stars to shine, and rivers to flow, so has he made men and women to converse with one another, and to his glory. Our tongue is the glory of our frame, and there would be no glory in its being forever dumb. The monks of La Trappe, who maintain perpetual silence, do no more than the rocks among which they labour. When God makes bells, he means to ring them.

It may be thought to be a desirable thing that some should speak less, but it is still more desirable that they should speak better. When the tongue indites a good matter, it is no fault if it is nimble as the pen of a ready writer. (Ps. 45:1) It is not the quantity, it is the quality, of what we say, which ought to be considered.

Now, observe that evidently the spouse held with her companions frequent fellowship — "The companions hearken to thy voice." She frequently conversed with them. I hope it is so among those of you who dwell in this part of Christ's garden. It should be so: "Then they that feared the Lord spake often one to another" (Mal. 3:16); they had not now and then a crack, now and then the passing of the time of day, but they held frequent converse. Heaven will consist largely in the communion of saints, and if we would enjoy heaven below, we must carry out the words of the creed in our practice — "I believe in the communion of saints." Let us show that we do believe in it. Some people sit still in their pews till the time to go, and then walk down the aisle in majestic isolation, as if they were animated statues. Do children thus come in and out of their father's house with never a word for their brothers and sisters? I know professors who float through life like icebergs from whom it is safest to keep clear: surely these do not partake of the spirit of Christ. It is well when such icebergs are drawn into the Gulf Stream of divine love, and melt away into Christ and his people. There should be among those who are children of the common Father a mutual love, and they show this by frequent commerce in their precious things, making a sacred barter with one another. I like to hear them making sacred exchanges, one mentioning his trials, another quoting his deliverances; one telling how God has answered prayer, and another recording how the Word of God has come to him with power. Such converse ought to be as usual as the talk of children in one family.

Next, it should be willing and influential; for if you notice, it is said here: "Thou that dwellest in the gardens, the companions hearken to thy voice." They do not merely hear it, and say to themselves, "I wish she would be quiet", but they hearken, they lend an ear, and they listen gladly. I know some Christians whose lips feed many. I could mention brothers and sisters who drop pearls from their lips whenever they speak. We still have among us Chrysostoms, or men of golden mouths; you cannot be with them for half an hour without being enriched. Their anointing is evident, for it spreads to all around them. When the Spirit of God makes our communications sweet, then the more of them the better! I like to get sometimes under the shadow of God's best people, the fathers in Israel, and hear what they have to say to the honour of the name of the Lord. We who are young men feel gladdened by the testimonies of the ancients; and as for the babes in grace, they look up to the grey-beards and gather strength from their words of experience and grace. If there are any here whose language is such that others delight to listen to it, it is to such that my text is especially addressed; and when I come to open up the later part of it, I want you that have honeyed tongues, I want you who are listened to with pleasure, to notice how the Beloved says to you, "The companions hearken to thy voice: cause me to hear it." Give your Lord a share of your sweet utterances; let your Saviour's ear be charmed as well as your companions' ears. Come, speak to him as well as to your brethren, and, if there is music in your voice, let that music be for the Well-beloved as well as for your fellow-servants. This is the very heart of the matter. I cannot help alluding to it even before we have fairly reached that part of the text. The converse of the bride in the gardens was constant, and it was greatly esteemed by those who enjoyed it.

I gather from the text, rather by implication than otherwise, that the converse was commendable, for the bridegroom does not say to the spouse, "Thou that dwellest in the gardens, thy companions hear too much of thy voice." No; he evidently mentions the fact with approval, because he draws an argument from it as to why he also should hear that self-same voice.

Brethren, I leave it to you to judge whether your communications with one another are always such as they should be. Are they always worthy of you? What communications have you had this morning? Can I make a guess? — "Nice and fresh this morning." "Quite a change in the weather." Is not this the style? How often we instruct each other about what we all know! When it rains so as to soak our garments, we gravely tell each other that it is very wet. Yes, and the sunshine is all we are eager to communicate the wonderful information that it is warm! Dear me, what instructors of our generation we are! Could we not contrive to change the subject? Is it because we have nothing to say of love, and grace, and truth, that we meet and part without learning or teaching anything? Perhaps so. I wish we had a little more small change of heavenly converse: we have our crowns and sovereigns for the pulpit, we need groats and pence for common talk, all stamped with the image and superscription of the King of heaven. O Holy Spirit, enrich us after this sort! May our communications be such that, if Jesus himself were near, we might not be ashamed for him to hear our voices. Brethren, make your conversation such that it may be commended by Christ himself.

These communications were, no doubt, very beneficial. "As iron sharpeneth iron, so does a man's countenance his friend." (Prov. 27:17) Oh, what a comfort it is to drop in on a cheerful person when you yourself are heavy! What ballast it puts into your ship when you are a little too merry to meet with one in sore travail who bids you share his burden and emulate his faith. We are all the better, believe me, when our Lord praises us, because the companions hearken to our voices.

In fact, our communications with one another ought to be preparatory to higher communication still. The converse of saints on earth should be a rehearsal for their everlasting communion in heaven. We should begin here to be to one another what we hope to be to one another world without end. And is it not pleasant to rise from communion with your brethren into communion with the Bridegroom? To have such talk with one another, that, at last, we perceive that truly our fellowship is with the Father and with his Son, Jesus Christ? We thought that we only communed with our brethren; but, lo, we see that the Lord himself is here: do not our hearts burn within us? (Lk. 24:32) We two are talking of him, and now we see that he himself is here, opening to us the Scriptures, and opening our hearts to receive those Scriptures in the power of them. Beloved, let us try, if we cannot make it so, that as we dwell together as church members, and work together in one common vineyard, we may be always making our fellowship with each other a grand staircase of fellowship with the King himself. Let us so talk that we may expect to meet Jesus while we are talking. How sweet to hear and see the Master in the servant, the Bridegroom in the bridegroom's friend, the Head in the members, the Shepherd in the sheep, the Christ in every Christian! Thus may we rise upon the wings of hallowed fellowship with holy ones to yet more hallowed fellowship with the Holy One of Israel.

Thus have we meditated upon two things: we have noted the appointed residence and the recorded converse. We know what we are talking about!

III. Now we come to the pith of the text: INVITED FELLOWSHIP — "The companions hear thy voice: cause me to hear it."

It is beautiful to hear the Beloved say, in effect, "I am going away from you, and you see me no more; but I shall see you: do not forget me. Though you will not hear my voice with your bodily ears, I shall hear your voices: therefore speak to me. Unseen, I shall feed among the lilies; unperceived, I shall walk the garden in the cool of the day: when you are talking to others, do not forget me. Sometimes we will turn aside, and when you have shut the door, and no eye can see, or ear can hear, then let me hear your voice: it has music in it for my heart, for I died to give you life. Let me hear the voice of your prayer, and praise, and love."

Now, I note concerning this invitation, first of all, that it is very loving and condescending to us that the Lord should wish to hear our voice. I do not wonder that some of you love to hear my voice because the Holy Spirit has blessed it to your conversion: but what good has Jesus ever derived from any of us? Is it not marvellous that he, the infinitely blessed, should want to hear our voices, when all that he has heard from us has been begging, sighing, and a few poor broken hymns? You do not want to hear a beggar's voice, do you? I expect if the man you have helped a score of times should be tomorrow morning at your door, you would say, "Dear, dear; there is that man again!" Might not the Well-beloved say the same of you? "There she is again: come on the same errand. Come to confess some new faults, or ask fresh favours." But instead of being tired of us, our Lord says, "Let me hear thy voice." O loving Bridegroom! Must he not love us very truly to ask us to speak with him? See, he asks as though he begged it of us as a favour, "Let me hear thy voice. Thy companions hearken": let me take a share in their fellowship, for they find your voice pleasant, and let it be a pleasure also to me. Come; do not deny me, your heart's best beloved! Do not be silent to me! Come; speak to me with your own sweet mouth."

It is condescending and gracious, and yet how natural it is! How like Christ! Love ever seeks the company of that which it loves. What would a husband say if his wife were seen to be chatty and cheerful to everybody else, but never spoke to him? I cannot suppose such a case; it would make too sorrowful a household. I should pity the poor, broken-hearted man who is forced to say, "My beloved, others hear your voice, and admire it; will you not speak to me, my husband?" O believer, will you let the Lord Jesus, as it were, with tears in his eye, say to you, "You talk to everybody but to me; you lay yourself out to please everybody but me: you are a charming companion to everybody but me"? Oh, our Beloved, how badly we have treated you! How much we have slighted you! In looking back, I fear there are many of us who must feel as if this gentle word of the Lord has also a sharp side to it. I do remember my faults this day. The text goes like a dagger to my soul, for I have spoken all day long to others, and have had scarcely a word for him whom my soul loves. Let us mend our converse, and henceforth show our Lord a truer love.

We may truly add that this invitation to fellowship is a blessed and profitable request. We shall find it so if we carry it out, especially those of us who are called by God to use our voices for him among the crowds of our companions. I address some brothers and sisters here who are preachers and teachers. What a relief it is when you have been letting the companions hear your voice, to stop a bit and let Jesus hear it! What a rest to leave the congregation for the closet, to get away from where they criticise you to one who delights in you. What a relief, I say! And what a help to our hearts! Jesus gives us sweet returns if we commune with him, and just what speakers greatly need. The apostles said that they would give themselves to the word of God and to prayer. (Acts 2:42) Yes, we must put those two things together. We shall never totally handle the Word of God without prayer. When we pray, we are taught how to speak the Word to others. Salvation and supplication make a blessed pair. Put the two together, so that when you speak to others about salvation, you do it after having baptised your own soul into supplication. "The companions hear thy voice: cause me to hear it" (Song 8:13): before you speak with them, speak to me: while you are still speaking with them, still speak with me; and when your speaking to men is over, return to your rest, and again speak with me.

This invitation is a many-sided one; for when the bridegroom says, "Cause me to hear it", he means that she should speak to him in all sorts of ways. Frequently, we should be heard in praise. If you have been praising the Lord in the audience of others, turn aside and praise him to his face. Sing your song to your Beloved himself. Get into a quiet place and sing where only he can hear. I wish we had more of that kind of music, which does not care for any other audience than God. Oh, my God, may my heart find you, and every string shall have its attribute to sing, while my whole being shall extol you, my Lord! The blessed Virgin had none with her but Elizabeth when she sang, "My soul doth magnify the Lord, and my spirit doth rejoice in God my Saviour." (Lk. 1:46) Oh, let the Lord hear your voice! Get up early to be alone with him. So let it be with all your complaints and petitions, and let them be for Jesus only. Too often, we fill our fellow creature's ear with the sad tale of all our care. Why not tell the Lord about it, and have done with it? We should employ our time far more profitably if, instead of murmuring in the tent, we enquired in the Temple.

Speak with Jesus Christ, dear friends, in little broken sentences, by way of frequent ejaculation. The best of Christian fellowship may be carried on in single syllables. When, in the middle of business, you can whisper, "My Lord and my God!" you can dart a glance upward, heave a sigh, or let fall a tear, and know that Jesus will hear your voice! When nobody observes the motion of your lips, you may be saying, "My Beloved, be near me now!" This is the kind of fellowship which your Saviour asks of you: he says, "The companions hear thy voice: cause me to hear it." Be sure that when you speak with others, you also speak with me.

This is such a blessed invitation that I think, dear friends, we ought to avail ourselves of it at once. Come, what say you? The best Beloved asks us to speak with him, what shall we say at once? Think for an instant! What shall I say? Perhaps I have the start of you, because I have my word ready here it is — "Make haste, my beloved, and be thou like to a roe or to a young hart upon the mountains of spices." "Why," say you, "that is what the church said in the last verse of the Song." Exactly so, and that is what we may wisely say at this moment. We cannot improve upon it. "Come quickly; even so, come quickly, Lord Jesus." Often and often, then, when you are about your business, say, "Come, Lord Jesus! Come quickly! "It is a sweet frame of mind to be in to be willing to invite Christ to come; and whenever you cannot do so let it be a warning to you that you are in dangerous waters. I can imagine a man in business calling himself a Christian about to engage in a doubtful transaction: how is he to discern the danger? Let him ask the Lord Jesus Christ to come while he is doing it. "Oh dear no", cries one, "I had rather he should not come until that matter had been finished and forgotten." Then be you sure that you are moving in the wrong direction. Suppose you think of going to a certain place of amusement about which you have a question, it is easy to decide it thus: When you take your seat your first thing should be to bow your head and ask for a blessing, and then say, "Lord, here I sit waiting for thine appearing." "Oh," say you, "I should not want the Lord to come there." Of course you would not. Then do not go where you could not wish your Lord to find you. My text may thus be a monitor to you, to keep you from the paths of the destroyer. Jesus says, "Let me hear thy voice," and let thy voice utter these desires — "Even so, come quickly; come, Lord Jesus!"

Alas, time reproves me; I must hasten on.

IV. I have a fourth head, which shall be very briefly handled. I find according to the Hebrew that the text has in it a REQUESTED TESTIMONY.

According to learned interpreters, the Hebrew runs thus — "Cause to hear me." Now, that may mean what I have said, "Cause me to hear"; but it may also mean, "Cause them to hear me." Now hear; you that are in Christ's garden: make those who dwell in that garden with you to hear from you much about HIM. In the church, everyone has a right to talk about the Head of the church. Some of our brethren in this Tabernacle kindly undertake to speak to individuals about their souls, and now and then they receive very sharp rebuffs.

What right has he to put such a question? How dare he intrude with personal remarks? What! Is the man poaching? No, these are the Lord's preserves; and the Lord's gamekeepers have a right to do as they are bidden by him. They are not poaching in this place, for they are on the Master's own land. Anywhere inside these four walls you may speak to anybody about Christ, and no man may forbid you. Speak lovingly and tenderly and prudently; but certainly the law of the house is that here we may speak about the Lord of the house. There are some other things you may not talk about, but about the Lord Jesus you may speak as much as you will. In the garden, at any rate, if not in the wild wilderness, let the Rose of Sharon be sweetly spoken of. Let his name be as ointment poured forth (Song 1:3) in all the church of God.

Again, you, according to the text, are one that can make people hear, so that "the companions hearken to thy voice"; then make them to hear of Jesus. You have the gift of speech: use it for Christ crucified. I always feel regret when a powerful speaker takes up any other cause but that of my Lord. Time was, when I used to wish that Milton had been a preacher, and, instead of writing a poem, had proclaimed the gospel to the multitude. I know better now, for I perceive that God does not use learning and eloquence so much as knowledge of Christ and plain speech; but still, I am jealous of anyone who can speak well, that he should not give my Lord the use of his tongue. Well-trained tongues are rare things, and they should be all consecrated to Christ's glory. If you can speak to the companions — make them hear about Christ: if you can speak well, make them hear attractive words about Christ.

If you do not speak about Christ to strangers, speak to your companions. They will listen to you; therefore let them hearken to the word of the Lord. I have heard of men who called themselves Christians, who yet never spoke to their children about their souls, never spoke to their servants or to their workpeople about Jesus and his love. This is to murder souls. If tongues can bless and do not, then they, in effect, curse men by their silence. If you have a voice, make the name of Jesus to be sounded out all around you. Many are the voices that strike the ear: the world is full of din, even to distraction, yet the name which is above all other names is scarcely heard. I pray you, my brethren, you that are like silver bells, ring out that name o'er hill and dale. As with a clear call, trumpet the saving name of Jesus till the deaf hear its sound. Whatever is left out of your testimony, be sure that Christ crucified is first and last in it.

Love Christ and live Christ; think of Christ and speak of Christ. When people go away from hearing you preach, they should say this, "He kept to his subject: he knew nothing but Jesus." It is bad when a man has to say of preachers, "They have taken away my Lord, and I know not where they have laid him." (Jn. 20:13) Yet in certain sermons, you meet with a little about everything except the one thing. They offer us what we do not need; but the need of the soul is not supplied. Oh, my brethren, cause Christ to be heard. Hammer on that anvil always: if you make no music but that of the harmonious blacksmith it will suffice. Ring it out with sturdy blows — "Jesus, Jesus, Jesus, crucified." Hammer away at that. "Now you are on the right string, man," said the Duke of Argyle, when the preacher came to speak on the Lord Jesus. It needed no duke to certify that. Harp on that string. Make Jesus to be as commonly known as now he is commonly unknown. So may God bless you as long as you dwell in these gardens, till the day break and the shadows flee away! Amen.

83. A CALL TO COMMUNION

PREACHED AT THE METROPOLITAN TABERNACLE

"Thou that dwellest in the gardens, the companions hearken to thy voice: cause me to hear it. Make haste, my beloved, and be thou like to a roe or to a young hart upon the mountains of spices." (Song of Solomon 8:13-14)

To those of you, beloved, who are about to gather around the Lord's Table, and join in observing the Lord's Supper, I shall chiefly direct my address tonight. The last two verses of the Song of Solomon furnish us with my text. The former of these verses we take to be the voice of Jesus to his Church, and the latter the response of the Church to her Lord. The two petitions are reciprocal. Christ seeks communion with his Church, and, indeed, with one and all of his redeemed family. His love then kindles her affection, and constrains her to pine and pant for his presence. So she desires to have communion with him, a desire echoed in the breast of every faithful disciple of Jesus. To both of these cravings I would invite your attention; but the limit of our time leads me to speak chiefly on the first:

JESUS INVITES HIS PEOPLE TO FELLOWSHIP WITH HIMSELF. "Thou that dwellest in the gardens."

How shall we appropriate this to ourselves? Believers dwell in the Church of God. They do not merely come into the garden to walk along its pathways, but they abide there. True saints are not satisfied with the formal salutations of their fellow-citizens; in the household of faith, there is thorough heartiness. Our choicest friendships, and our most cherished relationships, are cemented within her borders. Delightfully, Dr. Watts comments in his paraphrase of Psalm 23:

My shepherd will supply my need,
Jehovah is his name;
In pastures fresh he makes me feed,
Beside the living stream.

He brings my wandering spirit back
When I forsake his ways;
And leads me, for his mercy's sake,
In paths of truth and grace.

When I walk through the shades of death,
Thy presence is my stay;
A word of thy supporting breath
Drives all my fears away.

Thy hand, in sight of all my foes,
Doth still my table spread;
My cup with blessings overflows,
Thine oil anoints my head.

The sure provisions of my God
Attend me all my days:
O may thy house be mine abode,
And all my work be praise!

There would I find a settled rest,
While others go and come;
No more a stranger or a guest,
But like a child at home.

In his connection with the Church of God, the Christian discovers his chief solace and comfort. It is not merely a tabernacle or temporary hospice to him, but is a substantial mansion, a permanent dwelling-place. (Jn. 14:2-3) The churches of God are compared with gardens, gardens full of flowers, plantations where the graces of the Spirit bud and blossom, and yield a sweet perfume; where the fruits of the Spirit are produced in rich luxuriance, to the honour and glory of the One who planted the vines and tends the flowers. May this church ever be a garden, not a pathless waste overgrown with the briars of division, and not a swamp covered with the pestilential waters of heresy, but a garden where God himself may delight to walk as he did in Eden of old (Gen. 3:8), and where good men find congenial company in the fellowship of saints!

"Thou that dwellest in the gardens." The address, we thus take, as given to those of you who frequent the courts of the Lord's house, and the place where his honour dwells (Ps. 26:8), where Jesus says to you, "The companions hear your voice." You are accustomed to hold conversation with your fellow-Christians; you talk together along the way; you sit in your houses and speak of Jesus. Full often, his name is sweetly echoed on your tongue. Some of you [preachers] address your friends from the pulpit, lifting up holy hands (1 Tim. 2:8), and admonishing them concerning their duty and their privilege. Others of you find pleasant associates in the Sunday school, the Bible class, or the Catechism class. You let your companions hear your voice. None of God's children are born dumb; they all have a voice, and they all like to hold sweet converse with one another. The Lord, then, puts it on this basis. Since the members of the church, who are your companions, hear your voice, then "Cause *me* to hear it." Christ himself would taste of your honey and eat of your honeycomb (Song 4:11, 5:1); he would come into the garden and not only talk with your companions and with you, but he wants to hear you talk to him. Take, then, the latter clause in the former of these verses as an exhortation from our Lord. "Cause *me* to hear it." Does it not become us, brethren, whenever we lift up our voice in the sanctuary, to make a direct aim of causing Christ to hear our voice? In the service of song, what is more sweet or comely than to sing a hymn to Jesus? I like to hear the great assembly chanting some well-known psalm or hymn of praise. It is refreshing to listen to the strains of melody till the music steals through every pulse of one's nature, and language fades beneath its potent spell. And is it not a little inspiring to mingle our voices and make them blend with the multitude?

But is it not possible, dear friends, when often singing a hymn, through, observant of the tune, the words, or the tide of sound that floats on our ears, when we are totally oblivious of the worship that we are supposed to be offering to the Redeemer of our souls? Ought we not to be chiefly intent on adoring Christ with the most grateful homage? Should we not lay all our praises at *his* feet? Have we no plaintive notes to hang like flowers of yew and cypress on his cross? Have we no jubilant airs that well might rise to flaming ranks of seraphim, as we hail "the head once crowned with thorns", and which "is crowned with glory now"? Let our songs be like the frankincense made of all kinds of goodly perfumes. Let us not burn them, as though they were only meant to waste their odours, but let us breathe them out to him. Let us bring them to the brazen altar (that brazen altar is a type of Christ), and lay our praises before him, as the priest of old when they put the perfume into the golden censer. (Ex. 39:38)

In prayer, too, dear friends, we use our voice, but is it not sometimes the case that we forget that our main intention should be to cause Christ to hear our voice? There is a nervous apprehension that, in the presence of the assembly, your words are falling on some critical ears; and if some more gifted brother has led the devotion just before you, a fear lest you should fail to edify the people of God as he did will haunt your breast. Perhaps you turn censor on yourself, groan over sentences that limp from your lips, reflect on the lack of rhythm in your utterance, blame yourself for the lack of beauty in your expressions, and account your feeble part in the sacred service as more like the chattering of a crane or of a swallow than the supplication of a saint. Oh, brethren, would it not be well to shake off these silly thoughts of charming the outward ear, and study only to find acceptance with our Saviour? Remember, that all you have to do is cause Christ to hear your prayer. Just recede from the crowd that is listening to you, and resort to him. Be content to let others think what they will. Your petitions are not presented to them. What matters whether they like or dislike them? But oh, be sure that you are simple and sincere in seeking your Lord! Let your talk be with your heavenly Lover. To him, let your request be preferred. See to it that your entreaty enters into his ear. If your supplication meets with acceptance from him, neither the outer crowd nor your nearer comrades need disconcert you.

Not less, beloved, in the common occurrences and frequent anxieties of our ordinary life, would it not be well for us to try and cause Christ to hear our voice? We are all of us likely, at times, to fall into the evil habit of murmuring, Peevishness may seem a petty fault to your own fancy, but it really is a frightful plague to your family and your friends. Making mountains of molehills, a man can raise a prodigious tumult over a paltry trouble. You go from house to house in quest of sympathy. Then the companions hear your voice, and perhaps it would be better if they didn't hear it quite so often! Might it not be wiser and more welcome to cause Christ to hear it? The disciples of John, when their master was cruelly beheaded, took up his body and went and told Jesus. (Mk. 6:29-30) That was wise; they sought him out for sympathy, who could also give them succour. If you took your troubles straight away to the throne of grace, it would look as if you believed that God could help you. Then, in some new distress, when you come to offer an earnest prayer rather than make a fretful complaint, you might expect to speed better than if you had first bewailed your hard lot in the presence of your fellow-creatures, before you resorted to the mercy-seat and sought help from God. "Cause *me* to hear thy voice", says Jesus. "Come, my child, come, come away from all the other children, for they can only give you cold pity; come to my bosom, come to my heart, come and tell your troubles to me, Your companions hear your voice; cause *me* to hear it."

Sometimes, we get farther beyond the mere heaving of distress to the forlorn heaviness of despair. Yes, the child of God may be brought to the borders of despair. Did you ever notice, in reading Psalm 107, how, in one verse, David describes the Lord's redeemed people as wandering in the wilderness in *a solitary way,* and how, in another verse, he says that God pours contempt on princes, and causes them to wander in a wilderness where there is no *way*? The expressions are very similar, but the difference is very striking. The choicest of saints have, at times, been led through such dark paths that they could not see a spark of their own light, and yet there was light in them for all that dreary experience. I do not know whether a book by Timothy Rogers on *Trouble of the Mind and the disease of Melancholy* (1691) ever came your way. That good man was for twenty-three years without the slightest hope of his own acceptance with God.

Though a mighty preacher of the Puritan days, under whose ministry many souls were converted, he was not able to get so much as a single ray of light himself. Yet he came out, at length, into clear and cloudless brightness, and wrote a narrative of his own experience for the comfort of those tried believers who might be in similar dismay and despondency. You might be brought into the same condition. If you are, hear the voice of Jesus saying to you, "Cause *me* to hear your moaning." What a potent spell there is in the cry of a child when it breaks on a mother's ear! When those windows are open on week-nights, we can hardly hear ourselves speak because of the rumbling of the traffic; but if, on a sudden, the dull monotony of that ceaseless noise were broken by the shrill scream of a child, we should probably all hear it; but the mother, if there, would distinguish it as that of her own bairn, and run swiftly into the street to its rescue. I would be bound to say she would hear and know the voice! Above all the heavy-leaden sound of the busy thoroughfare, the shriek of distress would be sure to reach some ear, and if none other, certainly the sharp ear of a parent. At dead of night, the moan of her child will quickly wake a mother from the soundest sleep. Is the little one sick upstairs in a room overhead, the weary mother will wake in wild alarm at the faintest cry of the one whom she accounts dear to her as her own life, and doubly dear now that it is a sufferer. She sleeps with one ear open when her child is so sadly afflicted. Thus, beloved, it is with Jesus, if our heart says, "My voice, I will make him to hear; I will not rest till he listens to my groans! To him, I will tell my hopeless state; and I will pour out my complaint before him." Then it will be well with us. Jesus likes to hear his people's voice; to him their sighs and tears never come amiss. For him, there is music in a groan and beauty in a tear; so tender are his sympathies. Not but what, as I can well believe, there are other notes he far prefers. He would — and he told it us once, and he told it for all time — he would that his joy should remain in us, and that our joy might be full. (Jn. 15:11) Whenever, in the full assurance of faith, you realise your interest in his blessed Person, his mediatorial work, and all his holy offices, I pray you speak it out, and cause him to hear your hymns and hallelujahs. Whenever your heart is full of gratitude for preservation from harm, or deliverance from danger, do not impart all your lively emotions to your companions, but tell it all to Jesus. Speak it out in simple language, and pile up your unpolished words, as the patriarchs in days of yore did their unhewn stones for an altar of memorial to the Lord who had appeared to them. When your heart swells high with strong desire, with a fervent zeal for the promotion of his kingdom, and with a vow of consecration nestling in your breast, though not pronounced by your lips, offer it to him, and cause him to hear it.

I would, dear friend, I could bring myself, and you with me, into a more thorough acquaintance with Jesus, and a more intimate fellowship with him. He is a real Person, not merely the personification of sentiments we fondly cherish. His life and death are not merely doctrines, but we are his disciples whom he has called to be his followers. His doings and his sayings do not merely recur to us like a dream, in which we mistake fancy for fact. Our present apprehension of his *real presence* is not the fiction of the wafer which cannot see or hear, and is, at best, a fancy without faculties; but it is that of a friend unseen, though not unknown, with whom, creatures as we are, we can and do hold communion. We can talk with him as a man speaks to his friend, and we believe, and are sure, that we can as certainly cause him to hear our voice as I am now able to make my voice heard in this assembly.

Having thus explained what is meant by causing Christ to hear your voice, I think I need hardly urge you to respond to so tender a request. "Cause *me* to hear it." Can you deny your Saviour the sweet satisfaction he seeks? 'Tis but little; it costs you nothing; it will even profit you. So will you, then, refuse him? You have asked him sometimes whether he will be a stranger to his own flesh; and he now puts the same question to you. He is your Husband; will you give him no love-tokens? He is your Brother; have you no tender, fraternal words for him? He is your Head; and though you are but a feeble

member of his body, will you refrain from
those functions which suit you? He bought you with
his precious blood; can you not give him some, at least, of your heart's best thoughts? Remember, he pleads, and uses his voice for you; will you not use your voice for him? He stands at the door of your heart, my brother, and knocks (Rev. 3:20); will you be so slothful as not to open it to him? Dear sister, perhaps you have been for weeks without his company, and he says to you tonight, "My head is wet with dew, and my locks with the drops of the night; open to me, my beloved, open to me." (Song 5:2) 'Tis the voice of your Beloved who speaks; shall not your heart open at once?

Do you say, "My voice is so hoarse, so hoarse with sorrow, that it cannot please him"? No, but it is music to his ear, though it is jarring enough to your own. Sometimes, there is more harmony in the voice of the tried believer than of those who are thriving. There is a meekness in the one which makes it more chaste and more charming. At any rate, your Lord asks you to let him hear your voice; so then, be it harsh or harmonious, speak to him out of the fullness of your heart. Oh, but you say that your voice is defiled through sin, and, therefore, so discordant that nothing you could speak would please the great Master. Try it, my friend, for he knows best. Or perhaps you have reasoned thus with yourself: "My heart is feeble, and my articulation very weak; had I the devout fervour of old George Herbert, or the heavenly rapture of Samuel Rutherford, or the sacred passion of Madam Guyon [Jeanne Marie B. de la Mothe], I would give myself no rest day or night from talking in songs or in sighs to the Well-beloved of my soul. But, ah me, silence were sweeter than such poor speech as mine! The Master looks wistfully at you, as it seems to me, and says, "Comparing yourselves among yourselves, you are not wise." He tells you to take with you words, and gives you the words to take — plaintive words or words of pleading, words of petition or words of promise, out of the depths a piercing cry, or up to the heavens a shout of triumph — are they not all given us that we may adopt them, make them our own, and use them? What excuse, then, when he says, "Cause me to hear thy voice."

Well now, I need not detain you much longer, for the latter words of this text requires no expounding, as it is your own response to your Lord. Brothers and sisters in Christ, I am sure that the language of your heart to your Lord and Master would go something like this: "Lord, I cannot come to you unless you come to me. So far removed am I, and so unfit to travel, that you must stoop from your throne of glory to visit me, or else it is not possible for you to hear my voice." Is not your heart all aglow at the thought of fellowship with him? Do you not feel so hungry and so thirsty after him that these hasty words just suit you: "Make haste, my Beloved"? You call him *Beloved*, for the affection you cherish toward him is sincere and fervent. You call him *My Beloved*, for you are conscious that you have a vital interest in him, and your earnest cry to him is "Make haste". Every true lover of Jesus is eager, anxious, and can brook no delay in her quest for communion. "Make haste" is her perpetual moan. "Even so, come Lord Jesus", is the last prayer in the Apocalypse. (Rev 22:20) Well enough it is the last prayer of the Canticles! It is always the first and the last prayer of the true believer. "Come quickly, and make no tarrying, O my Lord!" In view of the Second Advent, Christians always want the Lord Jesus to return. Oh, when will you come, blessed Jesus, to scatter the shades of darkness, to cast down the idols from their thrones, and to take to yourself your great power and reign? Come quickly, come quickly, Lord Jesus! And, no less in desiring present sweet communion with him by his spiritual presence, we say, "Come at once, gracious Jesus; come like the hart, which seems to fly from crag to crag, and leaps from peak to peak. Come like the young roe, which, at a bound, seems to be in sight, scarcely taking leap after leap, but at one bound appears on the mountain top." Do you not see, brother, what the meaning of it is? It is a prayer that Christ would come at one bound into your heart tonight. Do you say, "I feel so dead"? In one moment, you can feel full of life. "Oh", but you say, "I am at a distance from God!" Just as those poor mariners on the Sea of Galilee came immediately to land when Christ came into the ship (Mk. 7:47-51), so will you be, in an instant, close to Jesus if he but speaks the word. So I close these meditations with a prayer of Dr. Watts:

Draw me away from flesh and sense,
One sovereign word can draw me thence;
I would obey the voice divine,
And all inferior joys resign.

Be earth with all her scenes withdrawn,
Let noise and vanity begone;
In secret silence of the mind
My heaven, and there my God, I find.

Alas for the careless and the ungodly! There is nothing in these yearnings of the soul to interest or edify them. But by the very lack of concern they feel, they may learn that the Lord has made a difference between his people and the Egyptians. And if there is an anxious hearer in this throng — one who longs to be saved, let me not sit down without repeating the invitation, and pressing it to his acceptance, "Believe in the Lord Jesus Christ, and thou shalt be saved." (Acts 16:31) Trust your soul into Christ's hands, and he will save you tonight. Your sins shall be forgiven you (Mat. 9:2; Mk. 2:5), and the Saviour's voice shall bid you to be of good cheer, and go in peace, [an invitation reissued by John Morrison in his paraphrase of Hosea 6:1-3:]

Come, let us to the Lord our God
With contrite hearts return;
Our God is gracious, nor will leave
The desolate to mourn.

His voice commands the tempest forth
And stills the stormy wave;
And though His arm be strong to smite,
'Tis also strong to save.

Our hearts, if God we seek to know,
Shall know Him, and rejoice;
His coming like the morn shall be,
Like morning songs his voice.

84. COME, MY BELOVED!

NO. 2360

AT THE METROPOLITAN TABERNACLE, NEWINGTON
ON LORD'S-DAY EVENING, MARCH 4TH, 1888

"Make haste, my beloved, and be thou like to a roe or to a young hart upon the mountain of spices." (Song of Solomon 8:14)

THE Song of Songs describes the love of Jesus Christ for his people, and it ends with an intense desire on the part of the Church that the Lord Jesus would come back to her. The last word of the lover to the beloved one is in effect, "Speed your return; make haste and come back." Is it not somewhat singular that, as the last verse of the Book of love has this note in it, so too the last verses of the whole Book of God, which I may also call a Book of love, having that same thought in them? At the twentieth verse of the last chapter of the Revelation, we read, "He which testifieth these things saith, 'Surely I come quickly.' Amen. Even so, come, Lord Jesus." The Song of love, and the Book of love, has, in almost the selfsame way, a strong desire for Christ's speedy return.

Dear friends, are your hearts in tune with that desire? They ought to be. Yet have not some of you almost forgotten that Jesus is to come a second time? Refresh your memories. Others of you, who know that he will come, have you not thought of it as a doctrine that could be laid by on the shelf? Have you not been without any desire for his glorious appearing? Is this right? The Song of Solomon is the central Book of the Bible; it is the innermost shrine of divine revelation, the holy of holies of Scripture; and if you are living in communion with God, you will love that Book, you will catch its spirit, and you will be inclined to cry with the spouse, "Make haste, my beloved." If you have no longing for Christ's appearance, no desire for his speedy return, surely your heart is sick, and your love is faint. I fear that you are getting into a lukewarm state. I believe that our relationship to the Second Advent of Christ may be used as a thermometer with which to tell the degree of our spiritual heat. If we have strong desires, longing desires, burning desires, for the coming of the Lord, we may hope that it is well with us; but if we have no such desires, I think, at best, we must be somewhat careless. Perhaps, to take the worst view of our case, we are sadly declining in grace.

I. Well now, to come to our text, I want you to notice, firstly, WHAT THE CHURCH HERE CALLS HER LORD — "Make haste, *my beloved.*"

I have only a few words on this point. I am hardly going to preach tonight, but just talk familiarly to you; and I want you to let your hearts talk. Observe, the spouse first calls her Lord, "Beloved," and then, "My Beloved."

Christ is our *Beloved*. This is a word of affection; and our Lord Jesus Christ is the object of affection for us. If you read the Bible, especially if you read the New Testament, and study the life of Christ, and yet only admire it, and say to yourself, "Jesus Christ was a wonderful being", you do not know him yet, and have only a very indistinct idea of him. If, after reading that life, you sit down, and dissect it, and say to yourself, coolly, calmly, deliberately, "So far as is practicable, I will try and imitate Christ", you do not yet know him; you have not come near the real Christ as yet. If any one should say, "I am near the fire", and yet he is not warm, I should question the truth of his words; and though he might say, "I can see the fire; I can tell you the appearance of the coals; I can describe the lambent flames that play about the stove", yet. if he were not warmed at all, I should still think he was mistaken, or there was some medium that interposed between him and the fire at which he said he was looking. But when you really come to see Jesus, and say, "I love him; my heart yearns toward him; my delight is in him; he has won my love, and holds it in his own heart", then you begin to know him. Brethren, true religion has many sides to it; true religion is practical, it is also contemplative; but it is not true religion at all if it is not full of love and affection. Jesus must reign in your heart, or else, though you may give him what place you like in your head, you have not really received him. To Jesus, beyond all others, is applicable this title of the Beloved, for those who know him love him. Yes, if ever love had emphasis in it, it is the love that true believers give to Christ; and we do well when we sing with the young William Featherstone,

I love thee because thou hast first lovèd me,
And purchased my pardon on Calvary's tree;
I love thee for wearing the thorns on Thy brow;
If ever I loved thee, my Jesus, 'tis now.

I will love thee in life, I will love thee in death,
And praise thee as long as thou lendest me breath;
And say when the death-dew lies cold on my brow,
If ever I loved thee, my Jesus, 'tis now.

We may also go beyond that point, as the hymn does, and say,

In mansions of glory and endless delight,
I'll ever adore thee in heaven so bright;
I'll sing with the glittering crown on my brow;
If ever I loved thee, my Jesus, 'tis now.

Our love for Jesus begins with trust. We experience his goodness, and then we love him in return. "We love him because he first loved us." (1 Jn. 4:19) They say that love is blind; I should think it is from what I have seen of it in some people; but love for Christ might have ten thousand eyes, and yet be justified in loving him. The more you see him, the more you know him, the more you live with him the more reason you have for loving him. There will never come a time in which you will have to question whether you were right to surrender your heart to him; but even throughout the eternal ages you shall, in the felicities of his blessed company, feel that you were, in fact, more than justified in calling him your Beloved.

That is the first part of the name the spouse gives to her Lord; no, not the *first*; the first part of the name is "*my*", for she calls him "*my Beloved*."

Brethren, this signifies appropriation; so the two words together mean affection and appropriation: "My Beloved." If nobody else loves him, I do. This is a distinguishing affection; and I love him because he belongs to me; he is mine, he has given himself to me; and I have chosen him because he first chose me; he is "my Beloved." I am not ashamed to put him in front of all others; and when men say, "What is thy Beloved more than another beloved? (Song 5:9), "I can tell them that "My Beloved" is more than all the earthly beloveds put together. It is a delightful thing to get hold of Christ with both hands, as Thomas did when he said, "My Lord and my God." (Jn. 20:28) There he held him with a double-handed grip, and would not let him go. It is sweet and saving even to come into contact with him, as the woman did who touched the fringe of his garment (Mat. 9:20); but, oh, to take him up in your arms, to hold him with both hands, and say, "This Christ is mine; by a daring faith, warranted by the Word of God, I take this Christ to be mine, to have and to hold, for better or worse. And neither life nor death shall ever part me from him who is 'my Beloved.'" Now, there is a sweet name for the Lord Jesus Christ. My dear hearers, can you speak of Jesus in that way, "My Beloved"? Someone who can, by the Spirit of God, say this, has uttered two words that have more eloquence in them than there is in all the orations of Demosthenes. He who cannot truly say this, though he may speak with the tongues of men and of angels, yet, since he hath not this charity, this divine love in his heart, it profits him nothing. Oh, that every one of you could say, "My Beloved! My Beloved!"

Do you all really know what saving faith is? It is the appropriation to one's own self of Christ in his true and proper character, as God has revealed him. Can you make this appropriation? "Oh" says one, "I am afraid I should be stealing salvation if I did!" Listen: so long as you can get Christ anyhow, you may have him. There is never any stealing of what is freely given. The difficulty is not about any rights that you have, for you have no rights whatever in this matter, but come and take what God gives to you, though you have no claim to it. Soul, take Christ tonight, and if you take him, you will never lose him. I was going to say, if you even steal him, so long as you take him to yourself, he will never withdraw himself from your grasp. It is written, "Him that cometh to me, I will in no wise cast out." (Jn. 6:37) Some come properly, and Christ does not cast them out; but there are some who come improperly, coming, as it were, limping on a wooden leg, or perhaps only creeping or crawling. It doesn't matter how you come to Christ; as long as you really come to him, he will never cast you out. Get to him anyway you can; and if you once come to him, you may plead that blessed promise of his: "Him that cometh to me I will in no wise cast out."

I told you before that, some years ago, I felt a great depression of spirit; I knew whom I had believed, but, somehow, I could not get the comfort out of the truth I preached. I even began to wonder whether I was really saved; and, having a holiday, and being away from home, I went to the Wesleyan Chapel, and a local preacher was occupying the pulpit that morning. While he preached a sermon full of the gospel, the tears flowed from my eye, and I was in such a perfect delirium of joy on hearing the gospel, which I so seldom have an opportunity of doing, that I said, "Oh, yes, there is spiritual life within me, for the gospel can touch my heart, and stir my soul." When I went to thank the good man for his sermon, he looked at me, and he could hardly believe his eyes. He said, "Are you not Mr. Spurgeon?" I replied, "Yes." "Dear, dear", said he, "why, that is your sermon that I preached this morning!" Yes, I knew it was, and that was one reason why I was so comforted by it, because I felt that I could take my own medicine, and said to myself, "There now, that which I have seen to have a certain effect on others has had the same effect on me." I asked the preacher to my inn to dinner, and we rejoiced together to think that he should have been led to give the people one of my sermons so that I should be fed out of my own cupboard. I know this, that whatever I may be, there is nothing that moves me like the gospel of Christ. Do not many of you feel just as I do?

II. Now, I will lead you on to the second division of my subject. I have shown you what the Church calls her Lord; now, in the second place, I will tell you FROM WHERE SHE CALLS HIM — "Make haste, my beloved, and be thou like to a roe or to a young hart upon the mountains of spices."

What does that mean? She cries to him to come from the place where he now is, which she calls "the mountains of spices."

Readers of the Song of Solomon know that there are four mountains spoken of in the Song. The first set of mountains is mentioned in the seventeenth verse of the second chapter of the Song, where we read of the *mountains of division:* "Until the day break, and the shadows flee away, turn, my beloved, and be thou like a roe or a young hart upon the mountains of Bether", or the mountains of division, the divided crags, or the mountains that divide. Well now, beloved, this was Christ's first coming. There were mountains of division; our sins and God's justice, like great mountains, divided us. How could God's love ever come to us, or how could we get to it? There were mountains of division; and, as we looked at them, we said, "They are impassable; nobody can ever climb those lofty crags, or scale those awful precipices, or cross those dread abysses. These mountains effectively separate a guilty soul from a holy God; and, my brethren, there was no way over those hills till Jesus came like a roe or a young hart. Roes and harts can stand on crags where men's heads turn giddy, and they fall; and our Divine Master was able to stand where we could not. He came leaping over the mountains of our sins, and over the hills of divine justice, and came even to us, and opened up a way over the mountains of Bether, the mountains of division, by which God comes to us and we come to God; and now, instead of division, there is a sacred union.

That was Christ's first coming, over the mountains of division. But there were other mountains beside those, which you read of a little further on in the Song; these were *the mountains of the leopards*, the dens of the lions. Turn to the fourth chapter, at the eighth verse: "Come with me from Lebanon, my spouse, with me from Lebanon: look from the top of Amana, from the top of Shenir and Hermon, from the lions' dens, from the mountains of the leopards." When Christ came the first time, he met with fierce opposition from sin and death and hell. These were the lions; these were the leopards; and our great Champion had to go hunting them, and they hunted him. You know how these grim lions met him, and how they tore him; they rent his hands, and his feet, and his side. Do you not remember how that great lion of the pit came leaping on him, how he received him on his breast like a greater Samson; and though he fell in the death-struggle, he tore that lion asunder, as though it had been a kid, and cast him down? As for his other enemies, he could truly say, "O death, where is thy sting? O grave, where is thy victory? (1 Cor. 15:55) Our Well-beloved came to us, over the mountains of the leopards and the dens of the lions, more than conqueror through the greatness of his love. Do you not see him as he comes from Edom, with dyed garments from Bozrah, travelling in the greatness of his strength, speaking in righteousness, mighty to save? (Is. 63:1) In spite of all opposition, Jesus finished the work of our redemption. So he came to us, over the mountains of separation, and over the mountains of the leopards.

But there is a third mountain mentioned in this wonderful poetic Book, and that is, *the mountain of myrrh*. In the sixth chapter at the second verse, it says, "My beloved is gone down into his garden, to the beds of spices, to feed in the gardens, and to gather lilies." It is called a garden, but in the sixth verse of the fourth chapter it is called a mountain — "Until the day break, and the shadows flee away, I will get me to the mountain of myrrh, and to the hill of frankincense." You know the story well. After Jesus had come over the mountains of our sins, after he had killed the lions and the leopards that stood in our way, he gave up his soul into his Father's hands, and loving friends took his body and wrapped it in white linen, and Joseph of Arimathea and Nicodemus brought myrrh and aloes to preserve his blessed body, that matchless casket of a perfect soul. And having wrapped him up, they laid him in a new tomb, which thus became the garden or mountain of myrrh. A bitter thing was that grave where he buried all our sin, that grave out of which he came victorious over death, that grave out of which he rose that he might justify his people. That was the mountain of myrrh to which he went for a very brief season. Scarcely three days was he there; but I think I can hear his Church standing at the tomb, and saying, "Make haste, my beloved! Be thou like a roe, or a young hart, and come quickly from thy sleep with the dead in the mountains of myrrh." It was but a short time that he was there, even as he said to his disciples, "A little while, and ye shall not see me; and again a little while, and ye shall see me." (Jn. 16:16) Soon was that slumber over, and when he woke, as Samson carried away the gate of Gaza, so Christ arose, and took up the gates of death, posts and bar and all, and carried them away, and neither death nor hell can ever bring them back again. By the resurrection of Christ, the tomb was opened, never to be closed again.

The "mountain of myrrh" is the third that is mentioned in the Song; but our text refers to *"the mountains of spices."* I am not stretching this passage, or drawing a lesson where there is none; the mountains of spices are those places where Jesus dwells at this very moment at the right hand of God. It is from there that we now call him with the spouse when she said, "Make haste, my beloved, and be thou like to a roe or to a young hart upon the mountains of spices.

What are these spices? Are they not Christ's infinite merits, which perfume heaven and earth? The foul corruption of our sins is not perceptible because of the mountains of spices. One single sin would be vile enough to pollute a universe; what, then, if all our sins were put together? Behold this wondrous sanitary power of divine grace; these mountains of spices more than nullify the foulness of our sins. Christ's merit is perpetually before the eye of his Father, so that no longer does he perceive our sins.

What shall I say next of these mountains of spices? Are they not our Lord's perpetual and prevailing prayers? He intercedes for the people before the throne of God. He is that great angel from whose swinging censer there goes up continually the incense of intercession. The prayers of saints are presented by him to his Father with all his own merit added to them. These are the mountains of spices, Christ's infinite merits, and his ceaseless prayers, his undying supplications to the great Father on behalf of all his people.

In consequence of this, I think I may say that the praises of his glorified people, the sweet music of the harps of the redeemed, the everlasting symphonies of the spirits of just men made perfect, and cleansed by his atoning blood, are not these as sweet spices before God? Yes, all heaven is perfumed with everything that is precious and acceptable, full of a sweet savour to God, and a delightful fragrance to all his people. Now, this is where Jesus is now; not here in this foul, polluted world, but up yonder as he rests in the mountains of spices; and the prayer of his Church continually is: "Come, my Beloved! Make haste, my Beloved! Be thou like to a roe or to a young hart upon the mountains of spices."

III. That brings me to what is really the gist, the main point, the arrowhead of the text. We have noticed what the Church calls her Lord, and from where she calls him; now, thirdly, note HOW SHE CALLS HIM. She says, "Make haste, my Beloved, make haste."

Why is it that all the Church of God, and each individual Christian in particular, is found anxious for the speedy coming of our Lord Jesus Christ? I think, surely, that *this is the result of true love.* Does not love always wish to see the object on which its heart is fixed? When your dearest one parts from you for a while, do you not always long for a speedy return? The parting is painful; it is bitter indeed if you did not expect to meet again soon. So you say, "Do not be absent longer than you are forced to be. Come home as speedily as you can." Where there is great love, there gets to be great longing; and that longing sometimes becomes so vehement as to be well-nigh impatient. May not the Church that mourns her absent Lord sigh and cry till he returns? Is not this the very language of intense love — "Make haste, my Beloved, and return to me"? If we love our Lord, we will long for his appearing (2 Tim. 4:8) Are you sure of this, for it is the natural result of ardent affection.

But, notwithstanding this, beloved, we sometimes need certain incentives to stir up our souls to cry for our Lord's return. One reason that ought to make the believer long for Christ's coming is that *it will end this conflict.* Our lot is cast in a wretched time when many things are said and done that grieve and vex God's Holy Spirit, and all who are in sympathy with him. Sometimes, it is false doctrine that is proclaimed; and if you preach the truth, they smite you on the mouth, and then you say to yourself, "Would God our Lord come!" At other times, it is sheer blasphemy that is uttered, when men say, "The Lord has delayed his coming" (2 Pet. 3:3-7), or when they talk as if he were not Lord, as if his gospel were no gospel, and his salvation worn out. Then we say, "Make no tarrying, O our God! (Ps. 40:17) Come, Lord, and tarry not!" We grow almost impatient then for his coming.

And, dear friend, when you see the oppression of the poor, when you hear the cry of the needy, when you know that many of them are ground down to bitter poverty, and yet are struggling hard to earn a bare pittance, you say, "Lord, will this state of things always exist? Shall not these wrongs be righted? Oh, that he would come, who will judge the people righteously, and vindicate the cause of the poor and the oppressed!"

Then we look even on the professing church, and we see how lukewarm it is, how honeycombed it is with heresy and worldliness, and how often the church that ought to honour Christ insults him, and he is wounded in the house of his friends. (Zech. 13:6) We say, "Will not this evil soon be at an end? Will not the conflict speedily be over? "Oh, how have I stood, in the midst of the battle, when the deadly shafts have flown about me on the right hand and on the left, and, wounded full sore, and I cried, "Will not the King himself soon come, and shall I not before long hear the sound of those blessed feet, whose every step means victory, and whose presence is eternal life?" Come, Lord! Make haste, my Beloved! Come to the rescue of your weak and feeble servants; come, come, come, we beseech you!" Put yourself into this great fight for the faith; and if you have to bear the brunt of the battle, you will soon be as eager as I am that Jesus should make haste, and come to your relief. You will also cry "Make haste, my Beloved" when you think what wonders he will perform at his coming.

What will Christ do at his coming? *He will raise the dead.* My eye shall see him in that day. "I know that my Redeemer liveth, and that he shall stand at the latter day upon the earth, and though after my skin worms destroy this body, yet in my flesh shall I see God; whom I shall see for myself, and mine eyes shall behold, and not another". (Job 19:25-27) When Christ shall come the second time, and that blast, of which we sang just now, "the loudest and the last", shall ring through earth and heaven, then shall the dead arise. There are newly-made graves; the mourners' tears are not yet wiped away. There are the graves of many that have gone home long ago, and we remember them, and say, "Would God that Christ would come, and spoil death of these precious relics! Oh, that he would reanimate these bodies, and call together the dry bones, and bid them live!" (Ezek. 37:5) Come, Lord! Come, Lord, make no tarrying, we beseech you!

And when he shall come, beloved, remember that *then shall be the time of the glory of his people:* "Then shall the righteous shine forth as the sun in the kingdom of their Father." (Mat. 13:43) Slander shall be rolled away in the day of Christ's coming. The wicked shall awake to everlasting contempt, but the righteous to an everlasting justification. (Dan. 12:2) They shall be cleared of every accusation in that day, and then they shall sit on the throne with their Lord. They were with him in his humiliation; they shall be with him in his glory. They, too, were despised and rejected of men, as he was; but, in that day, none shall dare to despise them, for every saint shall be seen to be a king, and a son of the King. Oh, the glory that awaits his people in the day of his coming! It does not yet appear what we shall be: but we know that, when he shall appear, we shall be like him; for we shall see him as he is." (1 Jn. 3:2) Well may the child of God say, "Make haste, my Beloved!" Oh, for the sheathing of the sword, and the waving of the palm! Oh, for the drying of the tear, and the handling of the harp of gold! Oh, for the ending of doubt and trouble, and the beginning of everlasting enjoyment and eternal serenity at the right hand of the Ever-blessed One!

Still, there is another reason why we say, "Make haste, my Beloved." It is this. We desire to share in Christ's glory; but *our chief desire is that our Lord may be glorified.* I do believe I have the support of every Christian heart when I say that we would a thousand times rather that Christ were glorified than that we should be honoured. Many years ago, after the Surrey Music Hall accident, I well-nigh lost my reason through distress of heart. I was broken down in spirit, and thought that, perhaps, I might never preach again. I was only a young man, and it was a great sorrow that crushed me into the dust through that terrible accident; but one passage of Scripture brought me recovery in a moment. I was alone, and as I was thinking, this text came to my mind, "Him hath God exalted with his right hand to be a Prince and a Saviour" (Acts 5:31), and I said to myself, "Is that so? Is Jesus Christ exalted? Then I do not care if I die in a ditch. If Christ is exalted to be a Prince and a Saviour, that is enough for me." I distinctly recollect remembering what is recorded of some of Napoleon's soldiers, who were well-near cut to pieces, lying dying, bleeding, suffering, agonising on the battle-field. But when the Emperor rode by, every man lifted himself up as best he could, some resting on the only arm that was left, just to look at him once more, and shout, *Vive l'Empereur!* The Emperor had come along; he was all right, and that was enough for his faithful followers. I think that I felt just like that; whatever happened to me, it was true of Christ — "Him hath God exalted with his right hand to be a Prince and a Saviour, for to give repentance to Israel, and forgiveness of sins." (Acts 5:31) Never mind what becomes of the man, the king lives and reigns, and Jesus Christ is glorified; and so long as that is the case, what matters what becomes of us? I think I can say for you, as well as for myself, that, if there is anything in this world that will glorify Christ, you will make no hesitation about the bargain. If it will glorify Christ, you say, let it come. Though your name should be cast out as evil, and your body should left unburied, to be gnawed by dogs, what does it matters so long as he who loved us, and gave himself for us, should ride on conquering and to conquer in the midst of the sons of men? (Rev. 6:2)

To every loyal soldier of King Jesus, this is the best thought in connection with his Second Advent, that, when he comes, it will be to be admired in his saints, and glorified in all those that believe. Then there shall be universal acclamations to him, and his enemies shall hide their heads with shame and dismay. Oh, what will they do then? What will they do in the day of his appearing? They also will live again, and what will they do in that day? Judas, where are you? Come here, man! Sell your Lord again for thirty pieces of silver! What does he say? Why, he flees, and wishes he could again go out and destroy himself; but that is impossible. Now Pilate, vacillating Pilate, wash your hands in water and say, "I am innocent of the blood of this just person." There is no water for him to wash his hands in, and he dare not again perform that wicked farce. And now, you who cried, "Crucify him, crucify him", lift up your voices again if you dare! Not a dog will move his tongue; but hearken, they have found their tongues, and what do they say? They are imploring the hills to fall on them, and they are calling on the rocks to hide them. (Rev. 6:15) The King has not put his hand on his sword, and he has not sent out his lightnings to scatter you; why do you flee so, you craven cowards? Hear their bitter wail: "O rocks and hills, hide us from the face, from the face, from the face, of him that sits upon the throne!" It is the face of Jesus, which they were bidden to look on, that they might live; but now, in another state, they dare not look on that face of placid love which, in that day, shall be sterner than the frowning brow of vengeance itself. Yes, they flee, they flee! But you who have trusted Christ, you whom he has saved, you will draw near to him and shout his praises; you will delight in him, for it shall be your heaven to bless him forever and ever. Oh, yes, great Master: "Make haste, my beloved, and be thou like to a roe or to a young hart upon the mountains of spices." And all his saints, with one voice and heart, will say, "Amen."

Oh, that you, who have never trusted him, would trust him now; and if you do trust him, you shall live with him forever and ever. God grant it! Amen.

Made in United States
Troutdale, OR
06/29/2024

20890776R00370